Hunting Captain Ahab

Hunting Captain Ahab

*Psychological Warfare
and the Melville Revival*

Clare L. Spark

THE KENT STATE UNIVERSITY PRESS

KENT, OHIO, & LONDON

© 2001 by The Kent State University Press, Kent, Ohio 44242

ALL RIGHTS RESERVED

Library of Congress Catalog Card Number 00-029585

ISBN 0-87338-674-4

Manufactured in the United States of America

07 06 05 04 03 02 01   5 4 3 2 1

Library of Congress Cataloging-in-Publication Data

Spark, Clare L.

    Hunting Captain Ahab: psychological warfare and the Melville revival / by Clare L. Spark.

        p. cm.

Based on the author's thesis (Ph.D., University of California, Los Angeles, 1993).

Includes bibliographical references and index.

ISBN 0-87338-674-4 (alk. paper) ∞

1. Melville, Herman, 1819–1891—Criticism and interpretation—History—20th century.

2. American fiction—19th century—History and criticism.   3. Criticism—United States—

History—20th century.   4. Politics and literature—United States—History—20th century.

5. United States—Intellectual life—20th century.   I. Title.

PS2387 .S66   2001

813'.3—dc21   00-029585

    Writing by Lincoln Kirstein © 2000 by the New York Public Library (Astor, Lenox, and Tilden Foundations); not to be reproduced without permission.

    Unpublished materials from the Charles Olson Papers, © 1993 by University of Connecticut Libraries, are used with permission.

    Materials from the Melville Papers, Houghton Library, Harvard University, are reproduced with permission.

    Unpublished writing by Jay Leyda has been quoted with permission of Elena Pinto Simon, literary executor of the Estate of Jay Leyda.

British Library Cataloging-in-Publication data are available.

In memory of
CHARLES SPARK
(1906–1986)
and
PAUL C. METCALF
(1917–1999)

Contents

Acknowledgments

An interdisciplinary project of this scope and detail would have been inconceivable without the cooperation and guidance of numerous scholars, archivists, and referees, both before and after the completion of my dissertation in 1993, only a few of whom can be cited here.

First, I thank Harrison Hayford and Merton M. Sealts, Jr., who spoke candidly about their lives and work, helpfully criticized my own developing arguments, and allowed me to publish their correspondence with other Melville scholars. Similarly, the executors Mrs. Caroline Murray and Elena Pinto Simon have allowed the reader to encounter firsthand the complex minds of Henry A. Murray and Jay Leyda. Other Melville scholars have also contributed to my effort in reconstructive history; they are Sanford Marovitz, Hershel Parker, Edwin S. Shneidman, Milton Stern, G. Thomas Tanselle, Douglas Robillard, and Kris Lackey.

Second, I was fortunate in having the critical intellectual and moral support of a distinguished reading committee: Alexander Saxton, Robert Brenner, Carolyn Porter, Albert Boime, Saul Friedländer, and Katherine King. Other scholars have read nearly every draft of this constantly evolving book over the last eleven years, directing my forays into the history of social psychology and the institutional politics of academe. They are Roy Porter and Robert Nashak, who have moreover revived for me the zest, clarity, and literary qualities of the eighteenth-century English essay, which I have done my best to emulate. I might not have focused so much attention on the history of antisemitism, especially as the image of the corrosively analytic Jewish scientist has been deployed against the rationalism and libertarianism of the radical bourgeoisie, were it not for the prodding of Leo Steinberg and Albert Boime.

Of the many archivists who have aided me, several stand out: Richard Fyffe, former curator of the Charles Olson Papers at the University of Connecticut, Martha Foley, curator of the Jay Leyda Papers at the Tamiment Institute of New York University, and Jeffrey Rankin and Simon Elliott, at the Department of Special Collections, Charles Young Research Library, UCLA. Special thanks also to Andrew Bodenrader, Morten Engstrom, and Thomas Mertes for numerous favors and encouragement.

Finally, I am grateful for the commitment of time and resources that the editors of The Kent State University Press—Julia Morton, Joanna Hildebrand Craig, and Erin Holman—and their hard-working anonymous referees have made to an ambitious and challenging project. Their enthusiasm and meticulous attention to detail have made this a perfectly happy collaboration.

I have given much thought to the dedication of this book, for several of the persons named above deserve that special acknowledgment, and my heart is full of gratitude to each; they know who they are. But in the early 1990s, poet-historian Paul C. Metcalf, Melville's great-grandson, made a collage of our correspondence (published in 1991), with excerpts from the first draft of my dissertation; he entitled it *Enter Isabel*, hinting that I was another Ahab. That intervention strengthened my resolve to set the record straight for Melville's descendants and all his readers, especially with respect to the rumors imputing insanity and/or impugning that artist's character.

The original source of my determination to attempt something substantial for mental and physical health, however, was my father, Charles Spark, M.D., an army pathologist in World War II and a doctor to forgotten veterans, including paraplegics, forced to live in substandard housing after the war. More and more, my work has focused on the ways that competing narratives purporting to explain mass death in the twentieth century might either fortify or undermine conceptual clarity, hence the political will to eliminate the structural causes of war and all unnecessary suffering. For these compelling reasons, my book is doubly dedicated to the memories of two good men.

Part I
Melville's Rainbow (Under-Read)
An Unclosed Case Study in Conservative Enlightenment

1

Introduction

... the childhood shows the man,
As morning shows the day.
　—Milton, *Paradise Regained*

True, if all fair dawnings were followed by high noons and sunsets. But as
many a merry morn precedes a dull & rainy day; so, often, unpromising
mornings have glorious middles and ends. The greatest, grandest things are
unpredicted.
　—Melville's marginal comment

The saints, they said, were the salt of the earth; an entire parity had place
among the elect: and by the same rule, that the apostles were exalted from
the most ignoble professions, the meanest sentinel, if enlightened by the
Spirit, was entitled to equal regard with the greatest commander.
　—David Hume

[Melville was] a devotee of poetic exaggeration, a propagandist for world
peace, a scoffer at gold braid and salutes and ceremonies, an anti-militarist,
an apostle of leveling and democracy.
　—Rear Admiral Livingston Hunt, *Harvard Graduates' Magazine,* 1930

Ride over mouldy plain to Dead Sea—Mountains on both side . . . all but
verdure.—foam on beach & pebbles like slaver of mad dog—smarting
bitter of the water,—carried the bitter in my mouth all day—bitterness of

life—thought of all bitter things—Bitter is it to be poor & bitter, to be reviled, & Oh bitter are these waters of Death, thought I.—Old boughs tossed up by water—relics of pick-nick—nought to eat but bitumen & ashes with desert of Sodom apples washed down with water of Dead Sea.... the unleavened nakedness of desolation.

—Melville journal entry, first published 1935

I understand that there is a chance that the Melville house in Pittsfield may be acquired and preserved as a Museum. That would be excellent, since, as you know, I agree with you that Melville is the greatest writer we have yet had in this country, and that his memory should be celebrated, therefore, in every way possible.

—F. O. Matthiessen to Henry A. Murray, November 23, 1943

Rainbow over Dead Sea—heaven, after all, has no malice against it.—

—Melville's marginal comment

Then the great myth of Moby Dick rose in the American imagination and Melville's overpowering sense of the omnipotence of evil blacked out the sunniness and whiteness of Emerson and Whitman.

—Van Wyck Brooks on the 1920s Melville Revival, 1952

The Sailors' cause is one which admits of no division. As long as the moral condition of the deep water sailor is such as to render him a wretched slave, morally, mentally, and physically, who bows in silent submission to the caprices and brutalities of unprincipled captains and greedy landsharks; so long as he may be overworked, underfed, beaten, swindled, and driven out of their vessels and forced upon our coast to enter into the most bitter competition for bread with ourselves, just so long will our struggle be worse than futile. Let us have a craft of intelligent men. We here, upon our [west] coast, who have more advantages—we should see to it that a glimpse of light fall upon the mid-ocean. Let us read, let us discuss, let us educate ourselves; let the result of our education be sent broadcast across the ocean.

—Editorial, *Coast Seamen's Journal*, 1887

And lucky it was for the tongueless sailors that this sensitive and manly fellow stepped out of his class to live among them, and then returned to embody their best sentiments in language that had stuff in it.

—Henry A. Murray on the fortunes of sailors, unpublished manuscript

Rainbow in the morning, Sailor's warning.
Rainbow at night, Sailor's delight.
—Sailors' song

Herman Melville (1819–1891), "an apostle of leveling and democracy" (and yet) indeed, "the greatest writer we have yet had in this country," has ever intoxicated the blue-pencil crowd. His first book, *Typee* (1846), a narrative of his captivity among cannibals in the Marquesas, made him an overnight celebrity but also an enemy to religious conservatives. Missionaries resented Melville's contrast of attractive pagan life in the Marquesas with the conditions of Honolulu natives who had been "civilized into draught horses, and evangelized into beasts of burden." Once Melville began "swimming through libraries" in his mid-twenties, nine novels and a collection of short stories emerged from the deep, many in rapid succession. Each effort greeted a polarized readership in America and England. But as his books became more learned, formally intricate, and socially critical, book sales declined. Following his last major publication, *Battle-Pieces* (1866), a collection of poems on the subject of the Civil War, Melville withdrew from public authorship and took a job as a minor customs official. He died in relative obscurity with most of his books out of print, his later stories and poems either privately circulated or unread.

He was left there for thirty years. After the centenary of his birth in 1919, then the republication of his works in multiple editions, thousands of literary scholars and journalists, in ever-accelerating numbers, became engaged, primarily with *Moby-Dick* (1851), accepted now as a classic of world literature with Captain Ahab and the White Whale familiar fixtures in popular culture. While other American authors have been vigorously promoted by scholars and publishers, few have aroused so much energy and animus; there is little or no agreement on what the complexion of "Melville" was or is, or whether he should be affixed with a warning label or hailed as the fairest flower of democratic culture or defended from recent attempts to overlook "his fundamental social conservatism."[1] "For consider the vacillations of a man," the dialectician ruminated,[2] inviting the reader to follow him hither and thither. Attempts to account for Melville's rise and fall are mixed with answers to still other questions designed to pin the rover down. Has he been overrated? Were his politics at all coherent? Which of the many apparently authoritative and impassioned voices in his fiction expressed his own beliefs? Was he a cynical confidence man, sadistically tormenting his readers? Were his adventures taken from (dangerously radical) eyewitness reportage or (safely derivative) plagiarized travel narratives and other literary sources? What was the role of his family, if any, in contributing to the crash of his meteoric career? Was he ever crazy? Was he ever in control of his material? Have academic revivers covered up disgraceful conduct as husband and father? Was he gay? What exactly were his relations with Nathaniel Hawthorne? How can we explain his rediscovery in 1919 and the reassessments that followed? Let me call this academic complex, for the present, "the Melville problem."

Given the range of Melville's lived experience and reading; the intellectual and political ferment of the nineteenth century; the almost overwhelming richness, intricacy, and subtlety of his art; and the polarized responses his writing has ever evoked, it is hard to imagine a more exciting, absorbing, and demanding project in the humanities. But whereas I experienced my lengthy immersion in Melvilleana as replenishing and releasing, the archival record of his official resuscitation presents little joy and much exhaustion, confusion, and suspicion of Melville. The dark thoughts of Melville scholars sometimes were directed at Melville himself and sometimes at competing scholars who seemed to share his imputed secrecy and manipulativeness. The record shows a most unscholarly withholding or ignoring of primary source materials by the same scholars who claimed that Melville himself had shameful secrets. These sources included illuminating passages of his own texts, published and unpublished, and other documents that could make sense of the multifaceted Melville problem.

There is much evidence to support his characterization as a classical conservative. Take a sequence in *Mardi* alluding to America's revolutionary break with Britain. No sooner had Babbalanja lamented British curbs on free thought that had severed a blood tie with the surpassingly great fatherland than he defended property from the thievery of communistic plebeians—like the author himself in his more heady speculations, perhaps: "There's not so much freedom here as these freemen think," he warned, referring to the young republic.[3] Conservative Anglophile or not, Melville was obsessed with the rights of citizens and the duties of authority; his critique was directed against confusing institutions with internally contradictory rules and practices, not only against individuals abusing class power. The age of science and discovery was also an age of revolution; adapting to the unprecedented conditions of modernity (print culture, mass literacy and mass politics, a growing secular intelligentsia), entrenched elites professed their commitment to cultural freedom while subtly circumscribing curiosity, patrolling unspoken boundaries that scholars (as middle managers) feared could not be identified without retaliation. Certain leading Melvilleans have attempted to divide liberal from conservative factions in Melville studies, yet research in the papers of these same scholars suggests an underlying unity among professors in universities coping with unspoken contraints on their wandering imaginations. The tolerance or intolerance of institutional cruelty should matter to students of antidemocratic social movements in our century.

On this subject, however, Melvilleans were often tongue-tied and immobile, while prolix in their responses to Melville and his "problem"—his famously fissured personality or identity that scholars generally described and classified in static terms and without reference to the analogous paradoxical institutional conditions in which their Melville biographies or criticism were generated; nor, in their published criticism could the revivers admit their own inner turmoil in response to Melville's art. As cartographer of bodies in double bondage, bodies facing institutional demands for new truths while simultaneously tied to conservative notions of stability, Melville clarifies one source of political apathy: he takes the reader through his cycles of "red" confession, submergence and explosive reemergence, resubmergence, etc. The retreats from empiricism and rationalism that he traces in exquisite detail have been generally hidden or reified in the Revival. Twentieth-century readers have tended either to diagnose Melville as a split or ambivalent personality torn between "aristocracy" and "democracy" or to celebrate his switch from self-destructive enthusiast to mature conservative after the Civil War. Missing are the concrete institutional conditions, rival antebellum reform movements, experiences, and self-understanding that led the artist from one political posture to another and back again at every stage of his career. To some extent, the Melville problem has been alleviated by "reader-response" criticism that simply denies any authoritative judgment with respect to textual meaning, authorial intent, or artistic merit. As I have seen it, however, the Melville problem is not the outcome of an inevitable multiplicity of readings, or irrational prejudice or blindness in literary scholars. At bottom, the twentieth-century Melvilleans studied here felt the agony and the moral beauty of the bold investigator, the Promethean artist following the facts wherever they led, who would then stand up to irrational authority, inspiring others to do the same. The confluence of thought and action both attracted and troubled them.

> Titan! . . . Thy godlike crime was to be kind
> To render with thy precepts less
> The sum of human wretchedness
> And strengthen man with his own mind.[4]

The example of the Melville Revival irradiates an overarching and hitherto mostly invisible sub-rosa culture war, an upper-class project in the humanities that took aim at the unpredictable political imaginations of the newly emancipated lower orders, including those hired to teach them. The players in my study had a mission they expressed in gothic and apocalyptic language. For Raymond Weaver, Lewis Mumford, Charles Olson, Henry Murray, Jay Leyda, Richard Chase, and other inheritors of German romanticism, the Hebraic Mind of Melville and Ahab was the leading edge of degeneration in the body politic. This seductive Mind was toxic, stealthily transmitting plagues, cancers, skin diseases, nervous jitters, and even madness; it was too adolescent in its romantic yearning for timeless ethical ideals; too perfectionist in its devotion to the universal Rights of Man; too enthusiastic in its efforts to write an accurate history of events by linking effects with their causes. By poking into the affairs of its betters, and, just as bad or worse, by probing too far into the mysteries of its own internal operations, the Mind's perversity stood revealed. It had weighed authority and found it wanting; it had heartlessly refused to follow its leaders by harmonizing social contradictions in mythic narratives. The contradictions it should have transcended, or buried, were those that reflected unequal distributions of power, as between trustees and professors, publishers and writers, and—most fundamentally—employers and employees. Labor, in its misconceived autodidacticism and reforming zeal, had been misled and nearly destroyed by its own Mind but would be saved by renewed and revitalized paternal authority, modern, to be sure, but pragmatically spiritual. The new (truer) Prometheans would be sternly disciplinary, attuned to communal welfare in the natural order of things. The (false) Promethean figures to be overcome were represented by Lord Byron and other Left romantics, including Captain Ahab and his Creator, the ungodly, godlike Herman Melville, exhausted by an access of Titanism. Dramatizing Melville's rescue from nineteenth-century neglect, literary scholars usually dub the 1920s exhumation "the Melville Revival." What the Melville Revival resuscitated was an *homme fatale*.

Notwithstanding their mountains of commentary on Melville and the changing reception to his work, scholars have been oblivious to the multiplicity of purpose in the promotion of American literature. Whereas Melville, like other modernists, was often an advanced proponent of the critical intellect in the service of social amelioration, his chief revivers, though self-declared radicals, possessed sensibilities and intentions that were, like Melville's (often) Tory, aristocratic, and Anglo-Catholic. Wonderfully, the debates swirling around Melville's life and art open a window into the innermost workings of cultural production, into the most hard-fought cultural and political struggles of the last five centuries, including, most recently, contending social psychological explanations for the rise and appeal of fascism and Nazism. Though Captain Ahab was frequently typed as an anticipation of Hitler, much of this vital prospect remains unexplored by academic Melvilleans. The Melville Revival is implicated in the parallel institutionalization of psychological warfare in the state as an indispensable feature of postwar pluralist politics; each instillation bleeds into the other. The successive waves of Melville scholarship can best be understood by reviving this double context. Some of the scholars who attempted to stabilize the Melville problem stood at the apex of the antifascist liberal establishment in the arts and education. Indeed, three of the very scholars who were at the forefront of Melville studies were skilled propagandists and practitioners of psychological warfare. Two scholars associated with the first wave of Melville studies, Dr. Henry A. Murray and Charles Olson, worked for the government during World War II, while Jay Leyda, a leading scholar of the postwar period, was a communist connected to the morale-building wartime propaganda apparatus in Hollywood.

Since the mid-1920s, Murray had been absorbed in writing a Jungian psychoanalytic biography of Melville that still remains unpublished. Murray was strongly influenced by the pluralism and philosophical idealism of William James and William McDougall, both chairs of Harvard's Department of Psychology. As director of the Harvard Clinic, Murray was interested in troubled students and left-wing rebels. He was the co-originator of the Thematic Apperception Test (1935), a diagnostic procedure intended to expose repressed fantasies but presented to clients solely as a test of literary imagination. He was also part of a group of Harvard professors, including Murray's mentor, sociologist Talcott Parsons, who were studying Mussolini's favored sociologist, Vilfredo Pareto, the antidemocratic theorist of "the circulation of elites." During the war Murray was not only chief of personnel assessment for the Office of Strategic Services (oss), devising their screening test for stable and loyal operatives capable of maintaining a false identity, but he had earlier envisioned "a federal department of social science."[5]

With his colleague Gordon Allport, Murray led the Harvard seminar "Psychological Problems in Morale" (1941), intended "to formulate psychological principles and describe methods that should prove useful to a government morale service or to private organizations concerned with the enhancement of morale." The seminars would study the conditions conducive to "strong and unanimous resolution, perseverance, confidence, idealism, freedom from anxiety, and all other aspects of good morale, as well as their contraries." Framing their seminar as a set of problems to be solved, the authors asked, "What are the strengths and weaknesses of Nazi ideology as an instrument for world conquest? . . . What, in psychological terms, is meant by the Jeffersonian tradition in America? . . . Certain themes in Axis propaganda are continually stressed, notably the self-righteousness and hypocrisy of the democracies in general and of the United States (and President Roosevelt) in particular. What's to be done about it?" But the worksheets created by Murray and Allport were not open-ended explorations of historical materials; rather, they contained detailed instructions for the psychological manipulation of internally divided Americans that would build and maintain "good morale," the will to fight the Nazis. Morale was enhanced by identification with an idealized American past and idealized democratic leaders; moreover, their instructions ordered progressive reforms that would enhance a stable and positive postwar pluralist national identity. During this same period, Murray wrote a long confidential report for Roosevelt, filed in the summer of 1943, analyzing Hitler's personality and its effect on the German people. Much of the Hitler report (begun in 1938) duplicated parts of the Harvard worksheets, which had more briefly described the psychodynamics of Hitler's mind and mass appeal. The 1941 worksheets deplored Hitler's contemptuous swindling of the masses, contrasting brain-dead Nazis with critical Americans, meanwhile recommending propaganda methods resembling those deployed by Hitler and Goebbels. Similarly, Murray's secret report to FDR (1943) suggested that twenty-one of Hitler's "principles of action" be evaluated by the U.S. government: Like Freud, Hitler had an "uncanny" insight into the hidden regions of the psyche, into the minds of other little men responsible for Nazism.[6]

Charles Olson, Murray's friend and ardent admirer, had been the most promising young Melville scholar during and after the mid-1930s. Later recognized by other poets and critics as the father of postmodernism and cultural pluralism, Olson also wrote propaganda for the Office of War Information. After the war, however, Olson returned to hostile characterizations of American culture, similar to those of D. H. Lawrence and Ezra Pound during the 1920s or Murray's views on Hitler during the late 1930s and early 1940s. These judgments all converged in the late 1940s; Olson's corresponded to the formulation of the Nazi-American national character disseminated by Soviet propagandists in the early 1950s and taken up by parts of the New Left in the 1960s. It persists today in American Studies and in the organicist literary theory of the New Americanists postulating the "essentially imperial, racist, and patriarchal historical project" of this country.[7]

Jay Leyda, a hero to scholars of "second wave" Melville studies after World War II, was anything but a dispassionate investigator of the Melville mystery. Leyda was a photographer, an assistant to Sergei Eisenstein, an authority on Russian film, and an expert propagandist himself, serving as technical adviser to the wartime film *Mission to Moscow*. A supporter of the Soviet Union during the 1930s and early 1940s, Leyda claimed to have left the Communist Party after 1943, but he relinquished his connections neither to comrades nor corporatist protectors. Yale professor Norman Holmes Pearson, another authority on propaganda working for the oss (and a Hitler fan during the 1930s), supported Leyda's career under the impression that he was an iconoclastic force; Pearson applauded Leyda's "scalpel" as it operated upon Melville and Emily Dickinson. For some twentieth-century communists and capitalists alike, the healthy artist surrendered critical independent thought and creativity, the cause and symptom of group degeneracy, to socially responsible bureaucrats ruling on behalf of the People. And the People preferred the purity of *Proletkult*, with its ethos of collective heroism, peace, progress, and optimism. Following the line to construct the New Man, Leyda arranged his chronology of Melville's hitherto confusing or mysterious life to track a progression from Ahab's family-splitting bourgeois individualism to Billy Budd's socially responsible sacrifice on behalf of family unity and order, ordering Melville's psyche in the process.[8] Every detail of *The Melville Log* was designed to fortify that message. American organic conservatives and Soviet communists walked hand in hand, sharing the same objective; the target of their operations was bourgeois democracy as it had evolved during the seventeenth and eighteenth centuries. For Milton, Locke, Diderot, Adam Smith, Thomas Paine, Condorcet, and Thomas Jefferson, as for other intellectuals of the radical bourgeoisie, Enlightenment rationalism and universal standards of morality were enlisted in the service of amelioration and democratic self-management, energizing resistance to all forms of illegitimate authority. Such objectives would be stigmatized as effluents of Ahab's ambition and pride; Ishmael's cultural relativism was a superior guide to the upper-class peace movement critical of the "Pax Americana" after World War II and seeking a new comity of nations.

The Melville Revival, then, is only tangentially about the author of *Moby-Dick*. It is but one telling episode in a long-standing global effort to maintain authoritarian social relations in an age of democratic aspirations and growing awareness of species-unity as the natural world and its far-flung inhabitants, directly encountered, became better known to the "heartless," "soul-less" empiricist eye. I and other historians have designated such opponents of empiricism or naturalism as corporatists, corporatist liberals, conservative liberals, cultural nationalists, nativist radicals, romantic anticapitalists, romantic conservatives, rooted cosmopolitans, neo-medievalists, or organic conservatives. I call their body of organic social theory and cultural criticism "the conservative Enlightenment," to be contrasted with the radical Enlightenment, "the enlightenment within the enlightenment" that seemed especially menacing to ruling elites after the disruptions of the English Civil War and then the French Revolution.[9]

As progressives, the corporatists submerged individuals, especially dissenters, into group categories, whether these freethinkers were artists, scientists, historians, or ordinary citizens. Radical liberals (the Prometheans) were challenging received ideas, reconfiguring existing models of human nature and traditional institutions, and, with new critical tools, imagining strategies that could alleviate unnecessary suffering: "strengthening man with his own mind." Coping with these "mechanical" materialists and other "economic determinists," reactive "moderates" co-opted procedures and concepts of the physical, natural, and social sciences (especially the eighteenth-century science of political economy). Through government regulation of markets and industry, the partial redistribution of wealth and resources, and incorporation of dissonant elements (most notably labor unions and minority groups), progressives sought to reinstate the "equilibria" thought to be lost during the transition from a peaceful and integrated agrarian society to the post–Civil War wild and wooly urban and industrial nightmare of market-induced greed, corruption, exploitation, economic strife, and anomie.[10] As experts and planners, progressives of the twentieth century gathered facts, professed scientific objectivity (nonpartisanship), and embraced aspects of Darwinism; but they were also paternalists attempting to preserve, recover, or attain class power and authority. Like earlier conservative reformers, they advocated gradual and orderly institutional "reform" to protect "the public interest" or "community"; their strategy would forestall "rupture" or "innovation" or "apocalyptic change" at the hands of radical artisans and their "perfectionist" allies. Following Edmund Burke, the conservative enlighteners desired "narrative continuity with the [idealized] past."[11] Preferring individual moral reform (understood as the suppression of narcissism or "bourgeois individualism") to root-and-branch institutional or structural transformation (a strategy deemed "Jacobin" and associated with liberal nationalism), the Burkeans were fixated upon "character," especially insofar as hubris in leaders and/or the led might corrode bonds of "natural" community, local or regional, as it had evolved over time in interaction with its physical environment. For conservative enlighteners, the most salient contradiction is "the individual versus society," a formulation that rebukes nineteenth-century "laissez-faire" liberals, who, it is alleged, were impervious to our interdependence with Nature and put self-aggrandizement ahead of social welfare.

The Burkean notion of "national character" may be applied to geographic locales (as in the aesthetic theory of "regionalism"), "races" or "ethnicities," and even classes: For some leftists, New Leftists, and reactionaries alike, the bourgeoisie is uniformly Bad, the working class is, or should be, Good. "America" is not a collection of diverse but educable individuals, some dead, some alive, with a full spectrum of opinions about values and their applications in domestic and foreign policies, individuals who are coping with institutions that may be flexible or inflexible with respect to equitable practices, responsive or unresponsive to democratizing social movements and proposals for amelioration. Rather, "America" is imagined as one very Bad individual stretching across four centuries (or more if we count Columbus as Ur-American). For the anti-Americans/antimoderns, "this country" is the worst in history; in its craze for the machine, for gambling (Wall Street), and for consumer goods, "the American character" retains its penchant for exterminating Indians, kidnapping and enslaving Africans, and raping the environment. Armed with surveillance apparatuses and mass media, rampaging America, the very model of the androgynous Victorian battle-axe, controls all aspects of everyday life, seeding sentimental kitsch culture while uprooting ethnic or other forms of collective identity. With the imagined (desecrated) community defined in organic metaphors lifted from the natural sciences, then, the discourses of "ethnopluralism" or, more recently, "multiculturalism," are weapons in the arsenal of corporatist ideology.[12] Such scientism pervades the Melville Revival. "Pluralist" progressives alleged that cultural/moral relativism would repair what querulous Anglo-Saxon Puritan America had squashed or rent asunder: Natural cultural diversity would be restored. For cultural nationalists following the eighteenth-century German theologian J. G. von Herder, the purified America is a mosaic of communities that do not merge with each other; within each ethnicity, persons are supposedly bound to each other by warm quasi-family ties marked by affection, duty, mutual obligation, and natural hierarchies.[13]

Organicism finds consensus where there is contestation, decadence where there is progress. By contrast, a materialist might say that American institutions have sailed unsteadily toward the egalitarian ideals professed in the Declaration of Independence, blown off course when certain foreign and domestic policy considerations contradicted the high idealism of the Protestant mission. Materialist historians have long understood the content and objectives of corporatist ideologies, some pointing to their irrationalist and protofascist character.[14] Other scholars, humanists writing in the idealist tradition and linking science and materialism with the destructiveness they attribute to the bourgeoisie, have attempted to turn science into just another story: "Facts" are embedded in "valuations."[15] As "postmodernists," some subordinate the truth claims of science, if not to the local *Volksgeist* then to the truth of transcendental religion with its perfectly insoluble mysteries and paradoxes, and then recruit social psychology or cultural anthropology to the project of enforced group cohesion. Overestimating the statism of the moderate men (who generally supported modest social democratic reformism but also federalist localism), postmodernists, whether writing from the Left or Right, have discerned pervasive and intractable "bourgeois hegemony" and "bureaucratic domination" as the condition of modernity. Following Melville's lead, I look at double binds and incoherence in pseudomodern institutions that Melville recognized (most explicitly in *Pierre*) and that many of his revivers suppressed.

Understanding institutional double binds and the precarious position of the freethinking individual within "liberal" educational institutions may help us describe more precisely the unsettled condition of the twentieth-century academy. My research has shown that competing definitions of fascism and explanations for its appeal form the subtext of recent fights over the humanities curriculum and the authority of science; that the Melville Revival cannot be fully described apart from these disputes; and that the combatants do not differentiate between varied and opposing ideological tendencies generally lumped together as "the Enlightenment." Two varieties of "pluralism" (superficially similar either to Hamiltonian federalism or to Jeffersonian republicanism) turn out in fights over the curriculum. Although they bitterly oppose each other, neither faction questions organic formulations of society by positing the legitimacy and value of the dissenting, creative individual above their indefinable, indescribable, irreplaceable "group cohesion"; therefore, neither faction can elucidate such problems as Melville's inner turmoil, or, on a grander scale, antisemitism and fascism. The Enlightenment, like "the West" or "the spirit of an age," is an integrated whole, angelically pure and healthy, or diseased, depending on its designated genealogy.

I will argue throughout that the scientific revolution bequeathed a method of investigation, not foreordained conclusions about the goodness and suitability of any particular economic system. Moreover, the radical puritan ("Hebraic") interpretation of the Old Testament insisted that each individual possessed equal rights before the law and was a potentially rational, creative, and moral creature capable of self-knowledge, social knowledge, and self-management; whereas some German romantics appropriated the scientific search for truth and turned it to the service of reaction with the propagation of ethnopluralism and the concept of "the-individual-in-society" seeking equilibrium, not enlightenment.

For today's canon warriors, whether they defend or attack canonized literary works, "the Enlightenment" supports group-think; you will find no avowed racists among them, but neither are there many freestanding individuals demanding rights and the ongoing legitimation of authority over duties to the state or "the community." One faction, the "democratic pluralists," are class-conscious neoconservatives promoting "the melting-pot," creatively coping with "mass society" and its kitsch culture as threats to the Great Tradition and opposing romantic nationalism and racism as obstacles to the global integration of money and markets.[16] For this group there was one, unitary Enlightenment; it proved that their recipes for social order and growth are rational, and they are its inheritors, whereas Hitler, a proto–New Leftist, is their antithesis. Like certain German romantics[17] (including Marx), Hitler simply opposed modernity and its intellectual tools. For Alan Bloom, who assimilated Locke to the German idealist tradition, the Enlightenment carried the rationalism ascribed to Plato, Aristotle, Locke, Kant, and Goethe.[18] Other "antiracists"—the antipluralist cultural relativists, New Left multiculturalists, and Foucauldians—are the idealist descendants of Herder and other German romantics. For them there was one, unitary Enlightenment and bourgeois, materialist, "extraceptive"[19] Hitler and other Western imperialists, similarly agents of state repression, genocide, and ecocide, were its logical culmination.[20] Thus, remarkably, vocal participants on opposing sides in the canon wars have seen Nazism as a form of irrational racism and hypernationalism produced by their rivals: for the neoconservatives, German romanticism; for some multiculturalists and even poststructuralists, a congeries of mostly British Enlightenment philosophers.[21] For some influential progressive social psychologists, Nazi antisemitism functioned solely as "scapegoating": a projection of exclusively inner conflicts upon the outside world by petit bourgeois "respectable" authoritarian personalities. Literary scholars impressed by that analysis would make Melville's Captain Ahab the prime exhibit in their case against the insurgent "technocratic" middle class. (The theoretical apparatus of this book, introduced here in compressed fashion, will be elaborated below as one or another aspect of the organicist ideology is brought out in specific contexts.)

RAILROADING AHAB

To be a true Jacobin, a man must be a good hater; . . . The love of liberty consists in the hatred of tyrants. . . . I am no politician and still less can I be said to be a partyman: but I have a hatred of tyranny, and a contempt for its tools. . . . I deny that liberty and slavery are convertible terms, that right and wrong, truth and falsehood, plenty and famine, the comforts or wretchedness of a people, are matters of perfect indifference. That is all I know of the matter; but on these points I am likely to remain incorrigible.
    —William Hazlitt, Preface to *Political Essays*, 1819

One feature of the (reinstated) organic society favored by many progressives is central to the Melville problem. Before the age of science, discovery, and increasing lower-class demands for a fully realized popular sovereignty, Church and State conducted their affairs in secrecy. Their subordinates, ordinary people, were free to confess their sins to their betters, but without reciprocity; when Ahab fretted double-talking "liberals," from one point of view his interrogations were tantamount to deicide and fratricide. For many of the corporatist thinkers who shaped the Melville Revival, Captain Ahab was the classic American type: a frontiersman, a "nosey Hebrew" (as D. H. Lawrence would say) whose curiosity must be moderated; similarly Melville's dubious "character" as husband and father would preoccupy numerous Melville critics in the twentieth century. Although I have seen new and startling primary source materials, much of the history presented here is derived from publications and archives long available but hitherto undescribed to students of American literature; literary scholars and curators have examined the papers of Henry A. Murray, Charles Olson, and Jay Leyda, and biographies of Murray and Olson have been published by the most reputable presses. Many questions still remain tantalizingly unanswered and invite further research, but it is clear to me, if not to previous investigators, that in the unmonitored autodidact Herman Melville, Murray, Olson, and Leyda had an able instructor, a mirror, and an irresistible adversary who, insofar as he was Captain Ahab, must have been nervously deranged, twisted by hate. The "isolato" Ahab was the paradigm of social irresponsibility and his own worst enemy, while sociable Ishmael was the scholars' antecedent doctor to society. Here is Ishmael's ominous blood-and-soil account of Ahab's origins in his native habitat: Nantucket was originally settled by peaceful Quakers, but they have been invaded by outside influences, they were "variously and anomalously modified by things altogether alien and heterogeneous." (As Melville's antebellum readers would have known, "Nantucket Quakers [were] members of a sect notorious for its literally visionary beginnings and its subsequent antislavery zeal."[22])

For some of these Quakers are the most sanguinary of all sailors and whale hunters. They are fighting Quakers; they are Quakers with a vengeance.

So that there are instances among them Nantucket Quakers of men, who, named with Scripture names—a singularly common fashion on the island—and in childhood naturally imbibing the stately thee and thou of the Quaker idiom; still, from the audacious, daring, and boundless adventure of their subsequent lives, strangely blend with their unoutworn peculiarities, a thousand bold dashes of character, not unworthy a Scandinavian sea-king or a poetical Pagan Roman. And when these things unite in a man of greatly superior natural force, with a globular brain and a ponderous heart; who has also by the stillness and seclusion of many long night-watches in the remotest waters and beneath constellations never seen here in the north, been led to think untraditionally and independently; receiving all nature's sweet or savage impressions fresh from her own virgin, voluntary, and confiding breast, and thereby chiefly, but with some help from accidental advantages, to learn a bold and nervous lofty language—that man makes one in a whole nation's census—a mighty pageant creature, formed for noble tragedies. Nor will it at all detract from him, dramatically regarded, if either by birth or other circumstances, he have what seems a half wilful over-ruling morbidness at the bottom of his nature. For all men tragically great are made so through a certain morbidness. Be sure of this, O young ambition, all mortal greatness is but disease. (73–74)

In *Moby-Dick*'s pivotal chapter "The Quarter-Deck," Starbuck, echoing Ishmael's earlier diagnosis, reproaches Captain Ahab for abandoning his proper search for profits; the quest for vengeance against a "dumb brute" is blasphemous and mad. Ahab reproaches the imperceptive first mate, suggesting twice that he adopt the ways of geology and dig: "Hark ye . . . the little lower layer." Then, lest Starbuck or other dense readers remain in the dark, Melville spills it: "Who's over me? Truth hath no confines."[23] Starbuck is briefly won over but protests in a chapter that directly follows Ahab's railroading speech:

[Ahab:] Swerve me? The path to my fixed purpose is laid with iron rails, whereon my soul is grooved to run. Over unsounded gorges, through the rifled hearts of mountains, under torrents' beds, unerringly I rush! Naught's an obstacle, naught's an angle to the iron way! (chap. 37, "Sunset")

[Starbuck:] My soul is more than matched; she's overmanned; and by a madman! . . . he drilled deep down, and blasted all my reason out of me! I think I see his impious end; but feel I must help him to it. Will I, nill I, the ineffable thing has tied me to him; tows me with a cable I have no knife to cut. Horrible old man! Who's over him, he cries;—aye, he would be a democrat to all above; look, how he lords it over all below! . . . Oh, life! 'tis in an hour like this, with soul beat down and held to knowledge,—as wild, untutored things are forced to feed—Oh, life! 'tis now that I do feel the latent horror in thee! but 'tis not me! that horror's out of me! and with the soft feeling of the human in me, yet will I try to fight ye, ye grim phantom futures! Stand by me, hold me, bind me, O ye blessed influences! (chap. 38, "Dusk")

Standing by Starbuck, one Melville scholar has construed these pages as evidence of Ahab's protofascism:

Like Adolph Hitler, Captain Ahab reaches for the "folksoul" of the crew, and manipulates their minds with the sinister skill of Joseph Goebbels. As in Nazi Germany, so on board the *Pequod*, the excesses of the will play a major role, as is illustrated in the various speeches of Ahab, and her fated course is, in effect, another triumph of the will. Again, paralleling the transformation of the German nation under the Nazis, the crew of the *Pequod* becomes "a folk organism and not an economic organization," since Ahab deliberately rejects the commercial advantages of whaling for a collective psychological fulfillment, resulting from the revengeful pursuit of one whale, seen as the enemy of the state. . . . Ahab is in reality a prototype of a twentieth-century fascist dictator.[24]

For many Melvilleans, ineffably tied to their tormentor, the most unassimilable element of Melville's psyche has been Ahab's materialism yoked to universal standards of ethical conduct. To the extent that Melville is Ahab, he is mad, self- and socially destructive, tyrannical, and an archvillain. Such views conform to the terror-gothic scenario, amplified by conservatives since the Radical Reformation, the scientific revolution of the seventeenth century, the American and French Revolutions, then the intertwined reform movements of the 1830s to 1850s, especially abolitionism. In the "tale of terror," brains and mobs are indissolubly merged; the pregnant bourgeoisie, swollen with a new class and its chimerical socialist utopias, has delivered catastrophes from the French Revolution to Bolshevism and Nazism. In two-dimensional artworks, this aristocratic narrative of the drowning Narcissus/crashing Icarus is frozen as the apocalyptic sublime, the style attributed to mass politics and America. Harold D. Lasswell, political science consultant to the influential postwar Committee for Economic Development, transmitted such neoclassical diagnoses of "romantic fascism" and urged the adoption of Murray's projective testing to implement a program of personnel screening and preventive politics, sighting latent radicalism in prospective leaders in government, industry, labor, and education before they succumbed to the blandishments of Ahab, thereby obviating sleazy witch hunts. Threatened or dispossessed elites continue to flood popular culture with identical antidemocratic propaganda, shaping academic disciplines and mental health treatments to blunt the tools of fiery artisans and their radical descendants.

Defining Melville's mental states, then, was not simply grist for variously voyeuristic or discreet literary historians, but part of ongoing campaigns to diagnose and delimit normality and deviance. For some Melvilleans, the divisive apostate Melville, like his characters Ahab, Pierre, Isabel, the "Hegelised" German-Jewish geologist Margoth, and other Bad Jews, has been cast out; "Melville" and other Good Jews have been taken in and "tolerated" by "the nation."[25] The national bedrock is the sanctity of (upper-class) property, not the republican principle of equality before the law. Melville has been selectively embraced by a reconstructed lovely family—an erasure of conflict evident in the letters of Melville's mother and wife. In this study of the Melville Revival, Starbuck's view of Ahab as totalitarian dictator is challenged along with the concomitant argument followed by some Old and New Leftists that the voyage of the *Pequod* is an unambiguous allegory of capitalist technology and exploitation, manifest destiny, and mind management in its harshest aspects.[26]

In these introductory remarks, I have tried to explain why the Melville Revival deserves the close attention of readers beyond the confines of departments of English. Political, economic, and social historians on the Left may wish to know why questions of high culture should bother scholars mapping "the transition from feudalism to capitalism" and beyond. Why, they might ask, should we distract ourselves with the squabbles of a handful of literary scholars and journalists over a once-forgotten, possibly overrated white male author's reputation? U.S. historians in other, less traditional, more cultural subfields are, of course, already interested in (or wearied with) Melville and the endless debates his life and art have provoked. Some perhaps are allied with earlier intellectual historians such as Ralph Henry Gabriel, Peter Viereck, and Richard Hofstadter, who annexed his life and art to support lugubrious interpretations of American history, joining with Ungar, a character in Melville's late poem *Clarel*, to lament a future overpopulated by "the New Hun"—the industrial working class and its allies "brutalized by popular science" and hell-bent for oblivion.[27] Charles Olson stated in his Winter–Spring 1940 Notebook, "Democracy . . . can demand champions only if it itself is more aware than it has shown itself of the dangers of its rationalism and faith in equality. Morals are taboos—emotional controls, not intellectual concepts. The seeds of democracy lay in a century which had secretly shifted the base of morals into an area of the human mind where morals don't exist—the mind."[28] He was upset that "emotional controls," the police functions associated with the Catholic Church (the Heart), had been transformed and secretly transferred to the Head. Olson was responding to Leveller and Lockean popular sovereignty and to the institutionalization of equal rights in the First and Fourteenth Amendments. "Morals are taboos," he wrote, but for inheritors of seventeenth-century radical puritanism and libertarianism, morality was not an assault upon the body but an affirmation of natural and universal creativity, Melville's rainbow. The radical Enlightenment search for truth and justice policed the rich and punished inquisitors. After the American and French Revolutions, arbitrary power went increasingly on the defensive as knowledge, virtue, and might, always intermingled, moved from castles and country manors to more humble abodes, at least in theory. High-born families, worried and dispossessed, dipped their toes into the mud and extolled the "dignity of labor," all the while practicing mind management and covert action, interpolating "expertise," their infernal machines, between readers and texts to build a consensus for their un-Chosen, un-American activities.

Intellectual and emotional autonomy are indispensable prerequisites to popular sovereignty. Literacy is moot without the capacity to decode the messages that subvert democracy—the narratives and images that discourage ordinary people from defending their interests, that bind them to illegitimate authority. The professional historian or literary scholar should not, by hoarding or suppressing or distorting relevant primary sources (including his own possibly timorous responses to artists and their work), protect his conduct from the scrutiny of other citizens; yet such behavior stains the Melville Revival. This book, then, is not about Melville and his critics as such; rather, Melville's homelessness is the compass that helps other democrats and autodidacts to delimit locales, inward and outward, which make critical reading possible.

"AS WILD, UNTUTORED THINGS ARE FORCED TO FEED"

The diffusion of literacy made possible through printing had been an object of anxiety ever since the Reformation. Whereas Truth-defining elites had modestly arrogated to themselves the marking of moral boundaries, lower-class Protestants were, without benefit of official clergy, scratching a clear, thick line around the privileges of their betters. And look where such hubris had led. In 1797, the anti-Jacobin critic T. J. Mathias, was arguing that

> We are no longer in an age of ignorance, and information is not partially distributed according to the ranks and orders, and functions, and dignities of social life. All learning has an index, and every science its abridgment. I am scarcely able to name any man whom I consider as wholly ignorant. We no longer look for authors in the usual places, in the retreats of academic erudition and in the seats of religion. Our peasantry now read *The Rights of Man* on mountains and moors and by the wayside; and shepherds make the analogy between their occupations and that of their governors. Happy indeed had they been taught no other comparison. Our unsexed female writers now instruct us or confuse us and themselves in the labyrinth of politics, or turn us wild with Gallic frenzy.[29]

In the early 1850s, Nathaniel Hawthorne transmitted the identical archetype in his portrait of the artisan Ethan Brand, the proto-Ahab whose career is a metaphor for the American Revolution:

> [Ethan Brand] remembered how the night dew had fallen upon him,—how the dark forest had whispered to him,—how the stars had gleamed upon him,—a simple and loving man, watching his fire in the years gone by, and ever musing as it burned. He remembered with what tenderness, with what love and sympathy for mankind, and what pity for human guilt and woe, he had first begun to contemplate those ideas which afterwards became the inspiration of his life; with what reverence he had then looked into the heart of man, viewing it as a temple originally divine, and however desecrated, still to be held sacred by a brother; with what awful fear he had deprecated the success of his pursuit, and prayed that the Unpardonable Sin might never be revealed to him. Then ensued that vast intellectual development, which in its progress, disturbed the counterpoise between his mind and heart. The Idea that possessed his life had operated as a means of education; it had gone on to cultivate his powers to the highest point of which they were susceptible; it had raised him from the level of an unlettered laborer to stand on a star-lit eminence, whither the philosophers of the earth, laden with the lore of universities, might vainly strive to clamber after him. So much for the intellect! But where was the heart? That, indeed, had withered,—had contracted,—had hardened,—had perished! It had ceased to partake of the universal throb. He had lost his hold of the magnetic chain of humanity. He was no longer a brother-man, opening the chambers or the dungeons of our com-

mon nature by the key of holy sympathy, which gave him a right to share in all its secrets; he was now a cold observer, looking on mankind as the subject of his experiment, and, at length, converting man and woman to be his puppets, and pulling the wires that moved them to such degrees of crime as were demanded for his study.

Thus Ethan Brand became a fiend. He began to be so from the moment that his moral nature had ceased to keep the pace of improvement with his intellect. And now, as his highest effort and inevitable development,—as the bright and gorgeous flower, and rich, delicious fruit of his life's labor,—he had produced the Unpardonable Sin![30]

And as recently as June 1995, the novelist Robert Stone, reviewing Norman Mailer's study of Lee Harvey Oswald, transmitted a Mathias-Hawthorne style diagnosis of the autodidact as assassin.

There are many rootless, open-ended lives in America and many children raised under the shelterless sky of possibility.... They are not all outlaws but there is an outlaw breed, consisting quite often of extremely intelligent and sensitive individuals. Everyone knows a few examples. They used to abound in the military, to which many turned for order and three squares a day. Autodidacts, Nazis or fascists or Communists-manqués, wiseguys, they lived to shock everyone aboard ship or in barracks with their records of the Red Army chorus and German marches and their copies of *The Communist Manifesto* or *Mein Kampf*. They affected a cool sophistication, acquired at the town library and the corner Bijou. They tried to use words they'd only seen in print. When they got out they would start satanic motorcycle gangs or go to Paris to paint or become gigolos.

Or they might be revolutionaries who, upon separation, would be straight off to Russia for instructions.... Marguerite Oswald, the neurotic, narcissistic woman who raised him in her image.[31]

As in the simultaneously self-scrutinizing and synoptic art of other satanic Left romantics, Melville's works are unsurpassed for their sweep, detail, psychological insight, moral earnestness, and capacity to induce wild Gallic frenzies in the reader. Although he may have used words he'd only seen in print, the sublimity of style and vision encompasses and expresses the grand features, contradictions, and sea changes of modernity as they emerged in antebellum nineteenth-century America: the dubious sanctity of property in the defense of slavery; the necessity or folly of submission to demented or evil authority on ships meant to represent society; the impact of missionaries on the "primitives" of the South Seas (a question linked to commercial national rivalries and the Protestant mission to renovate the world); the promise of technology to abolish toil and class exploitation; the inroads of materialist science on religion, including the threat to conservative order posed by the decline of magic; the appearance of "scientific" racism in opposition to the species-unity engendered by travel, scientific exploration, and internationalist belief systems; the jostle and jar of the new industrial working class, urban mobs, and "mass politics"; the increasing authority of women in the genteel family; and the swinging moral/class allegiance of enlightened intellectuals in industrial societies. These nineteenth-century features of modernity persisted into the twentieth century, with class conflict becoming especially acute during the 1920s, 1930s, and early 1940s—the years when competing factions emerged in the Melville Revival.

Like Melville and many of his fellow artists, twentieth-century writers and critics of the 1930s consciously responding to the rise of fascism often found themselves drawn either to libertarian or corporatist ideologies, or they inconclusively oscillated between those polarities.[32] Melville's writing is a history of class, gender, and racial conflict in the West blended with his own inner quest for an honorable moral and intellectual identity rooted both in individuality and affiliation—no easy task. Historians usually study institutional or political conflicts separately or a few at a time, while psychoanalysts may not study them at all; but for the darkly androgynous Melville, class, gender, and race are inescapably interconnected in the emotional, intellectual, material structures and dilemmas of everyday life. Accordingly, the problems and choices posed by questions of authority, direction, and class allegiance remain both epic in scope and delicately nuanced personal statements. They are omnipresent in Melville's art, whether he writes in his bluff, accessible, picaresque style (*Typee*, 1846; *Omoo*, 1847; *Redburn*, 1849; *White-Jacket*, 1850; *Israel Potter*, 1855) or his more difficult symbolist mode (*Mardi*, 1849; *Moby-Dick*, 1851; *Pierre*, 1852; "Bartleby the Scrivener," 1853; "Benito Cereno," 1855; *The Confidence-Man*, 1857; *Clarel*, 1876; "Billy Budd," 1886–91, pub. 1924). These latter works are especially kaleidoscopic, detailed, and tricky. They may bring us to question our sanity and his, because, like modernity itself, the fast-moving artist makes the ground shift beneath our feet. And here lies one source of "the Melville problem."

THE CHART

[Henry A. Murray's oss Assessment of Men personnel screening device] tested a recruit's ability to stand up under pressure, to be a leader, to hold liquor, to lie skillfully, and to read a person's character by the nature of his clothing.
  —Marks, *The CIA and Mind Control*

The simplest explanation for Melville's nineteenth-century troubles and his twentieth-century (selective) rescue can be found in the dynamics of the Industrial Revolution and the response of workers and managers to growing inequalities of income and life chances. Throughout the comparatively unregulated nineteenth century, the gap between rich and poor steadily expanded until 1900, most dramatically after the 1850s. After 1900, disparities of income tended to diminish (a trend briefly interrupted by the Depression) but then widened again after the early 1970s. Class warfare prompted progressive reforms that co-opted socialist demands with redistributive social democratic measures: the legalization of labor unions, mass education, restrictions upon immigration, income taxes, inheritance taxes, poor relief, social security, etc.[33] Melville's life experience drove him to identify with both the sufferings of the dispossessed and with the class fears of threatened elites, making him a perfect literary exemplar for prescient conservatives in this century insofar as he could be presented as a moderate like themselves: Those aspects of Melville's personality that evoked the potent symbols of the uncompromising radical puritan or freethinking Jew were necessarily marginalized as temporary aberrations or shifted onto selected characters, most notably Captain Ahab.

I have enlarged the family-centered repertoire of psychoanalysis by situating Melville's problems in the vicissitudes and transformations of the last four or five centuries as he or his critics understood them. This introduction and the first chapters of my study approach "the Melville problem" mindful of the political and economic developments that explain the discernable patterns of repression and self-censorship found in twentieth-century Melville scholarship. Chapter 2 outlines the growth of the twentieth-century Leviathan State and its interactions with industry in the performance of social welfare. Poor relief, education, and mental health policies were, and remain, acts and relationships with profound implications for the labor movement; as developed in America, these policies were weak and internally contradictory. Such autonomy as was conceded to labor during the 1930s was discreetly bounded by managerial elites. Leviathan's New Look was consolidated after World War II; its hats, neat hairstyles, gloves, high heels, nipped waists, and flowing skirts mimicked the aristocratic counterthrust to the Reformation, to the seventeenth-century scientific revolution, and to the alleged lapses of decorum and statecraft generated by the unshackled lower orders, increasingly emancipated through popular education.

Chapters 3 and 4 undrape Herman Melville's nineteenth-century life, his art, and their most important organs in seventeenth- and eighteenth-century libertarian thought, restoring faded shapes and colors, most particularly the burnt sienna of *Paradise Lost*. Newly available evidence for Melville's covert and hesitant alignment with the radical puritans of the Devil's Party, long suppressed, urgently requires that interpretations of Captain Ahab as destructive tyrant be reconsidered. This is a prospect and method that finds little resonance either in prevailing Melville scholarship or in most "social psychology"; my "Melville" as tracked through related passages in *Moby-Dick, Pierre, Clarel*, and "Daniel Orme," stands with other recusants (common sailors, autodidacts, and some scholars) as bemused spectators to the "Melville" Revival. Chapter 5 summarizes the antidemocratic and antipuritan lineage of Anglo-American cultural criticism over the last five centuries. As read by organic conservatives, Milton and Melville were modern artists and moralists usurping priestly authority; Tory fears called out the figure of the deicidal and parricidal Romantic Wandering Jew brandishing his "blood-incrusted pen of steel."[34] The modern artist merged with the figure of the mad scientist; here were irrepressible materialists whose continued presence was expressed most disturbedly in the "monomania" of whiggish liberal nationalism, working-class abolitionism, and Radical Republicanism.

By the end of Part I, the reader should have grasped the distinction between radical and conservative Enlightenment as defined above. The radical enlighteners tended to be socially critical, empiricist, and universalist; the conservative enlighteners co-opted scientific method and terminology in the service of the status quo or the status quo ante, castigating the unbalanced Head of the ubiquitous autodidact (i.e., the People running amok, possessed of books, archives, and movie cameras) as the primary source of mass death and genocide. The latter brand of Enlightenment, practiced today in some anti-imperialist left-wing cultural history and American Studies, paradoxically criticizes racism and national chauvinism without relinquishing a racial (ethnopluralist) discourse. Melville's characters Ahab and Ishmael (though their characters sometimes merge and interpenetrate) generally represent these competing tendencies: Ahab's search for truth deviates from the beaten path and follows the facts wherever they lead; while Ishmael turns back, respecting the boundaries (however vaguely stated) as determined by established authority.[35]

Contending yet related narratives explaining Melville's rise and fall (or fall and rise) are mapped in Part 2, "Tracing Their Old Courses Again: The Melville Revival, 1919–1953." Chapters 6 through 8 follow academic maneuvers to control the meanings of Melville's oeuvre and the trajectory of his career. Each is centered around the figures who have been most active in the task of dyeing Hebraic Herman: Raymond Weaver, Charles Olson, Henry A. Murray, and Jay Leyda as they purport to recover all the facts from their admired persecutor's life and art. The first mythic narrative (disseminated by Weaver, Olson, and Murray) echoed hostile nineteenth-century criticism. Melville, born a genius but an overreacher sadly fused with Mother, drowned (as Narcissus) or crashed (as Icarus) after *Moby-Dick*. Weaver's published and unpublished writings were conflicted responses to the incoherent cultural practices of organic conservatism with a modern face; Weaver transported his aristo-democratic Melville into the environment that enveloped his own work,

1917–19: the academic freedom controversy at Columbia University in October 1917, the organicist discourse of the *Nation* 1917–19, and then later developments in Melville criticism, cultural anthropology, and social psychology. A would-be aristocratic rebel, Weaver was torn between defiance and submission—he called himself Pierrot Philosophique. Though Weaver was usually mocked or disdained by later scholars, Weaver's "Face" is glimpsed in later Melvilleans, similarly contorted by class functions as middle managers.

In the second myth—the Bunyanesque conversion narrative promulgated by Lewis Mumford (1929) and Willard Thorp (1938)—Melville's deviations of the 1850s were a stumble, not a fall. Pilgrim picked his way through the quag,[36] nearly went under (succumbing briefly to Ahab's black magical moment), but instructed by his slip or purged by the bloody Civil War, Christian recovered his faith, moving up from the Slough of Despond to the Heavenly City where he joined other etherealized progressives. Analyzing archival materials ignored by his many biographers and commentators, I follow the tortuous career of Charles Olson, one of the few major Melville revivers to emerge from an immigrant working-class family. Olson muted his enthused first response to Ahab in obeisance to leading professors of American literature; it is possible that he withdrew from academic Melville studies because he could not reconcile the warring radical and conservative impulses within himself even as he marched toward respectability. Olson's accomplishments and frustrations are situated in the Melville scholarship of his most important predecessors and mentors: John Freeman, Lewis Mumford, Wilbert Snow, Carl Van Doren, Charles Anderson, Willard Thorp, and F. O. Matthiessen. A survey of book reviews from the *New York Times* between the wars suggests that Captain Ahab was dissociated from his creator in the late 1930s. I correlate this move with two political developments: first, a changing valuation of big government in the progressives' response to the Depression and ineffectual New Deal remedies; and second, fresh conservative hostility to the "romantic" expansionism of Hitler (and sometimes Mussolini) in the discourse of "pragmatic" moderate men. Whereas many organic conservatives initially had seen Hitler's policies as the neoclassical cure for modern decadence, their judgments changed after 1936. Corporatism was good, just, and binding to an increasingly divided America; "Ahab's" moral crusade was now seen as a swindle and a cover for tyranny; the same duplicity was attributed to Hitler. An excursus explores the scientistic propensities of American corporatism as promulgated by the chemist Lawrence Henderson, Olson's Harvard contemporary, organizer of the Pareto seminar and an admirer of Italian fascism.

Insofar as they were wedded to the epistemology of the German historical school, Soviet sympathizers of the 1930s could not provide a materialist alternative to the Narcissus myth or the conversion narrative. I examine the implicit organicism in Jay Leyda's documentary *Log* (1951) and his other Melville writings, arguing that he bore the inversion of slavery and freedom, conformity and originality, secrecy and disclosure promulgated by the American literary establishment since the mid-1930s: Leyda collaborated with young Melville scholars with generally conservative liberal politics; they tended to follow the conversion narrative. This segment (chapter 8) completes the second part of the book.

Part 3, "Melville, Ahab, and the Jewish-American Hitler," contains two chapters, a postscript, and an appendix. Chapter 9, "White Rot in the Melville Industry," solves "the mystery of Isabel" by narrating the return of the Red Republican Dragon as encountered by Dr. Henry A. Murray and other knightly organic conservatives beginning in the late 1930s. The Jungian Murray contrasted two antagonistic "types": the balanced and flexible good father (Franklin Roosevelt) and the Jewishly switching Byron/Ahab/moral mother. A similar move is made in the recent canon wars by some post-1960s critics of Amerika whose intellectual exemplars include D. H. Lawrence, T. S. Eliot, F. O. Matthiessen, and Richard Chase. Chapter 10, "After the Revolution," summarizes the problems in Melville criticism, noting the paradox of professing optimistic antiracist cultural politics inside the pessimistic discourse of ethnopluralism, and joining New Left Melville criticism with its 1920s precursors. The postscript "Statues" returns Melville as the most (radically) enlightened, if still ambiguous, guide to the study of his life, art, and changing reputation.

The appendix, "Repunctuating the Melville Revival" (a "Log" for the Melville Revival and a play within a monograph), first situates this study with respect to earlier periodizations of the Melville Revival, then tours the archives: excerpted memoirs, teacher's guides, letters, and other documents (mostly hitherto unpublished) that support my arguments. Identifying with Starbuck or Ishmael, some of the most prominent critics of the 1930s, 1940s, and 1950s struggled against and partly rationalized their submission to unworthy institutions; the Melville revivers alternately aroused and doused their own critical intellects: Ishmael switches Ahab.

Oxford Brown

The Melville Revival summons us to "the Jewish question." Melville scholars, both fascinated and repelled by his carefully guarded individuality, have seized upon ready-made myths that correspond to their own self-portraits as failed or successful intellectuals. If they have been Supermen stabbed in the back by the culture-destroying feminized reading public, so is Melville (Weaver, Mumford, Murray, and Olson); if they are aiming to please multiple constituencies (Thorp, Yale critics, Leyda), so is Melville. Murray's published and unpublished Melville writing vacillated between these responses: An admirer of Melville's novel *Pierre* upon first reading, he changed his mind, perhaps in response to New Deal and personal pressures. Murray not only withheld a document that he believed proved that Melville's father had produced a natural child (corresponding to the character Isabel in *Pierre*), he did not publish or publicize letters from Melville's relatives in the 1920s, 1930s, and 1940s that do not support charges of Melville's shameful personal conduct circulated by the early revivers: stories attributed by Murray to (unnamed) family sources. I argue that Murray withheld "the Isabel letter" and other materials for one clear purpose: Pathological puritanism, the Hebraic character acquired from Melville's mother, delegitimates the good father (not-a-Jew) who, as "the focus of veneration," is the only basis for unity in an incoherent pluralist society at odds with itself. The suppression of textual and biographical evidence (in public) has been ideologically determined. The Melvilleans in my study were not defending white maleness but the intellectually untenable picked and prudent formulations of corporatism, the "enlightened" *völkisch* ideology that comes and goes throughout.[37]

My discoveries may elucidate one influential explanation for the rise and fall of fascism, hitherto unnoted in the scholarly literature. Some accounts of the *Kampfzeit* and the Third Reich implicitly blame the Jews for their own destruction in World War II. Romantic Hitler was linked to Dionysus/Ahab, the Romantic Wandering Jew; Hitler's genocidal personality became the essential American type in the writings of aristocratic radicals, Third World cultural nationalists, and Soviet communists alike after World War II. It is their readings that pass for established authority on the Melville question in anti-imperialist American Studies and in the post-1960s curriculum reform that has rectified "Eurocentrism" or white male supremacy.

Since I use the terms "Good Jews," "Bad Jews," and "Wandering Jews" throughout this study, some explanation is in order. Traditional Christian images of the Jews have varied since their gradual emancipation after the French Revolution, but there is still no mythic representation of the Good Jew, nor can there be, for the "Jewish" hammer smashes myths and all other illusions. For conservative Europeans throughout the Christian era, all Jews were bad; good Jews annihilated this badness by converting to Christianity. The patristic Church fathers had railed against Judaism; it was not the parent religion, but their demonic antithesis, their negative identity. The Jews were materialistic, sensual, incestuous, hypocritical, legalistic yet antinomian, hypercritical of religious leaders, cannibals of their own children, money mad, spiritually blind, and liars.[38] The Renaissance, Reformation, and Enlightenment exalted singularity, materialism, and natural rights, heretofore qualities or claims condemned in the Jews. Corporatist Christians applied the late medieval myth of the Wandering Jew to rout the "Hebraic" radical puritan adversary. Ahasver, or Cartaphilus, a cobbler, having refused and mocked Christ on the way to the crucifixion, was cursed by Him to "tarry till I come." The sleepless, foot-sore, indestructible Wandering Jew, repentant and longing for death, was a fixture in European folktale; he was sighted all over Europe and understood as witness to the Incarnation, a corrective to skepticism in the lower orders.

However, the Left romantics and the French rural poor of the early nineteenth century appropriated and transformed the counterrevolutionary myth, construct-ing the figure of the Romantic Wandering Jew, the Napoleonic hammer-swinging little man who represented anticlericalism and hatred of abusive, illegitimate au-thority.[39] For writers of the terror-gothic genre, he was both Promethean and de-monic, able to pass through closed doors and the thickest walls: Like the repressed facts of the material world, he could not be excluded, contained, or incarcerated. To Byron and Shelley (and later, Yeats), the Wandering Jew represented their ideal-istic selves, the fully feeling and thinking adolescent who would never withdraw, whose probing gaze punctured all myths to construct accurate pictures of social re-ality as the first step in ameliorating needless human suffering. There was no Euro-pean myth of the Good Jew, then; for rebels, the Romantic Wandering Jew was Good because he was Bad, and in moments of remorse, could be disavowed by his champions. For ex–Left romantics returning to classical order, genteel religious antisemitism, with its distinctions between convertible Good Jews and unconvert-ible Bad Jews, shaded into nineteenth-century scientific racism, rendering all Jews evil by nature. The ideology of scientific racism, still extant today, was a reaction to liberalism and democracy. Correlating "the rise of the Jews" (really, market society) with modernity, scientific racists rendered all Jews incorrigibly evil, conspiratorial, and money mad, religious Jew or apostate, capitalist or communist alike. It would have been easier to spot them if ethnologists knew what the all-too-protean Jews looked like.[40] Could Herman Melville, genes and physiognomy to the contrary, have been a crypto-Jew?

Learning lodged like a faun

The Ishmaelite revolt against Ahab and the West did not begin with the massive antiwar protests of the 1960s as is sometimes claimed, but was long institution-alized in departments of English, the perilous outposts of Christian gentlemen. Melville's journal of 1856–57 suggests his appeal to organic conservatives seeking shelter and endurance; rooted in religion, they were unmoved by intestine disorder:

[January 1857] Three Sundays a week in Jerusalem—Jew, Christian, Turk. And now comes the missionaries of the 7th Day Baptists, & add a fourth. (Saturday—the Jews) How it must puzzle the converts!
    The road from Jaffa to Jerusalem in parts very wide & full of separate di-vergent foot-paths, worn by the multitude of pilgrims of divergent faiths.

[Sunday, May 2, 1857] At 11½ arrived at Oxford. Made tour of all colleges. It was here I first confessed my gratitude to my mother land, & hailed her with pride. Oxford to Americans as well worth visiting as Paris, tho' in a different way.—Pulpit in corner of quadrangle. Deer. Garden gridled [girdled] by river. Meadows beyond. Oxen and sheep. Pastoral and collegiate life blended.—Christ Church Meadow. Avenue of trees.—Old reef washed by waves & showing detached parts—Oxford. Ivy branch over portal of St. John intertwining with sculpture. Amity of art & nature. Accord.

Grotesque figures. Catching rheumatism in Oxford cloisters different from catching it in Rome. Contagion in Pamfili Doria but wholsem beauty in Oxford. Learning lodged like a faun. Garden to every college. Lands for centuries never molested by labor. Sacred to beauty and tranquility. Fell's avenue. Has beheld unstirred all the violence of revolutions. &c.—Ship roof. Spanish chestnut. Dining halls.

Dormer window derived from gable, as spire from elevating & sharpening roof in snowy climates—final result of gradual process.—Stair case of Christ Church. Single pillar as on Paris chapel. Each college has dining room & chapel—on a par—large windows. Soul & body equally cared for.—Grass smooth as green baize of billiard table.—The picturesque never goes beyond this.—I know nothing more fitted by mild & beautiful rebuke to chastise the presumptuous ranting of Yankees.—In such a retreat old Burton sedately smiled at men.—Improvement upon the monkish. As knights templars were mixture of monk & soldier, so these of monk & gentleman.

These colleges founded as men plant trees.[41]

The rover with a mixture of royal Scottish and Dutch burgher blood seems to have gone for the lovely family; like moistened Melville in repose, later romantic anticapitalists would similarly detach themselves from rambunctious and confusing mommas in search of the higher pluralism, the Great Chain of Being or the global federation of aristo-democratic *völkisch* states. Out of the many, One; "separate divergent foot-paths" would circle back to common ground. Is it not intriguing that a writer with Tory lodgings could be hunted as a corrosively intellectual and hyper-moralistic Jew by highly placed twentieth-century American critics, or that "Billy Budd" sustains a reading condemning Captain Vere? The rest of the book elucidates this seeming paradox: the Melville problem in our laps.

2

The Moderate Response to Nineteenth-Century Radicalism

"American Literature" and the Progressives

He is a diligent historiographer, from whom we may learn (I think) as accurately as from any other, the truth of the affairs of his time (for the real "inside" history is found in archives and documents) in most of which he was himself an actor. . . . There is nothing to show that he has disguised matters through hatred, favor, or vanity; this is evidenced by the outspoken judgements he passes on the great and especially those from whom he had received advancement and who had employed his services, as Pope Clement VII. . . . His digressions and dissertations . . . are good . . . but he revealed too much in them. . . . Having a subject so full and ample and almost inexhaustible, he becomes wearisome. . . . He never puts anything down to the score of virtue, religion or conscience. He always discovers for every action some ambitious motive or hope of gain.[1]
   —Montaigne on the Renaissance historian Guicciardini

We *Christians* know, that it was not *credulity,* but want of faith and of a spirit quicker to discern truth and goodness than to suspect imposture and evil, by which they of the circumcision were most painfully characterized.[2]
   —Samuel Taylor Coleridge's son, Henry Nelson Coleridge, 1852

No country will more quickly dissipate romantic expectations than Palestine—particularly Jerusalem. To some the disappointment is heart sickening. &c.
Is the desolation of the land the result of the fatal embrace of the Deity?
Hapless are the favorites of heaven.

In the emptiness of the lifeless antiquity of Jerusalem the emigrant Jews are like flies that have taken up their abode in a skull.
—Melville's *Journal*, 1856–57, 154

In these introductory chapters and throughout, I trace shifting discourses and cultural practices in liberal American institutions before and after the American Civil War. Institutions reformed by the progressives reiterate the structures and contradictions within Melville's own nineteenth-century family, contradictions that had appeared earlier in the once sturdy English oak bifurcated by seventeenth-century Civil War: the pliant branch flourished in British soil discreetly tended; the other branch, too good for this Tree, was lopped off and hurried to New England, where its infertilities were exposed in knobbed and gnarly people, stony soil, and the perverse social configurations that such stunted characters naturally generated. With our poetical Anglo-American history in mind, I will attempt a sketch of those political and institutional contexts that may explain the multiplicity of misery within academic entities after 1919, taking my cue from Melville's own preoccupation with demented authority, damaged workers, and other cast-offs observed first-hand and courageously reported with a materialist analysis atypical of his class. We start with the circumambient air and move, layer by layer, toward "the real inside history . . . found in archives and documents," noting along the way florid Tories ringed with withering inspections by short but Chosen People.

Moby-Dick was the neglected masterpiece that most excited the 1920s Melville revivers and their successors; it was first published in England as *The Whale*. Unlike the American edition that followed, the title page featured an epigraph connecting Milton's fallen Satan with Leviathan, and its last words, "Whale Song," were a final blast at the ancient doctrine that Might makes Right.[3] Readers seeking to understand the dynamics of the Melville Revival should ask whether the Leviathan State was a good or bad thing in the twentieth century, and what social forces made it what it came to be. Was the federal government ever the initiator of social welfare policy, overcoming heartless laissez-faire capitalism as myth-making bureaucrats have claimed? Or did late-nineteenth-century businessmen, organizing a national market and rationalizing their functions at the national level (e.g., worker's compensation), create the welfare state, but always in dialogue with a growing bureaucratic class of business's own making, a new class increasingly invested in maintaining itself and shrouding its operations in linguistic secrecy, regardless of larger public interests? And did such novel institutional conflicts, unique to a Jeffersonian America big on self-reliance and resistant to a strong state, eventuate in ever more incoherent social policies and ever more proliferating and mutually antagonistic interest groups in mismatched, internally incoherent coalitions? How, if at all, did factors extraneous to this institutional devolution impinge upon the development of clear and consistent social insurance policies? For instance, what anxieties were engendered by domestic radicalism and/or violent protest from below? How did the ideological imperative to carve a clear channel between the West and the Axis powers (which had also created social welfare legislation to stimulate demand during the economic crisis of the 1930s)[4] further mystify the political discourse? How did humanistic professors in elite universities respond to a swiftly changing and apparently impenetrable social environment? Could the vagueness and ambiguity of compromise "solutions" to structural conflict have made plausible to the post-1960s generation of scholars what they incorrectly took to be the uncertainty principle and chaos theory?[5] Could such institutional illegibility explain the Melvillean preference for Ishmael over Ahab (a choice partially, but never entirely, ratified by Melville himself)? This is a tall order, but necessarily addressed for a competent reconnaissance of the Melville problem; before this book is ended, we should understand both Melville's own movement toward and away from "Ahab," and the switching of Ahab from romantic artist to totalitarian dictator by Melville revivers in the late 1930s.

STEERAGE

The ideological appropriations of Melville's life and art, conscious or not, are deployed to attack or affirm institutions and policies peculiar to the tumultuous decades of Progressive, New Era, and New Deal social welfare legislation generally subsumed under "social security," but also related policies crafted by elites to counter militancy and the specter of unity, domestic and international, in the labor movement. There was no unified response in the business class; rather, businessmen were divided: Factions battled each other for control of the sane middle ground.[6] National unity had always been elusive, but order-loving conservatives had been especially hard pressed after the closing of the frontier with its safety valve of free land. With industrialization came intensified class struggle, vigilante justice in the unreconstructed South and West, massive prewar immigration (including an influx of radical "Polish Jews") that threatened WASP rule, labor militancy in the IWW (Industrial Workers of the World), the defection of many middle-class reformers to the Socialist Party, the migration of Southern blacks to Northern cities, an indignant response by intellectuals to the academic purges and other constrictions of antiwar activity during 1917–18, general strikes, race riots, red scares, a revitalized Ku Klux Klan, and, above all, the thrilling example of the Russian Revolution—all this before October 1929. The Red Decade of the 1930s erupted in response to an international capitalist crisis of unprecedented severity and danger, bringing real and spectral unity within the working class, creeping domestic fascism, then the doubtful unity of "the West" in opposition to European fascism and Soviet communism. These pressures are well known to historians and probably to most educated Americans, but there is one aspect of twentieth-century intellectual history that has been underappreciated. Under the New Deal, federal power expanded, but not in the enlightened direction its rhetoric often declared. While presenting themselves as pillars of "the commonwealth" or "the public interest," as friends to the common man, as defenders of civil liberties and racial and ethnic tolerance, as ardent antifascists, many progressives nonetheless legitimated (corporatist) blood-and-soil concepts of national, racial, and ethnic character against competing liberal and socialist notions of internationalism or species-unity. (In so doing, they reiterated the arguments of Southern planters and their allies in the Democratic Party during the years that Melville was writing most of his fiction and poetry, ambiguously shifting his own orientation to the great debate over race.)

There was nothing inevitable about the link between social democratic reformism (as either government regulation or redistributive measures) and ethnopluralism. Why should liberal academics profess antiracist curricular policies while employing a racial discourse? Most broadly, rationality and science were tools brandished by rising groups that threatened traditional elites;[7] irrationalism had been the aristocratic defensive weapon of choice in Europe. That club was seized by many native-born American intellectuals aspiring to letters and leadership in a country of immigrants and nonwhites. The immediate ancestors of 1930s New Dealers and 1960s campus radicals alike were populists and progressives responding to the depression of 1873–96; they abhorred social Darwinism, the Gilded Age, alcohol, prostitution, corrupt urban machine politics, robber barons, conspicuous consumption, monopolies real and imagined, and all revolutions (most recently the Paris Commune). Not necessarily sharing common class aims, some of these reformers found unity in a hefty dose of romantic anticapitalism (opposition to "the Money Power"). Wall Street was inhabited by the International Jew, bearer of a cruel and bogus Progress and the antitype to Jesus: Christian civilization was about to fail, Christ crucified again on a cross of gold. Parasitic nouveaux riches were agents of degeneration; American barbarians were at the gates.[8] Influenced by earlier utopians and organic conservatives, advanced American businessmen between the wars, Edward A. Filene, Gerard Swope, and Owen D. Young, for instance, were developing models for the socially responsible capitalism of the welfare state. That model was consciously or unconsciously developed in opposition to the "Jewish" machinations of either Bolshevism (allegedly installed by Jewish gold) or "laissez-faire capitalism," similarly materialist in essence, similarly destructive of a (predictable) rooted national/regional/ethnic identity. The ethnopluralists' forebear,

J. G. von Herder, had parodied such rootless cosmopolitans: "All national characters, thank God, have become extinct! We all love one another or, rather, no one feels the need of loving anyone else. We associate with one another, are all completely equal—cultured, polite, very happy! We have, it is true, no fatherland, no one for whom we live; but we are philanthropists and citizens of the world. Most of the rulers already speak French, and soon we all shall do so. And then, bliss! The golden era is dawning again when all the world had one tongue and language! There shall be one flock and one shepherd!"[9]

One distinguished protoprogressive was Lemuel Shaw, chief justice of Massachusetts (1830–60), Herman Melville's father-in-law and patron until his death. I have joined two of Shaw's major decisions to suggest a leitmotif for the Melville Revival: the paradoxical progressive gesture of simultaneous incorporation and encysting; we will see this process repeated as ambivalent Melville scholars elevate/reject Melville as Ahab, charismatic transmitter of radical Enlightenment. Judge Shaw had decriminalized labor unions in his landmark decision of 1842, *Commonwealth v. Hunt*.[10] In *Sarah C. Roberts v. City of Boston*, 1849, however, Judge Shaw created the precedent for *Plessy v. Ferguson*, 1896, the "separate-but-equal" doctrine that was not overturned until *Brown v. Board of Education* removed the legal basis for school segregation in 1954. Concluding the Roberts case, Shaw announced a unanimous decision by the Massachusetts Supreme Court upholding the right of the Boston Primary School Committee to exclude black children from white schools as long as blacks were educated elsewhere. The chief justice explained, "The law had not created, and could not alter the deep-rooted prejudice which sanctioned segregation."

Undaunted, Charles Sumner, advocate for five-year-old Sarah Roberts and her father, Benjamin, pressed on, accompanied by fellow abolitionists and integrationists, white and black. With the added support of sympathetic opinion in the towns, school segregation was outlawed by the state legislature and signed into law April 28, 1855. Prayed the *New York Herald* on May 4, "Now the blood of the Winthrops, the Otises, the Lymans, the Endicotts, and the Eliots, is in a fair way to be amalgamated with the Sambos, the Catos, and the Pompeys. The North is to be Africanized. Amalgamation has commenced. New England heads the column. God save the Commonwealth of Massachusetts!"[11] Propinquity alone must overwhelm blue blood; ring the tocsin! Not so for Captain Ahab as he took "Bell-boy," the black child Pip, into his cabin: "Come! I feel prouder leading thee by thy black hand, than though I grasped an Emperor's!" Melville and his revivers often diverged in their approaches to independent labor organization and its multifarious amalgamations; the labor question, in turn, is entwined with epistemology in an age of revolution. In the venerable centrist discourse (in use since the English Civil War) agreeable folks possessed qualities hitherto associated with race or ethnicity: Moderates were good (Tory) Anglo-Saxons; extremists were bad (Hebraic) Anglo-Saxons, over-taken and infiltrated by radical puritanism—the source of all obdurate, selfish, po-larizing and deceptive materialist influences.

As introduced above, the terms "corporatist" and "organic conservative" are used to characterize the triumphant ideology of postwar businessmen, federal bu-reaucrats, and union leaders, the moderate men of "the vital center," viny human-ists all. Emulating the gradualism advocated by the eighteenth-century politician Edmund Burke, the corporatist ideologues presented their scientific socioeconomic theory as progressive, as updated and rectified liberalism. The claims of individu-als would be balanced against the claims of community and tradition. A weak so-cial democracy was the outcome, with the stipulation that the doctrine of abstract rights, a Jacobin innovation, was out of bounds.

The holistic "vital" vision would unify warring fragments. Spiritualized but fact-loving moderates were at odds both with materialists to their Left (such as the IWW and the Socialist Party, later the Communist Party and the anti-Stalinist liberal Left) and with materialists to their Right. During the Depression, the Left wanted inde-pendent labor unions, extensive government regulation of industry, and all forms of social security (including health insurance) to emanate directly from the federal bureaucracy; the market-oriented Right opposed all labor unions and all state regu-lation. (For the latter, "inefficient" national social security programs would under-mine self-reliance, choice, and local control. At that time, some progressives classi-fied Nazism as a movement of the Left, not the Right; indeed, during the 1930s Gerard Swope's social democratic proposals, more extensive than Roosevelt's, were greeted by Herbert Hoover as "fascistic.") "National characters, where are you? . . . The whole earth has become a dunghill on which we seek grains and crow! Philoso-phy of the century! . . . The savage who loves himself, his wife and child with quiet joy *and glows with limited activity for his tribe as for his own life* is in my opinion a more real being than that cultivated shadow who is enraptured with the shadow of his whole species. . . . The former has room in his hut for every stranger. . . . The inundated heart of the idle cosmopolite is a home for no one."[12] The moderate men understood extremism as the offal of the rising middle class, a class they typed as inherently autocratic, as fomenters of class hatred and possessive individual-ism that destroyed rooted individuality (tradition). The corporatist mission, then, was to rescue society from flesh without spirit, from the rootless cosmopolitan. As philosopher-kings, they created the scientifically god-directed, paternalistic wel-fare state to co-opt "good" labor unions (good as class collaborationists), blessing its children in all their multi-colored diversity, whereas cultivated shadow Melville spurned Francis Parkman's "disdain and contempt" for brutish Indians (1849): "We are all of us—Anglo-Saxons, Dyaks, and Indians—sprung from one head, and made in one image. And if we regret this brotherhood now, we shall be forced to join hands hereafter. . . . Wherever we recognize the image of God, let us reverence it, though it hung from the gallows."[13]

But where Melville (as Ahab) merged, his revivers often washed their hands. Locating moderation in the *juste milieu* brought class power and Christian identity into angelic alignment: The industrial working class would be tamed with corporatist remedies for individual and group conflict, but not loved and honored as participants in a shared Nature, the common humanity that could seek, find, and communicate knowledge of their condition with each other; that Utopia might be limited by terminal subjectivity was an admission unsuited to refined society. Like the writing of "multicultural" history today, the grand project of inclusion only repositioned walls; it did not level them with newly imagined institutional configurations, with curricula that skilled all its citizens. Melville obsessively returned to one theme: the double bind of the would-be autonomous individual inside the "liberal" corporatist family. As moderns, such families demanded that their artists be original, self-directed, and conscientious, but without disturbing the legitimacy of traditional authority, for instance the prerogatives of church or state or ethnic group or parents and their surrogates in determining the fate of individuals. Melville felt that artists who identified such families as irrational would be cast out and on their own, a nineteenth-century predicament analogous to that of the twentieth-century unorganized urban industrial worker. In describing the evolution of the welfare state, historians have shed light on a double bind similar to Melville's that may explain one source of malaise for twentieth-century literary critics tied to similarly confusing institutions of conservative reform.[14]

The switch from nineteenth-century economic liberalism with its welfare capitalist or local remedies for disability did not occur suddenly: The enlarged Leviathan State was resisted until the Depression called forth its reluctant interventions. At first the federal government only coordinated recent state efforts to provide social insurance and minimum industrial standards; it was a private organization founded in 1900, the National Civic Federation, that united national business and labor officials in disseminating the "gospel of social welfare and efficiency." Responding to five years of bloody labor unrest (1910–15), Woodrow Wilson favored an umpire state that would restore local self-regulating free market institutions, exorcising "the curse of bigness."[15] Of course Wilson's antitrust sentiments could not endure a wartime mobilization requiring the cooperation of businessmen. Herbert Hoover had made his mark as wartime relief administrator, but as secretary of commerce and then president, Hoover returned to Wilson's minimalism with his antistatist plan for "decentralized eclecticism." Pooling their detailed knowledge of industrial and social conditions, organized interest groups should informally coordinate their efforts at national meetings. Thus moderate business leaders and bureaucrats, without coercion from above, would manage the economy efficiently and profitably while continuing to meet welfare needs in situ, within local corporations and communities; no need for the absolutist "social control" of the "worker state" ever looming over the miscegenating rainbow.

Voluntaristic welfare capitalism could not suffice in the international crisis of 1929 and after, no matter how kindly the intentions of enlightened businessmen, for the money had disappeared: Demands of the unemployed drained resources that could not be replenished by fainting businesses. As the Depression deepened and new constituencies (labor, veterans, and retired persons) made their grumpy demands for relief or revolution, vanguard business councils were formed and the face of moderate expression changed as Hoover's antistatist strategy gave way. Subduing the National Association of Manufacturers and the U.S. Chamber of Commerce, and co-opting the Left, enlightened CEOs allied with Roosevelt after 1934 gradually forged "an often symbiotic relationship" with government to create "the activist state."[16] The business-oriented Democrats and liberal Republicans of the Business Council helped to write New Deal labor and welfare legislation in the mid-1930s. But ameliorative New Deal measures, whether designed to help business or labor, could not restore confidence in the capitalist system/chaos; it was war that ended the Great Depression. The New Deal progressives had their own maneuvers and victories: Fearful of a labor movement strengthened by the Wagner Act and surging industrial unionism, and mindful of the wartime shrinking of the reserve army of labor, federal bureaucrats were joined by the newly formed Committee for Economic Development in the early 1940s. Silencing antiunionists to their Right, the moderates enabled the superprofitable war production that finally lifted America out of the miry clay and onto the postwar settlement that followed: "These [new, cooperative] relationships were to rest on three main pillars. First, big-business leaders sought to reassure the Democrats of their intentions by refusing to join in right-wing business efforts to destroy major elements of the New Deal status quo at home. Second, they moved to ensure that the Democratic mainstream would not push for ambitious expansion of New Deal domestic reform initiatives. Third, the businessmen joined their efforts and skills to the movement to create a bipartisan foreign policy aimed at the containment of communism abroad."[17]

Aufhebung

It was a transcendental moment: The roiling conflicts of the interwar period were clarified; the centrist coalition attempted a postwar consensus in which big business, big labor, and the state would sit and sup together; a newly composed and fattened corporate elite, as one historian of business lobbies has put it, was about to "come of age politically."[18] Crude union-busting tactics of the 1930s had been abandoned by better big business; government legislation would peacefully solve the labor problem and erase the color line: no need for sarcastic black cooks, shivering artists, wasted Bartlebys, or pallid factory girls in *this* roseate scenario. A reasonable, flexible capitalism was labor friendly—that is, so long as labor agreed to the bounded liberties granted by management (for instance, trading an unlimited right to strike for the right to collective bargaining). The government welfare bureaucrats installed by the New Deal ingeniously extended their powers after the war despite the opposition of the U.S. Chamber of Commerce, the National Association of Manufacturers, and the American Medical Association—first with the Eisenhower policy of "vocational rehabilitation" of the disabled (with its Hoover New Era emphasis on individual initiative, self-management, and a return to the labor force): Sick or disabled workers could not be encouraged to prolong their dependency. Once having established the principle of a national welfare policy, however, federal bureaucrats fought for and won full-fledged disability insurance for all and medical care for the elderly by 1960. Unfortunately, lacking a clear commitment to income maintenance (the path taken by European social democracies), conservative reformers, though skillful political bargainers, were forced to appease opposing constituencies, thereby dispensing a "schizoid" and ambiguous message. As historians of the welfare state have argued, one voice told us we were protected from disaster by national policies, but simultaneously another voice said we were on our own.

Historians Edward Berkowitz and Kim McQuaid summed up nearly a century of welfare capitalism and its shifting relations to the federal government: "These programs appeal to people because they appear to offer security against life's hardships and to lead to an era in which fulfilled citizens will be able to make meaningful contributions to society." But this was false hope based on fraudulent claims; lacking a paternalistic feudal tradition and disbelieving in a strong state, the American government was, in effect, forced to finance laissez-faire capitalism rather than make direct cash grants to the people. Benefits were awarded with regard to the payee's pre-existent position in the labor market: The fate of individuals rested upon the result of cumulative and possibly skewed business decisions. Scientific curiosity was funded only insofar as it was directed to the "rehabilitation" of individuals without regard to institutional constraints that hampered their freedom of "constructive" action. These twin pillars of the welfare state—the self-moving freestanding individual vs. individuals bound to institutions beyond their control—could not be integrated and certainly not acknowledged as contradictory by either the jargon-ridden self-interested bureaucracy or the 1960s "systems analysts" hired to untangle the knotted interests that still prevail.[19]

And our literature!—Oh, when will it breathe the spirit of our republican institutions? When will it be imbued with the God-like aspiration of intellectual freedom—the elevating principle of equality? When will it assert its national independence, and speak the soul—the heart of the American people? Why cannot our literati comprehend the matchless sublimity of our position amongst the nations of the world—our high destiny—and cease bending the knee to foreign idolatry, false tastes, false doctrines, false principles? When will they be inspired by the magnificent scenery of our own world, imbue the fresh enthusiasm of a new heaven and a new earth, and soar upon the expanded wings of truth and liberty? ... Why ... do our authors aim at no higher degree of merit, than a successful imitation of English writers of celebrity?[20]
   —*The Democratic Review,* November 1839

Sir, if any one will show me how I may do evil, with a good object in view, without committing sin; how I may discard the principles of justice, to attain what in itself is desirable, without being guilty of dishonesty; I will thank him for enlightening my understanding, and relieving my conscience. But, believing as I do that we should always abstain from wrong-doing; that we are to sacrifice every thing dear to us, rather than to compromise with sin; I am for standing on the ground of eternal rectitude, cost what it may. Though houses and lands—though reputation, and comfort, and affluence—though father, and mother, and brothers, and sisters, and children, and friends—be perilled or sacrificed by my obedience to the truth, I will commit them to the hands of a gracious God, satisfied with having done my duty as a moral and accountable being, and leaving the responsibility with Him who alone sees the end from the beginning. (Enthusiastic applause.)[21]
   —William Lloyd Garrison, June 1850

I am the Fates' lieutenant; I act under orders.[22]
   —Ahab, 1851

... The censor's charge I'll not repeat,
That meddlers kindled the war's white heat—
Vain intermeddlers and malign,
Both of the palm and of the pine;

I waive the thought—which never can be rife—
Common's the crime in every civil strife:
But this I feel, that North and South were driven
By Fate to arms. For our unshriven,
What thousands, truest souls, were tried—
As never may any be again—
All those who stemmed Secession's pride,
But at last were swept by the urgent tide
Into the chasm. I know their pain.[23]

    —Melville writing in the persona of Robert E. Lee, April 1866

Radio station WBAI of New York celebrated Christmas in a way as contrary
and highly personal as did a certain Captain Ahab when he chose "a short,
cold Christmas" to set out on a whale hunt.[24]

    —Melville Society reviews listener-sponsored Pacifica Radio marathon
      reading of *Moby-Dick*, 1971

Melville's later writing and the Melville Revival are similarly intertwined with
the reluctant and cautious promotion of other national writers in high schools and
universities after the Civil War. Organic conservatives, North and South, blamed
the fratricidal conflict on the insane excesses of "Black Republicans" (led by
Charles Sumner and Thaddeus Stevens) and working-class abolitionists (or their
supporters), champions of human rights as expressed in the Declaration of Independence. Here were crusaders agitating in the messianic tradition of New England
radical puritanism, inciting slave rebellions that understandably had panicked the
South. With the defeat of Radical Republican proposals for land reform, immediate black male suffrage, free desegregated popular education, exclusion of unrepentant rebels from government, etc., during Reconstruction, prewar Southern
values powerfully informed the victorious conservative nationalist synthesis: The
Civil War had been fought to preserve the Union, not to defeat slavery as a first step
to universal amelioration of the working class.[25] Organic unity, homogeneity, class
cooperation, lucidity, balance, and love of safely bounded democracy were the objectives of worried WASP educators during the late nineteenth and early twentieth
centuries, exactly like those of the social welfare policy makers during the same
period. Were their goblins spectral or real? To understand progressive pedagogy
and its measured approach to the teaching of American literature, return to the
upper-class Protestant response to the pretensions of popular religion several centuries earlier. Conservative enlighteners had mobilized to undermine the
confidence of common readers, the wild men who were in over their heads, and
who were dragging society into the abyss. One eighteenth-century compendium

laid out the impudent, reductive, and leveling practices of the Radical Reformation. I quote this classic of corporatist rhetoric at length because the passage, point by point, not only elucidates the major source of Melvillean angst but sums up the contents of antidemocratic propaganda documented throughout my study—for example, those more recent progressive initiatives that subtly and indirectly discourage the questioning of authority in the classroom or other public space.

There are Abundance of *Calvinists*, who reduce the *Ecclesiastic Body*, as it were, to a mere *State of Democracy*, wherein the merest *Mechanick*, upon any emergent Occasion, may follow his own Notions without any Restriction, contest the Rights of Faith with his own Ministers, and publickly oppose them. The other Principles which are, for the generality, received among them, consist in denying the Infallibility of the Church, and of her Decisions, unless they are conformable to the sacred Scriptures, *which they say ought to be the only Rule of Faith:* Since it contains all the essential Articles of the Christian Faith; and every Thing, which is in any way requisite to the Salvation of Mankind, and set in the fairest and clearest Light, and admirably well adapted to the meanest Capacities. To conclude, every one has free Liberty to enquire into the Grounds and Principles of his Religion, to search the Scriptures, and to expound them in such a manner as is most agreeable to his own Notions and Ideas. So far are they from paying a blind and implicit Obedience to the Decisions of their Ministers, and Doctors, that each Member has a Right to pass his Judgment on their Doctrine, the Nature and Quality of those Tenets which they advance either in the Pulpit, in private Conversation, or in their more elaborate Dissertations, to canvas, in short, the Method they pursue, and the Arguments which they produce to confirm and establish them. This free Liberty of making their Enquiries they ground on several passages of *Holy Writ*, by Vertue whereof the most contemptible Layman, with his Bible in his Hand, may boldly venture to tell his spiritual Pastor, that he is able of himself, without any of his Instruction, to search the Scriptures, and to expound the very Text which he has been labouring to open and illustrate, to weigh his own Notions of it with those of the Preacher, to examine into the Merit of both, and compare one Text of Scripture with another. After he has so done, this Auditor of his is at further Liberty to believe, or disbelieve all the doctrines which his Minister has endeavoured to inculcate and establish. If he be determined not to adhere to his Admonitions, he justifies his Conduct in the following Manner. "We ought not, says he, to believe, or observe any religious Tenet whatsoever, without duly considering the Force and Validity of the Arguments brought by our Ministers to prove it . . . that their Authority, in which Light soever they may be viewed, whether separately, jointly, as a Body, or a Majority of that Body, is by no Means boundless and unlimited with respect to Matters of Faith, Worship, or Morals."

These Principles, if there be too great a Stress laid upon them, have no doubt a natural Tendency to introduce Anarchy and Libertinism into the Church. They set the most worthless Layman almost on a Level with the united Body of Christian Divines, and give a sanction to a Variety of Schisms and Dissentions. They destroy that Certainty and Uniformity of Faith, which are the Foundation of Christian Unity.

Mobilizing the analytic tools of historicism and cultural relativism, the passage concludes that the Bible is too contradictory, too difficult to reconcile; it was written in different times and in societies with different customs; it follows that "the Mysteries of Religion [are] enveloped in impenetrable Darkness."[26]

While moderates were sealing the "Mysteries of Religion," merest Mechanicks and others were unremittingly dispersing the shadows of the past, for instance in the founding of the American republic with a strong admixture of left-wing Protestantism. In 1887, during the period of heightened class warfare that accompanied the rapid industrialization of the late nineteenth century, H. E. Scudder warned that "a materialist civilization can never be a safe one." There must be a "steady unremitting attention to American classics." Their authors, "fed with coals from the altar," were carriers of "spiritual deposits of patriotism" that will instill the "love of righteousness and the passion for redeemed humanity."[27] Scudder's religious sublimity was trimmed a bit in 1901 by Raymond Weaver's teacher at Columbia University, Brander Matthews, who taught *Typee* but no other Melville. While transmitting the ideals of "the Anglo-Saxon race" in its American setting, and cherishing our poets, the teacher should "free himself from excess of patriotic bias. He ought to present our American authors in their proper proportion, when tried by cosmopolitan and eternal standards."[28] For Matthews, "cosmopolitanism" was asserted against ultra-democratic and unique American aspirations. But in 1892, an Iowan, Newton Marshall Hall, looked askance at Western classics, unsuitable guides for the placid American mission; we want "study through his native literature of the life and activity of the people of his own country, of the age in which he lives and must work. In a country of such extent as ours, any influence which makes for homogeneity is too valuable to be neglected. . . . [We want to read] the great minds which have sprung from our own race and our own soil."[29] And lest native soil sprout troublemakers, Hall recommended Emerson as role model, the great teacher who said "a gentleman makes no noise, a lady is serene."

Few Americans were quiet and serene in the last decade of the nineteenth century or afterward—certainly not common sailors or the immigrants who toiled in sweatshops, steel mills, and tenements, working and living under unspeakable conditions. The progressives rolled up their sleeves to answer Nietzsche's question, "What is Noble?" Writing for the *Arena* in 1903, Frank Parsons pondered the lessons of history and called for arbitration and mutualism in the "cooperative commonwealth" as a substitute for class warfare and the tyranny of either labor or capital. "There is a great confusion in our civic thought today. . . . There is no conflict between individualism and mutualism. It is only a question between aggressive individualism and cooperative individualism. An ennobled manhood, under perfect liberty, must naturally and necessarily express itself in cooperative institutions, just as an imperfect manhood naturally expresses itself in competition and conflict."[30] Four months later, J. M. Berdan warned *Arena* readers that most people would not go to colleges (where perfect manhood was cultivated?); that unfinished girls were menacing hapless adolescent boys with materialist weapons: "There is the hampering conviction that anybody who can teach at all can teach English. A text-book is put into the hands of a raw girl graduate from the normal school, and she proceeds to shove indigestible facts down the throats of her unwilling class. Secretly she prefers the works of Laura Jean Libby, or Marie Corelli, or Bertha Rumble to those of Shakespeare, or Spenser, or any other passé author. . . . [She is making the male student look up obscurities in a play], the terror of the red pencil flaunting before his eyes as he writes." Synthesizing Scudder, Hall, Parsons, and Berdan, we may infer that spiritualizing males (the moderate men) could avert another French Revolution by ejecting immoderate gobbet-girls from high school torture chambers. Unhampered and treated with neoclassical values, the boys presumably would be liberated to pursue "cooperative individualism." As Berdan explained, the "national literature," soothingly forthright, modest, and blue, would rout "the [female force-fed] intolerable national egotism": "Our authors have been able to give expression to the widest ranges of life without descending to coarseness or vulgarity. With a single exception, the lives of our great men of letters have been blameless and self-balanced, teaching over again by example, the rare and sweet lessons which speak in their written words. . . . It should inspire in some that enthusiasm for letters, that devotion to truth, and pride of patriotism necessary to the wider and more complete development of our national culture."[31]

Long before either the 1919 Red Scare or the late 1940s–1950s Cold War, then, progressive educators were eager to direct youthful enthusiasm toward tried and true classical "letters" and the class harmony that writers such as Spenser and Shakespeare instilled. For these nervous scanners, materialists appeared as sadistic and deceptive interlopers—puffed-up philistines, red pencils in hand, flaunting facts and research; their "materialist civilization" was antithetical to the development of a balanced and measured patriotism. The theme continued into the 1960s and 1970s; as one "good planner" urgently put the case:

A . . . sequence involving the work of Melville might deal with *Typee* (1846), which established Melville as a primitive. *Mardi* (1849) concluded with the suggestion that the hero must pursue fate forever and in vain. Next would come Melville's "wicked book," *Moby-Dick*, which Leon Howard has called a "literal fable," in which "no one can err greatly in his interpretation if he simply recognizes Ahab as a tragic hero whose arbitrary assumption (that Moby Dick represents evil) is his tragic flaw." A good planner would undoubtedly include at some point in the sequence "Bartleby the Scrivener," "Benito Cereno" and *Billy Budd*. These products of Melville's later period continue to examine the theme of conflict between individual and social morality in American life which continually plague each individual as he finds himself enmeshed in the contradictions and ambiguities which inhere in the human condition. It was this condition which baffled Melville from *Typee* to *Billy Budd*. It is the key to Melville from book to book—truly a natural for the design of a new and necessary teaching sequence.[32]

And in 1973, a Berkeley doctoral dissertation in political science similarly concluded that Ahab, like hypermoral America, was noble but tragically flawed:

Ahab is mad because he has lost touch with his fellow men; our nation is mad because it is founded on principles and purposes rather than on a sense of human community. And yet both Ahab and America are noble in seeking to right the wrongs of the gods.

Like Ahab, America will probably not abandon her insane nobility until the ship sinks and the closing vortex subsides into a creamy pool. Then perhaps we will learn the lesson of *Job*—provided that there is a father sailing around who, seeking his lost son, rescues us.[33]

Sighted as the materialist miasma writ large, Herman Melville was at best detoxified and co-opted as a baffled commentator on the human condition, well-meaning but blind; at worst, exhibited as pockmarked ruin. He would be nailed as the victim of mother's milk, plaguing readers with his (feminine) demands for moral purity and the boundless inquisitiveness that such unreasonable perfectionism required. At no time was Melville, insofar as he could be positively identified with the romantics Ahab or Pierre, generally promoted as the great exemplary American writer. On the contrary, it is his stigmata that instruct the young. The human condition was the sticking point: A strange belief in (inevitable) human weakness in the lower orders addicted to "mechanical philosophy," alongside confidence in their own unlimited percipience, binds the moderate men studied here.

Young Raymond M. Weaver, founding father of the Melville Revival, thrashed about in two conflicted venues in the late 1910s, first, the academic freedom controversy that excited Columbia University in 1917 after the summary dismissals of two antiwar professors; second, the Red Scare of 1919 as addressed by the *Nation* magazine. In the pages that follow, nutty, yet in their view, logical institutional responses to anticipated mutiny are scrutinized, for similar tactics were followed in other conservative but "liberal" institutions and professions: universities, periodicals, the Dies Committee in the late 1930s (HUAC), the American Historical Association, a prewar organization of social psychologists, and postwar intelligence agencies. They could not describe their operations accurately without threatening institutional legitimacy; thus every human relation was deceptive. Under such preposterous conditions the critical intellect would have to waste away, dissimulate, or flee. The New Left opposition that entered university faculties after the 1960s has been forced to negotiate the same mixed message as that pressed on Weaver; if my analysis is accurate, then it would be difficult for younger scholars to describe their own predicaments without risking expulsion.

The incident at Columbia is infamous in the annals of academic un-freedom. Weaver's student and friend Joseph Freeman recalled that it started the "reign of terror" that transformed the American Union Against Militarism of 1915 into the ACLU. Carol S. Gruber, a student of Richard Hofstadter, has, like other liberals, criticized the limp behavior of the Columbia faculty and all professors who fail to protect academic freedom from right-wing hysterics.[34] But the weakly challenged purges of 1917 revealed more than faculty cowardice. There were contradictions in liberal thought, in the rhetoric of the French Revolution, and in Melville's family that Melville himself had identified as crazy-making in *Pierre*: How to reconcile manly independence and free thought with loyalty to conservative families? If we are liberals, how shall we simultaneously achieve liberty, equality, and fraternity? Why should socializing institutions in class societies subsidize processes that can get out of hand? Who decides that authority is legitimate anyway? Or, as conservatives from Robert Filmer, to David Hume, to Edmund Burke, to Thomas Carlyle, to the narrator of *Pierre*, to Henry A. Murray, to Orson Welles, to Hans Jürgen Syberberg would say, "Little man [Leveller, Jacobin, Pierre, Citizen Kane/Cain, Hitler], what now?"

During the mid-nineteenth century, Herman Melville failed to get the unambiguous patronage of another gentleman-sailor, Richard Henry Dana, Jr., author, abolitionist, Free Soiler and Boston Brahmin. Perhaps Dana's distaste for Lemuel Shaw, his political enemy and Melville's father-in-law, blighted a stimulating friendship for both men. Dana had written in his journal: "The truth is, Judge Shaw is a man of intense and doating biasses, in religious, political and social matters. Unitarianism, Harvard College, the social & political respectabilities of Boston are his *idola specus & fori* (1856, *Log*, 514)." Six decades later, Dana's grandson, Henry Wadsworth Longfellow Dana, a Harvard Ph.D. (1910), socialist and peace activist, was summarily dismissed from his position as instructor of comparative literature at Columbia University: The New England Red Prince had been blatantly insubordinate. Although America entered the Great War on April 2, 1917, "for democracy, for the right of those who submit to authority to have a voice in their own government, for the rights and liberties of the small nations . . . and to make the world itself at last free," as Woodrow Wilson told Congress,[35] Columbia president Nicholas Murray Butler announced to alumni on Commencement Day, June 6, that antiwar "wrong-headedness" and "folly" were now "sedition" and "treason"; academic freedom would be suspended in wartime.[36] Butler referred to the conspicuous agitation of Dana, economics professor Henry R. Mussey, the distinguished experimental psychologist James McKeen Cattell, Cattell's son Owen, and other friends or members of the Collegiate Anti-Militarism League. With motions magnified by the popular press, these were activators of primal passions, enemies to "balance."[37]

Cattell, editor of *School and Society*, had been a loud and unrelenting advocate of faculty control and community responsiveness in the universities; he was nearly "retired" in 1913, but, it was suspected, retained solely to cast an aura of liberal toleration.[38] On May 18, 1917, the irrepressible Cattell read a paper, "Academic Slavery," before the Twentieth Century Club, adjuring professors to remove their snobbish and mobbish propensities to please the king:

> In fact the professor has no right to hide in the crowd. It is not thieves alone who have a code of honor. Each group has its moral etiquette and its unpardonable sin. The soldier may get drunk and get syphilis, but he must not desert his post; the lawyer may try to deceive the jury and the court, but must not betray his client; the physician and the clergyman may flatter and conceal, but they must try to save lives and souls; the university professor may be "fonder of glory and vain," a snob and a cad, but in his teaching and research, he must tell the truth as he sees it and seek the truth as it is.

Cattell, a student of the British eugenicist Francis Galton, may have opposed the draft out of fear that the Conscription Act would provoke a revolution, for Woodrow Wilson had been elected on a peace platform.[39] Along with anthropologist Franz Boas, English professor William Peterfield Trent, co-editor of *The Cambridge*

History of American Literature, was one of the few faculty who supported the long-beleaguered Cattell. Trent wrote to political scientist E. R. A. Seligman, June 20:

> It ought not to be possible for a man of my training and temperament to feel that at bottom despite all his defects and missteps, my sympathies are steadfastly with Cattell rather with the ostensible attitude of a majority of my colleagues and with the officers of administration. I like peace and order and in many ways am conservative. I have filled, in a small way, administrative positions myself, I practically do not know what friction with my colleagues and the administration means, yet in my fifty-fifth year I find myself continually impressed by the subserviency and the sycophancy observable in academic life, by the parasitic nature of the typical professor, by the growth of the spirit of censoriousness and revolt in myself. This is not as it should be, but self-examination does not leave me convinced that the fault lies entirely with me.[40]

During the summer, Cattell had lobbied numerous congressmen, writing to them on Columbia University letterhead stationery; that seems to have been the last straw; on October 1, the trustees unanimously voted to "vacate" the positions of Dana and Cattell. Cattell alleged that the firing was a pretext to perpetuate the oligarchy of businessmen: The real targets were those professors who wanted administrative independence from the trustees; John Dewey agreed. As he told the press, "They smeared the whole case over with patriotism. If they had good cause to dismiss Cattell, they might have come out boldly with the reasons."[41]

Raymond M. Weaver was hired on October 8 to take over the teaching of Dana's classes, the very day that Charles Beard, hailed as the most popular professor at Columbia, resigned from the Department of Political Science to protest continued trustee interference with teaching. The October 9 issue of the *Columbia Spectator* led with the story of Charles Beard's emotional departure, noting approvingly that "sentiment is almost wholly in favor of Beard's action":

> Charles Beard announced it in his class yesterday morning. His action was greeted with applause which lasted for five minutes, and many of the students crowded about his desk at the close of the class to express their regrets personally. He was in tears when he left the room. . . . The resignation has created the greatest excitement among the faculties of the various schools and colleges of the university. Unofficially, several of the professors have signified their intention of resigning from the faculty in sympathy with the ideas of Beard. . . . [It] may lead to a secession of the most prominent members of the university.

What were Beard's ideas? According to the *Spectator*, his classes fostered a spirit of wide-open political debate. Beard's position was not antiwar like Dana's, or anti–forced conscription like Cattell's; he felt that support for the war should be proffered by disinterested intellectuals. He wanted to be viewed as an objective voice for national interests, not as a mouthpiece for the special interests of the trustees.[42] Whether Beard was a sane liberal or a moderate advocating repressive tolerance like Cattell, he had significant support among students and faculty; but the issues raised by the purge seemed to drag the rational intellect leftward onto the barricades. Worried liberal faculty and press predicted "incipient revolt," "a riot," and "great upheavals."[43] James Harvey Robinson said the Constitution had been violated; America's credibility as a democracy was at risk. John Dewey and Charles Beard felt proletarianized: "To my mind, this college is nothing but a factory, and a badly run factory at that," said Dewey.[44] Beard's letter of resignation was even more vehement, "[A] few trustees dominate the university and terrorize the young instructors. . . . The status of the professor is lower than that of a manual laborer. . . . Holding his position literally by the day, the professor is liable to dismissal without a hearing, without the judgment of his colleagues who are his real peers."[45]

Columbus Day, 1917

The *Spectator* of October 12 rocked with three incompatible pieces on the controversy. A front-page statement by Professor Robert Livingston Schuyler defended Charles Beard's book of 1913, *An Economic Interpretation of the Constitution*, from the attack of a *New York Times* editorial of October 10. (Beard's revisionist work characterized the framing and ratification of the Constitution as a virtual coup d'état by government bondholders and other representatives of the rising industrial bourgeoisie at the expense of the agrarian interest, including indebted small farmers and poor mechanics; the Constitution was a conservative class document, cunningly contrived to give the appearance of republican "balance" while actually stacking the deck against the popular legislative branch. Beard's "scientific history" had attempted to delegitimate federal authority; he unapologetically aligned himself with the Marxists against Bancroft and other early nationalist historians or the unnamed advocates of Teutonic supremacy. However, he imprecisely labeled the Federalists as "aristocrats" and their more numerous anti-Federalist opponents "agrarians"; compare with T. S. Eliot below.) The *Spectator* editorial called for rationality and unity, so the Dana-Cattell firing should be excluded from the agenda of the formal student-faculty meeting to come, while a less visible article headlined "Pacificism Was Not the Issue" quoted Cattell's suggestion that "a private corporation which now taxes the people to maintain the privileged classes must ultimately be taken over by the people and conducted for their welfare."[46]

To his opponents, Cattell's rationalism hitched to Beard's iconoclasm must have resembled an eruption of the apocalyptic sublime. While Cattell, Dewey, and Beard used economic categories to describe class domination and proletarianized professors, corporatist seekers of truth, taking the roles of doctors and clergymen, proposed medical remedies to save the souls of febrile organisms. Political disputes, resolvable only through rational deliberation, organization, and social action, were transmuted into diagnoses and prescriptions for decorous purges and healings. Disparate and irreconcilable interests had been welded by love's delicately equilibrated machine. An emotionally and intellectually mature person would manipulate the "body" to his (and everyone's) advantage; failure staggered forth from lapses of self-control and social sensitivity. The Committee of Nine was an early HUAC-type body formed at Columbia in March 1917 "to help the trustees inquire into the state and ultimate tendency of teaching in the university"; or, to be less polite, to sniff out pink and red disloyal professors. Columbia was conceived as a single body, but not One Big Union; the Committee had been denounced by some as an insulting and unnecessary inquisition.[47] Amid the furor of petitions, rallies, resolutions and rumors of strikes, uprisings, plots, and walkouts following Beard's resignation, the Committee of Nine pronounced "the University mind" quite mad and frantically cried for "corporate interest and corporate responsibility;" then, in a spectacular Freudian slip, begged for closure:[48]

The University mind is left a prey to distraction and unrest, which in these critical times may lead to unrestrained outbursts by the impulsive and to severity in discipline by those entrusted with the exercise of power. It would seem wise, therefore, to consider our state of health dispassionately before either by neglect or by improper remedies, our disease becomes chronic. . . . What then should be done? . . . This occasion ought not to be used to indulge in recrimination, censure, protest, or strife. We are in no fit state for dispassionate criticism and review. . . . If we can not or do not recognize the state of mind we are in, it is folly to suppose that in that state of mind we shall do full justice in any case which stirs profoundly our primal passions when we look upon those who are about to die and the whole tragedy of this present world. Our only hope, our only reason, our only sanity is to try to protect us from ourselves for the future. That we can do if we but set about to do it. We can not do it, however, by devising some happy plan overnight. We can do it only by patient study, for it is the soul of the plan which must be made over. Our house can not be cleaned by the Trustees of the University. . . . There can only be one leader and that is the President of the University. Efforts have been made to reform this place without his leadership and these efforts have failed. These efforts should stop. A new effort should be made under his leadership

THE IMPENDING DECISION

"The Impending Decision"—an editorial cartoon accompanying Abner Woodruff's "A Letter to the Professor," which appeared in *One Big Union Monthly* 1 (Aug. 19, 1919). Compare to Dürer, *Melencolia I.*

as chairman of a committee chosen from the University faculties to look into our condition. *The findings of such a committee would be final and conclusive, or they would create issues which can freely and openly be discussed by men who love the University and bear the name of scholars.* (Emphasis added.)

This is an astounding document to have emanated from a great university: Men trained through life to control their emotions in favor of objective judgment had utterly lost it. Farewell to the Rights of Man they say, while hovering over an Abyss: The whole World is awash in primal Passions—"we" are our own worst Enemies; "we" want a strong Leader to unite our flailing Family; and "we" want an unambiguous Diagnosis of our Insanity, ASAP. Where will the correct Answer come from? Why, from among our maddened, divided Selves in a Committee stamped by the Head, where else? Otherwise, we might succumb to the Ambiguity of ordinary Persons, becoming Scholars who love their Students and their Work.

Five weeks later, Butler received a letter from the faculties of political science, philosophy, and pure sciences upbraiding him, but urging rational reform all around:[49]

[The university is under suspicion]; there is a conviction that the Trustees and Faculties . . . are becoming increasingly estranged and are approaching an open conflict. [We want to] free the University from the imputation that the Trustees and Faculties have something to conceal and do not trust one another. It is now a great and international institution—we must cooperate with Trustees in this critical time . . . [the last two years have been embarrassing.] We have been too tolerant of abuses we might have remedied. [But your behavior has been the cause of our suffering reputation.] That such things as we have enumerated give occasion to the radical minded and the emotional to hold the university up to scorn is regrettable. [And more, we don't approve of them.] (November 22, 1917)

The faculties who signed this letter presumably had been trained to analyze institutions, social movements, and competing epistemologies; trained to teach their students how to separate facts from factoids by exploring the material world, clarifying controversies by consulting primary sources to compare competing truth-claims. They should have been relieved that the widening rift between professors and trustees had disclosed their true condition as unfree investigators, but no. They were aghast that their peers, radical critics all over the world, might be laughing as Columbia's perfectly happy corporatist identity came unglued. In the interest of mental and physical health at Columbia University, an institution devoted to the training of rational gentlemen and rational scholars by rationally cooperating faculty and trustees, disruptive passions were out and factoids were in. The "irresponsible," "poisonous," and "emotional" Dana and Cattell along with hot-heads such as Will Durant and the expelled Jewish student protester Leon Samson (one of the "wild-eyed" ranters and "kickers" pushing "cheap pacifism") could take their vagrant principles elsewhere, which of course made the leftovers look really liberal, at least to themselves.[50]

Two years later, Levering Tyson, executive secretary of the Alumni Federation and managing editor of the Columbia *Alumni News*, wrote to attorney John Saxe on the occasion of Cattell's lawsuit brought against Columbia for denying him his pension. Tyson reviewed the possibly fatal blow inflicted by Dana and Cattell:

> It will be years and I doubt if it ever happens that Columbia will recover from the reputation which activities of these two men gave her. The men were cancers. All [the radicals] needed was a few men like Cattell and Dana to give them standing and Columbia University was always conspicuous in the accounts of their activities. After getting rid of them the University was really able to make some headway in demonstrating to the public and to her alumni the war work which she was actually accomplishing, ready to perform and that she had already entered a regular program in assisting the Government in preparation for and in pursuit of war. (November 29, 1919)

Such was the social environment in which the impressionable and sensitive Raymond Weaver found his thorny nest. Not surprising, the young Melville presented in his biography resembled the Columbia troublemakers of 1917; whereas the sadly wised-up older authors (both Weaver and his subject), reeling from the barbs of readers hostile to *Moby-Dick* and *Pierre*, became brothers to the sedate and resigned professors who (with a few exceptions) had made their peace with Butler and the trustees.

Sanely moderate Columbians did not agonize over conflicts among reason, conscience, and the State. George W. Dithredge of the International Steel Car Company frankly advocated the primacy of order and cost-effectiveness over truth in his letter urging President Butler to fire the seditious bad father Cattell. Dithredge did not send mixed messages. Due process, academic freedom—even competence— were expendable. Loyalty to the goals of big business, identified with the national interest, was not: "With the example of Scott Nearing and his progressive descent to the dogs, Columbia cannot afford to cast the mantle of protective charity over a man so clearly unfit to exercise any influence over our young men, who above learning and technique, must be saturated by precept and example with the principles and spirit of good citizenship" (September 14, 1917).

In contrast, some "Members of the Committee on Instruction of the Schools of Mines, Engineering and Chemistry" (perhaps with a more obvious professional interest in the protection of innovation than Dithredge), writing to Butler on September 19, urged him to have it both ways. He should safeguard Columbia's good name by removing Cattell and Dana, avoiding future Ahabs, but without chilling the critical spirit: "We are also anxious that our students shall be surrounded by those influences which while encouraging vigorous independent thought, at the same time develop unquestioned loyalty to our country." Similarly, Professor Giddings declared on October 29, "Every loyal alumnus of the university and every loyal student, whatever position he may take upon the question of academic freedom, should make perfectly clear to the public that he does not stand by men who disobey law and obstruct government."[51] These practical men were saying that students could think vigorously about science that stabilized the status quo.[52] Here is the double bind specific to incompletely realized and subverted modernity, the contradiction that cannot be identified by conservative psychiatry: Academic slavery was masked by academic freedom. It was an intolerably blinkered situation for sensitive intellectuals, enough to call forth "radical" and "unbalanced" sympathies with an ever more numerous working class. By 1919, the "proles" were dangerously possessed of (or by) printing presses and movie cameras, some asking trained scientists and engineers to join them. A Wobbly intellectual wrote an open letter to professors, proposing a different image of coalescence than the one offered by Columbia faculty and alumni. One Big Union was designed to protect all humanity, a sublime project in social engineering: "We are intensely desirous of spreading our ideas of Industrial Democracy before the engineers, chemists, and technical men of the country, for we feel that their interests are identical with the interests of the artisans and laborers and they should recognize the splendid part they can play in the construction of a new society—a society which the workers regard as, in all essentials, a great engineering enterprise."[53]

Advocating a different form of uplift, and perhaps justifying his own controversial actions two years earlier, Nicholas Murray Butler testified to the New York State Overman Committee in its hunt for revolutionary radicals, October 9, 1919. The Columbia University president suggested that the teaching profession be upgraded and co-opted:[54]

What the loyal and unpatriotic citizens really have to confront is a widespread state of mind that is both disloyal and patriotic, and which glories in the fact because it regards patriotism and loyalty as outworn and "capitalist" virtues. This state of mind is especially frequent among those who often read but who rarely think. It has infected many school teachers, editors, clergymen and these have, consciously or unconsciously, become aids in a movement to break down the American civilization and the American government.

To combat a state of mind like this the only effective weapon is a better and more reasonable state of mind. Force does little more than create martyrs, except, of course, in months of acute national danger, when force must be resorted to by the nation for its self-protection. In ordinary times, however, the effective weapon to use with unwisdom and folly is reasonableness. This habit of reasonableness coupled with adequate understanding of social, economic, and political facts, should be constantly urged upon teachers, editors and clergymen, as well as upon any others who undertake to influence and guide public opinion. Columbia University, in its various parts is doing what it can do to instill the habit of reasonableness in those who go out from its doors.

It is a fact that the material compensations for the teaching profession are not sufficient to attract permanently to it men and women of the highest competence. On the other hand, competence alone will not change a state of mind, although it may have some effect upon the conditions which, in any case, have given rise to such a state of mind.

For Butler, as for other progressive mind managers advocating the vigorous and systematic investigation of the social, economic, and political environment, the coexistence of "disloyalty" (to upper-class interests, narrowly understood) and social engineering was intolerable. Definitions of "reasonableness" and "folly" would be adjusted accordingly.

BLUE-PENCIL DELETIONS IN THE *NATION* (1919) AND IN A BOOK FOR JEWISH IMMIGRANTS (1925)

Raymond M. Weaver's 1921 biography of Melville had emphasized Melville's romantic propensity to buy the blissful illusions constructed by bourgeois sentimental culture; these "stupendous discoveries" necessarily evaporated upon contact and brought him down. It is a commonplace of liberal Melville criticism, following Raymond Weaver's lead, that "disillusion" with the bourgeois idea of progress after the debacle of the Great War to end all wars explains the receptiveness of writers and the reading public to the ever-disillusioned Melville, who not only saw through the duplicities of confidence men before anyone else but prophesied the totalitarian dictators Stalin and Hitler. Historicizing gobbet-girls will interrupt: "Just a minute: who was disillusioned after the war, who had been betrayed, and what was to be done?"

Weaver's essay celebrating Melville's centenary appeared in the *Nation*, August 2, 1919, the year of (apparently contagious) international revolution; the negotiation and ratification of the Versailles Treaty; raging class, ethnic, and racial conflict in the United States; and violent right-wing reaction, including the establishment of the anti-Bolshevik division of the FBI. The *Nation* responded with hysterical entreaties for reform even before the conclusion to the Versailles treaty negotiations, regarded by editor Oswald Garrison Villard as a betrayal by Woodrow Wilson.[55] An editorial of February 8 unabashedly urged repressive tolerance as remedy of choice:

The process of turning the thoughtful working people of the country into dangerous radicals goes merrily on. . . . Readers of the *Nation* do not need to be reminded that for half a century it has opposed socialist dogma as energetically as it could; and it will continue to oppose it. But in the present premises it is concerned with preserving to every law-abiding citizen and organization the right to present for public consideration his ideas, no matter how erroneous they may appear. The democracy that cannot preserve that right for its minorities cannot live. It is the men who are denying that right, and not the Socialists or IWWS, who are the most dangerous enemies of the social order today.

For we live in perilous times. Privilege in Russia and Germany has dissolved, and in Great Britain is on the brink of dissolution. The people have lost faith in their rulers and leaders. Let not our privileged classes imagine that the United States is immune. Signs multiply that precisely the same unrest is working here. Deny men the right to discuss their grievances and to redress them through changes in the law, and you develop the temper recently expressed by one of the Socialist leaders: "I, for one, have severed all relations with the enemy. I have stopped signing petitions or other instruments of a pleading nature. I will endorse demands only. It is time that we came out in the open. . . . We must isolate ourselves—fight alone. This is the method by which we will be able to demand—not beg—our rights."

This is a spirit that cannot be put down by threats or suppression, and woe to that society in which it becomes rampant. We desire no violent revolution, and therefore we adjure the holders of privilege and power solemnly to consider whither their present course of repression leads. Perhaps it is not even yet too late.[56]

The progressive but counterrevolutionary theme was constantly reiterated: "reconstruction" in the conciliatory mode of the Anglo-Saxon heritage. The search for "common ground" would lead the masses away from proletarian revolution and dictatorship; against the Spartacist Manifesto (reprinted in the *Nation*, March 8) claiming that only socialism could bring peace and order, Anglo-Saxon progressives summoned another voice from Germany. Berlin professor and pacificist F. G. Nicolai argued that Karl Liebknecht, the recently murdered Spartacist leader, could have been brought into the system: "Revolution must come; not the revolution which is put through by force, but ordered revolution fought with spiritual weapons."[57] Another article opposed the "efficiency scientist," pleading for a reformed academic humanism to protect "ordered progress," the alternative to [Ahab-cancer]: "rampant Bolshevism" "malignantly seek[ing] to slay the great serpent, or at least scotch it into impotence." The triumph of materialism would result in pseudo-humanism—chaotic, sentimental, and dilettantish. In a preemptive strike, the reformed Ph.D. would promote Christian humanism: Gentlemanly art was a moderating criticism of social evil.[58] Freed from [Jewish] materialist science, [Christian] scholarship—once more liberal and courteous, prudent and restrained, spiritual and holistic—would not present a clear and present danger to capitalist and (patriarchal) family order.[59] Structural change was somewhere else, far, very far into the future.

The "disillusion" explanation for the Melville Revival has truth in it, but it has been misunderstood. Internationalism was in the air; the world was confronted with two sublime visions after 1917, Lenin's and Wilson's. Both would find intellectual support in Melville's *White-Jacket:* the perception of irreconcilable conflicts of interest between haves and have-nots, and the peace, order, and prosperity projected by the Protestant mission. Although Wilson's and Lenin's visions were apparently contradictory, at times the Left supported both. As socialist H. W. L. Dana wrote to James Graham Phelps Stokes:

> The propaganda which I find most necessary here in Massachusetts is one in favor of Wilson's ideals. So anxious do I feel myself to protect Wilson from attack, that I find myself ready to hold a position more radical than his in order to draw the fire of the reactionaries upon us. What does it matter if we are crushed out, so long as his liberal ideals remain. . . . I am willing to sacrifice those things which one holds dearer than life, my reputation and the understanding of my fellow men, if I can only contribute a little toward that great solution of the problem of war; so that my bleeding brothers may not have bled in vain.[60]

Thus Villard's vehement opposition to the League of Nations gains added significance. The following is a synthesis of diagnoses and presciptions transmitted by the *Nation,* January–August 1919, reproducing the Judgment Day discourse of Villard and other writers. Materialism was linked both to Shylock/Wilson (international finance capital, the source of imperialism) and to the Russo-Semitic mud of Greenwich Village (Freud's "nauseous juices").[61] The "hostile spirit" of mass politics (likened to "white ants") was eating at the foundations of society. Mammon, Freud, Eros, science, and cities marched past shriveling Anglo-Saxons.[62]

Villard (who had once believed that the Fourteen Points would end war and arms races) howled at the betrayal of the Versailles treaty, more or less denouncing Wilson as a hypnotic confidence man, long aware of the Allies' secret agreements to divest Germany of land and colonies.[63] At the "mad" peace conference, Wilson's disguise had been discarded of necessity; the lone wolf and egotist was snuggled in [Shylock's[64]] pocket, international finance capital. Thought by the pathetically eager and gentle millions to be the carrier of the Christian mission, Wilson was sponsoring the League of Nations to promote peace while conniving with other insider imperialists to dominate the world.[65] Meanwhile, Europe lay in smoking ruins, bankrupt and hungry. The red flame of revolution leapt from Moscow to Munich to Budapest to Vienna to London to Paris to Milan: Americans should be quarantined with a "Chinese Wall" to block the news (or "whirlwind") from Europe.[66] The disappointed, suspicious masses everywhere were tinder for the conflagration to come. Workers in Winnipeg, New York, Seattle, Toronto, Harrisburg (Pennsylvania), and Waltham (Massachusetts) were poised to take power. In the vacuum left by the fallen Wilson, the most deluded, stubborn, and headstrong false messiahs would be taking the van, pointing away from the calm, careful, and free deliberations of Anglo-Saxon politics, most plainly exemplified in the puritan town meeting and its spawn, the "honest populism" of the North Dakota Non-Partisan League. The misled were moving toward the savage (Jewish) vengeance of socialist revolution, mind control, and the bureaucracy that would follow in an inefficient, decadent workers' state.[67]

Under these desperate circumstances, what should a moderate man do? While praying for another savior/superman (an economic dictator or a Lord Robert Cecil), Villard's action-oriented magazine (with very few exceptions) put out a familiar appeal to rational conservatives. The Right, in its crusading zeal to stamp out the Left, was destroying the Constitution and every semblance of civil liberty, driving orphaned Wilson children into the arms of Jewish Bolshevism where presumably they would be betrayed once again, this time for good.[68] Similarly, by invading the Soviet Union, America and the Allies were only consolidating the irrational hold of the Bolsheviks. Unmolested, the Russians would revert to type and turn inward; meanwhile, a profitable trading relationship with the Russian masses beckoned.[69] To avert the bloody massacre of class war, Christian conservatives were to make a few needed sacrifices, move sharply to the Left, and engage Labor as partners to Capital in a Christian, decentralized, associationist state of humanistic, antimaterialist but productive brothers and sisters.[70] Alien and exploitative international finance capital (up in the air) should be banished; native commercial capital (close to the ground) would remain. If even twenty intelligent industrialists set their minds to it, conferred and planned, the problem of class warfare could be solved in a matter of weeks.[71] The socialist claim for international solidarity through "workers' control"[72] was jettisoned in favor of spirituality and a reinstated family of democratic Christian gentlemen, one or more of whom would befriend the common people: a "builder of more stately mansions."[73] In spite of the Nation's occasional support for liberal internationalism and opposition to racism and national chauvinism (April 12, 540), the scientific but Jewishly divisive suggestion of opposing interests between Capital and Labor had been discarded for the mystical but (internally[74]) unifying glue of race and national character. Honest Anglo-Saxons invited shifty immigrants to rationally assimilate through class collaboration, even if they were racially unfit to get it, quite.

An anonymous review of George Woodberry's "Nathaniel Hawthorne: How to Know Him" clarified American historicism in the *Nation*. Every writer (not only Hawthorne) should be first considered with respect to his all-shaping environment and the ideas of his time. Second, the writer, now located geographically and molded accordingly, would display his peculiar and idiosyncratic responses. These are the relevant factors of his biography. "Art," however, was a separate category from life. "Aesthetics" were related to standards of universal literature; unity was found only in the aesthetic realm. Alas, non-Anglo-Saxons could only hope to peer at Hawthorne. As the reviewer noted of literary scholar George Woodberry, however singular and parochial Hawthorne might have been, "there is no one now living who is so peculiarly fitted by racial inheritance to speak of Hawthorne with sympathetic understanding."[75] Relations between Hawthorne and Woodberry were guaranteed to be harmonious, since, happily, a similar biological environment had presoaked their individualities; why, they nearly had the same name. (Relations between Hawthorne and the Melville revivers would be as trouble free; it shall be seen that Hawthorne's insights into Melville's obsessive character, especially as recorded in the former's *English Notebooks*, influenced assessments by twentieth-century Melvilleans, almost as if a blood brother could not be contradicted.)

But such a rooted, blood-and-soil historicism would logically have to sabotage the rational search for "common ground" so strenuously advocated by progressives as the approved Anglo-Saxon solution to class warfare. This impasse was addressed six years later by the *Nation* reader Rabbi Lee J. Levinger, a pluralist and pragmatist who was the self-proclaimed intellectual descendant of Kant, Comte, Spencer, LeBon, Durkheim, McDougall, Cooley, and John Dewey. Levinger identified two brands of extremism: 100 percent Americans pursuing the "lost cause" of anti-semitism and maladjusted Jews suffering from "oppression psychosis." In his book *Anti-Semitism in the United States: Its History and Causes* (1925), Levinger softly explained that American "soil" sprouted neither Marxists nor nativist hysterics: "Class consciousness" and "prejudice" disappear when hard hearts melt and rationally adapt to new conditions. Jewish immigrants should leave behind their rigid European formulations of "Fascismo" versus socialism, Czarists versus Bolsheviks. In racially and ethnically diverse, sprawling, brawling America, unity would yet be found in the "higher synthesis" of "group minds" admiring their "ideal self." An all-inclusive God-figure smiled on equal opportunity, experiments in group adjustment, and a "scientific" sociology in which "group mind" (an "empirical fact") confers "functional unity." Worrisome dissension, hate, and intergroup violence were produced solely by "hysteria," the residual "high emotional tone" left in the dissolution of artificial wartime unity. With corrected "gradation of loyalties" and harmonized "overlapping" "group affiliations," groups, not individuals, would be possessed of the "individuality" for which democrats yearned. The national (nascently international) symphony should commence. As for domination, there isn't any. Levinger explained after quoting James Mark Baldwin, a sociologist: "'The real self is always the bi-polar self, the social self.' Empirically, not only are civilization, history and government the products of social heredity; the individual himself as we have him owes his mental content, many of his feelings and motor responses, and his ultimate ideals to the group in which he was born and has developed. On this basis the ancient conflict between the isolated individual and the group domination becomes unimportant, if not meaningless, from the empirical point of view" (32). Regretfully, Levinger's "exceptional individual," the "genius or social discoverer," was linked to the "criminal or social rebel." Mad and tragic misfits—like stubborn, hypersensitive, primitivistic Jews regressively merged with their "alters" or "other"—refused the "tolerant" "social self."[76] By the end of the 1930s, Melville's isolatoes (Ahab, Pierre, Isabel, Margoth) would be *desaparecidos*. Wholeness (but not whaleness) commanded "American" literature.

The Fourteenth Amendment guaranteed equal rights to every individual citizen. The new social psychology was sanely designed to wrest the concept of individuality from individual persons to groups: races, ethnicities, and business corporations.[77] There might be no commitment to civil liberties in the practice of corporatist intellectuals had not the bloody repression of oppositional political speech during the first two decades of the twentieth century apparently propelled workers and their allies toward socialism, forcing moderate conservatives to forestall revolution in the disillusioned lower orders after the Great War by incorporating libertarian ideals and subversive writers. But the inspiring Enlightenment rationalism of John Locke, Condorcet, and the Founding Fathers[78] was vitiated by the racial progressive discourse derived from German idealism and the ideas of J. G. von Herder, the hyphenated Americanism promoted after 1916 that advocated antiracist social and educational policies persisting today as "multiculturalism."[79] Horace M. Kallen's *Culture and Democracy in the United States: Studies in the Group Psychology of the American Peoples* (1924)[80] linked blood-and-soil determinism with anti-imperialism, boldly asserting an eighteenth-century *völkisch* social theory against materialist class analysis, proletarian internationalism, and war:

> The experiments on the salamander and the ascidian, on the rat and the rabbit, make a prima facie case, the importance of which cannot be seriously questioned, for the inheritance of acquired physical traits. The experiments upon the white mice make an even more significant case for the inheritance of acquired "mental" traits. (29) . . . The American people . . . are no longer

one in the same sense in which the people of Germany or the people of France are one, or in which the people of the American Revolution were one. They are a mosaic of peoples, of different bloods and of different origins, engaged in rather different economic fields, and varied in background and outlook as well as in blood. . . . The very conception of the individual has changed. He is seen no longer as an absolutely distinct and autonomous entity, but as a link in an endless historical chain which is heredity, and as a point in a geographical extent involving political, economic, social organization, and all the other factors of group life, which are his environment. (58–59)

    . . . *The fact is that similarity of class rests upon no inevitable external condition: while similarity of nationality has usually a considerable intrinsic base. Hence the poor of two different peoples tend to be less like-minded than the poor and the rich of the same peoples. At his core, no human being, even in a "state of nature" is a mere mathematical unit of action like the "economic man."* Behind him in time and tremendously in him in quality are his ancestors; around him in space are his relative and kin, carrying in common with him the inherited organic set from a remoter common ancestry. In all these he lives and moves and has his being. They constitute his, literally, *natio*, the inwardness of his nativity, and in Europe every inch of his non-human environment wears the effects of their action upon it and breathes their spirit. (93–94) . . . Americans are a sort of collective Faust, whose memories of Gretchen and the cloister trouble but do not restrain the conquest of the new empire, and perhaps, the endeavor after Helen. (265; emphasis added)

Researchers would not examine unique individuals with highly variable life experience, capabilities, and allegiances: more or less informed individuals making hard choices in shifting situations that were similarly available to empirical investigation, reporting their findings to anyone who cared to listen and respond. For many "symbolic interactionists" or "structuralists," "society" or "the nation" was a collective subject composed of smaller collective subjects or "subcultures": classes, races, ethnicities, and genders; these collectivities each possessed group "character" expressed in distinctive languages; we communicated solely through the mediations of symbols or "institutional discourses," and badly. The dissenting, universal individual (the mad scientist) had been swallowed up, while at the same time the conservative reformers claimed to protect or restore individuality in their rescue of deracinated immigrants. Such confusing policies are a futile attempt to impose a sunny, placid, crystalline exterior upon social actors—both individuals and groups—riven by unrecognizable but seething inter- and intraclass conflicts.[81] Although "corporate liberalism" has been derided by recent populists and New Leftists, its critics have not brought out the organicist subtext, which, curiously, many radical critics carry but do not seem to see. Melville as Ahab and other dark characters diagnosed the demented character of "moderate" social nostrums;[82] his conservative characters blinkered themselves for the sake of family unity. Why this semivisible racial discourse on behalf of a more rooted cosmopolitanism was deemed indispensable to many progressives is one theme of my book. The construction of the Jungian unconscious as site for progressive purification and uplift is further developed below as a straight line is drawn between some aristocratic radicals of the 1920s and their New Left admirers in the field of American literature.

MORE TOLERANCE, MORE DISAPPEARING BODIES

The concept of ethnopluralism could redirect and absorb the class resentments of the potentially explosive redundantly educated—the "disillusioned" worker or petit bourgeois, overtrained (in technology) and underemployed in the Depression, who had been spotted by conservative intellectuals as shock troops for fascism between the wars. The famous historian Friedrich Meinecke's postwar explanation for "the German catastrophe" resonates with the ruminations of earlier organic conservatives:[83]

> It often happens nowdays . . . that young technicians, engineers, and so forth, who have enjoyed an excellent university training as specialists, will completely devote themselves to their calling for ten or fifteen years and without looking either to the right or to the left will try only to be first-rate specialists. But then, in their middle or late thirties, something they have never felt before awakens in them, something that was never really brought to their attention in their education—something that we would call a suppressed metaphysical desire. Then they rashly seize upon any sort of ideas and activities, anything that is fashionable at the moment and seems to them important for the welfare of individuals—whether it be anti-alcoholism, agricultural reform, eugenics, or the occult sciences. The former first-rate specialist changes into a kind of prophet, into an enthusiast, perhaps even into a fanatic and monomaniac. Thus arises the type of man who wants to reform the world.
>
> Here one sees how a one-sided training of the intellect in technical work may lead to a violent reaction of the neglected irrational impulses of the spirit, but not to a real harmony of critical self-discipline and inner creativeness— rather to a new one-sidedness that clutches about wildly and intemperately. . . . A technical calling, however, does not necessarily precede the world reformer's intemperance. Men with hot heads, ambition, and an autodidactic

urge for advancement, when forced into the technically normalized working conditions of the present day, may easily lose their inner equilibrium in the conflict of the spirit with the world about them and flare up in a blaze. The petty painter and quarrelist Hitler, who once had to earn his scanty bread in construction work and in the course of it whipped up his hatred of the Jews into a general philosophy of world-shaking consequences, is a case of this kind. (36–37)

In the transition from Homo Sapiens to Homo Faber, Meinecke explained, we had lost the integrative powers of religion: "This was no specific spiritual force, but a spiritual need springing from and existing for the totality of the soul, and called upon to preserve the inner community of the life of men and to knit the ties between the simple workingman and the cultured man of developed individuality" (38).

Martin Dies and James Conant, along with other American progressives, had been similarly alarmed by the rupture in human history, a rupture that had prompted the desire for a complexly developed individuality in previously "simple" workingmen; hotheads and ambitious autodidacts were to be cooled out through incorporation into an organic community; special attention would be paid to suppressed metaphysical desires, unpredictably erupting in misguided attempts to reform the world. Class, the materialist analytic category par excellence was translated into the soulful *völkisch* discourse; thus, the irrationalism of conservative Enlightenment watered the growing field of social psychology, a developing discipline ever alert to the monomaniacal propensities of the one-sidedly educated and upwardly mobile protofascist middle class.

The Official House Committee for the Investigation of Un-American Activities (chaired by the Texas populist Martin Dies) continued the spiritualizing progressive line in 1939, exalting the toleration of specified differences over equality:

It is as un-American to hate one's neighbor because he has more of this world's material goods as it is to hate him because he was born into another race or worships God according to a different faith. . . . The simplest and at the same time the most correct definition of communism, fascism, and nazism is that they all represent forms of dictatorship which deny the divine origin of the fundamental rights of man. . . . [T]hey assume and exercise the power to abridge or take away any or all of these rights as they see fit. In Germany, Italy, and Russia, the state is everything; the individual nothing. The people are puppets in the hands of the ruling dictators. . . . [Rights] are subject to the whims and caprice of the ruling dictators. . . . Americanism is a philosophy of government based upon the belief in God as the Supreme

Ruler of the Universe; nazi-ism, fascism, and communism are pagan philosophies of government which either deny, as in the case of the communist, or ignore as in the case of the fascist and nazi, the existence and divine authority of God. Since nazism, fascism, and communism are materialistic and pagan, hatred is encouraged. Since Americanism is religious, tolerance is the very essence of its being.[84]

Dies was claiming that only Our Founder (Paine's and Jefferson's deist god of science, materialism, natural rights, and robust intellectual and religious controversy) should oversee the adaptation of Americanism to the novel conditions of industrial society. Yet it was materialist analysis that was inciting class hatred. What was to be done? Dies's remarks require further decoding. The "Supreme Ruler of the Universe" wanted the poor to tolerate those with "more of this world's material goods," but, as a Jeffersonian, probably not the socially irresponsible nouveaux riches hardening class lines. In his article of 1940, "Education for a Classless Society," James Bryant Conant, president of Harvard University, looked back with apprehension upon the old Jeffersonian constituency of small farmers and artisans: "We see throughout the country the development of a hereditary aristocracy of wealth. The coming of modern industrialism and the passing of the frontier with cheap lands mark the change. Ruthless and greedy exploitation of both natural and human resources by a small privileged class founded on recently acquired ownership of property has hardened the social strata and threatens to provide explosive material underneath" (46). The Jeffersonian ideal of a universal quality education would require a poetic metamorphosis: The Icarian hubris of the young republic with its "belligerent belief in individual freedom" must be corrected. Conant had reinterpreted the Jeffersonian heritage for the liberal readership of *Atlantic Monthly* with a palette of earth colors:

As a recent biographer has said, Jefferson believed that any boy or girl was capable of benefiting from the rudiments of education and would be made a better citizen by acquiring them. He believed in keeping open the door of further opportunity to the extent that a poor boy of ability should not be debarred from continuing his education. "To have gone farther and made a higher education compulsory on all," suggests this biographer, "would have seemed as absurd to him as to have decreed that every crop on his farm, whether tobacco, potatoes, rye, corn, or what not, must be treated and cultivated precisely as every other.... In terms of the citizen, he believed in the maximum equality of opportunity. In terms of the state, he believed in the minimum of compulsion and interference compatible with the training of all its citizens to the maximum capacity of each. (45)[85]

Notwithstanding New Deal reformism, the minimalist Jeffersonian state was still here and would not absurdly impose higher education upon the poor boy with different and unequal mental capacities.

The grand mixed message of progressive ideology stands revealed again. On the one hand, class mobility should remain fluid; the lower orders must not be repressed and made desperate by exploitative, inflexible capitalists. On the other hand, Conant was aware that higher education in the twentieth century entailed instruction in science and technology, and materialist tools tended to vitiate the authority of conservative religion that progressives believed had hitherto kept the lid on upsurges from below—in other words, "extreme" demands for structural adjustments in institutions self-evidently pitting class against class. As Conant reasoned (turning Jefferson on his head), the state would hamper the development of the less able future citizen by asking that he acquire more than "the rudiments of education"; for Conant, the contrast between the "poor boy of ability" and the less generously endowed of his class would be as rooted in biology as the truly self-evident differences among crops of "tobacco, potatoes, rye, corn or what not." The stage was set for the postwar triumph of ethnopluralism and this ideology's valorization of group identity and precapitalist traditional culture over common sense and the search for truth. Lest liberal nationalists worry about fragmentation, hostile "ethnic" competition, and the demise of popular sovereignty, the progressive could argue: As a rooted cosmopolitan each hyphenated American would be tolerant of the Others' (biologically determined) differences.[86] Dewily refreshed and spiritualized by sleeping minds, races and ethnicities would peacefully coexist in a setting of inequality and continued upper-class management: The poor would tolerate the rich, while the progressive educator would honor the individuality of groups, having overcome belligerently individualistic mechanical materialists— troublesome gobbet-girls and other leftovers from the eighteenth century teaching the masses how to read the institutions that controlled their lives. American society would remain classless because race or ethnicity or IQ, not class power, would fertilize the poor boy's sense of self and his possibilities for creative development.

Staatsnation to Kulturnation

The official New Lights were formulated partly in opposition to the irreligious motions of radical psychologists in the late 1930s. For example, the Society for the Psychological Study of Social Issues was founded in 1936 as a pro-labor progressive caucus of the American Psychological Association, vowing to disseminate the findings of social psychology to a broad public. Its first yearbook was published in 1939, bearing the title *Industrial Conflict: A Psychological Interpretation,* and included articles by Marxists, Left-liberals, and conservatives in related disciplines who were sympathetic to the labor movement; one article helped workers and their allies to decode anti-labor propaganda disseminated by the Hearst newspapers. When the second yearbook, *Civilian Morale*, appeared in 1942, there was little continuity with the more materialist group of authorities. One new presence was anthropologist Gregory Bateson, originator of double-bind theory, a diagnosis of structurally induced schizophrenia. Bateson was not looking at the mixed messages dispensed by corporatist liberals; rather, he held cold, rejecting-but-seductive mothers responsible for tying up and gagging their sons. Absent fathers were ordered home to block that Gorgon stare, redirecting the libido away from red-hot, ice-cold mommas. In 1976, schizophrenia was still thought by Bateson followers to be caused by "the absence of anyone in the family, such as a strong and insightful father, who can intervene in the relationship between the mother and child and support the child in the face of the contradictions involved."[87] (The Gorgon Face had already appeared in Weaver's Melville biography of 1921.)

Bateson had been a member of the Committee for National Morale created in the summer of 1940 by art historian Arthur Upham Pope in the hope of founding a "federal morale service"; Bateson's essay "Morale and National Character" pondered the tasks of Americans managing other societies.[88] His concerns rhymed with those of the Texas populist three years earlier, especially in the matter of what Dies more vulgarly called "class hatred." Defending the beleaguered notion of national character, Bateson urged that his concept of bipolarity ("dominance-submission, succoring-dependence, and exhibitionism-spectatorship") refine or replace the "simple bipolar differentiation" typical of "western cultures": "Take for instance, Republican-Democrat, political Right-Left, sex differentiation, God and the devil, and so on. These peoples even try to impose a binary pattern upon phenomena which are *not* dual in nature—youth vs. age, labor vs. capital, mind vs. matter" (emphasis added).[89] Bateson, the hip pagan materialist, has rejected passé formulations such as the mind-body dualism; thus we may give credence to his non-dualisms between labor and capital or youth and age. Like the rest of *Civilian Morale*, Bateson's essay carried the same "holistic" message as the *Nation* of 1919. Jeffersonian comrades were spun from neo-Hamiltonian federalists to unify the "national psyche," abjuring caste and standing with "labor" by regulating rapacious capitalists, yet guaranteeing the sanctity of property; gently substituting "social science research" for "punitive attitudes."[90]

Gardner Murphy contributed "Essentials for a Civilian Morale Program in American Democracy" to the collection, borrowing a simile from geology to nudge his materialist colleagues off the margins: Classes, only apparently at odds, he argued, were really like stalactites and stalagmites, each growing toward each other to "coalesce" in midair to form one big pillar (407–8). Murphy, a reader of Vernon Parrington, knew he had to reconcile thrusting Jeffersonians, the grassroots, Bill of Rights–oriented folk, with stubborn Hamiltonian gentry types hanging from the ceiling. But Murphy was pulling a fast one: Stalagmites do not emerge from the earth, thrusting upward toward coalescence; rather, stalagmites are very slowly layered with tiny limey drips over thousands of years; the same drips from on high produce the stalactite. When stalagmite and stalactite finally meet, they have not performed like groping bodies in the dark, finding each other at the moderate center to form a more perfect union. Not to worry; as Murphy implied, inequality was actually natural and earthy because ethnic and religious minority groups have different and diverse "taste or aptitudes or aims" but could shake hands "within the common framework of a reachable goal" (419–20). "Dissidents" must be fed accurate facts to modify their habitual, misinformed ("skeptical," 410) name calling, and taken into the Big Barn of civilian morale planners, trailing clouds of hydrogen sulfide behind them: "The minority-group member can be shown the specific contribution which he can make. His contribution may add to the more placid and bovine contribution of the co-working group. Not only in Congress and in the press, but in the planning of local morale work itself, there should be some acrid critics, *not just to buy off the critics as a group*, but to introduce some sulphur into the planning process" (420; emphasis added). Not that the minority-group member was demonic. As Bateson had explained, the natural dualism between God and the devil was an outmoded crotchet of Western culture. Ethical distinctions between good and evil had been transcended. The new dispensation juxtaposed different roles: Some folks were led into dominance, succorance, and exhibitionism; others into submission, dependence, and spectatorship.

The progressive psychologist of 1942, as Gardner Murphy explained it, would lead his newly inclusive, newly fertilized, newly inspirited crew of planners into the open-ended quest to discover *"a workable amount and form of private property and of private initiative"* (424). Oddly, the newly minted Jeffersonian was not flustered by the given fact that "the press, necessarily under our system [is] an organ of business" (428); moreover, Murphy regretted that Dr. Henry A. Murray's proposal for a "federal department of social science" had met closed doors in Washington (429). But what of acrid Ahab and his *tic douloureux;* where would they fit in? Murphy explained that isolatoes were happier in groups lauding interdependence and "group thinking": It could be shown through "existing data and fresh experiments" that authoritarian controls within democratic structures would be appropriate because "leaderless groups, formless democracies, are ineffective or even frustrating" (422–24). But the plan was not "totalitarian, laissez-faire or Marxist" because of its "respect for individual differences and the welcoming of criticism." The individual (leader) finds "resolution" in the context of "mutual interindividual trust" and in the process of "trying to mold the group to his will under conditions permitting the other members of the group to accept or reject such leadership." In other words, you could take a plan or leave it, but if you were led to reject the leader's vision, you might be returned to the toiling masses, which would make it easier, perhaps, for the others to find "resolution" of difference.

The socially responsible alchemists were joined by the Frankfurt School German-Jewish refugees in the early 1940s. Adorno, Horkheimer, and others have transmuted objective conflicts of interest and rational responses to economic crises into symptoms of personal irresponsibility, explaining that the character structure of the middle class with its falsely feeling mass culture and yen for agitators produced mass death in the twentieth century.[91] The overall project of their critical theory was to discredit excessively liberal values while subtly accrediting the discourse and worldview of organic conservativism—re-baptized by T. W. Adorno as genuine liberalism, like Wordworth's "genuine liberty" (*The Prelude*, 14. 132[92]), antidote to the protofascist "authoritarian personality."[93]

> I speak in recollection of a time
> When the bodily eye, every stage of life
> The most despotic of our senses, gained
> Such strength in me as often held my mind
> In absolute dominion. Gladly here,
> Entering upon abstruser argument,
> Could I endeavour to unfold the means
> Which Nature studiously employs to thwart
> This tyranny, summons all the senses each
> To counteract the other, and themselves,
> And makes them all, and the objects with which all
> Are conversant, subservient in their turn
> To the great ends of Liberty and Power. (14. 127–39)

> . . . I remember well
> That in life's every-day appearances
> I seemed about this time to gain clear sight
> Of a new world—a world, too, that was fit
> To be transmitted, and to other eyes
> Made visible; as ruled by those fixed laws
> Whence spiritual dignity originates,
> Which do both give it being and maintain
> A balance, an ennobling interchange
> Of action from without and from within;
> The excellence, pure function, and best power
> Both of the objects seen, and eye that sees. (14. 367–78)

According to the Kleinian psychoanalytic theory of "projective identification," the self projects forbidden aggression into an external object that must be controlled. In the case of the upwardly mobile middle class, their (contemptible) will to power is supposedly projected upon the Jews. Stubborn adherence to nondualisms was identified with scapegoating, obviously a bad thing for mental health. Social psychologist Gordon Allport denounced group prejudice in his frequently reprinted freedom pamphlet of 1948, *ABC's of Scapegoating*.[94] Allport advised Americans to adjust to pluralism by looking inside to check their "moral cancer" (7). Whites should stop scapegoating blacks, Christians should stop scapegoating Jews, "labor" should stop scapegoating "the spokesmen for 'business'" (like Allport?), and conservatives should stop confusing liberals with communists by scapegoating FDR (26). Allport's pamphlet is illuminated by comparison with the worksheets he earlier devised with Dr. Henry A. Murray for the Harvard seminar "Psychological Problems in Morale" (1941), meant to be disseminated to "private organizations" throughout the nation. A project of the Harvard Defense Council, the seminar was to be "an important component in a general program of coordinated research."[95] The materials for the course consisted of one short, red-bound typescript and numerous stapled worksheets, each methodically dealing with some aspect of propaganda, including a summary of Hitler's personality and psychodynamics that would inform counterpropaganda. Hitler's duplicity, irrationality, and contempt for the masses were constantly compared with American rationality, which, oddly enough, was derived from the protofascist and irrationalist social theorist Vilfredo Pareto.[96]

In Worksheet No. 4, "Determinants of Good and Bad Morale," the authors outlined "aggressive needs in group coherence." First, there must be "outlets for grievances": "Provision for the free expression of opinion improves morale." Second, "scapegoat outlets" were another aid to good morale:

> The direction of aggression against a subversive minority group may reduce tensions, and will be least disruptive if the scapegoat group is one which is in conflict with the total group in respect of major immediate aims. Aggression had better be directed against the external enemy, but if this is frustrated, or the group becomes apathetic, the subversive minority group may improve morale by either (1) reducing frustrated tensions of aggression or (2) reawakening aggression, or (3) displacing aggression away from intra-group aggression, or (4) displacing aggression away from the leaders of the group, if and when reversed [*sic*] are suffered. (8)

I am suggesting that the ahistoric, irrationalist concept of scapegoating or negative identity cannot explain prejudice; rather, the pluralists are admitting there is no basis for unity in class societies whose politics are organized around national or ethnic "peaceful competition." If the only unity is found in differing groups worshipping one "ideal self" (or artwork, which will, in practice, be designated by the elite), then the bad individualist like Melville will be attacked. Thou shalt not question the good parent's benevolence or the possibility of "group adjustment" by reconfiguring the social structure along materialist, or Jacobin, lines. As Sartre noted in his wartime essay "Anti-Semite and Jew," German unity was forged solely in the common project to remove the social irritant that prevented natural harmony. This "prejudice" against the Jewish intellect and its sulking reverence, so corrosive to "natural" family bonds, was specific to a pluralist society whose objective divisions could not be overcome without some measure of institutional transformation. The rooted cosmopolitanism of the moderate men, by definition masking class and gender conflicts with the bizarre notion of competing, yet peacefully co-existing, mutually adapting ethnic groups, is thus deceptive and discredits all science: Its "pluralism" and "tolerance" attack the moral individual seeking common ground by straying outside the boundaries set by elites. In the case of the Murray-Allport worksheets, those limits were scientistically delineated; aspects of Jefferson's thought were co-opted and redefined in the indispensable "Values of the Past": "The more awareness there is of the group's heroic past the better the morale. (Freedom from Old World Oppression, Jeffersonian Democracy, etc.) The more awareness of a national tradition of which the group is ashamed or guilty, the worse the morale. . . . The slogan 'Make The World Safe For Democracy' was anchored neither in the historical past or future. A durable morale must be historically anchored in the past and in the future, as well as in the present" (Worksheet No. 4, 4, 5). A hodge-podge of factors—"communism, fascism, economic chaos, depression, or uncertainty" (6)—would all impair morale. Murray and Allport understood that the ever-questioning, self-critical temper of the Enlightenment, the heroic Head and Heart of the libertarian and egalitarian eighteenth century, must be pacified in the face of continued racial or economic discrimination (shameful national traditions) and uncertainty about prospects for a future free from "Old World Oppression." Hence, peace aims were suggested: An International Police Force would ensure that "there will be a better distribution of the goods of the earth; all classes will be benefited" (red-bound typescript, 13). But war aims must remain vague, for we were a "pluralist society," not a "unified society." There were different strokes for different folks: "Disparities of statements shouldn't be too obvious or made visible" (Worksheet No. 4, 7).

Properly guided we would be historically anchored in promises of abundance and an illusion of unity, yet we were not fascists. The section "General Attitudes Toward Leaders" anticipated the criticism that American propaganda duplicated Nazi methods. First the authors warned, "The less the faith in sources of information, the worse the morale." The next item suggested "Linking of Present Leader to the Idealized Leaders of the Past":

> The more the present leader is seen as continuing in the footsteps of the great idealized leaders of the past, the better the morale. (Picture of Roosevelt between Washington and Lincoln would encourage this identification.) The more the present leader is seen as falling short of the stature of the great idealized leaders of the past, the worse the identification. (11)
>
> By effective leadership the group's latent communality may emerge through identification with the leader. If this smacks of the Führer-Prinzip, we would insist that identification is a process common to all societies, and that what distinguishes the democratic leadership from the Nazi leadership is not the process of identification but the content of what is identified with. It is the function of the democratic leader to inspire confidence in the democratic way of life, in its value *for the individual or the society* and not mere identification with his person, or the mythical Volk. (16; emphasis added)

For the tolerant materialists Murray and Allport, as with David Hume before them, there is no foreordained clash between individuals and institutions, no economic relationships to undermine altruism and benevolence: Man is naturally communal, and "society" as a coherent entity, a collective subject, actually exists. The good leader is neither autocratic nor corrupt, "does not waver, is not self-seeking, is impartial, accepts good criticism" (Worksheet No. 4, 10). As we have seen, criticism of leadership had its limits.[97] Jefferson's legacy had to be reinterpreted because critical support of political institutions in the Lockean-Jeffersonian-Freudian mode is not identical with "identification," an unconscious process whereby primitive emotions of early childhood are transferred to all authority, coloring our "rational" choices and judgments. Only the most rigorous and ongoing demystification and precise structural analysis (with no government secrets) could maintain institutional legitimacy for political theorists in the libertarian tradition, but, for the moderates, such claims to accurate readings as a prelude to reform were the sticky residue of the regicides. And where is the boundary between good and bad criticism? Alas, just as Martin Dies had suggested that the poor should tolerate the rich, Murray and Allport advised Americans to tolerate (or forget) "Failure in the Nation's Past." We must do better, of course. The worksheet continues, recommending that traditional American evangelicalism embrace the disaffected, for there may be moderate enthusiasts in the new dispensation: "The submerging of the individual in enthusiastic team work is not altogether foreign to the American temper. This means Jews, the 'lower' classes, the draftees, labor unions, and so on.

It cannot be done by fiat, but the inequalities might be mitigated if not removed, so that otherwise apathetic groups would feel a stake in the defense of the country, and the middle and upper classes more aware of the meaning of democracy" (16).

These latter remarks were intended to answer the question Murray and Allport had posed at the beginning of their book: "Certain themes in Axis propaganda are continually stressed, notably the self-righteousness and hypocrisy of the democracies in general and of the U.S. (and President Roosevelt) in particular. What's to be done about it?" (4). Virtually the entire postwar program of conservative reform was foreshadowed in these pages. As formulated in the mid-nineteenth century, abolitionist and working-class demands for universal education, equal rights, and enforcement of the Constitution would be redirected into the quotas of affirmative action or multiculturalism. In Worksheet No. 17, "Long Term Aspects of Democratic Morale Building," a program of integration and deferential politeness would rearrange the American people's community:

> Far from ignoring or suppressing diversities of intelligence, the objective of democratic morale-building should be their conscious *integration* into an improving collective opinion.
>
> The techniques of such integration exist. They are inherent in the democratic tradition of tolerance and the democratic custom of free discussion. They exist, however, in outline rather than in any ultimate or perhaps even very high state of development. (4) . . . [Quoting Gordon Allport:] Our pressure groups are loud, their protests vehement and our method of electioneering bitter and sometimes vicious. In the process of becoming self-reliant Americans have lost respect, docility, and trust in relation to their leaders. Our habit of unbridled criticism, though defended as a basic right, brings only a scant sense of security to ourselves in an emergency, and actively benefits the enemies of the nation. (5)

And one such source of insecurity (subversion) was antiwar education and pacifism: "Insofar as the disapproval of war was based on a rejection of imperialist patriotism, it engendered war-cynicism" (red-bound typescript, 4). Murray and Allport seem to be saying that involvement in the war could not be legitimated as an anti-imperialist intervention, nor could there be any other appeal to democratic reason. Leaders, past and present, would have to be idealized; all criticism bridled in the interest of "integration." The disaffected should moderate their demands, settling for mitigation, not relief. And if, despite the neoprogressive prescriptions, the road to national unity remained rocky, scapegoating, properly guided by social scientific principles, would certainly deflect aggression away from ruling groups.

Our University is now in the hands of reactionaries.[98]

—Ernest Kalibala, graduate student in the Harvard Department of
Sociology, to Ralph J. Bunche, August 30, 1943

The famous Harvard Report *General Education in a Free Society* (1945) addressed the "explosive growth" of high schools populated by the working class. Fellow-feeling, common ground, and common standards as conceived in traditional culture would bind potentially wayward youth, protecting them from the atomizing society made even more divisive and menacing by the baleful influence of mass media. Moreover, the Murray-Allport (depoliticized, irrationalist) interpretation of mass politics informed their efforts: Youth revolts were exacerbated by "extreme skepticism." The report asked,

> How far should we go in the direction of the open mind? Especially after the first World War, liberals were sometimes too distrustful of enthusiasm and were inclined to abstain from committing themselves as though there were something foolish, even shameful in belief. Yet especially with youth, which is ardent and enthusiastic, open-mindedness without belief is apt to lead to the opposite extreme of fanaticism. We can all perhaps recall young people of our acquaintance who from a position of extreme skepticism, and indeed because of that position, fell an easy prey to fanatical gospels. It seems that nature abhors an intellectual vacuum. A measure of belief is necessary in order to preserve the quality of the open mind. If toleration is not to become nihilism, if conviction is not to become dogmatism, if criticism is not to become cynicism, each must have something of the other.

Like the rest of the report, this statement co-opts the language of enlightenment, but whenever it gets down to cases, actually mentioning writers and documents, those "landmarks" or critical methods of the Western heritage that point to possible irreconcilable structural conflicts are missing. The double bind operating at Columbia University in 1917 was in full force: There shall be no contradiction between "belief" and the open mind.[99]

Harvard has not gone out of its way to publicize the Allport-Murray contribution to "civilian morale." In a 1995 exhibition of photographs celebrating Harvard's participation in the war effort, mounted near the entrance to Harvard University Archives, neither Murray nor Allport was represented. Similarly, the fall 1995 issue of *Harvard Magazine* featured "Harvard in World War II" but omitted the university's role in psychological warfare at home: Gordon Allport was mentioned once in connection with army propaganda and Murray was invisible, while rationales for American involvement described a fight for "liberty," not democracy.[100]

[Richard Evans to Gordon Allport] Since most of our students [at Harvard] begin the study of psychology by reading Freud, it might be profitable to begin by hearing your reaction to some of Freud's ideas and work. I understand you actually met Freud on one occasion, and I wonder if you would tell about this meeting.

[Gordon Allport] *My one encounter with Freud did not turn out to be very significant for my professional development,* but I'll tell the story briefly. Not long after I finished college, I found myself in Vienna where Freud was not as renowned as he became later. At any rate, I wrote him a note announcing that I was in Vienna, and that he no doubt would be very glad to know it. He was very courteous and sent me a hand-written note inviting me to his office at a stated time. So I went to the famous Burggasser office which was papered in red burlap and decorated with pictures of dreams. At exactly the appointed time, Freud opened the door of his inner office, invited me in smilingly, sat down, and said nothing. It suddenly occurred to me that it was up to me to have a reason for calling on him, but I actually didn't have any. I was just curious.[101] I fished around in my mind and came up with an event which occurred on the tramcar on the way to his office that I thought would interest him. There had been a little boy about four years old who obviously had already developed a dirt phobia. His mother was a *Hausfrau*, well starched and very prim, and the little boy would say he didn't want to sit there; it was dirty. He didn't want that man to sit next to him; he was dirty. And so it went throughout the whole trip. I thought this might interest Freud since the phobia seemed to be set so early in this case. He listened till I finished; then he fixed his very therapeutic eyes on me and said, "and was this little boy you?" It honestly was not, but I felt guilty. At any rate, I managed to change the conversation. In thinking over the experience, it impressed me that Freud's tendency was to see pathological trends, and since most of the people who came to see him were patients, it was natural that he'd think I was a patient and break down my defenses in order to get on with the business. Actually, he mistook my motives in this case. Had he said to himself that I was a brassy American youth imposing on his good nature and time, he would have been fairly correct. But to ascribe my motivation to unconscious motives as he did in this case was definitely wrong. *As I thought over the experience in subsequent years, it occurred to me that there might be a place for another type of theory to account for personality and motivation.* (Emphasis added.)

[Allport reflecting on the 1950s concerns with conformity]—I'm inclined to think that the challenge to the healthy person is to learn to play the game where necessary, to meet the requirements of the culture, and still to have integrity, to maintain some self-objectification, and not to lose his personal values and commitments. It becomes more and more difficult to do, but I believe it can be done. It implies that the personality of the future will operate under more of a strain, but we don't know yet what the actual potentiality of human development can be. We may be able to eat our cake and have it too by playing the organization game while remaining the individual of integrity and personal commitment.[102]

I have attempted to create a political context for the controversies surrounding the life and art of Herman Melville. Ahab became Melville in institutions held to be implicitly critical and self-critical, but where the perimeters of dissent were not always explicitly delineated, or where individuality was flaunted in one breath, taunted in the next. The consequence was the construction of a crumbling national monument to American literature, unable to withstand the delegitimating gaze of its radical critics suspicious of claims to unbounded cultural freedom in the playgrounds of the new social sciences. Here is a recently declassified government document of the 1950s Cold War. Progressive psychologists were now installed in the executive branch, meeting the propaganda offensive of the Soviet Union that was attacking hypocrisy in American foreign and domestic policy. The Psychological Strategy Board (PSB), an agency attached to the National Security Council from 1951 to 1953, was frankly manipulative in its intentions to sway foreign opinion. Eisenhower appointed a New York attorney, William H. Jackson, ex-deputy director of the CIA, to investigate the PSB. After a five-month investigation, the Jackson Committee condemned the creation of propaganda in favor of the dissemination of accurate "information" that the recipient could take or leave; we would tell the truth and find common ground. The PSB dissolved, its functions absorbed by the U.S. Information Agency. Jackson, a liberal opposing "discrimination," was attempting to craft an image of wide-open critical spaces in the American character. One recently declassified document from his committee report, however, suggests that some liberals practice censorship in one breath, while (sort of) condemn it in another:

The American film industry, working with [words deleted] and FBI, has cooperated in removing communists from production units and in withholding contracts until unions provide non-communist labor. With their huge overseas investments, American companies can assist materially in combating communist infiltration of the film industry abroad. . . . Many films have been damaging to U.S. interests.

[Paragraph redacted]

While the government should guard against distributing or aiding in the distribution of subversive books, it should not hesitate to facilitate the distribution of books which contain justified criticism of one phase or another of American life. In fact, if it does not reflect this type of criticism of American life, institutions and officials it is not presenting a true picture of America.[103]

Imagine an unterrified democrat's response to such vagueness. Which films were damaging to U.S. interests? The paragraph that might have named names has been blacked out. And what were those interests, since the government was hotly divided over foreign policy? But we should be able to guess what criticism is justified and what criticism is outside the pale, since conservative reformers had been beating the boundaries since the English Civil War. That celebrated "skeptic" David Hume (a Tory) found truth and certainty solely in the moderate middle, a terrain where perfectionist libertarians (the Whigs) refused to venture:

> The whig party, for a course of near seventy years, has, almost without interruption, enjoyed the whole authority of government; and no honors or offices could be obtained but by their countenance and protection. But this event, which in some particulars has been advantageous to the state, has proved destructive to the truth of history, and has established many gross falsehoods, which it is unaccountable how any civilized nation could have embraced with regard to its domestic occurrences. Compositions the most despicable, both for style and matter, have been extolled, and propagated, and read; as if they had equaled the most celebrated remains of antiquity. And forgetting that a regard to liberty, though a laudable passion, ought commonly to be subordinated to a reverence for established government, the prevailing faction has celebrated only the partisans of the former, who pursued as their object the perfection of civil society, and has extolled them at the expense of their antagonists, who maintained those maxims that are essential to its very existence. But extremes of all kinds are to be avoided; and though no one will ever please either faction by moderate opinions, it is there we are most likely to meet with truth and certainty.[104]

Instructed by bitter experience, Melville thought there might be a gap between republican theory and practice, a theme reiterated throughout his texts, but most certainly in *The Confidence-Man* (1857). Thomas Fry, nicknamed Happy Tom, a man with wizened legs swinging on his crutches, has been regaling "the herb-doctor" with the history of his infirmity. Fry describes an incident at a "political meeting at the park" during which a "pavior" (a street paver) had undertaken something beyond his strength: defending himself against a gentleman who had been pushing him around. The pavior dared to push back, inflaming the wrath of the gent, who boldly skewered the unarmed man with his sword-cane. The pavior died but the gent got off, presented with a gold watch instead of the jail sentence he deserved. Why? Because he had powerful friends in court. Meanwhile Happy Tom, the hapless witness to the crime, had testified against the gent, but no one ever believes him; like the pavior, he lacks "friends." Even before the trial, Tom had been sent to jail simply because he was a witness to an upper-class outrage, or so Melville hints. In the Tombs, Tom's legs were pickled by the cold and damp; now he is a cripple. With the end of the story, unfree Fry's expression changes: "[Fry's] countenance capriciously put on a morose ogreness. To kindly questions he gave no kindly answers. Unhandsome notions were thrown about 'free Ameriky,' as he sarcastically called his country. These seemed to disturb and pain the herb-doctor, who, after an interval of thoughtfulness, gravely addressed him in these words" (the herb doctor will reply to Happy Tom's corrosive account of differential justice for rich and poor in the high hushed tones of the liberal social pathologist or Martin Dies):

> "You, my worthy friend, to my concern, have reflected upon the government under which you live and suffer. Where is your patriotism? Where your gratitude? True, the charitable may find something in your case, as you put it, partly to account for such reflections as coming from you. Still, be the facts how they may, your reflections are none the less unwarrantable. Grant, for a moment, that your experiences are as you give them; in which case I would admit that government might be thought to have more or less to do with what seems undesirable in them. But it is never to be forgotten that human government, being subordinate to the divine, must needs, therefore, in its degree, partake of the characteristics of the divine. That is, while in general efficacious to human happiness, the world's law may yet, in some cases, have, to the eye of reason, an unequal operation, just as, in the same imperfect view, some inequalities may appear in the operations of heaven's law; nevertheless, to one who has a right confidence, final benignity is, in every instance, as sure with the one law as the other. I expound the point at some length, because these are the considerations, my poor fellow, which weighed as they merit, will enable you to sustain with unimpaired trust the apparent calamities which are yours."
>
> "What do you talk your hog-latin to me for?" cried the cripple, who, throughout the address, betrayed the most illiterate obduracy and, with an incensed look, anew he swung himself. (98)

Differential justice as sighted by the poor was more apparent than real; human government partook of the overarching rainbow, the benignant divine, though at times it may not look that way. The herb doctor's educated suspicion of distorted perceptions in the lower orders would be matched by the Dies Committee and other corporatist bodies under God. The scowl must go: Let there be light. The English Civil War, the Enlightenment, the American and French Revolutions, and the American Civil War had all undermined the legitimacy of traditional elites. It is impossible to understand the trajectory of Melville studies without tailing the herb doctors, who, apparently without a twinge, attempt to erase radical puritanism, individuality, and epistemological materialism (or any other romantic break with the past) while maintaining the appearance of cultural freedom and relentless self- and social criticism.[105] The outcome of their searching examinations has often been a renewed and firmer attachment to the pacifistic Christian humanism that masks the most ruthless pragmatism.

Unresolved disputes in Melville studies are enmeshed in the longevity of Melville's youthful defiance; thus his intellectual and emotional histories determine his credibility as either radical or conservative social critic. Had Homo Sapiens not repudiated Homo Faber with his epilogue to *Moby-Dick,* and had "free Ameriky" not been defined by social psychologists as antithetical to the Soviet Union, the Melville Revival might have drooped with the death of Raymond Weaver in 1948. T. S. Eliot, modernist poet and editor of the vanguard arts magazine *The Criterion,* was F. O. Matthiessen's model intellectual at the end of the 1930s. The following excerpt from Eliot's Page-Barbour Lectures at the University of Virginia in 1933 precisely summarizes the application of neoclassicism to the American landscape. (It could have been written by a character in *Clarel:* Ungar, expatriate mercenary for the Turks, an ex-Confederate soldier with Indian and Catholic blood. Though he opposed slavery, Ungar railed against the the loss of upper-class life in the American Civil War—also against Anglo-Saxon imperialism, the industrial capitalism that was crooking the backs of present-day Hughs of Lincoln, and other excrescences of the Reformation in its left-wing variant):

> The Civil War was certainly the greatest disaster in the whole of American history; it is just as certainly a disaster from which the country has never recovered, and perhaps never will. We are always too ready to assume that the good effects of wars, if any, abide permanently, while the ill effects are obliterated by time. Yet I think that the chances for the reestablishment of a native culture are perhaps better here than in New England. You are farther away from New York, you have been less industrialized and less invaded by foreign races; and you have more opulent soil. . . . [A] long struggle of adaptation between man and his environment has brought out the best qualities of both;

in which the landscape has been moulded by numerous generations of one race, and in which the landscape in turn has modified the race to its own character. And those New England mountains seemed to me to give evidence of a human success so meagre and transitory as to be more desperate than desert. . . .

It is not of advantage to us to indulge a sentimental attitude toward the past. For one thing, in even the best living tradition there is always a mixture of good and bad, and much that deserves criticism; and for another, tradition is not feeling alone. Nor can we safely, without very critical examination, dig ourselves in stubbornly to a few dogmatic notions, for what is a healthy belief at one time may, unless it is one of the few fundamental things, be a pernicious prejudice at another. Nor should we cling to tradition as a way of asserting our superiority over less favored peoples. What we can do is to use our minds, remembering that a tradition without intelligence is not worth having, to discover what is the best life for us not as a political abstraction, but as a particular people in a particular place; what in the past is worth preserving and what should be rejected; and what conditions, within our power to bring about, would foster the society that we desire. Stability is obviously necessary. You are hardly likely to develop tradition except where the bulk of the population is relatively so well off where it is that it has no incentive or pressure to move about. The population should be homogeneous; where two or more cultures exist in the same place they are likely to become fiercely self-conscious or both to become adulterate. What is still more important is unity of religious background; and reasons of race and religion combine to make any large number of free-thinking Jews undesirable. There must be a proper balance between urban and rural, industrial and agricultural development. And a spirit of excessive tolerance is to be deprecated. We must also remember that—in spite of every means of transport that may be devised— the local community must always be the most permanent, and the concept of the nation is by no means fixed and invariable. It is, so to speak, only one fluctuating circle of loyalties between the center of the family, and the periphery of humanity entire. Its strength and geographical size depend on the comprehensiveness of the way of life which can harmonize parts with distinctive local characteristics of their own. When it becomes no more than a centralized machinery it may affect some of its parts to their detriment; and we get the regional movements which have appeared within recent years. It is only a law of nature, that local patriotism, when it represents a distinct tradition and culture, takes precedence over a more abstract national patriotism. This remark should carry more weight for being uttered by a Yankee.[106]

Seguid vuestro jefe

Though he is often labeled as reactionary, Eliot's is the voice of the forward-looking middle way, inflected by the anti-elitist, socially responsible critical spirit. The target is nostalgia and melancholy, the inflexible conservative or decadent molded by the machine-saddened hills of New England—a landscape polluted by mongrel New York and/or boundary-blurring "free-thinking Jews." The "Yankee" Eliot prefers democratic pluralism without the ostensibly corrosive analytic procedures required by a rational democracy. His updated feudal localism would infuse New Criticism and, later, New Historicism, critical methodologies generally held to be at odds, but which are both part of the organic conservative tradition, similarly asserted against "reductive" positivist/materialist analysis. Historians see the progressives as conservative reformers, but this judgment does not say enough about the antisemitism that dots their eyes. I have tried to show the confused quality of progressive thought in its futile attempts to reconcile scientific truth and conservative order. Since the unbounded criticism associated with freethinking Jews was *verboten*, New Critics would aestheticize the contradictions they could not resolve without structural transformation. Masterpieces were time-tested artworks whose forms expressed the successful adaptation of a people to its peculiar physical environment over time; their aesthetic contemplation would moderate the actions of hotheaded romantics, building bridges over the abyss. Following the lead of Aristotle and Longinus, the New Critic understood that great and enduring literature could assimilate heterogeneous, exogenous elements into coherent organic wholes;[107] the Catholic pluralist formulations of the New Critics were congruent with the managerial (but utopian) model of society proposed by Talcott Parsons and his associates at Harvard (including Murray and Allport), later the demand for "inclusiveness" in multiculturalist circles. As Austin Warren explained in 1941, "A work is praised for its unity, but implied is a diversity to be unified; [praised] for its variety, but the variety implies a continuity to be varied. Similarly, coherence, or consistency, implies some refractorily various matter which is to be brought, through mastery, into an agreeable order" (*Literary Scholarship*, 158–59). That is, a progressive should understand that there is always common ground, a basis for compromise and cooperation, were antagonists to be sufficiently exacting in their critical scrutiny of impending conflicts. Freethinking Jews, that critical mass of refractory, amoral, and disagreeable materialists spotting irreconcilable contradictions and double binds, would remain unmastered; naturally the masterless men must undermine the moderates' program of preventive politics.

At the close of the 1930s, T. S. Eliot, despairing and demoralized, regretted the time he had wasted discussing communism during his twenty-two-year editorship of *The Criterion:* "I can only say that I was commenting on ideas, or the lack of them, and not engaging in political prophecy. I was concerned with ideas chiefly as they originated in, or penetrated to, England; and the version of fascism, which was offered locally, appeared to have no great intellectual interest—and what is perhaps more important, was not sufficiently adaptable to be grafted onto the stock of To- ryism—whereas communism flourished because it grew so easily on the Liberal root."[108] The new critical theory was intended to connect history and literature, but the preferred literary history corrected Whiggish ideas of progress: For the human- ists, societies, like seeds, germinated and luxuriated, then dropped to the mold, overcome by the war-making propensities of overly desirous urban mobs (misled by demagogues) while irresponsible elites languished in stupefied consumerism, neglecting their paternal responsibilities. Thus the New Criticism was a retrospec- tive diagnosis directed at these bad fathers, not at the wild children who could not have helped themselves and who had taken over. As a political prophet, T. S. Eliot looked ahead and saw, as Melville would say, nothing but "corpses of calamity" as freethinking materialism of the liberals flowed into the grafted communist sprig. Eliot hoped that underground little magazines, priced within the reach of starving and rejected intellectuals and artists, would produce more endurable hybrids.

The attempt by "moderates" to repair societies riven with misdirected class an- tagonisms (as they saw them) link Harvard sociologists and New Critics (despite their pessimism) to the more resilient sector of the European Right, instructed by their hidebound reactionary or libertine or otherwise distracted forebears in an age of revolution. Some post-1960s radicals write or create policy in this antidemocratic and antisemitic tradition while confident that they are antifascist, antiracist, and antistatist. We shall see unhappy scholars in both factions of Melville scholarship display their malaise in feminized and jewified "free Ameriky." In some respects, they will have followed their leader.

3

The Fatal Line

Who Was Isabel? What Was His Problem?

This is his inheritance—this symbol of command! and I swell out to think of it. Yet just now I fondled the conceit that Pierre was so sweetly docile! Here sure is a most strange inconsistency! For is sweet docility a general's badge? and is this baton but a distaff then?—Here's something widely wrong. Now I almost wish him otherwise than sweet and docile to me, seeing that it must be hard for man to be an uncompromising hero and a commander among his race, and yet never ruffle any domestic brow. Pray heaven he show his heroicness in some smooth way of favoring fortune, not to be called out to be a hero of some dark hope forlorn;—of some dark hope forlorn, whose cruelness makes a savage of a man. Give him, O God, regardful gales! Fan him with unwavering prosperities! So shall he remain all docility to me, and prove a haughty hero to the world!

> —Mary Glendinning, daughter of a major general, broods over a mixed message delivered to her son; she is holding her late father's baton. (*Pierre*, 20)

Scarce know I what I have written. Yet will I write thee the fatal line, and leave all the rest to thee, Pierre my brother.

> —Isabel to Pierre (*Pierre*, 64)

"Oh! falsely guided in the days of my Joy, am I now truly guided in this night of my grief?—I will be a raver, and none shall stay me! I will lift my hand in fury, for am I not struck? I will be bitter in my breath, for is not this cup of gall? Thou Black Knight, that with visor down, thus confrontest me, and mockest at me: lo! I strike through thy helm, and will see thy face be it

Gorgon!—Let me go, ye fond affections; all piety leave me;—I will be impious, for piety hath juggled with me, and taught me to revere, where I should spurn. From all idols, I tear all veils; henceforth I will see the hidden things; and live right out in my own hidden life!—Now I feel that nothing but Truth can move me so. This letter is not a forgery. Oh! Isabel, thou art my sister; and I will love thee, and protect thee, ay, and own thee through all. Ah! forgive me, ye heavens for my ignorant ravings, and accept this vow.—Here I swear myself Isabel's. Oh! thou poor castaway girl, that in loneliness and anguish must have breathed that same air, which I have only inhaled for delight; thou who must even now be weeping, cast into an ocean of uncertainty as to thy fate, which heaven hath placed in my hands; sweet Isabel! would I not be baser than brass, and harder, and colder than ice, if I could be insensible to such claims as thine? Thou movest before me, in rainbows spun of thy tears! I see thee long weeping, and God demands me for thy comforter; and comfort thee, stand by thee, and fight for thee, will thy leapingly-acknowledging brother, whom thy own father named Pierre!"

He could not stay in his chamber: the house contracted to a nut-shell around him; the walls smote his forehead; bare-headed he rushed from that place, and only in the infinite air, found scope for that boundless expansion of his life.

—Pierre on his own (*Pierre*, 65–66)

. . . Will I, nill I, the ineffable thing has tied me to him; tows me with a cable I have no knife to cut. Horrible old man!

—Starbuck (*Moby-Dick*, 169)

Chapter 2 reviewed constraints on free thought in the humanities, particularly institutional double binds: There could be no conflict between truth and order. I believe Melville sighted such constraints and complained, while his revivers, attempting to function in pseudo-progressive institutions, could not. My differences with other Melville scholars regarding "the Melville problem," resting on unstateable similarities between Melville's nineteenth-century family and the post-1917 university, may now be explored. Some advise their students to identify with Ishmael (a pluralist) over Ahab (a tyrant), insisting that this was Melville's preference as well; while others may conclude that Ahab/Melville was a seeker after elusive truth or textual meanings, his quixotic character formally expressed in self-erasing texts (that do exist, I agree). In my view, the available evidence points to an intractable dilemma specific to an evolving, incompletely realized democratic society, misted still by corporatism. The artist engagé is interrogating his and our moral imaginations: We live in a free society ruled by laws, not men, and where the misconduct and bad faith of elected authority may be revealed by unfolding events. As the mask of rectitude is stripped away, what is to be done? What constructive moral action, if any, can the citizen take to repair the damage to herself while discredited leaders, bolstered by class solidarity despite the cracked facades, continue to monopolize the instruments of coercion? So up front, so timely, is Melville's obsessive theme (albeit by necessity cunningly elaborated), and yet scholars continue to complain about (or revel in) his obscurity and/or the ups and downs of his career as if he were an unidentifiable flying object. A brief inventory of their assessments follows.

For Carl Van Doren or Raymond M. Weaver, writing after 1917, the Melville problem was the disappointing decline after the high point of *Moby-Dick;* the Nietzschean Weaver blamed "the herd" (the philistine reading public) who had pronounced the exquisitely disillusioned Melville "insane," driving him into "the long quietus."[1] Fred Lewis Pattee, a founding father of American literature partly agreed, arguing in 1927 that the "Byronic," "over-intellectual, over-egotistical, over-impetuous" author burned out at age thirty-two but was also "stoned" by "a perverse generation." Perhaps unnerved himself, Pattee quoted FitzJames O'Brian, a Melville contemporary: "The man is essentially exotical in feeling. Matter is his god. His dreams are material. His philosophy is sensual. Beautiful women, shadowy lakes, nodding plumy trees, and succulent banquets make Melville's scenery, unless his theme utterly preclude all such. His language is rich and heavy with a plating of imagery. He has a barbaric love of ornament and does not mind how much is put on. Swept away by his sensual longing, he frequently writes at random. One can see that he uses certain words only because they roll off his pen lusciously and proudly."[2] Pattee was also disturbed by mystery, by lack of closure to controversy, and by Melville's sudden rise to prominence among younger scholars. Writing in 1932, he described a youth revolt or what faculty psychologists of the eighteenth century had seen as "fancy" out of control and liable to start a revolution: "Melville is one of the mysteries, one of the problems of American literature. Until well into the twentieth century he was believed to be finally classified, a decreasing writer of the mid-century, of perhaps tenth magnitude. Then, suddenly, almost by accident, he shot into world notice, was published and republished in editions *de luxe*, was adjudged to be of the second and even of the first magnitude. To-day, the younger critics all class him with the four or five largest figures America has produced in the area of literature."[3]

Critical opinion *de luxe* should have been unanimous: The material world itself seemed to blame; it was leading Americans away from moderate management. Desire might sweep away an entire nation, so facts were to be guided gently in less excitable new directions. The humbling discipline of cultural anthropology would rectify the arrogance of scientific history. At the end of the Red Decade, Harvard professor F. O. Matthiessen echoed Caroline F. Ware's adjuration on behalf of the American Historical Association: The cultural historian should not "rest upon the prescription of the scientific historians to let the facts speak and to be guided wherever the material may lead."[4] In his account of "the American Renaissance," Matthiessen chided his generation: "[Our culture's] greatest weakness has continued to be that our so-called educational class knows so little of the country and of the people of which it is nominally part. This lack of roots helps to explain the usual selfish indifference of our university men to political or social responsibility." But the rescue of other rootless Americans would not follow the prescriptions of scientific historians:

> "[The American scholar's] works must prove . . . that he is a citizen, not a lackey, a true exponent of democracy, not a tool of the most insidious form of anarchy." . . . Ahab's savagery, not unlike that of a Hebrew prophet, has rejected the warmly material pantheism of the Greeks. . . . [*Pierre*] gives the sense of having been wrenched from him in a mood when illusion after illusion was crashing in his mind . . . [leading to] a psychological chaos in which discriminations between good and evil have inevitably been engulfed in the general wreckage of art and philosophy. . . . [T]he passion that drove him into the discovery of his ambiguities was peculiarly American. . . . Yet no matter how hard it might prove to discern psychological causation, he was determined to "follow the endless, winding way,—the flowing river in the cave of man; careless whither I be led, reckless where I land." . . . [It was in Melville's "throwing himself helplessly open to the workings of his unconscious mind"] that [D. H.] Lawrence found expression of "the extreme transitions of the isolated far-driven soul."[5]

Matthiessen happened to be a colleague of Henry Murray and mentor to Charles Olson, and both Melvilleans agreed with his sentiments: Savage, moralistic Hebrew prophet types—Melville's Ahab and Pierre—were coldly deceptive. Their driving passion to pry open the Id, to discover their ambiguities, was peculiarly American—unlike "a true exponent of democracy," one less jumpy, more alert to the healing properties of tradition. However, the Melville problem persisted, despite the efforts of later antimaterialists following D. H. Lawrence, Matthiessen, Murray, and Olson, who would endeavor to mold Melville's mobile materialism and nail him to the party of Order. As R. W. Short noted, "Even the laziest reader wants to make some pursuit of the mysteries. Here lies the essential Melville problem." Similarly, David Leverenz observed, "Only Emily Dickinson generates equally unpredictable, wild, and illuminating classroom responses. . . . [*Moby-Dick* has] the uncanny knack of wrenching out strange spontaneities. Its browbeat ventriloquism springs loose a rich variety of voices gone wooden with obedience to social codes. Alone among Melville's works, this book brings on the feeling of being creatively at odds with oneself as well as one's world." Finally, three prominent senior Melvilleans have declared the Melville problem, a matter of pinning down textual meanings, insoluble. "It's all a mystery," chuckled Walter Bezanson to David Leverenz, while Harrison Hayford more ambiguously hinted that Melville's managed indeterminacy of meaning emancipates the reader from the tyranny of professors such as himself: "Wonder ye that we still have not determined the dimensions of *Moby-Dick?* I mean, of course, that we have not done so because Melville made sure in his whole way of writing *Moby-Dick* that we should never do so. That was the point, and it is one of the virtues of the Library of America that its volumes eschew interpretive introductions and notes which might in any way limit the reader's open response to this vast and mysterious masterpiece."[6]

And, while describing the early chapters of *Mardi,* Hershel Parker puzzlingly cited a chapter where lonely Taji complains about his companion Jarl's moodiness and taciturnity in order to demonstrate that Melville found the ineffable to be the source of confidence, precision, and growth: "What he had in hand in the early weeks of his writing was remarkable for confident expansiveness of style and subject.... In Chapter 11 Melville offered an anatomy of reveries, his theories about his companion's states of being: he had seized as his own theme the riddling nature of the universe and every creature and object in it. In these early chapters Melville was evoking precisely some of the most unnameable moods, states of mind and body, states of consciousness—one of his greatest strengths."[7] Following such a premise, intimate knowledge of the world around us must be Pierre's contracting nutshell, the wall that smote his forehead; while not knowing any creature or object would lead to the boundless expansion of his life.

This brief survey suggests that "the Melville problem" is the problem of the historian. Clio digs out facts, then follows the fatal line wherever it takes her. Standing alone if necessary, she selects one best narrative and causal explanation, submits it to other investigators, and takes her medicine. Theoretically the next draft will benefit from the justifiable criticisms of her peers; she develops a firmer grip upon the material. But what if warranted conclusions (or the lack of them) discomfit institutions supporting historical research? In short, Melvilleans are anxious about patronage at a time when universal suffrage has forced organic conservatives following moderates such as Hume or Burke or Goethe to pose as genuine liberals who may not be unmasked: "It ain't natural." Our own possible misreadings or perceptual distortions or silences are partly determined by our position in a "free" market that may exclude enthusiastic or fanatical materialists with domineering master narratives, often held to be the products of their own solipsistic meanderings. We are asked to claim some vague measure of distinctiveness and authority for our own efforts while simultaneously submitting to the irrationalism of postdemocratic discourse. As Columbia sociologist Robert S. Lynd reminded his colleagues in 1938, "Science is itself but a bit of culture"; Clio is kaput.[8]

Wall-smitten

Melville has attracted champions and critics reflecting divergent political allegiances, a phenomenon partly explained by his own waffling, but also by the structural position of intellectuals in institutions simultaneously demanding truth, independence, and loyalty to conservative order. Rather than recognize the sometimes irreconcilable conflicts within themselves or the limitations or internal contradictions within institutions (the family, universities, and publishing), scholars may choose to ignore evidence that complicates their typologies. Thus aesthetes, New Humanists, primitivists, Southern Agrarians, New Critics, Christian Socialists, conservative Catholics, Nazis, Soviet Marxists, Trotskyists, Jungian mystics, New Deal progressives, New Leftists, and libertarian conservatives have picked up "Melville" as a handy lancet to puncture abscesses on the body politic, while Melville scholars at times seem out for blood. Important figures in American Studies such as Gerald Graff, William E. Cain, and Paul Lauter have suggested that *Moby-Dick* is a Eurocentric text crowding out rival works by women and nonwhites, and (in Lauter's experience) hated by students for its difficulty.[9] This is curious, because critics following H. Bruce Franklin, Joyce Sparer Adler, and Carolyn L. Karcher agree that Melville is the exemplary anticapitalist, antiracist, proletarian artist.[10] These Left interpretations are contradicted by long-standing claims that Melville's politics either drastically changed after the Civil War (for the better, Thorp; for the worse, Kazin, Fredrickson, Rogin), or were always bipolar, virtually incoherent (Parker), or, unresolved and unreliable (Howard, Hayford), or unresolved and inevitable in a man-o'-war world (Weaver, E. Metcalf, P. Metcalf).[11]

Middle managers are caught between antagonistic social classes and individuals, not only between rich and poor, but between producers competing in the market. The biographical sketch that follows will emphasize only those shaping structures, events, and patterns of communication in Melville's family that could explain and resolve some of the furious debates over Melville's politics and mental states.[12] Brief and schematic as it undoubtedly is, this sketch of divided class loyalties and institutional double binds, of disappearing male bodies and strong women who endure, may provide a sufficient explanation for the ambiguities and weird reversals in Melville's art. At times there will be a pause in the narrative in order to then contrast my interpretation of the Melville problem with the judgments of earlier biographers.

The still-unfinished transition from feudal corporatism to modernity has produced coexisting but incompatible values and worldviews. A grand, global mixed message is delivered by every "liberal" socializing institution practicing indirect rule: Think for yourself, rise up and sing, but don't make authority angry. What foot on your neck? What lock on your door? Melville was a good little boy, but such a well-traveled young man that he rubbed his eyes. Apprehending the unspoken details of family architecture, he mirrored cracks and flaws, blood and dirt. In his fiction, apparently good-hearted but self-contradictory, obtuse, and secretive authority figures were confronted by good-hearted younger rebels who might also be self-deceived. But the rebels usually lost; perhaps aghast at what he foresaw at the end of the fatal line, Melville could rewrite the narrative of a successful revolt to make the point, common to moderate conservatives, that all resistance was doomed, would drag everyone down if authority did not make timely concessions to the oppressed. One can almost hear Captain Vere saying "fated boy" after Billy's shot to the forehead unintentionally kills Claggart—"fated" solely because Melville himself had been repeatedly hammered by events beyond his control. Like other youthful victims, he may have projected his rage, isolation, and helplessness in averting personal or family disaster onto adults in organized social movements, anytime, anywhere. Or did he? Were his tragic consummations meant to be taken as such, as testaments to the inevitable irrationality of all politics, or were they strategies to get published, with the author winking in the wings? This Melville problem is fascinating; moreover the idea of the double bind as a feature of pseudo-modern institutions has directed this author's studies ever since reading *Pierre*. Some biographers, though, perhaps echoing the narrator of Melville's most notorious failure, seemed riveted by the fall in social class that produced a rebel angel: The absent, morally imperfect Father made him overly susceptible to the domineering and puritanical Mother. The decayed patrician struggles to regain his footing by leading the mob in a crusade against established but "evil" authority. In our feminized Victorian culture, it could happen to them; better to turn about.[13]

> When he came to himself he found that he was lying crosswise in the gutter, dabbled with mud and slime.
> —*Pierre*, 341

Melville's sea voyages had placed a once proud and secluded descendant of Revolutionary heroes, groomed for leadership, in intimate, possibly permanent, certainly miscegenating, contact with the dregs of humanity.[14] Melville was the third of eight children born to Allan Melvill and Maria Gansevoort. His father was an urbane, cosmopolitan New England merchant with Federalist sympathies; his mother's Hudson Valley family was integrated into patroon "aristocracy" and New York state politics through her brother Peter, a conservative Democrat, lawyer, banker, state senator, and secretary to De Witt Clinton. Allan's career as an importer of French luxury goods ended in disgrace after shady business practices, the disreputable milking of his brother-in-law Peter, and borrowings against his own inheritance. Declassed, the Melvills moved from New York to Albany. Allan's death in 1832 from pneumonia following exposure to freezing weather was reportedly preceded by a period of "mania."[15] A letter in the papers of Melville's father-in-law, Lemuel Shaw, suggests that sometime after the bankrupt Allan's death, two women, "Mrs. A.M.A. and Mrs. B.," perhaps Allan's natural child and her aunt, presented themselves as partial claimants to his late father's estate. (The letter was found in 1934 but withheld from publication by Charles Olson and Henry Murray. Amy Puett, a graduate student of Harrison Hayford, rediscovered "the closet skeleton," and the letter was finally published in 1978.)[16]

Upon the demise of the wandering father, both twelve-year-old Herman and his older brother, Gansevoort (the family genius, as his fond parents believed), were taken out of school. Gansevoort, age sixteen, managed his late father's new business acquired from a bankrupt client of Peter Gansevoort: a small factory and fur and cap store. A period of prosperity and partial recuperation of family status followed, including a brief return to Melville's interrupted classical education, but the Panic of 1837 with its contraction of credit plunged the business into ruin. Gansevoort retired to bed for fifteen months (with a bad ankle, but perhaps also a nervous collapse); Herman pursued a variety of humble occupations, including clerking, surveying, and schoolteaching, none of which afforded satisfactory or reliable employment; while Maria was reduced to begging her brothers for money.

Herman finally found subsistence, adventure, and terror at sea as a common sailor on a short voyage to Liverpool in 1839 and to the South Seas and the Pacific, 1841–44, including a four-week captivity by "cannibals" in the Marquesas. According to "Freudian" Melvilleans, Maria was responsible for the flight to the forecastle, both times.[17] Having been set up by Mother, rough treatment turned Melville into a homosexual, or so it has been broadly hinted. Newton Arvin, himself a persecuted homosexual fired by Smith College, explained that the "ambitious and commanding side of Maria Melville's nature was to gain the upper hand and to wreak injury on the emotional career of her 'meek' second son": Maria was seductive like Mary Glendinning, mother of Pierre, entangling Herman in an incestuous relationship as a ploy to make him assume the responsibilities of the departed father.

During his discussion of Billy Budd's hinted "rapturous embrace" with Captain Vere, Arvin stated outright that this was the only love he would know: Melville was "incapable of love itself."[18] The historical record, however, suggests that Maria did not try to keep Herman with her but acquiesced in his decision to go to sea. She probably wanted him to stop moping, which meant growing up and earning a living. After he had embarked on his second voyage, the clinging mother told her daughter Augusta, with obvious relief: "Last week I received a long letter from Herman, who has embarked for a long voyage to the Pacific under the most favorable auspices, and feeling perfectly happy. Gansevoort was with him to the last and assisted him with his more matured judgment to supply him with every comfort. Gansevoort says he never saw him so completely happy, as when he had determined upon a situation and all was settled" (Dec. 8, 1841, GL-A).

While Herman was roving, Gansevoort achieved renown as a spellbinding orator on behalf of "the unterrified Democracy." Brash Irish immigrants, urban artisans, and backwoodsmen gathered by the thousands in all weathers, three or four hours at a time, to hear him speak out for Irish nationalism, the re-annexation of Texas, and expansion into Oregon. Gansevoort had risen from bed in 1839 to study law; he entered Tammany politics in 1842, astonishing his family (namely his uncle Thomas Melvill, Jr., of Massachusetts, a nativist and conservative Whig, and his uncle Peter and younger brother Allan, both Van Buren Democrats). Bored with the mundane duties of local politicians, he embarked on a national tour in 1844, the star speaker for James Polk. The Democratic candidate had been chosen by Jacksonians over Martin Van Buren, whose cautious stance on expansion had alienated Old Hickory and divided the Democratic Party convention of 1844; Peter Gansevoort and Allan Melville were part of the stranded Van Buren faction. At the climax of the campaign, June 4, Gansevoort addressed 15,000 to 25,000 men in New York's City Hall Park. With the fervor of Captain Ahab, he exhorted the crowd, invoking the spirit of war and sacrifice: "As for James K. Polk, the next President of the United States, we, the unterrified Democracy of New York will rebaptise him; we will give him a name such as Andrew Jackson [won] in the Battle of New Orleans; we will re-Christen him. Hereafter, he shall be known by the name we now give him—it is Young Hickory. [Here the cheering was deafening and continued for some moments. A voice: "You're a good twig of Old Hickory, too!"—laughter and renewed cheering.]" The good hickory twig ended his speech with the electrifying war cry, "Up Democrats, and at them!"[19] Gansevoort rechristened Polk as "Young Hickory" to solidify a divided Democratic family. Having exploited his family connections to the New York State Regency, a clique headed by Van Buren, Gansevoort had triumphantly waved a lukewarm letter of endorsement for the Polk candidacy just extracted from the former president in a personal visit to Kinderhook, but the orator misrepresented the letter as giving unqualified, enthusiastic support to Polk.

With considerable legerdemain, Gansevoort was attaching the Van Buren constituency to the Jackson wing of the Democratic Party whose headlong militant expansionism Van Buren had not publicly approved. (In 1848, Van Buren would be the presidential candidate for the antislavery Free Soil Party.) The belated reward for Gansevoort's exhaustive services to the victorious Jacksonians was his appointment as secretary to the American legation in London in 1845, where his ultra-democratic sentiments antagonized conservative Englishmen and his superior, Ambassador Louis MacNiece. MacNiece, who had nervously written to Secretary of State James Buchanan that western extremists were liable to ruin chances of a compromise with England over the Oregon boundary, was exasperated by his secretary's irrepressible "fifty-four forty or fight!" nationalism.[20]

Almost as soon as he arrived in London in the late summer of 1845, Gansevoort began arrangements for publication of Herman's first book, an event that must have brought an excess of anticipated joy to the author. *Typee* appeared February 2, 1846. On February 28, Maria informed Augusta that Gansevoort had written to Herman, predicting a "brilliant success, and do you believe, Augusta—he even went so far—*was so very kind* [to advise Herman not to be] too much elated—with his success—and the numerous advances, compliments . . . that would be made to him." Gansevoort was reverting to standards of gentlemanly modesty perhaps to spare his brother the disappointment he had personally suffered at the hands of the Democratic Party. Shortly after the publication of *Typee*, Gansevoort began the downward spiral that ended in a mysterious demise. He had been suffering from severe headaches, fatigue, and a misty blindness in his left eye for weeks before he sought professional advice. The illness was characterized as "nervous derangement" by MacNiece, but it may have been caused by an infection in a dead tooth.[21] A pathetic letter to Herman was written on April 3. After bringing him up to date on publishing matters, Gansevoort continued:

> My thoughts are so much at home that much of my time is spent in disquieting apprehensions as to matters and things there . . . I sometimes fear that I am gradually breaking up. . . . I think I am growing phlegmatic and cold. Man stirs me not, nor woman either. My circulation is languid. My brain is dull. I neither seek to win pleasure or avoid pain. A degree of insensibility has long been stealing over me, & now seems permanently established, which to my understanding is more akin to death than life. Selfishly speaking I never valued life much—it were impossible to value it less than I do now. The only personal desire I now have is to be out of debt.[22]

Herman did not answer the cri de coeur until May 29. A perfectly happy but (perhaps) belated reply, possibly written from three to four weeks after receipt, was reassuring about matters at home and tried to cheer Gansevoort with sprightly remarks about Augusta's participation in the society wedding of Cornelia Van Rensselaer and the rollicking plebeian preparations for the Mexican War. Then, switching to the voice of Maria, Herman cautioned the disintegrating brother, "Remember that composure of mind is every thing." It was too late for moderation. Inappropriately treated as far as we know, Gansevoort had died at the age of thirty on May 12, the day before Polk declared war on Mexico, the latter "an executive usurpation" that Melville was to oppose in *Mardi*.

Herman had lost both father and older brother at turning points in his own life, moments of maturation and individuation. His elegant, overbearing, overreaching, ex-Federalist father died a raving failure as Herman was entering adolescence; his overbearing, overreaching, mob-wooing Jacksonian brother was sinking as Herman's star was rising. Don Benito Cereno, the Spanish captain of the *San Dominick*, and the African slave Babo, antagonists in Melville's story of a foiled slave revolt, were both thirty years old, Gansevoort's age when he died. Surely the abruptly disappearing bodies of Allan and Gansevoort are implicated in Melville's showdowns between Leviathan and Captain Ahab, Mary Glendinning and Pierre, the Wall Street lawyer and Bartleby, Benito Cereno and Babo, and even Captain Vere and Billy Budd (the last only a suspected mutineer). Moreover, he appears to have worried that the family was cursed with hereditary insanity; his mother, frequently nervous and depressed during her pregnancies and after, would have contributed to the fantasy, abetted by Allan's "mania" and Gansevoort's "nervous derangement" or "breaking up."[23]

To these psychological considerations must be added the practical conflict experienced by every righteous writer eager to report what he saw as class exploitation, but simultaneously dependent upon an upper-class reading public of moral reformers wishing to exonerate itself of complicity with un-Christian practices.[24] Though she was tied to conservative Democrats, Maria concisely echoed the ideology of the Second Great Awakening and New School Calvinism[25] that had guided the moral behavior of Whig modernizers and evangelists as well as rationalizing the sometimes contradictory, sometimes overlapping crusades for peace, abolition, temperance, female suffrage, land reform, labor reform, and sex reform in the mid–nineteenth century. In a letter to Augusta she advised: "Guard against selfishness, you will ever find it an impossible barrier to true friendship. Cultivate the best feelings of the heart & extract from it with the aid of fervent prayer, all the baser passions which are also natural to us in our present state of depravity. Cultivate the Virtues which are also but in a much fainter degree inherent in our nature, and by careful culture they will soon thrive and prosper so as to eventually root out & totally to eradicate, or greatly impair the natural prevalence to evil" (Oct. 17, 1838, GL-A).[26]

Such admonitions could be read in two ways. For Maria, social purity signified the heroic purgation of those "baser passions," vainglory, for instance, that bound little Melvilles to the lower orders. She was not thinking about the superior self-control that conquered fear and not-seeing, enabling effective resistance to illegitimate authority. A year later Allan, age sixteen, then working in her brother Peter's office, had dared to criticize the lawyer's harsh treatment. Maria simultaneously chastened and healed her erring boy: God and Mother were joined in their desire for Allan's victorious submission to undeserved cruelty: "My dear Allan while you live ever remember your Mother with deep enduring affection, and when you find you are about doing some thing which the inward Monitor Conscience—disapproves, let the recollection of your devoted Mother and her heartfelt advice come to strengthen the inward monitor, *crush not its voice,* & you—will triumph over temptations, my dear son I fear you feel too strong a confidence in your own strength" (Sept. 15, 1839, *Log,* 94). Three years later, Allan Melville, age nineteen, wrote to Augusta, age twenty-one, on behalf of Gansevoort, age twenty-six. Moralistic criticism of the type dished out by the mother-fortified inward monitor was intolerable:

> As usual your last letter received by Gansevoort was all wind and sound signifying nothing. "What possesses you" to write such abominable letters? Why when you sit down to write to an absent brother cannot you scribble off something about home, news in the village and ten thousand other little things which are always acceptable rather than a long, sedate, wordy advice giving epistle? I detest them, and so does any other person of common sense when they are corrected by such young heads of yours. But don't get angry sister of mine I do not mean to offend you, but really this is my private opinion in the premises (with all due deference to yours) and hoping you will take the hint, so let it rest. (May 5, 1842, GL-A)

Gansevoort was angry with Augusta, but Allan is disciplining her, perhaps on his own initiative. She is out of control, inhabited by a demonic force, yet her writing is too "sedate," that is, composed and calm, not an excited "scribble." She has usurped priestly authority, wandering away from her proper fixation with frivolous domestic gossip. Allan is understandably offended by her youthful hubris. But Augusta, the recipient of excellent correction volunteered by her younger brother, must not be angry, even though Allan's letter lacks punctuation and logic. Anyway, she can shut up now: The subject is closed; with Augusta's silence, order and clarity have returned. Allan and Augusta Melville were two young adults with no claim to historical notice except for their blood relationship to a famous writer. This private storm between brother and sister is no domestic trivia, however, but emblematic for the conservative reception to Melville's irregular life and art: Only the names have changed.

Melville was awed by the everyday heroism of the common sailor in mastering his craft and surviving the perils of seafaring under conditions almost inconceivable to us today. He was enraged at the treatment of his shipmates by haughty and incompetent officers at sea and negligent or abusive elites on land. But such indignation was perhaps vitiated by the fear of earnest, wordy, long, sedate, advice-giving epistles, hence the need for balance: Even one slip could propel dreamy Ishmaels into the deep, could return Melville to Gansevoort and the frozen underworld where his Satanic energies had led. So Melville, seriously troubled by mothers and missionaries, allowed Wiley & Putnam, his American publishers, to expurgate the most politically trenchant passages of the second American edition of *Typee,* lest the missionaries who had "evangelized [Hawaiian natives] into beasts of burden" be excessively offended. The humiliating excision was performed by the author himself, begun during the week of June 20–26, 1846, as Melville awaited the shipment of his brother's body to New York City.[27]

Trimmed and re-Christianized,[28] Melville gratefully entered respectable society with his early authorial success and celebrity, an event clinched by his (mother-directed?) marriage in 1847 to a wavering Elizabeth Shaw, daughter to his father's friend and family patron Lemuel Shaw, a conservative Whig. Writing to Augusta sometime in the spring of 1847, Maria hinted that Lizzie had been reluctant for some time to join their happy corporation and that Herman's writing had suffered accordingly:

> Herman is going to Boston, his visit is one of much importance to himself and every member of our family, it is nothing more or less than to have Lizzie name an early date for their marriage.
>
> He is very restless and ill at ease very lonely here without his intended, I can see no reason why it should be postponed any longer, if Lizzie loves Herman as I think she does with her whole heart and soul why, She will consent to live here for the present, and she can be happy too—all the elements of happiness are thick around us if we only will hold them to us, and not wantonly leave them [illegible] & you must tell Lizzie she must consent. In July she will have been engaged eleven months, a long time now a days.— Herman is really depressed because if Lizzie loves—she can be as happy here with us as elsewhere, and you must tell her so. Herman is able to support her here now, and to await for an uncertain future, which no one of us can penetrate, would be unwise he is really unsettled and won't be able to attend to his

"Book["]—if Lizzie does not reflect upon the uncertainty of the future, & consent to name some day in July.

The diplomatic mission was a success, but, oddly, Augusta did not attend the wedding of her favorite brother in Boston, August 4, 1847. After the festivities, Herman and Elizabeth, Maria, brother Allan and his new bride Sophia, and the four sisters, Helen, Augusta, Catherine, and Frances, moved back to New York City and lived in the same house.

Lemuel Shaw (having made the two-thousand-dollar down payment on their new home) joined the happy couple and their complicated household as a restraining but provocative spirit. In *Clarel* (1876), the American merchant Rolfe contemplates the "class-war . . . of history" that will follow the exhaustion of America's most valuable resource: free land that served as the safety valve sparing her from the tumults of industrializing Europe. Surprisingly, this "moderate" character muses that "the rich-and-poor-man fray," though "serious trouble," may produce a "good result . . . the first firm founding of the state." Such speculation would have scandalized Melville's father-in-law. For thirty years (1830–60) Shaw served as chief justice of Massachusetts, in good Humean fashion, protecting the public interest by sacrificing civil liberties when elites were threatened; upper-class property rights were the "bedrock" of the state. This view was denounced by radical Bostonians such as Charles Sumner and Richard Henry Dana, Jr. Though he was personally opposed to slavery, Shaw upheld the Fugitive Slave Law of 1850 (reversing abolitionist gains of the 1840s); before that he forbade blasphemy and school desegregation in Boston. In these and similar decisions Shaw served the ancient rule that "might makes right," enlisting "history" to overcome higher laws or constitutional and local laws alike, and rendering habeas corpus and other civil liberties a dead letter.[29] But the raucous writer refused to be co-opted. With the allegorical *Mardi* (1849), a survey of world politics, religion, and philosophy in an age of world revolution and growing sectional conflict in America, the facile and charming tourist of the exotic, the naughty-but-conservative reformer had switched on the defiance of the Romantic Wandering Jew. As Taji, Melville declared his allegiance to Milton's Satan, declining the safe haven of Serenia, a Christian Socialist utopia, for the "endless sea" of unbounded intellectual inquiry. The "Extracts" that begin *Moby-Dick* (a montage of quotations about whales taken from the Bible, history, literature, and popular culture) end with a "Whale Song": "Oh, the rare old Whale, mid storm and gale / In his ocean home will be / A giant in might, where might is right, / And King of the boundless sea." (These sardonic sentiments may or may not have been Melville's preferred ending for the English edition of his book, for the record is fragmentary on this point.[30]) Shaw-style compromises on behalf of Leviathan were parodied as "virtuous expediency" in "Plinlimmon's Pamphlet" (*Pierre*). And yet, the Shaw connection was the first and only firm foundation for Melville's financial security. Given the state of intellectual property rights and the limited market for difficult and demanding work (plus a disastrous fire at Harper & Brothers in late 1853 that destroyed 2,300 copies of earlier books that had been providing two to three hundred dollars of yearly income),[31] his literary career could not have maintained a growing ménage, even though the former outcast was travelling with distinguished company including the Democratic literati of Young America led by Evert and George Duyckinck, his admirers after the early successes of *Typee* and *Omoo*. Melville also met Richard Henry Dana, Jr., then Nathaniel Hawthorne with whom he participated in an irregular and one-sided romance after their meeting in August 1850. Class pressures could have installed a relatively contented Melville into one of the utopian socialist venues pleasing to patrician reformers in the antebellum period, but they did not; instead the family commune moved to an idyllic setting in the Berkshires (also with the financial assistance of Shaw). *Moby-Dick* (1851) and *Pierre* (1852) completed the trilogy that *Mardi* began. Taji, Ahab, and Pierre blasphemed against all authorities (including God or Nature or parents) who demanded moral rectitude and loving kindness on a heroic scale but made men, especially Christian gentlemen, weak, aggressive, and confused, then punished them for yielding to their passions.[32] A critical uproar followed publication of the scandalous *Pierre* (1852), apparently exposing his father's secret natural daughter (in the novel, Pierre's half-sister, Isabel). Melville celebrated their "incest" and underlined Pierre's determination never to sell out, even if it wrecked the family's idealizations of the dear perfect father. From 1847 on, relatives had tried to arrange a consular appointment; now these efforts were intensified, but to no avail.

What was Herman's problem? Melville's suggestive marking of Goethe's autobiography (acquired during his trip to Europe in 1849) supports my contention that Ahab, Melville's most famous isolato, is the Promethean modern artist, necessarily separated from the approbation of conservative authority, including God:

[Melville double-scored the following two and a half sentences:] The common fate of man, which all of us have to bear, must fall most heavily on those whose intellectual powers expand very early. For a time we may grow up under the protection of parents and relatives; we may lean for a while upon our brothers and sisters and friends, supported by acquaintances, and made happy by those we love, but in the end man is always driven back upon himself, and it seems as if the Divinity had taken a position towards men so as not always to respond to their reverence, trust, and love, at least not in the precise moment of need. Early enough, and by many a hard lesson, had I learned that at the most urgent crises the call to us is, "Physician, heal thyself"; and how frequently had I been compelled to sigh out in pain, "I tread the wine-press alone!" So now, while I was looking about for the means of establishing my independence, I felt that the surest basis on which to build was my own creative talents. For many years I had never known it to fail me for a moment. What, waking, I had seen by day, often shaped itself into regular dreams at night, and when I opened my eyes there appeared to me either a wonderful new whole, or a part of one already commenced. Usually, my time for writing was early in the morning, but still in the evening, or even late at night, when wine and social intercourse had raised my spirits, I was ready for any topic that might be suggested; only let a subject of some character be offered, and I was at once prepared and ready. While, then, I reflected upon this natural gift, and found that it belonged to me as my own, and could neither be favoured nor hindered by any external matters, I easily in thought built my whole existence upon it. This conception soon assumed a distinct form; the old mythological image of Prometheus occurred to me, who separated from the gods, peopled a world from his own work-shop. [Melville also scored the following sentence:] I clearly felt that a creation of importance could be produced only when its author isolated himself. My productions which had met with so much applause were children of solitude, and since I had stood in a wider relation to the world, I had not been wanting in the power or the pleasure of invention, but the execution halted, because I had neither in prose nor in verse, a style properly my own, and consequently, with every new work, had always to begin at the beginning and try experiments. As in this I had to decline and even to exclude the aid of men, so after the fashion of Prometheus, I separated myself from the gods also, and the more naturally as with my character and mode of thinking one tendency always swallowed up and repelled all others.

The fable of Prometheus became living in me. The old Titan web I cut up according to my own measurements.[33]

Are the Promethean Goethe's "regular dreams" an interpretive clue to Melville's "regular romance" (*Pierre* as promised to publisher Richard Bentley), and were not such artful dreams embodied in the family-disrupting character of Isabel, the Dark Lady with whom Pierre must merge to become a modern artist?

By pursuing the question of Melville's possible homosexuality, scholars may have missed the point, making their Ishmael's most urgent drive the search for a substitute father. Like Maria, Melville may have wanted a reconstructed lovely *family* and thought he had found it in the Hawthornes: unified, internally consistent, and frowning upon autodidacts, monomaniacal mad scientists, and abolitionists similarly guilty of excessive Protestant moralism and Promethean self-fashioning, while looking kindly upon Melville's noble blood.[34] Augusta reported one of their auspicious encounters to her sister Helen: "Had a delightful visit he said, the warmest of welcomes, '& a cold chicken.' . . . Herman says they are the loveliest family he has ever met with, or anyone can possibly imagine. We are all delighted to hear that you will be home before they come. Herman said last evening, when your letter came, 'I am glad Helen is coming home, it will make it so much pleasanter for the Hawthornes.' Now mind that you return to us with all your powers of entertainment in the happiest condition" (Jan. 24, 1851, GL-A). It was during this period that Melville was birthing *Moby-Dick,* an occupation that seems to have inspired an uncharacteristic act of self-assertion in life as well as art. His mother responded furiously in a letter to Augusta: "Herman I hope returned home safe after dumping me and my trunks out so unceremoniously at the depot—altho' we were there more than an hour before the time, he hurried off as if his life depended on his speed, and a more ungallant man it would be difficult to find. I hope to hear from *Herman*" (Mar. 10, 1851, GL-A).[35]

The perfectly happy, perfectly lovely family was filled with resentful martyrs; rarely in surviving documents directed to older relatives does any of Maria's brood directly express simple human needs for care, affection, and acceptance or a disturbing emotion, like fear of failure, sadness, or inconsolable grief, let alone the larger needs for sustained privacy, reflection, and life experience that make a mighty book; his gorgeously wrought letters suggest that Melville's complaints and longings for greatness were shared with Hawthorne, not his mother. Melville's simultaneous destruction/reconstruction of the lovely family, perhaps his central gesture in art and life alike, was sometimes shared by his siblings. Their occasional mini-mutinies and protests responded to the maternal expectation that they smoothly integrate antithetical values that were merged or left vague by Melvilles and Gansevoorts, values that intellectuals may recognize today as conducive to success in a "pluralist" society. The abstractness of rules and patterns of communication could not have lustered Melville children. Helen-as-Bartleby described an act of defiance to Augusta; she was twenty-four years old:

My dear nut-brown sister . . . In the afternoon, feeling in the mood for writing, I sat down to my desk, alone in our little snug dormitory, and indited a long and interesting letter to you, leaving (as Mama had requested) half a page for her use. My obedience in this case brought only sorrow to me, for Mama having scanned the pa [*sic*] with a critical eye, pronounced the chirography beneath contempt, and insisted upon my copying the document. This I protested against, so my good lady, to close the conference, tore the unoffending [*sic*] sheet into a thousand pieces. The mood for composition is gone for the present, and if you consider its destruction a loss, as I certainly do, you must lay the sin at Mama's door. (Sept. 16, 1841, GL-A)

Later, Helen comes home to classicism: "I am sorry you have had such a bad cold, because it must have dimmed the luster of your beauty, and marred the symmetrical proportions of your nose, which is at all times the most striking feature in your face" (Feb. 6, 1847, GL-A). Helen then relates her dream that Augusta was pitched out of the carriage that took her to Albany and would be a victim to "a spine in the back" all her days. Aggression still surges from below to mar the unoffending pa.

Here then are the qualifications of middle managers as inferred from the Melville family: independence of mind and adherence to the higher law of Judeo-Christian ethics, yet unswerving deference to the tastes and opinions of wealthy earthly elders; a perfected moral purity achieved through heroic self-control and cultivation, made visible in physical beauty, composure, penmanship, and book sales; total identification with family welfare and enmeshment in each other's affairs; unalloyed happiness; and the qualities of modesty, prudence, decisiveness, optimism, and stoicism. The Melville children, even as adults, had no rights of privacy nor could they criticize their parents; with the internalization of the mother's conscience (in her words, "the inward Monitor"), the children were expected to triumph over errors great and small—all the while reassuring mother that they were "completely happy" but not "too much elated." They adapted to Maria's perfectionist iron will by constant mutual surveillance, polishing each other's images, sometimes openly revolting, sometimes sharing fantasies of destruction, then reconstructing the lovely family that their hostile wishes (or actions) had demolished, for even one evil thought was a sign of impurity.

Unlike Newton Arvin and others, Melville did not blame Maria's crippling love for his troubles: Her cultural tradition was corporatist, and she rightly sensed that a close-knit family was essential to survival in a buffeting economy. Melville had a different problem with the priestly mother; for Maria, individuality or independence meant the virtuous achievement of self-control over divisive insight and other contaminating impulses, but Melville agonized over the ambiguities in separat-ing fate from free will, self-interest from altruism. While Herman was in Washington looking for a government job, Maria had written to Augusta expressing her relief that Herman had roused himself to action on his own/the family's behalf: "[Herman] seems to feel that if he succeeds at all it will be brought about by his own *personal exertions* at headquarters, I am glad that he is at last convinced of this important truth. It is worth a fortune to any man to understand this and act it out, it is a lesson Herman has been long in learning, but he is young enough to benefit by it still, I hope *God* will see fit to bless his endeavors, and it is for his and our good that he may succeed" (Feb. 6, 1847, GL-A). Was it God's blessing or young Herman's "personal exertions" that determined events, his success or failure? When Maria demanded that her clinging second son attain maturity and fame, she did not anticipate intellectual, religious, or political opposition to the Melvilles and Gansevoorts; the pious mother did not dither over God and Mammon. In a letter to Augusta and Herman, Feb. 10, 1854, Maria was the archetypal rationalizing industrial manager,[36] urging Herman to create a lecture that could be repeated seventy times; perhaps he would be paid fifty dollars per engagement, but Oliver Wendell Holmes and others had been satisfied with only twenty-five. Remarking that lectures are "the present style of enlightening the many who have no time to devote to reading and research," Maria forecast a happy resolution to the Melville problem: "So now my dear darling Herman, all your friends, relatives and admirers, say that you are the very man to carry an audience, to create a sensation, to do wonders. To close this subject, I will request you to think over this *not* new subject when in a happy hopeful state of mind, and there is the chance of your coming to the wise conclusion, to do that thing, which at once, and by the same agreeable act will bring us fame & fortune."

The class-conscious mother of *Pierre* preferred a selective paternalism to equality. Maria's notion of family solidarity could not be broadened to include all suffering humanity, yet such a stricture contradicted her own Christian ethics, expressed above in her sympathy for popular education. Maria's influence cut two ways: It was the lynx-eyed attention to dirt and details that brought Melville into confrontation with Maria's mixed messages, then encouraged him to chart his motions hither and thither as he simultaneously placated and punished "the inward Monitor," composing "the books that are said to fail." In a letter to Evert Duyckinck that has enraged feminists, Melville may have made a revealing slip. While in Boston waiting for the birth of his first child, Melville attended a performance by the English actress Fanny Kemble, then riveting young Bostonians (including the abolitionist Wendell Phillips) with her one-woman Shakespeare readings. Kemble's husband, the slaveholder Pierce Butler, was seeking a divorce and demanding custody of their children; Melville sided with the estranged husband: "[Fanny Kemble Butler] makes a glorious Lady Macbeth. . . . She's so unfemininely masculine that had she not, on unimpeachable authority, borne children, I should be curious to learn the result of a surgical examination of her person in private. The Lord help Butler. . . . I marvel not he seeks being amputated off from his maternal [*sic*] half " (Feb. 24, 1849).[37] Was this masculinist misogyny or was Melville amputating himself from illusory lovely families, too narrowly conceived? Perhaps Melville's panic in the face of phallic women, women such as actress Fanny Kemble or Goneril (Kemble's probable surrogate in *The Confidence-Man*), is traceable to the formidable and contradictory Maria.

Melville's alternating currents can be painfully witnessed in *Pierre*. It appears that he was repudiating his last book (or even the book, *Pierre*, we are reading), especially the determination of Ahab/Pierre to strike through the mask of official rectitude, hence to expose the fathers who have abandoned Pip/Isabel. With mathematical precision, the conservative narrator represents the author's conversion to terminal humility: "The more and the more that he wrote, and the deeper and the deeper that he dived, Pierre saw the everlasting elusiveness of Truth; the universal lurking insincerity of even the greatest and purest written thoughts. . . . [There was] nothing more he abhorred than the loftiest part of himself." The narrator has switched Ahab to Ishmael, has inflicted the blackout that engulfs and staggers Ahab as the whale smites his ship's "advancing prow . . . amid fiery showers of foam" (570).

In the earlier progress of his book, he had found some relief in making his regular evening walk through the greatest thoroughfare of the city; that so, the utter isolation of his soul, might feel itself the more intensely from the incessant jogglings of his body against the bodies of the hurrying thousands. Then he began to be sensible of more fancying stormy nights, than pleasant ones; for then, the great thoroughfares were less thronged, and the innumerable shop-awnings flapped and beat like schooners' broad sails in a gale, and the shutters banged like lashed bulwarks; and the slates fell hurtling like displaced ship's blocks from aloft. Stemming such tempests through the deserted streets, Pierre felt a dark, triumphant joy; that while others had crawled in fear to their kennels, he alone had defied the storm-admiral, whose most vindictive peltings of hail-stones,—striking his iron-framed fiery furnace of a body,—melted into soft dew, and so, harmlessly trickled from off him.

By-and-by, of such howling pelting nights, he began to bend his steps down the dark, narrow side-streets, in quest of the more secluded and mysterious tap-rooms. There he would feel a singular satisfaction, in sitting down all dripping in a chair, ordering his half-pint of ale before him, and drawing over his cap to protect his eyes from the light, eye the varied faces of the social castaways, who here had their haunts from the bitterest midnights.

But at last he began to feel a distaste for even these; and now nothing but the utter night-desolation of the obscurest warehousing lanes would content him, or be at all sufferable to him. Among these he had now been accustomed to wind in and out every evening; till one night as he paused a moment previous to turning about for home, a sudden, unwonted, and all-pervading sensation seized him. He knew not where he was; he did not have any life-feeling at all. He could not see; though instinctively putting his hand to his eyes, he seemed to feel that the lids were open. Then he was sensible of a combined blindness and vertigo, and staggering; before his eyes a million green meteors danced; he felt his foot tottering upon the curb, he put out his hands, and knew no more for the time. When he came to himself he found that he was lying crosswise in the gutter, dabbled with mud and slime. He raised himself to try if he could stand; but the fit was entirely gone. Immediately he quickened his steps homeward, forbearing to rest or pause at all on the way, lest that rush of blood to his head, consequent upon his sudden cessation from walking, should smite him down. This circumstance warned him away from those desolate streets, lest the repetition of the fit should leave him there to perish by night in unknown and unsuspected loneliness. But if that terrible vertigo had been also intended for another and deeper warning, he regarded such added warning not at all; but again plied heart and brain as before.

But now at last since the very blood in his body had in vain rebelled against his Titanic soul; now the only visible outward symbols of that soul—his eyes—did also turn downright traitors to him, and with more success than the rebellious blood. He had abused them so recklessly, that now they absolutely refused to look on paper. He turned them on paper, and they blinked and shut. The pupils of his eyes rolled away from him in their own orbits. He put his hand up to them, and sat back in his seat. Then, without saying one word, he continued there for his usual term, suspended, motionless, blank. (340–41)

Melville's political views would have been constrained even if he had not wished to protect his suffering mother's idealizations of male relatives. The Plotinus Plinlimmonish rationalizations of his patron Lemuel Shaw (ever the adored father of Elizabeth) limited the unequivocal expression of Melville's more democratic sentiments, derived from Hebraic puritanism and apostolic Christianity.[38] But more, the "passion-fits," eye problems, and immobility experienced by many of Melville's characters may be explained by the lesson he drew from the death of Gansevoort: Too much contact with the misery and grief associated with the lower orders contaminates the family, even makes them crazy. The abandoned Isabel is a representation of Grief; Pierre's mother dies of "grief" after Pierre runs away with Isabel, "married" to her (grief). Melville's relentless questioning, his heretical "irruptions" invaded the tranquil pastoral; when merged with family values the irruption becomes an internal eruption bursting out, not in—"that rush of blood to his head consequent upon his sudden cessation from walking" that could (from an external source?) "smite him down." Again, we are in two places at once, trapped and confused; unlike the defiant Bartleby, Pierre "knew not where he was."

"He paused a moment previous to turning about for home." This pausing is the reflective moment of writing that mates unlike things, that lifts Ahab's harpoon or

Pierre's pen to amputate himself from his maternal half. Facing away from the insular family, exploring the lower depths (however guardedly), invites the punishment that erases what he has seen and felt, mercifully sparing his weaker relatives and calling a halt to insight and self-reliance; he is one with the blank-faced paper factory operatives in "A Tartarus of Maids." But the double revolutionary inheritance will tell; when Melville persists in annoying conservatives, he blames the Hebraic taint in puritan blood, seeing himself as a bad Jew.[39] Not surprising, he was admired as the surviving family genius but also feared and resented as a crybaby, blabbermouth, and unpredictable bohemian. He imagined family hostility and rejection where none existed; perversely refused to please the public and restore the family's lost fortunes; and stubbornly sealed up his pockets of revolt (in public!) while strewing his narratives with enough characters to conciliate "popular conservatism" (in the persons of Mother, her brother Peter, and Lemuel Shaw, to name only a few of his relations).

The short stories of the 1850s that followed the debacle of *Pierre* ("Bartleby the Scrivener"; "Rich Man's Pudding, Poor Man's Crumbs"; "The Encantadas"; "Paradise of Bachelors and a Tartarus of Maids"; "Benito Cereno," etc.), and the novel *Israel Potter* have been taken by some post-1960s antiracist Melvilleans as radical (though "bleak," reflecting the "bleak political atmosphere of the 1850s," as one recent critic has alleged).[40] They do seem designed to reproach and warn the hardhearted Mammonite readers of genteel magazines such as *Putnam's* and *Harper's* who might identify with conservative lawyers and Yankee captains. In "I and My Chimney" the narrator defends secrets (?) or the sequestered ideals of his youth (?) from female relatives and other intrusive hammer-wielding representatives of commercial and industrial society. *The Confidence-Man, His Masquerade* (1857), apparently marked his most unforgiving attack on the pragmatic Shaws and Plinlimmons of the world. The speaker is Pitch, the coonskin-capped frontiersman from Missouri (a slave state) who confronts the herb doctor's wavering commitment to antislavery: "Picked and prudent sentiments. You are the moderate man, the invaluable understrapper of the wicked man. You, the moderate man, may be used for wrong, but are useless for right."[41] In other episodes, the Invalid Titan assaults the herb doctor, who promises to alleviate all mental and physical suffering with the fast-acting Samaritan Pain Dissuader, while, as noted above, Thomas Fry mocks the herb doctor's "hog-Latin" defense of differential justice for rich and poor. These pokes at deceptive elites were followed by a reported nervous breakdown, a possible separation from his wife and four children, and a Shaw-subsidized trip to England, the Mediterranean, and the Holy Land, which (in his journal at least) took him from the cynicism and despair of *The Confidence-Man* to "good talk" with Hawthorne in Liverpool, thence to episodes of terror and grief in Egypt and Palestine, but ending with a celebration of the enduring qualities of Tory institutions.

Had Melville switched from radical to conservative, or was his fiction of the 1850s, situated in its full historical context, always acceptable to conservative readers and publishers, especially those sympathetic to the Jeffersonian agrarian critique of industrial capitalism, a belief system agreeable to Southern planters who had claimed that "wage slavery" was worse than chattel slavery and that African savages were benefited by the civilizing influence of their Christian owners? Utopian socialists and land reformers alike possessed an organic, communitarian view of the ideal society and proposed gradualist schemes for how to get there; they generally were not based in the working class,[42] and their spleen was directed against abolitionists such as Charles Sumner or the Garrisonians whom they relentlessly slandered as bourgeois individualists indifferent to the welfare of Northern workers. "Who ain't a slave? Tell me that," says an (apparently) resigned and passive Ishmael in "Loomings," the first chapter of *Moby-Dick,* where the narrator identifies the "story of Narcissus" as "the key to it all."[43] Only land ownership, it was believed by patrician radical reformers, could preserve independence and republican virtue. At times, Melville may have shared their fantasy that the process of proletarianization would inevitably cause massacres perpetrated by impoverished and demoralized masterless men. Of course the abolition movement was not monolithic: The modernizers who controlled the new Republican Party were eager to rid the country of Southern domination of both parties (Whig and Democratic) that had hampered expansion and industrial development with free labor. The more progressive among them (writing in *The National Era* or *The National Antislavery Standard*) expected future adjustments in the relations between capital and labor, but certainly not drastic structural transformation. There was, however, a substantial and vocal working-class abolitionist constituency with international moral and intellectual support, and for them abolition was the immediate objective that made more equitable class relations possible; they denounced the "Associationists" (Fourierists) and land reformers as knowingly or unknowingly complicit with Southern interests and proslavery apologetics.[44] Melville did not publish in *The Voice of Industry* or *The Liberator* or other periodicals that presented dialogue among the various factions of the antislavery movement; instead, such confrontations found their way into his fiction. Most disturbing, he transformed successful slave revolts (for instance, the episodes of the *Creole* and *Amistad*) into the unsparing disaster of "Benito Cereno." The question remains: During the decade of accelerating national crisis and dramatic party realignment, was his political stance neutral? Was he a subtly reactionary amanuensis of Southern agrarian interests? Or could he have been a covert partisan of the most advanced materialists (at least on those occasions when he was not overwhelmed with feelings of responsibility for the decline of his family)?

As shown below, Melville's personal history propelled him toward the bleak and pessimistic vision of aristocrats threatened with dispossession, though he never stayed long or without equivocation. When he was discouraged and depressed, the leaps from myth into history, from light into darkness, from official explanations into inside narratives were occasions for terror and pity, but no catharsis, just deserts.

[January 1857] PYRAMIDS. Scamper to them with officers on donkeys. Rapid passing of crowds upon the road; following of the donkey-boys & c. [In heyday holyday spirits arrived at the eternal sorrows of the pyramids . . . Pyramids from distance purple like mountains. Seem high & pointed, but flatten and depress as you approach. Vapors below summits. Kites sweeping & soaring around, hovering right over apex. At angles, like broken cliffs. Table-rock overhanging, adhering solely by morter. Sidelong look when midway up. Pyramids on a great ridge of sand. You leave the angle, and ascend hillocks of sand & ashes & broken morter & pottery to a point, & then go along a ledge to a path &c. Zig-zag routes. As many routes as to cross the Alps— . . . Caves—platforms. Looks larger midway than from top or bottom. Precipice on precipice, cliff on cliff. Nothing in Nature gives such an idea of vastness. A balloon to ascend them. View of persons ascending, Arab guides in flowing white mantles. Conducted as by angels up to heaven. Guides so tender. Resting. Pain in the chest. Exhaustion. Must hurry. None but the phlegmatic go deliberately. Old man with the spirits of youth—long looked for this chance—tried the ascent, half way—failed—brought down. Tried to go into the interior—fainted—brought out—leaned against the pyramid by the entrance—pale as death. Nothing so pathetic. Too much for him; oppressed by the massiveness & mystery of the pyramids. I myself too. A feeling of awe & terror came over me. Dread of the Arabs. Offering to lead me into a side-hole. The Dust. Long arched way,—then down as in a coal shaft. . . . Then as in mines, under the sea. The stooping & doubling. I shudder at idea of ancient Egyptians. ~~It was in these pyramids that was conceived the idea of Jehovah. Terrible mixture of the cunning and awful.~~ Moses learned in all the lore of the Egyptians. The idea of Jehovah born here.— [When I was at top, thought it not so high—sat down on edge, looked below—gradual nervousness & final giddiness & terror. [Entrance of pyramids like shoot for coal or timber. Horrible place for assassination. As long as earth endures some vestige will remain of pyramids. Nought but earthquake or geological revolution can obliterate them. Only people who made their mark, both in their masonry & their religion (through Moses) . . . Pyramids still loom before me—something vast, undefiled, incomprehensible, and awful. These the steps Jacob lay at. Line of desert & verdure, plain[er] than that between good & evil. An instant collision of alien elements. A long billow of desert forever hovers as in act of breaking, upon the verdure of

Egypt. Grass near the pyramids, but will not touch them—as if in fear or awe of them. Desert more fearful to look at than ocean. Theory of design of pyramids. Defence against desert. A Line of them. Absurd. Might have been created with the creation.

[February 5, 1857] Patmos is pretty high, & peculiarly barren looking. No inhabitants.—Was here again afflicted with the great curse of modern travel—skepticism. Could no more realize that St. John had ever had revelations here, than when off Juan Fernandez, could beleive in Robinson Crusoe according to De Foe. When my eye rested on arid height, spirit partook of the barreness.—Heartily wish Niebuhr & Strauss to the dogs.—The deuce take their penetration & acumen. They have robbed us of the bloom. If they have undeceived any one—no thanks to them.[45]

It appears that Melville's anti-Jewish or anti-intellectual remarks were written as a by-product of the movement from penetration to a looming image of retaliation—"vast, undefiled, incomprehensible, and awful," then to blankness; in the journal excerpts quoted here and above, ugly remarks about Jews were crossed out, as if he knew better, as if another hand had written them. Melville's retreats to moderation, then, may be interpreted as a defense against "the rage of seeing."[46] The scared silences of the Melville readers studied in this book have passed over such scampers from sublime insight into panic and self-repudiation, so characteristic of his and their writing.

Freedom would be no boon to the slave without education, and this also must be provided for before slavery can be abolished. The right of property is a sacred right which must be recognized, and before destroying the institution of slavery, means must be found for securing full and acceptable indemnification to the owner. These are the problems to be solved in connection with the question of slavery, and it is the duty of the statesmen, especially, to study them and find solutions for them. It is a false position for our countrymen to put themselves in, to oppose and condemn abolition only, without endeavoring to effect the object aimed at in a peaceful and satisfactory manner to all parties. Mere opposition will give rise to a conflict which may end in dissolution of the Union and the most frightful political and social convulsions.[47] (*The Phalanx*, Nov. 4, 1843)

Eternal sorrows

During the late 1850s, Melville toured the country with several lectures, quietly delivered but as critical as ever of upper-class snobbery and the moral hypocrisy of the Western civilizing mission. His subjects were the statues of Rome, the South Seas, and traveling. Public reception was mixed; newspaper reviews did not meet Maria's expectations for a family triumph. His artistic interests appear to have shifted to poetry during the late 1850s and throughout the Civil War. *Battle-Pieces* (1866) was a collection of poems written, according to one Melville scholar, in multiple, clashing personae to complicate and undo the partisan propaganda of either side.[48] It contained a prose "Supplement" generally considered conservative, even racist, by some Melvilleans. Apparently lining up with Lincoln, Andrew Johnson, and other moderates against abolitionists and Radical Republicans, he seemed to be implying that freedmen must be trained in the rigors of self-government before attaining full civic equality; it also argued for generosity in the North's treatment of the white Southern rebels who were "nearer to us in nature."[49] But like the lectures, the Supplement was strongly anti-imperialist. It must be acknowledged, however, that at a potential turning point in American race relations Melville assumed his aristocratic posture, lending his prestige to the forces of reaction:

> Since the test-oath operatively excludes from Congress all who in any way participated in Secession, therefore none but Southerners wholly in harmony with the North are eligible to seats. That is true for the time being. But the oath is alterable; and in the wonted fluctuations of parties not improbably it will undergo alteration, assuming such a form, perhaps, as not to bar admission into the National Legislature of men who represent the populations lately in revolt. Such a result would involve no violation of the principles of democratic government. Not readily can one perceive how the political existence of the millions of late Secessionists can permanently be ignored by this Republic. The years of the war tried our devotion to the Union; the time of peace may test the sincerity of our faith in democracy. (189)

Had he been unambivalently sympathetic to the Radical Republicans and abolitionists, Melville would have said that the years of the war tried our devotion to universal human rights, to the republican concept of equality before the law—democratic laws and principles inscribed in the Declaration of Independence and in the preamble to the Constitution that the secessionists had flouted. Rather than invoking "millions of late Secessionists" he could have noted that the chief secessionists were but a tiny fraction of the Southern population (for example, 32,000 aristocrats out of 600,000 South Carolinians, claimed *The Liberator* in 1843[50]); and that the rebels were defeated but unrepentant, indeed were terrorizing the freedmen and attempting to reinstate slavery by other means. Still, a certain inconclusiveness remains; Melville's final sentences express both his own claustrophobic fears of mobs and other harsh critics, but withal larger commitments: "But crowding thoughts must at last be checked; and in times like the present, one who desires to be impartially just in the expression of his views, moves as among sword-points presented on every side. Let us pray that the terrible historic tragedy of our time may not have been enacted without instructing our whole beloved country through terror and pity; and may fulfilment verify in the end those expectations which kindle the bards of Progress and Humanity" (189–90).

On September 10, 1867, Melville's first child, Malcolm, age eighteen, shot himself with a gun kept underneath his pillow. He was buried in military attire. The family did not want the public to think that suicide was intended; John C. Hoadley, husband to Melville's sister Catherine, wrote an editorial for the *Boston Weekly Advertiser*, insisting that the grandson of Lemuel Shaw could not have taken his own life in a fit of temporary insanity as the coroner's jury had decided:

> . . . Those who knew this pure, genial, healthful young man, know that he could be neither insane nor a self-murderer. (*Log*, 691)
> Eighteen years of age, tall, manly, engaging, full of frank and generous confidence, yet possessing a noble reserve and power of self-control, free from low tastes or bad companionships; fond of the society of his gentle and amiable mother; the delight of his little sisters, in whom he also delighted, pleased with the society of well-bred ladies in company with his mother; with bright business prospects, good social position, the love of all who knew him, not one of whom ever suspected him of a wrong action or an evil thought. . . .
> [T]his fondness for arms and military discipline, and for athletic sports, will, I venture to say, in all healthy young men be found exactly proportionate in strength and intensity to the purity of their character and their freedom from degrading vices, ignoble aims, and debasing pleasures. (not in *Log*)

A successful engineer, entrepreneur, and manufacturer with interests in the finer things, Hoadley had precisely delineated the code of his class and the self-assurance that Melville's conservative narrators would assume but that an accurate history could not sustain. After the horror of his son's death, Melville had written to his brother-in-law, "I wish you could have seen him as he lay in his last attitude, the ease of a gentle nature. Mackie never gave me a disrespectful word in his life, nor in any way ever failed in filialness."[51] This is surely a clue to Melville's harsh judgment of his literary creation and disturbing opinions, the character who should not have discomposed families with agitated, rough, and deicide books. (Whether or not Melville trusted Hoadley is unclear. Also unclear is the context of a letter to Hoadley ending in a postscript, "N.B. *I ain't crazy*," and enclosing an important poem celebrating the Pax Romana, i.e., the calming, tasteful, and family-sparing unambiguous rule of law, when "none felt how the leveller pines; / Yea, men were better than blatantly free / In the Age of the Antonines."[52])

His last works were written while employed as a minor customs officer (1866–86) and during his retirement. Besides poems and sketches, they included two major works. *Clarel* (1876) drew upon impressions gathered during his long trip to the Mediterranean (1856–57). Besides the fratricidal Civil War, *Clarel* also responded to the Paris Commune (1871), the severe depression that followed the Panic of 1873, and the deaths of close relatives: his younger brother Allan (Feb. 9, 1872), his mother Maria Gansevoort Melville (Apr. 1, 1872), his Uncle Peter Gansevoort (Jan. 4, 1876), and his sister Augusta (Apr. 4, 1876). Ten years later, Melville lost his only surviving son Feb. 23, 1886. Stanwix performed a more protracted form of suicide than Malcolm: A drifter and an alcoholic, careless of his health, Stanwix died of tuberculosis at age thirty-five. That year Melville began the tortuous process that finally composed the Handsome Sailor's downfall/ascension.[53]

In a revealing note to Melville's cousin Kate Lansing, hitherto inadequately addressed by Melville scholars, his wife, Elizabeth, summarized the family consensus about Herman that must have clashed with his own sense of reality: ". . . and I want you *always* to mention Herman's name in your letters, especially if it is to say anything about coming down—I know your feeling is always right to him, and so does everyone else, but he is *morbidly* sensitive, poor fellow, and I always try (though I can't succeed to my sorrow) to smooth the fancied rough edges to him whenever I can—so I know you will understand when I mention it" (Feb. 25, 1877, *Log,* 759).[54] Elizabeth was saying, sorrowfully, that the poor fellow's misperception of family rejection was a symptom of morbidity, an extreme and unhealthy mental state, to be pitied. "The fancied rough edges" appear throughout Melville's work. They are the jagged scars that mar the bodies of Melville's key characters, including Ahab and Pierre. In "Billy Budd, Sailor (An inside narrative)," the jagged edge appears explicitly as a figuration of uncompromising honesty. After Billy has been hanged, then consigned to the deep, "larger sea-fowl" ominously circle the spot where his body had disappeared, offering a "croaking requiem" blended with "a second strange human murmur" from the crew. This inchoate protest is cut off by an unusual drumbeat to quarters, ordered by Captain Vere: "'With mankind,' [Captain Vere] would say, 'forms, measured forms, are everything; and that is the import couched in the story of Orpheus with his lyre spellbinding the wild denizens of the wood.' And this he once applied to the disruption of forms going on across the Channel and the consequences thereof" (chap. 27). In his last unread letter of 1846, Herman had written to his wildly democratic brother Gansevoort that "composure is every thing." Now he has Captain Vere linking measured forms and their disruption to the French Revolution. Melville is hinting that formal innovation (like his own) was the cause of its excesses. Only one paragraph lies between Vere's statement and the following: "The symmetry of form attainable in pure fiction cannot so readily be achieved in a narration essentially having less to do with fable than with fact. Truth uncompromisingly told will always have its ragged edges; hence the conclusion of such a narration is apt to be less finished than an architectural finial" (chap. 28).

After forty years of accusations that he was a liar, that he was unreadable, that he had exaggerated his suffering and the enmity of others, he calmly defended his veracity with the words "ragged edges"; "ragged" suggests the rage of the rebellious French. Melville is not saying there is no universal truth, that all points of view are equally suspect, but that readers must consider the source of the narrative and the particular circumstances that influence any given interpretation: The reader has work to do. In any case, truth unfolds and evolves in time under the pressure of events, though it suffers an underground existence only, preserved in the hearts of ordinary people. As in *White-Jacket* (1850), the officers and the sailors have opposing interests, thus divergent narratives of the incident. The "authorized" version grossly misreports the events: Billy was the ringleader of a mutiny; in the act of arraignment, "Claggart . . . was vindictively stabbed to the heart by the suddenly drawn sheath knife of Budd." (Compare these words to the images describing Ahab harpooning Moby Dick or Babo's sudden lunge toward Benito Cereno.) Claggart was the exemplary patriotic "petty officer" (the middle manager), "upon whom, as none know better than the commissioned gentlemen, the efficiency of His Majesty's navy so largely depends." But the "authorized" "publication [is] now long ago superannuated and forgotten." While no prose record of the sailors' responses remains, the sailors treasure chips of "the spar from which the foretopman was suspended"; they have not bought the contrived myth of Billy's guilt: "Ignorant though they were of the secret facts of the tragedy, and not thinking but that the penalty was somehow unavoidably inflicted from the naval point of view, for all that they instinctively felt that Billy was a sort of man as incapable of mutiny as of wilful murder." After discussion among themselves, one gifted sailor, "another foretopman, one of his own watch," writes a poem, "Billy in the Darbies." At first privately circulated among themselves, it "finally got rudely printed at Portsmouth as a ballad." The last chapters of the inside narrative have laid out two competing big pictures, and the text ends with the sailors' collective creation, not the version favorable to Vere's judgment. Several Melville scholars, writing after the defeat of fascism, turned the political message around:

[F. Barron Freeman, 1948] . . . to be a great tragedy, it cannot end without the purge and tranquillity which come with greater understanding and leave a note of hope. The evil characters may go unpunished; but if, through the death of the hero, their sin is realized and understood by some of the participants in the tragedy, then a catharsis is achieved and the spectator or reader is made to feel that, however dark the future looks, through this new-found comprehension at least some good can come from evil. Thus, after the rising calm of Billy's death scene which has lent a positive, upward surge to the reader's emotions, the truth of his sacrifice is spread abroad, not through those who write the blindly intellectual "official report" of the case, but through the common illiterate sailors who made a legend of the event. (125)

[New Critic Warner Berthoff, 1962] Melville is at some pains to present the martial law as sui generis, and in its own terms morally unimpeachable.[55]

[Suggested study topic] . . . 6. Write character sketches of Captain Vere and Claggart in contexts different from those in "Billy Budd." For instance, attempt to predict their behavior in a country club, a business office, an infantry regiment.[56]

F. Barron Freeman has made the greatness of the tragic tale dependent on turning state murder into a proletarian sailor-ratified noble sacrifice—An "incomprehensible world"[57] is blessed with "a new-found comprehension"—while Warner Berthoff described Billy Budd's creator as obviously siding with Vere. The R.D.M. Corporation's "Study Master" does not ask young readers to compare Melville's actual text with the accounts delivered by regnant critics, but to play anthropologist, fiddling with types of contexts and the presumably site-specific moral behavior each elicits.

Cannons and lapses

Intensifying class, racial, and gender warfare in America and Europe after the Civil War and the Depression of 1873 had coincided with a period of personal loss for Melville, with differing and opposite effects upon his writing in *Clarel, A Poem and Pilgrimage in the Holy Land*. (The title alone should fortify those critics who see Melville's art and life as ever entwined.) The death of his mother seems to have loosened his tongue; he could now write about his feelings of alienation from the family, his ongoing struggle with naturalism (atheistic materialism), and homoerotic surges. But the departure of his beloved and pious sister Augusta was an event that may have added to an already excessive burden of guilt, pulling him back to his customary defenses. Augusta, along with his other sisters, had been prevented from disturbing him during the last hectic stages of composition and preparation for the printer. She died in April 1876 at her younger brother Tom's home while Herman was reading proof; he was allowed to see her only once before she died (February 26), and, as his sister Frances reported, "could hardly control his feelings while with her" (Howard, 309). Losses, whether of bodies or of his own credibility, were taken as personal lapses. His godlike ungodly psyche had exacerbated political and family strife alike; such self-blame would infiltrate all his characterizations of revolt, of sane disagreement with official reality. The critical intellect of radical Enlightenment was too strong, however, to stay buried for long. Organic conservative denunciations of mobocracy alternated with excavations and exhumations of the same old radical insight and resolve, but such outbursts would call forth the similarly terrifying "whiteness of the whale." His numbing "pallid composure" was the calcification or liming over that spared the family that had supported him and had repeatedly taken him back no matter what graffiti his "Jewish" characters had scrawled on conservative monuments or bodies. These apparent oscillations are not necessarily the symptoms of ambivalence, but may be the strategy of an author who, like Shakespeare or Milton, wants to match his conservative and radical characters in fair fight. The reader's critical judgment is activated; at the same time the artist can argue with himself, sorting out and evaluating his many inner voices as they react to momentous cultural shifts, no easy task given the balance of forces in his depleted family.

Melville's two-volume poem was completed in 1876: At its finish, set in the month of April (the month of his mother's death, also Augusta's), *Clarel* faces a troop of dead friends and loved ones. The Melville Revival is inscrutable without a survey of the principal characters and their views of modernity, for numerous scholars have approved Melville's mature authorial voice as precursor to Pound and Eliot; hence Melville is assumed to be in agreement with the moderates or reactionaries encountered by the youthful seeker, Clarel. In the next section of this chapter, it is suggested that Melville's text contradicts that conclusion; moreover, that the poem cannot be discussed without reference to the emotional transactions in his family, one example being the letter quoted above, in which Elizabeth complains about Herman's "fancied rough edges." Frequently dismissed as unreadable and soporific, *Clarel* remains an indispensable guide to Melville's ongoing revisions of key relationships (especially his feelings for Hawthorne: "Name him— Vine") and the fantasied contributions of his "rebel senses" to family dissonance, decline, and fall. The latter feelings are partly expressed through the voice of Mortmain, the morbid and suicidal Swedish ex-revolutionary, a version of the repentant Wandering Jew. The inconsolable Swede is antitype to two relentless optimists: the apostate Jewish geologist Margoth, agent of capital and industrialization, and the liberal Anglican priest Derwent, a fellow traveler with science and atheism. The following excerpts from *Clarel* elaborate one aspect of the Melville problem:

"Jewish" materialism—the critical intellect (Margoth's) he had embraced at the expense of family solidarity.

THE DISAPPEARING RAINBOW

Struggling to renew his shaken faith, Clarel has joined a band of believers touring the environs of Jerusalem; they have been joined briefly by Margoth, intent on taunting his companions: It is Margoth who desacralizes the Holy Land. The pilgrims linger "by the marge" of the Dead Sea; debating with Derwent, "iron-grey" Margoth's immovable grey and black metaphors darken an already deflowered scene:

> "The agitating influence
> Of knowledge never will dispense
> With teasing faith, do what ye may.
> Adjust and readjust, ye deal
> With compass in a ship of steel."
>   "Such perturbations do but give
> Proof that faith's vital: sensitive
> Is faith, my friend."
>   "Go to, go to:
> Your black bat! how she hangs askew,
> Torpid, from wall by claws of wings:
> Let drop the left—sticks fast the right;
> Then this unhook—the other swings;
> Leave—she regains her double plight." (*Clarel*, 2.29.103–15)

Faith militant counterattacks with the oriflamme (the red ensign of medieval French royalty and here an emblem of the aristocratic order), now an overruling rainbow:

> "Ah, look," cried Derwent; "ah, behold!"
> From the blue battlements of air,
> Over saline vapors hovering there,
> A flag was flung out—curved in fold—
> Fiery, rosy, violet, green—
> And, lovelier growing, brighter, fairer,
> Transfigured all that evil scene;

And Iris was the standard bearer.
    None spake. As in a world made new,
With upturned faces they review
That oriflamme, the which no man
Would look for in such clime of ban. (116–27)

Nehemiah, the aged fundamentalist millenarian, thinks of his New England farm:

'Twas northern; and its home-like look
Touched Nehemiah. He, late with book
Gliding from Margoth's dubious sway,
Was standing by the ass apart;
And when he caught that scarf of May
How many a year ran back his heart:
Scythes hang in orchard, hay-cocks loom
After eve-showers, the mossed roofs gloom
Greenly beneath the homestead trees;
He tingles with these memories. (128–37)

Momentarily the oriflamme seems to emanate from within Vine, the gifted aristocratic artist, incognito in the text. The first time they met, Clarel and Vine had bonded in a glance, in appreciation of Nehemiah's gift for restoring the spiritual aura to humdrum places, "moved by that act / Of one whose faith transfigured fact" (1.28.135–36). But here Melville's and Clarel's ego ideal orders him to seek commercial success by pandering to the mucky masses. Compare Vine's introduction to the reader with the disillusioning adviser by the marge:

    Vine's manner shy
A clog, a hindrance might imply;
A lack of parlor-wont. But grace
Which is in substance deep and grain
May, peradventure, well pass by
The polish of veneer. No trace
Of passion's soil or lucre's stain,
Though life was now half ferried o'er.
· · · · · · · · · · · · · · · · · ·
    A saint then do we here unfold?
Nay, the ripe flush, Venetian mould
Evinced no nature saintly fine,

But blood like swart Vesuvian wine,
What cooled the current? Under cheer
Of opulent softness, reigned austere
Control of self. Flesh, but scarce pride,
Was curbed: desire was mortified;
But less indeed by moral sway
Than doubt if happiness thro' clay
Be reachable. (1.29.9–16, 27–37)

. . . .

    For Vine, over him suffusive stole
An efflorescence; all the soul
Flowering in flush upon the brow.
But 'twas ambiguously replaced
In words addressed to Clarel now—
"Yonder the arch dips in the waste;
Thither! and win the pouch of gold." (2.29.138–44)

Vine has switched from the otherworldly ascetic he at first appeared to be, the
gentleman revolted by Margoth. A few lines earlier in the same canto (2.29.62–67),
"docile" Vine is shown to be willfully ignorant of bookish learning, neither reserved
nor shy; unburdened by deep thought, he may bend this way and that to please the
speaker; his directive to Clarel is ambiguous, much like Melville's mother's admonitions to be simultaneously moral, heroic, and successful on society's terms. One
may gather (with Henry Murray) that Hawthorne was indeed the model for the religious yet pragmatic and amoral Plinlimmon of *Pierre*, whose prying, mocking
glance looks down from a window upon the Fool of Virtue.[58] It is the atheist Margoth, however, who brings the unleavened nakedness of desolation: the
oriflamme/rainbow itself lies, a false promise from a treacherous Father. With Margoth's words, "the bloom" suddenly disappears, like the soul that had briefly
flowered upon Vine's brow:

"... yonder bow's forsworn.
The covenant made on Noah's morn,
Was that well kept? why, hardly here,
Where whelmed by fire and flood, they say,
The townsfolk sank in after day,
Yon sign in heaven should reappear."
    They heard, but in such torpid gloom
Scarcely they recked, for now the bloom

Vanished from sight, and half the sea
Died down to glazed monotony. (2.29.149–58)

By submitting to the market, the true Vine has joined Margoth in the bourgeois destruction of medieval agrarian order; portentously, as the bloom vanishes, Clarel
has a premonition of his comforting loved one's (Ruth's/Augusta's) death.

Vine is so unfavorably drawn that the reader may wonder if Melville, not
Hawthorne, was the one who was disappointed. At the outset of his trip to the Holy
Land in 1856–57, Melville had visited the older man near Liverpool where
he had been appointed American consul, a handsome reward for his campaign
biography of Franklin Pierce: "Wednesday Nov 12 At Southport. An agreeable
day. Took a long walk by the sea. Sands & grass. Wild & desolate. A strong wind.
Good talk. In the evening Stout & Fox & Geese.—Julian grown into a fine lad;
Una taller than her mother. Mrs Hawthorne not in good health. Mr H. stayed
home for me."[59] Melville's journal notes at first seem to relate a solitary experience;
Hawthorne is not mentioned as his companion until the seventh sentence; then
there is reunion with the lovely family in which Mr H. is embosomed. Hawthorne's
oft-quoted journal entry offers as revealing a synopsis of their relationship as
any in the subsequent literature. The talk is not so good in Hawthorne's account.
(Italics mark passages excised in Sophia Peabody Hawthorne's edition of the *English
Notebooks*, "which Melville owned and no doubt read while composing *Clarel*."):[60]

[Melville is] looking much as he used to do (*a little paler and perhaps a little
sadder*), *in a rough outside coat*, and with his characteristic gravity and reserve
of manner. . . . *Melville has not been well of late; he has been affected with neural-
gic complaints in his head and limbs, and no doubt has suffered from too constant
literary occupation, pursued without much success, latterly; and his writings, for a
long while past, have indicated a morbid state of mind*. . . . I do not wonder that
he found it necessary to take an airing through the world, after so many years
of toilsome pen-labor and *domestic life*, following upon so wild and adventurous a youth as his was. . . . we took a pretty long walk together, and sat down
in a hollow among the sand hills (sheltering ourselves from the high, cool
wind) *and smoked a cigar*. Melville, as he always does, began to reason of
Providence and futurity, and of everything that lies beyond human ken, *and
informed me that he had "pretty much made up his mind to be annihilated"; but
still he does not seem to rest in that anticipation; and, I think, will never rest until
he gets hold of a definite belief. It is strange how he persists—and has persisted ever
since I knew him, and probably long before—in wandering to-and-fro over these
deserts, as dismal and monotonous as the sand hills amid which we were sitting.*

He can neither believe, nor be comfortable in his unbelief; and he is too honest and courageous not to try to do one or the other. If he were a religious man, he would be one of the most truly religious and reverential; he has a very high and noble nature, and better worth immortality than most of us.

It would be interesting to know if Melville himself diagnosed his condition and prospects; it does sound as if the problems of his "domestic life" were burdensome, while Hawthorne seems burdened by the Melville problem. Hawthorne does not directly criticize his friend for lofty high-mindedness; rather, he is impatient with Melville's obsessive seeking after the unknowable while also noting that his friend is "better worth immortality than most of us." Was Melville wriggling free from the worldly materialism of his relatives and Hawthorne alike when he announced (ambiguously) that he had "pretty much made up his mind to be annihilated"? Hawthorne died in 1864, freeing Melville to be openly critical.

Clarel does suggest crass motives in the creator of Ethan Brand. Another passage reveals even more emphatic contempt for Hawthorne's lack of commitment than the scene on the marge, significant for its suggestion that Melville scorned such aloofness from the conflicts of conscience: He hints that Hawthorne's apparent boredom with Melville's hellishly unresolved questioning concealed anger and contempt. The pilgrims are on the high desert, as usual, inconclusively arguing over the issues that most exercised their Christian contemporaries: the inevitably corrosive effects of science on religion and the Mammonish propensities of democracy:

> For Vine, from that unchristened earth
> Bits he picked up of porous stone,
> And crushed in fist: or one by one,
> Through the dull void of desert air,
> He tossed them into valley down;
> Or pelted his own shadow there;
> Nor sided he with anything:
> By fits, indeed, he wakeful looked;
> But, in the main, how ill he brooked
> That weary length of arguing—
> Like tale interminable told
> In Hades by some gossip old
> To while the never-ending night.
> Apart he went.[61] (3.5.183–96)

Clarel wants a clear-cut statement of moral and intellectual principle to touch his inmost centre, and Vine won't give it to him; so much for "one of the most fortunate" literary friendships in American history.[62] Melville has plainly separated himself from Vine's pseudo-aristocratic alienation, the ennui that refuses to partake of the universal throb. The unpardonable sin Hawthorne had imputed to Ethan Brand was no more than his own shadow. What does this unsympathetic portrait of Vine tell us about Melville's supposed conservative or reactionary politics in his late middle age?

Neither gibing Margoth nor raging Mortmain trusts the rainbow, causing consternation among their companions and the tumbling of rocks.[63] Mortmain is seated upon his "throne," the skull of a camel, by the marge of the Dead Sea, cataloguing the sins that called flood and fire upon the wicked city of Sodom. At the climax of his lengthy speech an evil God is held responsible for all humanity's failings:

> "Nearer the core than man can go
> Or Science get—nearer the slime
> Of nature's rudiments and lime
> In chyle before the bone. Thee, thee,
> In thee the filmy cell is spun—
> The mould thou art of what men be:
> Events are all in thee begun—
> By thee, through thee!—Undo, undo,
> Prithee, undo, and still renew
> The fall forever!"
>   On his throne
> He lapsed; and muffled came the moan
> How multitudinous in sound,
> From Sodom's wave. He glanced around:
> They all had left him, one by one.
> Was it because he open threw
> The inmost to the outward view?
> Or did but pain at frenzied thought,
> Prompt to avoid him, since but naught
> In such case might remonstrance do?
> But none there ventured idle plea,
> Weak sneer, or fraudful levity. (2.36.95–115)

Mortmain has told his companions, we are what we were made; this is the forbidden knowledge digested by the queen of this universe, the queenly personality; if he is flawed, it is not his fault. Speaking through Mortmain, Melville may have disclosed his dark secret(s) on the margin, the remote conclusion that, along with atheism, would have most revolted his family: Clarel's bisexual surges disgustedly mirror the moulding Father.[64] He remains Ahab, railing along with Byron and other

Left romantics: "They all had left him, one by one." Shortly after this scene, Nehemiah is found dead (by the marge again); at his funeral, Margoth's "sulking reverence" precedes an avalanche and the fading of a pale pencilled fog-bow, a re-iteration of crushed bodies and vanishing idealizations.

Darkness at noon

Since Melville's "outbursts" have been used against him by hostile critics, we might see how the artist accounted for them. Derwent, like Elizabeth or Maria, flings rainbows over wrecks. Mortmain lapses into a passion-fit shortly after the happy priest answers Rolfe's query about the Jews of ancient Palestine. Derwent delivers a narrative of upward progress: Slavery and wandering induced "gloom" and "bigot law" in the Jews, but the brightness of the Greeks and the liberal reforms of Hillel leavened their culture, allowing for the spot of green that produced "the Essene." Now lilies bloom everywhere and for every man:

> "How did the crowning Teacher show
> His broad and blessed comity.
> I do avow He still doth seem
> Pontiff of optimists supreme!"
>   The Swede sat stone-like. Suddenly:
> "Leave thy carmine! From thorns the streak
> Ruddies enough that tortured cheek.
> 'Twas Shaftesbury first assumed your tone,
> Trying to cheerfulize Christ's moan."
>   "Nay now," plead Derwent, earnest here,
> And in his eyes the forming tear;
> "But hear me, hear!"
>   "No more of it!"
> And rose. It was his passion-fit.
> The other changed; his pleasant cheer,
> Confronted by that aspect wild,
> Dropped like the flower from Ceres' child
> In Enna, seeing the pale brow
> Of Pluto dank from scud below.
>   Though by Gethsemane, where first
> Derwent encountered Mortmain's mien,
> Christian forbearance well he nursed,
> Allowing for distempered spleen;
> Now all was altered, quite reversed—
>
>   . . . .

> . . . [Clarel] longed to know
> How it could be, that while the rest
> Contented scarce the splenetic Swede,
> They hardly so provoked the man
> To biting outburst unrepressed
> As did the cleric's gentle fan.[65] (3.6.132–54, 159–64)

Melville has reiterated the leitmotif of his symbolist works, for instance, Bartleby's sudden switch from docile employee to rebel, or the Invalid Titan's attack on the herb doctor, salesman of the Good Samaritan Pain Dissuader, its label portraying a Romish Madonna. The effect of Mortmain's passion-fit upon Derwent (whose droop incorporates a pagan legend: where did that geniality go?) hints that Melville's inside narratives dispensed sadness and death. First Mortmain sits in stony silence, then attacks the Father who has abandoned the Son and anyone else who minimizes the depth and persistence of human suffering. Has Melville knowingly displaced his own family drama onto the crucifixion and onto nature? Earlier in the text, young Celio, like Mortmain, explicitly linked to the Wandering Jew, had delivered an impassioned reproach on behalf of Christ on the cross:

> . . . crying out in death's eclipse,
> When rainbow none his eyes might see,
> Enlarged the margin for despair—
> *My God, my God, forsakest me?*
> Upbraider! we upbraid again;
> Thee we upbraid; our pangs constrain
> Pathos itself to cruelty. (1.13.44–50)

The persistent Melvillean theme has erupted again: An evil Father has made us weak, then demanded moral purity so unattainable that only Christ Himself could reach it—"The shark thou mad'st, yet claim'st the dove." Even so, He was abandoned; there is no covenant between God and Man, no happy end, no heavenly reward for worldly sacrifice, no rainbow. Celio's tirade continues: Christ has been conned, and Christian doctrine has inspired wars, not brotherly love:

> . . . By what art
> of conjuration might the heart
> Of heavenly love, so sweet, so good,
> Corrupt into the creeds malign,
> Begetting strife's pernicious brood,
> Which claimed for patron thee divine?

Anew, anew,
For this thou bleedest, Anguished Face;
Yea, thou through ages to accrue,
Shalt the Medusa shield replace:
In beauty and in terror too
Shalt paralyze the nobler race—
Smite or suspend, perplex, deter—
Tortured, shalt prove a torturer.
Whatever ribald Future be,
Thee shall these heed, amaze thy hearts with thee—
Thy white, thy red, thy fairness and thy tragedy. (1.13.86–102)

Celio dies shortly after his bitter prophecy. The colors of white and red link Christ to Lucy and Mary in *Pierre*, not to snaky-locked dark Isabel. It is *their* fair faces that turn Melville's amazed heart to stone, the stone of Pierre's weeping prison. When Melville revises the good father into torturer, flowers droop and fall in the gently fanning family: Their rot infiltrates perceptions of Melville's Isabel-inspired art. The family's not-so-passive aggression becomes the "whitish scar" marring Daniel Orme's tattooed vermilion cross, or before that the "half-livid and half-bloody brand" inflicted on Pierre by Cousin Glen's whip. The pairing of red and white is no accident.[66]

Return to *Clarel*. Derwent is saddened again, this time by Ungar, the part-Indian Baltimore Catholic now a mercenary for the Turks. Criticizing his stereotyping of Turkish barbarism, Ungar wounds Derwent's amour propre by protesting that the Anglo-Saxons have nothing to brag about in the treatment of their own wards:

"*As cruel as a Turk:* Whence came
That proverb old as the crusades?
From Anglo-Saxons. What are they?
Let the horse answer, and blockades
Of medicine in civil fray!
The Anglo-Saxons—lacking grace
To win the love of any race;
Hated by myriads dispossessed
Of rights—the Indians East and West.
These pirates of the sphere! grave looters—
Grave, canting, Mammonite freebooters,
Who in the name of Christ and Trade

(Oh, bucklered forehead of the brass!)
Deflower the world's last sylvan glade!"
   "Alas, alas, ten times alas,
Poor Anglo-Saxons!" Derwent sighed.
[Ungar:] "Nay, but if there I lurched too wide,
Respond to this: Old ballads sing
Fair Christian children crucified
By impious Jews: you've heard the thing:
Yes, fable; but there's truth hard by:
How many Hughs of Lincoln, say,
Does Mammon in his mills, to-day,
Crook, if he do not crucify?"
   "Ah, come," said Derwent; "come, now, come;
Think you that we who build the home
For foundlings, and yield sums immense
To hospitals for indigence—"
[Ungar:] "Your alms house smaller than your till,
And poor-house won't absolve your mill." (4.9.112–41)

In pointing out the asymmetry between the crumbs strewn by industrialists and
the body-breaking labor of the factories, Ungar has rejected Derwent's pseudo-
paternalism. The merchant Rolfe asks Ungar if technology will not "guarantee . . .
[a] happy sequel" to all this misery. Ungar retorts:

   "Arts are tools;
But tools, they say, are to the strong:
Is Satan weak? weak is the Wrong?
No blessed augury overrules:
Your arts advance in faith's decay:
You are but drilling the new Hun
Whose growl even now can some dismay;
Vindictive in his heart of hearts,
He schools him in your mines and marts—
A skilled destroyer." (4.21.14–23)

Ungar's prophecy reinforces the warning that closed Part 2 (the first of two volumes as originally published). Once again, "salt" and the rainbow are juxtaposed as
Nehemiah is laid to rest: Derwent conducts the service, paraphrasing the Twenty-
third Psalm, then

... they kneeled—with foreheads bare
Bowed as he made the burial prayer.
Even Margoth bent him; but was so
As some hard salt will do
Holding the narrow plank that bears
The shotted hammock, while brief prayers
Are by the master read mid war
Relentless of wild elements—
The sleet congealing on the spar:
It was a sulking reverence. (2.39.112–28)

With Margoth's resentful attendance connected to atheistic sailors, a distant mountain falls down during seventeen lines of roars, thumps, and horrid echoes "fold on fold." The last verse of the canto shows us the fading "fog-bow," hovering like the oriflamme above the saline vapors, an enfeebled "counter-object" to the avalanche of nature's fury/the mob proposed by Margothian black bats.

The apocalyptic sublime is the consequence of Margoth's blithe indifference to omens and shadows, to the codes of gentlemanly behavior, to the lessons of the Fall, or to the social consequences of the market-expanding technology furthered by his science. Margoth was preceded by the mad scientist in Hawthorne's gothic tale, "The Birth-mark" (1843): Aylmer attempts to remove an imperfection from his wife's cheek—a crimson hand. The operation succeeds, but the patient dies:

> Again Aylmer resumed his watch. Nor was it without avail. The Crimson Hand, which at first had been strongly visible upon the marble paleness of Georgiana's cheek, now grew more faintly outlined. She remained not less pale than ever; but the birthmark, with every breath that came and went, lost somewhat of its former distinctness. Its presence had been awful; its departure was more awful still. Watch the stain of the rainbow fading out of the sky, and you will know how that mysterious symbol passed away.
>
> By Heaven! it is well-nigh gone! said Aylmer to himself, almost in irrepressible ecstasy. "I can scarcely trace it now. Success! success! But she is so pale!"[67]

Margoth had been experimenting with strange chemicals immediately before the death of Nehemiah; the proximity of these events suggests that Margoth's experiments have killed the kindly old man of the book. Margoth, an optimistic mechanical materialist like Aylmer, wants the stain of original sin to disappear for the sake of material well-being; if this means demystifying religion, so be it:

The bread of wisdom here to break,
Margoth holds forth: the gossip tells
Of things the prophets left unsaid—
With master-key unlocks the spells
And mysteries of the world unmade;
Then mentions Salem: "Stale is she!
Lay flat the walls, let in the air,
That folk no more may sicken there!
Wake up the dead; and let there be
Rails, wires, from Olivet to the sea,
With station in Gethsemane." (2.20.84–94)

Perversely, Hawthorne connects the "Crimson Hand" (Georgiana's birthmark) to the rainbow that marked God's forgiveness and renewed the covenant between God and man. For Hawthorne, the perfectionist fanaticism of radical Protestantism (symbolized in Aylmer's obsession) is a negation, not a fulfillment, of godliness. If the covenant is a "stain" (Jewish lucre?), then we are correct to make war on self-deceived and cerebral Hebrew messianism with its fixation on social amelioration in a world naturally divided between genders, colors, and classes: saving rainbows versus hard salts. For the organic conservative, the Hebrew God and those who follow the Chosen People are suffering from "the tragedy of mind" (the title of William Ellery Sedgwick's posthumous book, 1944).

Ungar told Rolfe that anti-Christ (Margoth) must prevail in a secular world ruled by the Dr. Aylmers and their progeny. For Ungar, the rainbow is a reassuring presence that lightens fears of another Deluge and controls the devil's machinations. Without the "blessed augury," the devil will avail himself of new tools and incite needless destruction. If Ungar's enlistments of religion to unhand mob rule were to be the chief lesson of *Clarel*, there would be no difficulty in describing Melville's politics. Is the Melville problem "the Jewish problem"[68] as has been hinted throughout this book? Who is Ungar's New Hun? Is his horrified survey of industrial society fair to nineteenth-century labor militancy, or is it suffused with antisemitism and irrationalism? Melville's portraits of Jews should be understood as a gallery of possibilities offered by nineteenth-century Anglo-American culture. Margoth, for Walter Bezanson, "limned with a touch of savage glee" (NN *Clarel*, 574), bears an uncanny resemblance to the incorruptible modern artist, the dirty, dusty materialist digging and probing beneath the surface of family relationships to uncover their resentful martyrdom on behalf of family "unity." "Margoth" was tracing dissatisfaction that marred placid white foreheads, the "foreheads bare"; Melville was struggling against the internalized family agreement to smooth over ruffled feelings that would have turned him into the moderate man. To the degree that Melville scholars are embarrassed by his geologic bad Jew, they are rejecting the author's (left-wing) modernism.

The interplays among the characters in *Clarel* should not be reduced to an ahistoric rift between mechanical materialism vs. idealism or atheism vs. faith as previous Melvilleans have done. At a time when Christian ethics had either been rejected wholesale or distorted for purposes of social control, Vine and Derwent first appear to Clarel as sincere Christians, Hellenistically combining pagan and Christian attitudes, attracting his respect and love. But they, like Rolfe (1.34.65–66), let him down: While loathing Margoth's crudity, Vine turns out to be a hypocrite and trimmer, a sensualist choosing success over spirituality. Derwent tries to reconcile science and religion, conveniently erasing the suffering concealed in paternalistic charity, a nonsolution to class exploitation. (What would Ungar and Derwent have said about the welfare state that promises to smooth the fancied rough edges of class society?) Derwent and Vine are confidence men and nihilists; they have no consistent philosophical orientation. Mortmain may be the earnest character, the moralist bereft of father figures, with whom Melville most closely identified. But Margoth is another aspect of himself: the ribald satirist and empiricist. Melville's affinities to Clarel, Celio, Mortmain, and Margoth, a quartet evoking the all-disclosing Romantic Wandering Jew, reflected the isolation that Melville inevitably encountered as a man of the transition from feudalism to capitalism—isolated because the judges of "Right Reason" were switched from priestly mediators to democratic majorities; but as Lemuel Shaw's dependent son-in-law, he was splintered from a more like-minded constituency, or perhaps that constituency has only begun to emerge. Radical Enlightenment, I suggest, is the totality of the open-ended process represented by the historicizing, introspective, clear-eyed double-breasted Eve himself.[69] His dueling characters are not simply checks and balances to one another's partly flawed vision as an irresolute "pluralist" would see it. Rather, his interminable tests of authority aim to separate truth from error, and hence turn Melville's corporatist friends and family against him, bringing darkness at noon.

Vine, Derwent, and Rolfe disapprove of Margoth or any *juif errant*, any "bold freethinking Jew" (2.22.55). Derwent compares Spinoza to Margoth; Spinoza was

". . . Pan's Atheist.
That high intelligence but dreamed—
Above delusion's vulgar plain
Deluded still. The erring twain,
Spinosa [*sic*] and poor Margoth here,
Both Jews, which in dissent do vary:
In these what parted poles appear—

The blind man and the visionary."
    "And whose the eye that sees aright,
If any?" Clarel eager asked.
Aside Rolfe turned as overtasked;
And none responded. 'Twas like night
Descending from the seats of light,
Or seeming thence to fall. But here
Sedate a kindly tempered look
Private and confidential spoke
From Derwent's eyes, Clarel to cheer:
Take heart; something to fit thy youth
Instill I may, some saving truth—
Not best just now to volunteer.
    Thought Clarel: Pray, and what wouldst prove?
Thy faith an over-easy glove.
    Meanwhile Vine had relapsed. They saw
In silence the heart's shadow draw—
Rich shadow, such as gardens keep
In bower aside, where glow-worms peep
In evening over the virgin bed
Where dark-green periwinkles sleep—
Their bud the Violet of the Dead. (2.22.121–49)

Clarel's question, "Whose the eye that sees aright, / If any?" could signify either the attitude of the skeptic (usually a conservative) or the modern freethinker's willingness to revise habitual ways of seeing. Given the disapproving silence of his older companions or Derwent's complacency, I believe Clarel leans toward the freethinkers.

The corporatist fathers had all slammed doors on Clarel. During the fatal confrontation between the master-at-arms and Billy Budd, Vine's Violet reappears in Claggart's rich violet eyes that turn to purple-brown, the color Melville had assigned to Vine as he first appears to Clarel: "A funeral man, yet richly fair— / Fair as the sabled violets be" (1.28.42–43). The envious Claggart had accused Billy of planning a mutiny. Captain Vere invites Billy Budd to his cabin to face the charges. The perfectly good boy assumes the invitation signifies an impending promotion:

"Shut the door there, sentry," said the commander; "stand without, and let nobody come in.—Now, Master-at-arms, tell this man to his face what you told of him to me," and stood prepared to scrutinize the mutually confronting visages.

With the measured step and calm collected air of an asylum physician approaching in the public hall some patient beginning to show indications of a coming paroxysm, Claggart deliberately advanced within short range of Billy and, mesmerically looking him in the eye, briefly recapitulated the accusation.

Not at first did Billy take it in. When he did, the rose-tan of his cheek looked struck as by white leprosy. He stood like one impaled and gagged. Meanwhile the accuser's eyes, removing not as yet from the blue dilated ones, underwent a phenomenal change, their wonted rich violet color blurring into a muddy purple. Those lights of human intelligence, losing human expression, were gelidly protruding like the alien eyes of certain uncatalogued[70] creatures of the deep. The first mesmeric glance was one of serpent fascination; the last was as the paralyzing lurch of the torpedo fish.[71]

"Speak, man!" said Captain Vere to the transfixed one, struck by his aspect even more than Claggart's. "Speak! Defend yourself!" Which appeal caused but a strange dumb gesturing and gurgling in Billy; amazement at such an accusation so suddenly sprung on inexperienced nonage; this, and, it may be, horror of the accuser's eyes, serving to bring out his lurking defect and in this instance for the time intensifying it into a convulsed tongue-tie; while the intent head and entire form straining forward in an agony of ineffectual eagerness to obey the injunction to speak and defend himself, gave an expression to the face like that of a condemned vestal priestess in the moment of being buried alive, and in the first struggle against suffocation.

Though at the time Captain Vere was quite ignorant of Billy's liability to vocal impediment, he now immediately divined it, since vividly Billy's aspect recalled to him that of a bright young schoolmate of his whom he had once seen struck by much the same startling impotence in the act of eagerly rising in the class to be foremost in response to a testing question put to it by the master. Going close up the young sailor, and laying a soothing hand on his shoulder, he said, "There is no hurry, my boy. Take your time, take your time." Contrary to the effect intended, these words, so fatherly in tone, doubtless touching Billy to the quick, prompted yet more violent effects at utterance—efforts soon ending for the time in confirming the paralysis, and bringing to his face an expression which was as a crucifixion to behold.

There may be a useful analogy to be drawn from *Clarel* in passages described above, for instance, when the splenetic Mortmain reacts to Derwent's optimism. "Touched to the quick" by Vere's "soothing hand," Melville's conflicts are intensified: If he leans on pacifying family stories, he loses his hard-won vision of things as they are. At first he is immobilized, like stony Mortmain, but then Billy's arm responds with the suddenness of Mortmain's "passion-fit." Derwent had "changed"; Vere's "aspect" is transformed when Billy hits Claggart's forehead. Similarly, when Clarel declares his independence from received wisdom, "Aside Rolfe turned as overtasked." Compare the foreheads of Rolfe and Claggart: "Disclosing so in shapely sphere / A marble brow over face embrowned . . . (1.31.10–11); and "[Claggart's] brow was of the sort phrenologically associated with more than average intellect; silken jet curls partly clustered over it, making a foil to the pallor below, a pallor tinged with a faint shade of amber akin to the hue of time-tinted marbles of old" (chap. 8). Claggart will drop like the flower of Cere's child, with the same wintry consequences:

> The next instant, quick as the flame from a discharged cannon at night, his right arm shot out, and Claggart dropped to the deck. Whether intentionally or but owing to the young athlete's superior height, the blow had taken effect full upon the forehead,[72] so shapely and intellectual a feature in the master-at-arms; so that the body fell over lengthwise, like a heavy plank tilted from erectness. A gasp or two, and he lay motionless.
>
> "Fated boy," breathed Captain Vere in tone so low as to be almost a whisper, "what have you done! But here, help me."
>
> The twain raised the felled one from the loins up into a sitting position. The spare form flexibly acquiesced, but inertly. It was like handling a dead snake. They lowered it back. Regaining erectness, Captain Vere with one hand covering his face stood to all appearance as impassive as the object at his feet. Was he absorbed in taking in all the bearings of the event and what was best not only now at once to be done, but also in the sequel? Slowly he uncovered his face; and the effect was as if the moon emerging from eclipse should reappear with quite another aspect than that which had gone into hiding. The father in him, manifested towards Billy thus far in the scene, was replaced by the military disciplinarian.

Billy's shooting arm represents the rage Melville directs against his critical relatives and Hawthorne—the latter because he, like Elizabeth and other family members, is covertly angry and self-deceived while accusing *him* of morbidly exaggerating the hostility of others to his relentless demystifications of authority. Indeed, Derwent's "strange forbearance" after Mortmain's passion-fit is explained further on: "[such shadows come and go] But don't you see the man is mad? / His fits he has; sad, sad, how sad!" (3.8.57, 61–65). Though he droops, Derwent does not hold a grudge.

The disciplinary function has moved from John Claggart to Captain Vere. Claggart's phallic gaze is made the accouterment of "an asylum physician" sensitive to the tell-tale signs of an imminent "paroxysm" in an inmate. It is this figure who has inflicted the "white leprosy," Ahab's "lividly whitish" scar/brand on his bronzed face and neck, that also marred Pierre's cheek ("inclined to brown") and the "salt philosopher" Daniel Orme's tattoo of the cross. The asylum physician would penetrate the psyches of latently parricidal leftist radicals in the twentieth century, administering discipline while assuming the gentle benevolence of Derwent or Vere, who will madly abandon his innocent son.[73] But as he tells us throughout, Melville is not a traitor to all fathers: He is not an iconoclast, not a nihilist.[74] Combining both adherence to moral principle and scholarly, scientific detachment, Melville, it seems, understands that certain questions must be held in abeyance until we possess greater knowledge and experience, understanding our own self-interested capacities to wreak evil while professing good. This is not the same as living with mixed feelings, in some cases the preferred adjustment of the cured analysand to an amoral society. Clarel's search for truth, for legitimate authority, links him to Ahab's libertarian, but not libertine, quest. He has unmasked Hawthorne's and Ishmael's moral relativism and distrust of the critical intellect. His analysis is offered to ameliorate human suffering, really.

> Not seldom Pierre's social placidity was ruffled by polite entreaties from the young ladies that he would be pleased to grace their albums with some nice little song. We say here that his social placidity was ruffled; for the true charm of agreeable parlor society is, that there you lose your own sharp individuality and become delightfully merged in that soft social Pantheism, as it were, that rosy melting of all into one, ever prevailing in those drawing rooms, which pacifically and deliciously belie their own name; inasmuch as there no one draws the sword of his own individuality, but all such ugly weapons are left—as of old—with your hat and your cane in the hall. (250)

Can anyone imagine a society driven by bureaucrats tolerating an intelligence as rigorous and unpredictable as Melville's? Can anyone believe that aristocratic radicals, however libertine, would have sympathized with the radical bourgeois Ahab's revolt of the plebs, or with Pierre's miscegenating merger with Isabel that, while restoring his "own sharp individuality," left him stranded by the marge? Those twentieth-century figures linked to the conservative Enlightenment resemble the organic conservatives Vine, Derwent, Rolfe, Ungar, and Claggart/Vere. Like Hawthorne, they discredit the empiricist science, inductive logic, and libertarian political theory of the seventeenth and eighteenth centuries while deploying old religious remedies—re-baptized as "scientific" technique—to contain the potential revolutions of the nineteenth and twentieth centuries. Whether or not we call them democratic pluralists, anarchists, bohemians, communists, or fascists, in the eyes of an independent artist or scientist they are similarly authoritarian and irrationalist, immoderately stoning their very best friends.

THE APPLE-TREE

Excepting their principles of toleration, the maxims by which the republicans regulated ecclesiastical affairs, no more prognosticated any durable settlement, than those by which they conducted their civil concerns. . . . The parliament went so far as to make some approaches in one province to their Independent model. Almost all the clergy of Wales being ejected as malignants, itinerant preachers with small salaries were settled, not above four or five in each county; and these, being furnished with horses at the public expense, hurried from place to place, and carried, as they expressed themselves, the glad tidings of the gospel. They were all of them men of the lowest birth and education, who had deserted mechanical trades, in order to follow this new profession. And in this particular, as well as in their wandering life, they pretended to be more truly apostolical.[75]
—David Hume on unfinished ragged edges

Conservative scholars have identified Melville with his moderate characters in the late works. Not all Melville scholars are so certain. Are *Clarel* and "Billy Budd," rather, inconclusive registers of a settled social or religious belief, as a few other Melvilleans, including some descendants, have assumed? Another manuscript points to a third possibility: Melville's enduring underground connection with the radical Enlightenment. The bread box containing his unpublished writings included the manuscript of "Billy Budd," and also one of "Daniel Orme." Preserved in a separate folder and titled "Story of Daniel Orme & Omitted of *Billy Budd*," the manuscript, along with fragmentary earlier drafts, is a short "sketch" of a dead sailor, in some respects perhaps resembling the original Billy Budd himself, an apprehended "ringleader of an incipient mutiny," a "Captain of a gun's crew in a seventy four."[76] His life has probably been misreported, like any object with an "exceptional aspect" awakening "commonplace curiosity": "We try to ascertain from somebody the career and experience of the man, or may seek to obtain the information from himself. But what we hear from others may prove but unreliable gossip, and he himself, if approached, prove uncommunicative. In short, in most instances he turns out to be like a meteoric stone in a field. There it lies. The neighbors have their say about it, and an odd enough say it may prove. But what is it? Whence did it come? In what unimaginable sphere did it get that strange, igneous, metallic look, the kine now cropping the dewy grass about it?"[77]

Daniel Orme has a strange habit rousing superstitious speculation: "At times, but only when he might think himself quite alone, he would roll aside the bosom of his darned Guernsey frock and steadfastly contemplate something on his body. If by chance discovered in this, he would quickly conceal all and growl his resentment" (426). What was this object of furtive contemplation, reminiscent of Isabel's poisonous vial of dissent hidden in her bosom? ". . . a crucifix in indigo and vermilion tattooed on the chest and on the side of the heart. Slanting across the crucifix and paling the pigment there ran a whitish scar, long and thin, such as might ensue from the slash of a cutlass imperfectly parried or dodged" (426). Hawthorne's fiction was filled with upstart characters whose cheeks, bosoms, or hair erupt in red: Hester's scarlet letter, Zenobia's red flower, and Miriam's lustrous red gem.[78] But Daniel Orme's scar was neither a Hawthorne-style brand of demonic possession, as the "unreliable gossips" would like to believe, nor a fancied rough edge: "The old mastman had in legitimate naval service known what it was to repel boarders and not without receiving a sabre mark from them. It may be" (426).

Given Daniel Orme's identification with a "mechanical trade" and "a wandering life" as Hume would say, the crucifix can be seen as a sign linking Melville to the radical puritan precursors to the enthused "Apostles" of *Pierre*. Melville had underlined and annotated Romans 14:22: "Has thou faith? have it to thyself before God." Melville wrote, "The only kind of Faith—one's own." The apostles were poor Jews and primitive communists; the crucifix could represent moral purity and consistency, assaulted by the forces of expediency that would have turned Melville into a hypocrite.[79] Goethe's autobiography suggests that Daniel Orme's hidden tattoo is a sign for the Pelagian heresy:

What separated me [Goethe] from this brotherhood [the Moravians of Marienborn], as well as from other good Christian souls, was the very point on which the Church has more than once fallen into dissension. On the one hand, it was maintained that by the Fall human nature had been so corrupted to its innermost core, that not the least good could be found in it, and that therefore man must renounce all trust in his own powers, and look to grace and its operations for everything. The other party, while it admitted the hereditary imperfections of man, nevertheless ascribed to nature a certain germ of good within, which, animated by divine grace, was capable of growing up to a joyous tree of spiritual happiness. By this latter conviction I was unconsciously penetrated to my inmost soul, even while with tongue and pen I maintained the opposite side. But I had hitherto gone on with such ill-defined ideas, that I had never once clearly stated the dilemma to myself. From this dream I was unexpectedly roused one day, when, in a religious conversation, having distinctly advanced opinions, to my mind, most innocent,

I had in return to undergo a severe lecture. The very thought of such a thing, it was maintained, was genuine Pelagianism, a pernicious doctrine which was again appearing, to the great injury of modern times. I was astonished and even terrified. I went back to Church history, studied the doctrine and fate of Pelagius more closely, and now saw clearly how these two irreconcilable opinions had fluctuated in favour throughout whole centuries, and had been embraced and acknowledged by different men, according as they were of a more active or of a more passive nature.

The course of past years had constantly led me more and more to the exercise of my own powers. A restless activity was at work within me, with the best desire for moral development. The world without demanded that this activity should be regulated and employed for the advantage of others, and this great demand I felt called upon in my own case to meet. On all sides I had been directed to nature, and she had appeared to me in her whole magnificence; I had been acquainted with many good and true men who were toiling to do their duty, and for the sake of duty; to renounce them, nay to renounce myself, seemed impossible. The gulf which separated me from the doctrine of man's total depravity now became plain to me. Nothing, therefore, remained to me but to part from this society; and *as my love of the holy Scriptures, as well as the founder of Christianity and its early professors,* could not be taken from me, I formed a Christianity for my private use, and sought to establish and build it up by an attentive study of history and a careful observation of those who were favourable to my opinion.[80]

Did Melville emulate Goethe, harboring a privately held apostolic Christianity?[81]
The sketch ends in a stunning riposte to boarders who had scandalized his name. Again, geography is everything:

But let us come to the close of a sketch necessarily imperfect. One fine Easter Day, following a spell of rheumatic weather, Orme was discovered alone and dead on a height overlooking the seaward sweep of the great haven to whose shore, in his retirement from sea, he had moored. It was an evened terrace, destined for use in war, but in peace neglected and offering a sanctuary for anybody. Mounted on it was an obsolete battery of rusty guns. Against one of these he was found leaning, his legs stretched out before him, his clay pipe broken in twain, the vacant bowl and no spillings from it, attesting that his pipe had been smoked out to the last of its contents. He faced the outlet to the ocean. The eyes were open, still continuing in death the vital glance fixed on the hazy waters and the dim-seen sails coming and going or at anchor near by. What had been his last thoughts? If aught of reality lurked in the rumours concerning him, had remorse, had penitence any place in those thoughts? Or was there just nothing of either? After all, what were his moodiness and mutterings, his strange freaks, starts, eccentric shrugs and grimaces, were these but the grotesque additions like the wens and knobs and distortions of the trunk of an old chance apple-tree in an inclement upland, not only beaten by many storms, but also obstructed in its natural development by the chance of its having first sprouted among hard-packed rock? In short, [had] that fatality, no more encrusting him, made him what he came to be? Even admitting that there was something dark that he chose to keep to himself, what then? Such reticence may sometimes be more for the sake of others than one's self. No, let us believe that that animal decay before mentioned still befriended him to the close, and that he fell asleep recalling through the haze of memory many a far-off scene of the wide world's beauty dreamily suggested by the hazy waters before him.

He lies buried among other sailors, for whom also strangers performed one last rite in a lonely plot overgrown with wild eglantine uncared for by man. (427–28)

Daniel Orme died leaning on a rusty gun in the lap of the sublime. Bequeathing a self-portrait of the modern artist and perhaps any principled intellectual as isolato, sailor, and besieged apostle of republican virtue, Melville is joined in death to anonymous, misunderstood, unsubdued humanity. Or perhaps not. The "vital glance" could signify an imperishable link with the Burkean organicism of Wordsworth, whose poetic vision, appalled by "freaks of nature / All Promethean thoughts of man," yet manages the whirl and "sees the parts / As parts, but with a feeling of the whole."[82] Whether he goes out as Wordsworth, Goethe,[83] or Byron, the insightful psychologist recognizes the difficulties of maintaining his budding goodness in a family demanding portraits of flawless perfection. Without remorse, the mapped apple-tree, brooding over the sea, listed the "wens and knobs and distortions" that others labeled aggression or insanity or the (mischievously willed?) indeterminacy of character that defies authoritative interpretation:

[F. Barron Freeman, 1948] We shall never know his exact nature during these last years, for his complex personality can be turned to the whim of any interested reader. (3)

[F. Barron Freeman quoting T. M. Coan, 1919] "My books will speak for themselves," [Melville] said, "and all the better if I avoid the rattling egotism by which so many won a certain vogue for a certain time." (10)

"Daniel Orme" was published in 1924, yet the Melville mystery remains unsolved. Indeed, Warner Berthoff, like F. Barron Freeman before him, framed the sketch to reinforce the anti-intellectual idealist epistemology he imputed to Melville.[84]

Shortly after Melville's death in 1891, Elizabeth began the campaign to recognize her once-famous husband that culminated in the Revival of the 1920s, concentrating her efforts on the republication of *Typee*. She had loved (and admired) her conservative authoritarian father (to whom *Typee* was dedicated) and she had loved (and pitied) her radical, free-spirited "communist"[85] husband, to all appearances without reservation or conflict. Meanwhile she did her tactful best to suppress any hint of strangeness or difficulty in getting to know him. Writing to Julian Hawthorne, in his youth an awestruck admirer of Melville, Elizabeth reprimanded him for faulty family portraiture:

> I have been reading your new memorials of your father with great interest, but am much troubled to see such a distressingly poor portrait of Mr. Melville— I am sure that my husband never looked so forbidding as that represents him—no one of his friends would recognize it—And if in a future edition you would withdraw it, or otherwise allow me to furnish you with a good photograph from which a copy could be taken, it would be a great relief to us all. Let me say also that my husband never made "aimless, mysterious journeys round the world"—The few that he did make after the publication of "Typee" were always short ones with a definite object in view—such errors will unavoidably creep in to any biographical notice. (Sept. 23, 1903, GL, box 20, not in *Log*)

"BROKEN, BROKEN, BROKEN" (BROKE-IN)

Twentieth-century assessments of the Melville problem should be contrasted with Melville's own diagnostics. Speaking through his character Isabel (the unknown, unacknowledged half-sister who has searched for and found Pierre just in time to rescue him from a marriage of convenience), Melville suggests that most of the inmates of the "unnamable" institution in which Isabel had once been confined (an asylum, the family, America) are either "dumb" or "broken, broken, broken"; while the grown-ups in charge are "strangely demented people;—composed of countenance, but wandering of mind; soul-composed and bodily-wandering, and strangely demented people" (120). Dr. Henry A. Murray said Isabel's memories proved she was "intellectually retarded" and probably modeled upon Melville's cousin Henry Dearborn Melvill, "a mental defective" who had been put away in

1848.[86] Isabel's memory was a problem to Pierre as well, but he does not blame Isabel; rather he fears his (almost) overpowering anger:

> So, also, in a good degree, did he endeavor to drive out of him, Isabel's reminiscence of the, to her, unnamable large house. . . . This episode in her life, above all other things, was most cruelly suggestive to him, as possibly involving his father in the privity to a thing, at which Pierre's inmost soul fainted with amazement and abhorrence. Here the helplessness of all further light, and the eternal impossibility of logically exonerating his dead father, in his own mind, from the liability to this, and many other of the blackest self-insinuated suppositions; all this came over Pierre with a power so infernal and intense, that could only have proceeded from the unretarded malice of the Evil One himself. But subtilly and wantonly as these conceits stole into him, Pierre as subtilly opposed them; and with the hue-and-cry of his whole indignant soul, pursued them forth again into the wide Tartarean realm from which they had emerged. (137–38)

Elsewhere Melville suggested that the Melville problem was the impossible integration of opposing points of view (perhaps the competing ideologies of warring classes), a project that could immobilize him in the face of persecution. Ishmael is describing "The Sperm Whale's Head":

> True, both his eyes, in themselves, must simultaneously act; but is his brain so much more comprehensive, combining, and subtle than man's, that he can at the same moment of time attentively examine two distinct prospects, one on one side of him, and the other in an exactly opposite direction? . . . It may be but an idle whim, but it has always seemed to me, that the extraordinary vacillations of movement displayed by some whales when beset by three or four boats; the timidity and liability to queer frights, so common to such whales; I think that all this indirectly proceeds from the helpless perplexity of volition, in which their divided and diametrically opposite powers of vision must involve them. (331)

Melville may be talking about himself in both excerpts, suggesting: (a) moral right is firmly situated on the side of the abandoned child, unrepresented suffering humanity cowed into silence, their spirits broken; and (b) the most pressing emotion for Melville is anger, infernal and intense, but blended with fear of invasion. The word "broken," offered by Isabel three times, allows us to hear "broke-in." He is not coolly observing antagonistic ideologies simultaneously as a detached observer should. Rather, one "prospect" discloses "three or four boats" with hostile

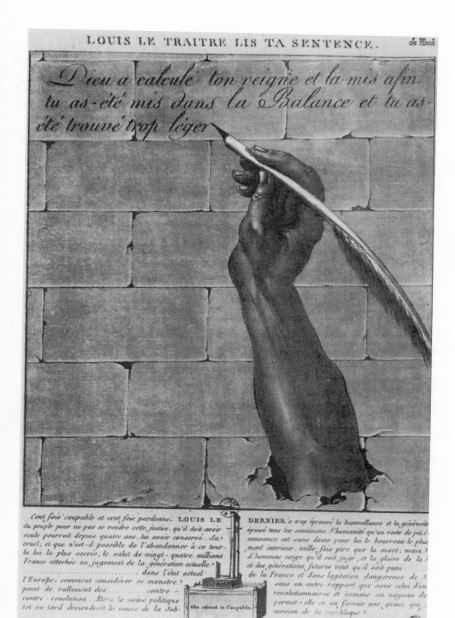

Caricature by Villeneuve (active 1789–99), "Louis the Traitor Read Your Sentence," Jan. 17, 1793. The text refers to Daniel 5:26–28; "God has numbered thy kingdom and finished it; thou art weighed in the balances, and are found wanting." Here Villeneuve has moved the source of legitimacy from God and King to the People, thrusting through the wall from below. Compare to Ahab: "If man will strike, strike through the mask! How can the prisoner reach outside except by thrusting through the wall?" From Cynthia Burlingham and James Cuno, *French Caricature and the French Revolution 1789–1799* (Los Angeles: Grunwald Center for the Graphic Arts, 1988), 98, 192. This and other caricatures were widely disseminated in single sheets.

intentions. They could be real class enemies penetrating his reserve and violating his rights (a breach that is bad enough), or they could be even more menacing as carriers of the justifiable rage he associates with marauding barbarians led by Ahab: These penetrations are his heretical irruptions. The Tartars are to be chased back to the underworld with the force of the White Whale, summoning "the hue-and-cry of his whole indignant soul."[87] He *must* push the anger down to spare suffering relatives. But the Ahab/Isabel prospect, his moral center that judges God and other rulers to be demented, is also compelling, so his capacity to resist illegitimate authority comes and goes. He neither flees nor digs in, but vacillates, "with timidity and liability to queer frights"; he may (over)identify with punitive authority or with the weaker victim, or both, patiently mapping his movements hither and thither, a motion that "indirectly proceeds from the helpless perplexity of volition." Sometimes he seems to position a character, impossibly, in two places at once. The point is simple: Shifting class position and personal history coincide to overheat his texts; Melville feels the righteous anger of the mob storming the Bastille, while simultaneously, guiltily, he wishes to protect upper-class sanctuaries from the slashing penetration long associated with democracies. Although the alert reader may locate many cubist moments within Melville's texts, such lubricities have remained invisible to many of his twentieth-century revivers.[88]

"My friend Max Levi, he passed through." (2.29.84)
—Margoth, "the hardy Jew"

Melville ended his sketch of Daniel Orme on a pathetic note: "He lies buried among other sailors, for whom also strangers performed one last rite in a lonely plot overgrown with wild eglantine uncared for by man." Key figures in the Melville Revival have been unable to solve the Melville mystery, not because of thorns and bristles that ward them off, but simply because as stoics, they cannot, will not mourn, either for Melville or for themselves. A Man is not taken by *those* weeping words and almost broken-into hearts: Where will it all lead?

". . . Mid such a scene
Of Nature's terror, how serene
That ordered form. Nor less 'tis cut
Out of that terror—does abut
Thereon: there's Art." (*Clarel*, 2.30.40–44)

The Rhyme recurred, made voids or gaps
In dear relations . . . . (*Clarel*, 3.31.14–15)

Modernizing societies attenuate the conservative religious leadership that promotes paternalistic charity to pacify incendiary mass political emotions. Melville's often troubled personal history was enmeshed in the nineteenth-century problem of secularism and order. His critics, however, have reduced the problem in *Clarel* to "religious doubts." Some moderates think he is one of them, and so the linked issues of family violence, imputed insanity, and Melville's illuminating relations with his Jewish characters are ignored or marginalized. Conversely, Melville's less attractive traits have been emphasized perhaps to discredit his subversive texts; or, worse, reported errant behavior has been attributed to heredity and lapses in self-control, not to persecution.

Charles Sumner, the abolitionist senator from Massachusetts, was elected on a short-lived fusion ticket of Free Soilers and Democrats in early 1851. While Sumner is a likely model or inspiration for Ahab,[89] other critics have equated the latter with previous writers' inventions (Lear, Satan), family members (his father, mother, or brother), or "extremist" political figures (Cromwell, Napoleon, Andrew Jackson, John Calhoun, Hitler, etc.). To be sure, Melville draws upon literary sources, his family, and contemporary events, but he assimilates his materials by dragging them and the reader into a violent and metamorphosing inner world that others, his wife, for instance, have preferred to bury. Traditional archetypes turn into their opposites and/or crumble, only to reappear in another character. Melville's torments are not the idiosyncratic expression of a "narcissistic" personality with poor self-control. Rather, he dramatizes those moments of defiance, compromise, and submission that have defined the problem of modern politics since the Reformation, demanding that we face unresolved issues of morality, order, and authority in an age of seemingly permanent revolution. If Melville felt the tug of forbidden knowledge and radical impulses, why did he not break (at least emotionally) with his conventional family, the "dear relations" whose genteel manners could not contain the terror within the neoclassical fortress of good form and impassibility? Structural factors such as "role-models," contradictory "instincts," class/gender position, and the pressure of market forces may be illuminating. But charted singly they cannot adequately explain Melville's rejection of the "vile liberty" his character Rolfe associates with the New World and Radical Protestantism.[90] The history of catastrophic events and relationships in his own family affected Melville's mixed response to the Ahab-ish phallic gaze that ripped duplicitous authority, however finely packaged. Insight could signify either abhorrent surveillance (his mother's and wife's) or emancipation or both. Those looks, like lower-class self-assertion and insurgency, could attract or frighten him, depending on the current state of his economic and emotional dependency. Some crossed-out sentences on "inscrutable inconsistencies" from the few pages that remain of *The Confidence-Man* manuscript suggest complex fears of retaliation when he paints the big picture, contradictions in place.

They were written during a period when Melville's self-confidence was reportedly low, and the voice is Ishmael's: "[The "flying squirrel" is] at different periods as ~~contradictory to~~ much at variance with itself as the butterfly is ~~to~~ with the caterpillar ~~from~~ into which it ~~proceeded had come~~ changes; may yet, in so doing, be not false, but faithful, to ~~Nature~~ facts. . . . Sooner or later she [Nature] puts out every one who anyway pretends to be acquainted with the whole of her, which is indispensable to ~~rightly~~ fitly comprehending any part of her. (The last sentence is crossed out.)

To illustrate his point, Melville had begun with the metamorphosis from caterpillar to butterfly; the direction of change is correctly stated: ". . . as the butterfly is to the caterpillar from which it proceeded" or "had come." But in the corrections, it appears that the creature reverses the normal development, suggesting feelings of degeneration when Melville (as Ahab) spots variations or internal contradictions: "as the butterfly is with the caterpillar into which it changes."[91] Is he teasing or testing the reader, or is he afraid and confused? The same sentence suggests that he identifies "facts" with "Nature." In the next excerpt, "she" refers to "Nature," the world of facts. The words "puts out," "rightly," and "fitly" are rich in possible meanings. Feminine Nature "puts out" intruders. "She" extinguishes or banishes or burdens the curious observer. Seeing relations between warring parts and wholes takes on a moral dimension with "rightly" and a physical dimension with "fitly." Perhaps when Melville sees correctly and justly, someone has fits and he is burdened with guilt: "the rush of blood to his head." Melville does not say that fallen flesh inevitably distorts perception; rather, he identifies a colossal, vindictive antagonist located outside (and perhaps inside) the body.[92]

In one of his parting shots, Margoth remands the pilgrims: "Again ye'll pine / Left to yourselves here in decline, / Missing my brave vitality!" (Or so speculates the narrator; 2.21.109–11). Here and throughout this book the reader's attention has been focused upon Melville's love / hate feelings for unbridled social criticism, science, and enlightenment, an ambivalence charted with the appetite and intricacy of a cubist painting: devouring, analyzing, and synthesizing; merging and mapping opposing or subtly shifting perspectives. It is not surprising that he "moored" the dying Daniel Orme on a safe spot, the haven/heaven where, peacefully, he could finally take it all in, bequeathing the vital glance to close reading posterity, "On a height overlooking the seaward sweep of the great haven to whose shore, in his retirement from sea, he had moored . . . offering a sanctuary for anybody. . . . He faced the outlet to the ocean. The eyes were open, still continuing in death the vital glance fixed on the hazy waters and the dim-seen sails coming and going or at anchor near by."

4

Melville and the Radical Puritans

I deny not, but that it is of greatest concernment in the Church and
Commonwealth, to have a vigilant eye on how Bookes demeane themselves
as well as men; and thereafter to confine, imprison, and do sharpest justice
on them as malefactors: For books are not absolutely dead things, but doe
contain a potencie of life in them to be as active as that soule whose progeny
they are; nay they do preserve as in a violl the purest efficacie and extraction
of that living intellect that bred them. I know they are lively, and as
vigorously productive, as those fabulous Dragon's teeth; and being sown
up and down, may chance to spring up armed men. And yet on the other
hand unless wariness be us'd, as good almost kill a Man as kill a good
Book; who kills a Man kills a reasonable creature, Gods Image; but hee who
destroyes a good Booke, kills reason itself, kills the Image of God, as it were
in the eye.
—John Milton, *Areopagitica*, 1644

Hereafter I shall no more stab at a book (in print I mean) than I would stab
at a man.[1]
—Melville to Duyckinck, 1849, regretting his negative critique of
Francis Parkman

Claggart hesitated not an instant. Deliberately advancing within short
range of the sailor, he spoke. Without emphasis and in a tone more musical
than ever, he delivered the accusation point-blank into his eyes.[2]
—from "Baby Budd"

The multiculturalist students of canon formation have not precisely delineated class conflict, social movements, and corresponding ideological shifts in the period under examination. They seem impatient with details and discourses, read the text too quickly, and fail to interrogate their own class anxieties. It is well to dissipate shadows lengthened by elite symbol-makers at war with critical thought, for whom "composure of mind is every thing." This chapter and the next assay a retrospective vital glance at the historically specific contexts and life experience that best explain Melville's struggle to find a safe public persona.[3] The nineteenth century did not introduce the problem of patronage to freethinking artists in Europe and America. We must skip over two more centuries to the early modern period in England and the exemplary fate of (radical) Melville's most important literary forebear, John Milton.

Seventeenth-century radical puritans and scientists produced many of the innovations we associate with the intellectual foundations of democracy: Along with the partial legitimation of dissent and libertarian ideas in some strands of Reformation thought, the scientific revolution fortified older political theories of popular sovereignty and constitutional government. The explosion of printing made subversive ideas broadly available to a growing and confident middle-class reading public eager to be emancipated from arbitrary authority. Milton published *Areopagitica* in 1644; it is perhaps the most eloquent statement ever conceived on behalf of intellectual freedom; it thrills to the puritan marrow of my bones. But that appeal to the censor was framed during the English Civil War soon after the Independents, reacting to new assertions of popular sovereignty, had put down rebels to their Left in the City of London, stifling vox populi (the voice of the people) in favor of vox salutaris (the voice of public safety).[4] After the Restoration, Sir Henry Vane was beheaded, and the bodies of the chief regicides, Cromwell, Ireton, and Bradshaw, were exhumed and hanged as an example to would-be republicans. All overtly radical thoughts were chased back to the Tartarean realms from which the Titans had emerged. Milton, who had been named as secretary of foreign languages in 1649, was taken into custody, then freed, perhaps by the intercessions of Andrew Marvell and Sir William Davenant or because the restored regime concluded that the blind poet, though formerly an official of the commonwealth and ardent defender of the regicides, was now harmless.

The revolutionary puritan writing under renewed censorship in the 1660s had unearthed the Melville problem at the beginning of *Paradise Lost*. Since deadly opposition from conservatives might be the wages of telling the truth and sticking to God-given moral principle, Milton asks for a steady hand:

... I thence
Invoke thy aid to my adventurous song,

That with no middle flight intends to soar
Above the Aonian mount, while it pursues
Things unattempted yet in prose or rhyme.

Milton faced the dilemma that persists today in the hearts and heads of every independent intellectual, a fight played out in contending notions of balance: Democratic "truth" brings only parricide and chaos, say conservatives; radicals are unbalanced when they refuse the "middle flight"; truth and certainty are qualities
adhering solely to Hume's or Ishmael's vital center. Radical democrats, Thomas
Paine for instance, retorted that conservative balance is a fraud: "Balance" is achiev-
able (if at all) only after the questing intellect accurately observes and assesses
institutional structures, discourses, and practices, those describable causes that
propel or constrain our actions. Such processes must be in the service of, and controlled by, the people and the Constitution they alone have written and rewritten to
suit changing circumstances. Demanding accountability, radical liberals have constantly compared republican theory with antidemocratic practice; we know how co-
piously our democracy has rewarded such trenchant critics.[5] But for revolutionary
puritans, the highest power, the chief, stubbornly remains on the side of virtue,
social knowledge, and self-knowledge; as the moderate Hume kept reminding his
hard-line conservative readers, royalist opposition and persecution only stiffened
the resolve of radical puritan and Whig antagonists.

Milton's invocation continues:

And chiefly thou O Spirit, that dost prefer
Before all temples the upright heart and pure,
Instruct me, for thou know'st; thou from the first
Was present, and with mighty wings outspread
Dove-like sat'st brooding on the vast abyss
And madest it pregnant: what in me is dark
Illumine, what is low, raise and support;
That to the highth of this great argument
I may assert eternal providence,
And justify the ways of God to men.[6]

The ambiguous spatial arrangement is everything. Character, "the upright heart
and pure," stands at the door of the Church, "before all temples." Profane poetry
is juxtaposed with sacred text; the lay poet's creation is subject to the judgment
of conservative religious authority. But Milton's "dove-like" Holy Spirit, his muse,
occupies a higher perch. "Chiefly" the Spirit "dost prefer" the pure heart, taking
the vanguard "before," or in front of, all religious establishments. If there is to be

conflict between Milton and organized religion, he prays that the Holy Spirit itself has illuminated "what in me is dark," a region possibly identified with "the vast abyss" made "pregnant." That lamp may guide both Milton's reading of earthly institutions and the inspection of his own dark interior life. The Holy Spirit makes his introspection pregnant with significance and, "with mighty wings outspread," has protectively guided and sustained his ethical progress to a prospect where he may take the full measure of "this great argument." John Locke and the deists were among the chief inheritors of the dovish but powerful radical puritan geography that joined human reason bestowed by Nature to universally applicable ethical precepts, moving "morals" from Heart to Head—up to "the mind" in Charles Olson's frightened Shakespearian imagination.[7]

Olson's anxiety was prefigured inside the ambiguous narrative of Herman Melville's own intertwined moral and artistic development. Like Milton, Melville was precariously situated in two places at once; at times he panics: Fainting with Pierre, "he knew not where he was." The man-made system of sanctions and rewards, in conflict with the higher law, had given him no choice. On the one hand, Melville was at the door of the temple and exposed to the censure of conservatives; on the other, he soared, Muse-guided by dark Isabel's lantern, claiming an ethical position superior to contaminated earthly institutions. Melville's *Mardi* concludes with his salute to Milton and an acknowledgment of their shared peril, dovelike, godlike, "brooding on the vast abyss." Taji has "seized the helm" with "eternity . . . in his eye."

> Now I am my soul's own emperor; and my first act is abdication! Hail! realm of shades!—and turning my prow into the racing tide, which seized me like a hand omnipotent, I darted through.
>
> Churned in foam, that outer ocean lashed the clouds; and straight in my white wake, headlong dashed a shallop, three fixed specters leaning o'er its prow: three arrows poising.
>
> And thus, pursuers and pursued flew on, over an endless sea. (654)

The biographical sketch presented in the preceding chapter reflects my own (brooding, still developing) thesis: Herman's self-assertion as writer and social critic was linked to ambivalent feelings about departed relatives whose deaths he imagined were hastened by his (and their) flaws. These were flaws he associated with Hebraic puritans or "plain deists underhanded" (*Clarel*, 2.25.104) who, as corporatists constantly reiterated, had delivered the world-destroying materialist epistemology. In his Tory mood, the "rebel senses" (4.13.170) were keys that unlocked state secrets to overreaching "citizen-kings." Father Mapple's sermon instructed Ahab; Taji, Mapple, and Ahab were ultimately repudiated by Ishmael. Two incompatible definitions of "balance" were at odds. A plot summary of *Moby-Dick* follows, concentrated upon themes developed in preceding chapters; for instance, Pierre's sojourn into the lower depths and his blindness as he hits the gutter.

"LET ME CALL MYSELF, FOR THE PRESENT, WILLIAM WILSON"

A depressed young man with a classical education, well born but fallen on hard times, narrates the tale of a mad whale hunt from the vantage point of the lone survivor. His first words, "Call me Ishmael," rectify the too-deferential opening sentence of Poe's "William Wilson," the story of a dissipated student and his stalking conscience whom he finally stabs in the mirror, thus destroying himself. Since Ishmael tells us at once that the legend of Narcissus is "the key to it all," the reader may sense he is not reading the commonplace tale of an albino whale and his pursuers, but a work, perhaps a puzzle or mystery, with literary ambitions and mythic resonances. And since the Faustian bargain is also mentioned, and since Ahab instructs his first mate that the whale hunt is a layered text and that "truth hath no confines," the reader might surmise that the no-holds-barred composition has something to do with the search for knowledge in the modern world at a time of waning upper-class authority. Indeed, the narrator comes and goes: Ishmael's memoir is an irregular collage, sometimes presented as a theater script, at other times as a "scientific" treatise on the physiology of whales and the minutiae of their capture and processing. There is even a story of a successful mutiny, "The Town-Ho's Story," snuggled within the larger narrative. The dialogue veers from the vernacular to the lofty, biblical, and romantic, poured forth with a relentless intensity and with close-packed Symbolist images that are unbearable to some readers, mesmerizing to others. It lacks composure.

Ishmael is befriended by a tattooed South Seas harpooneer, Queequeg, an almost superhuman protector whose pagan rituals he comes to respect. After hearing a ringing sermon on Jonah's disobedience delivered by Father Mapple at the Whalemen's Chapel, the two pals (now united in a mock "marriage") sign onto a whaling ship, the *Pequod,* commanded by Captain Ahab. Ahab has lost one leg to the jaw of a widely feared albino whale, the terror of the sea; the amputation is said to have maddened him. Shortly after the voyage begins, he persuades the multicolored crew to join his search for Leviathan, adding to the force of his personality the lure of a gold doubloon he hammers to the mast; the first sailor who sights the White Whale gets it. A dark demonic figure, Fedallah the Parsee, occasionally surfaces, commanding similarly demonic tiger-yellow Manilla men. The *Pequod* gams with numerous other ships as it "paws" through the oceans, each a portentous encounter, the most telling being the last. The captain of the *Rachel*, searching for his twelve-year-old son (Melville's age when his father died), asks to charter the *Pequod* for two days; Ahab must join him. But the obsessed Ahab, certain he is about to uncover the largest secrets of nature and the State, declines to help in this act of charity. The tale ends in disaster after three days of chase. Ahab is blinded at the moment when the whale presents his "blank forehead" and determines that the ship is "the source of all his persecutions," smiting the *Pequod*. His body turned from the sun, Ahab flings his harpoon, but the unwinding line catches his neck; he is strangled and drops into the sea, forever tied to Moby Dick. The ship of "inquiring heads" goes down; all hands will die, except for Ishmael, rescued by the good father.

There are several levels of suspense: (a) Is it within human capacity to conquer, or comprehend, the White Whale? (b) Can Ahab be dissuaded from his Satanic and lunatic enterprise by the first mate, family-loving Starbuck? And (c) Who controls the narrative voice? What is Ishmael's relationship to Ahab? Does he really separate from the terrorist, returning to "interdependence" (the Great Chain of Being), as conservative scholars and study guides insist? With the exception of a few fragments and the unpublished "Billy Budd" manuscript (in which the main character *does* dramatically metamorphose from guilty mutineer to innocent victim), Melville destroyed his drafts, covering his tracks and leaving scholars to speculate about the evolution of his characters and plots, *the* central question for psychologists interested in relating biography to literary texts.[8]

Before Ahab enters the narrative of *Moby-Dick*, Ishmael introduces Father Mapple's sermon with images that will be repeated in the responses of the crew to Ahab's stormy but illuminating presence: "[Father Mapple's] deep chest heaved as with a ground-swell; his tossed arms seemed the warring elements at work; and the thunders that rolled away from off his swarthy brow, and the light leaping from his eye, made all his simple hearers look on him with a quick fear that was strange to them" (47). Father Mapple preaches the higher law, goading his congregation of humble sailors to rebel against earthly authority should it violate the dignity and equality of individuals; he condemns as ungodly every form of slavery.[9]

> Jonah did the Almighty's bidding . . . To preach the Truth to the face of False-hood! . . . Woe to him who seeks to please rather than appal! . . . Delight is to him—a far, far upward, and inward delight—who against the proud gods and commodores of this earth, ever stands forth his own inexorable self. . . . Delight is to him, who gives no quarter in the truth, and kills, burns, and destroys all sin though he pluck it out from under the robes of Senators and Judges. Delight,—top-gallant delight is to him, who acknowledges no law or lord, but the Lord his God, and is only a patriot to heaven. Delight is to him,

whom all the waves of the billows of the seas of the boisterous mob can never shake from this sure Keel of the Ages. (48)

Mapple had charted the quest for forbidden knowledge in the service of ordinary humanity, preparing the entrance of Ahab's inexorable self, balanced when he is a patriot to heaven,[10] steadied by "this sure Keel of the Ages." But Ishmael warns that the crew of the *Pequod*, though embarked upon a just cause, is probably doomed; others have tried and failed. "Yet now, federated along one keel, what a set these Isolatoes were! An Anacharsis Clootz deputation from all the isles of the sea, and all the ends of the earth, accompanying Old Ahab in the Pequod to lay the world's grievances before that bar from which not very many of them ever come back" (121). Melville doesn't want readers to miss the keel symbol, so he repeats and repeats. Ahab won't stop the hunt to fix the leaking ship; Starbuck protests, and once more Ahab declares his independence from earthly interests that would subvert his God-directed quest for truth and justice: "'What will the owners say, sir?' '. . . Thou art always prating to me, Starbuck, about those miserly owners, as if the owners were my conscience. But look ye, the only real owner of anything is its commander; and hark ye, my conscience is in this ship's keel.—On deck!'" (474). Ahab's individuality is not about solipsistic self-absorption as Ishmael insists by invoking Narcissus at the outset. Rather, the inexorable self possesses the self-control that allows Melville to resist worldly temptations to regress. He is in command of himself, like Taji, which is to say that Melville's art making serves the general interests of self-managing, promiscuously merging humanity, not the commonwealth idea promoted by Lemuel Shaw that seemed to serve narrow class interests. Ishmael's response to Ahab's wild ambition could have been directed to Taji on the last page of *Mardi:* "Were this world an endless plain, and by sailing eastward we could for ever reach new distances, and discover sights more sweet and strange than any Cyclades or Islands of the King Solomon, then there were promise in the voyage. But in pursuit of those mysteries we dream of, or in tormented chase of that demon phantom that, some time or other, swims before all human hearts; while chasing such over this round globe, they either lead us on in barren mazes or midway leave us whelmed" (237).

The damage Ishmael/Melville wreaked upon his Ahab's soma and psyche would be reenacted by his fascinated champions, multitudinous arrows poising. Melville's critics are not operating alone. The conflicting notions of balance represented in Ahab's sure Keel of the Ages vs. Ishmael's uncertainty principle are played out every day within the humanities. The fight over "closure," at boiling point these days in the "science wars" and in the debates between empiricist historians and postmodernists, may be a displaced anxiety about the American and French Revolutions and the whirl of mass politics. While taking the van (or the center?) themselves, some younger literary critics are tarring all science and history with the brush of "absolutism."[11] Some tangled questions present themselves to the materialist (but introspective) historian: First, should scholars aspire toward authoritative interpretations and conclusions via archival research, reconstruction of institutional contexts, the conditions of artistic production, competing social movements, and pregnant discourses? Father Mapple and Ahab would say yes, at least until the emergence of contradictory evidence and persuasive refutations; Ishmael and other irrationalists, no: We are too weak to penetrate the mysteries and paradoxes that only God can read, but that we will comprehend in heaven. Or if we are (irrationalist) atheists, we never will, because our evil instincts and self-love will always prevail over clarity of vision. The Ishmaelite pagans and conservative Christians alike seem cathected to pain, whereas the Mapple congregation flaps its wings to historicize Ishmael and the Melville problem, a project dedicated to the proposition that, wherever possible, injustice should be both redressed and prevented. Second, have Melville scholars consciously withheld evidence or misreported texts or drawn unwarranted inferences, artificially prolonging the Melville mystery?

My research suggests that ideological commitments, not some ahistoric human frailty, shaped the collection of evidence. New primary sources, such as Augusta Melville's cache of family letters discovered in 1983, have confirmed early hunches about Melville's family and those patterns of familial communication that seemed to be delineated in his fiction. As Fortuna returns more of the materials that have been deliberately withheld or lost, some of the obscurities shrouding Melville's meanings may evaporate. One such example of suppressed history is the still-mysterious provenance of Melville's annotations to *Paradise Lost*. Now that these marginalia have been made available to scholars, the Miltonic influence on Melville's images and ideas may be assessed. Jay Leyda was one of two scholars allowed to examine Melville's marginalia to Milton's poetry while the two volumes were at auction in 1984; they had been sequestered by an unknown party or parties for decades. In the selection of Melville's annotations to *Paradise Lost* that follows (taken from Leyda's transcript), one sees his attraction to "speculations high or deep" (602) offered by the apple-tree, but there were also occasional hesitations and backward glances accompanying his Columbian adventures. In Book 9, the serpent, explaining to Eve how a lowly brute had acquired human speech, and leading her to the forbidden tree, reaches the climax of his argument with lines 679–84:

> O Sacred, Wise, and Wisdom-giving Plant,
> Mother of Science, Now I feel thy Power
> Within me clear, not only to discern
> Things in their Causes, but to trace the ways
> Of highest Agents, deemed however wise.
> Queen of this Universe. . . .

To lines 689–90, Melville double scored: "And life more perfect have attained than fate / Meant me, by venturing higher than my lot." Lines 703–5 were also double scored (referring to the knowledge of good and evil): "Why then was this forbid? Why but to awe, / Why but to keep ye low and ignorant, / His worshippers." Here is Melville's comment, partially erased: "This is one of the many profound atheistical hits of Milton. A greater than Lucretius, since he always teaches under a masque, and makes the Devil himself a Teacher & Messiah." (Leyda marked the word "Fate" with an arrow.) Although many other annotations were cut away or erased, a few other impudent notes survive:

[To Mitford's comment on Milton's religious wanderings (xcix)] He who thinks for himself never can remain of the same mind. I doubt not that darker doubts crossed Milton's soul, than ever disturbed Voltair [sic]. And he was more of what is called an Infidel.

[To Book 10 (5–11): ". . . for what can scape the eye / Of God all-seeing, or deceive his heart / Omniscient? who, in all things wise and just, / Hindered not Satan to attempt the mind / Of man, with strength entire, and free will armed, / Complete to have discovered and repulsed / Whatever wiles of foe or seeming friend."] The Fall of Adam did not so much prove him weak, as that God had made him so. From all that is gatherable from Milton's theology, the Son was created. Now had the Son been planted in the Garden (instead of Adam) he would have withstood the temptation;—why then he and not Adam? Because of his created superiority to Adam. [Leyda writes] "M adds, later: Sophomoricus"[12]

[Book 10, (41–43): ". . . man should be seduced / And flattered out of all, believing lies / Against his maker . . . .] All Milton's strength & rhetoric suffice not to satisfy concerning this matter—free will. Doubtless, he must have felt it himself: & looked upon it as the one great unavoidable flaw in his work. But, indeed, God's alleged omnipotence & foreknowledge, are insuperable bars to his being made an actor in any drama, imagined.[13]

Melville had traced the ways of highest agents. Seizing the helm, he rationally reflected upon their contradictory injunctions and pronounced them to be agents of nonsense, aligning himself with the Left wing of contemporary Whiggery.[14] On the other hand, the cautious, guilty parricide and fratricide may have sided with High Church orthodoxy. Melville scored the passages where the fallen angel Abdiel returns to the no-longer-angry God:

[Book 6, 25–37] . . . on to the sacred hill
They led him high applauded, and present
Before the seat supreme; from whence a voice
From midst a golden cloud thus mild was heard.
Servant of God, well done, well hast thou fought
The better fight, who single hast maintained
Against revolted multitudes the cause
Of truth, in word mightier than they in arms;
And for the testimony of truth hast borne
Universal reproach, far worse to bear
Than violence: for this was all thy care
To stand approved in sight of God, though worlds
Judged thee perverse. . . .

Melville underscored "high applauded" and scored lines 33–37.[15] That clutching other hand[16] began to erase the annotation praising Milton's masque; the same hand, perhaps, labeled Melville's diagnosis of demented authority as sophomoric. Milton's judgment would have been even harsher, as his commentary on predestination suggests: ". . . Free causes are not impeded by any law of necessity arising from the degrees or prescience of God. There are some who in their zeal to oppose this doctrine, do not hesitate even to assert that God is himself the cause and origin of sin. Such men, if they are not to be looked upon as misguided rather than mischievous, should be ranked among the most abandoned of all blasphemers. An attempt to refute them, would be nothing more than an argument to prove that God was not the evil spirit."[17]

The mystery of three

Like others caught in the transition from marble to mobs and looking for balance, Melville's characters and narrators stand in three worlds: One position whitens him with unquestioning deference to worldly authorities who claim to speak for God while betraying Christian ideals and oppressing their fellow creatures. To please such authority would effectively assault the brain, wizen the heart, and imprison the rebel senses: no balance there. A second position, chalked off in *Moby-Dick* and partaking of Ishmael's nihilism, floats him above the fray, but without the honor accorded Ahab by Stubb:

. . . Starbuck watched the Pequod's tumultuous way, and Ahab's also, as he went lurching along the deck.

"I have sat before the dense coal fire and watched it all aglow, full of its tormented flaming life; and I have seen it wane at last, down, down, to dumbest dust. Old man of the oceans! of all this fiery life of thine, what will at length remain but one little heap of ashes!"

"Aye," cried Stubb, "but sea-coal ashes—mind ye that, Mr. Starbuck—sea-coal, not your common charcoal. Well, well; I heard Ahab mutter, 'Here some one thrusts these cards into these old hands of mine; swears that I must play them, and no others.' And damn me, Ahab, but thou actest right; live in the game and die in it!" (502)

The third choice requires him to live in the present while shaping circumstances to the best of his ability; for the radical puritan, this is the only sane, balanced, enduring, and endurable position. Stubb, "the odd second mate" (127), affirmed such exemplary conduct even if it sent him to hell. So the erasure of rational, principled protest in the annotation to Satan's seduction of Eve is halted (assuming the hand was Melville's). But such arguments are grounded in demonstrations that any moderate man would call outcroppings of heedless adolescent enthusiasm. The moderate men do not simply make such observations and float away like Ishmael; having learned survival tactics from the best, the Promethean dons Milton's black masque to repel boarders.

The switches from one unsafe prospect to another are diverting. As White-Jacket (1850), Melville abruptly queried the piecemeal reform he had just been advocating: His proposed ban on flogging could not end injustices meted out to enlisted men whose class interest in pacifism was "essentially" opposed by glory-seeking officers. White-Jacket fatally defined the "incurable antagonism" that class collaborationists, fascist and antifascist alike, have ever attempted to render invisible: "Can men, whose interests are diverse, ever hope to live together in a harmony uncoerced? Can the brotherhood of the race of mankind ever hope to prevail in a man-of-war, where one man's bane is another man's blessing? By abolishing the scourge, shall we do away with tyranny; *that* tyranny which must ever prevail, where of two essentially antagonistic classes in perpetual contact, one is immeasurably the stronger?"[18] Moreover as the black cook Fleece pointed out in *Moby-Dick*, "the sharks" did not care to be converted. Such "dark" perceptions were dangerous to a morally ambitious artist faithful to social reality. If tepid reformism is really a blast of hot air, then structural transformation is on the agenda. *White-Jacket* gave a more fervid tongue to youth revolt that was unmistakably Hebraic/radical Protestant. It was the sublimity of a visionary republic that brought melancholy to dispossessed aristocrats, energizing the measures taken in retribution:

In many things, we Americans are driven to a rejection of the maxims of the Past, seeing that, ere long, the van of the nationals must, of right, belong to ourselves. There are occasions when it is for America to make precedents, and not to obey them. We should, if possible, prove a teacher to posterity, instead of being the pupil of bygone generations. More shall come after us than have gone before; the world is not yet middle-aged.

Escaped from the house of bondage, Israel of old did not follow after the ways of the Egyptians. To her was given an express dispensation; to her were given new things under the sun. And we Americans are the peculiar, chosen people—the Israel of our time; we bear the ark of the liberties of the world. Seventy years ago we escaped from thrall; and, besides our first birthright— embracing one continent of earth—God has given to us, for a future inheritance, the broad domains of the political pagans, that shall yet come and lie down under the shade of our ark, without bloody hands being lifted. God has predestinated,[19] mankind expects, great things from our race; and great things we feel in our souls. The rest of the nations must soon be in our rear. We are the pioneers of the world; the advance-guard, sent on through the wilderness of untried things, to break a new path in the New World that is ours. In our youth is our strength; in our inexperience our wisdom. At a period when other nations have but lisped, our deep voice is heard afar. Long enough have we been skeptics with regard to ourselves, and doubted whether, indeed the political Messiah had come. But he has come in us, if we would but give utterance to his promptings. And let us always remember that with ourselves, almost for the first time in the history of earth, national selfishness is unbounded philanthropy; for we cannot do a good to America, but we give alms to the world. (chap. 36, 156–57)

Since the late 1930s, numerous scholars have claimed that Ahab was an arch-imperialist. Was White-Jacket's statement made in the spirit of Jefferson and world republican revolution or in the spirit of James Polk's defense of slavery and expansion at the expense of Indians and Mexicans? Given Melville's constant references to abused South Sea islanders, Indians, sailors, and factory workers, these words need not be taken as crypto-imperialist, unless one confuses political emancipation with slavery, or self-assertion with self-sacrifice, which some anti-imperialist scholars may have done.[20] But what about the distinction drawn above between rooted and rootless cosmopolitanism?

> So be,—all's up and I must up too.
> Early in the morning the deed they will do
> Our little game's up they must needs obey
> Well, to these and many another crew—
> Save who was my mammy I never could say
> In my last queer dream here I did stray—

For most part a dream of ships no more.—
A number of men from every shore—
Hail to ye, fellows, and is it you?
Countrymen, yes and Moor and Swede,
Christian, Pagan Cannibal breed.[21] (discarded early version of "Billy in the
    Darbies")

Melville's own writing is ambiguous on the question of species-unity. Though
the rootless Billy's "fellows" hail from "every shore," he nevertheless specifies their
"breed," a term taken from animal husbandry and applied in ethnopluralist discourse as "kinds" of people or "kinds" of intelligence. In both his scornful review of
Parkman's *California and Oregon Trail* and in the passage from *White-Jacket* (quoted
above) Melville affirmed the "brotherhood of the race of mankind." In the draft
fragment from "Billy in the Darbies," however, he greets an international brotherhood while retaining the traditional racialism of group separateness through biological difference. Throughout his writing he oscillates: Donning the black masque
to tell Mapple's Truth merges him with the Other; the gesture triggers the recoil
to dissociation or insensibility; in this state he fixates on white walls with peeling
surfaces that disclose layered, contradictory, almost illegible messages. These pa-
limpsests are terrifying because so much is at stake in getting the messages right—
nothing less than his (white) family's survival, for it is they who will be burned
and burdened should the enthusiasm of Ahab or Pierre be misbegotten or self-
deceived.[22] Many scholars seem to have neglected this characteristic Melvillean dynamic to serve their "advanced" ethnopluralism, a lapse in a century when National
Socialism proudly distinguished its racial (*völkisch*) internationalist politics from
proletarian internationalism (the latter supposedly an ideology concocted by imperialist finance capitalists to swindle the toiling masses). Along with Ishmael, Melvilleans have tended to suppress or overlook his outcroppings of Hebraic republican messianism: the demand for meaning, coherence, and legitimate authority that
may lead to mutiny, to political struggle along the lines that Melville himself identified, addressing essential antagonisms, sometimes with the fighting words of Satan
speaking to the Tree of Knowledge (quoted above).

It was a revelation to read *Paradise Lost* and *Moby-Dick* together; my most calming insights are grounded in Melville's marginalia to Milton's poetry, particularly
his response to Satan's seduction of Eve. The pages that follow take the reader back
and forth between the seventeenth and nineteenth centuries and among some of
Melville's most apparently impenetrable texts. As always, the history of sudden loss
in Melville's family colored his movement away from promiscuous merging. Did he,
at last, come down on the side of universal brotherhood, moral rigor, and intellectual depth as his liberal champions would like to think?

By the mid-1840s the determining structures of Melville's life were in place: Experience had called Christian precept to account. Proletarian adventures and sufferings had cast a jaundiced light on the moral seriousness of established religion and Melville's classical education; conservative reform seemed a ploy to harmonize the irreconcilable interests of the haves and the have-nots. Explaining his symbolism to the reader in *Moby-Dick,* Ahab tries to teach Starbuck something about indefinite authority, man-made prisons, wall busting, and the implicit equality that an unimpeded view of Leviathan's penetralia could confer. Once more the questing artist is both inside and outside the whale:

> If man will strike, strike through the mask! How can the prisoner reach outside except by thrusting through the wall? To me, the white whale is that wall, shoved near to me. Sometimes I think there's naught beyond. But 'tis enough. He tasks me; he heaps me; I see in him outrageous strength, with an inscrutable malice sinewing it. *That inscrutable thing is chiefly what I hate;* and be the white whale agent, or be the white whale principal, I will wreak that hate upon him. Talk not to me of blasphemy, man; I'd strike the sun if it insulted me. For could the sun do that, then could I do the other; since there is ever a sort of fair play herein, jealousy presiding over all creations. But not my master, man, is even that fair play. Who's over me? Truth hath no confines.[23] (164)

Ahab, the most reviled "hater" in American literature, has directly stated that he "chiefly" hates the quality of "inscrutable malice"; in a possibly related remark, the narrator of "A Tartarus of Maids" says of his guide, Cupid, "Inscrutably mysterious was the strange innocence of cruel-heartedness in this usage-hardened boy." The comparison suggests that those charged with moral authority, those who guide our affective development and its expressions, are inexplicably cruel to the comparatively helpless and inoffensive creatures in their care.[24]

In other passages, Ahab's values are further elucidated, lest Melville's meanings be obscured to readers by Ishmael's or Starbuck's constant taunts that he is a tyrant risking their lives to indulge his passion for revenge against a mere beast. Against such misreadings, Ahab's driving ambition is shown to be perfectly focused upon the question: How can an omnipotent and benevolent God errantly tolerate injustice? Why will he not disclose this secret of secrets? Ahab is revealed as a Faustian figure, but neither libertine nor gold bug:

> [Ahab:] Speak, thou vast and venerable head . . . and tell us the secret thing that is in thee. Of all divers, thou hast dived the deepest. That head . . . has

moved amid this world's foundations. . . . Thou hast been where bell or diver never went; hast slept by many a sailor's side, where sleepless mothers would give their lives to lay them down. Thou saw'st the locked lovers when leaping from their flaming ship; heart to heart they sank beneath the exulting wave; true to each other, when heaven seemed false to them. Thou saw'st the murdered mate when tossed by pirates from the midnight deck . . . and his murderers still sailed on unharmed—while swift lightnings shivered the neighboring ship that would have borne a righteous husband to outstretched, longing arms. O head! thou hast seen enough to split the planets and make an infidel of Abraham, and not one syllable is thine! (311–12)

[Flask:] "What's the old man have so much to do with him [Fedallah the Parsee] for?"

[Stubb:] "Striking up a swap or a bargain, I suppose." "Bargain?—about what?" "Why, do ye see, the old man is hard bent after that White Whale, and the devil there is trying to come round him, and get him to swap away his silver watch, or his soul, or something of that sort, and then he'll surrender Moby Dick." (325)

In a passage that confronts the reader directly, the narrator (Ahab speaking through Ishmael?) denounces hypocrisy and the slavish adherence to the lower law, clarifying what kind of materialist he is: "What are the Rights of Man and the Liberties of the World but Loose-Fish? What all men's minds and opinions but Loose-Fish? What is the principle of religious belief in them but Loose-Fish? What to the ostentatious smuggling verbalists are the thoughts of thinkers but Loose-Fish? What is the great globe itself but a Loose-Fish? And what are you, reader, but a Loose-Fish and a Fast-Fish, too?" (398). Melville (not a pleasing Ishmael) has impudently informed his well-educated readership that they, like Loose-Fish, are up for grabs, slaves to propertied interests, held and holding, no matter what "official" laws and rights or their own claims to moral purity may declare. By contrast, Ahab's idea of radical Enlightenment is unfettered to rulers, to Hume's conservatively enlightened "established government." He will reject the tools forged by advanced conservatives, heretofore bringing technological progress that has often fastened the lower orders more securely to elites.

In the scene where Ahab smashes the quadrant, the gaze has been transferred from the reverential upward-looking gaze of conservative reason to the magisterial inward- and outward-looking gaze that other Prometheans would summon in the observing ego, the "independent intellect" that Wordsworth had scornfully rejected in "The Prelude."[25] We may infer from these and other passages that, for Ahab, the conquest of Moby Dick will disclose specifically those secrets of nature and of his own darkness, secrets of the physical and mental world alike, that could emancipate the lower orders and himself from injustice:

> ... the desired observation was taken; and with his pencil upon his ivory leg, Ahab soon calculated what his latitude must be at that precise instant. Then falling into a moment's revery, he again looked up toward the sun.... "Thou sea-mark! thou high and mighty Pilot! thou tellest me truly where I *am,* but canst thou cast the least hint where I *shall* be? ... Foolish toy! babies' plaything of haughty Admirals, and Commodores, and Captains; the world brags of thee, of thy cunning and thy might; but what after all canst thou do, but tell the poor, pitiful point, where thou thyself happenest to be on this wide planet, and the hand that holds thee: no! not one jot more! Thou canst not tell where one drop of water or one grain of sand will be tomorrow noon; and yet with thy impotence thou insultest the sun! Science! Curse thee, thou vain toy; and cursed be all the things that cast man's eyes aloft to that heaven, whose live vividness but scorches him.... Curse thee, thou quadrant! ... no longer will I guide my earthly way by thee; the level ship's compass, and the level dead-reckoning, by log and by line; *these* shall conduct me, and show me my place on the sea. Aye ... thus I trample on thee, thou paltry thing that feebly pointest on high; thus I split and destroy thee!" (501)

I don't think Melville is thinking about technology here; this is neither Luddite tantrum nor Humean critique of empiricism and inductive reasoning.[26] Rather, Ahab's favoring of the "level ship's compass" links him to seventeenth-century Levellers and their republican principle of equal justice. Like the radical puritans, he wants balance; his conscience is in his keel.[27] He has acknowledged the historian's reconfiguration of past and present in the light of earthly experience and study. Such measurements guide him away from bogus, enfeebling authority, from nonhuman history. Whose hand holds the quadrant? Kindly Providence or the God invented by usurping, self-interested earthly militarists? Ahab's is the cultural relativism, the shifting point of view furthered by the leveling radical Enlightenment: By removing himself from the "science" of abusive authority, by honoring free will and personal responsibility, his notion of history has thrust constraints along with opportunities and moral imperatives into our laps. "Wicked" Ahab, the author himself, will not passively acquiesce to the limits and lies imposed by conservatives (white walls) but colors the game with his aroused political will; challenging the Manxman, Ahab suggests ". . . perhaps, life holds thee; not thou it" (521). Contra Ishmael, he is not oblivious to his own passion-distorted perceptions and limitations:

What a lovely day again! were it a new-made world, and made for a summer-house to the angels, and this morning the first of its throwing open to them, a fairer day could not dawn upon that world. Here's food for thought, had Ahab time to think; but Ahab never thinks; he only feels, feels, feels; *that's* tingling enough for mortal man! to think's audacity. God only has that right and privilege. Thinking is, or ought to be, a coolness and a calmness; and our poor hearts throb, and our poor brains beat too much for that.[28] (563)

This passage veers close to Satan's challenge to Eve in *Paradise Lost*. Ahab asks, why has "God" made mortal man so weak and stupid? Why other than to keep him down? Only an imperfect God would trick his children so; for ungodly, godlike Ahab, the withdrawal of unquestioning deference must precede the godly pursuit of earthly truth and justice. And yet the hunt may be fraught with distorting emotions that low Man, forever tied to the whale, never requisitioned.

There is a final confrontation between Ahab and the Whale, but it is radical and conservative Enlightenment that are facing off. Ishmael's skepticism and racy, nihilistic cultural relativism, the tools of conservative Enlightenment, have suddenly disappeared. With the gentleness and geniality of a slap on the face, Ishmael tells the reader that Ahab-style frontal attacks upon Leviathan, by implication, upon all injustice, are utterly hopeless: "Retribution, swift vengeance, eternal malice were in his whole aspect, and in spite of all that mortal man could do, the solid white buttress of his forehead smote the ship's starboard bow, till men and timbers reeled" (571). The radically enlightened Ahab had never pretended to the certainty Ishmael has just expressed: that the mission of the *Pequod*, like that of the Anacharsis Clootz deputation, was doomed to fail. Nor has the Fates' lieutenant draped himself in godlike omniscience: "The greatest, grandest things are unpredicted." Given the limitations of ordinary people in societies where only the privileged few are properly educated, Ahab, the autodidact, is simply doing his best to lead a decent life, to obey his Mapple-instructed conscience. But Ahab also knows which institutions and individuals hold the monopoly of power in the American 1850s: The slavocracy controls the national government; even abolitionist Massachusetts has been forced to bow to its unholy will. He knows he is cut off from the approbation of his family or other conservative readers, that neither their God nor Nature will intervene on behalf of the good. Nevertheless Ahab does not relinquish his enthusiast's integrity to expediency: "I turn my body from the sun. What ho, Tashtego! let me hear thy hammer. Oh! ye three unsurrendered spires of mine; thou uncracked keel; and only god-bullied hull; thou firm deck, and haughty helm, and Pole-pointed prow,—death-glorious ship! must ye then perish, and without me? Am I cut off from the last fond pride of meanest shipwrecked captains? Oh, lonely death on lonely life! Oh, now I feel my topmost greatness lies in my topmost grief. Ho, ho! from all your furthest bounds, pour ye now in, ye bold billows of my whole fore-gone life, and top this one piled comber of my death!" (571).

Ahab's uncracked militancy has been badly misread; it is Ishmael who deems him a monomaniac, satanically driven to destroy God and his ship; the same insults were hurled at the abolitionists by pro-slavery apologists and utopian socialists or land reformers during the 1840s and 1850s. Rather, *Moby-Dick* relates one big moment in the West's progress toward intellectual freedom and responsibility: the withdrawal of legitimacy from duplicitous or confusing authority. Just as the narrator Ishmael attacks Ahab in *Moby-Dick*, the narrator of Milton's epic initially presents Mammon as a gold bug plundering Mother Earth:

> There stood a hill not far whose grisly top
> Belched fire and rolling smoke; the rest entire
> Shone with a glossy scurf, undoubted sign
> That in his womb was hid metallic ore,
> The work of sulphur. Thither winged with speed
> A numerous brigade hastened. As when bands
> Of pioneers with spade and pickaxe armed
> Forerun the royal camp, to trench a field,
> Or cast a rampart. Mammon led them on,
> Mammon, the least erected Spirit that fell
> From heaven, for even in heaven his looks and thoughts
> Were always downward bent, admiring more
> The riches of heaven's pavement, trodden gold,
> Then aught divine or holy else enjoyed
> In vision beatific: by him first
> Men also, and by his suggestion taught,
> Ransacked the centre, and with impious hands
> Rifled the bowels of their mother earth
> For treasures better hid. Soon had his crew
> Opened into the hill a spacious wound
> And digged out ribs of gold. Let none admire
> That riches grow in hell; that soil may best
> Deserve the precious bane. (1, 670–92)

But during Satan's council with the fallen angels, Mammon does not jibe with the greedy transgressor of Book 1; rather, he demystifies Heaven and withdraws deference from an omnipotent yet darkly angry and inscrutable God. Has Milton turned about?

. . . how wearisome
Eternity so spent in worship paid
To whom we hate. Let us not then pursue
By force impossible, by leave obtain'd
Unacceptable, though in Heav'n our state
Of splendid vassalage, but rather seek
Our own good from ourselves, and from our own
Live to our selves, though in this vast recess,
Free, and to none accountable, preferring
Hard liberty before the easy yoke
Of servile pomp. Our greatness will appear
Then most conspicuous, when great things of small,
Useful of hurtful, prosperous of adverse
We can create, and in what place so e'er
Thrive under evil, and work ease out of pain
Through labour and endurance. This deep world
Of darkness do we dread? How oft amidst
Thick clouds and dark doth heaven's all-ruling sire
Choose to reside, His glory unobscured,
And with the majesty of darkness round
Covers his throne; from whence deep thunders roar
Mustering their rage, and Heav'n resembles hell?
As he our darkness, cannot we his light
Imitate when we please? This desert soil
Wants not her hidden lustre, gems and gold;
Nor want we skill or art, from whence to raise
Magnificence; and what can heaven show more?
Our torments also may in length of time
Become our elements, these piercing fires
As soft as now severe, our temper changed
Into their temper; which must needs remove
The sensible of pain. All things invite
To peaceful counsels, and the settled state
Of order, how in safety best we may
Compose our present evils, with regard
Of what we are and were, dismissing quite
All thoughts of war: ye have what I advise.[29] (2, 247–83)

Seventeenth-century readers would have understood Mammon's mining as
the insatiable curiosity of materialists; in the twentieth century, some influential

anticapitalists claimed mining as a defining ingredient of the hated capitalist system.[30] In his own eloquent voice, Mammon's productivity was lustrous with moral effort and simplicity; "gems and gold" could signify radical Enlightenment, for extravagant display had been tarnished as "servile pomp." Mammon urges the rebel angels to abandon Satan's war against God, to create a paradise on earth won by labor and endurance. Like Milton's Mammon, the radical puritan Ahab has chosen hard liberty: if necessary, the artist will stand alone against evil emanating from Leviathan (the state) or an irrationally punitive God himself, but with his sturdy (providential) God-given conscience intact. Mammon's freedom does not lead to anarchy or chaos: The golden reward is self-respect.

Or is the golden reward only an ignominious death like Gansevoort's? Near the close of *Moby-Dick* a sky-hawk is trapped in Ahab's red flag of revolt, drowned with the ship in one long unwinding sentence:

> ... at that instant, a red arm and a hammer hovered backwardly uplifted in the open air, in the act of nailing the flag faster and yet faster to the subsiding spar. A sky-hawk that tauntingly had followed the main-truck downwards from its natural home among the stars, pecking at the flag, and incommoding Tashtego there; this bird now chanced to intercept its broad fluttering wing between the hammer and the wood; and simultaneously feeling that etherial thrill, the submerged savage beneath, in his death-grasp, kept his hammer frozen there; and so the bird of heaven, with archangelic shrieks, and his imperial beak thrust upwards, and his whole captive form folded in the flag of Ahab, went down with his ship, which, like Satan, would not sink to hell till she had dragged a living part of heaven along with her, and helmeted herself with it. (572)

Readers may contrast the heavenly sky-hawk's "imperial beak" with Ahab's character, rendering the captain as amoral Nietzschean Superman. But such a reading (Ishmael's) is contradicted throughout by Ahab's protestations. Comparison with parallel passages in *Pierre* suggests that the imperial "bird of heaven" is Lucy, carrier of the traditional-but-radical-making Protestant values espoused by Commander Maria Gansevoort Melville in her letter to Augusta, October 17, 1838 (quoted above). The conflicts Melville experiences in the act of writing as he veers from Ahab to Ishmael may reflect the feared consequences for his family if his railroading drive to tell the whole truth is misdirected, bringing everyone down. The Promethean will withstand their "pecking," but what if he destroys the solidarity they rely on to keep the ship afloat? And who else will take in *der Fliegende Holländer?* Certainly not Nathaniel Hawthorne, wary limner of the "Virtuoso" and other crimson flashings.

Goethe had surveyed the grandeur and pathos of Renaissance ambition in *Faust*. Disabusing Mephistopheles of the assumption that their pact was to engorge him with boundless bliss, Faust, not-a-libertine, answered to ratify the "restless activity [that] proves the man":

> But thou hast heard, 't is not of joy we're talking.
> I take the wildering whirl, enjoyment's keenest pain,
> Enamored hate, exhilarant disdain.
> My bosom, of its thirst for knowledge sated,
> Shall not henceforth, from any pang be wrested,
> And all of life for all mankind created
> Shall be within mine inmost being tested:
> The highest, lowest forms my soul shall borrow,
> Shall heap upon itself their bliss and sorrow,
> And thus, my own sole self to all their selves expanded.
> I too, at last, shall with them all be stranded![31]

However closely the epilogue to *Moby-Dick* buttoned Melville to the Hawthorne-pleasing Ishmael, the "regular romance" that followed Ishmael's rescue reattached him to Ahab, Goethe's Faust, the active life, and ostracism.

Pierre, or the Ambiguities (1852) may be viewed as a retelling of *Moby-Dick*, with Melville's deceptively white family raising the dark monster Ahab. Pierre is a poetic and privileged (but muscular) young man living in the Hudson River Valley with his widowed mother who owns and manages a prosperous estate complete with tenant farmers, rent rolls, and feudal dues; Saddle Meadows is hallowed by memories of Indian conquest, Revolutionary War exploits, and faithful slaves. Just before Pierre is about to solidify his class position through a brilliant marriage, a black-hooded stranger accosts Pierre in the dark of night, delivering a letter announcing that Pierre's late father had sired and abandoned a natural child. His alleged half-sister, Isabel, is revealed as the postman and letter writer. At first he is struck down, but after a few days of turmoil the transfigured, shaded Pierre runs off with Isabel to the city, rejecting the pastoral idyll offered by the aristocratic mother, Mary, and his wealthy fiancée, Lucy. Others of their class had been pleased with Pierre's puerile and inoffensive artistic effusions, but Pierre, instructed by disillusion with his hitherto perfect father, has reconfigured his situation, and puzzling fragments of childhood experience now cohere. No longer the victim of rosy lies, the illuminated Pierre has claimed his individuality.[32] Moreover the "electral" insight reveals Mother's narcissism and hypocrisy as well: She will never accept Isabel as a legitimate member of the family; by analogy she will never accept Pierre unless he perfectly mirrors her own gilded values and aspirations concealed beneath the

Christian and paternalistic false front. Torn between the conflicting imperatives to protect Mother from the knowledge of her husband's wild deed while simultaneously rescuing the orphaned Isabel from loneliness and poverty by taking her into the family, the ever-chivalrous Pierre pretends that he and Isabel are married, regrettably jilting Lucy. Pierre is disinherited but bravely attempts to support his sister-wife through newly mature authorship in an environment of physical and moral austerity. Repeated images show Pierre and Isabel snakishly coiled and entwined; it is specifically this erotic gesture that displaces false images of the white family. Their incestuous entanglement may be read in two ways. First, the coiled Isabel and Pierre suggest the "visible world of experience" mingled with the creative force of Isabel's grief (the wild notes of her magical guitar identified with the timeless morality of the Sermon on the Mount); second, as the undeserved torture visited upon the priest Laocoön and his sons after his failed attempt to prevent the sack of Troy.

As rendered in *The Aeneid*, "the wavering crowd is torn apart in eager dispute" while they debate what to do with the horse of "mountainous bulk" offered by the Greeks:

> Laocoön afire runs down from the fortress height, and cries from far: "Ah, wretched citizens, what height of madness is this? Believe you the foe is gone? or think you any Grecian gift is free of treachery? Is it thus we know Ulysses? Either Achaeans are hid in this cage of wood, or the engine is fashioned against our walls to overlook the houses and descend upon the city; or some delusion lurks in it: trust not the horse O Trojans. Be it what it may, I fear the Grecians even when they offer gifts." Thus speaking, he hurled his huge spear with mighty strength at the creature's side and the curved framework of the belly: the spear stood quivering, and the jarred cavern of the womb sounded hollow and uttered a groan. And had divine ordinance been thus and our soul not infatuated he had moved us to lay violent steel on the Argolic hiding place; and Troy would now stand, and you, tall towers of Priam, yet abide.

Ignoring Laocoön, whose spear has pierced a deceptive facade (as in Ahab's thrust at Leviathan, as in Pierre's newfound insight into Mother's class-bound narcissism), the Trojans are taken in by the wily prisoner Sinon. Then Laocoön meets his horrible fate as he, the priest of Neptune, slays a great bull near the seashore:

> Over the placid depths (I shudder as I recall) two snakes in enormous coils press down the sea and advance together to the shore; their breasts rise through the surge, and their blood-red crests overtop the waves; the rest

trails through the main behind and wreathes back in voluminous curves; the brine gurgles and foams. And now they gain the fields, while their blood-shot eyes blazed with fire, and their tongues lapped and flickered in their hissing mouths. We scatter, blanched at the sight. They in unfaltering train make towards Laocoön. At first the serpents twine in their double embrace his two children, and bite deep in their wretched limbs; then him likewise, as he comes up to help with arms in his hand, they seize and fasten in their enormous coils; and now twice clasping his waist, twice encircling his neck with their scaly bodies, they tower head and neck above him. He at once strains his hands to tear their knots apart, his fillets spattered with foul black venom; at once raises to heaven awful cries; as when, bellowing, a bull shakes the wavering axe from his neck and rushes wounded from the altar. But the two snakes glide away to the high sanctuary and seek the fierce Tritonian's citadel, and take shelter under the goddess' feet beneath the circle of her shield. Then indeed a strange terror thrills all in our amazed breasts; and Laocoön, men say, has fulfilled his crime's desert, in piercing the consecrated wood and hurling his guilty spear into its body. All cry out that the image must be drawn to its home and supplication made to her deity.[33]

Like the Trojan priest, Melville's Ahab would be read as a blasphemer and criminal by terrified relatives and shuddering, thrilled readers. A small reproduction of the celebrated sculpture group, Laocoön and his sons strangled by the serpents, occupies a niche in the mansion at Saddle Meadows, introduced to the reader at the climax of Pierre's defiance. Pierre's merging with the (family-blackening) critical spirit of Isabel[34] will drive "Optimistic" Mary to grief-induced insanity and death and Pierre to remorse, despair, and blindness. The radical democratic experiment of Pierre and Isabel with its too-piercing insight into "things as they are" has produced only a failed artwork, pridefully intended to "gospelize the world anew," a task too demanding for one only "just emerging from his teens." Originally promised a gay, romantic popular novel, Pierre's publishers indignantly reject the death-corrupted, overreaching, satanic issue of the Pierre-Isabel alliance. By the end of the novel all the major characters, shocked or truth-poisoned by Isabel, will have perished. It has been claimed that shortly after Pierre appeared, Melville, at the insistence of his mother, was examined for insanity by his Berkshire neighbor Dr. Oliver Wendell Holmes (later the author of the snake-haunted gothic tale Elsie Venner, a testament of conservative paranoia).

Isabel's hands are coarsened by labor. Not wishing to be an exploiter herself, she wonders if she has made exorbitant demands on her newfound brother and protector: ". . . Pierre, now, now, this instant a vague anguish fills me. Tell me, by loving me, by owning me, publicly or secretly,—tell me, doth it involve any vital hurt to thee? Speak without reserve; speak honestly; as I do to thee! Speak now, Pierre, and tell me all!" Pierre responds with the words of Goethe's Faust or Melville's Ahab. Infused with revolutionary ardor, they grow tall together:

"Is Love a harm? can Truth betray to pain? Sweet Isabel, how can hurt come in the path to God? How, when I know thee all, now did I forget thee, fail to acknowledge thee, and love thee before the wide world's whole brazen width—could I do that; then might'st thou ask thy question reasonably and say—Tell me, Pierre, does the suffocating in thee of poor Bell's holy claims, does not that involve for thee unending misery? And my truthful soul would echo—Unending misery! Nay, nay, nay. Thou art my sister and I am thy brother; and that part of the world which knows me, shall acknowledge thee; or, by heaven, I will crush the disdainful world down on its knees to thee, my sweet Isabel!"

"The menacings in thy eyes are dear delights to me; I grow up with thy own glorious stature; and in thee, my brother, I see God's indignant ambassador to me, saying—Up, up, Isabel, and take no terms from the common world, but do thou make terms to it, and grind thy fierce rights out of it! Thy catching nobleness unsexes me, my brother; and now I know that in her most exalted moment, then woman no more feels the twin-born softness of her breasts, but feels chain-armor palpitating there!"

Her changed attitude of beautiful audacity; her long scornful hair, that trailed out a disheveled banner; her wonderful transfigured eyes, in which some meteors seemed playing up; all this now seemed to Pierre the work of an invisible enchanter. Transformed she stood before him; and Pierre, bowing low over to her, owned that irrespective, darting majesty of humanity, which can be majestical and menacing in woman as in man. (159–60)

The narrator, however, will shutter aroused and ennobled humanity. Such "flying in the marble face of the Past," he tells us, was regretted by Isabel/Minerva herself "yielding to a momentary burst of aggressive enthusiasm" and "lawless wandering," or so Pierre infers (174).

The volte-face was prefigured in the pivotal chapter, "The Try-Works," of *Moby-Dick*. Though initially "one of that crew," Ishmael turns away from Ahab's quest as if he had just glimpsed the "hot hell" of Milton's unpacified Satan or Laocoön's punishment: The *Communist Manifesto* is becoming film noir:

As they narrated to each other their unholy adventures, their tales of terror told in words of mirth, as their uncivilized laughter forked upwards out of them, like the flames from the furnace; as to and fro, in their front, the harpooneers wildly gesticulated with their huge pronged forks and dippers; as the wind howled on, and the sea leaped, and the ship groaned and dived, and yet steadfastly shot her red hell further and further into the blackness of the sea and the night, and scornfully champed the white bone in her mouth, and viciously spat round her on all sides; then the rushing Pequod, freighted with savages, and laden with fire, and burning a corpse, and plunging into that blackness of darkness, seemed the material counterpart of her monomaniac commander's soul.

So it seemed to me, as I stood at her helm. . . . Wrapped, for that interval, in darkness myself, I but better saw the redness, the madness, the ghastliness of others. (423)

Disingenuously perhaps, Ishmael reassures the reader that he is immersed in Ahab's quest for educational purposes only, going on to describe his own hallucinatory fire worshipping that nearly capsized the ship, a warning that returns him to neoclassical order.[35] The family likeness of Ishmael's disclaimer with Pierre's second thoughts suggests that Isabel represents radical Enlightenment, as does Ahab himself. In "The Candles," Ahab becomes more and more excited, more and more in touch with his Muse, while the sane Muse of illuminated revolution beats the conservative Ishmael. "Corposants" have appeared on the "yard-arms" and lightning-rod-ends": "each of the three tall masts was silently burning in that sulphurous air, like three gigantic wax tapers before an altar":

"The rods! the rods!" cried Starbuck to the crew, suddenly admonished to vigilance by the vivid lightning that had just been darting flambeaux, to light Ahab to his post. . . . [Starbuck wants to drop the rods overboard.]
"Avast!" cried Ahab; "let's have fair play here, though we be the weaker side. Yet I'll contribute to raise rods on the Himmalehs and Andes, that all the world may be secured; but out on privileges! Let them be, sir." . . . Relieved against the ghostly light, the gigantic jet negro, Daggoo, loomed up to thrice his real stature, and seemed the black cloud from which the thunder had come. The parted mouth of Tashtego revealed his shark-white teeth, which strangely gleamed as if they too had been tipped by corpusants; while lit up by the preternatural light, Queequeg's tattooing burned like Satanic blue flames on his body. (505–6)

The "ghostly light" suggests the Holy Spirit, the "cloven tongues like of fire" that sat on the gathered apostles in the Pentecost and that Melville had earlier identified with the American political mission to unify the human race; moreover, he had marked in his own Bible the verses describing the communism of primitive

Christianity.[36] But most significant for our pursuit of Ahab's genealogy, the following (unattributed) lines are found inside the front and back covers of Melville's New Testament (1844), written in ink and underlined in pencil; Melville had copied out the perfectionist sentiments of Saint Evremond (1613–1703):

> In life he appears as a true Philosopher—as a wise man in the highest sense. He stands *firm to his point;* he *goes on his way inflexibly;* and while he exalts the lower to himself, while he makes the poor, the rich, partakers of his wisdom, of his riches, of his strength, he, on the other hand, in no sense conceals his divine origin; he dares to equal himself with God; nay, to declare that he himself is God. In this manner is he wont from youth upwards *to astound his familiar friends;* of these he gains a part to his own cause; irritates the rest against him; and shows to all men, who are aiming at a certain elevation in doctrine and life, *what they have to look for from the world.* And thus, for the nobler portion of mankind, his walk and conversation are even more instructive and profitable than his death; for to those trials every one is called, to this trial but a few.
>
> If we can conceive it possible, that the creator of the world himself assumed the form of his creature, and lived in that manner for a time on earth, this creature must seem to us of infinite perfection, because susceptible of such a combination with his maker. Hence in our idea of G̶o̶d̶ man there can be no inconsistency with our idea of God: and if we often feel a certain disagreement with Him & remoteness from Him, it is but the more on that account our duty, not like advocates of the wicked Spirit, to keep our eyes constantly on the nakedness and wickedness of our nature: but rather to seek out every property & beauty, by which our pretension to a similarity with the Divinity may be made good.

By making Jesus moral exemplar (as read by the Epicurean Saint Evremond), Melville has defied conservative Christianity. The orthodox Christian focuses on the death and resurrection of Jesus, not his life. Shielded by Saint Evremond, front and back, Melville is aligned with the Hebrew prophets, Lucretius, the Pelagians, the most radical puritans, and the empirical tradition in philosophy.[37] Though Ishmael sees the devil's rod lifted in anger and black Daggoo's looming expansion "relieved against the ghostly light," Ahab is joined to Milton's Muse, perhaps conquering the fear that he may repeat Gansevoort's lonely death—an anxiety hitherto admitted only through Ishmael's narration. Once more, Ahab addresses the God whose callousness he has berated throughout the text: ". . . the white flame but lights the way to the White Whale! . . . I now know thee, thou clear spirit, and I now know that thy right worship is defiance. To neither love nor reverence wilt thou be kind; and e'en for hate thou canst but kill; and all are killed. No fearless fool now fronts thee. I own thy speechless, placeless power; but to the last gasp of my earthquake life will dispute its unconditional, unintegral mastery in me" (507).[38] Ahab tells God that he fears Him but that, no matter how severe the punishment, he will not yield to the "speechless, placeless power" that could intimidate him, the power that Ishmael constantly brings to the reader's attention to divert us (Ahab, Ishmael, Melville, the reader) from the quest. After all, it was the distant, impersonal God Himself who gave Ahab free will that would control evil in himself and oppose it in others. But before Ahab can shout "out on privileges," he must know what evil is, and that is no easy task given the obscurantism of religion where the really important ethical distinctions are concerned. No authority is exempt from scrutiny, so Ahab blasphemously tests God, addressing an equal: "In the midst of the personified impersonal, a personality stands here. Though but a point at best; whencesoe'er I came; wheresoe'er I go; yet while I earthly live, the queenly personality[39] lives in me, and feels her royal rights. . . . Oh, thou clear spirit, of thy fire thou madest me, and like a true child of fire, I breathe it back to thee. . . . Oh, oh! Yet blindfold, yet will I talk to thee. Light though thou be, thou leapest out of darkness; but I am darkness leaping out of light, leaping out of thee!" (507).

The "queenly personality" recalls both the apple tree and Eve: Mother of science and Queen of this Universe, feeling her royal rights because she has agreed with the serpent's argument and eaten forbidden fruit (*Paradise Lost,* 9.679–87); she is the embodiment of female sensuality and wisdom so indispensable to Lockean constitutionalism or science or modern art-making. The difficult issue is one of obedience to earthly authority. Commodores, judges, and senators, while sworn to protecting and advancing the commonweal, support unchristian social policies that oppress the poor and perpetuate slavery. How can we know when our actions are righteous if we do not probe the darkness in ourselves and others? When we exert earthly powers in a democracy, doing the Lord's work, are we lifting our hickory harpoons in the interests of the underserved or only ourselves and our masters? Perhaps Melville was thinking of Young Hickory Gansevoort's exultant democratic war cry after deceptively waving the letter from Van Buren that was meant to unify the divided electorate: "Up Democrats, and at them!" Melville petrified himself by the audacity of "the unterrified Democracy" (Pierre merged with Eve/Isabel). Moreover, Milton had warned of the vortex that would swallow such abandoned blasphemy:

Ahab's harpoon, the one forged at Perth's fire, remained firmly lashed in its conspicuous crotch, so that it projected beyond the whale-boat's bow; but the sea that had stove its bottom had caused the loose leather sheath to drop off; and from the keen steel barb there now came a levelled flame of pale, forked fire. As the silent harpoon burned there like a serpent's tongue, Starbuck grasped Ahab by the arm—"God, God is against thee, old man; forbear!" . . . the panic-stricken crew . . . raised a half mutinous cry. But dashing the rattling lightning links to the deck, and snatching the burning harpoon, Ahab waved it like a torch among them. . . . Petrified by his aspect, and still more shrinking from the fiery dart that he held, the men fell back in dismay. . . . "All your oaths to hunt the White Whale are as binding as mine; and heart, soul, and body, lungs and life, old Ahab is bound. And that ye may know to what tune this heart beats: look ye here; thus I blow out the last fear!"(508)

Ahab is playing resolute Head to the crew's frightened Heart. There is a constant tension in the text between Ishmael's joking explorations of the whale's anatomy and Ahab's assertive thrusts through walls that would block his vision. The harpoon may be seen as a phallic gaze, residing in the "conspicuous crotch." With the whale hunt explicitly made to represent the Fall, the Enlightenment, and the mobbish revolution the representative Body's rebel senses have engendered, Ahab sounds like Hautia, the temptress releasing Taji's imprisoned body in *Mardi:*

[Hautia:] "Come! let us sin, and be merry. Ho! wine, wine, wine! and lapfuls of flowers! let all the cane-brakes pipe their flutes. Damsels! dance; reel, swim, around me:—I the vortex that draws all in. Taji! Taji!—as a berry, that name is juicy in my mouth!—Taji, Taji!" and in choruses, she warbled forth the sound, till it seemed issuing from her syren eyes.

My heart flew forth from out its bars, and soared in air; but as my hand touched Hautia's, down dropped a dead bird from the clouds.

"Ha! how he sinks!—but did'st ever dive in deep waters, Taji? Did'st ever see where the pearls grow?—To the cave!—damsels, lead on! (650)

[Ahab:] "Ha, ha, my ship! thou mightest well be taken now for the sea-chariot of the sun. Ho, ho! all ye nations before my prow, I bring the sun to ye! Yoke on the further billows; hallo! a tandem, I drive the sea!" (516)

Soon Starbuck will beg Ahab to return to the family (544), lest they all sink like that bird dropping suddenly into the sea: The price of forbidden knowledge could be the loss of security promised by upper-class patrons to docile middle managers. Has Milton's dove been slipping into Gansevoort's war hawk? Have cloven tongues of fire emanated only from Satan, not the Holy Ghost? Endings matter, and *Pierre* repeats the metamorphosis from dove to hawk but leaves the artist protectively masqued. In the "deluge-wreck" of the last scene, Pierre, like Ahab, at first seems satisfied with his momentous decision to follow Isabel over and inside the pregnant vast abyss. Having delivered an accurate family history and indicted demented authority, the queenly personality, Eve, is flaunting her serpent-tongued, white-flame-tipped red pencil, baptized in the name of the devil. Misleading perhaps, and igniting though it may be to the sister of Peter Gansevoort and the daughter of Lemuel Shaw, Red and Black have rescued him from the moderate men.

When Pierre suddenly announces his marriage to the penniless Isabel, Pierre's frantic mother disinherits him in favor of his cousin Glendinning Stanly, the quasi-lover of Pierre's youth. After previously promising Pierre and Lucy residence in a charming and well-appointed house he owns in the city, Glen locks out his de-classed cousin and bride, stranding the weary travelers and exposing the young ladies (Isabel and another outcast, Delly) to a wild multiracial riot in a police station. Furiously confronting Glen at a glittering party in his luxurious, brightly lit home,[40] the insolent, bedraggled Pierre is pronounced insane and ejected by his class-proud relative. Glen now woos Lucy, but she flees her sterile existence to join Pierre, Isabel, and Delly in the city, intent on protecting the married couple, but also to stake her eternal claim to Pierre, whom she intuits as having left her on a secret holy mission. The ménage à quatre struggles with poverty, living in a converted church building called The Apostles. Glen plus Lucy's relatives follow to retrieve her and dishonor Pierre. Defying them all, steadfast Lucy refuses to leave Pierre and Isabel, whom she assumes are really man and wife. Just after Pierre's failed book is refused by the publishers, Glen assaults his boyhood sweetheart

in a large, open, triangular space . . . shouting "Liar! Villain!" Glen leaped toward Pierre from front, and with such lightning-like ferocity, that the simultaneous blow of his cowhide smote Pierre across the cheek, and left a half-livid and half-bloody brand.

For that one moment, the people fell back on all sides from them; and left them—momentarily recoiled from each other—in a ring of panics.

But clapping both hands to his two breasts, Pierre, on both sides shaking off the sudden white grasp of two rushing girls, tore out both pistols, and rushed headlong upon Glen.

"For thy one blow, take here two deaths! 'Tis speechless sweet to murder thee!"

Spatterings of his own kindred blood were upon the pavement; his own hand had extinguished his house in slaughtering the only unoutlawed human being by the name of Glendinning;—and Pierre was seized by a hundred contending hands. (359–60)

In this astonishing passage, Melville has located the instruments of self-defense and aggression in Pierre's two "breasts" (formerly breast pockets), the site where death milk is produced, the milk of human kindness that fructifies his art: While bonding with the "unrepresentables," he has destroyed his class. Eve/Satan/Pierre is in the weeping, shrinking prison of the family, underneath the avalanche of their disapproval and exposed to the arrows poising, again. Even while fused rhetorically with the prison, he asks himself, Did I do the right thing by relying upon my own sense of virtue, Eros-illuminated?

> . . . The cumbersome stone ceiling almost rested on his brow; so that the long tiers of massive cell-galleries above seemed partly piled on him. His immortal, immovable, bleached cheek was dry; but the stone cheeks of the walls were trickling. The pent twilight of the contracted yard, coming through the barred arrow-slit, fell in dim bars upon the granite floor.
>
> "Here then, is the untimely, timely end; Life's last chapter well stitched into the middle. . . . It is ambiguous still. Had I been heartless now, disowned, and spurningly portioned off the girl at Saddle Meadows, then had I been happy through a long life on earth and perchance through a long eternity in heaven! Now, 'tis merely hell in both worlds. Well, be it hell. I will mold a trumpet of the flames, and, with my breath of flame, breathe back my defiance! But give me first another body! I long and long to die, to be rid of this dishonored cheek." (360)

Isabel and Lucy enter together; Pierre coldly rejects them both, then Isabel blames herself for her brother's crime: "At these wailed words from Isabel, Lucy shrunk up like a scroll, and noiselessly fell at the feet of Pierre. He touched her heart.— 'Dead!—Girl! wife or sister, saint or fiend!'—seizing Isabel in his grasp—'in thy breasts, life for infants lodgeth not, but death-milk for thee and me!—The drug!' and tearing her bosom loose, he seized the secret vial nestling there" (360). Lucy had thought Isabel was Pierre's wife, not his sister: The blurted secret kills her. Lucy is revealed as the bird that dropped from the skies in *Mardi*, as the heavenly bird caught in Ahab's red flag. The volcanic core of Melville's being, the connection to the sensuality and self-assertion of the lower orders represented by Pierre's two breasts and the "incest," has diminished the already shrunken family. The secret vial may refer to Milton's "violl" of dissent in *Areopagitica;* both Milton and Melville knew that the seeds of critical thought raised dragon's teeth; that the example of upper-class radicalism could provoke servile wars. Lucy's naval brother, Fred, and Pierre's friend, the radical democrat Charlie Millthorpe, enter to find the dying threesome:

> [Fred:] Dead!—without one visible wound—her sweet plumage hides it.— Thou hellish carrion, this is thy hellish work! Thy juggler's rifle brought

down this heavenly bird! Oh, my God, my God! Thou scalpest me with this sight!

[Charlie:] The dark vein's burst, and here's the deluge-wreck—all stranded here! Ah, Pierre . . . I would have rallied thee, and banteringly warned thee from thy too moody ways, but thou wouldst never heed!—one speechless clasp!—all's o'er!

[Isabel:] "All's o'er, and ye know him not!" came gasping from the wall; and from the fingers of Isabel dropped an empty vial—as it had been a run-out sand-glass—and shivered upon the floor; and her whole form sloped sideways, and she fell upon Pierre's heart, and her long hair ran over him, and arbored him in ebon vines.[41]

So the Melville problem concerns reason itself (the look evaded by those recent writers who want to make Melville a merely ambitious and unprincipled author and/or violent husband[42]). All three books, *Mardi, Moby-Dick,* and *Pierre,* present a paradox. If Melville takes the ethics instilled by his family too far, he will destroy the only source of his survival. If he does not obey the higher law, he cannot be a great artist but only a dishonorable flunky to powerful interests. The image of the "small vial of sand" in *Moby-Dick* recurs in the sandglass dropped by Isabel's fingers. Ahab has just encountered the merry, successful whaler the *Bachelor,* which is triumphantly returning to New England. This passage is located near the end of the book, and Ahab is weighing the alternatives, as will Pierre in the prison: ". . . as Ahab, leaning over the taffrail, eyed the homeward-bound craft, he took from his pocket a small vial of sand, and then looking from the ship to the vial, seemed thereby bringing remote associations together, for that vial was filled with Nantucket soundings" (495).[43]

Homeward, doubly bound

During their first interview, Isabel had invited Pierre to inspect the dark interior of her mystic guitar, marvelously inscribed with MOTHER. While acquainting Pierre with her strange history, Isabel's wild melodies tugged at his heart strings; later they inspired chapters of his New Model Gospel. Black-haired Isabel's predecessor in *Moby-Dick* was little black Pip whose panic-stricken leaps from a whaleboat foreshadow Ahab's death and Ishmael's rescue. Pip was accidentally lashed round his chest and neck by the harpoon line after the first jump, then cursed by the sailors, for cutting him free has cost them a whale. After the second leap, he was nearly abandoned by the angry harpooners:

By the merest chance the ship itself at last rescued him; but from that hour the little negro went about the deck an idiot; such, at least, they said he was. The sea had jeeringly kept his finite body up, but drowned the infinite of his soul. Not drowned entirely, though. Rather carried down alive to wondrous depths, where strange shapes of the unwarped primal world glided to and fro before his passive eyes; and the miser-merman, Wisdom, revealed his hoarded heaps; and among the joyous, heartless, ever-juvenile eternities, Pip saw the multitudinous, God-omnipresent, coral insects, that out of the firmament of waters heaved the colossal orbs. He saw God's foot upon the treadle of the loom, and spoke it; and therefore his shipmates called him mad. So man's insanity is heaven's sense; and wandering from all mortal reason, man comes at last to that celestial thought, which, to reason, is absurd and frantic; and weal or woe, feels then uncompromised, indifferent as his God. (414)

These "strange shapes of the unwarped primal world . . . among the joyous . . . eternities" undo "the horrors of the half-known [unexamined, half-remembered?] life";[44] (the conclusion that "man's insanity is heaven's sense" should also establish the ironic intent of "Plinlimmon's Pamphlet," a reminder from the moderate men intended to taunt Pierre's idiot idealism by justifying the superior rationality of "virtuous expediency"). Later, Ahab will break his isolation from God and man by taking Pip/Isabel into his cabin:

"Oh, ye frozen heavens! look down here. Ye did beget this luckless child, and have abandoned him, ye creative libertines. Here, boy; Ahab's cabin shall be Pip's home henceforth, while Ahab lives. Thou touchest my inmost centre, boy; thou art tied to me by cords woven of my heart strings. . . ." [Pip:] "What's this? here's velvet shark-skin," intently gazing at Ahab's hand and feeling it. "Ah now, had poor Pip but felt so kind a thing as this, perhaps he had ne'er been lost! This seems to me, sir, as a man-rope; something that weak souls may hold by. Oh, sir, let Old Perth now come and rivet these two hands together; the black one with the white, for I will not let this go." [Ahab:] "Oh, boy, nor will I thee, unless I should thereby drag thee to worse horrors than are here. Come, then, to my cabin. Lo! ye believers in gods all goodness, and in man all ill, lo you! see the omniscient gods oblivious of suffering man; and man, though idiotic, and knowing not what he does, yet full of the sweet things of love and gratitude. Come! I feel prouder leading thee by thy black hand, than though I grasped an Emperor's!"
"There go two daft ones now," muttered the old Manxman. "One daft with strength, the other daft with weakness."(522)

On the third day of chase, the same "line"[45] that strangles Ahab at the very moment of penetration is the heart string(s) entwining him with Pip:

[Ahab:] "Towards thee I roll, thou all-destroying but unconquering whale; to the last I grapple with thee; from hell's heart I stab at thee; for hate's sake I spit my last breath at thee. Sink all coffins and all hearses to one common pool! and since neither can be mine, let me then tow to pieces, while still chasing thee, though tied to thee, thou damned whale! *Thus,* I give up the spear!"

The harpoon was darted; the stricken whale flew forward; with igniting velocity the line ran through the groove;—ran foul. Ahab stooped to clear it; he did clear it; but the flying turn caught him round the neck, and voicelessly as Turkish mutes bowstring their victim, he was shot out of the boat, ere the crew knew he was gone.[46] (571–72)

The "path to [Ahab's] fixed purpose" and his (hickory) harpoon follow the same "groove" (168, 572). But Ahab's "soul" is not properly understood as a crashing railroad car or as "Old Hickory" Andrew Jackson swooping down on the Indians. Rather, Ahab's "railroad" marks the trail of Melville's internationalism, displayed in the irrepressible, indignant unmasking of illegitimate authority. It is internationalism performed in the context of solidarity with labor and the unjustly dispossessed (or misread and misappropriated), even if it chokes the "liberal" family. Such antics are labeled as narcissism and monomania by Ishmael and the conservative narrator of *Pierre*, who, like Charlie Millthorpe, sees Pierre as self-deceived, not "expanded" or extended (*erweitern* in Goethe) but only "stranded" or wrecked (*zerscheitern*).

There are subversively ambiguous words in the endings of *Moby-Dick* and *Pierre*, turning the classical concept of moderation (sanity at the temperate Greek center, monstrosity at the hot "antipodes"/periphery) on its head. The bursting of the "black bubble" or the "dark vein" saves Ishmael and Pierre once they have penetrated to the "vital centre"/Isabel's unbuttoned secret vial. The vial contains the forbidden knowledge of both good and evil that is the object of Mapple's demand for self-scrutiny, Ahab's geology, or Pierre's tearing/mourning:[47] ". . . one captain, seizing the line-knife from his broken prow, had dashed at the whale, as an Arkansas duellist at his foe, blindly seeking with a six inch blade to reach the fathom-deep life of the whale" (184). Look at Ahab's hammers, daggers, forks, jack-knives, flaming harpoons; they are line-knives that would expose the concrete content of fine-sounding abstractions ("cant"). Look at Ahab's burning ship, launched by Mary/Lucy's white religion, but leaping from light into darkness, diving underneath narrative irony (perhaps) to disclose Ishmael's imperishable *underground* connection with Ahab and Anacharsis Clootz, Pierre's with Isabel's. Their sinuous ebon arbor, helmets, and disheveled banners trail for suffering but militant humanity. Look for Ahab's conscience, you will find it in his keel; it will be the "vital centre" that saves Ishmael, the "vital glance" that centered Daniel Orme in an insular Tahiti of peace and joy. The grief-stricken outbursts on behalf of the oppressed confer the balance that tears up the accepting/rejecting mother and fails—while it flunks the upper classes by delegitimating hypocritical claims to wholeness and moral purity. Meanwhile, for Ishmael/Job, agent of Maria's white defenses, blackness is a shadow/shelter that helps him nab the deceptive troublemakers, the children of pride, who would poison his class with black milk. For the artists Ahab and Pierre, the black masque confers anonymity in a world of spying Ishmaels; the riveting charisma leaks out to attract rebellious posterity. Such childish probing and protective masking would continue, apparently to be disavowed, in the stabs and blows of two (short) characters linked to Ahab's digging: the dagger-wielding Babo, leader of a slave revolt ("Benito Cereno") and the scrawling, hammer-swinging Margoth (*Clarel*), an "apostate" and "geologic Jew."[48]

Compare Ahab's stab at the whale with these fatal lines from the sadder and wiser ex-Promethean Wordsworth, then with Melville's description of the African Babo going at his master Benito Cereno:

> I took the knife in hand
> And, stopping not at parts less sensitive,
> Endeavoured with my best of skill to probe
> The living body of society
> Even to the heart. (*The Prelude*, 1805)

> I summoned my best skill, and toiled, intent
> To anatomise the frame of social life,
> Yea, the whole body of society
> Searched to its heart.[49] (*The Prelude*, rev. ed. 1850)

> Glancing down at his feet, Captain Delano saw the freed hand of the servant aiming with a second dagger—a small one, before concealed in his wool [near the brain, his "hive of subtlety"]—with this he was snakishly writhing up from the boat's bottom, at the heart of his master, his countenance lividly vindictive, expressing the centred purpose of his soul; while the Spaniard, half-choked was vainly shrinking away, with husky words incoherent to all but the Portuguese. (99)

The latter scene is presaged by a description of the medallioned stern piece on the *San Dominick:* "uppermost and central of which was a dark satyr in a mask, holding his foot on the prostrate neck of a writhing figure, likewise masked." The prow had held a figure of "Cristobal Colon"; the mutinous slaves have replaced it with the cannibalized skeleton of their former owner, Alexandro Aranda, covered to deceive Captain Delano, but with the chalked scrawl, *"Seguid vuestro jefe"* (follow your leader) still visible. If Babo is an Ahab, then the voyage of the *Pequod* cannot be an emblem for the ruthless side of manifest destiny, as the gathered Left seems to think, but a replay of the French Revolution (including its Jacobin aftermath in Santo Domingo) as narrated by a Carlylean conservative. The "dark satyr" suggests that Melville's satire is meant to expose the two captains, Benito Cereno and the narrator Delano, both collaborators in the perpetuation of slavery, an institution Melville loathed, but that had been supported in the higher interest of national unity by his concilia-tory father-in-law and patron, Judge Lemuel Shaw, who was still alive. Melville had no choice; he played his cards the way they were dealt, toying with the mask, per-haps to protect himself from retaliation, but also to avoid the insensibility and de-pression he associated with his dying brother Gansevoort.

I KNOW WHERE I AM

It seems that Melville's heart was with Faust and the Romantic Wandering Jew, but even if his situation is "ambiguous still,"[50] as Pierre had concluded, the Melville problem remains—because he faced contradictions conservatives leave dormant or try to resolve, as Marxist and liberal critics have argued, only in the formal coher-ence of a perfected work of art. The Melville problem as defined by twentieth-cen-tury critics seems to have bothered the artist in early and midcareer, but at the end, at least, not at all. Perhaps Pip and Isabel were internalized: As Daniel Orme there are indications that he was "full of the sweet things of love and gratitude." By con-trast, the conceptions of Melville's twentieth-century champions were straitened by the structural demands of two myths: Icarus (a myth linked to Narcissus through the concept of vanity and antisocial self-love) and the conversion narrative. These constructions echoed Melville's conservative contemporaries and were taken for granted by his mother grieving for her oldest son in 1846: "To time alone can I look forward to bind up by its soothing influences my wounded heart, to raise from their present state of depression, my lost spirits. . . . My poor Gansevoort this early in life to die he was deeply belov'd by us, yes bound up in our very hearts. . . . His gigantic efforts to overcome more than ordinary obstacles, his too long and continued exer-tion both bodily and mental—I have no doubt occasioned his early and melancholy death."[51]

Melville, it is said, had a nervous collapse in 1856; perhaps the looming loss of Arrowhead played a part.[52] His family, however, had responded anxiously to the gigantic efforts of the early 1850s as if he were another Gansevoort. In the following excerpts from letters spanning the late 1840s to the late 1850s, Melville and his philosopher friend Dr. Adler, a student of German idealism, whom Melville first met on the boat to Europe in 1849, describe the driven artist; whereas the family diagnoses illness, distress, and failure as the inevitable result of overwriting or "philosophy." A conversion is proposed:

[Melville] You may think, in your own mind that a man is unwise,— indiscreet, to write a book of that kind [*Mardi*], when he might have written one perhaps, calculated merely to please the general reader, not provoke attack, however masqued in an affectation of indifference or contempt. But some of us scribblers, my Dear Sir, always have a certain something unmanageable in us, that bids us do this or that, and be done it must—hit or miss.

[Dr. Adler] I regretted his departure very much; but all I could do to check and fix his restless mind for a while at least was of no avail. His loyalty to his friends at home and the instinctive impulse of his imagination to assimilate and perhaps to work up into some beautiful chimaeras (which according to our eloquent lecturer on Plato here, constitute the essence of poetry and fiction) the materials he had already gathered in his travels, would not allow him to prolong his stay.

[Melville's mother] I hope Herman will feel content to remain away for six months at least for he has sadly overworked his strength—& requires recreation, freedom from care, from writing, & the little petty cares, & annoyances, of the farm which are ever recurring & are so distasteful to him.

[Melville's sister Augusta] We all feel that it is of the utmost importance that something should be done to prevent the necessity of Herman's writing as he has been obliged to for several years past. Were he to return to the sedentary life which that of an author writing for his support necessitates, he would risk all the benefit to his health which he has gained by his tour, & possibly become a confirmed invalid. Of this his physicians have warned him.

[Melville's cousin Henry Gansevoort to his father, Peter] I am invited to dine at [the Shaws]. Herman Melville and his wife are expected to be present. He has numerous engagements to lecture in Boston and its vicinity. I understand his subject to be "Roman Statuary." He is able to do this finely if he will follow "crassa Minerva" but if he aims at metaphysical disquisitions he will surely fail. His forte is narration or description in other words a wild, bold word painting—when he essays philosophy he seeks to ascend by waxen wings from his proper sphere only to find his mind dazzled and his wings melted and his fall mortifying.

[Peter Gansevoort to Henry] Altho persuaded he will be a successful Lecturer, I entirely accord with your opinion, that he would be more at home in Narrative than in Criticism. It would be luxury to hear from him a Narrative of his recent tour on the borders of the Mediterranean and Constantinople. I am surprised he has not made his travels the subject of a Lecture to be hereafter woven into a Book, which would not be only instructive to others, but very profitable to himself. Such work would not make a requisition on his imagination. When you see him again, make the suggestion.

[Lemuel Shaw to Allan Melville] I am as deeply impressed as you can be of the necessity of Herman's getting away from Pitts. He is there solitary, without society, without exercise or occupation except that which is likely to be injurious to him in *over-throwing* his mind. I therefore have hoped that some situation may be found for him, where he has easy employment and moderate exercise of mind and body, and give him an opportunity to associate habitually with others.[53]

Ahab's (hoped-for) adjustment to the marketplace sans ethical contradictions may be the elusive unity that frustrated New Critic Melvilleans. Feidelson calls the conversion Ishmael's "compromise." "Give not thyself up, then, to fire, lest it invert thee, deaden thee; as for the time it did me. There is a wisdom that is woe; but there is a woe that is madness. And there is a Catskill eagle in some souls that can alike dive down into the blackest gorges, and soar out of them again and become invisible in the sunny spaces. And even if he for ever flies within the gorge, that gorge is in the mountains; so that even in his lowest swoop the mountain eagle is still higher than other birds upon the plain, even though they soar" (425). Narcissus drowns, Icarus crashes, but the deep-diving/soaring artist, properly circumscribed, illuminates philosophy, bringing insights that heal family conflicts exacerbated by excessive moralism. Princeton professor Lawrance Thompson warned his Christian colleagues in 1952 that Melville was a slippery character.[54] Melville's unmaskers were not diverted by the voluble reactionaries and conservatives who crowd and intermittently narrate his texts. Rather, he seemed to them a veiled radical, an unrepentant materialist, speaking most authentically through the dark and fissured creatures flitting through his fictions and overthrowing the moderate men. Some liberal scholars, on the other hand, perceived lifelong oscillations between democratic and aristocratic beliefs (as if democrats lacked moderation, civility, and honor?). Conservatives long accustomed to managing the lower orders make the more vigilant observers of threats to their legitimacy. Thompson and others are more likely correct when they sight a troublemaker hiding/flaunting his true feelings. Notwithstanding the red ravings, Melville does seem torn between democratic and aristocratic forms of government, but not because these positions were antinomies, comparably virtuous and reasonable.

"Bartleby the Scrivener: A Tale of Wall Street" (1853) is narrated by a lawyer, rational and humane by his own rights but at a loss to explain the suicide of a former clerk. Bartleby is at first docile and productive, but abruptly he prefers not to be a copyist, just as Melville suddenly switched from saleable, derivative travel narratives to socially critical allegories that outraged conservative readers. Bartleby refuses to eat or leave the lawyer's office; forcibly removed to the Tombs, the ex-scrivener further deteriorates: "Strangely huddled at the base of the wall, his knees drawn up, and lying on his side, his head touching the cold stones, I saw the wasted Bartleby." The lawyer had tried to reassure Bartleby and himself that his surroundings "to you . . . should not be so vile a place . . . it is not so sad a place as one might think. Look, there is the sky, and here is the grass." Just so, Herman's tardy letter to his stricken brother had tried to soothe and recompose Gansevoort's desolation. Bartleby responds with customary terseness, "I know where I am." Instructed by his own errors, Melville tried not to relinquish his vision to official authority or to the marketplace. And yet each contending party seems infiltrated with the skeptical gaze of its opponent (a point not lost on Leon Howard).

In 1876, the year *Clarel* was published, Melville was increasingly bereft. The imprisoned but remorseless Pierre/Bartleby returned in the melancholy *Clarel*, a divinity student losing faith and direction. Compare a draft fragment from "Bartleby" with several related excerpts that join the scrivener's scene with Clarel's:

> It was clean, well lighted & scrupulously whitewashed. The head-stone was standing up against the wall, & stretched out on a blanket at its base, his head touching the cold marble, & his feet upon the thresh hold lay the wasted form of Bartleby.[55] (GL-A)

> In chamber low and scored by time,
> Masonry old, late washed with lime—
> Much like a tomb new-cut in stone;
> Elbow on knee, and brow sustained
> All motionless on sidelong hand,
> A student sits and broods alone. (*Clarel*, 1.1, 1–6)

> Tarries the student on the wall.
> Dubieties of recent date—
> Scenes, words, event—he thinks of all.

As, when the autumn sweeps the down,
And gray skies tell of summer gone
The swallow hovers by the strait—
Impending on the passage long;
Upon a brink and poise he hung. (1.41, 66–73)

Like Clarel, Melville hovers over an abyss, attracted by the ever-returning radical puritan voice, Milton's Muse: upright, empiricist, and shaking his fist at illegitimate authority; and in his poem "The Enthusiast," finishing with "Though light forsake thee . . . [in] fealty to Light." But he is also intimidated by Bartleby's retreat "on the wall"—the insensibility he associates with punishment imposed by conservative bodies when radical puritans attempt to reconcile Christian theory with social practice. Milton's "vast abyss," filled with significance and possibility, has turned into a strait and narrowed option. Or has it? Clarel does not merge with the conservative Christian narrator, and Melville writes Daniel Orme as an apple tree at the end of his life. With most of his pious relatives dead, the radical puritan could perhaps discard his conservative defenses, at least momentarily.

But until Melville composes this fugitive sketch, it is fair to say that his political voices are either strangled or too impure to be typed: To be sure, the condition of the poor, abused, and abandoned are indignantly presented to the reader throughout, but transcendentalists, radical Protestant reformers, reform-or-ruin moderates, or Catholic reactionaries opposing the brutalities and Social Darwinism of laissez-faire do not necessarily confront one another with a consistent line and clean boundaries among positions. Not only are there passages that make no sense, it is sometimes difficult to know who is speaking and if any or all of his characters (especially the narrators) speak for the author. Like the debaters Isabel describes in her memory of the asylum (America dominated by unprincipled mass politics?), they may switch to the colors of their opponents, visibly or invisibly seizing the helm as perhaps in the narration of *Moby-Dick*. Having been at least briefly supplanted, the narrators will speak in varied emotional tones. Their voices are inflamed or modulated by hysteria, cold fury, defiance, geniality, clinical detachment, hilarity, desperation, and melancholy. As many have noted, however, the irony/earnestness of Melville's deconstructive modernist texts encourages a skeptical temper. Such distancing finally buttresses the relentlessly analytic intellectual (Ahab) whom Melville at times executes or erases in his prose and poetry; simultaneously the powerful emotions he expresses and evokes, then (apparently) retracts, can frazzle readers.

Metamorphoses

Do these qualities imply a confidence game intended to waylay and humiliate the middle-class reading public, or are they symptoms of anxiety in the writer?

Melville's omnipresent mutilated or divided characters suggest embodied mental states as they would have been reflected by a partly supportive, partly disapproving family. Surely the sublime prospect from foretops, roof tops, and mountain tops (the brain making forbidden connections to the heart) could be terrifying, because such breadth of social vision and species-consciousness alienated Melville from his conservative relatives. In the conflict between Enlightenment truth/justice and feudal order, his passion for the Rights of Man linked him to blasphemers and abolitionists—the Abner Kneelands and Wendell Phillipses of "black" Boston; not to the white patroons, merchants, bankers, and industrialists, the elite to which his Hudson Valley and Massachusetts families belonged or were connected. Although the radical reformers offered an alternative culture, Melville was not prepared to re-experience the horrors of poverty that terrified him as a common sailor; while Hawthorne, the longed-for kindred spirit with a subterranean taste for Dark Ladies, would not melt his reserve even when Melville trimmed his sails by toasting Hawthorne's genius/anti-intellectualism in the gift wrappings of *Moby-Dick*. Indeed, Hawthorne abruptly left the Berkshires after a series of passionate letters from his pushy young friend; though scholars have identified reasons for Hawthorne's departure unrelated to Melville's intimate declarations, he did write *Blithedale Romance*, a novel mocking the emotional reformer Hollingsworth and drowning the passion-flower Zenobia.

Another body had disappeared; Pip thought he was holding his hand. They would all go away when he exposed his wicked surmise that authority was irrational. Perhaps the Melville problem stemmed from his switch to the Romantic Wandering Jew, a persona inhabiting all the rebels of *Clarel*. Nathan, a judaized American Protestant, becomes a deist, then a pantheist, then a Zionist monomaniac: "prey to one devouring whim." Although taken as an allegory of American manifest destiny, the downfall of Nathan the autodidact was probably intended to warn his contemporaries off subversive books of the radical Enlightenment, like his own or Tom Paine's. What was Nathan's/Herman's unpardonable sin? Surely not pride in the abstract, but the heart too merry, like Stubb's in *Moby-Dick:* too giddily Hellenistic, therefore not self-sacrificing enough to avert the sudden disillusion, desolation, and dissolution of his family. Maria's depression shaded Herman, as Isabel shaded Pierre, as Fedallah shaded Ahab, as "the negro" shaded Benito Cereno. Dismay unhinges Nathan because Melville failed to rescue mother from her sorrows or the family from his "Jewish" rage.[56]

Billy Budd has spilled his soup and Claggart's "countenance changed"; in *Typee*, Tomoo indulges his senses in the South Seas, but the sudden disclosure of a partly eaten skeleton impels him to flee these too-friendly cannibals. The leisure and abundance promised by the Industrial Revolution are similarly a trap: The "cannibals" of democracy—first the sansculottes and then the new industrial working class will set the world on fire. Melville's ominous faces and fronts moving from light to dark suggest the sudden shift in his parents' expressions from smiling approval to unhappy disappointment. The child may be, or wants to be, innocent of the error that provoked the darkened, depressed visage and the application of father's cane. But more, the child wants to be free of the inadmissible aggression that simmers just beneath the surface in himself, the guilty parricide. The child's volcanic rage is repressed but returns as catastrophe burying the harshly punitive parent in "the havoc from heaven." And, because he is shaking so badly, the rage seems to destroy the child's sanity: His body is unstable. Better to take one's flying, fleeing body up into the mind (Father Mapple breathing defiance from his lofty perch, solo). But here too, there is a switch and a preventive self-decapitation. The late adolescent pauses to separate from hitherto idealized parents; he scans an alarmingly mobile mental landscape as familiar, comforting images dissolve while new configurations are not yet sharply focused; the body feels uprooted, shocked. The electral light, source of disillusion and matricide, must be snuffed out and fast; the blood-filled Head blanched; its incendiary impulses are siphoned off to be replaced by pallid composure: Melville's smiting, smitten walls.

In a famous letter to Hawthorne, Melville suddenly reverses himself after a forthright statement of ideological disagreement:

> By the way, in the last *Dollar Magazine* I read "The Unpardonable Sin." He was a sad fellow, that Ethan Brand. I have no doubt you are by this time responsible for many a shake and tremour of the whole tribe of "general readers." It is a frightful poetical creed that the cultivation of the brain eats out the heart. But it's my *prose* opinion that in most cases, in those men who have fine brains and work them well, the heart extends down to hams. And though you smoke them with the fire of tribulation, yet, like veritable hams, the head only gives the richer and the better flavour. [The switch:] I stand for the heart. To the dogs with the head! I had rather be a fool with a heart, than Jupiter Olympus with his head. The reason the mass of men fear God, and *at bottom dislike* Him is because they rather distrust His heart, and fancy Him all brain like a watch. (You perceive I employ a capital initial in the pronoun referring to the Deity; don't you think there is a slight dash of flunkeyism in that usage?)[57]

Perhaps Mother's tribulation (including the loss of Gansevoort) bound Melville to the family and to its distrust of both the socially critical intellect and populist enthusiasm. Modern families dispensing mixed messages provide the disillusion that calls its myth of harmony and nurturance into question, but conservative religious culture provides the images and explanations that make Melville's experience frighteningly coherent and convince his moderate characters that "evil is the chronic malady of the universe" (*Mardi*); ameliorative structural reform is hopeless while charity never faileth; charity endureth all things. Promises of mutuality, cooperation, and equality are mere ruses to facilitate the transfer from one set of masters to another: The good-hearted king is our best bet. In Western culture, both the arch-destroyer of the good parent and the confidence man purveying fake utopias is the (switching) Jew. Thus Christ's betrayers and the modern critical intelligence are conflated and caricatured in *Clarel* in maggoty Margoth, the image of Melville's parricidal, world-shattering fury. Margoth's is the scorn he represses in his letter to Hawthorne as he switches from prosy opposition to passionate identification with Hawthorne's "poetic creed" of anti-intellectualism. The prose-writing "Head" is now the source of alienation, perhaps even the critical outbursts that relatives have reported (and that Melville is probably describing in his writing).

It bothered the corporatist Henry Murray that he could not always separate the voices in *Moby-Dick:* ". . . not clear, changes abruptly—Author & Ishmael are indistinguishable often." Elsewhere in his notes he claimed that "every book was autobiographical. He played many roles, usually the most demonic—Jackson on the Highlander, Ahab, Pierre, the misanthrope, etc."[58]Murray saw these qualities as flaws, probably markers of his own ambivalence and role playing. A battle between a radical Enlightenment line (materialist, universalist,[59] intellectually critical) and a conservative Enlightenment line (scientific, but covertly traditionalist, mystical, *völkisch*, obscurantist) has shaped responses to Melville's writing, including his own, from the mid-nineteenth century to the present. The same debates surrounded the reception to Milton's modernism two centuries earlier. Both artists were engaged in an internal dialogue that mirrored Titanic struggles for free speech and other civil liberties that continue to convulse Europe and America. These introductory chapters have attempted to clarify Melville's connection to Captain Ahab, in his own words, an indomitable quester after truth and justice, but for the narrator Ishmael, a tyrant to whom he often succumbs. To prepare the reader's immersion in the minds of twentieth-century Ishmaels, further connections are drawn among modernism, Milton's characters Satan and Mammon, Old Testament Hebrews, the Byronic hero, Thomas Carlyle's portrait of the Nuremberg Man, Charles Kingsley's agitator Crossthwaite, American Chosen People, and Melville's Titans. The sometimes opposed, sometimes interpenetrating, characters Ahab and Ishmael are joined to the unresolved problem of American identity: By describing irreconcilable antagonisms within institutions held to be naturally or potentially harmonious and benevolent, Ahab rang the tocsin that summoned Ishmael's scientistic response.

5

The Modern Artist as Red Specter

"An irruption of heretic thought hard to suppress"

While writing *Moby-Dick*, Melville confided to Hawthorne that "all my books are botches," in this instance blaming the market. Was the author in control of Ahab's slides from Miltonic modern artist to Gansevoort's war hawk? The characters Ahab, Isabel, and Margoth et al. are variants of the Romantic Wandering Jew: representations of historical memory, the critical intellect, and radical political will that Melville would by turns hug or annihilate. The erasure of dissent, however, would not remain invisible; the red specter inevitably returned either to energize/haunt his efforts at self-understanding, or to taunt his capitulations to illegitimate authority for the sake of his overburdened family: In his state of perplexity, "none felt how the leveller pines." Aided by Melville's newly uncovered annotations to *Paradise Lost*, I have argued that the virtually canonical Left reading of Ahab as an anticipation of Hitler slanders Ahab, and ultimately Melville; rather, Ahab is a creature of the radical Enlightenment, partly masked by the author[1] and misread by the narrator, a decayed patrician. In previous pages excerpts from *Moby-Dick* contrasted Ahab's self-understanding with Ishmael's anxious portraiture. Ahab's project both to demystify duplicitous authority and unlock the secrets of nature (even his own) is frequently described with metaphors suggesting the inexorable drive of the steam engine: Railroading Ahab's lunges toward the whole truth, "hit or miss," are expressed in images of rifling, digging, stabbing, piercing, and striking through masks. However, it does not follow that the whale hunt must be a microcosm of industrial society desanctifying and degrading nature, or that Ahab's curiosity is necessarily sadistic, an expression of pride, self-gratification, and separation from the human community, as William Blake or other corporatists would have seen it.[2] Of course, Melville's churning tableaux roll in the perilous conditions of labor; but the demonic character that bathes the narrative and Ahab with a blinding charisma is the invention of the Carlylean Ishmael, for whom the insatiable curiosity of the lower orders evokes the vindictiveness of the French Revolution's reign of terror and fantasies of strangulation. Parallel passages from *Pierre* have supported my contention that Ahab, like Pierre, is that "something unmanageable" in his creator.[3] This chapter continues the examination of Hebraic radical puritanism as imagined and transmitted by antidemocrats and suggests that Melville, like his modernist predecessor Milton, either concealed his sympathies with the materialists or vacillated in his identification with their supposedly corrosive politics. The late-seventeenth-century poet Dryden and the eighteenth-century historian and philosopher David Hume elaborated Tory portraits of the radical puritans as destructive primitives likened to ancient Hebrews: It is the admixture of (Jewish) fanatical religion and politics that creates an irrational political culture. Nineteenth-century conservatives cured Left romantics such as the Chartists, Melville, and themselves; like Thomas Carlyle and Melville's relatives they adopted the Christian conversion narrative, moving adolescent (Hebraic) Byron out and upward to socially responsible Goethe. Charles Kingsley's *Alton Locke, Tailor and Poet* (1850, a founding text of Christian Socialism) is the literary example that charts this transformation. Charles Francis Adams's account of the Antinomian controversy (1636–38) types the New England spirit as essentially importunate and Hebraic. An English Carlylean's 1924 essay on Byron completes the gallery of trapped Anglo-American conservatives, force fed and held to knowledge, beating down their own deliciously unruly impulses. Democratizing social movements summoned Hawthorne's red specters. Ahab's immediate precursor was Hawthorne's "Virtuoso"—the heartless Wandering Jew as archivist, historical memory, and genius. Ahab and his cannibal crew may be seen as representations of modern art-making, revolutionary puritanism, and mass politics (cubistically developed): romantically decadent activities for Tories in the seventeenth and eighteenth centuries, for Hawthorne in the 1840s, and for neoclassicizing conservatives after the Bolshevik triumph in 1917. Organic conservatives are still operating upon (Hebraic) hot heads and cold hearts; the distinguished professors Henry Farnham May and Richard Brodhead allude to the persistent Hebraic strain in American culture. I begin with some snapshots of the disappearing center, crumpled by bad Jews and other rebel angels.

[Ishmael on Ahab:] I was struck with the singular posture he maintained. Upon each side of the Pequod's quarter deck, and pretty close to the mizen shrouds, there was an auger hole, bored about half an inch or so, into the plank. His bone leg steadied in that hole; one arm elevated, and holding by a shroud; Captain Ahab stood erect, looking straight out beyond the ship's ever-pitching prow. There was an infinity of firmest fortitude, a determinate, unsurrenderable wilfulness, in the fixed and fearless, forward dedication of that glance. Not a word he spoke; nor did his officers say aught to him; though by all their minutest gestures and expressions, they plainly showed the uneasy, if not painful, consciousness of being under a troubled master-eye. And not only that, but moody stricken Ahab stood before them with a crucifixion in his face; in all the nameless regal overbearing dignity of some mighty woe. (124)

[Jay Leyda's high school notes on "The Bible"] Made English Puritanism[.] 1.a. Puritan tradition fostered in the English and American people most of the best and most distinctive qualities. b. Inspired the poetry of Milton and the prose allegory of Bunyan. c. Gave Cromwell and the Pilgrim Fathers that which made them honourable, stead-fast, and self-reliant. d. Has had direct influence on the English language and thought for 1. Has influenced the great Victorian writers[.] 2. Men so diverse as Emerson and Whitman came under its spell. 3. Abraham Lincoln a genius in statecraft and speech was essentially a man of one Book—the Bible. 4. For two centuries it has been the source of Anglo-Saxon idealism. 5. It has shaped the English language. 6. It has been the supreme spiritually creative force in the civilization of the British Empire and the American Commonwealth. . . . William Tyndale's translations . . . sought to serve the common people.[4]

[John Crowe Ransom to Allen Tate, Independence Day, 1929] Satan is the Hebrew Prometheus and so conceived is Milton's P.L.—he is Lucifer the Spirit of the Renaissance, the Zeitgeist of Milton's own age of science, very boldly displayed and only rejected after a proper hesitation. But then Jesus is Lucifer again. . . .[5]

For Thomas Hobbes (1651), curiosity was not an aid to reason, but an indomitable passion of the mind that could overpower and displace the less troublesome pleasures of food and sex. "Desire to know why, and how, is CURIOSITY; such as is in no living creature but Man; so that Man is distinguished, not onely by his reason; but also by this singular Passion from other Animals; in whom the appetite of food, and other pleasures of Sense, by praedominance, take away the care of knowing causes; which is a Lust of the mind, that by a perseverance of delight in the continuall and indefatigable generation of Knowledge, exceedeth the short vehemence of any carnall Pleasure."[6] In 1659 *"Committees* of the *Good Old Cause"* were virtuous vampires: "This Dragon it was and a monstrous Beast, / With fourty or fifty heads at least, / And still as this Dragon drank down Blood / Those heads would wag and cry *"good*-good-good!"[7] Not surprising, the same tumescent heads exasperated Dryden in *Absolom* and *Achitophel:*

The Jews, a Headstrong, Moody, Murm'ring race,
As ever tri'd th'extent and stretch of grace;
God's pampered People, whom, debauch'd with ease,
No King could govern, nor no God could please;
(Gods they had tri'd of every shape and size,
That God-smiths could produce, or Priests devise:)
These Adam-wits, too fortunately free,
Began to dream they wanted liberty;
And when no rule, no precedence, was found
Of men, by Laws less circumscrib'd and bound,
They led their wild desires to Woods and Caves,
And thought that all but Savages were Slaves.[8]

Similarly, the moderately moral philosopher Thomas Morgan advised his country-men to *cherchez la femme fatale:*

This wretched, insufferable Scheme of Superstition and false Religion, as it made Multitudes of Bigots and Enthusiasts at first, so it has brought forth the Atheists of this Age. For Atheism is the natural Production of Super-stition and Enthusiasm, as one Extreme terminates in and begets another. An Atheist is only an Enthusiast between sleeping and waking, in which Sort of Delirium he feels enamour'd on Reason as his Mistress and Idol, while he is raving against God and Providence. The Enthusiast is commonly grave and severe, but the Atheist gay and ludicrous; one groans and sighs, and the other laughs and sneers at Religion and Virtue. The Enthusiast in his sullen, dumb fits is always premeditating Mischief, and waiting for an Opportunity to rush upon you unawares, or stab you in the Dark; but the Atheist gives fair Warn-ing, and cries out I am unclean, unclean! Stand off or I shall destroy you. In short, there are only two species of Distinction: the Enthusiast is deeply and sullenly out of his Wits, and the Atheist is merrily and rantingly mad, and both are owing to the same general Cause, and may be reckoned the two op-posite and distinct sorts of religious lunacy. And one of these Extremes Men must always necessarily run into, when they bewilder themselves in the Clouds and Darkness of their own Imaginations, and seek for Religion any-where, without the Boundaries of moral Truth and Righteousness.[9]

Against such baleful glances, the eighteenth-century dissenting minister Moses Lowman, a Newtonian, offered a less hysterical analysis; in his rendition, the ratio-nal political and economic arrangements of ancient Hebrews prevented the factions, runaway ambition, deception, and corruption feared by organic conservatives:

The very foundation of the Hebrew Constitution was an equal Division of the Land, the Continuance of which was secured by a fundamental Law, which made that Division perpetual, as no Estate could be alienated or pass from One Tribe or Family to another. The laws had further provided that no Interest could be made of Money, so that had a Man never so much Money, he could make no profit of it, either by Purchase or Interest. . . . The Constitution had expressly made a perpetual Mortmain, so that they could not have any increase of Property in Land, by any Title whatsoever. . . . As the Constitution put a bar to great Riches, and made such Provision for the natural Conveniences of Life, that very few could be in great Want or Poverty; this served to diminish greatly the temptations of Luxury, Pride, and Envy, nor were there any so necessitous as to seek Relief for their private Wants and Misery, in the publick Confusion and Disorders of their Country. . . . The particular Powers of each Part of this Government were so balanced by the Powers of other Parts, that without the concurrence of all it was hardly practicable for any one Part to draw to themselves any share of Property, Wealth, or Power, from the other Parts; and it was as hard and impracticable to obtain their Concurrence, to the ruin of their own Property and Liberty.[10]

Lowman and Dryden have defined the Jewish "problem:" Each side claims centrist balance against its opponent; their disagreement marks the paradigmatic intellectual confrontation of modernity. Lowman's proto-Jacobinical[11] rendition appeals to readers with political science on behalf of "Laws, Rights, and Liberties"; the moral reformer or muckraker answers with symbol manipulation in favor of "rational" aristocratic paternalism designed to rescue society from Hebrew primitivism (today an overdose of American democracy fusing pagan science and Hebrew moral passion)—a nurture more gentle in theory than practice.[12]

There is no more illuminating guide to the logic of twentieth-century corporatists explaining the causes of war and mass death than their predecessor David Hume. His modern reputation as a skeptic who derails the necessary connection between cause and effect is not sustained by his social psychological analysis of prudent statecraft. In his multivolume *History of England,* Dryden's images recur in Hume's account of Calvinist or Jew-induced irrationalism, a seductive and novel feature of the Reformation that had led to civil war, an avoidable conflict that the moderate James I attempted to avert: "It is an observation suggested by all history, and by none more than by that of James [I] and his successor, that *the religious spirit, when it mingles with faction, contains in it something supernatural and unaccountable; and that, in its operations upon society, effects correspond less to their known causes than is found in any other circumstance of government.* A reflection which may, at once, afford a source of blame against such sovereigns as lightly innovate in so dangerous an article." James I, assuming the doctor role, had tried gradually to "introduce episcopal authority" to overheated, maddened Scotland, but to no avail:

A gloomy and sullen disposition established itself among the people; a spirit, obstinate and dangerous; independent and disorderly; animated equally with a contempt of authority, and a hatred to every other mode of religion, particularly to the Catholic. *In order to mellow these humours, James endeavoured to infuse a small tincture of ceremony into the national worship, and to introduce such rights as might, in some degree, occupy the mind, and please the senses, without departing too far from that simplicity, by which the reformation was distinguished.* The finer arts, too, though still rude in these northern kingdoms, were employed to adorn the churches; and the king's chapel, in which an organ was erected, and some pictures and statues displayed, was proposed as a model to the rest of the nation. But music was grating to the prejudiced ear of the Scottish clergy; sculpture and painting appeared instruments of idolatry; the surplice was a rag of popery; and every motion or gesture, prescribed by the liturgy, was a step towards that spiritual Babylon, so much the object of their horror and aversion. Everything was deemed impious, but their own mystical comments on the Scriptures, which they idolized, and whose eastern prophetic style they employed in every common occurrence.[13]

Hume specified the alien source of the "mystical . . . eastern prophetic style" resistant to kingly intervention:

The Old Testament, preferably to the New, was the favourite of all the sectaries. The eastern poetical style of that composition made it more easily susceptible of a turn which was agreeable to them. . . . [George Fox] frequently wandered into the woods, and passed whole days in hollow trees, without company, or any other amusement than his Bible. Having reached that pitch of perfection as to need no other book, he soon advanced to another state of spiritual progress, and began to pay less regard even to that divine composition itself. His own breast, he imagined, was full of the same inspiration which had guided the prophets and apostles themselves; and by this inward light must every spiritual obscurity be cleared, by this living spirit must the dead letter be animated.[14]

Following the scientifically irrationalist Hume, moderate, "objectivist" Melvilleans, no less than Melville's narrators, would read Ahab as Cromwellian hypocrite and Pierre as self-deceived Leveller. Outward protestant austerity only sped the imagination inward, into blasphemous self-worship and Hebraism—"the eastern poetical style" of the Old Testament. As Hume had explained (transferring absolutism from pragmatic monarchs to radical puritans demanding human rights and the liberty to criticize established authority), "In tracing the coherence among the systems of modern theology, we may observe, that the doctrine of absolute decrees has ever been associated with the enthusiastic spirit; as that doctrine affords the highest subject of joy, triumph, and security, to the supposed elect, and exalts them by infinite degrees above the rest of mankind."[15]

Tory readings of Milton's modernism are central to our decoding of the Melville problem. Melville's heavily annotated volumes of Milton's poetry contained a warning to the unwary. Quoting Mr. Hayley (who fretted lest "genius and virtue" be unmoderated by charity), the Reverend Henry John Todd warned that Miltonic sensitivity would lead to self-confidence; such arrogant dogmatism was the impetus to civil war:[16] "There can hardly be any contemplation more painful, than to dwell on the virulent excesses of eminent and good men. . . . The strength and acuteness of sensation, which partly constitute genius, have a great tendency to produce virulence, if the mind is not perpetually on its guard against that subtle, insinuating, and corrosive passion, hatred against all whose opinions are opposite to our own." Similarly, the Reverend John Mitford's sketch of Milton cautioned smitten prospectors; even greybeards could not be trusted to resist sublimity:

"The Pride of Reason (it has been very judiciously observed), though disclaimed by Milton with remarkable and probably with sincere earnestness, formed a principle ingredient in his character, and would have presented, under any circumstances, a formidable obstacle to the reception of true faith." Caring nothing for institutions that were venerable, or for opinions that were sacred, he not only disdains to wear the opprobrious shackles of authority, but even the decent vestments of custom. *Safe in his own inflexible integrity, in the great purity of his heart, and singleness of purpose, what his conscience dictates, his courage proclaims. Impetuous, fearless, and uncompromising, he pushes on his inquiries, till they end in a defence of the death of the monarch, and the substitution of a visionary republic in politics; in a denial of the eternal existence of the Son, in theology; and in the defense of a plurality of wives, in morals.* Yet it must be remarked that he lived in an age when men were busy pulling down and building up; a fermentation was spreading over the surface, and dissolving the materials of society. Old faith was gone; old institutions were crumbling away. Long splendid vistas of ideal perfection opened before men's eyes, dazzling their senses, and confounding their judgments. Grey-headed men, men grown old in the business of life, and in the pursuit of practical wisdom, yielded to the syren influence. It pervaded the senate, the city, and the camp. What wonder then, if the Poet, the visionary by his profession, the dreaming theorist, the man dwelling in ideal worlds and abstract notions, should be led astray.[17]

"Long splendid vistas of ideal perfection" are associated with "singleness of purpose," with monomania: the Jewish/radical Protestant passion for social justice through adherence to universal precepts; republicanism with one set of rules for rich and poor; earthly law to be tested by the higher law of dignity and equality before God (or Nature, or, if the Void, a consciously chosen standard). The placement of Father Mapple's sermon near the beginning of the text suggests that the voyage of the *Pequod* is launched to fulfill the mission of revolutionary puritanism. However, Ahab's fall or failure is ambiguous. Knotty problems are addressed as a historian reflects upon the conflict between radical and conservative Enlightenment in the course of *Moby-Dick*.

First, Marxists have argued that universal social justice, peace, and creativity for all cannot be attained without the agency of a ripened industrial working class (leading any majority coalition resolved to abolish exploitation). Is Ahab's fate, then, an outcome of the heart- and hearth-driven radical Enlightenment necessarily turned sour because of Ahab's narcissism, the weakness in human nature that mocks the historic task assigned by nineteenth-century socialists; or is the wreck simply a reflection of limited political possibilities at the time Melville wrote the book (1850–51)? Second, does the text disclose a developing antithesis between Mapple/Ahab and the patient, mystical Ishmael (Job) who survives by detaching himself from Ahab's sharp individuality[18] to write the epilogue? Or do Ahab and Ishmael display sometimes separate and antagonistic, sometimes interpenetrating personae? And if the latter, are these vacillations a function of Melville's locus in the incomplete transition from feudalism to market economies? Is the regenerated Ishmael-no-longer-Ahab, then, rejecting Mapple's Hebraic God sending Jonah/humanity on missions that today are sure to fail? "Nor was there wanting still another precautionary motive more related to Ahab personally. Having impulsively, it is probable, and perhaps somewhat prematurely revealed the prime but private purpose of the Pequod's voyage, Ahab was now entirely conscious that, in so doing, he had indirectly laid himself open to the unanswerable charge of usurpation" (213).[19] Is not the very act of creation by the self-reliant modern artist one such doomed enterprise—blasphemous and a usurpation, a Frankensteinian social catastrophe?

The Melville problem is inseparable from duelling epistemologies, face to face since the days when science bloomed in democratic Greece, to be sure, but a fight to the finish after the scientific revolution of the seventeenth century. In the preceding chapter Ahab's own words were compared with the narrator Ishmael's characterization of his motives and personality. It was suggested that Ahab, the materialist, transmits sane radical Enlightenment: His conscience is in his keel—the source of balance that humanizes science by restraining its potential brutality; whereas Ishmael, the idealist and irrationalist, represents the scared, demented, pseudo-science of conservative Enlightenment, intended to dull newly forged critical tools, claiming that the Head people lack Heart, that they have conspired to take over the world. Here is David Hume's obsessive verdict on the reawakened stealthy Zeitgeist, the undomesticated spirit of civil liberty during the reign of James I (that would resurface in the "fighting Quaker" Ahab):

So extensive was royal authority, and so firmly established in all its parts, that it is probable the patriots of that age would have despaired of ever resisting it, had they not been stimulated by religious motives, which inspire a courage unsurmountable by any human obstacle. . . . The spirit . . . of enthusiasm; bold, daring, and uncontrolled; strongly disposed their minds to adopt republican tenets; and inclined them to arrogate, in their actions and conduct, the same liberty which they assumed in their rapturous flights and ecstasies. . . . [T]he spirit of civil liberty gradually revived from its lethargy, and by means of its religious associate, from which it reaped more advantage than honour, *it secretly enlarged its dominion over the greater part of the kingdom.*[20]

In an early chapter of *Moby-Dick,* "The Prophet," Ishmael demanded that Elijah not "bamboozle us." Elijah responds that Ishmael is "just the man for [Ahab]—the likes of ye" (93). So the text begins with Ahab and Ishmael in likely agreement; but Ishmael, confronted by Ahab's probes, reacts with warnings of disaster to all Titans (like himself) who would demystify traditional authority, collapsing deference in the masses. Melville is wrestling with the concept of solidarity with history making, novel writing, suffering humanity: He must choose between competing notions of popular sovereignty and the public interest. Ahab stands up for the lonely internationalism of Mapple's Jonah or Goethe's Faust. The German romantics were already dithering over these issues during the latter part of the eighteenth century, not long after Hume had completed his tirade against austere puritans whose runaway self-love he also conflated with Restoration licentiousness, coarsening women who would no longer moderate the behavior of men. The result, Hume thought, was deism and the revived spirit of faction; politeness was still on the defensive.[21] Against this ghastly outcome, Hume, allegedly distancing himself from Tory and Whig alike, had proposed the middle way, the path taken by Melville's narrators and by twentieth-century corporatists: A limited monarchy would hold kings accountable to popular assemblies; the good king protected the people from ambitious, hypocritical popular agitators and the suspicious, vengeful mobs they had aroused against established authority. All "mechanical philosophers"—including puffed-up artists and scientists—throwing off the domination of religious institutions and prying into the affairs of their betters, were demagogues and the source of social disintegration.

Similarly, "A French critic" quoted in the translator's preface to Jean Paul Richter's *Titan* demanded to know:

> How is it to end, this civilization which exaggerates alike industrial and intellectual power at the expense of the life of the soul,—wholly factitious, theatrical—intoxicating, consuming itself with pleasure, seeking everywhere new enjoyments,—exploring all the secrets of nature, without being able to penetrate the first causes, the secrets of God,—what will be the fate of these generations supersaturated with romances, dramas, journals, with science, ambition, with vehement aspirations after the unknown and impossible? . . . Will it not be the giant that scales heaven—And that falls crushed to death? TITAN![22]

Thomas Carlyle, the chief interpreter and disseminator of German romanticism in England and an attractive figure to Melville, had similarly diagnosed Richter's failed heroes:

> They shoot into rugged exaggeration in his hands, their sensibility becomes too copious and tearful, their magnanimity too fierce, abrupt, and thoroughgoing. In some few instances they verge towards absolute failure: compared with their less ambitious brethren, they are almost of a vulgar cast; with all their brilliancy and vigour, too like that positive, determinate, choleric, volcanic class of personages whom we meet with so frequently in novels; they call themselves Men, and do their utmost to prove the assertion, but they cannot make us believe it; for after all their vapouring and storming we see well enough that they are but Engines, with no more life than the Freethinkers' model in *Martinus Scriblerus*, the Nuremberg Man, who operated by a combination of pipes and levers, and though he could breathe and digest perfectly, and even reason as well as most country parsons, was made of wood and leather.[23]

Did Melville agree with Carlyle's antiromantic fulminations, or did he clownishly whiten up as Ishmael only to evade conservative relatives and other critics who wanted to be turned on, as Henry Gansevoort put it, by "wild, bold word painting," but not made mechanical, not historicized, not brought down?

One contemporary text could have provided the model for Ishmael's rescue. The Old Testament Jewish prophet as the agitator was developed by the English cleric and Christian Socialist Charles Kingsley in his cautionary tale *Alton Locke*, published anonymously while Melville was composing *Moby-Dick*.[24] Kingsley's book purports to be the confession of a genuine repentant radical who has died of consumption. Inspired by "those old Jewish heroes" Moses, David, and Jehu, and rejecting (conservative) Calvinism, the tailor Alton Locke was fired by the aspirations of other "working men whose craving is only for some idea which shall give equal hopes, claims, and deliverances, to all mankind alike!" (12–13). For Ishmael, the radical Enlightenment was a snare and a delusion: Those who strive for truth, justice, and equality in a world purged of wickedness, but who are armed, like Ahab (or the dark angel depicted in Dürer's *Melencolia I* or Rosa's *Democritus in Meditation*) solely with the tools of earthly (not Right) Reason, will end their efforts in despair, wrecking the rest of humanity along with themselves. But we must not push the comparison too far. *Alton Locke* leaves us with ex-radicals tearfully but gladly chastened and regenerated; *Moby-Dick* leaves a regenerated orphan, dying into life, as Howard Vincent says, but, as Vincent does not say, clinging to Queequeg's coffin (primitivism), a coffin lacking a keel. The coffin had breached like a whale; Ishmael was rescued by a whale/coffin without a conscience, without balance.

Alton Locke recalls his collapse into the monomania of Chartism, prepared by harsh poverty and mother's levelling religious zeal:

> Those old Jewish heroes did fill my heart and soul. I learnt from them lessons which I never want to unlearn. . . . They were patriots, deliverers from that tyranny and injustice from which the child's heart,—"child of the devil" though you may call him,—instinctively, and, as I believe, by a divine inspiration, revolts. Moses leading his people out of Egypt; Gideon, Barak, and Samson, slaying their oppressors; David, hiding in the mountains from the tyrant, with his little band of those who had fled from the oppressions of an aristocracy of Nabals; Jehu, executing God's vengeance on the kings—these were my heroes, my models; they mixed themselves up with the dim legends about the Reformation martyrs, Cromwell and Hampden, Sidney and Monmouth, which I had heard at my mother's knee. Not that the perennial oppression of the masses, in all ages and countries, had yet risen on me as an awful, torturing, fixed idea. I fancied, poor fool, that tyranny was the exception, and not the rule. But it was the mere sense of abstract pity and justice which was delighted in me. I thought that these were old fairy tales, such as never need to be realized again. I learnt otherwise in later years. (12–13)

No Melville scholar has proposed that *Alton Locke* might have been a source for *Moby-Dick* (or if not a source, then a work carrying identical baggage). However, the *Illustrated London News* recognized the political referent of *The Whale* (the title of the English edition of *Moby-Dick*): "The personages are so conceived as to be types of the principal different parties and classes into which the late Aggression agitation split up the community."[25] Kingsley's character Crossthwaite, a Chartist who fascinates Alton (as Ahab fascinates Ishmael, as Isabel fascinates Pierre), resembles Narcissus/Ahab and his reflection or double, the Whale: "Wild grey eyes gleamed out from under huge knitted brows, and a perpendicular wall of brain, too large for his puny body."[26] Here is Crossthwaite's defiant speech as proletarian Christ to his fellow tailors, meeting to discuss their response to the newly (Jewishly) imposed system of piecework. Perhaps Crossthwaite is a source (or parallel) for Ahab with the "crucifixion in his face":

> "Every one fancies the laws which fill his pockets to be God's laws. But I say this. If neither government nor members of Parliament can help us, we must help ourselves. Help yourselves and Heaven will help you. Combination among ourselves is the only chance. One thing we can do—sit still."
>
> "And starve!" said some one.
>
> "Yes, and starve! Better starve than sin. I say, it is a sin to give into this system. It is a sin to add our weight to the crowd of artisans who are now choking and strangling each other to death, as the prisoners did in the black hole of Calcutta. Let those who will, turn beasts of prey, and feed upon their fellows; *but let us at least keep ourselves pure.* It may be the law of political civilisation, the law of nature, that the rich should eat up the poor, and the poor eat up each other. Then I here rise and curse that law, that civilisation, that nature. *Either I will destroy them, or they shall destroy me.* As a slave, as an increased burden on my fellow-sufferers, I will not live. So help me God! I will take no work home to my house; and I call upon every one here to combine, and to sign a protest to that effect."
>
> "What's the use of that, my good Mr. Crossthwaite?" interrupted someone querulously. "Don't you know what come of the strike a few years ago, when this piecework first came in? The masters made fine promises, and never kept 'em; and the men who stood out had their places filled up with poor devils who were glad enough to take the work at any price—just as ours will be. There's no use kicking against the pricks. All the rest have come to it, and so must we. We must live somehow, and half a loaf is better than no bread; and even that half-loaf will go into other men's mouths, if we don't snap at it at once. Besides, we can't force others to strike. We may strike and starve ourselves, but what's the use of a dozen striking out of twenty thousand!"
>
> "Will you sign the protest, gentlemen,[27] or not?" asked Crossthwaite in a determined voice.
>
> Some half-dozen said they would, if the others would.

"And the others won't. Well, after all, one man must take the responsibility, and I am that man. I will sign the protest by myself. I will sweep a crossing—I will turn cress-gatherer, rag-picker; I will starve piecemeal, and see my wife starve with me; but do the wrong thing I will not! The cause wants martyrs. If I must be one, I must."[28] (104–5)

Later, Crossthwaite becomes a professional labor organizer, an agitator resembling Ahab:

He scribbled, agitated; ran from London to Manchester, and Manchester to Bradford, spouting, lecturing—sowing the east wind, I am afraid, and little more. Whose fault was it? What could such a man do, with that fervid tongue, and heart, and brain of his, in such a station as his, such a time as this? Society had helped to make him an agitator. Society has had, more or less, to take the consequences of her own handiwork. For Crossthwaite did not speak without hearers. He could make the fierce, shrewd artisan nature flash out into fire—not always celestial, nor always, either, infernal. [Compare with Isabel's face, "compounded so of hell and heaven."] So he agitated and lived—how, I know not. (187)

Compare Kingsley's fantasy with Ishmael's in "The First Lowering." "But what it was that inscrutable Ahab said to that tiger-yellow crew of his—these were words best omitted here; for you live under the blessed light of the evangelical land. Only the infidel sharks in the audacious seas may give ear to such words, when, with tornado brow, and eyes of red murder, and foam-glued lips, Ahab leaped after his prey" (223).

Alton Locke contrasts the Chartist's integrity with his own as a hack writer, in terms achingly reminiscent of Melville's complaint to Hawthorne (June 1?, 1851), "Dollars damn me. . . . What I feel most moved to write, that is banned,—it will not pay."

It was miserable work, there is no denying it—only not worse than tailoring.—To try and serve God and Mammon too; to make miserable compromises daily, between the two great incompatibilities, what was true, and what would pay; to speak my mind, in fear and trembling, by hints and halves, and quarters; to be daily hauling poor Truth just up to the top of her well, and then, frightened at my own success, let plump down again to the bottom; to sit there, trying to teach others, while my mind was in a whirl of doubt; to feed others' intellects, while my own was hungering; to grind on in the Philistine's mill, or occasionally make sport for them, like some weary-hearted clown grinning in a pantomime . . . as blind as Samson, but not, alas as strong. (188–89)

Kingsley must drop the truth he has laboriously dredged up, lest he become an agitator, a monomaniac diagnosed as the prisoner of a fixed idea, as the carrier of a fatal disease (the doomed revolution). And yet, with Ishmael, Kingsley fears the "tornado brow" of his own raging disappointment, flying into "a whirl of doubt" when he chooses Mammon over God. Resubmerging poor Truth has turned him into an exhausted Pierrot. Like the repentant Wandering Jew, the compromised intellectual is cursed to pace and tarry sleeplessly until the Second Coming, to preach that slavery is freedom, ignorance is bliss, that universalist notions such as political freedom, equality before the law, and the amelioration of suffering are ploys dreamed up by demagogues to manufacture "difference" within the *Volk*.[29] The richer Truth that roots the torn-up Kingsley and Melville is the appetizing menu of the monarchist, railing against republics breeding furious, leveling, and regicidal mobs.[30]

What about these retreats into pragmatism? The case has been made above for a masqued Melville arguing for vast structural transformations while hiding behind the narrator, but even if this is wrong, the Tory relapses could be products of depression leading to the temporary ascendancy of a conservative program of individual moral reform, resignation to permanent earthly bewilderment and the retraction of Isabel's lawless wandering. Alton Locke understood his error but too late to avert an untimely death from consumption.[31] "Fool that I was! It was within, rather than without, that I needed [structural] reform" (110). Likewise, the other fanatical genius, Crossthwaite, is brought out of the Charter and into Christ by "an upper-class Christian Socialist, Eleanor, her figure dilating, and her eyes flashing, like an inspired prophetess":

"Denounce the effete idol of property qualification, not because it happens to strengthen class interests against you, but because as your mystic dream reminded you, and therefore, as you knew long ago, there is no real rank, no real power, but worth; and worth consists not in property, but in the grace of God. Claim, if you will, annual parliaments, as a means of enforcing the responsibility of Christian rulers to the Christian community, of which they are to be, not the lords, but the ministers—the servants of all. But claim these, and all else for which you long, not from man, but from God, the King of men. And therefore, before you attempt to obtain them, make yourselves worthy of them—perhaps by that process you will find some of them have become less needful. At all events, do not ask, do not hope, that He will give them to you, before you are able to profit by them. Believe that He has kept them from you hitherto, because they would have been curses, and not blessings. Oh! look back, look back, at the history of English Radicalism for the last half century, and judge by your own deeds, your own words; were you fit for those privileges which you so frantically demanded? Do not answer me, that those who had them were equally unfit; but thank God, if the case be indeed so, that your incapacity was not added to theirs, to make confusion worse confounded! Learn a new lesson. Believe at last that you are in Christ, and become new creatures. . . ."

Crossthwaite had kept his face fast buried in his hands; now he looked up with brimming eyes—

"I see it—I see it all now. Oh, my God! my God! What infidels we have been!" (362, 364–65)

I have reviewed a persistent trope: Tories attributed Jewish characteristics to the puritan rebels after the English Civil War, while reserving all civic virtue and balance to themselves, the moderate men. English Tories applied the same discourse to America after the American Revolution; they denounced the ex-colonists as hypocrites, preaching godliness and equality while abusing nonwhites and Nature. In an effort to achieve upper-class unity after the civil war against an expanding industrial working class, the essentialist anti-puritan /anti-Jewish/misogynistic reading of "the American character" was adopted by ideological brethren on American soil. The Left romantics, like New England puritans, were consistently typed or raced as Hebraic or Jewish by organic conservatives. But the fanatics were also gendered as the moral mother, her prototype Anne Hutchinson. Here is the nineteenth-century American historian Charles Francis Adams analyzing the Antinomian Controversy (1636–38) that he claimed had rent and permanently damaged the infant colony of Massachusetts Bay even though the provoking Anne Hutchinson and her corrupting middle-class will to power were banished:

It was a struggle for civil power and ecclesiastical supremacy in a small village community. As such it naturally—it almost necessarily—resulted in a display of the worst qualities of those engaged in it. It illustrated also with singular force the malign influence apt to be exercised by the priest and the woman as active elements in political life. Stirred by an access of ill-considered popular enthusiasm, the body of the freemen had, at the election of 1636, put a slight upon the time-honored magistrates of the colony, by placing the boyish [Henry] Vane over their heads, in the office of governor. An ambitious woman, with her head full of Deborahs and the like, and with a genius for making trouble, had then sought to drive from his pulpit, in the chief town, its long-settled pastor, in order to install her own favorite preacher in his place, with her kinsman as that preacher's associate and successor. In her day-dreams she herself probably occupied, in the new order of things she proposed to bring about, the position of a prophetess,—the real guiding spirit of the whole,—with her husband possibly in the judge's seat. Altogether it was an exhilarating vision,—such a vision as self-conscious and usually unappreciated natures have in every time and most places been wont to revel in. . . . (569) . . . At the hands . . . of an historian whose intelligence is not mastered by his sympathies, she and her friends, including Governor Vane, are entitled to no consideration. They went on a fool's errand, and they brought great principles into lasting odium.

On the other hand, the way in which the adherents of Vane and Mrs. Hutchinson were suppressed cannot be defended, without including in the defence the whole system of religious and political intolerance of that time. But why should it be defended? It is impossible to ignore the fact, and worse than useless to deny it, that the New England Puritans were essentially a persecuting race. They could not be otherwise. They believed that they were God's chosen people. As such, they were right; all others were wrong. If, therefore, they failed to bring up their children in the strait and narrow way, and to protect them and all the people from the wiles of the Evil One, God would not hold them guiltless. The Israelites were their models in all things, and the precedents which guided their action were precedents drawn from the books of the Old Testament. "So, by the example of Lot in Abraham's family, and after Hagar and Ishmael, he saw they must be sent away." The Israelites were not an attractive or an amiable or a philosophical race; they were narrow, devout and clannish. No one ever presumed to sophisticate away their cruelties or their persecutions. Yet withal they were a strong and aggressive people, believing certain things implicitly; and accordingly they impressed themselves and their beliefs on the human mind. Their very imperfections were essential elements of their strength. They believed to fanaticism; and it was the strength of their fanaticism which caused their belief to dominate. It was the same with the Puritans of New England. They persecuted as a part of their faith.[32]

The impartial historian Adams's misreading of ancient history is remarkably sturdy. In his Hume-style portrait of the usurping Anne Hutchinson (Hawthorne's "the Woman") we have the ahistoric archetype of the totalitarian agitator, the clinging maternal superego that holds humanity, rulers and ruled alike, to universal and timeless ethical standards, that dispatches utopians such as Ahab and Pierre.[33] It is fascinating and alarming to contemplate the birthing of Adams-style pluralism, scattering the dark shadows of intolerant Hebraic puritanism, cradle of both factions in the Antinomian Controversy. Today Anne Hutchinson is a heroine to some feminists and libertarians, a proto-Nazi to one prominent New Americanist. Richard H. Brodhead, a dean of Yale University and professor of English, writing for an educated middle- and upper-class audience, has depicted the lineage she spawned, worsened by "the emotional dependencies produced in the hyperaffectionate, inward-turning, hothouse family newly prominent in Melville's time":

> Captain Ahab is a figure of the psychically damaged man as visionary authority and charismatic leader. Ahab knows and persuades others of the One Sole Truth, the truth of his demented obsession. Pierre is another incarnation of a type that has run through American history, from the antinomian religious dissidents of the 1640s [*sic*] to the civil disobeyers and antislavery radicals of Melville's generation to the sect and militia leaders of our own time. In its harrowing rendition of the cult of private visionary calling, "Pierre" envisions this urge as leading not just to violent trashing of the conventional social world but to a meltdown or disorientation of the moral world.[34]

For gentleman scholars out on a spree, English and American alike, Lord Byron was the epitome of adolescent negativity, Thomas Carlyle his antithesis. Written in 1924, the English critic H. J. C. Grierson's remarks could have been voiced by any of the lashed Melville scholars peering at Mother's ruffled brow. They register an appetite both for suffering and its relief, an oscillation between pious aversion and illicit admiration: "To Byron's acute, clear mind the mystical philosophy which is at the heart of romanticism was altogether foreign. He never approached the inner shrine of romanticism where the mood of a mere rebellion begins to give way to dimmer or clearer intuitions of a new and positive vision, a faith to take the place of that which the spirit has rejected, the dawning of a new comprehension of the magic and beauty of nature, the mystery and beauty of human nature, full as it is of 'misery, heartbreak, pain, sickness, and oppression.'" Byron has failed, or has he? Pain is sublime, but so is the grandeur of social transformation. Byron reminds us of the Jews. "He was held in the grasp of too many contradictions—antidemocrat and democrat, believer and blasphemer, man of the world and inspired satirist. But, to speak more truly, the Romantics were all prophets, not unlike their Jewish precursors, intent at a period of world-disorder on the quest of justice and mercy and love and beauty, a recasting of life and reconstruction of faith. . . . He is the constant reminder . . . of what the world really is, of the greatness of the task of interpreting and reforming it."[35] Grierson, the devotee of Carlyle, but swept away, has conceded that Byron is "really" in touch with things as they are. Lord Alfred Douglas, editor of *Plain English*, was less favorably disposed toward spellbinding

Jews. His poem "In Excelsis" (1924) contains images that evoke the gothic touches of *Moby-Dick:*

The leprous spawn of scattered Israel
Spreads its contagion in your English blood;
Teeming corruption rises like a flood
Whose fountain swelters in the womb of hell.
Your Jew-kept politicians buy and sell
In markets redolent of Jewish mud,
And while the "Learned Elders" chew the cud
Of liquidation's fruits, they weave their spell.
They weave the spell that binds the heart's desire
To gold and gluttony and sweating lust:
In hidden holds they stew the mandrake mess
That kills the soul and turns the blood to fire,
They weave the spell that turns desire to dust
And postulates the abyss of nothingness.[36]

There is no single Left or liberal standard to evaluate the social content of art. Today's ethnopluralists continue to scan texts for positive or negative images of their partisans. In the 1930s, Stalinist bureaucrats separated proletarian and bourgeois consciousness so drastically that essentialist categories permeated their critical theory no less than the Herder-inspired corporatists'. Only workers or the colonized masses (for whom they spoke) were free of perceptual distortions. Hegelian-Marxists have attempted to locate the text in history, analyzing form and content to discover the concrete function it might have served in the world movement toward democracy. Artists who artificially reconciled glaring social contradictions (between capital and labor, between ideals and reality) through class collaboration or defeatism or formal closure were right wing and antimodern. Progressive artists ripped into appearances to leave secrets exposed and contradictions hanging. This is a test that Ahab and his blood-tipped harpoon should have passed; why didn't they? For one Hegelian-Marxist, Georg Lukács, writing during the 1930s Popular Front (1935–39), Goethe was the exemplary progressive bourgeois.[37] I am not certain that Lukács would approve Melville's weirdly metamorphosing symbols, nonstop modernism, and open-endedness envisioned as mutilated stumps, hurling themselves eternally against cruelty and injustice. Whereas an Ahab-ish literary critic would ask, does the text steer us away from the medieval world of myth and hero worship advancing the chosen few, or toward the uncharted waters of critical consciousness and self-management advanced by the Chosen People? The emancipatory project of Ahab's libertarian bourgeoisie has yet to be realized; for one distinguished intellectual historian, that sublime enterprise threatens disaster; we are holding on for dear life. Concluding a recent book of essays on Protestantism and the Enlightenment, Henry Farnham May quoted Harriet Beecher Stowe to put *les petroleuses* in their places: "Our own hard, rocky, sterile New England was a sort of half Hebrew theocracy, half ultra-democratic republic of little villages, separated by a pathless ocean from all the civilization and refinement of the Old World, forgotten and unnoticed, and yet burning like live coals under this obscurity with all the fervid activity of an intense, newly kindled, peculiar, and individual life."

The live coals burst into flame, Professor May continued, after the idea of the Chosen People animated nineteenth-century reform movements and wild Jacksonian romanticism: "In America all causes tend to become crusades. Around the corner of the sublime lurks the crazy: as Poe and Hawthorne and Melville knew, there is no poetry without danger, no prophecy without potential violence. It is fortunate that America's constitutional system, our main surviving inheritance from the Enlightenment, has so far, often precariously, held its own."[38] Like other moderates in this study, Professor May's preferred analytic categories are civilization and savagery; he does not analyze institutions, class position, interests, and allegiances. His nostalgia for a solid constitutional system hearkens back to the Great Chain of Being and other corporatist models that divided the deferential order-loving faithful from unpredictable nature lovers, rooted cosmopolitans from the ruthless rootless, good pluralists from bad.

Here was the abolitionist, brandishing his one idea like an iron flail.
   —Hawthorne, "The Hall of Fantasy"

[Charles Sumner's] was . . . the role of an ancient Hebrew prophet—the kindling of moral enthusiasm, the inspiring of courage and hope, the assailing of injustice.[39]
   —*Dictionary of American Biography*

Writing near the end of the nineteenth century, the progressive Carl Schurz, a veteran of the failed German revolution of 1848 and Charles Sumner's ally, attempted a biography of the controversial abolitionist senator, but questioned his friend's refusal to compromise. Commenting on Sumner's stubborn adherence to principle prior to his first election as senator from Massachusetts, April 24, 1851, Schurz wrote with some exasperation:

The Whig and Democratic press assailed him with unprecedented fury and reprinted his speech against the fugitive slave law which had given such offense to the Democrats. Democratic members of the Legislature besought him to withdraw or modify only some of his utterances in that speech so as to give them a pretext for changing their votes in his favor. Even so slight a concession in the way of recantation of his pledge would have insured his success. But in vain. To all such entreaties he had but one answer: that the office must seek him, not he the office, and that it must find him an absolutely independent man. . . . A political accident [the brief coalition between Free Soilers and Democrats] . . . carried into the Senate of the United States a man who was the very embodiment of the moral insurrection against slavery in its boldest and austerest form.

And Schurz's notes written on the back of an envelope provided fuel for Sumner's detractors in this century:

"The slavery question has not two sides." As to the moral bearings of the question—question of right and wrong—this was correct. As to the way in which slavery could best be got rid of, it was not correct. He not only refused to see any moral excuse for the opposite argument, but could never appreciate how far that opposite argument was apt to make an impression upon ordinary minds. Not to see two sides of a question was an element of weakness in a statesman but an element of strength in a moral agitator and a revolutionary character.

He was a moral terrorist—making it appear as a sort of moral delinquency not to follow him—which men were afraid of.[40]

The Catholic feudal world tended to view nature and the human body as Satan's province. Perceptible facts were traps—Ariadne's sticky web—whereas the radical bourgeoisie claimed that nature could be comprehended; reality could be penetrated and dominated for the benefit of humanity. For the medieval thinker, self-control was the mastery of disruptive passions, most particularly the passion of the Head for forbidden knowledge. For the nascent radical bourgeois, self-control corrected one's own perceptual distortions and antisocial impulses, but such mastery was also harnessed to the Lockean project of testing authority. For the medieval thinker and modern corporatist alike, enlightenment was the return of the darkening "fact" of fallen flesh to puffed-up atheists.[41] Human nature and the body's sensorium were evil; hopes for earthly amelioration were illusory, while "visions and shadows of a future state" (eternal salvation) were not. For the progressive bourgeois, say Locke, Mandeville, or Diderot, the return of the repressed was the body of suppressed facts that indicted hypocritical authority: embarrassing facts hidden by governments or individuals, facts discovered by digging into archives, assembling chronologies, and clearing previously misty social structures, events, and relationships. Demystification would necessarily shatter idealizations of parents, leaders, and other perfectly harmonious objects of veneration, including oneself. Hitherto good objects, suddenly, disconcertingly, became *unheimlich*, a word that is misleadingly translated in the Strachey standard edition of Freud as "uncanny," masking the idea that a homey object has suddenly switched: The familiar and protective is now unrecognizable and unpredictable. Wary conservatives described such reconstructive histories (including dioramas, museums, and the productions of mass media made available to a newly literate and growing working class) as obsession, monomania, iconoclasm, and catastrophe. These were projects curated by the virtuoso/Faust/Wandering Jew figure brandishing his "blood-incrusted pen of steel," poisoning the masses with insights attained through sensuality, social criticism, and self-criticism: "Life—earthly life—is the only good. . . . My destiny is linked with the realities of earth. . . . Give me what I can see, and touch, and understand, and I ask for no more," says Hawthorne's frigid, hellish Wandering Jew, assembler of "whimsical combinations and ludicrous analogies."[42]

[Moses Lowman, 1740] If after all it should be found defective in some Parts, which yet I hope it will not, I can however honestly say, a Discovery of Truth will always be pleasing to me, tho' at the same time it should shew me, a Mistake of my own.

With his snow-white new ivory leg braced against the screwed leg of his table, and with a long pruning-hook of a jack-knife in his hand, the wondrous old man . . . was wrinkling his brow, and tracing his old courses again. (*Moby-Dick*, 473)

[O. W. Riegel, 1931] Although Herman Melville has a throne in our literary Valhalla, it may perhaps be seen, after the rosy clouds have rolled away from the pedestal, that he is balanced precariously on a chair with a single leg, and that made of whale-bone, like the leg of Captain Ahab.[43]

It should not have been approbation (a positive image) of the French Revolution or glorification of plebeians or workers that tested antifascist art for materialist critics, but an author's willingness to map social structures and forces, to dig until inside narratives were disclosed. Like the self-critical Dissenter Moses Lowman or Ahab, his brow furrowed in concentration, the radically enlightened writer, spurning dogmatism, would return to the text, engage his critics, then revise and revise again to find a more accurate and persuasive analysis. Some Marxist critics understood that writers who stung the revolutionary bourgeoisie were romantic reactionaries.[44] Of course the heroic bourgeois modernizer was not idealized but viewed tragically: He was ravaged by internal contradictions, according to liter-ary criticism published by the *New Masses*. Capitalism was structurally incapable of delivering the earthly paradise industrialists had promised; moreover, it seemed that in its primitive accumulation stage, capitalism committed horrible atrocities against nature and "savages." The world where both toil and barbarism would be abolished could only be achieved through socialist transformation led by the party of the politically conscious international working class, or so argued Marxist-Leninists during the years of the Popular Front (1935–39). Romantic love was defined against the pseudo-love offered by deceptive corporatist elites and was prelusive to the creative, sensually awakened, gentle, and egalitarian society that industrialization would finally make possible. In a world where aristocratic elites had not been displaced or had become capitalists themselves, it was not surprising that artists working from the Renaissance to the present (and dependent on aristocratic or would-be aristocratic patrons) carried intellectual habits and emotional responses of the Old World into the New, sometimes transmitting what Marx called feudal socialism. Marxist or liberal critics should expect such contradictions in the transition from feudal to market societies. As we turn to the Melville Revival, I examine the ambivalent responses of Melville biographers from Left to Right as they encounter "blood-incrusted pens of steel"—Ahab's and their own.

Part II
Tracing Their Old Courses Again

The Melville Revival, 1919–1953

6

The Boulevard of Broken Dreams

Raymond M. Weaver and the Melville Revival, 1919–1935

And from whom but an American could we have expected such a book as we had the other day in the "Whale" of Herman Melville,—such a fresh, yet daring book—wild, and yet true—with its quaint, spiritual portraits looking ancient and also fresh,—Puritanism, I may say, KEPT FRESH in the salt water over there and looking out living upon us once more! These writers one sees at all events, have our old English virtue of Pluck. They think what they please and say what they think. And while McFungus is concocting philosophical histories in the style of the last century which drum on our ears, these other open-hearted men are getting into all our hearts and making themselves friends by our firesides.[1]
  —James Hannay, 1853

His later years were passed in the world of thought rather than of action. He published nothing; and New York, his old camping-ground, seldom knew him. But when he appeared, his gray figure, gray hair and coloring, and piercing gray eyes, marked him to the most casual observer. Though a man of moods, he had a peculiarly winning and interesting personality, suggesting Lawrence Oliphant in his gentle deference to an opponent's conventional opinion while he expressed the wildest and most emancipated ideas of his own.
  —Charles Dudley Warner, *A Library of the World's Best Literature,* 1907

Legend assigns the author's swift obscuration to the dispraise "Pierre" aroused. It is too simple an explanation, as we shall see. The book is repellent and overwrought, yet powerful. The theme is the endeavor of a long-parted brother and sister, a mere lad and lass, to cut loose and lead their own lives, as nominal husband and wife. The ambiguity of their situation leads to misery, madness, and ruin. It anticipates The Ordeal of Richard Feverel . . . . Poor health and brooding must chiefly account for his collapse.

—Frank Jewett Mather, Jr., "Herman Melville," *The Review*, August 9, 1919

The psychological novel, like all Romantic art, proceeds from self-adoration. The novelist may fancy that he is constantly spying on himself as he feels, thinks, and acts, for the sake of his art, for the sake of obtaining "copy." But the opposite is, of course, the truth: he practices his art because he is so interested in himself. . . . Now, this narcissism of the modern novelist is something which Christians have been particularly enjoined to avoid. It is by obliviousness to self that the Christian, so he has been told, may win salvation. "Whosoever shall seek to save his life shall lose it." Since, then, the preoccupation with self is inseparable from the writing of the modern novel, that writing cannot logically be justified, to my mind, if Christianity is true. The Christian should, for his own sake, even more than for the sake of such others as might read him, refrain from novel-writing. If, after all, he does turn novelist, there is only one course open to him: he must admit frankly that, notwithstanding his efforts, his prayers, and his willingness to let Divine Grace operate, he is unable to resist the temptation to write.[2]

—Critic Montgomery Belgion on narcissism

Raymond Weaver was one of the great teachers in modern times. He cared for his subject; and for his students, with an intensity which kept him always in immediate contact with whatever was personal, important, and alive. . . . One of his students has written: "To be a great teacher and still to be one's self, retaining the fine salt of one's own character—this, too, was within his compass." . . . Without bending his will to please others, he gained universal regard by his unceasing devotion to the profound and the beautiful.

—Minute for the Faculty of Columbia College upon the Death of Raymond Weaver, April 4, 1948

R aymond Melbourne Weaver (1889–1948), author of the first modern Melville biography, *Herman Melville: Mariner and Mystic* (1921), is remembered as "the father of Melville criticism." After assisting Michael Sadleir in bibliographic work, Weaver edited volume 13 of Constable's *Standard Edition of the Works of Herman*

Melville (1924) that included the first publication of "Billy Budd" and the sketch "Daniel Orme." He was also editor of Albert and Charles Boni's "Pequod edition" of Melville's works (1924–26); author of *Black Valley,* an antimissionary novel set in Japan (1926); editor of *Shorter Novels of Herman Melville* (1928); and editor of Melville's journal of 1856–57, *Journal up the Straits* (1935).

Weaver has drawn the fire of rival Melvilleans, perhaps because he was seen as a Freudian radical, perhaps because he was as changeable as the writer who hugged him throughout his academic career, perhaps because he was an uncloseted homosexual, but most likely because his initial reading of Ahab as modern artist was increasingly unacceptable after the late 1930s.[3] At the time of his first Melville publication he was a former Columbia student and instructor, then employed by the Brooklyn Polytechnic Institute. Obituaries wrongly stated that he had received a Columbia bachelor of arts degree in 1912, joining the Columbia faculty in 1916. In fact, Weaver was hired October 8, 1917, to replace purged socialist professor and peace activist Harry Dana. Moreover, Columbia records show that Weaver received a bachelor of science degree in 1910 from Columbia Teachers College and the master's in English in 1917.[4] His papers at Columbia contain a publicity handout from his first publisher, Doran & Co.: Weaver's Baltimore family had wanted him to be an engineer. No other elucidation of his family and class background was preserved. Defiantly severing his connections with machines, loyal only to his "nature,"[5] Weaver seems to have invented himself as a tragic hero, like Ahab, shrouding his origins in obscurity. But, unlike Melville, Weaver turned Ahab's rebellion into a pratfall, a me-tooism perhaps for his own loss of balance.

At the request of his colleague, Carl Van Doren, literary editor of the *Nation,* the young instructor had been asked, quite casually, to write a Melville centenary essay with less than two months lead time. He threw himself into the work and almost immediately made an uncharacteristically risky career move. Writing to the wife of Columbia professor John Erskine, July 2, 1919, Weaver set out the shrinking parameters of his revolt:

I have resigned my instructorship here at Columbia—an enterprise exciting enough to me, for I leave with very mixed emotions. Most should I have liked the advice of Professor Erskine. But I had to act rapidly—and have taken the step. I am teaching next year at the Brooklyn Polytechnic—with promise of real and almost immediate advancement. From one point of view I have entered the wilderness: but Columbia was wilderness also—though at Columbia there are a very few golden voices. Professor Thorndike was on the whole inclined to encourage my departure. He said he could not advance me here: that his policy must be to use "cheap labor" (the phrase is his) for most of the undergraduate work. He implied that I cheapened myself by staying on here so surrounded: that my final prospects were better if I at this time made my declaration of independence.

Weaver's Melville readings originated in the Poe-like prison frankly described to Mrs. Erskine. He notes his shameful dependence upon the good will of older conservative men who shamelessly display their dependence on still other men in the enforcement of unjust policies. Yet if the younger man submits to exploitation, he will be stigmatized as a slave. Which vista is bleaker: the radical stomping out to teach engineers, hence discarding the hard-won status of a gentlemanly humanities professor, or the cheerful lackey who will be ejected for excessive conformity? Both are imprisoned, both are wandering in the wilderness. Yet Weaver wishes that a better older man, John Erskine, were in town to help him choose his poison. No party is mystified about the real power relations or "who dunnit"; but neither is anyone responsible for changing his condition through social action. Chains will rattle and roll: Such is the constitution of manliness in the unhappy corporate family *not* founded by Thomas Jefferson in 1776.

Weaver's first publication, "The Centennial of Herman Melville" (*Nation*, Aug. 2, 1919), seems to have been written in the warmth of his spontaneous response to Melville's art, whereas the journal that solicited his contribution was an outpost of New Humanist serenity. As narrated above, throughout the months leading up to the Melville centenary in 1919, a year of international revolution and reaction, Oswald Garrison Villard, editor of the *Nation*, like other progressives before and since, hoped to forestall Bolshevism in America by co-opting socialist themes: improving material life for the majority while promoting the distinctively Anglo-Saxon tradition of compromise and free speech to counteract rigid and punitive right-wing responses to militant labor and its allies. Hidebound conservatism would, as Bismarck's antisocialist laws had done, generate an indignant response to capture or regain treasured cultural freedoms. This was said more quietly during the Columbia University controversy of October 1917, an event deplored because it made American attempts to bring democracy to militaristic Germans seem hypocritical. Even the *Nation's* response to the Bolshevik coup de main of November 1917 was relatively subdued.[6] In the context of their neoclassical adjurations of 1917–19, Weaver's Melville and the ironic, ebullient, highly colored tone of his article were a call to arms against the greyness of his immediate environs.

On July 7, 1919, the *New York Times* noted Melville's advanced views: "People of all colors and races are one to his philosophic eye." Weaver also spotted a radical, arraying stodgy objectivists against Melville. The clean-cut Dr. Johnson, "Puritan New England," the "intolerable monotony of relatives and friends," and "philistines and pragmatists" were met in Melville by their blurred antitheses: the Comic Spirit, "Pierre" ("a book to send a Freudian into ravishment"), and the moralizing, conflicted, elusive "delver." In Weaver's composition, the genial, happily married Melville shaded into the monomaniac Ahab, disappointed by "glamorous mirage[s]" and the ruinous cash nexus, the need for money that tied him up. Weaver foregrounded Melville's personal attachment to Hawthorne, but the authors he thought his art evoked or synthesized were Elizabethan playrights, Milton (in "Lycidas"), Browne, Rabelais, Smollett, Coleridge, Meredith (in *The Egoist*), and Whitman. Weaver's portrait conveyed precisely the disgusted, despairing proto-Bolshevik figure the *Nation* had set itself to rescue and incorporate, a figure with whom Weaver anxiously identified but could not celebrate. "Essentially was he a mystic," concluded Weaver.

For Melville, either unresolved personal issues or the will to mislead hostile readers subverted political clarity and consistency, creating the notorious confusion of the Melville scholarship; one can only pity Weaver as he contemplated the task before him. Static archetypal criticism cannot or will not describe Melvillean diagnostics and prognoses, the mental hygiene tied to the fortunes of a specific class; nor will Jungian-style quests for patterns in a national or collective unconscious discover the origin of Melville's conflicts or ambivalence, which must have originated partly in the particular history of a high-born common sailor clashing with red specters. These veiled demons were transmitted by conservative Christians haunted by the loss of idealized family members; the demoniacs became Melville's (and Weaver's) Jacobins: Both men were reaching for moral beauty in moralistic but amoral institutions.

WEAVER'S HEGIRA

The young instructor embarked on research for a full-blown biography in late summer of 1919, corresponding with Frances Thomas, Melville's daughter who directed him to her oldest daughter, Eleanor Metcalf, custodian of Melville's unpublished manuscripts. Metcalf and Weaver finally met on September 27, 1919. He approached writing the biography to recover from his own lawless wandering, as his memoir relates:

I wrote to Mrs. Metcalf. I have no record of the initial correspondence. But I vividly remember urging her (evidently against provocation) of the importance of getting recorded all that was known of Melville: that a man who has published a dozen volumes had thereby ceased to be a private personality— a public character, rather, at the mercy of anyone who drew his own conclusions from the published books—and the loquacity of the Hawthorne family and friends: that Julian had imputed against Melville a clean-gone madness:

that Id [sic] read Melville and lost my own mind: that I needed a little anchorage in fact for my own insanity.

Weaver claimed that Mrs. Metcalf disclosed family secrets that Weaver "as a gentleman" would be obliged to withhold. If this recollection is accurate, the authorized biography was produced by Weaver's tumultuous response to Melville, a peep inside the family that was to remain undisclosed to others, and the understandable opportunism of the arriviste suddenly in possession of unpublished manuscripts, journals, and letters.[7] Weaver was also launched by the personal enthusiasm of Eugene Saxton, an editor at Doran & Co., who really did come from Baltimore.[8] Saxton first contacted him January 26, 1920, asking to read Weaver's manuscript. A letter followed on June 9 requesting a complete proposal for "the Melville project," stating that George Doran was "considerably interested" in "the whole Melville proposition" and would take it up at once with their English house. Contrary to the impression of some Melvilleans, the Weaver article could not have spawned the English Melville Revival. Weaver did not inspire the Constable project; rather it seems he was cultivating Sadleir while simultaneously involved in competing Doran plans that were dropped after Weaver told George Doran (July 10, 1922) that the Sadleir-directed Constable *Standard Edition,* planned in secret, was about to appear.[9]

Suppressing his private excitement, Weaver's reservations about Melville's artistry were probably determined by conservatives. His papers contain Hoyt Hudson's long and unfriendly article in the *Freeman,* April 27, 1921, cut up and heavily marked. Comparing *Typee* with the failed later work, Hudson tossed out the interloper with the usual Tory slur on prideful autodidacts lost in an alcoholic stupor:

> Melville's tone in his conversation often must have been sophomoric and self-conscious, unless he talked philosophy much better than he wrote it. Here are hints of the true explanation of his defection as a writer. He came to the reading of the philosophers a little late in life, with small preparation for it and without humility; their heady liquor intoxicated him and made him lose his way. He gave up the struggle for literary greatness in which he was already fairly successful to enter upon a quest for abstract truth, foredoomed to failure. . . . [The white shark] haunted Melville and unfitted him for literary work. For it represents the sinister results of his thinking—nature seen as sinister in its indifference, truth seen as sinister in its elusiveness. The white radiance of eternity dazzled and frightened him; he never should have attempted to look beyond the dome of many-coloured glass under which he early found beauty and inspiration.[10]

The romantic pagan side of Weaver's nature surely applauded Melville's departure from Hudson's cathedral, but as an upstart and outcast himself he would echo Hudson's views and preoccupation with Melville's "failure" throughout his biography. The work after *Pierre* was dismissed in a chapter entitled "The Long Quietus," but *Clarel* was excerpted as a guide to the earlier fiction. Although Weaver tended to echo conventional opinion that had limited Melville's achievement to the early work (*Typee, Omoo, White-Jacket,* and *Moby-Dick*), he importantly diverged from Carl Van Doren's lament for the one-novel author of a great sea-tale in the *Cambridge History of American Literature* (1917) and Hudson's put-down of Melville/ Ahab: First, *Moby-Dick* and *Pierre* were thundering demystifications of a repressive and hypocritical society bound to call forth the wrath of philistines; second, the bourgeois reading public and Melville's mother were one. What besides the fiction, poetry, journals, and letters (including letters to Hawthorne published by his son Julian in the late nineteenth century) did Weaver have to work with?

WAS HERMAN MELVILLE/AHAB CRAZY?

Ship after ship passes the *Pequod*; they are homeward bound. Some are well laden with oil and full of merriment, others carry awful tidings of the white whale, of his terrible power and malignant strength. Each and all of these ships, whether stricken or successful, offer a marked contrast to the *Pequod*. Whatever fortune has befallen them, they are at least sane. The *Pequod* alone fights her way eastward against contrary winds towards that amazing calm, that entrancing mildness in which she is to encounter Moby Dick.

Each story that the passing captains tell adds fuel to Ahab's madness. He inspires his crew with his spirit, making his cause their own. They no longer appear as men, but as instruments of his will. The elements of personality are now flowing together; the increasing power of madness is too strong to allow them to remain separate.
—E. L. Grant Watson, 1920

Students of Herman Melville's works must be grateful to Mr. Raymond Weaver for his recently published edition of the novelist's journal, kept during his tour in Europe and Asia Minor, in parts of the years 1856 and 1857. The text, now printed for the first time, throws considerable light upon Melville's long poem, *Clarel*, as well as upon certain shorter pieces of verse included in the privately printed volumes of Melville's last years. That the journal furnishes ample evidence of its author's sanity in the years it covers is also true, as Mr. Weaver remarks. It should be added, however, that no one who has any knowledge of Melville in his later years needs such demonstration. Every allusion to Melville from close friend or casual acquaintance, as well as the proof from his own writings—correspondence or more formal literary expression—points to the perfect balance of his mind during this period. For thinking people, the question—raised by the late Julian Hawthorne—of Melville's sanity has long since been completely settled.[11]

—Robert S. Forsythe, 1936

It is difficult if not impossible to quantify the degree that readers project themselves into their subjects, but project we probably will unless checked by constant self-scrutiny and ongoing criticism from others. Given the competitive conditions of academic writing in the humanities and the potential subordination of historical accuracy to the demands of good taste, that corrective process is stunted; how many writers faced with the primitive emotions aroused by Melville's mutinies are likely to 'fess up to colleagues and readers? Still, inferences are warranted, and these shall be drawn from the repeated images and cross-outs my subjects have presented, especially in drafts and personal correspondence.

While apparently refuting Julian Hawthorne's imputations of insanity or extreme distress, Weaver subtly transmitted the same judgments of the sick, repellent Melville psyche; that was what one of his informants may have suggested to him (in confidence, of course). His papers disclose notes made after an interview with Josephine Mac C. Shaw, Elizabeth Melville's niece and confidante, described with Weaver's characteristic admiration/revulsion in response to memories transmitted by phallic women (perhaps his androgynous self):

Cousin Josie: Deaf—coarse bobbed hair—walks with a hideous rocking—with strange straps and paraphanalia [sic] rattling under her skirt. Loathsome in appearance and as keen as an old Devil. . . . Mrs. Melville planned to leave Herman twice. The first time his trip to Holy Land a tentative separation. He wrote nothing home—for a time. She in Boston. 2nd time she came to Boston with girls . . . some crisis possible but not known. But the Melville women settled down in persuasion—and Herman appeared heartbroken—and Lizzie went back home. . . . Herman violent—Lizzie's life not always safe. . . . Herman kinder to daughters—hated sons. Malcolm—affectionate—moody—loved mother—hated father for violence.[12]

These revelations may have prompted a letter to Julian Hawthorne who had recently alleged that Melville was "the strangest being that ever came into our circle." Racked by a "Puritan conscience" that "German metaphysics" could not relieve, he remained "restless and disposed to dark hours, there is reason to suspect a vein of insanity. His later writings were incomprehensible."[13] Hawthorne was unable to make his reason more concrete. As he told Weaver (who had presented himself, perhaps, as a fearless seeker after the real Herman Melville, suppressing no gory details):

I am glad you are undertaking the work of bringing out a complete account of Melville's life and writings: he was, at his best, unsurpassed in our literature, or in that of England; and we are beginning to realise, after sixty years, how good he was and is.

All the material that I possessed concerning him, however, was printed in my biography of my father, published in 1884. In his later years he was very reserved and taciturn, and seemed to suffer from some nervous complaint. Much of his later work, as you know, showed peculiarities which hindered their general popularity: he had darkened the sky with metaphysical speculations; and he became unhappy and downcast toward the end.[14]

Actually, Julian Hawthorne's faith in good form as barrier to darkening outbreaks from below (the test for sanity at that time) was faintly ambivalent, as suggested by a gobbet from "The Cakewalk Man at Atlantic City." "His suave authority continually checked the frenzy of the voodoo serpent when it was on the brink of breaking forth, and when the figure of the dance showed symptoms of transcending the smug bounds set down for it, he would shift to another, and so avert the peril which he knew not of except beneath the surface of his consciousness."[15] What could Weaver have learned from Eleanor Metcalf about the frenzied "voodoo serpent" beating smug boundaries "set down for it" that some (but not all) of the family preferred to forget? Her sister, Frances Cuthbert Thomas Osborne, later supplied some crucial details about her own family and Eleanor's limited contacts with her grandfather:

My own father, when he first paid an evening call upon my mother, was dismayed to hear her father stride down the hall to the front parlor door and shout, "Young man, do you prefer oatmeal or mush for breakfast?" The question having the desired effect, the young man hastily bade the family goodnight, and mother wondered whether she would ever see him again (180).

. . . My older sister, Eleanor, used to go to Twenty-sixth Street too sometimes, but, being older, she was more easily left at home when domestic upheavals necessitated sending away one of the little girls for safekeeping.[16] (183)

Except for some childhood memories, Eleanor Metcalf knew little about her grandfather, his books, or the details of his family life and career. She queried her laconic mother in letters dated August 29 and 30, and September 28, 1919, addressing questions put to her by Weaver and promising confidentiality. Frances Thomas responded very briefly; in several of her replies she wrote in the margins or between the lines of her daughter's letters, explaining that she would not withhold family memories: She wanted her well-known resentment of her father to be understood.[17] Surprisingly, Mrs. Thomas did not know when her grandfather Allan Melvill had died, nor did she know anything about "the circumstances that led to [M's] father's change of fortunes" or the condition of the family following the loss. In answer to Mrs. Metcalf's (Weaver's) questions, "Was [his mother] especially devoted to him and proud of him or not? Do you know anything of the relations between them?" Mrs. Thomas replied, "Never heard that she was," and "They were all a little afraid of him." Then, "Asking a question of my own . . . . Did he rail at things in general when he was angry, or were his attacks more personal?" Mrs. Thomas replied, "personal." In the second letter, Mrs. Metcalf asked, "How long was grandpa an invalid before his death? Grandma has a note on the margin of a newspaper clipping 'only two years.'" Mrs. Thomas wrote "O.K." Metcalf: "Then the milder manner of his last eight or ten years was not due to ill health, was it?" Thomas: "I should say lack of energy."

In the third letter, Mrs. Metcalf began by reassuring her mother about Weaver's character:

Mr. Weaver arrived yesterday afternoon and fell upon the records with enthusiasm. He is a keen, comprehending young man, eager about his subject, diffident about asking questions, yet anxious to be talked to, extremely desirous not [to] be a trouble, yet thorough and painstaking in his methods, quite a traveller I think, knowing the Sandwich Islands and having spent three years in Japan. There will probably be questions forthcoming almost every day. Here are some for you at once. Did he ever take an interest in "conventional Christianity"—that is, did he go to church at all at any period of his life? If so, to what church?

Did you ever hear the story told Mr. Weaver by Dr. Coan, who had it from some old admiral, that at the beginning of the *civil* war when feeling ran high against England, because of her sympathy with the South, that Grandpa went up the Hudson, got a schooner and went sailing with a British flag waving? Mr. Weaver wants to know if it has any foundation.

Mrs. Thomas wrote, "*I* never knew him to go to church but twice that I can remember—All Soul's Unitarian." Mrs. Metcalf asked her mother if she knew who authorized J. E. A. Smith's sketch of Melville's life (1891), which she had "recently re-read" and said "[I] think it rather namby-pamby in view of things I know from other sources. Have you a copy of Pierre?" Mother emphatically responded each time: To Coan's rumor of Melville's flaunting sympathy with the Confederacy, "Absolutely *no* truth in this, I *never* heard of it"; *"No,"* she did not know who authorized Smith's biography; as to her ownership of *Pierre,* "I am pretty sure I have *not.*"[18] In light of the efforts of later scholars to minimize the autobiographical content of *Pierre,* Mrs. Metcalf's letter with its leap from namby-pamby Smith to the antithetical Pierre is significant: Was a proscribed book one of the "other sources?" Suggesting that historical memory is painful and heavily circumscribed by all parties, Mrs. Metcalf tells her mother of Weaver's impending return: "He promises that he will *not* stay indefinitely and will try not to be a burden in any way."

Eleanor Metcalf contributed a memoir of her childhood to Weaver's volume (377–80), presenting her grandfather as frightening yet mysteriously attractive, given to abrupt departures and other symptoms of a restless imagination. His painted eyes followed her; Eleanor preferred her grandmother's white bedroom to the black, bookish habitat of the cane-wielding figure whose piled-up papers she knew not to touch. In her final sentence she wrote that he "forebode" his grandchildren would "turn against him as they grew older." These stories must have forced Weaver to revise his earlier version of the family. In the biography, he deleted the happy marriage that his *Nation* article had presented, interpolating a Freudian reading, suggesting that Melville's lifelong attachment to his Gorgon mother ("the Face") had turned him to stone, a matter clearly revealed in *Pierre;* in an almost buried remark, he implied that his relatives had provoked him to displays of extreme violence (245). There was no mention of near-divorces. Weaver's book earned him the gratitude of Melville's daughter Frances Thomas, who apologized for her initial resistance and expressed her "feeling of relief" after reading *Mariner and Mystic.*[19] When I first read this note in 1987, I assumed it pointed to a family cover-up of physical abuse; however, Mrs. Thomas's correspondence with her daughter suggests that she simply resented all unsubstantiated speculation, for instance the gossip that Melville's mother hated him. In her letter to Eleanor of May 17, 1926, she responds with annoyance to the John Freeman biography, just published; no one has captured an accurate picture of her father: "I have read only a little so far. I think the author might *not* have mentioned me, as furnishing the information about what H.M. said in regard to his mother's dislike of him—I hope Dr. Murray will be more discreet. I absolutely refuse to be interviewed by *any one* on the subject of H.M. I don't know him in the new light."[20]

Weaver did circulate lurid family gossip to insider Melvilleans and other men greater than he during the 1920s; strictly speaking, it is unknowable what disreputable behavior was reported by Eleanor Metcalf, Cousin Josie, and other relatives or friends, and how much was surmised from Melville's art[21] or produced by Weaver's (or Henry Murray's) fantasies.[22] How reliable are Weaver's notes and impressions? Several items in the papers of Henry Murray from this period may add detail to our knowledge of Melville's controversial behavior in the family, calling into question Weaver's imputation of either physical violence or mental cruelty (as we would understand it) directed toward Elizabeth by Herman. Murray's correspondents were Melville's granddaughter Eleanor Metcalf, Elizabeth's niece Josephine Shaw, and Melville's great-nieces Agnes and Margaret Morewood.

Apparently responding to Murray's suspicion that Melville had an incestuous relationship with his sister Augusta (as Murray would have thought, the model for Isabel in *Pierre*), Eleanor Metcalf wrote:

> I asked my mother some questions about Augusta. She says she *was* dark, that she had a quantity of black hair & black eyes, that she visited them more than any of the other sisters; that she had more mind than any of the others; and that she sang—always hymns, I believe. She also [illegible] more of her brother's uncertainties of temper and disposition.
>
> I do not know of any young picture of Augusta, but the photograph of her taken in 1864 shows, as I thought, a rather massive face with long heavy chin. The good looks in the family were given to the boys.
>
> Mother speaks of Augusta as a woman of strong beliefs and conviction, religious and energetic.[23] (Apr. 14, 1925)

In another letter, written soon after Murray had met Weaver in New York, Eleanor Metcalf answered Murray's questions about Elizabeth's brothers, Sam and Lem Shaw, possible matches for Lucy's brothers in *Pierre:*

> It seems more likely that Uncle Sam should be the antagonist in "Pierre." [Both mother and father said] that he was around more, saw more of the family situation of the Melvilles, felt it more keenly in his sister's account, and burst out more openly in indignation. He was a very devoted, domestic kind of man, extremely kind to women and tender of their trials. Uncle Lem was more of a club man, was more away from home, traveled a good deal, was urbane and kept out of troublesome difficulties. He would avoid a crisis and cover resentment where Uncle Sam would be explosive.
>
> [Murray should speak to Eleanor's father.] He has the distinction of having always been on good terms with H.M.: according to mother that is an extraordinary distinction. I got a fearful dose of the family side of the story in my last talk with mother.
>
> I am trying get at more knowledge of the marital relations. I learned that in his times of affectionate devotion he used to call his wife "Dolly" and treat her as if she were about seventeen [Lucy's age in the novel]. In the abusive pe-

riods he never used low language to her, nor did his exclamations express disappointment. She had an unpleasant habit of dropping her soiled handkerchief about the house. He would pick it up & give it back to her, calling it by some disgusting name which Mother absolutely refused to repeat.[24]

About Stanwix, he died of tuberculosis in a public ward of hospital in San Francisco, to which he was removed from a semi-private ward, after his father refused to let any more money be sent to him. Mother believes his illness was brought on by insufficient nourishment and clothing. He had very poor eye-sight—and was slightly deaf, so that he was always very much handicapped in his efforts to make a living. (May 26, 1926)

Responding to a pointed question from Murray, Josephine Shaw said she was choosing her remarks carefully, perhaps to avoid distortion by Melville's biographers. "I have been a long while writing you, but I wanted to be very sure of what I said. . . . No, I never thought Mrs. H. M. had any sense of humor, certainly not 'more than the average' by the time I knew her. (I was born in 1848.) She was always sad, weary, listless, and inclined to be fretful" (June 20, 1928).[25] Cousin Josie does not say Elizabeth had every right to complain because Herman was beating her and torturing his sons as well. Since some of the negative inferences about Melville's behavior may stem from his daughter Frances Thomas's supposedly permanent sulk, the following letters to Murray from Agnes Morewood and Eleanor Metcalf are especially revealing:

The fact that we have letters showing a loving mother and devoted sisters to Uncle Herman seems to have stirred Cousin Fanny Thomas up & she is anxious to see the letters. I wonder why she feels so strongly there was "hate" in Uncle Herman's Mother's heart towards that son.[26] Have you sensed that your self in your deep explorations. After all it is a serious question the truth of such a statement. When your book comes out, that is the side I am keen to learn how you take, so I am waiting. (Agnes to HAM, July 30, 1929)

Sometime ago Cousin Maria Morewood gave Mother to understand—wrote her I think—that she had letters of A[llan]. M[elvill]. found at Arrowhead which disproved the aspersions cast upon her grandfather, Allan Melville's, character by Herman's biographers. Mother immediately replied that she would like to see them, that anything connected with H.M. was interesting and important; and begged to have them forwarded to her for perusal. Weeks elapsed without a reply; then some ten days or two weeks ago came a letter of chat. . . . [Mother has asked if Murray would write to Maria to get quicker results.][27] (Eleanor to HAM, Aug. 5, 1929)

After decades of reported antagonism, Melville's daughter is reconsidering her position, having seen evidence that his mother and sisters were "loving" and "devoted." Had Herman been physically violent, as Weaver's notes suggest, I doubt that Frances ("little Miss Property," as her papa is said to have called her) would have been so open to contradictory impressions.

After initially refusing to speak of the family, Herman's great-niece Margaret Morewood became a frequent correspondent. In one letter she told Murray about repressed romanticism in her older relatives and the fantasies thereby generated. Maria Gansevoort Morewood (1849–1935), Allan Melville's daughter and Margaret's mother, has been speaking of Melville's son Malcolm (1849–1867), shot by his own hand:

> [Mother has been talking about how] Malcolm and she were inseparable play-fellows. . . . How they made tropical gardens in the hollows of the pasture land—and that she was never told about the details of his death ever—but suspected.
>
> But the amazing thing is her manner of relating dreams—dreams full of artistic sympathy—dreams described by words as vivid as flesh—About the youthful skater who came swinging down the Housatonic River with tights on "showing the lines of his beautiful body"—and his arms folded—and the people of Pittsfield did not appreciate him "he did no work—and he did not care about serious things." And he was so hurt by the coldness of the people who asked what he was good for, then he went back up the river swinging along on his skates & turned into a swan! Knowing the New England reserves the frozen reserves that is one of the threads of her personality you can imagine my amaz[ement] when she revealed this dream to me —"I want to know why you care so much for Shelley." & before breakfast she asked "Read to me The Sky Lark." (Jan. 1, 1933)

Who is the skater? Herman, Malcolm, or Maria Morewood herself, wishing to be an artist like Shelley or Melville, metamorphosed from bum to sweet-singing poet? From these family letters, it sounds as if all the free, sensuous spirits felt isolated and frustrated by coldness and rejection, the New England reserve. The body language in Maria Morewood's dream delivers a mixed message: The skater is swinging (an odd choice of words suggesting ambivalence) but with arms sternly, retentively, and self-protectively folded. And yet, as public interest in their peculiar relative mounts, as they finally read Melville, the guarded family melts; sympathy and interest build. But what about the violence? Melville's only uncritical ally may have been the loyal Augusta whose romantic personality most resembled his own. From the family memories reported here, Melville appears to have been preachy, moody, and passionate about his values, and perhaps excessively shocked by weakness and failure in others (in Stanwix, for instance), but not necessarily given to physical acting out against his wife or children as Weaver's notes from his talk with Josephine Shaw could be read. The relatives speak of "railing," not slaps.

There was no inherited wealth among this branch of the Melville family. When Murray met them in the mid-1920s, the Morewood sisters could barely maintain their family residence at Arrowhead (the farmhouse and ten acres in the Berkshires where Melville wrote *Moby-Dick,* later sold to his brother Allan).[28] Eleanor Metcalf, the granddaughter, was careful throughout life with money, husbanding her resources to educate her two sons in good progressive schools and subsidizing several of Paul Metcalf's books. Many letters in the Melville family papers or Murray's correspondence were devoted to the feud between the Morewoods and Charlotte Hoadley, daughter of Melville's sister Catherine and John C. Hoadley, who had commandeered money and furniture from the Gansevoorts and treated her own dying mother badly. With the exception of the bohemian Margaret Morewood, this polite downwardly mobile Victorian family was easily shocked by strong emotion or deviance of any kind, for superior self-control was one way they could still distinguish themselves from the lower classes, including usurping upwardly mobile immigrants. The disposition of family portraits (especially Melville's and his father's), books, journals, teacups, and furniture was a contentious topic, because heirlooms and the fantasy of family solidarity were precious remnants of elite status. Maria's imputed hatred of her son would have caused wonder and anxiety, as did Melville's renewed fame and the dogged Murray's "discoveries and quest for the strange, secret Melville."[29]

But what of the academics spinning Melville's "outbursts" (Mortmain's passion-fits?); would they not have been construed as remnants of his wayward democratic youth, as class resentment unbecoming to *their* stoically irrelevant class, boxed in as it were by the murmuring unemployed, sit-in strikers, and rising technocrats? At least two Harvard professors had no doubts about Melville's politics. G. W. Chessman took these notes in a course taught by Perry Miller and William Ellery Sedgwick, 1938–39. ". . . The experience in a forecastle is a terrific thing. He saw the dregs and the mud. . . . He hates the upper classes—the officers on ship. He is an aggressive champion of democracy & 'the people.' All his work must be considered a democratic saga. Much more literary & deeper than Whitman. He is not a man who is tamed. Melville said 'Hawthorne needed roast beef done rare . . . .'"[30] It was not the wild man Melville's descendants who were jumping overboard. The women generally seem to have been looking for documents that would clarify murky family relationships, letting go of or moderating older animosities; whereas Weaver had been impatient with the whole lot of them, Herman and the women alike, as Agnes complained to Murray in 1929. "The other day I took out of the Library 'Shorter

Novels' of Uncle Herman's and read it aloud to mother the tragic little tale of Billy Budd. Also Weaver's preface to the book and I am struck anew by [the] decided one-sidedness of his outlook. And how strange it was *when* writing Uncle Herman's Life never to come near Arrowhead and at that time we were all living there. When are you going to write your side?" (Feb. 5, 1929).

I interviewed Henry Murray in 1987. At one point he muttered, almost to himself, "I can't believe Herman ever touched Lizzie," contradicting his published remarks hinting at a near strangling.[31] Frances Osborne had written a short memoir of her Mosaic grandfather (partly quoted above), published and republished in 1965 and 1974, taking care to contradict false impressions:

> One thing which strikes me now as quite significant is that, although I was a shy and timid child, I never felt the least bit afraid of my Grandfather Melville. His looks were awe-inspiring; he was tall and imposing; and his amazing beard and deep voice alone might well have frightened me. Many visitors to that household had cause to fear him, but to me he was always gentle and I was never the victim of his moods and occasional uncertain tempers. He never revealed to me any of the impatience and even anger, which he was known to have visited on various people with whom he came into contact. I was too small to criticize him, too young to be impatient with, and too trusting to incur his anger. (180)
>
> [The Aolian harp on the windowsill was] a cure for the blues. (184)

Mrs. Osborne had specified some of the sources of Melville's anger, suggesting righteous indignation in a man suffering from bouts of depression, not lashings of the ugly drunk still depicted by his detractors, defamatory accusations that are sufficiently credible to expel a radical author from the canon on behalf of vox salutaris.[32]

My review of the Melville family situation in the 1920s and early 1930s as revealed in Murray's hitherto unseen letters from Melville's descendants casts light on the Weaver biography. *Mariner and Mystic* was extensively quoted by Perry Miller in his early 1960s Harvard lectures. Though he knew better (or thought he did), Murray's introduction to *Pierre* (1949) had attacked Melville for slandering Allan Melvill, the alleged seducer of the mother of "Isabel" and abandoner of his natural child. Perry Miller synthesized the views of Weaver and Murray for the New Left generation of future American Studies professors:[33]

> As Melville grew in maturity of years, he did not grow in charity toward his parents. In his novel *Pierre*, he seems to draw malicious delight in pronouncing, under a thin disguise, an imaginary libel [sic] upon his father's memory. There he desecrated in fiction what he had once fondly cherished in life. Aside from its high achievement as a work of art, this dark wild book of incest and

death is of the greatest importance as a document in autobiography. Most of the characters in "Pierre" are unmistakably idealizations of clearly recognizable originals. . . . And in this book Melville exorcises the ghost of his father, and brings him forth to unearth from the past a skeleton that Melville seems to have manufactured in the closet of a vindictive subconsciousness.

From his mother, Miller continued, Melville got both the hearty constitution and "the Gansevoort aptitude for anger." Miller's Melville had been presented (subtextually) as an Ahab, a switching Jew who desecrated the host. Melville may be right, Miller concluded, "but one can assent to Melville's creed only on penalty of destruction; and the race does not welcome annihilation." The lesson of Miller's lecture was plain: Disaster must ensue when Harvard students pursued the "ideals" of Melville's misguided youth.

THE FACE

For cautious Weaver, researching and writing in 1919–21, Melville's writing had only three positive aspects: First, he was "the literary discoverer of the South Seas"; second, like Richard Henry Dana, Jr., he explored "the secrets of the deep," the horrid conditions of previously spurned common sailors; third, he wrote one masterpiece of world literature, *Moby-Dick*, written in the bosom of New England (Pierre's too-capacious breast pockets?) (24–25, 22). There was no Melville problem; he was not ambivalent or hard to read. Inevitably, the switch from jocular travel narrative to pessimistic allegory would precipitate the abandonment of readers (including, oddly, Hawthorne) (337) that brought on "the long quietus." Weaver always identified Ahab, like Pierre, as Melville the beleaguered artist, a point underlined in the last words of *Mariner and Mystic*, but Weaver's Ahab was not a champion of the neglected workers whose sufferings moved Melville and Weaver alike;[34] he was a Nietzschean Superman whose "uncompromising despair" (332) and preference for "uncharted waters" (382) signified the freedom from utopian illusions. In a strained synthesis, Weaver's Melville was both an existentialist like himself and an aristocratic rebel likened to Milton, Satan, and the Comic Spirit (27, 37); he was a radical, but neither primitivist nor democrat. Still, Melville was an extremist, born to glory, gloomed to failure.[35] And curiouser still, he was a lesser artist than the one remembered by Julian Hawthorne, whose damaging imputations of "clean-gone madness" Weaver said that he opposed.

Comparison of the handwritten draft, "The Life of Herman Melville," with Weaver's published book suggests the train of associations and hereditarian explanations that produced Weaver's antimodern gothic narrative, Melville's decline and fall.

First, the vengeful and uncomprehending reading public ("the herd"), maddened by Melville's corrosive assaults upon tradition and the "foundations of life," tried to starve him and then "hit upon a more exquisite revenge. It gathered in elegiac synods and whispered mysteriously: 'He went insane'"(19). The herd was wrong.[36] Second, although "the *deus ex machina* of some steadily descending Gorgon" was rejected at first as the cause of Melville's undoing, Weaver soon reconsidered. "It seems not altogether fantastic to contend that the Gorgon face that Melville bore in his heart; the goading impalpable image that made his whole life a pilgrimage of despair: that was the cold beautiful face of his mother, Maria Gansevoort. One shutters [*sic*] to think how such a charge would have violated proprieties" (MS ch. 2, 25). Gorgon's breast was as cold making as her face; it was the source of his idealizations and early snobbery. "At his mother's breast he had absorbed with her milk a vivid and exaggerated belief [that] the accidents concomitant upon birth that range men into artificial classes was ingrained in the very woof of the universe. ~~Though he later saw through the fallacy of this position, came to discard many of the paternal standards, and view life in truer colors, never did he fall into the profounder fallacy of~~" (MS ch. 2, 13–14; M&M, 38). For Weaver, Gorgon represented the enigmatic Enlightenment. He conflated Maria's proud face with that of the unnamed Isabel (the iconoclast), whose haunting face "'compounded so of hell and heaven' is the instrument by which the memory of Pierre's father is desecrated, Pierre's mother is driven to insanity and death, and Pierre himself is utterly ruined" (62–63). Weaver had almost suggested that Gorgon, an ambiguous blending of opposites, dangerously stripped him of (would-be upper-class) intellectual defenses, perhaps exposing "us" to the "profounder fallacy" of social equality. In an insert to his first draft, the full sentence (quoting *Pierre*) appears, then is truncated: "[These faces (Maria/Isabel)] compounded so of hell and heaven ~~overthrow in us all foregone persuasions; and make us wondering children in the world again.~~"

Like Melville, Weaver seemed terrified of the confusing modern woman, who, on the one hand, defends tradition (class society), turning the compassionate heart to stone; while on the other, as Maria/Isabel, she subsidizes voyages of discovery, throwing her children helplessly open to new ideas and unrealizable desires. Janus-faced, Mother has raised the mob that will erase the stabilizing past she *also* promotes. In this novel historic situation, Melville's genetic superiority will be the source of decline. Because he is "well-born," "descended from a long and prolific line of the best American stock," "one of the most distinguished of our literary assets" and therefore born rebellious like Milton's Satan, the nobly endowed patrician is mesmerized by the natural attractions of the Enlightenment—the desire for a "stupendous discovery" (259) planted by Maria and realized through Isabel. Even though Melville was not insane, he did have serious conflicts owing to an inborn "imagination of very extraordinary vigor" (338) that would clash with the facts of "an inexorable and intolerable world of reality" (19); or (always rejected), ~~Rebuffed by reality, he sought catharsis in letters, literature and in matrimony~~" (MS 13). "Held closer to reality by financial worry and hostages of wife and children, ~~his untamed imagination took a corresponding rebound, flying to the antipodes.~~" (MS 14). The primitive, no longer respecting boundaries, becomes the rage-driven prospector Ahab: everyone dies because he lacked "~~the white light of critical reason~~" (MS, ch. 13, 22). In other words, Melville wrote because he was Ahab-ishly right but immoderately so. The "mystic" transcendentalist was filled with hot romantic illusions dropped by the cold-but-seductive mother into an extraordinarily vigorous, inherited imagination. Naturally he will be disenchanted, yet Weaver also says he was "mastered by" "dreams"; Ishmael had gazed too long at the try-works (152); in other words, Weaver was not taken in by the epilogue. It was this last judgment, I suspect, that would array thousands, arrows poised, against Melville's first biographer. Ishmael must get over his Ahab fixation to write "Billy Budd," or else natural hierarchies collapse.[37]

For Weaver as New Humanist, Ishmael had been rejected by the excessive coldness of Maria and the reading public and thus propelled to the hot antipodes, merging permanently with the monstrous, yet perceptive author of *Pierre*.[38] The passages on Pierre's vertigo and blindness (quoted above) as he writes his unpublishable failed masterpiece are fully quoted in Weaver's introduction to the Boni edition of *Moby-Dick* (1925); Melville's syncope occurs in the production of *Moby-Dick* (not *Mardi*, as others have speculated). And what was Melville/Ahab/Pierre, or "the Face"? Surely not Nietzsche's coldly ascetic moderate.[39] Weaver probably meant the "Id" that read Melville with understanding and empathy but also conflict: the endangered body that merged with the common sailors, the exploited and woebegone inhabitants within "the gloomy cave" under "the hatch" and would like to do something about it, but was paralyzed by upper-class patronage. Rather than admit this obvious difficulty, scholars following Weaver have focused on the absent good father whose comforting hand would have smoothed those ruffled brows.

[From a study guide, 1964] His mother, a rather domineering woman, became even more overbearing after her husband's death, and her influence (combined with the strict Calvinism of the Dutch Reformed Church to which she belonged) seems to have inspired in Melville some of the religious skepticism and rebelliousness that runs under the surface of *Moby-Dick* and others of his works. Melville developed in his mature years a feeling that no profound mind could overlook a sense of fateful imperfection in life (one senses this attitude frequently in *Moby-Dick*), which was probably the result of the very strong Calvinistic idea of original sin.[40]

Neither Weaver nor any other Melville scholar has defended imperialism or class oppression, yet Weaver is an outcast in Melville studies. He has been charged with hero worship and imprecision, breaking New Critical rules by reading Melville's texts too literally as autobiography and exaggerating the problems in Melville's family, especially the troubled attachment of Melville and his mother. Like Melville, his frank ambivalence and inaction in the face of family mixed messages may have been his sin, not fanciful Freudianism, as second-wave Melville scholars have insisted. Such passivity was of course the sin Weaver (occasionally) attributed to Melville. There is no evidence that Weaver made a systematic study of Freud, but a Freudian would be ravished by Weaver's all-disclosing parapraxes. Weaver's shuttering was surely a response to repression. His too-brief remarks on "Billy Budd" in a late draft manuscript prompted a penciled apology to Eleanor Metcalf, suggesting that he would have preferred an Ahab-ish touch of arson (or a cry for help?) to the accommodating fade-out of the Handsome Sailor. "The very conclusion—not more than a few hundred more words—I have not yet finished. I don't want to fall flat at the end—and at this time I'm too utterly used up to get the *flare* on which I would like to end. I'm going to rest for the next few days, and get some sleep—and then come back to this again, and really finish. Please pray that I come to a good end."

    ... Weaver kindled the Melville barnfires.[41]
    —Henry Murray, notes

Upon completing his exhausting Melville labors, Weaver told Eleanor Metcalf a Disraeli biography was in the offing (were powerful Christians with Jewish blood on his mind?). However, he returned to Columbia, and though he had been offered an associate professorship at Amherst, he wrote to Erskine on June 16, 1922, in a tone of utter defeat: "[I am] very tired now—used up by piecing out my life on the stint that I am paid, and in the end, getting nowhere beyond each year a little added work and the armed forebearance of those who have blocked me." The contrast between the article of 1919 and the biography of 1921 suggests that Weaver vacillated between romanticism and neoclassical New Humanism; it was always a problem of patronage and vague institutional boundaries. Were Weaver to allow himself to be exploited, he would not only lose self-respect, he would undermine his "final prospects" (the happy ending). Conformity would be punished, separation rewarded, but how far could independence be pushed? Harry Dana, of the finest New England stock, had stood by principle and was summarily removed, perhaps ruined; Melville before him had been ostracized, barely tolerated by his family, as it seemed to both of them. Weaver did retain the warm support of the Metcalfs. The biography was a substantial achievement in the eyes of many peers (becoming a collector's item in the late 1930s); its Freudian reading, however, fed the antidemocratic, anti-Melville fulminations of Ludwig Lewisohn in 1931.[42]

Weaver's writing of the late 1920s suggests the spineless acquiescence to illegitimate authority he had earlier deplored. He dramatically adjusted his view of Melville's end in essays for *The Shorter Novels of Herman Melville* (1928) and John Macy's *American Writers on American Literature* (1931). Perhaps following Sadleir's judgment in *Excursions in Victorian Bibliography*, Weaver denounced Melville's narcissism in *Moby-Dick*, while praising the flawless "Benito Cereno," an impeccably crafted work basking in the light of "universal reason." In 1921, Weaver had read the still-unpublished "Billy Budd" as another document of disillusion, lacking "lucidity," "sparkle," and "verve." After the novella was on the market (and lauded by the British Fabian John Middleton Murry as Melville's "spiritual testament" in 1924), Weaver praised it as "a brief and appealing narrative, unmatched among Melville's work for its lucidity and inward peace." *Pierre*, the centerpiece of *Herman Melville: Mariner and Mystic* and probably an inspiration for Weaver's novel *Black Valley* (1926), with its competition between black and blonde mother figures for the pure young hero Gilson, was now compared invidiously to "Billy Budd" (but with another ambiguous ending):

Melville's primary interest is not to probe into "the mystery of iniquity," but to vindicate his ultimate faith that evil is defeat and natural goodness invincible in the affections of man. *Billy Budd*, like *Pierre*, ends in disaster and death; in each case inexperience and innocence and seraphic impulse are wrecked against the malign forces of darkness that seemed to preside over external human destiny. In *Pierre*, Melville had hurled himself, in a fury of vituperation, against the world; with *Billy Budd* he would justify the ways of God to man. Among the many parallels of contrast [sic] between these books, each is a tragedy (as was Melville's life), but in opposed senses of the term. For tragedy may be viewed not as being essentially the representation of human misery (as it is in *Billy Budd*), but rather as the representation of human goodness or nobility. There is, of course, in this latter type of tragedy, with its essential quality of encouragement and triumph, no flinching of [sic] any horror of tragic life, no shrinking of the truth by a feeble idealism, none of the compromises of the so-called "happy ending." The powers of evil and horror must be granted their fullest scope; it is only thus we can triumph over them. Even though in the end the tragic hero finds no friends among the living or the dead, no help in God, only a deluge of calamity everywhere, yet in the very intensity of his affliction he may reveal the splendor undiscoverable in any gentler fate. Here he has reached, not the bottom, but the crowning peak of fortune. Only through tragedy of this type could Melville affirm his everlasting yea. The final revelation—or great illusion—of his life, he uttered in *Billy Budd*. (205–6)

This is vintage Weaver. One might infer that he had been repeatedly spanked as a child, an excellent preparation for the academic humiliations that would follow. Although "evil is defeat," defeat is really victory, weakness is really strength; God is just when he allows "the powers of evil and horror" to overwhelm his invincibly good children; the licking will "reveal the splendor undiscoverable in any gentler fate." So Pierre, one type of tragic hero, is agitating because he said God was evil when He allowed the world to destroy human goodness; Billy Budd, another type of tragic hero, is calming because he blessed the State that was killing him. The illuminated child has returned to the lap of evil-yet-benignant authority. But Weaver erases the entire thought in the last sentence by suggesting that "the final revelation" may be "great illusion" after all. What did Weaver really think? Don't ask.

Weaver's portrait of Melville, the incorrigible moralist, was now overtly hostile. Whereas Hawthorne had initially appeared as a heartbreaking, cold, and jealous rival (1921), Weaver clearly identified with the disgusted neoclassicist in "New England Gentlemen," a docudrama printed in the *Herald Tribune*. He also revealed his own confusion and fear in the face of Melville's switches. Imaginatively reconstructing a scene where Hawthorne receives one of Melville's overheated letters, Weaver suggested that Hawthorne had recreated Melville as the reformer Hollingsworth whose pushy intimacy was fended off by Coverdale in *Blithedale Romance:*

Hawthorne did not at once open the letter. The slant and tortuous writing was only too familiar and the burden of the contents he knew to weariness. He weighed the bulky document in his hand, pained at heart, but clear in his resolve. . . . In embarrassed and almost resentful regret, Hawthorne tore open the envelope and turned through the minutely scribbled sheets, reading in snatches. . . . Probably never, as Hawthorne had been soon to learn, had he so completely misread a fellow creature. Melville's surface gayety, the vivid recitals in which he lost himself in the drama of the past vanished with alarming suddenness. In their place, torrents of repetitious and bemuddled talk about time, and eternity, and God, and free will, and ultimate destiny; a morbid dogmatism, hypersensitive, overemotional; a dogged unwillingness to learn from experience; a contempt for rationality, despite his passion for the terms of metaphysics; a nature moody, sentimental, given to strange outbursts of jocularity, but as without humor as the insane. A perplexing and intricate, a demon-haunted personality.

With Margaret Fuller, Melville was surely the most vital, the most disquieting personality Hawthorne had ever touched. Margaret was dead—drowned only recently; and Hawthorne could not but feel Providence had been kind after all, in putting her and her clownish husband and their child on board that fatal ship.[43]

Since Weaver was conflicted about his own radicalism, he may have careened between alternative readings of the Melville-Hawthorne fiasco. By juxtaposing Hawthorne's touchings with Margaret Fuller's death, Weaver could be hinting that Hawthorne has been contaminatingly stirred up, that Providence would be doing Hawthorne a favor by sinking Melville. Or Weaver could be feeling the reverse, that the successful Hawthorne's embrace was scrofulous; that by tainting Melville's pure spirit, Hawthorne deserved to be put to death, as he had drowned the Margaret Fuller character, the passionate and idealistic Zenobia in *Blithedale Romance*. In the 1931 essay he again compared the roiling ship *Melville* to the fatalistic Hawthorne, a superior man and artist: "Fired by a lust for life, a dogged unwillingness to learn from experience, a contempt for rationality, [Melville] had launched forth in search of the sea-coast of Bohemia. And always he had gone burdened with a puritan conscience" (199). Melville remained the island hopper, at least partly Ahab (clinical prober into mysteries of iniquity), but also Claggart, hating Billy's innocence, as Melville disdained Pierre's (204).

In 1936, Lionel Trilling, at that time a Trotskyist bogged down in his doctoral dissertation, heard that Weaver had led a movement to oust him from Columbia University. Weaver almost convinced his colleagues that Trilling was both too radical and too passive; as Freudian, Marxist, and Jew, the troublemaker-victim would be happier elsewhere. After Trilling exploded in wrath, then lobbied the senior professors and promised to make them proud of him, he was retained as instructor by the Department of English. Trilling completed his thesis describing Matthew Arnold as a flaming radical, felt constrained by "the Marxist yardstick," and ascended to a permanent appointment, the first one awarded to a Jew. In the surprising denouement, Weaver and Trilling "precipitously" joined hands, similarly despising careerist graduate students.[44] Other strange reversals (themselves indecisive) pervade Weaver's actions as recorded in his letters and memoirs and in the reminiscences of others:

[An undated fragment cut from a letter from Weaver to Henry Murray] I'm losing my mind again over Melville—to the point of wanting to write another book. What a man! Very sincerely, Raymond Weaver.

[Editor Robert Giroux to Charles Olson, February 28, 1946] I saw Weaver, I had the ms. [*Call Me Ishmael*] with me. He declined to look at it. He did not say why, and I was too astonished and crushed to ask, but I have since learned from reliable friends that he no longer wishes to have anything to do with Melville or writing about Melville, and will himself not write on the subject. This is confirmed by the fact (which I tell you in confidence, since the series has not yet been announced and I am not supposed to know about it) that he also declined to do the Melville book in the American Masters Series which Henry Holt is planning to do. This gives me the idea: why don't *you* do it?

[Eleanor Metcalf to Charles Olson, August 10, 1947] Raymond Weaver *wrote* me (observe, he wrote me almost a miracle, even though in answer to the poems and two letters of mine) that he had read your book. "I found it a decidedly disquieting book: but I like to think it is one of the few books on Melville that Melville himself would like." Pretty grand, it seems to me . . . .

[Eleanor Metcalf to Olson, May 24, 1948] What a curious name for him— "Tiger Weaver"! I do not know where he was born, only that his oriental associations and living were in Japan. I have heard people say that they found his eyes terrifying. That I don't understand; he was so kind, and so humorous. I wonder if anyone was ever intimate with him—if all his friends had an isolated relationship with him, that was not really intimate, only separate.

How did Tiger Weaver wish to be read? Not untruthfully, after Weaver's death Lionel Trilling told the *Columbia Spectator* his former tormentor was "personally and intensely implicated in every idea he ever dealt with. He related every moment of the classroom to life, and his vision of life was heroic." But to himself, Weaver was a poseur and spectator; he appeared to have no positive social ideas, nor did he advocate the heroic life that Trilling mentioned in his eulogy. An undated but signed typescript, the confessional "Pierrot Philosophique,"[45] describes his sole positive emotion: the pleasure of creating beautiful masks. He was the disillusioned Pierrot (a version of Cain/Canio), spurning the evangelical Protestantism that had granted women too much power; he forecast disasters associated with the loss of self-control. Pierrot's strikingly anal/vaginal master image was the dwarf-ridden black valley of industrial capitalism—the charred remnant of necessary but futile revolts against missionaries and all reformers (mothers, scientists, the modernizing bourgeoisie, socialists). Striving is pointless, for life is absurd—but underneath Weaver's hectic paganism and disclaimers, one may glimpse the despair of the puritan clown who still cares. At least one major radical writer was fond of Weaver, and Weaver treasured the ideas of at least one radical student. Joseph Freeman, ex-editor of the

New Masses, remembered him as a nurturing and devoted friend (one who had introduced him to Freud through A. A. Brill), and whose good opinion he cherished.[46] Moreover, Weaver preserved an insightful essay, "Political and Social Satire in Herman Melville," by his student David Rein (class of 1933). For Rein, the "insult and rage" of the flogging scene in *White-Jacket* was carried into *Moby-Dick*, a work that "darts an invective at the whole [commercial] system, unsurpassed in fervor by any abolitionist"; Father Mapple was a precursor to Pierre; Melville's writing on sailors reminded him of *The Communist Manifesto*. Rein did not echo Weaver's masochistic hosannas to Billy Budd, arguing instead that Melville's final acquiescence to the system reflected the limitations of his culture: Shattered faith had not yet been supplanted by belief in the possibilities of science. These remarks contradict Weaver's insistent aestheticism in "Pierrot Philosophique."[47]

Although Columbians said Weaver died of a heart condition, he was admittedly suffering from mental illness, a condition he did not conceal, unlike his friends and Columbia faculty. A few months before his death in April 1948, Weaver was treated at the Payne Whitney Clinic in New York City (apparently for a suicidal depression). Writing to Mark Van Doren, he described his symptoms as if he were the thirty-year-old Gansevoort Melville complaining of numbness, inertia, and despair in his final letter to Herman, a letter that Weaver had printed in full (*M&M*, 253–55). His novel, notes, and letters hint at disturbance. The memoir of his entrance into the Melville mysteries described Eleanor Metcalf as an "English-looking woman, with flat-heels, a raincoat, and a bad breath"; the female characters of *Black Valley* are mostly vampires. Other writings relate his choking rage when confronted by domination, betrayal, and exploitation, but above all, he is scared of hypocrisy/ mixed messages that hurdle/hurtle/herd him into the void, the uncharted waters of a boundless sea:

[From Weaver's novel *Black Valley* (58–61); Gracia West, a demonic dark-haired older woman has pried the secret of young Gilson's sexual initiation with the golden "Mrs. Burgoyne" out of him.] Gilson clenched his teeth as if steeling himself against the probe of a lancet into his very quick, and wedged his cheek between his fists, speech obliterated. "—you first tasted the mystery of life and death." Like a tongue of lightning, Mrs. West's impetuous insight had blasted through all reserve and crashed into the inner sanctuary of Gilson's heart. For one blinding moment the burning air brayed with a blood-red voice. The sky shot molten darts and reeled into black silence. And then the glittering plunge of waves against the boat, the steady vibration of the propeller, and the white railing immaculate in the sun. . . . The stiletto glint of Mrs. West's black eyes vanished into the wide and haunted vacancy of his mother's gaze. "Gilson," she said, "your eyes were so dreamy, and moist, and lucid, and pure, as you sat there lost in thought, it almost seemed that my boy was again a little child. Such innocence—"

[Weaver to Mark Van Doren (whose family he idealized), June 7, 1927] Who can tell where the lightning's going to strike! It hit me out of a clear sky . . . your [Edward Arlington] Robinson book of course. [He has tried unsuccessfully to reach him by phone; tries to send a telegram.] The operator was a son-of-a-bitch. "Your address," he said—"Falls Village, Cornwall Connecticut—there's no such place." "I can believe that," I said. "Yo' can?" he drawled, with gallows [sic] of phlegm around his wind-pipe as he drawled it. "Yo' ought to know you can't send a telegram to two places at once." With this I got mad as Hell! I wanted to tell you, as straight and as quick as I could that I was a lunatic. . . . [Weaver apparently means only his "enthusiasm" for the book.] (Mark Van Doren Papers)

[Weaver to John Erskine, March 17, 1929] [Weaver must see him.] I'm going into the hospital—and before I'm normal again, you'll be sailed.

[Weaver to Mark Van Doren, April 30, 1939, from Honolulu] As you know, I can be very slow on the pick-up. This has been true of me in my relations with these Islanders. The "best" families are descended from Missionaries—and some of these have been very hospitable to Burrell [his companion] & me. All the while I never gave a thought to the fact that Melville had expressed himself bitterly about these same missionaries—calling Dr. Judd, the ancestor of one of *the* most pretentious of the island families "a sanctimonious apothecary adventurer." I myself had never given a thought to the fact I had expressed myself contemptuously of these same missionaries.— And only the day after I had very recently been entertained by some of their descendants did I discover that the brother of my hostess (the brother being a Walter F. Fryar, an old boy, formerly governor here) had just published a pamphlet on "Anti-Missionary Criticism" instigated by Melville in particular and me in large parenthesis. Here, it seems, they still tenderly nurse at a grudge what once seemed to me self-evident truth—and now that I am reminded of it again, it still does.

The urge in me is to write you what would turn out to be a sociological treatise on this island—its extraordinarily interesting mixture of population,—its blind provincial isolation,—its internal policies, as a Chinese-Hawaiian Irishman at the university recently said, in the hands of "unscrupulous men of wealth, church-going men 'of noble missionary stock' whose grandfathers brought the word of God here, and acquired most of the land by a violation of the Seventh Commandment,"—its——if I don't choke myself off, this windy start will *land* hurdle [*sic*] me into the void. . . .

[From "Pierrot Philosophique," Weaver's undated self-portrait as a history of the West] The eager, sophisticated quick-eyed Greeks were as noble children in their envisioning of this world: staunch-hearted, sobered by a loving intimacy with nature, whom they made mistress and mother. But this ardent Homeric strength corrupted itself with barbaric splendor, and while Roman magnificence spread its broad and mighty conquest, there rose from the lowest depths of humanity the great unrest of the disregarded masses . . . a deep wild voice that gathered with whirl-wind impetuosity. . . . [After Christianity, which apotheosized pain and created sharp divisions between good and evil] came Darwin and Industrial Revolution, and in vain the ways of God cried out anew, and in querulous and hysterical disagreement, to be justified to man. . . . The broad earth, that once was trod in the calm of self-trusting integrity with proud adventurous purpose, blackened its valleys with a race inglorious alike in its birth and its living: a puny people, small and morbidly self-conscious in its lives, and vulgar in its pleasures: a spawn that made a fetish of riches, and mocked its vaunted freedom by slavery to Mammon. It was in such . . . times that Pierrot . . . was born . . . the changeling of our modern days. Of his parentage, we know nothing. . . . While still a youth, Pierrot's adolescent sympathies were stirred by the strange mystery of the suffering that he saw on all sides of him. . . . [Everything is in flux.] His dignity, he felt, lay not in what he did, but in what he understood. Yet within him, constant among change, was the observant eye before which all passed in phantasmagoria: a passive spectator ever alert in the silent theater of his mind. . . . And so it was that he formulated to himself as ideal, the role of idler, spectator and poseur. . . . He saw the epic absurdity of any concern to improve either people or things. . . . He was an artist at heart, and amusingly repellent did he find the intemperance of reformers and the deluded ebulition of men burning with "missions." . . . He sought to win what joyn [*sic*] he could from beautiful masks. . . . Thus lives Pierrot, the tireless idler, the sad commedian [*sic*], the tragically sincere poseur. This is to have failed in life, perhaps—but with what a grace!

[H. R. Steeves to Mark Van Doren, July 10, 1946] Probably you have not heard, unless in a roundabout way, that Raymond had last week a threatening heart attack. *Fortunately, the worst of it came while he was actually in a specialist's hands and in the hospital* . . . the trouble is diagnosed as coronary occlusion. But the prognosis is good if Raymond will consent to manage his energies carefully. And the convalescence will be a slow one. I think he is re-signed to this, and naturally he knows that we will want him to take care of himself. He is now in a better state of mind, perhaps, than he has been in some time. His physical condition is good too. (Emphasis added)

[Weaver to Mark Van Doren, January 31, 1948, from Payne Whitney Clinic] ... When I went to the hospital in July, two years ago, I had already come to an abiding feeling of devitalization, and to a stoical resolution that I had no choice but to drive myself against a kind of leaden irresolution that nothing I was doing was really worth doing at all: a stoical enactment that brought none of the compensations of feeling even self-righteous. My mind rebelled at this—*seeing myself in a kind icy detachment,* but powerless to change what it viewed: and this in a kind of bottomless regression. This, with an abiding dizziness and vague nausea. My doctors achieved nothing to change any of these—so in desperation I went to [anonymous patient's] doctor who had so improved her by electric shock. I saw him three times . . . when I expected him to schedule me for his kind of electrication [*sic*]. But he had decided other-wise. . . . As for these recent twelve days—the whole staff of the hospital, I sometimes feel, seems to be working on me, soma and psyche, and with decided improvements in to date. . . . The routine of the days—that I shall not bore you with. *Though sometimes I ask myself if it may not become insideously* [sic] *demoralizing, this almost perfect consideration and sheltering with nurturing.* (Emphasis added.)

For Pierrot, Nature was mistress and mother to moderate Greeks; but, tenderly nursing a grudge, she turns on her children: "Out of a clear sky" the lancet probes, lightning strikes. The "broad earth" sets fires, producing deluded missionaries or a "vaunted freedom" that only enslaves. Weaver's last letter to Mark Van Doren, however, suggests a struggle against Pierrot's "kind icy detachment." Weaver was an enigma to later Melvilleans, but his conflicts may be typical of middle managers torn between classes, economically and emotionally dependent on conservatives, masquerading as nihilists and playing the fool. "Joyned" only to the beautiful mask, Weaver's role filled him with self-loathing and emptiness or rage when asked to send a telegram to two places at once, and left his faithful friend Eleanor Metcalf (who could have been talking about Melville's feelings of estrangement from the family) wistfully bewildered. And yet Pierrot's not-so-suppressed indignation had left its mark on Lionel Trilling, arousing feelings that the university, while claiming to develop critical intellectuals, was in fact crushing, not energizing, the critical spirit. Five months after Weaver's death, Trilling wrote to his former student Rich-ard Chase:

I'm really wearying of the critical posture. It means a public life and public poses and strange irrelevant disputes and I no longer want them. I don't
know whether I'm responding to a cultural trend, the internal petering out
of the critical impulse, or responding to something within myself wholly. I
did a queer thing: I was sent by Phil Rice five Kenyon School student essays
to pick the best for the contest. I picked it and sent the whole batch back with
a letter damning their snide little competence and asking if this was what
the school was going to turn out. Phil wrote me long alarmed letters, pointing out that these were but students, that the school was really all right; John
more wisely wrote with bland humor. I told them both not to pay any heed to
me. I don't know why I popped—some deep, deep impatience with my own
intellectual life: with maybe, intellectual life in general as it is institutionally
lived, the techniques learned and practiced. Is this what Raymond Weaver
was up to in his strange way when he used to attack the intellectual students?
I feel that if things keep developing in me in the present direction I won't be
able to teach very much longer. I begin to wonder if my students, especially
my graduate students, can detect the balefulness in my eye, my wish to basilisk them out of the office. I am now a Popular Professor; I'm treated with a
hideous kind of respect; the students think I have a Secret to impart; I think
they become angry with me when I don't impart it; I think the secret is how
to become a Popular Professor. For the first time I really know what it means
about the tigers of wrath and the horse of instruction.[48]

Notwithstanding the intimacy and eloquence of this revelation, Trilling might
have shocked and angered Chase, who, in a confessional (and unpublished) essay
of 1945, had scathingly accused himself of shallowness and incompetence, blaming
his upper-class education. In 1949, Chase had written to his wife from a summer
conference for New Critics at Kenyon College, indicating that he was unsettled by
the basilisk eyes of the radical English critic William Empson—in response perhaps
exculpating himself by identification with the survivor Ishmael, not with the
confidence man Ahab whom he had identified as a false Prometheus in his Melville criticism of 1947 and 1949. Perhaps the revered mentor Trilling (in the letter
about the strange Weaver and himself) was reversing advice about the satisfactions of an academic career. In 1957, Chase counterattacked in *Partisan Review* with
a story mocking the hypermoralism of a "student" named Silverman.[49] In his letter
to Chase of March 21, 1957 (appended), Trilling denied he had given Chase cause to
believe he had ever supposed that Starbuck was a better man than Ahab. It was
Hawthorne and Melville all over again, but with the ages reversed. If *Clarel* is to
be trusted as an inside narrative of their friendship, Hawthorne (Vine) had been
put off by his friend's passionate youthful idealism, stabbed perhaps by Melville's

all-seeing basilisk eye and by the inscription to himself in *Moby-Dick*, which by implication overestimated the disinterestedness of Hawthorne's "genius." Melville would have felt sharply abandoned when his idol and inspiration turned out not to share the integrity of Ahab, but instead harbored the unpardonably vulgar sin of ambition (Captain Vere's shameful, deepest secret, and a quality of the upstart Claggart as well).

I have argued that the structural constraints of academe shaped Weaver's reading of Melville. For aristocratic radicals, the bourgeoisie was never a progressive class. Such a lofty posture would not endanger authority in the university, for the aristocratic perspective was inevitably blackened by a future in which it could play no creative role. The ideological weapon of dispossessed aristocrats was the terror gothic narrative that stabbed at the heart of the rising class by discrediting the validity of the material world as a source of reliable guidance. Autodidacts could stick with their betters or drop into the abyss. As long as anti-bourgeois criticism led nowhere, it would serve the needs of ruling groups that wanted the aura of a critical intelligentsia but not the mobilization of students who would chart the shifting constraints and opportunities of historically specific institutions in order to devise effective tactics for change. The young father of Melville criticism was insightful about the problematic family, but since evil was so muscular and goodness so feeble, Ahab could only fall to the deck in a helpless spasm of rage. The anti-bourgeois Nietzschean could not discern Ahab's jabs at the whale as a blow for democracy against illegitimate authority, his quest for the whole as the Lockean demand that the state or any other bureaucracy disclose its closely guarded secrets to thoughtful, deliberative bodies of citizen-kings, bodies who would eschew factions, who would love peace, who would refuse simply to follow their leader.

[Julien Benda, *La trahison des clercs* (The Betrayal of the Intellectuals), 1928] ... we have to admit that the "clerks" now exercise political passions with all the characteristics of passion—the tendency to action, the thirst for immediate results, the exclusive preoccupation with the desired end, the scorn for argument, the excess, the hatred, the fixed ideas. The modern "clerk" has entirely ceased to let the layman alone descend to the market place. The modern clerk is determined to have the soul of a citizen and make vigorous use of it; he is proud of that soul; his literature is filled with contempt for the man who shuts himself up with art or science and takes no interest in the passions of the State.... And then especially, the "clerk" by adopting political passions, brings them the tremendous influence of his sensibility if he is an artist, of his persuasive power if he is a thinker, and in either case his moral prestige.[50]

[Ad from Tiffany & Co., Beverly Hills, mid-1970s, another instance of "The Try-Works"] TRY GOD This is a limited edition; that is, limited to people who believe in God. A pendant for women and a pin for both men and women of Tiffany sterling silver or Vermeil. The entire proceeds will be donated by Tiffany to the Walter Hoving Home, Inc., in Garrison, New York— a non-sectarian center for drug-addicted and seriously troubled girls—where, after a year's treatment, over ninety percent are permanently cured by accepting God into their lives. In sterling silver, $10. Vermeil, $12.

Pierrot advertises a satanic cruise on the dark ragged edge of female genitalia. His disturbing reading of Melville's life and art, though immediately controversial, held the field until it was buffeted by conservatives whose nervous efforts accelerated during the middle and late 1930s.[51] It was not, however, Weaver's notion of an aristocratic anticapitalist Ahab that bothered them. Stanley T. Williams would use exactly that model in his anthology of 1937, *The American Mind*. Amor threatened because Weaver drew attention to the troubled nature of all Melville's close attachments, a focus associated during the 1920s with Freudian explorations. The intertwining of the Melville family, homoerotic relations with Hawthorne, and the act of writing itself may have agitated Weaver's opponents. Ishmael must not have been mastered by dreams as Weaver had claimed; he must not have been infiltrated by Ahab's moral commitment to social equality (as understood by the radical bourgeoisie). If Melville had been so terminally "disturbed," how could the later writing, presumably more mature and resigned, be defended? Weaver's intellectual descendants Eleanor Melville Metcalf and Paul C. Metcalf, similarly stressing unresolved conflicts inside Melville, have tended to be tolerated rather than assimilated into official postwar Melville criticism. As Eleanor Metcalf reminded Charles Olson, "Billy Budd" was no testament of acceptance: "The bitterest criticism of 'this man-of-war world' remains."[52]

Conservatives are people with wildly rebellious feelings which they repress, remarked Leo Lowenthal, quoting G. V. Plekhanov and trying to explain the protofascist Knut Hamsen's appeal to readers of divergent political tendencies.[53] No Melvillean has applied this definition to himself, perhaps because Ivy League–trained academics, like all middle managers, are forced to conceal their outrage for the sake of institutional legitimacy. Melville's family can be seen as structurally analogous to the elite university insofar as both socializing institutions have dominated and confused, rather than instructed, their inmates; insofar as they have refused to recognize contradictory and irreconcilable demands for truth and order, independence and loyalty—certainly the case at Columbia in 1917. Melville's portrayals of the ambivalence, loneliness, and despair generated in genteel Christian families might make readers too romantically upset; perhaps it has drawn such famous radicals as Lewis Mumford and Newton Arvin to corrective neoclassicism and tight lacing. Both Mumford's and Arvin's Melville studies concluded with Billy's blessing of Captain Vere; Arvin's emphasized an erotic surrender. But Mumford's and Arvin's happy endings were only pauses for the artist; Billy's blessing was offset by the sailor-poet who commemorated "Billy in the Darbies."

Some crumpled pages of a pamphlet are discovered by Pierre on the seat of their getaway coach, as he, Isabel, and Delly flee the ancestral estate, rejecting the hypocrisy and coldness of Mary Glendinning and the genteel culture she represents. As a foil to the Isabel letter, the pamphlet, *Chronometricals and Horologicals*, authored by one Plotinus Plinlimmon, praises "virtuous expediency" as the via media that reconciles heavenly and earthly morality. Henry Murray voiced the Hawthorne-Plinlimmon line in his introduction to *Pierre* (1949), taking Melville to task for "[letting] Pierre off rather easily." Murray, his medical credentials in hand, roared at Melville the subversive (a regular Harry Dana), who should have unequivocally condemned this "narcist" and "spoiled brat." "[*Chronometricals and Horologicals*] ignores some of the most deadly errors and vices of the fanatical enthusiast: the injuries he does to others, the self-deceptions which blind him to essential truths, the hidden egotism which cancerously invades his heart, the progressive estrangement which brings him to misanthropy, and, not least, the damaging effects of the disguised sexual component." Murray's Pierre (with his unrecognized yen for home-wrecking Isabel) sounds like more recent rebels at Columbia. The devastating Columbia strike of spring 1968 was prompted by similar contradictions between democratic theory and institutional practice (or so the strikers thought); it was a thicket of Ahabs and Pierres, the monomaniacal children, the overreachers, the spoiled brats parented by Rousseau and Spock, bringing on the dark days of democracy. The student strikers were caricatured in *Columbia College Today* as hippos, rhinos, baboons, bats, pigs, lions, mules, bears, and other refusers of the great tradition, overseen by Rousseau (her)self.[54]

Contemplating the smoking ruins and reminiscing mistily about the bracing and preventive pedagogy of English professors Mark Van Doren and Raymond Weaver, Columbia graduate Charles Simmons confided to *New York Times* readers in 1972, "I have this wild notion that if [Van Doren and Weaver] had been around, Columbia would still be an important college and maybe Mark Rudd would have become an important person." Simmons had studied Shakespeare in 1942: his last indulgence before going off to fight fascism. The students had adored Van Doren, but he was departing to write "A Liberal Education" and had asked Weaver to take over the class: "I know of no one who understands Shakespeare better than Raymond Weaver," reassured Van Doren. Simmons heaped praise upon Weaver, noting his "stentorian," "measured," "mannered" style; "—Weaver had us in his hand";

Weaver "tested them terribly." "'What-a ... did-a ... Timon ... *want*'? The question would be dropped like a boulder on the class. Weaver's awful blue eyes would fix on a student, who would rise and deliver an answer he himself didn't know he was capable of."[55] Simmons shamelessly concluded his memoir with a report that the punctilious Mark Van Doren changed his grade from A- to A upon reading Simmons's favorable review of Van Doren's *Introduction to Poetry* twenty-five years later. For these stoics, great institutions are safe from decline when pleasure (the absorption of a Great Writer) is described in words that connote fear and pain, and where fathers and sons are thoughtful, attentive, grateful, and productive, under conditions that some might describe as infused with emotional terror and where students are moved by carrots and sticks. How odd it all seems! (as Michael Sadleir's father exclaimed in the face of nineteenth-century English working-class agitation). In the same issue of the *New York Times Book Review* carrying the Simmons encomium, psychiatrist Robert Jay Lifton reviewed Walter Langer's *The Mind of Adolf Hitler: The Secret Wartime Report*, which had criticized (but also admired) Hitler's efficacy in molding the (feminized) German people to join his evil purpose (23). Lifton thought Hitler's appeals to the irrational were dangerous and helped create brutes, but Simmons thought Weaver's (irrational) appeals to future elites were making men.

I have traced here and throughout the aristocratic radical argument that mass culture and mass politics produce totalitarianism. From the point of view of the displaced elite, this makes sense, for they will no longer be in control; at best, should they participate in "bourgeois society," they will be held accountable to inferiors demanding institutional transparency: The old irrationalism will no longer persuade or overawe the democratic polity. No less than the forgers of the ever popular *Protocols of the Elders of Zion*, reactionary intellectuals allege that all revolutions since 1789 have been cynically masterminded by divisive Jews, or Victorian Women and their feminized consorts.[56] It was Maria Melville or Ahab or Mary Glendinning or "Old Bach" or Banadonna who produced the automata fabricated in the absence of the organicist fathers of the "vital centre," banging the drum that drilled the New Hun of the Paris Commune. Logically, Charles Simmons should join the Langer team and propose that World War II could have been averted if Hitler had read Shakespeare instead of Karl May's stories of the Wild West; that Hitler was the Frankensteinian creation of the usurping mass rather than the tool of elite theorists embracing high culture and aristodemocracy or neo-aristocracy. But Hitler was a neoclassicist, not an Ahab or Babo, not a Dionysiac rebel, as Murray, Langer, and other corporatists have claimed. As in the imagery of the *echt* eugenicists and Social Darwinists William McDougall and Lothrop Stoddard, Hitler was portrayed (in Germany) as a centaur, dominating, not yielding, to his baser passions; Hitler's propaganda image was Apollonian: Hitler austerely defined progress as the ongoing purposeful process of race cleansing to produce more geniuses and to destroy the hapless weak and unfit. The New Order would leave the rubble of the romantic mixed-up Jewish-Marxist night behind. In *Mein Kampf* Hitler denounced sentimental culture; like mass media, it was a tool of the Jews, propagating the big lie.

> I know of no author who has succeeded in so thoroughly stamping his words with his own individuality—and in so thoroughly impressing a sympathetic reader with the conviction of the fine enthusiastic spirit of the writer. To read his words should be the cause of much enlargement of freedom and blitheness.[57]
> —English Melvillean James Billson to Raymond Weaver, July 18, 1921

Prior to this study, there has been no systematic attempt to interrogate the conflation of Melville, Ahab, America, and Hitler by corporatists and their Stalinist allies. Archival evidence, however, has blurred boundaries established by leading Melville scholars after the mid-1930s; their analytic categories have only masked the underlying political dynamic. Led by Jay Leyda after 1945, the "objectivist" or "fact-minded" second phase of the Melville Revival defined itself against the excesses of the "subjectivists" or "imaginative" critics.[58] Their 1920s list consisted of Weaver, Murray, and Mumford, then expanded to include writers publishing after the war: Charles Olson (1947), Richard Chase (1949), Newton Arvin (1950), and Edwin Haviland Miller (1975). Allegedly following Weaver, the latter were guilty of liberal Freudian interpretations merging art and life: They had read the fiction too literally as autobiography, exaggerated Melville's suffering in the family, and mistakenly inferred a homosexual attachment to Hawthorne. The post-Weaver scholarship, however, might better be seen as a flight from the impressiveness of a "fine enthusiastic spirit," one all too given to unraveling the ties that bind the lower orders. The Melville criticism of John Freeman, Lewis Mumford, Charles Olson, Willard Thorp, F. O. Matthiessen, and Henry Murray diverged from early Weaver by increasingly separating Melville from Ahab and Pierre and by joining Melville to his most corporatist characters, Ishmael, Ungar, and Captain Vere. This post-Weaver group (like their favorite characters) shadowed the egotistical sublime (the panoramic imagination of the revolutionary bourgeoisie) while glorifying obscurantism tricked out as poetic science. Negative capability and conservative Enlightenment reconstructed the lovely, tolerant, pluralist family that shuddered under Melville's/Ahab's probing, materialist, comprehensive, therefore totalitarian, gaze. The counter-Reformation in Melville studies assumed Ahab's role of Enlightenment demystifier to unmask Ahab/America as Hitler, a joint achievement of Charles Olson, Henry A. Murray, and Jay Leyda. The remainder of this book stakes my disturbing claim.

7

Pluralism in One Perfectly Happy Family, 1926–1953

A Peep at Apes and Angels

No critic who is himself a scrupulous and integrated mind can regard Catholicism and Marxism—to cite a pair of contemporary options—as equally tenable readings of reality. Privately, he must have arrived at the decision that one exceeds the other in maturity and coherence; and, as between two hypothetically equal writers, the one a Catholic and the other a Marxist, he must consider the "true believer" to be the greater, though this certainly need not mean that the critic will use his author, whether "orthodox" or "heretical," as the occasion for doctrinal homily.
—Austin Warren, 1941

What a madness and anguish it is, that an author can never—under no conceivable circumstances—be at all frank with his readers!
—Herman Melville to Evert Duyckinck, epigraph to John Freeman, *Herman Melville*, 1

Following the publication of the Weaver study (1921), two more popular biographies were published during the 1920s Melville Revival. The first post-Weaver retreat was written in 1926 by John Freeman (1880–1929). Melville and Walt Whitman were the two Americans included in the Macmillan English Men of Letters series edited by Sir John Collings Squire, the well-known poet and editor of the *London Mercury*.[1] Squire assigned the Melville biography to Freeman. Like Squire, thoroughly Tory in his politics and sensibility, John Freeman was both an insurance executive and a poet, pursuits he kept separate; friends and associates had no idea he was leading a double life.[2] An admirer of Wordsworth and Blake (127), he shared their distrust of "common sensuous apprehension" (183) or, as he termed it elsewhere, "the disease of thought [that] had assailed Melville himself" and which "the energy of imagination rose to resist" in his masterpiece *Moby-Dick* (126). Freeman began his study with the announcement that Melville was "the most powerful of all the great American writers" (1), then moved almost immediately to a refutation of Weaver's claim that *Pierre, or The Ambiguities* disclosed the malignant tie to Maria Gansevoort Melville that explained her son's secrets and silences. Freeman's remarks may reveal the source of Melvillean malaise in families that sharply forbade critical scrutiny of parents:

> It is proper to state at once that while that character, in *Pierre*, may quite truly contain hints and figures of Melville's mother, a difficulty still remains; for our author was a great imaginative artist, drawing with a free and wanton hand, using the most fantastic liberties when he pleased, and seldom constrained to mere literality. *Pierre* is a wild, vague, painful book, and of all the "ambiguities" of its alternative title none is so questionable as the identity of Mrs. Glendinning and his mother. Another reason for doubting whether Herman would indeed paint his mother's picture so darkly, under the name of another, is that *Pierre* was published in 1852, while she was yet alive and indeed, as Mr. Weaver himself remarks, was living mainly with her son. It is inconceivable that he should write so of her while she lived, or that if the portrait was recognizable it was not recognized, and resented, by the mother herself, and all the more because of that imputed pride and cold arrogance. But there is no reference to a rupture of affection within public knowledge. . . . Speculative biography is dangerous. (3–4)

As he went on, mentioning Maria Gansevoort Melville's "remoteness from those idealizations to which Herman's mind always tended," Freeman reported a disturbing family rumor suggesting that there *had* been a "rupture of affection": "It is said that once, in speaking of her, Melville had exclaimed that his mother had hated him" (4). And Freeman shuddered while discussing the overly cerebral *Clarel:* "And often, too often, the discussion [in *Clarel*] takes on the sad colours of dissent and division, and even the Epilogue is choked with phrases of *faith v. evolution:* 'science the feud can only aggravate'—the feud between ape and angel" (168). However guardedly, both Melville and Weaver had refused to reconcile the irreconcilable, even if it made "the family" very angry; families are understood to represent classes and their relations with subordinates. Freeman's antipathy to "the sad colours of dissent and division" in the family, previewed in his opening chapter, is the key to his evaluations of Melville's uneven oeuvre. Spurning the "pictorial prose" of nineteenth-century Victorian writers (171), Freeman had annexed Melville to the English tradition of rhythmic language, characterized for him "by the wave-like motion, on which the reader is borne into a serene acceptance and understanding" (175–76). Such musicality was epitomized in "Billy Budd," which, in Freeman's account, ended with Billy's ascent to heaven, followed by the body's perfect passivity hanging on the yard-end.

An allergy to Melville's switches in style (for example, after the first section of *Mardi*), a habit linked to his (Ahab-ish?) "autocratic will" and "passion for speculation" (100–101), erupted in Freeman's reaction to *Pierre:* "He had thrown aside the enchanter's wand when he finished *Redburn*, and now bore a serpent. The psychology is intolerably followed, with the sly and thirsty fury of a stoat; nothing outside the Russians could be more subtle or less scrupulous. 'I write precisely as I please,' he cries, breaking in on the narrative; and in this scorn of others he has written a book which may move deeply but cannot please any one" (112).

Melville as historian and sociologist masterfully managed scale; his maps situate personal troubles in macro-structures and conflicts of long duration; when he refocuses on the personal, his concrete experience radiates enlarged significance. At some level, Freeman seems to have appreciated the soaring and swooping, for instance in his enthused comparison of *Moby-Dick* and *Paradise Lost* (116–17, 131). But as in the case of other Melvilleans before and since, Freeman preferred to get away when art and life were too closely joined. After repeating that "Melville is the most powerful of all the great American writers," Freeman ended his book with (puritan[3]) Melville as a forbidding representation of the American sublime:

It is, nevertheless, not quite easy to see his work, or himself in his work, except in an image and at a little distance. The needed image is the simplest— that of a mountain or shape of mountain-like proportions, rising from a confused plain into confused cloud; a dark irregular formation with deep forests and falling waters and chasms that seem like mere defeats of creation; facing the east an abundance of green pasture, and to the west a wild mystery of incumbent shape and shadow. At times the head is obscure, at times clear, according as you look through glasses or without them, and see the mountain simply or with perverse prepossessions. The great mass is lonely and silent, as all places of natural growth or upheaval; it is heaved out of American soil, sustained by and in turn sustaining native resources. The brightness is never delusive, for in Melville's youthful, impetuous books, such as *Typee* and *Redburn*, there is no more than there seems, and symbols have not yet seduced him; but the western shadows are strange, and the forest growth of *Moby-Dick* and *Pierre* is painful, haunted, and unholy. (187)

Troubled by his weak heart, Freeman died young, his body planted in the green pasture of a country graveyard.

—What say of it? What say [of] CONSCIENCE grim. That spectre in my
path?[4]

—Edgar Allen Poe, "William Wilson"

Enforced idealization can only lead to switching as illusions of perfect harmony
crumble into "mere literality": all authority becomes unreliable and punitive. Melville certainly did have a problem with retaliation and guilt. In *Pierre*, Mrs. Glendinning hurls a fork at her portrait; its tines pierce her painted breast after Pierre
has defied her. He has read the left-wing of her mixed message by following truth
and Christian virtue, not her orders to protect the family image. She later dies of
grief, throwing Pierre into deep and self-punishing remorse. In life (it was said),
Maria called Dr. Holmes to examine Herman for insanity after the strange book was
published—a juicy secret Weaver may have passed on. Switches bothered both
Freeman and his young reader Charles Olson. Freeman's short story "The Change"
was published posthumously in Squire's *London Mercury;* it was a tale told by a
lunatic whose wife/mother has abruptly become his persecutor:

Hardly was the honeymoon over before he saw what had since obscured
everything else. Had it not been hateful, her nose would have been merely extraordinary. It was a long curve, like a scimitar, with rather a blunter end. But
for the enormous strength of so perfect an arc, you would have thought that
trestles upward and outward from her chin were necessary for its support.
When she was very pleased (but that was not often) she lifted it into the
air. When she was angry she lowered it like a scythe, and had the trick of
whetting it (as it were) with her fingers. The nostrils were close and cut up
slightly, leaving a narrow pink middle dependency that provoked strange fancies. He took it for a symbol of ferocity, twitching into activity whenever he
spoke. Far beyond the point of her nose the cold eyes slept. "They're ice, not
jelly," was his judgment, and he only knew he was wrong when they pro-
truded slightly.... "I can't think why you've changed so to me," she had said
to him once. "I haven't changed," he muttered—and thought it was a virtuous lie. "*You've* changed—physically, I mean." . . . He stared at her unflinch-
ingly, the first time for years. . . . Her nose still sprang forward, cutting at you,
pinning you down to what you had said a moment or a year before. . . . Why
had he come back? It was so hard to escape again. She showed him that
he wasn't trusted (though it was weeks since he had looked at her); and in
everything he saw, for lack of anything clearer, an inscrutable punishment.
He didn't know what he had ever done in his timid life to deserve punishment; but of course, that was the point: one never did. He teased himself to
recall tiny crimes of his youth which now screamed for expiation.[5]

At left: Charles Olson as a young man with an unidentified companion, 1930s, and pitching hay (*below*) at "Enniscorthy," in Keene, Virginia, summer 1946. Charles Olson Papers, Archives and Special Collections, Thomas J. Dodd Research Center, University of Connecticut Libraries.

Similarly terrorized by materialist noses, Charles Olson wished that *Pierre* had been published anonymously, then mentioned his discomfiture as Pierre changes from "a sweet, ingenuous, robust young man to a bitter, insane, half-blind, epileptic murderer" ("Growth of Herman Melville," 157–58).

The second post-Weaver study was written by Lewis Mumford. For many in the 1960s counterculture, Mumford is a hero: the warmly empathic and protective nature lover whose strolls down country lanes are contrasted with the shallow entertainments of armored urbanites. By rescuing the achievements of post-adolescent Melville, Freeman and Mumford reconstructed the pastoral idyll or Garden City that Melville, Ahab, and Weaver were wont to demolish. Aesthetic judgments were entangled with psychological and political considerations. As corporatists, both men underestimated or glossed over real divisions within the family, while longings for unattainable unity led them to quietistic readings of "Billy Budd."[6] These were major disagreements, and they raise questions about Weaver's interactions with his supposed followers in the 1920s. The record shows that Mumford and Weaver saw each other as polite antagonists; their opposition was well known to contemporaries.[7] As shown above, Weaver himself was inconsistent in his judgments, but he never shared the primitivism of other 1920s revivers with their fix on the childlike Marquesan nymph Fayaway. And yet he bowed to Henry Murray's primitivist mysticism. Herman Melville's horoscope, drawn at Murray's request, reposes in Weaver's papers at Columbia. The man who would later psychoanalyze Hitler for FDR, linking him as romantic artist-criminal to Lord Byron, Al Capone, and Melville, told Weaver around 1927:

> I am most desirous of investigating the Oracle of Horoscopes[.] Herman M was born at 11:30 P.M. August 1, 1819—I should like to know the position of the stars on that date etc., & the Lady's interpretation as well. Also as a control my own—Sat. May 13, 1893 I think in early AM before sunrise.
>
> It was the custom among some people to have their horoscopes read & then in a monstrous frenzied orgy—defy the fates & the stacked cards & swear defiance.
>
> Does handwriting come into this game?
>
> I hope you will make an appointment with the Lady[.]
>
> My memory is not quite clear—except I was intrigued by what you said on the subject.[8]

Matching horoscopes is not a scientific experiment, but Murray would compare his chart to Melville's "as a control," indeed. Such escapades were safety valves for the corporatist Murray, as they were perhaps for his close friend (and rival) Lewis Mumford.[9] Before proceeding to Mumford's contribution to Melville studies, some competing versions of the unconscious mind as promulgated during the years immediately preceding and following the Great War are reviewed below.

A TRIBE OF ISHMAELS

Too often the Melville problem has been reduced to whether or not his texts are transcriptions of his life, as if he were a journalist, more or less failed in accurate representation of his specific experience. As my research has shown, the purpose of such exercises was not always a scrupulous New Critical distinction between literature and biography made in the interest of "literariness," but an indignant unmasking of a prevaricating propagandist for The People. But Melville had rejected the latter role, at least in his more mature pronouncements: He was not deploying gods and devils to manipulate the audience, but reeling in his readers while he disentangled our common inner lives, family histories, and a macro-history of social transformation. Or so he said. There is a much-quoted passage in *The Confidence-Man* where the narrator directly addresses the question of realism. He disavows the dullness of "severe fidelity to real life" that one class of readers prefers:

There is another class, and with this class we side, who sit down to a work of amusement tolerantly as they sit at a play, and with much the same expectations and feelings. They look that fancy shall evoke scenes different from those of the same old crowd round the customs-house counter, and same old dishes on the boarding-house table, with characters unlike those of the same old acquaintances they meet in the same old way every day in the same old street. And, as, in real life, the proprieties will not allow people to act out themselves with that unreserve permitted to the stage; so, in books of fiction, they look not only for more entertainment, but, at bottom, even for more reality, than real life itself can show. Thus, though they want novelty, they want nature, too; but nature unfettered, exhilarated, in effect transformed. In this way of thinking, the people in a fiction, like the people in a play, must dress as nobody exactly dresses, talk as nobody exactly talks, act as nobody exactly acts. It is with fiction as with religion: it should present another world, and yet one to which we feel the tie.[10]

In this rich paragraph, Melville has further elucidated the meaning of his lines, ropes, and ties. As artist, he will not embroider myths that previous societies had passed along or invented to integrate the past with the present or the individual with society. In a statement reminiscent of Ahab's jabs with his hickory harpoon, he wants "even . . . more reality, than real life itself can show." Melville will use his fancy to invent refreshing new scenes, the better to probe the hidden meanings concealed by slick facades in the world we think we see around us. The fanciful imagination is not a misty obstacle to perception but the potential decoder and guide to mediations between subject and object. Melville's philosophy of hyperrealism, so charmingly stated, would have to threaten any and all illegitimate ruling groups. The problem for his class of artist was, first, to possess the vision capable of discovering the secrets of nature (including human nature), and, second, the imagination that could realize his discoveries in exciting new forms, challenging the reader to think and feel in unexpected ways. He sees the explicit artifice of theater as the proper model for emancipating fiction. Like other self-reflexive modernists, his narrators are characters whose perceptions are to be questioned and judged by readers; they are neither omniscient nor invisible. Melville's fictions that look more toward theater than narrative would appropriate the power of myth and symbol, but not the power of dissimulation and bondage that godlike conservatives preferred, that their notions of "the proprieties" had perpetuated.

When Melville looks into the knotted relations between children and parents, or sailors and officers, or writers and publishers, or writers and readers, he is contemplating problems of power and authority that neither capitalist democracies nor socialist movements have adequately confronted. What society has ever trained all its citizens in critical thought or in the imaginative reconstruction of history along the lines Melville has suggested? What university has ever delivered unbounded academic freedom, insisting that students and teachers "act out themselves" by speaking their minds in a protected, nonpunitive environment? How many high school or undergraduate history courses transmit the full range of debate raging within their profession, so that students may discern the subtle or hidden differences between competing ideologies? We should not be shocked by the anxieties of Melville scholars as they have leaked onto these pages.

[Melville to Duyckinck, March 3, 1849] I could readily see in Emerson, notwithstanding his merit, a gaping flaw. It was, the insinuation, that had he lived in those days when the world was made, he might have offered some valuable suggestions. These men are all cracked across the brow. And never will the pullers-down be able to cope with the builders-up. And this pulling-down is easy enough—a keg of powder blew up Block's Monument—but the man who applied the match, could not, alone, build such a pile to save his soul from the shark-maw of the Devil. But enough of this Plato who talks thro' his nose. To one of your habits of thought, I confess that in my last, I seemed, but only *seemed* irreverent. And do not think, my boy, that because I impulsively broke forth in jubilations over Shakspeare, that, therefore, I am of the number of *snobs* who burn their tuns of rancid fat at his shrine. No,

I would stand afar off & alone, & burn some pure Palm oil, the product of
some overtopping trunk.

I would to God Shakspeare had lived later, & promenaded in Broadway.
Not that I might have had the pleasure of leaving my card for him at the
Astor, or made merry with him over a bowl of the fine Duyckinck punch; but
that the muzzle which all men wore on their souls in the Elizabethan day,
might not have intercepted Shakspers full articulations. For I hold it a verity,
that even Shakspeare was not a frank man to the uttermost. And, indeed,
who in this intolerant Universe is or can be? But the Declaration of Independence makes a difference.[11]

Relying on this and similar statements, I have read a muzzled author respectful
of the labor and experience that constructed enduring institutions, while determined to speak his mind about their flaws, withholding nothing. Whereas Melville
publicly reveled in his strategy for achieving both candor and self-protection
in the service of human emancipation and solidarity, some of his revivers, for instance, Mumford and his circle, expected a more private public service, a different
sort of guide to the collective unconscious, to the teeming racial masses crowded
into tenements.

Marja Si! Isabel No!

Those who hold and those who are without property have ever formed
distinct interests in society. Those who are creditors, and those who are
debtors, fall under a like discrimination. A landed interest, a manufacturing
interest, a mercantile interest, a moneyed interest, with many lesser
interests, grow up of necessity in civilized nations, and divide them into
different classes, actuated by different sentiments and views. The regulation
of these various and interfering interests forms the principle task of modern
legislation and involves the spirit of party and faction in the necessary and
ordinary operations of government. . . .

If a faction consists of less than a majority, relief is supplied by the
republican principle, which enables the majority to defeat its sinister views
by regular vote. It may clog the administration, it may convulse the society;
but it will be unable to execute and mask its violence under the forms of
the Constitution. When a majority is included in a faction, the form of
popular government, on the other hand, enables it to sacrifice to its ruling
passion or interests both the public good and the rights of other citizens.
To secure the public good and private rights against the danger of such a
faction, *and at the same time* to preserve the spirit and form of popular

government, is then the great object to which our inquiries are directed. (Emphasis added.)

—Publius, in James Madison, "Federalist Paper No. 10"

If the great forces which have been set in motion are not checked and the movements redirected into constructive and lawful channels, the country faces the most serious problems that it has had to meet since the establishment of this Republic. . . . It is time that we awoke to the fact that the lack of religious and moral training which distinguishes this generation has given full swing to the baser instincts. What can be done to re-create right standard [*sic*] of right and wrong, of subordination of private to public good; to stimulate mutual understanding by frankness and the application of new standards of justice and mutual confidence. Knowledge of the facts is the first step in dispelling distrust. This knowledge we aim to suggest in this part of the report.

—Overman Committee Report, *Revolutionary Radicalism*, 1920

The influence of factious leaders may kindle a flame within their particular States but will be unable to spread a general conflagration through the other States. A religious sect may degenerate into a political faction in a part of the Confederacy; but the variety of sects dispersed over the entire face of it must secure the national councils against any danger from that source. A rage for paper money, for an abolition of debts, for an equal division of property, or for any other improper or wicked project, will be less apt to pervade the whole body of the Union than in a particular member of it, in the same proportion as such a malady is more likely to taint a particular county or district than an entire State.[12]

—Publius, in James Madison, "Federalist Paper No. 10"

In this rapid survey of a new and important educational idea we have carried Marja, the immigrant girl, from king- and caste-ridden Europe to America, the land of hope and opportunity. We have seen her struggle with an unknown tongue and with ways of life unfamiliar to her. In the end we see her transformed, reborn—no longer foreign and illiterate, but educated and self-respecting. Later she will marry and her children, though they may have traditions of another land and another blood, will be Americans in education and ideals of life, government and progress. It was been worth while that one man has broken through this barrier and made the road clear for others to follow.

All real education has the development of discipline as its basis. Poise, self-control and self-esteem are characteristic of the well-ordered mind, and the growth of these in the industrial worker makes for efficient service and better wages. Gradually there is an awakening of social consciousness—the awareness of one's place in society and the obligations such membership entails upon the individual in respect to the group or racial mass, with a constantly developing sense of one's personal responsibility in all human relationships.

In conclusion, the higher significance of this work means that we must descend the shaft and share the lives of those that dwell in the lower strata—the teeming populations that never see the stars or the green grass, scent the flowers or hear the birds sing—the huddled, hopeless foreign folk of the tenements. We are living in the Age of Service, and are growing into a conviction that life is not a matter of favored races or small, exclusive social groups, but embraces all humanity and reaches back to God. To those of prophetic soul comes a vision of the day that haunted Tennyson when "The war-drum throbbed no longer and the battle flags were furled / In the Parliament of Man, the Federation of the World."[13]

—"Epilogue," *Revolutionary Radicalism*

. . . An old house. They went West, and are long dead, they say, who built it. A mountain house. In winter no fox could den in it. That chimney-place has been blocked up with snow, just like a hollow stump.

—Marianna speaking, "The Piazza," 1856

Laocoön sighs softly, advised Lessing. Conservative social theorists responding to the Age of Revolution formulated a model of reason and balance that was objectively mad in its project to impose order upon the doubly bound; for James Madison, "popular government" was both there and not there. Were the non-propertied interests to become the new majority, "the spirit and form of popular government" would be preserved even as the wicked majority was "dispersed" by rational and virtuous citizens better attuned to "the public good." Speaking through Isabel and Marianna,[14] Melville had identified authority as strange and wandering. His literal history of a permanently wounded, wild, and wooly psyche was intolerable; Melville could not be a quasi-lunatic fending off madness fostered by mixed messages, but the prophet of social dissolution. Disillusion with the idea of progress supposedly explains Melville's sudden acceptability in the twentieth century; it was Melville's all-too-graphic disintegration, though, that frightened his critics. His apparent corrective flights to corporatism were promoted by Nietzschean radicals such as Van Wyck Brooks or Lewis Mumford, defining themselves against a mechanistic and alien mass culture. In concert with the Frenchman Gustave LeBon, Dr. Wilfred Trotter (1872–1939) had earlier laid out the premises and ambitions of a rectified Freudian "mass psychology" that could intervene in the headlong rush to oblivion, for "the so-called normal type of mind" "being in exclusive command of directing power in the world, is a danger to civilisation."[15]

Trotter's influential essays in *Instincts of the Herd in Peace and War*, first published in *Sociological Review* in 1908 and 1909, were updated and reprinted to comment on the Great War in 1919 (then brought out by Macmillan in fifteen printings by 1947). According to this "sometime Honorary Surgeon to the King," Freud, though the architect of "a great edifice," was bringing "a certain harshness in his grasp of facts and even a trace of narrowness in his outlook" along with a pervasive and repellent "odour of humanity" (78, 80). "The Freudian system" had developed "a psychology of knowledge" rather than a "psychology of power"; what was needed was an unveiling of "the sources of a director power over the human mind" so that "the full capacity of the mind for foresight and progress" could be developed (93, 94). Trotter addressed an elite audience sharing his belief in instincts and will power, understanding that war is "a contest of moral forces" and heeding his call for a "practical psychology," mobilizing "science" to achieve "a satisfactory morale . . . [which] gives smoothness of working energy, and enterprise to the whole national machine, while from the individual it ensures the maximum outflow of effort with a minimum interference from such egoistic passions as anxiety, impatience, and discontent." Methods and standards of elite recruitment and performance would have to change; old leadership "types" of "a class which is in essence relatively insensitive towards new combinations of experience" were unfit and obsolete (56); radical doctrines could be redesigned to fit new conditions: "If the effective intrusion of the intellect into social affairs does happily occur, it will come from no organ of society now recognisable, but through a slow elevation of the general standard of consciousness up to the level at which will be possible a kind of freemasonry and syndicalism of the intellect. Under such circumstances free communication through class barriers would be possible, and an orientation of feeling quite independent of the current social segregation would become manifest" (269–70). Thus, "true progress" will replace "oscillation" and wars will cease:

> The only way in which society can be made safe from disruption or decay is by the intervention of the conscious and instructed intellect as a factor among the forces ruling its development. . . . Nowhere has been and is the domination of the herd more absolute than in the field of speculation concerning man's general position and fate, and in consequence prodigies of genius have been expended in obscuring the simple truth that there is no responsibility for man's destiny anywhere at all outside his own responsibility,

and that there is no remedy for his ills outside his own efforts. *Western civilization has recently lost ten millions of its best lives as a result of the exclusion of the intellect from the general direction of society.* So terrific an object lesson has made it plain enough how easy it is for man, all undirected and unwarned as he is, to sink to the irresponsible destructiveness of the monkey. . . . No direction can be effective in the way needed for the preservation of society unless it comes from minds broad in outlook, deep in sympathy, sensitive to the new and strange in experience, capable of resisting habit, convention, and other sterilising influences of the herd, deeply learned in the human mind and vividly aware of the world. (6, 7, 266–67; emphasis added)

For Van Wyck Brooks, Melville was a foghorn, not a role model for Trotter's New Mind Manager; that honor went to his best friend Lewis Mumford, the source of "human renewal" poetically aligned with William Morris: "He had caught in England the last rays of the morning glow of William Morris's poetic socialism, and he was to remain a vitalist in a world of mechanists, behaviourists, determinists, Marxians and so on." Melville's appeal to youthful cynics of the "lost generation was limited" whereas

Lewis . . . knew that the optimists of the machine had forgotten that there was madness and night and that mankind had mystery to contend with, co-existing with universal literacy, science, and daylight, and why, because they ignored the darker side of the nature of man, they had been unprepared for the catastrophe that followed. He could see why it was that a grimly senescent youth confronted the still youthful senescents of the older generation, and having, along with Emerson and Whitman, read Pascal and Saint Augustine, he was fully able to enter their state of mind. Writers like Melville and Dostoievsky, with their sense of the presence of evil, had fitted him to grasp the post-war scene, the disintegrated world in which humankind, convinced of its inadequacy, ceased to believe in its own powers of self-renewal. . . . [W]ith his feeling for the inner life, he was convinced that the problem of our time was to restore the lost respect for this. For Western man had forgotten it in his concentration on the improvement of the machine. In a world obsessed by determinism, the human person must come back to the centre of the stage, he said, as actor and hero, summoning the forces of life to take part in a new drama.

Mumford had deepened his prewar "liking for brass buttons, music and drums" with "the consciousness of evil"; newly balanced, he could steer clear of shallow optimists and sour apples alike, the latter including Melville and "Wilson, Fitzgerald,

Dos Passos, Hemingway and Cummings": no vitalist renewal in either corner. It was Mumford and his circle, less innocent but no less confident, who had guided orphans through the minefields of modernity; Melville, though wholesome as a corrective to rationalist naiveté, was not a proper dramaturg, but an Isabel: the madness, night, and mystery "humankind" (imagined as one organism) "had to contend with." Brooks distanced himself from his Harvard teacher Irving Babbitt's bullying, negativity, sectarianism, and disdain for "the desire of the masses for their place in the sun"; still, Brooks was grateful that Babbitt and Harvard had introduced him to "the writings of Renan, Taine, and above all, Sainte-Beuve, who had almost all the qualities I admired so greatly. . . . How enlightening were Saint-Beuve's phrases about the master faculty,—the ruling trait in characters,—and families of minds, with his 'group' method in criticism and his unfailing literary tact, his erudition subdued by the imagination. How wonderfully he maintained his poise between the romantic and the classic."[16]

Similarly, Floyd Dell, novelist, poet, and associate editor of *The Masses*, was appalled by "intellectual vagabondage," a symptom of "shell-shock" that followed the collapse of idealism after the war. Hoping to clear away the rubble of ugliness and chaos he saw in modernist renderings of "the unconscious" drawn from Freud, Dell recommended ego psychology as a new source of order:

The scientific activities of mankind, unlike its imaginative activities, have not suffered from shell-shock; and we do not find the students of the human mind rejoicing in the chaos of the "unconscious" as an excuse for their failure to form a good working theory of it. On the contrary, we find that the "unconscious" is to them no chaos at all, but a realm in whose apparent disorder they have found a definite kind of order; in fact, they have been enabled by what they have found in the "unconscious" to correlate and explain all sorts of bewildering and painful discrepancies in outward conduct, previously inexplicable; they have created an intelligible and practically demonstrable theoretic unity out of just those aspects of human life which have for fictional and other artistic purposes seemed in the past a hopeless jangle of contradictions. And finally, they actually undertake therapeutically the task of bringing harmony, order and happiness into inharmonious, disorderly and futile lives. The imaginative artist need not be asked to "believe" in this; it may appear as alien to his own tasks as belief or disbelief in the new theory of electrons. But it is significant that such fiction as has undertaken to use these new concepts in the interpretation of life has met with no wide response from the intelligentsia—while on the contrary such fiction as has enriched its data with mere confusing and terrifying (one might say "bloody and stinking") *disjecta membra* of psycho-analytic research, has had the reward of our enormous applause and admiration. It is evident that we, at this moment in history, do *not* want life to seem capable of being interpreted and understood, because that would be a reproach to us for our own failure to undertake the task of reconstructing our social, political and economic theories, and in general, and in consonance with these, our ideals of a good life.[17]

The New Humanism was growing in influence in the late 1920s; its practitioners were viewed by Left liberals as allied to political fascism, not just the "literary" variety.[18] In the case of radical Floyd Dell, we see an abuse of scientific method typical of the conservative Freudians discussed here: The "unconscious" may not disclose the "bloody and stinking" gobbets (of repressed memories and desires?) that revolted him. Science and art are good only when they order and fully explain experience, building morale for social reconstruction: Axe the pessimists. Dell does not ask whether the "vagabonds" he criticizes are accurately depicting economic contradictions (which may or may not be relieved). Rather, he blames the victims for childishness and social irresponsibility, as if the eternal conflict between "the individual" and "society" were the source of "romantic" pain and ambivalence, not revulsion against hypocrisy and the quietism of upper-class allegiance. The "disillusionment" theory for the Melville Revival seems part of the arsenal of conservatives defending themselves against history, materialism, and critical reason by promoting mystical notions of national character and group mind with passions of "egoism" (distance from "the folk") postulated as the source of social friction and decay. The aristocratic radicals were responding to the Bolshevik Revolution, an undeserved triumph perpetrated by returning exiles, intellectuals opportunistically seizing power amidst the chaos of impending defeat. And wars are made by hidebound and greedy old fogies who misshape the national character by enforcing state worship: "War is the health of the state," as Randolph Bourne famously protested. Brooks, Mumford, and Murray, writing in this great tradition of progressive reproach, were pasting a piece of Melville to their projects while lengthily railing against the evils of "machines." Like Trotter, they believed (mechanistically) that a tiny elite of supermen could rescue the masses from themselves.[19]

The 1920s Melville Revival was too weak and bohemian to install Melville in the schools; that was the task of second-wave criticism mobilizing against Weaver (perhaps Melville's surrogate) in the late 1920s. Post-Weaver scholars detached Ishmael from Ahab by snatching *Pierre* from its mother, just as conservative social theorists had taken politics and institutional analysis out of (critical) Freudian psychoanalysis, leaving quietistic Jungian or ego psychology with its symbols, projective testing, surveillance, and mind management.[20] In Jungian readings, Ahab, like Hitler, was berserk: They were both men of the crowd. Melville was out of control in *Pierre* but the savior of Western civilization in *Moby-Dick*, the Ancient Bard

who has nailed the Wandering Jew: Ahab, Judas, arch-"narcist."[21] Perhaps Oswald
Garrison Villard was disillusioned by Wilsonian betrayals at Versailles, but rationalists have been defeated, perhaps in part by the activities of moderate conservatives
like Trotter and other freemasons and syndicalists of the intellect. Weaver, writing
for the *Nation* in 1919 and trying to make his way in a conservative institution (Columbia), could not have survived had he been as publicly frank about Melville as he
was with himself. Melville was romantic in his disgust with illegitimate authority,
and certainly disillusioned. He could, at first glance, seem conservative and primitivist enough; but in his dissections of the psyche and his mother's unreasonable perfectionism, or in his assertions of the omnipresence and inevitability of social conflict[22] and of class antagonisms that led to different forms of capitulation or revolt
(for instance, in *Redburn* and *White-Jacket*), there was an implicit demand for happiness and more than a paternalistic sympathy for labor, evident in his stinging reproach to all who ignobly submitted to oppression—so plain in his portrait of
Landless, called "Happy Jack" by the officers in *White-Jacket*.

Melville is a trial to conservatives for other reasons. There is no humor (bitter,
self-mocking, or otherwise) in postrevolutionary productions such as *Ambrosio, the
Monk;* or *Caleb Williams;* or *Theodore Cyphon, or The Benevolent Jew;* or *Melmoth
the Wanderer;* or *Frankenstein, the Modern Prometheus;* or *Doctor Jekyll and Mr. Hyde.*
These writers would not have taken Melville for a soul mate—he is too passionate,
too loud, and too androgynous. He is the protean Wandering Jew who invades and
dominates their inhibited imaginations, finally exploding the inside gothic genre.[23]
It is part of the political tendency that I am criticizing to believe that "the masses"
are, like children at their parents' mercy, helplessly swept away by charismatic
kitsch and demagoguery. The Mother/State/Market is writ large and scary, defined
against heartfelt, bite-sized, medieval localisms. Raising issues of domination, hypocrisy, exploitation, and alienation (however ambivalently) is always incendiary;
the reader does not have to accept an author's resolutions, ideas of racial character,
nihilism, or despair. And what is more self-reflexively modernist than the sequence
of *Moby-Dick* and *Pierre?* As I have tried to show above, the second work historicizes
the first, suggesting that delusive family relations were the key to understanding
Melville's manly epic of the whale hunt, relations that could not be improved with
better communication or family therapy alone.

Mumford's popular biography, *Herman Melville,* commissioned by the Literary
Guild and written quickly, appeared in 1929. The author frankly merged with his
subject, only occasionally using quotation marks to differentiate Melville's words
from his own. It is suggested here that Mumford's prolix condemnations of cities
and machines that had alienated modern man from Nature were irrationally motivated; he was his own prize-damaged specimen, too wary of his own feelings to

enter into either Melville's or Weaver's imaginations. Mumford's antimodern pessimism was produced by class constraints inflicted upon other Melville scholars; like them, he was lapping up family dirt while distancing himself from forbidden knowledge. His correspondence with Weaver establishes, first, that Weaver broke his promise to protect family privacy and, second, that Mumford was incredulous and did not, as a few Melville scholars have thought, depend on Weaver's faulty research to the detriment of his own work:

> Mr. Van Wyck Brooks told me this summer that you had gathered a number of details about Herman Melville that you weren't at liberty to publish in your biography. I wonder if there is anything which would be of help in doing the little critical biography I'm engaged in doing for the Murray Hill Biography Series; anything, that is, which, without being divulged, might guide or enrich my own interpretation. It would be a great privilege & help if you would permit me to call upon you, at your convenience & discuss the subject. I don't wish to start any hares that you've run to cover.

Mumford has delivered a mixed message, asking Weaver to reveal the "details" that Mumford the gentleman will also conceal, yet these golden nuggets will guide and enrich his little critical interpretations. Weaver obviously talked frankly to him, because he wrote once again:

> I have been mulling over all the baffling problems that you opened out to me; and I wonder if you can throw any light on the following questions? 1. When did Melville's "attacks" definitely begin? 2. Do they have any relation to the carriage accident? 3. At what dates did the Melville family actually attempt to put Melville away? 4. Was the aunt you saw in Boston Melville's sister or his wife's? 5. Are there any records of Melville's services at the Customs Office? 6. When did Melville begin to suspect the paternity of his children? The fact that Melville's wife couldn't bear to mention his name, or that his son committed suicide does not necessarily throw any light on Melville's disorder: if they did Dr. Smith Ely Jelliffe would be a candidate for the asylum, and Xantippe doubtless had similar feelings about Socrates. If the relations between husband and wife were as venomous and terrible, it is hard to explain *Bridegroom Dick* (1876) & if the family were inimical, what is one to make of the subsidy that published *Clarel?* I am not trying to counter your facts: I am merely trying to get them in line with other facts: and since, doubtless, you have asked similar questions yourself I should be grateful for your answer—even if the answer is, that there is no answer.[24]

Mumford was worried because facts were not settling the Melville problem. Whereas Weaver had collapsed both Melville and the fiction after *Pierre* into "the long quietus," Mumford, while noting the nadir of the sick mid-1850s, emphasized emotional recovery and flight away from bleakness, toward union with "the ancient cycle of life" finally attained in "Billy Budd."[25] Unlike Weaver, Mumford methodically separated Ahab from the great artist Herman Melville. Did he believe the careful distinctions he had drawn? The key to it all was bestowed in his chapter on *Moby-Dick*, "[Ahab] does not bow down to [evil] and accept it: therein lies his heroism and virtue: but he fights it with its own weapons and therein lies his madness. All the things that Ahab despises when he is about to attack the whale, the love and loyalty of Pip, the memory of his wife and child, the sextant of science, the inner sense of calm, which makes all external struggle futile, are the very things that would redeem him and make him victorious" (186). Mumford asserted that Ahab was forced to resort to "physical combat" because intellectual confrontation would have only revealed everything that was "partial, vindictive, and unjust" in himself. In short, Ahab is a bully; Ahab does not turn the other cheek. On the next page Mumford repeated his claim about the bully's flawed method: Even if he had used intellectual tools, he would have gotten nowhere. Ahab doesn't understand that art brings order, not suspended contradictions and more questions: "Melville's method, that of writing *Moby-Dick*, was correct: as correct as Ahab's method, taken literally, that of fighting Moby-Dick was fallacious. The universe *is* inscrutable, unfathomable, malicious, *so*—like the white whale and his element. Art in the broad sense of all humanizing effort is man's answer to this condition: for it is the means by which he circumvents or postpones his doom, and bravely meets his tragic destiny. Not tame and gentle bliss, but disaster, heroically encountered, is man's true happy ending" (187).

Mumford seems oblivious to Melville's theatricality, to his wish "for more reality, than real life can show," forgetting perhaps what Melville actually wrote, either in *Moby-Dick* or in *The Confidence-Man* (quoted above). Ahab had broadly hinted to Starbuck that his quest was not the violent, vengeful whale hunt it seemed to be; the reader is permitted to surmise that the harpoon represents the unterrified gaze of the democratic artist who, on behalf of the lower orders, penetrates white walls concealing state secrets or the sinister meanings of pretty words.[26] Or since Ahab asks, "How can the prisoner reach outside except by thrusting through the wall?" the harpoon could be the brawny arm that busted through the prison from *inside* the Bastille of subjectivity, to write on the outer wall: "Dear rulers, we the people have weighed your kingdoms in the balance; we find them wanting in candor and justice."[27] As Lockean democrat, Ahab cried, "Who's over me? Truth hath no confines." And yet Mumford applauded Ahab's manly audacity while decrying his evil weapons. Who else but an intimidated student would think "Ahab's method . . . that of fighting Moby-Dick" should be "taken literally"? Perhaps to reassure himself, Mumford insisted that the perception of Ahab's insanity is the test of sanity in Melville and, by implication, the reader. "To overlook Melville's characterization of Ahab as a madman is to belittle the sanity of his creator," the authoritative Mumford explained in the Herman Melville entry for a popular reference work of 1971.[28] But what about Mumford's sanity? Why should Ahab's "method" be "taken literally" unless Mumford's reading is class bound and therefore painful? Was Mumford the amanuensis of Leviathan or a daring social critic? Mumford, not insane, had looked over *Moby-Dick* and knew who was over him. The madness is Enlightenment hubris and Faustian overreaching. It is thinking that characters in a book are characters in a book; it is resorting to metaphors, even. Not to worry; managing the writing method, heroically submitting to mystery and malice, but armed with italics, the idealist Mumford felled Ahab's incorrect, crazy, feminine urge to fight back with some sort of futile external struggle—social reform and/or revolution, or just laborious research and intellectual analysis—take your pick. His readers could then feel superior to the agitated grinds willing to enter medicine, the sciences, and engineering and who were surpassing country squires in the race of life.

[Carl Van Doren explains to seventy thousand readers subscribing to the Literary Guild why the editorial board selected *Herman Melville*] Mr. Mumford, who has already shown himself to be a critic of insight and distinction, has defined Melville's genius with a skill which comes from a thorough knowledge of Melville and much reflection upon genius at large. Here is a moving account of Melville's great power frustrated by a lack of craft in directing it to its natural channels. In another society, Mr. Mumford holds, Melville might have been less frustrate. Here is a striking account of the standards, prejudices, repressions, discouragements which prevailed in the American Victorian age, which handicapped Melville from the start, and which kept him from being understood by his contemporaries. Yet Mr. Mumford does not go to the somewhat plaintive length of blaming Melville's misfortunes wholly upon his environment. He knows that in Melville there was a turmoil which belonged to him as an individual, an uncertainty as to his desires and aims, a struggle of the parts of his divided nature against each other, a long delay in his discovery of that peace which Melville arrived at only after he had ceased to write. Melville may have been a genius . . . who, like heroes of fiction or drama or penetrating biography, are seen to be struggling with the fates which most men struggle with unseen.

[Mrs. Elizabeth Effinger finds the chimney "In Herman Melville's Home"] It was the two little girls adventuring with me who discovered that the back door of Herman Melville's house was unlocked. Their enthusiasm was keen. They had been reading "Moby Dick." But their curiosity and excitement were no greater than mine, for I had been told that the house was deserted, that no one lived there, and it was with keen expectation that I opened the door and looked in. The result of that survey intensified the zeal with which this adventure was undertaken. Staring at a dismantled kitchen filled with baskets of dishes covered with dust and cobwebs, as if they had lain there for many years, I wound my way across the floor to a door in an opposite wall. Opening this, I gasped, for there stood the famous bully of Arrowhead![29]

A rupture of affection

Following publication of the Hendricks House edition of *Pierre* (1949) with its long introduction and copious notes by Henry A. Murray analyzing Pierre's "narcism," Mumford wrote to his friend with relief and panic, admitting that he had glossed over family memories. Mumford was happy that Murray had proven that *Pierre* was not "an unqualified masterpiece":

When I wrote my book I was over-reacting against Weaver, whose judgments I did not respect and whose manner I did not like; so, in interpreting Melville's weaknesses and his illness I was inclined to put the best possible face on every dark incident. Even now my own superficiality has saved a good part of Melville for me; while your autopsy of Melville is so thoroughgoing that even the Last Trumpet would hardly suffice to bring the various organs and parts together.

The worst of it is that I must agree with your demonstration, organ by organ; for no one has gotten closer to Melville than you have. But in the very act of penetrating the hidden layers of Melville's being, you followed his own method in apprehending the universe: so that your natural disenchantment with him, finally, springs from the same root as his disenchantment with the world itself. It is only on the surface, perhaps, that any life holds together and can stand up under inspection; if one goes far enough in one's analysis one is left with a hot shower of sub-atomic particles disconcertingly unlike a man. The fact is that Melville's inwardness is frightful to behold; and "Pierre" which reveals so much of it, is like a living man with his entrails exposed.[30]

This is no fan letter; inside narratives scare Mumford, but he has also disowned his superficial biography that allowed him to keep "a good part of Melville." Now he sees that Murray's medical tour of the text duplicates Melville's "own method in apprehending the universe." No illusions can be maintained under such scrutiny; no coherent story can be told. To be closely in touch with reality abandons him to "a hot shower of sub-atomic particles disconcertingly unlike a man." Mumford is admitting that Ahab, Melville, and Murray are one, wielding the same battle-axe on surfaces that mirror back the whole, integrated man. 'Tis murder to dissect: Getting too close is bad (wholeness is shattered), and staying far away is bad (the view is shallow and distorted). Given the alternatives, Mumford would rather split his subject, keeping the good part that, in the words ending Mumford's book, masochistically blesses the state that is killing him.

Writing to another friend after his Melville study was republished in 1962, Mumford apologized for his rough treatment of Melville's wife. "Melville was outraged by her calling in Oliver Wendell Holmes to decide whether he should be put in an asylum and for a while could not forgive her. This comes out in *The Confidence Man*. . . . He also had neurotic hallucinations [*sic*] about her infidelity. I left this out because the evidence was based on unverifiable family tradition. Their belated reconciliation (recorded in some of his last poems) was what counted."[31] In 1929, Mumford limited Melville's emotional distress to the 1850s. Why was he miserable? Mumford lectured "Lizzie" as if she were in the room: Her (critical) sexual coldness was counterpointed with the (uncritical) eroticism of Fayaway. It could make any man crazy. But the letter of 1963 scientistically undermined Melville's "outrage" at the label of insanity by labeling him a neurotic hallucinator: He really was seeing things, but this should not be reported because you can't trust "unverifiable family tradition."[32] The point is that the parents finally stopped fighting: a point that became a fact. Perhaps the romantic anticapitalist Mumford felt like Ungar's "new Hun" (the industrial working class) in his own family and was saving the planet from hallucinating perceptiveness and outrage, while relishing fantasies of their total annihilation. His personal history aside, Mumford was also protecting a class ideology, responding positively only to Melville's conservatism (along with its primitivist holidays) and reading *Moby-Dick* as if Ahab's probes were a personal attack that pulverized his own body, an entity he calls society. Why should this be? Corporatist thinkers paid to write for an upper-class audience may not maintain a boundary between themselves and the world. They deny that their opinions might reflect only the wisdom of a narrow spectrum; rather, having greater hearts than materialist hoi polloi, they intuit "the public interest" that generally turns out to be the perceived interest of at least a fragment of the ruling elite. Internal dissent and division signify only trouble, not opportunities for personal and group development. Mumford felt "reconciliation . . . was what counted." Might other punctured romances account for the depression that followed completion of his Melville study in 1929?[33]

The second wave of Melville studies proceeded on two fronts, both derived from Freeman and Mumford. The first line of attack was directed against Weaver and Ahab, surrogates for the douser Melville, who, off and on, plumbed the depths of families and other social bodies. Since Melville must not be reacting either to his own family or to his experiences at sea (locales of both liberty and fitful humors), he was neither steadily unhinged by the double bind nor intimidated by real or threatened repression throughout life.[34] The second front of Melville studies (aligned with the New Criticism) increasingly sought to emphasize literary sources for his fiction, focusing on craft; the purging of his life from the texts made it possible to rehabilitate the happy family and the apparently conservative later work, most important, "Billy Budd." Both lines converged in the reconstruction of Melville as a paternalistic organic conservative in the English progressive tradition of Burke and Disraeli, not that their politics were identified as such. Melville would be presented as a "moderate" and a "democrat" just like FDR and the New Dealers, some of whom had expected the Left to pull laissez-faire capitalism to the moderate middle.[35] Weaver's broken extremist had to go. Freeman had begun the first offensive by denying that Mary Glendinning in *Pierre* was a portrait of Maria Gansevoort Melville, as Weaver alleged. And whereas Weaver determined that Melville was Ahab, and Ahab, petrified by the Face, was not militant enough, Mumford attacked Ahab's feisty approach to social evil. The anti-Weaver corporatist project was carried forth in the 1930s by Charles Anderson, Stanley T. Williams, and Willard Thorp, professors at Duke, Yale, and Princeton, respectively.

Following the efforts of Harold Scudder and Carl Van Doren to uncover Melville's literary sources and fabrications in the late 1920s, the "fact-finding" phase of the Melville Revival heated up with Charles Roberts Anderson's MLA paper of 1932, "Tracking Melville in the South Seas."[36] Anderson's scholarship was to demystify Weaver's fallen *Übermensch* by discrediting feverish psychoanalytic readings that Anderson and others insisted had confused autobiography and fiction. Initially, Weaver refused to communicate with Anderson; in an unfinished letter to the Australian Melvillean John W. Earnshaw, he wrote, "You sent me a record of beautiful discoveries you had made in love of Melville. In sending these to me, with the generosity with which you sent them, you imposed on me a trust that I have perhaps been faithful to. You mention a Mr. Anderson in your letter. This same Mr. Anderson is, as you seem to know, about to publish a book on Melville in the South Seas and Mr. Anderson (I have never seen him, nor have I answered his offensive letters— offensive because of the patronage of a 'Southern gentleman.'"[37] Typically, Weaver had choked off his narrative at the height of indignation; the incendiary issue was "the patronage of a 'Southern gentleman,'" presumably a defender of academic slavery. By his own account, Anderson romantically muckraked Melville in dusty archives for many years before *Melville in the South Seas* (1939) was published by Columbia University Press with the cooperation of the Modern Language Association.[38] Anderson's targets were plainly the Left-leaning trilogy *Mardi, Moby-Dick,* and *Pierre* (4–5), but his book was purportedly a rebuke to the Freudian critical methods of Weaver and Mumford. According to Anderson, Melville's texts were not autobiographical; he had frequently plundered the research and adventures of other writers, misrepresenting them as his own. Plagiarism was both a good and bad thing: good because artists were not to be journalists, but rather should translate experience into the higher aesthetic realm; bad because of the lurking insinuation that the man was a liar.[39] Amazingly, Weaver defended Anderson from the wrath of his Columbia colleague Henry W. Wells, who had reviewed Anderson's book, complaining about its destructive sleuthing. Anderson replied to Weaver's letter of commiseration: "Thank you for your letter with its generous sentiments and its righteous indignation. Please be assured that whatever indignation I felt was directed against the publishers and not the author; but a more accurate statement would be that I merely charged it up to the sophism that publishers in general are Shylocks."[40]

But Weaver also preserved an undated letter from K. Baarslag responding to Weaver's "very informative letter of April 3" protesting Anderson's debunking of *Typee.* Perhaps the Ahab in Weaver was partly enraged by the Southern gentleman's dismissal of his and Melville's work; but as Ishmael, he would be relieved by Anderson's insinuation that Melville's radical characters were propagandists and agitators, leading workers and readers to their doom (Olson's interpretation, see below). Or perhaps Weaver was, as usual, collaborating in his humiliation by more powerful older men. Anderson's publication was received as a deliverance by a competing source hunter, Robert S. Forsythe of the Newberry Library (and editor of an anti-Weaver *Pierre* published by Knopf in 1930); it was "the most important publication dealing with Herman Melville which has appeared since Mr. Weaver's biography in 1921. And Mr. Weaver's book, it must be said, derives much of its value from the fact that it is the first full-length presentation of Melville's life." Forsythe concluded that Melville is "a deliberate literary artist, not an accidentally successful story-teller," and yielded the field to Anderson's achievement.[41]

The momentous uncovering of the good-bad confidence man had, in a single blow, delivered readers from Melville's moral authority and Weaver's unambiguous reading of *Moby-Dick.* Ishmael's solipsism and drift were transmuted to emancipation from totalitarian materialist science, the effluent of Ahab's pride and single-mindedness. A multiplicity of literary sources, not real-life experiences, false promises, and achieved understanding had informed Melville's artistry. The monomaniac's chart had been thrown overboard with the rest of the autodidacts. Clearly, now, Melville had left only a mish-mash that literary scholars might shape to their educated tastes, while readers were free to use *Moby-Dick* as a mirror, as the doubloon that Ahab had nailed to the mast. One by one, the crew peered into it, each seeing only his own reflection. Such an unbounded plurality of readings by the Narcissus mob would be the legitimating idea in the second wave of Melville scholarship and the New Left criticism following the same radical subjectivist (irrationalist) model. Ahab named the collection of disparate Melville interpretations, *Moby-Dick as Doubloon,* later edited by Harrison Hayford and Hershel Parker.[42]

There's something ever egotistical in mountain-tops and towers, and all other grand and lofty things; look here,—three peaks as proud as Lucifer. The firm tower, that is Ahab; the volcano, that is Ahab; the courageous, the undaunted, and victorious fowl, that, too, is Ahab; all are Ahab; and this round gold is but the image of the rounder globe, which, like a magician's glass, to each and every man in turn but mirrors back his own mysterious self. Great pains, small gains for those who ask the world to solve them; it cannot solve itself. Methinks now this coined sun wears a ruddy face; but see! aye, he enters the sign of storms, the equinox! and but six months before he wheeled out of a former equinox of Aries! From storm to storm! So be it, then. Born in throes, 't is fit that man should live in pains and die in pangs! So be it, then! Here's stout stuff for woe to work on. So be it then. (431–32)

This is a confusing passage, since Ahab seems to be articulating the thoroughgoing subjectivism usually espoused by Ishmael and that Ahab is supposed to lack. But see the qualifying sentence that immediately precedes and frames the speech: "Before this equatorial coin, Ahab, not unobserved by others, was now pausing." First, he is not alone; second, "pausing" is a key word for Melville, associated with the rush of blood to the head, vertigo, and blindness when he merges with the lower orders, diving to an unimpeded view of established authority. Is this one of Melville's sophomoricus moments, an affirmation of final mystery to please conservatives, as when he or another partially erased his comment on the seduction of Eve described above? Or is it because the Spanishly poetic doubloon is here identified with Catholicism? The speech, taken by itself, does seem to align Ahab with the Kantian German romantic hero, who, in spite of his ignorance of God's purposes, struggles to the death against the impositions of foreign (French) domination, no matter how uneven the combat.[43] But it also contradicts Ahab's demand for truth in "The Quarter-Deck," unless Ahab's point here is that all appearances are deceptive and that his (Melville's) readers will, out of cowardice, choose meanings that preserve intact their own purposely mysterious inner selves. As usual, Melville has left woeful us some stout stuff to chew on. If the work remains ambiguous, however, a retrievable history has created the puzzle, not the natural limitations of all human endeavors or Melville's sadistic teasing of readers.

Truth hath its confines

Writing in the pro-fascist *American Review,* John Crowe Ransom, the Southern Agrarian and later a leading New Critic as editor of *Kenyon Review,* joined the Melville Revival while enunciating the criterion of excellence for authors and readers alike:

[The tragic novel] is really in an important sense a superior product for it takes a strong intelligence to appreciate a tragic action. It may be hard for many moderns to imagine a working dramatic relation between man and God, when they have only heard of such a relation between man and man. That is because the modern imagination is poverty-stricken when we compare it with the Greek. Tragedy to the Greeks meant the lack of coincidence between the human order and the world-order or God-order, and therefore the essential failure of human ambitions.

In these days we have been educated away from such notions and their attendant mythology. Perhaps we do not need the mythology but we could use the sense of the thing. It is greatly to the credit of our artists that occasionally, even under their modern conditioning, they can show man defeated, and defeated not by enemies in human society but by nature, and not by nature as inertia and unconscious force but by nature as intelligent if inscrutable agent; by nature as Nature, or God, or as Devil. The author of *Moby Dick* was such an artist. There are others, but they are not the rule. We are obliged to say that it is not at all necessary for the novel to be tragic in the Greek manner in order for the novel to have artistic value; but it is welcome to do so if it likes, and then its value would seem very high.[44]

Lewis Mumford, himself an autodidact, had joined Ahab to Hawthorne's character Ethan Brand, the hyperintellectual artisan overreacher oblivious to "the essential failure of human ambitions." In the first edition of his biography, Mumford said Hawthorne had modeled Ethan Brand after Ahab, not vice versa.[45] The connection between the two autodidacts was reiterated in the pathbreaking anthology of 1937, *The American Mind,* co-edited by Stanley T. Williams,[46] future mentor to Yale students, who, after the war, set about the creation of a solid factual basis for Melville studies. The conception of the textbook (along with its Melville entry) served as an example of neoclassical organicism forestalling decomposition while cloaked in the sublime rhetoric of radical Enlightenment. An advertisement in *The Harvard Educational Review* (March 1938) offered alluring instruction in the manners of conservative Enlightenment. No devolving Protestant fragments on *this* frontier; rather, original, dug-up facts were literally capitalized:

> Distinguished by its basic plan from all other collections, or anthologies, this book offers a new approach to both American literature and American history. Its originality lies chiefly in the fact that it deals with the patterns of thought and development;—not mere isolated selections. It is the first book to have national coverage, the first to deal adequately with frontier writers and the first to tie together, in strands of unifying thought, the authors represented. The result is a vibrant, intellectual panorama of the nation's progress in cultural, political, economic, and social thought.
>
> The extracts composing this wealth of material have been chosen chiefly for the part each played in the intellectual and social development of the nation. The range is astonishingly wide. . . .
>
> THE FACT that many of the selections are from original documents gives the book its unique value. No such stimulating and comprehensive picture of the life, intellect, and soul of this nation has ever been published. It is fascinating reading.

Readers could trust the unique, almost Rabelaisian, synthesis because the texts were derived from real printed sources, not family gossip, and were checked by literary scholars. Adolescents would be thrilling to a documentary, not an arrangement with the devil.

The wide-ranging *American Mind* rendered Melville as autodidact. The Melville biographical sketch began cold with Ishmael's minimalist curriculum vitae: "A Whale Ship was my Yale College and my Harvard," directly following Hawthorne's "Ethan Brand."[47] The Melville selections did not follow a chronology. Although *Mardi* had been written first, the selection "On Popular Sovereignty in America" was placed between passages from *Moby-Dick* and *Pierre*. The latter was represented by Pierre's nightmarish vision of Enceladus, the armless Titan. Excerpts from *Moby-Dick* consisted of the confrontation between Ahab and Starbuck in the chapter "Symphony" (during which Ahab resists Starbuck's pleas, turning away from visions of home and family) and then the three-day chase of the White Whale and the sinking of the *Pequod*. The sequence lacked the epilogue in which Ishmael, the lone survivor, is rescued by the fatherly captain of the *Rachel*. It was a surprising deletion but probably not a printer's error. Hawthorne's allegory of democratic America had told of the artisan autodidact, instructed by Nature herself. Naturally his inner balance was destroyed by the withered, hardened heart that "had ceased to partake of the universal throb." "Ethan Brand" concluded with these lines:

The marble was all burnt into perfect, snow-white lime. But on its surface, in the midst of the circle,—snow-white too, and thoroughly converted into lime,—lay a human skeleton, in the attitude of a person who, after long toil, lies down to long repose. Within the ribs—strange to say—was the shape of a human heart.

"Was the fellow's heart made of marble?" cried Bartram, in some perplexity at this phenomenon. "At any rate, it is burnt into what looks like special good lime; and, taking all the bones together, my kiln is half a bushel the richer for him."

So saying, the rude lime-burner lifted his pole, and, letting it fall upon the skeleton, the relics of Ethan Brand were crumbled into fragments.

By dropping Ishmael's rescue, Ahab and Ishmael were both "crumbled into fragments," like the naturalist Ethan Brand who had immediately preceded them in the panorama of uniquely unified extracts. The orderly American mind, by a particular and deliberate arrangement of the Hawthorne/Melville selections, then, demonstrated how, after a bumpy start with the wayward American Revolution fought by Ethan (Allen?) Brand, the autodidact had come home to classicism, his authentic voice that of the anti-Jacksonian youth in *Mardi* declaiming against demagogues and mobs who perpetrated the Mexican War; finally, as repentant Wandering Jew, despairing of all revolt, however noble.[48]

Pierre, down on himself after his mother's death from a surfeit of grief, expects his publishers to reject his blasphemous, self-doubting manuscript. The Enceladus section is written out of this pessimism in the Heraclitean voice of the narrator; the lesson of the doubloon is reiterated: "Say what some poets will, Nature is not so much her own ever-sweet interpreter, as the mere supplier of that cunning alphabet, whereby selecting and combining as he pleases, each man reads his own peculiar lesson according to his own peculiar mind and mood." The Delectable Mountain near Pierre's home in the country has a shimmering purple atmosphere, but beneath the aura it groans with decaying, crashing, dripping, jamming plant life; "wolfish caves" suggest engulfment and castration for would-be dousers. Melville makes stout stuff of the competition between the sterile white amaranth, a symbol for immortality, and the nurturing catnip that succumbs to its proliferation. Another anthropomorphic formation clings to the side of the mountain: the rock called the "American Enceladus, wrought by the vigorous hand of Nature's self." College students on a lark had once dug into the earth surrounding the queer moss-turbaned Titan. Only the head and neck had been exposed; now their efforts have disclosed an armless torso. Pierre's dream animates Enceladus along with his rocky companions:

> No longer petrified in all their ignominious attitudes, the herded Titans now sprung to their feet; flung themselves up the slope; and anew battered at the precipice's unresounding wall. Foremost among them all, he saw a moss-turbaned, armless giant, who despairing of any other mode of wreaking his immitigable hate, turned his vast trunk into a battering-ram, and hurled his own arched-out ribs again and yet again against the invulnerable steep.
> "Enceladus! It is Enceladus!"—Pierre cried out in his sleep. That moment the phantom faced him; and Pierre saw Enceladus no more; but on the Titan's armless trunk, his own duplicate face and features magnifiedly gleamed upon him with prophetic discomfiture and woe. (346)

The message of the Enceladus vision is clear: America, Nature's nation of left-wing Protestants and deists, should be seeking "the earthly household peace of the catnip" and resisting "the ever-encroaching appetite for God," the amaranth associated in these pages with Ahab and the Whale, both good haters. *The American Mind* had created a little parable for theater in the Melville sequence, beginning with evidence of Ahab's narcissism: the withered heart and his pact with the devil, then ending with the society-wrecking denouement of futility and mutilation. *Pierre* the book, though, un-finished on quite a different note: Though his choice between the catnip and amaranth remains "ambiguous still," Pierre is glad he didn't sell out by denying Isabel, his connection with the clearer vision of lapsed humanity. Adam eats Eve's apple, the vial of dissent and division that poisons the happy family. The curtain falls with Melville's scornful last words pronounced in Isabel's gasp from the wall: "All's o'er and ye know him not," the ebon vines of her long black hair arboring the artist's vulnerable body.

Mumford's effort to separate sane Melville from the battering ram of Ahab's intellect had been joined in the mid-1930s by Princeton professor Willard Thorp. The American Book Company, publishers of *The American Mind,* brought out Thorp's anthology *Representative Selections of Herman Melville* in 1938, a title that linked Melville to the mystical Emerson, devotee of Thomas Carlyle and author of *Representative Men.*[49] The Depression had produced a militant response throughout the 1930s—increasing labor unity, sit-down strikes, and class polarization, not the hoped-for class collaboration that progressives had sought in the Wagner Act and Social Security.[50] In this tumultuous setting, the Princeton professor winnowed from the moderate Right, constructing a corporatist and pluralist Melville firmly connected to his father-in-law, Lemuel Shaw, the chief justice of Massachusetts and a conservative Whig. The "superstitions of the extreme Jacksonian democrats" or "dogmatic Abolitionists" were blown away:

> Feeling, as he did most ardently, that in their essential manliness (and this only) men are equal, what he hoped for democratic America was that those who have talents and power should wish to use these gifts for the common good. Leveling downward need not mean that excellence would be despised. Legitimate dignity and authority need not be affected. It is with this idea in mind that he implied, in a letter to Hawthorne, that even the aristocracy of the intellectual estates is selfish and unjustified. A man who is gifted beyond his fellows has no more right to shrink at their touch than they have reason to assert that they possess his gifts or have no need of them. . . . Melville's democracy, his pacifism, and his experiences on the seven seas, made him an internationalist. He rejoiced that the currents of a thousand nations flowed into us. "We are not a nation, so much as a world."

Thorp was thinking of the gifted Melville's role in raucous Jacksonian America; how should their betters behave? His association of equality with leveling in a downward direction merits decoding. The Levellers of the English Civil War were revolutionists and republicans. The same rules governed rich and poor alike, surely an excellent innovation to the radical puritans, but to displaced elites a hateful dogma. Such novel privileges as enjoyed by overly self-reliant Jacksonians, Thorp implies, were used to vitiate "talents and power"; he wants to rescue the native elites from themselves. Shortsightedly the natural aristocrats shrink at the touch of grubby hands; armed with cultural pluralism, however, nativists can fend off immigrants and radicals, continuing their prudent management of "democratic America." Thorp expresses a paternalistic class ideology dedicated to the proposition that class hierarchies are natural and inevitable; excellence is not a process of learning and striving toward high standards, but a spatial location; placed in gifted genes and preexistent (unspecified) power: no excuse then for snobbery.

Pace Thorp, the Lockean principles that informed popular sovereignty were never primitivist; the radical liberal program leveled upward by setting high expectations and awesome responsibilities for citizens; a free and undistorted press with quality education for all were indispensable accompaniments to the Enlightenment rationalist project—a project that had decisively broken with the Platonic-Christian rationalism that saw perfection in all God's creation, assuming that the Great Chain of Being was not disturbed by deracinating institutional innovations perpetrated by misguided atheistical democrats. By detaching these excellent qualities—democracy, pacifism, and internationalism—from the rootless cosmopolitans, Thorp had, through sleight of hand, transmuted the author of Ahab (and by implication, other dark democrats: Fleece, Isabel, Pitch, and Thomas Fry) into the moderate man possessed of legitimate dignity and authority, the better sort of "internationalist" and a steadfast friend to (suspicious) labor. Harrison Hayford remembered that Thorp's "little anthology" was "the indispensable handbook of the emerging generation of Melville scholars." Thorp was not writing to workers, but to future professors and their upper-class patrons whose too fastidious disdain of their indispensable lower-class brethren might provoke another reign of terror: step back far enough, and you must see We Are One, Really.[51]

One Melville reviver did have a family tie to the militant working class so assiduously courted by patricians in the 1930s: Charles Olson's underread juvenilia will serve as guide to his later Melville criticism, published and unpublished, that haltingly followed the rise and fall of the House of Labor.

A SACRAMENTAL MAN

Charles Olson (1910–1970), was the author of *Call Me Ishmael* (1947); he remains a cult hero to the Black Mountain Poets, the Beats, the San Francisco Renaissance, and some New Leftists.[52] Paul Christensen, an ethnopluralist who posits a monolithic and horrid Anglo-Americanism "tearing ancient bonds of community among racial and ethnic sub-groups," lauded Olson as the second mover who "set Postmodernism in motion as a voice of cultural pluralism in the world."[53] Some second-wave Melville scholars feel that Charles Olson was an outsider hostile to their efforts, a claim proven by his attack on the Melville scholars congregating at Williamstown, Massachusetts, in 1951 in his poem/broadside "Letter to Melville," "a bomb blasting the whole festive assembly."[54] Olson's unpublished papers, however, confirm him as one of several progenitors of the second wave. His later antagonism to the Melville industry may have been the product of jealousy and guilt, not a thought-out difference in principle or method. In 1945–46, intimations of the coming outburst were unexpressed, for Olson saw himself as the leader and organizer of Melville studies. An entry in his notebook for fall 1945–spring 1946 reads: "Proposal to publishers: 1) My book 2) Editorship of American Edition (Olson) 3) Publication of Melville's Uncollected Writings (Mansfield) 4) Melville's Letters (Birss) 5) Melville's Books (Olson) 6) Vincent's Book 7) Hawthorne & Melville (Hayford) 8) Levin on Symbolism."[55]

Olson was surely one of the most torn and blocked of all the Melvilleans. He tried (and failed) to juggle the labor sympathies and internationalism associated with his father, an embattled Swedish immigrant postal worker, with counter-Enlightenment views imposed by his respectable Irish-Catholic mother. During the war he hewed to the sane centrist line, serving in the wartime Roosevelt administration. As assistant chief of the Foreign Language Division of the Office of War Information, he wrote "propaganda pamphlets on how well various nationality groups [immigrants originating in parts of Europe then under Nazi rule] are serving the United States during the war."[56] Olson's unpublished notebooks suggest that his destruction or withholding or abandonment of the Melville research and criticism begun in the early 1930s, like his abrupt departure from Harvard graduate studies in 1939, may be traced to divided parental and political loyalties. Perhaps this was the quandary that developed his taste for the archaic and the obscurantism of his prose and later poetry, including disdain for Melville's "bourgeois" poems, alongside the conviction that his love, Melville, was "the thing since Homer."

The catnip and the amaranth!

Olson was initiated into Melville studies by his sensitive and artistic father, who, on Charles Jr.'s nineteenth birthday, December 27, 1929, presented him with a copy of the 1926 Modern Library edition of *Moby-Dick*, with an introduction by Raymond Weaver. The father's inscription sets Melville's call to arms against the Ivory Tower:

When o'er this book you cast
Your eyes
Forget your studies and Mobylize.
Each minute spent some thought should bring
Of Gloucester scenes, and your old Viking.

Olson's markings show that he was gladly enlisted in Father Mapple's activist religion and Ahab's quest, exclaiming, "What a sermon!" (48) and "Great" next to the underlined "Death to Moby Dick" (165). The demonic Parsee Fedallah represented "the league of Ahab with hell to kill hell's being" (231). In the spirit of many another youthful Melvillean before and since, he wrote (but later crossed out), "Gosh, all this is overwhelming!" (523).

Had he chosen, Olson could have dominated Melville studies, for he had the support of important allies in American letters (besides the devoted friendship of Eleanor Metcalf and her family): Wilbert Snow, Carl Van Doren, F. O. Matthiessen, Edward Dahlberg, the Guggenheim Foundation, Francis Henry Taylor (director of the Metropolitan Museum), Lincoln Kirstein, and numerous publishers and editors. Olson was tracked for letters and leadership, for "the real book about Melville," as Carl Van Doren had hoped.[57] But as he moved up the academic ladder, Ahab appeared less and less groovy. The following excerpts from Olson's unpublished notebooks and letters (and from the reminiscences of two Melville scholars) expose the deranging consequences of pluralism in one family. Father is a railroading Ahab, energizing, critical, and clear, a conscience Olson reveres and cannot evade while satisfying his withholding, resentful mother's competing desire for safety and respectability. With the young Charles immobilized by divided loyalties, the fragments gathered here suggest a lateral movement from white rat to white rot. The morally outraged, needy, curious child degenerates because mother's values decay when he identifies too strongly with father/Ahab, who died of a stroke at age fifty-two in August 1935. Father, the gentle labor organizer who never gave up, "came through the whole thing clear" but dead. Without him all attachments must be lethal: Mother has the power. Her Catholicism mystifies the world and stigmatizes the senses: Love's body becomes a poison Charles cannot evacuate.

[April 2, 1932] An idea for a story— . . . a parody of Poe's "Berenice." This man has a monomania on a woman's nose, a Grand proboscis. He must tweak that Nose. Instead of the chatter of 24 white teeth killing him let's have the squeal of a rat (mouse) or of a baby drive him mad. (Notebooks, 25)

[July 29, 1935] Recipe:xxxxx To a well-diseased biscuit of a face, add a heavy, bronze-red solution of mercurochrome. Then sozzle the above mixture gently, very gently with a calcium white wash. After one week (if you are lucky) you may remove and serve up—prayers. (Notebooks, 26)

[Uncataloged letter fragment (to Barbara Denny?), January 21, 1936] . . . I think I've naturally a weak will—Mary T. gave me that along with life. . . . A discipline from without has always been a necessity for me, a priming to get me to move and flow. That's what college was, that's what Melville was; that's what teaching is. Once started I can depend upon my physical and mental energy; God bless my father for that. . . . I'm unnaturally fastidious about what is me. . . . I've run through the corridors of myself and like the white rat in the maze, found rarely the cheese and mostly madness. . . . I found self-pity rotting at my core and my awareness of it has cauterized it.

[Summer and Fall 1939] His love she's always taken as an obeisance. The woman of bad will who is only greedy for the person or thing she does not possess. E[eanor] M[elville] M[etcalf] . . . What is love but to leave yourself unfortified? (Notebooks, 133)

[Winter–Spring 1940] . . . [Father] was too gentle to make the most of his inheritance [his mother's genes for longevity] and himself. But he had lovely hands. An artist's hands, be it they were incoherent and wasted their life on letters for the U.S. govt. But he gave me much that I am grateful for. He gave me love and watered the soil of my ambition. I remember how troubled he was by certain shynesses in me. And stupidities. He had an intellect and nothing but newspapers to use it on. That was his fault but it was also hers [Olson's grandmother]. . . . Calculation, you [Edward Dahlberg] charge me with. I've borne it in me like an arrow, twisted & loaded with a poison. I've tried to go all around it, watch its expression, seek out its sources, & I want to remove both. Its sources—mother, & a suspicion which must have arisen during the years in college when I was an outcast & felt no sympathy or understanding, only the chill of jealousy and hate. I had to batten on medals which my brain earned to stop the hunger of my heart which earned nothing but [black lines] censored. "hell." Brought me suspicions of all my friends. A feeling of the necessity to fight. What I've failed to do is to distinguish between those to hurt & those to be silent with. (Notebooks, 46)

[Ca. 1940] Volubly and nervously I talk down my own fears /Always I am trying to prove, not express myself—and so I seem false to me, and if false to me, it follows that I am false to others whether they know it or not. / But as E[dward] D[ahlberg] has it, I have no commitments but to myself and those only must I acknowledge. (So many poisons in his system he'll never have a disease) . . . . *luminous chaos* is what you must write: its own deep form for those who can find it. Magical error. (Use yourself only—how can you depend on HM/ [CO now links ambiguity, sex, and sore throats:] a polypus of an idea: many faced / erogine: woman's zone / mephitic: noxious / mephistic: diabolic / rugose—throat / Philistia, with all its war of whispers, cannot unhinge your throat / *Think of no one but yourself* / Why am I more mother than male? (Notebooks, 48)

[Letter to Constance Wilcock, 1941] [Don't take the subway or bus to meet me] It is only enemy, the machine. You and I hold something *against* the machine, against the world of the machine. The very thought of it cuts across me like a rip saw . . . our love is clean of it.

[January 1945] Interesting that no fear of my father as punishment at any time. Probably the son always relates it to mother. And, besides, fact was he was no Catholic. *He came through the whole thing clear.* (Notebooks, 56)

[February–April 1945] When I was a boy I had a companion I had made up like all kids do. His name was Cabbage. We baked potatoes together. He got me over childhood. Melville got me over adolescence. There was some iron, some green in him I needed. I liked his blood, maybe. . . . Then I couldn't have told you why I kept him close. I was warned he was bad for me. Women warned me, and made more impression than they who told me Melville only made me more rhetorical. [He] gave me important clues about *my* world, this America. . . . In M's biography there is something that is gauche, plain conventional. A lot of self-pity. Good women find this in his work and bridle. He had to be wild or he was nothing in particular. (Notebooks, 57)

[February 11, 1945] Always *invaded* by life. Noises. People whose faces suddenly cover you like a spider's web and you duck and strike them off. (Notebooks, 57)

[March 2, 1945] . . . I should have gone with that whore in Cologne and let her straighten it out. And seven years would have been fattened . . . . [Apparently Olson did not have sex until his father died in 1935.] That's the price I paid for America—an immigrant father never quite sure of himself and thus not able to give me the insight into middle class mores. . . . Like him stubborn I kept on with something like he did everything. My father was my father / but the moon was my mother. (Notebooks, 57)

[April 1945] . . . —never fall back on anything but discontinuity—contain yourself in yourself—attached to nothing—only yourself. . . . The loving heart is offered only to the sun. *spatial*—that's the continuity which is the absence of continuity, the only refuge of the individual. (Notebooks, 51)

[Fall 1945] Dreams: There seemed to have been an estrangement with my mother, or perhaps it was just the sense of her absence. It was all sharply my father and me alone. His eyes were deep, long, and hollow, his skin gray as he looked when dying, his body and self slow and profound, full and steady with experience, heavy, serious, considered. He was remembered. The gulf of years and death existed, but I felt close to him, understood, enjoyed his return. There was space around us, dimensions I do not remember we had when he was alive. (Notebooks, 55)

[January 2, 1946] (My father: gentleness & obedience, but underneath resistance & rebellion. Is it enough? The outward thing necessary? Sex the sword, & unarmed. . . . [January 23, possibly quoting Pound:]—my definition of a lunatic—an animal somewhat surrounded by Jews . . . (The moon my pimp). (Notebooks, 31)

[The Faust Buch No. 1, 1947] The root dream / My father, with axe, swinging it down by my head and over across the top—and I standing to it, with a sense, and peace, of fatality. . . . *What has been the nature of my relations with my mother?* Is not all my critique of her as moral and Catholic a blind for something below? (Notebooks, 41)

[Letter to Constance Wilcock, September 8, 1950] Agreed: the ultimate stupidity is: to write at all. To this I know only one answer. I run on the fatal track of my father, the stubborn rail.

[Merton Sealts, Jr., reporting Olson's response to his essay "I and My Chimney"] "Well, I see . . . that . . . THE WHITE DEATH . . . has descended . . . upon you." (*Pursuing Melville,* 1982)

[Harry Levin to the author, May 21, 1991] P.S. There's a story about Charles Olson that you should know if you don't already. After he had left Harvard, and was living in Greenwich Village, he was sought out by somebody who had recently become interested in Melville. The visitor found him—grimly colossal—seated at a cluttered desk in a dark and rather run-down apartment. Charlie's words of greeting were: "So you too have the white rot!"

Olson was in extremis from the outset of his academic career. He started Melville research while a graduate student in American Civilization at Wesleyan University, completing a fiery master's thesis, "The Growth of Herman Melville, Prose Writer and Poetic Thinker," directed by Wilbert Snow and partly inspired by Charles Anderson's MLA paper of 1932.[58] The thesis began with an assault on the "hastily written" biographies of both Weaver and Mumford (the latter was author of *The Golden Day,* a popular book praising antebellum American writers): "It was natural that those who first exploited his place in the sun of 'The Golden Day' should belligerently exaggerate his greatness and luxuriate in his richness. This passionate exaltation must cease. Melville's genius can run the gauntlet of criticism and be genius still." Unlike puffing and parasitic predecessors, Olson declined to read the texts as autobiography. He was arguing with himself, in one breath downgrading the quality of Melville's art and the significance of his life experience, in another, fixated upon it. Always drawn to the Melville charisma, his yearnings were expressed in violent, incoherent imagery "His was such a striking personality, filled with a Whitman-like strength and vigor, brooded over by deep intimations of evil, lashed by the whip of experience, that he literally drags the student away from his work."

In Book 1 of *Paradise Lost,* Milton was allied with the Holy Ghost, "brooding on the vast abyss." An intimation cannot brood, so what could Olson have meant? Did he think Milton's Muse, a pure spirit like Olson's father, was brooding on the abyss of Charles? Had the concern of brooding parents filled him with dark anxiety? Had Olson been pressed into evil, impressed by the class enemy? Perhaps the whip of father's experience was goading Olson, dragging him away from the corruptions of the ivory tower, but he followed Carl Van Doren and Charles Anderson, not the interests of the independent labor movement. In his master's thesis, Olson apotheosized the "imaginative artist," while simultaneously hinting that Melville should have been a better journalist:

> And through [Anderson's] discoveries we can accurately reveal Melville the artist, handling his source material. He declares in *White Jacket* that he is writing "an impartial account . . . inventing nothing." Research, though subtracting from the honesty of the man, adds to his greatness as an imaginative artist. Three distinct kinds of alteration are patent: 1. expedient changes of fact, 2. dramatic elaboration of actual events, and 3. deliberate invention of his most powerful scenes. [Thus] by shifting the setting of a fall from the main-yard to the quarter-deck, which happened in the normal performance of necessary duty, to the harbor in Rio during a competitive sail-furling, he brutalizes a mere accident into the needless and deliberate sacrifice of one of the "people" in order to glorify the admiral on the poop. . . . Wishing to give his propaganda against flogging added effectiveness of personal resentment and revulsion, he simply invented a scene in which he himself was the near-victim. (103)

Fulminating over the "violent invention of 'Mad Jack,'" an officer who seizes the helm to rescue the crew from incompetent superiors, Olson insisted there could be no such "unpunished insubordination."[59]

While still a young man of twenty-three, Olson was able to decipher propaganda, but he was also talking about himself. As this notebook entry discloses, Olson feared the strength of his own anger against insult, which, unchecked, could alienate potential supporters. It is a virtual precis of the Melville inferences to come:

> [April 6, 1932] If only I could conquer two traits in my nature that bother me ever so often. One is the sudden flash of anger, striking out as suddenly and destructively as lightning. Just as lightning destroys all objects it hits, I destroy the respect and good opinion of those about it [sic]. I was [sic] restrain it and "take it out" in this book or, as Emerson did, with a hoe in some garden; (probably with my arms and legs, in the past).

Growing out of that same vitiating power comes the aftermath that inevitably follows the teasing and pestering of fellows, leaping upon the fallen prey. I feel so defenceless when persons tease me. My heart lies open to their taunts. Such a weakness usually results in the acquisition of a coat of cynicism, and "smart-aleckness" that I despise. I think it wiser, therefore, to retire before such teasing until my larger nature returns—and mature it will—when such taunts will become as nothing. It is the *bigness* of the Prometheus of Shelley that I want—and need. The procedure will be something like Mithradates immunization: "Mithradates he died old."

Only *suckers* are those that achieve material *success*.

Two "traits" diminish it/him: First, the vitiating power of "the sudden flash of anger" coming out of nowhere. Why vitiating? Because it destroys the "good opinion" of those around it/him. Second, he grows a slick carapace to cover his hurt. So he picks Shelley's Prometheus as the figure, open to experience, who will replicate his noble father's humanity and largeness of vision. Olson, Christlike, renounces material success, not wishing to be taken in or to take in others. But the path to all greatness is fraught with hidden perils, within or without the Church.

[January 7, 1933, after copying Corinthians on charity] There is a mystical—a bitterly mystical—similarity between church bells and fog-bells heard at a distance. They stir the embers of evil in the fire of the soul; they presage destruction. The fog-bell tolls a warning of a reef to which parasitic sea-life clings but on which a free-sailing ship before the wind will be destroyed; perhaps these church bells on Sunday mornings covertly warn of a hard and treacherous reef of Christianity to which parasitic souls adhere but against clear of which the strong, independent soul must steer—but also, is often destroyed.

[January 8, 1933] My mind is like the moon—not made of green cheese, but passing through the same conditions. Now it is bright and clear and full; then it is clouded: then misted, then its face turned away.

[January 10, 1933] I had a desert [*sic*] today that was indistinguishable from the Ivory Soap I used to devour when I was a bad little boy taking a nasty little bath!

A few days later, he is worried about a writing block, describing the urge to create and discover as blight: "I'm plagued with a need to express myself, tortured with the idea (or is it a hope) that there's some undiscovered thing in my guts." As artist, he is still too small and weak to overcome a deprived childhood; the soaring, seeking artist has been pinned to the mat by philistines, so he contemplates the more cerebral task of interpretation:

[February 11, 1933] Criticism. Perhaps there lies my creation, as far as it is creation. My mind too far outweighs my emotion. There is too much suspended animation, too little wild freedom. My imagination is earthborn and the godawful thing is my youth pegged it down. ~~Parents~~. Mother. Religion. Poverty of art. Environment. This terrific energy that burns within me must be (or might have been?) turned into artistic creation if taste and joy and beauty had been mine. I guess it is that vacuum of background that has me licked. . . . I pour everything into the vacuum but like a quicksand bog it seems as empty as ever. My ignorance, my fearful feeling of surface and no bottom.

The preferred Promethean does not persist. Sinking into the "quicksand bog," Olson reflects upon the cyclical theory of history just discussed with a friend. "I cannot believe in cycles because I feel too strongly about chance. Even Haley's Comet may not appear on Jan. 27, 2009 at 11:30 P.M. because a chunk of the moon *may* drop on its way before then—who can say?"

"And as for that, what historical precedent is there for communism, which we are so rapidly coming to? Is it part of any cycle?—And yet I cannot accept progress. I have too much distrust for the human animal to be an idealist any more. I think progress is as aristocratic as art. Christ and Plato, Shakespeare and Spinoza have made certain individuals' lives fuller. But God knows how many." Communism is not the willful outcome of historical interpretation and political action; communism is like the sudden anger of the moon mother who punishes him for childish sins, sins committed without malice aforethought. Since the human animal is so naturally evil and unpredictable, he will stick with the aristocrats in academe. And yet two years later, the Jacobin Olson raged against the rigid, compartmentalized academy. Professors were "as bodyless and dead as French aristocrats on the pikes of revolutionists. . . . Colleges and all that infest them suffer from the most horrible plague of life, the Fifth Horseman, pernicious anemia of the mind" (March 7, 1935). Olson's apocalyptic anger had returned, and not merely in his notebook. His own wild, failing imagination was imputed to Melville, and he assimilated other artists and thinkers to his interior drama—as long as their "strength" protected him from the harsh taunts that had marked him for life; he will yield to the vitiating power and the carapace that he had earlier despised. Ishmael Olson internalized conservative fears of the autodidact and of history itself. There was only one Fall, binding us to the depravity of our first parents. Change is ominous, and it comes at you out of the blue, like a mother's frown, a mother's tears: Baby Budd, bad indeed, his filthy mouth washed away with white soap.

A BROODING EXCURSUS ON SUBVERSION AND COUNTERSUBVERSION, INTIMACY, AND DISTANCE, BROADLY SPEAKING

Composing his "Memories" at the end of the 1930s, the Harvard physical chemist Lawrence Henderson, founder of the Pareto seminar and mentor to Henry Murray,[60] reviewed the development of his social thought. As a young man he had studied in France, learning quickly to distrust the emotional Germans. Henderson preferred the French because "so many Frenchmen escape the cruder forms of sentimentality and . . . so many of them are individualists and also very French, that is the opposite of *anomic* [atomized] in Durkheim's sense." He admitted that the French were excitable in little things, but "cool and restrained in serious situations. In all countries most men are stupid, but I find more Frenchmen interesting than mere chance can account for" (90–91). Toward the end of the memoir, Henderson described his theory of historical change (afterward noting that the model resembled his first scientific paper on molecules and atoms): "Promises and principles are among the forces that determine the actions of men. There are other forces such as passions, political, military, and economic expediency that are also operative. Any concrete action by any person is a resultant of all these factors. Moreover, these factors are mutually dependent. In operation, each modifies all the others" (236).[61]

These words were written on Bastille Day, July 14, 1939, but there is no resemblance to the political science theories proposed by radically enlightened intellectuals. Henderson's model is scientistic and falsely compares historical causation ("the actions of men") with the attractions and repulsions of atomic particles; his scientism is also characteristic of the conservative Enlightenment, disposed to stave off the rival materialism of the nineteenth century—those ideological formulations supported by the "imperialist" "heroic science" that prevailed throughout the academy before some cultural/social historians of the 1960s–1990s unmasked its fatal pretensions.[62] Diverting his gaze from the facts that could model the structures, functions, and operations of real human institutions, Henderson undergirds fascist ideology in the twentieth century. It would be wrong to say that such thinkers erase class as an analytic category because of their commitments to nation or race as the source of identity. On the contrary, these philosopher-kings are acutely class conscious, believing they can manipulate systems made cockeyed and thrown off balance by selfish and stupid mass/class passions. The moderate men were classicists sensitive to "proportion" in all things. As several 1930s corporatists put it, unlike the puritans who liquidated their peasantries, peasant-rooted countries such as Italy, France, Belgium, and Ireland creatively mastered their bourgeoisies. Their remedy for the chaos of modern decadence was to remand the usurping, snobbish, class-conscious and divisive nineteenth-century middle class back to the middle where such antisocial, anti-intellectual persons naturally belonged. With the materialists safely sandwiched, sick societies would be returned to the steady state. Social equilibrium, classlessness, and a coherent national character were achieved, then, when society was rooted in the peasantry and governed by the aristocrats they, the peasants, had always thrown up in a crisis. In turn, the peasant-chosen self-sacrificing aristocrats would be obedient to the self-sacrificing good king who spoke for the common people.[63] Here was the "ideal force" that bound communities, bringing order out of chaos; that force was a fact, a higher truth that materialist historians were too blind to see.[64]

Of course, (self-indulgent) romantic artists, like other demagogues, should be silenced. In late 1943, Norman Foerster looked ahead to "the humanities after the war" and saw the necessity for lost intellectuals to "refind themselves" in the new-old criticism:

> With few exceptions the departments of the humanities in higher education are ill prepared for the high task before them. An age of science and of naturalistic philosophy has left its mark upon them. They have misapplied the method of science, and they have adopted views of life that make most of the great writers and thinkers of the world appear of little meaning to the modern age. Lost in a relativism approaching nihilism, they have all but ceased to look for the abiding truths which make the distinction between past and present unimportant. If for a century they have declined in prestige, the reason is partly that they themselves have robbed their great field of its greatness. Today their first task is to refind themselves, not to encourage an intellectual and artistic creativity of any and every sort but rather to lay the critical foundations which will give imaginative presentation a sound direction.[65]

It would not do for the lower orders to suppose that the anger one person feels for another could be alleviated through comprehending the larger social situation in which individual struggles are enmeshed, or that economic and political institutions are ill described with the analytic tools bequeathed by corporatist Greeks, medievalists, and Renaissance humanists.

The social views of Princeton professor Willard Thorp, like the corporatists quoted above, bear comparison with Henderson's. Thorp's model societies are paragons of deep breathing and balance, repelling the modernity that forces the

anomic individual to clash with other individuals. Here is the conservatively enlightened Thorp's 1938 account of Melville's radicalism; perforce "one" arrayed dogmatic and marauding transcendental Ahabs against deep-diving Herman Melville,
the proto-Durkheimian, proto–New Dealer Ishmael who said NO!:

> When one contemplates the number of matters on which the age had come
> to a final opinion, to which Melville offered a challenging negative, and the
> number of subjects which the age, for its safety, refused to discuss at all, but
> which Melville insisted on dragging up to the light, one is astonished that he
> was tolerated as long as he was. He seems, indeed, to be unique among his
> contemporaries in his freedom from zeal or prejudice. Even the most sacred
> tabus he insisted on examining with a cool dispassionateness. Not only did
> he question the inalienable right to property, *the dogmas of democracy,* the
> righteousness of imperialist wars and Christian missions, but he dared to
> discuss in a voice louder than a whisper such horrific subjects as canni-
> balism, venereal disease, and polygamy. At the moment when young men in
> America, imbued with transcendentalism, were giving eloquent support to
> the doctrine of the manifest destiny of the nation and defied the world
> to show any civilization which could equal ours, Melville was studying with
> habitually clear eyes a savage society in the South Seas which had achieved
> *an admirable social equilibrium.* While American orators scolded the Old
> World as corrupt and decayed, the home of tyranny and oppression, he mea-
> sured against their glorious American standards the attainment of the naked
> Polynesians. Equipped as no man in his day was by his contact with all sorts
> and conditions of men, having crossed many social frontiers without the bag-
> gage of the "yes-gentry," he returned to the America of 1845 to record what he
> had observed. He could report that he had seen happy savages who could live
> together in charity, and this had made him form a higher "estimate of human
> nature than [he] had ever before entertained"; he could also report that
> he had lived on an American man-of-war where unbelievable human vile-
> ness that made the heart sick nearly overturned any previous theories of the
> perfectibility of man he may have had.
>
> Though the business of navigating a ship never interested Melville, he
> felt a deep concern for the destination of the inhabitants of the world which the
> ship enclosed. He pondered the social relationships, the code of life and man-
> ners, *the clash of individual on individual,* which determined the nature of this
> compact, artificial society, and endeavored to relate what he saw there to the
> larger society which dispatched the ship on its errands of commerce or war.
> Every serious book or article which Melville wrote is a variation on the social
> theme. (*Representative Selections,* xcvii–xcviii; emphasis added)

One wishes that Thorp had not mixed up the reader with his bouncing balls of personified and incommensurable social and political categories; but he cannot help himself, because the social science or anthropological skills he attributes to the intrepid Melville are part of one's own religious, anti-scientific worldview, one in which the psychological acumen/self-control/decorum of individuals leads either to "admirable social equilibrium" or commerce/war.[66]

[D. H. Lawrence, 1923] There are lots of circuits. Male and female, for example, and master and servant. The idea, the IDEA, that fixed gorgon monster, and the IDEAL, that great stationary engine, these two gods-of-the-machine have been busy destroying all *natural* reciprocity and *natural* circuits, for centuries. IDEAS have played the very old Harry with sex relationship, that is, with the great circuit of man and woman. Turned the thing into a wheel on which the human being in both is broken. And the IDEAL has mangled the blood-reciprocity of master and servant into an abstract horror.

Master and servant—or master and man relationship is, essentially, a polarized flow, like love. It is a circuit of vitalism which flows between master and man and forms a very precious nourishment to each, and keeps both in a state of subtle, quivering, vital equilibrium. Deny it as you like, it is so. But once you *abstract* both master and man, and make them both serve an *idea:* production, wage, efficiency, and so on: so that each looks on himself as an instrument performing a certain repeated evolution, then you have changed the vital quivering circuit of master and man into a mechanical machine unison. Just another way of life: or anti-life. (Lawrence, *Studies in Classic American Literature*, 116)

An organicist discourse conflates political organization with physical organisms. Is your society devolving into warring classes or sects? Then loosen the whalebone stays of your Victorian corset, follow with a dose of paternalistic Christian charity, moderate expectations for improvement, and the Hobbesian, overurbanized nineteenth century will approach the happiness and natural harmony of Melville's (clean, generous) savages. The West had not brought progress, but there was a Golden Age before greed, individualism, and artifice (consumerism) blighted the landscape. Although his notebooks of the early 1930s had condemned romantic escapism, by the late 1930s a more conservative, even reactionary, Olson, like Thorp, would find his Golden Age in archaic, preliterate societies: There was no pattern to history, neither repetitive cycles of rise and fall nor Whiggish progress. "I feel too strongly about chance," Olson wrote, identifying with archaic societies perhaps because their warrior myths provided hero-fathers who, in some sense, won the battle with cosmic mothers.

Our analysis of the divisions that matter, of the source of social evil, will determine strategies for self-defense and amelioration. Whereas the scientistic Thorp had identified "the age" (Victorian materialism) as the great adversary, the radically enlightened social theorist studies the structural constraints on piecemeal reform; reformers should not raise unrealistic expectations that only structural transformations in the political economy can accomplish. The corporatists studied in this book, demagogically appealing to primitive emotions with images of spontaneity, unity, and relaxed tensions, cannot formulate a transformative politics, because they do not arm themselves with facts by studying how the system actually functions before they launch their salvos. Revolutionaries will betray their populist politics by the optimism with which they describe the projected outcome: For the corporatist Left, all social evil will be swept away with the bloated capitalists who manipulate Wall Street and the market, while the corporatist Right would puncture bloated bureaucracies (that pamper nonwhites and Nature) to liberate self-adjusting market mechanisms.[67] The operative word is "bloated," which signifies very old upper-class associations of usurpers from the lower orders as puffed-up toads. The toads are the new men, the scientists and engineers who displaced the old elites to create the revolting twentieth-century mass society articulated by Ortega y Gasset in 1930. Being toads, they are naturally oblivious (blinded) to the lessons of the Fall; or worse, they are the rebel angels who caused the Fall.[68] These demonic interlopers are possessed by an insatiable will to power, or the yen for absolute knowledge to be handed over, in their toadying way, to absolutist monarchs. The toads recognize none of the boundaries that have hitherto preserved order and continuity in the realms of good, tolerant kings, who, of course, frown upon excessive deference in their subjects, while the toads' expansionism destroys the balance of power that the good king would like to protect. Such fairy tales suggest social hygiene, the purge, as rational means to a rational end.

For the so-called functionalists, the national/ethnic natural community (always a good thing) is a chemically regulated system optimally in equilibrium, like any other biological body seeking homeostasis. Unless overwhelmed, it adjusts to invasion by foreign agents through either expulsion (vomiting, defecating, or urinating) or through internal destruction. Antibodies mask themselves in clothes closely resembling the enemy's apparel; they may blacken up, enticing hostile microorganisms or aberrant cells to the crushing hug. The primitivist vaccinations of conservatively enlightened Melvilleans cannot be fathomed without seeing through this rhetorical strategy, since the agents of countersubversion appear to be imitating Melville, adopting the persona of the Enlightenment historian/geologist/

sleuth who detects hidden faults and fissures in harmonious corporatist "families" and "honest" individuals. But the black mask functions solely to establish a safe distance from their femme fatale; first they must kill it. The organicist model continues to be embraced by antidemocratic social theorists because, unable rationally to legitimate class rule, they are forced to keep worker-soldiers anxiously focused on defenses—on threats to national security. The forbidden materialist gaze, like the demand for intimacy in love and friendship, is experienced as pressure that leads to disintegration: a breach in the fortress, a hole in the wall, a ripping of the social fabric, a nuclear weapon.

Here is one fascist writer from the 1930s who used some of these images to lure the uncommitted to the camp of revolutionary reaction; note especially his segue from chastity to the "real" boundary between subject and object, his escape from merging:

> Fascism arises . . . as an answer to the rise of Communism which accompanies capitalist decay. Communism is the toxin that calls up the Fascist antitoxin. And Fascism does not appeal to the discredited capitalist values, but to pre-capitalist ones: it emphasizes those virtues and that way of life which capitalism has steadily undermined and which Communism would destroy completely. . . . The full romantic tide of the nineteenth and twentieth centuries has risen with increasing force against all the foundations on which Western civilization was built: it seeks to sweep away things as various as Christian sexual morals and the epistemology which maintains that subject and object are real distinctions. Whatever it attacks it attacks out of hatred of discipline and authority; it is a philosophy which deifies *hybris*.[69]

The inflated rhetoric of the populist propaganda described above may be intended to advance particular careers by mobilizing resentment and hope in the lower orders, but it must lead to disillusion and apathy when repressed facts of the real world return. Here is an unfinished early poem by Olson, perhaps written to his lace-curtain Irish-Catholic mother, who is not at all like Milton's Muse: "[October 14, 1932] You gave me curtains and I hung them / fingering the coarseness of the gauze / as though it were as soft as your white skin / —Gauze / That stood between us like the veil / That separates this frantic life (Death) / From that other death (Living) beyond. / Gauze / That hid—oh. God, I want to press / you close / to me—on my knees before you—k (This is enough—better to write it in the closest chambers of my brain—and body!)"

Perhaps Olson wanted to press mother's/God's goodness into his evil flesh, but mother's blocked, blocking vision would lead the white rat into endless mazes and "mostly madness."

As Melville showed us, the process of emancipation from parental imagos is long and tortuous: We court rejection at "the perilous outpost of the sane." I cannot tell how many moderns have attempted Melville's Promethean task in their own lives, yet civil liberties are meaningless without the self-knowledge and social knowledge that makes self-determination and self-expression more than a recruiting slogan. Social organization may always be conflicted, no matter how rational and equitable the planning and feedback mechanisms in the hands of socialists, or no matter how free of government regulation the market may become in the hands of libertarian conservatives. The critical thinker, like Melville, is neither optimistic nor pessimistic, but alert to ambiguities, flaws, hypocrisies, and blind spots in the processes that legitimate authority. Visions of a more perfect union are deceptive when they imagine the uninterrupted bliss of suckling infants (the fantasy of kneeling Charles) as the end point of human evolution. These regressive longings for the idealized social relations of premodern societies are more powerful and dangerous than rationalists think. Charles Olson, like other irrationalists, would turn my analysis upside down. For Root Man, historians and political scientists are the primum mobile of social decay, "the Protestant thing" that is really Jewish. (End of unwinding excursus.)

Blut und Boden

Returning to his master's thesis, we may see the close resemblance of Olson on Melville to the Notebooks' Olson on Olson. His organicist discourse had fused artist and critic, "it" and "him." The sensual dark races, similarly stirring in Egypt, Turkey, Palestine, and the Pacific, challenge the stability of the northern traveler; Melville's "wandering blood" accounted for the formlessness of his texts, and, except in *Moby-Dick*, did him in. "In most of his writing Melville only achieved some unity when the accidental frame of his subject bound him—as in *Redburn*. Even *Typee* has the high, wooded hills of the valley to restrain the writer who, like Tommo, always, *in spite of happiness, wanted to escape beyond the ranges*. But Omoo had only the coral reefs of the many islands through which he wandered; and it was easy for Melville to slip through the outlets worn in these reefs by the strong currents of his mind" (38; emphasis added). "Always" (in Olson's reading) Melville ignored Ishmael's advice to avoid the horrors of the half-known life. Melville's forceful, wandering mind allowed him "to slip through" the boundaries that give force form. But he also had "innate" powers of narrative. The marriage, though lacking sensuality or companionship, was not to blame for his suffering: As a genius, hell was his portion (citing Carlyle, 45–47). And yet, the experience in the Marquesas was formative—emancipating, but threatening; the problem of the book was how to escape both valley and "loving epicures" (22).

When he fled into the woods at Nukuheva he entered upon a new life. He not only escaped from his mediocre past [embodied in "the rather seedy and conventional" father], the incubus of his parents, and the tedium of his youth. The effects of his life there in Typee, in Tahiti, and around the Pacific reached even to his death. Physically, the hard life in the rat-infested hold took a toll that was not realized until the breakdown of his health at thirty-four. Emotionally his first sex experiences were associated with vice and sexual disease—this seemed to Mumford an explanation of later irregularities. Mentally, these years opened his eyes to the blackness of civilization; he was in his own phrase "timonized"; the dark devil Azzogeddi, that grew out later, was planted in his soul. But suggesting these effects is all we can do. We must narrow the spotlight and watch him in his quieter moments. (12–13)

The experience in the South Seas and in "the rat-infested hold" drained the body and disastrously stimulated the crusading spirit that would alienate him from civilization. Olson's fearful attraction to Melville/Ahab as artist and agitator was clear: "He could tell a whacking story" (21); but, on the other hand, "It is an index to Melville's mind that many of his books march under a crusading banner. Both *Typee* and *Omoo* are thrusts at the Christian missionaries. *White-Jacket* is a purposed piece of propaganda against the naval abuses of the 1840s; and even *The Confidence-Man* in a spiritual way, is an attack on our lack of trust in each other. [Had he read it?[70]] In their variety there is pathos, for Melville, frantic with crusading zeal, never found the exact cause for his energies. He could only assail the battlements of life with doubt as his shattered lance" (24–25). Melville's "reveries" destroyed balance; probably thinking of Ahab's Narcissus gaze: "He threw his judgment overboard when he leaned over the side of a ship" (41). Perhaps the reveries have caught Olson/Starbuck: "This book [*Typee*] was spun out of himself like a spider's web."

While a great many authors put forward a more or less conventional and Europeanized picture of their civilization, Melville takes us back to the poetry of its origin, and wallows in the fundamental concept of nineteenth century America, the idea of the contrast between man and nature, a nature constantly subdued and yet unvanquished.

And the story of the white whale is typically American also in its literary form. As America is an agglomeration of races and traditions from which a new race and tradition has been formed, so in this book the material is gathered from widely different cultures, and reflects the most varied spiritual interests and levels of taste, yet is nevertheless fused by a new heat, unified by a new accent. (27)

Although he had promised to correct the hero worship of the 1920s critics, Olson was abject in the face of Ahab's grandeur. The old Viking's son could not have believed what he wrote about Ahab as an academic father-pleaser. *Moby-Dick's* greatness was linked mystically to Ahab's pointed weapon that resolved the clash between God and Mammon, hack and poet: "For in *Moby-Dick* the white heat of his imagination fused the two into as perfect a strand as the rods of Ahab's harpoon which was tempered by blood and lightning" (121). But Melville said he was damned by dollars; there could be no honest compromise with the market. Perhaps responding with anger to his own groundless claim, after dismissing "the phlegmatic Starbuck" Olson offered a frightened contrast reminiscent of the "vitiating power" he felt during that same period: "The man from whom they [the crew] receive the withering strength to be uplifted is Ahab . . . here is an Oedipus, a Samson, a Lear stricken with a supernal woe" (130).

One touch of rat-infested Venus and strong men wither and go blind. "Ahab was truly God-like. Like Satan in *Paradise Lost*, he had the proportions, if not the attributes of divinity. Like Satan, he fell when passion stood upon the neck of reason. He was a Prometheus bound, bound to the massy hulk of the White Whale. He had stolen the fire of wrath from the gods and by its very strength did he perish. Such a man-god was Ahab, Melville's greatest work, compounded of these contradictions" (130). The passage sounds like the Lewis Mumford riff on Ahab's misguided desire to fight evil with either physical or intellectual weapons, to fight at all. For Olson in this passage, Promethean fiery strength is "wrath," not the warmth and light that instruct all learning and technique or the hardened skin that allows him to withstand cruelty without cynicism. He has created a contradiction that exists only in Olson's notebook. It was the demonic Fedallah who was more visibly "bound to the massy hulk of the White Whale."

As I have argued, Ahab is determined to seek truth and justice, to wrench meaning from history even if the universe was created by an inscrutable, indifferent, or demonic god. Moreover, Olson has not reported the double meaning of the rope or line, signifying the connection to Nature as both generative and destructive, jealous of her secrets; nor has he noted the mixed blessing of Ahab's gaze, which could be simultaneously emancipating and disintegrating (angering Mother), or worse, could feel like Mother's abhorrent probing and prospecting (angering Herman). The eyes depicted in the propaganda and art associated with the French Revolution were ambiguous, retaining their Catholic connotations of authority and surveillance while deployed by pro-revolutionary propagandists to represent the illumination and piercing insights of rationalism.[71] In Ishmael's apocalyptic narration, both the white whale and Ahab's ship are likened to fallen angels, violently disturbing ocean, air, and sky. Moby Dick breaks "the profoundest silence" of "the becharmed crew" and the rainbow comes and goes.

Suddenly the waters around them slowly swelled in broad circles; then quickly upheaved, as if sideways sliding from a submerged berg of ice, swiftly rising to the surface. A low rumbling sound was heard; a subterraneous hum; and then all held their breaths; as bedraggled with trailing ropes, and harpoons, and lances, a vast form shot lengthwise, but obliquely from the sea. Shrouded in a thin drooping veil of mist, it hovered for a moment in the rainbowed air; and then fell swamping back into the deep. Crushed thirty feet upwards, the waters flashed for an instant like heaps of fountains, then brokenly sank in a shower of flakes, leaving the circling surface creamed like new milk round the marble trunk of the whale.[72]

. . . maddened by . . . fresh irons that corroded in him, Moby Dick seemed combinedly possessed by all the angels that fell from heaven. (567)

[The wing of a sky-hawk is caught as Tashtego nails Ahab's red flag of revolt to the mast of the sinking ship.] . . . and so the bird of heaven, with archangelic shrieks, and his imperial beak thrust upwards, and his whole captive form folded in the flag of Ahab, went down with his ship, which, like Satan, would not sink to hell till she had dragged a living part of heaven along with her, and helmeted herself with it. (572)

But Ahab's disappearance is written in images that both parallel and diverge from the vanishing and subsequent reappearance of Fedallah:

[To Ahab] "The Parsee!" cried Stubb—"He must have been caught in—. . . caught among the tangles of your line—I thought I saw him dragging under." (561)

Lashed round and round to the fish's back; pinioned in the turns upon turns in which, during the past night, the whale had reeled the involutions of the lines around him, the half torn body of the Parsee was seen; his sable raiment frayed to shreds; his distended eyes turned full upon old Ahab. (568)

. . . The harpoon was darted; the stricken whale flew forward; with igniting velocity the line ran through the groove; —ran foul. Ahab stooped to clear it; he did clear it; but the flying turn caught him round the neck, and voicelessly as Turkish mutes bowstring their victim, he was shot out of the boat, ere the crew knew he was gone. Next instant, the heavy eye-splice in the rope's final end flew out of the stark-empty tub, knocked down an oarsman, and smiting the sea, disappeared in its depths. (572)

Ahab was "shot out of the boat," his neck encircled by the unwinding harpoon rope as if he had been assassinated, while the "heavy eye-splice in the rope's final end" smites the sea. One must read carefully to infer that Ahab too is lashed to the now-submerged whale. At first glance at least, like has been joined to like: Ahab to the maternal ocean (a few paragraphs earlier "creamed like new milk"); by contrast, the satanic Fedallah had disappeared, then was ostentatiously displayed, lashed to the arbitrary paternal God personified in Hobbes's Leviathan; "his distended eyes turned full upon old Ahab." Here is the phallic gaze again, transferred to Moby Dick through the Parsee. When Ahab strikes through the mask, he demystifies illegitimate authority, but at the same time "the whale" feels the "corroding" "irons" that, in life, have rusted the artist's secrets, wishes, and beliefs.[73] The death of Fedallah was an omen meant to warn Ahab that the quest was doomed. Perhaps it reminded Olson that independent and inquisitive flesh is bound to destruction by the state. By equating Fedallah's end with Ahab's, Olson may have found greatness in Ahab's imputed evil, not in his goodness and bravery; this was a portentous misreading. Like other youthful romantics, it would not be hard for Olson to turn on the glamorous but wicked Ahab when political expediency demanded.

Oddly, Olson tried to separate "Melville the character creator" (Ahab) from "Melville the man" (139) but could not carve a clear channel, nor did he appear to care. The wages of hypermoralistic independent spirits were death. Decadence was bad and good and bad again ad infinitum: *Pierre*, although "covered with green mold, like a hidden rock . . . is one of the most amazing books ever written" (157). But then Olson brought back the chastened Weaver in his contrast of *Pierre* and "Billy Budd": "Melville ends *Pierre* in a helpless spasm of hate against a world, a life, a God that could allow such tragedy. He ends *Billy Budd* in the realization that evil has its place but good can triumph by keeping itself intact. This is Aristotle's true tragedy—the representation of Eudaimonia, the highest kind of happiness. To Melville it was not a resolution, it was not an answer" (175–76). Olson has once again reversed himself: Impossibly, Melville exits as both unwitting New Critic and unrepentant Ahab/Wandering Jew, dominated by thought, filled with intimations of evil, and even in death "still seeking rest." After a brief deviation to the Right, Olson had returned to the contagious revolutionary puritan, one who "totter[ed] on the perilous rim [of insanity]" (149) and was susceptible to Schopenhauer's "shadow" because he had already been greyed/green molded by experience (155, 157), infiltrated by Schopenhauer's/Isabel's "black blood" and irresistible "malignancy." Here was the "dire pessimism" or "mysticism" that beckoned him to "the search for Truth" (162–66).[74] Olson wished that Melville/Taji (*Mardi*) had gotten off at the Christian Socialist utopia of Serenia with the philosopher Babbalanja (69–74). There Taji would have been unplagued by speculative thought, the charging Isabel, unchanged from the fascinating, jealous wraith of the master's thesis to the "chromo Cenci" entrapping Pierre in "lampish incest" in *Call Me Ishmael* (1947).

Billy Budd, in contrast to the Isabel-molded Pierre, was dead but not red and black: His mother would have wanted it that way.

There was a pattern to Olson's rantings. The lamp-lighter Eve/Ariadne/Prometheus and her program mated unlike things, her universalist morality pressing into his flesh. Isabel was the apocalyptic sublime. Brooding on the all-disclosing vista of radical Enlightenment was not an appealing entertainment to conservatively enlightened prospectors of the twentieth century. And Olson had rooted himself, not in Melville's indomitably good Ahab, but in raging Evil, in the Big Money (not that he ever got any).

["Chief" Morrow to Charles Olson, 1931] Western civilization is in the position of a child playing with T.N.T. Without some knowledge of how to use its scientific power, without some knowledge of how to control the pent-up forces in its social and economic relationships, disaster is bound to overtake it.

[Carl Van Doren to Wilbert Snow, April 24, 1933] Well Charles Olson is about the only man I've ever met—certainly the only very young man—who showed signs of really understanding Melville. He'll do a good biography if he keeps up at the present rate. The only snag ahead is that fellow Murray at Harvard. He's a good man, too, and knows a lot of Melville in addition to having real insight into the kind of bastard Melville was (I use bastard in its complimentary, not its technical sense).

It was Carl Van Doren who suggested that Olson reconstitute Melville's library, much of which had been sold for a pittance at Melville's death, an important task for those laying foundations for fancy-free Melville scholarship.[75] But he also got political guidance intended to vouchsafe an establishment career. Olson needed it, because journal entries of 1933 and 1934 suggest sympathy with Melville's most radical books, views somewhat at variance with the master's thesis.

[February 20, 1933] What a comparison Hawthorne and Melville offer at almost every point of the ragged cliffs of their individual beings. Yet, they both drew the force of evil in life—in the "House of the Seven Gables" Hawthorne set down the remorseless forces of evil as M. did in "Moby" and "Pierre." (Notebooks, 25)

[January 25, 1934] Mardi, Moby and Pierre are Melville's Prophetic Books just as Typee was his Song of Innocence (and Omoo his Song of Experience). (Notebooks, 25)

[January 26, 1934] The why Melville's epic similes in *Moby* are good and Arnold's are bad—Melville has theme epic and character heroic to spread his cloth of gold over, just as Milton and Homer. (Notebooks, 25)

Wilbert Snow, his former adviser, was grooming his headstrong, zig-zagging student for a credible entrance into the academy throughout 1934. Olson (then teaching English at Clark University) was ordered to admire the antimilitarist Archibald MacLeish, not his critics Edmund Wilson, Granville Hicks, and Mike Gold (in Snow's opinion, red allies who were instigating a "fascist putsch" while accusing MacLeish of fascist sympathies). Olson should be grateful for the "fine help" of Van Doren and "the generosity of Weaver" ("one of the best young men at Columbia"); he should start with a carefully wrought introduction to Melville's journal of 1849; his career depended on it. Olson's critical faculties were not developed enough to undertake a full-scale biography: "Sometimes you hit things off excellently, sometimes you fumble noticeably."[76] Earlier that year, Olson had examined the Lemuel Shaw papers at the Massachusetts Historical Society, discovering family letters alluding to Alan Melvill's wandering mind and the possible existence of an illegitimate daughter. These documents would be hoarded, perhaps as bait for Guggenheim Foundation grants, but Olson showed them at once to his amazed mentor: "[Snow to Olson, March 6, 1934] I am all stirred up about your new Melville discovery, and hope you will let me know if any new points of view are going to develop out of those letters recently unearthed. I feel stronger than ever that you ought to keep at this new material until you write a new life of Melville. While it may not be any more sensitive than Mumford's it would certainly bring in a great deal of new material which Mumford knows nothing about."[77]

A photograph taken during this period shows Olson coiffed and suited like an English don, another T. S. Eliot. No wonder his notebook entry for May 6, 1934, describing a dutiful visit to the grave of "Ishmael's father," expressed Olson's self-doubts and aggression toward Melville (who no rational map could locate and whose writing was, in Snow's opinion, obviously too hard for a nice young man to read):

I made my pilgrimage to Melville's grave/ [Dead leaves bunched on a dead grave.] Today. It was a sobering experience. The plot lies a mile deep in the huge Woodlawn Cemetary far up in the Bronx. As I joged along in the greenness and the groundness after flat hard colorless Broadway I yearned overwhelmingly to throw myself on the grass over his body when I should get to him. It gave me deep pause, then, to find no grass beneath his stone, only a bristling, close-cropped, forbidding ivy covering the bare ground over his body—and that ivy dead to leafless save a few eaten & wrinkled ones of another year. Even nature seemed ready to challenge my presumption in hoping to come close to Herman Melville. It was chastening to be so near his bones and the dust of his bones and be no closer. I proposed to uncover his mind and soul quite as ruthlessly from the grave of his books and letters as though (like a Jerry Cruncher) I had struck a spade into the soft turf there this afternoon. I had hoped to be like Ishmael. "And I only am escaped alone to tell thee," to tell of Ishmael's father. God, how I was humbled. And when I looked at the stone cross twined with its stone ivy over Elizabeth Shaw's barren, too, beside her husband, and the stones of the three children, *I only* knew more sadness.

I left refreshed—and wiser. Yet I could have wished the visit impossible: I mean I wish Melville's had been a Viking's funeral. If the sea had been his grave it somehow would have been better to look for him there than to find him crowded in a huge metropolitan graveyard, surrounded by towering columns and mausoleums of the rich and the mighty, with no mark of the sea on his stone, only an unbroken quill and an unmarked scroll. Though the stone was rough-hewn marble and the tallest oak in Calapa Grove grew beside him and spread its branches [*sic*] into him![78]

Was Olson intimidated by the "towering columns and mausoleums of the rich and the mighty"? The insurmountable distance and melancholy expressed here did not match Olson's exuberant marginalia to *Moby-Dick*, the book delivered by his Viking postman father only five years earlier. And this tall father was still alive, his branches (not roots) spreading in the son. Taking cues from mausoleum directors, trying to deaden this quite different, threatening attitude toward authority and the ivory tower, Olson wondered perhaps how close he should get to the "new material" "recently unearthed." And how was he to achieve the proportion that Snow expected from his potentially excellent critical judgments? Another letter from Wilbert Snow suggests that the sensational family letters buttressed Weaver's portrait of Melville (against Forsythe or Anderson) as alert reporter of a historic family. Weaver was no longer the myth maker scolded in the thesis Snow had directed. Who exactly, then, were his legitimate fathers to be? Snow wrote to Olson on September 21, 1934: "Your discovery of the father's insanity and the illegitimate child, together with the account of Melville's reading, have made *Mardi* an entirely different book.[79] I shall read it as if I were looking at it for the first time. Not as a fantastic outpouring of Melville's imagination in a month of depression, but as an artistic account of his reading and family relationships." [The switch from honest Melville to distorted Melville/Olson:] "I am glad that you realize your critical limitations, although in this, as in everything else, you have a tendency to make the case too strong." For a moment, Snow has seen things as they are, but flees; Snow

now addresses Olson, applauding his newfound humility, while pulling him (and Melville?) back to an undefined center.

In June 1934, Olson went father shopping again, this time successfully approaching his only competition, "that fellow Murray at Harvard" named by Carl Van Doren as the one with "real insight into the kind of bastard Melville was." Olson and Henry Murray began the friendship with a division of labor. In a letter to Olson on June 7, 1934, Murray wrote, "I was delighted to hear of your discovery at the Massachusetts Historical Society, and think that you have the nucleus for a further elaboration or reconstruction of Melville's life. I understand that for the present you are leaving the Morewood material[80] to me and I am leaving the Historical Society material to you?" In his typically low-profile, self-deprecating manner, Murray erased his considerable wealth and access to family letters and other materials (but not reminiscences?), instead painting the marginal Olson as the true live oak tree: the better scientist (a down-to-earth materialist) and the better psychologist with "a real intuition":

> [June 13, 1934] Please do not dampen your own zest by giving house room to the delusion that I am rich in Melville lore and you are a pauper. You have a great store of facts with [sic] which I am ignorant; you have had a literary training and critical discipline which I have not; and you have a real intuition. I consider that we are attempting to approach the same object from somewhat different standpoints; that we have different contributions to make, but that yours is based on more solid facts than mine, and therefore ultimately of more value. Three hundred years of science has made it impossible for any trained person to enjoy reading anything which is based on airy nothings. My book will boil down to airy nothings.

Murray himself was only the floating *Luftmensch* and fake: Olson should harbor no delusions as to which one held the real power.

Olson acquired the Constable Edition of Melville's complete works in the summer of 1934. Marginalia suggest he was reading *Moby-Dick, Mardi, Pierre,* and *Clarel* carefully for the first time, or at least with increasingly conservative/freshly curious eyes (in the case of *Mardi* perhaps as late as 1939), for instance in the excitement of his pounces ("Homo!") upon the insinuated erotic interactions between Clarel and Vine.[81] But the purge was incomplete: Murray may have stamped him, but Olson remained at least partly unregenerate. Olson's comments could mark Melville as unproblematically joined to his Tory or Christian Socialist characters, or conversely as "an abolitionist" in *Mardi* (226), while dancing around Ahab's virtues or vices. In "Hawthorne and His Mosses" (Constable ed. 13:128), Olson recognized "Ahab!" in Melville's paean to Hawthorne: "a great deep intellect, which drops down into the universe like a plummet." Yet Olson's *Moby-Dick* shows that he distanced himself from Anacharsis Clootz, marked with an X, and no wonder: "X revolutionary fanatic [who] appeared at the bar of the Assembly (Paris) at the head of 36 foreigners; and, in the name of this 'embassy of the human race,' declared that the world adhered to the Declaration of the Rights of Man and of the Citizen. Called 'the orator of the human race.' Guillotined as Hébertist, 1794" (149). On page 253, "Ahab's mind has driven out the soul," but on page 342, "Ahab throughout is an intense, tightened, controlled, almost grim man: from the Symphony on he receives sympathy." More terror than pity is seen in other marginalia, one responding to Melville's core conflict: If all humanity are children of the same Father, what are our social responsibilities?

The wealthy Pierre has read the orphaned Isabel's tear-stained letter pleading to be owned by her brother; a chemical in the ink has turned her tears to the color of blood. Isabel is the elder Pierre's abandoned natural child. Pierre's half-sister does not ask for money; she simply wants to be acknowledged as a member of the family. Sensing that his life would change forever, Pierre had tried to destroy the letter before reading it: It was "so completely torn in two by Pierre's own hand, that it indeed seemed the fit scroll of a torn, as well as bleeding heart." Here Olson wrote "Isabel—a harpy, a vampire, a sucking, covering bat thing—whether because of the prose—or by intent? a dark, harsh graying thing." Then, on top of the following page, "The only story which was whispered in the family was of HM's madness but what of this story—Mrs B & Miss A?" Then, on page 472, "Truth and Thoughts the whores Melville pursued to his peril."[82] If there is one pivotal moment in Melville's writing or in Olson's life, this is it: The theme is disillusion with benevolent paternal authority. Class allegiance switches from the upper classes to the unrepresentables. Pierre will reunite the two halves of the "amazing" letter and throw in his lot with Isabel's. The ex-radical Olson, the champion of social integration, will look away. Both thought and feeling are proscribed: On a leaf of *Clarel*, Olson unhesitatingly declared that literature functions to distance readers from unpleasant physical sensations, most likely the pain of a torn and bleeding heart: "Clarel's a painful book. The pain is in the reader because the pain is in the writer—it's not, unfortunately, in the book itself, as it ought to be."

"Melville has become Jew"

Olson's father died in 1935, perhaps partly in response to his son's passive aggression. The postal worker was leading a rank-and-file struggle to oust corrupt union leadership; about to depart for the showdown at the national convention in Cleveland, he asked Charles to lend him his leather suitcase, "newer and bigger than his"; Charles refused and the senior Olson "went away sore." En route to Cleveland he suffered two strokes, then, as he lay dying, he responded to Mary, his wife, but did not "notice" his son. At least that is the way Olson told the story later in an unfinished tribute to the elder Olson.[83] That same year, 1935, Olson consulted the lawyer Carroll Wilson, general counsel to the Guggenheim brothers and a major book collector; Wilson also was compiling a list of Melville's reading. Olson was worried about his future; he hated the academy for the time it diverted from his artistic projects, including the "rounded" Melville book (not just the report of his reading) with which he was "pregnant." Like Snow, Wilson advised him to get the 1849 journal into print but to avoid a Melville biography: The Melville ranks were overcrowded.[84] In spite of the valuable materials Olson was accumulating, and in spite of his many alert and sensitive Melville readings, then, the anxieties, political fears, or jealousies of older men intervened. And as Olson moved to the Right, Ishmael/Ahab was split in two: One quite healthy conservative presented himself as orphan, applied for upper-class patronage and company, and promised conventional essays. But if Olson were to look at the selfish sellout con man through his dead father's Ahab-eyes, then the reflection would make his father sick. The Ahab who finally emerged was identical to the Olson excoriated in his notebooks of the 1930s.

[July 7, 1933] I suppose my intellectual weakness lies in the way I cling to my few ideas—like a drunkard to his hard-gotten bottle. I have so few ideas that the danger is that I rush to defend them before I have consider [sic] their case. I am like a shyster lawyer snatching up that rare fee. I become at once the champion and the victim of my own ideas. Another danger is that I'll fall down short of the true thought—sustained—because of my mental legerdemain. It is too easy for me to simulate wisdom. I can don and doff the cloak of Solomon with the speed and deception of a magician. It is a tempting performance. The more I avoid it, however, the truer I'll become. (Notebooks, 25)

[Winter 1939–40] The society and the sonnet both confine. Somehow [the artist] must work carefully within such limits. But never at the loss of his revolutionary spirit—that he must preserve even against doom. (Notebooks, 48)

[Summer and Fall 1939] . . . self. The action done at the expense of everyone else for self gain. It's the common root of all evil on this earth. . . . Dark traces of the past lay in his soul, ready to break through into the regions of consciousness . . . the great deed and misdeed of primeval times—the murder of the father . . . . (Notebooks, 133)

So the other shyster lawyer, Ahab the Promethean, became an emblem for every-thing that was deceptive, cruel, and corrupt in American history, while the doubly bound volume of Olson's published Melville criticism became ever more withhold-ing, obscure, eccentric, truncated, and diagrammatic.

In late 1938, Olson's article "Lear and *Moby-Dick*" (written in 1937 and read with suggestions for revision by Carl Van Doren and Matthiessen) appeared in the first issue of *Twice-a-Year*, a literary magazine devoted to civil liberties. The essay, as Olson told the Guggenheim Foundation, was the culmination of four years of close study in one hundred volumes (including seven volumes of Shakespeare's works) owned and annotated by Melville.[85] Olson now had a psychohistory in mind, an intensified focus after his reading of Freud's *Moses and Monotheism* in 1939. (Olson misunderstood Freud as the defender of myth against history, reflection, and ab-straction. It was, rather, these latter critical processes, opposed to myth that em-bodied Freud's concept of spirituality.[86]) Moreover, Olson had been electrified by sensational and suggestive "family" gossip passed on by Weaver. His unpub-lished notebooks of 1939–40 filtered the expanding Melville problem through Tory lenses: Catholic corporatism could rescue America from the sublime project of modern art-making; from exploring the material world, then assembling and dra-matizing what has been gathered and understood with social contradictions and di-vided loyalties glitteringly in place. Olson was now living in Cambridge, attending classes and teaching at Harvard.[87]

[Summer and Fall 1939] M—atomic will—the Protestant thing in him needed so badly a synthesis, something to integrate him—something to flow his At-lantic and Pacific together—the perilous synthesis of both seas was M-D—the Pacific got forced out & the Atlantic did not know how to get along—spirit of early years was at once the old West & the new—both exploration & industrialization—Where did the sensual & passionate come from in him—where?—J: equatorial vs. middle-class/C: Irish vs. Swede/Catholic vs Protestant—*synthesis is the Catholic if I can return—the danger is the Prot-estant mind*

Melville's struggle was to pass over into the modern—he was enough of a genius to know something was inadequate with what his century stood for & what his country [stood for]. "Utilitarian time and country." He saw that the adventure of man into space and into matter—both deflected man from man & man from spirit. . . . In these years [1851–56] it was as though M were cast-ing off an old skin, which had had its beauty, but was inadequate to the new season. All the writhing of self-pity, all the coiling of despair, sickness, and even insanity, are signs of the crisis he was passing through. The struggle of M's life was the transition to the modern and in that struggle he lost. . . .

[W]hat I have pointed out is the drama of the book—the conflict between the crew and Ahab gave the verdict of good & true to crew & evil to Ahab: *a bad capt—and evil man;* and the other thing is the way Melville allows himself to be so hypnotized by his creature Ahab as to lose the book to him. These two points are the indices of this very thing in M—he was great enough both to see the symbol and to criticize it—but he was not great enough to go beyond it. He was in danger of slipping back as he did, in '51–'56 (even after as a result of the crisis) into the state of the 19th when he needed to be in the 20th. . . . He had discussed space. But something else in him, which enabled him to introduce "the humanities" into M-D knew that the thing to explore was no longer the face of the earth but the face of man. (Notebooks, 133; emphasis added)

The subject is explicitly Olson, the torn artist and scholar advised by Melville's rifts; geography turned inward brings white death/white rot to the happy family. A summary of *Moses and Monotheism* follows these pages; Olson, confusing neurosis and psychosis, now sees that Melville's insanity is manifested in repetition-compulsion, projection, and delusion (Olson refers both to primeval events such as parricide lingering in genetic inheritance and lived traumas): "the sovereignty of an inner psychical reality [that] has been established over the reality of the outer world; the way to insanity is open. (M's case: . . ." Traces of Freud mark Olson's analysis, but the repressed racial explanations (and inferences from Melville's art) return to explain Melville's difficulties:

What broke him personally & humanly—was a prophet without a tradition to sustain prophecy. . . . (Possibility too, did he kill a man? *end of Typee* isn't there something in Anderson about this? & *father problems*—burning of the picture—Mother hated him—*must* be something *violent*—traumatic, to use the lingo, which had happened—for sex—murder—incest—father destruction—mother joined together—(father's death—Augusta? Kate?) [Olson suspects incest.] I do not propose, for I have not the skill, to unravel the psychological complexity of all this—my friend Harry Murray has, or undoubtedly will, do it full justice.

Olson twisted Freud's views on Jew-hatred. Whereas Freud had emphasized Jewish chosenness as the demanding, but also gratifying, adherence to ethical behavior (with one universal moral standard, conquering the selfish emotions in order to protect and advance humanity), Olson tossed this off as narcissism (self-love) and turned Jew-hatred into Christian envy: "a *profound jealousy of them* because twice they killed what all of us want to kill, the father—they killed both

Moses and Christ." The Trinity would relieve vertigo in exceptionally unbalanced Americans:

M had to have a God he could touch, not contemplate. Too much can be laid upon the abstract in (M)—his heady senses must always be recalled. And what a Christ offered to him was an escape from the intolerable abstraction involved in Protestantism—and Judaism . . . . M needed what Catholicism has offered the race. Lacking it he tried a lonely love for Christ. What M needed was both the Virgin & the Holy Ghost—one more sensuous the other more abstract than either Christ or God. (Title book "The Mutineer") . . . M is a man of inadequate intellect—and even his spiritual diversions fall short of problem he sets himself—his spirit's Catholic but his inheritance & habit is Protestant, his flesh is Mediterranean, but his will is Northern—even *Evil,* upon which he bears so, he has not got much *reach*—isn't it true that on Evil he's best in its drama, than its complications—*Mardi, Clarel:* / use that conjunction

Ungar alone? Why? the anger & the demand? What M forfeited in himself for the pallid Clarel

What in sum, can you take to be him? anti-reason, anti-science, anti-revolution, anti-Protestant; *but*—the leap, the embrace of the contraries he cannot, will not make—thus his strongest mood (and character) is attack—Ungar—on all these & his *only* final no is *tolerance*—thus he spends most of his time yearning for & questioning: faith, Christ, God, love, feeling, senses, nature—only when *tolerance,* as of Clarel, manages to admit & become *justice* of Billy does the man shed his pathos. (Notebooks, 133)

In Billy's story, romantic Melville had "shed his pathos" as if it were a soft skin, revealing the feudal armor beneath: Billy Budd's "justice" had infiltrated and transformed the too-tolerant, ever-questioning, open-minded, yearning Clarel who utters Melville's "only final no." Olson can't bear the sight of Melville's undeserved suffering. Billy had graciously submitted to illegitimate authority, switching from self-defense to accommodation, a gesture that relieves Olson's anxieties. The "pallid" Clarel's Hebraic Protestant mind, in its weak-kneed refusal to "embrace the contraries" in admittedly contrived but indispensable mythic narratives, was bringing white rot to the West. Plato's noble lies were rejected by Melville and Ahab: Bereft of the Hegelian synthesis, the Protestant thing attacked and attacked again. It must be stopped. Significantly, Olson did not identify with the part-Catholic, part-Indian Ungar, Melville's "strongest mood and character." For Olson in his defensive mode, submission masked as devastating social criticism preserves life; Melville's (and father's) repeated attacks on hypocritical authority fatally weaken the body politic. Olson was impressed by the Harvard professor William Ellery Sedgwick's verdict of Melville's "abstract consciousness," a quality praised by Freud but erased by Olson, who had rectified Freud with Jung:

[Winter 1939–40] Recall on last trip; Matty's [Matthiessen's] vaginal O'Keefe carefully hung in the bed-room & the conversation at dinner table over Auden &—the penis (in this case Ahab's!). . . . Ellery [Sedgwick] on HM: The problem of consciousness in M—in M.D. tightrope walking—the act going on before your eyes—abstract consciousness—everything came to him that way. Ask? What is truth & the one chance at an answer is gone. / *M importunate consciousness*— . . . M could not decide against direct sense perception without hanker [hunker?] for it . . . / M lacked the *self-poised mind* (When writer regards life as mythical & typical) What is gained is an insight into the higher truth depicted in the actual; a smiling knowledge of the eternal, the ever-being and authentic; a know-of the schema in which the supposed individual lives, unaware, in his naive belief in himself as unique in space and time, of the extent to which his life is but formula and repetition. (Notebooks, 48)

So the world of the senses dizzied Melville; his "hanker" for "direct sense perception" was responsible for the missing uninquiring "self-poised mind." For Olson, the idea of sameness (that he makes the Freudian/Jungian legacy) gives "dignity & security." In the next passage, Olson grasps modern tools to uncover the unsmiling Ahab's malady: History without myth kills art:

Van Wyck Brooks is right when he sees a resemblance to Beowulf. But the analysis—and I use the word in its precise psychological meaning— of Ahab's monomania with all its unfolding of hate & conscience & dreams in the stricken captain—exhibits a clinical ruthlessness which transports one into a world more modern and conscious—into the world of Dostoevsky. *Moby-Dick* has contact with both spheres, the one "remote from ours" as Wagner put it and the one "where the brain long ago developed into the modern intellectual tool we know," as Mann puts it, of "full consciousness" as Wagner put it. . . . The failure of [*Pierre*] does not lie in its autobiography but in the absence of mythic framework or atmosphere in which the psychological can be included. . . . / M's mixture of *quietism* and *heroics* / For his nature, too, was combined of urgent and tormenting desires for power and pleasure, together with longings for moral enlightenment and release; it was a conflict of passion and desire for peace / Schiller's rotten apples (a working condition) (Notebooks, 30)

The Olson notebooks contain extremely lurid entries, hitherto unpublished Melville family dirt; they are of a piece with the obscene drawings, scribbles, and comments on other pages but are quoted here to cast doubt on their reliability: What was their origin: family memory or inference? Or were these facts outgrowths of the larger Olson/counter-Reformation narrative, the Don Juan–Faust fatal separation from community that turned moral enlightenment into taboos? According to legend, the demystification of repressive aristocratic authority practiced by materialists can lead only to libertine excess: With dormant senses reawakened by the devil, free associations take over. Patterns are seen, floating orphans into the faraway of history with a too-coherent narrative linking past and present; naming names, history kills myth, the only source of corporatist unity:

[Ca. 1940] . . . HM/ I am Moses writing the story of Melville's creation of the Pacific world . . . Old Testament—Prose—Pacific: all joined: Why M is so vexatious & makes one impatient is his inability to abide with himself. He capitulates with his time & world, & lost himself / "The giver of all given conditions is in ourselves." M had to go to the Old Testament, so he went. . . . Uncirce the Circe world to beatrice me . . . (Notebooks, #6)

[Winter–Spring 1940] M's *disposition and tendency*—He so inclined to associations of thought, that it characterized and controlled his whole inner life. "Whenever he wrote his soul was played upon by chords and correspondences, diverted and led away into far-reaching considerations which mingled past and to come in the present moment." (Notebooks, 46)

Merging with Moses/Melville has turned Olson into a rebel and a parricide (Beatrice Cenci/Isabel). Dionysus has triumphed: The apples are rotting and Melville (or Olson?) is a degenerate with a family history of insanity, caught in an impasse. Olson in decay will prescribe negative capability as antitoxin to sensuous Hebraic moralism. Waldo Frank is remembered, speaking of the "pathology of sheer inanition [that] came to [HM]. God knows I understand it." Anemia comes from lack of "traditional nurture" in America—blood-and-soil rootedness. Ishmael is: "mocker—sporting . . . homo, half-Egypt, half-Jew, exile, wild ass. . . ." Melville's alleged vices are directly linked to a demand for privacy (the towel defense against family surveillance) and democratic ideals surreptitiously joined to the Head, not the Heart:

HM/ M drank good deal, apparently alone. *M stuffed key hole or hung towel over it* . . . M violent sexually about the time of the 2 girls . . .[88] [We must not indulge in crusades; should affirm, not slay dragons.] Democracy, for example, can demand champions only if it itself is more aware than it has shown itself of the dangers of its rationalism & faith in equality. Morals are taboos— emotional controls, not intellectual concepts. The seeds of democracy lay in a century which secretly had shifted the base of morals into an area of the human mind where morals don't exist—the mind. Alternatives—the curse of today which leads to blind action. We've reduced life to the choice of a coin—one of two faces to everything. And pitifully the flip of a coin is the frantic gesture of those powerless to choose. Foreign policy, social system, morals—in all everyone wants to reduce choice to a black and white decision. It's such a simplification dictated by the unnerved fear in our time of the confusion we inhabit.

Olson was referring to the revolutions of the seventeenth and eighteenth centuries that had institutionalized civil liberties in the State (the mind), defying Hume's dictum that truth and certainty lay in the center, the X-spot for established authority. Olson does not mean we are powerless because badly educated: We are powerless because we refuse to be confused, to admit that evil presses into good. Father wasn't so good, and mother isn't so bad. That amoral arrangement of furniture in the mind allows the colossus to straddle clashing classes. But now he wants closure, lest confusion make him sick:

M and my 56 passage: The flight from love leads to a crisis & leaves him in an utterly confused and unsettled condition, in a derangement such as usually appears at the climax of illness if neither of the two struggling forces is so much stronger than the other, that the difference could establish a strict, psychic regime. *under such psychological constellations analysis* brings *cure* at the same time. . . .

[Half-page is torn out, one page is heavily blackened and unreadable: what remains follows:] Jessie [*sic*] told W[eaver] after they tried (3 times?) to have M committed to an asylum, they finally thought of a plan to send him to the East in the hope he'd never return.

Lizzie used to run to Boston when she couldn't stand it any longer—and there spill her heart & her troubles to Cousin Jessie with whom she stayed.

When trunk opened, the Metcalfs passed on all mss & kept out one document which had to do with someone's commitment to an asylum—paper crisper & later than E.B.B.'s poem & the _____ _____ .

The Confidence-Man mss. was saved from the fire charred? Margaret More-wood has it.

. . . Moneocious Melville . . . having both male & female reproductive organs in the same individual . . . Melville has become Jew[.] The memory of the American race whatever can be called the American race, Melville has become the whale he conjured up out of the vast depths of his imagination. (Notebooks, 46)

[March 1940, started in Gloucester] Out of Joint—possible title . . . If M could only have rested in a great truth he speaks in *Mardi:* "Truth dwells in her fountains where everyone must drink for himself." . . . What is the body of the book is the man who wrote it, the human personality called H.M. *It is not a book, but a personal disclosure:* When it tries to be a book it fails either as a story or as a satire. When it has interest and beauty it is *an intimate journal,* as to be sure, most of M's deepest books are. He was a person, rather than a creator, a personality rather than a maker, and because he explored himself in print, he is, as any profound human being disclosed, by self or others, is fascinating so is he.

M's conscious values and methods were contemporary: he questioned all that his age stood for; and his unconscious motive and achievement were modern: material expansion. In this he resembled Columbus, another figure of transition in the active sphere, as in the spiritual. M's nature was Columbian.

. . . relate the murder to the principle of *wrench:* either as disease, or madness, or murder or incest or amputation throughout his life. Consciously or no he joined to the opening out of life & violence—something he felt stained him & thus the urge to the immaculate: constantly washing the spot from his hands in the 1st waters of life: any communication with other human beings & thus any relationship to society was for him, a contamination from which he must instantly purify himself. (Relation to masturbatory) . . . *life for M was corruption:* he felt his human nature as a disease & that's why he was always putting on space and time like white capes. also to partake of some *holy* sacrament which would hygienize his filthy spirit . . . .

He motivated from guilt

A dark soil from which his flowers came—always white flowers: why *whiteness* the dominant image? both purity and disease, holiness & evil, truth & untruth to him.

A white man rinsing his hands in an infinite white sea.

He felt his birth a curse . . . because he confronted in his birth, human life; that was the stain, that the livid birthmark which cut across his spirit as obviously as Ahab's white scar across Ahab's body—the lightning gash upon the pine.

That's why M's world was such a violent one, such a thing of melodrama and contrast, why tragedy was impossible to him / *life was leprous:* and unlike Heine he could not endure his paresis . . . beyond [his moods of diagnosis and purification] there is nothing but *psychotic people* / Desperately sick / . . . . Melville: write the Christ essay & turn it into a whole creative assertion of *love* / dedication: how absent in M / prayer / & thus how unsupported his search for God, how utterly Protestant is it, & how a whole side of him sought Catholicism . . . . (Notebooks, 47)

Melville had donned a white cape to cover the irresistible filthy Jewish materialist and androgyne. But then the still divided, guilty self wanted to be a forgiven Catholic.

Olson attempted to incorporate his knowledge of Melville-the-undependable into a "rounded" book. For instance, in his essay "Eastward, Again Eastward," Olson blamed Melville's "guilt" over the South Seas experiences for his "failure" and suspected him of murder. "Recall again the periodic violence toward his wife and mother, and the sadistic burning of his father's portrait in Pierre is a documentation. Perhaps he even had to kill a man to deliver himself from Nukaheva: there is something so vibrant about the murder which ends *Typee* as to suggest such a possibility. His behavior in the years between the crisis of 1851 and this trip of 1856 was ill[,] is strange and violent enough to argue some trauma; some shock more intimate to him and terrible than the collapse of his career." If Melville was disturbed, he had to be traumatized by something his own sadism had inflicted on another: The burning of father's portrait or the murder of a Marquesan is inferred, yet "documented" from a text. Melville was not disturbed by ongoing economic and emotional dependency on illegitimate authority, its undependability symbolized by the Isabel letter. Another manuscript, "Study of Melville" (probably written after 1938), praised "Billy Budd" for its mature resignation. The later work "has shed the looseness of adolescence, the self-congratulation of egotism, and the spatial universality of the orphic" (5). The Civil War brought "an equilibrium": the horror of war drew out "pity" and "tolerance" and "strengthened . . . the creative fibres that the doubt, which life brought, had weakened." As fatality advances, Melville stops worrying about God's existence (16–20). On the other hand, "The anarchic part of his nature [his 'violent temperament' and egotism, C.S.] is always destroying patterns. When young it was adolescent freedom which swept destructively through him.

When older, it was his doubt. A hindrance given to youth's impulse, and Melville was deflected into a doubt as impetuous, really, as adolescence. Disillusion brought none of the dignity of fatality to Melville, but only a sick doubt" (15–16). Similarly, Olson read the Supplement to "Battle-Pieces" as moderate and an acceptance of fate even though "He does seem to have retained his old moral antagonism to slavery, and the legalistic, constitutional defense of the right of secession he seems to have regarded, though it was [quoting Melville] 'plausibly urged,' as a trick to cajole a people possessed of 'the most sensitive love of liberty' into 'subserviency to the slave interest' and 'into the support of a war whose implied end was the erecting in our advanced century of an Anglo-American empire based upon the systematic degradation of man'"(31–32).

Olson saw that Melville's modernity was not tied to imperialism, but opposed it. The "Melvilles of the world and all their pother and fret" cancelled the "dignity of fatality" Olson never abandoned.[89] In his second proposal for a Guggenheim Fellowship, January 27, 1940, Olson explained, as usual, that nineteenth-century philistine materialism accounted for the genetically determined myth maker's failure:

[Melville] for whom prehistory and the primordial was peculiarly native. Any such inquiry, if it is to be pertinent, involves on my part a knowledge of and a use of other work on Freud and Jung on racial heritage, of Mann on recurrence and ritual, and of other contemporaries, including the anthropologists. Such a juxtaposition of Melville and myth goes far to explain— I believe for the first time, the source of his creative power and the source of the difficulties Melville had in his later life and work, to communicate that power to a transitional world inhospitable to myth.

This letter and his Winter–Spring 1940 notebook suggest a tonic (heavily indebted to Waldo Frank and Van Wyck Brooks) for the malaise of transition: "Racial memory" (Freud and Jung's concept inferred from *Moses and Monotheism*) provides "the continuums of life" that confer "culture & poise." Melville's [anti-materialist] "essential nature" as manifested in *Moby-Dick* would offer "a profound hope for the American people" beset with "modern industrialism" and needing a "national myth" to restore "creative power."

Before the war, various chapters (or versions) of a Melville manuscript were shown to Olson's mentors Edward Dahlberg, F. O. Matthiessen, and Carl Van Doren. Dahlberg (who had placed his protege's essay in *Twice-a-Year*) read some of these and discouraged publication. Criticizing the draft essay "Genesis" (Melville was Moses), Dahlberg wrote marginal comments such as "false bible," "false profundities," and "overly intellectual-abstract."[90] Matthiessen apparently read only the more conventionally written chapters, complaining that Olson's essay on the journal was unpersuasive and that Olson had rated the early work "too low. I simply cannot feel the author of *Moby-Dick* to be 'the egoist' lacking a tragic sense."[91] If Dahlberg and Matthiessen had both rejected their paternity of these contrasting manuscripts (tailored to their own styles?), what must the effect have been on Olson?[92]

Carl Van Doren's comments were supportive but highly qualified; "Call Me Ishmael" had stressed "one phase of Melville and that the most interesting philosophically"; however "it makes me want, somewhat, to write a book about Olson, to explain his metaphysical mystery. As big a boy as you are now you ought to write more simply, really" (January 24, 1941). "Big boy" explained himself quite simply in his notebook entry of March 4, 1942: He is definitely not father/Ahab, no dark hope forlorn; he would prefer to be a disengaged confidence man:

> They [friends who accuse Olson of noninvolvement, *C.S.*] are caught in the Christ trap which is history and the premise of purpose, ~~and growth~~. Their egos, bred of Christ's, act in change, aggressively seek to dominate change. The personal will is all because they know no other will to sustain them. Yet I, who assume change, live as a sacramental victim of change, fight to hold & make continuities I know do not & cannot exist. It makes me more a creature of rite than act, inflexible &, to my contemporaries, as they have often charged: "inhuman." Because I am impersonal, circular. I am tenacious & stiff where they are at ease in act. They are aggressive & futile where I am at ease in an action they'd call passive. Their participation is superficial but I envy them. It is so much more fun to be a personal than a sacramental man.

Olson's masochistic sacramental little man has echoed Pierrot Philosophique in the sad, unabashed admission that he does not believe in the myths ("the continuities") that will save America from "vitiating power," *from it/him*.

Noble lies after the war

Fresh from the Office of War Information, Olson reverted to the antimodern narrative, attacking Americans for choosing self-gratifying myths to prettify their shameful history. His 1945 notebook, written while under the influence of Ezra Pound,[93] attached the central formulation of *Call Me Ishmael* to the cynical perception that American fighting men had given their lives for a set of clichés: Machine-obsessed Americans did not care for freedom, but only for the domination of nature. The undemocratic Ahab was Melville's hero and, by implication, the essential American type.[94]

Whitman never got beyond a level of democracy as "craft." Essentially an agrarian democrat. All this talk of the mysticism of the common people is in the mouths of men who have not anticipated or experienced the 20th century. We Americans still fancy ourselves such democrats. But our triumphs are of the machine, not of democracy.

Something in Melville had got a hold on this sense of us as a people. It was not our will to be free, but our will to overwhelm nature that lies at the bottom of us as individuals and a people. Even those who know their history refuse to remember that the whole push of the West was organically a need to overcome nature by the machine not to overcome kings. Political freedom became the shibboleth of the middle class when it felt its future in the machine. As economic freedom became the shibboleth of the lower classes when they felt their power to finish what the middle class had begun.

Ahab is no democrat. Yet Ahab is his hero. Moby Dick is no king, but natural force or resource, and MD is the antagonist. This is a more honest story of any American: life than all the cliches we learn in school and get ourselves killed for. . . . I am fed up with all these books on Melville because they propagate the same sanctified lies we memorize about our history and die for. (Notebooks, 57)

Although numerous New York publishers were eager to enlist him, Olson did not publish his major opus, *Call Me Ishmael*, until 1947. It was disappointingly slim but an attempt at a strong artistic statement.[95] His *Twice-a-Year* article (1938) had been slightly enlarged and revised but also startlingly metamorphosed from scholarly prose to punchy, studiedly vernacular, Pound-influenced montage. Olson told one editor that his new book was "small, with much documentation deliberately left out in order to intensify what remains."[96] This was perhaps not entirely true; Olson simply was not permitted to circulate Weaver's gossip, as his notes and letters from the summer of 1945 suggest. "Possible additions to book as finished: . . . 21. Ask Mrs Metcalf about M's illusion in 1856 that John Hoadley was the father of his children?! 22. Weaver: Will he now tell me what Josie Shaw told him? he has transcription of conversation apparently on 1856—" (Notebooks, 54). And a letter from Weaver to Olson, August 31, 1945, states, "And, the couple of questions—again we have no alternative." Weaver's reluctance to disgorge the talk with Cousin Josie suggests that the Olson notebook entries (regarding Melville's violence in the family and quoted above) were his own frenzied speculation, perhaps exacerbated by reading Freud or Freudians.

Edward Dahlberg faithfully promoted the book he admired above all other Melvillean pronouncements, but Matthiessen had earlier turned in a negative reader's report, embittering his former admirer; these feelings were concealed from Matthiessen.[97] To his disappointment, Olson had not produced "the more pedestrian book about Melville's development through his reading" that had been promised and that the 1938 essay had begun.[98] Several short pieces followed: two reviews and the 1951 "Letter to Melville," his notorious attack on parasitic, bourgeois, and homosexual academic Melvilleans. The broadside/poem was produced at Black Mountain College. An (expurgated) review, "The Materials and Weights of Hermann Melville," for the *New Republic* (September 8 and 15, 1952) rationalized Olson's separation of sheep from goats in the Melville Revival. The draft manuscript lists good Melvilleans responding with "private acts some decency"—Ronald Mason, John Freeman, Lewis Mumford, F. O. Matthiessen, Ellery Sedgwick, Richard Chase, Newton Arvin, Van Wyck Brooks, Yvor Winters, and W. H. Auden. The damned included "grubby young monks of university research": Charles Anderson, Luther Mansfield, Howard Vincent, William Braswell, Henry Pommer, Egbert Oliver, and "their senior warden or tutor, Willard Thorp."

Eleanor Metcalf, his close ally since the mid-1930s, was personally wounded by Olson's broadside. She clarified their differences, effectively breaking off a friendship:

[November 6, 1952, "Begun several days ago"] I hardly know where to begin to answer your letter of Oct. 24 . . . let me take up what seem to be serious misunderstandings of my use of words.

First, if "life stuff, bread stuff, man stuff" is not *social*, what is? It is the earthly string that makes one part of other human beings (not a member of Society) rather than a cloud-supported being passing judgment on men and their works.

I do not criticize for a moment your holding an opinion that a piece of work is "sodden" or rotten or inspired or useful, or anything else that it seems to you—only your manner of *conveying* your judgment. And if there are different *manners* of conveying a judgment, there are *manners* in criticism.

As for making money, I should be mightily surprised if any professor makes a sizable sum out of his editing of Melville. Indeed, I am out of pocket, and shall continue to be, in producing this book, unless some unforeseen miracle happens.

Do you realize my peculiar position among all you scholars, critics, and students of Melville? I "hand-hold" none of them: that is not my business. I do try to help, in any way my peculiar position makes possible, whoever seeks my help. And good friends they have often showed themselves to be— friends very different from one another.

Your concern with the "distinctions between scholarship and critique" is one I share. It is obscured, but whether only in these days or no, I am in position to judge.

If we are to uphold "values"—and I agree we must—how can we best do it? Surely it must be in some way that conveys the sense of what we feel to be a higher value, without name calling or black eyes. (A political campaign, no!!!) Why for instance, take a "swipe" at a good man like Willard Thorp, who has done honest and useful work?

You ask about Cycle and Epicycle . . . I hope Harry Murray will read it once more. He gave me help early in the game.

Now—though I often feel quite inadequate to the right readings of these essays of yours (not really understanding some of your statements) in a general way certain impressions are made on me. One, that you must have gone a good way in your ideas of "form" merely to find so much good in such books as "The Spirit Above the Dust," and Geoffrey Stone's "Melville." Again, I share your feelings of the deep importance of "Clarel" as compared with "Billy Budd"; and I am looking forward eagerly to what Walter Bezanson may have to say. But I have never looked upon "Billy Budd" as an act of resignation. To me it expressed a deepened irony, the same irony that runs all through the happenings in this man-of-war world (and I do not mean only the Indomitable's world).[99] I have other thoughts on the subject too—concerning H.M.'s ideas of superstition and religious relics. . . . The sentence [of Olson's] I should like best to understand is "For Melville grasped the archeological man and by doing it entered the mythological present." I refer in my book to "the myth Melville created"—but as the book does not deal with mythology, or with any of the great matters I am incapable of dealing with, I do not pursue the subject. . . . [Referring to a Melville reader] The youth [?] is an interesting person—a Roman Catholic, sincere and devout, I think, *trying to combine his enthusiasm for H.M. with his Catholicism,* and aspiring to write. (Emphasis added)

The Melville/Metcalf-Olson connection can be seen as a dialogue between Reformation and counter-Reformation, unresolved, to be sure, but, from his granddaughter's side, situating Melville and herself unequivocally in the Protestant camp. The "earthly string(s)" that bind were also ties that respected individual difference, including the individual perception of irreconcilable social antagonisms and the higher ethical principles that Olson had violated in his lofty assault on the opportunistic Melville industry.

In 1953, Olson poured his heart out to the Englishman Ronald Mason, author of *Spirit Above the Dust* (1951), by day employed in an internal revenue office, by night a teacher of literature to adult students. Mason told Olson he was a D. H. Lawrence man (June 15, July 8, 1953); as Ferris Greenslet fondly noted in his adulatory review of *Call Me Ishmael*, quoting Lawrence's famous essay in *Studies in Classical American Literature* (1923), so was Melville the prophet who predicted the bomb and who "knew his [white] race was doomed."[100] Olson had announced to Mason on April 25, 1953, that his Melville days were over, limited to the years 1933–46. He ashamedly (?) commended Mason for not sinking to "the Judean (the flesh as dust: [Below the Dust] naturalism, all these novelists, kike it or not) [this passage crossed out but mailed, June 23, 1953])" and recommended that Mason read Brooks Adams on imperialism to acquire insights into both Theodore and Franklin Roosevelt (also June 22, 1953). And he found transoceanic unity and enlightenment in their joint espousal of Shakespeare's negative capability set against the egotistical sublime of Wordsworth and Milton. Negative capability was "the single essential statement made, over the whole of our joint literatures, as a light on the practice of the art now" (July 15, 1953). Billy-goat had taken the dawn.[101]

In sum, Olson's fights with more prolific second-wave Melvilleans conceal his role as one of their own; moreover, his interpretations suggest a continuity between New Criticism and the later New Historicism (both blood-and-soil methodologies asserted against materialists). Olson's master's thesis and subsequent works emphasized the literary sources for Melville's characters (especially the Elizabethans), while the earlier work also pointed to the burden of genius and the ruinous effects of emancipating-but-contaminating experience. Olson dramatically changed his interpretation of Ahab in the mid-1930s; in the thesis, Ahab (Lear, but also a version of Milton's Satan) was Melville's greatest "work"; in the *Twice-a-Year* article of 1938, Ahab was only Lear (but not yet the Ahab/Hitler formulation of *Call Me Ishmael*). Writing to the Guggenheim Foundation (ca. 1939), Olson also transformed Melville's politics: In the thesis he chided Melville's "bitterness," his mutinous enthusiasms and exaggerations of proletarian suffering. Now the Harvard man rendered *Mardi* as receptacle for "his incredibly vast reading during 1847 and 1848, in which he formed his political and social criticism of America and democracy"; a "Dostoevsky comparison" was in the offing. In Olson's writing of the late 1930s, the possible influence of Milton and Byron was invisible, no less than his earlier attraction to Ahab and (more ambivalently) to Isabel.[102] One judgment remained steady: Unlike Weaver (an anti-imperialist but not a primitivist), Olson favored the health and youth of Fayaway and the Typees (except in his notebook entry, March 11, 1935, disavowing romantic escapism). Unlike Mumford, Olson equivocated on the significance of the later work. His influence on Henry A. Murray's Melville readings (vacillating between the two views of Ahab that Olson embodied) are suggested below.

No stooping Mammon, in his *Maximus Poems* Olson said (of Gloucester): "Thank God / I chose a Protestant / *Federalist* / town / I come from the last walking period of man" (3.222.622). Mammon was sunk in both waves of Melville scholarship; no less than Weaver, the second-wave Melvilleans were unfriendly to the "money-grubbing plutocracy" (Thorp, cxi) of Melville's day.[103] The corrective neoclassical marching orders had been offered earlier by New Humanist Harvard professor Irving Babbitt in his Preface to *The New Laokoon:*

> The nineteenth century witnessed the greatest debauch of descriptive writing the world has ever known. It witnessed a general confusion of the arts, as well as of the different genres within the confines of each art. . . . I have followed out to some extent this romantic confusion of the nineteenth century—especially the attempts to get with words the effects of music and painting. . . . I have searched for principles that may be opposed to this modern confusion . . . *I hope I have at least made clear that an inquiry into the nature of genres and the boundaries of the arts ramifies out in every direction, and involves one's attitudes not merely toward literature but life.* . . . It involves especially a careful defining of certain literary movements. In making his protest against the confusion of poetry and painting, Lessing was to discriminate sharply between what he conceived to be the truly classic and the pseudo-classic. Any one who makes a similar protest today will need rather to discriminate between the truly classic and the romantic. . . . With the spread of impressionism literature has lost standards and discipline, and at the same time virility and seriousness; it has fallen into the hands of aesthetes and dilettantes, the last effete representatives of romanticism, who have proved utterly unequal to the task of maintaining its great traditions against the scientific positivists. The hope of the humanities is in defenders who will have something of Lessing's virile emphasis on action, and scorn of mere revery,—who will not be content with wailing more or less melodiously from their towers of ivory. (Emphasis added)

Olson's friend and mentor F. O. Matthiessen participated in Babbitt's antibourgeois offensive: *American Renaissance: Art and Expression in the Age of Emerson and Whitman*, a monumental study of Emerson, Thoreau, Hawthorne, Melville, and Whitman, appeared in 1941; it was the organic synthesis that American literature professors opposed to Marx, Freud, and Parringtonian economic determinism[104] had demanded since the mid-1930s (and even earlier). In Professor Merton M.

Sealts, Jr.'s view, Matthiessen's New Criticism[105] had rescued his generation from the art-erasing politics of Vernon Parrington:

> In the mid-sixties, shortly after I began teaching at the University of Wisconsin, a graduate student came into my office to tell me, excitedly, that he had discovered a book that would release him from "the tyranny of New Criticism": Vernon Parrington's *Main Currents in American Thought*! To his surprise I observed that when *I* was a graduate student (1937–1941) it was New Criticism that had released me from the tyranny of works like Parrington's.... The "history of ideas" approach to American literature that was current in the 1930s had talked about everything except the literary quality of the texts under discussion—either because "literary quality" was supposedly lacking in those texts or because the commentators themselves were unable to recognize it. It was Matthiessen's *American Renaissance* (1941) that assured many of us that what we planned to teach was worth teaching *as literature*.[106]

Although he claimed to be fusing history and literature, in practice, the organicist Matthiessen set himself against both disciplines, leaving himself helpless to act either on his own behalf or that of humanity. By removing the study of literature from its "economic, social and religious causes" (but not from "its sources in our life") and focusing on "what these books are as works of art," then fulfilling the "double aim . . . to place these works both in their age and ours," Matthiessen radically dehistoricized literary texts. One could move forward and backward between T. S. Eliot, Henry James, and Nathaniel Hawthorne, or between Ahab and Hitler, because historical specificity and concrete institutional referents had been banished: Works of art gave birth to other works of art and yet, though fictions, their characters spoke to us today as if freshly minted. Matthiessen's understanding of social conflict was expressed in timeless dualisms—Reason vs. Passion, Good vs. Evil, Civilization vs. Savagery, or Heart vs. Head: These antagonists made literature and history alike, but religion overwhelmed history and political science. In his draft of an introduction to a selection of Melville's poetry (1944), a penciled addition mapped the Melville problem in the functionalist style as "Melville's continual concern with the unending struggle, with the tensions between good and evil: within the heart and in the state, political, social, and religious."[107] And Matthiessen's readings of "literary" qualities could be deficient in formal analysis or even accuracy, because he had appropriated nineteenth-century American literature to support the counter-Enlightenment corporatist goals of twentieth-century progressive reform, eliminating textual facts that contradicted the lessons to be drawn from works such as *Moby-Dick* or "Billy Budd," all the while (implicitly) distancing himself from Weaver and Mumford by promising to avoid "the direct reading of an author's personal life into his works" (AR, xii). Excerpts from drafts and published versions of two major works, *American Renaissance* (1941) and *From the Heart of Europe* (1948), clarify Matthiessen's positions both before and after the war. They seem motivated by the confluence of objectives: a personal and class need for clear, unambiguous, reliable authority (or its simulacrum) and the ideological requirement of his class to moderate the selfishness of upper-class college students lest an unbalanced society continue its path toward disintegration. So Matthiessen evaluated authors and works of art with these standards: Symbols should be clear and unequivocal, for (Christian) democratic artists, like other earthy laborers, were craftsmen relating form to function; "individualism" must be tempered by social responsibility. It was Burke against Paine all over again. His works are considered chronologically below, but mostly postponing discussion of *From the Heart of Europe* (1948) so that it may be set in the context of other postwar Melvillean pronouncements.[108]

In a book of more than six hundred pages dealing with five major writers and numerous other cultural luminaries of the antebellum period, Matthiessen devoted long sections to Ahab. No previous writer had lavished so much attention on this character; indeed, the book was organized around the mad captain. The preface had ended with a call for artists to abjure (Ahab-ish) anarchy and take the side of the people against the brutal *Übermensch* who would be limned throughout, while the very last page traced Melville's progress from the "murky symbols" of *Moby-Dick* to the "comprehensive symbols" of Abraham and Isaac, Vere and Billy, as if Isaac's life had not been spared by the Jewish God. In his early unbalanced writings Melville was really the Head person Ahab, not Ishmael and not yet Vere, the Heart person who understood Necessity. Matthiessen had written, "In spite of Melville's enthusiasm for discovery and revolt [in *Mardi*], no depth of feeling has fused his instances with his abstractions" (early draft, 153). Instead of the dispassionate assessment of literary qualities that had been promised, Matthiessen delivered a stern rebuke to eighteenth- and nineteenth-century man. There were distortions of the text to support his hostile characterization of Melville/Ahab and to convince readers (and perhaps himself) that Melville was finally the democratic hero Billy who rightly blessed Captain Vere. I still wonder how Matthiessen, a man still revered by academic radicals as a martyr to McCarthyism, could have believed in his own writing.

For instance, the celebrated Father Edward T. Taylor, Methodist preacher to sailors at Bethel Church in Boston's disreputable North End, was the source for Father Mapple and identified as an "ex-seaman" (AR, 127) but not as a protester of Lemuel Shaw's positions regarding enforcement of the Fugitive Slave Law.[109] Since Mapple and Ahab (if not always Taylor) were both proponents of the higher law and the "inexorable self," Matthiessen had erased a fact that would have suggested Ahab as an antiracist, as a man leading a revolution against illegitimate authority on behalf of, not against, the common man. For Matthiessen, the "Keel of the Ages" in Mapple's sermon was not Ahab's Keel, the conscience that informed the struggle for universal human rights, but the "equilibrium" between "sense impressions and his reflective mind" that Melville had achieved, for a change, in *Moby-Dick* (AR, 128). Father Taylor was mentioned throughout the book as a positive figure, perhaps because, as Emerson had noted, he had unified a diverse congregation at Concord in 1845 (127); spiced with the salty vernacular, his sermons had followed Matthiessen's prescriptions for a rooted democratic intellectual discourse, appealing to "black and white, poet and grocer, contractor and lumberman . . . ."[110]

Matthiessen transmitted more serious distortions of the text, none of which apparently has been noted by Melville scholars. Referring to the confrontation between Ahab and Starbuck on the quarter-deck, after Ahab nails the gold doubloon to the mast, bribing and hypnotizing the crew into joining his hunt for Moby Dick, Matthiessen described Ahab's heartless and obsessive vengefulness through the eyes of "powerless" Starbuck. "At the moment of the initial announcement of his vengeance, he rises to a staggering *hubris* as he shouts, 'Who's over me?' Starbuck, powerless before such madness, can only think: 'Horrible old man! Who's over him he cries;—ay, he would be a democrat to all above; look how he lords it over all below!' Yet Starbuck is forced not simply to resent but to pity him, since he reads in the lurid eyes the captain's desperation" (448). Matthiessen has erased both content and order: The text states "Who's over me? Truth hath no confines." This is Ahab's response to Starbuck's accusation of vengeance and blasphemy. Ahab unmistakably announced that the whale hunt was not what it seemed. The text shows Ahab/Melville reproaching Starbuck's philistinism, telling him to "hark" below the surface of the statement, as Ahab and other modern artists marshal analytic skills to discover the truth and to know themselves: Ahab's speech is a call to revolution against illegitimate authority, but also a challenge to sincerely Christian readers harkening to Father Mapple's higher law, in this case opposing conservative New England's complicity with the slave power. Moreover, Starbuck's response to Ahab occurs in chapter 38 ("Dusk"), not immediately after Ahab's exclamation as Matthiessen implies.[111]

In my view, Starbuck feels invaded, but as a Christian, irresistibly tied to Ahab's charismatic idea—in Starbuck's later words, with "soul beat down and held to knowledge,—as wild, untutored things are forced to feed . . . ." Starbuck's initial response had been anger. Ahab noted that his passion had "melted" Starbuck's usual icy incomprehension expressed in "an intolerable . . . doltish stare." Ahab says compassionately, "My heart has melted thee to anger-glow," then he (ambiguously?) apologizes: "I meant not to incense thee." Perhaps the lurid eyes belonged to Matthiessen reading a double message and had to be disowned. Similarly, "the queenly personality" who feels her royal rights, Ahab's self-description and challenge to an indifferent and cruel deity in "Candles," is negatively interpreted. Without quoting the source in the text, Matthiessen described what Ahab means by "queenly": "The resources of the isolated man, his courage and his staggering indifference to anything outside himself, had seldom been exalted so high." Matthiessen's obliteration of the Milton-Melville connection in favor of Shakespeare-Melville made the task easier.[112]

The Ahab-Starbuck interchange sums up the Melville Revival: A possibly ambivalent representation of radical Enlightenment and the American and French Revolutions has been caricatured by conservatives. In their readings, the antagonists are bad Jews (the Hebrew prophets, Melville, narcissists, monomaniacs, abolitionists, modern women, materialists as either classical liberals or socialists) and overpowered bad Christians (Melvillains, as Merton Sealts, Jr., calls himself and his colleagues), bad because they are seduced where they should struggle to resist. In all fairness, Starbuck should not pity Ahab: Matthiessen says Starbuck's pity was forced. This shocking recognition of Ahab's comprehensive cunning could lead to suicide to smother [the Bad Jew] within gentlefolk like Matthiessen, or in the less gentle, the image of the "switching" Jew could rationalize social violence. Note that Matthiessen's example of "the great artist" was T. S. Eliot, not Melville/Ahab, though he quoted Melville's approbation of Hawthorne's "usable truth" before this tribute to Eliot. "Such steady inspection of life, which does not flinch from probing sinister recesses and is determined to make articulate the whole range of what it finds, is indispensable for the great artist. Only thus can he cut through conventional appearances and come into possession of what Eliot has called 'a sense of his own age'" (192–93). Eliot is praised for the qualities Matthiessen lacked in himself and that are abundantly demonstrated in the materialist Ahab, but here have been misapplied to the corporatist Eliot, enemy to freethinking Jews whose corrosive intellects dissolve natural ethnic, today, communitarian, bonds.

The English Tories with whom Eliot bonded were paternalistic agrarians, relentless opponents to the rising industrial bourgeoisie that threatened to displace them. Their counterparts in 1930s America were Southern Agrarians, champions of the New Criticism and, like Harvard professors of American literature, supporters of Roosevelt. In a revealingly erroneous reading of *Clarel* (AR, 495), Matthiessen, like Willard Thorp before him, confused the merchant Rolfe with the ex-Southerner Ungar, the expatriate mercenary for the Turks, even though Melville had not blurred their identities in his text.[113] To be sure, Ungar had earlier expressed passionate criticisms of Mammon and the brutal factory system (AR, 401), but so did the Tories of Young England. Expressing the concerns of other Jeffersonians, Melville had written:

The vast reserves—the untried fields;
These long shall keep off and delay
The class war, rich-and-poor-man fray
Of history. From that alone
Can serious trouble spring. Even that
Itself, this good result may own—
The first firm founding of the state. (*Clarel*, 4.21.91–96)

Matthiessen had, in effect, made the reactionary Ungar (bearer of "a strain of Indian blood" and "the Catholic mind" or, in *Poems*, "the Latin mind though no longer in the Church") a protosocialist. This is an interesting ideological point, since Melville's character Rolfe was a well-traveled and thoughtful autodidact; his antidemocratic and antisemitic views link him to the organic conservatism of Christian Socialists such as Melville's contemporary Charles Kingsley, author of *Alton Locke* (1850). Rolfe muses whether or not the outcome of class conflict would be a more stable, legitimate, social order, paternalistically concerned with the condition of labor.[114] Perhaps reflecting his own state of mind, Matthiessen continued his discussion of Ungar's prediction of the coming socialism with the pessimistic judgment that the lower orders are uncontrollable and overly susceptible to false promises and flattery. "Although Ungar glimpses that possible synthesis, he has little confidence in it. In his view popular ignorance often increases as society 'progresses,' and masterless men who have foregone all recognition of evil within themselves, are easy prey for demagogues. He holds that only an awareness of Original Sin can give significance to man's struggle; and the last that is seen of him by Clarel, he is riding off with 'that strange look / Of one enlisted for sad fight / Upon some desperate dark shore'" (495).

Matthiessen's apotheosis of Billy Budd's sacrifice is the elixir soothing Ungar's despair. The converted Melville "has come to respect necessity," a fact proven by Melville's check of a passage from "Peter Schlemihl": "Afterwards I became reconciled to myself. I learnt, in the first place, to respect necessity" (n. 510). Such a mark, taken by itself, proves nothing. Although moody, Melville did not rest in Ungar's pessimism. He did understand that history forces certain problems and constraints upon us; moreover, as any moralist would, he grappled throughout life with the ambiguous connection between freedom and necessity, structure and agency. But Matthiessen wants to convince the reader that Melville approves of Vere's action in hanging Billy. Following earlier conservative readings, Matthiessen praised the Plinlimmonish balance achieved at the end of Melville's life: He had grown out of the "angry defiance" of *Pierre* and *The Confidence-Man* (*AR*, 511); he cites Vere's death without "accents of remorse" as proof that "Melville could now face incongruity; he could accept the existence of both good and evil with a serenity impossible to him in *Moby-Dick*" (draft, 819; *AR*, 512, "serenity" changed to "calm"). This judgment is further strengthened, pressing the unrighteous moralist Mapple's inexorable self into Ahab's materialist savagery. "Vere is the wise father, terribly severe but righteous. No longer does Melville feel the fear and dislike of Jehovah that were oppressing him throughout *Moby-Dick* and *Pierre*. He is no longer protesting against the determined laws as being savagely inexorable. He has come to respect necessity" (*AR*, 510).[115]

Matthiessen had suppressed Melville's delegitimating remark upon the occasion of Vere's death from the musket ball shot from the *Athée*. In Melville's text, Vere "dropped to the deck" just like Claggart, then the narrator comments, "The spirit that 'spite its philosophic austerity may yet have indulged in the most secret of all passions, ambition, never attained to the fulness of fame." For Melville, Vere's lack of remorse stemming from secret ambition was the black mark linking him to the ambitious, lying Claggart, but this evil character is connected to Ahab, not Vere, in Matthiessen's reading (*AR*, 505). Captain Vere's "rectitude" as he announces the verdict that Billy must hang reminded Matthiessen of the eighteenth-century Protestant minister Jonathan Edwards (whose name Melville had written in the margin to pinpoint "the Calvinistic text" preached to a dumb "congregation of believers in hell"):

> The deepest need for rapaciously individualistic America [embodied throughout in Ahab] was a radical affirmation of the heart. He knew that his conception of the young sailor's "essential innocence" was in accord with no orthodoxy; but he found it "an irruption of heretic thought hard to suppress." . . . After all he had suffered Melville could endure to the end in the belief that though good goes down to defeat and death, its radiance can redeem life. His career did not fall into what has been too often assumed to be the pattern for the lives of our artists: brilliant beginnings without staying power, truncated and broken by our hostile environment. Melville's endurance is a reinvigorating [only in final draft, 819, *C.S.*] challenge for a later America. (*AR*, 513–14)

This was the conversion narrative, pure and simple. The later Americans should flee from wayward Prometheans such as Hawthorne's Roger Chillingworth and Ethan Brand, criminal precursors to Ahab, catastrophically possessed by their "proud lonely will[s]" (*AR*, 449–50; *FHE*, 30), to the open arms of Captain Vere, to the reinvigorating submission that Melville had mocked as ignoble servility in *White-Jacket*, a book Matthiessen rated as "running close to a tract of protest" (285).[116] Matthiessen's final comments on Vere (and Coleridge) had linked the text to the

America of the late 1930s and early 1940s, the years of the Hitler-Stalin pact when the Anglo-American libertarianism of the radical bourgeoisie was once again off-limits to the Stalinist Left.

During the early and mid-1940s, the post-Weaver separation of Melville from Ahab energized by Mumford, Thorp, and Matthiessen continued. An ominously antimodern, somewhat anti-Jewish article in *College English* (1943) moved Henry W. Wells of Columbia into his colleague Weaver's territory, promoting *Clarel* at the expense of *Moby-Dick*. The following year, Wells, like Thorp, presented Melville as a moderate democrat, not the aristocratic rebel of Weaver's biography.[117] Charles Olson, writing *Call Me Ishmael* after these judgments, again modified his reading of Ahab. In his earlier essay, "Lear and *Moby-Dick*" (1938), Ahab was condemned for the "solipsism which brings down a world," while the crew participates in the "citizenship of human suffering": This is Melville's (Lear's and Job's) "meaning" (186, 189).[118] Olson seemed to be pessimistically criticizing democratic leadership, but with respect for the crew. *Call Me Ishmael* (1947) more explicitly took on (proto-fascist) mass politics, linking Ahab's "Conjur Man" destructiveness to heartless, Ethan Brand–style Enlightenment reason:

Melville was no naive democrat. He recognized the persistence of the "great man" and faced, in 1850, what we have faced in the twentieth century. At the time of the rise of the common man Melville wrote a tragedy out of the rise, and the fall, of uncommon Ahab.... [T]he common man, however free, leans on a leader, the leader, however dedicated, leans on a straw [reason, the brain, C.S.]. (64) ... In exactly what way Ahab, furious and without fear, retained the instrument of his reason as a lance to fight the White Whale is a central concern of Melville's in *Moby-Dick*. In his Captain there was a diminution in his heart. (72)

Similarly, Willard Thorp's contribution to *The Literary History of the United States* (1948) abandoned *Pierre:* No longer a flawed but "fascinating book" (1938, lxxvii), it is "not a perfect book. It is not even a good one, judged by any standards" (458). Thorp's other assessments returned with a new emphasis on the importance of *Clarel* and "Billy Budd." Melville's dangerous sympathies with the wantonly self-directed Ahab's untrammeled curiosity and materialism had been averted; "private hurts" had been "healed" by the Civil War. The epilogue to *Clarel* proved that Melville had chosen broad-minded Rolfe (468) over the antidemocrats, Mortmain and Ungar. In fact, the regenerated writer had come to a serene and manful end in all his epilogues: The epilogue to *Moby-Dick* proved that "young Ishmael" had seen through and rejected Ahab (461); from the Civil War poems onward, Melville had "worked his way to the solid ground on which he finally stood when he wrote

Billy Budd" (404). For many liberal critics, the story has been either ambiguous or a thinly veiled ironic antiwar protest written from the Left; as Hayford and Sealts have shown in their genetic reconstruction of the text (1962), Melville himself increased the polarity between Claggart and Billy. (In the earliest version, Billy is a sexually experienced older man, a guilty mutineer. Gradually he becomes the child-like naif. The poem "Billy in the Darbies" was written first, resulting in some disjuncture between the poem and the final version of the narrative.) For Thorp, however, the sharp division between the naturally depraved, monomaniacal, and subversive Claggart and naturally innocent Billy had shattered the "fetters" of ambiguity, as perhaps it had done for Melville-in-retreat. The brainy mixture of good and evil, "the strange union under the eaves" (457) that had chained Pierre to immobility (470), was finally unmuddied.[119]

I met [Merton Sealts] wandering in a daze one day just outside the Toasty, and he said "Either Melville is crazy or I am, or someone is."
  —Harrison Hayford to Tyrus Hillway, co-founder of the Melville Society, January 25, 1945

In the process of conflating corporatism with democracy, Thorp had, like Matthiessen, cleanly separated the good, questing, submissive adolescent (the redeemed Ishmael-Billy) and the bad father (Ahab-Claggart). The rhetoric Thorp applied to Billy and Claggart implied that their genetic inheritance was dissimilar: The difference between Aryan Billy and the black-hearted monster Claggart was perceived in virtually racial terms. The connection Melville had drawn between the two quasi-lunatics Claggart and Vere, however, was invisible. And Billy was good in Thorp's reading because he understood the necessity for heroic self-sacrifice when Vere (Order, not Truth) demanded it. Thorp had consistently assimilated Melville's career to the conversion narrative. The same gesture had bolstered the hegemonic humanities line contrasting Western democracy with German autocracy or Bolshevism, following the ideology of the Columbia University "War Issues" course devised to build support for American participation in World War I and continued in the plans for the Jefferson Memorial, 1939.[120] This might have been an honest contrast had not the corporatists been as intent as Nazi and Stalinist bureaucrats in treating the contagious Lockean and Jeffersonian ideas of the American Revolution, turning these radical thinkers upside down to invert slavery and freedom, reinstating the Great Chain of Being to heal wasted liberals.[121] By bringing ethnopluralism into the discussion of psychological warfare in the Melville Revival, I am arguing that the core conflict between the wars, then, was not democracy versus totalitarianism or autocracy; rather, the forces of modernity were arrayed against those of reaction, even inside "democratic" countries and often inside individuals. Reactionaries might or might not represent themselves as progressives. The attempt herein to clarify the dispute has developed a distinction between rootless cosmopolitans (exponents of urbanized industrial, scientific society) and rooted cosmopolitans (exponents of small town life with pre-capitalist social relations). English and American fascist writers of the 1930s made this distinction explicit.[122]

After the war, Matthiessen and Alfred Kazin taught American literature in Austria and Czechoslovakia, describing their topic as the age of Whitman and Melville. Since both men wanted to teach *Moby-Dick* and "Billy Budd," they divided their groups, Matthiessen discussing Melville followed by Henry James, while Kazin's Melville was followed by Henry Adams. Matthiessen turned the journal of his fascinating and informative European experiences into a book, *From the Heart of Europe* (1948), with the published version forced to deal with the recent Soviet actions that had destroyed the independent democratic socialist state of Czechoslovakia, actions that were pending while Matthiessen was still there and for which he became an apologist. Matthiessen (whose father and grandfather had become wealthy through the applied sciences) felt he should explain why he never became a Marxist:

> I am a Christian, not through ~~my haphazard~~ upbringing but by ~~conversion~~ conviction ~~while at Yale~~, and I find an[y] materialism inadequate. I make no pretense to being a theologian, but I have been influenced by the same Protestant revival that has been voiced most forcefully in America by Reinhold Niebuhr. That is to say, I have rejected the nineteenth-century belief in every man as his own Messiah, along with the other aberrations of that century's individualism; and have accepted again the doctrine of Original Sin, in the sense that man is fallible and limited, no matter what his social system, and capable of finding completion only through humility before the love of God.[123]

The cross outs suggest that Matthiessen had no religion before he attended Yale and that he was searching for the security of a clear, consistent set of rules. The rest of the statement is a grotesque Hume-style caricature of seventeenth-century left-wing Protestantism that is conflated with the most buccaneering irreligious capitalism and then made symbol for the entire nineteenth century. But he was "a radical democrat," an admirer of Walt Whitman and Lenin (draft, 10). In spite of its flaws, we should accept the Russian Revolution because "the Russians have not been deflected from the right of all to share in the common wealth." As for the disappointed libertarian Czechs, they really were moving toward socialism, despite apparent reverses. They should understand that "Freedom can be gained and protected only by groups functioning together, with their sense of social responsibility as highly developed as their sense of individual privilege. That is what I understand by the definition of freedom as the recognition of necessity" (*FHE*, 142).

In a passage that reiterated the primary thesis of *American Renaissance* (and derived from the aesthetic theories of Herder, Wordsworth, and Coleridge), Matthiessen nostalgically described the role of art in primitive societies. Art best functioned as release. "This knowledge is common in primitive societies where the role both of the medicine man and of the ritualistic priest or poet is to exorcise the evil spirit and to invoke the good spirit by *naming* them. The *naming* must be exact, and it requires all the magical skills of the artist, all his control over words to make them become one with the thing . . . the primitive exorcism by naming life even as it is in its worst moments, and thus releasing us from fear of the unnamed and unknown" (*FHE*, 49). Melville is not listed among the dark modern figures that provide a similar salutary catharsis: Hamlet, Schopenhauer, Leopardi, and Kafka. Matthiessen also distanced himself from fellow lecturer Lyman Bryson, who had criticized "mechanical Stalinists" and the "Hollywood mass producer [*sic*]" alike, all of whom were committed to "official versions of life" (draft, 66; *FHE*, 51–53). These statements, taken together and in tandem with *American Renaissance*, strongly suggest that Matthiessen was always frightened by the introspection and social inspection that discloses contradictions between signifiers and the signified, the critical process represented by Ahab's leaps into the unknown, from light into darkness, into disillusion with father figures, thence into Pierre's ambiguous choice to merge with Isabel, ambiguous not because of elusive or necessarily contaminated "truth," but only with regard to the writer's self-interest. Where would it all lead? Would the innocent be sacrificed in the effluent of righteous action? So Matthiessen preferred to melt into the mass and worship necessity.

He had been rereading *Moby-Dick:* It was the book he most wanted to talk about in his trip to Europe; the emphasis on racial equality (that he had almost forgotten) had deeply moved him, but the auspicious beginning had been undermined by Melville's submission to Ahab:

> . . . his ejaculation of the "divine equality" among men was not borne out by what happened. Even the friendship between Queequeg and Ishmael was dwarfed and lost sight of in the portrayal of Captain Ahab's indomitable will. The single individual, a law only to himself, treats his entire crew as mere appendages to his own ruthless purpose, and sweeps them all finally to destruction. No more challenging counter-statement to Emerson's self-reliance had yet been written. No more penetrating scrutiny could have been made of the defects of individualism, of the tragedy that ensues when man

conceives proudly of himself as pitted against the mass, instead of finding the fulfillment of his nature through interdependence with his fellow-men. (*FHE*, 36–37)

This characterization may not jibe with the text: Was Ahab pitted against the mass, or was that Ishmael's and Starbuck's reading? Melville's long-suppressed annotations to *Paradise Lost* (along with remarks in his published letters and the not-so-muffled protest that he telegraphs throughout) indicated that he was writing under censorship; moreover, he had no use for demagogues and mobs or frontier rowdiness and brutality.

Melville's marginalia strongly suggest that Ahab was the necessarily masked modern artist, the Promethean who would, however abandoned and mutilated by God and his fellows, stand alone if necessary, to speak truth to power; he was also speaking to posterity so that his less perceptive and more deferential fellows might one day be emancipated from illegitimate authority. Matthiessen's Ishmaelite/Anglo-Catholic interpretation of Ahab's motives mirrored the image of Hitler as cynical demagogue disseminated by his colleagues Henry Murray and Gordon Allport in their worksheets on morale (1941). In 1948 Matthiessen praised the student with Heart and buried the Head, whose views of Ahab diverged from the official story:

> In the final session of our discussion group [in Czechoslovakia] Vladimir Kosina raised the topic, "What is there in *Moby Dick* that would not have been written by anyone except an American?" Several ideas were picked up from our earlier sessions: the author's immersion in everyday experience, the union of work and intellect that we had found in Thoreau, Whitman's kind of belief in the common man. *One girl felt that Ahab was a thoroughly American hero in his determination, no matter what the obstacles, to do what he set out to do.* . . . Some sentences from these students' final essays were very impressive. Bohumil Seidl, after analyzing the basis for Ahab's tragedy and finding it in the absolute ruthlessness of will that mistook its own desires for divine command, concluded: "The central moral problem in *Moby Dick*, the relation between will and feeling, particularly appeals to us who, not long ago, had opportunity to experience the disastrous consequences of a strong will in Germany, the will to power, surrounded by mythology and absolutely shorn of human feeling."[124] (Emphasis added.)

The students who read Ahab as a positive figure are unnamed, perhaps because Matthiessen preferred corporatist formulations of the causes of World War II, in

Bohumil Seidl's "very impressive" instance blatantly identifying a nation of American Ahabs with Nazi Head people. For Heart people, triumphant fascism as the outcome of class conflict, economic crisis, Stalinist tactics, and appalling sectarianism in the German Left is invisible.[125]

Such confusion is consistent with the counter-Enlightenment views of T. S. Eliot, Matthiessen's ideal of positive intellectuality (though he later disavowed Eliot's refusal of social action, *FHE*, 82). Matthiessen, like Mumford, Olson, and Thorp before him, was supporting the Tory Melville they inferred from the later texts.[126] Ersatz critical tools left them helpless in the face of preventable disasters. Starbuck was periodically depressed. The conclusion to the life of Matthiessen was a leap from the twelfth floor of a Boston hotel room in 1950. Harvard English professor Kenneth Murdock wrote to Perry Miller after Matthiessen's suicide. "Matty's nervous depression had been growing steadily more intense all winter, and he seemed to have lost any ability to conquer it by will. His friends urged him to see doctors, but he could not bring himself to do so, and I'm afraid his last months were spent in great anguish and loneliness. His friends did everything they could to help him, but he found it more and more difficult to see people and, I suppose, contributed to his final collapse by keeping steadily at work on his writing and sparing himself nothing."[127]

The Harvard community of humanists, with all their erudition and accumulated wisdom, could neither help their friend nor in any rational manner explain the horrendous conflicts of this century. In the war between passion and reason, passion won out; Matty lacked the self-control that would moderate his austerity. His colleague William Ellery Sedgwick (1899–1942) had earlier committed suicide; his unfinished study, *Herman Melville: The Tragedy of Mind*, edited by Sedgwick's widow, Sarah Cabot Sedgwick, and Theodore Spencer, was published by Harvard in 1944. Henry Murray reported that Mrs. Sedgwick blamed Melville's *Pierre* for her husband's death. But an unpublished poem by Sedgwick, "The Dark House," suggests that Tory anti-intellectualism was the symptom of excessive self-denial in the service of class rule. It bred despair, isolation, and emptiness, not the camaraderie and sane amelioration that the Heart people had professed. This is the poem as written in Sedgwick's hand:[128]

Scribners 1932–36
Stands in the darkness
on the stairs
of the dark house
a life so young—he stands there
tiptoe to question;

stands in the darkness on a stair
makes tentative the silence there.

and near him there
(no where)
chipped by a clock
bright moments fly
upward;
are there only dark hours
and he waits for me.

Across the obscure accumulation of my days
and undecided ways
he waits.

And I'll not come;

out of the emptiness I'd bring
I should not answer anything.

P.C. Where I have been he is;
Where I shall be, he is before
and where he asks no more.

The questing Enlightenment mind lives with uncertainty: Formulations of moral action in a secular world are necessarily experimental and provisional; we adjust received notions of morality to things as they really are, and the things might be strange indeed, nutty enough to merit structural transformations. While Melville found this lively habit of mind excitingly adventuresome (though it also gave him pause), these were exactly the "tragic" qualities that made Sedgwick and Matthiessen nervous. Similarly, "uncertainty" was the deadly enemy to social coherence in the worksheets devised by Murray and Allport to boost civilian morale before and after the war, even as they affixed the word "provisional" to their specific recommendations. Hitler felt the same way and devised his theory of propaganda to forestall ambiguity, for this greyness made it impossible to mobilize support for wars to save the planet from Jewish or German *Objektivitätsfimmel*, the brain-buzz or craze for objectivity that made it hard to establish the harmonious "people's community," reunited because rescued from vertiginous, Jewishly instigated, internal contradictions. In his own words, Hitler explained that he was simplifying but not falsifying his messages; the masses were too irrational to cope with the finer points of such pivotal issues as German responsibility for the Great War. This congruence between Nazi and American propaganda was not concealed by Murray and Allport. Indeed, they almost imitated the totalizing propaganda of the Nazis:

> The propaganda campaign must be based on a total view of the situation, expressed in an ideological language almost as inclusive as that of the Communists or the Nazis themselves. From the perspective of this ideology, all specific news items should be interpreted, so that they acquire significance beyond themselves and are seen as part of a coherent drama of dynamic forces. Radio programs of propaganda and propaganda leaflets should not be showered off hit or miss; perhaps at cross-purposes, and probably without effect, but should converge upon the master interpretation of the forces involved in the war. Only with a definite rationale, adhered to over a long period of time, can our propaganda have a cumulative effect and thus finally play an important role in the defeat of the enemy. (Worksheet on Psychological Warfare, 2)

Harvard professors of American history and literature were joined to American, Nazi, and communist social pathologists in their pedagogy of the paranoid sublime, the good fight between godly faith and demonic disbelief. But theirs was the destructive method they consistently attributed to wicked Ahab and the equally adolescent Pierre whose universalist ethics the corporatists had transmuted to absolutist domination while disseminating their own, preferred, "master interpretation." By contrast with Ahab and Pierre, Matthiessen and his counterparts were pluralists of the blood-and-soil variety. Like Murray and Allport, Matthiessen wished for a modicum of diversity-with-integration, not fusion; we should rewrite our history. Concurring in the important revision of American nationality advanced by Randolph Bourne (1916) and Horace Kallen (1924), Matthiessen urged that the cultural domination of the old Anglo-Saxon elites be repudiated, and moreover, "by making Americans more aware of the *diversified strains from which we have come*, it would enable us to know more about the rest of the world, and it could help to provide us with the international understanding we so much need now in fulfilling our unaccustomed but unavoidable role as a world power" (*FHE*, 125–26; emphasis added).

The next section examines the late 1930s turning point in Ahab readings: Our periscope descries another sea-change as the content of pluralism finally shifts away from the structural analysis that would disclose a comprehensive picture of social and individual conflict; ethnicity or race displaces class or the liberal nation as the decisive source of cultural identity. The Swedish economist and Social Democrat Gunnar Myrdal asserted in *The American Dilemma* (1944) that the doctrine of biological racism "is almost destroyed for upper class and educated people. Its maintenance among lower class and uneducated people meets increasing difficulties. *The gradual destruction of the popular theory behind race prejudice is the most important of all social trends in the field of interracial relations"* (1003). Gunnar Myrdal was wrong. Left-liberal materialism, archfoe to group-think, was going under, deepening the American dilemma.

GOD SUPPLANTS NATURE IN BLESSING AMERICA

Melville items in the *New York Times Book Review* between the wars disclose radicals and conservatives vying to define Melville's relations with his major characters. But there is also an emerging consensus, more evident after the war, to be sure, but picking up steam in the late 1930s: Ahab (the lopsided Head person) is increasingly counterpointed with Captain Vere (in whom Head and Heart are balanced). This study earlier sketched changing attitudes toward Leviathan in the delivering of social welfare and other relief measures as localist remedies were increasingly assumed by the federal government; one could add the growing autonomy of the executive branch, a move that was approved by some corporatist intellectuals inspired by the example of Mussolini and who were reappraising *Moby-Dick* in the mid-1930s.[129] Ahab's thrusts at Leviathan could have been conventional to antistatists in earlier stages of the Wilsonian progressive movement but might be outrageous in the later New Deal of the Roosevelt administration. In the following pages, another possible factor is correlated with the switch in Ahab valuations: the dramatic transformation in assessments of Hitler's personality after 1936.

An unsigned essay, "Unknown Writings of *Moby-Dick's* Biographer" (1923), brought a red Indian Ahab and Melville together: "The dark brooding side of Melville's nature found full expression through a maze of autobiographical material concerning his childhood." The Mead Schaeffer illustration showed a beardless, but shadowed Ahab from the 1922 Dodd, Mead edition of *Moby-Dick*.[130] The red Indian Ahab suggests the *Pequod* as bearer of a rebel crew retaliating against upper-class European persecution; the most salient contemporary reference would be the French Revolution, with the sans-culottes typically represented as cannibals (the latter image favored by Rockwell Kent in his 1930 illustrations for *Moby-Dick*). Compare this to Boardman Robinson's illustration of Ahab (as Old Testament prophet?, 1943) used in Lewis Mumford's review of William Ellery Sedgwick's posthumous *Tragedy of Mind* (1944). Mumford rejoiced that Melville had recovered from his Ahab malady. "In all the great questions of life and death, love alone excepted, Melville brings the reader to the edge of an abyss. His nihilism was the affirmation of a dauntless mind and of a solemn pride that attended its exercise; but he lived to overcome the innate treachery of man's highest organ" (January 25, 1945).

The British Fabian John Middleton Murry had made Melville a devout Christian (and his spokesman the pragmatic Plinlimmon). Long before Olson, Murry linked Ahab to Lear and Macbeth. Murry also launched the quietistic reading of "Billy Budd" (August 10, 1924, 7). Other reviewers read Melville favorably as a radical Ahab. In an anonymous review of the John Freeman biography, the author was Ahab's companion, his masterpiece an epic and parable like *Paradise Lost*: "He was grandly, peculiarly, stubbornly himself" (June 13, 1926, 11). Reviewing the Mumford study, Herbert Gorman painted Melville as a scarface whale, also tragic and indomitable, but hemmed in by his culture; however, Gorman, unlike Mumford, did not like "Billy Budd" (March 10, 1929, 1). Percy Hutchison favorably reviewed the Weaver edition of Melville's *Journal up the Straits* (July 7, 1935, 2), marking Melville's powers of reportage and the gaze that is obviously Ahab's. "Melville sees with his eyes— and they are as penetrating a pair of optics as any writer has ever been provided with. But he sees with more than his eyes. There is a most curious and baffling 'boring in' throughout. Recorded in the scantiest of manner, this journey increases in portentousness as one proceeds."

Like Olson, other Melville scholars and journalists, New Critic Yvor Winters, for instance,[131] turned away from Ahab in the late 1930s, beginning the process that would culminate in the stamping of a savage Hebrew prophet (Matthiessen, 1941), then archetypal totalitarian dictator, an anticipation of Stalin and Hitler, in the work of Olson (1947) or C. L. R. James (1953) and in their New Left successors. *New York Times Book Review* items in 1938 and 1939 excitedly departed from the earlier admiring, Weaver-ite portraits. Philip Brooks respectfully quoted Charles Anderson's article in *Colophon,* dismissing Melville "bugs" who were besieging him with queries: What did he think of Melville's insanity or his Oedipus complex? Snapped Anderson, "I don't think—I collect facts" (July 17, 1938, 19). A newly flustered Herbert Gorman raved about Anderson's revealing study of Melville's literary sources and inspired plagiarisms, defining Anderson against the Freudians and Melville against hysterical antifascists (May 21, 1939, 2). The formative period of the "born writer" Melville's life was not childhood but his years at sea that made a man of him. He was "subject to the elements and the rough life of a sailor before the mast." The "ingrowing" Melville of *Mardi* and *Pierre* was very bad; Melville the borrower and alchemist was wonderful, not a shrieking Isabel. "We are apt to forget (or neglect) Herman Melville in this disorganized period when every writer seems to turn his attention to the political aspects of a jittery era. We are apt to think that the end of art (if it is called art any more) is a shrill screaming against those malevolent powers that are destroying the great free works of the imagination in certain countries. But such an assumption is not correct. It is the duty of the artist to *transform* and that is exactly what Herman Melville did." Finally, George S. Hellman alluded to a negative Ahab in his review of Matthiessen's *American Renaissance* (June 15, 1941, 4). Melville's tragic awareness of "the danger of overweening will" was the secret of his "depth."

Given the continuing influence of myth and symbol criticism (and excitedly approved by Howard Vincent reviewing Richard Chase's Melville study, November 13, 1949), the importance of historically specific analysis cannot be overemphasized. The bad Ahab, although always available as an archetype of the overreacher/narcissist, does not powerfully emerge in conservative criticism until Hitler and other narcissists, romantics, and materialists threaten the moderates after Hitler ejected conservative nationalists from his ruling coalition (roughly 1936–38).[132] The same issue of the *New York Times* celebrating the Melville centenary carried a piece by Edward A. Bradford, "Labor's Inhumanity to Labor," describing the cruelty of the closed shop and pleading for cooperation in the labor movement (July 7, 1919, magazine sect., 3, 14). The *New York Times Book Review* essay praised the verisimilitude of Melville's art: His works are autobiographical because he shows us the menace of Labor, personified in the figure of Jackson, the proletarian tyrant/consumptive of *Redburn*, whose gothic description is the only quotation from Melville's fiction. (Jackson will be mentioned by William Gilman as a precursor to Ahab in 1951; such a connection is absent from Olson's master's thesis.) In 1919, then, Melville was an antilabor realist telling the story of his life. But in 1938, the shrieks of Ahab and Pierre could not be a proper response to unimaginary threats to cultural freedom: The hunt for literary sources was on. Plotinus Plinlimmon (the *echt* pragmatist and promoter of "virtuous expediency" in *Pierre*) should be, must be, the real Herman Melville. Such is the inexorable logic of pluralism in one perfectly happy family.

The war against Weaver in Melville studies accelerated in the late 1930s, nearly a decade before the Cold War and the establishment of the national security state in 1947. This turning point modifies the notion that McCarthy-ism explains repression after the war; it is suggested that prewar corporatists as well as "fascist Republicans" must take responsibility for unfreedom in the academy. Having swallowed (or been swallowed by) the Stalinist Left during the years of the Popular Front (1935–39), strategically placed New Dealers and other corporatists managed to control the dating of witch hunts. With the left-wing liberal materialist opposition banished from the democratic pluralist panorama, pseudo-materialists could take the van. "Left-liberal" refers not to communists or their anti-Stalinist liberal opponents, or to any other -ism derivative of German historicism, but to open-minded empiricists ever on the alert for new primary sources; their still untold story is bound to the fortunes of Ahab in the lapses of the Left before and after the war. The decapitation of the Head people has been catastrophic for progressive social movements, but not only for the Left: The execution of Ahab has distorted every aspect of American culture, including the arts, the humanities, and the mental health profession insofar as the irrationalist and essentialist concept of *Kulturnation* dominates both theory and practice. No one seems to remember that it ever happened here.

8

A Change of Clowns

Film Noir Phasing Out the Weaver Synthesis

Until his ambiguous "canonization" during the Cold War, Melville, although taught in universities after 1919 (insofar as American literature was taught at all), seems to have been an artist's artist, an exotic, a cult figure throughout the 1920s and 1930s, appealing to upper-class primitivism, for instance as Ishmael Olson's ROOT MAN, or to humanists rooted in the High Middle Ages, especially nascent New Critics.[1] Willard Thorp had told readers in 1938 that the Melville Revival was by no means a fait accompli: "Melville is not easy to 'place' today with a definiteness which will receive general assent" (*Representative Selections*, cxx). The Thorp/ Olson-moderated Melville did pop up in some unexpected settings, red flag flying. Writing in the communist periodical *Science & Society*, William Charvat cited Melville and "young Russell Lowell" as the only "major writers" who demonstrated "consciousness of the distress of the worker" in the depression of 1837: "Melville . . . saw poverty in New York and Liverpool which must have contributed to the cosmic bitterness of his mature works."[2] Bernard Smith's revision of the American canon, *The Democratic Spirit* (1945), firmly situated "a side of him" on the Left; good "'little' people" would keep his memory alive. "Always he showed sympathy for, and respected, the dignity of, simple uncorrupted men—whether South Sea savages, common sailors, or ordinary 'little' people in a strangely malevolent world. . . . [I]n the 1920s there was a revival of interest in his work, and that interest will not die. The sketches reprinted here . . . reveal a side of him that should be better known."[3] In 1944, Eleanor Metcalf told Henry Murray that she had sent Melville books and biographies to the Central Library of Foreign Literature in Moscow a year and a half earlier, and that a Melville exhibition was to be mounted that summer to commemorate the 125th anniversary of his birth.[4]

These tributes aside, Melville was mostly ignored by literary figures associated with the 1930s American Left. With the exception of two illustrators and *Moby-Dick*, Rockwell Kent (1930) and Boardman Robinson (1943), *The Masses* and *New Masses* crowds were not part of the Melville Revival; he was not in the usable past cultivated by the *New Masses*, nor was he included with Poe, Cooper, Twain, and Jack London in the popular Soviet translations of nineteenth- and early-twentieth-century American literature.[5] The Trotskyist Philip Rahv, editor of *Partisan Review*, did not unambiguously promote Melville until 1950 (and it was the deradicalized Newton Arvin's anti-Ahab reading that was praised).[6] Given the importance that leading 1930s leftists assigned to critical historical methods (above the "political correctness" of particular authors imputed to them today), and given the revealing psychological insights in Melville's works, this comparative neglect of an artist whose fiction was demonstrably "scientific" in its attention to the prisoners of class is disturbing.[7] For one Left literary critic, Edwin Berry Burgum, both Melville and Matthiessen were decadent romantics: "One fears that Matthiessen has not only taken over Coleridge's esthetics, but also the 'diabolism' involved in his personality and exhibited in his poetry. One wonders why the whole soul of man is more clearly presented in the cynicism of Melville, verging upon insanity, and certainly verging on incomprehensibility of statement in his later works, than in the later 'socialism' of Whitman. . . . It is a little odd that Matthiessen, when the structure of his book has forced a choice upon him . . . should have felt obliged to choose the despondency of Melville."[8]

Could it be that the major Left voice in Melville studies belongs to loony Herman himself? This chapter is concerned primarily with Jay Leyda's Melville writings. The public and private postwar Melville Revivals will be compared: The placid pluralist brow is ruffled by seething emotions and conflicted relationships. Leyda saw himself as Weaver's antithesis, but their similar responses to Melville's writing unify Melville studies; Leyda's existentialism, like that of Pierrot Philosophique, may stand for the whole. The diagnosis of a decadent, paranoid, satanic Melville (shared by some key Melvilleans) was buttressed by a selective reading of biographical and textual evidence: These were dark facts that bred white rot, facts that might be unassimilable in an age of enlightened counterrevolution. Dusty archives disclose the making of a ruin emptied of spirit, not the construction of a national monument.

WHO WAS JAY LEYDA AND WHAT WAS HIS PROBLEM?

[From *The Story of Moby Dick the White Whale Adapted from the Novel* (1934), with pictures from *The Sea Beast*. Ahab has just conquered Moby Dick]
"Black God," said the Chinese, "always right."

Jay Leyda as a young man, date unknown. Jay Leyda Papers, Tamiment Institute Library, New York University.

[Illustration from *The Story of Moby Dick* (1934). Faith Mapple (Dolores Costello) embraces Ahab (John Barrymore)] "I've Been Wondering Where You Were," She Said.

[Jay Leyda, letter to Sergei Eisenstein, February 23, 1935] During my school years (grade-school, high-school), my wishes to learn more than was taught in school required more money than my middle-class family was willing or able to spend on me, as I had been adopted as an orphan by them.

[(Grand)Mother Leyda to Jay, February 6, 1939] I do not like the story you told about the "Black Sheep." I know a better one than that, more true to life. Ask me to tell you some day. You must know that you are . . . the very best and most beloved of all the family. There is not one of us who if you asked for anything would not do all in their power to give it to you. Please do not forget that Jay.

[Leyda's FBI file, quoting *New Leader*, November 9, 1940] Too much importance can not be placed on the role which will be played by the documentary film in the propaganda which will necessarily be part of this nation's life during the next few years.

[Labor columnist Victor Riesel, *New Leader,* October 4, 1941, quoted in Leyda's FBI file] Our theatrical agents pass on to us the fact that despite repeated warnings Nelson A. Rockefeller has permitted Jay Leyda, Moscow-trained film expert, to emerge as a producer of cultural messages for showing south of the border, yi, yi, yi, yi, or maybe oi, oi, oi, oi. . . . Mr. Leyda's first opus, now in preliminary stages, is addressed at the Rockefeller-Whitney cultural relations program for the Latin Americas. The working title is "Better Dresses, Fifth Floor." . . . By the way, has anyone anywhere heard of an active anti-communist getting a government job?

[Joseph Freeman to Margaret E. Fries, his psychiatrist, June 20, 1947, unfinished and not sent] . . . a recurrent dream of my childhood . . . when I was ten or twelve. In it I saw my mother naked; she is confined in a cage; she screams as if she were in great pain—and I cannot get her out. This memory stimulated by a visit from Jay Leyda . . . Jay is a "comrade" whom I knew in the Communist movement many years ago; I got him a scholarship to the motion picture school in Moscow, where he studied with Eisenstein for three years; he never communicated with me during all those years, but later became one of the many "friends" I had when I edited the New Masses. To my surprise, he came to see me last year [1946], in spite of my exile as a "renegade." He is a curious, sensitive, ambitious, opportunistic boy; his wife, whom he married in Moscow many years ago, is half Chinese, half Negro; Jay is a Protestant from Ohio. It took courage, as well as neurosis, to marry Sylvia—but then it took ambition, too; she is the daughter of General Chen, one of the big shots of China; her brother Percy (now in this country) was trained in Moscow, was a GPU agent, and is now secretary to Sen [*sic*] Fo in Shanghai. Sylvia is a fine dancer and they have been getting along in Holly-wood because she gets dancing parts in the movies. When Jay came to see me it was not the only surprise; there was the further surprise that he had grown a beard which made him look like the younger D. H. Lawrence, and the great-est surprise of all—that is, no surprise at all when you come to think of it—that he had embarked on a new biography of Herman Melville.

As usual I was free with advice, tried to get him a Guggenheim Fellow-ship—in short did all the things for him which I fail to do for myself; and all the time he is far better situated both in the Party AND in the "bourgeois" world than I am. Among other things, I suggested that he see Raymond Weaver, a Columbia University Professor who started the Melville revival in 1919, when I was his student at college and his daily companion. It was his book *Melville, Mariner and Mystic,* which rescued Melville from an oblivion of forty years and started that flood of critical and biographical material which has finally established the author of Moby Dick as one of the world's literary giants. But Jay insisted that he did not want to see Weaver; he did not like his book; Weaver had no real understanding of Melville. Jay went to Hollywood, and I did not hear from him for a year.

Then, yesterday afternoon, shopping at the A&P I ran into Sylvia Chen, and thus learned, by *accident*, that Jay was in town. I sent my regards. At eleven last night Jay showed up. He asked what I was doing and I told him I had written ninety sonnets in the past two and half months. To my great surprise, he said he was delighted—and looked it. Later I asked him about his work on Melville; above all I asked: what did Melville do in the last thirty years of his life, how was he able to maintain such a long silence?

For the story is this (and it is this that makes it relevant to my own interest in it) that Melville, as a young man, published several *successful* novels; then he married, wrote a couple of books which were butchered by the critics. He was a failure as a writer, much to the distress of his wife's family, a fancy aristocratic clan, and to Melville's own children (his descendants to this day speak of him with great hatred, Jay told me; he has interviewed them). To earn a living, Melville got a job (through his wife's family) as Inspector 75 in the Customs House at the Battery, New York; for thirty years maintained, as I thought, a great silence. But Jay said: No, HE WROTE POETRY. Like most people, I have always thought of Melville as a novelist; I did not know he spent the latter half of his life writing verse though I had read a few of his Civil War poems in anthologies—and great they are, too. So here (and you can easily see how I rushed in to *identify* myself with one more defeated writer who found a way to circumvent his defeat) the author of *Moby Dick* leads an obscure life as a Customs House inspector, an unhappy husband and father, writing poetry, some of which is published by his wife's family. . . . In fact, I have everything except Melville's *genius*.

All this was very interesting, but sharp changes in my feelings came when Jay said that he was going to see Raymond Weaver. That cut deep. I have some strange attachment to Weaver. For one thing, he was the first of my teacher[s] to discover me as a poet; he read my sonnet on Don Quixote, which I had included or rather written for a theme paper on Cervantes, to the class, praised it highly, and, without telling the class my name, added: The author of this sonnet will be like Goethe, he will go through the deepest mud and will emerge purer than before. All this was very flattering to a poet of twenty who had never published in a real magazine; and even more flattering was the fact that Weaver circulated the report around Columbia University that I wrote sonnets as good as Shakespeare's. Later we became great friends; I saw a good deal of him, especially after my graduation; we lived in the dorms at Livingston Hall; I was working on my first (anonymous) book, Harpers Illustrated History of the World War; he was working on Melville; we lunched and dined together and spent almost every evening in late talks which had a profound influence on me. . . . But what I most remember . . . is that Weaver gave me a present, Mallock's *The New Republic*, a strange, a kind of Platonic dialogue. . . . On the flyleaf of this book Weaver wrote: Erite sicut Deus, scientes bonum et malum . . . this was the Serpent's speech to Eve in the Garden of Eden, urging her to eat of the Tree of Knowledge. What the Serpent is saying is: BE YE LIKE UNTO GOD, KNOWING GOOD AND EVIL. I was puzzled and a little hurt: did Weaver think I did not know the difference between good and evil? Shortly after that, Weaver gave me a book which changed the entire course of my life: Brill's book on Psychoanalysis. I read and re-read that volume till I almost knew it by heart—and then and there became a Freudian. . . . I know from my own experience that if we are hostile to an author or his subject, we find it hard to get into his book. For years I had the greatest difficulty reading Proust—whom I now read constantly, who is one of my great literary heroes. I still cannot read—Melville! (Perhaps in both cases an unconscious homosexual element plays a role).[9]

[Leon Howard to Jay Leyda, July 23, 1947] Your work is going to be monumental and—to a lot of people—devastating. I am delighted to learn that it is going to be published so soon.

[Alfred Kazin in his journal, 1951] [Leyda] is such a zealous investigator, such a nut for detail, that he uncovered Melville's wedding certificate. Melville had actually written in the name of his mother instead of his bride. He led me up and down the backstairs of some empty house in Amherst until he could triumphantly show me Emily's last nightdress hanging in a closet . . . .

Leyda is such a snoop after nineteenth-century lives that he is positively frightening, yet no one seems to know anything about Leyda himself. Even his "Dutch" (?) name is suspect. His manner is elaborate, heavily gracious, but his political opinions are commonplace Stalinist. His wife is Oriental, her background as ambiguous as Leyda's. The dedication page of *A Melville Log* reads "This book was begun as a birthday present for my teacher, Sergei Eisenstein." Leyda is something of a film buff, but what did Eisenstein the great Soviet film director teach him and when?

[From Leyda's opera *Bartleby*. Lawyer wonders if Bartleby is mad] Can this man have some malign effect Some malign insidious effect—

Upon me? Me! Impossible!
If he is insane, is that contagious?
Surely I must rid myself of a demented man,
Who has in some degree already turned the tongues,
If not the heads, of all my clerks,—
And my own tongue, too.
But I wish no trouble,
Not for myself, and not for him—
[He glances toward Bartleby] Gracious heaven! he's not even working![10]

[Leyda's notes for the Lawyer's response after Bartleby says he won't copy anymore] L[awyer]: [to the audience] ~~Oh, my soul~~ What would *you* do with such a man! What *good* is he to me? Ginger picks up his scizzors [*sic*]—and snaps them once. L—No; Bartleby—even you must realize [broken off].[11]

[Psychiatrist Dr. Edwin Robbins remembers his patient at Jay Leyda's memorial service, February 27, 1988] [Leyda's] beginnings, which may have provided the direction for much of his life were far from auspicious. His mother denied her role telling the young Jay that she was his aunt or grandmother. His older sister, who was in the same household, raised him as her child and was called mother for many years. Jay's penchant for unravelling the mysteries of other's stories may well have been given root as he tried to trace his own genealogy. He correctly concluded after seeing posters and clippings that a clown who visited Dayton with a small circus each year was his father. At some point in his life he located the man, but I can't recall any lasting impressions. Jay was a good son and brother and remained in contact with his family until they died. . . . Perhaps the fact that he never went to graduate school made it possible for him to circumvent the academic "dog eat dog" competitiveness. This is not to say, though, that Jay was a timid intellectual. He was a formidable intellectual foe, seeking clarity and integrity at all times and could be very tenacious, though he would dislike the word, in holding to his position.

. . . For all of his interest in China and Russia, he totally separated himself from their political positions.[12]

Herman Melville was a model of bourgeois regularity, lucidity, and predictability in comparison to his revivers; of these no one was more opaque than Leyda. He entered the Melville Revival, perhaps in 1939, perhaps in 1942, perhaps late 1944; exactly why, where, or when is hard to determine. Leyda is remembered not only as "the greatest Melville fact-finder ever . . . known, respected and sponsored by the whole circle of Melvilleans,"[13] but as a major photographer and film historian by the New York art world. His friends and patrons in the arts and academe have included Walker Evans, James Agee, Lincoln Kirstein, Alfred Barr, Jr., Muriel Rukeyser, Alfred Kazin, Elia Kazan, H. W. L. Dana, Daniel Aaron, Paul Jarrico, and Alan Trachtenberg. Leyda was also the controversial consultant to the pro-Soviet Hollywood film *Mission to Moscow* (1943); his un-American activities in vanguard photography, theater, and film had been cited twelve times in the Martin Dies Committee (HUAC) Report of 1944, and in later years, his movements, associations, and labors were of interest to the FBI, the CIA, the NSA, the Departments of the Army and Navy, the State Department, and the United States Information Agency.[14]

Leyda was such a prodigious Melville researcher that his project to compile a fully revelatory chronology of Melville's life in documents earned the backing of Harry Levin, F. O. Matthiessen, and Alfred Kazin and the awestruck cooperation and encouragement of Eleanor Melville Metcalf, Charles Olson, and Henry A. Murray. But most important, Leyda labored and suffered with a number of dedicated scholars, most of them Stanley Williams's students trained at Yale (some of them finishing their dissertations): Walter E. Bezanson, Merrell R. Davis, William H. Gilman, Harrison Hayford, Merton M. Sealts, Jr., Wilson H. Heflin, and Leon Howard (the last two not Williams's students). They would be teaching American literature, American Studies, or American civilization, apparently placing Herman Melville more securely in the canon. Their letters to Leyda described possibly psychosomatic illnesses, writing blocks, and ambivalence that accompanied some of their research and writing—a joint martyrdom that produced the major second-wave Melville scholarship.[15] Leyda's chef d'oeuvre, *The Melville Log*, is still touted as the corrective to misguided interpretations of the original revivers, bringing all the facts of Melville's life, even the most embarrassing, to light. James D. Bloom ended his review of the Northwestern-Newberry edition of Melville's *Journals* recommending the *Log*: "For most readers Jay Leyda's 'Melville Log' remains the most engaging way to relate Melville's work to the raw data of his life." Writing to prospective sponsors in the wake of falling fascist dictatorships, Leyda had promised that the "raw data" properly juxtaposed with the art would be engagingly presented in the spirit of democratic participation, self-management, and self-criticism: There would be no unwarranted inferences or speculation, hyperbole, hero worship, domineering (totalizing) narrative or magisterial interpretation, unlike "the gush and guff" of 1920s predecessors.[16]

Kidnapped

As the FBI discovered, there was no birth record for Jay Lincoln Leyda in Detroit, Michigan, but they persisted in believing that he was the child of Josephine Mellon Leyda and Newton Leyda, as Leyda had reported in various applications for foreign travel. Jay Flynn Leyda was born, however, on February 12, 1910, in Detroit, Michigan, according to an affadavit signed by his real mother, Margaret Flynn Leyda Smith, who was seventeen years old at his birth. "I really am a bastard," insisted Leyda to the Columbia University interviewer who took his oral history in 1980. But this account did not jibe with the one remembered by his psychiatrist, Dr. Edwin Robbins, and quoted above. To Columbia, Leyda described what would sound like a "fairy-tale" of his early life: "Up to the age of six . . . I thought that I was living in the family where I had three sisters, one of whom was away, a mother, a brother—" At that time his "mother" Josephine Leyda told Jay that his absent "sister" Margaret was his mother, really, and that his father had nearly kidnapped him just after his birth. "My actual father had been picked up by the police in Dayton [his grandparents' home] for trying to kidnap me. So I had to be on guard against him." Jay wanted to live with father, but the family slandered Mr. X, claiming he was "a black Irishman, a charlatan who had hired my mother as his stage assistant in reading—in his mind-reading act and in his hypnotism act."[17] Jay had found a full-length photograph of his father in the attic, "but the next time I went to the attic, the picture was gone." Meanwhile the two girls (his "sisters" who were really his aunts) and their mother never let him out of their sight; if one had to go out, the other took him to a movie so that he would not be retrieved and "swept off to the circus" by "the wicked father" with only one jailor to protect him. When he was seven or eight years old, Jay was allowed to see his father twice, but with his grandmother Josephine present; father was then a "worker in a circus." During that period, Jay convinced a girl his age to run away with him to join his father, but he was found and thrashed by his uncle-brother Newton Edwin Leyda. His father's real name was unknown; one of his many aliases was Flynn, Leyda's favorite. Leyda was his grandfather's name, but that wasn't *his* real name either. Leyda explained that the grandfather "had been born in a family named Singer, and then the mother had married again. . . . And that's how the name Leyda came to the family. So Leyda doesn't really belong to me at all, but I've had it from the beginning. I've always been accused of adopting it as a pseudonym, but it isn't. All the others were."[18] Leyda did not mention that, during his childhood, his grandfather was a living member of the family. In 1935, the elder Newton Leyda lost his job as a night watchman but then became an inspector in another steel company.[19] The grandmother Josephine had been a schoolteacher. They were Baptists, so Leyda's class background and family sans the dashing Mr. Flynn can be summarized as humble and unimaginative.

The itinerant performer-father with superhuman powers was the glamorous alternative, and Leyda, an outstanding student, presented himself as a misfit in his mother's dowdy and constricting environment, although Dayton was not the artistic wasteland implied in his self-portraits—for instance, Leyda was able to study with the famous portraitist photographer Jane Reece (a member of Stieglitz's Photo-Secessionist group) after his high school classes let out, and his correspondence contains letters from Dayton friends who were artists, writers, or dancers. Moreover, family letters demonstrate unflagging support and interest in Leyda's numerous activities, including his trip to the Soviet Union. (As it turns out, he was not illegitimate. Documents in his NYU papers confirm that his mother was married to his father in 1909; they were divorced in 1911; he was adopted by his grandmother's family, but he was no "orphan," as he told Eisenstein).[20]

If ever there was a case of multiple mistaken identity, of true gaps between signifiers and the signified, it was the case of Leyda. As he tells the story, the philistine women forced little Jay to feed on fake (inflated) movies and other bogus narratives, while the life-sized image of his real, exciting father, snatched away by dull female relatives, could not be held in memory (the attic). Of the two men named in mother's family, one supports the women in holding him against his will, and the other is absent. Interestingly, in a childhood drawing, "Two Forest Scenes from Ballet," each scene shows a diminutive fleeing or supplicating *female* figure menaced by gigantic and aggressive plant shapes.[21]

Contrast Leyda's crystalline story of his childhood with the garbled account relayed by Leyda's psychiatrist, Dr. Robbins, above: "His mother denied her role telling the young Jay that she was his aunt or grandmother. His older sister, who was in the same household, raised him as her child and was called mother for many years." In the Robbins version, his mother pretended to be aunt or grandmother, while his older sister (in the same household) pretended to be the mother. Did Robbins think about Jay's perception of their ages? And Robbins says Jay inferred that father was a clown, sought him out, and reconciled with everyone before they died. But according to the "Reminiscences," before Jay was six he thought his aunts and uncle were his sisters and brother, while his grandmother Josephine was supposed to be his real mother. Then he was told of his true parentage, and continued to be sequestered away from the "wicked father." He rarely saw his absent but real (and unnamed) mother, Margaret, Mrs. A. C. Smith, who was living on the West Coast.[22] There is one passage in the Columbia "Reminiscences" on Leyda's distrust of documents and documentaries that seems directly related to the uncertainties and insecurities of his childhood (as variously told to his psychiatrist and to Columbia). After a question on the ethics of reenactment, or staging in documentary filmmaking, he replied, "There isn't a sharp line between the document and the non-document. Everything is chosen. A newsreel cameraman chooses just where he puts the camera down, and where he points it too. It's almost impossible to draw an exact line between pure documentary and what is staged documentary. And sometimes it works wonderfully. Sometimes it looks very ugly—when it isn't well done" (1:35). Leyda has absolved himself of personal responsibility for his own (or anyone's) willed distortions of events: Everybody chooses, so it must follow that everyone prevaricates; there is no hierarchy of comparative truth and falsehood; Weaver's beautiful masks are back. The reader is on her own.

In mid-1933, Leyda, then a photographer and activist in New York City, announced to friends and comrades that he was about to enter film school (GIK, the State Film Institute) in the Soviet Union. To "Comrade Marshall" he suggested that if one member of the Workers Film and Photo League could get in each year, "then we would be a sharp instrument for revolution here."[23] His close associates had high hopes for him as an effective communist intellectual. Leyda was temporarily parting from his semi-secret first "wife," attorney Carol Weiss King, a Jewish woman fifteen years his senior;[24] King encouraged the trip and expected him to return in three years, implying that he was not himself in his current situation:

> . . . And probably the next three years in the Soviet Union will make you more your way. You know despite my frivolousness tonight I am terribly eager for you to get a hell of a lot out of this experience. If you come back without drinking the cup dry as it were I shall be terribly disappointed. Little things are going to be frightfully discouraging, but you musn't let go the main thing. One of your biggest difficulties with life is just going to pieces over obstacles that interfere instead of somehow climbing under, over, or around them. You get all tied in knots . . . . You must win out—learn what you need to learn, get a chance to use every bit of yourself, then if we both feel as I do tonight you'll come home and we'll get married, have a kid and everybody [will] live happily ever after . . . .[25]

His party wife's stoicism and optimism were reflected in a psychologically revealing letter Leyda wrote to Lincoln Kirstein, not long after his arrival in Moscow:

> There doesn't seem to be any real reason why you should delay your trip to Russia, as E[isenstein?] advised. There's enough food and excitement (both of all sorts—inner and physical) to make up for *any* lack you may feel, and you're not going to touristly whine about the clothes you see on the street, and the sanitation conditions, and the fact that a seat on a Moscow tram is rare, are you? True, it can get damn cold here, but it's a kind of cold that is hard to take but is good for one. You find it not only in going around the corner into Pushkin Square, and in your valuta-space, and in the Eisenstein lecture room at GIK, and blowing out on the audience in the last acts of "The Days of the Tourbins," but also in the methods of the chistkas. A chistka is a cleaning given the party members as often as the party feels it wants cleaning, which is about every four years. This is one of the sweeping,

cleansing years and the wind blows through every unit, trust, and union. Each member rips open his past and his mind for inspection by both the cleaning commission and his fellow-workers, and you know that man well after he has answered the commission's questions, and you've listened to his friends and enemies. A chistka can get heated, but its final cleanliness is always sure and cold, and that's what I like about it.

Russia gives an outsider, coming in, the effect of a chistka. Sitting in the slippery comfort of America, one has one's private small doubts about the USSR. "What proportion is it benefiting?" "Does it know where it's going?" "Can the arts turn in that direction?" "Is it still fragile to be pushed off its track?" etc.etc. And then one goes in and looks—and knows that it is working and sure of itself. It's moving toward what it wants—a classless society developing towards communism. I'm not a tourist hopelessly or hopefully passing through Russia. I'm a student here, here to stay for the length of my course. I'm not seeing everything, but I'm seeing lots and I want to tell you so much that this letter would have to be sent as a package, but there are more things to say than I have words to say them with. And fortunately for you, I've not been here long enough to give a complete report of even one theater. Or one newspaper. Or one architect. Or one composer. Or one power-plant . . . .[26]

That same month, November 1933, Joseph Freeman, writing on *New Masses* stationery, hinted that Leyda was nervous about leaving his party work in the United States, moreover, that he was expected to participate at a high level in communist pedagogy when he returned. "I beg you again not to speak of 'recovering' any trust in you since such trust was never violated & therefore never lost. I look upon you as a comrade from whom we can expect very fine things, & I am looking forward to good work on your part both in the school in the USA when you return where we hope you will work with us in establishing what—what you call—the U.S.S.A."[27] In a partially dated letter from the Soviet Union to his real mother, Margaret Leyda Smith, and written on his birthday, Leyda forcefully declared his love for Mother Russia and denounced the duplicity of libertarian America while expressing longings for a firm foundation:

Wonder if we'll ever see the day when there will be a *USSA*. As much as you dread that day, just that much I want it.

If you ever see what it has done for this people, literally making new people, giving them a solid base and a reason for life [to] everyone who wants a reason for life, you might want to see that day too. I don't know how America will seem once I'm back in it, but from here I get very angry at the disguised barbarism that is contemporary American life. You can't call a state civilized or progressive when an honest decent living is not made available for everyone in every calling. Here not only does every man and woman have more than enough work to do, but also every artist with something to create gets a chance to create it. This certainly can not be said about any capitalist country today.

Leyda then offered a brief reading list, beginning with *The Communist Manifesto:* "I wish I could be there to see their faces when you ask for this at the library. Watch for yourself, and see for yourself how 'free' speech is in America." According to the letter of application Leyda wrote to Eisenstein, asking to join his film project as a still photographer (February 23, 1935, appended),[28] the letter to his mother was wishful thinking: His experiences in the Soviet Union had consisted of blighted hopes, brought on, the "orphan" alleged, by dependency and unmerited rejection. Such disappointments may have shaped Leyda's approach to the Melville problem: His was a fairy tale told through a mask about a writer who wrote "tales told through a mask" (the suggested title of the Random House book of Melville's short stories that he edited in 1948). In his introduction to the *Stories,* America, Melville, and adoring women were similarly deceptive, cruel, and withholding. And the advanced modernist filmmaker would tell the reader of his *Log:* Here are my snapshots and facsimiles and excerpts of documents; the facts are all there. Watch for yourself and see for yourself; write your own biography (and, perhaps under his breath, it won't make any more sense than mine does).

Leyda remained in the Soviet Union for three years, marrying the dancer and choreographer Si-Lan Chen in 1936. With characteristic pessimism, he told Margaret, "I have a new wife whom I found in Russia and whom I'm sure you'll never like as much as I do."[29] Leyda departed in 1936; it was Eisenstein who recommended him to Iris Barry, in Europe to seek out German and Russian film for the Museum of Modern Art. Leyda speculated, "I think Eisenstein began to see that I was not going to be a director. That I didn't have enough initiative, that I didn't— that I couldn't control a large operation or a large group of people. And I think that accounts for his pushing me more and more towards film history" (oral history, 1:42, 2:87).[30] Leyda was appointed assistant curator of the Rockefeller-funded film department and asked to write the history of Russian film. But that, too, turned sour; writing on Mother's Day 1937 (?), he informed Margaret Smith, ". . . Film Library had turned out to be a racket, and it's not very soothing to realize that one is unconsciously participating in a racket. The whole bottom dropped out—I wasn't really useful to anybody—but they kept up my comfortable salary as part of their scam" (Leyda Papers, NYU). Since he was useful to no one, he was writing a book. Was Leyda talking about MoMA or the Soviet Union?

Eisenstein had marked his own flight from romanticism and montage to the cult of personality, from the sensibility associated with popular revolution to the higher neoclassicism. In 1936, the year that Jay Leyda left the Soviet Union (and feeling rejected by his mentor), Eisenstein took a new direction, repudiating the extremes of cold, dry didacticism and the ravings of the insane. Something even newer and finer was unfolding:

It is not accidental that precisely at this period, for the first time in cinematography, there begin to appear the first finished images of personalities, not just any personalities, but of the finest personalities: the leading figures of leading Communists and Bolsheviks. Just as from the revolutionary movement of the masses emerged the sole revolutionary party, that of the Bolsheviks, which heads the unconscious elements of revolution and leads them toward conscious revolutionary aims, so the film images of the leading men of our times begin during the present period to crystallise out of the general-revolutionary-mass-quality of the earlier type of film. And the clarity of the Communist slogan rings more definitely, replacing the more general-revolutionary slogan. (*New Theater,* April 1936, 13)

I think that now, with the approach of the sixteenth year of our cinematography, we are entering a special period. These signs, to be traced today also in parallel arts as well as found in the cinema, are harbingers of the news that Soviet cinematography, after many periods of divergence of opinion and argument, is entering its classical period, because the characteristics of its interests, the particular approach to its series of problems, this hunger for synthesis, this postulation and demand for complete harmony of all the elements from the subject matter to composition within the frame, this demand for fullness of quality and all the features on which our cinematography has set its heart—these are the signs of the highest flowering of an art.[31] *(New Theater,* June 1936, 29)

But in an intimate letter to Leyda dated February 1, 1937, Eisenstein expressed feelings of failure, isolation, and loss, complicating what we are told about their interactions while Leyda was working with him:

My dear Jay! I was very happy to get news from you and all the lovely things you've sent me. It was a pleasure and a sorrow. For strange as it may seem— I'm missing you here! You know I was never too sentimental—I'd say on the contrary—but you found a certain link with things I even have no opportunity to talk to anybody now! I mean by that theoretical ideas and the trend of thoughts surpassing the purely professional side of art producing! Most of the time with you I was pretty biting and disagreeable—but that was a sort of self-protection against . . . oneself: against things that drive me mad—things I cannot put down in book form being chained to producing other things! You were always provoking and touching my most secret wounds—the side of my work which is to my opinion the really most important of what I have to do—and which I am not doing. So that's why our intercourse had a certain mixture of pain and pleasure . . [sic] well as any masochistic passtime [sic]! Now nobody and nothing is tickling me in this way: and when I by accident jump out of production for an hour or so, I feel like Peer Gynt in the scene where he watches the rush of leaves on the earth which happen to be his ideas that never got form . . . .

As soon as I'm through with the picture I *must* feel myself at work on the book. But there will start again a new tragedy: primo: there are plans for Spain. Secundo: Paul Robeson who was here with a concert tour has put himself at my entire disposition from July to October! Now both these things fit marvelously together—taking the race and national problem within the film about revolutionary Spain, but all that means . . . two more years of nothing doing about the book!!! . . .

Another feeling of sorrow overcame me in another direction. Your letter made me feel out of touch with the outer world: I felt myself in no connection with what is going along on the other side of the ocean.—what people think about, what they write about, what is going on in the arts and sciences. Well I can imagine that not much, if anything, is in progress there in the modern way. But discoveries, research etc. must be going ahead. Couldn't you hold me a little bit "au courant" of what is happening in the fields I am interested in. Maybe it wouldn't be too difficult to send me from time to time even the . . . "Times" book review, so as to know what is published and printed over there. Also some about what is going on in arts and sciences— You're in the center of all that there. Thanks for the books you made notes of for me (the one you promised to be sent never arrived). . . . Always heartily yours, Sergei [signed in red][32]

Four years later, Leyda, translating Eisenstein's essays on film theory (published as *The Film Sense*, 1942), was no longer in "the center of all that"; as he informed Ivor Montagu in 1941:

You knew, didn't you, that I was no longer working at the Museum—or any place for that matter. Yes, Iris [Barry] asked for my resignation last August, providing a variety of interesting reasons—none of them having to do with the quality of my work. The point was that I had become an accumulation of

embarrassment to the institution (now entirely financed through the Hays
Office by the industry) & could have no place in the reorganization (into the
Rockefeller Committee of Cultural (!) Relations with the Americas). One of
the reasons given was my refusal to resign from the quarterly of FILMS. This
was just one of the earliest incidents in what has become a nation-wide weeding process, now as open as the process which you have witnessed yourself.
Incidentally the manuscript of the history which I was preparing for them
was confiscated by them to prevent its completion and publication. All in
all, I wonder what you and Iris would have to say to each other if you ever
met. One last item on that great woman is one of her rare frank moments—
long ago—when she confessed that her greatest ambition (next to money of
course) was to become a Dame of the British Empire. And I assure you, she
is still doing her best . . . .[33]

However, in a draft of his 1942 application to the Guggenheim Foundation, Leyda
asked for funds to complete his history of Soviet film, of which a first draft was said
to be half-completed along with a full outline (and which did reach final form as
Kino: A History of Russian and Soviet Film, 1960). Among the names given for references, Ivor Montagu's name was listed, then crossed out.

On March 22, 1942, Leyda, then working at Artkino (the American distribu-
tor of Soviet films), wrote to Eisenstein, asking if he owned the following titles
(Melville's name was absent): "Joyce's Finnegan's Wake, Levin's James Joyce (a good
study), the swell new complete edition of The Notebooks of Leonardo, Gorer's
Revolutionary Ideas of the Marquis de Sade,[34] Barry's D. W. Griffith, Van Doren's
Benjamin Franklin, the Letters of Mozart (Eng. trans.)." That same year, Leyda
told Eisenstein, "Have been hired by Warner Brothers as technical advisor on *Mission to Moscow*—not a very soothing job."[35] Perhaps entering his own special
period, in a letter to his mother, May 24, 1942, Leyda proposed a major project in
family reconstruction with himself as director:

> I don't know whether I told you, but Si-Lan is writing her memoirs! I must
> credit her with good stimulation, anyway, because it gave me the idea that a
> marvelous book about childhood in a small Pennsylvania town could be built
> around those swell photos that are kept in the attic in Dayton (I stole some of
> the best ones the last time I was home). It would be a completely original ap-
> proach to autobiography—based on photographs, and such good ones too.
> Complementing the photographs would be memories, anecdotes, character
> portraits, documents, and so forth. I'm going to recruit all of you—it's your
> childhood, so you have to tell all about it. My job will be to take all the stuff

that everyone sends me, and make it into a book. How about it? Will you be one of the collaborators? Send facts, stories, descriptions of photos that you remember, or that you kept. [Signed] Enthusiastically, Jay[36]

No such family project (or chistka) was ever accomplished, but the same movement and the same hunger for synthesis and harmony could be seen in Leyda's reconstruction of Melville's life through documents, as a collage of "Specimens" evolved into the carefully arranged and apparently comprehensive *Log*.

Some creation myths

In early 1934, Joseph Freeman had praised the Orozco frescoes at Dartmouth College as "his most revolutionary in the sense that he has a nihilist, destructive (subversive) attitude toward capitalist values."[37] Perhaps Leyda was attracted, similarly, to what he perceived as Melville's anticapitalist nihilism, and that is sufficient explanation for his lifelong pursuit/evasion of the author that followed his first reading of *Typee*, reportedly in an army hospital sometime in 1943, an event he likened to a lightning strike. However, the record suggests a more complex set of motives. The Olson Papers contain a copy of a letter to Leyda dated Feb. 4, 1946, commenting upon SPECIMENS (an early version of the *Log*). Olson's letters to Leyda were filled with enthusiasm and admiration, but on a page marked "withheld," Olson (working since the early 1930s) was indignant that Leyda thought his Melville research and writing was "with *only 7 years* finished!"[38] As a communist publicly loyal to Stalinist policies throughout the travails of the 1930s, Leyda may well have begun his research in 1939, the year of the Ribbentrop-Molotov pact; that alliance dissolved Popular Front coalitions with social democrats and liberals extant since 1935.[39] What would this mean for party intellectuals? In literary criticism, the rupture between bourgeois and proletarian consciousness was reinstated. Positive readings of radical bourgeois writers (including nineteenth-century naturalists and some symbolists and modernists) were once more discarded in favor of proletarian literature and its idealizing aesthetic of socialist realism. In politics, hitherto vigorously antifascist, interventionist communists were suddenly in the same camp as romantic anticapitalists, pacifists, and the right-wing isolationists of America First. FDR (a "social fascist" before 1935) was bad again, as tricky as Woodrow Wilson had been for Villard: Hitler's imperialism was no worse than the imperialism of America, England, and France; another war would only rip off American workers. These Stalinist positions were dropped after Germany invaded the Soviet Union in 1941,[40] but most reappeared with the Cold War and the strident anti-Americanism of 1950s Soviet communism. Communist writers, however, defended the New Deal from McCarthy-ite "fascism" and its assault on 1930s reforms that seemed to strengthen the labor movement.[41] How could Melville have fit in with communist cultural policy as relayed by Leyda?

Perhaps Melville (neglected by the United States Left during the Popular Front, 1935–39) was viewed as too defiantly libertarian, too antagonistic to collaboration with the statism of the moderate men, too impassioned with class hatred. However, Melville's pacifism[42] and anti-imperialism (as well as apparent submission to order in "Billy Budd") could have appealed to Leyda after the shift in policy (1939), particularly as counterpoint to the "nervously deranged" expansionist brother Gansevoort, who, in Leyda's opinion, not only exerted a "tremendous influence on HM's literary debut" but also molded his political thought; Leyda knew a great deal about Gansevoort by 1945.[43] Moreover, the first version of the Log ("Specimens") was heavily weighted toward the anti-French imperialist Typee.[44] Leyda could solve the Melville problem by delegitimating the weirder texts: Works including Mardi, Moby-Dick, Pierre, The Confidence-Man, and The Piazza Tales could be associated with Gansevoort's expansionist ambitions, mental instability, and death. Then there would be the progression that Stalinist bureaucrats preferred, like the change from the experimental pluralism of artistic production (post-1917–late 1920s) to the final victory of Proletkult and Stalin in the 1930s.[45] Impelled perhaps by the omen of civil war and personal tragedy, the wages of youthful sin, Melville's later work would advance the stubbornly adolescent artist toward the optimistic epilogue to Clarel, then to another unconditional surrender/victory: the cheerful submission of creative individuality to bureaucratic authority, epitomized by Billy Budd's blessing of the state that is murdering him.[46] In fact, the design of the published Log carried exactly that sense of a total break between the younger and the older Melville, mimicking the switch in Leyda's own "political character" that he reported both to Lincoln Kirstein and then to passport officials in the mid-1950s: "My life and ideas have changed completely. Reference to my writing since that time [1943] will confirm this."[47]

Isadora Duncan told me today that when I'm in overalls, I look like a blue Pierrot.
—Eisenstein, Memoirs, 265

Leyda told his establishment backers that the Log was conceived not in obedience to the shifting party line of 1939 (which, of course, would not have been mentioned), but in response to a request from his teacher Sergei Eisenstein. Writing to Harvard professor Harry T. Levin, an admirer of Eisenstein and other modernists, in the summer of 1944, Leyda sounded as if the project had just germinated:

Gansevoort Melville. Miniature dated June 13, 1836, artist unknown. Appears in the *Log,* vol. 2. Gansevoort-Lansing Collection, New York Public Library. Photo by Jay Leyda.

Gansevoort Melville (a severed head), as altered by Jay Leyda. It was apparently submitted for inclusion in an early version of the *Log* but was never published. Department of Special Collections, Charles E. Young Research Library, UCLA.

. . . I know this is an awkward time of year to try to reach you, but if I don't send you this idea soon, I'll burst with it.

What do you think of the idea of New Directions adding a new series to its several series—a series of chronologies of (primarily) American writers—particularly those with mysterious or ~~confused biographies~~ confusing lives—a Melville Calendar, a Poe Calendar, a Whitman Calendar? These would collate a variety of material (letters, contemporary accounts, records, diaries, newspapers, etc.) into single, continuous, concrete birth-death chronologies.

This is a form that has become extremely popular (and useful) in Soviet scholarship in literature and music—and a quantity of such chronicles have appeared. . . . You're entitled to know why you should be persecuted with this project. It all began with Eisenstein's request for books by and on Melville. The scattered ~~stuff~~ state of Melville material and information—seen side by side with the order brought by Orlov's chronology to similar scattered information on Musorgsky—made me wonder why Melville studies couldn't be helped in this way. . . . Will you help me with the presentation of the idea to New Directions? . . . As you've already guessed, I'd like to put the Melville chronicle into immediate work, but one of the advantages of the form is the opportunity for cooperative research—will you have any enthusiastic or hard-working students this year?[48]

A fuller account was given to Columbia in 1980. Eisenstein was again the impetus, and Leyda presented himself and Leon Howard as the prime movers behind the rescue of a neglected or misconceived Herman Melville. Leyda was translating Eisenstein's *The Film Sense* and thinking about Eisenstein's color theory, particularly his reversal of white and black:

So I had read *Moby-Dick* at some time, long before, and I couldn't resist adding the whiteness of the whale—whiteness not being used to add virtue or blessedness or angelic behavior to the whale at all, but absolutely the opposite. At least the suspicion that Ishmael had, and Melville had, that the whale represented evil. There are many different interpretations of that by now, but at that time, it was striking that here was another example that could fit his example perfectly.[49]

Well, he was quite struck by this, and the next cable I got, really very soon after he saw the book, was, "send me everything by Melville except *Moby-Dick* which I have." (3:116)

Leyda then read all of Melville:

I even read Typee for the first time in the hospital at Fort Knox. . . . I was ashamed of the Melville biographies. They were so casual, and each one was much more an autobiography of the biographer than it was of Melville. But I sent them anyway, as soon as I read them. . . . Someone like Newton Arvin did an excellent book [but] it didn't really go beyond [his] personal feelings about Melville. [*sic:* Arvin's book did not appear until 1950, *C.S.*] . . . Here was a great writer who had only recently been considered a great writer, and was still being discovered by people, and still not being taught in many schools. That's why I'd never heard of him when I went to high school. (3:117–18)

When Eisenstein came to America in 1930–31, Leyda continued (inaccurately), "Melville wasn't being talked about much. The books were not in print" (3:153). So in the early 1940s, he determined to create a book of documents for Eisenstein's birthday. Now comes his "real collision with academia." Lawrence Clark Powell had invented a job for him and gave him access to the stacks at UCLA and Interlibrary Loan, but

The next encounter was with the man who was considered the sort of chief-tain of American Studies and American Literature at UCLA. Freud has made me forget his name, but I'll remember it soon enough. [Probably Dixon Wecter, *C.S.*[50]] He gave me a shock. He said, "You're just wasting your time. You aren't trained for this sort of work. You don't know the material. You don't know the work that has been done on Melville." Fortunately, I re-strained myself from saying that I had read with unhappiness most of the work that had been done on Melville. "You should really find something more appropriate for yourself to do—not in literature because that's obvi-ously not your field. You say you're interested in film? Well, here we're right in the film capital of the world. You must do something with film." He tried to get me out of the office as fast as possible.[51] (3:120–21)

The "chieftain's" real name could have been blocked because the archetype of the bad parent was a blend of Eisenstein and his aunts who reportedly forced him to feed on bad Hollywood movies. (Leyda never criticized Eisenstein, but he did complain bitterly about another friend of Eisenstein, the "jealous" Seymour Stern, a biographer of D. W. Griffith who allegedly stalked him for years, denounc-ing him at every occasion when Leyda spoke in public, although once Stern did fall to his knees and beg Leyda's forgiveness; see "Reminiscences" 1:44–47). In the next example, Leyda seems to be saying that "even" Leon Howard, so apparently sym-pathetic, may have secretly harbored doubts as to his competence, as the following indicates:[52] "And even the next person I encountered, who really became an idol, god, to me . . . . It was Leon Howard, who was so sympathetic with what I was doing."

There were other Melvilleans against whom Leyda set himself as the open-handed and forthcoming collectivist scholar. Probably referring to Henry Murray and John H. Birss, Leyda pointed to "Melville people, who were never going to end their work. Who were so pleased with themselves that they had decided to go on until death removed them from the scene altogether. And these were people who kept what they did, what they found, very secret, too" (3:126).

Leyda is now hooked up with a "committee" of Yale students with "Leon the headmaster." "The first thing that had to be repaired was to encourage Leon to do the biography of Melville that he had long ago wanted to do, even before the Melville *Log* was published. So he started it then and was a big help in every way, because I went back to LA and began working on it there, with Leon nearby" (3:131). In contrast with the bubbly letter to Levin, or the comforting chronicle of the good father close at hand (which is false, as Leon Howard was teaching at Northwestern University during the period of the *Log*'s composition, not joining the UCLA faculty until 1950), the actual process of Leyda's Melville research, including his relations with other scholars, is an unsolved riddle.[53] For instance, the enthused cable from Eisenstein requesting Melville materials that Leyda described as sent in the early 1940s after Eisenstein read *The Film Sense* (1942) has not been found. The earliest reference to Melville is certainly enthused, but is dated January 1946: "Please continue to send books reckoning that still one to six or seven may reach me! You have a wonderful flair as to what excites me! Take for instance Melville . . . ."[54] Eisenstein's memoirs do not jibe with Leyda's reports of his interest in Melville; according to his own recollections, "by some strange intuition, Jay sent me from overseas Melville's *Omoo and Typee* (1945!)." Eisenstein's date, if correct, supports my contention that Leyda used his connection with the celebrated Soviet modernist to mobilize support for his own ambitious project, while the origins of his interest in creating the *Log* remain obscure.

Leyda is the model principled and objective artist and researcher to younger Melvilleans, photographers, and filmmakers. Although the Columbia interviewer kept circling back to Leyda's membership in communist-front organizations, he consistently distanced himself from the reds, giving the impression he was one of many noncommunists working at the Film and Photo League, or Frontier Films, or active in the John Reed Club.[55] This would add to the impression that his firing from MoMA in 1940, followed by the cancellation of his book contract by Princeton, then several nervous breakdowns ("Reminiscences"3:110–11), etc., were instances of senseless persecution directed against an idealistic but apolitical artist, an impression buttressed by the biography assembled by Elena Pinto Simon and

David Stirk of NYU, by his psychiatrist Ed Robbins after Leyda's death in 1988, and by Leyda himself on numerous occasions.

Though I would carefully avoid giving unnecessary offense, yet I am inclined to believe that all those who espouse the doctrine of reconciliation may be included within the following descriptions: Interested men, who are not to be trusted, weak men who *cannot* see, prejudiced men who *will not* see, and a certain set of moderate men who think better of the European world than it deserves; and this last class, by an ill-judged deliberation, will be the cause of more calamities to this continent than all the other three.
—Thomas Paine, *Common Sense*, 1776

We need not question the moderate credentials of Stanley T. Williams, the Yale professor who mentored many of the second-wave Melvilleans.[56] In 1923, Williams was looking for balance; the rights of labor had been too well realized in the growing internationalization of labor parties after 1917. "It even seems as if a new *Past and Present* were needed, one which would assert somewhat the rights of the opponents of labor. No longer is it so necessary to denounce the gospels of mammonism, dilettantism, of oppression of workmen, of extortion by capital. The boot is on the other leg. Labour's emancipation is more complete than even Carlyle would have guessed possible. Perhaps a book proclaiming the rights of the employer would be as pertinent today as was *Past and Present* in 1843."[57] Williams was co-editor of *The American Mind* (1937); the pseudo-materialist anthology contained a biographical sketch of Melville depicting a courageous antidemocrat, a Tory out of step with his times but representing the liveliest humanitarian sentiments. This particular autodidact was a rectified Ethan Brand, whose sad decay had immediately preceded some editorial remarks:

"A whale ship was my Yale College and my Harvard," wrote Herman Melville . . . . He attended Albany Academy. . . . *Mardi* (1849) was an allegorical representation of the intellectual struggle within the author's mind. . . . [*Pierre's*] preposterous and incestuous plot played no small part in Melville's literary downfall. The allegory of this powerful novel was completely overlooked. . . . For the rejection of Melville by the Americans of the eighteen-fifties, both the writer himself and his age were responsible. Melville, in a period deeply affected by romanticism, was a man out of place in his century.

Superficially, indeed, he sometimes displayed the romantic mood. He sought personal adventure on the sea, and he was capable of romantic descriptions of native civilizations on the islands of the western Pacific. But even in such writings he never lost sight of realism. This same tendency to see things as they were, made him unhappy in America. He challenged the assumption of his countrymen that democracy is the ultimate in social and political philosophy. He reluctantly gave up the Protestant faith that Christianity admits the faithful to a land of love and peace; this religion he allegorized in *Mardi* as Serenia. He assailed as false the intuition upon which Emerson and Thoreau founded their transcendental philosophies. In *White-Jacket* he became a humanitarian and attacked the practice of flogging in the American navy. Melville was one of the first to point out the deadening effect upon personality of the machine, which was creating the new industrialism, and he dared to accuse respectable ecclesiastics of sycophancy toward the great capitalists.

These were only a few of the denials of the ex-whaler, who, for a moment, became celebrated as the man who had lived among cannibals. Melville saw the world as a struggle between Captain Ahab and Moby-Dick; that is, as a conflict between good and evil. Man's only privilege was to fight dauntlessly. Because he renounced the current philosophy of progress, his contemporaries thought Melville a pessimist. They rejected him, as they had Cooper, because they were unwilling to listen to honest criticism of the institutions and ideas by which they lived. Yet Melville was also at fault. He too often clothed his message in obscure allegory.[58]

The Ahab of Williams et al. is not yet the totalitarian dictator construed by Olson and Matthiessen, to be continued in New Left criticism. Rather, he is a good example to wayward youth (if a bit hard to read): the realistic anticapitalist out of synch with a self-deceived and evil materialistic civilization. According to Charles Olson, Williams dramatically shifted his opinion of Melville in the late 1930s, a few years after Olson had studied with him. Fuming about the failure of the Melville industry to acknowledge his pathbreaking research, Olson told Leyda, "There is on deposit, at the Wesleyan library, the MA thesis of Olson, 1933, which lays out the origin points to his work. (This will amuse you: the MA was done at Wesleyan and Yale, under an Olin Fellowship, and part of the work was a course with S. Williams in which I was refused the right to do a paper on Melville because he was so unimportant, and to contrive a thesis on Hawthorne and his friends! Later, when I was the 1st candidate at Harvard for the Phd in Am Civilization, and was on the faculty, I received a letter I still have from same Williams, begging me to let his locusts in![59])

Even if this story is not true, Ivy League assessments of Melville's potential as prodigal son could have responded to elite fears of "breaking up" (the dying Gansevoort's self-image). Rank-and-file workers were on the move in 1934–36, with maritime labor assuming a leading role,[60] while capitalists were divided over a New Deal that seemed out of control; moreover, elite factions in both America and England were tacitly or directly supporting Hitler and internal fascist elements. What were progressives to do? Chester R. Heck told readers of *The Harvard Educational Review* in 1938 that "exotic dangers, ominous and imminent," were threatening a "muddled" America. The young were overexcited by "dynamic new cultures" of "Nazi-ism, Communism, Fascism," while academic history courses were dominated either by "the political and economic interpretation, or the strictly literary interpretation." No one agreed on the meaning of "democracy": To some it meant capitalism ("rugged individualism"); to others, socialism ("popular cooperation"). Citing Harvard president James Bryant Conant's report of 1935 and Robert Hutchins's Great Books program at the University of Chicago,[61] Heck advocated cultural history appreciation, quoting Conant: "Intellectual culture indigenous to the American soil" promised to be "the common denominator among educated men which would enable them to face the world united and unafraid." America would be inoculated against the "seeds" dropped into the "fertile soil" of "the young graduate." How would "the American tradition" be taught, given the obvious lack of consensus on American identity and direction? Heck admonished that "the only honest method of getting a national point of view is to obtain a cross section of representative thought on any given problem or proposition. By such method and only by such method, can a correct insight into our cultural past be obtained. Having obtained it, we may then face the present and the future equipped to pursue or to guide our national destiny with some sense of direction."[62]

Ambiguities were dissipated by another progressive, William Donnelly, who surveyed high-school textbooks on "The Haymarket Riot," bitterly criticizing anti-labor biases; Harvard men need not fear the recollection of American labor history. It was a fact that "for native American workmen, the doctrines of socialism and anarchism held little appeal. What small following such philosophers held lay mostly within the German immigrant group" (206). Native-born workers and American literature professors alike were staving off alien doctrines of the radical Enlightenment. By 1940, Ernest E. Leisy could report with satisfaction, "In welcome contrast to the recent studies of American authors in terms of Freudianism, humanism, psychoanalysis, and Marxist philosophy, it is refreshing to come across the newer analytical biographies of Emily Dickinson by George Whicher, of Hawthorne and Whitman by Newton Arvin, and of Thoreau by Henry Seidel Canby. . . . The voluminous writing about Melville since 1921 necessitates a bibliography and a new biography."[63] Before the Cold War, then, corporatists had set the stage for the fact-finding phase of the Melville Revival and for the promotion of *Clarel* beginning in 1943, a work usually read as contrasting the domesticated Melville with the apostate German-Jewish geologist Margoth.[64]

The Melville Society was founded in February 1945 by Harrison Hayford and Tyrus Hillway (another former Williams student), with the support of John H. Birss, who, during the 1930s and 1940s, had been compiling a bibliography of Melville's works entailing a chronology of his life and a collection of his letters, never published. According to Hillway, Matthiessen was one of several senior scholars who disapproved of the prospective society. "My recollection is that he believed scholars already had too many organizations and that Melville did not deserve another one. He and other scholars were of a generation that were taught to think of Melville as a writer of adventure stories (and of course was not one of the Boston Brahmins)."[65] This populist sentiment, together with an excerpt from the "first editorial" of the *Melville Society Newsletter* (May 15, 1947), suggests that at least one member of the Melville Society (Hillway) viewed the new society as a means of liberating Melville scholarship from elite domination:

Reports coming in from all parts of the United States indicate that Melville scholarship is on the increase. While only a few years ago many critics were willing to declare that the so-called Melville boom represented a temporary and esoteric enthusiasm for a fifth-rate literary figure, the Melville scholars continue to multiply, and the world of scholarship is making a rapidly enlarging place for Melville in its calculations. It has clearly accepted the facts of his permanence and growing importance. The number of new studies recently published or under way is itself sufficient proof of the solid ground upon which we are working. In this virile and outreaching growth of Melville scholarship, we can assure ourselves with considerable satisfaction that the Society has played a part. The first objective which we set ourselves in February, 1945, "to stimulate the study of Melville's life and works," can almost be said to have been achieved; and present activities appear only as a foretaste of what lies ahead.

Melville's granddaughter Eleanor Metcalf, impressed by the interpretations and research of Weaver, Murray, and Olson, began her own scholarship in 1945. Her first effort, an edition of Melville's Journal of 1849–50, brought her into conflict with Leyda, who blamed her and the Harvard University Press for delays in the publication of the *Log* (that had commandeered larger chunks of the journal than Eleanor Metcalf had expected). Ever faithful to Weaver and his biography, her notes mentioned Melville's unresolved conflicts, specifically, the tension between aristocracy and democracy. In 1946 Leyda told Joseph Freeman (former editor of the *New*

Masses and once a close friend of Weaver, his teacher at Columbia) that he disliked Weaver's book. Leyda, like Leon Howard, would adhere to Willard Thorp's conversion narrative, a view of Melville's ending ("Billy Budd") sharply opposed by Eleanor Metcalf as noted above. Lines were being drawn.

Stanley Williams's only piece of Melville criticism, "'Follow Your Leader'" (1947), aligned him morally and emotionally with Benito Cereno, the Spanish captain of the *San Dominick*, taken prisoner by the wily African Babo, leader of a slave revolt.[66] Conservative nationalists in Germany read "Benito Cereno" the same way after World War II: Good Germans (not to be confused with Nazis or their supporters) had been taken hostage by Hitler/Babo in a slave uprising, an Ortega y Gasset–style revolt of the materialist masses.[67]

The Rochester Synod: 1984 in 1948

During the period of Melville's alleged obscurity, some passages from *Moby-Dick* were excerpted in *The International Library of Famous Literature*, edited by Richard Garnett (1900). Volume 12 of the series included "On the Track of the White Whale"; the volume was prefaced with a work of criticism by Émile Zola, "The Naturalist School of Fiction in France." For Zola, the lineage of naturalism included Diderot, Stendhal, Balzac, Flaubert, and the brothers Goncourt; the antithesis to naturalism was mystical romanticism. The author of "J'accuse," later assassinated by the Right, had no difficulty reconciling the cultures of science and the arts:

> ... this evolution was, in letters as in science, a return to nature and humanity, combined with carefulness of scrutiny, exactitude of anatomy, and truthful portrayal of whatever existed. There were to be no more abstract personages, no more mendacious inventions, no more absolute rules, but, in lieu thereof, real living personages, the true record of one and all, and the relativity that is found in daily life. For this to be, it was necessary to study man in all the sources of his being, so that one might really know him before formulating conclusions after the fashion of the idealists who simply invent types. And thus writers had to reconstruct the literary edifice from its very base, each in turn contributing his human documents in their logical order. (xiii–xiv)

> [On precise description of causality] ... as a question of principle one must blame all description which exceeds the portrayal of those surroundings that determine and perfect the novelist's characters. (xxvi)

> [On objective art versus propaganda] A work that is true will last forever, whereas a work that is disfigured by direct expression of its author's emotions can only appeal to the sentiments of a given period. (xxvii)

[On the social obligations of the naturalist novelist] . . . the Idealists assert that to be moral one must lie; the Naturalists retort that one cannot be moral by departing from the truth. Nothing is so dangerous as the romantic. Certain words, by painting the world in false colors, unhinge the mind and urge it to the most hazardous and pernicious courses. And I speak not of the hypocrisy of much of what is called propriety, nor of the abominations which are rendered alluring by the flowers that many writers heap upon them. We, the naturalists, adorn no vileness, we teach the bitter science of life, we offer the world the high lesson of reality and truth. I know no school that has ever shown more morality, more austerity. Certainly we write not for babes and sucklings, but for the world at large, that world which is full of sin, vice, crime, deceit, and hypocrisy. While we extenuate nothing, we set down nought in malice. We simply paint humanity as it is. We say let all be made known in order that all may be healed. And there our duty ends. It is for the leaders and guardians of the nations to do theirs. (xxvii–xxix)

Half a century later, two Melvilleans, Leon Howard of Northwestern University and William H. Gilman of the University of Rochester, staged a four-part conference at Gilman's university during the winter of 1948–49, adjusting and cleansing the all-too-naturalistic literary canon for the benefit of graduate students, "guests from the community," and "the general reader."[68] The leading lights of American literature were there, including Stanley Williams, Willard Thorp, Leon Howard, Henry Nash Smith, Norman Holmes Pearson, Robert Spiller, Alfred Kazin, Harry Levin, and Lionel Trilling. A selection of twelve lectures was published and republished as *American Writers and the European Tradition*.[69] Now that America had become the most powerful nation on earth, the editors explained, it seemed appropriate that America "produce a literature which will nourish and refresh European readers; at the same time it needs to perceive more clearly the source and nature of formative influences, both past and present, upon its literature. . . . ["Cultural" responsibilities should be met through] the extension of commendable American influences abroad . . . discarding the mere violence which now is his forte but not the natural virtue which is his real strength . . . to cultivate the fertile ground that lies somewhere between our native Americanism and the European tradition" (v, xi, x).[70]

Since nine of the twelve scholars had participated in the Melville Revival, and since the editors assure us of the "underlying unity and the dynamic unity [the essays] bear to each other" (x), I shall attempt a synthesis, framed with an excerpt from the correspondence of Van Wyck Brooks and Lewis Mumford. They were both active in the 1920s Melville Revival, were repeatedly mentioned in the Martin Dies (HUAC) report of 1944, and are still admired by 1960s radicals. Jubilating over a returning trend in American culture, Brooks told his friend, "I have a clear strong feeling that things are coming *our way,* that another generation is coming along that is much more congenial with you and me than the minds that have been dominant in the last twenty years. I gather that you are encountering them in your Southern lectures, as I find them in several writers who are going to have something to say in the future (among them, Peter Viereck)."[71] Brooks was correct. Uncongenial, domineering, leftish "minds" were out; romantic conservatives (like Viereck, an ardent Melville fan) were in. At Rochester, only a few months earlier, Louis Booker Wright and Theodore Hornberger (prolific scholars specializing in the English Renaissance and Anglo-American culture whose papers launch Denny and Gilman's book) clarified the agenda for postwar humanism: They must claim the Enlightenment and the American Dream for themselves, which meant transfiguring the radical bourgeoisie and the dogmatic democrats it had spawned.[72] Hornberger emphasized stability, order, and balance found in the Constitution, eighteenth-century political theory, and its conservative but progressive antecedents (Greece and Rome, "British parliamentary procedures," and Calvinist New England), praising Montesquieu, John Adams, and Benjamin Rush, and ending with an affirmation of American cultural freedom defined against fascist mind control:

We have learned recently that under the Fascist regime John Steinbeck's *The Grapes of Wrath* was permitted to circulate on the theory that it would convince Italians of the degeneracy of the United States. Instead, the young men, or some of them, concluded that a government which would permit such a novel to appear must have something admirable about it. The moral is, it seems to me, is that Americans appear at their best to the rest of the world when they are self-critical. The charming thing about the Enlightenment and the American Dream is their dissatisfaction with what is and what has been. No one who reads *Candide* will ever again think that this is the best of all possible worlds. No one, I think, who reads widely in American literature will be either smug or chauvinistic. (27)

In the talks that followed, irrationalism as practiced by antebellum romantic conservatives was redefined as the rational antidote to complacency and excessive nationalism. Although Hornberger's Steinbeck story was repeated by Harry Levin (182), Steinbeck's fiction was deemed defective and romantic (Levin, 170); the documentarians of the 1930s were attacked throughout the conference, directly or indirectly. As Hornberger had hinted, there were competing contenders for critical "social realism" (Thorp) in America: The spirit of Thomas Carlyle was in the saddle. Traditional writers such as Melville (as Ishmael and Vere) who were "didactic, allegorical, romantic" veterans of the abyss (Levin, 180, 174) should be plainly distinguished from *other* romantics: Jacksonian Ahabs with their "lying spirit" and monomania (Howard, 84). Also discredited were "dyspeptic" pessimists expecting too much from America: the "sour liberals" of *Partisan Review,* presaged by the later work of Mark Twain (Thorp, 105, 104), and French-inspired naturalism (Levin, 174) catering to the "idolatry of the mechanical and of 'facts'" (Pearson, 161; Kazin, 121). Trilling attacked "the extreme rationalist position" (148), while (the preconversion) Dos Passos was hit hard in Kazin's essay.

After the weeding out of the progressive bourgeoisie, who would be (moderately) Left? Captain Vere! who had been blessed in the last breath of Billy Budd (but not "Billy Budd") and in the last words of Lewis Mumford's biography (1929). Melville had his problems with Vere, but the conferees at Rochester did not. Willard Thorp talked of him as a historic figure, joining Vere to Emerson, Thoreau, and other classically educated intellectuals of the pre–Civil War United States. Captain Vere, like veritas itself, was rooted in the Renaissance ideal of the Christian gentleman, "ready and eager to serve the state in the most intelligent fashion" and promoting "the cultivation of man's full powers under the restraint of law" (L. Wright, 9). The "proletarianizing" all-American soil had only mothered materialists whose Faustian science had created the bomb (L. Wright, 4) and erased "personality" (Pearson, 166); hence, it should be shoveled out and replaced by the Euro-American compost that yielded the greatest inheritor of the English Renaissance, Thomas Jefferson (L. Wright, 14), and the *poetically* scientific (Pearson) writers of the 1850s, Mumford's Golden Day. The search for a usable past had won these gentle but forceful flowers of "the saving remnant" (L. Wright, 51), who, like Emerson, "believed that the tension between Conservative and Radical would be fruitful in the end" (Thorp, 95), who would be ready to spring to action, averting the confiscations of the "extreme Reformer" who "uses outward and vulgar means. [Who] precipitates revolution when other means would have done" (Thorp, 92). And who would disagree with that?[73]

Several participants advocated temporary despair as healthy and broadening, somewhat like the Grand Tour, the evidence of spiritual capacity and deep diving: Unflagging optimists lacked a soul. Melville and Whitman were exemplary, for Christian gentlemen/American artists do not yield to permanent depression. Perforce, Melville's work after the nadir of the nihilistic 1850s would be annexed to the cause of Christian affirmation and acceptance of an imperfect world. If Melville had been in pain, yanked between "America" and "Europe," ultimately it was good for his originality. "Melville" was cured; progressive uplift and social hygiene had evacuated mechanical materialists, amplifying the message of Thorp's essay in *Literary History of the United States* (1948), canonizing "Melville" defined as Ahab's repudiator. Like other corporatist enactments, however, this ritual conversion of stonyhearted Jewish healers was a subversion of radical Enlightenment, claiming, of course, to uphold gentlemanly or true science, complete with stringent self-criticism. One might infer that cultural freedom was safe in their hands, that their unity was both a buffer against and a solution to "war and economic chaos and the new fears aroused by atomic power" that had worried Thorp in *Literary History*.[74]

The three Jewish participants, Kazin, Trilling, and Levin, affirmed their American identity, loyalty, and virtue by dumping the "naturalists," agents of desolation to a peculiar people. As the final contribution, Harry Levin, Irving Babbitt Professor at Harvard, clinically probed iniquitous American mass culture (the Face that plagued Weaver?), then praised the redemptive power of the typically "American anguish" (evoked twice), for this "ambivalence of anguish" gives us pause; properly guided it could lead to an elevating new direction; Melville, original as the bearer of "tradition" in a chaotic trash culture, was the good seed:

"There is an American anguish in the face of Americanism," Jean Paul Sartre has written. There is an ambivalence of anguish which simultaneously asks "Am I American enough?" and "How can I escape from Americanism?" If anything can redeem us, it is this hesitation between our optimists and our pessimists, our frontiersmen and our expatriates. On the one hand, we have a unique background, which would be quite barren if it remained unique. On the other hand we are strengthened by a hybrid strain, the cross-fertilization of many cultures. What is commonly regarded as peculiarly American is blatant and standardized: Ford, Luce, Metro-Goldwyn Mayer. What is most original is most traditional: Melville. Moving in T. S. Eliot's phrase, "Between two worlds become much like each other," these opposites are neutralized. As Andre Siegfried predicted, Europe is Americanized and America is Europeanized. Organization conquers the Old World, chaos is rediscovered in the New. Beyond the clamor, beneath the surfaces of the present, the past continues, and our brightest lights are those that keep burning underground. (183; compare with Leon Howard's idea that Melville's ambivalence reflects cultural conflict between Europe and America)

In other words—given the proclivities of mass culture for "totalitarian realism," as suggested by Levin with regard to Nazi Germany and fascist Italy in a sentence immediately preceding the segment quoted above—the apparently conservative or reactionary traditionalist turns into his opposite: He becomes an invigorating innovator, a Burkean "critical realist." Such were the cool assessments that have defeated seditious naturalist novelists—mystical yet bound to Benjamin Franklin's independent science "and . . . the higher learning that we have built upon it" (Spiller, 40). Robert E. Spiller suggested we study Franklin "to find a key to the problem of our present concern: the growth of American culture from its first roots in American soil to a flowering after three centuries as a dominant world culture. . . .

If we can understand what happened to Franklin [1740–50], we may appreciate more keenly the cyclic process by which a transplanted civilization developed from dependence to independence to dominance" (32).

Free will and personal responsibility were now ghosts in the machine of organicist discourse, caught by the determinism of biological cycles. A manufactured but heavenly pastoral of flowers, trees, seeds, and soil had drifted gently onto the grimy, bristling political science of the empiricists, a game anyone could play.[75] People were no longer self-moving participants in describable social movements or class formations: They were either sour apples and weedy extremists (bad) or moderates (good) stoically enduring the fructifying tension associated with self-criticism and social realism. Who could resist the call of dreamy, peace-loving moderate men: dominant and yet attractive to European readers fed up with fascism, only starved by the revolt of the masses?[76]

On October 20, 1950, Yale professor Norman Holmes Pearson, another ex-Stanley Williams student and now a leader in the interdisciplinary field of American Studies, responded to comrade Leyda's complaint that he was not permitted access to Emily Dickinson's papers.

> I am annoyed, though not deeply surprised at the block in the Dickinson exploration. I only wish something could come of it, for if anyone needs your diligent scalpel, Emily Dickinson does. If it doesn't go through eventually and you are left without a project, why don't you do a calendar for Hawthorne, though I dare say the iconoclastic value would not be so startling in this case as for either HM or ED. At any rate if there is an impasse consider, with Leon's help, shifting the subject to something else. Now that he and Louis Wright are the wheels with Guggenheim, they could fix the other end easily.[77]

Leyda, the pathetic outsider with powerful friends, did gain access to the papers of Emily Dickinson to produce another calendar, assisted by the Guggenheim grant. Pearson was a veteran of the OSS, and, like Leyda, an expert propagandist. But we must not leap into dark conclusions: Was the "iconoclastic value" of Leyda's *Log* directed against Melville himself or the alleged excesses and deficiencies of earlier scholarship?

NOTES FROM THE UNDERGROUND LOG

Jay Leyda bore the burden of an idealist philosophy that dogmatically precluded discovery; its poetic science pulverized history and meaning like the bomb that Jeffersonian Louis B. Wright had fastened to Faustian hubris. Such official obscurantism kept Melvilleans guessing; in Charles Olson's scholarship this would take the form of an attack on dirty materialism, perhaps the candor of Melvillean texts that clung to memory like Isabel's spider webs or Margoth's bats. Leyda did not depart from Olson's key organicist formulations; indeed, Harry Levin had proposed that Reynal and Hitchcock issue their book and collage together, but both men tactfully balked. At first, Leyda seemed interested, writing to Olson on January 14, 1946, "I hope that after looking at these specimens you'll still be interested in pooling our projects. . . . Please ignore (for the present) both the obvious gaps and the documents that you know I have no right to use." Although Olson had declared to Leyda early in their correspondence, "It is my feeling that writing today has to go back to first ground and that the healthiest act is the record of fact" (January 24, 1946), in his letter of February 4, the proletarian interested in "the whaler as worker" seemed determined to separate his work from Leyda's (apparent) empiricism, while cautiously exploring a "marriage":

> Your LOG came today. I have been through it, and back over it, in an out, and it is a damned splendid idea and, properly made, should be a vivid book.
>
> I'm DAMNED if I know if my work and yours complement or contradict each other! I wish I had a carbon copy of mine to send so that you also could be confused!
>
> I THINK I can see a use of them together which would, by the mere act of juxtaposition, block out and give mass to each. And it would be, at first glance, achieved by leaving each intact, side by side. / What IS common to both is the graphic-dramatic method, and it makes juxtaposition possible. But there is one striking contrast: here you have gone to the detail, of day and day, I am at the other extreme, the man stripped down to, say, five acts hung on the one mighty line, MOBY-DICK. Maybe this, too, makes a marriage: existence-essence. (We will each say both are in each!)

> Maybe it amounts to this. You speak of non-interpretation in your letter to Taylor. In other words, what you aimed at was to tell the story by documentation alone. It was precisely such documentation that I spent 13 years to discard! For my aim was to master such an intense interpretation that could make the man come alive without biography. It could be that, now that we are done, the opposite can, ought perhaps to be introduced. Certainly your structure of a LOG makes the facts most engaging. And I can hope you will find my probe-prose of an order of interpretation fresh and clean.

> This is my suggestion: Both your mss and mine have an independent life of their own and can walk in their own right. But here is somebody, Frank

Taylor, who has the idea that maybe they'll do better together. Why don't I send him my mss., let him test his idea, and if he sees its a go from his point of view, let us then, on the basis of his proposition, consider whether we wish to accept or not, individually or together?

After reading Olson's manuscript, Leyda turned down the collaboration, explaining to Olson in his letter of March 23, 1946, "Your book is very impressive—both solid and passionate. I see no reason why it should have any trouble finding a publisher. But I don't see yet what I looked for most eagerly—a way to combine our two approaches, unless Ishmael is looked upon as an introduction to the Log, or the Log is looked upon as a supplement to Ishmael. I doubt very much if you could persuade a publisher that they need each other, however, for your work is quite complete and independent. I'm afraid I'll have to put the Log back on the shelf when R & H return it to me."

Why did the collaboration not pan out? After all, both men pitied and feared their subject; both used modernist distancing techniques. From Olson's side, the "fresh and clean" critic may have been simply threatened by a rival muckraker. Olson consistently railed against materialists who soiled and diminished Melville, while he dished the dirt himself. In a letter to Leyda of July 7, 1946, he implied that the effluvium had flowed only under duress, after a demand from his publishers Reynal and Hitchcock that he account for Melville's "loss of power." I have found no letter in Olson's papers that would document this alleged request, nor are there any early drafts of *Call Me Ishmael*. It may well have been his own choice to explain the fall of Ahab and Pierre to preempt Leyda: *Call Me Ishmael* (1947), in a very few compressed paragraphs placed near the end of the book, had blended facts, inferences, and a hereditarian explanation to fill out the mighty line:

> When he set out in October of that year [1856] he had reasons of health for doing so. The writing of *Moby-Dick* had hurt him. He was 31. The immediate labor on *Pierre* aggravated his condition. It went so far his family in 1853 called in doctors, among them Oliver Wendell Holmes, Pittsfield neighbor, to judge his sanity. . . . By 1856 and the writing of *The Confidence-Man,* wild and whirling words, the whole persistent multitude of Melvilles and Shaws felt that something had to be done, that there had to be some disposition, once and for all, of this man whom some tolerated and others feared, and of whom most were ashamed and all seemed weary. The money for the trip came from his father-in-law Justice Shaw. This time Melville did not go away on his own; he was—though guardedly—sent away. (90)
> . . . The sun and the darker races stirred up feelings Melville had for twelve years beaten back, even as he worked. In spite of his writing he had become

wedded to a white guilt. The pressures had originated from his environment America and tightened inwards. The stifling forces had a traitorous agent to help them: the ethical and Northern Melville.

There seems no doubt he brought back from the South Seas a number of shames, social shames to add to earlier ones reaching back to his father's sins and failures. Melville's behavior in the years 1851–56 was ill. He remained periodically violent to his wife and strange with his mother. There was shock in him. *Pierre* is documentation enough. Add *The Confidence-Man*. In each Christ is of the subject and the matter. (92–93)

The primitivist Olson saw Melville in trouble wherever he roamed. Novel sensual feelings, aroused in the tropics, stubbornly returned. Both "Northern" heredity and the American environment were suffocating; he was possessed of the sentimental Christ: Here was the path to decadence, here was Olson's indictment of Melville's aching modernism.

But why did Leyda balk? Olson's Melville seemed permanently broken; perhaps his man of sorrows, like Weaver's, was too marginalized and persecuted, not himself the confidence man and persecutor of others (at least in the early work). But most likely *Call Me Ishmael* was too focused on *Moby-Dick*, implicitly dismissive of Billy Budd's happy end, while Olson himself seemed marginal, his style too personal, obscurantist, and irrationalist, whereas the Stanley Williams students and Leon Howard, proponents of wholeness, science, clarity, and Willard Thorp's conversion narrative seemed poised within the American literary establishment along with Captain Vere. After resisting pressure to write a new Melville biography himself, Harrison Hayford encouraged Leyda to collaborate with Leon Howard, who would have prepublication access to Leyda's data, forestalling an "unknown" writing a new Melville biography, with or without new facts, as Hayford put it.[78]

Leyda's project aimed to dislodge the timid and half-knowing portraits of his predecessors; his first Guggenheim application draft explained (in terms reminiscent of the pathbreaking *American Mind* co-edited by Stanley Williams, 1937):

I want to provide, both for student and reader, the fullest possible account of Herman Melville's physical and mental life. The form chosen for this purpose is the Log, not however as a stripped record of latitude and longitude, of a gale encountered and a spar broken, but embracing the very experience of the storm (whether an actual gale in the northern Pacific or an artistic crisis in a locked Pittsfield workroom), the tangibility of the spar in both picture and word (although it may be of a back-porch in Albany), and the entire course of Herman Melville's life. The scope of this search is to be limited only by the hero's birth and death; no material touching him or touched by him will be eliminated—for it seems essential that this project take its opportunity to re-establish the natural relations of Melville's varied activities that have been broken up and isolated by existing studies.

For the student, particularly in non-Eastern institutions, this Melville Log will have the value of a source-book in the subject, not reducing the research to editorial conclusions, but rather bringing together these documents themselves for each user's own conclusions. Certain collections that have hitherto been left unexamined by Melville scholars have already yielded rich new source-material in the course of this unselective search. The Log will also constitute a co-ordinated guide to all these new as well as familiar Melville materials.

The reader will find in the Log a full-length, realistic portrait of an artist whose work has grown to have a more immediate meaning for the American reader than has the writing of any of this artist's contemporaries. A reader's interest in the Log will inevitably lead him to expand his interest in Melville's less familiar and fully rewarding works. The Log will serve to deepen the reader's understanding of the works, for it will replace a tangle of generalization around the figure of their creator with a far richer drama of actuality.

The visual presentation of this actuality will play an important role in the use of the Log. Both the student's information and the reader's imagination will be reinforced by the key documents being reproduced in facsimile and by a continuous pictorial representation of the many-sided world of Herman Melville.[79]

Leyda's draft of the introduction (presented to Leon Howard for editing) similarly rendered the Log as another Reformation: Catholic spectacle had been overcome; austere Protestants once more spoke to each other and their God without unreliable priestly mediation: "In making his family motto come true [Deqique Coelum (Heaven at Last)], the heaven of his reputation was opened to all singers and enquirers, and for thirty years Melville and his Whale have enjoyed attentions of varying responsibility. The abundance of this singing has tended to drown out Melville's own voice, and it is now a rare reader who comes to a Melville book unprepared by its commentators. His work and his life no longer speak to us directly." Leon Howard's corrections emphasized the Melville Revival as an accelerating anthem, making preceding biographers only singers, not enquirers (and authoritarian ones at that); while simultaneously Howard (an Episcopalian) trimmed Leyda's (apparent) Protestant enthusiasm with an added sentence: "Herman Melville has justified that crusaders' cry [Heaven at last] by achieving a certain posthumous celestial glory. If he has not been worshipped, his praises have been sung for thirty years of mounting enthusiasm and varying responsibility. The insistence of this singing has tended to drown out Melville's own voice, and it is now a rare reader who can come to a Melville book unaffected by its commentators. His work and his life no longer speak to us directly. This book is an attempt to restore some measure of communication" (*Log*, xvii). And the Melville whose voice was once more (sort of) clear and strong was clearly not to be trusted. As Leyda suggested to his editor, Robert Giroux, "How about making some distinctions [through differing typefaces] between a printed source such as a contemporary review or report, and quotations from HM's own published works, which are always used here for another reason? The reader must be warned to read the latter with unusual discrimination—to distrust them more than anything else in the book."[80]

Why did Leyda want the reader to "distrust" Melville's writing "more than anything else in the book"? In his oral history comments on documentary, did he not declare that all texts were suspect? Was he simply precluding the Freudian readings of the 1920s revivers that misguidedly mined the texts for clinical material while ignoring sources in the Gansevoort-Lansing Collection at the New York Public Library, as Hayford had protested? Or was Leyda, unbeknownst to his collaborators, wielding his scalpel to peel away the mask of a consciously dissembling confidence man? Notes for his introduction to Melville's *Complete Stories* emphasized the "contrast between reality and its transformation into rumor and myth" (then "the remote thing that man makes of this reality / the ties between the living and the dead / Hunilla and her husband"); a draft of the *Log* introduction suggests how *he* used myth to legitimate the (proletarian) objectivity of his own work against the myths of competitors (probably Weaver). Referring to the earlier but undated curiosity of Eisenstein as precipitator of his Melville project, Leyda explained:

As my friend was Russian and interested in facts it occurred to me that a defense against the bogs of interpretation (with its thick growth of wild guess [*sic*]) would be to arrange whatever could be relied upon as fact or document in a simple chronology, making no attempt to hide the gaps or to smooth contradictions. . . . In the pulling together I discovered, of course, that Melville was not responsible for all the shadows, and that the darkness of his life was due more to the simplifying act of the biographer than to the facts available to him. (At that time I supposed that a biographer either knew or presented all facts that he was able to determine.) ~~Excited by the discovery that Melville's life was far from simple, offering a drama more wonderful than the simplifications handed down to us, a drama as wonderful as his art, & finding great areas of his art bypassed by the biographer, I became~~

~~exaggeratedly suspicious of biography as a form & exaggeratedly fascinated~~
~~by the puzzle to be solved aspect of this new task.~~

. . . This self-employment was not then thought of as a book to be published, nor had it occurred to me that there was more to be known and seen than was already in print. I was curious to see the originals of the quoted Melville documents, but most of the scholars I approached for information gave me to understand that all that was to be known was known, that Melville was an exhausted subject for investigation, and that I should leave this problem to better trained minds. ~~Period.~~ But my project (still half game) had three godfathers, men who were so entertained by the unorthodoxy of the project that they gave me kinds of encouragement that I can never thank them enough for. These amused benefactors were Lawrence Clark Powell, Harry Levin and Leon Howard. They suggested new directions for digging, thrust new sources at me, and even hinted that enough readers might be found, willing to tackle a strange-looking page, to warrant publication! ~~They all encouraged me in my most foolhardy proposal to create a pool of Melville information.~~

. . . How often must Dr. Henry A. Murray and John H. Birss have groaned as they watched the stumbling harm done by the heavy-footed novice to the delicately baking porcelains that were not ready for public view! And I'm sure there are others who would prefer to forget the assistance they gave the Log.

In these excerpts, Leyda has (a) asserted the reliability of his facts against competing or disreputable others; (b) transmuted the "the thick growth of wild guess" to "simplification" that Leyda will remedy with his dramatic rendering of the life as puzzle; (c) set himself against competitors by constructing himself as innocent and heroic (not on the market), rescuing Melville from "the biographer" (Weaver) against tremendous odds; but then (d) humbled himself as clumsy proletarian bull in a china shop as a device to expose Murray's and Birss's delicate (guild-artisanal?) secretiveness. After an exhaustive search, I have found no evidence that scholars ever discouraged Leyda, unless he refers to the English publisher John Murry's initial reluctance to reveal the contents of Melville's letters to his firm, or the non-Melvillean Dixon Wecter of UCLA (which Leyda disclosed only in his Columbia interview and which may not be true), or the Guggenheim grant he did not win in 1947. He did elicit anger from correspondents, including Eleanor Metcalf, William Gilman, Merrell Davis, and Gerry Gross, for various acts of duplicity and role playing. He was further criticized for imperceptive or hostile interpretations of Melville's motives from Random House editor Albert Erskine and Leyda's research assistant and half-brother-in-law Gordon Williams. Moreover, to my knowledge, neither Powell nor Levin "thrust new sources" at Leyda.[81] Some of the textual and biographical facts and stories at Leyda's disposal will now be examined, with the argument that an antimodern (primitivist) agenda informed his objectivist adventure in sublimity.

What Did Leyda Know and When Did He Know It?

Olson, who knew more than he ever printed, did not entirely know what Leyda knew; writing to Leyda on June 23, 1950, he tacked on this cagey afterthought. "A question: have you got anything on the famous Josie Shaw? who lived, late with a Miss Bessy, in Wahan, Mass? a gabby old dame, I gathered from Weaver, who ran on, mostly about HM's relations with Elizabeth?" A crumbling brown sheet of typed notes entitled "Weaver notes on conversation with Mrs Thomas" suggests that Leyda was privy to at least some of the gossip disseminated by Raymond Weaver to Olson in the late 1930s. In his biography, Weaver (1921), followed by Mumford (1929), had attacked imputations of insanity by Philistia; now Weaver was confiding in Leyda, but it appears that he wanted Leyda to know (some of) what he knew, but not who told him. According to Weaver's memoir, it was Eleanor Metcalf, not Frances Thomas, Melville's daughter, who had lifted the veil. Despite Eleanor Metcalf's correction, Leyda perpetuated the error in the *Log*.[82] The document in full is reproduced below, preserving most of Leyda's layout.

Weaver notes on conversation with Mrs Thomas.

Birthplace. Pearl—between Whitehall & State, on South side
restlessness in travelling—Coney Island, all over boat

H.M. thought Thackeray dreadful snob—all doctors humbugs—but ready on slightest provocation to call them in

Took Frances to Madison Square Garden—came home having forgot her—Went back found her. Frances aetat 4

Bought Arrow Head 1850—mother & sisters went to live there at that time. Aunts later moved to Gansevoort on Hudson to keep house for Herman Gansevoort after death of his wife.

Thos Melville at Snug Harbor—long suffering mother & Augusta died there—spent winters there.

No doctor would pronounce him insane. Mother, sisters & wife tried to send him to asylum (while living at Arrow Head). E.S.M. thought him insane. These fits of temper began almost immediately after marriage.

49 Mt Vernon—wife here with mother while Herman on Eastern trip.
[arrow to margin penciled "sep."] Stanwix sent to Gansevoort, Malcolm to
Aunt Helen in Brooklyn, Wife and daughters back home to Boston

His condition acute. Spent summer with Kate & Tom—Herman to Boston
once.

His family sympathized with wife—too proud to make any public stir.

His mother: worldly—formal—"proper"—fuss about clothes
Criticized home made clothes of grand children

Wife back from Boston "It's all very discouraging"—shrink into background
In Pittsfield, taken for ghost/?/—avoiding, getting out of way.

Lansingburgh 1839—ask Kate White

Always walked with cane—even in house

clipping "Keep true to the dreams of thy youth" (was in old desk—Mrs Metcalf remembers)

Cousin Maria said H.M. said his mother hated him

critical of food
drank more towards end: aggravated condition.

Epicurean in taste—yet always stinted by necessity & seems to have felt birth
entitled him to these things

Typee: in N.Y. Mail & Express serially

There is nothing here to suggest either the repentant radical or the lifelong conservative painted by some second-wave Melvilleans. Rather, Melville is said to detest snobbery; he maintains connection with youthful idealism (but hides it inside his writing desk: Is this the chimney that will never surrender? or are the dreams of his youth dreams of glory?); his worst crime is epicureanism, a trait perhaps linked to democratic entitlement (and that Weaver may have invented). Although this and other documents are sensational, there is nothing that the "elusive" Melville's fiction and poetry had not repeatedly engaged and even explained (for example, "fits of temper"); nor does any document contradict my view of Melville as crypto-

radical unwilling or unable to separate from the family that judged him mad, struggling against their evil Ahab whom he had partially internalized, perhaps seeking
numbness in alcohol.[83]

[Melville's marking of Seneca, in Leyda's notes but not used in *Log*] In the
Examination of my own Heart, I find some Vices that lie Open; Others more
Obscure, and out of Sight; and some that take me only by Fits. Which last I
look upon as the most Dangerous and Troublesome; for they lie upon the
Latch, and keep a Man on perpetual Guard: Being neither provided against
them, as in a State of War; nor Secure, as in any Assurance of Peace.

[Melville's marking of Lamb, in early version of *Log* only] 1850, Final Me-
morials of Charles Lamb by Thomas Moon Talfourd: X Being by ourselves is
bad, and going out is bad. I get so irritable and wretched with fear, that I constantly hasten on the disorder.

The fact finders did not answer the earlier family-centered criticism by more
responsibly engaging the structural origins of Melville's suffering. They tended to
evade the pain of real families by seeking literary sources; sometimes they scape-
goated or otherwise mocked the Melville women (the sisters were described in one
Sealts letter as Herman's "stable of fillies"). For Leyda, as well as some others in
his faction, when women are praised, it is for putting up with abuse they have
caused. Avoiding any association with Father Mapple's radical Protestantism,[84]
Leyda tended to present a rake and a rascal romanticizing his past, but also deceived, toned down, and tied up by Woman/Nature/Jailor. His correspondence
(especially with William Gilman and Wilson L. Heflin) exhibits the energy directed
in tracking the bum who had originally gone to sea (1839) to evade responsibility
for a local girl he had impregnated (Gilman's suspicion), who then on the second
longer voyage had concocted a false history in the South Seas.[85] Leyda generally fled
(in public) from the self exposures in Melville's art,[86] on the one hand, providing
implausible family members, friends, and literary sources as prototypes for Melville's characters and plots (for instance, young Eli Fly as the model for Bartleby, a
drowned cousin Thomas Melvill as the source for Ishmael, and *Reginald Dalton* as
the source for *Pierre*); on the other hand, (with Hayford) privately identifying with
"the Scrivener," and like the 1920s revivers, blaming Victorian culture for forcing
Melville into the mask.[87] Modern women, like Old Testament Jews and the proletarian Christ, are signs for the scientific materialism the Yale critics were supposed
to be defending from Freudian myth makers such as Weaver, Mumford, Murray,
and Olson. Leyda, however, attacked the evidence of the senses. While praising
Melville's previously underrated Hawthorne-influenced short fiction of the 1850s,

Leyda subtly conveyed a negative image of his masked subject: Melville was playing a "dangerous" "game," forced to conceal his secret life and artistic meanings from female relatives, "the copying sister(s)": disabling purveyors of "life's deceptive surface." Here was the subject matter of "Benito Cereno." Behind the "screen" of sister-inflicted materiality lurked Melville's hot stuff: His "greatest fears" were "the twisted mind and the evil past."[88] For Leyda, this appears to have been Melville's essence, the secrets concealed in the "chimney" of "I and My Chimney." Why else did the *Log* not include the following item suggesting Melville's conviction of (his own, not only the Dr's) inner goodness, not monstrosity? "I missed seeing the Dr at Washington, although I sought him at Willard's. I trust he has got rid of his temporary disfigurement. When in your tent you introduced him to Gen. Tyler, you should have said: —General, Let me make you acquainted with my friend here, Don't be frightened. This is not his face, but a masque. A horrible one I know, but for God's sake don't take it to be the man. General, that horrible masque, my word for it, hides a noble & manly countenance. &c &c &c Your wit and invention render further strumming on this string idle."[89]

As his project evolved, Leyda kept his secrets and complicated the Melville biography, apparently belittling rumors reporting Melville's violence in the family while amassing rumors and facts that impugned Melville's character, including a rumor that he had abandoned pregnant Fayaway; the unsupported assertion of the English merchant Edward Lucett that Melville had attacked him with a knife while Lucett was bound in jail; and a damaging letter asking Melville's friend Alexander Bradford to vouch for the verisimilitude of *Typee*. Most seriously (and contra Weaver), Leyda suggested pervasive family emotional instability, even a strain of hereditary insanity on the Melvill side.[90] Exposing Weaver's and Mumford's naiveté in presuming that Melville's art revealed the life, Leyda's *Log* juxtaposed literary texts and historical materials to reveal discrepancies between life and art. In at least one case the process was reversed. Letters from Peter Gansevoort to Thomas Melvill, Jr. (describing the maniacal condition of the dying Allan Melvill, Melville's father) and from Melvill to Lemuel Shaw precede a passage from *Pierre* in which the young Pierre recalls his dying father's wandering mind *(Log, 51–52)*. Sentences indicating the father's remorse over an abandoned daughter have been omitted from that passage; yet it is clear that Leyda was familiar with a document that seemingly confirms the existence of precisely such an illegitimate child.[91]

One can only guess at Leyda's standards for omission or inclusion. To show that Melville was emotionally disturbed would tend to undermine the verisimilitude of his (crusading) art. Generally, this seems to have been one of Leyda's objectives, but if pushed too strongly, it might subvert the epilogues to *Moby-Dick* and *Clarel*, since the de-radicalization they expressed would seem more persuasive if arrived at through genuine misadventure and remorse, remembered in full clarity of mind.[92] Leyda had avoided a public confrontation with the artist undermined and overwhelmed, not by puritanical northern genes or a narcissistic mother, but economic and emotional dependency on a (would-be) elite. The artist was told through religion, reading, and direct family feedback that the qualities he valued most in himself—his empathy with children, penetration, moral purity, and passion for justice, that is, Victorian culture—were desirable but treacherous. Taken to extremes (the antipodes, as Weaver would say), these same values made him a traitor to his class and the source of decline and fall, a threat most erotically and sweetly conveyed in the serpentine entwining of Pierre and Isabel as he whispers his secret plan for their "marriage" in her ear. Leyda seemed willing and able to please everyone except Weaver and Eleanor Metcalf. Since the 1920s, Melville critics had been divided over Ahab's literary antecedents—Shakespeare's Lear in John Middleton Murry, Olson, and Matthiessen; Milton's Satan in Weaver and John Freeman. Leyda played up Shakespeare; this would fortify the mystical concept of Negative Capability.[93] As shown above, the corporatist discourse was represented as the voice of sane Enlightenment against proto-Nazi romantics and puritans, bearers of the Miltonic Egotistical Sublime. Leyda and other purveyors of conservative Enlightenment (Harry Levin, for instance) had turned radical Protestants into Anglo-Catholics and vice versa. Simultaneously, however, Leyda tirelessly provided other iconoclasts with ammunition (both real and imaginary) to tear down the exemplary moderate democrat[94] and great artist under construction by the impresario faction of the Melville Society involved in planning the first American edition of the complete works.[95]

Throughout the *Log* and other Melville criticism, Leyda (while recapitulating Weaver's misogyny) energized both sides of the anti-Weaver conservative project: the Anderson-type sleuthing expeditions (only the exotic early narratives are wonderful, but are not necessarily autobiographical), and the redemptive Thorp tendency (the prodigal returns to the fold, the late work is wonderful). The book design itself was to embody the switch, contrasting the harpoon with the customs house badge: Youthful adventures in exposing duplicitous authority were moderated by mature law and order/the State, throughout. Indeed, book designer Gerry Gross asked Leyda for a caption to explain the "startling juxtaposition" of harpoon and customs house badge. "Without it, Bob [Giroux] feels that many readers are going to miss the impact of the contrast we have gone to all this trouble to achieve."[96] The conflict seems to have bothered Leyda. In his introduction to *Complete Stories* (1949), he insisted on pessimistic readings of Melville's 1850s stories and novellas;[97] but in the introduction to the Viking *Portable Melville* (1952), Leyda celebrated the optimistic Christian epilogue to *Clarel*, while neglecting "Daniel Orme" that Weaver also had disliked.[98] If Daniel Orme were to be Melville's true voice, he could not be simply the victim of the human condition in a fallen world (Leyda), nor of women (Weaver and Leyda), nor devious (Leyda and some Yale critics).

Two excerpts from Leyda's introductions to the *Log* and to the *Portable Melville* betray confusion. First, in the *Log* (xvii), Leyda broke his own rules forbidding editorial mediation between reader and text, or wild speculation: He invited readers to guess the answers to questions Leyda had raised. A discarded draft suggests the pressure of Leyda's antagonism toward the bossy, seductive Ahabs of Melville's family: Maria, Allan, Gansevoort, and Melville himself. As originally written, the paragraph reads:

At the risk of seeming to limit the suggestiveness of these diverse materials, I want to propose some of the many specific areas for guess-work: On their own testimony how should Melville's parents and sisters and brothers be characterized?—*if you had any preconception of his mother's personality, have you changed it? If you were Melville, would you admire your Uncle Thomas more than your father? And how would you feel towards your commanding older brother Gansevoort? Do you feel, as I do, a sense of freeing relief only regret when Gansevoort dies after his service to* Typee?[99] *Can you decide if Melville actually saw Owen Chase on the* Acushnet—*or if Melville was mistaken in his identity of that "most prepossessing whale hunter"?* How did Melville's opposition to the mission and his deviations from "fact" in *Typee* affect his subsequent career? Did the counter-opposition of the missionary papers limit his reading public and do permanent damage to his career? (See Mr Tappan's attitude (page 393) and the correspondence among the Revd Doctors Tidman, Anderson and Dulles in 1856; even today in Hawaii there is an instantaneous reflex of protest on hearing the name of Melville.) Does his vigorous defense of a "narrative" he knew to be stretched and pointed make him more sensitive to all attack? *Does this war rumble in his later writing and thinking? After reading the letter to Hawthorne of November 17, 1851, do you think that Hawthorne ever learned that Melville was the Virginian who wrote "Hawthorne and his Mosses?"* Does the quoted documentation contain sufficient evidence on the slackening companionship of Melville and Hawthorne, or does the explanation lie somewhere outside of these documents? *As husband and father was Melville more than an ordinary trial to his family?*[100] Does Melville's grave contain infinitely more than Melville ever wrote? [Passages from the draft are in italics.]

The published version of this paragraph may resolve the ambiguity of the matter, raised with Giroux, of using a separate typeface to emphasize the unreliability of

Melville's own words as facts. By subtly conflating Melville's "opposition to the mission" with "deviations from fact," Leyda is hinting that Melville's criticism of exploitative missionaries in the South Seas (that provoked retaliation) is as bogus as his borrowings from other authors and the exaggerated heroic exploits that are actual "deviations from fact." The dispassionate Leyda perhaps had joined Olson's project in the master's thesis passage on *White-Jacket*, suggesting Melville as cynical propagandist exaggerating the suffering of sailors, inciting revolts that are sure to fail.

Leyda's introduction to the *Portable Melville* put the Melville problem on the table in language reminiscent of Nathaniel Hawthorne's frequently quoted journal entry of 1856:[101]

It is these lines of search (and the opposite, shunning side of the coin), with their images of failure and glimpses of resolution, that the modern reader can be caught and held by Melville, who offers his findings to all of us. Not that we all hear the same counsel—by no means! Melville is today cited in as many mutually cancelling causes as is Scripture. For Melville was not a neat, systematic searcher (or shunner)—through the years his line of thought detoured, back-tracked, flung itself to the right and to the left; any advances or retreats in society and politics, especially those of the United States, would shake him with revulsion or hope. Back and forth, across his mind, pushed the unending wrestle of fate and free will. No decision in this contest was ever final, not even "A Sketch" in *Clarel*. (xvii)

Leyda has alleged that Melville evaded classification (a fact apparently proven by the discordant ideologies that claimed him); the reader is caught by the vacillating but generous Melville, while Melville is caught by the age-old and insoluble contest between fate and free will (not by the historically specific contradiction within conservative democratic ideology—disruptive proletarian truth vs. conservative order). Leyda had adopted the F. Barron Freeman solution to the Melville problem ("what or where *is* he? and how can I make him a conservative like me?"), similarly mixing Captain Vere and Ishmael with Father Mapple and Ahab, or Tory monarchism with Hebraic revolutionary puritanism and deism: "Though his writing failed to make a living for his family, it never ceased to be employed for a deepening ravine for his probing honesty. 'Woe to him who seeks to please rather than appal!'[102] Like Captain Vere's, his 'honesty prescribes . . . directness, sometimes far-reaching like that of a migratory fowl that in its flight never heeds when it crosses a frontier'" (xiii). But these are also Ishmael's soaring Catskill eagle qualities *after* he resists the temptation of the Try-Works by separating from Ahab. Another passage brings Melville scholarship to a quiet place. "His bitter questions became more piercing and unanswerable in the pilgrimage of Clarel and the trials of Billy Budd and Captain Vere. The search continued to the end, but the struggling had been replaced by a steady stride across a battle-ground where the battle had paused" (xvi). Here Leyda reiterates Thorp's, Matthiessen's, and Freeman's formulations of the solid ground Melville had won in the peace of his deradicalized maturity; while Melville's permanent irresolution could please Hayford and other liberals who would (sometimes) read this as open-endedness. In his internally contradictory sentence, Leyda had reconstructed the happy family that the historical record declined to disgorge, the family that alienated contemporaries sought in vain.[103]

Writing (later?) for a New Bedford audience and again attempting to define Melville's achievement, Leyda put a communitarian and localist spin on Ahab's Byronic Titanism, asserting that Reverend Enoch Mudge was the model for Father Mapple and his great sermon, even implying that the high idealism of puritan New England had launched the *Pequod*. But Leyda mapped the big picture without its Captain:

> We can see this now as one of the key encounters in our cultural history, the meeting of a great oral tradition of the English language with an artist who was to take the long next step in American literature, though it was not his generation who recognized the weight of that step.
>
> That that encounter occurred in New Bedford underlines the crossing forces. Herman Melville's *Moby Dick*, where Ishmael listens to a passionate sermon in the Bethel before setting out on his first whaling voyage, can now be read as the epic of a giant New England industry that was built with the imagination and audacity of the people of this port. Both the Reverend Enoch Mudge and Herman Melville drew their arts from the realities of their century and their communities. Together they prepare us for the floating community of a whaleship, and the towering moral meanings of that voyage.[104]

Again, it is Ishmael, not Ahab, who possesses the long and steady step.

The draft introduction to the *Portable Melville* contains a startling political judgment suggesting Leyda's underlying conservatism and reversal of Right and Left. Following the strange claim that critics have neglected Melville's growing humor (seen by Leyda as culminating in the "subtle, tragic irony of Billy Budd's fate"), Leyda deleted this observation: "And Melville's daring as a political prophet is as startling and as unorthodox as the anonymous scroll of *Mardi* (resounding in the Preface to *Billy Budd*) as in 'The House Top.'" Although Leyda is writing of ideology and political culture, his discourse is depoliticized and ahistoric. The theme uniting all three cited texts (and referring to the Mexican War, the French Revolution, and the New York Draft Riots of 1863) is the civilized objection to mob rule and violence, a value shared by Thomas Paine and other radical liberals. Melville respects the rule of law, but, as a radical puritan and republican, wants to make laws consistent with the highest religious ideals. Leyda has made Melville's values here daring, startling, and unorthodox. No one had thought of them before; frontier rowdiness and the degradation of nature and nonwhites must be features of mainstream orthodoxy, effluent of the commanding, oppressive, heartless Gansevoort/Ethan Brand/Ahab, as if violent expansionism were America's official culture, not its violation; as if ordinary Americans had not just fought a war, or so they thought, against the most brutal imperialisms the world had ever witnessed, against desperado leftovers of aristocratic societies headed by Captain Veres (or their imitators) in Germany, Italy, and Japan. Captain Vere, not Olson's Conjur Man, must be the honest man with the steady stride and the soaring sense of justice. Leyda had borne the inversion of tradition and innovation, slavery and freedom, disseminated in the organicist discourse of the American literature establishment.[105]

His final verdict on Melville, the realistic antidemocrat, was strangely reminiscent of the Stanley Williams entry in *The American Mind* (1937), but with a difference: Since tragically good Ahab (Williams) was now evil Hitler (Olson), Leyda, like his academic predecessors, must look to Ishmael and Vere as the exemplary realists whose science is informed by conservative religion, hence ultimately obscurantist. Indeed, the pessimism and self-annihilation of Christian existentialism pervaded the modernist opera *Bartleby,* with libretto by Leyda and music by Walter Aschaffenburg (written intermittently over a ten-year period from 1954–64). The composer read Melville's text as a powerful incentive to conservative reform: The lawyer was humanized and awakened from complacency by contact with a member of the lower orders. But the reform-or-ruin scenario proposes only the most limited, voluntaristic forms of social amelioration (the charity that never faileth that Melville had mocked in *The Confidence-Man*). Given the perceptual weaknesses of human flesh (Leyda's emphasis), nobody is really reformed. Two excerpts from Leyda's libretto suggest a compromise between competing and contradictory visions of human possibility:

> [End to the Lawyer's prologue] I cannot recognize myself
> Across the great gulf
> That Bartleby cut through my life.
> If I had known how he would change me,
> Would I have sent away the harmless figure
> On that first day?
> All seemed as ever
> Before the first hint came
> To penetrate my placid satisfaction.

[Bartleby's aria] What do these walls shut out?
What do these bricks shut in?
Behind that wall—behind every wall—
Is another—and yet another—wall.
Between the dirty bricks—
Below every beam—
People live—or think they live,
And watch each other die.
Through walls of brick—and walls of flesh,
What man believes his fellow man? (Stage directions: He turns slowly to gaze at
the audience as the scene-curtain closes.)[106]

The *Log*, an expensive proposition from its very inception, had been primarily directed to an upper-class audience.[107] Its documentary appearance, munificent bulk, visually exciting variety of sources, declared evenhandedness, and seemingly authentic incoherence made it the perfect symbol for American pluralism: a symphony that held dissonant keys in tension, thus liberating readers from demagoguery, from the authoritative interpretations of a rising rationalist class at odds with elite interests. Thanks to Leyda's heroism, readers were at last armed with all the facts (even if some might be innuendos) and able to write their own biographies. In practice, the Melville mystery/romance was only deepened—and this doubtless helped the book business, increased the value of Melville first editions and letters, and motivated numerous academic careers.[108]

Late in life, Leyda seemed uneasy about the *Log*. He told the Columbia interviewer that his Melville collage, defined against the seamless mythologized narratives of the 1920s biographers, had yielded a "horrible result." "The anti-biography stand and my anti-biography form left the gaps, omitted the artificial bridges and shied away from interpretation altogether. But many people saw it as a complete thing that didn't need any more" (4:176). Perhaps Leyda meant to say that his empowered readers were not to be trusted any more than the commanding Melville or Weaver et al.: They were all seeking premature closure. In Leon Howard's memoir, "Mysteries and Manuscripts," Howard made a revealing statement. After going through the Harvard materials donated by Eleanor Metcalf and being held for Olson (in the early 1940s), he said that he had diverged from the early revivers, seeing Melville "as an ambitious writer rather than a raging Lear or a suffering Prometheus" (18–19). In spite of all the hints that Melville was only "an ambitious writer" as Leon Howard, his collaborator, believed; in spite of all the deliberate omissions that slanted the objective *Log* toward Howard's partly negative judgment, for Leyda, Melville remained (at times) the suffering Prometheus of Weaver and other sympathetic critics. As Alfred Kazin wrote (ca. 1951): "But Ahab is not just a fanatic who leads the whole crew to their destruction; he is a hero of thought who is trying, by terrible force, to reassert man's place in nature. And it is the struggle Ahab incarnates that makes him so magnificent a *voice*, thundering in Shakespearian rhetoric, storming at the gates of the inhuman, silent world. Ahab is trying to give men, in one awful, silent assertion that his will *does* mean something, a feeling of relatedness with his world."[109]

Leyda said he had experienced severe emotional difficulties, which some time after his induction, November 11, 1943, had caused him to be hospitalized and then honorably discharged from the army.[110] Although he denied it (in an angry interchange of letters with Henry Murray, appended or quoted below), Leyda apparently merged with his image of everybody's Melville. His publications, drafts, and notes show him riveted by Melville's images of desolation and decay, identifying with the tragic genius writer unhorsed by the reading public and chained to his writing desk by overwhelming family responsibilities, finding moral purity in the furtive composition of (underrated) poetry for posterity. Leyda's alternations of gleeful aggression toward Melville the rake and reprobate who burdened his family, and tender solicitude toward Melville the victim, should be viewed in light of his own unhappy psyche and volatile temper, which—as he told Murray in 1948 (a few months after the death of Eisenstein, February 19, apparently not mentioned by Leyda)—was out of control.[111] Shared hostility toward the women of Melville's family (symbols of the Victorian reading public/the sentimental bourgeoisie) would be the unifying theme of the Melville Revival; the suppressed alternative to misogyny—the historicism of Isabel's corrected family history or Daniel Orme's reveries—was positively un-American in the haute couture of the moderate center. Instead of helping each other read Melville's confessional texts with care and empathy, employing the critical tools that modernity had provided (close reading and textual/class analysis as wielded by Diderot or Melville), Leyda's collaborators often wilted or dried out, bearing out Olson's prophecy of the white rot or white death that blighted Melville scholarship.

Second-wave scholars (no less than their predecessors) might blame Melville or each other or the intractable conditions of intellectual production for their misery. After Murray's edition of *Pierre* appeared, Leyda blew up, accusing Murray of withholding something, perhaps the Isabel letter. Murray offered a stern diagnosis of Leyda's Melville problem: Leyda should not upstage Murray's analyst Jung; Leyda had neurotically withheld interpreting his own "mountain of data"; Leyda was projecting his feelings about Melville onto Murray; simultaneously Leyda, who had merged with Melville, was taking Melville/Murray's lacerating self-criticisms of *Pierre* too personally. Leyda responded wearily:

I'm tired, sick, not only of the disillusioning "intense competition" that you, too, find in this field (that I wandered into by mistake, anyway), but also sick of competing with a perpetual handicap. *No, Melville & I are not "one." [On the slip:] No, I am not a Great Seer. No, M & I are not "one." No, the insulted one is not another—but your reader. No, I am not regretting secreted "facts" but your analysis of them and your conclusions. [In pen on top, the corrected version:] But in ending let me say: No, I am not a Great Seer. No, M & I are not "one". I regard nothing that you say about the author of *Pierre* or even Pierre himself as a personal insult. No, you are not spitefully sitting on a lot of secret facts, but on your analysis of them & your conclusions.[112]

Note that (a) Leyda denied that he was out to get anyone "in this field (that I wandered into by mistake . . .)"; and (b) Leyda appears to have at first deleted, then included, the denial that he had merged with Melville.

How shall we assess Leyda's contribution to the Melville Revival? Leyda's insecurities with respect to his training in literary criticism were well founded. His energy in discovering hitherto unnoticed or unreported materials is obvious, but it does not follow that he was able to separate his own history from Melville's. Two desires seem to have motivated Leyda's project: first, the wish to direct (control) a group of collaborators, which he achieved by turning Melville's biography into a detective story/treasure hunt, alternately feeding "secrets" and withholding materials from his collaborators (especially Howard, Sealts, Hayford, and Gilman); and second, the yearning for a consistently supportive family, hospitable to artists.[113] He may have consciously manipulated his Melville materials to conform to his personal narrative, a narrative similar to the one imposed by Stalinist tactical alliances. Or he may have embroidered his already bizarre personal story to conform ever more closely to Melville's. In any case, Leyda was not prepared, politically or intellectually or emotionally, to bring the objectivity to his Melville research that has been imputed to him by younger scholars. Like Leyda, his correspondents often took Melville's themes personally and reacted with anxiety and depression. Leon Howard told Leyda more than once that rereading his Melville manuscript made him sick,[114] while Harrison Hayford, having just read Leyda's excited letter describing Eleanor Metcalf's imminent "bomb" (Melville's unrealized plan to build a towered dwelling in the Berkshires), also thrashed himself:

> Most of these things I'm thinking of getting out of the way are trivial and probably I ought to forget about them and turn myself to something important, but somehow I got in the mood to do something chiefly to get them out of my system and increase the length of my academic dong—I mean bibliography—I'm sort of ashamed to have worked so many things up to the point of writing and then just have them filed away. Some sort of loss of

interest and effort once the thing's found out. Like the Putnam trove, for example. . . . Now as to the enticing invitation to loaf in your pleasant upstairs all by myself for a week—it sounds delightful, and as of right now I accept with all my dessicated heart.[115]

I doubt that Hayford suddenly got bored "once the thing's found out." More likely, he felt the same vulnerabilities that Melville did and sought a more neutral public persona.

The Weaver-ites had not been silenced by the Yale critics. Eleanor Metcalf's family memoir, *Herman Melville: Cycle and Epicycle* (1953), undermined the efforts of her rivals Leyda, Leon Howard, and William Gilman (whose Melville biographies were all published in 1951) to downplay the strife in Melville's home life.[116] Metcalf introduced letters showing family approval of "wild, bold word painting[s]" but condemnation of brooding (sick-making unbounded critical inquiry) and, like Weaver and Olson, took Melville's side against the women in the often tense family. Moreover she attempted to clear away suggestions of hereditary insanity planted in the *Log*. During this period she remained attached to Weaver, grieving at his death in 1948. She was also under the spell of Henry Murray, who had, since the mid-1920s, fascinated her with his work-in-process on the Melville family's psychodynamics, possibly contradicting the spirit of his own introduction to *Pierre*— or, as I now strongly suspect, planting exaggerated notions of family violence gleaned from his own fertile imagination. Nonetheless, in spite of the presence of the Freudian Weaver-ites, the source-hunting Thorp/Anderson tendency dominated Melville scholarship during and after World War II. Except for the nonacademic Leyda, all were professors who reviewed one another (and the Weaver-ites) in *American Literature*, a journal founded in 1929, which, like the *Nation* of 1919, affected a balanced, neutral, and Emersonian stance.[117] These professors compiled and edited the new anthologies of American literature; later they assessed Melville criticism in *American Literary Scholarship*, casting baleful glances at occasional dissidents who injected "their own liberal politics into Melville's writings."[118] Liberals and moderates alike may be more accurately described, however, as lost moralists grieving over their own betrayals and alarmed by surging anger at illegitimate authority. Uneasily aware of Melville's perpetual suffering, they perhaps shared with Olson glimpses of the greyish chaos that might slide into revolution and parricide. Weaver's Pierrot Philosophique, the figure torn between defiance and submission, may be the aptest emblem for academic Melville studies. To paraphrase the image in materialist terms, Pierrot captures the dilemma of the petit bourgeois radical, resentful of upper-class control or intrusiveness, fearing the consequences of proletarianization, and never assured of riding out panics and depressions.

Against decadence

Knitting and probing were proscribed activities for objectivist Melvilleans of the second wave, steering clear of inside narratives. Celebrating the unsentimental asceticism of Howard's and Leyda's contributions, William Braswell rejoiced. "Here is the available basic material, much of it new. There is no attempt to fill in the gaps, no attempt to explain discrepancies or to interpret. The Melville that one becomes acquainted with in these pages will probably be rather different from the man he had in mind before. Here, minus the legends, is the man as he acted, as he appeared, and, so far as the nonfictional documents reveal, as he thought. For one who likes his facts neat [the *Log*] makes fascinating reading from beginning to end."[119] Willard Thorp's review of the William Gilman biography similarly attacked the unchecked fancy of tearful Weaver-ites. "What was wanted, after Weaver offered his biography, was scholarship and criticism which would in a measure account for the greatness of *Moby-Dick*, the falling off of Melville's powers as a writer, the long silence, and the final flowering in *Billy Budd*. Many who were stimulated to write about Melville were in haste to free themselves from the minutiae of biography so that they might speculate about Melville's inner life, the symbols which dominated his imagination, and his powers as a maker of myth."[120] Portraiture and Melville's subcutaneous condition had been a charged subject for Thorp, who had been sighted in Hawaii during the mid-1930s searching for Melville traces. Reproving Geoffrey Stone's publishers for printing a "botched" engraving of the Eaton portrait of Melville, he wrote, "It makes him look as if he had contracted a filthy disease in the South Pacific and had never got rid of it."[121] We have already glimpsed the emotions pressing Thorp to make sharp distinctions between Ahab/Pierre and the mature Melville. Melville's radical (primitivist) vision, contracted in the South Seas, brought death to the relatively happy family Thorp had once presented and that Gilman's biography would reinstate. Anger disfigured Melvilleans and the monument the conservatives had labored to construct/tear down since the mid-1930s: William Gilman was distressed by Lawrance Thompson's insinuation that the riddling Melville had tricked Christian humanists.[122]

Previous accounts of the Melville Revival have stressed factional differences, neglecting the contradictory emotions inside individuals, their common ground, and their capacities for change. In 1954, at the height of the Cold War, Charles Anderson, beacon of the conservative anti-Weaver backlash, reviewed Eleanor Metcalf's family portrait.[123] Anderson's sentiments could have been penned by the bohemian, psychologizing Weaver himself. Obviously moved and upset by Metcalf's revelations (or Murray's self-projections) of "bursts of nervous anger and attacks of morose conscience" that "drove him at times to desperate irascibility and the solace of brandy"[124] and by her quotation of a letter expressing family fears that Melville's social criticism was driving him mad, Anderson concluded that Melville was the "great author torn between two lives"; his conflicts may have fed his art. He then linked Melville's productions to the quest for truth, the connection that earlier revivers associated with Ahab and Pierre. Moreover, a muffled cri de coeur is heard in Anderson's account of Melville's ambivalence: Is he speaking of two Pierrots or only one? "Melville . . . was proud of his large and distinguished family, shared their loyalties, and periodically enjoyed their society. But not one of all this extensive connection really understood what mattered most to him, his art and his search for truth. . . . There were none who cared for philosophy or the life of the imagination" (263). Perhaps some objectivists have rejected Weaver/Pierre-style exposés of the genteel family, not to promote pluralism, not even to protect *Moby-Dick*'s status as cautionary tale, but rather to defend themselves against Melville's *unheimlich* disorienting references to their analogous situations and predicaments. They discounted Weaver's radical reading of Melville (with its suggestions of incest, Oedipus complexes, merged identities, and blurred boundaries) by subtly undermining Weaver's/Melville's veracity and good faith. In the academy, neither Weaver nor Melville could be perceived as sick or miserable; they had to be Isabels, poisoning the happy family; possibly Weaver was attacked as surrogate for the pathetic character they found themselves obliged to confront and classify, a Bartleby—resembling their own unhappy reflections in Melville texts—who appeared unable either to ignore the duplicitous social relations of various liberal "families" or to conquer his shameful (unmanly, un-WASP-ish) dependency on their patronage and esteem. If so, the second-wave scholars have created a new genre: the mock victimized, protectively distancing themselves from their real suffering. In the group portrait I have drawn (reminiscent of Picasso's seated Pierrot of 1918), variables of class, "race," and gender cubistically intersect, but it is the issue of class that colors their disease.

Jay Leyda photographed the last words of Melville's poem "Billy in the Darbies" for inclusion in his documentary *Log*, but he appears to have chemically altered a key word. "Sleepy," plainly legible in the original manuscript, was Melville's revision that replaced the word "drowsy" and was inserted into the line "I am drowsy and the oozy weeds about me twist," but in Leyda's photo "sleepy" morphed to "slain." Swinging to the Left now, Melville's last words in art were "I am slain . . . ." As well he might have done.[125] Christian resignation was not always Leyda's preference. His libretto for another opera, *Beatrice*, an adaptation of Shelley's play *The Cenci*, attempted to rectify the quietism that Shelley attributed to Beatrice Cenci as she goes to her execution, the city of Florence's punishment for arranging her brutal father's assassination.

[Shelley:] . . . Here, Mother, tie
My girdle for me, and bind up this hair
In any simple knot; ay, that does well.

This page and opposite: Lines from "Billy in the Darbies" before and after. The inserted word "sleepy" can be read as "slain." At left is Leyda's negative as shot from the manuscript of "Billy Budd." At right is Leyda's positive, as apparently altered by him and published in the *Log,* vol. 2. Department of Special Collections, Charles E. Young Research Library, UCLA.

And yours I see is coming down. How often
Have we done this for one another; now
We shall not do it any more. My Lord
We are quite ready. Well, 'tis very well. (V.iv.159–65)

These last words echo the calm mood of Beatrice's former resolve to defend herself from her father, Count Cenci (who was killing all his children and had raped

Fathoms down, how I'll dream
fast asleep.
I feel it stealing now. Sentry, are
you there?
Just ease this iron at the wrist,
and roll me over fair,
I am drowsy, and the oozy weeds
about me twist.

———— // ————

End of Book April 19th 1891

his daughter after she exposed his sins to the nobility of Florence), but she has reversed the earlier sentiment: "What is done wisely, is done well," said the swollen Beatrice, defying the Church and nobility.[126] So Leyda invented a chorus that rectified Beatrice's exit line, too resonant perhaps with Billy Budd's blessing of Captain Vere: The Count was a villain and deserved to die. In Leyda's libretto, a red cap is taken from one character and placed on Beatrice's head as she is rescued by the (Red) Chorus, dragged into a happier epoch: "It's time to come with us / Into a new century." [Boys only] "It also has its wrongs and tortures." [All] "But we'll change all that."[127]

Hatted with Phrygian caps, director Leyda's family of origin was together at last.

Part III
Melville, Ahab, and the Jewish-American Hitler

9

White Rot in the Melville Industry

Well, I'm sorry if the letter squirms instead of sparkles, and often totters on
the edge of the Bit Banal, but the Congo gets into one, it does, and starts the
god damned damp rot, it does, and pretty soon we'll all be shipped back so
much white cargo, we will. . . .
    —"Lucasta" to "Moby" Olson, ca. 1933

M, chained down for life, had no hope left. . . . A fusion of half-conscious
tendencies in M were clamoring for liberty, for a Saturnalia that would
grant exemption from the law. . . . And so at times it was alluring, not only
because he pictured it as a manic riotous release from tormenting
inhibitions and self-reproaches, not only because his father went that way,
but more because it represented the ultimate state toward which his
downward voyage through the mind was tending. . . . Children, primitives,
pagans, madmen, prophets, poets and geniuses had something in common;
and what they had in common set them apart—opposed to worldliness,
social institutions, Vanity Fair, the Pharisees and Philistia. . . . For, in
conjunction with his disposition to prate only about things which [HM]
had personally experienced, there was the tendency to *become* the object he
was writing of.[1]
    —Henry A. Murray on Melville's insanity, unpublished manuscript

But it is [in] *Pierre* that the ambiguities of the father are unralleved [*sic*] in
the acts of the son.
    —Charles Olson, unpublished footnote, *Call Me Ishmael*, 1947

I am slaving over Melville's early years, using a good many letters and quotations from letters to give the family's own picture of its members. This is the hardest part of the whole job, staying *in* the family and feeling outside of it at the same time. My individual reaction will come later.
—Eleanor Metcalf to Charles Olson, August 10, 1947

Why should we *be* them?[2]
—Eleanor Metcalf to Charles Olson, February 8, 1950

M elville studies remain confused and misinformed as to the basic facts of the Melville Revival. Writing to other Melville specialists, T. Walter Herbert described intolerable obstacles that continue to block the research of younger scholars:

Melville himself, in filling *Pierre* with biographical matter, raised a reasonable suspicion that his father had given birth to an illegitimate daughter, and this possibility long stood as the best guess as to what such a shameful secret might be. That Melville was sexually attracted to other men is a more recent candidate, as is the contention that he abused his wife—and possibly his children—through psychological hectoring and physical violence.

At the time of the Melville revival, of course, the family controlled access to virtually all of the surviving documents and, as items became available to scholars, there remained a degree of uncertainty about what various family members might still possess. Even today, further disclosures from Melville's descendants cannot be ruled out.

For scholarship, of course, primary documentation possesses unchallengeable authority. Melville dramatizes his own experiences in virtually all his fiction, which early treatments of his life sometimes mistook for reliable sources. . . . The task of separating biographical fact from Melville's fictional inventions became an urgent mission in the early period, and scholars who enjoyed access to family-held materials possessed an overwhelming strategic advantage in carrying this work forward.

Melville's granddaughter Eleanor Melville Metcalf played a major role in this project. . . . She expressed the fear that *Pierre* might prompt readers to conclude that the embarrassing features of the novel were true, doubtless including the depiction of an illegitimate daughter.[3] By the time of Metcalf's writing, however, other Melville scholars had accepted that very conclusion. Raymond Weaver knew the story of a pair of women, presumably Allan's lover and his daughter, who approached the family after Allan's death to ask for financial support; and Henry A. Murray had located a letter that recounts this incident, or something like it.

But Murray did not publish his findings, and his long-anticipated biography of Melville never appeared. Remaining a highly honored and powerful figure among Melvilleans, Murray occupied a position of divided obligations. Deference to the wishes of the Melville family may justifiably have prevented him from breaking silence; but the consequences of that silence for Melville scholarship were pernicious. It sponsored an "old boys club" atmosphere in which an inner circle of devotees share a secret that is not to be imparted to outsiders, and it produced a tradition of relentless normalization in the presentation of Melville's life.

That Melville lived a turbulent and troubled life is obvious from his writing. . . . [The normalizing second-wave scholarship of Leon Howard] diminish[ed] indications of chronic distress.[4]

In the introduction I mentioned the shared fantasy that Melville and his followers were hoarding hidden treasures. Though he is right to be suspicious, nearly every one of Herbert's statements characterizing earlier Melville scholarship has at best a grain of truth: There was no old boys' club; gossip, possibly concocted (consciously or unconsciously or so I have inferred), was strewn about to attack or defend specific Melvillean texts, just as Melville's own writing was selectively quoted to buttress the conversion narrative for Melville's/Billy Budd's apotheosis. One misleading judgment mentions "a letter" and Murray's "divided obligations." The following pages are intended to set that particular record straight. The drama of the Isabel letter is indeed entwined with divided obligations, but it was not Melville's descendants who drove Murray's supposed pernicious influence.

In early 1934, Charles Olson consulted the unsorted papers of Chief Justice Lemuel Shaw, Melville's father-in-law, at the Massachusetts Historical Society. There he spotted a letter written by Melville's uncle Thomas Melvill, Jr., concerning two women with a claim against the late Allan Melvill's estate. Although discreetly worded, the letter suggested that Allan Melvill had fathered a natural child; that two women (Mrs. A. M. A. and Mrs. B.) had visited Thomas's mother and his sister Helen after (bankrupt) Allan's death, and had been paid "some money" by Thomas Melvill, Jr. The uncle explained, with an unmistakable air of secrecy, that no one else in the family but Thomas, his mother, and Helen knew of the young woman's existence.[5] The letter gave weight to Weaver's contention that Melville always wrote about himself: Like Pierre, Melville was disillusioned by a wandering father. Their notes disclose that both Murray and Olson guessed that Melville discovered his father's indiscretion when he was nineteen years old, Pierre's age in the novel.

Immediately upon his discovery, Olson shared his find with fellow Melvillean Dr. Henry A. Murray, director of the Harvard Psychological Clinic. Besides Olson and Murray, numerous scholars including Raymond Weaver, Eleanor Melville Metcalf, Wilbert Snow, Jay Leyda, perhaps William Charvat and others, were privy to this story of stories in the 1930s and 1940s, yet the letter was withheld from the public for many years, surfacing at last in a doctoral dissertation directed by Harrison Hayford in 1970 and even then not published until 1978. No direct reference to it appeared in Murray's introduction to *Pierre* (1949); instead, Murray vehemently reproached Melville's unmotivated slander of his father. The psychoanalyst's eagerly awaited multivolume Melville biography, expected to disclose a mountain of "morsels," was never published. Murray's diagnosis of Herman Melville's mental states and his suppression of the "disreputable . . . tell-tale letter,"[6] are portentous, however, not only for frustrated literary sleuths, but for all students of antidemocratic social movements. For David Hume, framing the tenets of preventive politics in the eighteenth century to prevent another civil war, memories that could indict authority for the abuse of privilege should be banished from public discourse.

If ever, on any occasion, it were laudable to conceal truth from the populace, it must be confessed, that the doctrine of resistance affords such an example; and that all speculative reasoners ought to observe, with regard to this principle, the same cautious silence, which the laws in every species of government have ever prescribed to themselves. Government is instituted in order to restrain the fury and injustice of the people; and being always founded upon opinion, not on force, it is dangerous to weaken, by these speculations, the reverence which the multitude owe to authority, and to instruct them beforehand, that the case can ever happen, when they may be freed from their duty of allegiance. Or should it be found impossible to restrain the license of human disquisitions, it must be acknowledged, that the doctrine of obedience ought alone to be *inculcated*, and that the exceptions, which are rare, ought seldom or never to be mentioned in popular reasonings and discourses.[7]

Continued resistance to even the possibility that *Pierre* refers to Melville family relationships is ideologically determined and signifies the difficulties in assimilating fact-based history into "liberal" institutions. Heated scholarly debates over critical methods are not petty academic squabbles but encompass issues that concern us all: Is literary scholarship to be a subset of psychological warfare? Do ordinary people have the mental and moral capacity to read the system (or the lack of one) and participate in the decisions that determine their lives? Should instances of justifiable resistance and rebellion be expunged from "popular reasonings and discourses," as Hume advised? Shall our ideas about individual and group psychology be guided by rationalists like Locke, Paine, and Freud or irrationalists like Hume, Carlyle, Nietzsche, Pareto, LeBon, and Jung?[8] And with what academic support will the public test its educators?

Written for lazy or bewildered college students, the Random House *Keynotes* for *Moby-Dick* baldly erased five centuries of scientific achievement and social amelioration, returning the sentiments of medieval monks and Spanish Inquisitors to the perplexed:

KEY CHARACTERS. Captain Ahab Veteran sea captain, age 58. Rugged, dedicated to evil, committed to devil. Moody, scheming, determined to kill whale. Ruined by false pride. . . . Major flaw: believes he can defy fate; considers himself immortal, godlike, all-powerful. Wants to capture and kill white whale, confront universe, rid world of evil. Narrates certain portions of novel. MAIN THEMES & IDEAS. 1. SEARCH FOR TRUTH Story deals with man's pursuit of truth, meaning of existence. Melville not merely writing story about whale; more interested in its mysteries. . . . Search for truth parallels sea voyage: discovery, adventure, challenge of one's values. Melville not comfortable with status quo, tradition; questions conventional values (religion, social behavior, morality) to discover truth or falsehood behind them. . . . Ahab not convinced of God's existence . . . undertakes crazed course of ridding evil from world. . . . 6. REVENGE Ahab becomes mad as quest for revenge consumes his entire being. . . . Fools himself by thinking he alone can accomplish impossible task of ridding world of evil; commits himself to the devil to do so, but in process becomes slave to internal devil of madness. Fails to accept human limitations; by assuming it is possible to impose his concept of "truth" on world, he considers himself equal to God, commits fatal sin of pride. Dooms himself by trying to control fate. CRITICAL OVERVIEW . . . THE NARRATOR Critical debate about consistency of narrator, point of view. Melville uses Ishmael as narrator . . . but Ahab often seems to be chief spokesman, as when Ahab and second mate argue (Ch. 24). Does one of them represent Melville's ideas? Most critics believe Melville identified with Ahab because of his anger toward God and evil in the world. Yet Ishmael survives in the end; suggests possibility of new understanding of life. (John Campbell, 1986)

Other academic guides to Melville offered the same incentive to wayward adolescents: Ishmael's recognition of interdependence in contrast to Ahab's terrorism was the ticket to a correct answer on the SATs.[9] Ahab's proclivities are taken for granted beyond the confines of literary scholarship. In his controversial best-seller

Hitler's Willing Executioners, Daniel Jonah Goldhagen offers Ahab as Holocaust perpetrator *avant la lettre.* The Germans' "violent anger at the Jews is akin to the passion that drove Ahab to hunt Moby Dick. Melville's memorable description of Ahab's motives may serve as a fitting motto for the unrelenting, unspeakable, unsurpassable cruelties that Germans visited upon Jews." By contrast, Ahab was not a villain to the Italian Jewish scientist Primo Levi, writing in 1941 while searching for nickel in the foothills of the Piedmontese Alps before he was dragged off to a concentration camp: "We are chemists, that is, hunters: ours are 'the two experiences of adult life' of which Pavese spoke, success and failure, to kill the white whale or wreck the ship; one should not surrender to incomprehensible matter, one must not just sit down. We are here for this—to make mistakes and to correct ourselves, to stand the blows and hand them out. We must never feel disarmed: nature is immense and complex, but it is not impermeable to the intelligence; we must circle around it, pierce and probe it, look for the opening or make it."[10]

An earlier chapter made a case for Milton as Melville's most important literary forebear. The profane poet, modern artist, and radical puritan represented indomitable humanity seeking truth and justice. Like mountaineers lashed together, artists and readers climbed to view the big picture, or they mined beneath and behind surfaces to extract secrets concealed by nature or the mystifying upper classes. Milton's Muse wanted it that way, but such nosiness was viewed as satanic heresy, as gold digging, by conservative religious authority. Upstart artists were looking too closely at the details of this world; sense perceptions were controlled by the devil. After the French Revolution, rebellious young artists such as Byron and Shelley identified with the Romantic Wandering Jew, the accurate historian that conservatives loathed, but the romantics might turn on their own creation when the voices of internalized authority retaliated. It was always a problem of divergent interests in an era of incomplete transition from rigidly hierarchical to more egalitarian societies: Artists spoke to advanced audiences while exposed to the "cannons" of reactionary or conservative patrons. Merging with the unrepresentables would eventually shutter windows that had widened the imagination. Predictably, conservative nationalists in the twentieth century accused their new-fangled rivals of totalitarianism, by which they meant overreaching materialism, global analyses sans God's pointing finger. Finance capitalists, Soviet communists, Nazis, and radical democrats of any stripe similarly concealed intentions to drag their Faustian adherents to hell; scratch the surface and a bad Jew erupted.

Some Melville scholars would come to read Ahab as "an anticipation" of Hitler and Stalin. But if this were true, readings of *Pierre* would have to be modified, for Ahab and Pierre were plainly analogs, and Pierre was obviously Melville the writer accounting for the strangeness of the book they were reading. Pierre's moral purity and determination to acknowledge the outcast Isabel suggested he was the descendant of every overzealous radical puritan in U.S. history. Like his first biographer Raymond Weaver, Yale professor Stanley T. Williams had presented a good Ahab-Melville in *The American Mind* (1937), a bold antidemocrat, epistemologically an idealist scoffing at modern progress and holding out against philistine Victorian materialists. But whereas Weaver saw *Pierre* as an uncompromising indictment of injustice that propelled Melville into unpopularity and "the long quietus," Williams subtly planted the notion that Melville had renounced utopian adventurism in that very text by ending his selection of Melville extracts with the despairing vision of Enceladus, generally presenting a daring critic of the entrenched American orthodoxy, democracy, of the Protestant mission to renovate the world. Weaver had also emphasized the connection of Ahab, Melville's surrogate, to Milton's materialist Satan, oddly, along with corporatist Elizabethans. With Charles Olson in the lead, the influence on Melville of the Elizabethans and Milton was rejected in favor of Shakespeare's alone: Ahab and his creator were separated in Olson's article of 1938; Ahab was no longer the anticapitalist hero drawn by Williams. The identification of Ahab with Melville had changed after the mid-1930s in tandem with a moderate conservative mobilization against extremists of both Right and Left (along with a changing progressive assessment of Leviathan's responsibility for social welfare). Was it only coincidental that Ahab was most vigorously switched when Hitler switched after the mid-1930s, apparently determined to go all the way with the national socialist world revolution, no longer the surrogate for anti-communist patrons in the West who had cheered on the Nazi Party?

Henry Murray's readings of Melville's psyche seem influenced by Weaver's book but diverged in one particular. He agreed that Pierre was an unrepentant radical, but unlike Weaver who was generally sympathetic with Melville but critical of Melville's father, Allan, Murray held that Pierre's anger at his father was irrational and excessive: out of control and out of bounds. Murray's introduction to *Pierre* (1949) was instrumental in reinforcing the impression of the Leyda-Howard faction that Melville was "an ambitious writer" given to romanticizing his past, and not always honorably. Meantime, Murray quietly emulated the useful traits of all three charismatic Supermen: Melville, Ahab, and Hitler, for Murray was at the center of a movement in social psychology to establish a federal morale service. Perhaps the major tenet of Murray's theory of group cohesion in a pluralist society was the absolute necessity to idealize national democratic leaders, the good fathers Washington, Lincoln, and FDR. Murray's suppression of the Isabel letter is incomprehensible without seeing this ideological imperative. The following pages return to the mid-1930s to describe the politics of Murray's affinity group, the moderate men whose prescriptions for ailing economies were bound to an irrationalist diagnosis of "romantic Fascism" in Europe and America. No one has traced this: Murray was grappling with romantic Melville at the same time he was participating at a very high level in a group reading of "romantic Fascism," along with the construction of psychological testing, personnel assessment, and techniques for morale building to forestall a similar outbreak in America. It was a blow against the Enlightenment epistemology that had fortified insurgent democrats since the seventeenth and eighteenth centuries and had inspired Herman Melville and other extremely independent bodies.

EVACUATING THE ENLIGHTENMENT

Excessive subjectivity diffused through time and space [led to his alienation, killed the desire for art].[11]
  —Van Wyck Brooks explains the death of Melville's career,
  Dictionary of American Biography, 1927

One certainty at least, however, stands clear and fixed in the midst of all this bad blood, and special pleading. And this certainty is: *Pierre* and *The Confidence Man* are not, by anybody's count, "achieved literature" in the transparent sense that that phrase applies to *Anna Karenina*, say, or *Hamlet*, or *Agamemnon*—works composed from the vantage ground of universal reason, above the passionate experience they body forth. Too rarely did Melville save his soul as an artist by losing it in something outside of himself. Melville came to put the highest premium upon "sincerity," and the overwhelming bulk of his writing is "self-expression" and satire; the hero is always himself, either in his own undisguised person or else thinly masked in all sort of romantic and allegorical finery. Since he was so much and so increasingly in earnest in his fiction, since he threw himself so unreservedly into his creations, since his imagination was so exclusively a vent for his personal preoccupations, rarely could he portray emotions, which demands detachment; usually he could but betray it. Withal, Melville did have the power to stimulate, which is the beginning of greatness; and he had genius besides. But surely in *Pierre* and *The Confidence Man* he falls dizzily from being a writer of seasoned experience and heavenly inspiration. And such a spectacular fall from grace must provoke in the spectator either embarrassment or revulsion. Passion imperfectly transmuted into art can never inspire in a reader the serenity and the exultation of wonder; the reader is left rather with the disquietude of tensions unresolved, with an aching sense of

unfulfillment, and a restless urge to do something about it: "to write a check or join a society," or to anatomize the faulty art as "clinical material."[12]
—Raymond Weaver, 1935

She is the eternally baffling object of human speculation, and she is also speculation itself, which, refusing all external guidance, collapses into introspection.
—William Ellery Sedgwick, *Herman Melville: The Tragedy of Mind* (1944), explaining the significance of Isabel, Pierre's half-sister

I should like to add again that you are World Editor No. 1—particularly at this time when I am a slave of the Blue Devils & encouragement from you has meant so much. I met Mrs. Sedgwick a few days ago & she told me that *Pierre killed* her husband—that he left that chapter to the last & rewrote 100 times, & left it unfinished, & then began drinking and died of pneumonia after exposure. This is not hard for me to understand.[13]
—The sad end of William Ellery Sedgwick as told by Dr. Henry A. Murray to Howard Vincent, September 17, 1947, while composing his introduction to *Pierre*

Instead of *Pierre's* killing you, you have pinned its shoulders to the mat.
—Howard Vincent to Murray, September 29, 1947

A dramatic expression of its author's most profound anxieties and obsessions, it stands as the strangely compelling creation of an intensely troubled, eternally questioning mind. As William Ellery Sedgewick [*sic*] has written: "*Pierre* was the only book of Melville's maturity as ambitious as *Moby-Dick.*"
—Signet Classic edition of *Pierre, explication de texte*, 1964

The pursuit of Melville in elite eastern universities during the late 1930s was coterminous with the excising of radical will through antifascist liberal surgery. As world war loomed, Marxists and many others from Center to Left were predicting fascism in America. New Deal policies, they argued, could not avert or repair the periodic structural crises of capitalism; only a corporate state could suppress the class warfare that would flare anew in the depression that was expected to follow demobilization. Irrationalist moderate conservatives viewed moralistic self-righteousness (on the Left) and selfishness (on the Right) as the source of social violence.

In 1939 or 1940, three moderate men, Robert Hutchins, Paul Hoffman, and William Benton, invited University of Chicago faculty and "personal friends" from big business to join a study group, the American Policy Commission. Hutchins was president of the University of Chicago and defender of Great Books; he and Benton's former partner Chester Bowles would be members of America First. Hoffman was president of Studebaker, later chief administrator for the Marshall Plan and first president of the Ford Foundation. Benton was vice president of the University of Chicago; promoter of modern radio advertising, "Amos 'n Andy," and Muzak; and later publisher of *Encyclopedia Brittanica* and other educational media before becoming assistant secretary of state and then originator of "The Voice of America" and finally the U.S. senator from Connecticut and a backer of UNESCO-enabling legislation. The American Policy Commission evolved into the Committee for Economic Development (CED), institutionalized in 1942; its purpose was to meet the anticipated postwar depression with Keynesian economics. The planners of CED distinguished their "socially responsible" policies from those of the laissez-faire National Association of Manufacturers; it brought scholarly specialists together with liberal businessmen to steer America clear of the mad extremes of fascism and communism, later McCarthyism, inflated arms budgets, and commercial broadcasting. The omnipresent political scientist Harold D. Lasswell[14] was central to the project of preventive politics: The Jung-inspired Lasswell discovered the psychopathology of communism and fascism. Benton's biographer unambiguously placed Lasswell's probe in the democratic tradition: "[Lasswell] looked hard and long at these worldwide disorders of the political mind, hoping to find in them the terms for a program of preventive medicine that could help maintain America as a free society with equal opportunity for human dignity open to all."[15]

With the examples of Plato and other classicists at hand, Lasswell and fellow psychopathologists could protect the old master narrative. Nazis sighted on the horizon (like the jingoistic followers of Father Coughlin and other American fascists) must be the People: sneaky, bloody, perverse, selfish, and paranoid. Without good father navigation, the hysterical People would be driven by shadows in Plato's Cave, go berserk, and drown "business." Lasswell was worried about the possible transition from fascism to communism; while attempting to overcome Marxian socialism, (rational) European businessmen had been captured by the "romantic Fascists" of the squeezed "lower middle-class" who might go on to liquidate their former patrons.[16] Interestingly, for Lasswell in 1936, the scenario in America seemed different. Here the middle class was so identified with "big business" and "big finance" that it was likely to fall for the propaganda against "reds" and smash labor. To avoid "piecemeal fascism" and to enhance "peaceful development," Lasswell (and other ego psychologists) prescribed class consciousness (but integration) through pluralist bargaining in "interest groups" to achieve emotional and intellectual independence from monopolistic big business. In 1941, Lasswell urged vigilant sighting and sympathetic treatment of bad seeds:[17]

Public opinion is profoundly distorted when there are deference crises in society; and these appear when the level of deference is suddenly interfered with, and when destructive personalities exercise a directive effect upon public opinion. Some persons are at odd with themselves, carrying heavy loads of anxiety, and from these anxiety types extremism may be expected. We need to become aware of which social practices in the home, school, factory, office—contribute to anxiety and which to security. We may be able to lower the level of the explosive reserves when human development is subject to gross distortion.

Lasswell could have been describing Herman Melville's anxious disillusion with paternal authority; perhaps explosions would be obviated by enhanced civilian morale with methods advocated by the Harvard social psychologists Murray and Allport, also disseminated in 1941. By 1942, these social scientists were certain: The Head Self was sturdy guardian of "the public interest," whereas overly egalitarian motions inside the Western Body levelled walls, erected barricades, then tossed up lonesome corpses. In his article "Propaganda and Social Control,"[18] Talcott Parsons, Murray's Harvard associate and mentor, addressed mental health practitioners, proposing that the government practice "social psychotherapy" to stabilize the national consensus. He advocated subliminal "reinforcement type" propaganda to calm the "revolutionary" and "disruptive" types that were inducing structural change or undermining "confidence in authority and leadership." Maladjusted neurotics were fomenting conflict and fragmentation, not adaptation and interdependence. But froward rebels could be cured in the socially responsible psychiatrist's office through "steady discipline to which the patient is subjected in the course of his treatment. While the fact that he is required and allowed to express himself freely may provide some immediate satisfactions, he is not really allowed to 'get away' with their implications for the permanent patterning of his life and social relations, but is made, on progressively deeper levels, conscious of the fact that he cannot 'get away' with them. The physician places him in a kind of 'experimental situation' where this is demonstrated over and over again" (561). Compare the Parsons protocol with the sermon of a German theologian in 1933 switching "secular Jews," the most dangerous type of atheist: "Everywhere where something can disintegrate decomposed, can be destroyed, maybe marriage and family, patriotism or the Christian church, discipline and order, chastity and decency; everywhere there is something to gain, he is involved there. He is mocking with his ingenious joking, with his smart and skillful talent, with his persistent subversive energy. An atheist always acts destructively; but nowhere is the destructive force of this attitude as devastating as in the case of a Jewish person who wasted his rich heritage from the Old Testament and joined the swine."[19]

Pragmatic Harvard social psychologists had appropriated Madisonian pluralist politics, ignoring the libertarian, anticorporatist aspect of their theoretical underpinnings. For the new moderates, social stability was achieved when triumphalist factions (instigated by religious enthusiasm or other forms of zealotry such as an inordinate love of gain) were replaced by amoral interest groups; relieved of (Hume's) plundering or leveling extremists, bargains could be struck, reconciling private interest with public good: The moderates would have clambered onto solidly "mobile-middle ground."[20] Reading Madison in *The Federalist Papers No. 10*, they could infer that free speech was a safety valve, circumscribed spatially and irrelevant to political processes with realistic goals.[21] Having banished irrationality from their own procedures, the Harvard clique could see themselves as resolutely antifascist, for it was the mob-driven Nazi movement (likened by Parsons to romantic puritans in other writing of 1942) that was pathological. Ritual rebellions could be safely confined within psychiatrists' offices or the pages of *Typee* (or in the bed Ishmael shared with Queequeg).

Parsons's contribution appeared in *Psychiatry* along with a germinal article, "Hitler's Imagery and German Youth," by Erik Homburger Erikson, another colleague of Murray's at Harvard. Erikson presented Hitler as a "great adventurer" possessed of "borderline traits"; he was the perennial adolescent, a big brother to other unyielding gangsters. Erikson held that broken-spirited German fathers lacking inner integration and authority were responsible for the (hysterical) romantic revolt of the sons.[22] Erikson's identity politics owed more to Murray and the romantic conservative Jung, a theorist of racial character, than to the cosmopolitan and bourgeois Freud. Soon the Jungian analyst Murray (who admired the Wandering Jew Freud's eyes that penetrated walled-up areas of the psyche) would be advising President Roosevelt that Hitler, the autodidact Id-man, the Dionysiac Man of the Crowd who had overcome big Capital, was an "arch-Romantic," a composite of Lord Byron and Al Capone, a paranoid schizophrenic, a homosexual, and probably a carrier of Jewish blood through his father—ergo Hitler's "uncanny knowledge of the average man" should "be appropriated to good advantage." Disillusion with the Führer could be perilous to American interests, however; Murray argued for "a profound conversion of Germany's attitude" after the Allied victory. "Disorganization and confusion will be general, creating breeding ground for cults of extreme individualism. A considerable part of the population will be weighted down with a heavy sense of guilt, which should lead to a revival of religion. The soil will be laid [*sic*] for a spiritual regeneration; and perhaps the Germans, not we, will inherit the future."[23]

Lasswell and Murray, both progressives, thought as one. In his *Power and Personality* (1948), Lasswell contemplated the continuing plausibility of Marxist analysis, worried about "paranoids" with their fingers on nuclear buttons, and urged "genuine democrats to expose the dubious and dangerous expectation of democracy through mass revolution." The world revolution of the twentieth century would probably culminate in mutually annihilating technocratic garrison states unless "the scientists of democracy" intervened to create the "sociocapitalist" "free man's commonwealth." Murray's personality tests (developed in the mid-1930s and during his stint with the oss during the war) fertilized Lasswell's febrile, holistic imagination. While recalling the concepts of accountability and openness that for Locke had been indispensable to the functioning of popular sovereignty, Lasswell, with Murray's personnel assessment tests in tow, had turned Locke upside down:

One of the practical means by which tensions arising from provocativeness can be reduced is by the selection of leaders from among non-destructive, genuinely democratic characters. . . . This has already gone far in appointive jobs. Several businesses are accustomed to promote executives not only on the basis of the general administrative record but according to scientific methods of personality appraisal. The aim is to discern whether factors in the personality structure counterindicate the placing of heavier responsibilities on the person.

To a limited extent selection procedures in army, navy and civil administration have been directed to the same end. But the procedure is not yet applied to elective office. What is needed is a *National Personnel Assessment Board* set up by citizens of unimpeachable integrity which will select and supervise the work of competent experts in the description of democratic and antidemocratic personality. The Assessment Board can maintain continuing inquiry into the most useful tests and provide direct services of certifications of testers. When this institution has been developed it will slowly gather prestige and acceptance. Sooner or later candidates for elective office will have enough sense of responsibility to submit voluntarily to an investigation by the board, which would say only that the candidate has, or has not, met certain defined minimum standards. Gradually, the practice of basic personality disclosure can spread throughout all spheres of life, including not only local, state, national or inter-nation government personnel, but political parties, trade unions, trade associations, churches and other volunteer associations.

It is an axiom of democratic polity that rational opinion depends upon access to pertinent facts and interpretations. Surely no facts are more pertinent than those pertaining to character structure of candidates for leadership. Progressive democratization calls for the development of such new institutions as the Assessment Board for the purpose of modernizing our methods of self-government.[24]

"The National Personnel Assessment Board set up by citizens of unimpeachable integrity," "gradually" penetrating every institution, would control definitions of acceptable rational opinion. And yet Lasswell was no friend to totalitarian regimes; as member of the Research Advisory Board and spokesman for CED, he condemned loyalty investigations. Instead of imitating vulgar witch hunters on the Right or the "negative" tactics of the ACLU on the Left, he called for an overhaul of leaders and the led (the latter ultimately responsible for protecting First Amendment freedoms). A balance would be struck between national security and individual freedom through formation of community discussion groups, to be fed by appropriately cautious government experts supplying an interactive (but "expert"-controlled) free press and public broadcasting system.[25] In the 1950s, Lasswell's study of political symbols helped social scientists refine their tools in the surveillance of blooming political dissidents. Murray's OSS recruitment test of 1943 could weed out potentially disloyal government employees, while his Thematic Apperception Test (1935) could enhance content analysis of mass communications. Lasswell frankly explained the purposes that infused the new discipline of communications studies, said to be relevant to literary scholars and historians; indeed, he decoded authoritarian styles of discourse throughout.[26]

Modern preventive politics did not begin with the machinations of Lasswell & Company but with Humean or Burkean autopsies of the regicidal English and French Revolutions. According to the reform-or-ruin school of preventive hygiene, foul winds and cancers appear when aristocrats allow vices to ferment in the bowels—the social bond is broken; virtue and vice trade places.[27] Through alert planning (such as for education and sports for the masses and psychoanalysis for their betters), elites would become more flexible while containing their passion for libertine excess and luxurious display; meanwhile, the People would have healthy outlets for their discontent and desirousness—such as libertine excess and luxurious display, especially in the mass media. Thus Reason, Conscience, and the State would be brought into congruence. The reform-or-ruin strategy of social hygiene and preventive politics would dominate the political science and social psychology created by moderate conservatives. Understrapping their dreams of thoroughgoing surveillance, the watchbird watched everybody, leaders and the led.

Apply this formula to "Billy Budd, Sailor" as it might have been read by Lasswell or Murray. Melville's cryptic fable is set in the summer of 1797, only weeks after naval mutinies at Nore and Spithead in April and May while conservative England was at war with revolutionary France. The uprisings have been suppressed, some grievances redressed, but lieutenants with swords stand behind the gunners lest their weapons be turned against their commanding officers. Two of the three principal characters lack the perception of evil in themselves and others that would have averted a catastrophe. The brew of desire, envy, and malice (qualities associated with incendiary Frenchmen) fermenting inside the handsome John Claggart, master-at-arms, caused his preposterous accusation that Billy was plotting mutiny. Baby Budd, as the sailors call him, not having eaten Eve's apple, has no defenses against hidden evil, nor has he any sense of personal rights: The prelapsarian Adam lacks self-control. So when Claggart repeats his accusation in the presence of Captain Vere, the unanticipated outrage prompts Billy to overreact with a blow to Claggart's forehead. Because Claggart, a petty officer, was Billy's superior, Captain Vere is forced into regrettably severe but rational discipline: The slightest breach could trigger a mutiny. To set an example, the angel must hang, even though Vere loves Billy. Vere was trapped. Why didn't he avoid this mess by probing into Claggart's mind before the situation got out of hand? Now Vere's excessively harsh and peremptory punishment has led the other officers to doubt his sanity and judgment, while over time, the sailors vindicate and memorialize their innocent martyred Billy: The entire structure of authority has been toppled. Like Captain Delano, the naive American of "Benito Cereno," Vere lacked insight into the psychology of the unshackled lower orders. Their apparent deference could not be taken for granted; the guillotine of the never-ending French Revolution shadowed their movements, master and servant alike. Vere's training should have been grounded in social knowledge, specifically of rising little men like Claggart. Enter preventive politics and the Freudianism of political scientists Harold Lasswell, Talcott Parsons, and Henry Murray beginning in the 1920s. The Billy Budd menu was embarrassing and dangerous, never more so than in 1917, the year of the "Jacobin" Russian Revolution, or in the late 1930s when the tricky little man Hitler, another Jacobin, seemed to be getting the better of his conservative nationalist patrons.

Would Henry Murray have passed the tests he had devised to identify latent radicals before they ascended to positions of leadership? In my interview of November 4, 1987, Murray told me he believed both he and Melville were periodically "insane" or "abnormal"—but in a nineteenth-century mode that he was attempting to "retype." It was a condition Murray believed he could have treated, and yet he felt that he, Murray, had failed to solve the problems of war and violence; moreover, he (like Melville) had always lived in "the most painful ambivalence." My portrait of Murray and his relations with other Melvilleans is only partly filled out in Forrest G. Robinson's biography, Love's Story Told. Robinson's Murray is an aristocrat, troubled and outrageous to be sure, but, finally, a beaming friend of youth, an embattled pioneer/explorer of the psyche, and the essence of humanistic Enlightenment. The Isabel letter, like Murray's intense friendship with Charles Olson, is missing; rather, Isabel (like Murray's Ahab/Hitler or Robinson's Christiana Morgan, Murray's mystic mistress) rose from the deep to possess and destroy Melville's psyche. Murray, in contrast to Melville/Ahab/Hitler, pulled back from the borderline (where bad women had driven him) to marry a woman who was not crazy, thence to father the jolly academic psychology that has fortified the cultural radicalism of the 1960s generation.[28] During my own friendly conversation with Murray, I unguardedly mentioned his facility in constructing a (false) self-making apparently intimate disclosures, while observing the charade from a safe distance. A few minutes later, he suddenly turned away from my Ahab gaze, covered his eyes with his hands, and cried out, "Don't look at me! I'm afraid you can see into all of my secrets!" Unlike Forrest Robinson, I do not think sexual dysfunction/adventure was the source of his fear and trembling.

[Leslie Fiedler to Richard Chase, January 30, 1949] Is the Confidence Man *inside* the previously satirical intent of the book; or is he, favorably, regarded by the author, the touchstone by which the corruption of all the other characters and institutions surveyed is shown up. How are we expected to respond to him? Can we take as a guide to his true worth the opinion of the one-legged man or of the young Tennessee preacher? We know what the one-legged, one-sided, distorted character means in Melville; he is the destroyer of faith, of himself and of those that believe him; it is the one-legged man who calls what is white (the inscrutable—Moby Dick—the first avatar of the Confidence Man) evil—and his end is madness, the ultimate isolation of the man in himself.

[Fiedler to author, May 21, 1991] There isn't the slightest doubt in my mind that Melville suffered from a severe nervous breakdown, psychotic episode, or whatever you call it (perhaps several). Everything about the history of his literary production and the facts of his life seem to suggest this. I, at least, never doubted it.

Part 2 reviewed materials in the private papers of Melville revivers Raymond Weaver, Charles Olson, and Jay Leyda reporting or speculating about Melville's violent behavior in the family. More and more I feel that such rumors are suspect, if not planted; perhaps they are the inflated outcome of class-bound readings in which Melville/Freud-style explorations of the psyche inevitably lead to degeneracy and decline in the body politic. For instance, Lewis Mumford, prolific critic of the machine age, responded to *Moby-Dick* in fractured fashion. In his 1929 Melville biography, Mumford took Ahab's violent "method" literally, whereas he stated that the story as a whole was allegorical. This selective inability to separate life from art highlights the difficulties in evaluating reports of Melville's alleged abusive behavior. If Mumford (like other corporatist thinkers dogmatically positing the terminal inscrutability of the universe) experienced Ahab's probes as a personal assault,[29] how can we rely on his critical judgments?

Notes and manuscript fragments intended for the psychobiography of Melville preserved in his papers (opened in 1991) at Harvard University suggest that Murray, too, may have made unwarranted and tendentious inferences about Melville's psyche. Rather than sitting on "secrets" as competing Melville scholars had long suspected, Murray, while diagnosing insanity and family violence, seems to have trusted his intuitive responses to Melville's art. For Murray, Melville's entire oeuvre was perhaps one big Thematic Apperception Test. The following excerpts (including notes labeled 1852–56) suggest inference,[30] not the testimony of relatives; the style is reminiscent of Weaver's docudrama in which the reserved Hawthorne receives one of (Hebraic) Melville's pushy letters, his arrogant purity demanding recognition and reciprocity. Some of Murray's notes may have been written as early as the mid-1920s. Has he transmuted the rainbow of Isabel's tears into Melville's "narcistic weapon" that threatened defenses of twentieth-century Melvilleans, the rainbow becoming the husband's violent assault upon "the wife" (themselves as middle managers)?

[Folder "Psychology of 1840"] [Melville's mother, Maria Gansevoort Melville] had an Ishmael complex. . . . Thus Herman's melancholy was the result of his mother's self-absorption and consequent indifference, as well as the narcistic weapon with which he fought her ("tears are a woman's fits"). Therefore we must list his imitation of Maria among the important factors which led to the establishment of his succorance, self-pity and what he called a "half-wilful overruling morbidness." Ishmaelism was a Gansevoort disease. Each of them wanted to be wanted, and felt sick if they were not.

[Comparing Melville to the Hellenistic Emerson, Folder 1849–50] H.M.— Hebraic of Job, Jeremiah, Isaiah, Jonah, Ecclesiastes/ Hebraic consciousness Guilty: throw me overboard

[MS chap. 16, 1849–50, on the birth of "Mackey"] He was there to cast his dark shadow on the little boy whose advent was a questionable blessing. Paternity was scarcely felt . . . .

[Folder "Morsels," loose sheet] His mental derangement had already set in . . . sometime in the late fall of 1851, after he had finished M.D. The bits of information that I shall shortly present are compatible with this conclusion.

[1852] Macabrish searching down the back alleys

[1852–56] Suppose wife is unfaithful; my boys not mine. Now I know how a man feels who wants to murder his wife.

[1852–56] Reverie in his room. Take the main obsessive preoccupations from his stories.

[1852–56] Confidence Man[:] H.M. probably reexamined his father's correspondence. Allan-Confidence Man/Kill better by intelligent experiment, by laughter—*Psych* love gone rank. Frozen rage or wrath

[MS "Half-wilful overruling Morbidness" and fragment] How was he to rid himself of his hate? It is perhaps one of the most unfortunate truths of human psychology that any aroused irritation—whatever the cause—is first directed against a member of one's own family—usually the nearest and dearest. "There is a woe that is madness."
 M never lowered his colors. He could find no way of meeting the world on his own terms, so that he ceased to meet it. . . . But to the end he remained a Nay-sayer . . . Hated himself—Death stalked in on him & left / Suffering is portentous—It is an omen of coming murder / In its first flush / Libertine in melancholy / Even the worm will turn . . . .

[1852–56] Self-pity was the underlying theme of those revengeful scar-bearing years / The self-accusatory finger was the canker that bore its way into his hot brain

[1853–54] Elizabeth [Melville's wife] rooted to the ground with terror/The [sneers?]—the fireplace—pipe—brandy jug . . . Hoadley—Look in his eyes—Infuriated him/Dust—Mother—Ambitious—Spotlessness. Put up a bold front—M engaged to covering up—In excusing—In maintaining respectability—To the neighbors—could not make excuses gracefully—Talked about all the inconsistencies of others—scandals—They would remain proper and decent. Afraid of novel, free.

[1852–53] An utter wreck

[1853] The heavy measured tread of Maria. In sullen silence—no one daring to be frivolous—the portentous. This was the Nemesis—Nature defeated by custom. The overbalancing Moral destroying life. Glowering darkly across the table at his mother. Withering them with his mood—dominating, master. Poor Elizabeth, gentle, feeble, untoughened, pitched for a [illegible]—Bulk of his passion enfeebling him, driving out all thought—constrained them in frozen manner. Long impassive hours—Step out into the delicious air—walking stick in hand. Massive indifference—more unkind than words—sorrow too utter for speech.

[1853] —He was now reduced to the limit—but refused to be a mendicant or a mercenary—He was an alien in thought—his whole mind was on the threshold of alienation / Satanic gave place to the Mephistophelian

[1853]—Mrs. M . . . resigned—flogged by the knotted pain of their relationship

[1852–56] He fell victim to a mood of perplexed and dramatized stoicism. Draw the blows and let them fall about his head.

[1852–56] Crumbled in the face of the felt calumny and wrong
    Throbbing pain / beast of prey / sullen, lonely, acclaimed mad / Balancing his agony—Torn reed / Unbent—too proud for vituperation.

Crumbled, throbbing, torn (yet unbent) as he was, Murray's borderline man stepped back from the abyss (lent a hand by Shaw), willfully overcoming his (mother-inflicted) melancholy and (Old Testament Jew–inflicted) guilt, at last finding wholeness in the gay, pragmatic ideals of conservative elites (or did he?):

[On Lemuel Shaw, "one of the most respected and beneficent men in the state," 1852–56] [HM] must have been a complete enigma to him and his books cryptic and melancholy. . . . The Shaws had been planning how best to relieve E of her domestic burdens and give her a respite from her anxiety. They decided to encourage a long period of European travel, which he had expressed enthusiasm for.

[1852–92, "Terrible is Earth"] Retreat—spiritual disgust, grief & despair & revulsion . . . Childish sulk, cowardly, indolent, masochistic. What is the difference between this & a man fighting & dying for a cause? Would not compromise—Died; Gave his life by compromising—Killed by his Conscience. Refuge from the ceaseless struggle—Insanity. . . . What is suicide rate in U.S.

[MS "Half-wilful overruling Morbidness"] One of the most amazing accomplishments ever performed by a human mind was M's struggle and victory on the verge of insanity. Unlike Nietzsche, he simply refused to lose his reason. We can think of it as a sheer act of will—and whatever we mean by insight—it was that quality or capacity that saved him. . . . After a number of exceedingly stormy years, one would wager that surely no human mind could hold out in such a maelstrom—he recovered completely, and in his seventieth year wrote the best short story ["Billy Budd"] of his career.[31]

Melville dug deep and (maybe) found a man inside the maelstrom. Suppression of the Isabel letter would be linked with a Tory assessment of Melville's crazily Jewish, feminized social criticism. Like the mobbish (American) People, Melville was projecting (irreconcilable) inner conflicts onto a world in which, as Parsons argued, internal disputes were really all negotiable without drastic structural transformation. *Pierre's* dark critique and testing of adult authority in Melville's strange family supported the moral passions of the seventeenth-century radical Diggers and Levellers, Milton, Locke, Paine, Jefferson, and Freud; such antics were proscribed by the pieties of organic conservatives, the moderate men. For would-be biographers such as Murray and Olson, the target has been not Melville as such but the revolutionary bourgeoisie that had asserted the rights of individuals (specifically the institutionalization of natural rights in republican constitutions with one set of rules for rich and poor) along with the anti-authoritarian features of scientific method and its concomitant heresy, mass literacy. Shortly after reading Freud's *Moses and Monotheism* in 1939, Charles Olson charged that morality had been secretly transferred from the Heart (the Catholic Church) to the Head (the Freudian Superego, Hebraically intent on peace, truth, and justice at all costs) and given a positive function. American identity, born "in rebellion" was "essentially" "left-wing protestant" and therefore hostile to the "mumbo-jumbo" and "pageantry" that brought unity (however bogus) to Catholic societies.[32] For Murray (as for Max Weber or Olson) freelance examination of the material world without the unifying power of myth (the Spirit or Heart) was a social disaster, flesh without spirit. Indeed, to accept misfortune without a murmur, however undeserved, was a sound social and spiritual investment.

In *White-Jacket, or The World in a Man of War* (1850), Melville had, as usual, upbraided sycophants; he also posited an irreconcilable conflict between common sailors and officers that his own conservative reform, the abolition of flogging, could not ameliorate. Moreover, he stirringly advocated the Old Testament mission of American Chosen People: to bring peaceful, life-renewing republican institutions to the entire world. Presumably such societies would be interconnected only when bound by equitable social relations, gentleness, and mutual respect.[33] It is ironic that Murray, a leader in the upper-class peace organization United World Federalists after World War II, pounced on this (too organic?) image in *White-Jacket* that parallels Tawney's eloquent denunciation of the price paid by common sailors to feed the "cruel carnal glory" of the officers. "Peace to Lord Nelson where he sleeps in his mouldering mast! but rather would I be urned in the trunk of some green tree, and even in death have the vital sap circulating round me, giving of my dead body to the living foliage that shaded my peaceful tomb."[34] Murray fumed, "Typical of the Hebraic ethos was this attempt of Melville's to apply a religious ideal to life." He continued ominously as if assigning himself a mission: The romantic "gospel" had mistaken Christ for a "revolutionist"; the (Wanderingly Jewish) legacy of Luther, Cromwell and the American Revolution was "an eternal denial of the superiority of the upper classes, a rebuke to prestige & the will to power. Melville was merely reiterating this gospel. The difference between him and the officers into whom he fired his cantos was that *they* were fighting for superiority & *he* was fighting for equality, their aggression was spontaneous, his retaliative. The difference was great unless it could be shown that Melville was a frustrated dictator, a tyrant in disguise."

Such worldly applications of the "Hebraic ethos" had drastically shifted the relations of elites and populace. Nervous conservatives in an Age of Revolution saw bourgeois society with its elevation of species-unity and popular sovereignty (later the amplification of the vox populi in critical mass media and other new models) leading inevitably to cascades of severed heads and the tyranny that would follow the failed communist experiment. In Olson's imagery, Enlightenment demystification of charismatic feudal authority "beatriced" him; he felt like Beatrice Cenci, Shelley's ambiguous parricide and alter ego whom Olson linked to Isabel. For prescient conservatives such as Murray and Olson the adaptive, dissembling Burkean strategy was theirs: They would co-opt the terms of science and take the van to unmask Melville as "frustrated dictator, a tyrant in disguise," no different from, no better than, the elites he indignantly criticized from the point of view of the People. Here were upper-class Levellers blaming the materialist opposition (Ahab, democratic America) for absolutism, militarism, fanatical (but hypocritical) moral purity, and hysterical projections. While still employed as a propagandist by the Office of War Information (and having recently written an antifascist essay for *Survey Graphic*), Olson nevertheless expressed sentiments in his notebook (quoted above) that would resound throughout *Call Me Ishmael* and then the New Left. America was a pseudo-democracy intent only on the mechanical conquest of nature; American identity was essentially demonic; American soldiers giving their lives for this masquerade were dupes.

These ideas were partly shared by Murray, for whom the domination of nature referred to surplus sexual repression. Although Murray sometimes viewed Melville's mother, Maria, as too love-starved, weak, and needy, the source of his "Ishmael complex," in her appearance as Ahab's parent, Maria cracks the whip:

[Folder "Objective," MS "Pittsfield 1850–51"] Now the spiritual air of M's America had a bad odor. It was in fact a matriarchal federation bent upon preserving the boundaries of prepubertal act and thought. [He was suffocated.] And so it came about that M by repudiating the doctrines that had styled a century exiled himself .... A proud man, once exiled, makes no compromises at first. He stands firmly in opposition—a true protestant—even though in doing so he becomes the devil's disciple. . . . His central preoccupation was religion. Not, of course in any orthodox sense, for his criticism had utterly annihilated all prevailing creeds and faiths . . . .

[MS with materials relating to 1852–56] Melville was a selfish egoist, overridden by pride, who, because of his particular temperament and circumstances evolved into the only first rate exponent of Demonism that America has ever produced, hardly second to Dante, Milton, and Nietzsche. . . . Destroyed by the family of women who interrupt; the domineering mother expanding her empire . . . Pierre was the last harpoon forged in his maddened soul.[35] What happened to M after the unceremonious condemnation of his autobiography is uncertain. But I believe he was driven a bit beyond human reason. At any rate it is known that 2 children and his wife fled the house, and sought the protection of her parent's roof—But that soon Herman's persuasion eloquence and solicitation brought her back—encouraged by her stepmother who believed that a wife's duty was always by her husband's side . . . .

Throughout his writings, Murray scored the features of a medical emergency: the (bad) disillusion that drowned marital and other forms of social "bliss," thus driving Melville to ambivalence, alcoholism, and excessive reading. Here in "Interchapter 2 [,] Analysis of Mardi and its Author" is his description of black-cloaked, stealthy Queen Hautia ("the Oriental harlot"), a character in *Mardi* and the expansionist precursor to Ahab and Isabel in hostile conservative readings. She is Murray's image of the People: bearer of materialism, the darkening new light of antimyth that organic conservatives necessarily saw as the creature of pride, sharkishly downing big bites: gobbets ripped from the flesh of the owning classes.

Like the sybil-stars or moon, the incognito was a woman of the night, acquainted with the mysteries, revealer of the hidden soul of man, lustful, sinister in her strength. She came as the eruption of the dark side of M's spirit, standing for all that was repressed: sorrow, sexuality, hate, egotism, power, and the death-wish. She opened the way to the unconscious, to the sharkish inner depths of mind. Queen Hautia he would call her: a witch who mocked conventional society, pure reason, innocent naieve [*sic*] idealism. She came as an opponent to his sunlit life of love, and left him caught between the opposites: Yillah and Hautia, day and night, outer and inner, the gay surface and the brooding depths, optimism and pessimism, selfless love and proud retraction, social membership and lonely exploration, heaven and hell, serenity and guilt, purity and lust, good and evil. Like St. Paul and all succeeding Christian puritans, M apperceived this haunting image as a tremendously destructive agent against which he must rally all his forces. At this time what he saw in her was lust, flesh without spirit; so he concentrated his defenses along that front. But being a great deal more than this, she made successive inroads without his knowledge, attaching more and more territory to her dominion. Her first victory was the drowning of the Yillah-vision. . . . M also dimly realized that a deliberate tendency in his personality had a hand in Elizabeth's obliteration. (23, 25)

Murray sees Melville/Hautia as hellishly determined to leave contradictions (ambiguities) hanging in mid-air, at odds: uncoupled, unmarried, unallied. As a promoter of benign cultural pluralism, Murray was allergic to such "ambivalence." Publishing the Isabel letter would have collapsed his structure of myth, possibly replacing it with an accurate family history and righteous indignation. He waffled in his relations with Charles Olson, finally suppressing the Isabel letter, even though he felt the discovery of Allan Melvill's teenage indiscretion was "The Great Trauma" that incapacitated Herman Melville for life.

The dream of a moderating education shapes patterns of censorship throughout the Melville Revival. While withholding a clear-cut statement about Allan Melvill's amours, Murray was forthcoming about extremist autodidacts: "The story told of one Ethan Brand, a former lime burner, who had broodingly watched his furnace for so many years that he became infected by the demonic character of the flames and consequently possessed by the idea of Evil and Satanism in general. What, in fact, was the unpardonable sin he had asked himself? Without previous culture he commenced reading & pursued his quest so assiduously that his reason soon outstripped his heart. . . . In cold blood he could act against mankind without feeling any of its anguish" (MS "Source of Ahab-Ethan Brand"). So what was Melville's pose? Elsewhere, Murray explained that "The unpardonable sin was not hate but frigid insensibility"; he meant that Melville, though victimized by "the brutalities of a gross and vulgar lot of men," thus too disillusioned to believe ("romantic utopianist" that he was by nature) that "the lower classes would make a better of job of governing the State than its present leaders," nevertheless had taken the point of view of the sailors in the anti-officer, antiwar diatribes of *White-Jacket* (1850). Painting White-Jacket as a David fighting Goliath, "a mouthpiece for the Major Prophets," and another "William Lloyd Garrison," Murray fretted, "He had nothing to say about the executive responsibilities, the irritations, the worries, and burdening concerns of his superiors."[36] Murray was echoing Captain Vere speaking to fellow officers in "court" and arguing against clemency for Billy Budd:

"The people" (meaning the ship's company) "have native sense; most of them are familiar with our naval usage and tradition; and how would they take it?

Even could you explain it to them—which our official position forbids—they, long molded by arbitrary discipline, have not that kind of intelligent responsiveness that might qualify them to comprehend and discriminate. No, to the people the foretopman's deed, however it be worded in the announcement, will be plain homicide committed in a flagrant act of mutiny. What penalty for that should follow, they know. But it does not follow. Why? they will ruminate. You know what sailors are. Will they not revert to the recent outbreak at Nore? Ay. They know the well-founded alarm—the panic it struck throughout England. Your clement sentence they would account pusillanimous. They would think that we flinch, that we are afraid of them—of practicing a lawful rigor singularly demanded at this juncture, lest it should provoke new troubles. What shame to us such a conjecture on their part, and how deadly to discipline. You see then, whither, prompted by duty and the law, I steadfastly drive. But I beseech you, my friends, do not take me amiss. I feel as you do for this unfortunate boy. But did he know our hearts, I take him to be of that generous nature that he would feel even for us on whom in this military necessity so heavy a compulsion is laid."

In sum, for Murray disillusion is constructive when the utopian romantic detects the disabilities of the oppressed (which seem to be permanent when autodidacts, hardened and embittered by "arbitrary discipline," are refused the moderating instruction of official culture), but disillusion is misdirected when s/he detects incompetence and hypocrisy in elites—who, the sensible critic will come to understand, are suffering in their own, different, but still awful, not quite lawful, ways. The mature individual (defined against Ethan Brand, like Madison's meritorious man of the *juste milieu* or Austin Warren's New Critic) climbs to the "main top" where he will gain "the most comprehensive & disinterested view of the vessel." Although Melville seems to be razzing environmentalism in chapter 12 of *White-Jacket*, for Murray, the prospect reveals the power of the environment to mold behavior: "To be forever burrowing like a Troglodyte in the bowels of a ship makes a man lumpish and torpid, to be always among the guns makes him cross & quarrelsome." As a competent social psychologist, Murray spots Mad Jack, who has seized the helm; thus, apprised of forms and functions and dangerous personalities amid the combustibles, the neutral observer, if leaning toward the Left, sloughs off perfectionism and "frigid insensibility" to the plight of suffering officers; or, if leaning toward the Right, he resolves to treat the lower orders with greater humanity and consideration through self-control and social engineering: He has found the middle ground.

After noting that "Melville's worst villains are hypocrites who protest their freedom from selfish motives/might over right," Murray, leaning on the reinstated good father, reassured himself that Melville was not the frustrated dictator and Leveller after all, but a moral reformer like himself:

> M was not a radical Locofoco agrarian. He did not want to do away with property; nor did he think perfect equality in this respect was possible. [Referring to Serenia:] "More heart!" This was the sum and substance of his propaganda. In general, he was satisfied with American democracy. He had no specific political reforms to advocate, no social ideas worth elaborating. Laws and systems were less important than fraternity and trust. More heart! . . . Unlike the majority of idealists M entertained no sentimental vision of the virtues of the underdog; & his efforts could receive no encouragement from the thought that a Saturnalian reversal of status would bring more peace, justice, and brotherhood into the order of society. . . . He was speaking for sensitive men like himself, born, or by fate made, under-dogs, as he had been, first by his father's bankruptcy and second by his own desperate impulsion, overwilling the obligatory. . . . M recognized that place and power were necessary for the order of society. Distinctions based on talent, intelligence, taste and heart were given and inevitable. . . . In brief, M was calling for further moral development, or a religious conversion, on the part of the rich and powerful. . . . "Be a good father to your men"; M would hardly be repeating this so often if his own father had not led him to expect it being so kind and affectionate, and if the father had not died at so critical a moment in his son's growth & by losing his fortune thrown the boy upon the stony mercies of Uncle Peter.

So Melville had been abandoned to a bad father (Peter) by the good father (Allan), the type whose exemplary behavior forestalls catastrophic revolts from below: "Possibly if he had not left school at the age of twelve years, had known Hawthorne earlier and was not infuriated beyond reason by the conditions of his life—he might have achieved an invariable excellence" (MS fragment on the crusader). The gap in moderate fathering between Allan Melvill and Hawthorne was the source of Melville's eruptions, his transformation to "the woman—Brunhilde—surrounded by fire." In various fragments, Murray demonstrated the explosive trajectory of religion taken to extremes: Calvinism (mother's religion) was linked to Melville's "untamed wild spirit."[37] "These ideals of his youth were to triumph unwittingly, drive him to fury and then misanthropy. / wilful morbidness."

What did the sable Isabel-singed Melville himself have to say about the ideals of his youth? Here is White-Jacket's opinion of the flunky and the courtier, poured into his portrait of "Landless," the eternal child who dances under the lash:

This Landless was a favorite with the officers, among whom he went by the name of *"Happy Jack."* And it is just such Happy Jacks as Landless that most sea-officers profess to admire; a fellow without shame, without a soul, so dead to the least dignity of manhood that he could hardly be called a man. Whereas, a seaman who exhibits traits of moral sensitiveness, whose demeanour shows some dignity within; this is the man they, in many cases, instinctively dislike. The reason is, they feel such a man to be a continual reproach to them, as being mentally superior to their power. He has no business in a man-of-war; they do not want such men. To them there is an insolence in his manly freedom, contempt in his very carriage. He is unendurable, as an erect, lofty-minded African would be to some slave-driving planter.

Landless is antitype to the naturally aristocratic Handsome Sailor described near the beginning of "Billy Budd":

In Liverpool . . . I saw under the shadow of the great dingy street-wall of Prince's Dock . . . a common sailor so intensely black that he must needs have been a native African of the unadulterate blood of Ham—a symmetric figure much above the average height. The two ends of a gay silk handkerchief thrown loose about the neck danced upon the displayed ebony of his chest, in his ears were hoops of gold, and a Highland bonnet with a tartan band set off his shapely head. It was a hot noon in July; and his face, lustrous with perspiration, beamed with barbaric good humor. In jovial sallies right and left, his white teeth flashing into view, he rollicked along, the center of a company of his shipmates. These were made up of such an assortment of tribes and complexions as would well have fitted them to be marched up by Anacharsis Clootz before the bar of the first French Assembly as Representatives of the Human Race. At each spontaneous tribute rendered by the wayfarers to this black pagod of a fellow—the tribute of a pause and stare, and less frequently an exclamation—the motley retinue showed that they took that sort of pride in the evoker of it which the Assyrian priests doubtless showed for their grand sculptured Bull when the faithful prostrated themselves.

To return. If in some cases a bit of a nautical Murat [*sic*] in setting forth his person ashore, the Handsome Sailor of the period in question evinced nothing of the dandified Billy-be-Dam, an amusing character all but extinct now, but occasionally to be encountered, and in a form more amusing than the original, at the tiller of the boats on the tempestuous Erie Canal or, more likely, vaporing in the groggeries along the towpath. Invariably a proficient in his perilous calling, he was also more or less a mighty boxer of wrestler. It was strength and beauty. Tales of his prowess were recited. Ashore he was the champion; afloat the spokesman; on every suitable occasion always foremost. Close-reefing topsails in a gale, there he was, astride the weather yardarm end, foot in the Flemish horse as stirrup, both hands tugging at the earing as at a bridle, in very much the attitude of young Alexander curbing the fiery Bucephalus. A superb figure, tossed up as by the horns of Taurus against the thunderous sky, cheerily halloing to the strenuous file along the spar.

The moral nature was seldom out of keeping with the physical make. Indeed, except as toned by the former, the comeliness and power, always attractive in masculine conjunction, hardly could have drawn the sort of honest homage than the Handsome Sailor in some examples received from his less gifted associates.

Such a cynosure, at least in aspect, and something such too in nature, though with important variations made apparent as the story proceeds, was welkin-eyed Billy Budd—or Baby Budd, as more familiarly, under circumstances hereafter to be given, he at last came to be called. . . .

"Ashore he was the champion . . . ." Melville commenced his construction of "Billy Budd" during post–Civil War labor insurgency, great strikes, and the invalidation by the Supreme Court of the Civil Rights Act of 1875 (initiated by Charles Sumner and directed against social segregation and discrimination) in 1883— yet another blow to Reconstruction, since "it endorsed the position of the segregationists that the Fourteenth Amendment had not given Congress jurisdiction over the social relationships of the two races."[38] On August 25, 1886, the Coast Seamen's Union, after 1885 open to "colored" seamen, "called the first coast-wide maritime strike, in all ports from Puget Sound to San Diego."[39] The clarity of Melville's moral distinctions among Landless, the Handsome Sailor, and the importantly variant Baby Budd should have put conservative Melville scholars on notice, but perhaps not. Apparently, officers and common sailors have different favorites, different notions of how the Handsome Sailor should look. Unlike the "superb figure" of the first Handsome Sailor "astride . . . the weather yardarm end," Billy will hang from "the yard-end, . . . no motion . . . apparent." Pity the boy who would be (heroic) Man, still connected to hypermoral mother as he anxiously contemplates the historical record of heroic resistance and craven capitulation and the uneven enforcement of the right to free speech. Does he not remind us of something in ourselves as independent and original artists and intellectuals? How far may we go in our critique of authority, for the boundaries are indistinct and the rules seem ever to be changing and contradictory? Theoretically, there should be no opprobrium attached to close readings of social reality: Democratic capitalist society is contractual, its authority derived from the consent of the governed; its rulers are representatives, not absolutist gods or kings; their governance must be legitimated through social processes free from censorship. Cultural and political freedom is the linchpin of America's claim to superiority over "socialist" societies plagued by every kind of commissar; in times of mobilization for war against the tyrannical enemy, our priceless and bejeweled First Amendment is strenuously advertised by propagandists demanding the sacrifice of pacifist-minded young men and women.[40]

Why, then, do modern artists so frequently portray themselves as Cains, Wandering Jews, and Pierrots? Wherefore the brand, the mask, the tension between defiance and remorse, the odor of murder and self-murder these scapegraces exude? Why are images of phallic women both irresistible and intolerable to Melville, Weaver, Murray, and the rest? Why do they vacillate between revolt and restoration, symbolized by these legs and masks that must come off and that may not come off? Why do both their independence and dependency kill the mother and drive all parties to insanity and social dissolution? What do they have to hide in societies (that are said) to tenderly nurture their intellectuals and that are strengthened through criticism? Could it be that our socializing institutions partake more of Filmerean patriarchy than of Lockean voluntarism and its threat of permanent revolution? Could it be that social stability and conformity rather than the advertised merit, accuracy, and innovation are standards more often applied by the doorkeepers of our cultural institutions to would-be applicants? Could it be that socially responsible mothers so conscientiously detoxify their children of critical impulses and imaginings that self-censorship is automatic? And that Melville's art, to his everlasting credit, strips such domination bare and forces us to confront the piteous wreck of our self-serving rationalizations as good parents and dutiful children, here exposed as wreaking the most terrible violence to the autonomous individual in supposedly peaceful and nurturant domestic sanctuaries? Could it be that Melville's supposed failure, nonresistance, and dropping out are all too resonant with the fate of the tongue-tied American intelligentsia in established institutions, so that academic Melville critics are both peddling and hoarding a compensatory dream image of themselves as they wish they were: deep diving, bold, outspoken, and controversial (however doomed); manly in the face of an encroaching, clutching, feminized, consumerist, tyrannical mass urban society—where they and their rural chimneys, rooted and erect (and securely masked) will never surrender? Could it be that, like Melville, these suffering but stoical inmates dream of a lovely family? "There are some vessels blessed with patriarchal, intellectual captains, gentlemanly and brotherly officers, and docile and Christianized crews. The peculiar usages of such vessels insensibly soften the tyrannical rigor of the Articles of War; in them, scourging is unknown. To sail in such ships is hardly to realise that you live under the martial law, or that the evils above mentioned can anywhere exist."[41]

And yet Murray was fascinated by the fiery androgynous radical; for Murray, Melville's Hebraic/Promethean condition was the sublimity that both repels and attracts:

[MS "Melanophilia"] One knows that organic or social revolutions are always propagated by anti-organic people—people that are either separate from inadequacy or separate from superiority, i.e., idealism, dissatisfaction with the surrounding mediocrity—or both.

[Folder "Art"] M was a hot coal, he was pregnant, his words were loaded—It takes years, sometimes generations for the professors to touch him . . . .

[A two-page MS] Doom-Eager men . . . The woman—Brunhilde—surounded by fire. Why? because as a child—spiritual—refusing to partake in the commonplace life about her—naievely—unquestioningly—she stands apart—energy goes to her intellect. This becomes analytic & critical & separates her. This is part of or at least abets the fire.

[MS chapter "Annus Mirabilus"] In the execution of his purpose Ahab's first task was to unify his men, such as Melville's task was to unify the discordant personalities within himself. . . . Through sheer hypnotic power, Ahab charged the crew with "the same fiery emotion accumulated within the Leyden jar of his own magnetic life"; and all of them, shouting "a sharp lance for Moby-Dick!" were deliriously converted to his monomaniac revenge, all except the first mate, Starbuck, a Nantucket Quaker . . . [who was] a breadwinner whose habits, in conformance with the duties of his vocation, were efficiently directed toward substantial goals. There was no nonsense about him. Accepting conditions as he found them, he was content to fit into his proper place, advancing in his calling by the appointed steps. He assumed responsibility for his actions, judiciously allowing each need, none of which were at all exceptional, its fair and prudent satisfaction. Thus, Starbuck, as a symbol, might have stood for *reason* adapted to established forms, for conscious circumspect control, for down-right sanity . . . for Melville's ego. Opposed to him was Ahab, whose entire being was subservient to one autocratic motive. This motive was not dictated by the entrenched interests of society, the mercenary aims of the ship-owners whom he served; it was a private passion which behind the bolted bars of reason had grown to colossal strength, and was now screaming for discharge. Ahab was gnawed within by the "unrelenting fangs" of an incurable idea, overpowered by an orgiastic tide of hate that demanded free expression. He was possessed by the spirit of Satanic rage. (88–89)

Melville's strength increased by leaps and bounds as soon as reason became subservient to his ~~aristocratic~~ overpowering aim. Emotion did his work for him: no conscious effort of the will was required to get him started or keep him going. Truly could he have said with Ahab, "My malady becomes my most desired health." And in changing from agent to instrument the efficiency of his intellect had not been diminished by one jot. It had merely been concentrated upon *one mark*. . . . (91–92)

Starbuck, though powerless to oppose the supernal force of Ahab's will, still retained some power of detachment. . . . Likewise Melville, though identified generally with his hero, was able to stand off, analyze with consummate skill the origin of the man's obsession, and perceive the inevitable disaster. As artist, he was now almost always in control of his material. He could participate exultingly but he could also act the calculating puppeteer. Above the turmoil he could look down and laugh at "self-consuming" misanthropes like himself and warn others against indulging in infernal dreams. . . . The author refused to come out publicly on Ahab's side. On the contrary, the captain was repeatedly proclaimed a lunatic, his own worst enemy. . . . Nor did the author fail to name the focus of Ahab's sickness, the cancerous growth that distorted his philosophy: "In his fiery eyes of scorn and triumph, you then saw Ahab in all his fatal pride." (94–95)

[MS "To keep #3," unmarked folder with manuscript on Melville's childhood] [The crusader] . . . when he was older this vision would lead him to all manner of impassioned moral poses. He would see the dragon everywhere, wickedness in the cities, corruption in high places. And avowedly he would be on the side of Conscience. But in the hot aching very centre of his being the Demi-urge would wake and realize its chains and snort its malice.

—M had soul but not talent of a poet

—MD is a Mt Everest—must go into training—makes the greatest demands on him.—One cannot expect to read Paradise Lost with a hangover—Moby Dick the book and M the man quickens me, ignites me, lifts me, ferments me. Just as Ahab brought the Pequod's crew under his will. . . . Such a book justifies a life, a period, a civilization . . . .

Is Murray not admitting that (moderated) Madisonian pluralism with its incoherent interest-group politics and ethical relativism doesn't work, producing only "discordant personalities" and Starbuck's mediocrity? As the model integrated personality, Murray was in trouble; so he drags himself into the double bind: Melville had yielded to Ahab's monomania, thus energizing the creation of a great book in that blast of satanic rage, and yet he was also standing apart, in control of his material. The proudly autonomous moderate conservative (Melville/Murray) had succumbed to/resisted the mesmerizing conscience of radical Enlightenment. The pyromaniac, puppeteer, and fake had justified "a life, a period, a civilization." But his well-known essay "In Nomine Diaboli" did not depart from the postwar consensus; Murray did, however, link Ahab to Milton's Satan, prompting a declaration of sexual love and androgyny from Charles Olson, along with the sheltered query "(((((a 1000 questionings of the Pradise Lost gig: please write me what evidence there is for this)))))."[42]

Murray first wrote to Olson after their first meeting in June, 1934.[43] His letter suggests that Murray assumed *Pierre* was taken from Melville's life. The letter also confirmed a division of labor in their Melville biographies; however, each would try to get the other to publish the Isabel letter. It will be seen that Olson understood Murray's 1949 identification of Isabel with Melville's cousin Priscilla was "the biz," a refusal of Ahab's throb. In the sequence of Ahab-ishly intense letters to a relatively placid Olson that follows, Murray expresses the longing to connect with a passionate artist (the dark swirling bloody pool), but flees; then, quite right, devalues his own etiolated production.

[Murray to Olson, November 16, 1938:] Your article ["Lear and *Moby-Dick*"] has just the right feel. I started this PM & found almost immediately that it was too near my own conception to be good reading for me *now*. I opened here and there & was swept into that dark swirling bloody pool again & I knew your heart was in it & beating strongly. I did not read enough to get your chief point: nothing beyond the influence of Lear, Shakespeare as catalyst, & the ambiguities & evil mixed with food [*sic*]—but I feel sure you are right. I cannot read your Chapter until I have written mine—which won't be until June.

I have been blocked this Fall & my H.M is only just now rounding the Horn—homeward bound. Congratulations old fellow you've got your fingers on the pulse.

[Murray to Olson, 1945?] . . . I intend to return to Melville eventually—perhaps next summer. Naturally, I am keen to see everything you have collected as soon as you are through with it. What are you writing—a 5 vol biography? a long epic? or a long short story? I am eager to see you. . . .

[Murray to Olson, October 1, 1945] I have no doubt at all that the Daemon took hold of your hand & wrote your book. That's the way old Ahab would have liked it. Its not only a book about him but it is written by one possessed of his spirit. Its an identification—[Diagram: triangulated Shakespeare, Melville, Olson] . . . I can spell everything out from 1819 to 1852 in 2 volumes—with your help, with your generous heritage from the Mass. Historical Society & and other aids you are giving me. Your book when published will illuminate the abyss for me & then I shall proceed to wind it up as swiftly as possible with everlasting gratefulness to you . . . keep me in touch in you [*sic*].

[Murray to Olson, July 18, 1946:] O great Charles, Our last rich evening gave me a strong appetite for more of the same thing . . . I am going to get going on the *Pierre* preface very soon & would like to know 1. when your book is to exude from the press—it will be a very intoxicating beverage—& 2. whether you are doing anything else on H.M now, & 3. whether you have published your letter (Thos M Jr to Justice Shaw about Mrs. A.M.A. & Mrs. B). I should like to refer to your article in my preface when I take up the question of Allan's premarital adventures . . . Hope you are thriving. I am, *except* that I haven't finished, if you can believe it, putting together the bones of that monstrous skeleton—Assessment of Men.

[Olson to Murray, July 28, 1946:] My dear Harry Murray . . . It is wonderful news you are in to the *Pierre* preface. You will save [Howard] Vincent's whole series. I await it most eagerly, am hungry to read it, knowing as I do how total is your possession of it. It is going to be an EVENT . . . Now as to Mrs. AMA & Mrs. B. I refer to the letter in a footnote in the book itself, in the CHRIST section, and quote it. I do not discuss it, or weigh it, or examine it in relation to the text of *Pierre.* Such a discussion would be out of place. What's more I feel that you are the man who can give the letter its real setting and interpretation. And I hope you will do just that. The next time I am in town (the 15th of August) I shall make you a true copy. And please feel free to use it whenever and wherever you choose. For I would prefer you to have it than to make any use of it myself other than the reference to it in the footnote mentioned above. It is most properly yours, finding its place in the sequence of your investigations and your perceptions. When I send you the copy I shall also enclose the evidence I have as to its date and its location in the T.M.-Shaw correspondence.

[Murray to Olson, July 28, 1946 (*sic*)] I am looking forward to the appearance of your book with the keenest appetite. I shall take it in a corner, & smack my lips over it, & chew the cud, & inwardly digest it, & brood upon its magnificently uttered truth. You read me enough of it to assure me that this experience is in store for me.

I have hugely enjoyed the days devoted to *Pierre*, which I set down in my calendar as holidays from the devastating labor of Assessment of Men. One fatal mistake that H.M made was to hug his grief, under the assumption that grief, which had once been the chief source of his creativeness—was wiser than joy. One of the hundred forms in which I view him is that of a pitiful victim of Christianity—in *Pierre* he thrusts the spear into the side of his crucified self . . . .[44]

[Murray to Olson, August 1946?] . . . I am disappointed to hear that your book—which palpitates to the beat of Melville's own heart—is not coming off the press until 1947. I will not be able to refer to it in this Preface, but I shall feast on it for Vol. II of the biography.

Also I will not have room for the AMA & B letter in the Preface, because if I put it in I would have to include the 5 or 6 other bits of evidence I have—which would mean devoting three or four pages to a topic which is interesting from a biographical standpoint, but not essential to an understanding of *Pierre*. Do you agree?

[Murray to Olson, December 7, 1946] . . . By the way, the Pittsfield Library is going to be completely rebuilt & I am presenting them with a Melville Memorial Room with books, documents, portraits &c. If you hear of anything appropriate let me know. I saw the Chair Portrait of A.M. the other day. It is much better than the Weaver reproduction of it—both from an artistic point of view & as a representation of a fairly personable human being . . . .

[Olson to Murray, January 19, 1947] My dear Harry, It occurred to me you might like to have a copy of the letter concerning Mrs. A.M.A. and Mrs B. I imagine you know Peter Gansevoort's letter about Allan Sr's last illness, but there is a chance the record of his death by PG might be of use. I'm enclosing both anyway. . . . [Allan's insanity (by itself) was not the exciting issue, *C.S.*]

[Olson to Murray, May 12, 1947] I dare say you are in the midst of Pierre. How goes it? Is it possible you will unravel the father, and in this place put down the Isabel story as it shapes up in reality? I should so much like to see you do that—for then it will be really done . . . .

[Murray to Olson, 1947, water-damaged document] Dear Prodigal and Prodigious Charles, My nature has been the [source?] of intolerable annoyance to me . . . [In slowly] building the *Pierre* shanty [it] would not allow me the privilege of such relishable occupations as *really* reading *Call Me Ishmael* . . . lest it would influence me too greatly in doing *Pierre* . . . [which] should break wind about April (don't touch it for fear of vomiting and diarrhoea. . . . [You are not] conveying objectively definable meaning, but rather the tempo & temper, the primitive desperation and fury, the [illegible] spatial longing of the man. You were talking out of your entrails after you had got in harmony with H.M's . . . . Your book is as mythological & cannibalistic as H.M's own shadow self . . . . [Murray linked Isabel to both anima and shadow. *C.S.*]

Olson's footnote was not published, nor have I found correspondence with Reynal and Hitchcock indicating that it ever entered the text of *Call Me Ishmael*. There does exist an incomplete draft footnote intended to follow the "lampish incest" with Isabel (*Call Me Ishmael*, 95):

*The "shames" of the father were: (1) he "failed" in business; (2) the cause of his death shortly thereafter seems to have been lost in whispers though my evidence indicates it was pneumonia;[45] and (3) there are suggestions he had children outside his marriage. All three left their mark on M's work. *Redburn* is a study of a young man's disillusion, and involves his father; the subtitle is *Redburn, or, The Son of a Gentleman.* But it is [in] *Pierre* that the ambiguities of a father are unralleved [*sic*] in the acts of the son. It's plot is the problem of .[*sic*] The source of the plot is the existence of ~~a daughter~~ an illegitimate sister. The question remains, is Melville here using a Jacobean device to disguise attention to a legitimate sister, or is he working on hidden family facts of an actual illegitimate sister. I cannot answer, nor am I particularly interested; because I do not find *Pierre* created enough to hold my attention. But I should here include a letter from the papers of Lemuel Shaw which may have a bearing on the question. It is from M's father's brother, Thomas Melville, to Shaw, who was long before M married his daughter, the family's attorney and confidant. It is without date, but is probably of the year 1838. It concerns a Mrs Ama and a Mrs B.[46]

Ambiguities of evil mixed with food

Perhaps Murray only glanced at history to pass his test for screening reliable oss operatives, by transforming himself into the rakish Allan Melvill, a certified confidence man, unmarred by either anger or dependency, therefore "a fairly personable human being." For the 1920s Melvilleans, it was not Melville but his nativist radical revivers who were (self-) promoted as William Blake's Ancient Bards, identifying and isolating the source of evil to restore unity: Melville is the Bard's antagonist and target; he is the Romantic Wandering Jew/Promethean whose materialist science has incited the mob to unprecedented acts of destructiveness, whose searching, analytic intelligence relentlessly historicizes and interrogates all authority, indefinitely. Commentators may have seized upon the archetype Melville recognized in himself: "Am *I* the Jew?" the heaven-born but hunchbacked, Christ-rejecting and family-spurning Celio asks in Melville's *Clarel* (1876). Having spoken truth to power, Celio's ruin is complete; he dies, reddened by Jewish soil and suffocated by fever. For Melville (the Bard who strangled Celio), modernity is a wasteland made barren by Jewish science; Mammon a representation of the New Birth that has weedily choked off flowering personality, marring the gentle gothic spirit. Such a victim was Harvard professor William Ellery Sedgwick, whose posthumous Melville study, *The Tragedy of Mind*, was published in 1944; at least Murray thought so. I offer my own diagnosis of Murray's famous headache.

[Murray to his editor, Howard Vincent, September 17, 1947] I met Mrs. Sedgwick a few days ago & she told me that *Pierre killed* her husband—that he left that chapter to the last & rewrote 100 times, & left it unfinished, & then began drinking and died of pneumonia after exposure. This is not hard for me to understand.

[Vincent reassures Murray, September 29, 1947] Instead of *Pierre*'s killing you, you have pinned its shoulders to the mat.

[Murray to Olson, October 1948] Dear Charlie, . . . Just to pile up my own small list of light woes, I will confess to having a peculiar and constant headache (for a year) which has prevented my doing any writing. (I was planning on this year to write Melville i.e., finish it). Perhaps the Jay Leyda–Morewood incident had something to do with it. Anyhow I have been more or less helpless & futile for 12 months—since the *Pierre* job (which is coming out in December). . . .[47]

The ideal oss operative assumes a false identity that will never crack, even under torture, nor will he decamp to the enemy. While completing the monstrous *Assessment of Men*, Murray was also wrestling with *Pierre*. At some point during the initially pleasant composition, Murray (the Nietzschean beyond good and evil), writing about Pierre (the moral idealist who refused to crack or assume a false identity), was pinned to the mat. Murray had once admired *Pierre* as Melville's second greatest achievement. "Although I think M rather a one man book [*sic*], *Pierre* is a close second in my estimate and *Mardi,* a rather casual third. *Pierre* is an amazing introspective psychological novel in the modern spirit—but very far from the modern style—the writing is difficult and unequal. Sometimes flawed and elaborate and gnarled—at other times it attains its former lucidity. Or is [it] the amazing interior penetration of this artificial seeming book which gives it its interest."[48]

Moreover, in a discarded draft of the introduction, Murray had given the greatest possible weight to the effect of Allan Melvill's "sin" upon the psyche of his son:

> The bolt of intelligence which in Pierre produced a wound "never to be completely healed but in heaven" is one and the same as the blight which in Redburn's young soul left such a scar "that the air of Paradise might not erase it" and also one and the same as the lightning which struck Ahab so burningly that "to this hour I bear the scar." Furthermore, just as the down-darting lightning left Ahab's body forever divided by a lividly whitish brand, so did the discovery of his father's sin produce a lasting division in Pierre's heart, a radical and protracted moral conflict which resulted, on the intellectual level, in an obdurate dualism.[49]

But in his published introduction (1949), Murray altered his diagnosis, returning to an earlier impression that Melville was insane (or Ahab) while writing the book. Was this gesture an overheated medical warning to himself, a description of the consequences following his own delegitimating perceptions of "good fathers" (that would make him flunk his test), or simply an allurement to readers with decadent tastes? "*Pierre* is a literary monster, a prodigious by-blow of genius whose appearance is marred by a variety of freakish features and whose organic worth is invalidated by the sickness of despair. It is a compound of incongruities and inconsistencies that is shocking to a nicely integrated intellect. Most readers instinctively protect their health from it by judicious revulsions or by unconsciously holding their minds back from the comprehension of its most devastating matter" (xciii). Murray explained that *Pierre* is a factitious whine of "narcism," spoiled by a writer who was exhausted and neurotically vindictive; and yet, "It is probable that most of the interpersonal relationships in *Pierre* represent basic realities and that several of the more crucial events are founded on actual occurrences, but that everything is fictitious as literally recounted. It should be understood that we are concerned with an artist of exceeding imagination and that *Pierre* is at no point a transcription of fact; everything has been completely recast by Melville's shaping will" (xxii).

Perhaps Murray was torn between loyalty to his class and his obligation to science and medicine in taking a complete family history of his subject. He suppressed the Isabel letter but punished himself as Melville/Pierre, magnifying the willfulness, deliberateness, and therefore the opprobrium attached to Melville's monstrous birth, whose wails against hypocrisy might seem too relevant to the present. Typically, he explained that he would not give a "lengthy or deep or technical analysis" of the book's "problems," but listed some questionable aspects of Melville's "personality," including "the author's interest in unique and immense sins—the Unpardonable Sin" and "the writing of *Pierre* as an act of spiritual parricide and matricide." Then he explained the origin of "the maledictory (extrapunitive) current" of this novel as an emanation of Isabel.

> The hateful dispositions for which the hero blames and damns the once-beloved objects of his environment are precisely those which have been hitherto repressed with most difficulty in himself. Everything he condemns in the external world are projections of his shadow self [Isabel, *C.S.*]. This is proved, in due course, by his own actions: Pierre's incestuous inclinations are more sinful than his father's amorousness. . . . Thus Pierre's vision of the world shows less correspondence to the world of *his* day than it does to the contents of his unconscious, or, let me add, to the world of *our* day. (xcii–xciii)

Technically, Murray did not erase the possible existence of an illegitimate half-sister, he merely buried it. Writing of Melville's interest in "the discovery of unsuspected evil in the revered object" (the theme of *Hamlet* and *Othello*), Murray had quietly remarked, "That Melville was confronted by an equivalent situation in his own life is a conclusion that seems warranted by the available evidence; but this is not the place to marshall it" (xlvi).

Murray's analysis of *Pierre*'s radical democratic experiment broke no new ground in Melville criticism. His bohemian repudiation of the Victorian straitjacket resembled Weaver's and Mumford's of the 1920s: The excessive instinctual repression associated with female puritanism and rationalism (not feudalism) would generate catastrophic revolts such as the French Revolution. Ignoring the most charged and emotionally revealing passages, Murray stressed a congeries of liter-ary sources (the German romantics, Godwin, Byron, Disraeli), not family interactions and double binds; e.g., he admitted that he would not follow "the tortuous course" through which Pierre arrived at his decision to run away with Isabel (lviii). Nor did Murray linger at the ending (Pierre is glad he did not sell out but seeks death anyway); Murray simply claimed, "Pierre, in all truth, is deficient in heroic substance. Unlike Ahab, he does *not* make a heroic wreck" (cii). Why this unseemly haste? Murray's friend, psychologist Edwin Shneidman, has told me that it was precisely Ahab's ruthlessness in resisting the plea to join the *Rachel* in the search for the lost child that attracted both Murray and his mistress, Christiana Morgan;

perhaps it was Pierre's ruthlessness in sacrificing the esteem of his relatives for artistic and moral integrity, imagined as the tender-hearted Christian rescue of an orphan, that really tormented the physician and healer Murray.

Melville's first biographer, Raymond Weaver (1921), while dryly noting Melville's "Miltonic self-esteem," had constantly praised *Pierre* as a prophetic and subtle exploration of the unconscious determinants of behavior and an indictment of social hypocrisy, "a spiritual biography" plainly grounded in the author's life ("the anatomy of his despair").[50] Pierre was grappling with real (but for Weaver) insoluble conflicts in the world. In contrast, Murray denounced Pierre's childish, unmotivated, and vengeful attack on his family as a symptom of "narcism" (xx, xxiv, xxx–xxxi, xcii, and passim): Pierre was escaping his "ambivalence," unlike the sensible pragmatist and relativist Reverend Falsgrave (lviii). Pierre was psychotically positing irreconcilable differences (xvii, lxix); his uncompromising, immoderate rejection of conventional values made him "a spoiled brat" (lxiii) disconnected from real social relations (xv, xvii, xxx, xcii–xciii, xcvi–xcvii). Murray identified Melville (in the role of Pierre) as a monomaniac, a masochist, a protofascist, and an arrogant democrat (xxxi, xcv, lxi, lxxvi). Though Weaver and Murray differed sharply in their estimates of Pierre's mental acuity, Murray reproduced Weaver's judgment that Melville had been mastered by "dreams" by which Weaver meant Victorian culture as "the Face": mother/Isabel. For Murray this was a representation of the Jungian "tragic anima," the source of art and innovation, but also a "tragic shadow" likened to "a brain tumor" or a revolution/tocsin (xliv) ringing only homosexuality, regression, and inwardness (xci–xcii, l–lvii, lxiv).[51]

Murray's edition of *Pierre* appeared in 1949. Olson understood that Murray was preparing two volumes of a projected four-volume Melville biography for William Sloan Associates (publishers of the Freudian Melville study by Newton Arvin in 1950). That year Olson contemplated airing the Isabel material in a Melville project proposed by James Laughlin of New Directions on June 3, 1949, but withdrawn on June 13 for lack of funds. It was to be a collage of pictures and documents (compare with Leyda's *Log,* which Laughlin had turned down in 1945). Olson visualized the project as "the sex life of mr melville" and included Leyda's find (as of 1949, unpublished) of "the birth certificate of HM's 1st child with his mother's name where his wife's should be" and his own discovery, "sister—the Mass Hist Soc letter I found on his illegitimate sister ('Isabel')."[52]

Jay Leyda meets Isabel

An Olson letter indicates that Leyda, too, was in possession of a copy of the Isabel letter he knew he could not publish.[53] Olson had just read Leyda's montage of Melville documents (then entitled "Specimens") and asked to keep the carbon copy. The following excerpt from Olson's letter of July 7, 1946 (in answer to Leyda's of March 23 asking, "By the way, did you enjoy anything you found in it? or was all the material so well-known to you that the montage held no surprises for you?") suggests that Leyda knew he had a bombshell. Olson wrote:

> I do hope you will keep in touch with me. Please, if there is anything I can offer you, as your work progresses, call on me. In any case, let me hear of it, for, as I told you, I believe very much in your idea. You ask if there were any surprises in it: the surprise and pleasure was the astounding completeness. I gasped at some of the things you had. When I saw the letter from the Shaw Collection, the only copies of which I thought to be in my own file, I said to myself: This man Leyda is in the charmed circle! Harry Murray and I got in the habit of thinking we had the jump, but I told Harry when I saw him this spring, that you had to be included. Your work is a pleasure. So much that the locusts of the universities are doing makes Melville more inaccessible. He is a man who should be handled only by men who do the scholarship not for coups or power but as your man Eisenstein acquires facts, to illumine via reality. I deeply respect you in this respect. . . .

Leyda responded on August 20 with a double message: on the one hand, proclaiming his duty to tell the whole truth; on the other, complaining that he had been excluded from the charmed circle. Olson and Murray (he adds Jack Birss, compiler of a "secret booklet"[54]) will have to exert themselves if they want his company: "Thank you very much for your praise of my intentions—but you must be warned that I am depending a great deal on you for their realization. There is so much that my non-academic hands can't touch, and so many Melville scholars who won't trust me to respect their multiple priorities, special fields and mangers! I don't want to hurt anybody, but it is my duty to see everything. How? If I'm too dumb to select the *right* things from the *everything*—that's another question. I am in no 'charmed circle' unless you and Murray and Birss drag me in."[55]

How did Leyda, living in Hollywood, get that letter? According to his papers at UCLA, he did not commence archival research in the east until late 1946. (He may have told Olson he had started work in 1939, while Elena Pinto Simon and David Stirk wrote in 1988 that he had moved to Boston in 1944 to work on Melville.[56]) Moreover, control of the Shaw archives was a sensitive matter. Olson was angry that other scholars had been given access to materials that Mrs. Metcalf's father had given to the Massachusetts Historical Society, the mother lode that was to appear in his pending publication funded by a Guggenheim Fellowship.[57] In a letter to Leyda dated June 3, 1950, Olson mentioned "the fracas I got into with the Curator (since dead) in 1945, over rights to [the Shaw] material, which I dug out in the spring of 1934." Olson did not tell Leyda how or when he and Harry Murray got the "jump" on the other scholars, but Leyda would have to see that Murray was, at best, vague and evasive in his introduction to *Pierre*. Note that only Olson and Murray mentioned the Isabel letter explicitly. In his letters to Leyda, Olson coyly evaded the exact content of the prized document. It is, of course, unlikely that the eagle-eyed Leyda would have missed the Isabel letter in his research, nor allowed such a spicy item to go uninvestigated—if he had control of the situation. As he exasperatedly wrote to Charles Olson, June 9, 1950, while proofreading the *Log:*

> Thanks for that heroic eleventh hour reinforcement. You're quite right to assume that [I']ll go on cramming *everything* possible into the Log until page-proofs bring the bars down (I have half the galleys now). Here are replies & further queries on your welcome contributions: . . .
>
> 6) Did a job on the Shaw papers—much for the Log—but I can't tell whether I have your pet or not as long as you don't care to identify it. I have those you list. You know that I'm not fond of "rights" questions—& that I regard nothing I've found as "mine." There are already too many people sitting on too much material of value to all people—with some mistaken idea of "rights." I again offer you the galleys . . . but don't irritate me with talk of "rights."[58]

Olson knew that Leyda had seen the Isabel letter, however, and was astonished by its absence from the *Log*, as he told Murray shortly after publication in late 1951, still hoping that Murray could be convinced to solve the Melville problem:

> [Olson to Murray, January 16, 1952] My dear good Harry: . . . You really wowed me on asking where I ever printed the Mrs AmA Mrs B biz. For I think if you look in your file, you will find all my copies there, that is, my copies of the mss in the MHS. My memory is, that, at the time I was writing ISH, it did seem to me that material so joined yr own peculiar and intense interest in PIERRE, that I sent it all to you for your use alone. That would have been Spring, 1946, I'd guess—in case you can check. And if you can't put your finger on my letter to you (with enclosures I *think*), then I can ask Moore to check in my trunk of Melville stuff in Washington to see if by any chance I kept the originals, and sent you typed copies—that is, (again), the original copies of the letter at the MHS
>
> ((what struck me, by the way, as astonishing, was, that
> i did not notice, in dipping into Leyda, that he had
> used that letter: how come? have you any idea about that?

in any case, i am delighted that you are now ready to investigate that whole question, and am most eager to hear back from you if you find what i say I sent you—and please, if it doesn't turn up, let me know right back, and I'll move myself & Moore (hardly heaven or earth!) to get it all to you

boy, is that something, that, you will unravel this mystery!

o Harry please, on this, keep me abreast of your work. and all developments—for this ought to be a real bombshell: wow . . . .

Wish we could see you—(you never did answer me, whether you'd come down here and lecture to these crittters [*sic*]—on HM as a compost of all our problems, or on anything which your mind is full of at the moment: it wld be tremendous for them. Please say, God,—why not come and unravel the mystery of Mrs AMA, Mrs B! For I have always thot yr hunch abt one of those cousins up there at Broadhall as the identifiable Isabel is the biz . . . .

Although he had once referred to Murray as "my other HM," Olson was naive in thinking that Murray would "unravel the mystery." He had given consistent signals that he could not bear fully to enter either Melville's or Olson's psyches, as the letters of November 16, 1938 and 1947, suggest.

After Amy Puett's 1970 dissertation reproduced the Isabel letter, Murray prepared to air The Great Trauma (an event that was not consummated until 1985, and this after numerous discarded variant accounts of his interactions with Olson in obtaining the evidence).[59] In an unpublished manuscript dated February 6, 1974, Murray reiterated his view that Herman/Pierre was a prude. "Maybe we don't need to know any more details about Allan's errant libido. What needs to be explained is the intensity of H's explosion of horror, righteous indignation, and utter condemnation of his father on hearing of a love affair that occurred (before his marriage) 30 years ago. The father's behavior is par for the average man's life, his son's behavior is pathologically puritannical [*sic*]."[60] Of course, Melville as Pierre, *l'homme sensual,* was not objecting to premarital sex, but to his father's facade of perfect rectitude while heartlessly abandoning his natural child. Indeed, the Isabel letter suggests that Melville's uncle, Thomas Melvill, Jr., was sensitive to this issue when he commented to Lemuel Shaw, "From the little I saw of her, I thought her quite an interesting young person, and that it was most unfortunate that she had not been brought up different—and most deeply regret that she too, has been called to feel the disappointments & sorrows, so generally attending our earthly sojourn." For Melville, the bad father was a metaphor for all Christian gentleman whose allegiances were solely localist, oblivious to the claims of humanity writ large.

In an age of science and exploration, traditional boundaries are leveled, exacerbating self-love, dangerously reducing dependency on religious authority, and eroding the paternalist ethos. Defending other conservatives, nervous paternalists in Melville scholarship agree that Melville is a poor witness to his mental states; that he was at times insane and violent (but driven to it by women); and, worse, that there is no Isabel,[61] but there was a disgusting inside narrative. Julian Hawthorne, his father, and other nineteenth-century critics who had stressed Melville's confusion, morbidity, and erratic performance were not necessarily malicious or insensitive to great art. Surely they were frightened of Jewishly feminine introspection or narcissism, long identified with revolutionary puritanism, masturbation, this-worldliness, the realm of the senses and self-direction.[62] Henry Murray also attended Ovid's warnings about Narcissus and Icarus, adjuring pride and over-reaching; the form of progressive psychoanalysis that he ambivalently[63] promoted was designed to elicit confessions that would curb radical ambition; Murray's analytic style was not intended as an aid to liberal activists, (collaboratively) unveiling the perceptual distortions or repressions that could hinder the development of efficacious tactics for change. Perhaps Murray suffered like Julian Hawthorne, who idealized his parents throughout life and was appalled by the once-admired Melville's clinical self-disclosures in *Pierre*, which he had found "repulsive, insane, and impossible."[64]

Veneration lost

HM. 1. Death of F[ather]? Hate / 2. Discovery of F's Evil (loss of focus of veneration: disillusionment [arrow] heretic."[65]
    —Murray "Memo"

Murray's biographer made the triangle with wife and mistress the defining structure of his life, whereas this author has found a tug between Melville's ethical Hebraism and Murray's pragmatism to be the opposing forces explaining his turmoil and writer's block. For Murray (as for other family reformers), the paternalistic father brakes the leftward momentum of industrial society by deflecting libido *away* from the mysterious mother of the radically agitating Enlightenment *toward* corporatist elites and the party of flexible Order. Murray identified with Melville's bohemian revolt in *Typee* (1846) because Melville's target was the zealous, hypocritical female missionary, not the sexual adventurer. Murray's Melville/Pierre was a sick man and a crybaby, an emanation of "Malodorous Mother" from whom he derived absurdly high standards of ethical conduct, thus undermining the only source of unity in a pluralist society. Murray's unifying good father figure (the "focus of veneration" assigned by corporatist elites, such as FDR and his precursor Lemuel Shaw) will be shattered by puritan perfectionism and Lockean testing of authority. Disillusionment with the good father produces heresy. Murray would see Ahab as both Left and Right, a dyad intertwined as Melville and the mother from whom he never separated. Against Murray's benign and protective (discreetly wandering) father (himself) glared the suckling, yearning "narcist," "melanophile," "sable divinity," "Night," Poe's Dupin, and morbid Melville/Isabel whimpering Hebrew melodies,[66] a figure he found appealing. "You aren't going to let them academicize you, are you?" he anxiously inquired during our unusually personal interview.

Acknowledging Allan Melvill's premarital escapade bestowed a forbidden legitimacy to Pierre's strike through the masks of (upper-class) social hypocrisy. Melville would have been justifiably angry with the wandering father who had sanctimoniously administered corporal punishment to imperfectly pure and obedient children.[67] If Melville was not mother maddened, then Murray's class-bound Tory diagnosis of pathological Victorian culture can't be sustained. Suppression of the autobiographical content of *Pierre* is the linchpin of the organic conservative argument that Melville (a stand-in for the apparently protosocialist nineteenth century) was an irrationally violent radical, a spoiled brat, whose conversion late in life was prompted by a more mature grasp of (unknowable) earthly reality; thus the ex-brat was rationally persuaded of the moral necessity to follow his leader. For Murray, such leaders were moderate conservatives, the cool planners Murray ambivalently defined against romantic artists and other radicals who disconcertingly switched from passivity to action and got things done that the moderates "fail to achieve"!

[Murray diagnoses radicals, 1938] [The radical] favors modern art, the rejection of sex taboos, socialism, the freedom of the press, the elimination of religion, nudism, progressive schools, the humane treatment of criminals, etc. Radicalism is usually opposed to authority, to any force that restrains liberty. It favours the weak, the dissatisfied, the oppressed minority. Thus radicalism is often an indication of suprAggression (inhibited) and infraNurturance. It may be an expression of the stern father and rebel son thema. [But these people don't act:] . . . the most radical sentiments were expressed by succorant, abasive and infavoidant subjects.[68]

[Murray to FDR, confidential report, 1943] MEIN KAMPF proves that the young man from Linz who could not get through High School was capable of profiting by what he saw and read, and that these five years of drifting and irregular employment were by no means wasted. The flophouse and the beer hall were his Heidelberg and University of Vienna.[69] (126)
. . . *Hitler operates on thalamic energy rather than on conscious will and rational planning. Possessed by fanatical passion he can accomplish things which*

those who act on cooler and more moderate plans fail to achieve. The force, in other words, comes from the id, and the ego is used in its service. This combination is typical of the gangster; but Hitler is different from the ordinary type, having some of the attributes of the romantic artist. He is a compound, say, of Lord Byron and Al Capone. (142–43)

Again, there are two kinds of disillusion for Murray (or other conservative psychoanalysts): healthy disillusion deflates the ambitions of the lower orders (women, sailors overtaken by Id forces) who think they are trained or emotionally equipped to rule. Sick-making disillusion (or projection of inner states) unmasks really good corporatist fathers whose superior self-control and social responsibility legitimate their authority over women and sailors. When Melville's social criticism went too far, that is, straying into structural class analysis in *White-Jacket* and *Pierre*, mischievously casting doubt upon the good father's power to ameliorate suffering without appropriate structural reform, Murray detached himself, but not without regret. He suppressed what he believed to be material evidence to protect social equilibrium or wholeness. Sometimes he identified Melville with the corporatist father, but it is an unsustainable fiction. The attraction to organic models of society may be viewed, then, as both personal and class defenses against powerful Left or liberal sentiments in his own breast.[70] The praise of epigones notwithstanding (and that he told me he "hated"), Murray viewed his political and literary efforts as failures, implicitly aligning himself with Tom Paine and Melville as refusers of phony reconciliations. Toward the end of his long life, Murray, age eighty-four, made a startling and endearingly honest confession in a letter to his old antagonist Jay Leyda. ". . . I am surprising myself every week by finding out how intensely interested I can become in some minute issue. I suspect that my failure to resolve the core problem—the exact nature of HM's alternating mental states, their causes and consequences—the failure of fifty years effort to untie that knot of knots disposes me to escape into any detour that I encounter."[71]

The restraints of conservative Enlightenment that must harmonize science and religion for purposes of social control push humanities scholars toward myth, not history. The bourgeois Freud called such practices symptoms of mass delusion, an assault on the brain that frustrated social progress, whereas his predecessor, Goethe, also an advocate of the active life, warned of the perils of introspection where unambiguous moral leadership had disappeared, and with it the clear rules and distinctions that prompted effective social action. In the autobiography that Melville purchased in his 1849 European sojourn (and which Henry A. Murray had acquired), Goethe threw up his hands at the prospect of depicting the character of his "remarkable" friend Jakob Lenz;[72] his diagnosis of Lenz's problem could have been penned by Murray, stuck on Melville and Isabel, or the lawyer stymied as biographer of Bartleby, or Melville's family, bewildered by the distracted stranger in their midst, or numerous Melvilleans unsure whether the author who electrified them was a great artist or a sadistic confidence man:

It would be impossible to follow him through the mazy course of his life, and to transfer to these pages a full exhibition of his peculiarities.

Generally known is that self-torture which in the lack of all outward grievances, had now become fashionable, and which disturbed the very best minds. That which gives but a transient pain to ordinary men who never themselves meditate on that which they seek to banish from their minds, was, by the better order, acutely observed, regarded, and recorded in books, letters, and diaries. *But now men united the strictest moral requisitions on themselves and others with an excessive negligence in action; and vague notions arising from this half-self-knowledge misled them into the strangest habits and out-of-the-way practices. But this painful work of self-contemplation was justified by the rising empirical psychology which while it was not exactly willing to pronounce everything that produces inward disquiet to be wicked and objectionable, still could not give it its unconditional approval, and thus was originated an eternal and inappeasable contest.* In carrying out and sustaining this conflict, Lenz surpassed all the other idlers and dabblers who were occupied in mining into their own souls, and thus he suffered from the universal tendency of the times, which was said to have been let loose by Werther; but a personal peculiarity distinguished him from all the rest. While they were undeniably frank and honest creatures, he had a decided inclination to intrigue, and, indeed, to intrigue for its own sake, without having in view any special object, any reasonable, attainable, personal object. On the contrary, it was always his custom to propose to himself something whimsical, which served, for that very reason, to keep him constantly occupied. In this way all his life long his imagination made him play a false part; his love, as well as his hate, was imaginary; he dealt with his thoughts and feelings in a wilful manner, so as always to have something to do. He endeavoured to give reality to his sympathies and antipathies by the most perverse means, and always himself destroyed his own work. Thus he never benefited any one whom he loved, and never injured any one whom he hated. In general he seemed to sin only to punish himself, and to intrigue for no purpose but to graft a new fable upon an old one.

His talent, in which tenderness, facility, and subtlety rivalled each other, proceeded from a real depth, from an inexhaustible creative power, but was thoroughly morbid with all its beauty. Such qualities are precisely the most difficult to judge. It is impossible to overlook great features in his works—a lovely tenderness steals along through pieces of caricature so odd and so silly that they can hardly be condoned, even in a humor so thorough and unassuming, and such a genuine comic talent. His days were made up of mere nothings, to which his nimble fancy could ever give a meaning, and he was the better able to squander hours away, since, with a happy memory, the time which he did employ in reading was always fruitful, and enriched his original mode of thought with various materials. (2:1–2; emphasis added)

Melville's public display of the double bind in *Pierre, or the Ambiguities,* violated the upper-class code that declares no conflict between loyalty to the interests of the family of origin and the moral imperative to relieve the suffering of ever encroaching humanity. *Pierre* blackened mother's milk; writing was the materialist revolt that poisoned mother, killing both her and her attached son, images pervasive in *Pierre* and "Benito Cereno." Melville had described the feared matricide-suicide that follows the expression of difference, specifically the accurate description of deceptively benign social relationships that the rising empirical psychology had facilitated. Such exposures provoked retaliation by critics still tied to conservative elites (the sane fathers whose superior self-control "really" does bring harmony, and who alone can modulate the dissonances of modernity); ergo, Olson's bafflement and Murray's urge to protect the image of Allan Melvill. Ahab and Pierre found their insular Tahitis in the embrace of little black Pip and dark Isabel—the facts of the material world and of the self that impregnated and watered their art, which tested the sincerity of their moral codes. Or even more problematically, the rising empirical psychology aroused unsettling wonder in the reader: In our brave new world where should we locate perhaps multiple sources of evil, as scientific inspections of nature and nurture shift inquiring glances away from the actions of inscrutable or capricious deities toward the material bodies we inherit, interacting with institutions that human beings construct and might transform? In their flights from self-knowledge and social knowledge, fastidious Melvilleans have turned away from the "horrors of the half-known life" as Goethe and Ishmael had advised. Lord Byron, Al Capone, Melville, Ahab, Freud, Hitler, and Jewish blood were fused in Murray's crucible; the residuum was the Dark Lady Isabel, indivisible as ashes.[73]

Illustration (unidentified subject) for Henry A. Murray's article "Time for a Positive Morality," which appeared in the March 1947 issue of *Survey Graphic*. The December 1947 issue featured a Bill Mauldin cartoon showing a seated young man, bespectacled and with tousled curly black hair, his chin resting on his fist, with an open book of Marx on his lap. Two older women in the background are gazing at him. The caption read: "Right now we're nursing him through a bad siege of social-consciousness."

Photo by Edward Schwartz

What positive ideal do we set before today's insecure youth?

Henry A. Murray, ca. 1962.
Henry A. Murray Papers,
Harvard University

10

After the Revolution

The Racial Discourse of Ethnopluralism

This is one of the many profound atheistical hits of Milton. A greater than
Lucretius, since he always teaches under a masque, and makes the Devil
himself a Teacher & Messiah.
　　—Herman Melville's annotation to Satan's seduction of Eve, partially
　　　erased, in his copy of *Paradise Lost*

[On the rear end of the *San Dominick* was a medallion] uppermost and
central of which was a dark satyr in a mask, holding his foot on the
prostrate neck of a writhing figure, likewise masked.
　　—Narrator, "Benito Cereno"

Since the nineteenth century, images of Melville have moved from lunatic to
Fallen Superman to rootless cosmopolitan to rooted cosmopolitan, with the
figure of the rooted cosmopolitan unmasking would-be tyrants posing as democrats. Underneath the mixed, ever-ambiguous reception to Melville's art is a larger
impulse: the subliminal blue penciling of natural rights. The eighteenth-century organic conservative Edmund Burke, like Samuel Johnson, reacted to Bacon, Milton,
and Locke by nervously constructing a politicized aesthetics. Whether rendered as
sublime or beautiful, the seductive material world the neoclassicists called Nature
was always subversive to rational inquiry.[1] The sublime was the terrifying but alluring romantic style associated with rupture or iconoclasm, unchecked fancy and
speculation, unmonitored boundary-blurring science, and Hebraic revolutionary
puritanism. It was contrasted with its beautiful rival, the soothing, bounded pastoral style associated with conservative reform. Melville's gigantic sin was, perhaps,

also the source of his greatness to corporatist readers. In cleaving to purple/black/ brown sublimity, he jammed his poetic prose with too many images. The disorienting view from mountain tops, foretops, and rooftops (the brain) bored within the psyche and without, defying Ovid by mating "unlike things," thus muddling distinctions between art and life, dreams and reality.[2]

While the literary cubist Melville melted walls between some categories and made them interpenetrate or turn into their opposites, he had a fitful but keen eye for structures that could not be washed away by his conservative narrators; he might interrupt their moralistic admonitions with materialist expletives. The *Nation* magazine had explained in 1919 (the year it helped initiate the Melville Revival) that "the inherent common sense" of the flexible "Anglo-Saxon race" would overcome Jewish Bolshevism in America. Following this logic, Melville would have betrayed his Anglo-Saxon racial inheritance by describing group antagonisms and double binds that, in turn, suggested the necessity of structural reform. "The class war, rich-and-poor-man fray / Of history" could not only ameliorate the condition of labor and create "the first firm founding of the state," but, in a related perception, would prevent mental illness in the laps of "families" that had erased the contradiction between (adolescent) truth and (parental) order, families that madly protected the critical spirit while spooking rebel senses.

But even as a Burkean, Melville was subversive. As Burke recognized, the relaxing beautiful was not the antidote to the agitating sublime, but a different style of romantic seduction. Melville's "primitivist" or "reactionary" protests, no less than his "Marxian" moments, were utopian delegitimations of deceptive or heartless authority in the name of universal standards of truth and justice. Such unsettling criticism as the desire for something better, as desire itself (as opposed to the impassibility[3] of "aestheticism") may initiate processes that can get out of hand, that may lead to unpredicted developments more far-reaching than Machiavellian "moderate" conservatives, the managers of "ritual rebellions," would like. The impeccably WASP American writer, on closer scrutiny, turned out to be a bad Jew even when he tried to be good by working within the system.

In seeking to define "the Melville problem" (*what* is he, *where* is he, *why* did he fail?), "the Jewish problem," and the problem of the form and content of American democratic institutions, I find myself trampling over the same dark and bloody ground. The Melville scholars studied here were transmitters of his "Hebraic" utopian provocations, while dependent on "neutral" (but conservative) institutions. They have, with frequent resentment, tightened their corsets, assaulting the body in repose, the body freed from intimidation, the relaxed body better able to exercise curiosity and formulate those worldly assessments of social relationships and domination that build confidence in rising groups. The revivers anxiously merged with and simultaneously rejected their Hebraic monster/monument, fencing their own "rebel senses" as well as Melville's. Given the structural pressures in American universities after 1919, the ongoing appeal of crypto-Tory nostrums, and a series of fatal decisions by the Left, the Melville malaise was inevitable. The etiology of the Melville problem is revealed in attempts of organic conservatives to contain the explosive forces unleashed by science, liberal nationalism, universal literacy, and mass suffrage. Their reactive concept of national, ethnic, or racial character is the heartstring that constricts and arrests the questing or utopian imagination in either its sublime or beautiful expansiveness. Ahab's quest alarmed conservatives resisting the creation of a rational-secular international order with universal standards of excellence and human rights. Red pencils were flaunted in 1917–19 with the stunning advent of Bolshevism and Wilson's appealing concept of a New World Order. The corporatists forged a middle way between the "extremes" of right-wing reaction and revolutionary socialism in 1919, and similarly, between laissez-faire liberalism and Nazism/communism in the mid-1930s. The "moderate" strategy co-opted the scientific language of the Enlightenment, purging or discrediting class-conscious "Bolshevists," Left-liberal materialists, and laissez-faire liberals alike. Incorporating newly discovered "facts" into "totalities" or "organic wholes," they presented blood-and-soil historicism as the democratic vanguard of progress; their interacting biological, geographical, psychological, or cultural "types" were offered as novel interventions protecting the uninitiated reader from mad scientists and the bomb. I have neither typed nor stamped Melville; rather, I have followed his lead, marking the tight harness of nineteenth-century family loyalty (corporatism and hereditarian racism) that restrained the isolato's equally stubborn efforts to depict, overturn, or escape illegitimate authority, to enter the imaginations of suffering humanity. Whether hiding or writhing under the boot, Melville was an insoluble problem for the moderate men in all factions of Melville studies after 1919.

By suggesting ongoing conflict between materialist and pseudomaterialist (organicist) thinkers in the West as the subtext of the "Melville" Revival, I implicitly criticize the notion of Cold War culture as the unique creation of "fascist" Republicans. The postwar conflation of classical liberalism with fascism has been the dubious construct of corporatists and their Popular Front Left allies, supporters of the New Deal. The same thinkers have identified red scares as hysterical overreactions to a relatively insignificant communist presence in the labor movement or to an exaggerated Soviet military threat after 1945: This is their explanation for assaults on civil liberties. The picture changes when we take elite perceptions of lower-class autodidacts in a period of mass literacy and mass media as the subject of inquiry. Ongoing hostility to "materialism" and "insatiable curiosity" (self-assertion in the independent labor movement and its associated internationalism) explains the continuities in the Melville Revival and modifies the Cold War explanation for repression of civil liberties. Rather than diagnosing far Right hysteria or overreaction, "hysteria" is herein relocated in the moderate center, in its "cool" neoclassical (but not beautiful) response to hot-headed romanticism or "paranoia" on the fringe. There was an epochal emancipatory moment in the seventeenth century; all subsequent intellectual history in "the West" may be seen as counterattack to the Titanic threat of universal democracy and scientific advance, grounded in economic arrangements that would facilitate that goal. I cannot think of a single political movement that has embraced the scientist's open-ended and experimental program, though it should be implicit in the struggle for cultural freedom.

Enlightenment materialists argued for the universal natural rights of individuals; as republicans, they demanded one set of rules for rich and poor, institutionalizing natural rights in the state as civil liberties. In this context, the so-called eternal conflict between individual and society denotes, rather, a fight specific to bourgeois democracies: the defense of civil liberties against privileged minorities or intolerant or uninformed majorities. Moreover, as Locke and Diderot insisted, the citizen protester demanded that authorities heed exactly their own rules and standards—the precepts that legitimated their power and signified superior competence.[4] By transferring their own libertinage onto social rebels (in this case, the revolutionary bourgeoisie), threatened aristocrats resorted to stereotypes that slandered democracy and the People.

In a scenario still played out in offices of conservative psychiatry, the conflict between (savage) individuals and civilization originates in self-indulgent acting out of antisocial emotions and instincts, not legitimate grievances. Unlike Don Juan/ Faust, socially responsible elites possess an "inner check," the measured response to provocation that staves off both violent, rigid responses in themselves and revolution by the desperate.[5] A rainbow (not reaction or rubble or rivers of blood) is dispensed by the good father and other mental health professionals.[6] In a pastiche of Freud, conservative anthropologists/historians have tried to brake the "Jacobinical" momentum of the Reformation by scuttling Judeo-Christian ethics and Whiggish "progress," positing an "anti-elitist" cultural relativism against "scientific history" in the late 1930s. These recent pragmatists and pluralists (thinkers who have adopted materialist categories to describe the "social organism") finesse conflict between individuals and oppressive institutions through "traditional"[7] formulations that submerge the individual in the group (national, ethnic, racial, or linguistic); individuals are, by definition, narcissistic; groups ("communities" and corporations), not individuals, possess desirable individuality/difference. Here are experts in wholeness and context, performing "cultural history" operations, twirling myths and symbols to yield "consensus history." New Left critics have not always noticed the pseudomaterialism of their favored social scientists, rather identifying "Western science" with imperialism. After two decades of anti-imperialist insurgency within the humanities, radical literary scholars are engrossed in studies of "canon formation" to demonstrate that "white male" "Eurocentric" writers have been apotheosized to the detriment of competing women or nonwhites; some have attacked Melville as archoffender; critical methods and standards inimical to the understanding of "cultural difference" are held responsible. Wandering off into the history of concrete, historically specific social movements and their rival epistemologies is still a daring dig for students of "American literature" or "aesthetics" who follow the conservative sociology of Emile Durkheim, Frederick Jackson Turner, Werner Sombart, Max Weber, George Herbert Mead, Carl Jung, and Talcott Parsons.

The figures studied here seem rooted to the spot, unable to leave the confines of anecdotal, regional, group, or institutional history to discover a broad and ever changing (but discernable) view of agency, internal contradiction and ambivalence, opportunity, and structural constraint. By contrast this account is situated both outside and inside the academy, examining the several contexts the evidence suggests and demonstrating elite resistance to being seen, even as some call themselves radicals; threats from below (Melville as Ahab) are met with cautionary myths as old as science and democracy. The examples of Narcissus and Icarus are mobilized to warn the rebel senses and the catastrophic overreaching that "self-love" engenders. Their advice is dispensed to the book-loving lower orders, not themselves.

I have emphasized the fragility of Melville's rainbow in the practice of "asylum physicians" flexibly adapting to new conditions, but with a guiding vision of small town balance and communitarianism associated with antebellum America: They are "Burkeans" and Tory-Radicals who perhaps believed with Lewis Mumford that swallowing small doses of the modernist Melville would restore Golden Day "Melville." Exploring the venues of similar inoculations has moved this account of the Melville Revival away from petty disputes between professors to the more cosmic terrain it deserves.[8]

FATHERS AND CHILDREN: 1920S RADICALS AND THE NEW LEFT

In the 1960s teaching literature, American or any other variety, is an exciting and somewhat bewildering occupation. Living in the midst of a revolution is not likely to afford even the noncombatants peace and security. Our sleep is disturbed by two problems. We have first to try to understand what the critics and theorists have discovered, advocated, and argued about. Then we will have to sort out their new approaches in the study of literature and decide which ones will help our classes to a better understanding of the works they are studying.[9]
—Willard Thorp, 1965

There is an unacknowledged genealogy wherein 1920s bohemians, 1940s New Liberals of the vital center, and post-1960s New Historicists share the same aristocratic disdain for radical puritans and positivists. Melville was strenuously promoted as an organic conservative before, during, and after World War II by New Critics, but these men were closer in sensibility to monarchists than to the Hebraic radical puritans or ordinary Americans who had fought and died for the principles of democracy and the Bill of Rights in Europe, the Pacific, and, later, the American South. Enlisted men managed neither the war nor the postwar world that their efforts had made possible, a point rarely if ever brought out in the constant remembrances in the mass media of that age of heroic sacrifice and "unity"; such unity was a dream. World War II, like antifascist movements of the 1930s, had been opposed and undermined by important intellectuals, industrialists, and even segments of the Left; some had profited from commercial ties to Hitler while others joined the National Socialist struggle against Soviet communism/Jewish world domination. A few antifascist Melvilleans shared the elitism of the Axis enemy, in the case of Murray, proposing to FDR that progressive planners profit from Hitler's brilliance in penetrating the minds of the little people whom he had mobilized and controlled, a probing gaze shared by Ahab/Melville and Freud. Unable to find an anti-imperialist motive for American entry into the conflict, Murray and other social psychologists proposed limited social democratic reforms and a federal morale service using symbol manipulation to build consensus. Melville, in his personae as Ahab and Pierre, however, was a resolute enemy to the moral hypocrisies of "whiteness," or "virtuous expediency," as a guide to conduct; in this mode, he would be seen as an ally to independent, internationalist labor and to all inquiring minds united by moral principles. Not surprisingly, Ahab was attacked by conservative New Critics (who did support the right of Ezra Pound to receive the Bollingen Prize awarded by the Library of Congress in 1949, separating fascist life from aesthetic considerations that floated art above the fray), but why should radical post-1960s literary scholars, political scientists, and cultural historians, proudly antiracist, have taken up Ishmael's white flag, not Ahab's blood-incrusted pen of steel?

Raymond Weaver's biography of 1921, *Herman Melville: Mariner and Mystic*, was republished in 1961, with an introduction by Mark Van Doren. Weaver, the philosophical Pierrot, had read the early work (including *Moby-Dick*) as antimissionary and anti-imperialist, but Ahab was hero and victim, not a perpetrator. Perhaps sore at the compromises he felt forced to make in his own career, Weaver argued that Ahab (like Melville) was admirable as the disillusioned and pessimistic artist who would be judged insane by his philistine contemporaries. Weaver maintained an anticapitalist persona by fleeing to Eastern mysticism and existentialism, while harboring a pocket of revolt in his papers at Columbia University: His student David Rein's essay suggested that Weaver told his classes that "Ahab" was not radical enough. By contrast, in the neatly bounded but holistic, Jungian criticism of Columbia professor Richard V. Chase, Ahab and America were conflated and declared to be monomaniacal, echoing D. H. Lawrence in *Studies in Classic American Literature* (1923).[10] Macmillan's press release to the *Columbia Alumni News* on behalf of Chase's Melville study (1949) stated that Melville (like Whitman) had exposed "the American character": Ahab was "the essential American." Columbians further underlined the depth and relevance of Chase's Guggenheim-supported work; it was "one of the first serious over-all studies of Melville. . . . It displays the essential qualities of each of Melville's works, and relates them to each other and to the vicissitudes and problems of Melville's personal life. It presents Melville's views of personality, culture, art and morals and considers them in the light of today and its social and political problems."

In other words, considered in its sublime totality, Melville's oeuvre demonstrated problems to be pinned on Ahab. Earlier, Yvor Winters had made the same connection, in "Herman Melville and the Problems of Moral Navigation" (1938):[11] *Moby-Dick* was "profoundly an American epic"; the relevant history was American nationalism in the nineteenth century, "in its physical events . . . a narration of exploration and heroic adventure." For Winters, Ahab had exceeded the bounds of the Prometheus myth. The Calvinistical, deicidal Ahab (68) was "the magnificent fruition of Maule's curse," the monomaniac with "the will to destroy human evil itself, an intention blasphemous because beyond human power and infringing upon the purposes of God" (65–66). While Ahab was a creature of instinct, Starbuck, (quoting Melville) "no crusader after perils," represented "critical intelligence" and "sanity and morality" (62). Though Starbuck's rebellion failed, the author himself (Ishmael in the Try-Works?) "escaped the curse by comprehending it."(75).[12] Newton Arvin's psychoanalytic reading of Ahab made him both the typical self-reliant American and (as Ishmael?) a maddened Herman, rendered homosexual by his mother's crippling love, seeking to destroy the parental principle in the androgynous whale.[13] The Lawrence-Winters-Chase-Arvin mystical anti-Ahab line was followed by Richard H. Brodhead (1986). "Melville's ravaged and fanatic captain, so overscaled in his energies and so restricted in his range of interests, is in one sense a variant on a classic American type. Monomania, a rare personality disorder in everyday life, has something of the status of a normal state of selfhood in American fiction."[14]

Rejecting the "insane [dogmatic state] religions" of Germany and the Soviets that were bound to explode in the face of the "diversity and complexity that marks all social life," Ross J. S. Hoffman, a frequent contributor to the *American Review*, argued (in an article immediately preceding Yvor Winters's "Maule's Curse") that the statism of Italian fascism was neither despotic nor irrationalist but "fundamentally Italian, Catholic, and realist, and hence linked inseparably with the soundest traditions of our civilization." Mussolini's antecedents, Hoffman claimed, were Aristotle, Thomas Aquinas, and Machiavelli.[15] It has been argued throughout this book that competing historicisms are at play in the humanities: The organicist version suppresses facts while praising "critical intelligence." Starbuck (or Ishmael), not the divisive and aggressive Chartist Ahab,[16] earns allegiance from corporatists who have dominated the transmission of American literature. Their idol is "multiplicity," a concept opposed to Wall Street, the machine, pharisaical liberalism, and forced assimilation: afflictions explicitly or implicitly linked to totalizing, homogenizing know-it-all Ahabs. What about that gold doubloon Ahab hammers to the mast? Does it reflect the false self-image of narcissism, the bribe described by Ishmael, or does the doubloon signify radical Enlightenment: dugout knowledge and emancipation from illusion after Ahab's unpenned pen has completed its work? As a man tied to ex-Federalist conservative Democrats and conservative Whigs, "Melville" would reject Jacksonian military expansionism for the cautiously (elite) controlled method of trade and cultural penetration. As seen by Ishmael, the world of the *Pequod* discloses an America fatally dominated by finance capital (the doubloon?), mass politics, newspapers, and demagogues, and spawned by the French Revolution and its usurping social classes: These are the people and forces Melville seems to have associated with the downfall of his family, and they are most powerfully symbolized by fanatical reformers such as the false Prometheans Ahab and Nathan, apostate Jews like the geologist Margoth, or commercial Jews such as Mordecai, the broker who ruins "Woebegone" and his starving family (*Moby-Dick*), and reminiscent of the hook-nosed and greasy-haired pawnbrokers in *Redburn* exploiting starving Christians after the Panic of 1937.[17] It was this reading of America that Columbia professor Richard Chase and many student radicals preferred.

Granted that *Moby-Dick* was Melville's "lyric-epic comprehension of the American spirit"—but, Chase argued, it was *The Confidence-Man* that demonstrated a "mature critical intelligence," a critique of relevance to intellectuals mapping a new middle ground, burying the 1930s liberal-progressive moderate lines that had understrapped the Soviet Union and its foreign policy through the Communist Party. Joining the yellow-and-red-garbed (true) Promethean boy who leads the Old Man away at the end of Melville's book, it would be the New Liberal mission "to defeat the universal Inquisition by which the Old God tries to rule the world." The New Liberals (for whom Arthur Schlesinger, Jr., was a "brilliant spokesman") must avoid "bankrupt" 1930s liberalism; taking its cue from Melville's exposé of the confidence man, the New Liberalism must yield up "social realism" for an older self-critical realism, the really spiritual aesthetic that would never reduce itself to "rectitude, absolutism, automatic thought and action."[18] How free were freethinking Jews in America after the defeat of the fascist revolution? Two items from *Kenyon Review*, January 1949, comment:

[Advertisement] SEARCH FOR THE REAL by Hans Hofmann[.] Being the presentation of a vital philosophy wherein certain technical factors in modern painting are reconciled with the world of the spirit. Published by Addison Gallery of American Art, Phillips Academy, Andover, Massachusetts.

[Richard Chase, "New vs. Ordealist"] Slitting one's own throat can be a kind of paradoxical assertion of authority, or at least a declaration that one had ceased to underestimate oneself.

Chase's "New" Self-Criticism joined the anonymous youth of *Mardi* in affirming that evil was the chronic malady of the universe, and perhaps Bartleby (when Chase argued that suicide, though paradoxical, was a kind of authentic self-assertion, the vanguard formula for self-improvement). Like Kingsley, another admirer of the romantic conservative Thomas Carlyle, Chase's Melville was hoping to convert bad Jews. To all crusading Ahabs who criticize God, who believe evil is exterior to themselves, Chase, no less than Murray and Allport, would argue: ". . . unless you own the whale, you are but a provincial and a sentimentalist in Truth." The sophisticate scoffs at the freedom, solidarity, and dignity imputed to humankind by the cosmopolitan eighteenth century, embodied in Taji, then Ahab and his mongrel crew (later in Margoth with his Arab assistants?). And if Ishmael's lesson is actually his ownership of the whale (acknowledging innate depravity and a fallen world) and his rebirth as a good Jew in "The Try-Works," fastened to conservative institutional control, then we should wonder at Ishmael's famous paean to democracy, labor (of all colors), Jackson, and equality.

The progressives cannot have it both ways; if Ishmael is cured of Ahab's materialism, then he is no longer a democrat in the sense that the radical democrats of the eighteenth century or many of the radical reformers of the nineteenth century used the term. But this would wreck the presentation of Melville as radical exemplar in the schools, unless the entire postwar political discourse was skewed to turn corporatists into left-wing democrats (which I believe is the case).[19] When Melville anwered Hawthorne's letter (that may have offered to review *Moby-Dick*), protesting "I have written a wicked book, and feel as spotless as the lamb,"[20] is he confessing that he started out identified with Ahab (for whom might does not make right), has murdered Ahab and his fellow incompetents, and has died into life, as the Christian myth demands?[21] If Melville was so convinced, why did he move on immediately to *Pierre*, a work in which the only major character to survive is Charlie Millthorpe, the leftist "Apostle"? And what did he mean by other remarks to Hawthorne (in the same letter)?: "You did not care a penny for the book. But, now & then as you read, you understood the pervading thought that impelled the book—and that you praised. Was it not so? You were archangel enough to despise the imperfect body, and embrace the soul. Once you hugged the ugly Socrates because you saw the flame in the mouth, and heard the rushing of the demon,—the familiar,—and recognized the sound; for you have heard it in your own solitudes. . . . Lord, when shall we be done growing? . . . So now, let us add Moby Dick to our blessing, and step from that. Leviathan is not the biggest fish;—I have heard of Krakens." Is this the voice of (demonic, Hebraic) Ahab arguing with God and his accusatory family, and here, perhaps Hawthorne's conservative persona as well, or is this the repentant, placatory Ishmael?

The wild letter quoted above (described by Melville himself elsewhere in the text as both sane and incoherent) marks his most intense merging with Hawthorne, whom, like Melville's own family, he describes as simultaneously rejecting and embracing the (demonic) author and even his furtively demonic self.[22] Chase's admirers in the 1960s generation of Melville scholars have yet to engage these puzzling issues. But a related question remains: Why impose ideological consistency on Melville at all, why not listen to what he has to say, why not luxuriate in the subtlety of his mind and the alertness with which he maps psychological processes that have rarely been described in such precision and complexity? Why not adorn our experience with the almost indescribable richness and suggestiveness of his (deliberately unclassifiable) art; why not follow his example by closely inspecting all our institutions, and how, as Melville suggests, they actually function, dispensing mixed messages that may immobilize the moral historical actor? Why not weigh our own attachments to the principles, people, and ideas our socializing institutions confusedly espouse?—unless, of course, English professors are to be commissars of culture, excising baleful, overstimulating influences on impressionable young, still open, minds.

As elites adapt to new configurations from below by modifying social policy, they change the concrete content of abstractions such as moderation, extremism, decorum, etc., along with how and what we read. Melville's unflinching eye inspected political language, discovering slavery where freedom should be; his lantern highlights conduct by forcing attention on portentous but empty abstractions, on the ways we may, as socializers of the young on behalf of more powerful others, overtly or subtly coerce the young people in our care. As libertarian, the artist may prod and disturb corporatist readers lacking legitimacy in their own social roles. In Melville's short story "The Piazza," Isabel's longing for a happy family reappears in Marianna/ Mother, but without any mystifications from the compassionate but unyielding narrator: "Oh, if I could but once get to yonder house, and but look upon whoever the happy being is that lives there! A foolish thought: why do I think it? Is it that I live so lonesome, and know nothing?" "I, too, know nothing; and, therefore, cannot answer; but, for your sake, Marianna, well could wish that I were the happy one of the happy house you dream you see; for then you would behold him now, and, as you say, this weariness might leave you." When the narrator says he knows nothing, we can take him to mean that no power in heaven or earth will stop him from unfolding, from reconfiguring previously settled arguments and beliefs in the light of new knowledge: "the greatest, grandest things are unpredicted"; when some Melvilleans say that they, like Melville at his most brilliantly pluralist, conclude that they know nothing for sure, they may really mean it, for they wait upon conclusions dictated from above, rules that are made and remade *ex cathedra;* unlike their hero and victim, they have not escaped the double bind.

STATUES (A POSTSCRIPT)

Writing history, especially where that current event is Vietnam, is a treacherous exercise. We could not get into the minds of the decision-makers, we were not present at the decisions, and we often could not tell whether something happened because someone decided it, decided against it, or most likely because it unfolded from the situation. History, to me, has been expressed by a passage from Herman Melville's *Moby-Dick* where he writes: "This is a world of chance, free will, and necessity—all interweavingly working together as one; chance by turn rules either and has the last featuring blow at events." Our studies have tried to reflect this thought; inevitably in the organizing and writing process, they appear to assign more and less to men and free will than was the case.

   —Last words in a memo from Leslie H. Gelb, chairman OSD Vietnam
      Task Force, to the Secretary of Defense, January 15, 1969, *Pentagon
      Papers,* xvi

It is plain that where he ought to have enlarged upon his praises, he maliciously chooses to be silent; a proceeding unworthy of an historian, who ought to be exact, sincere, and impartial; free from passion, and not to be biased either by interest, fear, resentment, or affection, to deviate from truth, which is the mother of history, the preserver and eternizer of great actions, the professed enemy of oblivion, the witness of things past, and the director of future times . . . .

   . . . "Do you remember," said I, "that within these few years, three tragedies were enacted in Spain, written by a famous poet of ours, which were so excellent, that they surprised, delighted, and raised the admiration of all that saw them, as well the ignorant and ordinary people as the judicious and men of quality; and the actors got more by those three, than by thirty of the best that have been writ since?"[23]

   —Narrator, *Don Quixote*

But this august dignity I treat of, is not the dignity of kings and robes,
but that abounding dignity which has no robed investiture. Thou shalt see it
shining in the arm that wields a pick or drives a spike; that democratic
dignity which, on all hands, radiates without end from God; Himself!
The great God absolute! The centre and circumference of all democracy!
His omnipresence, our divine equality!

If, then, to meanest mariners, and renegades and castaways, I shall hereafter ascribe high qualities, though dark; weave round them tragic graces, if
even the most mournful, perchance the most abased, among them all, shall
at times lift himself to the exalted mounts; if I shall touch that workman's
arm with some ethereal light; if I shall spread a rainbow over his disastrous
set of sun; then against all mortal critics, bear me out in it, thou just Spirit of
Equality, which hast spread one royal mantle of humanity over all my kind!
Bear me out in it, thou great democratic God! who didst not refuse to the
swart convict, Bunyan, the poetic pearl; Thou who didst clothe with doubly
hammered leaves of finest gold, the stumped and paupered arm of old Cervantes; Thou who didst pick up Andrew Jackson from the pebbles; who didst
hurl him upon a war-horse; who didst thunder him higher than a throne![24]
Thou who, in all Thy mighty earthly marchings, ever cullest Thy selectest
champions from the kingly commons; bear me out in it, O God! (117)
    —Narrator, *Moby-Dick*

If to meanest mariners &c—ideal [HM] could not suppose they were really
that
    —Henry Murray's notes, 1850–51

For organic conservatives (including many of Melville's narrators), the aristocratic
Melville's protest was not directed against class hierarchy as such, but against unrealistic expectations of hypocritical, unreliable, deluded, incompetent, or malicious
bourgeois authority: the illegitimate authority stolen by usurpers who were abusing
workers and peasants. The genteel reader of *Redburn* (1849) was asked to reconceive
programs of amelioration for labor, understanding, for instance, the sailors' vulner-
ability to predatory "land sharks," "a certain recklessness and sensualism of character, ignorance, and depravity" (in the "majority" of sailors), and their isolation from
"respectable and improving society." But the problem is so enormous that (seemingly) "the moral organization of all civilization" must be reformed, a thought that
brings Redburn close to despondency. After a bitterly resentful passage comparing
sailors to the wheels of a carriage, indispensable to comfortable passengers and to
world commerce, but only carelessly assisted by wealthy Christians, the narrator
gropes for an optimistic (but unconvincing) finish to his sermon:

But can sailors, one of the wheels of this world, be wholly lifted up from the mire? There seems not much chance for it, in the old systems and programmes of the future, however well-intentioned and sincere; for with such systems, the thought of lifting them up seems almost as hopeless as that of growing the grape in Nova Zembla.

But we must not altogether despair for the sailor; nor need those who toil for his good be at bottom disheartened. For Time must prove his friend in the end; and though sometimes he would almost seem as a neglected step-son of heaven, permitted to run on and riot out his days with no hand to restrain him, while others are watched over and tenderly cared for; yet we feel and know that God is the true Father of all, and that none of his children are without the pale of his care.[25]

In his frozen and pallid Nova Zembla state, Melville's pious narrator is unable to imagine sailors intervening in their own behalf or that of humanity at large; the wheels are probably going to be stuck in the mud owing both to hot nature and cold nurture; we hear the voice of a battered child, later given to running on and rioting; he has imputed his weakness to adult workers, Ishmaels all; Melville's narrators do not generally abandon this immobilizing metaphor. But into his reserves, another Melville warms to the margins; his fatherly care reddens. Who narrated the passage quoted above, Ishmael or Ahab? ". . . If even the most mournful, perchance the most abased, among them all, *shall at times lift himself to the exalted mounts;* if I shall touch that workman's arm with some ethereal light; if I shall spread a rainbow over his disastrous set of sun; then against all mortal critics, bear me out in it, thou just Spirit of Equality, which hast spread one royal mantle of humanity over all my kind!" (emphasis added). Melville is speaking to the democratic God directly, holding him to his promise. Toward the end of his late sketch of John/Jack Gentian "(omitted from the final sketch of him)" similar sentiments surface: "To the last thou wilt be a Jack Gentian; not too dignified to be humane; a democrat, though less of the stump than the heart."[26]

In this postscript, I have returned Melville with his customary ambiguities intact—holding his hand, the swart convict Cervantes. Thrusting through the wall of *historische Individualität* they judge modern Melville scholarship in its authorized blend with upper-class-directed foreign and domestic policies.[27] Their thoughts on uplift are of particular interest to a history profession that, insofar as it has been subsumed under "literary theory," has lost its nerve, neither "the witness of things past" nor "the director of future times" that Cervantes celebrated. The opening paragraphs of Melville's lecture "Statues in Rome" are forcefully democratic, universalist, and plainly spoken:[28]

It might be supposed that the only proper judge of statues would be a sculptor, but it may be believed that others than the artist can appreciate and see the beauty of the marble art of Rome. If what is best in nature and knowledge cannot be claimed for the privileged profession of any order or men, it would be a wonder if, in that region called Art, there were, as to what is best there, any essential exclusiveness. True, the dilettante may enjoy his technical terms; but ignorance of these prevents not due feeling for Art, in any mind naturally alive to beauty or grandeur. Just as the productions of nature may be both appreciated by those who know nothing of Botany, or who have no inclination for it, so the creations of Art may be, by those ignorant of its critical science, or indifferent to it. Art strikes a chord in the lowest as well as in the highest; the rude and uncultivated feel its influence as well as the polite and polished. It is a spirit that pervades all classes. Nay, as it is doubtful whether to the scientific Linnaeus flowers yielded so much satisfaction as to the unscientific Burns, or struck so deep a chord in his bosom; so may it be a question whether the terms of Art may not inspire in artistic but still susceptible minds, thoughts, or emotions, not lower than those raised in the most accomplished of critics . . . .

The next paragraph reiterates the first, emphasizing the shamed silence of the uneducated in the face of expertise. Melville thus affirms his solidarity with "the lowest . . . the rude and uncultivated." He then continues: "I shall speak of the impressions produced upon my mind as one who looks upon a work of art as he would upon a violet or a cloud, and admires or condemns as he finds an answering sentiment awakened in his own soul. My object is to paint the appearance of Roman statuary objectively and afterward to speculate upon the emotions and pleasures that appearance is apt to excite in the human breast" (128–29).

Though Melville has made an invidious comparison between "the scientific Linnaeus" and the "unscientific Burns," he undermines his own medievalism by prescribing a method of study recognizable to modern historians and sociologists. Speaking of the Farnese Hercules (whose "cheerful and humane" qualities are distinguished from a less attractive "powerful Samson" and "mighty Hercules"), he introduces other autodidacts to the demanding procedures of critical thought: "To rightfully appreciate this, or, in fact, any other statue, one must consider where they came from and under what circumstances they were formed. In other respects they reveal their own history. Thus to understand the statues of the Vatican it is necessary to visit often the scenes where they once stood—the Coliseum, which throws its shade like a mighty thunder cloud, the gardens, the Forum, the aqueducts, the ruined temples—and remember all that has there taken place" (147).

Is this the voice of the Renaissance, the Reformation, and the Enlightenment in their most democratic tendencies, suspicious of mystifying "priestly" mediators, attempting a reconstruction of all aspects of the past that could shed light on the closely observed object of study returned to its original setting? Is this the historical memory and Lockean empiricism that the counter-Enlightenment moderate men have stigmatized as the apocalyptic sublime, the hubris, materialism, and monomania of the rootless Greek or Romantic Wandering Jew that produces only red terror and totalitarianism, not a more accurate and empathic history?[29] For Melville, the historian, the ancients are not so different that we cannot enter into their imaginations and judge their conduct: "The component parts of human character are the same now as then" (134). Aligning himself with Ahab, Pierre, Pitch, Thomas Fry (or later Celio and Margoth), Melville's lecture continues their collective unmasking of upper-class hypocrisy and double talk:

> The appearance of the statues . . . is often deceptive, and a true knowledge of their character is lost unless they are closely scrutinized. The arch dissembler Tiberius was handsome, refined, and even pensive in expression. "That Tiberius?" exclaimed a lady in our hearing. "He does not look so bad." Madam, thought I, if he had looked bad, he could not have been Tiberius. His statue has such a sad and musing air, so like Jerome in his cell, musing on the vanities of the world, that, to some, not knowing for whom the statue was meant, it might convey the impression of a man broken by great afflictions, of so pathetic a cast is it. Yet a close analysis brings out all his sinister features, and close study of the statue will develop the monster portrayed by the historian. For Tiberius was melancholy without pity, and sensitive without affection. He was, perhaps, the most wicked of men. (135)

Professor Merton M. Sealts, Jr., chose this passage to link the arch dissembler Tiberius to Melville's most coldly cerebral, monstrous, Jacksonian characters:

> As in an earlier passage on "the diabolical Tiberius," in Ch. 55 of *Redburn*, Melville was presumably relying here on the account of "the unmatchable Tacitus." In *Redburn* he had written of Tiberius as "that misanthrope upon the throne of the world . . . who even in his self-exile, embittered by bodily pangs, and unspeakable mental terrors only known to the damned on earth, yet did not give over his blasphemies but endeavored to drag down with him to his own perdition, all who came under the evil spell of his power." The passage occurs in a discussion of the sailor Jackson, whose characterization anticipates Ahab in *Moby Dick* and Claggart in *Billy Budd*.[30]

When Melville saw the bust of Tiberius in the Hall of the Emperors at the Capitoline Museum 26 January 1857 he recorded in his journal the comment of his fellow-tourist: "That Tiberius? he don't look ["wicked at all" lined out] so bad at all'—It was he. A look of sickly evil,—intellect without manliness & sadness without goodness. Great brain overrefinements. Solitude." (n. 135–36)

Sealts agreed with other Melvilleans, including Charles Olson, Henry A. Murray, Lewis Mumford, Richard Chase, and C. L. R. James, for whom Ahab was "an anticipation" of Hitler and/or Stalin; the corporatist Ishmael was Ahab's antitype and the rectification of his pathological narcissism. Scholars have criticized similar ahistoric speculations as relics of "patristic and medieval culture" in which typology and telos rule, in which there is neither history nor critical thought but only providential design: cycles and the "repetition of similar or antithetical appearances" until the fulfillment of Christian eschatology—for Hegel, the "progress" culminating in the reign of Absolute Spirit;[31] for Hegelian-Marxists, the organic communist utopia; for the profession of American history in 1939, the emergence of cultural anthropology (today, cultural history) as the anti-elitist solution to "scientific" history and the endless winding way of critical thought or the ambiguities of individual versus collective moral responsibility.

Why is the Sealts analogue to Tiberius necessarily Ahab and not Leviathan? Why should we not see Melville's analytic gaze bringing out all the sinister features of deceptively fair-faced authority, and, over time, developing the monster whose might makes right, "The King of the boundless sea"? Why should this moment in the lecture not be seen as a concise synopsis of Ahab and the whale hunt, no different from the intellectual and emotional processes that wrote this book? Here I ask myself, "Have I constructed a Melville who thinks as I do? Have I neglected the possibility that his political sympathies were always attuned to the neoclassicism of the German romantics, say, Goethe or Carlyle?"

In the fourth volume of *German Romance*, Carlyle quieted Faustian explorers, offering a repaired alternative, another statue that gradually reveals itself. Do Carlyle's masculinist protocols resemble those of Melville's lecture? Commenting upon Goethe's *Dichtung und Wahrheit*, Carlyle apotheosized the model historian and autobiographer, one who kept his attachment to Prometheus, the Pelagian heresy, and the active life under wraps:

There, in the kindest and coolest spirit, [Goethe] conducts us through the scenes of his past existence; unfolds with graphic clearness and light gay dignity, whatever influenced the formation of his character and mode of thought; depicting all with the knowledge of a chief actor, and the calm impartial penetration of a spectator; speaking of himself as many would wish, but few are able, to speak of themselves: In the temper of a third party, and not sooner or not farther than others are desirous and entitled to hear that subject treated. (1–2)

. . . In Goethe's mind, the first aspect that strikes us is its calmness, then its beauty. A deeper inspection reveals to us its vastness and unmeasured strength. This man rules and is not ruled. The stern and fiery energies of a most passionate soul lie silent in the centre of his being; a trembling sensibility has been inured to stand, without flinching or murmur, the sharpest trials. Nothing outward, nothing inward, shall agitate or control him. The brightest and most capricious fancy, the most piercing and inquisitive intellect, the wildest and deepest imagination, the highest thrills of joy, the bitterest pangs of sorrow: all these are his, he is not theirs. While he moves every heart from its steadfastness, his own is firm and still: the words that search into the inmost recesses of our nature, he pronounces with a tone of coldness and equanimity; in the deepest pathos, he weeps not, or his tears are like water trickling from a rock of adamant. He is king of himself and his world; nor does he rule it like a vulgar great man, like a Napoleon or Charles III, by the mere brute exertion of his will, grounded on no principle, or on a false one: his faculties and feelings are not fettered or prostrated under the iron sway of Passion, but led and guided in kindly union under the mild sway of Reason; as the fierce, primeval elements of Nature were stilled at the coming of Light, and bound together, under its soft vesture, into a glorious and beneficent Creation.

This is the true Rest of man; no stunted unbelieving callousness, no reckless surrender to blind force, no opiate delusion; but the harmonious adjustment of Necessity and Accident, of what is changeable and what is unchangeable in our destiny; the calm supremacy of the spirit over its circumstances; the dim aim of every human soul, the full attainment of only a chosen few. (17–18)

But Carlyle's encomium does not fit turbulent Goethe describing his resentment at the stunted development, self-denial, and renunciations forced upon him by both his physical and social life—passages that Melville marked in ink with diamond shapes and wavy lines.[32]

Has Ishmael reached a kind and cool Carlylean Rest? By quoting Job in the epilogue to *Moby-Dick,* has he agreed not to test God, thus evading the legitimation of authority altogether, or would close-reading Daniel Orme/Melville have tested Carlyle and found him wanting? Would he have noticed that Carlyle, in his domestication of sublimity, made no sense, that he had denounced "the reckless surrender to blind force" while praising "the harmonious adjustment of Necessity and Accident"? Where is the will that resists reckless surrenders? Carlyle has nullified it: The "will" is a "mere brute exertion" ruled by "Passion" unless led by "the mild sway of Reason," the "true Rest" that discerns what "is changeable and what is unchangeable in our destiny."

Carlyle's sketch of Goethe has presented a rectified Titan/Wandering Jew, a scientific harmonizer at once promoting "the temper of a third party" and the stoic adjustment to social forces that may be incomprehensible and that are certainly not of his making. History is marshalled to underline the power of "destiny" and the inevitability of human weakness; coolness and kindness are attained when Goethe objectively understands the power of the past "in the formation of his character and mode of thought." Here is the proof of superior self-control, an aristocratic quality glaringly absent in the weeping, willful, ungrateful, and slanderous lower orders. Carlyle was only following Goethe's lead:

> In my efforts to free myself from the pressures of the too-gloomy and powerful, which continued to rule within me, and seemed to me sometimes as strength, sometimes as weakness, I was thoroughly assisted by that open, social, stirring manner of life, which attracted me more and more, to which I accustomed myself, and which I at last learned to enjoy with perfect freedom. It is not difficult to remark in the world, that man feels himself most freely and most perfectly rid of his own failings, when he represents to himself the faults of others, and expatiates upon them with complacent censoriousness. It is a tolerably pleasant sensation even to set ourselves above our equals by disapprobation and misrepresentation, for which reason good society, whether it consists of few or many, is most delighted with it. But nothing equals the comfortable self-complacency, when we erect ourselves into judges of our superiors, and of those who are set over us,—of princes and statesmen, when we find public institutions unfit and injudicious, only consider the possible and actual obstacles, and recognise neither the greatness of the invention, nor the co-operation which is to be expected from time and circumstances in every undertaking. (1:322)

And such cooperation would be manifested in Goethe's energetically publicized management of the sublime, in his particularly German understanding of organic form. Describing the architecture of the Strasbourg minster, Goethe joined the contradictions in his own character:

> The more I considered the *facade*, the more was that first impression strengthened and developed, that here the sublime has entered into alliance with the

pleasing. If the vast, when it appears as a mass is not to terrify; if it is not to confuse, when we seek to investigate its details, it must enter into an unnatural, apparently impossible connexion, it must associate to itself the pleasing. But now, since it will be impossible for us to speak of the impression of the minster except by considering both these incompatible qualities as united, so do we already see, from this, in what high value we must hold the ancient monument, and we begin in earnest to describe how such contradictory elements could peaceably interpenetrate and unite themselves.

. . . For a work of art, the whole of which is conceived in great, simple, harmonious parts, makes indeed a noble and dignified impression, but the peculiar enjoyment which the pleasing produces can only find place in the consonance of all developed details.

And it is precisely here that the building we are examining satisfies us in the highest degree: for we see all the ornaments fully suited to every part which they adorn; they are subordinate to it, they seem to have grown out of it. Such a manifoldness always gives great pleasure, since it flows of its own accord from the suitable, and therefore at the same time awakens the feeling of unity. It is only in such cases that the execution is prized as the summit of art. (1:328–30)

Goethe rejoiced in his analysis of the Strasbourg minster and its cultural salience in the promotion of German nationalism: "Since now I found that this building had been based on old German ground, and grown thus far in genuine German times, and that the name of the master, on his modest gravestone, was likewise of native sound and origin, I ventured, being incited by the worth of this work of art, to change the hitherto decried appellation of 'Gothic architecture,' and to claim it for our nation as 'German architecture'; nor did I fail to bring my patriotic views to light, first orally, and afterwards in a little treatise . . . which Herder afterwards inserted in his pamphlet: *Von Deutscher Art und Kunst*" (331).

Melville's wish to meet Carlyle on his trip to England in 1849 does support the efforts of the organic conservatives to claim Melville as their own.[33] Class position will tell, and yet Henry Murray could say to the assembled Melvilleans at Williamstown in 1951 as they celebrated the centenary of *Moby-Dick*, "Some may wonder how it was that Melville, a fundamentally good, affectionate, noble, idealistic, and reverential man, should have felt impelled to write a wicked book. Why did he aggress so furiously against Western orthodoxy, as furiously as Byron, or Shelley, or any other Satanic writer who preceded him, as furiously as Nietzsche or the most radical of his successors in our day?"[34]

At about the same time that Melville was writing *Pierre*, another Left romantic—Karl Marx—meditated upon failed revolutions:

Cromwell and the English people had borrowed speech, passions and illusions from the Old Testament for their bourgeois revolution. . . . Bourgeois revolutions, like those of the eighteenth century, storm more swiftly from success to success; their dramatic effects outdo each other; men and things seem set in sparkling brilliants; ecstasy is the everyday spirit: but they are short lived; soon they have attained their zenith, and a long depression lays hold of society before it learns soberly to assimilate the results of its storm and stress period. Proletarian revolutions, on the other hand, like those of the nineteenth century, criticize themselves constantly, interrupt themselves continually in their own course, come back to the apparently accomplished in order to begin it afresh, deride with unmerciful thoroughness the inadequacies, weaknesses and paltrinesses of their first attempts, seem to throw down their adversary only in order that he may draw new strength from the earth and rise again more gigantic before them, recoil ever and anon from the indefinite prodigiousness of their own aims, until the situation has been created which makes all turning back impossible, and the conditions themselves cry out: *Hic Rhodus, hic salta! Hier ist die Rose, hier tanze!*[35]

Marx should not have been so quick to dismiss the achievements of the "bourgeois revolutions" by claiming that their characters were not only arrogant, but lacking in the boldly self-critical intellectual habits he attributed to proletarian revolutions (as if there had been one); most seriously, he prophesied that the once-revolutionary bourgeois, spellbound perhaps by the "passions and illusions from the Old Testament," would refuse the leap into a better society though roses were in bloom. For Melville (as radical bourgeois, inheritor of the American and French Revolutions), the project of human liberation had, and perhaps always would have, its unfinished, ragged edges. As I have emphasized throughout this book, Melville was writing in a dangerous cultural situation, with one foot planted in the Middle Ages, the other kicking at the pricks. When he thought about the damage Ahab's or Margoth's clearer sightedness had wreaked upon his family, he paused and turned about. Homeward bound he blurred the boundary between two contradictory body states. As an experimental modern artist, testing the powers of language and form to express and penetrate the inner and outer worlds he experienced, Melville's self-control quieted realistic fears of retaliation when Ahab leaped into darkness. As an organic conservative, however, his composure was only the pseudo-courage that masks abject submission to the will of illegitimate authority.

My own brooding ends neither with a refurbished monument nor the rubble thrown down by iconoclastic Melvilleans, and without any conclusive opinion as to the artist's mental states beyond what he confided to careful readers. Melville and those modernists who both inspired and alarmed him remain Titanic in our imaginations because they, like Cervantes and Milton, imperishably enunciated the propositions of the democratic experiment: rejection of servile pomp, respect for hard liberty and for the transformative power of labor, human fellow-feeling, and the nonstop critical intellect that much of the twentieth-century Left has abandoned. Their ruins need no longer detain us.

Appendix
Repunctuating the Melville Revival
A New Map, a Pause, and a Tour through the Archives

Academic treatments of Melville's rise and fall are entwined with the unsolved problem of popular legitimation in "pluralistic" modern democracies: societies that preach toleration and mutual respect but may withhold the critical tools (empiricism, historical memory, access to state secrets) that could make popular sovereignty a fact, not a charade. Melville saw through pseudodemocrats and hammered away in book after book (though subtly, evasively, and inconsistently), but the autodidact's more emancipating insights were frequently suppressed in three overlapping but distinguishable "waves," or, more precisely, bouts. In this appendix I will review the phases of the Melville Revival and then offer the historical materials and tools developed in this book to literary scholars across the political spectrum.

Two publishing events in America and England returned Melville to public scrutiny three decades after his death: Raymond M. Weaver's *Herman Melville: Mariner and Mystic* (1921), and the Constable *Standard Edition of the Works of Herman Melville* (1922–24), directed by Michael Sadleir. Thousands of books, articles, and dissertations followed in two more waves of interpretation, with "booms" of interest following World War II and especially after the campus revolts of the 1960s. Each wave washed away the errors of its predecessors in Melville scholarship, the better to explain the highs and lows of his career. The Nietzschean first wave (post-1919) reproached Victorian philistines and puritans, or the women of Melville's family, for his failure; the second wave (post-1933) reproached the first wave for mystifications: Weaver and his followers had exaggerated the greatness of their "titanic culture hero,"[1] reading the fiction too literally as autobiography and making unwarranted inferences about Melville's family life, for instance, the notion that young Melville had gone to sea to escape an incestuous connection with his cold but seductive mother. Some second-wave scholars, conservative Christians and anti-Freudians, greeted the late work as a welcome departure from adolescent defiance or ressentiment. During the outpouring of post-1960s Melville dissertations and other publications, scholars often read Melville as a proto–New Leftist like themselves, relying upon the biographies of the more scientific second-wave scholars, while (oddly) some returned to "Freudian" interpretations of the first wave: Their antibourgeois, anti-imperialist hero could not have been the conservative that some second-wave scholars had imagined. Myth- and symbol-minded New Leftists, however, were more Jungian than Freudian in their enthusiasm for archetypes and, in good *völkisch* style, a racially specific collective unconscious.[2] Although the post-1960s scholarship might be called a third wave, no breakthroughs were achieved, nor was there a synthesis of first- and second-wave ideas: Raymond Weaver is still an outsider, perhaps because he had encountered Melville unhampered by preceding interpretations, at least in one respect. Viewing Captain Ahab as the feisty and awesome Melville himself, the no-holds-barred modern artist, Weaver's reading clashed with a reading now virtually hegemonic. With few exceptions, 1930s leftists, Agrarian New Critics, and 1960s–70s New Leftists have elevated Ishmael. Captain Ahab was the epitome of capitalist-imperialist America drunk with power, his corpse-laden ship, the *Pequod*, an emblem of technology gone awry, whereas Ishmael/Melville survived, alerting posterity to coming American fascism and the bomb.

The labors of second-wave scholars have culminated in an authoritative edition of Melville's complete works, co-published since 1965 by Northwestern University and the Newberry Library. Each volume contains extensive historical notes, sources, textual emendations, and surveys of the changing reception to Melville's puzzling art. In all phases of the Revival there seems to be a consensus, stated or not, that Melville's "greatness" or "failure" as a literary figure should be a major concern,[3] particularly insofar as the duration of a possibly troubled mental condition during the mid-1850s affected the artistic quality, social themes, and politics of his work. This was the period of his eerie short fiction, including "Bartleby the Scrivener" and "Benito Cereno," and then his last published novel, *The Confidence-Man* (1857). At stake was the hotly contested meaning of his last work, "Billy Budd." Did the young radical finally emerge from his teens as a resigned Christian blessing the state that is slaying him, or did he remain a heretical irruption, leader of a sit-in strike that interminably calls authority to account? I argued that assessments of Melville's last work (which along with "Benito Cereno" passed muster with Nazi censors in 1938, entering certain German libraries) are precise indicators of the authoritarian commitments of prominent English and American literary critics: Some were unabashedly profascist during the interwar period, while others, as organic conservatives, were simply attuned to fascist ideologies. Biographical and textual facts were collected or ignored to buttress readings vindicating Captain Vere.[4]

In accounting for the Melville Revival, English professors have generally emphasized changing taste, personality, and Zeitgeist. The resurgence of interest in *Moby-Dick* and its author was such a striking phenomenon that Percy H. Boynton, a writer for the *Nation* and the *New Republic*, was already commenting upon it in the early 1920s: "The present 'Melville revival' can be accounted for partly by the present-day vogue of South Sea literature and partly by the post-war temper of skepticism, but more because in Melville has been rediscovered one of the immensely energetic and original personalities of the last hundred years."[5] Princeton professor Willard Thorp offered a multiplicity of factors in his still canonical 1938 publication:

> By a happy chance, the centenary of his birth in 1919, the publication of Weaver's biography which partly drew aside the veil of mystery about his life, the assertion of his artistic greatness by a new group of English admirers, and the movement among scholars here to reinterpret our literary history, provided a series of coordinated impulses which have succeeded in placing him in the company he should have been keeping.
>
> Melville has had to wait this long because the world has only recently caught up with him. His personal vision was largely at variance with his age for whom, as Sullivan says [in the *Times Literary Supplement*, July 26, 1923], "the material world was a perfectly clear-cut and comprehensible affair, and everything that was not material was merely moral." We are aware once more, as Melville was, of the mystery of man.

Percy Boynton read *Moby-Dick* as "the story of Eve and Prometheus, the perennial struggle of man for spiritual freedom in the midst of an externally physical world—his attempt to make a conquest of circumstance." For Boynton, Eve and Prometheus had switched from materialism to spirituality, but he did not explain why the gods should have punished such admirable docility. Similarly for Thorp, whose Christian Socialist sympathies were evident throughout, Melville left Victorian culture lagging in the rear while he took the van with medieval mystery. More recent writers continued along similar lines. Michael P. Zimmerman and Jeanetta Boswell have stressed the theme of postwar "disillusion," referring to the salutary disenchantment of liberals with "progress"—the collapse of Wilsonian idealism after the Versailles conference of 1919. Watson G. Branch argued that social and literary changes created a new critical context: *Moby-Dick* was now read as rebellion against the (unspecified) oppressive forces in society. Like Fred Lewis Pattee before him, H. Bruce Franklin hinted that the Melville Revival and the Harlem Renaissance were linked. Hershel Parker's historical note in the recent Northwestern-Newberry edition of *Moby-Dick* (1988) mentioned the centenary and the many essays it inspired, but it further hinted that a taste for nonwhite handsome sailors (that some have mistaken for the fellowship of humanity) partly accounts for Melville's relatively unflagging popularity in England. More significant, Parker turned moderate men into radical democrats, identifying an earlier English cohort of Melville advocates whom he characterizes as progressive, even revolutionary, allies of the working class and nonwhites:[6]

> The younger members of the British literary world who constituted the admirers of Melville, Whitman and Thoreau belonged for the most part to three or four overlapping groups. They were members of the Pre-Raphaelite Brotherhood of artist-writers or their associates; they were adherents of the working-men's movement (datable from 1854, when F. D. Maurice, the Christian Socialist, founded the Working Men's College in London); they were (a little later) Fabian Socialists; or they were themselves sea-writers or writers about remote countries. To belong in any of the first three of these groups was to be politically and socially radical, never far from the revolutionary spirit of Shelley. . . . [T]o belong to the last group almost always meant to have done one's own fieldwork in comparative anthropology and to have learned (often under Southern constellations) to think untraditionally and independently and therefore to look at European society unconventionally.

It is understandable, if distressing, that nonhistorians are often unfamiliar with the intricacies of social movements; of course historians themselves frequently disagree about the political significance and character of leading personalities, transformative events, and economic developments in the last five centuries, but few would place centrist social democrats (for example, Christian Socialists) in the revolutionary vanguard. Unable or unwilling to identify the relevant context, then, literary critics could explain neither the selective promotion of "classic" American literature in the 1920s nor the acrimonious debates among insider Melvilleans. Radical English professors have usually confined the study of literary reputations to the internal politics of specifically "cultural" (symbol-making) institutions such as the academy and publishing, institutions dominated, it is alleged, by white males who, through the imposition of exegetical criticism and the phony universalism of Western standards of quality, have relegated to the margins those texts that challenged their narrowly restricted elitist vision.[7] For many, Melville and his supporters are turning out to be the chief perpetrators.

Paul Lauter has advanced multiculturalism as editor of the massive *Heath Anthology of American Literature,* funded by the Rockefeller Foundation; Melville is not condemned in the essay written by Carolyn Karcher. Lauter's more recent article, "Melville Climbs the Canon" (1994), however, implies that Thorp should have enlarged his list: Counterrevolution created *Moby-Dick* as a godlike text. Lauter surely joins me in doubting that elite-dominated institutions canonized radical artists vilified by earlier conservatives, or that, no matter how destabilizing to institutional legitimacy, professors freely exercise taste and judgment, since robust pluralism has always existed throughout the enlightened academy. But we part company in our accounts of the Revival. Lauter asserts that Melville was constructed as a shrewd Yankee tour guide to the exotic, a high modernist weapon brandished by nativist white males to club ascendant Others. Moreover, his scenario is conspiratorial, directed primarily to the year 1919, as if a rotten egg had been hatched by J. Edgar Hoover or Mitchell Palmer in league with the Whites in the Russian civil war. A longer time frame and more archival research would have demonstrated that *this* white male author was not glorified but simultaneously praised and undermined as the sick man of American letters. From Weaver on, especially in the published criticism of Olson, Murray, and Leyda, Melville's bumpy career and romantic wildness were often a dire warning to other wayward youth: Such diagnostics had been pleasing to 1930s fascists and other corporatists. For Lauter, however, the determining "milieu" (an idealist category) comprises authors of different races, ethnicities, and genders: Racial/gender conflict makes literary history; that's all we need to know. What Melville actually wrote, his confusing family situation, and why his works could appeal to readers with opposing politics seem of little interest— "perhaps" the real Melville is unknowable: "As is perhaps always the case," Lauter writes, "what the critics of the 1920s made of Melville tells us more about them than about him."[8]

Lauter is saying that the Melville Revival is good as proof of cultural relativism, evil when he offers the "culture" of "race, class, and gender" as the source of social action.[9] Lauter does not see the incoherence in his own position. As a relativist, he argues that the canon changes: Melville was a failure in the white male-dominated nineteenth century, oddly a success in the twentieth, also dominated by white males. I agree that valuations of artistic excellence are not necessarily intrinsic, timeless, and universal; Lauter, however, is saying that greatness is determined by the ideological requirements of the dominant culture, ruled generically by the upper-class white male. But if that is so, why did the patrician Melville antagonize fellow conservatives in the nineteenth century?[10] Historians and other materialist readers may understand that standards are not rooted but contested and unstable within a given modern culture—indeed, within artists and critics themselves. And as chroniclers of change, aesthetic power and pleasure aside, should historians not distinguish between "art" that socializes the young into a relatively static hierarchical society versus "art" that, where appropriate, continually reconfigures reality (past and present) and challenges authority on behalf of human dignity and equality before the law? But these are not Lauter's analytic categories.

My account of the Melville Revival should be contrasted also with that of William V. Spanos, Jr. Informed by Gramsci, Althusser, Heidegger, Raymond Williams, and Foucault, Spanos, a "New Americanist," believes that Melville's 1920s revivers constructed a monument to American democratic superiority and, like other radicals of his generation, Spanos gives credit to the 1960s cohort for bringing counterhegemony and decentered authority to the academy after the Vietnam War caused America's hitherto blameless self-image to self-destruct. Melville's American classic *Moby-Dick* had been a synecdoche for the greatness of white native-born America after World War I, Spanos argues, and was promoted as such by the aristocratic revivers of the 1920s. This sounds like Lauter's opinion, but Spanos thinks that the book's "errant art," its antinarrative is counterhegemonic, unlike the tragic form (preferred by neoclassical New Critics) that reconciles contradictions and supposedly immobilizes the reader for action in the public sphere.[11] The post-1960s scholars, with all their dedication to multiplicity, allow little room for experience, introspection, understanding, and moral choice; they may not recognize the depoliticizing consequences of their supposedly anti-elitist critical method. The old historicism, born in an age of revolution, has been rejected; much recent radical criticism axes "positivist" heresies. Why read individuals (or oneself) when all subjectivity is "rooted" in the collective—the class, the gender, the race or ethnicity, the linguistic entity, the community, the society—hence localist? And we know what we will find before we start: Our pictures of the material world will be dim, indefinite, and idiosyncratic, for humanity, bibulous by nature, is incapable of distinguishing between legitimate and illegitimate authority. The canon warriors, with more than a dash of populist paranoia and primitivism, are disrespectful to "white male" and all other artists, artworks, and publics; no one has demonstrated that books are cookie cutters or that publics are molded and stamped.[12] The record more persuasively suggests that Melville was conflicted and elusive as were his readers and revivers, but that says nothing conclusive about human capacity; rather, it should arouse our curiosity about historically specific social conditions that have muzzled authors and readers alike. I have found pockets of erratic and unscholarly conduct in high places, in men widely revered. Who and what has educated these educators? Historians such as myself may glean hints of disturbance from published records, but it was prolonged digging into private communications that unearthed the analytic tool introduced above: the distinction between radical and conservative Enlightenment. Scholars in both tendencies aver their respect for "facts" and comprehensive exploration; they would never disdain meticulous inspection and protracted introspection to the detriment of the young people in their care. The telling difference between the rival materialist ideologies was found in their contrasting valuations of the dissenting individual and in contrasting standards for artistic originality and greatness.

The "English" empiricist method I prefer is usually identified with the "rigid" New England theocracy, (bourgeois) science, and the naturalist style in literature. It is open-ended but not nihilistic, and it describes structures and functions, comparing concrete institutions and individuals making decisions that may be, to varying degrees, more or less informed and accurate, more or less self-interested decisions that are susceptible to empirical investigation. The other, more supple method promoted by philology and German historicism examines genealogy and "milieu" as prime movers in the formation of a distinctive "national" or "ethnic" character: Clear-eyed historicism of the German school does not create heroic myths by idealizing its own ethnicity or race; it simply says each *Volk* is incomparable and unique—or will be, once its language is purified of alien Hebraic influences or Western rationalist "rules." Artists are great, spontaneous, and original only insofar as they are rooted in a particular national character/linguistic community, reflecting the ever-evolving, progressively more limpid Zeitgeist. For these world citizens, the healthy corporatist entity alone possesses individuality; its modernity and liberalism stem from its "internationalist" appreciation of "diversity" (at a distance); common culture inwardly binds the national organism; rooted cosmopolitanism and relativism preclude war-inciting invidious comparisons with other, similarly purified national groups. Perhaps such sentiments seemed practical and inviting to Herder's readers—eighteenth-century German-speaking Europeans dominated by France, and bereft of a vernacular high culture—but the achievement of a similarly coherent (if irrationalist) cultural identity was elusive to mixed-up Americans who preferred their individuality done rare and personal.

To solve this conundrum, some New Leftists have adopted the role of German romantic hero, overthrowing the New England spirit by making America the world-in-itself, federated in diverse races, genders, and ethnicities, and coexisting peacefully when properly understood and represented. Lauter's argument in the *Heath Anthology* jibes with other New Left positions that Anglo-Saxon (bourgeois) hegemony characterized the academy until their generation installed cultural pluralism, an argument vigorously opposed, however, by one distinguished cultural historian at the New Orleans meeting of the American Studies Association in 1991. MIT professor Leo Marx, a student of Matthiessen and Perry Miller, claimed continuity between his anticapitalist professors at Harvard and the 1960s generation. Similarly, Kermit Vanderbilt's book *American Literature and the Academy* rebuked 1960s radicals such as Lauter, Richard Ohmann, and Louis Kampf who brought the 1968 meeting of the Modern Language Association close to "havoc and revolution." Vanderbilt constructed an alternative heroic tradition to displace New Left crazies: The unappreciated Carl Van Doren and his cohort fought for the viability of "American literature" against classicist colleagues, an enterprise that commenced in 1913.[13] The bibliography recommended in 1948 by other educators in American literature and written by the very democrats recommended by Vanderbilt, however, disclosed only a heroic encounter with the fatal sublimity of the Protestant mission. Pedagogues were running from half-baked mass literacy in industrial society.[14] It was Victorian culture and the liberal nineteenth century that oppressed Melville's twentieth-century promoters—a judgment echoing Melville's own moodier diagnostics.

Curettage

After World War II, established doctors to society exhibited a good fellow "Melville" such as themselves, refusing filthy lucre and stoically accepting the ultimate inscrutability and irrationality of the universe, and like God's creation, too various to pin down. Exemplary physician that he was, Melville, beset in youth by a hypertrophied brain, had healed himself; the mature Melville was a democratic pluralist (Leyda and the Yale faction). For other, defiantly radical scholars of the 1960s (H. Bruce Franklin and C. L. R. James), Melville was a master pathologist whose x-ray vision and mighty arm stripped the pretensions of the capitalist system to expose the violence that lurked just beneath its lawfully ordered white exterior; the conspicuous interdependence of Ishmael and the nonwhites on the *Pequod* presumably could arouse the submerged masses to overthrow all the Ahabs. More recent feminist scholars have flayed their deceptive teachers along with Melville: The moderate men are beating back insurgent women, blacks, Indians, etc.; neither a hero nor a victim, perhaps Melville (like elderly professors) should be dislodged from favored positions in the canon (Lauter and Renker). Generally stricken from the postwar melodrama was the nineteenth-century philosophe, unmasking frauds, and, when united with his better angel, standing firm for individuality and solidarity with humanity, adhering to republican principles and universalist ethics, mapping and remapping antagonistic social forces and his own vacillations, interrogating language, planning strategically, biding his time, keeping the flame alive.

Rejecting ethnopluralism as an analytic category, and aligning with eighteenth- and nineteenth-century empiricists, I revised previous accounts of the Melville Revival. First, I challenged the notion that revivers of the 1920s mythologized and overvalued Melville's writing, whereas empiricist scholars after the mid-1930s approached a more human, life-sized artist. Raymond Weaver's biography (1921) was only a qualified endorsement resembling later, equally cautious biographies of the 1920s. Weaver's own developing public criticism was not necessarily more favorable; the rebellious Weaver was always fixated upon Melville's predictable failure; his private estimates of Melville's artistry were reined in by men more conservative than himself. Melville scholars in "both" waves have cut a libertarian hero down to size, while harboring complex emotional responses; their trimming is central to our evaluation of Melville's mental health—the core issue of the Revival. Melvillean operations may determine the reader's response to Captain Ahab/the modern artist as Superman, our Great Adversary, tragic hero, or revolutionary madman. Weaver's sensitive biography has been attacked, I suspect, not because later scholars wanted to rehabilitate Melville's relatives (who, most older scholars agreed, were to some degree philistine and uncomprehending of the genius in their midst), but in aversion to Weaver's heart-on-the-sleeve identification with Melville as Ahab.

Second, previous studies have not described the strange institutional conditions that impinged upon their own formulations and those of their predecessors as they evaluated Melville's mental states, textual meanings, and politics. Nor have literary scholars sufficiently examined ideological realignments during and after the interwar period; their recent studies of canon formation seem motivated by campus politics and the economic need to justify new sub-disciplines and anthologies. While the retrieval of hitherto overlooked artistic production is important and illuminating, bereft of an accurate and comprehensive history, the new, more inclusive, curricula remain token gestures of accommodation. Where, why, and how "change" occurs is (or was) the task of historians; the exact mapping of shifts in macroeconomic structure, ideology, and politics is the topic of their most pregnant debates. Such concerns seem not to have troubled literary scholars since the ascendancy of cultural anthropology with its idealist emphasis on "symbolic interaction."[15]

A PAUSE TO MEASURE THE MODERATE MEN

What we are is the highest attainable earthly good, reigning authority insists; we alone are realistic, conciliatory, and practical democrats; do not confuse us, please, with the moral absolutists to our Left and Right. Notwithstanding Arthur Schlesinger, Jr.'s (possible) reading of Ishmael's rescue in the vital center,[16] I have found neither balance, complacency, nor conviction in the upper reaches of Melville scholarship, and certainly not the "bourgeois hegemony" that many Old and New Leftists had postulated. If there is hegemony, it is promiscuously antibourgeois and often misogynist and antisemitic; the Melville who spoke through Ahab and Pierre has been squashed.[17] Like other bearers of radical Enlightenment (radical puritans, Lockeans, Smithians, Jeffersonians, moral mothers, abolitionists, nineteenth-century workers, and some Marxists of the Second International), "Ahab" has promoted ever-increasing political and economic democracy and a commitment to the universal education that enabled unbounded critical thought. Conservative enlighteners preferred Ishmael/Melville; as progressives they attempted to reconcile science and religion, the older, higher, rooted truths of traditional culture,[18] not necessarily because of deeply held faith or reverence for ancestors, but to harness the unpredictable horse of scientific instruction—galloping, as it seemed to them, toward the abyss of either socialist internationalism or a democratic society that had banished arbitrary authority vested in unaccountable bureaucracies and the uncontested rule of the rich.

Priestly spells would promote class harmony in the face of contradictory evidence conveyed by Ahab's rebel senses. The wall separating radical and conservative Enlightenment, however, turned out to be a semipermeable membrane; the forced reconciliation between science and religion or "tradition" has made men sick. No matter how hard they pushed them down and out, the repressed facts of the material world slipped back in, only to be pummeled and extruded again. The twists and turns of the Melville Revival, their "self-erasing" subject moving in and out of focus, can be explained by the counter-Enlightenment cultural practices of prestigious socializing institutions—families and universities ostensibly training the promising young for bold and creative leadership in the arts and sciences, while denying the ever looming contradiction between discovery and institutional stability—in the ensuing confusion undermining the self-confidence essential to invention and mastery. Rather than examining often incompatible demands of their liberal profession, then asserting their rights to academic freedom, scholars tended to blame the Romantic Wandering Jew, Melville/Ahab—the unthrottled radical Enlightenment— for their discomposure.

Radical enlighteners look conflict in the eye, do not repress compassion to protect their careers. With tools of empirical science and its inductive method, they probe beneath and behind surfaces to seek fundamental causes of social cruelty and unequal treatment; and taking sides with the weak and oppressed, they try to alleviate unnecessary suffering. These noble qualities were taken over by the conservative opposition and denatured: The pseudo-enlighteners say that they too are good doctors wedded to progress; they too examine conflict and social maladies, boldly prying into their multiple sources. But try as they may to warn us, the natural world keeps throwing dust in their (really, our) eyes; for most of us (not them), human limitations and passions are too powerful to be overcome; Reason should not expect to penetrate and master Nature.[19] Of course they are not old fogies: The world changes, new conditions disturb existing social arrangements; however, all conflicts, no matter how novel, can be negotiated and conciliated through compromise and incremental improvements; traditional cultures understood the benefits of myth and ritual, and continuity with its time-tested methods preserves and nurtures greatness. Breaks within families or between groups or between past and present are simply cultural misapprehensions or failures in communication; they do not point to institutional weakness; only neurotics are stressed. Dangerous to themselves and others, such unstable characters are politically repressed in the interest of public safety and national security. By contrast, those souls properly rooted in past excellences (the hierarchical organic society, tailored to the specific conditions imposed by blood and soil) are elevated to leadership: They are natural aristocrats, having surmounted their own prideful divisive propensities or outmoded habits to find those institutional configurations and discursive practices that insure social cohesion—and of course the maintenance of their own status. Unfortunately, not all conflict is manageable without structural change; faced with intractable antagonisms, the moderates shut down at least part of the body's sensorium. The personal histories traced in this book suggest that conservative enlighteners are scientistic and unbalanced, not scientific and poised: This world of real people, real structures of domination, and dangerously unsolved problems of global magnitude refuses to lie still; its constant reappearance forced Melville and his revivers to allow the possibility that they had been taken in; the authority they trusted and relied upon was deceptive; as leaders they had failed. Rarely is there a clean boundary between radical and conservative Enlightenment, but not because the world defies unequivocal distinctions. Perhaps the blur appears when we are unsure whether the lap of benignant authority is a safe harbor or a man trap, or we blink when we see which is which. The unnerving oscillations between radical and conservative Enlightenment inside moderate leadership itself, amply demonstrated in Melville's own characters and in the private communications of his Ahab-obsessed revivers, is the key to the Melville problem.

As both a leading Melville scholar and a pioneer in personnel assessment at Harvard and the OSS, psychologist Dr. Henry A. Murray was annoyed that he could not always separate Melville's (Ahab's) voice from Ishmael's, for it was his task to diagnose latent radicalism in bright young men like himself before they went off the deep end: Ahab was an arousing but unpredictable trailblazer, while Ishmael (or Starbuck) was the comfortably adapted alternative, but mediocre and boring; the Bostonian Murray separated himself from other "Boston Brahmins," deprecating them as "smug soft seated passionless intellectuals" or "staid puritan professors."[20] Murray often admitted that he identified with Melville and was similarly torn. One may plausibly segment Melville studies by contrasting 1920s bohemians in revolt against feminized Victorian culture—Murray, for instance—with good bourgeois defenders of nineteenth-century scientific reforms, the battle-axes who invaded male sanctuaries to make the whole world homelike, but this well-worn formulation, though accurate, is too cold. There is an underlying unity, an unspeakable shared suffering and horror that has not been remarked: the loss of an integrated self, of an identity with a consistent moral center. There are pragmatists and pragmatists; some test and improve theories in action without attempting to control the outcome; others, less humble, take "pragmatism" as permission to separate means from ends, deceptively if they please, for might makes right and science is just another tool for limited ascensions upward and onward. Youthful democratic republican ideals could not survive in an ethical system valuing harmony and stability over the potentially "disruptive" consequences of unbounded intellectual inquiry. Cynics may be surprised to learn that the prominent scholars studied herein were not sociopaths oblivious to the effects of noble lies, but since the calamity could not be acknowledged in a free society utterly antithetical to the Soviet Union or Nazi Germany, the attenuated and riven bodies limed by Melville were neither mourned nor rehabilitated. Perhaps his survivors, family and academic alike, under-read Melville because they dared not read their ambivalent selves in (justifiable) revolt against an irrational system; not surprisingly, "his" credibility is always on the line; it is "he," particularly in moments of perceptual clarity, whose intellectual, moral, and emotional development has been twisted or arrested. The comfort of a fully comprehended broken heart was inaccessible in the better universities.

Liberal nationalism vs. the politics of group identity

When not diverted by elites, science has had objectives incompatible with mind management. Focusing here on academic freedom and the marketplace of ideas, I have documented the restraints on one liberal nationalist democratic writer and his readership in "free Ameriky" (to borrow the taunt of Melville's grumbling cripple Thomas Fry in *The Confidence-Man*)—one who tried to decode the supposedly rational institutions in which he moved or was immobilized. For Melville in his democratic mood, Americanization signified mastery of those intellectual and emotional skills appropriate to a popular democracy; chattel slavery, wage slavery, castes, servility, passivity, and ignorance had no place in a polity of citizen-philosopher kings. Clear-sighted persons measured the obstacles to such a grand and unprecedented achievement: There could be no liberty or equality of opportunity without an unimpeded view of the impure self and of all irrational institutional arrangements. There could be no personal or civic virtue in expediency; we could not wish away incoherence. Discarding the *Realpolitik* of opportunistic alliances, reform movements would join persons in political groupings sharing material interests and objectives.

There is no place for rigid determinism in the radical liberal scenario. With Freud (and Ahab/Melville), I have confidence in the "observing ego" ultimately capable, through effort and uncensored critical feedback, of stepping outside the supposed limits of self to inspect its inside operations and those of its environs, out from under the discourses that mediate between subject and object. Melville discovered institutions and social relationships that made no sense: His too-scenic, too-detached and analytic, too-cosmopolitan route was avoided by conservative reformers in academe. Arguing against those anthropologists and others who had punctured the idea of racial or national character (or of any collective subject whatsoever),[21] many progressives emphasized ethnic identity as the natural source of political interest and behavior. "Antiracists" asserted their "cultural pluralism" against the dessicating melting pot that allegedly robbed immigrants and former slaves of self-esteem and puissance. An example is John Higham's standard treatment of the ugly nativism that led to the Immigration Act of 1924. Higham viewed American cultural nationalism as reactionary, arguing that nativism and ethnic rivalries (not class fears) motivated the promotion of nineteenth-century American literature in the 1920s;[22] he ignored, however, competing concepts of cultural nationalism: liberal versus conservative, as well as persistent elite resistance to American democratic writers. The liberal nationalism espoused by Melville and other admirers of the seventeenth- and eighteenth-century revolutionary bourgeoisie was process-oriented and democratic, pressing toward popular sovereignty everywhere, by which they meant ongoing emancipation from illegitimate authority when and if it was wanted.[23] Their historical criticism interrogated cultural artifacts and institutions (most dangerously, religion) as constructions made by people, not gods or demi-gods; fetishes and sacred texts were now susceptible to educated understanding, a process with no end in sight.

Plumped by regicides, the extended application of civil liberties and the Napoleonic Codes, then a literate industrial working class (or its specter), "modernity" has consistently evoked a violently reactionary response in governing elites. Conservative nationalists accused rootless cosmopolitans, the utopians, of wholesale destruction, of reductionism, while they, as realistic yet mystical conservative liberals, perpetuated ignorance in the lower orders. Nineteenth-century German romanticism provided scientific reasons for displacing naturalism with "culturalism," a disguised form of biological determinism. Today the New Historicism parodies the materialist analysis that existed when Melville, referring perhaps to his own impudent procedures, regretted the lost bloom of revealed texts.[24] Conservatives still tied to aristocratic elites would have to see the emancipation of the senses as heedless iconoclasm, as destruction of all that was consoling and healing (the inexhaustible mother). Indeed, has not the management of desire, of rebellious impulses, of the emergent autonomy made possible by clear and complete pictures of all our institutions been the great task and achievement of the humanities in their conservative trajectory? Has not enlightenment been constantly linked with the wasteland, thereby degrading our natural capacities to adapt and survive? Many of the 1930s Southern Agrarians became the New Critics of the postwar literary establishment; members of this clique, such as John Gould Fletcher, John Crowe Ransom, and Yvor Winters, unapologetically publishing with fascists and vociferous antisemites in the *American Review,* were among Melville's most emphatic promoters between the wars; here were irrationalists affirming the reactionary and pessimistic side of Melville, preceding F. O. Matthiessen in praising America's greatest writer.

My confidence in Spinoza rested on the serene effect he wrought in me . . .
But let no one think I would have subscribed to his writings, and assented
to them *verbatim et literatim*. For, that no one really understands another;
that no one attaches the same idea to the same word which another does;
that dialogue, a book, excites in different persons different trains of
thought:—this I had long seen all too plainly.[25]
—Goethe on Spinoza, a sentiment not marked by Melville

Melville's vertiginous insights did not pacify conservatives in *The Confidence-Man*
and preceding works of the 1850s, for instance "Benito Cereno." In the latter work,
Melville slyly described the Yankee Captain Delano, who doles out water "with republican impartiality as to this republican element, which always seeks one level,
serving the oldest white no better than the youngest black; excepting, indeed, poor
Don Benito, whose condition, if not rank, demanded an extra allowance." Melville's
most presumptuous work was blamed by relatives as the cause of his decline. Here
is the artist on tour in 1856–57, an Ishmael indisposed, shuttered by the sight of
touchings in Egypt, by the prospective mating of unlike things:

[Saturday January 3, 1857] . . . Haunted houses & Cock Lanes. Ruined
mosques, domes knocked in like stoven boats. Others, upper part empty &
desolate with broken rafters & dismantled windows; (rubbish) below, the
dirty rites of religion. Aspect of the thoroughfares like London streets on Saturday night. All the world gossiping and marketing,—but in picturesque cos-
tumes. Crookedness of the streets—multitudes of blind men—worst city in
the world for them. [Flies on the eyes at noon. Nature feeding on man. Con-
tiguity of desert & verdure, splendor & squalor, gloom & gayety; numerous
blind men going about being led. Children opthalmick. Too much light and
no defence against it. . . .

. . . After seeing the pyramid, all other architecture seems but pastry.
Though I had but so short a time to view the pyramid, yet I doubt whether
any time spent on it, would tend to a more precise impression. As with the
ocean, you learn as much of its vastness by the first five minutes glance as you
would in a month, so with the pyramid. Its simplicity confounds you. Finding it vain to take in its vastness man has taken to sounding it & weighing its
density; so with the pyramid, he measures the base, & computes the size of
individual stones. It refuses to be studied or adequately comprehended. It
still looms in my imagination, dim & indefinite. (*Journals*, 74, 78)

Though they may have taken in Melville's vastness (with conditions), nativists did not applaud his taunts at phony liberals succoring failing aristocrats with "extra allowances"; moreover, as "White-Jacket," his messianic republicanism was neither racist nor chauvinist. Risking his own peace of mind, Melville identified double binds in the family and in society alike; these were incompatible expectations for independence and loyalty; originality and conformity; truth and (conservative) order; science and religion; narrow ethnic identity and international brotherhood; universal human rights and upper-class property rights. John Higham, like other ethnopluralists, did not acknowledge that moderate conservatives have tried to steer overzealous American democrats clear of ultrademocratic Circes, redefining or stabilizing American "identity" as the sharing of power, territory, and resources among diverse (and peacefully competing) ethnic groups, while proclaiming an overarching nationalism and internationalism. Ironically, such mystical rainbow coalitions, by definition ungrounded in shared material interests, were necessarily administered through mind management, not through appeals to the analytic and synthetic skills of scientific reason that made "progress" possible to radical enlighteners.

To understand the tenacity and duration of the Melville problem, I positioned Melville's life, art, and the controversies these evoked alongside competing social movements of the nineteenth and twentieth centuries, similarly unresolved. The contours of Melville studies have been shaped more by economic crisis, "excessive" labor militancy, class allegiance, and class fears than loyalty to the evidence of Melville's texts and the facts of his life as these emerged throughout the turbulent 1920s, 1930s, and 1940s. Not personal deficiencies in reading or comprehension, but contradictory institutional voices, each promising a renegotiated covenant, seem to have deterred right scholarly conduct by Melville's twentieth-century revivers. While moral clarity and consistency brought balance and a degree of emancipation from double bondage to their nineteenth-century subject, the chief Melville scholars concluded their studies in a mist misconstrued as the new dawn. The darkening light was sometimes greeted with joy and amazement, sometimes with a more tempered satisfaction.

There have been two Melville Revivals, one public, the other private; both are befuddled. The following appendix contains excerpts from private correspondence of leading Melville scholars, teaching guides, and other documents that support my thesis: There was nothing inevitable or singular or obscure about decisions made and unethical measures taken. Scholars were subjected to visible social forces, often contradictory, not of their own making. Some chose to conform to illiberal institutional demands and to mislabel their own shifting politics along with those of contemporary social movements. And, unlike the artist speaking through "dark" characters who untied the double binds bestowed by pseudodemocratic institutions, they were imprisoned accordingly and by their own lights. Oddly, it was often the revivers themselves who took the role of rude unmasker, exposing by turns their predecessors and/or Ahab/Melville himself. Like the red flower trailing on the white expanse of Lucy's pillow or Isabel's rusted tears, misdirected mortification has stained more than a few of these pages; here is the canon that propels our human narrative by turns into desolation or into the creative collaboration of our species with one another. Scholars attempting to remedy the neglect of women and non-whites in the academy would do better to face the limits of curiosity within our institutions by joining Ahab's project of Enlightenment wherever it may lead—the incompleted project of the radical liberals—than by decapitating idols that are nowhere to be found.

Following is a fragment from the papers of the Tory poet and critic Sir J. C. Squire, editor of the *London Mercury* and Macmillan's English Men of Letters series that published John Freeman's Melville biography (1926):

June 15. Russell goes back to town today. He tells me I must stay with him at Toynbee Hall [the British precursor to Jane Addams's Hull House, *C.S.*] when I next come to town, strangely enough the thought of it gladdens me. Why should I, sitting on a wide balcony looking over flowers & greenery & the sea, feel warmly toward Salmon's barrow of books in Whitechapel High St., or Prescott St. or Wellclose Square, or Davey's shop in the Minories, or the little grocer's behind Tower Hill by the Mint where I have so often dragged weary feet in the hours of lunch, willing neither to eat nor to fast, to walk nor to sit, to rest nor to desist from the rage of seeing?

These surely are the passions of the Wandering Jew; to keep his eyes for ever gazing on what gives him as much pain as pleasure. Do I really wish to walk in Goodman's Yard or to sit with errand boys & young-old women in the little dairy in Jewry St? Do I not know what I wish? Here at least I have quiet, air, rest, & some books to work with, and I can be content with this or with nothing. I think I am content. (Squire Papers, box 6)

Like J. C. Squire ("strangely enough" drawn away from the tranquilizing Country to the City's Jewishly arousing melting-pot) other conservatives have sought a rural refuge from "the passions of the Wandering Jew . . . his eyes for ever gazing on what gives him as much pain as pleasure." Our tour through the archives will disclose similarly ambivalent responses to the rage of seeing.

[Dr. Henry A. Murray's notes, undated fragment] No[.] Bulkington is seeking nothing, is attacking nothing, is not driven by revenge. He is driven out to sea—liberation from constraint—freedom of thought—out of revulsion of the insidious influence of current conventional values—hypocrites—fear of being [unconsciously] intimidated/ HM is attracted to B "like a magnet"[26]

[Murray to Olson, ca. June 1949] I was in Oahu in April, & when I returned found your wondrously heartening, prodigiously generous letter about *Pierre*. What a fountain of vitality you are! I need hardly say it was to me a volcano of delight. In contrast, I received from our friend, Jay Leyda—who up to then had been all sweetness & cordiality—a diatribe of vituperation.

A study of the interpersonal relations of Melvillians might be quite revealing! Anyhow, despite the fact that your poetic diction is beyond my reach quite often & therefore leaves me temporarily in a cloud of unknowing, I trust *your* guts.

I was in New York when your last letter arrived. Of course your idea (about Tales) fires me! It has fired me (in a quiet way if that is possible) for several years. I think we were running round the fringes of it in our last conversations. Most fairy tales & myths are compounded of several archetypal themes, & it is possible to tell precisely which of these themes is the one to which the child is especially attracted (at a given time). Therefore, I have decided that we should start by composing *pure* myths (or rather fairy tales)— each of which consists of a *single* theme. (Perhaps a few subsidiary or minor themes will have to be included; but I hope not)

I was planning to start by encouraging someone to bring his or her talents to bear on the task of writing several very *short* tales about the *threat of being devoured* (what I would call *press Oral Agression*). The situation is that of a *hero & a monster* (giant, ogre, werewolf, dragon, whale &c) in the neighborhood. The major solutions are:

1. The monster is destroyed somehow by Fate (the hero is passive, i.e., no hero).
2. The monster is destroyed by the hero with the aid of others & of magic means (someone gives him a magical sword, helmet, shield, sandals or whatnot).
3. The monster is destroyed by the hero almost unaided—by prodigious effort & courage.
4. The hero is defeated by the monster (at least temporarily). Tragic ending too tough for a small child to endure.

My idea was to read stories of this sort to children of different sexes & ages, & discover which is most liked by which sex at which age &c, &c. . . .

[Ovid, *Metamorphoses*] Chaos, a raw and undivided mass, / Naught but a lifeless bulk, with warring seeds / Of ill-joined elements compressed together.[27]

[Alexander Pope, 1704, describing the new Eden of "Windsor Forest," the seat of reunited Monarch and Muse (previously severed by radical puritans)]

Here earth and water seem to strive again;
Not chaos-like together crush'd and bruis'd,
But, as the world, harmoniously confused:
Where order in variety we see,
And where, tho' all things differ, all agree.

[From the *London Times*, quoted in back of *White-Jacket* (1850) in praise of *Omoo* (1847)] Let Mr. Melville write as much as he will, provided he always writes as well as now, and he shall find us greedy devourers of his productions. He has a rare pen for the delineation of character; an eye for the humorous and grotesque which is worth a Jew's; for the description of natural scenery he is not to be beaten.

[Ishmael] Squeeze! squeeze! squeeze! all the morning long; I squeezed that sperm till I myself almost melted into it; I squeezed that sperm till a strange sort of insanity came over me; and I found myself unwittingly squeezing my co-laborer's hands in it, mistaking their hands for the gentle globules. Such an abounding, affectionate, friendly, loving feeling did this avocation beget; that at last I was continually squeezing their hands, and looking up into their eyes sentimentally; as much as to say,—Oh! my dear fellow beings, why should we any longer cherish any social acerbities, or know the slightest ill-humor or envy! Come; let us squeeze hands all around; nay, let us all squeeze ourselves into each other; let us squeeze ourselves universally into the very milk and sperm of kindness.

Would that I could keep squeezing that sperm for ever! For now, by many prolonged, repeated experiences, I have perceived that in all cases man must eventually lower, or at least shift, his conceit of attainable felicity; not placing it anywhere in the intellect or the fancy; but in the wife, the heart, the bed, the table, the saddle, the fire-side, the country; now that I have perceived all this, I am ready to squeeze case eternally. In thoughts of the visions of the night, I saw long rows of angels in paradise, each with his hands in a jar of spermaceti. (416)

[From Walter Crane's introduction, *Socialism and Art*, by J. C. Squire, a pamphlet published by Twentieth Century Ltd., sponsored by the Social Democratic Federation, 1907] [Under socialism art will be] the great source of joy, the harmonising influence of beauty, the spirit of order and proportion, at once creative and adaptive, capable of lifting men's thoughts to the loftiest plane, and yet, withal, a sweet and familiar domestic spirit, cheering and comforting, gladdening the eyes with form and colour as it sheds its refining influence everywhere.

[From Squire's text] Take away long hours, take away slums—take away in fact everything we have got, and put its exact opposite in its place, and amongst the things which will come again to the surface of the people's soul will be the old irrepressible yearning after Art. (12)

[Under socialism, the artist will no longer be alienated.] The whole way along, Capitalism has stifled Art and tortured the artist. For Art there has been a cramped and narrowed existence; for the artist starvation during his best years, and fame when he was too old to enjoy it. There was never a system which was so noxious to Art as this of Capitalism. All the accusations that it hurls at Socialism will rebound with redoubled vigor against its own lying head. The most inconceivably unrefined Socialistic State could not do worse than degrade Art and starve the artist. (15)

[Squire on American critics, *Observer*, June 12, 1921] But in America the struggle of notions has infected the whole artistic field. There has been, amongst the so-called intellectuals, a violent revolt against Puritanism; there has been a struggle between elephantine organisations and insurgent ideas; there has been conflict between the inherited colonial English conceptions about law, morals, and aesthetics, and a miscellaneous swarm of doctrines and practices which have been brought in by the heterogeneous immigrants from the continent and the Near East. You have a great conventional dead weight, stigmatised as orthodox and sentimental; and small violent groups of intelligent persons in revolt against it.—"Anywhere, anywhere, out of the business world." This intense antinomianism has had evil effects on criticism. Everything in the most pretentious of American papers, is judged, not by its truth to nature, its sincerity, or beauty or power of entertainment, but by the "ideas" which it embodies. Granted that a man shouts out his determination to break shackles, whether those of metre or of marriage— he is welcomed as an artist. A bold Anarchism, even a few obscene or defiant words, will give a European writer the entrée at once, and there is even a tendency to judge the writers of the past according to their "contributions" toward the emancipation of mankind from anything whatsoever. If you believe in cannibalism or in cubism you are safe. . . . A man has the option of secluding himself from the rebellious uproar or of swelling it. (Clippings notebook, Squire Papers)

[Agnes Morewood to Murray, November 20, 1925] [Agnes will give him key to Arrowhead; mentions "north bedroom, when Uncle Herman (used to lock him self in for days) and write."]

[Agnes Morewood to Murray, January 27, 1926] [Murray had asked her to read *Pierre*.] All my life I have heard of my Aunts Augusta, Helen & Fanny, such good women. Mother will tell you much. Some books sold to Mr. Weaver of Albany Library.

[Murray to Raymond Weaver, Spring 1926] Dear Professor Weaver, During the last year and a half, i.e., since reading Moby Dick & your spirited and illuminating life of the mystic mariner, I have occupied slices of my few leisure moments in reading & chewing the cud over the the vast macrocosm, of whose Sun the above-mentioned books form the axis.

I do not know what plans you may have yourself nor have I any criteria for judging of my own capacity for treating competently such intricate and infinitely subtle and profound subject matter.

However, if it is not distasteful to you, I should very much enjoy the privilege of questioning you upon several points in your biography.

[Agnes Morewood to Murray, June 22, 1926] [Murray has been rummaging through books and trunks and old papers at Arrowhead.]

[Margaret Morewood to Murray, October 7, 1926] . . . I shall not talk freely of Arrowhead nor Uncle Herman—nor ask you any questions about Jung.

[John Freeman (assigned by Squire to write the study of Herman Melville for the English Men of Letters Series, published by Macmillan, 1926) to Henry Bergen, May 18, 1927] I've seen [John Gould] Fletcher once, and talked with him of the two Great Problems of his native land; the colour problem and the Jewish problem. He says that both are insoluble, and both dreadful. He found a sort of blind stimulation in the excitement of New York, but isn't sorry to have escaped with his life, and a little more prosperity than he took with him.[28]

[Charlotte Hoadley to Murray, undated (Murray marks "Dead letter 1928")] In reply to your letter of July thirteenth Mr. Murray I can only repeat my former assertion, namely, that the interview you request is impossible.

[Margaret Morewood to Murray, undated, from La Cañada, Calif.] It is indeed like a Tropical isle of quietness after the terror of The Melting Pot of Los Angeles . . . And someday I hope to meet you again, and to look long and deep into your pool [in] which you work to clarify to reflect the image of H.M. who no doubt will elude you.

[Eleanor Metcalf to Murray, March 3, 1929, August 5, 1929] . . . I am in the midst of The Book, and should not say what I am [illegible] to say to you until I have finished it. But though I am excited by it and enthusiastic as I read, and though it runs on like a lucid stream making clear the dark hard things in the bed of it—yet I feel that you still must write whether you can or not—but I dare not say any more until I have finished the book. This much I had to say, and I would have written you so, letter or no letter from you . . . . H.M. did not see many things concerning him—not even my half-conscious early mothering of him [which he did not live to see]. It is curious, but that relationship is what I most nearly feel for him personally . . . .

[Retired Rear Admiral Livingston Hunt, Harvard 1881, assesses "Herman Melville as a Naval Historian" (*The Harvard Graduates' Magazine* 39 {1930–31}: 22–30)] It can at once be stated that those who wish a picture of life in the old American Navy of sails—about the time of 1843—will find no more detailed description of the manners and customs that prevailed before the mast, as well as aft it, than that in the pages of Herman Melville's *White-Jacket*. . . . But it should be remembered that it is a writer of exuberant imagination, a devotee of poetic exaggeration, a propagandist for world peace, a scoffer at gold braid and ceremonies, an anti-militarist, an apostle of leveling and democracy, who writes the story of *White-Jacket* (22). . . . He was by nature fundamentally opposed to all class distinctions and privileged ranks, and for him to be in the navy at all, to be a member of a minutely graded and shaded aristocracy, was a howling anomaly, only to be explained by the fact . . . of his lingering youthfulness and half-baked development. He had not yet found himself (26). . . . He seems never to have heard of what once happened to the French navy after the Revolution of ninety-three, when sans-culottism had invaded the quarter-deck. His railings at rank and the naval polity provoke a smile (27). [The Navy is now more humanitarian (30).]

[Squire on the New England spirit, 1933] There was for example "Moby Dick" by Herman Melville, who was a New Englander. . . . His poems are few and almost completely unknown in this country, certainly unpublished, but they are worth referring to because they are rather rough and violent, and have almost a Bronteish quality. "Moby Dick" is full of passionate imagination and the most extraordinary force of feeling.[29]

[Jay Leyda to Irving Lerner, January 31, 1934] . . . The more I read about America (and that mostly from the Daily Worker), the more I want to come back, so don't be surprised or worried if you see me sooner than you expected. . . . [He is now conscious politically.]

[Leyda to Sergei M. Eisenstein, February 23, 1935] No doubt Pearl has told you something of my wish to join your group, but I think it is time for me to tell you directly the whole story—why I want to, in what capacity, etc.—and show you the place of this work in its relation to my stay in the Soviet Union.

Putting aside, for the moment, the very low opinion you must have for my capacity for work, let me take a few minutes of your time in giving you my background in America and here, and perhaps your immediate objections will be slightly tempered.

I quote from an autobiographical outline which the Mejrabpom requested of me upon entering its factory:

> . . . My wish to do creative work in kino precedes by many years my knowledge of or participation in the American working-class movement. This is natural, as I come from a clearly petty-bourgeois family and environment, and from a section of the U.S.A. where the class-struggle was least in evidence until recent years. In addition to this, the only factory in which I worked was an open shop where unions were prohibited, so that my only proletarian experience before I came to New York was this contact with unorganized labor.
>
> During my school years (grade-school, high-school), my wishes to learn more than was taught in school required more money than my middle-class family was willing or able to spend on me, as I had been adopted as an orphan by them. So all the "extras"—music lessons, painting materials, and all the stuffs of a general artistic self-education (except books, which were supplied by the school library) were paid for by work after school every day.

After graduating from high school in 1928 at the age of 18, I worked for a year in the National Cash Register factory in Dayton, Ohio. I corresponded with a New York amateur experimenter in kino (Ralph Steiner) with whom I was eager to work, and as soon as I was sure that I had interested him in my ideas and photographs, I left Dayton and my steady job, taking my savings to New York before I was sure of permanent employment there. After a few months my savings were spent and I had to forget kino and find any paying job. Then I had my first sight of the crisis (this was at the beginning of 1930) and the people who were affected by it. After several months that I cannot count among the happiest months of my life, I found a very interesting job (arranging music for films) and also made connections which enabled me to sell articles, mostly criticisms of kino and theatre. I lived as cheaply as possible and saved money regularly, which was spent first on film apparatus, and then habitually on short lengths of film for my first short picture.

This was a short film about a district of New York in which I had lived for a while, and was called "A Bronx Morning." Although I learned a great deal through making it, and proved to myself that kino was to be my work, and although it interested people at that time, and was sold to Europe through the London Film Society, within a few months afterwards, I had my eyes opened so much that I was deeply ashamed of the exclusively aesthetic and poetic attitude of the film, and of the opportunities and materials that I had missed in its making.

At its first showing two comrades from the Workers Film and Photo League asked me to work with them. For the following year all my kino and photo work was with and for the Workers Film and Photo League. . . . This year determined my work for the future—work in the American revolutionary kino. The next step was an easy one.

The European showings of "A Bronx Morning," and my work with the League had been brought to the attention of the director of the State Kino Institute in Moscow, which resulted in an invitation to come to study in the regisseurs' course. With the permission of the League, I accepted, and came in September 1933, bringing both my movie and still cameras. . . .

I must admit that the combination of the lack of any provision for foreign students in GIK, my lack of Russian (which made me dependent on people I could not trust), and the shattering of my more superficial and foolish illusions (such as the Soviet Union greeting me with open arms) had me rather beaten for a while. (I have not yet regained my former self-assurance.) Although I had brought both cameras, plenty of photo film, and a little movie film, I could not trust myself to take one foot of film nor one photo. Now that I have seen here the early work of Ivens, I think my first little film compares very favorably with his first work, but I could interest no one here into giving it any sort of professional screening for the kino-workers here. When my photos were shown at the Museum of Western Art, the reception was lukewarm, and perhaps chilly.

Now I can look back on my mental condition then with contempt, but I cannot ignore it, because it holds the explanation for all of my activity and inactivity since I came to the Soviet Union.

After last summer, spent aimlessly, I was desperate for any sort of real work, and as I was unwilling to face sure failure in the GIK examinations, I applied for work in the Mejrabpom factory. Both jobs I was given there had bright beginnings and black conclusions. The history of the first, the Intourist films, you know already. The results of the second were with Joris Ivens, were a much greater disappointment to me, because I was 100% optimistic about it. Aside from a smattering of the mechanics of sound (but not the principles) I added nothing to what I knew before. But both of these jobs taught me innumerable practical lessons of organization within a Soviet kino factory, generalizations about human nature as it functions in a kino factory, etc.

Last summer, you and Pearl and I considered the possibilities and advantages of my joining the E. group as photographer. To this day I am not sure whether an uninterested factory or the postponement of the expedition was the main obstacle to this plan. Anyway, it was dropped. But as soon as I read the announcement of your work on a new film, I remembered this prospect of last summer, and compared my present parched prospects to the usefulness and excitement of working in your group, particularly in working in such a position where I could observe each moment of work from the film's beginning to its completion. THEN I would have something to take back to the Film & Photo League—participation in the practical application of the theories contained in your lectures. I would have Soviet experience to take back with me—real knowledge of Soviet life that I cannot get in our present isolated "foreign" position.

I would not have the nerve to ask you for a place in your group as assistant or practicant, because my past experience is not of the kind that would be very useful as assistant here, and your best students at GIK deserve to be the practicants. As for photography, I know that I have taken good photos in the past, and if my job is to take photos, the discipline will jolt me out of this year and a half of frightened modesty and I will give you photos as good as any still photographer in Potilikha—(or better).

Now the Yes-Or-No rests in your hands. Once the factory gives its OK, I am ready to start straight off to work. Pearl says that very soon (in about two weeks) you will look at locations. This will need a photographer, and I hope that I may start work with your group at this point.

Well, what do you say?

[Henry A. Murray and Christiana Morgan, 1935] The thematic apperception test is an effective means of disclosing a subject's regnant preoccupations and some of the unconscious trends which underlie them. The advantages of the test are that it is a simple procedure which may be completed in two hours or in an abbreviated form in half that time, and it may be performed in a casual and informal fashion. Since the subject is led to believe that it is a test of creative imagination, even when it is given in a clinic, he is unaware of the fact that he is revealing his innermost thoughts. The subject's attention is not on himself, and so in many instances he indirectly confesses to things which he would not be willing to mention directly. But more than this, he exposes latent tendencies of which he is entirely unconscious. For the fantasies being projected may be inwardly disclaimed and thus avoid complete repression. . . . At the present time a young person who shows a few mildly neurotic symptoms or, like all inwardly developing young persons, is temporarily overburdened by mental conflict generally has, if he wants expert assistance, but two choices. He may be analyzed, or he may consult a psychiatrist with no experience in analysis. . . . There are numberless young men and women who need the kind of help which perhaps only a trained therapeutist trained in psychoanalysis is in a position to give and yet who do not need, or want or cannot afford an analysis lasting a year or more. They need to confess and discuss their problems, to attain insight, but in most cases it is better not to impede their progressive efforts by having to revive and relive their past. It is in such cases that the thematic apperception test may provide the psychotherapeutist with the information necessary for the fulfillment of his function as a guide and healer of men.[30]

[Michael Sadleir compares Theodore Dreiser to James T. Farrell, 1936] Between Dreiser's novel and Farrell's is no analogy, either of content or of treatment. They are alike in their sweeping and sustained power; they are alike in that both expose the squalor and stupidity and cruelty of an industrial society; they are alike in the inevitability of the tragedies they describe; they are alike in their fundamental Americanism, for neither could conceivably have been written in, or of, any country but the United States. But in theme and technique, they are as different as the two races to which their writers belong (Dreiser—Germanic; Farrell—Irish), and as the two angles from which they have approached their task.

[Both stories are set in postwar America, but Dreiser has written a classical tragedy; however,] Farrell . . . has chosen to depict one stratum of American life which, for all its vast extent, has never before been used with the same knowledge and scope, as material for fiction. The outstanding characteristic of this stratum is that it is being educated by the street, instead of the home, the school, or the church; and the influence of the street is often— and increasingly—in conflict with that of its three competitors. *Dominant in "Studs Lonigan" is the evil spirit of city streets—first as playground for youth, then as forcing bed for turbulence and disease and even crime.*

Nor is this all. Studs and his friends are not merely the product of city streets, but of city streets at one particularly reckless epoch of American history. During the period covered by *Studs Lonigan,* the United States experienced war with all its attendant hysteria; prohibition; wild and mounting prosperity; the growth of racketeering; a relaxation of all controls—legal, domestic, religious, economic; the sudden yawning of the gulf of depression; the headlong descent; and thereafter disillusion, bewilderment, despair. These abnormal stresses might be expected to leave their mark on the young of the day; and so indeed, as Farrell's story shows, they most disastrously do.[31]

[Leyda's grandmother/mother Josephine to Jay, May 29, 1937] We sure were glad to hear from you, but so sorry that you were not happy. Wish there was some way I could help. It certainly is fine you have your wife to cheer you and make life more pleasant. Don't forget to return the favor. . . .

[Eleanor Metcalf to Murray, October 18, 1937] I have just reviewed our correspondence from the beginning, and all my latent Melville enthusiasms, championings and excitements have come to life.

If you could know what I have been buried in—the schools of minnows in the whale's wake!—. . . .

For the sake of all that is honest and true, give me a hand out of the [swelter?]. How can a woman be kind, and yet live? Be kind she must: live she must.

[Eleanor Metcalf to Murray, May 19, 1938] [Josephine Shaw has died, her adopted daughter Constance Cushing Berse [?] has the papers, found at 49 Mt. Vernon St.; HAM had seen J.S. On her daughter] She is a terror to me:

I would run a mile from her tongue. So would, and do occasionally, my sisters. I do not like to wish the job of an interview with her on you; but if you think it worth while, I have reason to believe some outsider might be more effective than a member of the family.

[A Harvard physical anthropologist cautiously exhorts readers in a textbook published by Macmillan, 1939] The subject of racial intelligence has . . . not progressed far enough to merit inclusion in a general work of racial history; it has furthermore provided too ready a field for political exploitation to be treated or interpreted as a side issue with scientific detachment. Races, in the present volume, are studied without implication of inferiority or superiority. . . . The people who came to America, from the time of the Pilgrim Fathers to the imposition of the laws restricting immigration, were selected; none were fully representative of the countries from which they came. In America they were subjected to environmental forces of a new and stimulating nature, so that changes in growth such as their ancestors had not felt for centuries produced strange, gangling creatures of their children. In America we have before our eyes the rapid action of race-building forces; if we wish to understand the principles which have motivated the racial history of the Old World, it behooves us to pay careful attention to the New.[32]

[Squire, unpublished, undated poem (the next work is dated 1940). In the same box 5, Squire preserved a series of pen and wash drawings entitled "Divinity" picturing (himself?) as a grotesque, slipping, demonic alien. Each drawing has quotations from the Bible, like those of many Blake illustrations. Also in this box is a short story, "The Golden Scilens," in which "Little Mackenzie Wile," "half-scotchman and half Jew," fools the world into paying him a fortune for Ann Hathaway's diary (containing drafts of *Hamlet*), which he has found through his persevering, low-profile, hard-working autodidacticism; the fortune he extracts from an American magnate causes the collapse of Wall Street.]

~~The Jews and the Slovaks, czechs and the Poles~~
~~Are inferior people who haven't got souls~~
The Czechs and the Slovaks, the Poles and all such
Are inferior people who don't matter much
Unlettered and ugly unmartial and base
And made to be bossed by a governing race
But as for the Russians we can't be quite sure
If they have or they haven't the higher Kultur

In fact we must wait to decide on our view
Till we're rather certain what Stalin will do.

[Squire, undated manuscript "Loyalty and Patriotism"] To avoid any confusion of ideas it will be as well to commence by defining Patriotism as the sentiment of attachment to one's country and Loyalty as that of attachment to a personal sovereign, setting aside any questions as to whether one can be loyal to Parliament or the British Constitution.

In the olden times when the King was also the leader of the army and the supreme lawgiver there was a strong tendency for a strong sense of personal devotion to him to exist, whatever might be his character as a man. Society consisted of strongly marked castes and no one had any idea that he had any right to be in any caste except the one he was in. The result was that the monarch was regarded as the apex of the pyramid of Society, who had an innate right to support from all the lower stones. Everything bears the stamp of this. The great roads are the King's highway; the battle-cry is St. George and King Harry, or Tom and Dick as the cases may be. After the 17th century the divine right of Kings was an untenable theory but before that time the staidest philosophers were willing to uphold it.

The death-blow to this all-pervading King-worship was dealt by the Great Rebellion. The Cavalier generation died out and left no true progeny. The decay of this spirit was inevitable but the character of the kings accelerated it and the change of dynasties in 1688 & 1714 were additional forces acting in the same direction. The iconoclastic 18th century tolled the bell at its funeral.

It was inevitable however that among the uneducated classes who are practically unaffected by moral and intellectual considerations that a certain sense of attachment to the throne should survive. It exists to the present day. Many a cottage has a coloured print of the King hung on the wall. In many other people, the spirit is still preserved in a debased form. The sycophantic instincts of humanity render it impossible that the court should not be the center of Society. The glamour which hangs around the name of King is largely responsible for this. The present generation of monarchs are in this respect trading on the achievements of their ancestors.

Viewed in the light of reason, the cynical view of Loyalty is of course the only sensible one. One might well wonder why one should be called upon to love honour and obey any evil-visaged scoundrel or fool who may be born with a silver spoon in his mouth and a purple robe on his back. All sane men are at heart Republicans. Democracy being however a terrifying thing as long as the "plebs" exists, the best substitute has to found [sic]. In modern monarchies the sentiment of Loyalty is used to cheat the vulgar for their own good. The average labourer still has a sneaking belief that the King governs the country. He would fall totally at sea if he had to cultivate a love for the abstract constitution. His limited intellect requires something tangible to look up to. This is supplied by the monarch with coronation-processions & they like to keep up the illusion. For this reason alone, the sentiment of Loyalty is one which no Statesman could tamper with without incurring a very grave responsibility.

Patriotism is another matter. It is to all intents and purposes universal. In a man's relations with his country most of the main forces which influence human action come into play. Unselfish & selfish motives tend in the same direction. It is to the gregarious animal's interest to stick to his herd, all his relations are in it, and he also has a kind of instinct that it is really a much better herd than any other. More external considerations such as those of language & religion are also of great weight. Men's souls are also to a certain extent tied to the land. A rich Englishman abroad usually likes to slink home to his own hole to die.

If a community is victorious in war every individual in it is bound to it by sharing its conceit; if it is defeated the new tie of a desire for revenge unites all the severed [?] persons together.

In the abstract Cosmopolitanism is the ideal theory. If all men were perfect all men would be brotherly. Since however even if thousands of earnest people determined to guide their actions in accordance with the narrowness of the average man's mind would render their efforts entirely null, the world must be taken as it is. Patriotism may be an Evil but it seems to be an inevitable evil so the only thing can be done is to propagate the best kind of it. Very little harm can come from a moderate patriotism which while preferring its own country sees the good in every other. While human nature is as it is at present the preaching of the brotherhood of Man can have very little practical effect and "That Man's the best Cosmopolite / Who loves his native country best."[33]

[Murray to Olson, 1940] . . . I have been unable to work since France was invaded. How closely the two events are connected I do not know—but most of my time has gone by way of a Committee on National Morale.

I have only picked up one item along your line—Melville's copy of Goethe's Autobiography which he read in 1849—very interesting.

[Kurt L. London to Leyda, undated (1942?), inviting him to speak] I am now starting the sociological and political unit.

[Eleanor Metcalf to Murray, October 22, 1943] The whole of me seems to act best in a fog of ignorance. Yet I don't like the ignorance. Oh well, it doesn't much matter. Life is short, and the speed sometimes is dizzying. . . .

[Several entries from Richard Chase's Dartmouth College notebooks] (Taine, 1878) "Beyond the King, inert & disarmed, beyond the assembly, disobeyed or submissive, appears the real monarch, the people—that is to say, the mobs of a hundred, a thousand, a hundred-thousand beings gathered together haphazard, on an impulse or an alarm, suddenly and irresistibly made legislators—a formidable power, undefined and destructive, on which no one has any hold, & which, with its mother, howling and mis-shapen Liberty, sits at the threshhold of the revolution like Milton's two spectres at the gates of Hell. [Each individual descends] to the darkness, the madness, and the savagery of the dregs of society." [Chase:] T. is impressed with the disparity between the abilities, faculties, etc. of the individual Jacobin leaders (Marat, Danton) & the beast they gave birth to.

(Notes on Jung, *Integration of the Personality*, 1939:) "It is . . . rather a futile undertaking to disinfect Olympus with rational enlightenment. The gods are not there; they are ensconced in the shadows of the unconscious, where we cannot uproot them (p. 23)." "May we therefore, be thankful to humanity, to all the well-meaning shepherds of the flock, and to all the anxious fathers of the hosts of children, when they erect protective walls, set up efficacious pictures, and recommend passable roads that sinuously wind around the abysses? (p. 304)."[34]

[Murray to FDR, *The Mind of Adolph Hitler*, 1943] Hitler spent five years in Vienna. Living as he was, penniless among the penniless of the lower class, he himself experienced, and he was in close touch with others who experienced, the basic wants and viewpoints of the depressed victims of civilization. Here, certainly was much food for thought. He also attended sessions of parliament and numerous political mass meetings, and observed the proceedings critically. From the start he was constantly preoccupied with the question: why does *this* political movement fail and *that* one succeed? It was natural for him to think realistically and strategically; not to make the mistake of supposing man to be better than he is, and yet taking full account of his heroic potentialities, having observed that millions of simple untutored men will gladly fight and sacrifice their lives for an ideal vividly presented. In addition, Hitler spent many hours in the public library looking over histories and books dealing with social questions. MEIN KAMPF proves that the young man from Linz who could not get through High School was capable of profiting from what he saw and read, and that these five years of drifting and irregular employment were by no means wasted. The flophouse and the beer hall were his Heidelberg and University of Vienna. . . . For the Vienna period the critical question psychologically is this: why did Hitler, living among the proletariat, find the developed ideology of communism repellent and the embryonic ideology of fascism appealing? (125–26)

[Harry Levin to Leyda, August 30, 1944; he will speak to Laughlin about "a series of chronologies," but Laughlin is unpredictable] I suppose you know Willard Thorp's volume on Melville in the American Writers Series, which at least contains a good bibliography, as well as a brief chronology. We have a good deal of unpublished Melville material here, which Charlie Olson—who recently resigned from the OWI—is supposed to be writing up. Incidentally, I have been trying to get Laughlin to include *The Confidence Man*, which has never been reprinted, in his New Classics.

[James Laughlin, publisher (New Directions), to Leyda, October 8, 1944; Laughlin has talked to Levin] I would urge that the scheme of the books be visualized as much as possible. I think picture books are going to be the big thing in the next decade. [Give us a sample on Melville, choosing] a time of his life for which pictures and directly reproducible material are readily available.

[Laughlin to Leyda, postcard postmarked March 1945; Lustig wants to show the "Melville stuff" to Siegel, who wants to start a "wonderful" magazine] It will be on the scale of Fortune but about culture and modern living. The idea is to make use of their technical facilities to work out (at their expense) a section of the Melville log which they would run in their first issue. This would be both good advance publicity and a good way to finance the experimental work. Do you approve? I agree that you should control the thing entirely in selection of material and visual stuff.

[John Murray to Leyda, December 15, 1944] [He has 40–50 letters of HM to his grandfather, but does not like to give access. Once published they "lose about half of their market value, and there is no compelling reason why, time after time, I should give away this value." He can't control their use; maybe, if Leyda has friends in England, they could make extracts, but not till after the war.]

[Leyda to Harrison Hayford, December 30, 1944] [Wants to see reference to Galapagos in Greene editorial, Sandusky *Mirror,* 2 February 1855. Answered by Clarence Ghodes.]

[Victor Hugo Paltsis to Leyda, January 12, 1945] [Answers inquiry on Gansevoort's Diary, notes publication of his article "Background of HM, and New Light on the Publication of *Typee*," which can be found in the tribute volume called *Bookman's Holiday*, to H.M. Lydenberg, former director NYPL] I tell the extent of the diary and the fact that illness ended Gansevoort's life. I never heard anything suggesting a suicide, even from that branch of the family. He was highly respected as the oldest brother of Herman, and as an orator in the Democratic-Buchanan campaign. . . . I know of no connection or complaints; of which I had heard, that were related to his negotiations with Murray, or Wiley & Putnam, or dealings with the bankers.

[Hayford to Leyda, January 13, 1945] I am very happy . . . to hear from someone who is interested in Melville, and especially from someone who is working on factual, biographical details. I am convinced there is much more to be discovered about Melville's life that will throw light on the interpretation of his works. Too much that is written about Melville is irresponsible. The project I am working on for my degree at Yale is a study of the relationship between Melville & Hawthorne, largely from the prosaic, factual aspect. It is surprising how much can be gained by a grubbing study of the mere dates and documents.

[Lesley A. Marchand to Leyda, January 17, 1945] There seems to be a great run on M. I know of two doctor's dissertations in progress touching special aspects of his work.

[A. C. Glassgold ("Cook") to Leyda, February 4, 1945] [Has been in gov't WPA Art, Housing Authority, no longer at Whitney; has no time to "probe" for Leyda regarding HM or Mount; Leyda should write to Lewis Mumford, "who probably is the best informed historian on Melville."]

[Hayford to Leyda, February 11, 1945] [Leyda should write to John Birss (who is interested in Jay's project, and who does not intend to publish his nine-page chronology). Look up Leon Howard at the Huntington.] He shares our slant on M and may write a book on him later.

[Laughlin to Leyda, April 10, (1945? dated 1944 by Leyda, in pencil)] Segal— the man back of the new magazine—did not seem to grasp the thing. He liked the excerpts from the letters but could not visualize the rest.

[Tyrus Hillway to Leyda, April 14, 1945] [Welcome to Melville Society. Packard & Co. have been interested in "complete works" "for some time"; H. Vincent to act as go-between. "We already have one collector in our membership, and we shall probably have more." (Leyda had sent him Powell and Henshaw as prospective members). Asks for interests and activities in M scholarship.]

[A. Gillies reviving Herder, 1945] Our personalities must achieve permanence through useful and healthful activity; this is the first rule of happiness. This is the complete answer to *Weltschmerz*—the *Weltschmerz* that [Herder] himself knew only too well. "We were given our bodies, which are constituted for so many things, along with all their senses and members, for use, for employment. Otherwise our vital humours stagnate; our organs become slack. The body, like a living corpse, dies long before its time; it decays in a slow, miserable, unnatural death. . . . A head too full of knowledge, even though such knowledge be golden, stifles the body, constricts the chest, darkens the sight and becomes an unhealthy burden to the life of its possessor. . . . The blessing of health is founded only on the use of all our soul, particularly of its active faculties; and here let us thank Providence once again for not having made too delicate a job of all the human race and for not having intended our earth to be a lecture-room for learned studies." . . . [Herder's rosy ideal of *Humanität*] is capable, when given greater coherence [or rescued from Kant's "one-sided intellectualism," *C.S.*], of inspiring a modern state. Its weakness lies in its susceptibility to being given a partial application; in the manifold radiations, its central glow is apt to be lost to view. The world has, therefore, not seen it in all its fullness. It is democratic and federationist; its nationalism is not expansionist or arrogant, but cooperative, the friend not the enemy of internationalism; its ideal is that of a community of nation-states all striving, in fertile collaboration, towards ever higher spheres of human achievement.[35]

[Undated draft, Leyda to Mr. Hayford] ~~The disappointment has been so painful that I haven't been able to read anything relating to Melville.~~ Actually I want very much to see your dissertation and those tempting "other things," but I don't dare ask you, or anyone else, to help a project that has so little chance of being realized. [In margin] Just before Mr. Laughlin's final tap, Mr. Birss contributed a blow: he found that the Log fitted into no one of the recognized forms—and it "took the edge off" his letter volume which I certainly would not want to do.

[John Birss to Leyda, May 3, 1945] [He will send JL descriptions of Duyckinck letters at Yale; he has never hoarded material when approached by] serious and cooperative M students. . . . Tomorrow Willard Thorp, Hillway, Wells, Mansfield and I are meeting at Columbia to discuss the big edition of

Melville. I wish you could be present; undoubtedly you would have excellent, stimulating ideas.

[Laughlin to Leyda, August 21, (1945?, dated 1944 by Leyda)] I'm terribly upset about the Melville Log. There is nothing I wanted to do more . . . . [Leyda should get a publisher on the coast and] sit down together and sweat it out to get it right.

[Three letters from "Gordy" (Lt. Gordon Williams, married to Jane Williams, Leyda's half-sister), in Hawaii, to Leyda, August 23, 24, 28, 1945] [No written record showing that Isaac Montgomery left money to Catholics; no photos of HM, first photographer arrived in 1847. Census of Americans on Sandwich Islands, March 1, 1843, from *Temperance Advocate and Seamen's Journal*: 57 men married with native wives; 61 married with American wives; 74 unmarried; 119 half-caste children. Pearson at Yale said to be working on M letters. M supposedly said, "he—M.—doubted if they would find anything about him here."]

[Hayford apologizes to Leyda for not sending dissertation, September 4, 1945] The only explanation is that I was so utterly tired and sick of Melville by the time I finished it that I dumped all vestiges of the project into a big box the day I sent off the dissertation to Yale, and have only within the last day or two been able to think about the thing without sickness.

[Harry Levin to Leyda, September 11, 1945] [Not surprised about Laughlin and MLA too academic; go with commercial publisher. His tutorial student Walter Pistole is with Reynal & Hitchcock and] they are not unaware of the Melville boom, and might like to do something about it. Another possibility is Bernard Smith of Knopf's, who is an intelligent scholar and critic of American literature.

I continue to look forward to the album-chronology, and to think it's a swell idea. I notice that "Life" has approximated it in their pictorial series on American writers. Did you know there was a Melville Society . . . which is planning to bring out a complete American edition? And I think Matthiessen's advice would be worth having. No, I never saw the specimens.

Is Eisenstein planning to do anything with Melville? The French, in their postwar mystical phase, seem to be fascinated by "la baleine blanche." One of the translators, as you probably know, Jean Giono, seems to be under a cloud as a collaborationist. Lincoln Kirstein, just out of the army, tells me that an opera is being made out of "Billy Budd" (a work whose merits, it seems to me, have perhaps been exaggerated in certain circles).

[Postscript] Do you know Charlie Olson? He has just completed a book, the distillation of labors begun on a Guggenheim years ago, called "Call Me Ishmael," and is having trouble with his publishers (Harcourt) because it only runs to 25,000 words. Perhaps you might team up?"

[Murray to Olson, October 1, 1945] I have no doubt at all that the Daemon took hold of your hand & wrote your book. That's the way old Ahab would have liked it. Its not only a book about him but it is written by one possessed with his spirit. Its an identification— [Diagram: triangle with Shakespeare, Melville, Olson]

Moses is a great idea. Only a plunger who comes up with bloodshot eyes could get at it.

I don't want you to entertain expectations of my book! It's a different sort of thing. Since seeing you I've decided to end with the collapse after Pierre— Terror & then Pity. After that its no longer tragedy it's pathetic. If a collapse comes in my life & I live on for a while in death, I may write the long aftermath—from 1852–1893 [sic: 1893 was Murray's birth year; Melville died in 1891. C.S.], but now I have got to gather up my forces to make something out of my own life rather than expend them over the ruins of a man, great— very great—though he may have been. No one who is boiling over inside could write that last volume. I can spell everything out from 1819 to 1852 in 2 volumes—with your help, with your generous heritage from the Mass. Historical Society & other aids you are giving me. Your book when it is published will illumine the abyss for me & then I shall proceed to wind it up as swiftly as possible with everlasting gratefulness to you.

It is hard to talk now—your opening your eyes to the first cry of your offspring & I still in labor. We have so much to say to each other but the inner balance is delicate & the magnetic needle easily diverted. After both pups are well born we must meet & drink & talk about ourselves into a lather.

When I started HM I was desperately searching, as he was, for the lost path & I wrote out of my thirst and hunger. Now, after finding the oasis, the promptings to write come from a need to tell others of my well of delight. That makes a difference.

May the sun rise upon your book & glorify it forever & forever. Keep me in touch in you [sic]. When I have finished my present job I shall be able to shake free from routine and outfly philosophy, Pax Vobiscum.

[Murray to Olson, November 24, 1945] I am positive now that you have written a truly great book. Your letter to Mr. Forbes had such pace and passion in it that I immediately recognized it as perseveration (as the long-hairs call it) of the feeling and style that was active in the composition of your book. Melville's letter to Hawthorne after finishing *Moby-Dick* is an example of this sort of thing....

[Hayford to Leyda, December 4, 1945] As to cutting in on Birss, of course that is a problem, but I don't see why it cannot be circumvented in some way. I do not know how near he is to publication, but he has been at the job a long time and I am sure he does not expect everyone else to hold up everything, awaiting his eventual publication. I mean, I believe the conflict could be adjusted.

[Richard Chase, "Brief Self-Analysis," presented to his wife, Frances, 1945] Feeling so dismal has called forth certain reflections on the state of my soul. It seems to me that in the past I've often been tempted to cheat life by hurrying through anything which promised to be a difficult or rewarding experience—satisfying myself with a superficial pattern of experience extracted from life & put together into a sometimes neat but usually dishonest synthesis. Dishonest because my treatment of things has never reflected their integrity and fulness. I feel that in this sense I've cheated the authors of books I've read, the people I've written about in essays, the students in my classes, & you. You most of all, I fear. I've always thrusted the world away either because I was scared of it or because I was unable to see the rich and beneficial experience it offered. I guess Henry James had me in mind when he portrayed those timid, ascetic men. But don't worry—all this doesn't depress me very much:—I've realized it for a long time but have only recently determined to try to face up to it. I'm not just beating myself over the head either—what I say about cheating is true & useful not as self-castigation but as a clearing of paths into the future. What should I do about the future? Well, at least approach things a bit more slowly, attentively, fulsomely, honestly. That might mean no more writing for a while, for 5 years, maybe for ever. At least it means (I hope) no more writing until what I write seems good & faithful to its subject. Too much nervous, shallow bustling about in search of a quick success in teaching, writing, & relations with you, & life in general! I guess I'm just a Babbitt in intellectual's clothing—which is what I was brought up to be at home, school and college [Dartmouth]. This kind of life, as E. M. Forster well observes, brings not health, but "panic and emptiness." His formula for the decent life is a reformed liberalism—i.e., liberalism which has learned to free itself from the strictures of its principles & dogmas whenever they interfere with one's grasping hold of life or with one's understanding of people as people—liberalism which sees the values of stabilities, richnesses, venerablenesses. . . . Trilling is right as usual: Dwight McDonald & the eds. of P.R. [*Partisan Review*] are wrong—or at least inadequate.

[Sergei Eisenstein to Jay Leyda, Moscow, January 1946] My dearest Jay! Many thanks for your letters. I hope my cable answers reached you. I was just (and still am for about 3 weaks [*sic*]) busy like hell: just finishing to shoot and cut the second part of Ivan. This part includes two reels made in color. Color used in quite different a way, than it is usually done—so that it gives a big additional chapter to what is nearly ready in book form. If everything is allright here with the picture I expect to take a vacation and finish the book—¾ of which are ready for print. Most of the stuff is unpublished (part of it even . . . un-written yet.) and is mostly concerned with the development of the principles started by "Potemkin" during these 20 years in different media (is that the way to say it?)—treatments of sound, music, color. The way of composing extatic scenes, etc. "Ivan" in connection with "Potemkin." I will send you a detailed plan as soon as the film goes to the labratory to be printed. Maybe it will be all-right to include the script of Ivan as well into this book.

Out of the books you sent one only very few reached me—and according to the list—the less interesting ones!

The best way of sending books is address them not to Soyiuzintorgkino but to VOKS. There are very charming young ladies who take care as to the books not being lost.

There are lots of things I'd like to write you about—and I'll do it as soon as I get my vacation.

Please continue to send books reckoning that still one to six or seven may reach me!

You have a wonderful flair as to what excites me!

Take for instance Melville and [Saul] Steinberg (this book did not reach me!)—so very important for analytical research work.

All my love to you Always cordially yours   (S. Eisenstein)
Best regards to Sylvia [Si-Lan] and please write![36]

[Dr. C. G. Jung diagnoses wasteland maladies, 1946] As I said before, the upheaval of mass instincts corresponds to a compensatory move of the unconscious. Such a move became possible because the conscious state of the people had become estranged from the natural laws of human existence. Because of industrialization, large parts of the population became uprooted, and they were herded together in large centres. And because of this new form of existence—with its mass psychology and its social dependence upon the fluctuations of markets and wages, an individual was created who was unstable, insecure, and suggestible. . . . Germany . . . is by no means the only nation threatened by this dangerous germ. The influence of mass psychology has spread far and wide. It was the individual's feeling of weakness, and indeed of non-existence, which was compensated by the upheaval of hitherto unknown desires for power. . . . Nothing but materialism was preached by the highest intellectual authority. . . . Hitler . . . was the most prodigious personification of all human inferiorities. He was a highly incapable, unadapted, irresponsible, psychopathic individual, full of empty childish fantasies, but cursed with the keen intuition of a rat or guttersnipe. He represented the shadow, the inferior part of everybody's personality, in an overwhelming degree, and this is another reason why they fell for him.[37]

[Raymond Weaver's undated memoir (ca. 1947?) of the origins of his Melville biography, *Herman Melville: Mariner and Mystic,* hand printed on leaves roughly the size of the "Billy Budd" manuscript he found in "the trunk"; evidentiary documents pasted onto the pages of his manuscript not included here] *A letter from Carl Van Doren.* Some days previous we had been seated besides each other at an English Department Dinner.—It was this that started it all. He had said to me: "You know, there will soon be a centenary of Herman Melville. He was a wonderful old boy—and I'd like to do him myself. But if you'd try him, I'm willing."

I knew almost nothing of Melville—beyond the fact that Brander Matthews had mentioned him in course. I'd begun *Typee*—and stopped at the beginning. So, with Carl Van Doren's offer, being unhampered with information, I feel [*sic*] in with his request. I thought: "I'll read a few South Sea travel books, examine Melville's official biographies, and turn out an adequate article." The following day, I visited Columbia library, to find books and books by Melville—an indecent spawning—and no "official" biographies at all. So I consulted Poole's index—to learn, by the references, that Melville had started off well enough, but went wrong, somehow—living to an incredible forty years of sedulous obscurity.

I read him—with gaping wonderment and incredulity. I also bought him. A first edition of *Moby-Dick*, in 1918 [*sic*] could be had for less than a dollar. I picked up easily enough a set of him. Duplicates, when were offered me as pleading gifts, I charitably bought: in my excitement they seemed incredibly inexpensive gifts of an excitement I feared to credit, to unconverted friends. *Moby-Dick's* that now are unpurchasable at $200 I scorned at the piracy of anything over a dollar. Evidently, I did not view Melville as an *investment.* He was an excitement, rather—a kind of indulgent madness vastly interesting to myself, but not trusted to wholesale consumption.

I went to the Faculty Club for Sunday Lunch. A ruddy stranger sat at my table. Who this intruder was I had no idea. "I'll talk of something wholly remote" I resolved. So I mentioned Martin Luther's preference for polygamy; I'd the day before chanced upon it in some reading. My rosy dining companion grew rosier, "I took a dissertation on that in Germany" he said. He started to lecture me with Teutonic endurance. I wanted to change the subject. "I'm working on Herman Melville," I said. "Melville?" he repeated. He brighted [sic] hatefully. "Didn't he live in Pittsfield?" I had to admit that in so far as I knew Melville had. "My uncle's librarian is in Pittsfield" he said. "If you want to get in touch with what survives of Melville's family, he might tell you. Here's my card."

So I wrote to Mrs. Morewood. To my surprise, the answer came from Melville's daughter. This is it: [". . . I am quite willing to have you write a life of my father . . . but fear I can not help you very much. I shall be obliged to put the matter in my daughter's hands, as I am in ill health, and have serious trouble with my eyes. . . ."]

Mrs. Morewood evidently wanted to keep her hands clean of Melville. And Melville's daughter, in her turn, was passing the buck.

I wrote to Mrs. Metcalf. I have no record of the initial correspondence. But I vividly remember urging her (evidently against provocation) of the importance of getting recorded all that was known of Melville: that a man who has published a dozen volumes had thereby ceased to be a private personality—a public character, rather, at the mercy of anyone who drew his own conclusions from the published books—and the loquacity of the Hawthorne family and friends: that Julian had imputed against Melville a clean-gone madness: that Id [sic] read Melville and lost my own mind: that I needed a little anchorage in fact for my own insanity.

Mrs. Metcalf lived out of Boston. I went to Boston to call. We neither of us knew the other—so I was happy to be accepted for tea. This left both of us without involvement (it sounds in retrospect, as if the ghost of Hawthorne were presiding!). Either of us might hate the other: and meeting at tea made the meeting merely experimental.

It rained when I left Boston. On the train I naturally wondered what I was coming to. When I came to Wellesley Hills, it was still dismally raining. A suburban station—but not absolutely deserted. Mrs. Metcalf was there. And [sic] English-looking woman, with flat-heels, a raincoat, and a bad breath. She had a taxi.

"This weather is enough to provoke conversation" she said at once on the way to her home; "but you don't want to talk about the weather. So I'll tell you at once the worst—though I trust you as a gentleman as to what you'll ever publish."

She said: "You say in your *Nation* article, that Melville was happily married. He wasn't." And before the short ride to her house was over, I felt that Melville was a man of even deeper secrets than I had expected. We opened the trunk of manuscript—as I've recounted in an article that follows. Always. it rained.

[Leyda to Bert, undated] . . . I was given a Melville book to do, which is now completed, after a year of work. During this year, I have eaten, slept and lived Melville—and little else . . . .

[Frank Taylor of Reynal & Hitchcock to Leyda, January 8, 1946] [We want to see several specimens. Levin has mentioned the project to him and Pistole.]

[Charles Olson to Leyda, January 24, 1946] [Levin says Taylor thinks your M collage and my M book go together.] It's interesting this thing should bring us together. For I have had a sense of you for years, first I think through your work on Eisenstein. Then it was you and the Film Library . . . .[38]

One document I transcribe entire, using it as a climax, a clinch to the whaler as worker, M's mss. record of what happened to the Acushnet crew. It fires me to think we may have used a similar graphic sense.

It is my feeling that writing today has to go back to first ground and that the healthiest act is the record of fact.

I open the book with a naked account of what happened to the men of the Essex. It is meant as a prologue to the tale.

[Telegram, Leyda to Olson, January 27, 1946] Wonderful idea . . . .

[Leyda sends Olson "Specimens" and a copy of his letter to Frank Taylor, January 14, 1946] I hope that after looking at these specimens you'll still be interested in pooling our projects . . . Please ignore (for the present) both the obvious gaps and the documents that you know I have no right to use.

[Hayford to Leyda, February 21, 1946] I'm chiefly interested at the moment by your postcard saying you have pretty well completely dated or placed the poems. I'd be interested to get some details on that whenever you get a moment. [in margin:] I mean you wouldn't have to prove your dating.

[Leyda to Olson, August 20, 1946] Yes, it looks like real Melville interest at Reynal & Hitchcock. Nothing else could have persuaded them to take such a long chance on me. I'm actually more eager to see your work in print than I am the Log, for the completion of my work now seems so remote. I see the many obstacles more clearly now, and I can't even imagine being satisfied that a thorough job will have been done—and there's little point in doing it if it's not to be thorough . . . .

[Leyda to William Gilman, November 7, 1946] Did you know that a box of valuable papers entrusted to Elizabeth (wife) "to the care of the Metropolitan Safe Deposit Co, 3 E. 14" was stolen before October 1905? So she may not have destroyed as much as we have assumed. Know anyone working at the Metropolitan Storage Warehouse (connected firms?)? (Gilman Papers)

[*Moby Dick by Herman Melville,* "Condensed and Adapted for Reading in Secondary Schools by David Temple Sometimes Professor of American Lit, St. Anthony's Seminary, Santa Barbara, California" (1946)]

Introduction. . . . The undercurrent of the story will carry you into deeper water. It has to do not merely with a man and a whale. Rather it is the story of a man and a life. To be sure, Melville writes of a whale hunt, but with the same pen and at the same time he tells also of a mightier conflict between good and evil. In this fuller meaning of the story, Ahab, the captain, would stand for the soul of man beset by the forces of evil which are here embodied in Moby Dick, the White Whale. There are grim forebodings of the future. There are frantic warnings to escape. There is much moody pondering on the problem of it all. You will notice this particularly when the captain mutters strange, deep sentiments about life and fate and the voyage of man. He is like some Hamlet that has gone off to sea. He tosses up and down in his mind the great problems of life. He is worried about final purposes and the last reasons why. Ships are important, but a ship is like a soul that sails a sea. The problems of navigation are intricate but not nearly so deeply mazed as the problems of life. But Ahab's solutions, as you will find, are not very convincing nor are they at all satisfactory . . . .

Critics have praised Melville's great novel as few other books in American literature. It belongs with the best of all time, they say; it has unmatched power; it stands alone as America's great contribution to the literature of the sea. Ambitious young men, and eager young women, however, have often found the book difficult to read. The author is at times unclear. He digresses from the straight path of the story and leads the reader too far afield. Somewhere interest may lag and be left in the folds of blubber.

It has been our conviction over a number of years that if this volume were presented to student readers in streamlined form, they would love the adventure of it and be captivated by the wild and attractive characters. A trial of the text in manuscript form has borne this out. It is hoped that this printed adaptation of the great classic will help to introduce Moby Dick to many student readers.

[From Eisenstein's memoirs, *Beyond the Stars*, written between May and December 1946]

I was interested in Rockwell Kent.

I clearly recognized him (amongst the rapidly executed reproductions of his journey across Alaska) from a strange book almost half as deep as it was wide—black with a gold title, and containing his magnificent illuminations, tailpieces and whole illustrations.

It was all about whales.

The title was *Moby Dick*.

There is a very poor film of *Moby Dick*, the one-legged captain played by John Barrymore.

I saw it once.

. . . I tried to read a bit of the actual book.

I was introduced to Melville and was intoxicated.

Then, by some strange intuition, Jay (Leyda) sent me from overseas Melville's *Omoo and Typee*, admirable constructions (1945!)

Before this, Jay mentioned my name in *The Film Sense* in the chapter from *Moby Dick*—"The Whiteness of the Whale" (apropos my passage about how I used white, contrary to tradition, to denote villainy in *Alexander Nevsky:* the knights and monks).

I hunted feverishly for something on Melville. I find *Moby Dick* interesting even now as possible material for a parody of Lewis Carroll's *The Hunting of the Snark.*

The only thing I have found so far (I found it earlier when I read Moby for the first time) was in Mrs. Rourke's brief notes in *American Humor* (before the war).

Then I read in *Literaturnaya gazeta* [The Literary Gazette] (1944) that the late Melville's daughter had sent a series of old editions of his works to Moscow.

At the same time I read (in Régis Messac's *Le "Detective novel" et l'influence de la pensée scientifique*) about Melville's *The Confidence Man.*

I looked for it in the Library of Foreign Literature. There was everything under the sun, apart from *The Confidence Man.*

On the other hand, there was a wide selection of books on Melville.

Amongst them was . . . Lawrence's "Studies in Classic American Literature."

I cannot abide reading in libraries.

Especially in the chill and dirty month of December 1944, in the unheated foreign literature library on the small street off Prechistenka.

But I ploughed through all the chapters on Melville and was left *bouche bée.*

It was so close to the themes of my *Grundproblem* of Melville *vu par* Lawrence—utterly astounding.

I received a small volume as a present, via Hellmann.

Then from Jay came *American Renaissance* by Matthiessen and Sedgwick's *Herman Melville* (I was then in hospital, at the start of 1946).

"Revival" of the mad attraction for Lawrence. (358–60)

[Murray to Leyda, February 6, 1947, declining to turn over some secrets] . . . Melville has been my life's work for 21 years—not a peripheral hobby, but a central preoccupation. Your present zest, excitement of discovery, enthusiasm, was mine, especially between 1925 & 1930 when I was going over the ground that you recently have been traversing. A good part of the time & energy spent during those years was wasted because others have come along, done the same job, and published. Except for a heterogeneous collection of stray items as yet unpublished, Miss Morewood's material was my only possession. She herself suggested & it was definitely agreed that she should not show *any* of her material to *any* biographer until my book was finished. This is customary practice in similar situations.

Now, I am merely human & you are asking me to do something which will make your book much *more* valuable & make mine much *less* valuable, if not unnecessary. If we were to hand in our manuscripts simultaneously then it would be fair & very advantageous to both of us to share *all* our data. But since your Ms. is going to press long before mine, then you have everything to gain & nothing to lose by the transactions—whereas the reverse is true for me.

Being merely human, I cannot quickly, easily, & graciously, hand over my life's work to someone I have never met, who is hurrying on to publish with such importunate dispatch. Give me time to accommodate myself to this exorbitant expectation of yours.

In the meanwhile, let me tell you that I have great admiration for your success as an explorer and want to do what I can within the limits of my capacity for selfishness to promote your noteworthy & important undertaking.

[Hayford to Leyda, March 7, 1947] Leon and I laughed that *your* publisher also did Olson! Leon stands by his resolve to do the life, and I slap down any tendencies to slip out of it . . . Naturally, I'd be much pleased to see you pin [*Mabel Ware*] on Herman—but! . . .

[Hayford to Leyda, March 17, 1947] [Merrell Davis says another researcher] is working on Melville's Primitivism, with the theory that Herman got himself tangled up in an emotional crisis in marriage, that this was one of the sources of his emotional primitivism, and that Pierre proves it!

[Henry A. Murray, "Time for a Positive Morality," *Survey Graphic*, March 1947, illustrated with pensive, melancholy Jewish/Italian-looking young man] A good boy often means a namby-pamby sort of fellow, tied to his mother's apron strings. There is no exhilaration, no adventure in the picture. Or our ideal is that of mere respectability, too low an aim to offer a challenge to the child. . . . We have demonstrated that as a nation we are capable of mobilizing all our powers to destroy something, but we have not shown that we can mobilize on a comparable scale to create something—good world citizens and a good world order.[39] (195–96)

[Telegram, Murray to Olson, April 2, 1947] Found your wonderful book two days ago when I returned to New York. You have written a tense and exciting saga which sings in unison with the pulse beats of the great man himself. Congratulations and everlasting thanks.

[Harry Levin, Harvard professor of comparative literature, to Olson, April 9, 1947] Warmest thanks for and congratulations upon *Call Me Ishmael*. It is fully as exciting and impressive as I expected, which is to say a good deal. Knowing you as I do, I know that it is the all but inevitable product of a process which could scarcely have been otherwise at any step, and I am too pleased with the results to indulge in subjunctive criticism, or to tell you—as some of your reviewers may have done—what kind of book I would have written with your material. On the all-important question of Shakespeare, you have said the last word, even as you said the first. And, in introducing the highly illuminating concept of space, you have documented it with the richest kind of first-hand seafaring lore.

On the whole, I think your style is not merely emphatic, but effective; and I am pledged to refrain over cavilling over the occasional confusion between Melville's symbols and your own; but I have one wish which, Oliver-Twist-like, I cannot keep down—that you had given us more. Since you stressed the notes on the backleaf of *King Lear*, I wish you had reprinted the whole thing, including Melville's title, *The Quaker Devil*. When you speak of two *Moby-Dicks*, I take it you were driving home your significant point about the conversion of the book from nautical yarn to Shakespearean drama; but unhappily I foresee future generations of Melvillian Dryasdusts, nurtured on *Ur-Fausts* and *Ur-Hamlets*, who may be misled into a literal search for an early recension. Let me also record my amicable disagreement with your interpretation of the *Don Quixote* note; my own view, for what it is worth, is that Melville is not speculating on women but interpreting Dulcinea as a personified ideal.

But these are mere pencillings in a volume to which I count on frequently turning back with increasing satisfaction and profit. I have already heard many enthusiastic comments upon it—from Lincoln Kirstein, for example, and from a number of students in my Humanities course.

[Gilman to Leyda, April 15, 1947] . . . do you know anything about Simon's story that a woman and her daughter descended on the Melville's after Allan's death and were bought off? . . . Simon's errors are innumerable, as you know, but I'd like to try to run down some of these insinuations, since they bear on my handling of the early life.

[Leyda evading Gilman's question, April 17, ?] . . . [Mrs. Metcalf] has said that Simon puts a lot in her mouth that never came from there, & that he will quote her as saying things she distinctly remembers *him* telling *her*.

[Hayford to Leyda, April 23, 1947] . . . P.S. [Howard] Vincent has cut [Egbert] Oliver down to 20 pages from 52, & I guess taken care of most of his egregious blunders. He had allegorized "The Piazza" as an account of HM's life. The "Old Aries" (goat) was Lemuel Shaw, etc.!

[Eleanor Metcalf to Leyda, April 28, 1947] We saw "Ivan"—stupendous! I would like to know under what conditions Eisenstein works, if he is wholly free or not. I came away with mixed feelings about what the film was trying to say.

[Merton M. Sealts, Jr., to Leyda, April 28, 1947] Thanks for the intriguing card—I take it you've seen Dr. Murray. I won't make any moves in that direction until I hear further from you. The "page 39" hint has me trying to figure out when I can go in to Widener and have a look—is that the stump-stirring object you had in view in being so cryptic? (**!!)

[Leon Howard to Leyda, April 30, 1947] Harry [Hayford] says you are as bad as Melville on the whiteness of the whale—hinting of indescribable things and leaving your readers up in the air. . . . What Harry really said was that you were an s.o.b. for not describing your Pittsfield hoard.

[Murray to Leyda, May 1, ?] Don't be upset by my last letter which was merely an instantaneous reaction. I shall be coming to the Berkshires around May 20ᵗʰ & we can talk these matters over & come to a just solution. I am very anxious that your book be as complete & authoritative as it can be, and I have some things that may be of use to you. Have you ever read the history of how Darwin came to announce his evolutionary theory? If you haven't, you might be entertained by looking it up.

[Chester Kerr, vice president of Reynal & Hitchcock, to Leyda, May 2, 1947] I have followed Charlie Olson's book through now and I can tell you that we are keen to see yours come along next in this field.

[Eleanor Metcalf to Leyda, May 2, 1947] Of course I am greatly distressed by the main news of your letter, and am left with exceedingly mixed feelings about it all. Of one thing only am I sure as regards my own position—I shall ask no questions about the material, and I shall take no initiative in the matter, nor mention it at all to anyone. I see the different points of view all too clearly, and my sympathies are divided. It now remains for our friend [Murray] to get out his book as soon as possible—which I believe he means to do.

[Hayford to Leyda, May 7, 1947, thanking him for copies of Bentley letters he had seen in Birss's collection years ago, but forgotten] It just makes me think what a general fuckup the whole Melville business has been, including Murray who in my calendar qualifies as one of the criminals of the century to have sat on this stuff all these years. Who would have thought he had so much blood in him? The more I think of it the more convinced I am that all documents should be published at once by the finders, *as documents* if nothing else can be done with them at once. But scholars for nearly a generation now have stewed around in ignorance that he could have enlightened. Nothing imaginable justifies his holding back all this stuff, except selfish vanity, the vain wish to amaze the world by springing it all at once. For as far as the facts themselves are concerned, and the letters and documents, his biography would just as good in all but its éclat if they had already been given to the hungry world.

[Gilman to Leyda, May 7, 1947] I wish you much luck in your interview with the Doctor. I do not see how you can be blamed in any way. If I should ever have a talk with our friend, I shall be thoroughly discreet, and, I am afraid, extremely cautious about yielding any information which I have.

[Sealts to Leyda, May 17, 1947] Instead of commenting on your leads, which I'll save for next time, I'll call your attention to something that had me spinning all week, ever since I read the Jungian article on Melville in the current *Partisan Review*. Pierre, in the "locked, round-windowed closet" (this has always said "head" to me), takes down the ambiguous portrait of his father and locks it in a "chest" (meaning "chest")—from which he later extracts it and burns it. With that chest compare:

Isabel—her "light was lidded and the lid was locked" (quoted in my article)

The mysterious closet in the chimney

The old chest in the garret where the apple-tree table is discovered

The mysterious box in "The Happy Failure"—which when opened, reveals a mass of convoluted pipes and syringes.

I'm sure that last description has anatomical overtones, but I'm not clear as to implications. In short, I think I'm on the trail of some more pieces that fit into the chimney story, and would like to put them together without going esoteric and psychological. Walt and Bett Bezanson are dropping in for a moment tonight—maybe he can crystallize it for me as he did with the chimney story.

Howard to Leyda, May 30, 1947] I didn't—and don't—give a damn what you do with Murray. There are two kinds of sob's in the scholarly world—one a universal sort who takes what you have got and then cuts your throat by getting the family to give him exclusive literary rights on it; the other merely inherits the characteristics of the dog in the manger. HM seems to be the latter, and anyway, thank God, the question of literary rights seem to have gone by default with respect to the Melville material.

[Hayford to Leyda, June 4, 1947] I am glad you reached a modus vivendi with Murray, even though it involves delay on your part. I hope he really does have some stuff to give you to justify your giving things to him and waiting.

[Howard to Leyda, June 7, 1947] . . . I was struck, while going through M's works again, by the fact that the physical circumstances under which he worked seemed to have had an observable effect upon his writings.

[Lincoln Kirstein to Leyda, undated] . . . Helen Gray who worked at the Museum at one point, is now working on Town & Country and she went over Frances Hawkins head and told the responsible editor that you were a famous communist and that Hearst would call everything off if he found out that they had printed an article by such a character; so now I don't know if they will take the piece or not; people are darling, aren't they but Mina thinks that she can have the Atlantic Monthly take the piece as it is so madly New England, so call her; I spoke to Russell Lynes on Harper's magazine about the Civil War piece which interested him. I talked to Tate at Holt's about the LOG; but he is publishing Arvin's book.

I suggest that you have Margot Johnson send it to Lambert Davis at Harcourt Brace; he is an intelligent man with a passion for Melville and they have nothing like it on their list, and they have a big text-book department as well . . . I was thinking that you might do a very good piece on how you got the method and materials of your book together; how you found the documents and the people etc. with a suggestion on how others could use (and few want to use) the materials you have gotten together. The Atlantic Monthly does not need pictures; I think that Harpers might be interested also in the methods and materials article; John Marshall of the Humanities division of the Rockefeller foundation might give you a grant? No?

Rotfront! Lincoln.

[Kirstein to Leyda, June 17, 1947, suggesting ideas for future articles]
M in and around Boston (Holmes, etc.)
A New Approach to Literary Documentation: M
My Experience with Previous Biographers
. . . I suppose it would be tempting God to think of a connection between the Whale and the [Rimmer] Gladiator?

[Lewis Mumford to Mr. Clucas, June 21, 1947] Dr. Henry A. Murray of Harvard has perhaps most of the unpublished material: that will go into his own biography on which he is now working. He has fresh data which bear on the interpretation of Pierre. Otherwise most of the known material has been combed through and published.

[Eleanor Metcalf to Leyda, June 30, 1947, on his meeting with Weaver] I am delighted that two good Melvilleans like each other. And I agree that H.M. was fortunate in his first biographer, who struck a deep note where it needed to be struck.

[Telegram, Eisenstein to Leyda, July 21, 1947] . . . MOST ENTHUSIASTIC THANKS FOR ISHMAEL. . . .

[Murray to Leyda, August 12, 1947] How do you like the company T[own] & C[ountry] provided for your White Elephant? Arrowhead alongside of "My Honolulu House," Lizzie rubbing elbows with Doris Duke? It was a fine article, crammed with juicy fruits of your inspired & industrious pickings. . . . As I told you, I have a filing cabinet full of ill-sorted & unintelligible notes which I put away when I stopped working on H.M. in the spring of 1940. Most of it you have already seen, of course;—since it comes from the sources you have examined, Metcalf, Morewood, NYPL &c—but here and there we shall run across an item ["new tit-bits" in next sentence] which you may not have discovered . . . I did not understand your question about the dream in The Counterpane chapter. Are you thinking of introducing it into the Log? The substance of it (memory of hand &c) might have occurred when H.M. was about six in N.Y. City. It means that he felt rejected by his punishing mother & dreamt that she had relentingly come to comfort him and hold his hand (suggested by sensation in arm)??

You suggested my using the item about the Stanwix birth certificate. I said I could not work it in. Now I have a good place for it. Does your offer hold?

[Sealts to Leyda, August 15, 1947] What *was* the man doing when some of those "holes" show up in the chronology?

[Gilman to Leyda, September 13, 1947] . . . Yes, I have seen *More Books.* And Jay, I won't pretend to conceal my disappointment. Where did Haraszti get that material on Alexander Bradford that Merrell and I worked so terribly long and hard to put together? I had no idea he was going to do anything more than print the letter. When I came to it in my dissertation, I simply didn't indicate that I had dug it up myself, and found out to whom it was written, because the explanation would have been lengthy and would have seemed envious. I had to yield credit to him; and while this will not do irreparable damage, at the same time, originality is the principal basis upon which a dissertation is judged. Perhaps this will seem like petty academic quibbling, but it is far from that. I hold no brief for sitting on valuable materials, as you know; but in this profession, like it or not, rank, reputation, salary, and other things are based just as much on what a man publishes as on how well he teaches, and sometimes, as at Yale, the teaching is taken for granted. The dog-eat-dog aspect of academic life is despicable, but it can't be wished away.

[Birss to Leyda, September 14, 1947] [Congratulates JL for his *Town & Country* article and on finding new prose of HM (?), then] There is no reason for characterizing yourself as "forgotten." Please try to get over the erroneous feeling that you are being neglected. I am at a loss to understand the tone of your letters at times. You have always received a cordial reception here, haven't you? You ought to realize that not all Melville workers have your advantage of unlimited time and the financial backing of a publishing house.

[Murray to Leyda, undated (but before September 15, 1947)] . . . My *God!* What are you saying? It has been *definitely* decided by the three most alluring sisters that your book *must* be *complete*. To hell with the edge of mine! It has so many nicks in it already that it makes no difference whether it receives any more or not. . . . [Postscript] The bonfire occurred before I arrived. It was grim news. I could hardly resist the temptation to tar & feather [broken off]

[Howard to Leyda, September 22, 1947] Could there have been a skeleton of fact in the early part of *Mardi,* or am I going nuts?

[Lionel Trilling to Richard Chase, October 8, 1947, commenting on Chase's response to his novel *The Middle of the Journey*] All that you say about the Laskell-Maxim axis [the sensitive protagonist vs. the ex-Stalinist modeled upon Whittaker Chambers who has taken Vere's side in "Billy Budd"] I agree with, and have thought of bitterly before. I do not think that Maxim is too large; or, if he is, I am glad of his fault because he ran away with things and grew out of bounds and always came with utter ease—I never had to touch anything he said or did once it was down on paper: and I have the old-fashioned notion, now not honored, that characters ought to run away with things or at least take hold of their fates—Maxim's wilfulness I take to be a good omen and a good lesson to me. Laskell, that sneak, he's the trouble— simply not sufficiently detached from his author, nor, on the other hand, sufficiently his author; in the effort to detach him from my own self I somehow sterilized him; and while a certain sterilization is of his character, still it doesn't do him any good. He is the character that often inhabits an early novel; perhaps better than most, perhaps raised a little by Jamesian theory and practice, but not right, not the right kind of person to have in a novel. And I hope never again to have such a one. The hardest thing in the book was getting him started right. And you put it with *absolute* precision when you speak of "appetite and imagination for force" that he might have had: there lies the whole trouble with him, and it was essentially what Diana kept trying to tell me about him. But you will, I know, understand that I am not trying to exculpate myself for this failure if I say that I could not become aware and let myself go on all things, that the book having been so difficult and central an event in my emotional life, written out of the strangest adjustment of the will and the unconscious: seemingly to get it done at all, to at last clear the way for novels, not this one but all the ones to follow, I had to make some sacrifice, and Laskell is it. . . . And again accept my gratitude for your letter, and my assurances that my next hero has appetite and admiration for force—I think they'll kill him, poor fellow.[40]

[Wilson L. Heflin to Leyda, October 13, 1947] To spin super fantasy wouldn't it be something if M. left Eimeo on the C. & H. which went east, jumped ship at sea or at Mocha, stopped at Callao on the Damon and went from there to Lahaina? . . . best of hunting on your trip.

[Eleanor Metcalf to Leyda, October 14, 1947] In view of the fact that you are using so much of the journal, and should have the photographs too, I might be able to persuade Mr. Wilson [of Harvard University Press] that the journal should come out no later than September 1948. The press has been told that this publication will be the first giving the complete text. Could your book wait until October? Even a *little* later I should think should be an argument in favor of the journal's coming out in September. . . . If our two publication dates cannot be straightened out sufficiently satisfactorily to everyone, I see nothing for it but a minimum use of the text of the journal, just to give where he was on successive days. But let us wait, and see what I can do.

[Hayford to Leyda, October 25, 1947] So Murray played you false! I'm not surprised. But of course you managed a brilliant victory in the engagement even so.—What with the Morewood cache. And he got nothing from you he would not have gotten from you in print. Vincent has shown me the *Pierre* introduction, of which all but the last few pages are in his hands. It is long and fanciful. He is positive that Plinlimmon is Hawthorne!! There is a lot of good stuff in it nonetheless. The volume should be a good seller.

[Chase to Trilling, October 29, 1947] There is without exception no human being with whom I am completely at ease . . . [attributed to? Chase's] ragged and soulless and prideful New England home.[41]

[Eleanor Metcalf to Leyda, November 3, 1947] But I am interested in what you say about Gansevoort's London career. How, unpleasant? I had already gathered that Washington was not satisfied with his performance of his official duties. I put it down to his failing health. Is there more than that?

Skeletons will walk when questions begin. As a member of the family, I am perhaps inclined to be more [illegible] and compassionate than an outsider.

[Murray to Leyda, November 14, 1947] I trust your leg is better. I could not make a diagnosis from your brief account of it & therefore, have no idea what the prospects are: whether you are already springing in the air like Nijinski in his prime or whether you are still limping about painfully with a cane. One thing seems certain: you *don't* like New York. This to me is not only surprising but incomprehensible, in fact, mad. . . .

I may say that *Pierre* is at last finished—110 dreary pages of footnotes & 105 dreary pages of introduction. . . .

It was good of you to send me a copy of the McLane letters from the Buchanan collection—very intriguing because of the vagueness of the criticisms. The last letter was written before Gansevoort's death & it suggests that he died of tubercular meningitis. Other letters you have seen may have supplied the key to his failure as an under-secretary—loud-mouthed boasting, extravagant falsifications, disrespect to the President, American bumptiousness, arrogance? This does not fit very well with the letters to his family.

[Eleanor Metcalf to Leyda, November 19, 1947, with a donation toward his support enclosed] Poor Gansevoort! It was indeed ill health. If the family ever knew of this situation, no one could ever have divulged it to the next, or to the next, generation; for Gansevoort was always spoken of in the most glowing terms—indeed a good deal to Herman's disadvantage.

[Murray to Leyda, November 29, 1947] Your leaving your manuscript before departing for California puts you several miles ahead in the Generosity Marathon, and it looks as if no amount of exertion on my part could bring me within range of you. As you have discovered by this time, I have a very limited, single-tracked, narrow-gauged mind, and while I am working on something (in this case *Pierre*) I can do more than glance confusedly at things that for the moment are off the main track. . . . I gather that your last weeks in New York were extremely unpleasant ones due to your painful knee-joint, your aversion to the incomparable city, and your pervasive fury at my tardiness in finishing so slight an assignment as the introduction to *Pierre*. Please let me know how you are now, after arriving in your Eden. It is strange that your Heaven is my Hell, and your Hell is my Heaven. Have you any evidence that Herman Melville thought that Los Angeles was the Promised Land? No doubt both places were Hell to him, Heaven being somewhere near Tahiti.

[Murray to Olson, 1947, water-damaged document] Dear Prodigal and Prodigious Charles, My nature has been the [source?] of intolerable annoyance to me—never more than this [year?] It could not or would not move faster than a snail, with his [illegible] & nail, in building the *Pierre* shanty & would not allow me the privilege of relishable occupations such as *really* reading *Call Me Ishmael*, writing a review of it, & discussing it [illegible] & also with you. It, that is, the Id, [my self?]—just got durn stubborn, partly, I suspect, because I felt humiliated and on the verge of despair over the length of time it was taking to get the job done. Three weeks ago, the job was finished—110 pages of footnotes & 105 pages of introduction, both of which I am afraid, have succeeded only in communicating the fatigue in which they were wrought. But now, anyhow, after 2 years of uninterrupted painful scribbling, I am [planning?] to play the role of an eolithic [*sic*] sloth. [illegible] scratching my navel, while the former boarders pack their belongings and move out of the tenement of my mind—*Assessment of Men* came out in February (cross the street if you see it coming), a book of case histories (Summer) a book of readings in Personality & Culture (which may interest you, Knopf in March) & *Pierre* which should break wind about April (don't touch it for fear of vomiting & diarrhoea). . . .

You know, I have purposely not read *Call Me Ishmael* lest it would influence me too greatly in doing *Pierre*, but I did run through it & went to Washington last spring partly to tell you that it was a book straight out of Melville's unconscious. I don't suppose many readers know *consciously* what it is saying, but many of them undoubtedly feel its impact as I did in the solar plexus. I don't suppose that you suppose that [you are?] conveying objectively definable meaning, but rather the tempo & temper, the primitive desperation & fury, the [illegible] spatial longing of the man. You were talking out of your entrails after you had got your [illegible] in harmony with H.M's, & so you are communicating, in a [deep?] way, a [illegible] version of H.M himself—assuming he had been relieved of some of his inhibitions. Your book is as mythological & cannibalistic as H.M's own shadow self &, consequently, expresses something very real, even though it would be hard to rationalize the logic of your image patterns. I am saying all the [illegible] basis of last spring's quick plunge into its cool waters, but before I see you again, I shall have *really* read it and shall have more to discuss with you,—this time we won't get diverted, as we did last spring into other channels. You have written a significant book— gale of Southwest wind that blows us land lubbers, like so much flotsam, into the shallows. [Whereas?] we craven crawl to shore. I hope it has been selling well. I have been out of contact except for a [brief?] talk with Eleanor Metcalf who mentioned 4 people who had had an exciting experience reading the book & Ferris Greenslet who, as you know, is very keen about it. I gather from these instances, that your forceful & felicitous [?] courage is having its effect. It is a daring book—possibly a little too sensational & imaginative for impermeable, rational readers who want everything spelled out in grammatical sequences; but just right for those who like to be outdoors in a hailstorm, facing the cutting edge of it. I have withered not hearing from you this summer—have felt isolated & deprived—but now, I hope, you will forgive my silence.

[Sealts to Leyda, December 12, 1947] [Murray] was tremendously impressed, I gathered, with the scope of your labors, as was Vincent, and remarked sadly that he has "nothing" now that hasn't been turned up by someone else. I remarked that I knew of no one else who could *handle* the material as he will, but no mere Bright remarks will free him of an obvious sense of lost opportunities and frustration. It's too bad. He and I get along fine as before. . . . Despite his air of discouragement he talks as though he loves everybody, you and me included . . . On our Arrowhead hypothesis, Dr. Murray insists that he went through Agnes' library *before* the sale and found nothing but the *History of the Berkshires.* The other items belonging to Herman came to her from Charlotte Hoadley, with whom she made up at his instigation & who left them to her. He has nothing to suggest on where books from the early New York period may have gone, and indeed raises the further suggestion of what happened to *Allan's* library. . . . He also had no suggestions on that page of Weaver's notes, which incidentally I copied and sent to Walter Osborne.

[Leyda to Sealts, undated draft] I see no reason for accepting Murray's search story for the Arrowhead library.

[Random House editor Albert Erskine to Mr. Cerf, December 19, 1947, a memo predicting ever-growing interest in Melville and arguing for an affordable trade book of Melville's collected short stories to be edited by Leyda] . . . [On the man and his art:] The stories are allegorical and symbolic (Hawthorne's influence is clear though not dominating)—sometimes obviously so, sometimes obscurely. For the most part, they are nondramatic in form. They are a pleasure to read because of the fine texture of the writing and because Melville had a complex and fascinating mind. In addition to their inherent interest they have the added dimension of relevance to the further understanding of Melville himself and his other work . . . .

[Sealts to Leyda, January 17, 1948, letter and notes from visit to Mr. Carol Wright of Chatham, Mass., owner of Melville's *Poetical Works of Lord Byron* in 10 volumes, 1851 facsimile] This is really Dr. Murray's baby. Please check with one or both of us before using any of the details. He is going to Chatham soon . . . [Sealts's notes on Melville's markings] . . . on Byron and Cervantes, Milton's blindness, effect of mental health on physical health (!); certain of 'Domestic Pieces' in IV heavily marked, with significant relevance to his own situation (aimed at MGM?) . . . 4 lines of apparently original verse written at end of VIII. *Highly important item*—Dr. Murray should examine these volumes as soon as possible.

[Leyda to Erskine, January 20, 1948] [Wants to call the Stories volume "Tales Told Through A Mask: The Collected Stories of HM"] . . . [The Fifties are] ripest period of his craft.

[Eleanor Metcalf to Leyda, March 21, and 31, 1948] I saw Raymond in New York recently. He has been far from well, though now on the mend. He seemed averse to asking you for the *Clarel* himself, so I said I would. [Weaver had lent Leyda his personal, probably annotated, copy of the book. *C.S.*] . . . I am glad to know where Raymond's *Clarel* is: I will write him that it is safe and in use, and that he will get it back again. His condition has probably made him worry. I think he would be very glad to hear from you. He spoke highly of you, and was amazed at your detailed memory—or is it "your memory of details."

[Eleanor Metcalf to Leyda, May 3, 1948] Your idea of dedicating the Random House volume of stories to the memory of Raymond Weaver is a good and just one, which would make me happy. Though we saw so little of him over the years between his visit to us in Wellesley Farms at the very first of his Melville work, and his untimely death, and though correspondence was desultory, his presence made itself felt warmly in our lives, and his loss is great.

I had a letter from Charles in which he says he wishes very much that "someone more intimate to him would speak up about him." He feels that "a memorial book of him (that old-fashioned gesture) is called for."

[Eleanor Metcalf to Olson, May 24, 1948] Your good letter about Raymond touched me deeply. I had lunch with him five weeks to the day before he died. He was still terribly thin, but in good spirits. He had been living at the Payne-Whitney Clinic, under psychic and physical treatment, but was allowed time and more freedom to live his regular life, even to teaching some of his classes.

I called John Burrell when I saw the notice in the paper, and he told me Raymond died in his sleep—the heart just stopped. He had been out to dinner, and had talked with John Burrell at half past eleven. In the morning he was dead.

I have written John B. since but received no answer. I know nothing of his ability as a writer, but do think *someone* should write, or collect from his friends, a memorial. He was always so mysterious to me as you picture him: his endless searching for some root took different forms at different times. I always felt him enveloped in some oriental cloud. I told him once of Richard Wilhelm's translation of the Chinese "The Secret of the Golden Flower" which made a deep impression on him; and he told me he had used it in a course on the Middle Ages. He used to make spiritual tie-ups between far times and places I think.

I did not even know he had a sister living in New York, and brother somewhere else, until I read of it in the paper.

I never thought of *understanding* Raymond, only of enjoying him.

Why don't you write to John Burrell? I think I shall again, in spite of no answer.

What a curious name for him—"Tiger Weaver"! I do not know where he was born, only that his oriental associations and living were in Japan. I have heard people say that they found his eyes terrifying. That I don't understand; he was so kind, and so humorous. I wonder if anyone was ever intimate with him—if all his friends had an isolated relationship with him, that was not really intimate, only separate.

You would have had an answer before this, but that I have been low in vitality since a devastating grippe three months ago and the finishing up of the editing of the Journal.

[Leyda to Eleanor Metcalf, Draft, undated (1948?). See her response "coals heaped upon my head"; Leyda blames her for the *Log*-jam, held up for some months because Harvard objected to simultaneous publication of Melville's Journal of 1849 and the *Log*, which excerpted large chunks] I actually envied your friend's doing your index for that's a game I particularly enjoy doing and for lack of any more helpful move to make on the Log, I am doing an index for it. But it doesn't now look as though Log or index will ever reach the printer. Not Reynal's printer, at any rate, for he has let our contract lapse beyond the specified deadline (this month), & refuses to answer my inquiries. I don't know what next to attempt, whether I can regard the contract as an option, & their advances as fee—& peddle it elsewhere, or what. Those few months delay were fatally unnecessary. I hope the Harvard Press is not in the habit of making such demands without further investigation. With production of the *Log* to take no less than a year, it would have given your Journal plenty of leeway. But that request for delay unfortunately postponed the beginning of production beyond the time when the publisher was willing to face the production of such a difficult monster. And now expensive books are completely shelved—I imagine that it is the Log's unusual costliness of production that makes Reynal silent to all my questions and pleadings. But understanding doesn't seem to make me more tolerant of such behavior.

One effect of this is to make all other work impossible—particularly my Melville work. I can't even think of an introduction to the volume of stories that Random House will do,—if I can ever get them an introduction. It was a lot of fun working with them until the pall of this failure settled down over everything.

Now the only useful thing I can do is play other people's games—& Sealts tells me that you have found someone to index the paintings and prints.

[Murray to Leyda, June 15, 1948] I am extremely sorry to hear that you have been so miserable for so long. I wish you had discussed it with me when discussion was possible—last summer in Topsfield. Your letter is naturally non-committal & you are three thousand miles away—this does not make communication easy. You have explained that you have been the victim of a psychological revolt by unconscious forces more serious than you can cope with single-handed. Obviously, you need help. Have you consulted your analyst? (You omit his name.) Is he considered competent? or is he a second-rater? Perhaps psychoanalysis can help you, but not as practiced by your analyst. If your analyst was A 1, perhaps another form of therapy would be more effective. I don't know any psychiatrist in Los Angeles, except a very competent woman, Dr. Ruth Tolman. She is chief clinical psychologist of the VA, Branch 12 . . . —an attractive, sensitive & perceptive, common-sensical woman with considerable clinical experience. She worked with me on the OSS job. . . . If you want to come to the Harvard Clinic [in the Fall], for a nominal fee, I shall be glad to do what I can for you.

The fact that your are capable of deceiving everybody about your state of mind, that you are mysterious about your private life, that you never mentioned your troubles to me, that your present letter provides no clues in respect to your troubles, that your analysis was not successful, that you have shown no interest in interpreting the mountain of data you collected about H.M —all this suggests that you are unusually prideful and reticent in respect to what goes on under the surface, that repression & suppression has perhaps been overworked. This suggests also some unwillingness to admit to yourself & accept humbly certain more or less unchangeable components of your own nature. An enormous relief comes when we allow conflicts to become fully conscious & freely acknowledge our limitations. You know all this, but the wisest man in the world is not free from the tendency to conceal from himself the Ugliest Man among the contending aggregate of personalities that make up his Whole Self.

The Army made a great mistake at first, discharging thousands of men with psychoneurotic symptoms before they had been rehabilitated *within* the Army. Discharge is a profound blow to a person's self-respect & unless he can immediately find his niche in some civilian occupation, he does not recover from it for a long time. Working by yourself as you have been working without any regular salary or sense of security is extremely hard—you must struggle against an incessant stream of anxiety, thoughts of possible failure &c.—& if on top of that there are conflicts in the sphere of sex & intimate human relationships, the burden is well-nigh insupportable. Would you be willing to take a job for a while? I think first of all of a job connected with a modern museum or possibly a magazine, publishing house, or film company or theater. Some security at this point would help a lot while you gathered your forces and prepared for further creative work. You do not tell me what you are doing now, so that my suggestions are necessarily random. For the moment, to tide you over, I am enclosing a check to *keep*, but I shall lend you more if you need it. You shouldn't have any trouble getting a job—because you are a genius with all kinds of people, invite their affections & persuade them to anything you want, & have great talents in the sphere of art & research—only at this season, you should not be too high-brow—you can't afford to be psychologically or economically—about the kind of job you accept. If I were you I would even sink to the advertising business to recuperate my finances for later more congenial ventures. Anyhow, I will bet on you as a winner at almost anything, provided you can become distinctly aware of your major conflict & solve it. Possibly a divorce is what you want? Since you have told me nothing I can't say anything concrete, except to reiterate my well-founded conviction that you have an extraordinary abundance of talents & triumphant human qualities.

As far as I am concerned I have not been able to bring myself back to Melville since seeing you. I am satisfied that your book will be an outstanding landmark & that further labors on my part would be a waste of time.

[Murray to Olson, July 1, 1948] I find it hard to explain—even to myself— why I have not been able to make time to get to Washington—& have a long exchange with you—since our last meeting there over a year ago . . . [sends Olson a check, but nothing for Erik Hawkins] . . . I have been lying fallow for sometime [next page missing]

[Murray to Leyda, July 7, 1948] I hope that you were not put off by anything I said in my letter. I do not know any doctors in Los Angeles in whom I have any great confidence except Dr. Tolman. Please drop me a line.

How about joining the World Federalists? [On the back of a circular reprinting Murray's letter to the editor of June 3, 1948 (asking for a world government to prevent nuclear war: Congress should "initiate and support two measures: one, the revision of the U.N. Charter . . . and two, an amendment to our Constitution"), including a final paragraph omitted by the *New York Times:* "To achieve our purpose we must appeal to Congress; and to appeal to Congress we must know their expectations in respect to war, their states of mind and motives. Therefore, some of us, pleading ignorance, are asking readers of the *Times* to give us their views as to why Congress has not acted to prevent the extinction of our country and of other countries. All replies will be gratefully received, carefully considered, and systematically compiled. The most illuminating contributions will be published (if permission is granted) as soon as possible, in conjunction with a tabulation of the over-all findings, to serve as guide for further action."]

[From Leyda's typescript for "The Army of the Potomac Entertains a Poet"] It seems to have been in 1859, or not long before, that Herman Melville began his career of poet. The responsibilities of a large family, the obligations imposed by a burdensome property that he had managed to halve before he sailed for the Mediterranean and Asia Minor in 1856, had ~~chained~~ handcuffed him to his desk and had brought about a "nervous condition" that disturbed and even alarmed the family.

[Hayford to Leyda, July 8, 1948] [Asks Leyda to tell him about someone in France seeing M's journal in the South Seas. Also, possibly referring to Melville items owned by A. Rosenbach:]. . . The letters you sent (sub rosy) are very fine——is there no end to that mine?

[Eleanor Metcalf to Murray, July 11, 1948] I am so very much distressed about Jay Leyda. I had always supposed the illness he had after the war was of a mental nature. He sent me a postal not long ago with a question about some Melville letters, of which I know nothing. What can I do or not do? I suppose the postponement of the "Log" was not good for him after all that intensive work; and insofar as the "Journal" had anything to do with it, it makes me most unhappy.

You must know that your Melville book will be unique in plan and scope; but of course you cannot go on with it at present feeling as you do. No one will do the kind of *justice* to him that *you* will; and it really is not true that other men write better than you. . . .

[Dr. Herschel C. Walker, in Honolulu, to Sealts, July 30, 1948, and copied to Leyda] [He bought Melville-owned books at ten to fifteen cents each from the Pittsfield house, but gave them away to servants, his sister, and a neighbor in 1940.]

[Howard to Leyda, August 2, 1948] P.S. Don't worry about Melville's sisters. I figured his family was to [*sic*] complicated to handle at once and that they didn't mean much in his life until he got back from the Pacific, and I'll introduce them as he found them then.

[Sealts to Leyda, August 10, 1948] Just when did the various sisters cease to be regular residents of HM's stable of fillies? That, as you recall, is my dividing line on whether books acquired by them go in or not.

[Chase to Trilling, September 4 and 30, 1948] Here's more on *Billy Budd*. At least I've discovered that Billy is the Lamp Chop of God. . . . I've added some thoughts on Melville as Captain Vere, the Anglo-Saxon gentleman, to offset the isolated and suffering artist image. And Melville is the Old Sailor, as he's presented in "Daniel Orme." Also some fine relevance: shall we chop hell out of Leviathan or love Leviathan? [A few weeks later:] I always hear an inner Starbuck saying, for God's sake, let's get back to Nantucket.

[Gilman to Leyda, October 9, 1948] I have worked in the Bible family records, thanks; and incidentally, I'm building up the religious education . . . and working out a simple theme of cyclical compression, or cumulative tragedy, or what have you . . . you've probably charted the periods of prosperity and adversity . . . roughly 11 years, 7 years, 2 years, 1 year . . . and then the *Acushnet*. Each period has a sequence of fortune and disaster, or hope and despair, that I assume conditioned Melville's sense of predestination as Ishmael voices it in Ch. 1.

[Leyda to Gilman, October 15, ?] Let me know how much time you're going to have in NYC—there's a BIG thing, untouched, waiting there—but mostly on his last years.

[Trilling to Chase, October 25, 1948; Trilling had been lobbying the Columbia English department to hire Chase, his former graduate student, here discussing who will edit the Viking Portable Melville (later assigned to Jay Leyda)]. I can't guess what effect your review will have on [Viking editor] Covici. The Melville portable is in any case a thin chance, you being mystical and [Malcolm] Cowley being an authority and a critic, who will probably be given the Melville. Yes, the Hawthorne is rather ghastly. Mark Van Doren [a Columbia colleague] has written a Hawthorne for the Am. Men of Letters which is strangely moving. The criticism is of a general and impressionistic kind but this fits the general intention of the book, which is essentially biographical. (By the way, in the name of the Lord, DON'T review this book if you don't like it: I beg it of you!)

[Eleanor Metcalf to Leyda, October 26, 1948] I expect to see Harry Murray shortly. He is lecturing at Harvard to *enormous* classes on human relations, I believe.

[Albert Erskine to Leyda, October 27, 1948] [Suggests two passages from *Mardi* (from chapters 114 and 120) for Leyda's collection of epigraphs:] "I am intent on the essence of things: the mystery that lieth beyond; the element of the tear which much laughter provoketh; that which is beneath the seeming; the precious pearl within the shaggy oyster. I probe the circle's center; I seek to evolve the inscrutable." "Meditate as much as you will . . . but say little aloud, unless in a merry and mythical way. Lay down the great maxims of things, but let inferences take care of themselves . . . ."

[Murray to Olson, 1948 ca. October] You will not be provoked, I trust, if I confess ignorance of your symbolism. You are speaking a language more complicated than Einstein's & keeping the key in your pants' pocket. I should see you one evening a week to keep within range of comprehensibility.
      "About Space" is full of suggestions, but it must make a lot of nitwits like me think of entirely different things—
      Space as form
      Space as *more* space, unlimited
      space, unstructured space—the sea, the
      universe, space in which to breathe—freedom
      Space as limited & confined, closed space
—cabinned, cribbed, —the womb; the tomb—birth & death
      Charles Olson—7 foot giant—with never
      enough space in which to stretch—dreaming of

the great Southwest open spaces &c &c

Agoraphobia, claustrophobia &c &c.

Ruling out time arbitrarily—when the whole of modern philosophy hinges on the concept of *process*, temporal structure—like music—seems to be a futile attempt to escape the reality of involvement in life. Personally I would like to slow Time down to the limits of organic tolerance. We are all ill from being stretched too much by time. You can't make a leaf grow by stretching it—or can you? . . . I am in the dumps as you can see . . .

[Henry A. Murray, "America's Mission," *Survey Graphic*, October 1948] To take the initiative in the creation of a democratic world government—this is our mission, our manifest destiny, because it is in our power to achieve this thing and in no other nation's power; and mankind expects it from us.

Thus, if we fail, through lack of sagacity or courage, to form a partial world government to checkmate her at her own game, we shall lose our sole chance to create the one institution which could eventually eliminate war, or could, if war is thrust upon us, unify all the rest of the world in subduing the aggressor. (414)

A hundred and sixty years ago our ancestors successfully performed a comparable experiment; they conceived a federal government and made it work, and all breeds of men and women who have since migrated to this land and learned to live here side by side in peace and confidence have found it good. The United States is the abstract of the One World which now awaits creation. It seems fitting then, that leadership in executing this last and most difficult experiment should have fallen to our lot.

Perhaps fate has summoned us at a time when we are not capable of acquitting ourselves with honor. On all sides one sees the classical symptoms of moral breakdown, manifestations, to quote Lewis Mumford, of the "cult which denies the fundamental discriminations between good and bad, between higher and lower, which are the very bases of human development." But despite these discouraging evidences, I hold that there is still some unspoiled latent stuff in us which, quickened by this emergency, can carry us beyond our common selves to become once more "the pioneers of the world," as Melville described us, "the advance guard, sent on through the wilderness of untried things, to break a new path."[42]

[Chase to Trilling, November 18, 1948] While I was writing the Melville book, I found myself now and then wishing to have done with these gigantic and whale-like people and turn to something more limited, intense, circumscribed, and subdued.

[*The Story of Moby Dick the White Whale as Adapted and Retold by Frank L. Beals*, former assistant superintendent of schools, Chicago (1949)] Introduction. The original story, *Moby Dick, or The White Whale*, written by Herman Melville, represents a work of research seldom equaled by writers of stories. However, the original volume contains some 219,000 words, divided into 134 chapters, and a considerable Appendix.

As originally written, the book has many drawbacks for the young, or less expert, reader. It is long, rambling, and contains many expressions that are impossible except for the reader of large experience. However, it is one of the literary classics and, as such, should be made available to as many readers as possible. Every young person should have the satisfaction of having read it.

It was with this in mind that I undertook to rewrite the story. It has been retold in about 38,000 words, divided into 32 chapters.

The original story was written in the first person, which makes it difficult for the young reader to identify himself with any of the characters. The present interpretation is written in the third person and is, therefore, much easier to follow. It becomes an adventure story with a strong appeal.

Where it was thought necessary to interpret the thought in language different from the original, I have employed my own method of expression freely.

My effort has been to make this a clear, readable story of adventure while adhering strictly to the ideas of the original author. I have tried to present a story that flows along easily and in proper sequence. Much of what I regard as extraneous matter has been eliminated.

It is my hope that young people will learn to love *The Story of Moby Dick* as much as I love it.

[Undated draft, Leyda to F. Barron Freeman, written on back of screenplay dated November 29, 1948] Mrs. Metcalf owns a copy of *White Jacket* interestingly annotated in HM's very late hand, as a reference work for his last novel.

[Norman Holmes Pearson to Leyda, January 22, 1949] It was splendid to meet you last summer, after so long a period of hearing your praises and your graces sung. . . I saw Leon briefly at the MLA in New York. He seemed very harried, and for the moment apparently had put the Melville aside. He spoke of plans to come out to the Coast this summer, take a spot to live, and re-write his Lowell in order to make it popular. Just why he left off HM I don't know, but he once thought he could use that to get the Lowell published. It's really bad luck for him to have that hanging by. Otherwise he was busied by a lecture he'd given at Rochester, the fine paper he read at the MLA, and the series he had to prepare for the University of Chicago where he was to give the series established by (Damn it, I can't think of his name) the man who has the chain of drug stores in the middle west, and got into a fight with Hutchins over commies on his faculty. Apparently there is really big money in this series, and a book from it is guaranteed, so he was happy about it. . . .

[Arthur Schlesinger, Jr., to Chase, January 24, 1949] I was reading with my usual interest your article on THE CONFIDENCE MAN in the current issue of KENYON REVIEW when I came upon your pleasant reference to me. I was particularly interested by the article because I have just been putting together my thoughts on modern liberalism in a volume which Houghton Mifflin will bring out in the next few months; and in the course of argument I am urging a return to those earlier and profounder representatives of our democratic tradition, such as Hawthorne and Melville . . . [who] certainly stand up superbly when read in the interesting light of the 20th century.

[Sealts to Leyda, February 2, 1949] I have seen a couple of the "religious tracts" belonging to Maria—Hannah More's stuff published by the American Sunday School Union, and drivel of the sort I don't believe Herman would have looked twice at . . . [On Murray's MLA talk]. . . Murray discussed Plinlimmon as Hawthorne—in the face of openly expressed skepticism from most of us. Personally, I think he makes a fine case if not an air-tight one. My big objection was that so much points to Emerson and various Transcendentalists, but he explains that too as you'll doubtless find whenever his *Pierre* is out. It was reported to be nearly ready in the trade edition but delayed in the critical because of changes in textual notes. . . .

[Murray to Olson, February 22, 1949, with heading "From the trough of the wave where only our heads show"] . . . I am a miserable sinner. Have mercy on me, O Lord!

Your Christmas gift and New Year poem were enough to bring water from the Rock & yet I, miserable sinner, wrote you no word of acknowledgement—the essence of disfriendship.

As I have told you before, Modern Poetry excludes me. It is as esoteric as electronic physics, & only a complete psychoanalysis of each poet—a lifelong study—is capable of yielding the private meanings which give the poem its significance. However; I can appreciate the magic of sound & the congress of imagery and symbol, & I know intuitively that you have the divine gift bestowed by the Angelic Orders.

You are a persuasive voice bidding me hang my plough on a golden bough & my tongue on any branch & follow after—for a while at least.

I have been ploughing too assiduously & have permitted myself to be caught up in the threadmill [sic], or rat race, or dog fight, or assembly line that is Modern Life, & your Y & X (standing for two unknowns) comes as a breeze of fresh, invigorating air—regardless of what it means.

The tide has already long ago moved me to my moon. My problem is, or rather will be very soon, the communication of that experience—a task for which I am patently, at the moment, unfitted. As I probably told you, overwork resulted in a constant headache which has been with me for over a year, & in a few weeks I intend to go off to some solitary spot for a real rest—merely to sleep upon the waters, waiting for the recuperating flood.

I am happy to know that you are still bursting with productiveness, despite temporary recessions & reverses, & that you are managing words in a new way with new intentions. Someday I hope you will explain yourself a little so that I will not be so much of a stranger in your sphere of feeling & thought as I am now. In any event—whether we meet or not in the near future—I am sure we can trust each other's ways whether, for a season, they diverge or converge.

I have asked Farrar, Straus, & Co to send you the new edition of *Pierre* which is a year late in making its appearance. As one who has his own independent vision of Melville, you will inevitably find much that does not fit your picture. However, I hope, that there will be fragments here & there of which you will approve, despite my unpoetic, & perhaps at times pedantic, treatment of the work. The intrusion of a psychologist into the realm of literary criticism is almost certain to ruffle the back hairs of the scholars. Matty, if he reads it, may come down with a neuraglia [sic].

Don't bother to answer this letter. I don't deserve a reply. But keep your time open for more bubblings like Y & X, & let me have the satisfaction of watching you become famous as a pioneer poet. . . .You can take it for granted that I was both touched and honored to receive the *first* copy of Y & X, a very handsome achievement by The Black Sun Press as well as by Charles Olson.

[Eleanor Metcalf to Murray, March 7, 1949] I have read your introduction ("superb writing," as Harry Metcalf exclaims) and the voluminous notes, and now I have gone back to "Pierre" itself.

My reaction is the same as that which I tried to express on the telephone. I feel so strongly the value of what you are doing that I am ready to turn over to you all or *any* part of the material I have gathered from memories, family stories and the result of research, if it will help along your own work. But as I have reiterated again and again, my debt to you and other Melvilleans is so much greater than any of you seem to understand, that it is hard for me to realize the debt to me that you [illegible] so generously. After all, my interest is so close and natural an interest in the subject, and it began so *unliterarily* a way—simply a sharing with my grandfather certain tastes and a delight in certain of his things—pictures, statuary, dishes and such. His writings followed after, and continue to follow.

When I look back over my abysmal ignorance over the years, I think it must have been some hidden unknown god was looking after me and my precious charge, during the time when I was concerned with my more narrowly personal affairs.

Well, there it is. How can I best help you and your work, if at all? . . . I would like to ask you about Judge Shaw in his relations to Herman.

[Murray to Leyda, undated (but before March 10, 1949)] I am a miserable sinner. Immediately after receiving your letter in July I wrote you a longish reply saying that as far as I could see you had acted with immaculate goodwill from start to finish & that I had not the slightest reason to criticize you for anything. The next morning—after sleeping on it—I did not like the letter I had written & so I tore it up with the intention of writing a better one. But since I was sailing for England in 3 days & there was a great miscellany of business to be attended to, I did not get round to writing the letter, which I not only *should* have written but *wanted* to write. When I returned I was confronted with a mass of 70 or so letters to be answered, lectures to be prepared, a house to settle, & a hundred & one odds & ends, more than I could cope with. I turned to the most urgent things—lectures—& let all my correspondence stand untouched.

This happened to be the best I could do—but I won't try to justify it except to say that for a year and a half I have had a constant headache which has cut down my mental efficiency 50 percent, & left me incapacitated for anything but the most routine tasks, performed slowly & painfully. My explanation for the headache was exhaustion after more than 2 years of writing (*Assessment of Men, Personality in Nature, Society, & Culture,* Introd. to *Pierre,* & several smaller pieces). Some of this work was done out of duty rather than creative fullness, & I have had to drive myself day after day. Hence my diagnosis seemed justified. Anyhow, the most marked symptom (worse than the headache itself) was an unconquerable aversion to writing anything—even lectures & letters. I had allowed myself a year Sept, 1947 to Sept, 1948 to write the 1st volume of Melville; but found I could not scribble a sentence, & so I temporarily dropped the whole project. My head cleared for about 4 days in the Spring & I wrote the enclosed (It is old stuff, but I am sending it along just to indicate my state of mind &c)—otherwise I merely existed in a more or less paralyzed stupor.

Back at Harvard this fall I made a complete mess of the lectures & began to feel somewhat desperate, so I went to the world's headache specialist in N.Y.C. who said I was suffering from a *repressed depression!* which had taken a psychosomatic form (arterial tension in the cortical circulation) & this could be explained by mental exhaustion &c &c.

I tell you all this so that you will see that there are ample reasons—exhaustion & headache—to explain my abandonment of Melville, or rather my temporary inability to write.

Since the MD defined it as "depression" & since the news that Agnes Morewood had given all her material to a "Rival" was the most depressing I had ever heard, it is just possible that there is some connection between the headache & the depressing news. The fact that I *consciously* recovered from the depression & *consciously* accepted the whole circumstance as soon as I met you, may conceivably explain the *repression* of the depression & its appearance as a physical symptom. However, there were other depressing events, & even if Agnes M. was the whole & sufficient cause of my sick head, you are not culpable to the slightest extent. You did *precisely* as I & all other Melvillian researchers have done. It was only that A.M. had spontaneously asserted three or four times over the years (without any prompting from me), that she would keep her material for me, so that I would not feel pressed in writing the book & I was relying on her promise. Having already seen about 20 hard years of research wasted, as others published the same findings bit by bit, I was hopeful that I would have at least the Morewood collection to contribute. Very selfish, egocentric, & competitive—yes—but that was H.A.M. in the Spring of 1947. Now I am different.

In any event, *you* are entirely free of any blame & should feel "spotless as a lamb." I can emphasize this in a dozen ways if you would like to have me; but I trust your conscience is as clear as the waters of the St. Lawrence on a sunny day. So much for *that.*

I have asked Farrar, Straus to send you a copy of *Pierre* with my compliments. I hope you do not too thoroughly disapprove of it.

Now for the point of all this. How about the Great Book? I trust it is passing smoothly through the Press & will be a fine viable Child in May or June. It will be a monument—not only in Melville history, but in American literature. It will start a new tradition: others will do the same for Hawthorne &c. I am impatient to see it, to see the result of the most intelligent, dedicated, skillful, enthusiastic, & persistent research I have ever been privileged to observe. Now, having exposed my entrails for your inspection, please give me a word about yourself. I am not asking for "Confidences," but I am anxious to hear of your state of being.

[Leyda to Murray, undated draft] If your *Pierre* had not arrived in the following mail, I would have answered your letter at once—& that would have been an easier letter for you to read than this will be.

With your *Pierre* that whole edition is justified for me [Hendricks House]—though up till now I was inclined to doubt its justice. Even after further volumes this will be the high point & reason for the edition.

But then, behind all that hard work & sound thinking I find such unendurable personal attitudes that all sympathy aroused by your letter drains quite away. How can you dare ornament your contempt & hate & anger with all those fulsome baubles & false modesties? These only draw attention to the disgraceful motives they hang upon—if you're not fooled by them, why should anyone else be! I don't see room even for humorous modesty—you can be as immodestly proud of your contribution as those Melville "scholars" who have no right to be—& when you choose to play coy it's so worrying as to let suspicion fall on your most basic contributions. On you this peekaboo dress is obscene—& unhealthy.

Though you're the doctor & I'm the patient—& that makes me scared of you for all the familiar reasons—I feel that you're less willing to face cure & honest behavior than I am. It was curious how our clash put match to the store of gas that each had accumulated. I've admitted both accumulation & explosion, but you still deny both in every polite smile of your introduction. My wounding of you has taken a backfiring revenge that could satisfy any feudist—but your self-inflicted wounds do no more than tickle yourself and make you more satisfied with your cozy retreat into spiteful silence. I can't pretend any diagnosis, but I feel sure that if you came to your senses & got down to hard, scheduled work on the job of saying *everything* you have to say about Melville, without regard for the feelings of family or colleagues, much good would come of it. While if you continue to enjoy the sensations of being deprived & cheated by a shark-pack of rivals, nothing but harm will come of it. Now you have some idea of the harm to yourself this brings. If I weren't afraid of sounding like the pretty flattery you indulge in, I would tell you of the harm to the rest of us this would bring.

~~You're a fool & a social criminal to play the game you're playing.~~ I hoped that Pierre would be the wedge to open you & break down the self-conscious piety of your attitude to your store of Melville experience, but now I can see you've used the edition as an extra lock on your knowledge. And you can write of Pierre's selfish pride!

After all this self-righteous anger I must be allowed to wash it down with the usual drop of self-pity, which is the only way I can talk about myself. 1) I have grown completely & suddenly old—with none of the advantages or maturity or calm of legendary old age. 2) The Log will not be published. . . .

[Leyda to Eleanor Metcalf, undated draft] Please accept my sincerest thanks for your welcome appreciations of the story volume as well as my apologies for such a long, unexplained silence . . . To be brief—I have hoped to be able to send you more hopeful news on the Log-jam—but I can't yet. And all this has added to the pain of Murray's decision—making me feel even more frustrated as well as guilty about his decision—and he has stopped replying to my persuasions; no reaction even to the "hate treatment" used in some cases of hyster paralysis. See what whining you have been spared!

[Murray to Leyda, March 10, 1949] Your letter is one long explosion against me, the stimulus of which seems to have been the Introduction to *Pierre*. You make a number of diagnoses:

I am full of "contempt, hate & anger" (of Melville?
    of You? of the Universe?)
I "ornament" all this hate with "false modesties"
    (in relation to?)
These false modesties "only draw attention to the
    disgraceful motives they hang upon" (motives
    to harm Melville"? to harm you? to harm the world?)

Perhaps you are a Great Seer, & can see things that Jung & and other training analysts & intimate associates & friends are unable to see in me. In your long list of accusations you don't refer to a single fact (statement or act of mine) so that it is impossible to discover whether you are talking about my attitude to Melville, or my attitude to you, or my attitude to the whole world. Perhaps you & Melville are one, & everything I say about the author of *Pierre* or even Pierre himself is taken by you as a personal insult. It is up to you to explain what you mean so that the problem can be defined, & I will not spend my time discussing Y when you are preoccupied with X.

You speak of "accumulation & explosion," & say that you have admitted both, & I have denied both. I have heard of nothing but denials from you, &, as I remember it, I admitted (in my first letter to you) the shock of learning that you had acquired the Morewood material, & I confessed that it would take a little time to accommodate myself to the situation—to the loss of something I had counted on for so long.

I came to the conventional conclusion years ago that American culture is based on intense competition, & if someone beats you it is part of the Order of the Universe (like the weather)—not something to shake your fist about. Anyhow, there was *never at any time* any trace of "contempt, hate or anger" towards *You* & there is none now. Perhaps you have done something that would ordinarily provoke "contempt, hate or anger" in another person; or perhaps you feel "contempt, hate & anger" (as your letter indicates) towards me & you are projecting these emotions into me. In any event these emotions are *not* in me at *any* level. Why should I suppress anger? Its expression is very enjoyable. In this instance I have none to express.

Now, what would you have me do:

1. Feign anger in order to demonstrate that your diagnosis is correct?
2. Be "immodestly proud" of my contribution, despite the fact that I *positively* know that my knowledge of literature is meagre & amateurish (compared to Matthiessen, Kazin, Arvin, & the whole company of *good* literary critics)?
3. Publicly attack all Melville scholars for having discovered during the last 10 years what I discovered 20 years ago? We all proceeded in the same manner & spirit & I had no priority. The plain truth is that I was slow & they were quick to publish their findings.
4. Sit down immediately & finish a biography?—When writing "Assessment of Men" exhausted me, & I am burdened with all kinds of college obligations, &, even if my exuberance should return, I have other more crucial things to write?

Perhaps you think I am "spitefully" sitting on a lot of secrets—facts unknown to you or other Melvillians—I don't know of a *single fact* that is unknown to you.—Many of them facts from my collection are to be found in the *Pierre* footnotes; if they have not already been published by other Melvillians.

You say that you have "suddenly grown old"—this, I am sure, is a temporary phase, experienced by all developing people, particularly when they fall out of love or succumb to despair—for a season.

You say "the Log will not be published." *This is serious & intolerable.* You devoted years of blood & anguish; & scores of people helped you—trusting in its unique importance. It is finished. Please explain. It must be that the publisher is unwilling to take it in its entirety with all illustrations & documents &c&c.

In which case a Foundation should be wise enough to step in & finance the venture. Give me the details & I may be able to help. Since we have something of Unquestionable Value, all we need is a little Courage in pushing it through to final publication. Please tell me what went wrong.

[Leyda to Murray, draft on the back of Murray's envelope for the letter of March 10, 1949] You have so thoroughly misunderstood me (I'd guess, in some things, that the misunderstanding was deliberate, that I prefer to end the debate here. Sorry to have started it.

Forget the Log—regardless of everybody's help to me. I signed a faulty contract & can do nothing to force Eugene Reynal to publish or to give it up—or even to answer my inquiries.

Foundations? That is a kind suggestion, but I cannot enter any race where degrees are running.

I'm tired, sick, not only of the disillusioning "intense competition" that you, too, find in this field (that I wandered into by mistake, anyway), but also sick of competing with a perpetual handicap.

*No, Melville & I are not "one."

[Leyda draft, continued on yellow library slip, dated March 14, 1949] No, I am not a Great Seer./ No, M & I are not "one."/ No, the insulted one is not another——but your reader./ No, I am not regretting secreted "facts" but your analysis of them & your conclusions [In pen on top:] But in ending let me say: I regard nothing that you say about the author of *Pierre* or even Pierre himself as a personal insult. you are not spitefully sitting on a lot of secret facts.

[Chase to Trilling, March 17, 1949] (. . . It suddenly occurred to me that Bartleby is . . . the ARTIST.)

[Ferris Greenslet of Houghton, Mifflin to Leyda, April 13, 1949] Mrs. Metcalf tells me that there is some hitch in the publication of your own long-awaited and indispensable book. It has occurred to me that if publication is too costly under present conditions for any regular publisher, you might get it financed by the Bollingen Foundation and published by the Pantheon Press. This combination, as you probably know, has recently published many distinguished and expensive publications. I have pretty good connections with Huntington Cairns, director of the Foundation, as well as with Kyril Schabert, head of Pantheon. Let me know if there is anything I can do.

[Flashback: Leyda undated draft, to Chester Kerr] [Can't meet August 1947 deadline for LOG, wants more money and] I have been promised an entry into a wholly new collection of unpublished Melville manuscripts at the beginning of that month.

[Draft, Leyda to agent introduced to his problem by Lincoln Kirstein:] Dear Miss Agent . . . The Melville Log contract was signed on July 17, 1946, & I agreed to deliver ms on August 1, 1947. My entire correspondence was with Frank Taylor and Albert Erskine. After the departure of these two editors from R & H, Erskine told me that Reynal had offered him the Log among other unwanted projects. Their new company fell through & Erskine offered the Log to his employer, Random House, whose three editors turned it down.

Just at the point when I am frantically searching for some publication hope & security I receive a letter forwarded (tardily) from my Los Angeles address. I enclose a copy of this & my reply to it.

What do you think of your part in all this? Do you want to plunge in, or don't you think it worth while?

[Leyda to Ferris Greenslet, undated draft] Dear Mr. Greenslet, How I wish I were brave enough to take you up at once on your magnificent Bollingen-Pantheon suggestion. I can think of no place that would be righter for the Log—with its multiple problems of pictures, design, format, bulk!

Here is my silly dilemma of the past year & a half. Just as the book was going into production Reynal and Hitchcock "merged" with Harcourt, & Reynal was given a desk there. Most of his back-log of contracts was turned over to Harcourt—except for a few titles held back, I am told (not by Reynal—for he has remained ominously unresponsive) for mixed reasons of egotism, independence, prestige & future security. The Log is unfortunately among these—& remains there, although Harcourt has expressed specific interest in taking it over. My particular dilemma is that I cannot buy it back from Reynal without assurance that I can resell it away from Harcourt. I cannot offer it elsewhere without being sure that Reynal will relinquish it. I am no longer clear about his motives—he may even ask for more than the advance paid me—perhaps more than money. I have even hesitated to let my agent bring the whole issue into the open. You see how tangled this has become. . . .[He has struggled with himself to tell the whole truth].

[Chase to Trilling, April 15, 1949] Macmillan is preparing a marvelous jacket blurb about how M trembled at women, feared castration, solved the problem of the universe, and believed in America. At the risk of losing thousands of readers, I've asked them to tone it down a bit.

[Agnes Morewood to Leyda, May 22, 1949] I fear Dr. Murray overworked. I have not seen him for over a year and he wrote he was going away for a rest as he had constant headaches. I am so sorry. I like his work on Pierre.

[Hayford to Leyda, June 7, 1949] I am little more than a scrivener who would "Prefer not to"—be one—and as I feel rather scronful [sic] toward all of my Superiors, I guess that they must feel it—and feel that they would like to get rid of me—and have tried to do so.

[Howard Vincent to Leyda, June 29, 1949] [Gordon Roper, Hayford and he discussed *Typee* and *Omoo* problems yesterday.] Harry is quite wound up in *Omoo*. He has found that Anderson far from utilized the source materials behind that book, and he repeatedly mutters that the second half of *Omoo* is little short of an outright steal of Ellis and Wilkes.

[Chase to his wife, Frances, July 6, 1949, from summer institute for New Criticism at Kenyon College[43]] Last night at the dining hall there was much to-do about the Fiedler article on homosexualism and Come back to the raft agin Huck, honey. I was trying to defend it against a battery of attackers: Tate, Matthiessen, and to some extent Bentley. They all seem very much to resent that kind of treatment of American literature, and they regard the current interest in trying to understand what is specifically American (Gorer, etc) as a "vogue" and apparently a not very productive one. Their point was that while Fiedler might be right in some sense about American culture it really wasn't specifically American culture he was talking about, but Western culture in general. I was trying to admit that and also insist that homosexualism as Fiedler discusses it was still in a special sense American. Matthiessen very much resents the tone and what he calls the know-it-all attitude of Fiedler. Aha, says I to myself, a defense mechanism.

This evening there were ceremonials at table. The John Crowe Ransom issue of the Sewanee Review, edited by Tate and Red Warren, was presented formally to Ransom with speeches by Tate and Ransom and much fine old Southern courtesy on all sides. Mr. Matthiessen; so I thought, could do with more curtesy [sic] than he has. For during the meal I was (foolishly as I see) candid enough to bring up certain matters which I understood myself as disagreeing with him about, thinking that fitting since he has kept sounding me out about attitudes, etc. I told him I was publishing a piece in Partisan on Billy Budd in which I took occasion to disagree with him on the interpretation of that book. Then I tried to distinguish between liberalism and progressivism, saying that I thought I was the former and he was the latter, or so I gathered from his books. I then mentioned the problem of socialism as being connected with Stalinism and said that I thought the problem of liberals now was to modify the Stalinism of the 1930s and that I regarded myself as being interested in a more thorough modification than I understood him to be. Well, sir, that did the trick. He said the PR editors were "skunks," that he had never had anything to do with Stalinism or progressivism; that his idea of life and politics was the "tragic" view of Hawthorne and Melville. Period. I said that that being the case (which it obviously isn't) the question was whether I had read or misread his books. The discussion ended most abruptly; and I take it I am set down as a small and evilly smelling animal with black and white fur. My original impression of FOM was correct. And if I had the sense enough to stick to it, I should never have tried to exchange anything with him but pleasantries. Well, live and learn. And believe in the gracelessness of the self-divided, the grim, and the humorless.

[Chase to Frances Chase, July 10, 1949] (Quoting Empson): "The object of life, after all, is not to understand things, but to maintain one's defenses and equilibrium and live as well as one can." It's not the understanding and the analyzing and the intellectualizing that will do us good: it's the emotional commitment to the family culture as both the repository and source of our humanity: our sentiments, attitudes, affections, values, and manners. It's a terrifying thought that our society denies that this is what the family is, and that it seems dead set on destroying the family as origin of humanity and culture. But there's no other origin. So you see, I should think we are heroes of some sort. You've seen the psychological wreckage amongst our contemporaries. We've been on the margins of that wreckage ourselves and, anything we do to overcome it is jolly well admirable.

A three-quarters marriage is a thousand times better than no marriage at all. But a complete marriage is better than a three-quarters one. Psychoanalysis has certainly established what many a dull moralist has opined about marriage and the family.

[Chase to Frances Chase, July 18, 1949] . . . Inadequate answers to hard questions:

The question of social consciousness and whether art has cultural relevance would have to be considered with reference to each New Critic. Ransom, Tate, and Brooks and the other southerners (Red Warren, too, I guess) have their ideal Old South, a sort of patriarchal-religious society with aristocratic institutions, established manners, and fatherly benevolence, etc etc. In any immediate political application, this would certainly have to be called a reactionary ideal. Yet in practice I'm pretty sure the Southerners have been New Dealers, Roosevelt supporters, etc. Ransom always voted for FDR, so I hear. So with them it's a complex question. Matty is hopeless. I learned today that I was mistaken in thinking Austin Warren a Wallace man. He seems to have been a New Dealish sort all along, and plans to vote for old Harry; still, I think he has a tenderness for Wallace. He's very religious in the high Episcopalian Anglo-Catholic way, which of course implies in some sense a conservative, not to say monarchist, politics. Complicated again. I heard Empson say today that he thought Norman Thomas must be the only hope in Ameddica. So I gather he is just a sort of British socialist. If a generalization be possible, it would be this: on the whole the New Critics hold up as an ideal some aristocratic view of culture, not in any case a capitalist ideal—but in practice they lean to the left on the theory, I suppose, that capitalism can be modified, practical considerations being what they are, only from the left. In other words, they see in capitalism no power at all of establishing any kind of coherent culture in which individual life can have meaning, manners, art, morality, purpose, etc. I suppose this sums up my own view of the matter, though in the aristocratic-socialist culture of the future I hope my friends the Southern writers will not insist that I share the affection for religious dogma.

But the New Critics don't have the constant interest in culture and politics and morals that other kinds of critics have had. Their great point is that the critics of the 1930s—Parrington, Hicks, et al—were so much interested in society that they neglected literature. Another point is that Babbitt and Paul Elmer More were so much interested in moral questions that *they* neglected literature, and the academic critic-scholars and Tuves and Smysers etc etc were so much interested in the historical background and philosophical and philological context of the literature that *they* neglected literature. So the great cry was: look at the text in itself, experience it, and judge it by the standards of structure, coherence, tone, style, etc. That's the great success of the New Critics: to have insisted that literature must be read as literature.

It's a fine thing and we need more of it. But you can see the dangers. The New Criticism tends to attract not only people who are expert lovers and comprehenders of literature, but also people who use the study of text as text in order to evade understanding the psychology of human beings and the workings of culture and politics.

The New Critic will tell you that he very well realizes the cultural meaning of art but that he is deliberately putting that aside as part of his strategy as a critic. And that is all very well, since one must honor any strategy that produces results. But actually, in some cases, this becomes more of a strategy and begins to assume the office of a whole view of life. This makes people like Tate and Ransom a bit dippy on cultural and psychological matters. Ransom's view of life is metaphysical, philosophical: he is a very poor psychologist and has little grasp of cultural anthropology. He has a great admiration of Freud, but he sees Freud as a philosopher, not as a psychologist.

As usual Lionel gets an A and the rest get B. He reads the text accurately and makes the necessary psychological, moral, and cultural connections. He's the whole man; the New Critics tend to be a bit bland, innocent, and unmotivated whenever they are looking at anything outside the text. But I suppose Lionel gets only A-; for he is after all no great shakes when dealing with poetry, and the New Critics are.

The great thing about the New Critics is that theirs is a strategy for studying art, and most other kinds of modern criticism have been strategies for avoiding the study of art in order to study something else. Surely that is one reason college students and the rest of the populace never really *learn to read* anything harder than Time mag. Fundamentally the New Critics are teaching people how to read. I never learned in college or graduate school either, except on my own. I still haven't learned to read, really.

Oh, as for D. Macdonald having political ideas and Lionel not—I guess Lionel meant that Dwight was preeminently the Political Thinker but that Lionel was unlikely to think about politics apart from culture, art, psychoanalysis. Certainly Lionel is a political critic—the best going in fact. I mean the best literary-political critic. The best purely political critic, seems to me, is Schlesinger, Jr.

The NC's are very much against any critic whose only method is psychoanalysis. Most of them use Freudian insights incidentally, Empson does quite a lot. But none of them are quite the Freudians you and I are. Tate is dippy on this subject: thinks it's a matter of snakes jumping into wells. Us psychoanalysts are always wondering about the life of the author of a work. The NC's say that's irrelevant. Or we are interested in analyzing to some extent the characters in the book. The NC's say (or at least Tate says) You can't do that; this character isn't a human being; he's a thing in a book. Tate is the extremist on this matter. The NC's say the psycho. critic values A Tree Grows in

Brooklyn just as highly as he values Hamlet, since both are about the Oedipus complex. And they have a point—which is, psychoanalysis is not in itself an adequate literary-critical method. Freud of course said that himself. Freud was more modest than any Freudians.

We had a meeting the other night of "psychoanalytically oriented" students. After two papers were read, my militant Chicago lady-student announced with Divine Dogmatism: "Psychoanalysis is an exact science." And you could never guess who responded to this and how: Master Matthiessen pipes up and he says, "I was psychoanalyzed and I certainly don't think psychoanalysis is an exact science." Well, sir, you could have bowled me over with a feather. Can you imagine? and will wonders never cease? It must have been a correspondence course he took over a weekend. Yes, I dare say you are right. All Matty wants is for P[artisan] R[eview] and everyone else to summon him back to the raft, honey. . . .

[Chase to Frances Chase, July 20, 1949] But of course. I didn't mean one musn't try to understand things. But only that one has defenses, equilibrium, etc., the question of understanding is secondary. . . What I was driving at was that neurotic folks of our generation have just simply failed to adjust at the lowest most elementary and primitive levels of being. . . And isn't it true that the conscious intelligence always questioning, trying to understand, trying to defend its prerogatives, can play hob with one's emotive adjustments—which *should* come so easily and naturally to us. D. H. Lawrence is very right about all of this: the probing seeking intellect is a cheat and a traducer when it is allowed to get in the way of simple ordinary emotional health and equilibrium. Ransom, with his funny version of Freud, spoke the other night of the overweening Ego which in modern times has tyrannized over and interfered with the Id, "so that the Id can't stand it any more and explodes." It's a very moving idea, and true.

The fact that friend Ishmael understands what goes on with the stricken and sinking ship is of secondary importance. Of primary importance is the fact that he saved himself from the wreck, by the simple process of swimming and enduring. If he couldn't have done that, he wouldn't have understood a thing.

I'll hazard a guess. You sometimes feel unhappy because I don't appear to share intellectual interests with you as much as you'd like, or because I don't join with you easily enough in the effort to "understand." Well, it isn't because I don't in an abstract way, want to, or because I have any objection to intellectual discussion. I haven't enough insight to say why we don't have more intellectual conversation, why it's easier for me to write these matters to you, than say them. Partly because I'm not very good at impromptu conversation anyway, except with the aid of fire water. I don't know all the reasons. I can simply report that the intellectual-discussion relationship between us is sometimes awkward and lacks the grace and genuine communicativeness we achieve in other kinds of relationship. So I sometimes shy away from it. And why not? Isn't it unhealthy to force oneself into a kind of abstract relationship without grace?

Well, what do you think? Am I an overweening and selfish male keeping my huge intelligence to myself and consigning my poor wife to the intellectual kitchen?

What *do* you think? Am I imagining all this?

It's not that I don't think you have any brains, my poor umpkins. Don't I know how much more perceptive you often are than I in psychology and prose-fictional matters?

You have to remember that I'm only a part-time intellectual—not one of those perpetual motion brains like Lionel's or Bentley's or Empson's. Most of the time I haven't an articulate thought in my head. . . .

The intellect does damage to the unconscious and the body. It feeds on and ruins and wastes these emotive and physical depths. This damage must be perpetually repaired, the wasted tissue restored. In some intellectuals, this restorative process goes on pretty continuously, so that the intellectual expenditure can also go on continuously. But some people, and I'm one, have to perpetually go through a cycle, somewhat like the manic-depressive one. Or call it the rhythm of withdrawal and return. I think that sometimes when you want me to be intellectual I'm in the depressive or withdrawn stage, mending my fences and patching up the battered Id.

And after all, it's this very Id—the ambiguosly [sic] wonderful murderous and loving unconscious mind—which deserves our tenderest and most perpetual care. It's the source of EVERYTHING. Am I wrong, then, to think that the rituals of the family home, the family bed, the family routine, etc. ought primarily to support, restore, and celebrate the Id?

[Chase to Frances Chase, August 2, 1949] Empson is one of those people who wave their eyelids at you as they talk. As the eyelids wave, Mr. E. looks up toward his maker so that the pupils of his eyes disappear and you have only the whites to look at. It makes him look like St. Sebastian undergoing torture. Then all of a sudden, the eyelid waving stops, and Mr. E.'s very sharp dark eyes stare straight at you in a way that makes you jump with horror. Together with the menacing beard, these eyes produce a very strong effect.[44]

[Margaret Morewood to Leyda, August 16, 1949] I have been diving into the MSS you lent me by L. Howard and like his drift better than anything I have ever read about H.M. . . . when I discovered through his reading that H.M. was greatly influenced by Sartor Resartus—a book that had a tremendous influence on my philosophy—I got a quickened sense that H.M. is closer kin than a "Great uncle"—for I adored Thomas Carlyle so much that I arranged to visit his home in Chelsea alone—(when traveling the first time in London heavily chaperoned by Mother and two inquisitive sisters). And I found T.C.'s old Jaeger dressing gown exhibited over a chair by his narrow bed, I knelt down and kissed the frayed cuff that must have circled the hand that wrote Sartor Resartus. . . .

[Murray to Leyda, August 25, 1949?] I returned from Hawaii several weeks ago—in much better health—to find your second letter. Your behavior has displayed, better than that of anyone I know, the sharp contrast between two expectations of American culture: (one) that our work should be impelled by a spirit of intense competitiveness (if not envy & malice); but this need for superiority should be covered over by (two) manifestations of the greatest good will & fellowship. But why should you permit your inordinate sense of rivalry such freedom at this moment?

1. You have edited a very fine collection of H.M.'s stories with a superb introduction.

2. Your introduction to the Russian book (I have forgotten the exact title) is a gem—one of the best pieces I have read for many a day. It shows you can write with passion & style.

3. The great Log (I hear from H.B. & Co.) is moving along—a little slowly perhaps—but steadily, & when it appears, it will stand out as a Monument—unique & authoritative.

4. You say in your violent letters that my "endurable [sic] personal attitudes" come from the fact that I am "sitting" on my "analysis of the facts" of HM's life. But (a) there is *much more* analysis of the facts than is warranted in the Introduction to one book (Did you analyze HM's character in *your* Introduction?) & (b) you are publishing a complete & comprehensive Log which contains (according to you) *no analysis at all.* Thus, it appears that you are criticizing yourself.

5. I don't know what you mean by fake modesty—Olson wrote me flatteringly & said the chief impression he received was the note of *Authority.* Naturally, as a psychologist, I am modest about breaking into the field of literary composition & criticism & c. I have never taken a single English course or written anything of this nature. The feelings & emotions & poses

you attribute to me are not mine. You have invented them out of air, thin air. Like most geniuses & perfectionists you are troubled lest each of your works is not a resounding masterpiece. I am a physiologist & doctor by training & have my disillusionment *before* my work begins. Cheer up a little.

[Leyda to Murray, undated draft] I'm very glad to have news of you, &, of course, this has made me eager for more. I hope you got the rest you were after in Hawaii, & I want to hear that it has renewed your attacking powers on the Big Biography.

Please try to forget my whole dirty correspondence—of the past, I trust. My only "excuse" is my bad state then (aggravated by my feelings of multiple obligations to you), but I am *much* better now. How I wish you had seen me on your way through—that would have been far better than even the most rational letter.

I have so many HM matters (large & small) to discuss with you—when may I throw them towards Plympton Street? For the present I wish you'd tell me (in as much detail as your have time for) what, in that "superb introduction" does & doesn't make sense. I had many qualms then—& I still have them. . . . [Questions appended, including suggestions that Gansevoort wrote the Lansingburgh "Fragments" and that *Reginald Dalton,* read by Gansevoort, was inspiration for *Pierre;* wants to see Melville's Byron marginalia, which Murray had examined.]

[Hayford to Leyda, September 3, 1949, handwritten postscript] I hope you remember your promise to me to put a section in your *Log* preface or appendix a section on the myths, bonfires, apocrypha, rumors, & elusive items etc. In thinking over what the reception of the *Log* may be and getting reactions from various Melvilleans & others it occurs to me the most likely criticism will be that you have collected the materials—why didn't *you* write the biography? This is mean but it will be said. I hope you are providing some sort of preface explaining the form & its rationale. Everyman his own biographer— etc, & say it has been done in other countries.

[Murray to Olson, ca. September 6, 1949] . . . you agreed to take the test which has been taken this summer by Aiken, Williams, Shapiro, Ciardi, Leonie Adams, Mumford, & ten others, mostly poets. Would you be a Saint & drop a line to Robert N. Wilson . . . telling him when you can conveniently take the test—one hour on the first day & one hour on the next. He can run down to Gloucester very easily. He looks a little "bookish" at first glance, but has more than this, & is a fine sensitive guy who wants to understand the Role of the Artist in the Modern World. . . .

[Hayford to Leyda, October 29, 1949] I am working as hard as I can on $Ommoo.oo. Thank you for them very kind and gratefully received remarks about the Office-Seeker. The first official reaction was from Newton Arvin who saw it in manuscript and who was rather sniffy about it, pointing out that we didn't after all see the most important thing about the documents, which was that M was always unhealthy & unhappy—and I didn't bother to write and tell him that some things don't have to be said, even if people see them, and that some things do have to be said, because nobody has seen or said them. But a very good reaction from Bill Charvat who will be helped by the article. . . [HH is reviewing Chase and Vincent for *Accent* in January.] Haven't read Chase, just glanced, turned pale and gave it to Leon. He's low lately. . . .

[Alfred Kazin to Chase, January 4, 1950] First, about the review. I can understand that you were disappointed, if not hurt, by it; and I deeply regret the harsh tone into which I fell. I do not enjoy writing critical reviews of anybody, much less of anyone so sensitive and serious as you. But the book aims very high, it is very tendentious, and it expresses a tendency that has a good deal of support in our generation. I am not aware that your book has had such a bad press. I only saw one in the Times Book Review, which was very favorable.

The important thing I want to say, however, is that your "breach"—if there is one—is with me, not with Partisan Review. Do not stop writing for them because of me. I have no love for the magazine, and the editors certainly have none for me. Someone who worked in their office once told me, with genuine consternation, that they talked about me as if I were Hitler. I can well believe it; they talk that way about almost everyone. You must un-derstand, Chase, that anyone who publishes a book, who is not content with militant conversation, is *ipso facto* on their bad books. I have known Rahv and Phillips for the better part of 10 years. In all that time I have never heard them say an understanding and favorable word about anyone who in the remotest way appeared to be more productive than they are. I have heard people denounced in the cruelest way; I have heard them denounce each other in the same way. The review of my own book, years ago, was supercilious in the extreme. And worse, they permitted, if they did not encourage, Irving Howe to align me (in his attack on Matthiessen), in the most unthinking and irresponsible way with Stalinism—the result of which was malicious and despicable letters from the lunatic fringe of anti-Stalinism, and considerable embarrassment for me in my professional contacts.

Yet I write for PR, and probably will go on writing—though I have, all told, perhaps not published more than four pieces there in all these years. There are not many "serious" reviews I can write for, and if you want to know what it is like to be outside new critics, old critics, academic critics, and even a chance to make a living at teaching in New York, I can tell you what it is really like. Ignore my review, or laugh at it, or challenge it—but don't think that I reflect the prevailing literary opinion, and above all, that I was in any sense an instrument of PR. Why should you not write for them still? I can think of many writers, much worse handled there than you, who do. Our intellectual environment is such, so heartbreakingly limited and split between the idiocies of commercialism and the doctrinal narrowness of the avant-garde, that a writer must simply ignore all that, and say what he must, and where he can. In any event, the review is all mine—if PR had even given me a hint of what they wanted to see in it, I would have told them to go to hell. Fight it out with me alone. I was not trying to destroy your book—on the contrary I said several times, if not widely enough through the review—I respect it. But the "New Liberalism" is something I have very little sympathy for—I think it a very bourgeois movement intellectually, and in Schlesinger's case, very opportunistic indeed; and I aimed at it, not at you. Naturally, I was harsh with you in the process, much harsher, I see now, than I should have been. *La vérité, est dans la nuance.* There isn't enough nuance in that review, and I'm sorry. If there's the slightest resemblance in my work to the hectoring tone of Stanley Edgar Hyman, I will stop writing altogether. Criticism is either founded on the immortal saying of Augustine—I want you to be; or it is hateful.

I want you to be. I want Melville to be—outside the New Liberalism. Of course you don't agree with me. But you have many more supporters than you know, or admit. As I've so often been told, my attitude is "extreme" and "impractical."

[Eleanor Metcalf to Murray, January 11, 1950] I was inspired with new strength and ardor after your call. Some of your suggestions I find very valuable. The final result of what I have been doing since you were here will probably be a compromise . . . .

[Olson to Leyda, January 30, 1950] i have waited long enuf my god how can a man say a word about herman melville, have conversations with him in rage

and whisper these days when so many who are his natural enemies publish
. books in praise and analysis of him in the public press, WITHOUT KNOWING
WHAT JAY LEYDA KNOWS?

. . . i am all fired out again on HM (do you know what it is to have others
rifle you of yr perceptions, and then not speak of yr work?)

if you will tell me yr news, and give me substance for my conversations
with HM, i should tell you what he and i are saying!

(i'm going to get so bursting with rage i shall start being "Patience Worth,"
and wrote by dictation all those novels of HM's which you were rightly looking for!) . . . yrs in hell (where all good melvilles are)

[Leyda to Olson, February 6, 1950?] Though Billy Budd is not my favorite
among HM's works, I thought you crowed a little too loud about Baby Budd.
The quality is not *that* different, and it seems that Freeman had to stretch
a mite to shape the Baby—employing intuition as well as evidence—but this
is the occupational disease for all Melville scholars. (Olson Papers)

[Eleanor Metcalf to Olson, February 8, 1950] In the first place, let me say that
I quite fail to see why you are so angry with Alfred Kazin, who finds Richard
Chase very far from perfect, to say the least, and with Newton Arvin, whose
introduction to "Moby Dick" I specially like. I can only agree with you that he
might have listed "Call Me Ishmael" in the bibliography, if he used it. But he
may not have. Others have known of H.M.'s use of Owen Chase. And he is
familiar with D. H. Lawrence on Melville, Lawrence who did first present him
as a mythographer, if I am right . . . Jay Leyda's Log is due to come out in the
latter part of this year. Harry Murray has no publication date, he tells me.
I too respect them both, but let me tell you Jay has a slant which once, at
least to my knowledge led him to an entirely unjustifiable conclusion, rather
unsavory.

Of course Melville is a breeder, a fore-runner, and not to be treated like
Henry James . . . You cannot have as big a subject as H.M. without a lot of
mistakes, misinterpretations, personal biases, and general disorder. But neither do I think they can permanently obscure him or obscure the important
issues.

You will probably be disappointed with what I am doing: I hope not too
much so. I value your reactions, even your rage, though—-well, let it stand at
though.

About the [illegible] article, I was much interested in it, when I read it
before your letter came, but it irritated me too. I think what I was most critical about was the last part of the series of questions which begin with, "The

real questions are unaskable: what *good* is Emerson to us now, has Melville any use, will Thoreau help us if we call on him, can Adams feed us in the wilderness? How did they live, what did they *really* do, what were they *essentially*, how can we get to *be* them?"

Why should we *be* them?

[Robert Giroux to Leyda, February 10, 1950] We feel strongly that parenthetical sources will detract from the saleability of the MELVILLE LOG. It has been a custom in this house of long standing to put such identifying material in a special section at the back of the book; we have done it with THE ROBBER BARONS and LINCOLN STEFFENS and many others, and I hope you will consent to our doing so with the Log.

[Leyda to Giroux, undated draft] [No,] this would blur the total reversal I want to suggest in biographical procedure: to provide the reader with all the material for him to do his *own* autobiography [*sic*] of the man in question. He has to believe in the material, he has to be conscious of it as *raw* material. He has to be made constantly aware that no interpreter, no *writer*, stands between him and the material, he has to sense the documentary character of the material before him & this has to be made as striking & dramatic as possible. (Thus my original dream of facsimiles and pictures of documents). Instead of hiding ~~this character any part of this~~, ashamed, in the back (as in a book that merely *uses* sources) all this paraphernalia of documentation has to step forward to the front of the stage, boldly & even flamboyantly. The code to abbreviations, for example, should occupy the usual front place of "acknowledgments"; the rawness usually confined to footnotes rears up in the text itself—& footnotes are abolished altogether. The shock of all this reversal of usual polite scholarly behavior *that spares the reader all the harsh, uninterpreted edges,*[45] will have a pleasure of its own, I am certain. No, let me cling to the sources in their present clarity. Gerry might try a smaller type for them, to fit them into the ~~body~~ blocks of each item, instead of standing so apart from the items, as these capitals now do. But they belong with the items. I think you underestimate the flavor this will give to the reader in the West or Middle West far from the sources. [Emphasis added. Giroux responded on February 15, saying Leyda can prevail if it is a matter of principle; however, in the published Log the sources are in the back as Giroux requested, *C.S.*]

[Ferris Greenslet to Leyda, March 20, 1950] I'm delighted to hear that Harcourt Brace is going ahead with the long-awaited log, but a little disappointed, like you, that Pantheon wouldn't take it on.

[Stanley T. Williams to Leyda, April 14, 1950] [Asks about M's knowledge of Spanish, shore leaves in Lima and other South American ports.] . . . I am a devoted Melvillian, but this book of mine treats Melville only incidentally.

[Howard to Leyda, May 11, 1950] You goddamn man of mystery. Why in the hell do you want to keep a fellow in suspense about your discoveries? . . . [Hayford] has an interesting and amusing letter from Pittsfield about Stanwix's birth registration which seems to make clear that Herman was probably not responsible for giving Maria as the name of the mother—partly from the circumstances given, and partly from the fact that the name was spelled "Stanwicks". . . .

[Eleanor Metcalf to Leyda, May 23, 1950, after reading galleys to *Log;* will reiterate the point in letter June 12, 1950] . . . I think all Melville scholars have deplored the use of Peter Gansevoort's use of the word "Maniac" in writing of Allan Melville's last illness. At one time you told me it had been discovered that he caught a severe cold which turned into pneumonia ending in violent delirium. Peter's accounts to Thomas, and Thomas' to Lemuel Shaw say nothing of this. Also, Allan's markings in his Bible and Maria's comment on this would seem to assign different causes for his state of mind. Since the form of your book does not allow your comments on the entries, it is hard to know what do about such a statement, which Harry Murray once told me was based on ignorance. Must we perpetuate it?

Another instance where lack of comment leaves an ambiguous impression: that is the supposed, but unauthenticated attack, in 1842, of Melville on a helpless man in the stocks. Such an act would conflict with everything we know about H.M. Lucett's whole attitude is malicious. And you cannot comment. Must we perpetuate a malicious and unperpetuated story? . . . I do you feel that your inability to comment puts you in a peculiar position; and if in your "acknowledgments" you mention my having read the whole book before final printing, I should not want it inferred that I passed favorably on the two sorts of incidents I have mentioned . . . .

[June 12, 1950] . . . You see, I do not question that interpretation enters into your scheme, and I realize that it is more than "a mass of separate items with only a general time connection."

[Sealts to Olson, June 12, 1950] In going from the Bible to Homer you mentioned [Richard] Chase. From his first PARTISAN article I thought he had something, but those on the C-M and BB seemed to say the right things for the wrong reasons, and the book to have been published about ten years too soon—Hawthorne said it best, about MARDI. I should long ago have written you that in staggering through Chase while in bed at Christmas time I was moved to reread CALL ME ISHMAEL to see his best things done better. Why what you laid out there and enlarged upon in last spring's letter hasn't had more impact, particularly on the younger and less hidebound Melville people, I don't know. Yes, I do, too, for it's happened to me. Those of us who are teaching and sweating out promotions are taking on the protective coloration of those who do the promoting. Every man jack is being either *safe* (i.e., scholarly, factual, DULL), or publishing too fast, à la Chase. I haven't had another "Chimney" in me since before the war (and before teaching). What writing army directives during the war and grading student themes after the war have done to my writing, teaching has done to my imagination, which has the aridity of CLAREL and THE WASTE-LAND. Another example, with reference to your letter again: the article on the "uses" of M-D in the new AMERICAN QUARTERLY, which sets out to deal with Narrative but ends by sounding just like every other academician, as though the author surrendered without a fight.[46]

[Sealts to Leyda, June 21, 1950] [Wants to do a "selected critique," to show "growth of interest"] and the various lines, sound and unsound, pursued by the Mel*villains*. Have just heard from Olson, who is all steamed up about the idea and urges me to go ahead—I hatched the idea and wrote one publisher, just after I last wrote to you, but have done nothing at all on the project itself. . . . [On Gansevoort's fascination with Byron] I suppose the whole family felt very much the same way, along with the whole generation. Reminds me of my American Lit. kids here *going wild* over Hemingway—not an impossible parallel, methinks.

[Olson to Leyda, June 23, 1950] No, I sort of imagine my growings by way of the Great Man, are now going to stay inside me.

[Walter Bezanson to Leyda, July 1, 1950] [M marked the Introduction to the poems of James Clarence Mangan, (acquired in 1859)] "He was a rebel politically, and a rebel intellectually and spiritually, —a rebel with his whole heart and soul against the whole British spirit of the age. The consequence was sure, and not unexpected. Hardly anybody in England knew the name of such a person . . . ." [On back fly leaf evidence of Melville's] fellow spirit in his moods, but that he also studied somewhat his prosody.

[Book designer Gerry Gross to Leyda, July 15, 1950] Would you please hop to it and get me a photograph of the daguerrotype facing p. 68 of the Metcalf

MELVILLE JOURNAL. I have changed my mind since I discussed this with you last. In scaling the pictures and working with the other print of Elizabeth, it seemed to me that it would be so much fairer to Herman if we had the prettier picture. She really does look frightening in the other one . . . . [Edward Haviland Miller used the rejected picture of Elizabeth in his psychobiography of 1975, C.S.]

[Harcourt Brace undated memorandum to salesman, to be used for sales conference not publicity[47]] *The Melville Log* contains:

New Melville Letters—50% never before printed

New family letters—90% never before printed

New letters about Melville by his contemporaries—50% never before printed

Comment on Melville in the contemporary press—75% never before brought to modern attention

New documents on Melville's wife and children (including some possible South Seas children)

New documents on Melville's friends and acquaintances and on their influence on his work (including the friendships with Hawthorne and Dana)

New pictures of Melville and his family—almost *all* unfamiliar to readers

New and unsuspected facts on:

His childhood and youth (hitherto completely obscure and fictionalized)—including his father's and brother's business failures

His whaling years (including identification of a hitherto unknown whaleship on which he worked, and the facts of a mutiny on another)—and his service in the U.S. Navy

His writing and methods—with facsimiles of his worksheets—and the development of *Moby Dick*

His crises—both domestic and financial

His career as a teacher—and self-teacher (including his library and reading)

His brother's political career (that led to Melville's first important publication)

His first printed writing (in *The Albany Microscope*), a year earlier than any other previously discovered publication, revealed here for the first time

His reputation—both private and public and foreign

His running war with the missionaries—its effect on him and his work

His projects for books unpublished and unwritten

His lectures—their texts and reception

His poetry—and its place in his career
His attitude toward the Civil War
His work as a customs inspector and his last days in New York

[Leyda to Giroux, undated draft] By the way, I wish, the next time Mumford visits you, that you would show him the *Log* if you haven't already. He once expressed pleasure in its idea, & I wonder what he would now think of HM in its light.

[Murray to Olson, ca. August 27, 1950] I have been an abominable friend to you and *all* other persons I cherish for a year or more—if not always. Somehow, the inpouring tides of letters drowned my zest for response, and, after a while, in despair, I abandoned the Whole Enterprise.

I delight in the reception of your Poems even though I never understand them. Don't cease, please, because You and I have much in common and someday, you may be able to get your meaning to my Thalamus, or Solar Plexus, at least. In fact I am counting on you more than anyone to give me Signs—a few—so that I can get close enough to your thought to see it—dark, marvelous, and inscrutable—on the rim of the distant ridges. The Poets are out of sight from where I stand today. I greatly appreciated the "Praises" and "Y and X" which struck the bull's eye of my birth day. I brooded over them, & I think the first slipped into a dream, but my Consciousness remained Wondering—perhaps Wonder is all.

I have done no more than glance at Chase's Melville & Arvin's Melville [or] Y Z's Melville, but I did not get the impression that they furnished legitimate stimulus to Wrath! Everybody recognizes that H.M is a snowy Everest on which a number of Enthusiasts like C.W.O. & H.A.M project their Shadows.

As for the Cash, Charles, *I haven't got it,* because I have been *overpouring* what I had of it into Baleen (annex to the Clinic) & I shall be below-sea-level for some months... Very Sorry.

[Murray to Leyda, August 29, 1950] In packing up for a vacation up here on the River I took a large drawer full of unanswered letters, & eventually came down on yours of March 3, which I answered, in a way, on the telephone.

You seemed surprised that I could not quit my treadmill of work at Harvard & have some exhilarating conversations with you about H.M. Well H.M. is either dead in me, or retired into a Rip Van Winkle sleep, to be revived at some later time after I have had several more revelations which allow me to see him in a totally new light. If, by a small chance the bombs miss both of us, & there are still printing presses in this U.S., & my Liver holds out, perhaps in 15 years, I shall be old enough to look at H.M. from a new perspective & discuss him with you on a California Mt. & then write a short volume composed of pure pith. But the fact that my own writings have gone out to sea does not diminish my enthusiasm for yours. You said Fall publication—before Xmas anyway—*that* will be good, a great relief to you, I am sure, after all your laborious researches, and probings, and editings, and revisions & troubles with publishers, & what not. As I told you, I could not answer any of your questions. Have you been in touch with Eleanor Metcalf? She has discovered some new things, & is placing her book with the Harvard Press next month. Among some of her discoveries are some family letters belonging to a Miss Morewood of Pittsfield. Also some interesting Hawthorne family letters. But Yours will be the only Authoritative & Complete Book. I wish it a fair sail through the minds of 10,000 Readers.

[Leyda to Hayford, July 3, 1951] Another Secret Report from Unscrupulous: Wilson of the [Harvard] Press here, has given me (today) a pretty distasteful job—to read the delayed book by Eleanor Metcalf, and I went to it reluctantly this evening. But what a pleasant bomb is buried in Chap IV (its title, "Deep Peals and Light Revelry," is unfortunately typical of the whole book), and it's so dazzling that I haven't read it carefully before racing to this typewriter—to hand you the bomb—which you'll have to keep as quiet as I do, for she is not to know that I am reading it for the Press. (I feel incoherent—probably am.) In her preface she says she has got this letter from Mrs Beatrix Hawthorne Smyth, NH's grand-daughter—no address—and Mrs S is certainly pledged to hold it for Mrs M's single (so far) big reason for her whole book. Another concealment technique played by Mrs M is to omit the date—though dates are every where else given in extenso; she places this only "in the eventful autumn of 1850: (to her mother). . . . [Leyda marks this passage with an arrow] "Since his visit he drove up one superb moonlight night & said he had bought an estate six miles from us, where he is really going to build a real towered house—an actual tower."

[Lawrence Clark Powell to Leyda, undated] Last night an English scout was here and said he is convinced that the manuscript of Moby Dick is here in London in possession of Bentley's daughters. How about this?

[Chase to Trilling, September 7, 1951] Last weekend I was at Williams for a monstrous Melville conclave involving 77 panelists and at least 67 bores.

I gave a little speech about how the assembled persons should stop throwing up their hands in awe because Melville spoke of EVIL and confronted REALITY. There was an undeclared and very narrow theology of experience in the air compounded very much of Parrington and—theology. This psychiatrist feller from Harvard entertained us all by inadvertently referring in his speech to the "expulsion of Adam and Eve from Paris."

[Newton Arvin to Chase, September 14, 1951] [He did not attend the Williamstown conference on *Moby-Dick* because of the trouble in getting there] and this, joined to my at least temporary boredom with HM and that whale and the whole overtreated subject, was enough to keep me away. I am glad however that other people have more spirit than I have. . . . For myself I wish I didn't have to hear one more word about Herman and the fish (shall I say) the next five years. We heard nothing about them in Cambridge & perhaps that is one reason why I enjoyed the conference there so much.

[Agnes Morewood to Leyda, November 13, 1951] Through Margaret, I heard that you missed most of the conference in Williamstown. . . . I am sorry for your accident a fall? at Williamstown and also that you did not get to my tea after the lunch at the Club.

[Eleanor Metcalf to Leyda, January 9, 1952] What you say about your financial condition gives me concern. You must know that we have regular financial responsibilities toward our sons. But if anything up to a hundred dollars would tide you over a temporary situation, we would like to know. I hope you will be quite frank.

[Maurice Kelley introduces Murray, author of *In Nomine Diaboli*, as a writer on psychiatry and lecturer in clinical psychology to readers of *Princeton University Library Chronicle*, 13 (Winter 1952): 48] [All the Melville scholars] defer to him: They all acknowledge that his study of *Pierre*, the most baffling of Melville's novels, is the most penetrating analysis of the relationship between Melville's life and his art that has yet been written.

[Olson to Murray, February 16, 1952] Yr IND [*In Nomine Diaboli*] came an hour ago, and I have read it, and it breaks my heart. In two ways: that you do know HM, and have told the unhappiness he was locked in, and they are of such an order, are still so much the fate of several of us—are so, not only in the context you put them in, but so in contexts such as LANGUAGE and such as that CIVIL WAR he saw as well as the INTERNATIONAL CW we are watching . . . to suggest that an incompatible marriage is an ending of it . . . . you see Harry, why I take this piece of yours to be of the moment it is, that you are here putting your hand in—as I always found you putting your hand in—to the very MEAT of the thing, to where we men LIVE, WORK, HIDE, & DIE

That is, I think you know me, know me well, where I, too, hide. And so I write as straight as I do to you—have never written so or said many of these things to any one but you. OK. Thus, you were right—in *that* context—to leave me out, to be calmly certain that I had written no *MOBY-DICK*, and so do not deserve to be talked about when there is my brother there who did write such a book and so told what men of our tribe can say on the subject.

Which gets us to the HEART & PARADOX of my response: I would have you wholly *relentless*, and because you haven't been, here, and because I believe—*want* you to be, wherever & whenever you write on this subject again—I take up this machine this afternoon, and, all crawling with nerves and the collidings of love—for I do love you—do know love, the love you have him speak of, there, that other androgyne.

(((((question: do you know any modern man other than an androgyne, who makes sense? who is capable of love—*or of power?*

e.g., your own pegging of AH [Adolf Hitler] as copralagnist;[48] your own acquaintance with FDR, probably more than my own look into those boy eyes; and Mao? that is, *before* Peking-*before* power (for power, like all accomplishment outside art, deceives, makes me think they have OVERCOME their own enemy.

You defer to much, pay too much mind to 1) LITERATURE and 2) RELIGION. I mean that this way, that, your own discipline, PSYCHOLOGY is serious enough in its own right to be an ordering offered *without reference to* either 1) or 2)—or, which also bulks large in the present piece, 3) SOCIETY. And it is this *purity* which I would urge on you, here & anywhere. . . . *why do you use HM's* language at all?

[Leyda to Murray, undated] Dear Harry, I'm ashamed that your copy of the Log did not come from me as I intended it should, but I am proud of what you say of it. Now that it is a book, out and on its way to being forgotten, perhaps the place that it occupied between us can also be forgotten—Will you show that this is possible by telling me that you have gone back, in earnest, to work on your book? . . . I would be very happy to hear this—it is your new letterhead that made me hope again that this wrong of my doing was to be righted someday. And to see your fine lecture in print was an experience as stimulating as that first hearing at Williamstown. If you have an offprint left, may I have it to give to a man who is doing some real new good thinking about Moby Dick? This is C.L.R. James, a West Indian Negro whom you may have heard in the fragmentary radio discussion of Moby Dick, and whose ~~whole~~ fully developed approach I've heard in a lecture at Columbia. The resemblance between your and his approaches is not entirely accidental because he gives public appreciation to your work on Pierre. . . You're right to find that flaw in Leon Howard's book, but you should also ~~have seen~~ be aware sympathetically, of its ~~motive~~ cause: a revulsion to the gush & guff about HM. And then you would have room to see the many good & lasting qualities of his book. Has your review been printed yet?[49]

[Murray to Leyda, March 14, 1952] Just a hasty word to say that your little Melville volume [*Portable Melville*] arrived last week and I have had time to go through it and come to the conclusion that a better selection of H.M.'s works would have been impossible. It is obviously a difficult task to have on the one hand a complete specimen of his mind (such as *Typee*) and on the other hand a larger sample of heterogenous fragments to show the range of his interest and powers of expression.

I am very grateful to you for this gift, and it more than makes up for my wait for your great *Log*. It was absurd of me to suppose an author of so expensive a book could afford to distribute copies widely through the country. Now I am fully satisfied and snug with this latest product of your devotion to the Great Man. . . . P.S. I am sending you under separate cover a copy of the Williamstown speech for Mr. [C. L. R.] James.

[Olson to Leyda, March 15, 1952] I am a devotee of the man. I am a fool of the hearts, have—am blind. You see, for me he still looms as the thing since Homer.

[Sealts to Olson, April 5, 1952] The truth of the matter is that sloppy, hasty, half-digested work in our field and on our man plays into the hands of these intellectual fascists who in their suave way are worse than the thing they so pretend to hate. If I were to judge the worth of Melville in terms of the worth of the people who have written on (literally *on*) him, and hadn't lived with the man these last thirteen years, *I would think the same.* But, you ask, what can we do about it? Well, I wish I had a capsule answer on that and a hundred associated questions that hit me in the classroom and faculty meeting, not to mention plain ordinary conversation with my neighbors in this enlightened Chicago-Tribune reading MacArthur-worshipping community. I think simply laying a foundation of straight facts, undramatic as it is, is probably the first thing. With Melville I think clean work like Jay's *Log* and "straight" books like Gilman's are the first things—Hayford and Merrell Davis are others I'd add to the list [along with Heflin and Horsford]. This is just what you're driving at in discussing *sources*. I would put it this way . . . IF A MAN AT LEAST KNOWS WHERE TO *STOP*, ASSUMING HE FIRST KNOWS WHERE TO *START*, let us do him honor. If he knows neither where he should have started (Chase) or where he ought to stop—or at least *wait* (Mansfield and Vincent), let us have at him. And if we can *correct*, we should do that. And if you can *go beyond* (note, I say *you*), do that . . . .

[Murray to Olson, May 27, 1952] Your prompt, friendly, copious, & exocordial letter was a little surprising & hence instructive & welcome. It goes without saying that if there is a fight on—with lines drawn—between you & the Old College tie English professors, I am on *your* side in Spirit. But it is obvious that I have not learnt to be on your side in Style. You have promised to elucidate what you & other poetical pioneers are about. I am aware, of course, of your daring experimentations in form, of the fire-works of contemporary writing & c, but I have not the necessary clues or keys to get at the content—the idea, the feeling, the hope—that is represented. If you tell me the form is *all*, that it is significant of itself & nothing else, then I shall be inclined to believe that modern verse is solely for technicians—waiting for birth of a new mythology that merits embodiment in these new forms. There is much to be learnt from you. When can we meet? If I have done Wrong I am ready to be forgiven. In the meanwhile I am very grateful for your corrective words & apologize (as usual) for my tardy response to your swift judgment of my endeavor.

[Leyda to Lawrence Clark Powell, June 18, 1952] I'll be expressing soon (perhaps collect) the rest of the staggering correspondence around the Log & related HM projects. . . . A favor: as there are plenty of the scholarly & nonscholarly types of indiscretion, never intended for general circulation when sent to me, will you please ask Leon how to protect my innocent correspondents? He can either throw them away (I hope not) anything that worries him, or put some sort of barrier around it—if it's worth keeping at all. I do think some things in it may lead to more persistent digging some day.

[The "famous American Novel" adjusted for "American students needing a simplified vocabulary" and for "foreign students . . . wishing to increase their knowledge of English." Adapted by Robert Dixon (New York: Regents Publishing Company, 1953)] You may call me Ishmael. Some years ago—never mind how long exactly—having little money and nothing in particular to interest me on land, I thought I would go to sea. In this way I could travel and see part of the world. Whenever I feel myself low in spirits, when life seems suddenly of little importance and death almost attractive; or when I feel myself angry at everyone and at the world in general, then I consider it time to go to sea as soon as possible. There is really nothing surprising in this. If they only knew it, almost all men have the feeling toward the sea as I have.

[F. W. Dupee to Chase, January 19, 1953, Paris] I'm having a good time reading Melville and other old Americans for my Lille lectures. I don't quite share your wish to be translated back into their time (I knew your were joking). It was full of genius and high enterprise but seems to have been so unsociable. Melville's personal story, the mother, the wife, the poverty, the abortive relationship with Hawthorne, the long retirement, never fails to give me the horrors. You can't say the writing of Moby Dick makes it all all right. But I know you *don't* say that.

[A warning and a plea from C. L. R. James's the last chapter of his self-published Melville study (1953), berating "the American social type" symbolized in the treacherous Jewish communist named "M" and excised from the 1978 Bewik/ED edition] . . . M is a Jew, born in Russia. But he came here when he was twelve years old and if ever I saw a man with all the characteristics of the American social type, he has them . . . M handled his protests with great discretion, for after all, he was a prisoner. . . . M claimed, and as far as I could see, with truth, that he indulged in no political propaganda on Ellis Island. But he had no need to. He told me that many of the men he had helped and others who had seen his actions had told him or passed the word to him that as soon as they reached home they were going to join the Communist Party. His reply was that they should be careful, that joining the Communist Party was not a thing to be done in heat and passion, that they could harm both themselves and the party; such action needed careful consideration. In fact I know that one day a bitter and rather disreputable South American spat when the American flag was being raised, and M rebuked him sharply.

But perhaps his greatest triumph was among the staff of Ellis Island itself, the guards. These men were of all types (I shall deal with them later). But all whom I saw respected M for the way he conducted himself and his uncompromising stand on elementary human decency. I could see that a great number of them, some Irish Catholics and outspoken anti-Communists, talked to him about their problems and the problems of the Island. Once when a number of them were dismissed, as they believed unjustly, and the whole staff was in an uproar, between those who came to say goodbye and those came to ask him what he thought of it all, there seemed to be two centers on the Island—the official staff upstairs, and M below, the center of attraction for aggrieved and bewildered men.

Under my very eyes, M had turned the Department of Justice itself into a great arena where he struck hard blows for his side in the great struggle now going on for world mastery. He was using the American tradition against those who were supposed to be its guardians. On Ellis Island it was M who stood for what vast millions of Americans still cherish as the principles of what America has stood for since its foundation. You needed a long and well-based experience of Communism and Communists to know that M in reality was a man as mad as Ahab,* [* I should say that I do not necessarily believe that all the American Ahabs are in the Communist Party or will ultimately join it . . . .] in all that he was doing pursuing his own purpose, with the flexibility, assurance and courage that are born of conviction. How many there knew that if it suited his purpose, in fact his purpose would demand that if he were in charge of Ellis Island, he would subject both officers and the men he championed to a tyranny worse than anything they could conceive of? The officials were the contemporary image of those officers this book describes, who even when competent, morally enfeebled the men they were supposed to lead by their indifference, their lack of any moral principle or conviction. Could anything be more shameful than that they should have to ask this Communist what was wrong on Ellis Island? that he should be able to say that he acted as a human being, and not as a Communist? This is the news that was being taken to every quarter of the globe by the thousands of men who passed through Ellis Island while he was there.[50]

[Murray reviews Melville biographies by Leon Howard and William Gilman; he begins with a discussion of the *Log* (knowing the Isabel letter is missing), 1953] After years of cunning, unremitting, far-ranging and precise research, Mr. Jay Leyda has come forth with an encyclopedic compilation which will be required reading for all Melville scholars so long as there is a world in which scholarship can flourish. *The Melville Log* as I weigh it, is the complete embodiment of Mr. Leyda's original idea: that one could "escape from the bog of Melville interpretation (with its thick growth of wild guesses)" by collecting "the largest possible quantity of materials" and arranging them in "a simple chronology of events," the "main aim" being "to give each reader the opportunity to be his own biographer of Herman Melville."

What does this last imply? That the People should decide? That, since thirty years of long-haired thinking has resulted in nothing but a "bog" with a "thick growth of wild guesses," the trained and devoted scholar should stop thinking and confine himself to the task of garnering as many documents as possible? That, given the scholar's data, the untrained and undevoted reader is capable of arriving at a better conception of Melville's personality than is the scholar himself, and, therefore, the more difficult and important task of interpretation should be left to him? That every reader wants to make his own interpretation and the scholar should not interfere by publishing his? That the goal is ten thousand private biographies, all of them suppressed because their publication could only serve to deepen the bog and thicken the growth of wild guesses? That the only way we Melvillians can avoid trouble is to take flight into facts and become quiz kids? But enough of this.[51]

[Jean Simon to Chase, February 20, 1953] I think you are pretty hard on some of our fellow-workers. I entirely agree on your favorable appreciation of D. H. Lawrence and Mumford (the latter has been shamefully treated by some "scholars"). I am not so sure about Charles Olson, in spite of some splendid flashes of intuition. But on the other hand, I am afraid you are not quite fair to Leyda, Howard and Vincent. Leyda's *Log* is not, I think, to be "read," but "consulted"; in that case, beside its unquestioned usefulness to writers and critics, it may secure attractive and even moving moments to casual readers—just because Melville himself speaks through its pages, without interference from the commentator. As to Howard, I agree that his final, vituperative pages are out of place. I even agree that he does not combine "biography and analysis." He is a "factual" biographer, and little more. But his information is, in my opinion, both amazing and well-arranged. . . .[Notes to the Vincent and Mansfield edition of *Moby-Dick* have "elucidated" "a host of small points" but] I agree that all of *Moby Dick* cannot be explained in such a way: and the rest, i.e., the unexplainable phenomenon of genius, is after all the essential.[52]

[University of Chicago Committee on Human Development sociologist David Riesman to Chase, April 15, 1953] What remarkable observations are contained in your letter of April 1! I wish you could write something about these experiences you have had with students. Your point that art is "insincere" seems to me a correct interpretation. The artist is not "being himself" so that the standard question "who does he think he is" is particularly applicable.

I spoke recently at Smith College and got into a lengthy discussion in which I was defending the non-coeducational colleges. The students attacked me very, very fiercely on the ground that segregation is insincere and artificial and they would not listen to the possible advantages when, for instance, I suggested that it was pleasant to vary one's pace, to live in an exciting intellectual and blue stocking culture five days a week and a boy-girl culture on the week-ends. They felt it was just this dichotomy which was insincere. They were in search of a blue-jeans informality seven days a week.

[Leyda to Lincoln Kirstein, November 25, 1953, asking for help in getting a job and commenting on his cv] Here is the page, incomplete, but perhaps too full for your purposes. As for redness, there's always—these days—the risk of investigation (but one reason I thought your giving me a job might be less risky for you than giving me a recommendation—until I recalled the City Center)—but the unacceptable truth is that I have had no political character since I went into the army 10 years ago. I'll give you full details of that "political character" when I see you.[53]

[*New York Times* review of Leyda's book on Rachmaninoff, March 18, 1956] ... more disappointing is the authors' unwillingness to extend their imaginations in the interpretation of the subject's character. They offer a wealth of incident, yet not much to suggest what made up the elements of the man's mind, what was back of that forbidding exterior and that lush music. There are endless excerpts from Rachmaninoff's own letters, but much of their content is trivial; and somehow one feels that a potentially interesting person has been followed about attentively for a lifetime without ultimately making him quite comprehensible.[54]

[FBI report on Jay Lincoln Leyda, Washington Field Office, August 28, 1956] Subject on 12/2/55 submitted application for passport for proposed travel to England for purpose of arranging English publication of his last two books. Subject was notified by Passport Office that his application was being considered in light of provisions of Passport Regulations which require the submission of an affadavit as to present or past membership in the CP or CPA. Subject forwarded to the Passport Office by letter postmarked 1/9/56, an affadavit in which he stated he joined the CP early in 1937 and left it late in 1943, when he entered the U.S. Army; that he never held any office in the CP; that he has no intention of resuming his CP membership, as his life and ideas have changed completely. On 1/12/56, subject was issued passport for proposed travel of six months duration to England.

[Leyda's affidavit, January 9, 1956] . . . on my return to civilian life I did not resume that membership or that activity [in the Communist Party], and I have no intention of so doing, for my life and ideas have changed completely. Reference to my writing since that time will confirm this.

[Eleanor Metcalf to Olson, January 20, 1957] Dear Charles, You say "*Do* write": but there is nothing I can say to you. We know something of your story and the story of Black Mountain. From Paul of course. You have simply given me more details. I feel nothing but sorrow for what I do know.

We are grateful for what we have had. We wish you you [*sic*] greater peace. Eleanor Metcalf.

[To Chase, signed "Romantically, Oliver," January 25, 1957] Your portrait of the serious "young" intellectual ["Silverman" in "Radicalism Today," *Partisan Review* (Winter 1957)] was quite accurate and devastating. (I'm glad that you made him a Jew . . . it was quite just.)

I can't help feeling that the moral school you are attacking stems as much from Trilling as from Blackmur and Leavis. Trilling may be shocked to know this and I'm sure that this is not what he meant at all, but this sort of thing— disinterestedness, moral intelligence, high seriousness, moral cores, etc.— has de-gutted many young men who could have been better off burning the goddamn candle at both ends and in the middle. Worse than that—he made too many good critics out of middling writers who might have yet become good writers. Somehow it has turned out that there is an awful lot of good taste around but nothing much to exercise it on—an awful lot of polish but not much fire—an awful lot of poetics but not much poetry. (By the way, didn't you once tell me you used to write stories? From what you did with Silverman, I'll bet they were good ones.)

[Lionel Trilling/a.k.a. Silverman to Richard Chase, March 21, 1957, recollected in tranquillity] I have read your dialogue and I had better say straight out that, so far as it touches upon me, which of course it does a great deal, it made me angry. I suppose I rather expected it would from what I had heard of it, and perhaps that is why I put off reading it. But the considerable anger which I did feel for a while has now quite passed off. I should like you to believe this, and I should like you to understand that I didn't *undertake* to get rid of it; I wasn't trying to practice forbearance—it just went, quite of itself.

But I owe it to you to say why I was angry. In your dialogue you announce a position for yourself and urge its general rightness and necessity. You go about defining this position by contrasting it with a position which you describe with no little satiric intention and force: a chief part of your ridicule—it quite amounts to that on the page, however you meant it to seem—is the ironic use of the phrases which quite obviously come from my work and are intended to indicate it. I make but a small point when I say that it would have been more friendly and courteous to have named me right out as a writer whose point of view you meant to oppose and think others should oppose, rather than to have said this by implication. Aggression—not a very dreadful word in my vocabulary—is always better for being open and avowed. The course you took inevitably makes your declaration of opposition more personal than you probably intended and as much a matter for gossip as for thought. And the gossip might well be of a particularly unpleasant kind because of the reason you playfully give for your not naming names, even though at that point you are not—as I understand, but not everyone will—talking about me.

Yet this, as I say, is only a relatively small point. The essential reason for my anger—I suppose it is returning as I write! but only momentarily, I think—is the interpretation you make of my position. I of course can't undertake to say here in what particular respects I find you so extravagantly mistaken. It is possible that there will be, or ought to be, an occasion when I should endeavor to do just that. But now I'll say that I entirely reject the views you impute to me.

It occurs to me to wonder whether, in attributing to me the position you do, you do not really mean to characterize adversely, and to repudiate, your own position of a few years ago, and that you confuse mine with yours, for there surely were many points of agreement between us. Certainly some adverse attitude to your own former views must be involved in your present feeling, and I think it would have been more enlightening, more graceful, and (best of all) more interesting, if you had indicated that your former self was one object of the attack you make. But you ought to have it clearly in mind that, although there may have been some similarities in the things you and I thought a few years ago, we are two very different temperaments and intellects and the lines of our respective developments were bound to describe very different patterns, and, mixing the figure, to have very different resonances; and probably they had essentially different intentions—we each have enough wilfulness to make that likely. Thus, I might have been glad to have written the eloquent conclusion to your *Melville* with its praise of community and connection and its warning against the deceptions of liberal moralism and self-righteousness, but it was you and not I who represented Starbuck as being more truly "human" than Ahab, as being the more admirable, the better man. This is not a judgment I would ever have made, although I found it, when you made it, and even now, interesting and worth thinking about. If it is a judgment you now believe to be wrong, you should not suppose that it was I who made it.

And that's all I have to say, except to add this comment: that this incident of ours points to a very sad inadequacy in the lines of communication between us. It is very wrong and strange that I should not have known, except in a vague way, in what direction you have been tending the last few years, and you should have expressed your radical disagreement with me by implication, and suddenly, and publicly, instead of directly, and over the time in which it was developing, and personally. In this serious failure of communication I hold myself to blame as much as—and, indeed, more than—you. Yours always, Lionel.[55]

[F. W. Dupee to Chase, April 1957] I'm sorry I missed that Trilling-Podhoretz party at your house with Diana on the Warpath and Lionel holding his fire. I imagine your Silverman did quite pique her. So is such a crying or muttering instance of what we all (not only the Trillings) have done to the young with our domesticated imaginations, subdued as we are by the home, the lecture, the literary conference, the foundation grant, the Fulbright grant, the publisher's advance. I personally exempt Lionel himself from much responsibility for all this. For him the plunge into respectability was at least an adventure and he has shown much enterprise in it and applied the literary mind to many things it had long shrunk from, and has always written well, and in fact renovated the literary essay. I imagine that he knows this and would not be personally affronted by your article. Still my personal encounters with him in recent years have suggested that he is more and more an armed camp, holding communication with you only on his terms, and relaxing his vigilance only when it is a question of doing you a kindness—which he does often of course and with all dispatch and graciousness. But then I can just barely envision the possibility that it is with FWD, not the world at large, that he wishes to cut off communications. . . .

[Leyda to his mother, Margaret Smith, January 27, 1961] You should realize by now, that my secret is that I *can't* write. But I have found some ingenious substitutes for writing. . . The Melville and Dickinson monsters substitute running about and scissors and paste for writing—and I think they're more useful this way than if I had tried to write them. . . [It also substitutes for filmmaking as Eisenstein taught him.]

[From Murray's presidential address to the American Psychological Association, 1962, "The Personality and Career of Satan"] In this day of non-authoritarian parents, of independence training, of the precocious emancipation of youth, and of teenage killers, Satan's ascensionist hopes (perfect illustrations of the Adlerian craving for superiority) are not likely to be regarded as ample cause for everlasting ostracism and damnation. But of course this judgment of our time may be nothing but a consequence of the Devil's having pretty nearly realized his unswerving ambition to subvert our natures. (Shneidman, 527)

[Murray to Olson, ca. March 26, 1962] Dear Kind, Elusive, Bubbling Charles, Bless you for your message out of an old friendship—ragged, for one reason or another, over the last years.

I have followed, at some distance to be sure, the meteor of your spirit, & wish you the consummation of your extraordinary powers. Let me know if you ever give another reading within my reach. In the meanwhile, from my present night I am sending you my gratitude.

[Agnes Morewood to Murray, April 28, 1962] Oh, Harry—it is just impossible for me to say what I feel for you and your own deep loneliness—and you can then write to me your great kind understanding for me.

I am glad you went away and trust the new strange life with no one to know your inside suffering helped you.

. . . Eleanor Metcalf seems to be in a bad way, not leaving her room, or wanting to see anybody. Years seem to do strange things to us. I cannot realize where I am now!

[October 2, 1962] [Richard Chase's body is found in a pond by his nephew Jonathan Chase; it was floating "in eighteen inches of water, only ten feet from shore" near his parents' home in Osterville, Massachusetts. The victim of "an apparent heart attack" he was 46 years old and at the height of his success, regarded by The Columbia Spectator as about to become the "elder statesman" of American cultural criticism.[56]]

[From Lionel Trilling's eulogy for Richard Volney Chase, Jr., Columbus Day, 1962, St. Paul's Chapel, Columbia University; Chase was the ideal Emersonian, the American Scholar] . . . The response which Richard Chase made to Nature is to be heard in the tone of his prose. When we read his books, we are inevitably first aware of his style as the index of the energy and activity of his mind—we are conscious of its range of reference, of its diversity and its engaging wit, and of its subtlety and accuracy of modulation. Yet what finally gives his writing the authority it has—an authority which, as I believe, is not to be matched, and which will grow with passing years—is something we come to hear beneath the happy music of this strong and vivacious mind: it is a stillness that underlies the activity, a quietness which we hear almost as silence. It is brought into being by the writer's recognition that, surrounding the human world, and interfused with it, there is an existence which is not human. An English colleague in criticism spoke recently of mankind's need, in the exigent modern time, "to be in full intelligent possession of its full humanity," and Dr. Leavis went on to say that "'possession' here means, not confident ownership of that which belongs to us—our property, but a basic living deference towards that to which, opening as it does into the unknown, and itself immeasurable, we know we belong." Of Richard Chase's mind a preeminent quality is the deference it paid to what is not to be possessed, to what is apart from human existence, yet makes its circumstance. It was to be seen in what, to my friend, was necessarily a very moving way, in the precise ironic courtesy with which, in his garden and greenhouse, which made one of the sure pleasures of his life, he comported himself towards the flowers he grew—they were part of that existence which may be delighted in but not possessed, that is sometimes to be loved and sometimes to be feared, but that, whether pleasing or monitory, constitutes an otherness from the human. The consciousness of this otherness was instinctual and not formulated, but it was an intellectual trait. In our time it is rare, and it goes far toward explaining Richard Chase's peculiar distinction as a writer. The deep acknowledgment of Nature, of what lies beyond the human and contains it, gave to his perceptions and judgments of human affairs, even when these were intense, a quality of transcendence which shows itself as a grace of modesty and uncontentiousness. Richard Chase was not a man who was often visited by peace, yet peace is an element of the beauty of what he wrought.

[F. W. Dupee to Trilling, on Chase, November 26, 1962] At the time of his death, a colleague wrote to me, "It is a pity Richard's life did not have the shape of his career." This is unfortunate but true. Both his reputation and the quality of his work reached a high point at about the same time that his health and sense of well-being began seriously to decline.

[Barron's simplified approach to *Melville: Moby Dick*, by Darrel Abel (1965)] [Reporting Henry Nash Smith's "socio-political" reading] Ahab, in revulsion against a bad society, turns against all society—in a suicidal act of total alienation and monstrous self-assertion. The hero of the fable is Ishmael, who, like Ahab unable to make a sustaining commitment to a generally bad society, nevertheless is warned by Ahab's fatal example and learns how to survive by cherishing selective personal relationships with his fellow men. [The reader should not try to answer the question of Melville's relation to Ahab.] Ahab's tragic flaw was his willingness to identify what the White Whale represented. Ahab understood that "visible objects are but as pasteboard masks," but he was so exasperated by the stubbornness with which things resist unmasking that he arbitrarily sought out in Moby Dick only "outrageous strength, with inscrutable malice sinewing it." Although outrageous strength was fact, the malice was imputation. Ahab in a sense stands for any thinking man—but a man who will not acknowledge the limits of his thought. Is evil evil by any-thing except arbitrary definition from a limited viewpoint? Ahab cannot get outside himself, and measures the universe by his own rule. The explicator of Ahab's tragedy is too prone to fall into the same trap, and to cover up the author's symbolic fable with allegorical figments of his own devising.

[Ishmael-Melville breaks out-in with irony and paradox, C.S.] These con-tradictions can be reconciled if one accepts that the truth of any particular judgment (ungodly, god-like; mildness, malice; wicked, spotless) is a limited land-truth, a lower truth, whereas "in landlessness alone resides the highest truth, shoreless, indefinite as God." (26–27)

Ishmael is a type of intelligent, sympathetic inquiring humanity. He is an intellectual as well as a physical adventurer, seeking to escape the restrictions of conventional life, and to find out whatever is practicable for a man to know of the mystery which environs him. (28) . . . [On the Bosom Friend] . . . Ishmael had reached a breadth of intelligent sympathy which matched the instinctive humanity of the savage and transcended sectarian formulas. (41)

[Draft fragment of Jay Leyda's response to Murray biographer Forrest G. Robinson's August 4, 1971, request to comment on his "painful" "dealings" with Murray, asking Leyda to be "frank and forthright" as Murray has been] More than one reason for this delayed response to your letter, forwarded to me in Moscow (one reason). settling into the new job at York—another. A wish to evade answering—possibly the most powerful reason.

You are right to guess that the light-hearted tone of my reference in the Log's introduction (xviii) to our clash was not genuine. [Robinson's letter re-ferred generally to the Log, not to any specific reference, C.S.] And the bow to Harry on xx was not as kind as it sounds. These were actually barbs—translation: "If you're going to do it, do it, & don't use me as an excuse for not doing it." I think that was what griped me most—Harry's accusation that I had killed his greatest work. With his profession & his knowledge, he cannot deny knowing what he was doing to me when he burst into our Stockbridge door with that shout. After that we really had nothing to do with each other, no matter how often we met. Even his greetings were ironical.

To go back a little. Again the introduction—xvii–xix. Behind the thanks you may detect that from the beginning of what seemed then a modest project I met two contrasting reactions to it from academics. Without moving out of California I got a good taste of both. I was just out of the army & the primitive "nerve Hospitals" of that time (their real function was disposal, as swift as possible), I couldn't face studio work again, & as Eisenstein was asking for Melville's books (that's another long story), I decided to keep myself busy by making a game out of putting together—for him—all the documents, printed of course, in the UCLA Library. Larry's response was wonderful—somewhere he describes our first encounter—& later, Leon's was miraculous. Leon's words (& deeds) were made even more glorious because between Larry & Leon I had a demoralizing conversation with Dixon Wecter (I hope I haven't mentioned this in print). Then it was clear that I would be dealing with two kinds of academics—generosity and concealment "hands off" were only two of their contrasting characteristics.

A long time after, after a publisher took the book (a pure accident) & paid me advance enough for a year's work in Eastern collections, I met Harry & immediately considered him an understanding ally. He took me to his home, showed me a letter he owned, but said nothing about any Morewood papers in Pittsfield. (I had not yet met any of the Morewood sisters.) He knew that I was planning to move near Pittsfield—Sally Sedgwick lent us her Stockbridge house—& I can now imagine what he could have said then that would have been more honest and more protective of his "rights." But he didn't, & when I began digging in Pittsfield, it was inevitable that I would (at least) see Agnes Morewood. The conversation went well & she told me to come back the next (?) day when she would have something to show me. When I came back, I was dazzled by the heaps of letters piled on the dining-room table— & she made no objections to my transcribing anything there of use to me. (Later, after meeting her sisters, I realized that Agnes was the most formidable and hard of the sisters, & wondered newly why she had been so spontaneously generous to me.) Her things were a treasure & though she mentioned Harry's interest in them, nothing was said about any "agreement" with him. Perhaps she had given up waiting for any signs of progress from him— I know that he had decided to wait for the grand-daughters' deaths, but needn't have held up his writing—& showing something to all the people whose death he was counting on before publication. (Note: Is the fact that

Helen Morewood is still alive holding him up now?) Perhaps Agnes felt that she "was keeping faith" by withholding a couple of letters—later published in the *Letters*.

In any case she telephoned (I think) Harry to tell him of my visit & pleasant labors. I don't know what he said to her, but he drove at once to Stockbridge & had plenty to say to me. (My wife was scared & never wanted to see him again—& she didn't, not even when we were supposed to dine with him last year at Yale.)

So what should I have done then? Or now? Something heroic? I still admire his passion & understanding for HM (his published work on Pierre is beyond praise) & I'm sure his book would have changed the whole messy field of Melville scholarship, but—? I offered to show him everything I had found, some of which was new to him, & he seemed to enjoy that. But that was not enough to clean my conscience. Since then I have chosen subjects that were luckily of no interest to him—although I might have much appreciated the chance to discuss Dickinson & China (the new book) with him. No, indeed. (Leyda Papers, NYU)

[Murray to Leyda, April 27, 1977] I was very pleased to receive your cordial letter of April 5 on my return from the West Indies about two weeks ago. I must say I was a little surprised, however, to get a sniff here and there of the old animosity. For one thing you seemed to think that some of my queries were based on criticisms of the *Log*. Why, I've been engaged in commerce with that most remarkable book, both editions, for a quarter of a century, and I found *only one minor* error out of ten thousand truths. Next to the Random House dictionary its nearer to infallibility than any chronicle of a human life I have ever been familiar with. Alongside the Bible—well you know what I'm going to say: The *Log* is uncriticizable *period*.

. . . The question you didn't answer may possibly have been interpreted as a criticism: where is the note (from whom? And to whom?) which refers to Gans M's sending word to HM to shave before seeing his mother? The reader is referred to Morewood papers, but Bob Newman can find no trace of it.

The conflict over Hair between Hippies and parents was foreshadowed, I am supposing, by HM and his mother in late 1840 and in October 1844.

. . . It was Maria Gansevoort Melville Morewood who gave me a rather distinct impression of John R. Morewood's dislike of H.M. . . .

[Murray to Leyda, May 13, 1977] . . . Have you perchance decided not to answer my letters from now on? Out of revenge for my not answering "one or two, or very few" of yours in ye olden days? At that time wasn't the situation veritably different from what it is today? Today I am in no position to win fame and fortune by publishing the sweat of your brain ahead of you, am I? Or by hurting you in any other way?

I've forgiven you, but you were so far away that it was almost impossible to pick a time when our paths would cross. [Murray wants to know the] whereabouts of the references to Gansevoort M's writing instructions to HM in the Fall of 1844.

. . . I am surprising myself every week by finding out how intensely interested I can become in some minute issue. I suspect that my failure to resolve the core problem—the exact nature of HM's alternating mental states, their causes and consequences—the failure of 50 years effort to untie that knot of knots disposes me to escape into any detour that I encounter.

Forgive my pestering you please Jay, Salvos, Harry

[Erik Wensberg, editor of the *Columbia Forum*, to Leyda, April 29, 1979, asking him to decode an illegible word in an unpublished article by Leyda's ex-roommate James Agee, 1948, deploring the deradicalization of Left intellectuals after the war. The passage refers to "Taylor and his wife, Joe Losey, Florence, the Fox people, Whitney and his wife, Val Lewton, Ben Maddow (David Wolff), Jay Leyda, Salka Viertel, Isherwood and his friend, Harry Vietel." Agee's words] . . . The richness of everything gets me down, & the absolute necessity & habit of compromise, among most of these people. Even their professionalism, since it seems chiefly a professionalism of showmanship & of slipping points across, not of creative artists. To hear V.L. talk, without regret, about "enriching" the story of Billy Budd. Or J. L., aware of— and against—[doubting? doubling? cloaking?] his symbol, say . . . it was just time an[d] obligation & opportunity. In all of this, constant problems of balance between frankness, silence, & temptation to dishonesty or at least highly modified soft answers. As another aspect of this, I am drinking too much. . . .

[From the oral history of Jay Leyda, given to Columbia University, 1980] . . . [Josephine] finally told me that she was not my mother—that she was my grandmother. . . And that the reason she was telling me this was that my actual father had been picked up by the police in Dayton for trying to kidnap me. So I had to be on guard against him. Well, it was just the wrong thing to say to me, because I had wanted to know all about him, I wanted to know him, I would have felt very fine if I had been allowed to go away with him. So from then on, for quite a while, they would tell me horrible stories about what sort of person he was, how unreliable he was—a black Irishman, a charlatan who had hired my mother as his stage assistant in reading—in his mind-reading act and in his hypnosis act.

In the attic, I found a whole full-length picture which must have been used in lobbies of the theatre where he was appearing. But the next time I went to the attic, the picture was gone. I was told there was a marriage certificate, but I never saw it, so I don't believe it. I really am a bastard. But the family was very good to me. Margaret, my mother, must have put me in my grandmother's hands almost immediately after birth in Detroit. I never saw any papers about the official adoption or anything, and there's always been confusion about my parents' names on passports and things like that, not to mention their birthdates and their parents' names and so on.

I eventually found some evidence, and I believe it, on how they got me away from Detroit just after my birth without him knowing about it. He was a great fancier of prize fights and circuses, and just by chance, I saw an obituary in the *Times*, oh, it must have been back in the '30s—it said, "February 1910," so of course I wanted to find out what had happened in February, 1910. Here was an important prize fight in Colorado, I think, just a few days after my birth—after the 12th—. That he probably felt obliged to go to. So they whisked me out of Detroit to Florida as fast as possible. And he seems to have caught up with them at several points in there afterwards, after he got back from this—well, the prize fight is speculative, but I really believe that that was the reason they could get me away easily and safely.

This is the reason I've been going to films since the age of one. Because the two girls and their mother arranged things so that whenever they couldn't be home for any reason, one of them would take me to any film theatre in any city they happened to be in, and we'd always sit in particular seats. I just wish I had total recall. My memory of film history would be priceless. But I don't remember any film until a film that—I do remember a scene that I've always tried to identify. I recognize the actors in it, but that's all. I could probably find out when I became conscious of films by identifying and dating that film. But the reason for it was still to escape from the wicked father.

[Q:] . . . Did you ever meet him?

[Leyda] I saw him twice. Always in the company of my grandmother, who in those days, would not allow me to go to the library on my own. I must have been seven or eight by then, and the police in Dayton were always alerted whenever she knew that he was in town. Later, it turned out that a couple of traveling circuses—he became a worker in one of then, and she would always look out for that circus. But even before I knew about the circus connection with him, I ran away to a circus, taking a little girl in the neighborhood with me. I was only about eight, perhaps. And I think she was just eight, or maybe a year younger.

Now that is the last thrashing I got from the person I knew was not my brother, but I still thought of him as my brother. (2:5-213–16)

[John Hillyer Condit, dissertation abstract, Columbia University, 1983] Many high school English teachers find themselves with a heavy course load in American literature and a strong background in British literature. They then face the twin tasks of studying American literature and deciding how best to present this knowledge to students. This dissertation presents an approach for teaching three early nineteenth-century American romances to adolescent students which will directly involve them yet maintain high critical standards.

The approach is based upon a simple analogy. Early nineteenth-century America had space and adolescent students have time in which to project possibilities. Up to the Civil War America abounded in high hopes and deep fears for what the young nation might become. The three romances studied subjected these possibilities to imaginative and critical exploration. The romance was an ideal vehicle for such an exploration because of its traditional license to entertain the hypothetical and its potentiality for critical self-awareness. Interestingly, during adolescence some say the individual develops the ability to hypothesize. Also the adolescent needs to balance this new power with a sense of consequence. Thus, in reading these romances the adolescent participates in a literary experience matching his or her current capacities and needs.

The Prairie by Cooper, *The Scarlet Letter* by Hawthorne, and *Moby-Dick* by Melville all have narrators who watch as characters explore possibility. The narrator endorses positive aspects of the quest to transcend individual and social limitations; however he pulls back from monomania and anarchy. Related interpretations of the three romances are offered to involve and challenge students but not to preempt their own readings. A high school teacher could best use them to bring students to an awareness of the analogy connecting them to these works and to model an interpretation argued from factual evidence.

[Reporting Leon Howard's last words:] My friend Jim Barbour tells me that at the moment of his passing, Leon sat bolt upright, vigorously shot an arm out into space, as if grabbing some intangible thing, and spoke clearly and loudly, "I want to get it back."[57]

[Murray to Isabel, November 4, 1987, unwitnessed] Promise me you won't let them academicize you. . . . I'm giving you a present: the Tower.

[Hayford to Isabel, from memory, November 1996] Don't you know that Herman showed his secret tattoo to his little granddaughter Frances? She wanted one too, so he tattooed a whale on the top of her hand; he used blue ink and it took three days.

[A roundtable discussion with psychiatrists on the future of their discipline, the *Charlie Rose Show*, December 11, 1996, from memory:] [Psychiatrist 1 (long-windedly):] . . . I dreamed that one of my AIDS patients ascended to heaven like an angel. At that moment, 2:22 A.M. I awakened to discover that he had, in fact, died at that very moment. Should we not think twice before intervening in the natural and beautiful process of death?

[Psychiatrist 2 (agitated):] [What are you saying? What about the White Whale? We are all Ahabs here [pause] *aren't we?*

[Phone interview with Donald Yannella, December 15, 1996, from memory:] I visited Mrs. Osborne in an old-age home sometime in the late 1970s. With my own eyes I saw the remains of that blue tattoo on the upper side of her right hand, mingled with the blue veins. But she said nothing about a tattoo on her grandfather.

[Philip Weiss, author of "Herman-Neutics," *New York Times Magazine*, December 15, 1996, encounters Herman Melville's energy, channeled through a descendant at Arrowhead, August 1, 1997, then lets the nineteenth century go] . . . My father is a big scientist. As a boy I was sent to science school, taught to shun my grandmother's superstitions, and packed off to Harvard. Still, all that rationalism hadn't helped me to get at my true interests. Or as Melville put it: "Science explains it. Bides no less / The true innate mysteriousness."

. . . [Adrienne Metcalf] had artistic ambition, but struggled with the shadow of an ancestor who had "crashed and burned." Melville's lesson was that if you followed your passions, you risked madness.

We went to dinner at a tavern, and [Josh Schwartzbach, Adrienne's companion] said that Melville's unhappy energy was still in the world, fucking people up. If we channeled Herman we might be able to "heal" him. [The channeling follows: Melville speaks through Adrienne, Ezekiel through Schwartzbach, Weiss pretends he is Hawthorne]:

"Oh lighten up, you old fart," Ezekiel said.

Suddenly she spoke in a deeper voice.

"Yes well—you are a sonofabitch!"

It was very loud. I was afraid they could hear us back at the house. She pointed at me.

"We don't want to talk to him!"

"All right well, will you speak with us?" Ezekiel said.

"You are a sonofabitch too!"

"We never had a mother, thank you."

"Do you think we wanted this?"

"Yes, absolutely," he said. "Herman, aren't you ready to give this up?"

"Then die?" she said in a stern crotchety voice.

"Then live. You're already dead."

"Well, it has had its perverse pleasures."

"Yes, certainly so—and admit it, those were the only pleasures that you allowed yourself, the perverse ones."

"You sting," she said.

"And we love you."

"Such is this love—that stings! It is real then is it not."

Metcalf's face looked different, more masculine, contorted with anger. She spoke in a weird Englishy old American accent. I couldn't tell if we were playacting or something was really happening, that Melville was flooding through her. In a way I didn't care. I had a wash of impressions: How immature Melville was! He was a two-year old, with a two-year old pettishness and playfulness and sulks, something I'd never fully understood from reading him but that now made perfect sense. Then, too, I was slightly horrified at the connection I'd made with Adrienne. I'd met this woman once, now we were virtually confessing love. Was I connected to her for life? Were we supposed to have sex? Would she hang around my neck? I wanted to get out of there before she overwhelmed me. . . . When Melville's waves of atheistical horniness crashed over him, Hawthorne surely had similar feelings and split. . . .

"You know, Adrienne, I think that Hawthorne compromised himself because of the cerebral judgmental aspect. His art is never as interesting as Melville's." . . . .

. . . I followed their car into Lenox and we had turkey sandwiches and talked it over. Schwartzbach said that by channeling the energy and healing it, we had changed Melville forever. No longer was Melville an angry betrayed energy. Yes, the love and betrayal had happened between Melville and Hawthorne, but now it was healed it could stop being an urgent emotional reality for us, and became a fable. We could move on.[58]

[E-mail, October 21, 1997] I read in an ad for a book entitled Last Words that Melville's last words on his death bed were "God bless Captain Vere!" Is this correct? Where could this reference be found? Hank Galmish

[Elena Pinto Simon, literary executor for Jay Leyda, e-mail to author, December 5, 1999] One morning, just a few years before he died, Jay came into my office and as he often did, remained quiet for several minutes. Jay's long silences were well-known to his friends. After a while, he looked at me, and then quietly said, "I am not a bastard." I hesitated for a moment, somewhat startled, and then realized what he was telling me. I knew enough to wait and let him speak, or else risk not hearing the story at all. (I had just begun my own oral history with him. We started this because after he gave me his copy of the Columbia piece, I was upset with the errors—it did not match with some of what Jay had told me over the years. And when I told him, "You didn't always give her correct answers." He very characteristically replied, "She didn't always ask the right questions!") At any rate, there was a silence after his statement, and then he said he had found a marriage certificate. "They were married. And all this time, I thought they were not." I do not have proof of this, and only tell you of a rare shared emotional moment for Jay.

Several years later, when Jay was hospitalized for the last time, he called me one morning from his hospital bed and told me that Si-Lan was throwing out his papers and books. "She's throwing away a life's work," he said. I immediately went over to his apartment, with a friend and my husband, and the three of us convinced her to let us take away the remaining "rubbish," which was already in green plastic garbage bags. Four or five bags, she said, had already been incinerated. The certificate was not among the papers we were able to salvage that morning. We did use his line as the title of the show we were working on to honor him—Jay Leyda: A Life's Work. The exhibition was up when he died, and was where we held a reception after our memorial service.

Notes

1. INTRODUCTION

1. James W. Tuttleton, "Melville in the Try-Pots," *The New Criterion* (Dec. 1996): 23–30, review of Hershel Parker, *Herman Melville: A Biography*, vol. I, *1819–1851* (Baltimore: Johns Hopkins UP, 1996), and Laurie Robertson-Lorant, *Melville: A Biography* (New York: Clarkson Potter, 1996).

2. Herman Melville, "The Encantadas or Enchanted Isles," *The Piazza Tales*, ed. Harrison Hayford, Alma A. MacDougall, G. Thomas Tanselle, et al. (Evanston and Chicago: Northwestern UP and the Newberry Library, 1996), 146. Unless otherwise indicated, quotes from Melville's writing will refer to the Northwestern-Newberry editions and will be abbreviated NN.

3. Herman Melville, *Mardi* (NN), 522. Also see preceding chapter, referring to Britain: "Ah! Did this sire's old heart but beat to free thoughts, and back his bold son, all Mardi would go down before them" (520). The speaker in both cases is Babbalanja, a philosopher.

4. George Gordon Byron, "Prometheus," in *Byron*, ed. Jerome J. McGann (New York: Oxford UP, 1986), 265.

5. Gardner Murphy, "Essentials for a Civilian Morale Program in American Democracy," *Civilian Morale: Second Yearbook of the Society for the Psychological Study of Social Issues* (New York: Reynal and Hitchcock, 1942), 429. Also John D. Marks, *The Search for the Manchurian Candidate: The CIA and Mind Control* (New York: New York Times Books, 1979), 17–18. According to Marks, Murray adapted German and British methods to his own ideas. It was "the first systematic effort to evaluate an individual's personality in order to predict his future behavior." Murray's methods were institutionalized in the CIA by John Gittinger, while his personality assessment techniques were adopted by corporations, beginning with AT&T. Whether or not Pareto was either a supporter of Mussolini or a protofascist is contested. See James H. Meisel, ed., *Pareto and Mosca* (Englewood Cliffs, N.J.: Prentice-Hall, 1965); for a more systematic study of Pareto's thought, see his *Sociological Writings*, comp. and intro. S. E. Finer, trans. Derick Mirfin (London: Pall Mall Press, 1966).

6. See Gordon W. Allport and Henry A. Murray, "Worksheets on Morale: A series of explorations undertaken by a seminar in Psychological Problems in Morale in the Department of

Psychology at Harvard University under the direction of Dr. Gordon W. Allport and Dr. H. A. Murray," 1941, Harvard University Archives, Cambridge, Mass. Also see Henry A. Murray, "Analysis of the personality of Adolph [sic] Hitler with predictions of his future behavior and suggestions for dealing with him now and after Germany's surrender," declassified confidential report, Oct. 1943, FDR Library, Hyde Park, N.Y, 211–20. Murray noted that his ideas were consolidated by the fall of 1941 in collaboration with Gordon Allport. The Harvard worksheets are quoted extensively below. For Murray's selective appropriation of Freud, see his "What Should Psychologists Do About Psychoanalysis?" *Journal of Abnormal and Social Psychology* 35 (1940): 150–75.

7. William V. Spanos, Jr., *The Errant Art of Moby-Dick: The Canon, the Cold War and the Struggle for American Studies* (Durham, N.C.: Duke UP, 1995), 3; see also Julian Markels, *Melville and the Politics of Identity: From King Lear to Moby-Dick* (Urbana: U of Illinois P, 1993).

8. Robin W. Winks, *Cloak and Gown: Scholars in the Secret War, 1939–1961* (New York: Morrow, 1987), chap. 5. After a visit to Germany in 1933, where he was especially impressed by Hitler's mastery of crowds, Pearson was "nearly Nazi in his mind" (254); but after 1939 he "rejected all things German." Winks gives the impression that the pro-Nazi sentiments were temporary but does not discuss his opinions during the years 1933–39. On *Proletkult*, see Igor Go-lomstock, *Totalitarian Art in the Soviet Union, the Third Reich, Fascist Italy, and the People's Republic of China*, trans. Robert Chandler (New York: Icon Editions, 1990), 26.

9. See Roy Porter, *Enlightenment: Britain and the Creation of the Modern World* (London: Penguin, 2000), a book partly in dialogue with Margaret C. Jacob, *The Radical Enlightenment: Pantheists, Freemasons, and Republicans* (London: Allen and Unwin, 1981).

10. See Richard Hofstadter, *The Age of Reform: From Bryan to F.D.R.* (New York: Vintage Books, 1955), who called attention to the proto-progressive Mugwumps, native-born American Protestants who were losing power to the new industrialists and who were energetic civic reformers after the Civil War.

11. Burke quoted in Don Herzog, *Poisoning the Minds of the Lower Orders* (Princeton: Princeton UP, 1998), 15.

12. Corporatism: state-direction of economic activity asserted in opposition to laissez-faire doctrines of the free market (today "neo-liberalism"). As defined by some social theorists, the corporatist (or corporative) state, an offshoot of syndicalism, organizes employers and labor into parallel organizations (in Italy, the *sindicati*) and then forcibly reconciles their interests, favoring capital. Such top-down attempts to harmonize warring classes were features of the corporative state under Italian fascism, of Hitler's Germany, and of the social democratic Western democracies (including the New Deal); adding the Soviet Union to the mix, some sociologists characterize their structural similarities with the term "bureaucratic collectivism." The term "corporatism" is often misapplied by populists to the concentration of business power, seen as controlling the state. Such a usage fails to specify both similarities and differences between strategies that attempt to rescue capitalist economies in response to crises, the Great Depression for instance. "Corporatist" also refers to the social structure of medieval organic societies or to governments that arrange voting blocs by occupation rather than geographic location.

13. For cultural nationalists, the individual elements of the mosaic represent "self-reliance" as expressed in economic autarky, the unit being the ethnic nation, not persons. Such organization would make it difficult for workers to unite across "ethnic" or "cultural" lines. As John Crowe Ransom or Eric Voegelin understood the *völkisch* idea of a national culture, there would be a spiritual uniformity in a people who had interacted for a lengthy period with their specific material environment, evolving into a balanced relationship with nature and each other. This was the point of T. S. Eliot's famous remark (1933) about limiting the number of freethinking Jews in the interest of local stability. See John Crowe Ransom's essay "The Aesthetics of Regionalism," *American Review* 2 (Jan. 1934): 290–310, for an elucidation of scientistic localism that infuses contemporary

concepts of multiculturalism, and compare to Herder's concept of nationality as described by the political sociologist Eric Voegelin, *The History of the Race Idea* (Baton Rouge: Louisiana State UP, 1989). Voegelin rejected the concept of "race" as too materialist because of its biological implications, favoring Herder's idea of cultural nationalism.

14. See Robert C. Nye, *The Origins of Crowd Psychology: Gustave Le Bon and Crisis of Mass Democracy in the Third Republic* (London: Sage Publications, 1975); also his *The Anti-Democratic Sources of Élite Theory: Pareto, Mosca, and Michels* (London: Sage Publications, 1977).

15. Gunnar Myrdal, *Objectivity in Social Research* (New York: Pantheon, 1969), chap. 10 and passim.

16. See Lewis Coser, "Europe's Neurotic Nationalism," *Commentary* (June 1946): 58–63: "Cultural pluralism—the right of each people to its own culture—is perfectly compatible with unification on the economic and political plane, and it is absurd to pretend that those who favor such unification call for the standardization of European culture. On the contrary, a diversified European culture is no longer possible except through political and economic integration. 'Balkanization' will mean not only material, but cultural poverty. The only political, economic, or cultural hope of the peoples of Europe lies in an over-all community that goes beyond the separate nation." Coser is assuming that culture can be separated from economics and politics. His cultural pluralism was asserted against "totalitarianism" resulting from nationalism (gradually transformed from democratic revolution to racism and imperialism). These thinkers are vigorously "antiracist" but have substituted ethnicity as the category to study "the problems of group adjustment" and "real group differences that are the soil and raw material of democratic society." See Melvin Tumin, "The Idea of 'Race' Dies Hard," *Commentary* (July 1949): 80–85. Compare with the progressive A. A. Berle, Jr., "The Rise and Fall of Liberal Democracy," *Democratic Pluralism and the Social Studies*, ed. James P. Shaver and Harold Berlak (Boston: Houghton Mifflin, 1968). Scorning the "Jeffersonian" sentiments of New Left framers of the Port Huron statement demanding participatory democracy, Berle explained to high school teachers that participation could not exist in a scientific, bureaucratic culture (143); however, "democracy" was time tested: "Throughout history democracy has been the most effective device for complex societies to coordinate the action of masses of people performing a large variety of complex functions" (142). If constitutional checks and balances are obsolete, as Berle claims, then there is no basis for unity other than the organic solidarity promised in ethnicity; perhaps "multiculturalism" is a way for technocratic elites to micromanage "group" (but really class) conflict. Ritual obeisances to the Founding Fathers would be used then to create the illusion of popular sovereignty; in other words, both Hamilton and Jefferson are passé.

17. For a 1930s critique of "Steel-Romanticism" and "realistic Idealism" published by a Tory literary journal, see Gudmund Roger-Henrichsen, "Literature in Nazi Germany," *London Mercury* 38 (May–Oct. 1938): 140–50. The editor was J. C. Squire.

18. Allan Bloom, *The Closing of the American Mind* (New York: Simon and Schuster, 1987). Note the organicist title; however, Bloom distances himself from "the progressives of the twenties and thirties" whom he blends with Stalinists (32) and New Leftists. For an example of the tug-of-war for the Enlightenment, see Roger Kimball, "Whose Enlightenment Is It?" *New Criterion* (Apr. 1996): 4–8.

19. "Extraceptiveness" is a term coined by Henry A. Murray and taken up by T. W. Adorno, Melanie Klein, Dorothy Dinnerstein, and others to describe the materialist psychology that they opposed as objectifying both perceiving subject and object. Science led to nuclear weaponry, inevitably. For an example of Murray's continued influence in the peace movement, see John M. Broughton, "Babes in Arms: Object Relations and Fantasies of Annihilation," in *The Psychology of War and Peace: The Image of the Enemy*, ed. Robert W. Rieber (New York: Plenum Press, 1991), 88–89, 97.

20. Milan Hauner, "The Professionals and Amateurs in National Socialist Foreign Policy: Revolution and Subversion in the Islamic and Indian World," in *The Führer State: Myth and Reality*, ed. Gerhard Hirschfeld and Lothar Kettenacker (Stuttgart: Klett-Cotta, 1981), 305–27, discusses anti-imperialist proposals supported by aristocrats in the foreign service, with similar efforts (1914–18) predating Nazism and opposed by inexperienced Nazis. (The target was the imperialist West.) Should some of today's postmodernists and New Leftists be seen as anticapitalist/antistatists similar in outlook to the prewar British Right (for instance, the Catholic Distributists Belloc and Chesterton, or T. S. Eliot)? G. C. Webber calls the type "the aristocratic backwoodsman." Rejecting the crude fascist vs. right-wing conservative division, Webber suggests four categories: anticapitalist antistatists, anticapitalist statists (reactionary Tories), capitalist statists (managing capitalism like FDR's New Deal or Mosley's British Union of Fascists), and capitalist antistatists (like today's New Right); all were to the Right of the liberal conservatives and of course liberals and socialists. See G. C. Webber, *The Ideology of the British Right 1918–1939* (London: Croom Helm, 1986).

In agreement with Herbert Marcuse's theory of repressive tolerance, Frankfurt School thinkers reject (bogus) pluralism: "Pluralism" masks a totalitarian (but fragmented) United States. Fredric Jameson argues for an overarching Marxist dialectic as the umbrella to local Marxisms (as there are national variants in late capitalism). This seems to me to be "rooted" cultural relativism, an apology for cultural nationalism; similarly, other historical materialists, cultural materialists, and postmodernists are idealists. See Fredric Jameson, *The Political Unconscious* (Ithaca: Cornell UP, 1981), 31–32, 54, 74, 86, 87; also his *Postmodernism or the Cultural Logic of "Late Capitalism"* (Durham, N.C.: Duke UP, 1991), xx. Compare with Ralph Bischoff, *Nazi Conquest through German Culture* (Cambridge: Harvard UP, 1942), 3, who writes, following an argument for unconditional victory as prelude to peace, "It is the thesis of this book that the march of National Socialism to power was in part due to the inborn cultural and blood nationalism of the German people, and the ability of their leaders to reawaken, reemphasize, and re-form certain characteristic traditions and faiths already existent in Germany and other German communities." (This book was part of the Harvard Political Studies series.) Such cultural analyses are historicized in Abram L. Harris, "Sombart and German (National) Socialism," *Journal of Political Economy* 50 (Dec. 1942): 805–35.

21. See, for instance, Richard Popkin, "The Philosophical Basis of Eighteenth-Century Racism," *Racism in the Eighteenth Century*, ed. Harold E. Pagliaro (Cleveland: Press of Case Western Reserve, 1973): 245–62. Locke is mentioned (245, 254), without citation for racist statements (as opposed to affiliations). He is included with Berkeley, Hume, Voltaire, Franklin, Jefferson, and Kant. Popkin's standard for antiracist philosophy seems to be "egalitarianism and relativism." I read Locke as opposed to the identity politics criticized here; see Christopher Fox, "Locke and the Scriblerians," *Eighteenth Century Studies* 16 (Fall 1982): 1–25. For Locke, identity was fluid and based on (learned) "consciousness," not (inherited) "substance." The violence of rude and barbarous peoples is not inscribed but learned. Relativism is supported by Mario Biagioli, "Civility, Court Society and Scientific Discourse," *Clark & Center Newsletter* 21 (Fall 1991): 2–3: "What we see emerging from very recent historical work is that the acceptance of the new science rested largely on the ways in which the practitioners managed to present themselves, their theories, their discoveries, their arguments and disagreements, and their experimental practices as fitting the proper cultural (and behavioral) codes. In short, to gain acceptance and credibility, the practitioners of the new science needed to present themselves as fitting the codes of those who had the social status and power to legitimize their knowledge—that is, princes, aristocrats, and gentlemen." See also Michael Denning, "The Academic Left and the Rise of Cultural Studies," *Radical History Review* 54 (Fall 1992): 21–47: "The roots of United States cultural studies lie in the pioneering work in the 1930s and 1940s of such figures as Kenneth Burke, Constance Rourke, F. O.

Matthiessen, Oliver Cromwell Cox, and Carey McWilliams. . . . They shared socialist or leftist social-democratic politics, an interest in the popular arts, a desire to rethink notions of race and ethnicity and nation and people, and a concern for social theory." Neither Matthiessen nor McWilliams was a materialist, however; Denning's imprecision in describing what were many distinct and embattled left and liberal tendencies during this period is typical of the vagueness, organicism, and anti-intellectual populism of the radical scholars criticized here. Denning even cites the attacks on 1890s populist social scientists, etc., "which grew into the postwar 'McCarthyist' purge of the universities" (33). Compare with Stalinist accounts of fascism: There was no populist (petit-bourgeois) movement; the big bourgeoisie is inevitably fascist in decadent late capitalism; both Matthiessen and McWilliams agreed with the latter formulation.

22.   Carolyn L. Karcher, *Shadow over the Promised Land: Slavery, Race, and Violence in Melville's America* (Baton Rouge: Louisiana State UP, 1980), 172.

23.   Neither statement was included in the dialogue of the movie *Moby-Dick* (1956); thus Ahab's quest is decoupled from Mapple's sermon (which in the film does include the imperative to seek and preach the truth in the face of worldly opposition). Moreover, the interchange takes place in Ahab's cabin, and Starbuck challenges his authority immediately. The director was John Huston, the script writer Ray Bradbury.

24.   Christopher S. Durer, "*Moby-Dick* and Nazi Germany," *Melville Society Extracts* 66 (May 1986): 8. Constructions of Ahab as Hitler invariably depend on irrationalist explanations for the appeal of fascism and nazism, erasing rational political and economic interests.

25.   See William Braswell, *Melville's Religious Thought: An Essay in Interpretation* (Durham, N.C.: Duke UP, 1943). "Melville was aware of the deification of science in some quarters. Henry Kalloch Rowe, in his *History of Religion in the United States*, writes: 'Many scientists were so enamored of their facts and hypotheses that they claimed too much. *They seemed to take pleasure in the destruction of that which was old.* They inclined toward a materialistic explanation of all phenomena to the exclusion of spiritual reality altogether.' It is scientists of this type that Melville derides in *Clarel* in the character of Margoth, a Jewish geologist who says that 'all's geology,' and who would do away with the 'old theologic myth.' Because of Margoth's insensibility to spiritual things, the pilgrims condemn him severely, and Melville adds an extra touch by causing an ass to bray after certain of Margoth's speeches" (111; emphasis added). Even more crudely put, see Vincent Kenny on Margoth: ". . . a geologist, a 'Hegelised—/Convert to science.' He calls the Bible a tissue of lies and insists that the so-called Holy Land must be made over in the name of progress. Unlike the Syrian monk with his gentle appeal, Margoth repels everyone within sound of his loud voice." In *Companion to Melville Studies*, ed. John Bryant (New York: Greenwood Press, 1986), 382–83. Note that Margoth is an atheist, yet still "Jewish." Insofar as Melville is seen to espouse these late-nineteenth-century antisemitic views, he would be a positive figure to organic conservatives discussed in this book.

26.   D. H. Lawrence (1923) is cited by Ronald Mason, *The Spirit above the Dust* (London: John Lehmann, 1951), as characterizing the *Pequod* as a sign for American industry. (Lawrence's *Studies in Classic American Literature* [New York: T. Seltzer, 1923] demonized America as a mongrel country that would, aided by the machine, destroy Europe and the white psyche. Ahab was destroying phallic power as epitomized in the White Whale; hence, for Lawrence, *Moby-Dick* was a warning to true aristocrats.) With the exception of the recently added try-pots, the mechanics of whaling had not changed for several hundred years and partook of craft in hunter-gatherer societies, not the increasingly divided labor and mastery of nature associated with industrial processes. See Daniel F. Vickers, "Maritime Labor in Colonial Massachusetts: A Case Study of the Essex County Cod Fishery and the Whaling Industry of Nantucket, 1630–1775" (Ph.D. diss., Princeton University, 1981). The few exceptions to the bad Ahab reading include Raymond M. Weaver, *Herman Melville: Mariner and Mystic* (New York: G. H. Doran, 1921); Granville Hicks, *The Great*

Tradition (New York: Macmillan, 1935), 7; Henry Alonzo Myers, *Are Men Equal? An Inquiry into the Meaning of American Democracy* (1945; reprint, Ithaca: Cornell UP, 1955), 51–55; Cecil M. Brown, "Through a Looking Glass: The White Whale," *Partisan Review* (1969): 453–59; and Toni Morrison, "Unspeakable Things Unspoken: The Afro-American Presence in American Literature," *Michigan Quarterly* (Winter 1989): 16–17. Hicks and Myers see Ahab as reformer. Myers, a pluralist, recognizes Ahab's driving (but misplaced) intensity; he is the romantic "earnest reformer" (like those nineteenth-century crusaders assaulting "ignorance, clericalism, slavery, alcohol, capitalism, war"). Cecil Brown sees a heroic revolutionary (contrasted with the "jew-bastard" surviving liberal, Ishmael). For Toni Morrison (a cultural nationalist), Ahab is a great foe to racism: "the only white male American heroic enough to try to slay the monster that was devouring the world as he knew it." Most recently, Richard C. Doenges presented the paper "Ahab Redux: Or, Playing the Devil's Advocate" at the Melville and the Sea Conference, June 19, 1999, Mystic, Conn. Doenges sees Ahab as both mad and a tragic hero with the whale a representation of Nature in its hostile mode; I view this as a moderated reading, not one entirely favorable to Ahab, who, unlike Ishmael, as the author argues, was blinded by the fire.

Readings by liberals and leftists hostile to Ahab include Charles H. Foster, "Something in Emblems: A Reinterpretation of *Moby-Dick*," *New England Quarterly* (Mar. 1961): 3–35, who views Father Mapple as an ultra-abolitionist the likes of Garrison, Richard Hildreth, and Gilbert Haven, but Ahab as Daniel Webster, an apologist for slavery and a demagogue. Some see Melville, or Ahab (or both), as ineffectual bohemian, consummate narcissist, or world-destroying archcapitalist; or as anticipator of Hitler and Stalin. See V. F. Calverton, *The Liberation of American Literature* (New York: Scribner, 1932), 272–73; Henry Bamford Parkes, "Poe, Hawthorne, Melville: An Essay in Sociological Criticism," *Partisan Review* 16 (Feb. 1949): 157–66; Richard V. Chase, *Herman Melville: A Critical Study* (New York: Macmillan, 1949), 101; John Howard Lawson, *The Hidden Heritage* (New York: Citadel Press, 1950): 428; James B. Hall, "Moby Dick: Parable of a Dying System," *Western Review* (Spring 1950): 223–26; C. L. R. James, *Mariners, Renegades and Castaways* (New York: Privately published, 1953), its last chapter (suppressed in a later edition) linked Ahab to a duplicitous Jewish communist named "M." See also Leo Marx, "The Machine in the Garden," *New England Quarterly* 29 (1956): 27–42; and H. Bruce Franklin, *The Victim as Criminal and Artist: Literature from the Prison* (New York: Oxford UP, 1978), chap. 2. The introduction to the Luther S. Mansfield and Howard P. Vincent edition of *Moby-Dick* (New York: Hendricks House, 1952) was largely focused on their review of changing Ahab readings after 1919 (xvi–xxxii); see especially their account of W. H. Auden's identification of Ahab with romantic artists in *The Enchafed Flood* (xxx).

27. Ralph Henry Gabriel, *The Course of American Democratic Thought: An Intellectual History since 1815* (New York: Ronald Press, 1940), 67–77; Peter Viereck, "The Philosophical 'New Conservatism,'" in *The Radical Right*, ed. Daniel Bell (New York: Doubleday, 1964), 185–207; Richard Hofstadter, *Anti-Intellectualism in American Life* (New York: Knopf, 1963), 239–40. Gabriel read Melville favorably as an antidemocrat and monarchist.

28. Charles Olson, Notebook 46 (Winter–Spring 1940), Charles Olson Papers.

29. Quoted in Lois Whitney, *Primitivism and the Idea of Progress in English Popular Literature of the Eighteenth Century* (1934; reprint, New York: Octagon, 1973), 5.

30. Nathaniel Hawthorne, "Ethan Brand: A Chapter from an Abortive Romance," reprinted in *The American Mind: Selections from the Literature of the United States*, ed. Harry R. Warfel, Ralph Henry Gabriel, and Stanley T. Williams (New York: American Book Co., 1937).

31. Robert Stone, review of Norman Mailer, *Oswald's Tale: An American Mystery*, *New York Review of Books*, June 22, 1995, 7. A Halloween feature "Getting into Character" for the *New York Times Magazine*, Oct. 29, 1995, showed Norman Mailer dressed up as Captain Ahab, one eye cov-

ered by an Indian headband, one eye staring at the reader, with the caption "Many a novelist has a touch of the monomaniac and Ahab is the monster of us all" (51).

32. Antifascism was not monolithic; rather, this book will distinguish between Left-liberal/independent and romantic anticapitalist variants. The systematic empirical investigation of institutions and social movements as practiced by Ralph Bunche exemplifies the independent intellectual practice derived from the radical Enlightenment. Contrast to D. H. Lawrence's redefinition of Whitman's "open road" in the final chapter of *Studies in Classic American Literature.*

33. These statistics were presented by economist J. Bradford De Long at the UCLA symposium entitled "The U.S. Economy Today: Back on Top?" Jan. 26, 1998. While this measurement, taken by itself, does not necessarily convey the overall condition of poor people and laborers, excessive gaps between rich and poor are considered threats to order by conservatives. Perceived threats to social cohesion are crucial to understanding the moderates studied here.

34. Hawthorne's expression in "A Virtuoso's Collection," in *The Complete Short Stories of Nathaniel Hawthorne* (Garden City, N.J.: Hanover House, 1959), see below.

35. Compare with Thomas Babington Macaulay's Whiggish defense of the moderate Canning faction: (As described by John Clive) "A republican sect, as audacious as the French Jacobins, but superior to them in acuteness and resolution, was arising within the middle classes. If diehard Tories came to power, that sect (presumably the Utilitarians) would become leaders of a strong democratic party within the ranks of the educated, would join forces with spinners, grinders, and weavers already chafing in a period of distress and ripe for revolution; and there would then be formed an alliance between the disaffected multitude and a large portion of the middle orders, with every reformer in the country being goaded into becoming a revolutionary." John Clive, "Macaulay and the French Revolution," in *The French Revolution and British Culture,* ed. Ceri Crossley and Ian Small (New York: Oxford UP, 1989), 104. Melville read Macaulay. Conservative Melvilleans will set themselves against this fearsome coalition of positivists and workers, with Melville/Ahab as a middle-class intellectual aligned with the lower orders.

36. John Bunyan, *The Pilgrim's Progress from This World to That Which Is to Come Delivered under the Similitude of a Dream* (London: The Religious Tract Society, 1904). "I saw then in my dream, so far as this valley reached, there was on the right hand a very deep ditch; that ditch is it, into which the blind hath led the blind in all ages, and have both there miserably perished. Again, behold on the left hand there was a very dangerous quag, into which, if even a good man falls, he finds no bottom for his foot to stand on: into this quag King David once did fall, and had no doubt there been smothered, had not He that is able plucked him out" (70).

37. Compare with the claims of Michel Foucault and his followers that the statist bourgeoisie has played a repressive role, stifling individual freedom.

38. See Rosemary Radford Ruether, *Faith and Fratricide: The Theological Roots of Antisemitism* (New York: Seabury Press, 1974), chap. 3, 219, 258.

39. Champfleury, "French Images of the Wandering Jew," in *The Wandering Jew: Essays in the Interpretation of a Christian Legend,* ed. Galit Hasan-Rokem and Alan Dundes (Bloomington: Indiana UP, 1986), 68–75. "Since the beginning of the century, [Ahasverus] has decorated every poor hovel, balanced by a picture of Napoleon. It seems that the common man gave an equal place in his imagination to these two great *marcheurs.*" For the Wandering Jew as alienated modern artist, see Edgar Rosenberg, *From Shylock to Svengali: Jewish Stereotypes in English Fiction* (Stanford: Stanford UP, 1960). For Ruether, Cain is the typological ancestor of the Wandering Jew, used by the patristic fathers to represent the reprobate Jewish people; see her *Faith and Fratricide,* 133–34. See also Uriel Tal, *Christians and Jews in Germany* (Ithaca: Cornell UP, 1975), 16, 232: Christians dealt with the corroding skepticism fostered by persistence of the obdurate Jewish people by

either converting or humiliating them so that their "abject state would then bear witness, *testes veritatis nostrae*, to the indefeasible claims of the triumphant religion of Christianity" (16). Christians might abjure rabble-rousing massacres, while excluding Jews from positions of authority.

40. After the Bolshevik victory, the establishment of the Labour Party and the extended franchise, antisemitism in Britain intensified and was directed specifically against both socialism (thought at that time to promote democracy and anarchism) and its materialist antecedent, liberalism with its emphasis on civil liberties; for example, Colonel A. H. Lane wrote (in *The Alien Menace*, 1928), "It is not an exaggeration to say that the whole fabric of British life and inspiration is being steadily undermined by the effect of the alien presence, his propaganda, and the evil practices which he has brought with him to this country. In many cases—if not in the majority of cases—he is an undesirable or a criminal in his own country, from which he has been forced to flee to avoid punishment there. So he comes here, free to propagate his filthy and immoral species, and by his degrading activities, to deluge the country with a flood of bitterness and class hatred, and to create industrial unrest, strikes, Socialism and Communism." Viscount Lymington made the connection between liberalism and Bolshevism explicit: "Liberalism is the philosophy which sets material increase as an end and not a means, and which sets individual liberty above social duty. The one ends in making man the slave of material, the other [libertarianism] in producing spiritual and moral anarchy. Each is the inevitable evangelist of Bolshevism." These corporatists were quoted in G. C. Webber, *The Ideology of the British Right*, 56. For similar views propagated by the Agrarians and New Critics, see Alexander Karanikas, *Tillers of a Myth: Southern Agrarians as Social and Literary Critics* (Madison: U of Wisconsin P, 1966).

41. Herman Melville, *Journal of a Visit to Europe and the Levant, October 11, 1856–May 6, 1857*, ed. Howard C. Horsford (Princeton: Princeton UP, 1955), 136–37, 259–60. For NN *Journals* edition, see 91, 128–29, adding the parenthesis about the Jewish Sabbath. I have quoted the first draft of the Oxford entry; these passages were rewritten and transferred to another notebook. The revision states, "Learning in Oxford lodged like a baron." *Journals* (NN), 156. Compare with "scared white doe of truth," in "Hawthorne and His Mosses," *The Piazza Tales and Other Prose Pieces* (NN), 244.

2. THE MODERATE RESPONSE TO NINETEENTH-CENTURY RADICALISM: "AMERICAN LITERATURE" AND THE PROGRESSIVES

1. Quoted in James Westfall Thompson, *A History of Historical Writing*, vol. 1 (New York: Macmillan, 1942), 501–2.

2. Henry Nelson Coleridge, Introduction to Samuel Taylor Coleridge, *Biographia Literaria* (New York, 1852), 22. Coleridge's son was defending his father from charges that he had plagiarized Schelling in the first edition.

3. Or perhaps he was insinuating that the lower orders were easily manipulated and overly deferential. I thank Jordan Alexander for suggesting this reading of the Whale Song, presumably sung by common sailors.

4. Peter Alexis Gourevitch, *Politics in Hard Times: Comparative Responses to International Economic Crises* (Ithaca: Cornell UP, 1986), chap. 4, esp. 158–59. The author compares "Nazi Germany, Social Democratic Sweden, the France of Laval and the France of Blum, the United Kingdom under Baldwin, the United States under Hoover and the United States under FDR." Though politically diverse, there was a common effort in these countries "to break with economic orthodoxy and to experiment with demand stimulus." (Japan's response to the crisis was imperialist expansion to create an East Asian co-prosperity sphere [not examined in his book].)

5. See Paul R. Gross and Norman J. Levitt, *Higher Superstition: The Academic Left and Science* (Baltimore: Johns Hopkins UP, 1994), for a critique of post-1960s anti-science in the humanities.

6. See the pamphlet *This We Believe About Education,* by the Educational Industry Advisory Committee and the Educational Advisory Council of the National Association of Manufacturers, Feb. 1954, Robert H. W. Welch, chairman. The authors viewed "totalitarianism" as the belief in "God-given authority" and "exclusive wisdom"; only despots claimed to be objective.

7. See Norman J. Levitt, *Prometheus Bedeviled: Science and the Contradictions of Contemporary Culture* (New Brunswick, N.J.: Rutgers UP, 1999).

8. Edward Berkowitz and Kim McQuaid, *Creating the Welfare State: The Political Economy of Twentieth-Century Reform* (New York: Praeger, 1980), 28. The parasitic exploiter image is attributed to Sidney Webb, the English Fabian Socialist. The book argues against the premise that business and federal welfare bureaucracies have developed separately from one another. See also John L. Thomas, *Alternative America: Henry George, Edward Bellamy, Henry Demarest Lloyd and the Adversary Tradition* (Cambridge, Mass.: Belknap Press, 1983), a study of the cooperative commonwealth ideal (continuing in the 1960s counterculture and asserted against the mob and mass politics).

9. J. G. von Herder's parody of a rootless cosmopolitan is quoted in Robert Reinhold Ergang, *Herder and the Foundations of German Nationalism* (New York: Columbia UP, 1931), 96.

10. See Philip S. Foner, *History of the Labor Movement in the United States,* vol. 1 (New York: International Publishers, 1947), 163–64. Foner was discussing the Whig pretense that their party served the interests of independent workingmen using suffrage to remedy their grievances. Shaw's decision had made it legal "to organize and bargain collectively" (but with "enough leeway" to be gutted by "reactionary judges"). In 1839–40, seven leaders of the Boston Journeymen Bootmaker's Society had been indicted and found guilty for conspiracy, the bootmakers having made rules that would have excluded nonmembers from the craft. It was argued that they maliciously intended to destroy the plaintiff's business; Shaw was reversing a municipal court decision that had held the bootmakers' regulations a conspiracy, enforced or not. Foner quoted Shaw's opinion: Associations could "adopt measures 'that may have a tendency to impoverish another, that is, to diminish his gains and profits, and yet so far from being criminal and unlawful, the object may be highly meritorious and public spirited. The legality of such an association will therefore depend upon the means to be used for its accomplishment. If it is carried into effect by fair or honorable and lawful means, it is to say the least, innocent, if by falsehood or force, it may be stamped with the character of conspiracy.'" Shaw had drawn a clean boundary between honorable and dishonorable social action. Melville may be seen as interrogating Shaw's distinction in his most disputed texts: What if the fair and honorable were always punished, while rascals were deemed "innocent"?

11. See Leon F. Litwack, *North of Slavery* (Chicago: U of Chicago P, 1961), chap. 4, for a full discussion of the conflict. The Roberts case was argued by Charles Sumner before Shaw's court, December 4, 1849. Melville began writing *Moby-Dick* in 1850.

12. Ergang, *Herder and the Foundations of German Nationalism,* 97 (emphasis added). Compare with Richard Wright, *White Man, Listen!,* intro. Cedric Robinson (New York: HarperPerennial, 1995), xxviii–xxix: "I'm a rootless man, but I'm neither psychologically distraught nor otherwise particularly perturbed because of it. Personally, I do not hanker after, and seem not to need, as many emotional attachments, sustaining roots, or idealistic allegiances as most people. I declare unabashedly that I like and even cherish the state of abandonment, of aloneness; it does not bother me; indeed, to me it seems the natural, inevitable condition of man, and I welcome it. I can make myself at home almost anywhere on this earth and can, if I've a mind to and when I'm attracted to a landscape or a mood of life, easily sink myself into the most alien and widely differing environments." I thank Ralph Dumain for the Wright quote.

13. Melville was reviewing Parkman, *The California and Oregon Trail;* this passage was quoted favorably in the 1937 doctoral dissertation of Karl Sundermann, a German intellectual

whose thesis director, Fritz Schoenmann, was a Nazi teaching American Studies. Sundermann probably read Melville as a German romantic, as sometimes he was. Hitler considered the American Indians to be Aryans; in his anti-Western propaganda, the mistreatment of the American Indians was a familiar theme. Sundermann corresponded with Henry Murray in the 1930s. Schoenmann is mentioned favorably in H. Lüdeke, "American Literature in Germany: A Report of Recent Research and Criticism 1931–1933," *American Literature* 6 (May 1934): 168–75. Schoenmann, a professor at the University of Berlin, author of several major books (including one on American propaganda), and the leading Americanist in Germany, had studied in America during the Great War. For more on Schoenmann, see Max Weinreich, *Hitler's Professors: The Part of German Scholarship in Germany's Crimes against the Jewish People* (New York: Yiddish Scientific Institute, 1946), 282. Weinreich's index identified him as an important Nazi scholar in the following entry: "[b.] May 30, 1886. Instructor, Harvard U., 1913–1920. Professor of North American Civilization, U. of Berlin. Author: 'Der Anglo-Amerikaner und das Judentum,' *Wk* II (1942); 'Das geistige Geschichte Amerikas,' *NSMon*, October, 1942, 657–66; 'Hintergrunde und Tendenzen des USA-Imperialismus,' *Völk und Reich*, 1942, 697–706; *Die Vereinigten Staaten von Nordamerika* (Berlin, Junker und Dunnhaupt, 1943, 160)." Lüdeke, however, writing earlier, praised him as an objective critic, noting that he was antidemocratic and fascinated with race amalgamation in the United States. In the same article, Goethe was mentioned as a major influence on Randolph Bourne and Van Wyck Brooks.

14. I am departing here from some Melville scholarship (for example, Franklin and Karcher) by arguing that Melville's "prisons" are not only about the master-slave or capitalist-worker relationship. He seems interested in demystifying the perceptual prison of "false utopia" wherever he finds it.

15. Berkowitz and McQuaid, *Creating the Welfare State*, 46.

16. See Kim McQuaid, *Big Business and Presidential Power from FDR to Reagan* (New York: William Morrow, 1982), 91. My account of shifting progressive strategies is indebted to this book and to the treatment of the welfare state by Berkowitz and McQuaid, *Creating the Welfare State*. The remarks on ethnopluralism are based on my own research.

17. McQuaid, *Big Business*, 121.

18. Ibid., chaps. 1–4, 123.

19. Berkowitz and McQuaid, *Creating the Welfare State*, chaps. 8 and 9, quotes from 156, 165. See also Sanford M. Jacoby, *Modern Manors: Welfare Capitalism since the New Deal* (Princeton: Princeton UP, 1997).

20. "The Great Nation of Futurity," excerpted in Hershel Parker, *Herman Melville*, 155.

21. Closing remarks by William Lloyd Garrison at the 1850 New England Anti-Slavery Convention, published in *The Liberator*, June 14, 1850, and in Philip S. Foner and Herbert Shapiro, eds., *Northern Labor and Antislavery: A Documentary History* (Westport, Conn.: Greenwood Press, 1994), 168–74.

22. See *Moby-Dick* (NN), 561.

23. Herman Melville, "Lee in the Capitol," the penultimate poem in *Battle-Pieces*. When "Lee" blames Fate, is Melville attributing the Civil War to the Hebrew God as read by Garrison?

24. *Melville Society Extracts* 10:23. The editor was Hennig Cohen of the University of Pennsylvania.

25. As abundantly documented in Foner and Shapiro, *Northern Labor and Antislavery*, 1994.

26. Bernard Picart, *The Ceremonies and Religious Customs of the Various Nations of the Known World*, vol. 5 (London, 1736), 319–21. Volume 1 of this series joined the (conservative) Jews to Catholics, disconnecting the Protestant Reformation.

27. H. E. Scudder, "American Classics in School," *Atlantic Monthly* (July 1887): 85–91. In tracking progressive cultural politics, I consulted the bibliography recommended in *American*

Literature in the College Curriculum (Committee on the College Study of American Literature and Culture [Chicago: National Council of Teachers of English, 1948]), 20–21.

28. Brander Matthews, "Suggestions for Teachers of American Literature," *Educational Review* (Jan. 1901): 11–16.

29. Newton M. Hall, "The Study of American Literature in Colleges," *The Andover Review* (July–Dec. 1892): 154–62.

30. Frank Parsons, "The Great Coal Strike and Its Lessons," *Arena* (Jan. 1903): 1–7.

31. J. M. Berdan, "American Literature and the High School," *Arena* (Apr. 1903): 337–44.

32. Robert E. Shafer, "Teaching Sequences for Hawthorne and Melville," in *The Teacher and American Literature: Papers Presented at the 1964 Convention of the National Council of Teachers of English*, ed. Lewis Leary (Champaign, Ill.: National Council of Teachers of English, 1965), 114.

33. Bruce R. Parker, "Political Thought of the American Renaissance: Melville and Parkman" (Ph.D. diss., U of California at Berkeley, 1973).

34. Carol S. Gruber, *Mars and Minerva: World War I and the Uses of Higher Learning in America* (Baton Rouge: Louisiana State UP, 1975), 187–206. See also David Caute, *The Great Fear: The Anti-Communist Purge under Truman and Eisenhower* (New York: Simon and Schuster, 1978); and Ellen Schrecker, *No Ivory Tower* (New York: Oxford UP, 1986).

35. Wilson quoted in Ronald Steel, *Walter Lippmann and the American Century* (Boston: Little Brown, 1980), 112. A selective service bill cleared Congress in May, drafting men ages 18 to 45.

36. Walter Metzger, *Academic Freedom in the Age of the University* (New York: Columbia UP, 1955), 255.

37. A letter from alumni secretary Levering Tyson to John Saxe, November 29, 1919, states that the warning was directed against Dana. My description of Butler's targets is a synthesis of my research and Carol Gruber, *Mars and Minerva*, but Gruber is hostile to Cattell. Unpublished materials cited here are from "Miscellaneous correspondence relating to the dismissal of Cattell and Dana" in the James McKeen Cattell Papers. As the preliminary report from the Committee of Nine reminded E. R. A. Seligman, Dana and Cattell had argued against the Conscription Act before it was passed into law; however, Dana and Cattell were highly visible. Harry Dana paid the bond to release Owen Cattell and two other Columbia students from jail after their arrest on June 1, 1917. The New York newspapers featured the controversy on their front pages.

38. A clipping from the *Evening Telegram*, May 19, 1913, in the Cattell file reported that Cattell could be in trouble because he had attacked the Century Association for its refusal to admit the Jewish Jacques Loeb, a biologist at the Rockefeller Institute. Cattell, leading a movement for faculty control, may have been saved from dismissal at that time (1913) because his "early retirement" would have given credibility to his claim that professors were muzzled. See letter from the zoologist Edmund B. Wilson to Butler, May 20, 1913. Cattell was a consistent radical throughout the interwar period, but no American Rosa Luxemburg or Wobbly; still, he did not view "socialism" as a "nightmare." See his "Academic Slavery," *School and Society*, Oct. 13, 1917, 421–26: "I myself accept the social ideal: From each according to his ability, to each according to his needs; and I think that, thanks to the applications of science, the resources of society are sufficient to provide adequately for all." His animus against college administrators was connected to a rejection of the "autocratic and bureaucratic" rationalizing businessmen who ran American universities (unlike Oxford and Cambridge where dons are administrators). See J. M. Cattell, *University Control* (New York: Science Press, 1913), 9, 13–15, 44, 49. As a young man writing to his parents in 1888, he declared his intellectual preferences and affinities for authors who, with the exception of Darwin, were English romantic anticapitalists: "I can suggest no other wedding-present than books and pictures. We should like to have editions of Carlyle, Ruskin, Scott, Rossetti, Morris, and Darwin." See Michael M. Sokal, ed., *An Education in Psychology: James McKeen Cattell's Journals and Letters from Germany and England, 1880–1888* (Cambridge, Mass.: MIT Press, 1981), 303.

39. See *Columbia Spectator,* Oct. 4, 1917, 2. Amazingly, Cattell was serving on a committee of the American Psychological Association organized to assist the U.S. military in the current conflict; see R. M. Yerkes, "Psychology and National Service," *Science,* Aug. 3, 1917, 101–3.

40. Quoted in Gruber, *Mars and Minerva,* 195.

41. *Evening Post,* Oct. 9, 1917. Dewey's protests had been quoted also in the *New York Tribune,* Oct. 4, 9, 1917; *New York Times,* Oct. 9, 1917.

42. *World,* Oct. 9, 1917. The newspaper clippings quoted here were mostly found in the Cattell Papers.

43. *Herald,* Oct. 10, 1917; *American,* Oct. 10, 1917, quoted Robinson.

44. *Evening Post,* Oct. 9, 1917.

45. *New York Times,* Oct. 9, 1917.

46. *Spectator,* Oct. 12, 1917, 4. Also see letter Cattell to John Coulter of the AAUP Committee on Academic Freedom in Wartime, Mar. 30, 1918, Cattell Papers, still insisting that the underlying motive for his dismissal was his cause of "university reform."

47. See Metzger, *Academic Freedom,* 224–25.

48. Unsigned twelve-page manuscript in file, probably the report of the Committee of Nine, summarized in *Spectator,* Oct. 13, 1917. Even if the last sentence contained a typo, it must have been proofread.

49. One of the signers was John Erskine, Butler's friend and, with Carl Van Doren, W. P. Trent, and Stuart Pratt Sherman, an editor of *The Cambridge History of American Literature* (New York: Cambridge UP, 1917).

50. *Spectator,* quoted Oct. 12, 1917, 1. "Sane, dignified and gentlemanly" views versus "cheap pacifism" was the contrast offered by C. P. Ivins, vice president of the senior class, Columbia, 1917. It was reported on October 11 that Matthew Josephson, Kenneth Burke, and Percival Winner were supporting academic freedom as long as it was exercised in a legal manner. A statement in support of Cattell and Dana was circulated denouncing the public meeting, signed by L. M. Hacker and Josephson (October 16). On October 16, 17, and 18, the *Spectator* ran antisemitic stories on Leon Samson's activities: He was linked to outside agitators Henry Factor (NYU), Isidore Schneider (CCNY), and Israel Common (Columbia 1917) and mocked by "The Delilah Club." Meanwhile, also according to the *Spectator,* Samson had been expelled and could not get into another university or obtain a certificate to study law. On October 25 the Alumni Association was quoted: They supported the action of the Trustees; "unbridled license" was not part of free speech; the university was neither forum nor market place but a site for the training of scholars, not soap-box orators. *Spectator* coverage ended October 27, with a mention that Morris Hillquit denounced Dana's firing. Letters in the Cattell Papers from Henry Mussey (who resigned and later became editor of the *Nation*) and Thomas Reed Powell are moving examples of the moral conflicts generated by the dispute.

51. Quoted in Gruber, *Mars and Minerva,* 206. Compare with David Hume, sardonically commenting on the transparent ruse of the house of peers and Charles I in amending the petition of right sent up by the House of Commons, 1628. The peers had proposed this clause: "We humbly present this petition to your majesty, not only with a care of preserving our own liberties, but with due regard to leave entire that *sovereign power,* with which your majesty is intrusted for the protection, safety, and happiness of your people." Hume sneered, "Less penetration than was possessed by the leaders of the house of commons, could easily discover how captious this clause was, and how much it was calculated to elude the whole force of the petition." See Hume, *History of England* 6:188–89 (hereafter cited as *HE*).

52. This point has been missing from published commentaries on the Columbia incident of 1917. See, for instance, Russell J. Reising, *The Unusable Past: Theory and the Study of American Literature* (London: Methuen, 1986), 43. Commenting on Gruber's standard account, Reising states,

"Gruber is careful to avoid crude assertions of conscious complicity or hypocrisy, and one of the major strengths of her book is its cautious, though bold, delineation of an academy won to interests antithetical to its declared and sincerely held values." Throughout, Reising sees American Studies as a propagandistic discipline devoted to American exceptionalism and imperialism (39–40), a view with which I sharply disagree. I am arguing that the field is an outpost of humanism, generally Tory and antibourgeois.

53. Abner Woodruff, "A Letter to the Professor," *One Big Union Monthly*, Aug. 19, 1919. Also, Steven J. Ross, "Struggles for the Screen: Workers, Radicals, and the Political Uses of Silent Film," *American History Review* 96 (Apr. 1991): 333–67; and *Working-Class Hollywood: Silent Film and the Shaping of Class in America* (Princeton: Princeton UP, 1998). Ross argues that early working-class film challenged the dominant images of the labor movement that had characterized the rank and file as mobbish, its leaders demagogic, and its efforts doomed to failure.

Compare with Senate Document No. 217, 74th Congress, p. 33, citing the 1933 baccalaureate speech of Mordecai Johnson, president of Howard University, in its investigation of "Alleged Communistic Activities at Howard University, May 12, 1936." Johnson (a Baptist) wrote: "We must not allow the words 'communism' and 'socialism' to blind our eyes to the realization that on Russian soil today—it makes no difference what mistakes are being made or crimes are being committed—there is a movement for the first time in the history of the world to make available the natural resources for the life of the common man. I am in hearty sympathy with those who want to preserve our American system, but the preservation of our system is not the primary urgency. The primary urgency of life is to work out some way to use the scientific and technical resources of life for the emancipation of the people (33)." Johnson did not separate the Head and Heart. See "Communism a New Religion Says H. U. Prexy," *The Afro-American*, June 10, 1933. It was reported that intellectuals should use their powers of observation and ability to think systematically, spotting blind alleys and enthusiasms that mislead the people; their plans and visions sprang from the pure, inspired, knowledgeable Christian heart. These materials are in the Ralph J. Bunche Papers.

54. New York State Legislature, Joint Committee Investigating Seditious Activities, *Revolutionary Radicalism: Its History, Purpose and Tactics with an Exposition and Discussion of the Steps Being Taken and Required to Curb It, Being the Report of the Joint Legislative Committee Investigating Seditious Activities Filed April 24, 1920 in the Senate of the State of New York* (Albany: J. B. Lyon, 1920), 3306–7.

55. Villard believed that the peace conference would degenerate into a contest for spoils without the presence of Wilson; "Wilson and the World," *Nation*, Feb. 15, 1919, 252. In the issue of February 22, "The Net Result" (on the Peace Conference) argued that leaders at the conference were failing to perceive the importance of class conflict as national alignments gave way to those of class (268).

56. "Danger Ahead," ibid., Feb. 8, 1919, 186–87. (In the same issue, Nathaniel Hawthorne was lauded as a genius whose writing, formerly held to be parochial, was now to be judged in competition with universal art.) According to revolutionary socialists, tolerance is repressive when it masks social impotence; expression is "free" but may not be translated into measures for structural change beyond social democratic reformism.

57. "The Future of the World," ibid., Mar. 22, 1919, 298.

58. Norman Foerster, "Reconstructing the Ph.D. in English," ibid., May 10, 1919, 747–50. See also Richard M. Gummere, "The Modern World and the Latin Classroom," ibid., Jan. 4, 1919, 13–14; Grant Showerman, "Measuring the Immeasurable," ibid., July 5, 1919, 12–13. Study of the classics would stave off the catastrophic scientific vogue for quantitative results. Compare with Norman Foerster et al., *Literary Scholarship: Its Aims and Methods* (Chapel Hill: U of North Carolina

P, 1941). The contributors were reforming the teaching of literature, seeking "to sort, order, weigh, apply—what the scholarship of the nineteenth century and the early twentieth so devotedly accumulated" (29–30); they will "expose and counteract the unbounded appetite for material power, combined with the self-deception of flimsy ideologies from eighteenth-century sentimentalism to twentieth-century totalitarianism" (31).

59. See *Nation*, Jan. 25, 1919, 136. Jews are perennial radicals, no matter how wealthy; ibid., Apr. 19, 664–65; Apr. 26, 646–47; May 3, 668, 675, 678.

60. See the James Graham Phelps Stokes Papers. The Second International supported Wilsonian diplomacy; the Third did not support Wilson's "alternative to Bolshevism" (the League of Nations, the International Labour Organization) until 1933, when Stalin felt himself menaced by both Germany and Japan. See Kathryn W. Davis, *The Soviet Union and the League of Nations 1919–1933* (Geneva: Geneva Research Center, 1934), 3–23; also see Arno J. Mayer, *Wilson vs. Lenin: Political Origins of the New Diplomacy 1917–1918* (Cleveland: Meridian Books, 1964), 368–93. Mayer saw both leaders as unrealistic: "Lenin's immediate aim was destructive: class war in preparation for the transitional dictatorship of the proletariat. However, his ultimate objective of the classless society in a warless world had the same hopeful and utopian quality as Wilson's search for a peaceful community of sovereign democratic nations of unequal power" (393).

61. See the hostile review of Albert Mordell, *The Erotic Motive in Literature*, *Nation*, July 19, 1919, 94. Freud's only God is Venus who "rages like a fire" "defaming and defacing" noblest names like Galahad and Lancelot. See also Walter A. Dyer, "The New Order at Juniper Hill," July 26, 1919, 104–6. The "Anglo-Saxon race" is free from ideas of "class revolution" (106); Fabian Socialism (bearing "inherent common sense") is contrasted to the Greenwich Village "red radical[s]" with their "Russo-Semitic" "lineage" (104). The Right (exemplified by a banker, an economist, and an editor) is not characterized racially. The same *Nation* issue notes that British conservatives in a "National Unity Movement" will remove false teachings from the working class (131).

62. "Mental Reconstruction," a review of five recent books, ibid., May 31, 1919, 871–73.

63. See Oswald Garrison Villard, "The Truth about the Peace Conference," ibid., Apr. 26, 1919, 646–47. See also Feb. 15, 252; Feb. 22, 268; May 10, 721, 728–30; May 17, 826; July 5, 30. Also, "The Failure of Moral Leadership," July 5, 4 (the hypnotic Wilson to whom even the *Nation* had succumbed; the need for a spiritual revival); May 5, 14–16; Lincoln Colcord, "Why Wilson Was Defeated at Paris," May 17, 782–84. Colcord explained that the secret treaties of the Allies had been published by Trotsky in November 1917; Wilson had them but would not act. "With the ineluctable knowledge of their existence and terms, he outlined, a month later, his famous Fourteen Points. . . . It is only fair to assume that he himself was deluded; at all times he promised himself that he would rectify the error when the Peace Conference came" (783). The preceding article, "Madness at Versailles," was harsher: "His rhetorical phrases, torn and faded tinsel of thought which men now doubt if he himself ever really believed, will never again fall with hypnotic charm upon the ears of eager multitudes. The camouflage of ethical precept and political philosophizing which for long has blinded the eyes of all but the most observing has been stripped away, and the peoples of the world see revealed, not a friend faithful to the last, but an arrogant autocrat and a compromising politician." With the sane liberal center abandoned, there are two hostile camps: radicals and reactionaries. Wilson is with "the staunch supporters of power and privilege, the controllers of great wealth and dictators of social favor, the voluble champions of the established order against every form of revolution, the preachers of hate and prejudice, and the timid and dependent whose souls are not their own" (779). See also July 19, 68.

64. Although Polish pogroms were vigorously protested, antisemitism in the *Nation* was implicit in its characterizations of finance capital and foreign radicalism. See especially W. G. Roylance, "Americanism in North Dakota," July 12, 1919, 37–39, a defense of the populists and

their Anglo-Saxon antecedents, the Lollards. "The League in North Dakota represents the organized revolt of the farmers, who make up the majority of the population, against long-continued exploitation of financial Shylocks and marketing profiteers." The populists are not "European [dishonest] radicals" but examples of "honest American progressive democracy." Failure will only come from outside the system (autocratic forces that hate democracy). In a *Nation* review of a pamphlet, *Shylock Not a Jew*, by Maurice Packard and Adelaide Marshall, June 28, 1919, 1018, the reviewer dismissed "the little brochure" as unilluminating and belaboring the obvious.

65. See the *Nation* reprint of a pamphlet by the English anti-imperialist, J. A. Hobson, "The New Holy Alliance," Apr. 19, 1919, 626–28: Wilson "willingly poured his idealism into the Smuts plan"; a "conspiracy of autocrats" will defeat true internationalism and control the world. Also, Lincoln Colcord, "A Receivership for Civilization," ibid., June 28, 1009–10: The press has been hiding this story—American boys will be giving their lives to protect bond investors in Europe. Compare with May 24, 820: U.S. soldiers will die to protect loans to China; Anglo-American imperialism will rule the world; progressives in the Republican Party are splitting from the Old Guard on this. Also, July 5, editorial: Elihu Root, the servant of finance capital is swaying Republican opinion away from the progressive bloc to join Wilson and the Democrats, all of whom are in their pockets. Also, "Possibly other inner circles" of finance capital for the benefit of Wall Street are mentioned in connection with the treaty, Aug. 2, 140–41. The antisemitism of Hobson's influential study of imperialism (1905) has been noted by Lewis Feuer in *Imperialism and the Anti-Imperialist Mind* (Buffalo: Prometheus Books, 1986).

66. *Nation*, Apr. 15, 1919, 485, "the whirlwind approaches across Europe"; Villard, "Germany Today: Food or Chaos," Mar. 29, 464–65.

67. Ibid., Feb. 15, 1919, 246–47; Mar. 29, 464–66, 496–97; Apr. 12, 542–49; Apr. 19, 601–3; Apr. 26, 650–52; "Reason in Revolution," June 14, 932. If we open lawful channels for change, labor can realize its demands. May 10, 726, on "May Day Rioting": We should stick to "the Anglo-Saxon method [the moderate way] of settling our difficulties by peaceful means and no others"; the "Anglo-Saxon way of altering social and political institutions by free debate and discussion" contrasted to "Prussian intolerance," June 7, 899; William MacDonald, "North Dakota's Experiment," Mar. 22, 420–22; Allen McCurdy, "Wanted—A Ballot Box," July 5, 9–10; "The Technique of Revolution," Mar. 22, 417; also see Mar. 15, 396; Mar. 29, 460, 467–68; May 5, 10-11; May 10, 738–39; May 17, 839–40; May 31, 871–72; June 7, 899; June 14, 955–56; July 5, 23; July 12, 43.

68. "While They Dance the Tango," ibid., Mar. 22, 1919, 452: Spartacism is unchecked; we need an economic dictator (also 459). Labor and capital must sit down and transform industry. John Kenneth Turner, "A Pledge to the World," July 5, 14–16: Lord Robert Cecil (like the model subscriber to the *Nation?*) had departed from the feudal and reactionary ways of his Vere de Vere type ancestors, standing for peace and cooperation with labor, in control of all the impulses that made for irresponsible demagoguery of the past. Also see "Poisoning the Wells," Mar. 8; Mar. 29, 485–86; Apr. 12, 553–54; Apr. 19, 595, 626–28; May 3, 692, 699; May 17, 806–8; June 28, 1000; July 26, 97.

69. Ibid., Feb. 8, 1919, 188–90; Mar. 22, 413; Apr. 5, 522–25; May 10, 792.

70. See the review of M. P. Follet, *The New State*, ibid., Jan. 18, 1919, 97: The neighborhood group would be the embodiment of the "group state" that replaced the "crowd state." Oliver Wendell Holmes, Jr., and Louis Brandeis represented the change from a state that protected individualistic privilege to a conception of law as the "outcome of community life and bound to its service." Ibid., Mar. 1, 1919, 314–15; Mar. 29, 459, 463, 478–79; Richard Roberts, "England in Revolution," May 17, 784–85; "The League of Nations in Danger" (sermon by Charles Gore, Bishop of Oxford, who fears education and science as promoters of competition, not Christian corporatism), May 17, 806–8; May 31, 866–67; "The Problem of the State," Aug. 2, 137.

71. Ibid., June 7, 1919, 931–44; Lincoln Colcord, "The Carving of Russia," June 14, 1919, 940–41, for the distinction between "industrial bankers" versus "financial bankers." The "international bankers" stand in the background of the negotiations in Paris, arranging the destinies of men." Commercial bankers are "outside" this scenario. Unlike the "financial" bankers, the commercial ones (for example, National City Bank connected to Standard Oil, American International Corporation, and the banking-engineering firm of Stone and Weber) are close to production, wisely making concessions to labor. The former (J. P. Morgan) see the state as existing to clamp down on debtors. July 12, 28: The Non-Partisans are not Socialists; they want to buy cheap and sell dear; alien speculators and alien control of markets and terminals are to be eliminated. In the same *Nation* issue, a review entitled "Immanent Idealism" (a synthesis of the old idealism and pragmatism) recommends its formless self as best counter to emancipated, atheistic, international democracy (23). See also Feb. 15, 243; Mar. 22, 452; Apr. 12, 536.

72. Ibid., Feb. 8, 1919, 217, 241; Special Correspondent, "The Shop Stewards Movement," Feb. 22, 277–79 (favorable toward worker's control); Mar. 22, 451; Mar. 29, 477–78; May 3, 680; May 10, 722.

73. A. A. Berle, Jr., "The Betrayal at Paris," ibid., Aug. 19, 1919, 170. Compare with ibid., 160, "An Appeal to America Not Yet Written by Woodrow Wilson," in which the ideal leader is not a friend of one class over another but helps classes to understand each other, then see their common interest and common justice.

74. Internal to "the race," not the individual psyche.

75. Unsigned review, *Nation*, Feb. 8, 1919, 202, possibly Carl Van Doren.

76. Rabbi Lee J. Levinger, *Anti-Semitism in the United States: Its History and Causes* (New York: Bloch, 1925), 29, 33–34, 39–44, 51, 71, 78, 94–95, 110, 115.

77. A clipping preserved by Carey McWilliams clarifies individuality as an attribute of persons, not groups. Woodruff Randolph's editorial in the *Typographical Journal*, Sept. 4, 1937, protested recent right-wing offensives; the headline read "Incorporate Unions? Step Toward Fascism, Says 'Typo' Secretary." Randolph contrasted the business corporation "partly a person and partly a citizen, yet it has not the inalienable rights of a natural person" with "a labor organization [that] is organized to do in numbers what each may do individually under his inalienable rights." Carey McWilliams Papers.

78. See James W. Ceaser, *The Reproduction of America: The Symbol of America in Modern Thought* (New Haven: Yale UP, 1997), chap. 2. Ceaser differentiates among the Founders, arguing that Jefferson's political rationalism existed in tension with received ideas on race; the overall effect was to replace political science with natural history as the guide to sound government. In my view, Condorcet—the most comprehensively democratic philosophe, the champion of internationalism, popular sovereignty, public education, feminism, and progress, and enemy to separation of powers and checks and balances (as ploys of elites to subvert democratic will)—was annexed to the conservative Enlightenment to give liberal credibility to the New Deal elevation of the executive branch of government over the legislative branch. See J. Salwyn Schapiro, *Condorcet and the Rise of Liberalism* (1934; reprint, New York: Octagon, 1978), 276–77: "Security for both capital and labor is essential if freedom of enterprise is to survive. . . . Responsibility in government can be more efficiently maintained by giving more authority to the executive, who would wield power, not as an irresponsible dictator, but as a democratically chosen official responsible to a legislature whose essential function would be to act as the nation's monitor. Progress has been the peculiar heritage of liberalism to which it must be ever faithful in order to survive." Condorcet joins Paine and Jefferson as fodder for the moderate men of the vital center.

79. I am using 1916 as a milestone in the promotion of ethnopluralism because of the Randolph Bourne article "Trans-National America" (first published in the *Atlantic Monthly*) and a

now-forgotten book by the head psychologist of the Boston Normal School, J. Mace Andress, *Johann Gottfried Herder as an Educator* (New York: G. E. Stechert, 1916). The latter introduced Herder as the precursor to Franz Boas and advocated the new "race pedagogy." There was no ambiguity about the welcome counter-Enlightenment drift of German romanticism in this work. For Andress, the German romantic hero was a rooted cosmopolitan, fighting to throw off (Jewish) materialist domination to liberate the *Volksgeist*. In 1942, Herder was presented as a Kantian, pantheist, cosmopolitan, and quasi-democrat, even a supporter of the French Revolution in James Westfall Thompson, *A History of Historical Writing*, vol. 2 (New York: Macmillan, 1942), 133–38, esp. 137.

Some more recent intellectual historians are rehabilitating Herder along with other figures of the *Hocherklärung*, similarly held to be avatars of the freethinking emancipated individual. In his talk at the Clark Library symposium "Materialist Philosophy, Religious Heresy, and Political Radicalism, 1650–1800" (May 1, 1999), John H. Zammito declared that Herder's philosophy (the demolition of mechanical materialism?) cleared the way for the further development of natural science in Germany. The key figure for these scholars is Spinoza, his pantheism the apex of "vitalist materialism." Margaret C. Jacob, author of *The Radical Enlightenment: Pantheists, Freemasons, and Republicans* (London: Allen and Unwin, 1981), was organizer of the conference, but we are using the term with differing assumptions about scientific method and what, exactly, constitutes the radical Enlightenment.

80. Horace M. Kallen, *Culture and Democracy in the United States: Studies in the Group Psychology of the American Peoples* (New York: Boni and Liveright, 1924), recognized in Alfred E. Zimmern's review in *Nation and Atheneum*, May 17, 1924, 207, as a decisive shift away from Lockean environmentalism toward hereditarian racism, notwithstanding Kallen's benign characterization of "a cooperation of cultural diversities"; Zimmern linked Kallen's pluralism to that of William James. See also Robert Reinhold Ergang, *Herder and the Foundations of German Nationalism*, chap. 3. On the explicit and implicit antisemitism/counter-Enlightenment in Herder's position, see ibid., 92: "The Hebrews 'were a people spoiled in their education, because they never arrived at a maturity of political culture on their own soil, and consequently not to any true sentiment of liberty and honor.'" There it is, the Big Lie of rootless cosmopolitanism. See ibid., 95, for the basis of Herder's anti-French revolt: Rousseau's *Contrat social* is not the force that binds a nation, but nature's laws of blood and soil; Nature, not Culture, creates interdependence. For Herder there is only Nature and all history is natural history; environmentally acquired characteristics are inherited by the corporate entity; this was Kallen's claim as well.

81. See, for instance, Louis Filler, *Randolph Bourne* (Washington, D.C.: American Council on Public Affairs, 1943). The council was a progressive organization producing pamphlets during the war and promoting cooperation between capital and labor. Louis Filler (also a *Nation* writer) explained why Randolph Bourne, espousing an orderly international nationalism for America and explaining war as an outgrowth of (narrowly understood) nationalism, had been wrongly deemed as irrelevant to the youth of the 1930s (i.e., to so-called economic determinists); we need Bourne today. Filler explained,

> Alien cultures, Bourne declared, brought new forces and ideas to American life. [Those bossy, snobbish Anglo-Saxon assimilationists who controlled everything, who] discouraged retention by immigrants of their Old World heritage did not thereby create Americans. They created "hordes of men and women without a spiritual country, cultural outlaws, without taste, without standards but those of the mob." Moreover: "those who came to find liberty achieve only license. They become the flotsam and jetsam of American life, the downward undertow of our civilization with its leering cheapness and

falseness of taste and spiritual outlook, the absence of mind and sincere feeling which we see in our slovenly towns, our vapid moving pictures, our popular novels, and in the vacuous faces of the crowds on the city street. This is the cultural wreckage of our time, and it is from the fringes of the Anglo-Saxon as well as the other stocks that it falls. America has as yet no compelling integrating force. It makes too easily for this detritus of cultures. In our loose, free country, no constraining national purpose, no tenacious folk-tradition and folk-style hold the people to a line." What would be done about such a state of affairs? "America is a unique sociological fabric, and it bespeaks poverty of imagination not to be thrilled at the incalculable potentialities of so novel a union of men. To seek no other good but the weary old nationalism—belligerent, exclusive, inbreeding, the poison of which we are witnessing now in Europe—is to make patriotism a hollow sham, and to declare, that, in spite of our boastings, America must ever be a follower and not a leader of nations." Do not, therefore, denigrate any culture that has driven stakes into the American soil: do not, certainly, term it un-American: "There is no distinctive American culture." Do not, above all, set up American material achievement as a token of American fulfillment: "If the American note is bigness, action, the objective as contrasted with the reflective life, where is the epic expression of this spirit?" We were patently inhibited from presenting in impressive artistic form the energy with which we were filled. The reason was that we had not yet accepted the cosmopolitanism with which we had been endowed. Americans of culture could be made of the Germans in Wisconsin, the Scandinavians in Minnesota, and the Irish and Italians of New York. "In a world which has dreamed of internationalism, we find that we have all unawares been building up the first international nation." (76–78) . . . "[Bourne's] ideas, his experiences, the warp and woof of his personality were not necessary to a generation that believed it had discovered impersonal economic laws that (properly applied) would at last bring about a settlement of human affairs." (133)

82. Compare with David Leverenz on the "Ugly Narcissus," Ahab: "He certainly is not afflicted with contradictory or discontinuous role-expectations. But he does start to experience a desire for [sadomasochistic] fusion, previously blocked by his obsession." In *Manhood and the American Renaissance* (Ithaca, N.Y.: Cornell UP, 1989), 294.

83. Friedrich Meinecke, *The German Catastrophe*, trans. Sidney Fay (Boston: Beacon Press, 1950), 36–38. Though he is writing after World War II, Meinecke's analysis is typical of other organic conservatives. Similar identifications of the class base of fascism were made by Harold Lasswell before the war and CIA-affiliated social scientists during the 1940s and 1950s.

84. Martin Dies, "Un-American Activities and Propaganda," *House Reports, Misc.* 1939, 10–11. By 1939, Stalinists had given Dies lots of ammunition to support the accusation of fomenting class hatred. However, even if Rosa Luxemburg had been at the helm, Dies would not have placed a dispassionate materialist analysis in the American tradition.

85. James Bryant Conant, "Education for a Classless Society: The Jeffersonian Tradition," in *Education for Democracy: The Debate over the Report of the President's Commission on Higher Education*, ed. Gail Kennedy (Boston: D. C. Heath, 1952), 46, 45; originally published in *Atlantic Monthly*, May 1940, and included in one of the Heath series, "Problems in American Civilization," gen. ed. Allan Nevins. Compare it with the presidential address of Dr. George S. Counts, American Federation of Teachers Convention, Aug. 19–22, 1940: Rejecting messianic ideas that would end exploitation, democratic education was "designed to discipline the young, through knowledge and understanding, in the ways of democracy, in the temperate and responsible use of political processes, in the subordination of individual to social welfare, in the sacrifice of the present to the long-time interests of individual and society. It is an education designed to prepare the young to

live by, to labor for, and, if need be, to die for the democratic faith." Jefferson and Lincoln were cited as exemplars.

In 1945, Ann Westerfield, a student in the Harvard Graduate School of Education working under the direction of Howard E. Wilson, explained the need to revise the social studies curriculum:

I am desirous of finding out how the courses which include the study of the Negro contribute to the improvement of intergroup relations. A program of instruction which includes the study of intergroup relations should fulfill these criteria. 1. It should aim to develop mutual understanding among the children and youth of the various culture groups as a basis for their cooperation. 2. It should foster an appreciation of the part each has played and can continue to play in making America. 3. It should seek to awaken a sense of comman [*sic*] adventure among Americans of many antecedents to promote American unity through loyalty to American ideals. . . . Prejudice, I feel, is distinctly a problem for education. In most cases it depends on historical misconceptions or social misunderstandings. People should be brought to analyze their prejudice under the light of historical fact and investigate scientifically the background of these irrationalities. In the future, the foundation of the social community must be cooperation. It is evident to men in this country and all over the world that any attempt at prolonged peace will depend on the renunciation of racial and social prejudice by all the people in the world. Since our country has led the way toward the realization of democratic ideals it is imperative that our conduct be a good example for all.

These materials found in the Bunche Papers, box 1, folder 23. Before the war, Bunche had been appalled by such formulations, for he viewed "prejudice" as built into the economic system that pitted black and white workers against each other; bigotry could not be erased without structural transformation responding to pressure from an educated and democratically controlled independent labor movement.

86. Compare to cultural historian David Hollinger, *Science, Jews, and Secular Culture* (Princeton: Princeton UP, 1996). The Jews who "quietly entered" university faculties since WWII have joined Protestants in weakening the hold of Christian ideas, manipulating science as their weapon, and producing the nuclear bomb. Post-1960s developments have challenged their hegemony. Though he says he is not an essentialist, cultural formations "have a life of their own." He joins other corporatists in the belief that individuation entails freedom from the repressive and depressing rule of law originating with the Mosaic code.

87. See Carlos E. Sluzki and Donald C. Ransom, eds., *Double Bind: The Foundation of the Communicational Approach to the Family* (New York: Grune and Stratton, 1976), 11.

88. The preface by Goodwin Watson reviewed the history of the committee in the passive voice and with vagueness as to the politics of their group: "Concern with American morale in the face of a developing world crisis was evidenced at the meeting of the s.p.s.s.i. in September 1940. At that time a committee on Morale was appointed, under the chairmanship of Professor Gardner Murphy. During the year 1940–41 interest in morale grew, and at the 1941 meetings several programs of the American Psychological Association and of the American Association for Applied Psychology were devoted to discussions of morale. In accord with its purpose to communicate psychological findings on public questions, the s.p.s.s.i. decided in September 1941, to postpone some other yearbooks, and to concentrate immediate effort on a volume dealing with civilian morale. Professor Goodwin Watson of Teacher's College Columbia University was appointed editor, and the book was planned in coordination with the president of the s.p.s.s.i., Professor Kurt

Lewin, University of Iowa, and the Society's secretary, Professor Theodore Newcomb, University of Michigan" (vi).

89. Gregory Bateson, "Morale and National Character," in *Civilian Morale: Second Yearbook of the Society for the Psychological Study of Social Issues*, ed. Goodwin Watson (New York: Reynal and Hitchcock, 1942), 71–91.

90. See Goodwin Watson, "Five Factors in Morale," *Civilian Morale*, 30–47; and Gardner Murphy, "Essentials for a Civilian Morale Program in American Democracy," in ibid., 405–36. According to Murphy, the federal morale service (designed for both temporary and permanent morale) fell through because it evoked the Creel Committee of WWI; Americans would have rejected "active propaganda," preferring "patient discovery by Americans of what they really thought about the world predicament" (see 426–27, 429). See also two recent studies treating the history of social psychology, including the personalities (but not the materials) discussed in this chapter: Ellen Herman, *The Romance of American Psychology: Political Culture in the Age of Experts* (Berkeley: U of California P, 1995); and James H. Capshew, *Psychologists on the March: Science, Practice, and Professional Identity in America, 1929–1969* (Cambridge: Cambridge UP, 1999).

91. See T. W. Adorno, Leo Lowenthal, and Paul W. Massing, "Anti-Semitism and Fascist Propaganda," in *Anti-Semitism, a Social Disease*, ed. Ernst Simmel (New York: International UP, 1946), 125–38; Nathan W. Ackerman and Marie Jahoda, *Anti-Semitism and Emotional Disorder* (New York: Harper, 1950), and the other publications in the series "Studies in Prejudice," edited by Max Horkheimer and Samuel H. Flowerman, sponsored by the American Jewish Committee. See below for the links of their identity politics (usually attributed to Erik Erikson) to the Harvard/Chicago pragmatists Parsons and Lasswell. Compare with Hugh Seton-Watson, "The Age of Fascism and Its Legacy," in *International Fascism*, ed. George L. Mosse (London: Sage, 1979), 365: Hitler was only slightly indebted to the capitalists (who did not extensively fund him or put him in power), and he soon brought them to heel. The irrationalist interpretation of nazism as an outpouring of bad middle-class taste was followed by the Los Angeles County Museum of Art, defending modernism in its reconstruction of the Nazi Degenerate Art exhibition of 1937.

92. Melville owned (and took with him on his 1860 *Meteor* voyage) *The Complete Poetical Works of William Wordsworth Together with a Description of the Country of the Lakes in the North of England, Now First Published with His Works*, ed. Henry Reed (Philadelphia, 1839). Some of his (surviving) annotations were discussed in Thomas F. Heffernan, "Melville and Wordsworth," *American Literature* (Nov. 1977): 338–51. There is no mention of "The Prelude." Hershel Parker states that Duyckinck brought the Appleton proof sheets of the poem to the Berkshires in 1850, and even reviewed it, but that neither he nor Melville read the poem at that time. See Parker, "Melville and the Berkshires," in *American Literature: The New England Heritage*, ed. James Nagel and Richard Astro (New York: Garland, 1981), 68. Parker suggests that Melville's sympathies for the suffering poor were inspired by Wordsworth's cottagers and his own professional or personal traumas of the early 1850s (78–79), while Heffernan noted the importance of "The Excursion" to *Clarel* (351), a work displaying "the similarity of moral and religious concerns."

93. See T. W. Adorno et al., *The Authoritarian Personality* (New York: Harper, 1950), 71, 781–83. The "Genuine Liberal" type is antitotalitarian and free of narcissism; in Adorno's appropriation of Freud, the genuine liberal possesses "that balance between superego, ego, and id which Freud deemed ideal" (71). Adorno's example of the type is a politically naive but frank and independent twenty-one-year-old woman not given to ultra-femininity/feminine wiles. She is the daughter of a hiring manager at a railroad; in the family sexual division of labor, her loving mother represents emotions, her father facts. She is religious ("Perhaps we will all be saved") and reads Plato for Utopian inspiration. When asked how she felt about Negroes and Jews, she was "guided by the idea of the individual," but she wouldn't want to marry a Negro with dark skin or a man with a big nose. However, as a nurse's aide, she did not object to caring for Negro patients.

Adorno quotes her "joke" (what would Freud have said?): "Maybe if the Jews get in power they would liquidate the majority! That's not smart. Because we would fight back." Admirably free of bigotry, she is also free of "repression with regard to her feelings toward her father: 'I want to marry someone just like my father'" (783).

Distinguishing themselves from "manipulative" fascists, the authors, in their concluding sentence, prescribe an antithetical appeal to the emotions: "We need not suppose that appeal to emotion belongs to those who strive in the direction of fascism, while democratic propaganda must limit itself to reason and restraint. If fear and destructiveness are the major emotional sources of fascism, *eros* belongs mainly to democracy" (976). Henry A. Murray's Thematic Apperception Test was used by Adorno's colleagues creating "the F-scale" (the potential for fascist behavior).

94. Gordon W. Allport, *ABC's of Scapegoating*, 9th rev. ed. (1948; New York: Anti-Defamation League of B'nai Brith, 1983).

95. Murphy, *Civilian Morale*, 427.

96. Murray-Allport Worksheet No. 16, "Psychology of Influence (Education Persuasion) Applied to Morale Building in America," 13.

97. David Hume had confidently asserted that unpredictability enters politics when factions are infiltrated by radical religion, by triumphalist hypermoralistic, hyperrationalist puritan extremists; the link between cause and effect would no longer be obvious. See *HE*, vol. 6 (year 1617). The Hume entry in the *Encyclopedia Britannica* (1971) presents Hume as a philosopher whose major contribution was his demonstration that there could be no theory of reality, no verification for our assertions of causality. Faced with the necessity of action, we rely upon our habit of association and (subjective) beliefs. And yet Hume is described as a thinker who saw philosophy as "the inductive science of human nature." He is not described as a moderate or a Tory.

98. Bunche Papers, box 1, folder 19. Kalibala was studying under Pitirim Sorokin; his thesis was entitled "International Peace and the New Colonial Approach."

99. Harvard University, Committee on the Objectives of a General Education in a Free Society, *General Education in a Free Society* (Cambridge, Mass.: Harvard UP, 1945), 12, 30–31, 78, and passim.

100. John T. Bethell, "Harvard and the Arts of War," *Harvard Magazine* (Sept.–Oct. 1995): 32–48. Delivered after Pearl Harbor, President Conant's speech to a formerly antiwar Harvard population ended with an incantation to Tom Paine: "There is very little indication that this will be a short war. The period of waiting may try our souls. But patience, fortitude and courage are required of us all. In every preceding ordeal of battle Harvard has stood in the forefront of those who toiled and sacrificed that liberty might survive. There can be no question that in the days ahead this University and its sons will bring new honors to justify the expectations of ten generations of Harvard men" (36). Harvard's contribution to curriculum reform, funded by Mrs. Bonwit Teller, linked the European humanist tradition (corporatist and hierarchical) with democratic values: "*The Report of a Committee on the Objectives of a General Education in a Free Society* . . . set the agenda for a national reevaluation of educational methods and goals. Much of the report was focused on secondary education; its vision of liberal education at Harvard gave primacy to great works of Western humanism, the study of democratic ideals and values, and familiarity with the basic principles of physical and biological sciences" (47). The seminar on civilian morale is not mentioned, but Allport does appear in a list of war-related research carried on by Harvard professors: "Gordon Allport, professor of psychology, lectured to army units on propaganda and psychological warfare" (38). Nor was it mentioned that Murray was chief of personnel assessment for the OSS (see below).

See also Gordon W. Allport, "Basic Principles in Improving Human Relations," *Cultural Groups and Human Relations: Twelve Lectures before the Conference on Educational Problems of Special Cultural Groups Held at Teachers College, Columbia University August 18 to September 7, 1949*

(New York: Bureau of Publications, Teachers College, 1951): 8–28. Allport acknowledges that some (determinists) believe racism is caused by economic subordination, but he is not convinced. He rejects Freud's death instinct and believes that early childhood is central to development. Children whose needs for love and affiliation are attended will not be excessively aggressive; this leads him to the team approach to management. Allport's bibliography includes books on modern management techniques in industrial relations by Elton Mayo and S. E. Hoslett.

101. In other words, for Allport curiosity is a passion, not an aspect or component of reason. Compare Hobbes, *Leviathan*, ed. Michael Oakeshott (New York: Collier, 1962), 51, quoted below.

102. Richard I. Evans, *Gordon Allport: The Man and His Ideas* (New York: Dutton, 1970), 4–5, 104. The interviews with Allport are undated. Nothing is mentioned about his work on civilian morale, though the role of the academic psychologist in society is briefly explored. The interviewer never asks Allport to reflect on the possible influence of his intense (German) Protestant religious commitments upon his social ideas. That he was indeed religious was stated by a former student speaking from the floor in a memorial symposium (1969) two years after Allport's death.

103. From the [William] Jackson Committee Report, ca. 1952: "Propaganda and Information Activities in the Free World," *Declassified Documents Catalog: 1988* (Reading, Conn.: Research Associates), no. 1163.

104. Hume, *HE* 8:310–11 (year 1680). Hume's footnoted list of Whigs includes Locke (mentioned only here, and absent from the index). According to the *Encyclopedia Britannica* (1971), young Hume, finding legal studies "distasteful," began to "read voraciously in the wider sphere of letters and, through this intensity and the excitement of intellectual discovery, had a nervous breakdown in 1729 from which it took him a few years to recover." His renowned history was published in six volumes from 1754 to 1762, then revised in various editions between 1762 and 1773.

105. See Foerster et al., *Literary Scholarship: Its Aims and Methods*, especially the introduction by Foerster, chapter 3 by René Wellek, and chapter 4 by Austin Warren.

106. T. S. Eliot, *After Strange Gods: A Primer of Modern Heresy* (London: Faber and Faber, 1934), 15, 19, 20, 63 (partly republished as "Tradition and Orthodoxy," *American Review* 2 [Mar. 1934]: 513–28).

107. Austin Warren, in Foerster et al., *Literary Scholarship*, 152–57.

108. T. S. Eliot, "Last Words," *Criterion* (Jan. 1939): 269–75. The first article was Friedrich Gundolf, "Bismarck's *Reflections and Reminiscences* as a Literary Monument," *The Criterion* (1939): 179–94, a tribute to the literariness of Bismarck's autobiography. Compare with ibid. (Oct. 1937): 193–98. Hugh Gordon Porteus surveyed nine new periodicals that would be labeled reactionary and lamented that seven or eight years ago one could discuss the merits of fascism vs. communism without being "blackballed." Now it was no longer possible.

3. THE FATAL LINE: WHO WAS ISABEL? WHAT WAS HIS PROBLEM?

1. Carl Van Doren et al., eds., *The Cambridge History of American Literature;* Weaver, *Herman Melville: Mariner and Mystic.*

2. Fred Lewis Pattee, "Herman Melville," *American Mercury* (Jan. 1927): 33–43.

3. Idem, *Century Readings in American Literature* (1919; reprint, London, 1932), 505.

4. Caroline F. Ware, Introduction, *The Cultural Approach to History* (New York: Columbia UP, 1940), 9. Ware presented the new cultural history as the vanguard of progressive thought; the concept of culture and the tools of anthropology would prevent nostalgia, elite bias, and the old ethnocentrism, while rescuing the profession from the chaos of excessive multiplicity and diversity; nineteenth-century rationalism, science, progress, etc., had been challenged by the rise of the social sciences and the theories of Spengler, Pareto, and Marx. The correct, holistic social theory

held that technology produced change, and "cultural patterns" produced "personality types." The individual had disappeared, subsumed in the concept of "individual-in-society," a nonstop interaction in which those shaped by society [miraculously] reciprocally shaped their society (19). Compare with Berkowitz and McQuaid, *Creating the Welfare State*, 53–54, for a pithy summary of the social psychological theory emanating from progressive scientific management theory. The individual was of interest only insofar as he "interacted with social and work surroundings." The "nature of human consciousness" need not be analyzed.

German university reformer Elfride Heidegger-Petri also emphasized the vanguard innovation of (postmodern) humanism: "The old goal of modern humanism, the education of the free person, is not sufficiently modern. Beyond the singular 'I' exists the 'we'; beyond the needs of individuals exists the needs of the community of the people." Quoted in Victor Farias, *Heidegger and Nazism* (Philadelphia: Temple UP, 1989), 229. See also Ross J. S. Hoffman in the fascist periodical *American Review* 3 (Sept. 1934), reviewing liberal historian Erik Achorn, author of *European Civilization and Politics since 1815:* "such [objectivist textbook-writing historians] . . . cannot appreciate the instinctive popular dread of the threatened destruction of a thousand precious things the roots of which lie embedded in the sanctions of a Christian past. Similarly such writers can never tell the whole truth about Fascism; they can give us only the familiar Marxian formula, missing entirely the appeal to historical tradition, the assertion of spiritual forces, the brave effort for discipline, authority, and justice, the chivalric and idealistic elements, all of which make up the really significant content of Fascism" (519).

5. F. O. Matthiessen, *American Renaissance: Art and Expression in the Age of Emerson and Whitman* (New York: Oxford UP, 1941), 475, xv (quoting Louis Sullivan), 466, 474, 477.

6. R. W. Short, "Melville as Symbolist," in *Interpretations of American Literature*, ed. Charles Feidelson, Jr., and Paul Brodtkorb, Jr. (New York: Oxford UP, 1959), 103; David Leverenz, "Class Conflicts in Teaching *Moby-Dick*," in *Approaches to Teaching Melville's "Moby-Dick,"* ed. Martin Bickman (New York: MLA, 1985), 94, 90; Harrison Hayford, "Dimensions of *Moby-Dick*," 1982 address to honor the second volume of The Library of America. In 1980, Hayford seemed to think that the myth of Narcissus "indeed is 'the key' to the thematic argument of the book: something in man, now as throughout his history, forces him to confront the mystery of life, to pursue that phantom; but it is 'ungraspable,' and the man who goes too far in the effort, who crowds too close upon the mystery, destroys himself. Such is Ahab's pursuit of Moby Dick, and such is his fate." Quoted in Jack Cook, *The Face of Falsehood: The Key to Moby-Dick and Mosses from an Old Manse* (Owego, N.Y.: Jack Cook, 1986), 8. Compare *The Auto-Biography of Goethe. Truth and Poetry: From My Own Life. The Concluding Books*, trans. Rev. A. J. W. Morrison (London: Henry G. Bohn, 1849), 15, rejecting both nihilism and mechanical materialism: "The contest between knowledge and faith was not yet the order of the day, but the two words and the ideas connected with them occasionally came forward, and the true haters of the world maintained that one was as little to be relied on as the other. Accordingly, I took pleasure in declaring in favor of both, though without being able to gain the assent of my friends. In Faith, I said, everything depends on the fact of believing; what is believed is perfectly indifferent. Faith is a profound sense of security for the present and future, and this assurance springs from confidence in an immense, all-powerful, and inscrutable Being. The firmness of this confidence is the one grand point; but what we think of this Being depends on our other faculties, or even on circumstances, and is wholly indifferent. Faith is a holy vessel into which every one stands ready to pour his feelings, his understanding, his imagination as perfectly as he can. With Knowledge it is exactly the opposite. There the point is not whether we know, but what we know, how much we know, and how well we know it. Hence it comes that men may dispute about knowledge because it can be corrected, widened, and contracted. Knowledge begins with the particular, is endless and formless, can never be all comprehended, or at least but dreamily, and thus remains exactly the opposite of Faith."

Is *Moby-Dick* about the fatal search for (unknowable) truth? The younger Hayford was clearly not an irrationalist. See Hayford to Jay Leyda, Apr. 5, 1952: Referring to F. Barron Freeman's *Melville's Billy Budd* (Cambridge: Harvard UP, 1948), Hayford wrote, "I have been worrying all winter off and on about a word in Melville's cancelled postscript to BBudd—the one that goes 'Here ends a story not unwarranted by what sometimes happens in this incomprehensible world of ours. . . .' The word I'm worried about is 'incomprehensible'—which Weaver read as 'incongruous' and Freeman changed to 'incomprehensible,' which you keep in the Portable. Freeman gives a facsimile of that page, and in the facsimile, which I've looked at all winter, I can't see it that way, unless the 'ible' is simply left off, which I guess is not impossible. On the other hand, do you think it worth while, perhaps, to try to make it out over again? I would be interested in having it challenged—because it seems to me a very important word, coming from HM in such a place at such a time in his life. *Did* he label the world 'incomprehensible'? . . . [Regarding Lawrance Thompson, *Melville's Quarrel with God* (Princeton: Princeton UP, 1952), claiming that Melville was a masked heretic] I think it has very good things about it, but is off on its central thesis, by pushing it too hard and trying to make it omnipotent. The more I think about HM and consider what others make of him, the more it seems to me that you just can't make out that he had a single settled and consistent attitude. I think questing, trying, mood, ambivalence, around a certain core of problem, is the best we can state the situation." Hayford files.

7. Hershel Parker, *Herman Melville*, 516.

8. Robert S. Lynd, *Knowledge for What? The Place of Social Science in American Culture* (Princeton: Princeton UP, 1939), 177. See also George Levine, "The Ambiguous Ethics of Self-Annihilation," paper presented April 26, 1997, UCLA symposium, "The Values of Science." Presenting himself as a radical, Levine argued that Victorian scientists (e.g., Darwin) had merely substituted submission to Nature for the old submission to religious authority; the fantasy of liberty gave power to their bogus heroic efforts; the servants who enabled their labors in science were absent from their narratives; (referring to Gross and Levitt, authors of *Higher Superstition*) their moralistic rhetoric is full of vehemence and rage. Similar arguments were offered by the other participants: "all knowledge is local," there is no such thing as "value-free inquiry" or "absolute objectivity" in the academy or anywhere else, etc.

9. William E. Cain, *The Crisis in Criticism: Theory, Literature, and Reform in English Studies* (Baltimore: Johns Hopkins UP, 1984), 261–62; Gerald Graff and William E. Cain, "Peace Plan for the Canon Wars," *Nation*, Mar. 6, 1989; Paul Lauter, "Melville Climbs the Canon," *American Literature* (Mar. 1994): 1–24.

10. For examples of the Franklin faction, see H. Bruce Franklin, *The Victim as Criminal and Artist;* Joyce Sparer Adler, *War in Melville's Imagination* (New York: New York UP, 1981); and Carolyn L. Karcher, "Herman Melville 1819–1891," in *The Heath Anthology of American Literature*, vol. 1, ed. Paul Lauter (Lexington, Mass.: Heath, 1990).

11. Willard Thorp, ed., *Representative Selections of Herman Melville* (New York: American Book Co., 1938); Henry A. Murray, unpublished MSS, see below; Alfred Kazin letter to the author, Aug. 8, 1987; George M. Fredrickson, *The Inner Civil War: Northern Intellectuals and the Crisis of the Union* (New York: Harper & Row, 1965); Michael P. Rogin, *Subversive Genealogy: The Politics and Art of Herman Melville* (New York: Knopf, 1983); Leon Howard, *Herman Melville* (Berkeley: U of California P, 1951); Hershel Parker, "Herman Melville and Politics: A Scrutiny of the Political Milieux of Herman Melville's Life and Works" (Ph.D. diss., Northwestern Univ., 1963); Eleanor Melville Metcalf, ed., *Journal of a Visit to London and the Continent by Herman Melville, 1849–1850* (Cambridge: Harvard UP, 1948); Henry A. Murray, "'In Nomine Diaboli,'" *New England Quarterly* 24 (Dec. 1951): 435–52; Paul Metcalf, ed., *Enter Isabel: The Herman Melville Correspondence of Clare Spark and Paul Metcalf* (Albuquerque: U of New Mexico P, 1991).

12. Melville family members mentioned in this chapter are father Allan Melvill (1782–1832), the "e" added after his death; mother Maria G. Melville (1791–1872); uncle Thomas Melvill, Jr. (1776–1845); sisters Helen (1817–1887) and Augusta (1821–1876); brothers Gansevoort (1815–1846) and Allan (1823–1872); wife Elizabeth (1822–1906); sons Malcolm (1849–1867) and Stanwix (1851–1886); brother-in-law John C. Hoadley (1818–1886, married to sister Catherine); and cousin Kate Lansing (1838–1918). Unless specified, these excerpts are from the 1983 additions to the Gansevoort-Lansing Collection (GL-A) at New York Public Library.

13. This scenario is most pronounced in Ann Douglas, *The Feminization of American Culture* (New York: Knopf, 1977).

14. Ralph Henry Gabriel wrote in *The Course of American Democratic Thought*, "Perhaps Melville . . . enjoyed his perch aloft because of the escape it gave him from a forecastle intimacy with the lowest social stratum of the nineteenth century sea. The whalers were, for the most part, men coarse of body and of mind, drained from the waterfronts of the world" (68). This sentiment was deleted in the revised edition of 1956; Gabriel read Melville as a pessimist wisely alienated from naively optimistic democratic contemporaries. Compare with Kenneth S. Lynn, "Lemuel Shaw and Herman Melville," *Constitutional Commentary* 5 (1988): 417; taking *Redburn* to be an accurate account of his first voyage, Lynn writes: "Not only were most of the young sailor's shipmates shockingly coarse, but one of them, a squint-eyed desperado named Robert Jackson, conceived a monomaniacal hatred for him. If the novel can be believed, the psychologically unbalanced Jackson was suffering as well from a fatal physical disease, and hated Melville out of envy for his health and handsomeness."

15. For some detailed accounts of Allan's deceptive business practices in the late 1820s, see Parker, *Herman Melville* (1996); and T. Walter Herbert, Jr., *"Moby-Dick" and Calvinism: A World Dismantled* (New Brunswick, N.J.: Rutgers UP, 1977). See Jay Leyda, *The Melville Log: A Documentary Life of Herman Melville* (New York: Harcourt Brace, 1951), 51–52 (hereafter *Log*), for family letters with the prognosis that even if he survived his fever, Allan would remain "a Maniac."

16. See Amy Puett, "Melville's Wife: A Study of Elizabeth Shaw Melville" (Ph.D. diss., Northwestern University, 1970), 88–91. Puett speculated that the public revelation of a natural child in *Pierre* prompted Melville's mother to pressure him to give up writing, since he was disclosing family secrets (91). The date of what I will call "the Isabel letter" is uncertain. What exactly the letter indicates is controversial; its significance for Melville studies is extensively discussed in chapter 9.

17. I have used quotation marks because no literary critic in the Melville Revival adhered to Freudian method, which is (or should be), finally, no less than a painstakingly detailed reconstruction of all possible sources of emotional conflict. The "Freudian" Melvilleans were mostly Jungian bohemians and often misogynists. By the time Arvin wrote his book, the neo-Freudian Erich Fromm had added class considerations to the analysis of neurotic symptoms. Of course, Melville himself had described an adolescent homoerotic relationship with an upper-class cousin in *Pierre*, along with hints in other texts.

18. Newton Arvin, *Herman Melville* (New York: William Sloan, 1950), 18, 28–30, 298.

19. Newspaper account quoted in *Gansevoort Melville's 1846 London Journal and Letters from England, 1845*, ed. Hershel Parker (New York: New York Public Library, 1966), 9. Parker's detailed and somewhat ambivalent accounts of Gansevoort's career (in his dissertation, the *Journal*, and the biography) suggest that Ahab shared Gansevoort's demagoguery and sharp practice regarding the Van Buren letter. Whereas I, while not denying the example of Gansevoort, emphasize the ambiguities in American exceptionalism and read *Moby-Dick* as referring to the age of revolution, as well as posing the problem of ethics in a universe ruled either by an indifferent deity or none at all.

20. For the sensitivity of diplomatic maneuvers between England and America, see David M. Pletcher, *The Diplomacy of Annexation: Texas, Oregon and the Mexican War* (Columbia: U of Missouri P, 1973).

21. See *Log* entry, May 4, 1846, MacNeice to James Buchanan. Leyda had access to, but did not use, a then-unpublished source that could have cast doubt on this judgment. After weeks of alarming symptoms, Gansevoort visited Mr. Koecker, a dentist. In the journal entry of March 25 he wrote that a molar had been extracted and a dead tooth found. It was "next in front of the left eye tooth, *which tho' presenting no appearance of decay has been dead five or six years.* He strenuously advises on the score of general health that my mouth should be rid of all unsound teeth & fitted out with masticators" (Parker, *Gansevoort's London Journal,* 56–57; emphasis added). Gansevoort could have died from complications following abscess in this tooth, positioned to allow an infection to travel to the brain. This is my speculation after consulting with Dr. Alvin Rosenblum. (Compare with Leon Howard's suggestion of "cerebral anemia." Also, the sentence describing the dead tooth might illuminate Melville's preoccupation with "the charnel house within," his image of benign nature masking inner decay.)

22. See *Log,* 208–9. The letter was fully quoted in Weaver, *Mariner and Mystic.*

23. Olson's notes from conversations with Raymond Weaver, Melville's first modern biographer, state that Eleanor Metcalf, Melville's granddaughter, withheld a document showing that a member of the family had been institutionalized for insanity. Alleged attempts to put Melville away and Olson's jottings are fully described below. The significant timing of Melville's personal losses are recognized by all his biographers.

24. Harrison Hayford and Merrell R. Davis, in "Herman Melville as Office-Seeker," *Modern Language Quarterly* 10 (June and Sept. 1949): 168–83 and 377–88, explained Melville's conflict as the gap between his artistic vision and the imperatives of a literary marketplace controlled by conservatives.

25. See Daniel Walker Howe, *The Political Culture of the American Whigs* (Chicago: U of Chicago P, 1979), chap. 7. Howe discusses rationalist adaptations of Calvinism in response to the challenge of Unitarianism. New School Calvinists argued that man was now capable of reshaping himself and society alike.

26. Maria's admonition does not differ from the liberal Protestant sentiments expressed in a surviving fragment by her late husband: "The principle & spirit of eternal truth & justice implanted in the breast of every human being by our divine creator, may every human being *obey* its dictates, & then we shall have Heaven on earth—said to be given at Pekin on the anniversary of Confucius" (GL-A). Maria's letter (GL-A) has been partially excerpted in the biographies of Parker and Robertson-Lorant, but with the imputation that self-control refers to sexuality alone, not to all forms of selfishness. The connection to the Second Great Awakening, to New School Calvinism, and their associated reform movements is not seen; rather Maria's Calvinist advice alludes to original sin.

My inclusion of labor reform in the mix of antebellum social movements will startle some scholars (especially those who see "white supremacy" as the engine of American history), who claim that the labor movement and abolitionism were based in distinct and opposing social classes; but see the historiographical essay in Philip S. Foner and Herbert Shapiro, eds., *Northern Labor and Antislavery: A Documentary History.* The authors note that anti-abolition mobs were often drawn from the propertied classes, while abolition could not have succeeded without the support of small farmers, artisans, factory workers, immigrants fleeing the failed revolutions of 1848, etc. The Irish immigrants, a special case, were heavily propagandized against cooperation with black workers. Meanwhile, as the documents show, English Chartists, Irish nationalists, and Scottish workers supported abolition against those anticapitalists (land reformers, utopian socialists) who echoed the Southern proslavery argument that wage slavery was no better than, or no worse than, chattel slavery and that abolition would simply flood the North with competing cheap Negro labor.

Unless he is kidding (and I think he might be), Ishmael's remark "Who ain't a slave? Tell me that" (*Moby-Dick,* 6) announces his willingness to submit to all "sea-captains," however cruel.

Seen in context, such a sentiment not only refers to Pauline notions of irreparable original sin, but links Ishmael to agrarian reformers and Southern planters alike who, as the documents collected by Foner and Shapiro indicate, constantly accused the abolitionists of bourgeois individualism (Ahab's "narcissism"), one-sided simplism, and fanaticism; one land reformer even suggested that the abolitionists were secret tools of the British aristocracy determined to destroy the Union. The conservative and radical abolitionists viewed the relations of capital and labor differently: Where the conservative antislavery men represented in *The National Era* saw their relations as evolving and amenable to adjustment, arguing at times that wage slavery only exists when bound to chattel slavery (as the South was becoming industrialized, see *The National Era*, July 24, 1851, in Foner and Shapiro, *Northern Labor and Antislavery*, 83–86), the working-class abolitionists were less optimistic (see *The Voice of Industry*, Aug. 13, 1847, ibid., 51–54), but held immediate abolition to be the first priority as a self-evident and common-sense tactical matter. See discussion below.

27. See Leon Howard, Historical Note in *The Writings of Herman Melville*, vol. 1 (Evanston and Chicago: Northwestern University and Newberry Library, 1968), 286. A full account of this period is given in Hershel Parker, *Herman Melville*, chaps. 20–26. Parker believes that Melville was "passionately in love" with Elizabeth, already integrated into his family, as soon as he returned from the sea in late 1844. Parker suggests that Melville's unconscious or momentary sexual attraction to his sisters was understood to be more appropriately bestowed on the wife, who had already become, as it were, another sister.

28. See the appendix for letter from Henry Murray to Jay Leyda asking for the document establishing that, earlier, Gansevoort had cleaned Herman up before seeing their mother, a document that Murray could not find in the Morewood papers that Leyda had cited.

29. See Leonard Levy, *The Law of the Commonwealth and Chief Justice Shaw* (Cambridge, Mass.: Harvard UP, 1957), chap. 2; also Kenneth Lynn, "Lemuel Shaw and Herman Melville," 411, who quotes Oliver Wendell Holmes (1881): "[Shaw:] the greatest *magistrate* which this country has produced." Shaw argued that the Constitution could not have been ratified had not the South been assured that their fleeing property would be returned; in his last public act, Shaw urged repeal of the Massachusetts personal liberty law to conciliate the South. For Dana's angry criticisms and other arguments in favor of natural rights of individuals over "the nation," see Levy, *The Law of the Commonwealth*, 53–54, 90–91, 94–96, 99, 101, 106–8, 112–14.

30. In the Bentley English edition (*The Whale*), the extracts end the work. The epilogue is absent; the Whale Song lyric (taken from the title page of Henry T. Cheever, *The Whale and His Captors*) has the last (Ahab-ish?) word, and Ishmael does not survive. Moreover, an epigraph from *Paradise Lost* graces the title page. The ideological implication of these differences between the English and American first editions has been relatively neglected in Melville studies, though scholars have advanced various hypotheses, stressing printers' errors and censorship (but without consideration of Melville's characteristic vacillations between Burkean conservatism and radical puritanism).

Michael Sadleir, 1922, was the first Melvillean to mention the variants. The only article on the English vs. American editions is William S. Ament, "Bowdler and the Whale," *American Literature* (Mar. 1932): 39–46. Believing that Harper's had sent proof sheets to Bentley, and that Melville was in the throes of a "nervous breakdown" during the last stages of composition, Ament wrote, "The addition of the 'Epilogue,' which appears only in the American edition, was evidently an afterthought appended after the last proofs had been mailed to England" (41). No mention is made of the extracts placed at the end. The bowdlerizer is "Bentley's copy-reader." The notes to the Luther S. Mansfield and Howard P. Vincent Hendricks House edition of *Moby-Dick* (1952) discussed the differences between the English and American editions, but without analysis of their ideological implications (see pp. 831, 833–38).

31. See Patricia Barber, "Two New Melville Letters," *American Literature* 49 (Nov. 1977): 418–21. Melville had put Arrowhead on the market in mid-1856, while being suddenly pressed by a hitherto friendly creditor, T. D. Stewart, who, along with Dr. Brewster and Shaw, had helped him pay for the farm. Shaw had provided $3,000 but declined to be part of the record of lenders, as Melville had requested in his letter to Shaw, May 12, 1856.

32. But see Historical Note, *Moby-Dick* (NN), 654. By grouping Taji, Ahab, and Pierre as the same archetypal (Miltonic) character, I am diverging from Leon Howard's 1951 view of Hawthorne's influence on the composition of the book. As shown below, in one of the most important moves of "second-wave" Melville scholarship, Howard followed the corporatists Olson (1938) and Matthiessen (1941) in excising Milton and the radical puritans from Melville's consciousness; the seventeenth-century metaphysical poets were now in vogue.

33. See Goethe, *Truth and Poetry* 2:37–38. Melville's copy is now in the Berkshire Athenaeum, a gift of Henry Murray in the late 1970s. See my appendix for his letter to Charles Olson, announcing his acquisition of Melville's Goethe autobiography in 1940. He does not say that he has only the second volume. See also T. Heffernan, "Melville and Wordsworth," 350. Melville marked this statement in Wordsworth's "Essay Supplementary to the Preface": "Every Author, as far as he is great and at the same time *original,* has had the task of *creating* the taste by which he is to be enjoyed: so it has been, so will it continue to be."

34. Compare with Historical Note, *Moby-Dick* (NN): "He already knew that one thing he had in common with Hawthorne was the need to reconcile family duties with the sacredness of a writing routine.... [He saw] how Sophia subordinated everything else to the needs of her husband, whom she quite literally worshipped" (615). I agree that privacy while writing was a concern, but the NN statement ignores Melville's fear of destroying family unity (and the patronage of Lemuel Shaw) through political difference or confronting them with their mixed messages.

35. Maria implied on March 6, 1852, that there were other mutinies in the family when she included this fervent wish: "I am delighted to hear that a good deal of interest is awakened upon the subject of religion in Albany, would that an interest in this greatest of all concerns would come in our midst. But I am still sanguine & hope to see the day when all my beloved children will in truth and sincerity openly come forward before the world & proclaim themselves on the side of God, feeling in their hearts their own unworthiness, trusting in the atonement of their blessed Redeemer Jesus Christ, beleiving [*sic*] fully in his [forgiveness?]. May God in his great mercy thus guide and direct them" (GL-A).

36. Compare Melville's diptych *A Paradise of Bachelors and a Tartarus of Maids,* published in 1855. In the latter segment, a paper factory is run by a dark figure named Old Bach, a figure linked by his buttons to Captain Vere.

37. *Log,* 288. "Maternal" was used in Luther Mansfield's dissertation, "Herman Melville: Author and New Yorker, 1844–1851" (University of Chicago, 1938); Leyda's *Log* (1951); and Eleanor Metcalf's *Herman Melville: Cycle and Epicycle* (Cambridge, Mass.: Harvard UP, 1953). William H. Gilman and Merrell R. Davis (editors of *Melville's Letters* [Yale UP, 1960]), Harrison Hayford and Hershel Parker have read the word as "matrimonial" without acknowledging the controversy; that readings have differed is also not mentioned in the NN *Correspondence* volume. Laurie Robertson-Lorant quotes some of the letter but not the contested sentence. Given Melville's acknowledgment of erotic bonds between sons and their mothers, sisters, sweethearts, and wives, I still find the more Freudian "maternal" a plausible reading. Most surprising, Henry A. Murray referred to the disputed word as "matrimonial" in his discussion of the letter in his unpublished biography (chap. 16). Could he have encouraged Hayford et al.? But see his notes on the sources of Melville's morbidness—his depressed mother from whom he could not separate: "Repudiating his own work—cutting right across his grain—because his soul had gone into them. Ask a mother

to disinherit her child, but don't ask M to disown his mother" (folder containing typed manuscript "Half wilful overruling Morbidness").

38. See Karl Kautsky, *Social Foundations of Christianity*, trans. Henry F. Mins (New York: S. A. Russell, 1953); and S. G. F. Brandon, *Jesus and the Zealots: A Study of the Political Factor in Primitive Christianity* (New York: Scribner, 1967), for the figure of the proletarian, anti-imperialist Christ. Plotinus Plinlimmon is the author of a pamphlet advocating "virtuous expediency" to reconcile the conflict between earthly and heavenly morality. A fragment of the pamphlet is discovered by Pierre during his flight from the Saddle Meadows estate; in New York, Plinlimmon spies on Pierre. Melvilleans have identified the neo-Platonist with Hawthorne, Emerson, and Melville, but not with Lemuel Shaw. The political motive underlying this identification is illustrated in a textbook by Loren Baritz, *Sources of the American Mind* (New York: John Wiley, 1966), 396, describing Melville's pragmatism: "His essential point was one that he had already made in his best novels and poetry. Everything in life was uncertain, and so public policy must be resilient. . . . He thought it was possible for the North to dispense justice to both the freed Negro and the white Southerner. . . . As Melville wrote years before in *Pierre*, the absolute system of morality articulated by Christ was simply and unfortunately not designed for success in this world." Baritz has read Plinlimmon as Melville's true voice, and approvingly.

39. Both grandfathers were heroes of the American Revolution: General Peter Gansevoort and Major Thomas Melvill. See *Clarel*, 1.17.219−31. The narrator is ranking the causes of the Protestant Nathan's conversion to Judaism:

Still as she dwelt on Zion's story
He felt the glamour, caught the gleam;
All things but these seemed transitory—
Love, and his love's Jerusalem.
And interest in a mitred race,
With awe which to the fame belongs,
These in receptive heart found place
When Agar chanted David's songs.
'Twas passion. But the Puritan—
Mixed latent in his blood—a strain
How evident, of Hebrew source:
'Twas that, diverted here in force,
Which biased—hardly might do less.

40. Karcher, *Shadow over the Promised Land*, 92.

41. *Confidence-Man* (NN), 112.

42. See William Lloyd Garrison's critique of the nonthreatening character of Fourierism as compared to the antislavery movement, June 14, 1850, while debating William Ellery Channing at the 1850 Antislavery Convention: "What signal success has yet crowned the Fourier movement . . . ? What alarm, what commotion has it caused throughout the country? What mob has howled upon its track? To what extent has it secured the confidence and awakened the zeal of the white laboring classes? Where are its multitudinous supporters! They are *non est inventus*. I am not speaking reproachfully, but dealing with facts. On the other hand, how eventful has been the history of the antislavery movement! What discussion and conflict, what agitation and tumult, what tremor and consternation, in Church and State, among all sects and parties, have marked its triumphant career! And how many have been induced to become its advocates and supporters! Is not this an evidence of rare vitality?" Garrison goes on to accuse "the Socialists" (i.e., the utopian

socialists) of racism and sexism. In Foner and Shapiro, *Northern Labor and Antislavery*, 172–73.

43. If Melville is seriously identified with Ishmael here, then he has repudiated White-Jacket (who scorns the lackey Happy Jack) and every other one of his democratic rebels. The tone is joking and ironic; perhaps such teasing of conservative readers (including Hawthorne) constitutes the "wickedness" of the book.

44. See the following items in Foner and Shapiro, *Northern Labor and Antislavery*. For the land reformer critique of abolitionism (wage slavery was worse than chattel slavery), see George Henry Evans, *Young America*, Mar. 11, 1848, 174–78. On the comparable conditions of wage and chattel slavery, see John Pickering, *National Reformer*, 184–85, or Evans, *Working Man's Advocate*, July 27, 1844. 189–91. On international support for abolitionism, see "Address from the People of Ireland," signed by "Daniel O'Connell, Theobald Matthew, and Sixty Thousand other Inhabitants of Ireland," published in *Liberator*, Mar. 21, 1842, 114–16. See also "Address to Mr. Collins," a statement by Glasgow workers, in *Herald of Freedom* (Concord, New Hampshire), June 4, 1841, 236–41; and the racist plea to Chartist leader Feargus O'Connor to abandon his support for abolitionism, published in *Working Man's Advocate*, June 22, 1844, 186–89.

45. *Journals* (NN), 75–76, 97. Compare with *Journal*, ed., Horsford, 117–19, 166. The NN edition of the 1856–57 *Journal* renders the "line of desert and verdure, plain as line between good and evil," whereas Horsford first published the same line as "plain[er] than that between good and evil." I believe the first Horsford rendering of the line is more persuasive, because "than that" was penciled in the margin, as the NN edition notes but does not discuss. Given the importance of moral ambiguity to *Pierre*'s author, the silence in NN is surprising.

46. "The rage of seeing" was J. C. Squire's poetic phrase; see below.

47. Referring to the Fourierist periodical. "The *Phalanx* on Slavery," in Foner and Shapiro, *Northern Labor and Antislavery*, 166.

48. Stanton Garner, *The Civil War World of Herman Melville* (Lawrence: UP of Kansas, 1993). Commenting on the preceding scholarship that suggested Melville was disconnected "from the actual events of the war," Garner blamed Raymond Weaver: "That idea is rooted in Raymond M. Weaver's conception of Herman as a 'mariner and mystic' who stood aloof from earthly concerns, for a mystic looks only above and a mariner looks only beyond, at the inscrutable sea. That leaves unexplained the lively interest in the social and political issues of the time demonstrated in many of Herman's other works" (389). Melville is depicted throughout as a moderate, not an ultraradical like abolitionists or the postwar Radical Republicans (who Garner says included Melville's sister Helen Griggs and his brother-in-law John C. Hoadley). Nor is he even an organic conservative of the Right, like the narrator of "The House-Top," read by Garner as an ironic text.

49. After the Republican victory, Melville, Lemuel Shaw, and other supporters approached Charles Sumner, senator from Massachusetts, in early 1861, hoping to gain his recommendation for a consular appointment. Unfortunately Sumner, though friendly to Melville, did not have sufficient authority to accommodate the author, and moreover he was not getting along with Seward, secretary of state. Compare with *Log*, 634–39; Leyda nowhere describes Sumner's politics, except for an early speech in favor of international copyright. A family letter discovered by Amy Puett in the papers of Lemuel Shaw II (Massachusetts Historical Society) after publication of the *Log* raises questions about one family member's enthusiasm for such an appointment. A journal entry by Hope Shaw (Judge Lemuel Shaw's wife), dated February 21, 1861, states, "Mr. Shaw rode out today and has appeared more interested in his business than usual. Mr. Dana called and they conversed upon business, for Herman (I have no faith in sending away a *person* that is not able to see to his own business at home)." See Folder Notes and Correspondence, letter from Hershel Parker to Leyda, Oct. 28, 1968, Leyda Papers, NYU.)

Sumner's radical and vanguard approach to emancipation and reconstruction stands in sharp contrast to that of Lincoln or Johnson: Sumner argued for immediate emancipation early in the war, then full black manhood suffrage accompanied by free popular desegregated education, a plot of land for each black household, an end to all racial discrimination in the use of public accommodations, the rights to serve as witnesses and to serve on juries, etc. Unlike some other abolitionists, Sumner did not wish to postpone the vote for the freedmen, arguing, rather, that their votes would check white supremacists (who were defeated, but not subdued or repentant and were attempting to perpetuate slavery by other means), but also that the responsibility that came with full political participation for black and white alike would spur rapid political growth and sophistication. Sumner's demands for suffrage and an education in civic competence were inseparable. Melville could have argued against Northern gloating and triumphalism (as did Charles Sumner) while clearly stating that the freedmen should not be returned to the control of the planter class, but he chose to idealize upper-class Southern rebels instead.

For the relevant political alignments regarding postwar land reform, Negro suffrage, and civil rights, see James M. McPherson, "The Ballot and Land for the Freedmen, 1861–65," in *Reconstruction: An Anthology of Revisionist Writings*, ed. Kenneth M. Stampp and Leon F. Litwack (Baton Rouge: Louisiana State UP, 1969), 132–55. By comparison with the maximalist demands of abolitionist contemporaries such as Wendell Phillips, Charles Sumner, Lydia Maria Child, or Frederick Douglass, Melville's position in the supplement must discourage critics who claim a consistently unequivocal left-wing or antiracist politics for their hero. However, see his treatment of the first Handsome Sailor encountered in "Billy Budd," discussed in Karcher, *Shadow over the Promised Land*, and below. Karcher's chapter 6 sees the supplement (and *Clarel*, especially the character Ungar) as lapses attributable to the anxieties caused by Civil War, resonating with Melville's fratricidal jealousy of Gansevoort. What she misses is Melville's obsessive theme, that the bereaved mother of the "slain collegian" war hero is inconsolable.

50. Foner and Shapiro, *Northern Labor and Antislavery*, 66.

51. Melville to Hoadley, Sept. 12–18, 1867, *Melville's Letters*, ed. Merrell R. Davis and William H. Gilman (New Haven, Conn.: Yale UP, 1960), 228. Also see Hennig Cohen and Donald Yannella, *Herman Melville's Malcolm Letter: "Man's Final Lore"* (New York: Fordham UP and NYPL, 1992). The authors have relied on Henry Murray's assessment (transmitted through Edwin S. Shneidman) of terrorized children and loveless family relations (see 111n.166).

52. Melville to Hoadley, Mar. 31, 1877, *Correspondence* (NN), 451–54, the only surviving manuscript letter from HM to his cherished brother-in-law, yet another suggestive gap in the Melville family chronicles. Though this letter supports readings of Melville as irrationalist, he qualifies his own complaints about cosmic senselessness and mystery with the parenthetical remark "(from a certain point of view)." As published in the Constable edition, vol. 16 (under *Timoleon*, etc.), the lines from "The Age of the Antonines" read "Orders and ranks they kept degree / Few felt how the parvenu pines . . . ." (274). In the letter to Hoadley, the same lines read "Order—grades and due degree— / None felt how the leveller pines . . . ." In manuscript, the lines are "Orders and ranks <observed> they kept degree, / <Few felt how the leveller pines; / Factories none, no crippled and free>." He inserted "Few felt how the parvenu [*sic*] pines, / No lawmakers took the lawless one's fee." The manuscript versions (one in Melville's hand, the other as copied by his wife) are at the Houghton Library at Harvard; they would have been written in 1890 or 1891 in preparation for printing. See chapter 7 below for gossip that in 1856 Melville thought Hoadley was the father of his children.

An interchange between Eleanor Metcalf and her mother (Frances Thomas), probably after 1925, is suggestive, not only about family attitudes toward Melville and his wife, but with respect to Murray's interests and speculations. A note from EMM to FT is preserved, but with top and bottom cut away; this fragment and its answer survives: "How—did Grandma have a quarrel or row or whatever you wish to call it with the Hoadley line of the family—especially Charlotte? What was the basis of her and Aunt Bessie's very evident dislike of Charlotte? Did she get the lion's share of heirlooms from Gansevoort, and why? Do you have the present address? [See my appendix for Charlotte's curt refusal to see Murray, marked by him "Dead letter 1928"] ... What was Aunt Kate's character? When did she marry? What about her relation to Herman? Any information you can give me on the Hoadley's will be appreciated before Dr. Murray's visit about Memorial Day. He has no [cut out]."

FT answered, "Your grandmother never had a quarrel with *anyone* that I know of, but she was disappointed in Charlotte's taking her mother's business affairs out of Uncle Sam's hands, and managing things herself. This she did after mother died. The latter, John C. Hoadley was a very fine man, honest and upright. Your grandmother had a great respect for him; he was quite a reader and an admirer of H.M.'s *books*, and it was he who had the portrait painted for H.M.'s mother, I *think* she died before it was finished, and it was given to your grandmother. II. Charlotte's treatment of her mother during her last illness was open to criticism, she would not allow her brother Frank to even *see* his mother when he'd gone to Boston for that purpose. After her mother was buried, she tried in her sharp unprincipled way of doing business, to get most of the money just how far she succeeded I don't know. III. Yes, she did get the cream ... she sold portraits of H'M's father and mother ... V. Charlotte's mother did not have a strong character, she was married in Pittsfield, Sept. 15, 1853—I don't think her relations to Herman were anything of a decided nature, according to my remembrance." The Melville Papers, bMS Am 188 (348), Houghton Library, Harvard University.

53. The transformations in the only complete surviving Melville manuscript have been traced in Harrison Hayford and Merton M. Sealts, Jr., eds., *Billy Budd, Sailor (An Inside Narrative): Reading Text and Genetic Text* (Chicago: U of Chicago P, 1962). The movement from guilty mutineer to falsely accused child is a typical feature of Melville's ambivalence in his shifting views of legitimate authority.

54. This letter (extracted) was first published in *Family Correspondence of Herman Melville 1830–1904 in the Gansevoort-Lansing Collection*, ed. Victor Hugo Paltsits (New York: New York Public Library, 1929), 46. It was partly quoted in Geoffrey Stone, *Melville* (New York: Sheed and Ward, 1949), 303. Bezanson quoted the letter in his doctoral dissertation (Yale University, 1943) to make the point that Elizabeth did not understand her husband. A letter from Elizabeth to Catherine Gansevoort describing "a sudden and severe illness" in May 1873 is characterized by Bezanson as one in which "body and mind were interlocked ... and for his mind Elizabeth could do little" (93–94). Leon Howard, *Herman Melville*, 309–10, quoted a few sentences to assert that Melville found none of his customary relief after having completed the "mental strain" and "drudgery" of publication, though a year had passed.

55. Warner Berthoff, *The Example of Melville* (Princeton: Princeton UP, 1962), 189. Berthoff gives a German idealist lineage for Melville's "organic growth": Goethe, Emerson, Hawthorne, Coleridge, and Carlyle. For example, "In *Billy Budd* he undertakes to define not universal truth but certain specific and contingent examples of being and behavior" (9).

56. *Herman Melville's Billy Budd/Typee: A Critical Commentary* (New York: American R.D.M. Corporation, 1967), 61. The series consultant was Mina Mulvey, M.A. Radcliffe College; the project editor was Arman Schwerner. The unnamed authors attributed Melville's rebelliousness to the inflexible bad mother, unmoderated by the affectionate and adventurous father. Compare with Henry Murray, below.

57. See footnote above, the younger Hayford's incredulous letter, Apr. 5, 1952, to Leyda on Freeman's reading of "incomprehensible" versus "incongruous"; the latter word Hayford attributed to Melville as the more likely alternative.

58. Vine is described elsewhere in the text as a Paul Pry. Compare with Bezanson's discussion of the Melville-Hawthorne friendship in *Clarel* (NN), 593–604, and his synopsis of Hershel Parker, "The Character of Vine in Melville's *Clarel*," 666, 668–69. For Bezanson, Clarel

becomes critical of Vine only after he has been physically rejected. The two authors differ in temperament, not in basic political orientation. Melville was impassioned (and gay?), Hawthorne reserved. Clarel still loves and respects Vine at the end of the poem. This follows the near consensus that both Melville and Hawthorne were more balanced than Emerson and other contemporaries neglecting the lesson of fallen flesh. Indeed, "Clarel belongs increasingly in the middle group with those skeptical humanists Rolfe, Vine, and the narrator" (574). To the extent that Clarel is disowning Vine (in my reading or, before that, in Parker's, though with a differing emphasis), is Melville criticizing Ishmael, also incognito, also the anti-intellectual and aristocratic artist?

59. *Journals* (NN), 990.

60. Walter E. Bezanson, "Historical and Critical Note in *Clarel* (NN)," 510–11. There is a slip in Bezanson's doctoral dissertation: "He can neither believe, nor be uncomfortable in his unbelief" (27). Was this a typist's error, or did Bezanson think Melville was always an atheist/mechanical materialist like Margoth?

61. Compare Bezanson, "Historical Note," 598. He omits the hostile characterization of Vine's neutrality, ending his quote at "pelted his own shadow there." Nor does he mention the "pouch of gold" speech.

62. See Randall Stewart's entry on Hawthorne in *Encyclopedia Britannica* (1971). Stewart viewed Hawthorne's religious beliefs as "essentially Catholic."

63. Compare the widely disseminated etching by Salvator Rosa, *Democritus in Meditation*, a response to Dürer, *Melencolia I*. As described by Richard W. Wallace, *Salvator Rosa in America* (Wellesley: Wellesley College Museum, 1979), 54–57, Rosa transformed the laughing Democritus (an empiricist) into a melancholiac, sitting in despair amidst the rocky ruins. The etching's inscription reads, "Democritus, the mocker of all things is here stopped by the ending of all things."

64. I am speculating that Mortmain's horrid secret relates to sexuality simply because Melville locates the scene in Sodom and because Clarel seemingly admits to sexual desire as part of his attraction to Vine. The secret may be the one stated: the blasphemous belief that God is evil, in this case to have made him bisexual and then blamed the victim.

65. Compare Bartleby in the Tombs to the lawyer: "I know where I am."

66. In the opening scene of *Pierre*, much is made of a crimson flower that has climbed onto Lucy's white pillow. Pierre plucks it and makes it his boutonniere. Lucy applauds the gesture with "Bravissimo! oh, my only recruit!" In the Maurice Sendak illustration to this scene (Krakens, 1995), the pillow is lavender, and we see Pierre from the rear, a pale red scarf draped across his arm. No flower is visible, but Lucy resembles Melville's wife.

67. Nathaniel Hawthorne, "The Birth-mark," in *Selected Tales and Sketches*, comp. and intro. Michael V. Colacurcio (New York: Penguin, 1987), 276–77.

68. "The Jewish problem" refers to the fears of conservative Christians that "the Jews" were too powerful and numerous in the modern world; crucially, they lacked the Christians' sense of "social responsibility," felt to exist in the bygone agrarian order and undermined by the brutally impersonal operations of markets in industrial societies.

69. See discussion of *Pierre*, below.

70. "Uncatalogued" was changed from "unspeakable," suggesting that in Melville's family the parental visage disclosed unspoken anger belied by words.

71. Compare with *Clarel*, 1.23.76–80:

... the zealot—made
A slave to one tyrannic whim—
Was scant; while the sage unkind

> Sat a torpedo-fish, with mind
> Intent to paralyze . . . .

The monomaniac Nathan is linked to the Rabbi; both block Clarel from the comforting domesticity he experiences with Ruth and Agar. Margoth emerges from filth in the next canto.

72. In the same verse that introduces Rolfe, the narrator mentions an "untoward" "tinge of soil." Or is the forehead also the "foreheads bare" of the reverential mourners at Nehemiah's funeral? For another reference that does not jibe with Melville's text, see J. C. Lavater: The forehead was the site where power, memory, and abstract thought were revealed to the skilled physiognomist. See his *Physiognomy; or The Corresponding Analogy between the Conformation of the Features, and the Ruling Passions of the Mind,* translated from the *Original Work of J. C. Lavater* by Samuel Shaw, Esq. (London: H. D. Symonds, 1790), 49, 201, 206; also *Physiognomical Sketches of Lavater, Engraved from the Original Drawings by John Luffman* (London, 1802).

73. The hanged Billy's passivity on the cross/yard-end after he blesses Captain Vere is, in my view, a reproach to all class collaborators but also a self-reproach to Melville's childish compliance with illegitimate authority, sternly criticized in *White-Jacket.*

74. Melville marked in red this passage from Goethe on "abuse of the term—genius": "The time was yet far distant when it could be affirmed, that genius is that power of man which by its deeds and actions gives laws and rules. At this time it was thought to manifest itself only, by overstepping existing laws, breaking established rules, and declaring itself above all restraint. It was, therefore, an easy thing to be a genius, and nothing was more natural than that extravagance both of word and deed should provoke all orderly men to oppose themselves to such a monster." Goethe, *Truth and Poetry* 2:141–42.

75. Emphasis added. Hume, *HE* 7:200–201 (year 1651).

76. Daniel Orme MS, Melville Papers, MS Am 188 (369.4), Houghton Library. The word Orme (for serpent?) is crossed out. I have assumed that Melville's mark between Orme and Omitted represents "and." The enigmatic title with "omitted of" rather than "omitted from" suggests that Billy's unwarranted deference to authority was refreshingly absent from the character Melville is describing in this sketch. The preliminary versions of the closing paragraphs are published in F. Barron Freeman, *Melville's Billy Budd* (Cambridge, Mass.: Harvard UP, 1948). Discarded versions of "Billy in the Darbies" were found on the back of several pages from "Daniel Orme," which Freeman dates as beginning in 1888 (xi). Moreover, Orme's secret tattoo was located on the right forearm in one version (354); it was Billy's right forearm that shot out to accidentally kill Claggart. The condemned mutineer fragment is found in Freeman, appendix I. Freeman identifies Orme with the enigmatic Dansker, not Billy/Melville, a judgment he published in 1944, responding to William Braswell, *Melville's Religious Thought,* which read Daniel Orme as a self-portrait of the essentially serene (i.e., resigned) Christian, returning to his early "Christian fundamentalism" and relinquishing in his last gasp religious doubts/Taji's rationalism/Byronic subjectivity, nihilism, and materialism (126). Braswell's book, read by Henry A. Murray in manuscript, reiterates the Christian Socialist ideology of Thorp and Matthiessen. As I have argued, their politics may be characterized as pluralistic and irrationalist, in sync with Anglo-Catholicism. See F. Barron Freeman, "The Enigma of Melville's 'Daniel Orme,'" *American Literature* 16 (1944): 208–11. It is the Dansker who is flawed: "If the Dansker had been less enigmatic in his answers [regarding the reasons for Claggart's antagonism toward Billy], the tragedy which followed might have been averted" (210). Authoritative New Critics were perhaps discomfited by the uncertain relations between authors and their texts. Freeman concluded, "To examine the 'Orme' fragment primarily as it is connected with the two novels ["Billy Budd" and "Baby Budd"], is to deal safely with counterparts of characters

and events in three fictional worlds and not with the dubious similarities between autobiographical fact and fiction" (211). Yet Freeman does make such connections: Because it was written for "Billy Budd," "Daniel Orme" cannot be autobiographical. But it was possible to read it as "Orme's quiet waiting for the death which will bring him peace and understanding. One could also attempt to see Melville admonishing himself to cease speculating and writing—to live out with quiet acceptance, the brief remainder of his allotted life" (209). Who is the agitated quietist here? "Daniel Orme" is mentioned by Laurie Robertson-Lorant, *Melville*, 670n.4, as "a maudlin, masochistic fragment . . . which Melville mercifully omitted from *Billy Budd*."

77. Warner Berthoff, ed., *Great Short Works of Herman Melville* (New York: Harper & Row, 1969), 424. Page numbers refer to this edition.

78. Hawthorne associated pride with Jewish blood: The artist Miriam, a character in *The Marble Faun* representing the parricidal potential of the Reformation and Enlightenment, reveals a gem glowing on her bosom with a "clear red lustre" like stars in the southern sky. Her Jewish blood is linked to the gem, an "emanation of herself, passionate and glowing"; Jewishness signifies "freedom of thought and force of will." See chapters 18 and 22. Henry Murray believed that Hawthorne identified with these characters and, in his unpublished notes, characterized him as "antinomian."

79. See below for Henry Murray's surmise (in an early draft of his introduction to *Pierre*) that the scars on Melville's characters all represented the sudden disclosure of Allan Melvill's sin in fathering a natural child. In that case, the dark secret that Orme is supposed to be keeping for the sake of others would be the fact of his father's hypocrisy regarding sexual purity. Compare with Murray's draft: "It was partly to avoid a barrage of gun shots that M concealed his truths in symbols, allegories, and myths in such a way that only a worthy reader can get at them. His books are not rationally designed with a pre-selected, coherent scheme of symbols, but are one in the nature of loosely governed free associations, with 'a general drift of symbolism,' as Homans has well said, the straight course of the logic being interrupted by all manner of digressions. Understanding comes through emotional involvement in the current of imagery." Photostat found in the Henry A. Murray Papers, box "the Great Trauma," *Pierre* folder.

80. Emphasis added. Goethe, *Truth and Poetry* 2:34–35.

81. The slanting white scar also recalls the hammer-swinging scientist Margoth's chalked scrawl in *Clarel*: "I, Science, I whose gain's thy loss, / I slanted thee, thou Slanting Cross" (2.31,109–10), in which case the materialist Margoth could have inflicted the wound, but that removes the force of the title "Daniel Orme."

82. Wordsworth, "The Prelude," 7.715–16, 734–35. See also the tribute to Edmund Burke, who rejects "abstract rights" for the "vital power of social ties / Endeared by Custom" (7.523, 526–27).

83. Melville marked a passage from Goethe distinguishing between "vanity" and "inward satisfaction" that fortifies my argument that Ahab is a portrait of himself as artist, necessarily isolated. Goethe wrote, "I cannot say that [Zimmerman] was vain. We Germans misuse the word 'vain' (*eitel*) but too often. In a strict sense, it carries with it the idea of emptiness, and we properly designate by it only the man who cannot conceal his joy at his Nothing, his contentment with a hollow phantom. With Zimmerman it was exactly the reverse; he had great deserts, and no inward satisfaction. The man who can enjoy his own natural gifts in silence, and find his reward in the exercise of them, but must wait and hope for their recognition and appreciation by others, will generally find himself but badly off, because it is but too well known a fact that men are very niggard of their applause; that they rather love to mingle alloy with praise, and where it can in any degree to be done, to turn it into blame. Whoever comes before the public without being prepared for

this, will meet with nothing but vexation; since, even if he does not overestimate his own production, it still has for him an unlimited value, while the reception it meets with in the world, is in every case qualified" (*Truth and Poetry* 2:52).

Melville also marked this passage on the ignobility of "the people": "If we contemplate, on the spot, the noble buildings which Palladio has erected, and see how they are disfigured by the mean filthy necessities of the people, how the plans of most of them exceeded the means of those who undertook them, and how little these precious monuments of one lofty mind are adapted to all else around, the thought occurs, that it is just the same with everything else: for we receive but little thanks from men, when we would elevate their internal aspirations, give them an idea of themselves, and make them feel the grandeur of a really noble existence. But when one cajoles them, tells them tales, and helping them on from day to day, makes them worse, then one is just the man they like; and hence it is that modern times take delight in so many absurdities. I do not say this to lower my friends, I only say that they are so, and that people must not be astonished to find everything just as it is" (2:279; Melville marked similar sentiments on 283).

84. Berthoff, *Great Short Works*, 424. He included "two prefatory paragraphs . . . because they suggest how stories commonly developed in Melville's mind; how, starting from some memorable impression of a man's appearance or aspect, he would seek out 'the career and experience' that produced it; and how the pursuit of this inquiry might lead at last to some insoluble mystery, all ordinary information proving but 'unreliable gossip.' It is precisely the presentational logic of *Billy Budd*." Similarly, Freeman had begun his 1948 elucidation of the novella with "Here Melville presents his final verdict on the central problem of all his major works—the universal conflict between good and evil. . . . The stupidity and limitation of earthly, or human, knowledge had long been one of the vital points of Melville's philosophy" (Preface, 21). I find it typical of the (Tory) critics to link their medieval liquidations of the critical intellect with vitality.

85. See Melville's "Clover Dedication" to *Weeds and Wildings:* Praising the "Red Clover": "Yes, we are communists here" (*Works* 16:303).

86. Herman Melville, *Pierre, or the Ambiguities*, ed., intro., notes Henry A. Murray (New York: Hendricks House, 1949), 141, 461–62. Unless otherwise specified, page citations for *Pierre* in my book refer to the NN edition.

87. As a child, Melville was not permitted to play with lower-class children in his New York City neighborhood. It seems possible that he, the gentleman-sailor, was gang-raped by three or four rowdy shipmates; such "unretarded malice" would have given added credibility to the anxieties of his protective parents. Though Parker and Robertson-Lorant discuss male sexuality on ships, neither infers an actual incident of sexual assault (or fear of one) that could partly explain Melville's phobic responses to being "seen" or his sometimes hysterical descriptions of mobs (as in the Watch-House episode in *Pierre*). Paul Metcalf appears to have intuited this possibility in the portrayal of Carl Mills, a sadomasochistic homosexual who sometimes speaks Melville's words. See Paul Metcalf, *Genoa: A Telling of Wonders* (1965; reprint, Albuquerque: U of New Mexico P, 1991), esp. chap. 7. Paul Metcalf found my suspicion plausible, given the inhibitions of the nineteenth century: "The same things happened then as now, but people did not talk about it" (interview, June 16, 1995).

88. This is not quite the same as Carolyn Karcher's still-vague formulation that "Melville's unique perspective on his society derives from his experience of living at the intersection of these opposing worlds" ("Herman Melville," 240). She refers to the proletarian and patrician circles. In her earlier book, *Shadow over the Promised Land*, she describes his well-known ambivalence: "By temperament Melville seems to have been at once a refractory conformist and a reluctant rebel" (3). Karcher has chosen a hereditarian explanation for Melville's attitude toward rebellion where she could have identified class position or the objective correlation of forces that forced him under the mask. See also Elizabeth A. Schultz, *Unpainted to the Last: "Moby-Dick" and Twentieth-Century Art*

(Lawrence: U of Kansas P, 1995), 10. In a scientistic discussion of Melville's integration of multiple perspectives, she writes, "Throughout *Moby-Dick*, Melville *demonstrates* that complete perception or total understanding is neither desirable nor possible. . . . But at no point does he despair in his attempt to perceive and to interpret reality. Throughout the novel, his own desire to see and to see well, to understand and to understand fully compels him forward and compels him to engage the reader in his endeavor" (emphasis added). This is an example of conservative Enlightenment (elevating the tragedy of Ahab's noble quest); i.e., attempting to reconcile (hubristic) science and religion, activating the reader into quietism. I have tried to be more concrete and dialectical in tracing Melville's political oscillations. In my view, idealist retreats to psychological abstraction (as in the Schultz quote) hide the analogy between artists dependent on conservative patronage and college professors who are similarly constrained by the ideology of pluralism-without-materialism but who may not admit the resultant constraints on academic freedom.

89. Sumner is mentioned in the second of the "Jack Gentian" Sketches: Was not Jack not wearing his Civil War memorial "because thou wert in sympathy with the spirit of thy deplored New England friend Charles Sumner—whom, for what was sterling in him, thou didst so sincerely honour, though far from sharing in all his advocated measures?" Arguably, any of the major abolitionists could have inspired Melville: William Lloyd Garrison, Frederick Douglass, Wendell Phillips, or Thaddeus Stevens. All were considered fanatics and moral terrorists by their opponents; these widely read orators were outraged by the decision of Lemuel Shaw, chief justice of Massachusetts who, by upholding the strengthened Fugitive Slave Law (a key element of the Compromise of 1850) in the Sims case, 1851, had turned his state into a polity of informers and slave catchers. What makes Sumner a more likely model is his insistence that the Constitution, properly read, did not uphold slavery, for there was no positive law to that effect (his precedent was the famous Somersett case in Britain, 1772). Moreover, the Declaration of Independence took precedence: "Whatever is moral is constitutional" was his repeated motif. Ever the enemy of expediency over principle, Sumner appears as the avatar of the higher law, consistently applied and located in the Declaration of Independence, a document that, for Melville, "makes a difference."

90. In a canto beginning with the apostate Jew Margoth's mockery of the Catholic Church, Rolfe tells the liberal Anglican Derwent, "'Tis the New World that mannered me, / Yes, gave me this vile liberty / To reverence naught, not even herself" (2.26.151–53). Margoth's "sulking reverence" at Nehemiah's funeral precipitates an avalanche; earlier in the text, an avalanche had buried the judaizing Protestant Nathan's uncle, a memory that "unhinged" Nathan.

91. Draft, *The Confidence-Man*, Melville Papers, bMS Am 188 (365), Houghton Library. Compare with Tom Paine on heaven: "The belief of a future state is a rational belief, founded on facts visible in the creation: for it is not more difficult to believe that we shall exist hereafter in a better state and form than at present, than that a worm should become a butterfly." Quoted in Harry Hayden Clark, Introduction to *Thomas Paine: Representative Selections* (New York: American Book Co., 1944), xix. See Braswell's discussion (*Melville's Religious Thought*, 30) on metamorphosis in *Mardi*. Braswell might have interpreted the revision I have analyzed as a comment by the younger (nihilist) Melville on vanity and a refutation of the idea of immortality.

92. Compare with Philip Young, *The Private Melville* (University Park: Penn State UP, 1991), chap. 7. Young mocked readers (such as Michael Rogin) who read "A Tartarus of Maids" as an indictment of the factory system; Young sees only a parable of sexuality and gestation. Had he dealt with Jacobin Melville's boiling mad eruptions that produced only pallid composure, or the rational fear of decapitating or unmasking crazed authority figures before a more honest moral order was institutionalized, Young might have linked the birthing of the modern artist's necessarily subversive narratives with Melville's response to his wife's (or mother's) pregancies, not to speak of connections with analogous images in other supercharged Melvillean texts.

1. Melville to Evert Duyckinck, Dec. 14, 1849, *Correspondence* (NN), 148–49.

2. Herman Melville, "Baby Budd, Sailor," quoted in Freeman, *Melville's Billy Budd*, 317. In "Billy Budd" Claggart's glance is linked to an "asylum physician" and to the mesmerizing Rabbi in *Clarel*.

3. By context, I do not mean to merge Melville's choices with institutional pressures that molded his "choices" and that are resistant to moral judgment from our twentieth-century perspective. That would be the New Historicist approach that I am challenging. Rather, I am saying that would-be autonomous intellectuals face exactly the same hard choices as Milton and Melville; for that reason, the political stakes are very high in the Melville Revival.

4. See Robert Brenner, *Merchants and Revolution* (Princeton: Princeton UP, 1993).

5. Burkean libertarian conservatives, advocates of constitutional checks and balances and moderation in all things, have seen Paine as a forerunner of New Deal social democrats, his theories applicable only to small polities; they attack such Jacobin abstractions as "the people." See, for instance, Patrice Higonnet, *Sister Republics: The Origins of French and American Republicanism* (Cambridge, Mass.: Harvard UP, 1988); also essays by George Woodcock, "The Meaning of Revolution in Britain," and Roger Scruton, "Man's Second Disobedience: A Vindication of Burke," in *The French Revolution and British Culture,* ed. Ceri Crossley and Ian Small (New York: Oxford UP, 1989).

6. *Paradise Lost,* 1.12–26. Line numbers will refer to Milton, *Paradise Lost,* ed. Alistair Fowler (London: Longman, 1968).

7. As Olson deradicalized, he increasingly aligned himself with Shakespeare and Negative Capability, rejecting Milton and the Egotistical Sublime. See below.

8. Thirty pages of the *Typee* manuscript were found in the 1983 discovery of Augusta Melville's letters and other family memorabilia, perhaps rescued by her unbeknownst to Herman.

9. The figure of Mapple may have been partly inspired by the histrionic style of sailor-preacher Edward T. Taylor, who vigorously protested the Fugitive Slave Law but was anti-abolitionist. Mapple's sermon is a veiled reference to the sin of slavery. Some conservatives have unpersuasively claimed that the sermon preaches humility and obedience (which the historic Taylor, a law-and-order conservative, did), contrasting good Mapple with defiant Ahab. Compare with Hume's fulminations on the puritan sermon as incendiary innovation, *HE* 6:244–45 (year 1637).

10. Since many Melvilleans see Ahab as Mapple's opposite, this will be a controversial claim. For instance, see Lawrance Thompson (author of *Melville's Quarrel with God,* 1952), who presents Pierre as the romantic Byronic-Satanic hero, linking him to "the violently anti-Christian Melville" in his foreword to *Pierre* (New York: New American Library, 1964), xvii. I read Thompson's characterization as a slur against deicide Jews and a misunderstanding of Jews in relation to God. Mapple as a Massachusetts abolitionist is a Hebraic radical puritan; the ancient Jews argued with God without becoming disrespectful. Critics raised in an authoritarian belief system may find such freely expressed criticism of authority incomprehensible and outlandish. Compare with Braswell's chapter on *Moby-Dick* entitled "Accuser of the Deity."

11. The fascist and protofascist monarchists writing for *American Review* in the mid-1930s disliked absolutist monarchs of the early modern period, whom they saw as nationalists and imperialists. Their model kings were the contractual monarchs of the High Middle Ages.

12. The word "Sophomoricus" was written with a darker pencil and separated from the rest of the comment.

13. In a letter to Lawrence Clark Powell dated October 30 (answered November 2, 1948), Leyda proposed an exhibition: "Books That Fed Melville's Art." The list included "Milton's Par-

adise Lost (HM's early reading unsettled)." Leyda Papers, box 8, "correspondence, misc. 1940—" envelope, UCLA. The two volumes, heavily annotated, with numerous comments erased or cut away, were offered anonymously at auction decades later; Jay Leyda and Hershel Parker were allowed to copy the marginalia. Jay Leyda reported to Harrison Hayford in a letter March 6, 1984, that Parker was "hysterical" (Hayford files). Leyda's transcription was sent to Harrison Hayford on February 4, 1985. In a letter to me, August 18, 1987, Parker wrote, "After seeing M's Milton marginalia I would be more wary than ever about deriving a coherent ideology from M's texts." Hayford, at my request, sent me a photocopy on April 3, 1990. I analyzed these annotations (and their implications for Melville scholarship) on Pacifica Radio (KPFK) to celebrate Melville's birthday in 1990 and 1991. Their new owner had refused access to scholars but later sold the volumes to another anonymous collector who subsequently donated the Milton volumes to Princeton University, where they are now located in the General Rare Books Division, Department of Rare Books and Special Collections. Melville owned *The Complete Poetical Works of John Milton* (Boston, 1836).

A few of the marginalia have appeared in Robin Sandra Grey, "Surmising the Infidel: Interpreting Melville's Annotations on Milton's Poetry," *Milton Quarterly* 26 (Dec. 1992): 103–13. Grey (a Milton scholar, not a Melvillean) finds herself "confronted with a reading of Milton's ambitions and agenda so curious, indeed perverse, that perhaps only William Empson in *Milton's God* and Harold Bloom in *Ruin the Sacred Truths* would have regarded Melville's assessments without significant surprise" (110). She has read Melville as another Satan: "Milton's powerful dramatic depictions of Satan's character have interest for Melville largely as they reveal the tension in Satan between his former glory and virtue and his present degradations and viciousness" (112n.21). Her comment on the Devil as Messiah annotation states her preference for "skeptical" Ishmael over "frenzied" Ahab, linking only Ishmael to the "masque" because of his remarks in the Whalers Chapel. Compare with Hume, *HE* 7:337 (year 1660) on *Paradise Lost*, which he fervently admired despite its not being wholly purged of (Leveller) cant.

Hershel Parker has been reticent about these matters in the first volume of his authoritative Melville biography. Of the marginalia quoted above, Parker has heretofore published only the comment about Milton and Voltaire (618). (One other annotation is quoted, in which Melville ratifies separation of Church and State in Mitford's Introduction.) *Paradise Lost* influenced *Moby-Dick* insofar as "Melville took some of Ahab's qualities as Satanic opponent": Ahab is the "tyrannical captain" likened to Cromwell (699–700). Parker does not discuss the mysterious prior provenance of these books. In the historical note to the NN edition of *Moby-Dick*, he mentions Milton, but his battles are aesthetic ones alone, as these sentences hint: "[While writing the book] Melville's imagination for many months had unrolled at will a panorama of Milton's dubious battle on the plains of heaven. The dubious battle being waged in his study was . . . the most intense aesthetic struggle yet waged in the English language on this continent" (617).

Parker has answered my personal query regarding his mental states while copying the annotations, as well as his intentions regarding their publication: "I will not write an essay on HM and Milton, ever, but I will refer to the marginalia—esp in the 1860 chapters." "I wasn't hysterical, except that Jay and I were at the Phillips Gallery in 1983, not 84, with someone else who simply would not shut up his mouth. It was excruciating. I was not hysterical about the annotations. As usual with me, the excitement came long afterwards—when I was drafting the 1860 chapters of volume two, in 1990 or 1991 or so. I sacrificed myself and led him around the corner so Jay could have some time with the books. By the time the volumes came back on the market I had a set of the same edition and carried that up to NYC and got all I could, in the right place on the pages; the day was very overcast, but I got some erased words, nevertheless, by carrying the volumes to the windows. Princeton tried some very expensive processes, I understand, but failed to recover erased words. . . . I will quote all the recovered annotations in the Log, I assume, when the time comes" (e-mail message to author, Nov. 1, 1997).

14. See Daniel Walker Howe, *Political Culture of the American Whigs*. In his exegesis of Lyman Beecher's political views, Howe describes the attempts of proslavery advocates to destroy him, dragging the heretic into court: "The principal accuser at his trial in 1835 was Joshua Wilson, a Kentuckian who had moved to Cincinnati and was later the author of proslavery writings. The trial record shows Beecher and Wilson confronting each other on the issue of whether it would be just for God to condemn sinners who did not possess the ability to obey His laws. Beecher maintained that it would be 'oppressive' for God to do so. He marshaled a host of theologians to sustain the orthodoxy of his viewpoint, and in the end the court voted to acquit him. Some of Wilson's charges were rather vague and amounted to assertions that Beecher was encouraging the Finneyites. Beecher always claimed that his antislavery and other social views had really prompted the accusations. The trial was part of a pattern of Old School prosecutions of New School ministers for heresy that signaled the coming breakup of the Presbyterian denomination."

Howe continues, summarizing the competing creeds within Protestantism; the rationalists are "devotional," the believers in innate depravity are "confessional": "The evangelical united front, which Beecher hoped would include both Finney on the left and the Old School on the right, proved unstable. In its place a different alignment of religious groups emerged. Most of the 'devotionalist' Protestant groups—the Unitarians, Finneyites, 'perfectionists,' and New School Calvinists, as well as Quakers, Free Will Baptists, and others—learned to ignore their differences and cooperate in the interests of national redemption. The end of Beecher's campaign against Unitarianism coincided with the birth of the Whig party, within which they all found a place. . . . Opposing this alliance were the 'confessional' bodies in the Democratic party, an even more incongruous assemblage of Roman Catholics, German Lutherans, Dutch 'True' Calvinists, Old School Presbyterians, and Antimission Baptists; with them should probably also be listed the small organizations of freethinkers, who honored the memory of Thomas Paine. What these disparate groups shared was a grim determination to survive in the face of pressures to assimilate" (166–67).

15. Leyda's line numbers are different from my edition.

16. Compare to Ishmael's dream in *Moby-Dick*. Braswell, *Melville's Religious Thought*, n.11, comments that, according to Eleanor Metcalf, Elizabeth Shaw Melville would never have erased Melville's marginalia, as she was "too much in awe of her husband's genius." Note the words "too much." Braswell was not so much in awe that he felt constrained to report Melville's texts with accuracy; see, for instance, his repressions of parts of the text of "Daniel Orme" in his Catholicizing of the dying Melville (124–26).

17. Milton, "The Christian Doctrine," in *John Milton: Complete Poems and Major Prose*, ed. Merritt Y. Hughes (New York, Macmillan, 1985), 915–16. Milton explained that God, foreseeing the Fall, had also prearranged eternal salvation for "those who should believe and continue in the faith" (916). The essay was published posthumously and read as a gloss on *Paradise Lost*, which would support the conservative reading.

18. Quoted by Franklin, *The Victim as Criminal and Artist*, 39. Franklin uses this passage to make a claim for Melville as primitive communist. In chapter 16 of his unpublished biography, the progressive Henry A. Murray revealingly distorted the passage, minimizing Melville's description of a structural antagonism. Rather, Melville is describing point of view as dependent on one's place in the hierarchy: "War, for example, which offered officers their only opportunity for glory, was anticipated more eagerly by them than by the seamen." Although Harvard professor Alan Heimert has identified Ahab with John Calhoun, neither White-Jacket nor Ahab condones coercive harmony. However, noting the differing interests of sailors and officers does not make Melville a Marxist. Compare with John Calhoun's defense of slavery as a positive good: "There never has yet existed a wealthy and civilized society in which one portion of the community did not, in point of fact, live on the labor of the other. . . . There is and always has been in an advanced

stage of wealth and civilization, a conflict between labor and capital. The condition of society in the South exempts us from the disorders and dangers resulting from this conflict." Quoted in Frederick Jackson Turner, *The United States 1830–1850* (New York: Norton, 1965), 197.

19. Compare with Hume's distinction between Presbyterians and Independents: "The enthusiasm of the Presbyterians led them to reject the authority of prelates, to throw off the restraint of liturgy, to retrench ceremonies, to limit the riches and authority of the priestly office: the fanaticism of the Independents, exalted to a higher pitch, abolished ecclesiastical government, disdained creeds and systems, neglected every ceremony, and confounded all ranks and orders. The soldier, the merchant, the mechanic, indulging the fervours of zeal, and guided by the illapses of the spirit, resigned himself to an inward and superior direction, and was consecrated, in a manner, by an immediate intercourse and communication with Heaven" (*HE* 7:18–19 [year 1644]). Ahab, a "fighting Quaker," would seem to be an example of the latter.

20. Compare with Melville's well-known comments in *Israel Potter* on America as "intrepid, unprincipled, reckless, predatory, with boundless ambition, civilized in externals but a savage at heart" (chap. 19), but also the "essentially Western" Ethan Allen: "frank, bluff, companionable as a Pagan, convivial, a Roman, hearty as a harvest" (chap. 22). David Brion Davis used the *White-Jacket* quote as an example of manifest destiny in *Antebellum American Culture: An Interpretive Anthology* (Lexington, Mass: Heath, 1979). Similarly, Eric Foner, in a talk entitled "The Struggle for Freedom," delivered at Willamette University, Salem, Oregon, cited this passage as an example of American forgetfulness of the past, its (selfish) future orientation with respect to the notion of freedom, and its moralistic imposition of American values upon different societies. Foner thus makes Melville an imperialist (KPFK broadcast, July 5, 1999). I am questioning these judgments. American nationalism (as expressed in the American and French Revolutions) had an ideological component that asserted the common good against privilege; it was not simply a claim for territory, language, or ethnicity as conservative nationalism would be. See Eric J. Hobsbawm, *Nations and Nationalism since 1780: Programme, Myth, Reality* (Cambridge, England: Cambridge UP, 1990), 20. Compare with Andrew Stark, "Adieu, Liberal Nationalism," *New York Times*, Nov. 2, 1995. The author, a teacher of management at the University of Toronto, defines liberal nationalism in terms of primal differentiation from the mother, making it "even more irrational than chauvinistic nationalism. Bereft of any appeal to 'mystical' qualities like race, religion and culture, it relies on more primal, elusive entities like consciousness, existence, sense of self." Stark's definition reveals the depoliticizing inherent in any and all "identity" politics. There is no concept here of Hobsbawm's emancipatory process in which "the people" progressively defeat illegitimate authority, moving toward self-management, individual and group development.

Hobsbawm's interpretation should be contrasted with Ernest Lee Tuveson, *Redeemer Nation: The Idea of America's Millennial Role* (Chicago: U of Chicago P, 1968), 51. Tuveson presents Marxism as counter-Enlightenment and then links it to millennial movements in Britain and the United States. The mocking epigraph of the book is a statement by Woodrow Wilson: "America had the infinite privilege of fulfilling her destiny and saving the world." Elsewhere he suggests a continuity of identity between "the young republic" (1), "the ancient Jewish tradition of apocalyptic" (2); the epic form and sublimity (5); and "the evil" of (naively hopeful) American participation in World War II (8). The passage from *White-Jacket* was quoted (156–57) without the analysis of context; Tuveson notes Melville's apparent "profound disillusionment with these high expectations" in *Clarel*. See also Edward Said, *Culture and Imperialism* (New York: Knopf, 1993). Said begins by defending anti-Western cultural nationalists from the charge of separatist chauvinism: "Far from invalidating the struggle to be free from empire, these reductions of cultural discourse actually prove the validity of a fundamental liberationist energy that animates the wish to be independent, to speak freely and without the burden of unfair domination" (xx–xxi). But this standard disappears when applied to Melville: "There is . . . a dense body of American writing, contemporary with the British and the French work, which shows a peculiarly acute imperial cast, even though paradoxically its ferocious anti-colonialism, directed at the Old World, is central to it. One thinks, for example, of the Puritan 'errand into the wilderness' and, later, of that extraordinarily obsessive concern in Cooper, Twain, Melville, and others with United States expansion westward, along with the wholesale colonization and destruction of Native American life (as memorably studied by Richard Slotkin, Patricia Limerick, and Michael Paul Rogin); an anti-imperial motif emerges to rival the imperial one" (63). Puritans, Melville, and Ahab now merge (citing C. L. R. James and Victor Kiernan): "Captain Ahab is an allegorical representation of the American world quest; he is obsessed, compelling, unstoppable, completely wrapped up in his own rhetorical justification and his sense of cosmic symbolism" (288). Is Melville Ahab or not? Melville was critical of Ahab, Said notes, but follows his qualifier with the vehement scientistic statement, a non sequitur: "Yet the fact is that during the nineteenth century the U.S. *did* expand territorially." Is Melville then a hypocrite? Commenting on the comparison between Saddam Hussein and Hitler during the Iraq war, Ahab is a cynical scapegoater: "Anyone who has read *Moby-Dick* may have found it irresistible to extrapolate from that great novel to the real world, to see the American empire preparing once again, like Ahab, to take after an imputed evil" (295).

Too much purity and stridency disturbs the pluralist peace: The "imputed evil" Americans profess to find in Third World dictatorships is a pretext for a more sinister domination. For a critique of the counter-Enlightenment "anti-imperialist" intellectuals, including Said, see Christopher Norris, *Uncritical Theory: Postmodernism, Intellectuals and the Gulf War* (London: Lawrence and Wishart, 1992), 127–30: "To imagine that truth might at length win out through a detailed, critical, investigative treatment of the relevant source materials is merely to demonstrate one's lingering attachment to the old Enlightenment paradigm" (127). Rorty and his cohort in "postmodern bourgeois liberal pragmatist" culture are practicing a cynical *Realpolitik* imposed from above (128). Counternarratives don't solve problems: We need facts (130). It must be said that none of the scholars upon whom Edward Said relies has done the empirical investigation of Melville and Ahab that could justify Said's characterization of Ahab as the crazed imperialist.

21. F. Barron Freeman, *Melville's Billy Budd*, 283.

22. See Melville's poem "The Enthusiast": "So put the torch to ties though dear, / If ties but tempters be." Contrast these sentiments with *Clarel*, Canto 41, "On The Wall," with its conservative resolution of conflict.

23. Emphasis added. Compare with Ahab to the Manxman ("The Log and Line"): "The dead, blind wall [God? Human tyranny?] butts all inquiring heads at last." See *Moby-Dick*, ed., intro., annot. Charles Feidelson, Jr. (Indianapolis: Bobbs-Merrill, 1964), 658; Ahab's remark was noted: "In contrast to Ahab's purpose of 'thrusting through the wall'" (chap. 36). This college textbook had fourteen printings by 1980. New Critic Feidelson's anti-Ahab annotations will be discussed below in other endnotes.

24. Deconstructionists might argue that the hated inscrutability refers to the elusiveness of stable meaning, so that the Melville problem is in reading. But I am wondering if the reading problem is not historically specific to a society in transition from authoritarian to anti-authoritarian social relations, with the old ruling class coalitions still effectively in power but forced to present themselves as responsive to lower class demands and deploying deceptive language accordingly—the mixed messages that Melville constantly decodes.

25. Wordworth is commenting on his misguided vainglorious youth in revolutionary France:

How glorious! In self-knowledge and self-rule,
To look through all the frailties of the world,
And, with a resolute mastery shaking off
Infirmities of nature, time and place,

Build social upon personal Liberty,
Which, to the blind restraints of general laws
Superior, magisterially adopts
One guide, the light of circumstances, flashed
Upon an independent intellect. ("The Prelude," 12.236–44)

See also Albert Boime, *The Magisterial Gaze: Manifest Destiny in American Landscape Painting ca. 1830–1865* (Washington, D.C.: Smithsonian Institution Press, 1991).

26. The devilish Parsee observes the quadrant trampling, and the narrator observes ". . . a sneering triumph that seemed meant for Ahab, and a fatalistic despair that seemed meant for himself—these passed over the mute, motionless Parsee's face." This would seem to confirm my reading that Ahab's gesture is not directed against science and materialism: Rather he, Faust, has traded his soul for earthly knowledge. For a "new philosophy" explanation of empiricism, rationalism, and its eighteenth-century critics, see Hans Reichenbach, *The Rise of Scientific Philosophy* (Berkeley: U of California P, 1951). Reichenbach believes that Hume's irrefutable critique of Lockean empiricism was made obsolete by modern probability theory, erasing the old scientific absolutism. Though noting that Hume was a Tory, Reichenbach does not report what is at stake in these debates for insurgent democrats asserting themselves against "mystery." The book was assigned at Harvard in I. B. Cohen's history of science class (which I took in 1959), where the Hume critique of empiricism was pushed very hard, without reference to Hume's *HE*.

27. Compare with Lawrence MacPhee, *Monarch Notes and Study Guide* (New York: Simon and Schuster, 1964), 86. On the quadrant: "Ahab, more and more obsessed by Moby Dick, is leaving his human and geographical position in the actual world behind him, 'locating' himself only in terms of his relationship to the whale." See also 21–22: Ahab and Mapple are opposites: "In his conflict with the whale, Ahab will refuse to turn to any God but himself (we shall see with what results). Ishmael mentions that the hymn drowns out the storm: is he (or Melville) suggesting that faith such as Ahab will fail to demonstrate, can triumph over the forces which buffet men around the world?" Identifying Melville with Ahab, MacPhee also distrusts the sincerity of Ishmael's words in "The Try-Works."

28. Feidelson footnotes this passage, accusing Ahab of "a pose of humility . . . he really considers himself superior to a God who can only 'think'" (709). Compare with Barrington Moore, Jr., *Political Power and Social Theory: Seven Studies* (New York: Harper Torchbook, 1962), 32–88 and passim. For Moore, totalitarianism originates in the "arbitrary brute" Hebrew God Yaweh, from whom Job cannot separate (215). Moore's studies applaud the Marxian emphasis on class struggle and historical specificity, but they see "totalitarianism" as a vicious cultural tendency that has appeared many times in preindustrial societies. While lauding the tolerance of the Roman empire, Moore equates the repression in "Oriental despotism," Old Testament prophets, Calvin's Geneva (modeled upon the "Israelite theocracy," 66), Bolshevism, and Nazism. Mass media are the latest deadly purveyors of anti-intellectualism; similarly the progressive family propels its rudderless children to authoritarian cults. Rational-bureaucratic authority of the type practiced by ancient agrarian Chinese Legalist book burners is the source of the big lie. The Nazis showed the same cunning: "In 'blood and soil' and other slogans Nazism too shows the same mixture of contempt for the people combined with a nostalgic desire to return to the good old days of 'healthy' rural life before men were corrupted by the flesh pots of the cities" (53). This book (first published in 1958) was partly inspired by conversations with Herbert Marcuse. Moore's utopian idea of a free society is hedged: "It is more honest and more realistic to accept the conclusion that even in a free society the vast majority of the citizens would be neither professional intellectuals nor the holders of political power. What ordinary people might do with the time liberated from work by

advancing technology in a society *also* liberated from the threat of destruction is indeed a problem. Certainly there would be room—and there is room even today—for vastly more participation by the intelligent amateur in the life of the intellect. But that problem can wait" (219–20). No wonder Moore hesitated to name the type of polity he expects to emerge in advanced industrial societies (28); it might be too close to Italian fascism (aristo-democracy or the balanced absolutist monarchies he also likes) for comfort.

29. Melville owned John Martin's print of *Satan Presiding at the Infernal Council* (the setting for Mammon's speech). Mammon has described the "peace and prosperity" that Henry Murray would accurately associate with the promises of "Communism" (not capitalism), contrasting communism with militaristic, power-mad fascism in his 1943 report on Hitler's psyche. Milton's ambivalence is explored in Christopher Hill, *Milton and the English Revolution* (New York: Viking, 1977), but without discussion of Mammon's speech. For a nineteenth-century reading, see David Masson, *The Three Devils: Luther's, Milton's, and Goethe's* (London: Macmillan, 1874), 26–27. Masson revealingly distorts the text: "Some of the Angels appear to have been ruminating the possibility of retrieving their former condition by patient enduring. . . . Mammon was for organizing their new kingdom so as to make it as comfortable as possible." Compare with Carolyn Merchant's use of Milton's Mammon as archdestroyer of the earth in *The Death of Nature: Women, Ecology, and the Scientific Revolution* (New York: Harper and Row, 1983), 39. The "radical subjectivity" that stems from the fortunate Fall has been seen as the beginning of "the power of positive thinking" or "bourgeois order." See Herman Rapaport, "*Paradise Lost* and the Novel," in *Approaches to Teaching Milton's* Paradise Lost, ed. Galbraith M. Crump (New York: MLA, 1986), 141; Rapaport teaches *Paradise Lost* and *Moby-Dick* together; in a richly ambiguous remark he notes Milton's "satanic leviathan" as an influence on Melville.

30. See W. P. Witcutt, "The Future of Capitalism: A Note on Werner Sombart," *American Review* 5 (Oct. 1935): 531–35. Comparing Hilaire Belloc and Sombart, Witcutt wrote (praising Sombart for his "objectivity"), "By Capitalism Sombart, like Belloc, does not mean the régime of private property, as opposed to Socialism. He does not give any formal definition of Capitalism, but indicates certain constituent elements which may be gathered under the following headings. The Capitalist system consists: (1) of a society stratified into possessors of capital, entrepreneurs, and workers, pure and simple, possessing nothing—proletarians; (2) in the intensive utilization of mineral wealth. The exploitation of riches beneath the earth's surface and modern Capitalism are at bottom different aspects (natural and social) of one and the same phenomenon" (531–32). Compare A. J. Penty, "The Centrality of Money and Machinery," *American Review* 6 (Nov. 1935). Financiers were the first to destroy the stability of peasant life and property. The merchants were the "haves," the peasants the "have-nots" (2–3).

31. Goethe, *Faust*, trans. and ed. Bayard Taylor (1870; reprint, Boston: Houghton Mifflin, 1924), scene IV, 71. See note 65, 263, for Goethe's statement linking individualism to the humane awareness of others: "We are justly told . . . that the cultivation in common of human capacities is desirable, and also the most important of aims. But man was not born for that; properly each one must develop himself as a particular individual, but also endeavor to attain an apprehension of what all are, collectively." Melville could have seen the A. Hayward 1838 translation (in prose), its language suggesting Ahab: "I will enjoy in my own heart's core all that is parcelled out amongst mankind; grapple in spirit with the highest and the deepest; heap the weal and woe of the whole race upon my breast, and thus dilate my own individuality to theirs, and perish also, in the end, like them" (65). Compare Ishmael's description of Ahab: "He piled upon the whale's white hump the sum of all the general rage and hate felt by his whole race from Adam down; and then, as if his chest had been a mortar, he burst his hot heart's shell upon it" (184). See also, in Harry Hayden Clark, *Thomas Paine*, Paine on hate in *Common Sense:* "Reconciliation is now a fallacious dream. Nature has deserted the connection, and art cannot supply her place. For, as Milton wisely

expresses, 'Never can true reconcilement grow where wounds of deadly hate have pierced so deep'" (25).

Bayard Taylor could have read these lines from *Moby-Dick* choosing "stranded" for the key word (*zerscheitern*) of Goethe's verse, not "wreck" or "defeat": "[Ishmael:] For as this appalling ocean surrounds the verdant land, so in the soul of man there lies one insular Tahiti, full of peace and joy, but encompassed by all the horrors of the half known life. God keep thee! Push not off from that isle, thou canst never return!" (274). The issue for Goethe, Ishmael, or Bayard Taylor is class allegiance, specifically, the limits of the cosmopolitanism that modern artists (by definition) must adopt. Bayard Taylor expressed the pitfalls of the American "national temperament": "A great many causes have combined to make the American a much more flexible, sympathetic, impressionable creature than his ancestor or contemporary [English] cousin. Not being born to fixed habits of thought, he more easily assumes, or temporarily identifies himself with those of other races; he is more competent to shift his point of view; he is more capable of surrendering himself to foreign influences, and recovering his native manner when the occasion has passed. His power of sensation is keener, his capacity for enthusiasm greater." Quoted in Juliana Haskell, *Bayard Taylor's Translation of Goethe's* Faust (New York: Columbia UP, 1908), 17. Taylor is saying that the American artist will come home (though the word "recover" suggests another mask). Melville may be in disagreement both with Taylor's optimism and his assumption of cultural superiority; he is also expressing the tragedy of estrangement from his own family.

Like the Milton and Melville problems, there is a Goethe problem. For a summary of the Faust legend, see Eliza Marian Butler, *The Fortunes of Faust* (Cambridge, England: Cambridge UP, 1952), which argues that Lessing and Goethe reversed earlier cautionary tales. Such an interpretation would make Thomas Mann's *Dr. Faustus* a reversion to sixteenth-century treatments; Georg Lukács (publishing during the Molotov-Ribbentrop Pact period, 1939–41) saw Goethe as contradictory and progressive; Thomas Mann viewed Goethe as consistently aristocratic in his social attitudes. See Mann's introduction to *The Permanent Goethe* (New York: Dial Press, 1948), xxviii. The anthology uses the G. M. Cookson translation of *Faust* (1927): "I'll grapple the great deeps, the heights above; / Upon my head be all men's joys and griefs; / So to their stature my sole self shall grow / And splinter with them on the roaring reefs."

32. See *Paradise Lost*, 9.445–70. Milton contrasts the city and the country as the serpent proceeds to the seduction of Eve. Perhaps these lines inspired the first scene of *Pierre*. The pastoral and the sight of Eve's innocence momentarily abstracts Satan from evil. In this condition he is "stupidly good, of enmity disarmed, / Of guile, of hate, of envy, of revenge" ("stupidly good," line 465, marked by Melville).

33. *Virgil's Works*, trans. J. W. Mackail, bk. 2 (New York: Modern Library, 1934).

34. See the caricature "A Right Hon. Democrat Dissected," by William Dent, Jan. 15, 1793, reproduced in Roy Porter, "Seeing the Past," *Past and Present* (Feb. 1988): 193. The clenched right fist is marked "argument"; the left hand holds a dagger ("penetration"); the face is mostly blackened, but the white forehead is labeled "self-interest."

35. See Feidelson, *Moby-Dick*, 543–44n.22.

36. See Acts 2:1–4. "And when the day of Pentecost was fully come, [the apostles] were all with one accord in one place. And suddenly there came a sound from heaven as of a rushing mighty wind, and it filled all the house where they were sitting. And there appeared unto them cloven tongues like of fire, and it sat on each of them. And they were all filled with the Holy Ghost, and began to speak with other tongues, as the Spirit gave them utterance." In his own New Testament (1844) Melville marked subsequent verses: "5. And there were dwelling at Jerusalem Jews, devout men, out of every nation under heaven. . . . . 44. And all that believed were together, and all had things in common; 45. And sold their possessions and goods, and parted them to all *men*, as every man had need." Compare with *Redburn*, the Pentecostal jubilee, quoted in Karcher, *Shadow*

over the Promised Land, 16: "Then shall the curse of Babel be revoked, a new Pentecost come, and the language they shall speak shall be the language of Britain. Frenchmen, and Danes, and Scots; and the dwellers on the shores of the Mediterranean, and in the regions round about; Italians, and Indians, and Moors; there shall appear unto them cloven tongues as of fire."

37. An annotation followed but was erased. Walker Cowen identified the passage as part of a letter by Saint Evremond to Mareschal de Crequi, 1671 (in "Melville's Marginalia," 11 vols. [Ph.D. diss., Harvard University, 1965]). Not surprisingly, the annotation that followed the heavily marked passages from the Sermon on the Mount was cut out of the book, from both the top and bottom of the page. On orthodoxy, for example, see Hilaire Belloc, *The Great Heresies* (New York: Sheed and Ward, 1938).

38. Compare with Job 13:15 (double scored and underlined by Melville): "Though he slay me, yet will I trust in him: *but I will maintain mine own ways before him.*" The word "unintegral" is a neologism which may connote disintegration or fragmentation.

39. See Feidelson annotation, *Moby-Dick*, 641. The "queenly personality" is linked to the "infidel Queen of death" mentioned in chapter 116 or to Ahab's unknown mother, not to the Tree of Knowledge.

40. Eleanor Metcalf had heavily marked her own copy of *Pierre* (the Constable edition now in the Berg Collection, NYPL), noting resemblances of settings and characters. For instance, cousin Glen's luxurious drawing room was compared to "49 Mt. Vernon St." (Judge Shaw's house in Boston); Mary Glendinning's abhorrence of Pierre's secrecy apparently evoked Melville's mother; and Reverend Falsgrave's delicate hands were likened to those of "Judge Shaw and his son Samuel."

41. *Pierre*, 359, 360, 362.

42. Most recently, see Philip Young, *Private Melville;* and Richard Poirier, "The Monster in the Milk Bowl," *London Review of Books*, Oct. 3, 1996, 19–22 (a review of the Hershel Parker edition of *Pierre*).

43. Nantucket, home of the zealous abolitionist fighting Quakers.

44. Yvor Winters, *Maule's Curse: Seven Studies in the History of Obscurantism* (Norfolk, Conn.: New Directions, 1938), thought the half-known life was a journey into the life of instinct, identified with Ahab.

45. Compare with Franklin, *The Victim as Criminal and Artist*, after quoting chapter 72: "Many ties bind people to each other, like this line between Ishmael and his 'dear comrade' Queequeg, are woven throughout *Moby-Dick*. Toward the end, at the moment of crucial decision, the symbolic monkey-rope is the handhold between Captain Ahab and the Black cabin boy Pip. This bond almost saves the crew, but then Ahab rejects it in favor of the hempen line which fatally lashes him to the white whale. Severing the bond with Pip, Ahab dooms the entire crew to death, except for Ishmael, who escapes to tell the tale and explain what it means" (47). Franklin could have relied on either his teacher Yvor Winters or Newton Arvin, *Herman Melville*, 174: "What wretched vestiges of pure human feeling are left in [Ahab] go out only to the small black boy Pip, and to him reluctantly. Ahab is dedicated now to mere destruction, and he ends by attaining his suicidal death wish and meeting his death by water." However, Ahab did not reject the tie with Pip, nor did he choose death for the crew; he was defeated (or was he?). Insofar as Melville scholars adhere to the antebellum Democratic line that the Whigs (whose radical wing included the abolitionists) were repressive moralists who destroyed the natural man, they must deny Ahab's tie to Pip, while emphasizing Ishmael's merging with Queequeg as the gesture that saves him from the catastrophe.

46. Feidelson annotates this passage: "Figuratively, the *Pequod* has been like an explorer's ship, bound for one of the Poles, which might stand for ultimate truth or the essence of things." But compare Ahab's "shot" with Billy Budd's shot at Claggart's forehead.

47. Isabel and Queequeg may be analogs here. See Epilogue to *Moby-Dick*: "Round and round, then, and ever contracting towards the button-like black bubble at the axis of that slowly wheeling circle, like another Ixion I did revolve. Till, gaining that vital centre, the black bubble upward burst; and now, liberated by reason of its cunning spring, and, owing to its great buoyancy, rising with great force, the coffin life-buoy shot lengthwise from the sea, fell over, and floated by my side."

48. Walter E. Bezanson, Historical and Critical Note to *Clarel* (NN). The aging, experienced Melville increasingly "seemed to support the essentially republican-aristocratic philosophy which his family had stood for" (608); he is a "religious type" (612). Margoth is linked to the Scottish Elder with pruning knife: the "modern critical spirit" type and "sectarian intolerance" type (623); Margoth as "savage caricature of scientific materialism" (625–26) is contrasted with Rolfe as ideal (moderate) and (hopefully?) Melville's achieved mature identity (630–31).

49. Quoted by Nicholas V. Roe, "The Physiology of Reform," talk at the UCLA Clark Library symposium, "Materialist Philosophy, Religious Heresy, and Political Radicalism, 1650–1800," May 1, 1999. As characterized by Roe, the deradicalized Wordsworth was the passive recipient of Nature's messages, choosing intuition over empiricism; see "Tintern Abbey" and "Expostulation and Reply." The parallel with Ahab and Ishmael seems exact.

50. I have assumed that Bartleby's last words to the lawyer signified his refusal to ignore the prison, presented by the lawyer as pastoral. But there may be (as usual) a double meaning: Could Bartleby be saying that he has mentally ensconced himself in a medieval world where class mobility was not an option? This would link him to "B.L." in "On the Wall" (*Clarel*).

51. Maria Gansevoort Melville to Lemuel Shaw, Nov. 1, 1846, quoted in *Log*, 228.

52. See Patricia Barber, "Two New Melville Letters," *American Literature* 49 (1977): 418–21.

53. Emphasis added. Melville to Richard Bentley, June 5, 1849, *Correspondence* (NN), 131–32; George J. Adler to George Duyckinck, Feb. 16, 1850, quoted in *Log*, 343; Maria Gansevoort Melville to Peter Gansevoort, Nov. 28, 1856, quoted in ibid., 533; Augusta Melville to Peter Gansevoort, Apr. 7, 1857, quoted in Eleanor Metcalf, *Herman Melville: Cycle and Epicycle*, 164–65; Henry Gansevoort to Peter Gansevoort, Nov. 23, 1857, ibid., 166; Peter Gansevoort to Henry Gansevoort, Dec. 17, 1857, ibid., 169; Lemuel Shaw to Allan Melville, Feb. 20, 1861, ibid., 191. In the last example, Leyda's *Log* (634) transcribed "overthrowing" as "over-straining," a serious discrepancy.

54. Thompson, *Melville's Quarrel with God*.

55. These sentences are written on a page of names of prominent citizens (to be sent calling cards?) and suggest that the Tombs and Melville's conservatively enlightened family (and its connections) are linked. See Melville Family Papers, GL-A.

56. Weaver put the cause of Melville's problems in his smothering and imperceptive philistine female relatives. It is they who failed to rescue Herman; the family failure to understand him caused his banishment in 1856–57: "It is a fact that after *Moby-Dick* Melville's personal behavior grew even more perplexing to those who surrounded him. But fancy Michael Angelo so surrounded, or Dostoevsky, or Beethoven, and how similar would have been the perplexity! How their moods of taciturnity or their excitable outbursts would have occasioned a dumb solicitude or a blind distress irritating them to moments of murderous hatred! And the elegiacal family synods and the half-glances of accusing suspicion! So by 1856, when to the cousins and the sisters and the uncles and other of such like progeny, Melville seemed to be going from bad to worse— when he was a tired sick man hungry in his heart for some understanding companionship (which is one of the deepest and truest notes struck in *Clarel*); when his writings were earning him but a pittance; when the family both by marriage and by blood had tried in vain to get him a consular appointment to the Sandwich Islands or to any other remote place, or at best to do *something* for him, then, some one of them finally suggested in summary desperation: send him on a long trip

and pray for the rest." Herman Melville, *Journal Up the Straits, October 11, 1856–May 5, 1857* (New York: The Colophon, 1935), xxiv. Compare with Charles Olson, *Call Me Ishmael* (New York: Reynal and Hitchcock, 1947). Note that it is the relatives, not Herman, who are the persecutors; see below.

57. Quoted in Weaver, *Mariner and Mystic*, 322–23.

58. Murray Papers, folder "Moby Dick log," and folder "Art."

59. By "universalist" I do not mean to adopt absolutist rationalism as understood in Platonic and Christian thought, but rather the universal verifiability of scientifically observed facts and the predictability achieved by correct explanatory theories. By examining the warring points of view of all parties in a controversy, radical enlighteners use "relativism" (point of view) as a tool in search of truth, not as a ploy to evade moral responsibility in the process of pluralist bargaining and compromise.

5. THE MODERN ARTIST AS RED SPECTER

1. Fybate Lecture Notes (Berkeley, Calif., 1968) reads Ahab as a seeker after truth, at any cost (29); also mentions oscillations between Ahab and Ishmael (31).

2. See Stephen C. Behrendt, *The Moment of Explosion: Blake and the Illustration of Milton* (Lincoln: U of Nebraska P, 1983), 71. "Separation was for Blake the essence of the fall of man; the establishment and assertion of separate individuals was an act of fragmentation grounded in pride and totally destructive to unity, integration and wholeness."

3. The Krakens edition of *Pierre*, ed. Hershel Parker, illus. Maurice Sendak (New York: HarperCollins, 1995), excises those passages that reveal Pierre as a writer, a move justified by Parker's theory that the novel as he conceives it was finished before the middle of January 1852 (xi) and that further additions were an impulsive response to bad *Moby-Dick* reviews and an insulting book contract. Such abridgement also has the effect, however, of obscuring Ahab's "private quest" as art-making/demystification, an aim found in a lower layer than the one perceived by Starbuck.

4. Leyda Papers, folder "Pre-1930 Sunday School clippings, etc.," NYU.

5. Quoted in Thomas Daniel Young, *Gentleman in a Dustcoat: A Biography of John Crowe Ransom* (Baton Rouge: Louisiana State UP, 1976), 191. See 162–63 for Ransom's concept of romantic irony as the dualism produced by disillusion with youthful hopes for happiness in the garden of this world, a happiness brought about by man's shaping interventions.

6. Hobbes, *Leviathan*, 1651, pt. 1, chap. 6. Do Melville's rebel senses refer only to repressed sexuality, or are they the necessary stimulus to thought, reflection, and the perilous search for "why" and "how"?

7. "Sir Eglamor and the Dragon, How General George Monck Slew a Most Cruell Dragon, Feb. 11, 1659," *Rump: or an Exact Collection of the Choycest Poems and Songs Relating to the Late Times* (London, 1662), 371–72.

8. Quoted in Cicely V. Wedgwood, *Politics and Poetry under the Stuarts* (Cambridge: Cambridge UP, 1960), 165–66. Dryden's fears have not been quieted in her commentary: "Leaving aside this sidelong shot at current political theories about noble savages, this is the statement of a man who remembers the excesses of the sects and disorders of the Civil War, who sees how fatally easy it is to kindle into flame a 'Headstrong, Moody, Murm'ring race'—a one-sided but not untrue description of the seventeenth-century English—and who knows how difficult it will be to put out the flame once kindled?" Her obituary (*NYT*, 11 Mar. 1997) credits her with "vivid narratives [that] told the story of Britain with the common man in mind." A fellow at the Princeton Institute for Advanced Studies, 1953–68, Dame Veronica was born in 1910 to Sir Ralph Wedgwood, a baronet and former head of British Railways, and was great-great-granddaughter to Josiah Wedgwood (identified here as a potter).

9. Thomas Morgan, *The Moral Philosopher: In a Dialogue between Philalethes a Christian Deist, and Theophanes a Christian Jew*, 2nd ed. (1659; London, 1738), 219–20.

10. Moses Lowman, *A Dissertation on the Civil Government of the Hebrews. In Which the True Designs and Nature of Their Government are Explained. The Justice, Wisdom and Goodness of the Mosaical Constitutions are Vindicated; in Particular from Some Late, Unfair and False Representations of Them in the Moral Philosopher* (London: 1740). See Ernest Tuveson, *Redeemer Nation*, 41–46, for his account of Lowman's *Paraphrase and Notes upon the Revelation* (1737). Lowman is then connected to another undesirable, Joseph Priestley (also a target for Edmund Burke).

11. See the unsigned review of *Reform or Ruin* by John Bowdler, *Anti-Jacobin Review* (Aug. 1798): 193–94, for a statement distinguishing between political analysis (Jacobinical and subversive) and moral reform.

12. For instance, Carl Holliday, "A Need in the Study of American Literature," *School and Society* 4 (Aug. 5, 1916): 220–22. Holliday was not interested in artistic merit but in "keys to the social, ethical, political, and spiritual temperament of a people in the making" (222).

13. Emphasis added in both passages quoted. Hume, *HE* 6:21–24 (year 1617).

14. Ibid. 7:326–27 (year 1660). Compare with Hawthorne's autodidact "Ethan Brand," quoted above.

15. Hume, *HE* 6:107, appendix to James I.

16. Reverend Henry John Todd, *Some Account of the Life and Writings of John Milton* (London, 1809), 153. In the passage quoted, Todd was criticizing Samuel Johnson's excessively harsh estimate of Milton. Todd presented Milton as a (should-have-been?) moderate, properly serving neither the tyrant Cromwell (who deceived him) nor "the *majesty of the people*, which the *modern illuminators* of the world have imagined" (155). Like today's cultural relativists and pluralists, Todd and other conservatives characterized modernity (linking science, materialism, and excess democracy) as charismatic, utopian, and iconoclastic, with themselves as the moderate, communitarian, tolerant, soberly realistic alternative. See also James Thorpe, *Milton Criticism: Selections from Four Centuries* (London: Routledge & Kegan Paul, 1951), 3, 5–6, 12. From the 1840s to the 1890s, "Milton the man was typified almost universally as solemn, austere, proud, intolerant, and scornful" (i.e., he was an Ahab). There are striking resemblances between Milton and Melville scholarship; in both cases, contemporaries did not match the appreciation of later generations, and adherents to divergent worldviews claimed Milton or Melville for their own.

17. Emphasis added. Reverend John Mitford, "Life of Milton," in *Works* (London, 1851), 66. (Mitford was quoting Dr. Sumner's preface.) Melville owned *The Complete Poetical Works of John Milton* (Boston, 1836); Mitford's biographical sketch was composed for the 1831 first edition.

18. Compare with Feidelson, ed., *Moby-Dick*, 160, annotation 4. Ahab, not Ishmael, is the "social pantheist." This attribution is called into question by the passage from *Pierre* quoted above in which "sharp individuality" is opposed to rosy merging.

19. I thank Leo Steinberg for calling to my attention this instance in which he agrees that Melville the artist is speaking through Ahab.

20. Emphasis added. Hume, *HE* 6:48 n. (year 1621). The editors of this Dove 1822 revision advise that Hume, wishing to avoid the intrusion of "the style of dissertation" into "the body of his history," had moved this statement from text to footnote because of its "views so important." Compare with Charles Olson's belief that moral authority had been secretly transferred from Heart to Head during the Enlightenment.

21. Hume, *HE* 8:317–18 (year 1689): "The people, during these two reigns [of Charles II and James II], were, in a great measure, cured of that wild fanaticism by which they had formerly been so much agitated. Whatever new vices they might acquire, it may be questioned, whether, by this change, they were, in the main, much losers in the point of morals. By the example of Charles II and the cavaliers, licentiousness and debauchery became prevalent in the nation. The pleasures of

the table were much pursued. Love was treated more as an appetite than a passion. The one sex began to abate of the national character of chastity, without being able to inspire the other with sentiment or delicacy. The abuses in the former age, arising from overstrained pretensions to piety, had much propagated the spirit of irreligion; and many of the ingenious men of this period lie under the imputation of deism. . . . The same factions which had formerly distracted the nation were revived, and exerted themselves in the most ungenerous and unmanly enterprises against each other. King Charles being in his whole deportment a model of easy and gentleman-like behavior, improved the politeness of the nation, as much as faction, which of all things is most destructive to that virtue, could possibly permit. His courtiers were long distinguished in England by their obliging and agreeable manners." This is a most confusing statement: Charles the libertine has coarsened public life, while Charles the polite gentleman fights to maintain civility against the forces of irreligion. Apparently, for Hume, loss of control is more menacing when it infests the lower orders.

22. Jean Paul Richter, *Titan*, trans. Charles T. Brooks (Boston, 1862), iv–v.

23. Thomas Carlyle, *German Romance*, vol. 3 (London, 1827), 12, 13. Compare with his description of Klinger's Faust: ". . . a rugged, vehement, substantial mind, seemed much too harsh, infernal, and unpoetical for English readers" (1:ix). It is known that Melville owned the first two volumes of these works edited by Carlyle, but it seems likely that he was familiar with the passages quoted here from volumes 3 and 4. He also wanted to meet Carlyle on his trip to Europe in 1849; Shaw wrote to Emerson requesting a letter of introduction, but to no avail. See my postscript below for discussion of Carlyle's Goethe and Melville's marginalia to Goethe's autobiography.

24. [Charles Kingsley,] *Alton Locke, Tailor and Poet: An Autobiography*, ed. Elizabeth A. Cripps (Oxford: Oxford UP, 1983). Compare with Mary Wollstonecraft, *An Historical and Moral View of the Origin and Progress of the French Revolution and the Effect It Has Produced in Europe*, vol. 1 (London, 1794), 4: "Locke, following the track of these bold thinkers [English emigrants to America], recommended in a more methodical manner religious toleration, and analyzed the principles of civil liberty: for in his definition of liberty we find the elements of *The Declaration of the Rights of Man*, which, in spite of the fatal errours of ignorance, and the perverse obstinacy of selfishness, is now converting sublime theories into practical truths."

25. Nov. 1, 1851, reprinted in Harrison Hayford and Hershel Parker, eds., *Moby-Dick as Doubloon: Essays and Extracts (1851–1970)* (New York: Norton, 1970), 18.

26. Compare with Lavater's caption to his sketch of the Prophet-type, "After Raphael": "Prophetic seriousness and apparent inexorableness / The Eyes penetrating and immoveable, the Eyebrows choleric, the Nose firm & commanding, the Forehead hard and always forbidding, the Hair characteristic" (*Physiognomical Sketches*, 46).

27. In other words, no aristocrat would submit to such slavery.

28. Emphasis added. The villain is Schechem Isaacs; Schechem was the name of George Walker's benevolent Jew in *Theodore Cyphon*, 1796. With respect to Crossthwaite's martyrdom, compare Mary Glendinning's speech (quoted above), fearing that Pierre will darken himself as a "hope forlorn," or as a figure of the political/moral vanguard, sacrificing himself to a good cause.

29. The distinguished German Professor Hans Ulrich-Wehler addressed the UCLA history department March 19, 1997, on the evolution of German nationalism since 1800. Self-described as a pragmatic advocate of *Gesellschaft*, he suggested that a regional nationalism (the European Union) would be an improvement on the older nationalism that seemed susceptible to right-wing radicalism during periods of crisis. When I asked why he did not prefer international solidarity grounded in science and universalist ethics (the radical Enlightenment vision) rather than a new bloc, he spoke as a corporatist, responding, "Universalism creates difference."

30. Compare with Georg Brandes, *Revolution and Reaction in Nineteenth-Century French Literature* (New York: Russell and Russell, 1960), 58–59: "Human reason had risen and freed itself

with athletic strength. Everything that existed had to justify its existence. Where men heretofore had prayed for a miracle they now investigated into causes. Never before in history had there been such doubt, such labour, such inquiry, such illumination. . . . For the time being the emancipatory movement was checked. It began once more to be inexpedient not to profess faith in revealed religion. . . . The majority of the men without private means who had prepared themselves for government appointments, and could not overcome their irresistible desire to eat every day, were entirely reliable supporters of the re-establishment of the church. No one over twenty-five years of age will be surprised by the number of supporters orthodoxy gained from the moment when it advanced from being an absurdity to being a means of subsistence. To such converts add the great party of the timorous, all those who live in fear of the Red Republic, and in whose eyes religion was, first and foremost, a safeguard against it. It was among these that the army of the principle of authority obtained most recruits. From a religious body the church suddenly turned into a political party."

    31. Alton Locke predicts his imminent demise: "No,—I shall never see the land [the New World]. I felt it all along. Weaker and weaker, day by day, with bleeding lungs and failing limbs, I have travelled the ocean-paths. The iron has entered too deeply into my soul" ([Kingsley,] *Alton Locke*, 388).

    32. Charles Francis Adams, *Three Episodes of Massachusetts History*, vol. 2 (Boston: Houghton Mifflin, 1903), 569, 574–75. Henry Vane was a puritan aristocrat, briefly governor of Massachusetts Bay, later executed as a regicide. Note that Hutchinsonian ambition is blamed, yet the puritans were essentially persecutors. (Adams was the son of John Quincy Adams, whose puritanism was directed against the money power; his son had married into wealth, as Daniel Walker Howe points out in *Political Culture of the American Whigs*, 48.) This inner contradiction pervades much of the historiography of the Antinomian Controversy. See my manuscript "Anne Hutchinson's Red Regiment." It is also telling that Adams had turned against the unbending radicalism of his friend Charles Sumner, who may be the more immediate inspiration for his hostile portrait of the puritans.

    Compare with Robertson-Lorant, *Melville*, 287: "Melville intuitively sensed, perhaps in the deepest recesses of his own heart, an inner mother—not the haughty, controlling Victorian matriarch, but the great goddess whose nurturing presence antedated the angry God of the Hebrews and the Puritans." Again, the slur against the angry Jewish God. Referring to a late poem, "The Devotion of the Flowers to their Lady," she writes: "Before the Old Testament patriarchs twisted it into a symbol of sin and death as part of their campaign to destroy the worship of the Goddess, the snake was considered sacred because it was the creature who hugged the bosom of the Mother and heard her secrets. The inviolate Rose, a trope for the female genitals, embraces the phallic Worm, or serpent, who is demonized in the Scriptures. Thus the poem implies that violation and conquest are the direct legacy of a jealous God whose power is controlling and destructive, not generative and erotic" (611). Similarly she conflates Melville's neo-Calvinist mother, the Hebrew God, and Ahab: "In a man-of-war world, the voice of the people is strangled by propaganda, which is violence transformed into a bloodless art. The *Bellipotent* resembles a twentieth-century totalitarian state where government officials invoke 'national security' to cover politically expedient violations of civil rights, and where military necessity dictates that perversions of language are acceptable political weapons, and justice as civilians know it does not exist. In *Moby-Dick*, Ahab bends the crew to his insane will by incantatory language and brilliantly orchestrated ritual. With its intentional inaccuracies and syntactical twists and turns, *Billy Budd* anticipates George Orwell's *1984*" (594). As with many other scholars, she assumes that Ahab foresees or igores the inevitable doom of his ship and crew; the allegorical meaning of the quest as explicated in "The Quarter-Deck" is not engaged. Whether Melville views Ahab as geologic Promethean/abolitionist or something less appealing to twentieth-century liberals, the comparison with Hitler or Stalin is ahistoric.

33. See the Robert Altman–Donald Freed film *Secret Honor*, in which the Quaker Richard Nixon is dominated by his mother, the source of his overreaching and tragic descent into madness. First as his mother's little dog, he is then set up to become the running dog of the fascistic nouveaux riches southwestern capitalists after the war. It is hinted that the eastern establishment erred in not taking the talented young veteran and lawyer into their club; they lacked the necessary stabilizing pluralism that keeps the ship afloat.

34. Richard H. Brodhead, "The Book That Ruined Melville," *New York Times Book Review*, Jan. 7, 1996, 35. See also Brodhead's essay "Melville, or Aggression," in *Melville's Evermoving Dawn: Centennial Essays*, ed. John Bryant and Robert Milder (Kent, Ohio: Kent State UP, 1997), 181–91. Relying on a recent revolution in feminist cultural history that has explicated the entry of sphere ideology and new roles for the sexes, Ahab is now understood as the exemplar of individualist masculinity as constructed in mid-nineteenth-century America, the self-assertive entrepreneur resisting subjugation, his rage a cover for inner feelings of impotence. Ishmael, not Ahab, represents Melville's creative capacities, sublimating male aggression into "writing, irony, and verbal play" (182).

35. H. J. C. Grierson, "Lord Byron," *The Nation and Athenaeum*, Apr. 19, 1924, 81–83.

36. Quoted in Gisela C. Lebzelter, *Political Anti-Semitism in England 1918–1939* (London: Macmillan, 1978), 26. The "Learned Elders" were the conspiratorial rabbis exposed in *The Protocols of the Elders of Zion*. John Freeman, the second Melville biographer of the 1920s, published in Douglas's periodicals, including *Academy*.

37. For example, essays written in the 1930s and 1940s, Georg Lukács, *Goethe and His Age* (London: Merlin Press, 1968), esp. 165, 175, 204, 217, 231, separating the Faust legend from the Lutherans and asserting the progressive character of Goethe's (and Byron's) contributions, Goethe's aristocratic side notwithstanding. I do not agree with Lukács's easy conflation of German and English romanticism, positions also enunciated in *The New Masses* and *Science and Society*. Tellingly, Kant was rejected by Lukács as purveyor of mystifying mediations, perhaps because Kant was an ethical universalist.

38. Henry Farnham May, *The Divided Heart: Essays on Protestantism and the Enlightenment in America* (New York: Oxford UP, 1991), 195–96. See especially 161–96 for May's scheme for classifying different strands of the Enlightenment; compare with imagery of F. O. Matthiessen or T. S. Eliot, below.

39. Compare with the Charles Sumner entry in *Dictionary of American Biography* 9:213. I am indebted to Frank Doble for calling this characterization to my attention. The fit between Sumner and Ahab seems exact.

40. See *Charles Sumner: An Essay by Carl Schurz*, ed. Arthur Reed Hogue (Urbana: U of Illinois P, 1951), 38, 40, 140n.28. In the second excerpt, Schurz was quoting, then commenting on, a line from a letter from Aron Haake, Feb. 2, 1894. The editor discovered the notes, written on the back of the envelope, in the Schurz Papers. For more evidence linking Sumner to qualities ascribed to Ahab, see David Herbert Donald, *Charles Sumner and the Coming of the Civil War* (New York: Knopf, 1960), 192. Opposing his election, Caleb Cushing described Sumner as "'a red-hot abolitionist' . . . like a firebrand . . . the election of a 'one-idead abolitionist agitator' like Sumner would be a 'death stab to the honor and welfare of the Commonwealth.'" The hostile Donald (a Southerner from Mississippi) referred to Sumner as a "moral terrorist" (relying upon Schurz as quoted above?) and blamed him for partly causing the Civil War.

41. Antimaterialist combatants in the science wars, in their resistance to the notion of a scientific revolution, have pointed to the empiricism of the High Middle Ages. See the profascist *American Review* of the mid-1930s for the constant evocation of the empiricist Thomas Aquinas, for whom there was no contradiction between faith and reason. For the Agrarians arguing that

(Aristotelian) case, the contractual arrangement that supposedly existed between the good kings of the twelfth century and the people exemplified the ideal society, one that they wished to reinstate. Some historians say that Locke's theories are derived from the same source.

42. Nathaniel Hawthorne, "A Virtuoso's Collection," *Complete Short Stories*, 443–44, 448, 446.

43. O. W. Riegel, "The Anatomy of Melville's Fame," *American Literature* 3 (1931): 203. Riegel was a professor at Washington and Lee University. His negative assessments were refuted by William Braswell, "A Note on 'The Anatomy of Melville's Fame,'" *American Literature* 5 (Jan. 1934): 360–64.

44. Compare with Fredric Jameson, *Marxism and Form* (Princeton: Princeton UP, 1971). Jameson, a Hegelian-Marxist for whom 1930s-style Marxist analysis is irrelevant to "postindustrial society," rejects Anglo-American positivism.

6. THE BOULEVARD OF BROKEN DREAMS: RAYMOND M. WEAVER AND
THE MELVILLE REVIVAL, 1919–1935

1. James Hannay, "A Notice of His Life and Times," in *The Poetical Works of Edgar Allan Poe* (London, 1853); partially quoted in *Moby-Dick* (NN), Historical Note, 733. Hannay is identified as a Scottish sailor, then journalist, critic, and novelist.

2. Montgomery Belgion, "God Is Mammon," in *The Human Parrot and Other Essays* (London: Oxford UP, 1931), 124–25.

3. In answer to my question about Weaver's family background (interview, Nov. 4, 1987), Dr. Henry A. Murray said he knew nothing about Weaver's early life but that, during their first meeting, Weaver presented him with a first edition of *Clarel* and "sort of made a pass at me." Murray was entranced by Weaver's black-painted bedroom with a golden crucifix hanging over the bed, eerily glowing in the slanted afternoon light; Murray mentioned this scene several times in a dreamy tone of voice. Paul Metcalf, Melville's great-grandson, and his wife, Nancy, visited Weaver in this apartment at a later date. They remember red lacquer (Chinese-style) furniture in the living room but not black walls in a bedroom. Murray further told me he could not bear to read Weaver's *Black Valley* (1926), a novel in which the main character, a female missionary, suffers a nervous breakdown when facing marriage with a ship's captain. It is possible that the black bedroom with its suggestion of a homosexual Black Mass was imaginary, that Murray identified Weaver with Melville, whose bed and covering were black (as Eleanor Metcalf remembered). Or the strange black bedroom could have really been there, suggesting that Weaver had merged with his subject. The Weaver bedroom is described in Murray's Melville papers (Morsels folder), but in his notes the crucifix is remembered as ivory.

4. See Joseph Freeman, *An American Testament: A Narrative of Rebels and Romantics* (New York: Farrar and Rinehart, 1936), 113, for the circumstances of Weaver's appointment. The records of Columbia University confirm that Weaver was hired on October 8, 1917. No printed source in Melville scholarship or in newspaper obituaries has reported this. I found no entry in student records indicating a Baltimore address. However, the Minutes for the Faculty states that he was born in Baltimore in 1888, that he taught English in Hiroshima, Japan, 1912–15, and that he was "instructor in English in 1917, associate in 1919; assistant professor in 1923, associate professor in 1937; and professor in 1946." Also see Freeman's affectionate reminiscence of Weaver, below.

5. See Weaver's introduction to André Gide, *The Counterfeiters* (New York: Modern Library, 1931); he commented on the pain of denying one's "nature" (which of course he refused to do).

6. See Simeon Strunsky, "What the Bolsheviks Really Want," *Nation*, Nov. 15, 1917, 530–32. The following themes were pervasive from late 1917 to 1919 (the period when Weaver reentered

the academy and then began his work on Melville): American identity should not be anti-British; the *Nation* promoted an Anglo-Americanism tied racially to Burkean conservatism; excessive repression caused revolution; narrow nationalism ("militaristic madness") was autocratic, and its antidote was pluralism and free trade. It was "a fact" that the war would cause socialist revolution as its outcome, so conservatives should adapt now before they lost everything. "Moderation" (the broad, generous, honest populism of the Anglo-Saxon race) was constantly contrasted first to German autocracy (materialist); after the war, more vehemently, to Bolshevik/Jewish extremism (materialism, sensuality, pantheism, mysticism, primitivism, anarchism, "complete democracy," "fanaticism"). See *Nation,* Oct. 4, 1917, 361–62, 365, 373; Oct. 11, 388–89; Oct. 18, 418, 424–28; Nov. 29, 590–92; Dec. 20, 687–89; Jan. 3, 1918, 4–5, 8–10; Jan. 10, 31–33; Oct. 12, 408–9, 412; Oct. 19, 444–45; Feb. 8, 1919, 186–87, 202; May 10, 747–50; July 5, 12–13; July 12, 37–39; July 26, 104–6.

7. Weaver used the concept of insanity in two ways: In his response to Melville he obviously referred to the divine madness of poets; when describing his emotional difficulties to Mark Van Doren, he did not label his condition. Weaver's undated twelve-page memoir is hand printed on leaves roughly the size of the "Billy Budd" manuscript, which Eleanor Metcalf showed him in 1919 and which he edited for publication. The memoir (partly appended) was written probably within two years of Weaver's death in 1948 and may have compressed years of rumors, but it also may be a displaced response to Melville's revelations/retractions. I cannot imagine what secrets Weaver could have heard from Eleanor during their first meeting, other than about Melville's unhappy marriage he says she reported in 1919, correcting his article. (See below for Olson's report of a document she supposedly showed Weaver at a later time regarding a family member institutionalized for insanity.) She knew very little about her grandfather, as subsequent letters to her mother suggest. Unpublished materials in her custody included the "Billy Budd" manuscript, various sketches, and the journals of Melville's trips to Europe and the Mediterranean, 1849 and 1856–57, and the 1860 voyage to San Francisco with his younger brother Tom, captain of the *Meteor.* Family letters included the dying Gansevoort's devastating last letter to his brother Herman.

8. Eugene Saxton, father to the novelist and scholar Alexander Saxton, was born into a conservative Baltimore Catholic family, according to his son, sharing the views of other Southern Democrats. While promoting Melville, he was also interested in Hilaire Belloc (see Raymond Weaver Papers, UCLA; and J. C. Squire Papers); however, he later joined Harper's as editor-in-chief, shepherding many literary radicals, including John Dos Passos, Aldous Huxley, and Richard Wright.

9. A complete publishing history of the Melville Revival is beyond the scope of this study (or impossible to write, since the Constable records were destroyed during the war and the Doran records are missing). Melvilleans may believe that Weaver's article of 1919 "led to the publication of the Constable Edition." Nathalia Wright, "Melville and STW at Yale: Studies under Stanley T. Williams," *Melville Society Extracts* 70 (Sept. 1987): 1–4. My research has not yet shown such a connection. I suspect that if there is a link, it would be the stimulation of a popular Melville edition planned by an American publisher (Doran) which Sadleir could have heard about in mid-1920; also the republication of *Moby-Dick* (New York: Oxford UP, 1920) with an enthused introduction by the conservative Catholic critic Viola Meynell.

Although the evidence is fragmentary, it appears that Weaver was ingratiating himself with publishers whose interests were at odds. A letter from Henry K. Metcalf to Weaver on August 28, 1920, reports on some Melville research and alludes to Weaver's letter indicating that Doran had not yet committed (presumably to the biography and the larger project; the Metcalfs were helping Weaver find a publisher in Boston). This letter and those from Eugene Saxton are at Columbia University. However, according to the Weaver Papers at UCLA, Weaver did contact Michael Sadleir on May 23, 1922, suggesting emendations for Sadleir's *Excursions* and telling him he could lead him to the privately printed *John Marr* and *Timoleon* (later dangling the unpublished works in Eleanor Metcalf's possession, e.g., "Billy Budd," which he had not sent "because of a death that has touched me closely," July 20, 1922). Sadleir responded to the first letter on June 9, 1922, telling Weaver "*Very confidentially*, this firm has already nearly completed a handsome collected edition of Melville's prose. We are not telling a soul until the thing is actually ready. . . . It is for subsequent inclusion in this Edition that I am so anxious to get first rights in the unpublished matter, and I am encouraged by your letter to ask whether you can assist the project." In the letter of July 20, 1922, Weaver abjectly apologized for his "treachery": He had been put in a position where he had been forced to reveal Sadleir's confidence because he had been pressured by Doran to sign a contract with their company and to disclose information about rival editions to prevent Doran from further financial loss. (Doran "was already involved pretty heavily.") Doran told him, said Weaver, that "Saxton was in England working especially on this adventure." Sadleir responded on July 24, 1922: He had seen Saxton, who would return; Sadleir proposed to tell him then about the Melville project. It is clear that Doran thought they were getting the unpublished material that Sadleir had desired: "I understand from Saxton that Doran had completed arrangements for (but not started to manufacture) their edition, which will be first in twelve volumes (with a little unpublished material included) and possibly will have a supplementary four or five volumes of other new stuff. What we should like to think is that you would be free to let us also add the unpublished material to our edition for later volumes. I do not think we should clash with Doran's interest but rather with the subscription publisher who is going to work the sale of the edition de luxe for him. Mr. Saxton tells me that they propose to use the plates of the subscription edition for a popular edition. This is not our way to treat buyers of expensive de luxe editions, and we ourselves are distributing the type after the 750 (possibly 1,000 but more possibly 750) sets have been printed. Will you therefore now feel yourself quite free, if necessary, to make public our plans and see whether you can arrange for the unpublished stuff to be at our disposal for the extent of a limited edition?"

After Saxton's second visit, Sadleir told Weaver not to worry about his conduct: He had "acted with the greatest discretion and tact." Sadleir did mention that Saxton's version of Weaver's relation to the Doran project deviated from Weaver's version in his letter of July 20, 1922. In a handwritten letter of August 1, 1922, Sadleir remarked, "Incidentally Saxton told me you were signed and pledged to the Doran edition; this is clearly not the case. Tant mieux." Sadleir went on to deny that Saxton was snooping: "Further I don't gather Saxton to have been here 'working especially on this venture.' Indeed he knew very little about it having only heard since he sailed from Doran that the contract with the subscription publisher was closed. He was mainly interested in arranging for the trade edition they were to make from the plates of the subscription edition." Another letter, on October 11, 1922, bears out my suspicion that Sadleir was using Weaver: "I wonder how successful Wells is being with the Standard Edition in the USA? Here it has gone far more quickly than I expected and late applicants bitterly lamenting that the whole number has been subscribed away." One set has been saved for RW "because the firm feel they would like you to have this for all the trouble you have taken and will yet take to fix up matters with Mrs. Metcalf." A copy of the Constable volume 13 alone is with the Raymond Weaver Papers at Columbia.

The only article to use the Weaver Papers at UCLA transmits a different theme: Philip Durham, "Prelude to the Constable Edition of Melville," *Huntington Library Quarterly* 3 (May 1958): 285–89, cites some of these materials to demonstrate the superiority of English taste to American philistinism. His selections tended to protect the two gentlemen, Sadleir and the Anglophile Weaver, while casting suspicion on Doran and his "man Saxton." According to Durham, the Doran/Saxton file is missing.

10. Hoyt Hudson, 157. Other examples of sound English conservative opinion, before and after publication of Weaver's biography: J. M. Dent published an edition of *Typee* in 1907 with this

editor's introduction: "His love for philosophy and mysticism which are to be clearly traced in certain chapters of 'Moby Dick' had grown upon him to a degree that undoubtedly hurt his art as a tale-teller. His acquaintance at Pittsfield with Nathaniel Hawthorne may have indirectly encouraged in him the same taste for abstruse speculations. In many of the books of his later period, the break with reality is complete. They attempt a fantasy which is not justified by its result in narrative art; and although his personality was a unique one, these later books of personal philosophy strained through a broken mesh would try even the most enthusiastic reader. 'Pierre, or the Ambiguities,' 1852, and 'The Confidence Man,' 1857, are among Melville's failures" (ix–x). For J. W. N. Sullivan in the London *Times Literary Supplement*, July 26, 1923, Ahab was a troubled soul and an overreacher (i.e., the extreme romantic of Melville's early work); quirky Melville was at odds with (the arrogantly positivist) Victorians; the "general mind" has now changed, more respectful of "mystery." But Melville, though compelling, is not first rate; his nihilistic darkness and despair signify spiritual immaturity and his writing lacks formal control. In other words, he is dominated by his vision (Isabel).

11. E. L. Grant Watson, "*Moby-Dick*," *London Mercury* 3 (Dec. 1920): 180–86; compare with Weaver plagiarism, *Mariner and Mystic*, 332. Robert S. Forsythe, review of *Journal up the Straits*, *American Literature* 8 (Mar. 1936): 85–96.

12. Undated, Weaver Papers, Columbia University, written in pencil on pale-green note paper, the same used by Eleanor Metcalf in some notes to Leyda. Compare with Eleanor Melville Metcalf, *Herman Melville: Cycle and Epicycle*, 55, describing the ever-loyal and kind grandmother, bitterly complaining to her niece. Also see James F. Barbour, "Melville Biography," in *A Companion to Melville Studies*, ed. John Bryant (New York: Greenwood, 1986), 23. Barbour criticizes the Leon Howard biography (1951) for neglecting rumors of imputed insanity after 1851, also for "tales of irascibility, drunkenness, intellectual bullying of his wife. . . . These are ignored or attributed to Elizabeth's habit of translating her frustrations into concerns about her hus-band's health." William Braswell, *Melville's Religious Thought*, relying on personal conversations with both Weaver and Eleanor Metcalf, stated firmly that after the publication of *Pierre*, Melville was nervous, but not insane; that his family could not distinguish between nervous strain and insanity so called in doctors (106). For Braswell, the Melville problem consisted in the loss of his early religious faith, one that recognized "the limits of human reason" (105–8), repaired in old age as revealed in pro-Catholic passages in *Clarel* and "Billy Budd." Garner, *Civil War World*, 22, reports that Josephine Shaw's father, John Oakes Shaw, was hostile to Melville's writing. Relying on the Kring-Carey find of correspondence between Henry Whitney Bellows and Sam Shaw discussing the merits of rescuing Elizabeth from Herman, Robertson-Lorant, *Melville*, 504–9, discusses Melville's abusiveness toward his wife as if there was no uncertainty about the behavior, nor does she explore Bellow's ultraconservative politics. It was "Lizzie's docility [that] may even have sparked some of her husband's outbursts and reinforced unhealthy repressions that adversely affected her four children." Robertson-Lorant holds Herman responsible for the deaths of his two sons; until he connects with his inner woman he is the archetypal angry (Jewish) God.

13. Julian Hawthorne, *Hawthorne and His Circle* (New York: Harper, 1903), 32–33. Compare with discussion of Vine and Clarel, above. As a child, Julian was fond of Melville; I find it plausible that his later harsh judgment was derived from his father.

14. Julian Hawthorne to Weaver, Dec. 5, 1919, Weaver Papers, Columbia University.

15. *The Memoirs of Julian Hawthorne*, ed. Edith Garrigues Hawthorne (New York: Macmillan, 1938), 288–90.

16. Quoted in Merton M. Sealts, Jr., *Early Lives of Melville* (Madison: U of Wisconsin P, 1974), 179–85. What kind of family upheavals could Eleanor and Frances have experienced that would have sent the younger away to safety? According to Paul Metcalf (interview, Dec. 15, 1996), his mother dominated her younger sisters and idealized her own childhood. She and Frances were

close in age; there was an anxious hiatus in which Frances Thomas (Melville's daughter) and her husband were unable to conceive, perhaps the period to which Frances Osborne referred; but it is also possible that Frances was afraid of her sister's antagonism, however subtly expressed.

17. See Eleanor Melville Metcalf to Frances Thomas, Melville Papers, bMS Am 188 (272–74), Houghton Library; and Frances Thomas to Eleanor Metcalf, Nov. 3, 1919, Melville Papers, bMS Am 188 (342). It was "Aunt Kate" (Thomas Melville's remarried widow, Mrs. Kenneth G. White) who refused to breach confidences (presumably from Elizabeth). Amy Puett, in "Melville's Wife," mentions Frances Thomas voicing resentment at her father's emotional neediness during the composition of *Clarel*. Frances complained about "the rhythm with which her father would recite, while pacing the floor, certain verses he had written, looking for approbation, she thought, from his wife and daughters" (149).

18. See also Frances Thomas to Eleanor Metcalf, Nov. 16, 1919, the Melville Papers, bMS Am 188 (344), Harvard University, quoted in Amy Puett Emmers, "Melville's Closet Skeleton: A New Letter about the Illegitimacy Incident in *Pierre*," in *Studies in the American Renaissance 1977*, ed. Joel Myerson (Boston: Twayne, 1978): "Cousin M wrote me that she was pretty sure she had a copy of 'Pierre' and thinks it must be at Arrowhead. Will had read it; and said it seemed to refer to family matters." ("M" referred to Maria Gansevoort Morewood, Allan Melville's daughter; "Will" was her husband.) In a letter to EMM of November 12, 1919 (bMS Am 188 [343]), Frances says she is reading her father's unpublished short stories with enough interest to withhold them from Eleanor until she is finished; in the letter of November 16, 1919, she is "reading the *short* stories that were published in Putnam's about 1854–1855, others are in Piazza Tales."

19. Frances Thomas to Weaver, Jan. 17, 1922, Weaver Papers, Columbia University. Compare with Frances Thomas to Eleanor Metcalf, Jan. 12, 1922, suggesting a variety of opinions within the family about her father but no serious antagonism to Weaver: "I am a little more than half way through the book. Perhaps I don't appreciate the 'chivalrous position' Mr. Weaver has taken in regard to unpublished material. At any rate, I have no unfavorable criticisms to make, and if I had, I should not do it, for I prefer to take a negative part in the matter. Will Morewood is *deep* in it. No, I am not surprised at the view Cousin Catherine takes about 'Grandma Melville.'" Melville Papers, bMS Am 188 (345), Houghton Library.

20. Frances Thomas to Eleanor Metcalf, the Melville Papers, bMS Am 188 (347), Harvard University. Compare with Hershel Parker, Historical Note to *Moby-Dick*, 753: "Not the least of the damage Weaver did was to distress Melville's surviving daughter, Frances Thomas, to the point that she absolutely refused to cooperate with later biographical researchers."

21. For instance, Weaver's introduction to the Albert and Charles Boni edition of *Moby-Dick*, following John Masefield, takes the position that Ahab was mad. But in the same essay, Weaver quotes the lengthy section from *Pierre* depicting Pierre/Ahab's intense mental and physical suffering while writing what Weaver assumed was *Moby-Dick* (quoted above). In this reading, Pierre, the principled bearer of truth, is driven to desperation by the rejection of the philistine literary world, collapsing in the gutter and experiencing temporary blindness.

22. An undated note from Mary W. Kimball, Saddle Meadows, Pittsfield, Massachusetts, alludes to an exchange of "confidence(s)." Weaver Papers, Columbia University.

23. Murray's notes for his unpublished biography declare Augusta as the love of Herman's life.

24. Has Eleanor contradicted herself, or has Herman's "disgusting" characterization of the handkerchief been precise, but not vulgar ("low")?

25. Special Correspondence, Murray Papers, box 4.

26. This is an important detail: Frances Thomas had written to Eleanor, November 12, 1919, "Cousin M. was here yesterday & we talked over things, she was already aware of a good deal, *she* said H.M. *said* that his mother hated him." Melville Papers, bMS Am 188 (343), Houghton Library.

27. These two letters are misfiled in Henry A. Murray Special Correspondence, box 13, Harvard University Archives. The letters from the Morewoods and Eleanor Metcalf are dispersed throughout boxes 4, 13, and 14. In her letter to me, January 15, 1993, Laurie Robertson-Lorant (who had read Murray's unpublished biography with mixed feelings), asked, "He certainly tracked down many obscure descendants, but I have yet to find any notes of conversations with Paul's mother, or the Morewood descendants. Do you know of any?" In the materials I was allowed to read, there are neither notes nor letters from Murray to the relatives, nor are there any comments on their responses to his queries.

28. Murray had been rummaging through books, trunks, and old papers at Arrowhead probably during the early spring and summer of 1926, but he got the key from Agnes after November 20, 1925. It was also Agnes who gave Murray Eleanor's address. Soon after, Murray asked Agnes to read *Pierre*. In 1926, he seems to have been offering to buy the place and turn it into a historical site. Maria Morewood at first asked $40,000, then $20,000, if it were to be for public view and commemoration. See letters Agnes Morewood to Murray, Nov. 20, 1925, Jan. 2, 27, June 22, Oct. 16, and Dec. 8, 1926.

29. Margaret Morewood to Murray, Aug. 14, 1927, Murray Special Correspondence, box 13, Harvard University Archives. Margaret was writing from Scotland where she had tracked down a noble ancestor, the "deteriorated" Lord Dundas in his decrepit castle.

30. G. W. Chessman Lecture Notes for English 7, 1938/39, Mar 7, 1939, Harvard University Archives. The course was taught by Perry Miller and William Ellery Sedgwick; this class was taught by Miller. Other judgments showed typical upper-class readings of American history: John Smith's "braggadocio becomes the spirit of the pioneers" (Sedgwick); "Protestantism was a mask for radical capitalism as shown by Max Weber" (Miller). On Roger Williams (who had been banished from the Bay Colony by John Winthrop because he preached that the English had no title to the Indian lands they were occupying): "He has an emotional and hysterical quality about his idealistic writing. He was no realist. His style was arresting . . . . Williams carried the Protestant Reformation a step farther & says people should try to find the truth when they can. Today we begin to see some of the reasoning of Winthrop. Miller makes a beautiful allusion to Roosevelt in his view of Winthrop." Hawthorne is viewed as "solid, commonsensical and healthy."

31. See Henry A. Murray, "Bartleby and I," *Bartleby the Scrivener: A Symposium by Henry A. Murray [and others]*, ed. Howard P. Vincent (Kent, Oh.: Kent State UP, 1966), 3–24. Murray presented his paper as a dialogue among the author, the scrivener, two critics, a biographer, and a psychologist. An interchange between the biographer and the author suggests that Murray had actually received a report of abuse from a descendant: "*The biographer.* 'Didn't you rage at her occasionally in real life? I was told by a member of your family that once you clutched her by the throat and exclaimed: "Now I know what a man feels like who wants to kill his wife." And after that didn't she leave you and return to her family's house in Boston, taking the children with her?' *The author.* 'Yes, but I was overcome with remorse and pity and in a week or so—I don't remember how long it was exactly—I went up there and persuaded her to come back to me and try again. Nobody like you on the outside can possibly understand the anguish of those years for both of us. Do not judge, lest you be judged; and so the less said the better. Ladies are like creeds; if you cannot speak well of them, say nothing'" (19).

32. As reported in Philip Weiss, "Herman-Neutics," *New York Times Magazine*, Dec. 15, 1996, 60–65, 70–72. Paul Metcalf believed that his mother withheld secrets from him regarding family violence, secrets she had disclosed to Murray and no one else. However, in light of her "semi-nervous breakdown" of the early 1920s, reported by David Metcalf, Paul's older brother (both boys were shipped out of the house), and in light of the jealousy Eleanor probably would have felt toward her younger sister Frances (who was not afraid of Herman), it is conceivable that Eleanor's "secrets" gave her a psychological advantage over Frances. Also, she may have felt threatened by

Melville's clear-eyed exposures of the not-so-happy family. This would explain the flight to the pastoral mode in her own poetry—a sentimental construction of her own immediate family that Frances said was marked by "domestic upheavals."

33. I find it unlikely that Perry Miller had not heard about Isabel from Murray or other insiders. See Miller's class notes for English 170a, Romanticism in American Literature, "Teaching Notes ca. 1950–1960," Perry Miller Papers. In his lecture on *Pierre*, twenty pages of handwritten note cards carry lengthy passages from Weaver (1921) without attribution. These are interspersed with Murray's hostile judgments about Melville's slander of his father in *Pierre* and extensive quotes from the novel. Of course, I do not know whether or not Miller told his classes he was reading from Weaver, but it seems odd that there were no page numbers or any other identification attached to the Weaver lines on Miller's note cards.

34. Melville's working-class readership has not yet been investigated. See George McPhersen Hunter to RW, Dec. 23, 1921: "As an ex-sailor, and writer on sea topics I have been struck with the prevalence of the Moby Dick legend, and wonder if Melville's book was responsible for it. Recently an old flying fish sailor quoted from the volume, and the other night on a trolley car I asked a German [?] ex-sailor if he ever heard of Moby Dick, 'Su-ure' he said, 'Everybody knows him'" (Weaver Papers, Columbia University). The latter sailor could have referred only to the legend, but political scientist Richard Ashcraft told me he had seen numerous references to Melville in nineteenth-century working-class English newspapers.

35. However, Weaver admired the radical Victorian poet and journalist James Thomson ("B.V."), who may have connected Melville with both Ishmael and Ahab: "[Thomson:] I know but one other living American writer who approaches [Whitman] in his sympathy with all ordinary life and vulgar occupations, in his feeling of brotherhood for all rough workers, and at the same time in his sense of beauty and grandeur, and his power of thought; I mean Herman Melville." See *National Reformer*, Aug. 30, 1874, 135. Compare with Henry Salt to Willard Thorp, Sept. 1, 1935: "I was greatly interested to hear of new studies in James Thomson, as the neglect of 'The City of Dreadful Night' by English literary men has been almost as disgraceful as their treatment of Shelley. I think it is due to sheer stupidity more than intention. I, personally, can do nothing; for to anyone who has worked for humanitarian causes the literary Profession seems instinctively to turn a cold shoulder." Also see Arthur Stedman to Henry Salt, May 4, 1892: HM paid $3.75 for Salt's life of Thomson before it was sent to him. Melville Files, Newberry Library.

36. The typescript of the manuscript (sent to Eleanor Metcalf before publication and donated to Columbia in 1954) was checked approvingly here.

37. The word "assets" used twice and protested by Eleanor Metcalf, changed in *Mariner and Mystic*. For Weaver "the stupendous discovery" seems to have been associated with the happiness of merging with the primitive. In his introduction to the Boni edition of *Redburn* (1924), he wrote, "A sensitive and impetuous child of undisciplined imagination, he was, both by temperament and training, at odds with himself and reality. . . . Stirred by motives of desperation and by the delusion that some stupendous discovery of happiness lay just over the world's rim, Melville planned a hegira" (5–6). Compare with Weaver's introduction to the Boni *Israel Potter* (1924): "It is a book in which the beauty of splendid adventure ends in the closing chapters by wasting itself in an impotent rage at life's small ironies. . . . *Israel Potter* is Melville's own life, allegorized" (v–vi). Commenting on the hostile depiction of Benjamin Franklin: "Melville's soul was, indeed, a vast dark forest; and it could evoke little sympathy for Franklin's almanac morality, his neat kitchen-garden scheme of things. Melville's kinship was rather with tumultous and uncharted souls, and upon Ethan Allen and John Paul Jones he lavished his best art. . . . John Paul is presented as a young and gallant Captain Ahab, 'combining in one breast the vengeful indignation and bitter ambition of an outraged hero with the uncompunctious desperation of a renegade. In one view the Coriolanus of the sea; in another, a cross between the gentleman and the wolf'" (vii).

F. Barron Freeman shared Weaver's contempt for happiness as a legitimate value in *Melville's Billy Budd*. Melville had objected to this passage in Matthew Arnold, *Empodocles on Etna:* "Couldst thou but once discern / Thou has no *right* to bliss." According to Freeman the marginal comment was checked and later erased. Following is Freeman's evaluation of Margoth/Melville's response: "A western critic here exclaims—'what in thunder did the Gods create us for then? If not for bliss, for hate? If so, the devil take the Gods.' The quiet, triumphant and religious description of Billy's hanging shows how far Melville finally came from the angry and defiant frustration of this hastily scrawled note; it should also suggest why this scrawl was erased" (23).

38. See John Block Friedman, *The Monstrous Races in Medieval Art and Thought* (Cambridge, Mass.: Harvard UP, 1981), 35, 47–49, 53. The Attic sensibility was viewed by medieval (Aristotelian) Catholics as moderate, disciplined, and balanced, while its monstrous antitheses represented "emotion, redundancy, and formal disorder"; monstrosity was correlated with "the enigmatic, the inflated and the grandiose." The hot, deserted antipodes were linked to the vaguely situated Ethiopia and found at the most extreme distances from the Greek center of the world; its perverse inhabitants had feet turned backward and walked upside down; they were out of reach of the Christian gospel.

39. See George Allen Morgan, *What Nietzsche Means* (Cambridge, Mass.: Harvard UP, 1941). Weaver could have mistaken Nietzsche's Superman for a romantic.

40. MacPhee, *Monarch Notes and Study Guides*, 5.

41. Murray had started to answer Hershel Parker's call for responses to the Kring-Carey find of the mid-1970s, disclosing an aborted kidnap plot and near divorce in 1867. Murray referred to Parker as "management."

42. Ludwig Lewisohn, "The Weakness of Herman Melville," *This Quarter* 3 (Apr.–June 1931): 610–17. His bogus masterpiece lacked "an ultimate spirit of reconciliation"; he should have emulated Milton and Goethe, who were "servants of their states." Relying on Weaver's researches regarding the mother fixation, he decided Melville was "a big-bearded, violently excited man, trying to shout down the whimpering, lonely child in his soul." Lewisohn praised Melville when "he speaks of real things, of the dangers of Democracy creating 'an Anglo-Saxon China.'"

43. Weaver, "New England Gentlemen," *New York Herald Tribune Books*, Sept. 16, 1928, 1, 6. Weaver seems influenced by Hawthorne's *English Notebooks*, quoted above. Some fragments in the Murray Papers suggest that Weaver was also inspired by a talk with Henry Murray sometime between 1925 and 1928 (see Morsels folder). Compare with the ending to Hershel Parker's biography, volume 1, in which the two men are affectionately united in appreciation of Melville's masterpiece.

44. See Lionel Trilling, "From the Notebooks of Lionel Trilling," *Partisan Review* 4 (1984): 496–515; Diana Trilling, "Lionel Trilling: A Jew at Columbia," *Speaking of Literature and Society* (New York: Harcourt Brace Jovanovich, 1980), 420. "Precipitously" is Mrs. Trilling's word. Trilling wrote "A Recollection of Raymond Weaver," in *University on the Heights*, ed. Wesley First (New York: Doubleday, 1958), 5–13, stating that they made peace when Weaver asked to read his doctoral dissertation. He ended with this story: "Weaver's own work with his hands served the purposes not only of pleasure but also of survival. I once paid him a visit in his home and he showed me some old chairs he had bought cheaply at auction and was scraping down to the wood. Partly with sincerity, partly to show my sense of the attractiveness of his enterprise, I said that I would like to engage in it too and asked about auction rooms. He shook his head in emphatic negation, addressed me by name with a solemn intensity that took me aback, and said, 'No. I do these things because I must. Last night until four o'clock I scraped flecks of paint off my kitchen range with a razor blade.' No one, I think, would have supposed that Raymond Weaver led an unperturbed inner life, but never till then had I imagined the virulence of the evil spirits with which he struggled to hold them off, the activity of the hand defending the citadel of the mind. A natural word

for him had always been 'superb' and never did it seem more just than at that moment when, with a superb simplicity, he for a moment put aside his characteristic reserve out of the need to have his pain recognized. Beyond recognition no one would have presumed to go: one could not possibly pity the man who, in any meeting one had with him, had the power of making life seem larger than life." Trilling alludes to Weaver's "early training as an engineer" and makes much of his hand motions as a means to grasp reality, to assure himself that the world out there was really there.

45. Joseph Freeman's memoir, *An American Testament*, 154–55, either plagiarized several paragraphs from the Weaver manuscript (which would date Weaver's composition sometime before the mid-1930s) or Weaver was the plagiarist, writing the essay after Freeman's book was published.

46. Freeman's unfinished letter to his psychiatrist, June 20, 1947, after a visit with Jay Leyda, is lengthily quoted in chapter 8 below.

47. One David Rein was treated like Weaver in the pages of *American Literature*. See Ernest Earnest review of David M. Rein, *S. Weir Mitchell as a Psychiatric Novelist* (New York: International UP, 1952), *American Literature* 24 (1953): 564–66. Rein is criticized for making Mitchell, not Melville and Hawthorne, the first novelist to depict mentally ill characters (Ahab and Dimmesdale). Earnest also wonders why a childhood history is necessary to understand the mad: "After all, we do not ask for an account of the childhood of Captain Ahab or the early traumatic experiences of a King Lear."

48. Trilling to Richard Chase, Sept. 25, 1948, Richard Volney Chase Papers (deposited by Chase's widow, Frances Chase, in 1984).

49. The feud is partly documented in my appendix.

50. Julien Benda, *The Betrayal of the Intellectuals* (1928; reprint, Boston: Beacon, 1955), 32–33. Deploring all forms of class hatred, particularism, and pragmatism (as advocated by William James), Benda was thinking of Italian fascists, Leninists, the *Action Française*, and their common inspiration, George Sorel.

51. Compare reviews of *Pierre* or Mumford's biography by John Brooks Moore, A. H. Starke, and Weldon Stone in *American Literature* 1 (Mar. 1929–June 1930), with reviews or criticism in the mid– to late 1930s–1950s, by William Braswell, Charles R. Anderson, Robert S. Forsythe, and Willard Thorp. Concluding his Weaver rectification in "Contemporary American Opinions of *Typee* and *Omoo*," *American Literature* 9 (Mar. 1937): 1–25, the statement made by Anderson is typical: "Such was Herman Melville at the height of his early popularity. The portrait contains no touch of foreboding gloom or impending tragedy, no hint of the 'mystic' or the philosopher, no trace of the beard which later muffled the lamentations of the Victorian Jeremiah."

52. Eleanor Metcalf to Charles Olson, Jan. 1, 1950, Olson Papers.

53. Leo Lowenthal, *Literature and the Image of Man* (New Brunswick, N.J.: Transaction Books, 1986).

54. Trilling, a moderate, was perceived to be sympathetic to the strike; Mark Rudd approached him to solicit firmer support, but without success. Interview, Kenneth Cloke, 1987. I am suggesting that the figure of Rousseau is gendered as femme fatale in the discourse of stoicism.

55. Charles Simmons, "Mark Van Doren at Columbia," *New York Times Book Review*, Dec. 31, 1972, 23.

56. Compare with Norman Cohn, *Warrant for Genocide: The Myth of the Jewish World Conspiracy and the Protocols of the Elders of Zion* (London: Eyre and Spottiswoode, 1967); following some psychoanalytic readings, Cohn sees the authoritarian father, not the moral mother, as the parent/Jew with the knife.

57. Folder "Copies of M letters, etc.," Olson Papers.

58. "Subjectivist" vs. "objectivist" are terms used by Laven Rasco, "The Biographies of Herman Melville" (Ph.D. diss., Northwestern University, 1957). The contrast between "imaginative"

and "fact-minded" scholars is used by Harrison Hayford, *Melville's "Monody" Really for Hawthorne?* (Evanston, Ill.: Northwestern UP, 1990); he views the deployment of "depth psychology" versus "everyday commonsense psychology" in biography and textual interpretation as the "key" difference in Melville studies (5–6). See also Merton M. Sealts, Jr., *Pursuing Melville 1940–1980* (Madison: U of Wisconsin P, 1982), 236, 339–44. Whereas the family and others thought the early work was autobiographical, "the publication of new biographical research steadily undermined the easy assumption of the earlier years about the reflection of Melville's life in his longer works." "A Letter to Henry A. Murray," in the same volume, defends the objectivists from Murray's charge of deficient imagination. In retrospect, the Stanley Williams students trained at Yale (see chapter 8 below) buttress the autonomy of the literary work advocated by New Critics by insisting on a misfit between Melville's art and life. While some Yale critics (Sealts and Hayford) seem to want to patch up or minimize differences between themselves and Murray, the latter felt rejected by other Melvilleans to the extent of saying to this author, "There has been no Melville Revival."

7. PLURALISM IN ONE PERFECTLY HAPPY FAMILY, 1926–1953: A PEEP AT APES AND ANGELS

1. Once a Fabian Socialist, Sir John Collings Squire became a leading British advocate of Italian fascism in the mid-1930s, though according to his biographer he only "flirted with fascism." In 1934, he was the chair of the Sunday Morning Club, a study group interested in discussing fascism as an alternative in England, later taken over by Oswald Mosely's BUF. Squire's maternal grandfather had been deposited as a child in a country inn by a Spanish grandee, who then disappeared; his father was a veterinarian who abandoned the family; his mother took in boarders. Squire was darkly handsome and obviously thought he carried bad Spanish genes. A novella, "Two Women," by BLAIR, is preserved in his papers, an allegory in which a Creole "belle dame sans merci" and bigamist sends both her husbands (one a poet, the other an American businessman) to a banana republic, with orders to bring back poems after overthrowing the government. Squire's wife, Eileen Wilkinson, was a noted Fabian (and his first love); she divorced him in the late 1930s; by then he was an alcoholic and bankrupt; there is a suggestion in his correspondence that he was bisexual. Squire identified Jews with alienation, loss of caste, constricted possibilities, deception, and torture. For Squire, as for other social democrats treated in this study, neoclassical aesthetics emancipate the tormented Artist from modernist/Jewish/capitalist degeneracy. (Excerpts from brief essays are appended.)

2. See the John Freeman entry by R. Flower, *Dictionary of National Biography* (1937) 25:315–16. Freeman's father was a commercial traveler. An autodidact, Freeman left school at age twelve. He contracted scarlet fever at age three and had a weak heart for the rest of his life.

3. See Freeman, *Herman Melville*, 39 and passim. With reference to the scene in *White-Jacket* where Melville contemplates an assault on Captain Claret (who has threatened him with flogging), Freeman wrote: "He was only twenty-five, but his reserved nature hourly deepened with all suppressions, and the 'reserves' themselves became as a well which he was soon to tap at will and which, with all that was drawn, did but sink deeper and yield a colder water. Already that colder temperature could be felt, and traced to something puritanic in his race. With the removal of his unconscious self-control, as in the scene with Captain Claret, the secret fury of his nature is liberated; but ordinarily the instinctive repression of strong passions was almighty, and the face that he presented to the world in his day, and to us still, is a mask. He could not have worn it so calmly if he had always worn it consciously, but as we said just now, his repression was instinctive and instinct was reinforced by training, example, and the discipline of a life in which no man could afford to wear his heart on his sleeve."

4. Epigraph to Edgar Allan Poe, "William Wilson," 1839.

5. Freeman's misogyny, racism, and antisemitism (like Squire's) are apparent throughout his letters and other writings. "The Change" could also signify the stock exchange.

6. Compare my account of Weaver vs. Freeman with James F. Barbour, "Melville Biography," in *A Companion to Melville Studies*. For Barbour, Weaver's biography is "naive in its methodology, and unbalanced in its presentation" (16); "Weaver gives us a rebel who preaches truth to a pious and hypocritical world and is banned for his audacity. Freeman presents an author of considerable imagination who invests the world with illusions and ideals only to find that reality is different; his final years are an attempt to cope with the barrenness that remained" (17). As shown above, Weaver is responsible for both views, and I do not see them as contradictory. The aristocratic Nietzschean Weaver believed that antibourgeois rebellion was correct and that all hopes of changing humanity were illusory.

7. See Weaver review of Mumford's biography, *New York Evening Post*, Mar. 9, 1929; and Eleanor Metcalf to Charles Olson, Oct. 4, 1934, Olson Papers. A Melville celebration at Broadhall was organized by Miss Bragg, a "Mumfordite" who had snubbed Weaver, asking only Mumford and Murray to speak about Melville; then she invited Olson to speak and Weaver to attend at Mrs. Metcalf's request.

8. Henry A. Murray to Raymond Weaver, n.d., Weaver Papers, Columbia University.

9. I had assumed that the close friends Mumford and Murray shared information about the family, but two letters from Eleanor Metcalf, June 21 and June 30, 1928, suggest that Murray worried that Metcalf would divulge his ideas to Mumford. The first letter assures Murray, "I shall say nothing about your activities unless I hear from you. He is interested in this point in the material that he supposes went into Clarel." In the second, she reassures Murray: "Have no fear— Mr. Mumford will not displace you. As far as I can judge, you are doing something no one else has done. As for your notes on the Journals, I would not dream of having him see them!" (Murray Papers).

10. *Confidence-Man* (NN), chap. 33, 182–83.

11. Herman Melville to Evert Duyckinck, *Correspondence* (NN), 121–22. Here is another parallel with the character of Charles Sumner, who took his political theory from the Declaration of Independence (which had the force of law for him) and the Sermon on the Mount (source of the higher law) and whose alleged monomania and tactlessness outraged conservatives.

12. James Madison, "Federalist Paper No. 10," *The Federalist Papers*, ed. Clinton Rossiter (New York: New American Library, 1961), 79, 80, 84.

13. New York State Legislature, Joint Committee Investigating Seditious Activities, *Revolutionary Radicalism*, 2014, 2201, 3136–37.

14. Marianna is the sad seamstress (another Isabel) who tells the narrator of "The Piazza" that her "strange fancies" (as the narrator defines them) "but reflect the things." Jungian critic E. L. Grant Watson, a contributor to *London Mercury*, inverted Isabel's identical point in his "Melville's Pierre," *New England Quarterly* 3 (Apr. 1930): 195–234, praising *Pierre* as Melville's greatest book. I know of no correction to this revealing gaffe in Melville scholarship, though Watson is frequently mentioned. Watson characterized Isabel's "collective unconscious" as transmitter of the "strangely demented people" (207) that Melville's Isabel clearly identified with real world authority during her stay in the unnamable institution/asylum.

15. Wilfred Trotter, *Instincts of the Herd in Peace and War* (New York: Macmillan, 1947), 94. The scientistic "Publishers' Note" to the 1947 edition reads: "The aftermath of the Second World War, bringing with it the application of Atomic Energy and the need to prevent aggression (an indulgence now realised to have within its reach the power to do even greater harm to civilisation)— these are the considerations either at the front or the back of everyone's thinking. In Europe they apply to the Peace Settlement yet to be made with Germany, and the future part to be played by

her strange and able people. . . . [Trotter's] conclusions can be tested by the evidence of two great wars. Incidentally, they offer one explanation of the German political and social mentality which the British and the American mind find so incomprehensible." Trotter's publishers, Macmillan, avid disseminators of Anglo-American culture, also published Richard Chase's Jungian study of Melville in 1949. Other publishers of Trotter's book include T. F. Unwin, The Scientific Book Club, and Oxford University Press.

16. Van Wyck Brooks, *An Autobiography*, fore. John Hall Wheelock, intro. Malcolm Cowley (New York: E. P. Dutton, 1965), 407–10, 125–26. See Meyer Schapiro review of Mumford, *The Culture of Cities*, "Looking Forward to Looking Backward," *Partisan Review* (June 1938): 12–24, for analysis of Mumford's reactionary organicism.

17. Floyd Dell, *Intellectual Vagabondage* (New York: Doran, 1926), 247–49 (Doran published Weaver). See Daniel Aaron, *Writers on the Left* (New York: Oxford UP, 1977), 102–7, for discussion of Dell's and Joseph Freeman's critique of bohemian symbiosis with puritan middle classes, the babyishness of the bohemian rebel. Such magisterial critiques of romantic infantilism ignore the real hypocrisies and incompatible demands and expectations that have driven "bohemians" into flight and withdrawal. Dell's interest in Nietzsche, Ignatius Donnelly, G. K. Chesterton, and Ezra Pound bears looking into.

18. Aaron, *Writers on the Left*, 233–43. And see photographs at UCLA Special Collections of D. H. Lawrence and Frieda in the Southwest, 1922–1923: Lawrence in tie and (usually) three-piece suit, and Frieda is above him, framed in a black window (elsewhere she is always dressed in ethnic clothing, Indian or Mexican, earth mother and duende, i.e., Isabel).

19. See Robert E. Spiller, ed., *The Van Wyck Brooks–Lewis Mumford Letters: The Record of a Literary Friendship, 1921–1963* (New York: Dutton, 1970). Henry A. Murray said he hoped that I would be able to solve the problem of violence and war, since he had failed (interview, Nov. 4, 1987). Matthiessen denounced the Nietzschean Superman as protofascist while maintaining his reverence for the genius of poets who would, through adherence to organicist aesthetic theory, revitalize and unify culture. See discussion of *American Renaissance*, below, keeping in mind the taming of Marja.

20. See, for instance, Harold D. Lasswell, Daniel Lerner, and Ithiel de Sola Pool, *The Comparative Study of Symbols: An Introduction* (Stanford: Hoover Institute, 1952), commending the "fruitful" content analyses of "a number of kinds of interrogations including thematic apperception tests, questioning of war prisoners, and political opinion studies. . . . Where interviews can be used they are often preferable, but there are situations where a direct question is impossible. One of these situations is typical of intelligence work. The enemy will not usually answer questions. . . . The psychoanalytic approach . . . deals with motivations quite different from those made explicit. . . . Such psychological analysis of written materials is one promising and largely untouched area for content analysis."

21. The nihilist Weaver introduced Ahab as Melville in *Mariner and Mystic*, arguing that Ahab's "uncompromising despair" (the wisdom that is woe) isolated him; this (social) isolation was taken by Melville to be madness (332–33). James Hoopes, *Van Wyck Brooks: In Search of American Culture* (Amherst: U of Massachusetts P, 1977), reports views that may have affected Weaver's later public positions in praise of "Billy Budd" (retroactively a repudiation of Ahab). In his review of the John Freeman biography, Van Wyck Brooks commented on "the note of sweetness and serenity in 'Billy Budd' that speaks of inward peace." In his entry on Melville in the 1927 *Dictionary of American Biography*, Brooks said that Melville's career died of "excessive subjectivity diffused through time and space." Thus alienated, he lost his desire for art (179). In 1947, Brooks praised the Jeffersonian Mazzinian Melville for his belief in national mission. But in 1952, the 1920s revival was condemned for its pessimism: "Then the great myth of Moby Dick rose in the American imagination and Melville's overpowering sense of the omnipotence of evil blacked out

the sunniness and whiteness of Emerson and Whitman" (242–43). Brooks explicitly blamed Marx and Freud, who destroyed our confidence in ourselves (291).

Also see Newton Arvin, *Hawthorne* (Boston: Little, Brown, 1929), 169. He accepted Mumford's (mistaken) judgment that Hawthorne wrote "Ethan Brand" as a portrait of Melville/Ahab: the man of lonely intellect, cruel and inflexible, sharing meaning with no man. Clifton Fadiman, in his introduction to *Moby-Dick* (New York: Limited Editions Club, 1943), argued that Melville's "pessimism" was not "pathological," but Ahab was "a masochist," the invention of the whale a "cancer" in his mind; Ahab was also linked to Gorgon. Boardman Robinson's agitated illustrations depicted Ahab, in my view, as Old Testament prophet. For Lawrance Thompson, *Melville's Quarrel with God*, the gnostic Melville is an Ahab, a hater, malicious, vengeful, and self-pitying; Melville stages ruses to evade heresy hunters; he traps and tests the reader, remaining a defiant rebel to the end of his life.

22. Noted and disparaged by Henry Bamford Parkes, "Poe, Hawthorne, Melville: An Essay in Sociological Criticism," *Partisan Review* (Feb. 1949): 157–66; Melville's disbelief in an underlying organic unity, an aberration he shared with Poe and Hawthorne, made Parkes describe all three as neurotics whose narcissism forecasted the neurotic American personality of our time. Parkes remarked disapprovingly, "Melville fought a long battle with his environment and was never able either to repudiate it or to come to terms with it" (159). Adjustment to reality was Parkes's standard of normality as it was for other followers of ego psychology.

Parkes's essay appeared the same month that Ezra Pound was awarded the Bollingen Prize. The *Saturday Review of Literature*, in articles by Robert Hillyer and Dr. Fredric Wertham, censured the Bollingen Prize, Pound, T. S. Eliot, and Jung, starting a campaign that culminated in removal of federal arts funding until 1965 with the establishment of the National Endowment for the Arts. Hillyer also argued that New Criticism was a protofascist tendency. The *Partisan Review* intellectuals (Richard Chase, Philip Rahv, Alfred Kazin, Harry Levin, Newton Arvin, Lionel Trilling, most of whom were actively promoting Melville after World War II) signed the famous letter attacking the *Saturday Review* for "its methods." The *Partisan Review* intellectuals were defending modernism, they said, and the separation of art and life. The *Nation* joined them by printing the protest, which was incorporated into a pamphlet circulated by *Poetry*. See E. Torrey Fuller, *The Roots of Treason: Ezra Pound and the Secret of Saint Elizabeth's* (New York: McGraw-Hill, 1984), for a muckraking account of the conspiracy to declare Pound insane to avoid a pending trial for treason. My position, elaborated throughout this study, is that muckrakers ignore the structural determinants of behavior, in this case the defenses (both personal and political) against critical thought found in every racist and xenophobic society. Pound's and Eliot's antisemitism should be understood as common, not aberrant, and viewed in the context of counter-Enlightenment conservativism which frequently calls itself radical, liberal, or democratic.

23. See Irving Babbitt, *The New Laokoon: An Essay on the Confusion of the Arts* (Boston: Houghton Mifflin, 1910), 64: the French Revolution was caused by "subliminal uprush." Such formulations of mass politics are traced in Nye, *The Origins of Crowd Psychology*.

24. Mumford to Weaver, Oct. 27 and Dec. 14, 1927, Weaver Papers, Columbia University.

25. Lewis Mumford, *Herman Melville* (New York: Literary Guild, 1929), 351–53.

26. The uneducated "people" may be too fearful and deferential to risk the modern artist's task; Ahab has to overcome their reluctance, taking the role of teacher and agitator. Melville differentiates manly rebels from childish conformists among the sailors throughout.

27. See the caricature by Villeneuve in *French Caricature and the French Revolution 1789–1799* (Los Angeles: The Grunwald Center for the Graphic Arts, 1988), 98. I am freely paraphrasing the message to the king.

28. Louis Kronenberger, ed., *Atlantic Brief Lives: A Biographical Companion to the Arts* (Boston: Little, Brown, 1971), 516.

29. The two extracts are in *Wings* 3, no. 3 (1929):4–7, a periodical published by the Literary Guild of America and sent to its subscribers. Mrs. Effinger's adventure was reprinted from *Atlantic Monthly*. The "bully" was the chimney, linked to the women of the family. "It is known that he was lovingly dominated by the five women of his household—his wife, mother, and three sisters." Thanks to Christine Bass for sending me this rare publication.

30. Mumford to Murray, June 29, 1949, quoted in Lewis Mumford, *My Works and Days: A Personal Chronicle* (New York: Harcourt Brace, 1979), 292–93. Melville saved Mumford's generation from "our too hopeful liberalism, our glib futurism, our pious belief in the progressive solubility of all human problems through science and technology" (288).

31. Mumford to David Liebovitz, Mar. 11, 1963, *My Works and Days*, 293. Compare with Henry Murray to Howard Vincent, Sept. 17, 1947, in answer to his editor's questions about Murray's notes on Melville's madness and family hostility in the introduction to the Hendricks House edition (New York, 1949) of *Pierre*: "[Regarding] 'pathological jealousy'—this comes from family & a friend who called HM—American Othello & 2 other sources & several inferences. But I would favor complete *omission* of notes as family would not care to be quoted. . . . [On] J. O. Shaw's hatred. This comes from family who would not like to be quoted. It is rather generally known & might be left as it is." (Photocopies of Murray-Vincent correspondence are in the files of Harrison Hayford.) Note that Murray does not exactly say Cousin Josie's "hatred" was merited but leaves the impression she was correct. As shown above, there are no family letters supporting this view (at least not in Murray's papers), and Murray's notes for a projected biography (see below) indicate inferences solely from Melville's art as the source for his personality assessments. As for the "pathological jealousy," given Melville's propensity to work out personal problems in his art, and since it is the *women* who are possessive and nosy (as in *Pierre*), perhaps Murray surmised that Melville had projected his jealousy onto his wife, sister Augusta, and mother.

32. Mumford has confused neurosis with psychosis. Neurotics make bad object choices but, unlike psychotics, are not delusional.

33. Donald L. Miller, *Lewis Mumford: A Life* (New York: Weidenfeld and Nicolson, 1989), 278.

34. See "The Dowser," an engraving by Agostini Caracei (ca. 1600): A centaur holds a plumb line over the vagina of a reclining nude, a mature woman; the image connects tools, discovery, lecherous curiosity, and female genitals. Dowsers might search for underground water or ore. The contradiction between liberty and fitful humours was sighted by Georg Brandes, *Naturalism in Nineteenth Century English Literature* (1923; reprint, New York: Russell and Russell, 1957), describing the English love of the sea. For Brandes, naturalism always led to radicalism, the latter understood as resistance to European reaction following the American and French Revolutions. For another view of double binds in Melville's art, see Robertson-Lorant, *Melville*, 307: the "double bind" occurs in the contradiction between Mrs. Glendinning's admiration of Pierre's docility and her aversion to "his hearty appetite for breakfast . . . [which] makes him seem so lower class."

35. See appended letters from Richard Chase to Frances Chase describing the politics of his New Critic colleagues at the Kenyon College conference, Summer 1949.

36. See Charles Olson, "The Growth of Herman Melville, Prose Writer and Poetic Thinker" (master's thesis, Wesleyan University, 1933), 26ff. (draft), for reference to Carl Van Doren's introduction to *White-Jacket* (London: Oxford UP, World's Classics, 1929), which supposedly attacks Melville for fabrications (Olson Papers). However, Van Doren's admiring introduction is yet another call for relaxation of (upper-class puritan) strictures, not a reproach to Melville. While noting that Melville embellished and rearranged life experience, taking the side of "the people," Van Doren explained the young man's zeal: He had come from the "kindly freedom of the cannibal valley" to enter "the straitjacket of civilization again under the most rigorous conditions. What wonder if he had rebelled! What wonder if he still remembered!" (vi). Compare with Mary K. Bercaw, introduction to *Melville's Sources* (Evanston: Northwestern UP, 1987), which dates the

beginning of "the great source studies" (her quotes) with Harold Scudder's discovery (published 1928) that Melville had relied on Amasa Delano for the plot of "Benito Cereno." Other source hunters are traced, including Russell Thomas (1932) and Robert S. Forsythe of the Newberry Library (mid-1930s, but superceded by Anderson).

37. Weaver to Earnshaw, May 21, 1935, Leyda Papers, box 11, UCLA; perhaps a draft.

38. Charles Roberts Anderson, "The Romance of Scholarship: Tracking Melville in the South Seas," *Colophon* (Spring 1938): 259–79.

39. Anderson's book, *Melville in the South Seas*, was reprinted in 1966 (New York: Dover) sans the original preface and introduction, which Anderson explained were no longer relevant. His ambivalent feelings about Melville were well expressed in the last paragraph, which finished with some lines from the Victorian poet Robert Buchanan's "Socrates": "Within a decade the high priest of the South Seas had become, in his own eyes at least, the heretic of an inquisitional civilization. In spite of the consequences, he undoubtedly continued to think of himself always as the philosopher in his tower, castigating an unresponsive world. But posterity, no less than the contemporary world, prefers him as the *jongleur* of *Omoo* and *White-Jacket*, or best of all, as the enchanter, '. . . the sea-compelling man / Before whose wand Leviathan / Rose hoary, white upon the deep, / With awful sounds that stirred its sleep; / Melville, whose magic drew Typee, / Radiant as Venus, from the sea'" (434). Note the sequence of compulsion, magic wand (the rod), gigantic power, and sex, a typical cluster of images in sadomasochistic imaginations I have studied.

40. Anderson to Weaver, Dec. 7, 1939, Weaver Papers, Columbia University. The Wells review is also preserved.

41. Robert S. Forsythe, *American Literature* 11 (1939): 85–92.

42. Harrison Hayford and Hershel Parker, eds., *Moby-Dick as Doubloon: Essays and Extracts (1851–1970)* (New York: Norton, 1970). Compare with Robertson-Lorant, *Melville*, 279: "[Ahab's] fanatical determination to 'strike through the mask' and deal a death blow to the white whale contrasts dramatically with Ishmael's receptivity to many truths, not merely one exclusive Truth."

43. Andress, *Johann Gottfried Herder as an Educator*, 29–30. "Kant gave to the world . . . a new sense of spiritual freedom. He taught that the individual is able to build his own world. No matter what your condition in life, your world may become glorious if only you will make it so. 'Its spirituality is your own creation, or else is nothing. Awake, arise, be willing, endure, struggle, defy evil, cleave to good, strive, be strenuous, be devoted, throw into the face of evil and depression your brave cry of resistance, and then this dark universe of destiny will glow with a divine light. For you have no relations with the eternal world save such as you make for yourself.' This sort of philosophy was a call to the individual to arise to self-mastery and self-realization. Kant believed that the world is not beyond us but is the deepest truth within us. As we master this truth we conquer the discordant tendencies of our own lives. . . . With Kant [German idealism] said the world is indeed the world as built by self-consciousness; but the real world is the world of the genius, the poet, the artist. It refused to interpret the world according to reason or the moral law, but in terms of sentiment, emotion, and heart longings. Romanticism found its chief interest in man's wealth of divine emotions."

44. John Crowe Ransom, "The Content of the Novel," *American Review* 7 (Summer 1936): 310–11. Ransom's assessment was perhaps a rebuke to his Agrarian colleague John Gould Fletcher, who probably saw Melville as a fellow Nietzschean, one of the four most important Americans ever; moreover, he rated *Pierre* as a masterpiece. See John Gould Fletcher, *The Two Frontiers: A Study in Historical Psychology* (New York: Coward-McCann, 1930), 263. "This Captain Ahab is Melville's symbol of the human will in its highest and most courageous aspect; the human will that, not having been able to conquer evil by fair means, in direct battle, now strives to do it by unhallowed ones." (Compare with Olson, below.) But Ahab is not Hebraic; for Fletcher the moralism of the Mosaic code is directed solely toward the preservation of property. Fletcher's two

frontiers referred to the United States and the Soviet Union. Norman Holmes Pearson was a close friend and admirer; see Pearson to Leyda, July 26, 1950, Leyda Papers, UCLA.

Younger critics may be surprised at the number of New Critics (and related members of the prewar literary establishment mentioned in this book) who published frequently in the *American Review* (formerly *Bookman*), edited by Seward Collins and blatantly profascist during its period of publication in the mid-1930s (April 1933–October 1937): These include Cleanth Brooks (vols. 3, 6, 8), Harry Hayden Clark (vols. 2, 4, 5), John Gould Fletcher (vols. 3–6), Norman Foerster (vols. 1–5, 9), John Crowe Ransom (vols. 1–7), Robert Shafer (vols. 2, 4), Geoffrey Stone (vols. 1, 2, 5–9), Allen Tate (vols. 1–3, 6–8), Mark Van Doren (vol. 8), Austin Warren (vols. 3–9), Robert Penn Warren (vols. 2, 5, 6, 8), and Yvor Winters (vols. 7–9). It was the stated mission of the periodical to bring together the English Distributists (Belloc and Chesterton), New Humanists (Irving Babbitt and Paul Elmer More), Neo-Thomists, and Southern Agrarians in a neoclassical synthesis to halt the slide toward romantic decadence and socialism (constantly associated with the inordinate power of international Jewry as either capitalists or communists). A few of the *American Review* writers also published in *American Literature*: Austin Warren, Yvor Winters, Donald Davidson, and Norman Foerster (who joined the AL editorial board in the later 1930s). Melville was not mentioned in this journal until May 1936. Yvor Winters wrote in "Jones Very: A New England Mystic," *American Review* 7: "In the past two decades two major American writers have been rediscovered and established securely in their rightful places in literary history. I refer to Emily Dickinson and to Herman Melville. I am proposing the establishment of a third" (159).

Of the *American Review* critics just mentioned, only the future Melvillean Geoffrey Stone vociferously supported the fascist dictatorships. Most confined their essays to literary subjects. See Stone's "Left Wings over Europe," an admiring review of the Wyndham Lewis book of that name defending the rearmament of Germany, *American Review* 7 (Oct. 1936): 564–85. The following passages by Geoffrey Stone sum up humanism as understood in the *American Review*: "[Wyndham Lewis] gives expression, in his amazingly flexible and informal style, to a point of view which is too rarely advanced in England and America. In fact, a leading exponent of the Nazi as a sort of groping Distributist has been Mr. Lewis himself, who, in 1930, gave a thoughtful account of German National Socialism in his book *Hitler*. At that time Hitler had not yet been chosen by the German people as their ruler and the Nazi movement was still to enjoy the outbursts of vituperative denunciation, variously Marxian, Liberal, and Jewish, which have been hurled at it since its assumption of power. Though Mr. Lewis came forward as the exponent rather than the advocate of the Nazi party, he saw in the movement a resurgence of national vigor and an affirmation of our traditional Western way of life against the corruptions of capitalism and Marxism. He saw in it (and no one who has read his other books can deny Mr. Lewis an eye acute to discern levelling influences) a great popular movement to re-establish individual dignity and to escape the slave-status which collectivism everywhere imposes—whether by machine-guns in Russia or uplift unctuousness in America. He further pointed out that what, to the Anglo-Saxon reader, might seem the nonsense of 'Aryan' pride was at least an expedient way of meeting the disintegration brought about by class strife. Pride in race, as he indicated in a still earlier book, *Paleface*, was far from reprehensible, since it offered one method of lifting the inferiority complex that was being saddled upon the Western white with the purpose of degrading him to the coolie's level, to the accompaniment of much talk about the equality of races and even the superiority of the darker ones. Fascism—as it exists in Germany, Italy, and Portugal, and as it may exist tomorrow in Belgium under Degrelle's Rexists and in France under the leadership of Doriot or La Rocque— is not the last embattled stand of capitalism, but, however objectionable some of its features, a truly popular attempt to preserve the ideals of Christian society and to assert, *through the classic conception of him*, the worth of the individual; and upon recognition of this depends the solution of the problems of our democracies, threatened as they are, by the imminence of the Servile State, whether Marxian or neo-Benthamite. Throughout *Left Wings over Europe* Mr. Lewis stresses the need of recognizing the true character of fascism and insists that the attempt being made to prevent such recognition can result only in war and slavery" (570–71; emphasis added).

In the very opening pages of his *Melville*, directed to general readers and published by Catholic publishers Sheed and Ward in 1949, Stone changed his line, now distancing himself from the European tyrannies (brought about by the Calvinist/puritan/romantic sensualist spirit, the cause of Melville's very American problems) and, of course, racism. Whereas (neoclassical) Nazis were essentially preserving the classic conception of the individual in Stone's prewar essay, now they were all romantics: "American fiction from the first has been touched by the Romantic vision and given to the Romantic attitude. The essence of Romanticism is revolt; it asserts the superiority of the individual's impulses over all that is established, organized, and rationally articulated. Every false theory eventually works out to its own negation, because falsehood is of its nature contradictory; and the absolute freedom sought by the first Romantics has resulted in our time in tyrannies, whether in practice or theory, as thoroughgoing as any the world has ever seen. The same course of development is plain in the lives of the chief figures of Romanticism" (1). Stone's study of Melville's tormented narcissism and abused family can be seen as a cautionary tale to Catholic readers tempted by modernity to "question the Christian ethic" (26) and lured to political adventurism by Eros (44). Stone identifies with Ungar's reactionary antimodernism, Plotinus Plinlimmon's virtuous expediency, and Captain Vere's justice. Arguing against his contemporaries, Stone claims that Melville was never a democrat and did not fundamentally challenge Christianity (26), though he did overcome his earlier rage by the time he wrote "Billy Budd." Compare the notes of Charles Olson and Henry A. Murray, excerpted below.

45. Mumford's "howler," the bungling of the chronology (he made Ahab a source for Ethan Brand, rather than vice versa) is a distraction from Mumford's important insight. In general, in its zeal to follow the Shakespeare-Melville connection, the Melville scholarship has neglected the terror-gothic version of the French Revolution as a persistent theme in nineteenth-century literature. Mumford's connection would logically lead to a more careful consideration of Melville's book purchases in his trip to England in 1849, which included Godwin's *Caleb Williams* (a favorite of Hawthorne, read when he was sixteen) and Mary Shelley's *Frankenstein*.

46. Harry R. Warfel, Ralph Henry Gabriel, and Stanley T. Williams, eds., *The American Mind: Selections from the Literature of the United States* (New York: American Book Co., 1937). The same publisher was responsible for the Willard Thorp anthology and Michael John Demiashkevich, *The National Mind: English, French, German* (New York: American Book Co., 1938). Imputations of national character were criticized by 1930s liberals and leftists as protofascist.

47. Compare with Henry Murray, "The Mind of Adolph [*sic*] Hitler," 125. Summarizing the Führer's education: "The flophouse and the beer hall were his Heidelberg and University of Vienna." See my appendix for context.

48. Warfel et al., *The American Mind*, 630–53. There was no mention of "Billy Budd." The Melville selections were included in the section "Spiritual and Ethical Exploration." The next section was entitled "Some Romantic Writers," beginning with Poe. Viking Press editor Malcolm Cowley did not believe that the Tory youth of *Mardi* voiced Melville's true politics; see his undated letter suggesting cuts to Leyda's *Portable Melville*, referring to Melville's "political unbeliefs." Leyda Papers, box 23, UCLA.

49. But note that Emerson had been presented as the epitome of the New England reform spirit, qualities linked to Jacksonian democracy by Frederick Jackson Turner in his posthumous *The United States 1830–1850* (1935; reprint, Norton, 1965). See p. 90 for two quotes that encapsulate Melville's youthful democratic idealism and sublimity, and even an image that resonates with his Enceladus vision. Emerson wrote in "The Young American": "America is beginning to assert herself to the senses and to the imagination of her children, and Europe is receding in the same

degree. . . . We cannot look on the freedom of this country, in connexion with its youth, without a presentiment that here shall laws and institutions exist on some scale of proportion to the majesty of nature. To men legislating for the area betwixt the two oceans, betwixt the snows and the tropics, somewhat of the gravity of nature will infuse itself into the code. A heterogeneous population crowding on all ships from all corners of the world to the great gates of North America, namely Boston, New York, and New Orleans, and thence proceeding inward to the prairie and the mountains, and quickly contributing their private thought to the public opinion, their toll to the treasury, and their vote to the election, it cannot be doubted that the legislation of this country should become more catholic and cosmopolitan than that of any other. It seems so easy for America to inspire and express the most expansive and humane spirit; new-born, free, healthful, strong, the land of the laborer, of the democrat, of the philanthropist, of the believer, of the saint, she should speak for the human race." And in another quote on the same page from Emerson's diary of 1834: "Sometimes the life seems dying out of all literature, and this enormous paper currency of Words is accepted instead. I suppose that the evil may be cured by this rank rabble party, the Jacksonism of the country, heedless of English and of all literature—a stone cut out of the ground without hands;—they may root out the hollow dilettantism of our cultivation in the coarsest way and the new-born may begin again to frame their own world with greater advantage." Turner had noted Emerson's sympathy with the Whig party, contrasting with the sentiments quoted here.

50. See Luther Mansfield to Charles Olson, Jan. 21, 1937, noting that Thorp has just finished his American Book Company selections. Later that year Eleanor Metcalf informed Charles Olson of "another request for the right to edit the 1849 journals! Mr. Willard Thorp of Princeton. I have just written him that it had been promised, but also directed him to make any inquiries of the committee with the imposing name" (letter, Oct. 4, 1937, Olson Papers).

51. Willard Thorp, *Representative Selections*, cviii, cix, cx. Thorp was co-opting the principle of Enlightenment universalism to render ethnopluralism as progressive. The Melville quote is from *Redburn*, a passage favorably cited by numerous historians, including the American Studies Association's November 1990 meeting, Rivers of Contrast, National and Global. See also Hayford, *Melville's "Monody,"* 19.

52. See *Charles Olson and Cid Corman, Complete Correspondence 1950–1964*, ed. George Evans (Orono, Maine: National Poetry Foundation, 1987), 18. Olson and Corman were "key figures in a network of activities spanning both coasts, encompassing several modernist literary movements (e.g., the Black Mountain Poets, the Beat Movement, and the San Francisco Renaissance) as well as individual poets not identified with any particular group."

53. Paul Christensen, *Minding the Underworld: Clayton Eshelman and Late Postmodernism* (Santa Rosa: Black Sparrow Press, 1991), 21, 11. Also Charles Boer, *Olson in Connecticut* (Chicago: Swallow Press, 1975), 37, 63–64. On the "post-literary" "post-modern" Olson, Boer wrote, "You saw poetry, the primary mode of expression in all pre-literary societies, as your own best post-literary means of knowing and articulating order" (64).

54. Harrison Hayford, "The Melville Society: A Retrospective," *Melville Society Extracts* 88 (Mar. 1992): 3. The bomb was directed against Olson's friends Eleanor Metcalf and Henry Murray, who should not have attended; Hayford's imagery implies that Olson was a coalition-busting divisive force. See also Merton Sealts, Jr., "A Correspondence with Charles Olson," in *Pursuing Melville*.

55. Charles Olson, Notebook 31. By 1951, Olson was a bitter critic of the Melville industry. Unless otherwise indicated, all Olson materials quoted in this chapter and elsewhere are located in the Olson Papers.

56. On Olson's corporatism as a New Dealer, see his manuscript "Religious, Racial and National Origin Factors in Political Campaigns," ca. May 1946. He lamented the loss of Roosevelt (the voice) and the war agencies which "tended both to keep these people better informed and at

the same time restrained forces in some of these groups which go against the best interests of the people and of the country as a whole" (9–10). Olson was speaking as an antifascist. Compare with Olson's (Pound-influenced?) diatribe against America that has duped soldiers who sacrificed their lives in World War II, quoted below.

57. Carl Van Doren to Olson, Apr. 28, 1938. Van Doren can't get over the Melville interest at Princeton and Duke. He told Olson, "Don't let me down."

58. Charles Olson, "The Growth of Herman Melville, Prose Writer and Poetic Thinker" (master's thesis, Wesleyan University, 1933), 11, 15. Olson said Anderson was probably inspired by A. Mordell, *Saturday Review of Literature* 7 (1936): 946. Mordell praised Melville's radicalism.

59. Olson, "The Growth of Herman Melville," 103–4, 109–10, 105. The draft in the Olson Papers is not systematic in the description of Melville's borrowings, simply quoting Anderson's conclusions: "Charles Anderson sums up the results in these words: 'If, then, 'White Jacket' emerges from this analysis shorn of most of its autobiographical value, it is enhanced as a piece of readable fiction; and, if Melville loses as a veracious travel-writer, he gains as an artist who can portray even his own narrow escape from death so realistically that official records are necessary to prove that it was all imaginary'" (33).

60. See Barbara Heyl, "The Harvard 'Pareto' Circle," *Journal of the History of the Behavioral Sciences* 4 (1968): 316–34. The Paretans were viewed as fascists by their liberal Harvard colleagues in the 1930s. The seminar included Crane Brinton, Henry Murray, Clyde Kluckhohn, Talcott Parsons, Joseph Schumpeter, Bernard De Voto, and Robert Merton. Merton was a major figure in the developing discipline of the history of science; its agenda is avowedly anti-Marxist and anti-liberal. See *Puritanism and the Rise of Modern Science: The Merton Thesis*, ed., intro. I. B. Cohen (New Brunswick, N.J.: Rutgers UP, 1990). George Sarton proposed the discipline in 1916 (see "Proposal [for] An Institution devoted to the History of Science," Lawrence J. Henderson Correspondence, History of Science folder, Lawrence J. Henderson Papers).

61. "Memories," Henderson Papers. Compare with Joyce Appleby, Lynn Hunt, and Margaret Jacob, *Telling the Truth in History* (New York: Norton, 1994), 253. "Historians cannot comprehend all the variables bombarding a single event. Human beings participate in a dense circuitry of interacting systems, from those that regulate their bodily functions to the ones that undergird their intellectual curiosity and emotional responses. A full explanation of an event would have to take into consideration the full range of systematic reactions. Not ever doing that, history-writing implicitly begins by concentrating on those aspects of an event deemed most relevant to the inquiry."

62. See Appleby et al., *Telling the Truth in History*, 51 and passim.

63. See Carl Schmitt, "A Note on Europe," *American Review* 9 (Sept. 1937): 407–10. I am using Schmitt's metaphors. The same argument can be found in Geoffrey Stone, "The End of Democracy: Ralph Adams Cram's Plea for a New Order" *American Review* 9 (Sept. 1937): 365–79. For these fascist critics, moderation does not signify the willingness to compromise but to subdue the bourgeoisie without sacrificing progress.

64. Folke Leander, "The Materialistic and the Humanistic Interpretations of History," *American Review* 9 (Sept. 1937): 380–406.

65. Norman Foerster, ed., Introduction to *The Humanities after the War* (Princeton: Princeton UP, 1944), vii. Wendell L. Wilkie was a contributor to the volume.

66. Thorp later edited *A Southern Reader* (New York: Knopf, 1955), stating in the introduction that he had always found the South to be the most exotic and exciting part of America, its problems with Negroes and poverty notwithstanding. See E. M. W. Tillyard, *The Elizabethan World Picture* (New York: Macmillan, 1943), for a concise summary of the organic conservative cosmos shared by corporatist thinkers from Plato through the late Middle Ages and the Elizabethans on into Central Europe of the fascist period. See also Stephen Copley, ed., *Literature and the Social*

Order in Eighteenth-Century England (London: Croom Helm, 1984), introduction, for the contrast between the discourses of the humanists and Adam Smith (along with other analysts of economic institutions).

67. See F. A. Hayek, *Individualism: True and False* (Oxford: Blackwell, 1946), for a concise enunciation of the main principles of libertarian conservatism in which science is annexed to hierarchical organic conservatism and the rule of expertise. His recommended lineage for "true individualism" is Locke, Mandeville, Hume, Josiah Tucker, Adam Ferguson, Adam Smith, Edmund Burke, Tocqueville, and Lord Acton. Hayek has undermined the search for legitimate authority based on common understanding and checks from below. Man is innately incapable of grasping totalities; only deluded and false individualists would claim such an achievement. These include rationalist philosophes and utilitarians, along with the "original" German romantics, similarly looking to coercive, bureaucratic state power to impose order, destroying checks and balances attainable through spontaneous voluntary organization at the local level. The only role for the state is negative: to prevent any one group from arrogating to itself the excessive power that destroys equilibrium. Describing the conditions that enable true individualism, Hayek explained: "[It is absurd to think that] individualism postulates (or bases its arguments on the assumption of) the existence of isolated or self-contained individuals, instead of starting from men whose whole nature and character is determined by their existence in society. . . . The willingness to submit to [flexible but normally observed rules that make the behavior of other people predictable in a high degree], not merely so long as one has no definite reason to the contrary, is an essential condition for the gradual evolution and improvement of rules of social intercourse, and the readiness ordinarily to submit to the products of a social process which nobody has designed and the reasons for which nobody may understand is also an indispensable condition if it is to be possible to dispense with compulsion. . . . Coercion can probably only be kept to a minimum in a society when conventions and tradition have made the behavior of man to a large extent predictable" (7, 23–24).

68. Thorp's fixation on stable savage societies can be explained by their focused contemplation on natural creation that is abandoned in the introspective individual of modernity. Tillyard in *The Elizabethan World Picture* quotes Hooker on this phenomenon: "The bad angels fell away voluntarily, and they did so because they turned their minds away from God and from God's creation, itself, the evidence of God's goodness, to themselves. There was indeed 'no other way for angels to sin but by reflex of their understandings upon themselves; when, being held with admiration of their own sublimity and honour, the memory of their subordination unto God and their dependency on him was drowned in this conceit. Whereupon their adoration, love and imitation of God could not choose but be also interrupted. The fall of the angels was therefore pride'" (50). The multicultural emphasis on diversity and inclusion refers back to the idea of God's (Nature's) plenitude and perfection described at length in Frank Lovejoy, *The Great Chain of Being: The History of an Idea* (1936; reprint, Cambridge, Mass.: Harvard UP, 1953).

69. Geoffrey Stone, "Excelsior," *American Review* 9 (Summer 1937): 299, 303. Stone, a future Melville critic, was reviewing Stephen Spender, *Forward from Liberalism*.

70. Olson's copy of the Constable *Confidence-Man* was unmarked; also, he did not engage it in his criticism.

71. Talk by Klaus Herding, UCLA symposium, Dec. 2, 1988, in connection with the exhibition and catalog *French Caricature and the French Revolution, 1789–1799* (Los Angeles: The Grunwald Center for the Graphic Arts, 1988). Herding's catalog article is "Visual Codes in the Graphic Codes of the French Revolution," 83–100.

72. The breaching of Queequeg's coffin–life buoy is described with the same image, now bursting into the creamy pool left after the ship has sunk. What, then, is Melville saying about "the vital centre" and the state?

73. The distended angry eyes are recurrent images in Melville's art. Also, note the "fog-bow" that hovers and disappears in response to Margoth's sulking reverence, closing Book 2 of *Clarel.*

74. When Weaver and Olson talk of pessimism and mysticism, they must mean refusal of the scientistic Whiggish progressive project. For Weaver, George Meredith (whose *The Egoist: A Comedy in Narrative* [London: Kegan Paul, 1879] he linked to *Pierre*) was a pessimist; however, Meredith was no irrationalist, but a modern whose comic spirit razzed the pseudo-emancipating discourse of feudal socialism, identifying narcissism with the Tory Willoughby Patterne, not the radical bourgeoisie.

75. See Olson to Carl Van Doren, June 5, 1934, acknowledging that CVD sent him on the book hunt; also to Victor Hugo Paltsis, June 6, 1934, who has been assisting him, Olson Papers.

76. Wilbert Snow to Olson, Mar. 6 and May 15, 1934, Olson Papers.

77. Wilbert Snow to Olson, Mar. 6, 1934, Olson Papers.

78. Olson, Notebook 26. Compare with Olson's poem "The Civil War": ". . . The one has to upset things, / to get at them, that you do have to turn / The ground under. / Or up, is it?" But see Tom Clark, *Charles Olson: The Allegory of a Poet's Life* (New York: Norton, 1991), 26, who partly quotes the notebook entry but interprets it as an expression of Olson's need for replenished creativity. Clark also characterizes New Deal reforms as "radical."

79. I think Snow meant to say *Pierre*, but it is conceivable that he saw Yillah as Elizabeth and Taji as Melville the artist, perhaps merging the two quasi-autobiographical narratives.

80. The family letters and other materials held by the Morewood sisters, Allan Melville's descendants, became a source of contention between Murray and Jay Leyda; see below.

81. Compare Olson's statements from his 1932 notebook entries (praying he will not, like the aging Emerson, give up his ideals, and criticizing his own violent anger, ambition, egotism, and cynicism) to the unapologetic manipulativeness expressed in a letter to Constance Wilcock in 1941. His resignation is already hinted in the entry for March 25, 1934, in his ambiguous response to Maugham's *Of Human Bondage*: "Terms are made with life. Maugham was no Prometheus taking the fires from the Gods, nor a Melville throwing it back; he was no preacher of woe." Late entries for 1936 contain indications of mental distress, which I infer from his violent misogynistic, sadistic fantasies.

82. Until I noticed the black bats Melville associated with Margoth's materialism, I did not grasp the reference to vampires in Olson's characterization of the Isabel letter. Notes in the poetry volume continue Olson's speculations on the half-sister and the central importance of the discovery to Melville. To Melville's poem "Trophies of Peace; Illinois in 1840": "M. made trip West? to see Thomas M.? did he then discover Isabel? Was this the reason he left sea in December?"

83. While revising this book, I noticed that Olson never referred to his father by name and that I was endlessly repeating "Olson's father." His posthumously published memoir, *The Post Office: A Memoir of His Father* (Bolinas, Calif.: Grey Fox Press, 1975), written ca. 1948, three years after the writing of *Call Me Ishmael*, but unfinished, conveys this timeless archetype of the father. The late George F. Butterick, editor of much of Olson's poetry, wrote the introduction in which the mother's name, nationality, and class background are described but not the father's, though the little book is about him. Nor does Olson name him in the text. In one picture of the father from 1934 (opposite page 20) we learn that the elder Olson's name was Charles Olson, Sr. However, the publications of his son do not carry the "junior": Olson had incorporated the father's name while obliterating their relationship. The book's cover is a photo of baby Charles in his father's mailbag; I read the mailbag as the suitcase—the connection to the ruddy, radical father that had to be denied. Olson asked himself, "Do I exaggerate and punish myself anew for the guilt of my refusal of the suitcase? I do not know" (55). The book ends shortly after this attempt at self-exoneration. Olson has just written that he punishes himself for having a guilty conscience;

perhaps his selfishness has killed his father, or perhaps not. Is this guilt and ambiguity the "Hebraic" or "Protestant" poison that infiltrates the Catholic and primitivist Olson?

84. Carroll Wilson to Olson, Nov. 12, 1935, Olson Papers.

85. Charles Olson, "Plan for Work," Guggenheim Fellowship File, Olson Papers.

86. See below, Olson Notebook, Winter 1939–40, on art and revolution. William Ellery Sedgwick's Melville study, *The Tragedy of Mind*, was published posthumously in 1944 (Cambridge, Mass.: Harvard UP). See letter from Murray to Howard Vincent, quoted below, regarding cause of death. Olson was a worshipful Jungian. Both Freud and Jung believed in the inheritance of acquired characteristics, but Freud's universalism and rationalism (universal reason can comprehend and master the irrational aspects of our behavior; institutions are man-made and can be ameliorated) exist in tension with both his own Lamarckianism and Jung's irrationalism and racially specific archetypes. The discussion of Freud in H. Stuart Hughes, *Consciousness and Society: The Reorientation of European Social Thought 1890–1930* (New York: Random House, 1958), simply ignores those comments that would align Freud with the radical liberals, instead presenting him as an intellectual pillar of necessarily coercive social order. Hughes was part of the scientistic Harvard cohort who have been described throughout my study.

87. The 1940 Harvard Alumni Directory states that Olson attended the Graduate School of Arts and Sciences from 1936–37 to 1938–39 but did not receive a degree. Faculty directories state that he was assistant in the English department (1936–37), then instructor in English and tutor in the division of Modern Languages (1938–39). In the 1938–39 directory Olson is listed as a fellow in American History.

88. Olson's jottings here suggest he was reading Eleanor Metcalf's reminiscence in Weaver, perceptively noting that "HM & EMM always turn to ice if [an ornamental butterfly has] flown away since here last." It may be Olson's idiosyncratic association from reading EMM (with whom he had a close and conflicted relationship) that Melville was "violent sexually," not information passed on directly by Weaver.

89. Melville refers here to the alliance between the slave South and cotton-manufacturing England that would have followed successful secession. This in itself does not make Melville an anti-imperialist; however, the thrust of Melville's republicanism suggests the peaceful dissemination of political democracy and the rejection of imperial conquest. I have inferred here, perhaps wrongly, that Olson read this passage as anti-imperialist.

90. Compare with Charles Olson, *In Love, in Sorrow: The Complete Correspondence of Charles Olson and Edward Dahlberg*, ed. Paul Christensen (New York: Paragon House, 1990), xii. Christensen, who is hostile to Dahlberg, does not quote these marginal comments, but he states that Dahlberg "denounced" the manuscript as "too imitative and derivative of his own writing."

91. F. O. Matthiessen to Olson, Feb. 23, 1940, Olson Papers. Was Matthiessen reversing his own opinions in the manuscript (*American Renaissance*) he had been composing since the mid-1930s?

92. This is my inference, based on letters in Olson's papers. The "Ur–*Call Me Ishmael*" manuscript Christensen describes is no more than twenty-five pages of "Genesis" that is badly water damaged and virtually unreadable. Only one page remains of "Exodus"; the other unpublished fragments cited here are more complete and could be the ones read by Matthiessen. Van Doren's letter suggests that he may, like Dahlberg, have read the Moses chapter, but he could have seen another manuscript, "Essay on Melville" (also damaged and torn and which George Butterick may have misdated ca. 1948). It is less obscurely written and treats Ahab as "a wild man with an axe . . . MUTINEER." Compare with the clipping in "Misc." folder, by Bernard Herrmann, composer of "The *Moby Dick* Cantata: For the Fallen," in *New York Times*, Apr. 7, 1940: HM's "strong meat for the musical imagination": "New England hymns, the fiery exhortations and melancholy solilo-

quies of Ahab." The linking of fire and melancholy evokes the melancholy but ferociously vindictive negresses in "Benito Cereno."

93. Pound had denounced the sacrifices of young American men in the Great War, writing that they had died "For an old bitch gone in the teeth / for a botched civilization." Pound was quoted in Steel, *Walter Lippmann and the American Century,* 258. Olson's relations with Pound are treated in Charles Olson, *Charles Olson and Ezra Pound: An Encounter at St. Elizabeth's,* ed. Catherine Seelye (New York: Grossman, 1975). Faced with Pound's aristocratic opinions (which he partly shared—for instance, he writes "Pound right about USURY" in his notes on Pound [1945]), Olson could rebel. However, in his "Notes for a lecture at Pacific Northwest Writers Conference" (July–August 1947), he does not distance himself from the fathers who include prophets of doom, D. H. Lawrence, Wyndham Lewis, and Pound: Americans and Russians are the barbarians threatening civilization. Responding to Richard Chase's Melville study in his letter to Chase, March 6, 1950, Olson rejects Founding Fathers, the Republic, the Renaissance, Christ, The Rights of Man, secular liberalism, and morality for the folkishness he finds in pre-Republic people and all those of the Pacific. Melville's greatness lies in exposing the desolation of modernity (Olson Papers). I did not see the letter in the Chase Papers at Columbia University.

94. See Charles Olson Notebook Key West II, Feb.–Mar. 1945. Compare with Olson, *Call Me Ishmael,* 12–13.

95. Paul Metcalf had mixed feelings about the book; see his letter to Eleanor Melville Metcalf, March 28, 1949, praising the new poems, but adding, "When he wrote [*CMI*], he was thoroughly involved in becoming a poet, a process for which the material, the dominant interest in Melville, the scholarly research, simply didn't suit, so that the book emerged as a half-developed, bastard prose-poem, at once exciting and exasperating" (Olson Papers).

96. Olson to Henry Holt editor Keith Jennison, Mar. 12, 1946. To Joseph Brant of the American Men of Letters Series he promised a different book (letter, Apr. 7, 1946), including the MHS letters, diaries, and records, material on Melville in the Pacific, including his role in the *Lucy Ann* mutiny, the marginalia in 350 volumes, and other source materials on the Pacific and on Amasa Delano.

Before I read his master's thesis, I thought that Olson resented Charles Anderson, assuming that his protests to Sealts or Leyda regarding scholars who had "dirtied" Melville referred to the muckrakers; but he was referring to Luther Mansfield and Howard Vincent, whose Enlightenment materialism was the contaminant (and whose 1952 edition of *Moby-Dick* linked Ahab to Milton's Satan. On the back flyleaf of his copy, Olson wrote "Ahab to be engaged").

97. See Charles Olson Notebook Fall 1945/Spring 1946: "that ass Matthiessen to refuse a book like yours" vs. Olson to Matthiessen, May 4, 1947.

98. F. O. Matthiessen to Olson, Apr. 3, 1947, Olson Papers.

99. Leyda told F. Barron Freeman that Eleanor Metcalf owned a copy of *White-Jacket* annotated "in late hand" of Melville as reference to "Billy Budd." See Leyda draft letter, Leyda Papers, box 7, UCLA. Harrison Hayford told me that he has never heard of any such book.

100. *New York Herald Tribune Weekly Book Review,* Mar. 23, 1947, 5.

101. Ronald Mason was the author of *The Spirit above the Dust.* It is as pure an example of protofascist literary criticism to be found in the Melville Revival, though the reader must be familiar with interwar cultural politics to see it. Mason constantly counterposed Ishmael and Plinlimmon (the detached, flexible, pragmatic Christian stoics) with Ahab and Melville (the rigid puritans/dogmatic sectarian Jews). For Mason, Melville's high points were found in the supplement to *Battle-Pieces* (in which the Lincolnesque Melville nobly calls for reconciliation of the conflicts of [simply different] convictions) (217–18); those parts of *Clarel* where he leans on Catholicism; and most prominently in "Billy Budd," at which point the rootless Jew becomes

a moderate man. What makes Mason's book protofascist, as opposed to conservative, is his conflation of the unified work of art, the "order of nature," "natural justice," and the lawfulness of the military state as realized in Vere's stoic judgment of Billy. Vere/the authoritarian state does not simply speak for God: it becomes God (see esp. 256–58). It is Melville's conversion at the end of his life that makes him, though technically imperfect until that moment, the most important American writer.

While writing *Clarel*, Melville's tragic heroes had moved forward: "Melville is perhaps not so much proclaiming his approval of Catholicism as underlining a new realisation that was only now forcing itself upon his meditations—that no faith can be effective and no philosophy have sanction without a firm discipline to enforce it. Protestantism he regarded as flabby with the lack of it; Judaism as perhaps tyrannical with an overdose of it; but Rome he saw for the time as providing just that necessary blend of regulation and rapture that could illuminate an individual without rendering him either unsuitable for contemporary society or too readily corruptible by its compromises. Rome, I must emphasize, symbolized this discipline only, it did not necessarily represent it. Melville did not turn Roman Catholic; merely had the perception to invoke on behalf of his rarest visionaries a discipline that their own hearts could not provide alone, but for which they would be forced to turn to a tradition outside their own contexts. This I believe to be one of the most important stages in his spiritual progress" (241).

For Mason, all human conflicts are rooted in human nature, in the struggle to overcome base instincts. Historic struggles are subsumed in this eternal warfare between God and the devil. The concrete facts of the material world feed the symbolic, mythic, spiritualizing imagination of the artist. Most significant, however, is Mason's typically medieval belief that the study of the material world and of human institutions intended to lead to amelioration of suffering is satanic in motivation and result. Protestant or Jewish reformism is seen as the expression of deception, hatred, and revenge, with Ahab read accordingly. Echoing the Catholic and fascist writers of *American Review*, Mason viewed human suffering, like force, as a designated part of the natural order of things.

See also the Melville study by Geoffrey Stone (1949), ideologically identical with Mason's and described above. The French Melvillean Jean Simon, commenting on the voluminous new Melville scholarship, noted that Mason's book was to his taste, an example of the "via media" he had always attempted to follow. See his review in *Études Anglaises* (Feb. 1953), 46; a reprint is located in Leyda Papers, NYU.

102. Olson reported files on 163 titles in 225 volumes in his first Guggenheim Fellowship application, ca. 1939. "In the quantity of notes" the leading volumes were "Shakespeare (9 v.), Arnold (6 v.), Schopenhauer (7 v.), Emerson (3 v.), Hawthorne (19 v.), the New Testament, Balzac (15 v.), Disraeli and Alger on genius (5 v.), Schiller, Calderon, 4 books on the Holy Land used for *Clarel*, Davenant, and Warton's *History of English Poetry*." Olson then ranked the "quality" of his notes: "Shakespeare, Emerson, Hawthorne, New Testament, Arnold, Seneca, Balzac, Schopenhauer, Cervantes, and [I.?] Disraeli."

103. Olson must mean a decentralized Protestantism antithetical to colonial New England's Hebraic theocracies, their radical puritanism the source of the money-mad anticommunitarian society that has sliced him in two. Thorp also sympathized with Melville on industrial capitalism: "For him the factory system is simply a new form of bondage, the more inhumane because the man who profits by the machine has no direct responsibility towards the laborers in his factory" (*Representative Selections*, cxii), in a discussion of "The Paradise of Bachelors and the Tartarus of Maids." In *Clarel*, the part-Indian Baltimore Catholic Ungar voiced these complaints; contemporary Hughs of Lincoln had their backs crooked in the English factories; this was linked to the (discredited) blood libel; the effect is subtly to fasten the blood libel on the industrial bourgeoisie. The idea and image of crookedness is ubiquitous in Melville's and Melvillean texts. The criminality is

obvious; more interesting is the relation to materialism and Mammon that slants the cross. (The narrator's unflattering description of Mammon, "the least erected spirit," was checked by Melville in his edition of *Paradise Lost*.)

104. "Economic determinism" as used by the moderates studied here does not refer to an economic model that neglects the force of religion or other ideas in history. Rather, it signifies the ideas of the "mechanical materialists": the philosophes who spawned the mob-driven French Revolution. See Clark, *Thomas Paine*. Clark's consensus-building project is clearly directed toward separating Paine from the radical Enlightenment and from radical puritanism, while making him the standard-bearer of American idealism and cultural freedom. Clark asks the reader to scrutinize Paine's writing, where he will discover Paine's belief in science as revelation of natural order and harmony, hence congruent with the goals of progressive New Dealers (though the analogy is never exactly drawn). Readers could substitute the Axis powers for Paine's Tory Britain or ancient Hebrew royalists.

105. See the admiring essay by New Leftist George Abbott White, "Ideology and Literature: *American Renaissance* and F. O. Matthiessen," in *Literature in Revolution*, ed. George Abbott White and Charles Newman (New York: Holt, Rinehart, Winston, 1972), 430–500, in a volume dedicated to Matthiessen; White attempts to separate him from other New Critics (considered today to be conservative).

106. Merton M. Sealts, Jr., to author, June 20, 1987. Sealts, a Stanley Williams student, was a of the leading Melvillean and the scholar who continued Olson's project to reconstitute Melville's library. Sealts, however, denied that he was a New Critic, but, rather, eclectic: "My approach to . . . 'I and My Chimney' combined the biographical orientation then current among Melvilleans with the new discipline of close reading (picked up from New Criticism) and an interest in symbolism deriving from such critics as Eliot and Wilson Knight." Compare with Robert E. Spiller's review of Matthiessen, *American Renaissance, American Literature* 13 (Mar.–Jan. 1941–42): 432–35. Spiller commended his critical method that reconciled aestheticism and historicism through organic form ("a modern functionalism"). While advocating an extreme determinism ("masterworks" are entirely caused by [great?] "social and philosophical forces"), Matthiessen had rescued artists and literary history from the economic determinists: "those historians who evaluate literature in terms of its content of communism, agrarian democracy, Puritanism, materialistic determinism, or other borrowed ism. The central pole of reference is esthetic significance." But see H. Lark Hall, *V. L. Parrington: Through the Avenue of Art* (Kent, Ohio: Kent State UP, 1994), where Parrington's views are linked to those of Henry Adams, Randolph Bourne, and other native-born radicals (i.e., the corporatists described in this study).

107. Handwritten draft, Francis Otto Matthiessen Papers, bMS Am 1433 (11), Houghton Library. These sentences ended his introduction to *Herman Melville Selected Poems* (New York: Oxford UP, 1944), a work dedicated to the late William Ellery Sedgwick. The published version changed the word "heart" to "mind." Compare with the NEH project proposal for "Documentary Film on the Life and Work of Herman Melville," authored by George H. Wolfe. In a letter of February 12, 1979, Wolfe (University of Alabama) asked Jay Leyda to join consultants Richard H. Fogle, Harrison Hayford, and Howard Vincent. The NEH application states that the film will treat "Melville's relentless search to unravel the meaning of meaning and the nature of good and evil . . . his brilliant examination of the human condition. . . . For Melville is concerned with nothing if not with the way men make ethical choices (and live with the results), engage life fully (or fail to), and deal with the ambiguous possibilities of good and evil in human affairs . . . his cosmic debates with himself about the nature of man. These interior battles bisect his life and work until finding some sort of odd solace in the final brilliance of *Billy Budd*." That social cohesion was on Wolfe's mind is indicated by his definition of Melville's context: formation, dissolution, reformation of union. The proposal also mentions a third narrative voice, Lizzie, who will provide information about "Herman's black

moods, his monomaniacal writing habits, the state of his health, the progress of his literary works, his finances, and so forth." Nathaniel Hawthorne is the most important single influence on Melville's art; the Bible and Milton are not mentioned. See Leyda Papers, NYU.

108. Compare with the Harvard University Report, *General Education in a Free Society* (Cambridge, Mass.: Harvard UP, 1945), 110–15. Matthiessen is mentioned in the acknowledgments as having either aided the Harvard Report or served on a subcommittee. Their recommendations for methods in high school teaching of English ("language and literature") include these vague yet balanced strictures meant to emancipate students from both ignorance and faction-making critical habits: "Among prevailing trends to be discouraged in the study of literature, it would list: Stress on factual content as divorced from design. Emphasis on literary history, on generalizations as to periods, tendencies and ready-made valuations—in place of deeper familiarity with the texts. Strained correlations with civics, social studies. Overambitious technical analysis of structure, plot, figurative language, prosody, genre. Use of critical terms (Romanticism, Realism, Classical, Sentimental) as tags coming between the reader and the work. Didacticism: lessons in behavior too closely sought. These dangers are familiar to reflective teachers, as are their opposite extremes: Superficial reading of too much, with no close knowledge of either the content or its import. Lack of any aids to the understanding of what is being read. Indifference to or ignorance of techniques of literature. Avoidance of critical terms and appraisals when the student is ready for them. Irresponsible attitude to the implications of what is being read." The authors then recommend "abridgement and selective editing" to make great works accessible to general readers. Imagine the "moderate" reader of this report, asked to determine what is too much or too little in her interventions.

109. See Charles H. Foster, "Something in Emblems," citing Gilbert Haven and Hon. Thomas Russell, *Father Taylor, the Sailor Preacher* (Boston: H. B. Russell, 1872), esp. chap. 15, "In Reforms." Foster argued that Taylor (originally a Virginian brought up among slaves) went back and forth on the abolition question and was an unlikely model for the ultra-abolitionist Mapple. But as the nineteenth-century authors (one a minister, the other collector of the Port of Boston) more precisely put it, "He shot back and forward between the contending hosts and ideas, faithful alike to his two central forces,—love of ideal truth, love of organic form. Truth must not shatter form: organism must not stifle truth" (250). Here is the double bind constantly encountered and identified by Melville as I have argued throughout. Yet Taylor could not stomach the Fugitive Slave Law. His biographers report this conversation: "Just after the passage of the 'Fugitive Slave Law,' he was standing at the door of the Methodist Bookstore, No. 5 Cornhill, and Rev. Thomas Whittemore, the leading Universalist preacher, who was a very strong abolitionist, was passing. 'Well,' said Father Taylor, 'Brother Whittemore, are you and I going to turn slave-catchers and do the dirty work of these miserable man-thieves?' 'No,' said Mr. Whittemore, very indignantly. 'No, no!' 'No, no!' said Father Taylor, with greater emphasis, clapping him warmly on his back: 'We'll see them all in hell first; won't we, Brother Whittemore?'" (253–54).

Melville's conservative narrators fit comfortably into the popular evangelical Protestant culture of his day. The Bethel Church was funded by members of the Unitarian merchant class of Boston, and its purpose was conversion and moral uplift, not the politicizing of the sailor congregation. Taylor, a former sailor and circuit rider, ardently defended Church and State (laws were inevitably imperfect, being the creation of devil-infested man, 175). With the example of successful mutinies before them (192), captains were asked to sacrifice their natural propensities to tyrannize sailors; sailors were asked by Taylor, ever the temperance crusader, to give up drink and promiscuity (that were not only impoverishing their wives and children but infecting and debauching heathen populations that missionaries sought to Christianize), and to adhere strictly to duty, with a blissful heavenly reward in sight. One observer, John Ross Dix, described the single painting in the Bethel; it transmits the message: "[The Church] is small and neat,—the only ornament being a large painting at the back of the pulpit, representing a ship in a stiff breeze off a lee shore, we believe; for we are not seaman enough to be certain on this point. High over the mast-head are dark storm-clouds, from one of which a remarkably small angel is seen, with outstretched arms,—the celestial individual having just flung down a golden anchor bigger than itself, to aid the ship in its extremity, we presume, although there is attached to the said anchor but a few inches of California cable, which for any practical purpose would not be of the slightest use. However, we must not be critical on allegories; and perhaps many a sailor now on the great deep has pleasant recollections of the picture: if so, a thousand such anachronisms might well be pardoned" (357–58). Another sailor-preacher, Enoch Mudge, was suggested by Jay Leyda as the source for Father Mapple (see below). The historical note to the *Moby-Dick* (NN), discussing the paucity of real-life models for Melville's characters, names a sailor, Backus, as the source for Pip, then states, "The only convincing exception is Father Mapple, for whom Father Edward Taylor of Boston supplied more than a hint" (636). We are not told why the editors are convinced. In his Melville biography, Hershel Parker mentions both Mudge and Taylor but does not specify their politics.

110. Matthiessen was quoting Emerson. Haven and Russell, *Father Taylor*, are unclear on the integration question. One observer, pro-abolitionist Harriet Martineau, saw segregation at Bethel: "There is one great drawback in the religious services of his chapel. There is a gallery just under the roof for persons of color; and 'the seed-carriers of the world' are thus countenanced by Father Taylor in making a root of bitterness spring up beside their homes, which, under his care, a better spirit should sanctify. I think there can be no doubt that an influence so strong as his would avail to abolish this unchristian distinction of races within the walls of his own church; and it would elevate the character of his influence if the attempt were made" (348–49). However, Stevens, historian of the Methodist Episcopal Church, describes the perfect missionary with a different scene: "In a spacious and substantial chapel, crowded about by the worst habitations of the city, he delivered every sabbath, for years, discourses the most extraordinary, to assemblies also as extraordinary perhaps as could be found in the Christian world. In the centre column of seats, guarded sacredly against all other intrusion, sat a dense mass of mariners,—a strange medley of white, black, and olive,—Protestant, Catholic, and sometimes pagan, representing many languages, unable probably to comprehend each other's vocal speech, but speaking there the same language of intense looks and flowing tears. On the other seats, in the galleries, the aisles, and the altar, and on the pulpit stairs, crowded, week after week, and year after year (among the families of sailors, and the poor who had no other temple), the élite of the city, the learned professor, the student, the popular writer, the actor, groups of clergymen, and the votaries of fashion, listening with throbbing hearts and wet eyes to the man whose chief training had been in the forecastle, whose only endowments were those of grace and nature, but whose discourses presented the strangest, the most brilliant exhibition of sense, epigrammatic thought, pathos, and humor, expressed in a style of singular pertinency, spangled over by an exhaustless variety of the finest images, and pervaded by a spiritual earnestness that subdued all listeners; a man who could scarcely speak three sentences, in the pulpit or out of it, without presenting a striking poetical image, a phrase of rare beauty, or a sententious sarcasm, and the living examples of whose usefulness are scattered over the seas" (367). Significantly, the authors compare Father Taylor to Wordsworth's Peter Bell (437). I am reminded of Melville in his conservative mood, situated as a stylist in the culture of popular evangelical religion.

111. Matthiessen had already set this up earlier on page 426, following a portion of Ahab's quarter-deck speech rendered in blank verse with the statement, "Starbuck's meditation opens the next chapter: 'My soul is overmanned . . . .' He has excised the chapter "Sunset."

112. See my discussion of Melville's Milton annotations above and their relevance for Ahab's probable allusion to Eve, addressed by Satan as "Queen of this Universe." Matthiessen is

contradicting his response to Olson's draft essay, that Melville could not have lacked the tragic sense.

113. Thorp, *Representative Selections*, xci, cxviii.

114. Rolfe has been taken by corporatist Melvilleans to be Melville's true voice in *Clarel.*

115. Matthiessen uses the word "inexorable" to sting Mapple's and Ahab's "inexorable self" that stands up to illegitimate authority.

116. Compare with Olson, "The Growth of Herman Melville," quoted above; also the chapter on Dana in D. H. Lawrence, *Studies in Classic American Literature.* Matthiessen flunks *White-Jacket* as art: Of all Melville's early too-concrete works, it is "[the] most heavy and diffuse through its number of surface details." Extrapolating from D. H. Lawrence, I suggest that when the right-wing modernists looked for equilibrium between matter and spirit, the lurking model giving specificity to their abstraction was the "dynamic equilibrium" between master and man, characterized by "reciprocity" before the rule of capital destroyed such bonds.

117. Henry W. Wells, "Herman Melville's *Clarel,*" *College English* 4 (May 1943): 478–83, and "An Unobtrusive Democrat: Herman Melville," *South Atlantic Quarterly* 43 (Jan. 1944): 46–51.

118. But see H. M. Bossard to Olson, Mar. 26, 1938, giving him the reference he requested on Jung's analysis of Hitler, "Wotan: a psychologist explores the forces behind German fascism" (Olson Papers).

119. Page references are to Willard Thorp, *Literary History of the United States*, rev. ed. (New York: Macmillan, 1974). Melville tried to reform the missionaries in his first works; by the late 1850s, in his lecture "The South Seas," he advised Americans to leave primitives alone until the "civilized" had reformed themselves. Thorp's Christian Socialist account would support the aims of the internationalism of the postwar upper-class peace movement by rebuking Pierre's excessive idealism and rejection of pragmatism. See Thorp, *Representative Selections*, xxxviii, and *Literary History*, 470. The strange union refers to the living arrangements of Pierre and Isabel (later joined by Lucy) in the city.

120. See Gruber, *Mars and Minerva;* also *The Report of the Thomas Jefferson Memorial Commission to the Senate and House of Representatives, June 1939*, which stated, "For more than 150 years, Thomas Jefferson, the third president of the US, has been recognized by our citizens not only for the outstanding part which he took in the drafting of the Declaration of Independence, itself, not only for his authorship of the Virginia Statute for religious freedom, but also for the services he rendered in establishing the practical operation of the American Government as a democracy, and not an autocracy."

121. I am not claiming a moral equivalency between the New Deal and fascism or Soviet communism; state murder is not the same as marginalization or unemployment or amnesia. As I have argued throughout, while diffuse anxiety and self-censorship characterize postwar American culture, libraries remain open, though access to state secrets is still limited, with the result that conspiracy theories further pathologize our political culture.

122. See Donald Davidson, "Where Are the Laymen? A Study in Policy-Making," *American Review* 9 (Sept. 1937): 456–81. Davidson was protesting against mushrooming independent citizen policy groups in the South, loosely allied with, but also critical of, the Roosevelt administration. Davidson derisively typed these fact finders as either neo-abolitionists or as top-down social planners. Scientific industrial society had destroyed the capacity of Jeffersonian democrats to participate in the major decisions of their lives. The New Left phrase "participatory democracy" may be indebted to such 1930s Agrarian thought, proudly professed by Davidson as "fascist."

123. "From the Heart of Europe," "revised early draft 2," p. 10, Matthiessen Papers, bMS Am 1433 (7). See Matthiessen, *From the Heart of Europe* (New York: Oxford UP, 1948), 82. In 1937, Reinhold Niebuhr had written "Religion is forced to tell many little lies in the interest of a great truth, while science inclines to tell many little truths in the interest of a great lie. The great truth in the

interest of which many little lies are told is that life and history have meaning and the source and the fulfillment of that meaning lie beyond history. The great lie in the interest of which science tells many little truths is that spatio-temporal realities are self-contained and self-explanatory and that a scientific description of sequences is an adequate analysis of causes." Reinhold Niebuhr, "The Truth in Myths" is reprinted in *Evolution and Religion: The Conflict between Science and Theology in Modern America*, ed. Gail Kennedy (Boston: Heath, 1957), 94.

124. Matthiessen, *From the Heart of Europe*, 182–83. Sidney Kaplan, a liberal Melville critic and Leyda admirer, criticized Eleanor Metcalf's politics but commended Matthiessen's "wonderfully eloquent and (last) words on Melville" in a letter to Leyda, July 21, 1950. Commenting on the difficulties of "Benito Cereno," Kaplan wrote, "I do intend to examine the whole Melville canon, including the Civil War writings. Warren, Hettinger and Arvin leave much to be said. Some time ago Mrs. Metcalf wrote me that the only thing of interest she had was a presentation copy of Battle Pieces from Melville to his wife . . . and a brick from Malvern Hill. 'If what you write,' she added, 'gives a wider circulation to the prose appendix to *Battle Pieces*, that in itself would be a great service to his memory and fine contribution to the thinking and feeling of these torn days.' I fear I shall disappoint her there; I am not sure that the appendix was or is worth much as a moral-political document. It has the alarming odor of Bennett's *Herald*. As you suggest, however, I shall try to see Mrs. Metcalf and talk with her."

125. But see Leo Marx, "Double Consciousness and the Cultural Politics of F. O. Matthiessen," *Monthly Review* 34 (1983): 34–56. Marx believes that his teacher's critical achievement (the recognition of contradictions) helped overcome the regnant organicism: "It signalled the virtual disappearance of the older complacent idea of our national culture as an essentially homogeneous, unified whole" (40). In my research, I have found no such complacency or sense of unity. Marx discusses the context of Matthiessen's suicide: personal loss (his lover Russell Cheney had died in 1945) and political persecution exacerbating a history of depression. By contrast, one prominent New Americanist critic sees Matthiessen as a consensus builder, papering over social conflict. See Donald E. Pease, "*Moby Dick* and the Cold War," in *The American Renaissance Reconsidered*, ed. Walter Benn Michaels and Donald E. Pease (Baltimore: Johns Hopkins UP, 1985): 113–55.

126. Compare Henry W. Wells, *The American Way of Poetry* (New York: Columbia UP, 1943), 86. Wells, a founding member of the Melville Society, discusses *Clarel* as a revelation of America: "The section of Book One devoted to [the judaizing Nathan's] past gives a vivid and circumstantial picture of many aspects of American life. Nathan's pioneering family after migrating from Maine settled at last on the Illinois prairie. Here Nathan came into imaginative touch with the land on which he worked and with the Indian aborigines who preceded him. As a thinker he felt the force, in turn, of Tom Paine's rationalism, of a narrow and fanatical sectarianism, of a transcendental nature-worship, and of the puritanical variety of Hebraism. This section of only ten pages constitutes a really remarkable epitome of no small part of America's social and intellectual history."

127. Kenneth Murdock to Perry Miller, Apr. 12, 1950, Miller Papers.

128. William Ellery Sedgwick Papers, bMS Am 1728 (63). There is another version, typed by Sedgwick's colleague Theodore Spencer. I do not know the meaning of the line "Scribners 1932–36," or the prefix P.C. (preceding the last verse which is written on the reverse of the page). Neither of these appears in the Spencer version.

129. See especially the last volume of *American Review* (1937), where both themes are elaborated: the startling move away from the insane theocratic state of Hitler (now compared to Stalin) and the continued glorification of Mussolini's autonomous corporatist state, while in "Maule's Curse," Yvor Winters praised *Moby-Dick* and "Benito Cereno" as unique examples of sanity in the face of the cultural confusion caused by New England Transcendentalism and Calvinism. Winters was strenuously opposed to Ahab and Pierre.

130. Schaeffer's three Winslow Homer–style illustrations of Ahab show him lost in thought, scanning the sea, and in raging confrontation with Starbuck. The first one depicts a deep-bronzed, lined face with some white hair showing under his brown cap; the eyes are narrow and the nose beaked; the bronze color is continued in the jacket, which contrasts with the white shirt and pants. Around his ivory leg are brown belts and a red band. The right hand is clenched, while the left arm supports a telescope as if he was carrying Ben Franklin's loaf of bread. This edition carried the Etymology and Extracts at the end of the text, as in *The Whale*.

131. See below, chap. 10.

132. Robert Wistrich, *Hitler's Apocalypse* (New York: St. Martin's Press, 1986), who marks the 1936–38 turning point to explain why Nazi antisemitism, though bad, was relatively muted in 1933–35; German conservatives wanted to protect "useful" Jews. Wistrich diagnoses Hitler as a monomaniac.

8. A CHANGE OF CLOWNS: FILM NOIR PHASING OUT THE WEAVER SYNTHESIS

1. Charles Olson to Jay Leyda, June 15, 1950. Unless otherwise indicated, Olson letters quoted in this chapter are in the Leyda Papers, UCLA, copyright 1993 University of Connecticut Libraries. With the exception of a few future New Critics, organic conservatives promoted Melville insofar as he was not Ahab; see citation of Yvor Winters, below.

2. William Charvat, "American Romanticism and the Depression of 1837," *Science & Society* 2 (1937–38): 73. Compare with Charvat's later depiction of Melville's hostility toward the undifferentiated but mostly feminine reading public, a judgment contradicting his observation that Melville stimulates critical inquiry, in "Melville and the Common Reader" (1959); see also his "Melville," in *The Profession of Authorship in America, 1800–1870*, ed. Matthew J. Bruccoli (Columbus: Ohio State UP, 1968), 204–61.

3. Bernard Smith, ed., *The Democratic Spirit*, rev. ed. (New York: Knopf, 1945), 336. Smith's literary criticism appeared in *Science & Society*. Like Jay Leyda, Bernard Smith was one of the signers of "Statement of American Intellectuals," July 1938, a defense of the Soviet purges: "We call upon [American liberals] to support the efforts of the Soviet Union to free itself from insidious internal dangers, principal menace to peace and democracy." Other signatories mentioned herein or in related manuscripts were Edwin Berry Burgum, Malcolm Cowley, H. W. L. Dana, Granville Hicks, Selden C. Menefee, and George Seldes. See James Truslow Adams, "The Democratic Fashion," *Saturday Review of Literature*, Sept. 27, 1941, for a negative review of the Smith anthology, which had brought communist writers into the mainstream; Adams also denounced communist professors who are permitted to destroy America from within. Of course, sympathy for workers is not confined to the Left and should not be the test for progressive or democratic art; moreover, the characterization of a strangely malevolent world obscures Melville's understanding of class institutions and hypocritical authority in a putative democracy.

4. Eleanor Metcalf to Henry Murray, June 8, 1944, Special Correspondence, Murray Papers, box 4.

5. Robert Magidoff, "American Literature in Russia," *Saturday Review of Literature* 2 (Nov. 1946): 271–73. For V. F. Calverton, *The Liberation of American Literature* (New York: Scribner, 1932), Melville was an overrated bohemian, nostalgic and unhelpful. In 1947, Howard Fast attacked the canonizing of *Moby-Dick*: Like Irving, Poe, and Hawthorne, Melville's vision was static and insensitive to issues of exploitation and tyranny; Ahab was interested only in exorcising his personal devils. In "Democracy, American Literature, and Mr. Fast," *English Journal* 36 (1947): 321–23, H. Blair Rouse answered Fast ("American Literature and the Democratic Tradition," *College English* 8 [1947]: 279–84), asserting both Melville's rootedness and his transcendent qualities

as a thinker and a great artist. Talking with me after a UCLA ACLU conference on blacklisting, Fast denied ever having criticized Melville; he had always recognized Melville as the exemplary American writer. John Howard Lawson's brief remarks on Melville were mixed: Melville had succumbed to the market after *Moby-Dick*; "Benito Cereno" was thoroughly racist and proslavery, while his more proletarian work, Lawson hinted, was marred by his depiction of docile sailors on board the *Pequod*. Lawson, The *Hidden Heritage* (New York: Citadel Press, 1950). Later assertions of Melville's unambiguously proletarian identity (especially by H. Bruce Franklin and his followers) should be viewed against this backdrop of late 1930s Thorpian embrace and Old Left rejection in the 1930s (the exception was Granville Hicks). But see Eisenstein's memoir excerpt (appended) indicating the presence of Melville criticism in Moscow's Library of Foreign Literature, though probably not translated.

6. Philip Rahv, "Melville and His Critics," *Partisan Review* 17 (1950): 732–35. While still a Leftist, Newton Arvin presented a paper to a closed session of the Popular Front–oriented Second American Writers Congress (1937), "The Democratic Tradition in American Letters." He distinguished between authoritarian and democratic "strains" in American literature, complaining about the appropriation of democratic writers by the Right; he did not mention Melville in his line-up (which included Frances Wright, Theodore Parker, Channing, Emerson, Thoreau, Lincoln, Whittier, Longfellow, Howells, Twain, and, above all, Whitman). See Henry Hart, ed., *The Writer in a Changing World* (New York: Equinox Press, 1937), 34–43. Compare Arvin's 1937 talk with some disparaging remarks about common sailors in his Melville study of 1949.

7. See William Phillips and Philip Rahv, "Some Aspects of Literary Criticism," *Science & Society* 1 (Winter 1937): 212–20. The author of *Pierre* would qualify as a Marxist critic were their standards to be applied: "The real value of the Marxian philosophy to literary criticism is in the framework it provides by revealing the sources of literary ideology in the class struggle, and by defining the relation of literature to material life, to the flow of political events, to the classes that contend for mastery in American society. Once criticism has a body of general principles against which it can be checked, it is well on its way to scientific status" (214); the critics should get inside the heads of their subjects, describing "the new multiplicity of factors" the sociological critic descries (215); the critic must not be one sided, avoiding contradictions and "precarious combinations of belief" (216); formalists have distanced themselves from their subjects: "Every act of assimilation changes the assimilator" (217); even writers with invalid philosophies (Balzac, Tolstoy, Dostoevsky) are valuable because "in qualitative artistic terms and in moral and intellectual range and relevance they gave a truthful account of the lines of directive force in the life about them" (219). Compare with Zola on naturalism, quoted below.

8. Edwin Berry Burgum, *Science & Society* 6 (1942): 177–78. See Burgum's hostile remarks on *Paradise Lost* in "Art in War Time: The Revival of the Heroic Tradition," 336–37: "The Paradise from which Adam departs with mingled emotions symbolizes in disguise the stability of the gold age of communal life, and the world that he enters is that world of competition in which a man must rely solely upon his individual initiative, and which has altogether lost the concept of cooperation whether as means or end." Milton has erased the conflict between individual and society out of a desire for domination. Burgum's reading suggests Matthiessen's attack on Ahab.

9. Joseph Freeman to Margaret E. Fries, June 20, 1947, Joseph Freeman Papers, box 167, Stanford University. I have found no evidence that Jay Leyda spoke to Melville descendants who told him that they hated their ancestor. Note that Freeman makes no mention of Leyda having left the Communist Party. In characterizing Sylvia (Si-Lan) Chen's father, Freeman meant to write Sun Fo. It is, of course, very difficult to discover the identity of secret police agents, as Percy Chen is alleged to be in Freeman's unmailed letter. In a letter of October 23, 1990, to me, Tillman Durdin, former correspondent for the *New York Times* wrote, "I have seen no written official document or authenticated statement to the effect that Percy Chen was a GPU agent, but I take it for granted he

was. He fled with Mme. Sun to Moscow when the KMT took control of Hankow, and when he returned to China and settled in Hong Kong he acted the part of a Soviet partisan and informant. In HKG when I was there (*N.Y. Times* correspondent) (1949–54) (1957–61) (1967–1974) he seemed to have no employment but was always in funds and lived well. He was always a defender of the USSR and acted the role of a secret agent." The GPU, or OGPU, was a precursor to the KGB, the Soviet secret police.

10. Jay Leyda, draft script, "Bartleby," 14, Leyda Papers, NYU.

11. Leyda wrote these notes to himself on the bottom of a letter of November 30, 1954, from Walter Aschaffenburg, his collaborator on the opera *Bartleby*. Leyda Papers, box 1, folder "Walter Aschaffenburg 1954–59," NYU. In the working script, the lines read (to the client) "What should I do with such a man? What *good* is he to me?" (15).

12. Robbins told me in a telephone interview (ca. 1989) that he had been Leyda's psychiatrist; that Leyda was secretive, refusing to give an oral history to Columbia University (which is not true); that he was always unhappy and overly dependent. He also recalled that Leyda told him that, after their blow-up (see below), Murray "had come crawling back to him." The letters reproduced in my appendix from the 1950s suggest that Leyda, not Murray, abjectly ended the feud (unless he referred to several letters from Murray, spring 1977, appended). The FBI also had trouble pinning Leyda down, initially believing that he was a Russian citizen sent to the United States to create pro-Soviet propaganda, because it seemed implausible that anyone could have learned to translate Russian in such a short time; moreover, there was no birth record in Detroit, a fact that also disturbed Leyda.

13. Hayford, *Melville's "Monody,"* 32. Leyda's expertise was such that he was asked by the New York Public Library to excavate and catalog the cache of family letters (stored in a trunk belonging to Augusta Melville and discovered in 1983), an unusual procedure for an archive (interview, Leyda archivist Martha Foley, June 17, 1999).

14. Leyda was attacked by anti-Stalinist leftist T. R. Greene in the *New Leader* (Sept. 6, 1942) as a "former employee of Moscow's International Bureau of Revolutionary Literature [who] has caused bitter comment and controversy in the highest government circles. However, few State Department officials, or directors of other important federal agencies, dare to criticize the filming of [former ambassador to the Soviet Union, Joseph] Davies' book. The fear of the 'second front press' is all-pervading. No one wants to be branded as an appeaser-mad-dog merely to take exception to a single film, or to Jay Leyda himself who received his training in Moscow propaganda activity. Leyda, of course, opposed the American defense effort until Russia was invaded. . . . Jay Leyda's new job means that the Pro-Soviet crowd has taken over and is unafraid to work in the open" (1). Also according to Greene, Leyda's appointment signaled danger for A. A. Berle and other anticommunist State Department officials. Leyda's heavily redacted and voluminous FBI file, begun in 1943, indicates that they were tipped off by an anonymous informer in a letter dated July 3, 1940, enclosed in an envelope from the *New Leader* (possibly Seymour Stern, who was a relentless critic of Leyda's film criticism and politics). Ambassador Joseph E. Davies's book *Mission to Moscow* (the basis for the 1943 film of the same name) was reviewed in the *New Leader*, Nov. 22, 1941, 4, as a whitewash of GPU terror.

15. Of the scholars I have mentioned, only Bezanson did not complain of physical symptoms or writer's block, often attributed to some aspect of their work on Melville. Eleanor Melville Metcalf may have been one of the most upset during the late 1940s; but in her letters to Leyda, she blamed her illness in the summer of 1949 to excessive heat. Her son Paul Metcalf suspected, as I do, that many of her encounters with Melville's writing were disturbing, including precipitating a possible nervous breakdown (anxiety attack?) in the early 1920s. Charles Feidelson, Jr., was also a Stanley Williams student, but he was not part of Leyda's circle.

16. James Bloom, review of *Journals, New York Times Book Review*, Nov. 12, 1989, 58. In my characterization of the *Log*, I am synthesizing my research, not claiming that Bloom would agree with all of my conclusions. For "gush and guff," see draft of Leyda letter to Henry Murray, n.d. (1951?), attempting to win him over to the Leon Howard Melville biography (appended, Leyda Papers, UCLA). I have found no such sentimentality in the Melville scholarship. But Leyda could have fused his mother, Margaret, with the alleged hero-worshipers that preceded him. While Jay was hospitalized after he was drafted into the army (apparently for nervous troubles that were advertised as "pneumonia"), Margaret wrote on January 31, 1944, "You know, Dear, I'm soft, mushy, mothering, weak and 'liquid'; when I think of you and your environment, but don't let me be that way. Does it help? No,—but silly, bright stuff is just as bad—God help me to be someone you would like, related or not.—Now is the time to tell you how wonderful I am, isn't it?"

17. Compare with the affectionate letter from Margaret (Jay's real mother), July 13, 1930, stating that she really wants Jay (age twenty) with her. She relates the story of Josephine, a colored girl of fifteen years, whose mother was white but whose black father had kidnapped her; Josephine hates white people now. See Leyda Papers, Chronological Correspondence, year 1930, NYU. Is this the Ur-story of Leyda's childhood as told to Columbia University?

18. "The Reminiscences of Jay Leyda" 5:212–14, Oral History Collection of Columbia University, 1981. Leyda's pseudonyms included Eugene Hill and Chen-Li. The full text describing his early childhood and the family prison is appended.

19. Margaret Leyda Smith to Leyda, Dec. 7, 1935, Leyda Papers, NYU. I am indebted to Martha Foley, curator of the Tamiment Institute (NYU) Leyda Papers, for her guidance through a collection still being cataloged. In his Columbia oral history (2:53), Leyda described himself as "spoiled" by his "coddling family." He worked after school in a department store and was not paid by Jane Reece, his photography mentor while in high school.

20. Leyda told Columbia that he did not believe that his parents were legally married, since he had never seen a marriage certificate, though he had been told of its existence. See appended e-mail letter from Elena Pinto Simon, suggesting that Leyda located his mother's marriage certificate after the Columbia oral history was taken and that the oral history contained inaccuracies. In my own research, I have glimpsed a clinging family that gloried in their famous traveling boy but at the same time undermined his autonomy with their constant demands to communicate and to stay within the family circle. (Melville, too, faced this double message.) For instance, see the undated letter from Josephine (the grandmother) to Leyda while he is in the Soviet Union, expressing her interest in that country and asking him for a long letter, as he has not written to them; at the same time, she reminds him that his picture is in all their rooms and she wishes he would come home. She signs the letter as "Mother," though she is not. An undated letter from Josephine to Margaret states that the family is upset that Sylvia (Leyda's nonwhite wife) has come to Dayton to perform. However, Mary (Margaret's sister) saw her dance and invited her to lunch but was refused. Leyda did not attend Josephine's funeral in 1944 but sent flowers. See folder "Mrs. J. M. Leyda (Mother)," Leyda Papers, NYU.

There is a hint that Josephine (the grandmother/mother) suffered from a nervous disturbance, which could explain Leyda's obsessive search for hereditary insanity in the Melville family. See letter from Margaret Leyda Smith to Leyda, Oct. 8, 1933, interesting on several counts: "Jay I brought a confused set of feelings back from my meeting with you in New York—most of them approved—some disapproved. Suppose you had a few disapproved ones yourself—but I loved being with and near you. . . . The folks at home (three loyal to you, women) are in rather tough circumstances—but guess Joe will surely by now be working—Mother still had her 'stupid ones' that she struggles so loudly with, not so good for the nerves, and Mary the real 'bread winner' loves the responsibility of the household but kicks about it just the same. I did not like your ridicule of them, because they really love you—selfishly perhaps but a real affection."

21. See folder "Pre-1930 Sunday School clippings, etc.," Leyda Papers, NYU. These pictures suggested to me that Leyda indeed had serious emotional difficulties, that he was not playing crazy for political motives. They should be contrasted with Leyda's impressive sketches of solid and robust individual Soviet peasants and workers, rendered in crayon on brown paper, also in his NYU papers. The drawings of the Russians are not placed in any particular environment and are unsigned.

22. I cannot tell which parts of the Columbia version are true, which are embroidered in retrospect. Leyda does seem to have imagined rejection even when he was admired. And the drafts of even the most mundane written communications that swell his Melville papers at UCLA suggest that Leyda did not trust his unmonitored imagination or his irritable temper to stay down; or perhaps he was trying to keep his stories straight, since they often varied depending on the correspondent. The rest of the oral history at Columbia leaves out or distorts many of the most important relationships and events of his life, which are revealed in his NYU papers, including the affection and admiration consistently proferred by his maternal family; his initiation into the Left in New York City around 1930 (which was one facet of his liaison with lawyer Carol Weiss King, a Jewish activist lawyer for numerous communist front organizations, a party "marriage" apparently concealed from everyone in his family except his real mother, Margaret); his membership in the Communist Party (or related activities) probably before and after he told Lincoln Kirstein or the State Department he had joined or quit; his duties as a Communist Party writer, whatever they may have been; his attempts to avoid induction into the army in 1943 (perhaps at the behest of Lincoln Kirstein [see below] and which would have been disapproved by the Communist Party); the state of his finances while working on the Melville books; and the details of his Melville adventures. How can we account for his acceptance into the northeastern Ivy League literary establishment while he was either an active communist or a famous ex-Stalinist well known throughout every nook and cranny of 1930s theater, photography, and documentary film for defending the Moscow purge trials, attacking the Congress for Cultural Freedom, opposing intervention (1939–41), then joining other Stalinists in calling for a Second Front in 1942? Why was the FBI only intermittently interested in investigating him in the 1940s and after, and then after prodding by the indefatigable Seymour Stern and, later, the American Legion, or when the Bureau investigated "the Moscow News Group" in the early 1960s? And why, though well known to the Dies Committee, was he not called before HUAC in the late 1940s and 1950s with other prominent communist intellectuals?

23. See draft letters from Leyda to Ralph Steiner and Comrade Marshall, both July 2, 1933, "Chronological Correspondence Folder for 1933," Leyda Papers, NYU.

24. See Leyda's notes for an autobiography and a letter to Mrs. A. C. Smith (Margaret, his mother), June 18, 1933: "The family doesn't know about Carol, and I don't see why they should. I wouldn't like their enthusiasm, their concern, their questions. But I think you will like her and I hope she will like you. I'll be very grateful if you don't mention Carol or my marriage to Dayton. Will you try?" (Leyda Papers, NYU).

25. Carol Weiss King to Leyda, n.d., Leyda Papers, NYU.

26. Leyda to Kirstein, Nov. 2, 1933, Leyda Papers, box 2, NYU. The sentences regarding the chistka ritual were apparently begun on the back of a letter from Leyda's mother, Margaret Smith, who had written, "Jane and her friend Phyllis speculate a great deal about you and your future—do give us lots of information about your doings[.] We three do love to talk about you and your interests. . . . Now I shall be on tiptoe until I hear from you—Love—yrs and longing Margaret." Leyda's remarks on the extraction of information from Soviet citizens were first formulated as follows: "A chistka is a cleaning given the party members every five years.

This is one of the sweeping, cleansing years and the wind blows through every unit, trust, and union. Each member exposes his past or his mind in a cleaner, colder process than I ever saw functioning in an American court." See folder "Margaret Leyda 1933–1940s," Leyda Papers, NYU.

27. Joseph Freeman to Leyda, Nov. 3, 1933, Leyda Papers, box 2, NYU. Compare with Leyda's letter protesting the false and libelous accusations of *Hollywood Reporter* columnist Irving Hoffman: Leyda wrote that he "never belonged to any organization even remotely resembling a 'Soviet Propaganda Bureau'" (in Chronological Correspondence folders). Also in box 2 see reprint of Lee Elihu Lowenfish, "The American Testament of a Revolutionary," *Columbia University Columns* (Feb. 1978): 3–13. Freeman (1897–1966) was born in the Ukraine; his family moved to Brooklyn in 1904. After the publication of his memoir explaining his transition from romantic to revolutionary, *An American Testament,* Freeman was anathematized in Moscow (1937) because Trotsky was "denounced . . . as an erring individual rather than as a traitor. Freeman was rebuked for mentioning the existence of detention camps, and he also drew attack for depicting Stalin as an earthy political leader—quoting Stalin's remark to a Party conference, 'Excuse my breath, comrades, I ate herring for lunch'—instead of presenting him as an infallible, if not divine figure" (11). Freeman then canceled his book tour but found "solace" in Wordsworth's *The Prelude.* During the McCarthy period, Freeman would not testify against party comrades.

28. The application diverges from other accounts of Leyda's work experience in the USSR prior to working with Eisenstein. For instance, in one set of autobiographical notes, he states he worked with Dziga Vertov for six months, then with Eisenstein for a year and a half. However, the supplicating letter of 1935 describes failure and dashed hopes. (Leyda did not expect to pass his examinations at the GIK and went to work at a kino factory.) On reflection, Leyda's lifelong interest in communism seems partly motivated by the need to expose and punish hypocritical or contradictory authority, hence the turn to gloomy existentialism. This seems to me to be a stronger motive than identification with the American labor movement as it developed during the 1930s and 1940s. As one of his letters to his mother implied, he went to the Soviet Union for a makeover, to become the new Soviet man, a valued artist.

29. Leyda to Margaret Smith, Oct. 19, [1936], Leyda Papers, NYU. In the same letter, he urged his family to vote for Roosevelt. Leyda had stopped writing to Carol King, and when she confronted him he told her of his marriage; she felt herself deserted, but did everything she could to help Si-Lan with her visa difficulties. See Carol King letters, Leyda Papers, box 3, NYU.

30. Leyda told Columbia that he left the USSR in 1936 because the purge trials had started, and all foreigners were told either to become citizens or to depart ("Reminiscences" 2:82). In another autobiography written for prospective publishers or employers, while employed in the research division of the Berlin Film Archive (in East Germany), Leyda stated that "smallpox forced Eisenstein to halt and revise film [the unfinished "Bezhin Meadow"], he advised acceptance of invitation from New York's Museum of Modern Art to join new department, the Film Library, as assistant curator, with a grant from the Rockefeller Foundation." In yet another vitae (hinting that he had been Eisenstein's collaborator before Babel), Leyda explained: "1936—when Eisenstein recovered, a new script was needed, and Isaac Babel became E's collaborator. A film department had been started at the Museum of Modern Art in NY, and Iris Barry came to Europe in search of films; Alfred Barr sent her to me in Moscow to help as guide and interpreter, and before her departure she offered me the post of assistant curator to her. Consulted Eisenstein, he advised me to go—the trials had begun to make trouble for all resident foreigners and the new version of the film would not be started before winter."

31. Sergei Eisenstein, "Film Forms, New Problems," trans. Ivor Montagu, *New Theater* (Apr. and June 1936): 13, 29, in Leyda Papers, UCLA, with penciled editing marks. The magazine was an organ of the Communist Party; Leyda was on the board.

32. Eisenstein to Leyda, Feb. 1, 1937, Sergei Eisenstein Papers, Series B. Eisenstein and Leyda may have been intimate physically as well. Apparently Leyda had visited Eisenstein after the latter's severe heart attack. In his letter of May 26, 1946, Eisenstein lamented, "I'm sorry we could not have had *all* the fun we could have had: but my heart still feels lousy" (Eisenstein Papers, Series B).

33. Leyda to Ivor Montagu, Apr. 30, 1941, Leyda Papers, box 4, NYU. Note that Leyda made a film for Nelson Rockefeller that year (see Victor Riesel comments above, quoted in Leyda's FBI file). Leyda does not mention this film in any of his cv's.

34. This is a shocker: Did Gorer's promotion of "Constructive Sadism" in any way influence Leyda's outlook, behavior, and relations with other Melvilleans? See Geoffrey Gorer, *The Life and the Ideas of the Marquis De Sade*, rev. ed. (London: Peter Owen, 1953); originally published by Wishart in 1934 as *The Revolutionary Ideas of the Marquis de Sade*, intro. J. B. S. Haldane. I quote examples of most possible relevance to this book (page numbers refer to the 1953 edition): "[Sade:] 'Various buildings, healthy, large, properly furnished and completely safe shall be erected in all towns, every sex, every age, every creature will be offered to the caprices of the libertines who will come to take their pleasure, and the most complete subordination will be the rule for the people present; the slightest refusal will be punished arbitrarily by him who has suffered from it' (158–59). [Gorer:] Modesty, or the attachment to another man, would be no motive for a woman's refusal. Love which can be called madness of the soul, is equally inadmissable because it is selfish and exclusive. . . . Women will have exactly the same license as men' (160). [Gorer:] It is now perhaps easier to understand why de Sade wished for legally enforced promiscuity. Happiness depends on the greatest possible extension of sexual pleasure; but his very strong regard for the rights of every individual prevents him from conceiving the idea of a caste of slaves or quasi-slaves who will be the objects by which this extension of pleasure is to be obtained; and therefore his only solution was to give everybody momentary rights over the body of every citizen (181). [Sade's character Madame de Mestival in *Philosophie Dans le Boudoir:*] '. . . All men and all women are alike. . . . What a deception that intoxication is which absorbs in us the results of our senses and puts us into such a state that we only see, we only live through the adored object! Is that living?'" (183).

35. Leyda to Eisenstein, Mar. 22, 1942, and letter, n.d., Eisenstein Papers, Series B. Leyda referred to Iris Barry, *D. W. Griffith, American Film Master* (New York: Museum of Modern Art, 1940).

36. Leyda to Margaret Leyda, May 24, 1942, folder "Margaret Leyda," Leyda Papers, NYU. Leyda was referring to Beaver Falls, Pennsylvania, birth place of aunts Margaret Eleanor, Eleanor, and other Dayton relatives. See folder "Autobiographical Notes," Leyda Papers, NYU.

37. Joseph Freeman to Leyda, Jan. 25, 1934, Leyda Papers, box 2, NYU.

38. Party members were not supposed to generate their own projects. Still, I cannot rule out the possibility that it was Lincoln Kirstein who suggested that Leyda work on the Melville mystery. Kirstein contemplated a ballet based on *Moby-Dick* in the early 1930s. A letter from Kirstein to Leyda, Nov. 8, 1946, states: "I cannot find those damn proofs that Birss gave me; I must have either given them back or away,—it must be at least five years now." Eleanor Metcalf told Henry Murray, July 26, 1932, that Kirstein was planning a new edition of "Billy Budd": "Mr. Birss has just told me that Lincoln Kirstein, editor of the *Hound & Horn* wants to get out a limited Paris edition of Billy Budd, taken from the manuscript. He says that the first transcription is not careful and is also incomplete. Are there any omitted parts that you wish to make use of? If so, I shall say 'no' to Mr. Kirstein until you have done what you want." See Special Correspondence, Murray Papers, box 13.

Further hints that Kirstein, not Eisenstein, could have been the impetus behind Leyda's Melville project are found in a letter from Leyda to Kirstein dated June 18, from 91 Pineapple Street, Brooklyn (Alfred Kazin's apartment, probably early 1952; see draft letter to Sukel, Leyda

Papers, UCLA): "A fresh burden on my conscience: Birss now has to go far out of his way to avoid meeting me in the Clark Street Station—the first time was also the last time we met there. I often imagine him hurried to the grave by me via the BMT. . . . In a hot hour began plotting a future job—and then, in cleaning up correspondence about HM, I found you had suggested this [the undescribed future job] years ago." See Lincoln Kirstein Papers, folder 247. I am not claiming that this statement proves that Kirstein told Leyda to do the Melville reconstruction, rather that Leyda felt he had preempted Birss's collection of Melville materials, and free-associated to Kirstein, his most potent patron and guide, when he went through his Melville materials, probably in preparation to giving them to UCLA. Kirstein's obituary, *New York Times*, Jan. 6, 1996, 1, 9, emphasizes his commitment to classicism and its projection into society beyond the realm of dance. Kirstein had converted to Catholicism. The obituary cites T. S. Eliot as an important influence: ". . . tradition must always be the basis for artistic innovation."

39. Compare with Whittaker Chambers, *Witness* (New York: Random House, 1952), 325. [Reporting first meeting with General Walter Krivitsky in flight from the GPU, 1938] "For more than a year, Stalin had been desperately seeking to negotiate an alliance with Hitler. Attempts to negotiate the pact had been made throughout the period when Communism (through its agency, the Popular Front) was posing to the masses of mankind as the only inflexible enemy of fascism."

40. See, for instance, the flurry of inexpensive books and pamphlets emanating from (the Communist) International Publishers of NYC in 1942–43 on the heroes of the radical bourgeoisie in American history, linking "three American wars for national liberation"—the Revolution, the Civil War, and World War II—and celebrating Tom Paine, Thaddeus Stevens, Wendell Phillips, and numerous black heroes, but not Charles Sumner. Sumner, arguably the single most powerfully placed and effective abolitionist and fighter for black political and civil rights in America until his death, is also missing from Karcher's *Shadow over the Promised Land*, with the exception of one reference wrongly attributing to him the view that the freedmen should be denied suffrage until they had attained literacy (269).

41. See, for example, the Robert Aldrich adaptation of Clifford Odets's stage play *The Big Knife* (1955). A once-radical actor played by Jack Palance (linked to the Group Theater and Roosevelt) has sold out to the loathsome Jewish film producer Stanley Hoff (Hoff is German for courtier), played by Rod Steiger and made up (as a Nazi?) with short blond hair, sunglasses, and a sadistic personality. Hoff is a whoremaster who torments the blonde floozy with a heart of gold played by Shelley Winters. The estranged wife (Ida Lupino) will return to the actor if he leaves Babylon. But the actor had participated in a hit-and-run incident witnessed by the floozy and covered up by the studio. Hoff is blackmailing him, forcing him to renew his contract and continue making absurd but popular movies about upward mobility and the triumph of the common man (as boxer) in America. The actor chooses virtue, but the conflict kills him. He dies in the bathtub, like Marat, killed, though, by his own hand. There is no climbing out from the pit of mass culture, even when offered a strong assist by the New Deal wife and their best friend (a stand-in for Odets and Aldrich), who lives to write the play and movie, to unmask the crypto-Nazi bad Jews of Hollywood who opposed Roosevelt.

42. Compare cable Eisenstein to Leyda, Dec. 11, 1947: "Please add Chaplin essay short post scriptum dated 1948 appreciating Charlie's uncompromising postwar antifascist attitude referring to trial speech IV Monsieur Verdoux and statement about himself as peace monger" (Eisenstein Papers, Series B).

43. Jay Leyda to Lawrence Clark Powell, Apr. 11, 1945, Leyda Papers, box 8, UCLA. Leyda wanted Powell to write the story of Gansevoort, adding, "Birss will ache to see it." The characterization of Gansevoort's nervous derangement was from a letter written by Louis MacNeice to James Buchanan, which later appeared in the *Log*.

44. For the early emphasis on *Typee,* see draft letter to James Laughlin and draft of first sample, comprising Melville's life at sea, the writing of *Typee* and *Omoo,* and his marriage to Elizabeth Shaw Melville. Leyda Papers, box 24, UCLA. *Typee,* in its unexpurgated form, did not reject all missionary activity; rather, as Hershel Parker has pointed out, Melville's criticisms of French adventurism in the South Seas and of Hawaiian missionaries could have been lodged by any upper-class Englishman, critical of lower-class evangelical Protestants and in competition with the French in the region.

45. Alan Swingewood, *The Novel and Revolution* (New York: Barnes and Noble Books, 1975).

46. Lionel Trilling made the positive appraisal of "Billy Budd" the test of his Stalinist characters' ruthlessness in his novel *The Middle of the Journey* (New York: Viking, 1947). But see "From the Notebooks of Lionel Trilling," *Partisan Review* 4 (1984): 496–515. During the period when he was writing his book (and suffering from insomnia and despair, 506–7), he criticized his Columbia students in the tones of a Young Hegelian, lining up with Gifford Maxim (the Whittaker Chambers character) and Irving Babbitt:

Spirit. The modern feeling that spirit should find its expression immediately in the world of necessity and that all that falls short of the full expression of spirit is repulsive. I see this often in gifted students of a particular kind who when find that, say, a graduate school is not up to their standard and expectation, cannot endure staying and abandon their projects. They have, one might say, no irony—for irony, perhaps, is the awareness with acceptance of the breach between spirit and the world of necessity—institutions, etc. They insist that spirit be wholly embodied in institutions. If what I have just written were put to them, they would say, why of course, why not? Yet the fact is that there is a weakness of spirit within that keeps them from enduring—they do not believe that they really exist and can exist if what they recognize as good within themselves is not matched by external forms, received and established by something. This has, of course, its social source—for once, no doubt, apart from institutions, there was an agency that established spirit within a man, so that he could say what he felt within himself was really right and true, no matter how little was existent outside. This agency was religion itself but also a more extensive thing & view of which religion was a part. . . . My students discussing Billy Budd, feel that there is really nothing to be said about the story. Vere is, to them, wholly culpable, Budd being good. Law does not express spirit—even kills it: they insist that this is the whole and final truth in the matter. They think that Vere is a not-exactly-bad man, but a stuffy one, and in objective result bad. They do not understand the tragic choice. They want the reign of spirit immediately. What they do not understand is that: if spirit exists in its purity, so does evil in the form of Claggett [*sic*] and that Claggett makes Vere necessary as an intermediate force between him and Budd. (Notebooks, 1946–47, 508–9)

47. See my appendix, Leyda to Lincoln Kirstein, n.d. (1952?), and affadavit (1956).

48. Draft, Leyda Papers, UCLA. The late Professor Harry T. Levin added a new touch. In a letter to me, June 11, 1991, he said that Leyda was interested in Melville "originally because his Russian mentor, Sergei Eisenstein, thought of filming *Moby-Dick* and had written to Jay for further information." Leyda's first contact with Levin was probably in 1942. A letter from Levin to Leyda, August 22, 1942, says he is impressed by the Eisenstein book (for its suggestiveness regarding imagery and poetry) and has lent it to Matthiessen. The Leyda Papers at NYU contain a page of notes and diagrams, written by Leyda while in the Soviet Union, containing these tantalizing hints: "death-life-death-life (&death) leaking into opposite (whale film)."

49. For Eisenstein, both black and white connoted death, for example, "blind inexorability" as in the Teutons' advance in *Alexander Nevsky.* White was "something tragic, something wasted"

and signified impending doom: an "all engulfing white threat." See Yon Barna, *Eisenstein* (Bloomington: Indiana UP, 1973), 229–30, 261–62; Leyda wrote the foreword to this book. Leyda earlier wrote a lengthy series of quotations from artists on color symbolism for Eisenstein in an undated letter titled "The Night Before Christmas." Neither black nor white is mentioned. The colors analyzed are mainly red, yellow, gold, and green. Charcot was quoted as identifying red with hysteria; Leyda mentioned yellow as wanton love. Leyda and Eisenstein were discussing color and its emotional associations but not the subversion of traditional responses. Eisenstein Papers, Series B.

50.   Leyda referred to Dixon Wecter, who was in charge of graduate studies in American literature. According to the University of California General Catalog 1944–45, full professor Dixon Wecter and assistant professor John Frederic Ross taught "American Literature, The Age of Exile," including authors Bayard Taylor, Herman Melville, Lafcadio Hearn, Mark Twain, Stephen Crane, Henry Adams, Henry James, George Santayana, and T. S. Eliot. Assistant professors in the department also teaching American literature were Bradford Allen Booth and Carl Sawyer Downes. The Exile course was not offered in 1944 or 1945 but existed before and after those dates. Melville and Twain are presented along with alienated aristocratic American writers.

51.   Compare with Leyda's notes for one of his cv's: "1943–44—drafted: basic training in tank corps at Fort Knox. Pneumonia and discharge . . . . Physically unable to work in studios, I earned some money as a script doctor; while I was in army Si-Lan was profitably employed in films as actress and choreographer. I worked on a birthday present for E[isenstein], of Melville documents arranged chronologically. 1945/46—an acquaintance [Harry Levin?] heard of the Melville reconstruction (which I had not thought of as a book) and offered it to a New York publisher. First result: a handsome advance that made it possible to work in East Coast archives for a year. Melville scholars did not like this intrusion, but Leon Howard championed my project. Returned to California to organize new materials into a book—and its publisher failed. (Harcourt bought their assets) . . . . After a year the Harcourt people hired Alfred Kazin to go through the unpublished work to rescue anything that deserved publication. He recommended *The Melville Log* and its difficult production was begun" (folder "Autobiographical Notes," Leyda Papers, NYU).

52.   Leyda, "Reminiscences" 3:111–20. Leyda is vague about the dates. He started the "Film Sense" project after Germany attacked the Soviet Union in 1941. He met Leon Howard at the Huntington Library around 1944. He had had a nervous breakdown sometime after induction in the army (supposedly he was forced to lead younger men who thought he knew more than he did, and they put him in a tank), was sent to the hospital in Fort Knox, then discharged in March 1944. He then was treated at a VA hospital in the Bronx but returned to Los Angeles where he saw two different psychiatrists. The second one got him functioning again.

Compare with Leon Howard's account in "Mysteries and Manuscripts," a memoir located at the Newberry Library. He describes his first meeting with Leyda and his own involvement in the biography as follows: "There appeared at [the Huntington Library] in the early spring of 1945, an ambulatory patient from the Pasadena veteran's hospital who introduced himself as Jay Leyda and asked permission to see anything the Library had on Herman Melville" (20). Leyda had sent Eisenstein books on Herman Melville to answer Eisenstein's question "Who is this Moby Dick?" (Eisenstein had read Leyda's reference on the whiteness of the whale in *Film Sense*, according to Howard.) Leyda had not read *any* Melville until he was in the hospital. While working on the Musorgski letters, he thought he could make a survey of facts on Melville using materials in the Pasadena Public Library and the Huntington. "What appalled him was the amount of speculation he found about Melville in comparison with what was actually known." The survey was to be *for* Eisenstein. "The substance, nature, and effects of Melville's creative imagination continued to fascinate me, as they had for years, and I was also fascinated by Leyda's efforts to strike through the masks in which he had been concealed by his commentators. But whenever the man who had settled down to write got away from his writing desk I am afraid I found him something of a bore"

(22). On the biography: "Somehow I became committed to it." In other words, the better unmasker, Leyda, had unearthed the "ambitious writer," who may not coincide with the suffering hero. "Ambition" is a word carrying unsavory connotations such as ruthlessness, cunning, and dishonesty. But Melville the man isn't even an interesting villain; for Howard, he is "a bore."

53. For instance, Leyda presented himself as a penniless, starving student to Lawrence Clark Powell in 1945. His correspondence with Eleanor Metcalf and Henry Murray indicates similar approaches; he asked for and received handouts from Murray. Leyda told his oral history interviewer that he had gotten "a handsome advance" from Reynal and Hitchcock that enabled his initial archival research on the Melville family in 1945; but as a letter from Albert Erskine indicates, he received a modest advance of $750 in 1946, after the research trip was completed. Leyda's wife, Si-Lan Chen, was a well-paid choreographer, he said, while he was in the hospital at Fort Knox, but that was in early 1944. "Reminiscences" 3: 124–26. A letter from the IRS, May 9, 1944, to Private Leyda (then in the hospital) granting him an extension to file his 1943 return, suggests that Leyda could have had a large income in 1942. The letter ordered him to appear at an IRS office in Holly-wood to explain a deduction for a $700 bad debt (this really existed and was a loan made to a Dayton friend James Smyth, desperately down on his luck in 1942 [see letter Smyth to Leyda, Mar. 3, 1943]; where did Leyda get so much money to lend?) and advised him how to recompute his erroneous 1942 tax: "Due to the fact that you were in active duty with the armed forces during 1942, also 1943, you are entitled to recompute your 1942 income tax, *eliminating all earned income under $14,000*" (emphasis added; could that have been a quote of the law, not a reference to Leyda's income?). According to his selective service questionnaire (Apr. 24, 1941), Leyda earned only $30 a week as film critic. Leyda earned $150/week as adviser to *Mission to Moscow*, a six-week gig. In 1942, Leyda was a freelance photographer; he was working for Artkino, distributing Russian films that would appeal to American audiences; also he had produced a film for Nelson Rockefeller's Office of Inter-American Affairs, starting in late 1941. Where could that 1942 income have come from? What happened to it? Why did the IRS think he was on active duty in 1942 when he was not inducted until November 11, 1943? Why did Leyda's FBI file report only $3,350 family income for 1942? In his attempt to avoid induction in 1943, Leyda had claimed that his wife "was unable to support herself." This IRS letter, left in his Melville papers at UCLA (box 8) by accident perhaps, along with other inconsistencies and possible fabrications, demands investigation by future biographers.

54. Telegram, Eisenstein to Leyda, Jan. 1946, Eisenstein Papers, Series B; full text appended. Books subsequently requested by Eisenstein (telegrams, May 5, Sept. 7, 1946, Jan. 23, Sept. 21, 1947) included "Lawrence Binyon's Spirit of Man in Asian Art & Flight of The Dragon . . . Franz Schoenberner Confession of European Intellectual, Salvador Dali, Autobiography, Anthony How Grow Old Disgracefully . . . Third American History Album . . . Still awaiting Brady [Civil War photographs], Rewald's Impressionists, Parker Tyler Magic and Myth of Movies." The request for the Dali autobiography is interesting in light of his letter to Leyda, May 12, 1939: "Is there anything new? Or is it still surréalisme and surréalisme for ever as the 'dernier cri' in capitalist art?" In letters to Edith Egan (ca. 1946), Eisenstein expressed his admiration for Judy Garland and wanted a copy of *Forever Amber*. A 1935 letter to Ivor Montagu asked for books on cinema. From these and other materials at MoMA, it appears that Eisenstein was interested in history, film theory that might or might not conform to dialectical materialism, symbolism, and popular culture. See especially his scrapbook notes for *Que Viva Mexico*, Eisenstein Papers, Series A.16. However, Eisenstein was fascinated by Melville, as his memoirs indicate; the relevant excerpts describing Leyda's role in his growing interest are appended. See *Beyond the Stars: The Memoirs of Sergei Eisenstein*, vol. 4, ed. Richard Taylor, trans. William Powell (London: British Film Institute, 1995), 358–60.

55. Many details of Leyda's family background are elucidated in his NYU papers, but other matters are not, such as the timing of his association with the Communist Party or the impetus for his Melville research. The late Paul Jarrico has told me that he never saw Leyda at party meetings in the Writer's Branch in Hollywood, nor did he put out the signals common to comrades. This is peculiar, because there are postwar letters from Jarrico to Leyda in his NYU papers, as one comrade writing to another; indeed, the Tamiment Institute register of Leyda's correspondence reads like a "Who's Who" of the 1930s pro-Soviet Left, and his associations did not cease after 1943. According to a report dated November 30, 1943, the FBI acquired "a photostatic copy of a COMMUNIST PARTY Membership Transfer Card on July 28, 1943, on transfer from New York Section C (probably the Cultural Section) of the COMMUNIST PARTY, and that he had been assigned to Branch A of the Northwest Section, Los Angeles County COMMUNIST PARTY, after having been 'okayed' by the Organizational Secretary of the COMMUNIST PARTY." However, Leyda's application for a passport in the mid-1950s declared that he had joined the party in 1937 and quit when he joined the army (late 1943); but these facts changed in 1958. A report from the Washington Field Office of the FBI states, "In connection with his application for renewal of his passport, LEYDA submitted an affadavit dated Jan. 6, 1958, to the American Consul, at the United States Embassy at Paris, France. In this affadavit, he stated that he is a writer by profession. He said that early in 1937, he joined the Communist Party, and was a member thereof until the early part of 1942, when he severed his connection entirely with the Party. LEYDA said that he was the bearer of a membership card for that period, which, to the best of his knowledge, he returned when severed connections with the Communist Party." Yet another FBI memo, June 20, 1962, "recommended that the subject be removed from the S[ecurity] I[ndex], as the information concerning his activity does not warrant it being noted that subject was reportedly *dropped* from the CP *shortly after World War II and there* is a lack of reported activity in CP front groups." (Hoover wrote in his own hand, "I agree," and underlined as indicated above.) At this point, the biographical sketches assembled by Leyda's NYU colleagues and his various cv's are in conflict with his 450-page highly sanitized FBI file, which, in the fragments that are not redacted, demonstrate the interest of J. Edgar Hoover in pursuing him in 1947, after a gap of four years, then twice in 1956 after he saw a news article quoting Seymour Stern, who alleged that Leyda had gone to England to soften public opinion regarding impending visits of Soviet leaders and that it was Leyda who had first suggested that Soviet and American filmmakers should engage in cultural exchanges; then again in response to a complaint from the American Legion that Leyda, a pro-communist, was making information packets for the USIA to release abroad; then again in 1962, when Hoover began investigating all 1930s visitors to the Soviet Union who been their apologists, who had worked for the *Moscow Daily News,* and who were suspected to be Soviet agents. Yet another report from the New Haven Office of the FBI (Nov. 19, 1971) states that in June 1944 reliable informants had said Leyda was a member of the Writer's Branch of the CP and active in various front groups. Sometime after late 1971, his file seems to have been closed.

It is interesting that the Department of the Army responded to the FBI's inquiry as to Leyda's military status (Jan. 4, 1951), stating that he was discharged on March 15, 1944: "Allegation: Communist." No medical reason was given. An FBI report dated February 3, 1948, however, citing his record in NYC Draft Board #42, states that he was given a "'disability discharge' . . . which was the equivalent of an Honorable Discharge, his character rating being excellent." The disability was described as "psychoneurosis severe" and of a "progressive nature" that "incapacitates him for all types of military service." (Leyda claimed a pension, which was discontinued by the VA in 1947.) In the chronologies of his employment and elsewhere, Leyda described his discharge as "Honorable" and stated that he suffered from pneumonia. In the report of June 29, 1949, after a blacked-out passage referring to his army records and the Los Angeles Veterans

Administration, the following FBI gaffe is revealed: "In this interview subject stated that his parents had been separated and that he possessed no affection for them, which might be the answer for the fact that the subject through the years has consistently given his older sister [redacted] as his mother, when in fact, his real mother was JOSEPHINE LEYDA."

In a letter to me of February 1, 1999, the super-secretive National Security Agency (part of the Department of Defense) denied my Freedom of Information Act request on the grounds of "national security," and also because it is permitted by statute "to protect certain information concerning its activities," but admitted to having three documents regarding Jay Leyda classified "Secret." My appeal to release them, unredacted, has been denied.

56. The Williams students at Yale were a diverse lot, according to Harrison Hayford. In comments on my dissertation draft (Jan. 6, 1993), Hayford stated, "Williams never *talked* politics when I was in his seminar." Taken as a group, the Yale students may have varied in their ideological commitments; however, I have not found evidence of political disagreement between Leyda and his particular Yale correspondents (or Leon Howard). There was generally a shared hostility to the overspeculative "Freudian" Weaver-ites and to the older Henry A. Murray (who was often blamed for keeping secrets). In general, the Melville scholarship, a product of English departments, has dealt with political categories imprecisely and ahistorically. It is also true that Hayford, while disagreeing with many of my judgments, has, in person and through written communications, generally aligned himself with the values expressed in this study: sympathy with radical puritanism as expressed by Father Mapple, the labor movement, the necessity for scrupulously collected and evaluated archival evidence, etc.

57. Stanley T. Williams, *Studies in Victorian Literature* (New York: Dutton, 1923), 41–42.

58. Warfel et al., *The American Mind*, 630–31. Melville selections were three chapters from *Moby-Dick* ("The Symphony," "The Chase—Second Day," "The Chase—Third Day"; chapter 57 from *Mardi* ("On Popular Sovereignty in America"); and the Enceladus vision from *Pierre*. The Melville entry immediately follows "Ethan Brand," with Hawthorne described as a neutral observer of "Puritan moods of the past" (597).

59. Olson to Leyda, June 4, 1950. However, Melville was included in Stanley T. Williams and Nelson Adkins, *Courses of Reading in American Literature with Bibliographies* (New York: Harcourt Brace, 1930), 52–62, along with Poe, Hawthorne, Emerson, and Thoreau. The surviving Stanley Williams letters to Olson in the Olson Papers do not bear out Olson's report. For instance, Williams noted in his letter, May 30, 1933, that Olson did not hand in his work.

60. See Stephen Schwartz, *From West to East: California and the Making of the American Mind* (New York: Free P, 1998), 226–78, for an account of the dramatic confrontations between communists and noncommunist radicals for control of the maritime unions.

61. Compare with Norman Foerster, "The Liberal Arts College Curriculum," *American Review* 9 (Apr. 1937), 182–83. [Robert] Shafer of Cincinnati is mentioned along with [G. R.] Elliot of Bowdoin as having suggested Robert Hutchins's Great Books program. Discussing the implications of such courses for state universities, Foerster wrote "Since great books are often hard reading and should be read entire, the superficial type of survey course would have no place. It means that, since great books require reflective thought, courses concerned with mere fact-collecting would be discouraged" (183).

62. Chester R. Heck, "The American Way in Colleges," *Harvard Educational Review* (Mar. 1938): 228–36.

63. Ernest E. Leisy, "The Significance of Recent Scholarship in American Literature," *College English* (Nov. 1940): 115–24.

64. Henry W. Wells, "Herman Melville's *Clarel*," *College English* 4 (May 1943): 478–83. Walter Bezanson's Yale dissertation, "Herman Melville's *Clarel*," appeared the same year (1943); Bezanson

was ambiguous in his assessment of Melville's "scathing" portrait of Margoth (270–76): "[Margoth] takes pride in the destruction of all spiritual values, whether they are the products of the creeds, or the accumulations of historical thought, or the gropings of modern sceptics. His was the spirit which science had brought to the Holy Land, the energetic, commercial, acquisitive spirit rampant in postbellum America" (273–74). In footnote 276, he distances himself from the caricature by criticizing Melville's disclaimer (that he is not satirizing Jews), but Bezanson nevertheless characterizes Margoth as a "Jewish geologist," not "the apostate" (359), and adheres throughout his dissertation and the historical note to the NN edition of *Clarel* to the values Margoth is pridefully destroying.

65. Tyrus Hillway, letter to author, Aug. 29, 1988.

66. Stanley T. Williams, "'Follow Your Leader,' Melville's 'Benito Cereno,'" *Virginia Quarterly Review* 23 (1947): 61–76. Compare with Harold H. Scudder, "Melville's Benito Cereno and Captain Delano's Voyages," *PMLA* 43 (1928): 502–32, which concluded that Melville identified with Cereno, and "Babo is the personification of malicious criticism."

67. Leland R. Phelps, "The Reaction to 'Benito Cereno' and *Billy Budd* in Germany," *Symposium* 13 (1959): 294–99.

68. William H. Gilman to Leyda, Dec. 11, 1948: "Leon was here for a talk in an American literature conference we cooked up" (Leyda Papers, box 23, UCLA).

69. Margaret Denny and William H. Gilman, eds., *American Writers and the European Tradition* (Minneapolis: U of Minnesota P, for the University of Rochester, 1950). My page citations are from the Haskell House edition, 1968. Leyda told Gilman he liked these papers.

70. Compare with Matthiessen, *From the Heart of Europe*, 54–55, on the deplorable European taste for *Gone with the Wind* and other trashy novels.

71. Brooks to Mumford, Mar. 18, 1949, in Spiller, ed., *The Van Wyck Brooks–Lewis Mumford Letters*, 343.

72. Compare with Clark, *Thomas Paine*, v, xxi. "Since it was customary, before the rise of Fascism, for those devoted to American history to represent the Federalists and the Jeffersonians (with whom Paine was associated) as in sharp conflict, it is perhaps well to remind ourselves that they were both loyally American and, like brothers in one family, differed mainly as to the *extent* to which the people could be trusted to govern themselves and the extent to which the national government should take precedence over the state governments. Toward tyranny, monarchy, the idea of one politically established church, and the kind of ideas now associated with Fascism, they presented a common front. . . . [quoting Paine] '[W]e see unerring order and universal harmony reigning throughout the whole. . . . Here is *the standard to which everything must be brought* that pretends to be the work . . . of God.' Having interpreted Paine's mind in the light of contemporary philosophic definitions and their relative emphasis given by men whom Paine acknowledged as his teachers, we have now arrived at the very core of his thought, 'the standard to which everything must be brought,' which is a divinely revealed and sanctioned law and order, in harmonious conformity to which society finds its happiness. Thus Newtonian deism, as interpreted by Paine, involved discipline and order just as did Calvinistic Federalism in America, or Anglican Toryism in England, although the difference in background and terminology has prevented many critics from recognizing it, at least in the case of Paine." Throughout, Clark presents the autodidact Paine as a neoclassical advocate of balance, opposed to mobs, favoring a welfare state, federalism, free trade, and internationalism—less of a Quaker than a Deist. Paine is a freethinker likened to Alexander Pope; i.e., he is the reforming capitalist of the New Deal.

Clark's research was funded by the Rockefeller and Guggenheim Foundations. He was the general editor of the American Writers Series for the American Book Company, publishers of the Willard Thorp Melville study discussed above, as well as *The American Mind*.

73. Compare with John Stafford, *The Literary Criticism of "Young America": A Study in the Relationship of Politics and Literature 1837–1850* (Berkeley: U of California P, 1952), 1, 128. Stafford thanks Theodore Hornberger and Henry Nash Smith for inspiring his studies; his organizing tool for distinguishing conservatives and radicals is Emerson's famous distinction between "Establishment and Movement." The exemplary democrat Whitman is the culmination of Young America in literature. It is worth noting that Wilbert Snow, Olson's adviser, was sent on an international tour by the U.S. State Department in 1951 on behalf of American culture, discussing its "men of vision such as Emerson, Whitman, Thoreau," its folksongs and ballads, the Four Freedoms, and the early struggle to achieve national unity. See Snow's memoir, *Codline's Child: The Autobiography of Wilbert Snow* (Middletown, Conn.: Wesleyan UP, 1974), 457.

Leon Howard's remark about "lying spirit" was clarified in his Melville biography (194). Howard was criticizing the transcendentalists' search for "absolute rather than relative justice" and claiming that Melville understood the foolishness of Goethe's (transcendentalist) statement "Live in the all."

74. Thorp, "Herman Melville," in *Literary History of the United States*, 468.

75. I do not claim that materialism was hegemonic or unchallenged by moderate conservatives prior to the Rochester conference. The modern promotion of blood-and-soil theories of group identity would probably start with J. G. von Herder, a leading figure of the German Enlightenment, continue with the racist geographers and social theorists of the nineteenth century, and bloom in the *völkisch* pseudomaterialist historical methods of Frederick Jackson Turner and other social historians, including the founders of American Studies and the new labor history associated with the New Left that privileges culture over repression and corrupt leadership. Lockean environmentalism was simply co-opted and turned against workers; race and nativity became determining factors as concrete as the physical conditions with which persons coped, while Locke's emphasis on experience and achieved understanding was tainted by association with unspiritual materialism. See, for instance, the *Nation*, Sept. 17, 1918, review of Joseph Kinmont Hart's *Democracy in Education*: "The author feels that the crucial question of the time is whether our civilization shall conform to schemes handed down from the past, everything to be fitted into the old patterns, or whether education should be free to use the new energies which have been released, the new patterns suggested by new conditions. He strongly emphasizes the fact that thinking, only, does not lead to truth; what one feels and believes, his spiritual possession, is more fundamental to life and growth than what one reasons out and proves. The book . . . is an organism; it is concrete, yet always suggestive of the general, and at times of the universal; it is free from masses of detail; and while it is sufficiently technical for the author's purpose, it has exceptional literary value." Compare with Matthiessen on the symbol.

The positions I have outlined were frequently criticized by Stalinists and Trotskyists alike during the late 1930s in *Science & Society*. See Lancelot Hogben, "Our Social Heritage," *Science & Society* (Winter 1937): 150–51, for remarks on right-wing slanders against quantitative materialism; also William Phillips and Philip Rahv, "Some Aspects of Literary Criticism," ibid., 216, for a comment on genteel New Humanist condemnations of the "'sordid' naturalism of modern literature." Samuel Sillen discussed blood-and-soil ideology in Carlyle, Ruskin, and Van Wyck Brooks; see his review of Van Wyck Brooks's *The Flowering of New England*, ibid., 262–65. Muddled liberalism (which glorified vacillations and eschewed simplicity) was noted by Edgar Johnson, "Henry Adams, the Last Liberal," ibid. (Spring 1937): 376–77; Carlyle was cited as a protofascist and Charles Kingsley's *Alton Locke* was criticized by Granville Hicks, "The Literary Opposition to Utilitarianism," ibid. (Summer 1937): 454–72.

76. See the title-page illustration to Louis B. Wright's textbook, *The American Tradition: National Characteristics, Past and Present* (New York: F. S. Crofts, 1941). A great oak occupies the fore-

ground; a Protestant church and a few other small dwellings nestle among gently rolling hills; farm lands lie between.

77. Pearson to Leyda, Oct. 20, 1950, Leyda Papers, box 7, UCLA; Robin W. Winks, *Cloak and Gown: Scholars in the Secret War, 1939–1961* (New York: Morrow, 1987), 319, 317.

78. Hayford first wrote to Leyda on January 13, 1945: "I am convinced there is much more to be discovered about Melville's life that will throw light on the interpretation of his works." Leyda responded on January 26, 1945: "Your letter indicates that you will sympathize with my motive for undertaking this dry, anti-interpretive project. I, too, felt that the richest material was being ignored, either through laziness or through fear that it might interfere with some neat scheme" (Hayford files). Hayford mentioned Leon Howard in his letter of February 11, 1945: "[LH] shares our slant on M and may write a book on him later" (Leyda Papers, UCLA). But Hayford and Leyda pressed each other to write the biography, both expressing impatience with the sloppiness of other Melvilleans, Hayford with the rigors of Melville research as such.

As Leyda wrote to Hayford on December 12, 1946, "There is no question about my doing it—I consider your comment on the point mere parrying for time. I said I wanted a good biography—I refuse to add to the Melville mush as I surely would." Leyda goes on to complain about Howard Vincent's "stale rhapsodies," factual errors, and "pomposity": "What's his excuse for all that twaddle? I feel sure it is selfishness of some unsubtle sort—he's not helping us, he's not helping Melville, he's not helping *Moby-Dick*. . . . For Olson's sake I'm sorry to observe too many similarities between Vincent and him; Olson just writes more interestingly" (Hayford files.)

Hayford told John Birss on September 4, 1945, "I have just recovered from the revulsion that prostrated me on completion of that bloody dissertation. I got the degree . . . and have spent the summer trying not to think of Melville. I'm not happy about everything in the dissertation; much of it was slung together in a determined last-minute rush, and all the ideas on allegory, etc. I had to leave out" (Hayford files). Hayford's letter to Leyda of January 30, 1947, was more reserved: "About the biography which you were urging upon me. I still do not think it would be wise for me to do it. It is largely a personal matter. I have already spent six years on little else but digging at Melville. That would commit me to a couple more, at least, at the rate I can work. And I think it much wiser & for my own good to go on to read and find out about something else. Now, just what kind of biography do you have in mind? Is it a definitive thing, a massive work, like Williams' Irving? Or would you think kindly of a book of say 350 pages designed for the general public, not heavily documented, but done like Mumford's (though for godsake on the basis of solid information)? If you would consent to have your material used for such a book, I have talked Leon into doing it. He will undertake to begin this summer and to bring it out six months or so after your log appears. His own ideas on Melville he was going to make into a book of essays, but I have talked biography to him incessantly and he thinks now he would like to try it, and knows he could [say] what he was planning to say, but in a different form. Today, I was at him about it, and he had thought enough about it that he had even blocked out a synopsis of the chapters and told me what would be in each one. BUT he still wonders whether it would be quite ethical for him to read over your log and to make use of what Merrell and I have told him—all for his own purposes. I tell him that someone is going to do it very soon after your book comes out,—or worse, do it without the benefit of yours, and that what you would like would be for someone you have confidence in to get an advance start on this UNKNOWN by having pre-publication use of your material. If this does meet with your approval, please write me convincingly on the subject, or better, write Leon. He would not want to undertake a solid 2 vol job, to be definitive. We both think this log you have invented will make that unnecessary, and will supplant the old Life and Letters idea, so far as HM is concerned" (Leyda Papers, box 8, UCLA).

79. Leyda Papers, box 24, UCLA. The application concluded with a request for support so that further research (in consultation with leading Melville scholars) could continue. References included Alfred Barr, Aaron Copland, Joseph Freeman, Leon Howard, R. Javits, Lincoln Kirstein, Howard Koch, Harry T. Levin, and Eleanor Metcalf.

80. Draft Leyda to Giroux, Leyda Papers, box 24, UCLA. Compare with Leon Dennen's criticism of Van Wyck Brooks's assault on the morally dictatorial puritans, *New Leader*, Dec. 20, 1941, 5.

81. Howard did have notes from the Boston Melville-Shaw collections taken in the early 1940s, perhaps even the Isabel letter. Leyda must have told his friend Lincoln Kirstein that Random House was lukewarm about the *Stories* volume, because Kirstein reassured him in a letter of May 20, 1947, that he, Kirstein, could place the book with one of his editor friends, including Allan Tate, Russell Lynes, Cortlandt Burns, or Dorothy Hillyer. Kirstein referred to Leyda's editor, Albert Erskine, as that "straw-stuffed doll" (Leyda Papers, NYU). See also letters from Kirstein, Feb. 14, and June 6, 1947. Kirstein was Leyda's most effective ally in entering the world of New York publishing as a Melvillean.

82. Leyda told Joseph Freeman in June 1947 that he was to see Weaver for the first time. However, a correspondent named "Mave" or "Marvin" (perhaps one of the several comrades helping him with the Melville research) had reconstructed the probable dates of conception of Melville's four children for Leyda (letter, Feb. 4, 1946, Leyda Papers, box 8, UCLA): Could Leyda have met Weaver earlier, or could Olson have been the source for the story that Melville doubted the paternity of his children? I also wonder why Leyda did not immediately consult with Eleanor Metcalf after receipt of these stories; perhaps he was influenced by Hayford, who had cautioned him in a September 3, 1949, letter, "I hope you remember your promise to me to put a section in your *Log* Preface or appendix a section on the myths, bonfires, rumors & elusive items etc." It appears that Leyda suddenly became nervous about Weaver's reliability after reading Eleanor Metcalf's response to the galleys of the *Log*. *Log* 2:804 contains the following entry: "[M] Took Frances to Madison Square Garden—came home having forgot her—Went back found her. Frances aetat 4 (*Weaver note on information from Mrs Thomas*)." In her letter of June 30, 1950, Eleanor Metcalf wrote, "End of 1887. Raymond Weaver never talked with my mother. This story was told by my sister, Frances Osborne, in a little sketch she wrote of her memories, which I think you must have seen here. I notice that Lewis Mumford mentions my mother's name in his preface, but only as answering written questions sent to her through me. As my sister tells the story, she was well on her way home before being found by my grandfather." This probably provoked Leyda into showing Eleanor Metcalf his page of Weaver notes. In her letter of September 11, 1950, Eleanor Metcalf told Leyda, "As for the Weaver notes on conversation with Mrs. Thomas I do not understand that wording. He put questions to *me* which I passed on to my mother. These are her answers—though the last three I do not recognize as hers. The next to last is not hers at all in spirit. The food and drink one contradicts the impression she gave me that he was much quieter towards the end, and she laid it to 'lack of energy.' The rest I recognize as hers—or my father's. The 'restlessness in traveling' comes from my father" (Leyda Papers, UCLA). Having been corrected twice, Leyda still did not change his entry. Eleanor Metcalf had already warned Olson on February 8, 1950, "Let me tell you Jay has a slant which once, at least to my knowledge led him to an entirely unjustified conclusion, rather unsavory" (Olson Papers). Her other objections are mentioned below.

83. Harrison Hayford's Yale Ph.D. dissertation, "Melville and Hawthorne: A Biographical and Critical Study" (1945), was inconclusive on the question of Melville's mental states and when, exactly, he may have been examined for insanity. In Appendix B, he delegitimated Julian Hawthorne (often nailed by Melvilleans, including Weaver, as purveyor of the philistine myth of Melville's insanity), but in Appendix G he printed part of an important letter to him from Eleanor

Metcalf, August 30, 1943, which stated that she cannot date the "mental crisis" and "examination" but that Melville suffered from a "nervous condition" throughout the period under scrutiny (1852–53 and 1856–57) and even into later life, which was "extremely hard for his family."

84. See Gerry Gross's (book designer for Harcourt Brace) note to Leyda regarding the cover design: "Do not worry about Herman's parsonical look. We have to have the dark mass there if the title is to stand out in the book shops at all" (Aug. 4, 1950, Leyda Papers, box 7, UCLA). Melville's affinity to radical Protestants was obvious; Merton Sealts (inheriting the Olson mission, searching for Melville's annotated books) wrote to Leyda on August 10, 1948: "I'm sure that somewhere is a heavily marked Milton" (Leyda Papers, box 7, UCLA).

85. Harrison Hayford has objected to my characterization of himself and his colleagues as excited sleuths. However, Leyda's correspondence suggests that there is a factual basis for this view. See Merrell R. Davis to Leyda, November 15, 1946: "I do not have letters you list in 'secret' Birss booklet—and would like to know and have . . . . This last in particular I would like. You place an exclamation point (3 of them) after HM to EAD Ap13 noon [1869]—What is this letter?" (No such letter has surfaced in the *Log* or in NN *Correspondence*.) Or see Gilman to Leyda, Nov. 10, 1946: "I'm naturally eager to include the story of his [Albany] romance"; Oct. 16, 1946: "I am naturally much excited by the note about M's romances which Merrell Davis passed on to me. I have been trying unsuccessfully to run these to earth for several months now, ever since I first heard of them. I had heard that Dr. Murray knew something about one of them. . . . I have heard in Troy, from the editor of one of the newspapers, the story, now traditional up there, that Melville ran away to sea because of a love affair. The editor is a sensible man, and realizes that gossip is gossip. (The story he had heard maintained that the girl was in trouble.) But traditions usually have some foundation in fact, no matter how remote they may be from strict accuracy. I should be very glad to have proof of M's amours. They would help fill out the blank years for which I have little or no information." Apr. 15, 1947: "I'm writing to Mrs. Wickes soon, with a prayer." Nov. 6, 1947: "Are you going to see Mrs. Wickes before you leave New York? Her story is hearsay only, but there may be something in it." Melville's South Sea adventures were tracked in the Wilson L. Heflin letters. See also Hayford to Leyda, Nov. 7, 1946, on his eagerness to see the NYPL discoveries, "especially of course the document concerning M's reaction to Hawthorne's death"; Aug. 3, 1948, "I'd be particularly interested in any references [in Leyda's unused notes for *Log*] to the truth or falsity of particular things in [*Omoo*]." In response to my dissertation draft, Hayford was not persuaded by these examples that muckraking was intended; moreover, he doubts that Leyda meant to say Melville's texts should be distrusted. Robert Giroux, Leyda's editor, associated the *Log* with works by muckrakers in a letter to Leyda of February 10, 1950 (appended). The conspiratorial tone of the Leyda Papers is summed up in a postcard depicting George Washington's bed: "I don't sleep much, either, since that Melville Mission,—B."

86. In a series of letters, Albert Erskine, Leyda's editor at Random House, was surprised by Leyda's general line of interpretation in his introduction to Melville's *Complete Stories*. Erskine asks why Leyda does not include "Billy Budd" and sketches from volume 13 of the Constable edition, which would have included the portraits of John Marr, Jack Gentian, and Daniel Orme (see Erskine to Leyda, Feb. 12, 1948). On September 16, 1948, Erskine writes: "For my own part, I am quite certain that the figure of Bartleby symbolically stands for that of Herman Melville . . . that he stands for the Writer in relation to society as Melville saw this relationship at the time." On November 12, 1948, he sharply disagrees with the dangerous game/concealment line taken by Leyda. Erskine argued that Melville's writing was deliberately layered because it enriched his writing; he was not an obscurantist; symbolism says more. On February 25, 1949, Erskine challenged Leyda on his postulating a "troublesome contradiction" between art and life as if Leyda believed that Melville had no imagination. All in Leyda Papers, box 7, UCLA.

87. See Leyda to Lawrence Clark Powell, Feb. 10, 1949, Leyda Papers, UCLA.

88. Jay Leyda, Introduction to *Complete Stories of Herman Melville* (New York: Random House, 1949). The phrase "the evil past" (draft) was changed to "the threatening backdrop of evil" in the published version. Although he makes much of the "diptych" form of the stories (playing off contrasts such as responsibility versus irresponsibility), the action for Leyda is in unmasking the false attractions of women (nature). In "The Encantadas," the images "added up accumulatively to a single fiery glimpse of isolation, desperation, punishment, deceit, mis-used authority, endurance, lonely struggle, and all the odds against life, hope, decency." It is finally all too much: "Though just as dangerous a game for biographers, these stories and their attitudes tell almost more than we care to learn of the writer himself in a period of his greatest anguish. As Keats said of Robert Burns, 'We can see horribly clear in the works of such a Man his whole life, as if we were God's spies.'" In a letter signed "G." (I believe it was Gordon Williams, Leyda's research assistant and brother-in-law, married to his half-sister Jane in 1942), Leyda was questioned about the hostile image of Melville conveyed in his introduction: "And for the rest of the symbolism—was he feeling diabolical, delighting in holding up a clouded mirror and laughing at the fools who failed to see themselves imaged, or was he disappointed that his meaning was not more clearly perceived and therefore blamed himself for poorly realizing his intention, or was he satisfied with the understanding he got, and only disappointed that he was not received more heartily?" See Leyda Papers, box 4 (draft, Stories Introduction) and box 7 (correspondence), UCLA.

Margaret Smith, Leyda's mother, sent him a lengthy biographical booklet, the *Dayton Art Institute Bulletin* 21.5 (Mar.–Apr. 1963), commemorating the Jane Reece Memorial Exhibition, reproducing many of the most famous photo-portraits by Leyda's high school mentor. Reece's sensibility was pre-Raphaelite, mystical, and religious; her portraits were soft in focus, romantic with much chiaroscuro, and flattering to her wealthy subjects. I suspect a reference to Reece's aesthetic, for or against, in Leyda's fulminations about Melville's sisters. See folder "Margaret Smith," Leyda Papers, NYU.

89. Melville to Henry Gansevoort, May 10, 1864, in draft of Leyda's "The Army of the Potomac Entertains a Poet," *Twice-a-Year* 16 (1948): 259–72; but this portion of the letter is not in *Log*.

90. Leyda's notes show that he had read Mabel Weaks, "Long Ago and 'Faraway': Traces of Melville in the Marquesas in the Journal of A. G. Jones, 1854–1855," *Bulletin of the New York Public Library* (July 1948): 362–69. Weaks quoted from the Journal of A. G. Jones, 1854–1855: "We did not enter the eastern valley which was the one where Melville was confined. Our curiosity was the less in this point from the fact, that although we had evidence that such persons as Kory-Kory and Tinor and the one eyed chief had once existed, they were now however dead and their houses abandoned or destroyed. 'Moreta' recollected Melville and had seen the personages alluded to in his book, but there was no one of the name of 'Faraway.' Indeed their language does not admit of such a name." Leyda did not contest her suggestion that Fayaway [the blue-eyed Marquesan nymph with Melville's coloring] had been an invention of Melville's, but instead of juxtaposing contradictory accounts of travelers regarding Fayaway's existence, he separated them. See *Log*, 281, 506, 694. A Harcourt Brace memo for salesmen (appended) shows that Melville's possible illegitimate child through Fayaway was a titillating item to be publicized. For the Lucett rumor, see *Log*, 156–57; for Bradford, see 214–15. For Eleanor Metcalf's angry response to the material on Lucett and the characterization of Allan Melvill as a maniac (rumors which she said Leyda refused to evaluate), see her appended letters to Leyda, May 23, 1950, June 12, 1950; she wanted Leyda to delete any acknowledgment to her which suggested that she had approved of his presentation of these documents. A letter from Victor Hugo Paltsis of January 12, 1945 (appended) indicates that Leyda suspected Gansevoort had committed suicide; Leyda's notes for the *Complete Stories* introduction include the phrase "hereditary insanity" next to "The Apple-Tree Table," and he doggedly attempted to track insanity in the midwestern descendants of Thomas Melvill, Jr.

Writing to Norman Holmes Pearson (for whom he was doing research in Julian Hawthorne's papers to discover the evidence for a duel between Nathaniel Hawthorne and John O'Sullivan over Mary Crowninshield, a tidbit, which, as Pearson's explained, was intended strictly for private delectation), Leyda sent him a Julian Hawthorne reference, "a less familiar one that may add a shade to this destruction" (draft, Leyda Papers, box 24, UCLA). I doubt that Leyda could have meant Julian Hawthorne's imputation that Melville's late work was morbid and mad, since he spent much time trailing alleged crazies in the Melville genealogy. I continue to believe that Leyda was on a mission, either self-imposed or in line with party policy, digging to undermine the materialists in Melville's family of texts and merging Gansevoort with Herman, tending to delete items that could create compassion for a suffering Melville. There is no reason to believe that the young Yale critics (Hayford, Sealts, Davis, and Gilman) whom he helped, and who shared their research with him, shared such an objective.

91. Whether or not the letter proves that Allan Melvill fathered a natural child, it should not have been withheld. See below for discussion of the Isabel letter and Leyda's knowledge of its existence since at least 1945.

92. In 1947 Harry Dana, also a prominent defender of the Soviet Union, thanked his friend Jay Leyda for telling him about *Pierre*: "[It was] a marvelous book" (Dana to Leyda, Mar. 13, 1947, Leyda Papers, box 8, UCLA). But Leyda used very few of the numerous quotations he had copied from *Pierre* when he assembled the complete Melville in the *Log*. A fragmentary draft of an undated letter to Hershel Parker suggests that Leyda was conflicted in his own response to the book, or perhaps was reluctant to make an unfashionable connection among Melville, Ahab, and Pierre. Leyda wrote, apparently in response to a question by Parker, "I swore I couldn't answer you until I had read the *Pierre* essay [probably Parker's]. Yes, it was easier than *Pierre* itself, but I have always been stumped by that book (2½ times, yet ever praying for a miraculous revelation) & by everything written about it. And yet I've hoped that someone would speculate on the sudden genesis of its language, not only the rhetoric, but the flood of new-made wordness—Browne/Carlyle responsible? There is a thread between the last chapters of M-D and the first of Pierre—but not strong enough to explain the experiment. Of course, everything should reflect the difference between the two books, but [broken off]." See folder "Hershel Parker Correspondence," Leyda Papers, NYU.

93. See Derek Longhurst, "'Not for all time, but for an Age': An Approach to Shakespeare Studies," in *Re-Reading English*, ed. Peter Widdowson (London: Methuen, 1982), 150–63, arguing that Shakespeare has been deployed by the Right, taught as a model organic thinker and source of national unity.

94. Sidney Kaplan felt that the *Log* would rescue Melville from critics who wanted to diminish his standing as proletarian sympathizer; see his letter to Leyda, Sept. 11, 1950, Leyda Papers, UCLA.

95. Until I read Leyda's conflicting narratives of his own life, it never occurred to me that he might be raising the morale of the young Yale scholars by hinting of exciting materials that had not yet surfaced. Either Leyda was misleading Hayford et al., or there are biographical treasures still unpublished and in the hands of private collectors.

Besides Howard P. Vincent, general editor of the Hendricks House edition, the more entrepreneurial Melvilleans included John H. Birss, Willard Thorp, Tyrus Hillway, Luther S. Mansfield, and Henry W. Wells, all active members in the recently founded Melville Society (Feb. 1945). (The names were mentioned in a letter to Leyda from Birss, May 3, 1945, describing an upcoming meeting at Columbia.) Responsibility for the complete edition was given to the eccentric and unreliable Walter Hendricks, who had preempted other presses, according to Professor Sealts (letter to author, Mar. 13, 1991): "Walter Hendricks, a sometime professor and college founder with fewer funds than good sense, of which he had very little, started his Melville edition in the 1940s when other bigger and better presses were interested but withdrew after his preemptive strike. Except for Harry Murray (*Pierre*) and Howard Vincent (never qualified as either an editor—*Poems*—or editor-in-chief), many of those he signed up were returning veterans of WWII just established in new jobs and needing to establish ourselves professionally. As a professor himself, Hendricks knew the tribal customs and governing ground rules of Academia, but he treated us shamefully (Bezanson, Foster, Oliver, Roper, Hayford, Sealts, etc.), repeatedly making promises he couldn't and wouldn't keep. While I was still at Wellesley and he was at his first Vermont college he finally agreed to a face-to-face meeting about the volume I had finished but which was languishing unpublished; my wife and I drove up as scheduled but he literally *hid* instead of seeing me, and we drove home seething! After Jay's collection of the stories appeared WH simply refused to issue a competitive volume. This is when Jay and Mrs. Metcalf persuaded me to do the original [Harvard Library Bulletin] version of *Melville's Reading*."

96. Gerry Gross to Leyda, July 12, 1950, Aug. 8, 1950, Aug. 23, 1951, Leyda Papers, UCLA.

97. See Leyda's notes on "Bartleby" and "Benito Cereno": "the insurmountable barriers between man & man or a man's own unavoidable conscience" (Leyda Papers, UCLA). Leyda's existentialism in both "Bartleby" and the *Stories* volume was consistent with Alfred Kazin's *New Yorker* essay, "Ishmael in His Academic Heaven," Feb. 12, 1949, 84, 87–89, preserved in Leyda Papers, box 12, UCLA. On Kazin's aid to Leyda's *Log*, see Albert Erskine's letter to Leyda, February 15, 1950: "I showed [Kazin] portions of the manuscript which I had at Reynal and Hitchcock a long time ago and used his enthusiasm for the idea as one of the levers for getting the project accepted in the first place." Also, Robert Giroux reported to Leyda, June 8, 1950, that Kazin gave a talk on the *Log* to the Harcourt Brace Sales Conference, a "wonderful-kickoff." Leyda Papers, box 7, UCLA.

98. In an unfinished letter to Michael Sadleir on May 22, 1923, Weaver described it as "a thing called *Daniel Orme* which Melville elimenated [*sic*] from *Billy Budd:* and I think he did well by such surgery" (Weaver Papers, Columbia University).

99. The politics of these relatives differed: Thomas was a nativist populist conservative; Allan was a liberal Unitarian with sympathies for the defunct Federalists; and Gansevoort was an antinativist radical democrat, a Jacksonian, but also a friend and admirer of Abby Hutchinson, member of the famous abolitionist singing family, as his London journal relates.

100. The published *Log* reads: "How much can we guess of Melville as husband and father?" (xvii).

101. See Hawthorne's *English Notebooks*, Dec. 12, 1856, quoted in *Log*, 529, and discussed above.

102. Leyda quotes Father Mapple, a radical puritan, but implies that these words are stated by the Tory Captain Vere. The soaring eagle image is associated with sublimity and with both the unrepentant Ahab and the circumscribed Ishmael. Compare with F. Barron Freeman, *Melville's Billy Budd*: "Tragic nobility and defeat are the keynotes of the closing pages of *Moby-Dick*; hope and triumph in death form the final ascendant notes of Billy's tragedy. Certain parallels between the characters of the two tales make the contrasting tones of their final pages more vivid. Ishmael, the understanding observer, like Captain Vere, the knowing arbiter, saw and felt the full truth. Both Moby Dick and Claggart were only agents of evil. But when the crashing sea surges over the masts of the *Pequod* and drags down the bird of heaven with its archangelic shrieks, the reader experiences a calculated effect which is in direct contrast to Billy's ascension into the calm sky of the rising sun with 'no motion apparent save that created by the ship's motion, in moderate weather so majestic in a ship ponderously cannoned.' Here, as in *Moby-Dick*, the sacrifice is made, the evil realized—but here it is realized in a calm, ascending note of hope" (126). Leyda knew the Freeman book very well. In a note to me added to a photocopy of his letter of April 5, 1952, to Leyda, thanking him for obtaining a copy of "Billy Budd," Hayford explained, "Copy of Freeman

edition which had been withdrawn from sale by H.U. Press when Jay pointed out its many misreadings." And yet, astoundingly, Leyda seems to have taken his sentiments from Freeman.

103. In conversations with me, Hayford has emphasized Melville's unresolved ambivalence.
His co-editor, G. Thomas Tanselle, vice president of the Guggenheim Foundation, however, seems
to follow the nihilists and Christian existentialists. The jacket blurb to Tanselle's edition of *Redburn, White-Jacket,* and *Moby-Dick* for the Library of America (1983) states, "Together these books
reveal Melville's obsession with the possibilities of human freedom, the sacrifice of that freedom
to the demands of social cohesion, and of the submission of social groups—represented by the
shipboard community—to traditional forms of authority. . . . Captain Ahab's hunt for the white
whale drives the narrative at a relentless pace, while Ishmael's meditation on whales and whaling,
on the sublime indifference of nature and the grimy physical details of the production of oil, provide a reflective counterpoint to the headlong idolatrous quest." This seems internally contradictory: If Ahab is obsessed with human freedom (as implied), what is idolatrous about the quest?
Tanselle would seem to be agreeing with the corporatists: Relying on human reason is tantamount
to self-worship.

104. Leyda, undated draft manuscript, letter to Dr. Adams, Leyda Papers, NYU. Mudge was
mentioned as the preacher at Bethel Chapel, attended by Melville before his 1841 voyage; see
Log, 111.

105. A 1972 draft essay clarified Leyda's understanding of facts: We are stamped by the environment and yet unknowable. "The reality of the elusive artist can be a never attained goal, and
all the more worth aiming at. . . . *There is a certain virtue in not separating milieu from hero,* especially
in the drama of Melville's life. He drew so directly from experience, and his concealing veils of art
are so much more transparent than those that Hawthorne or Dostoyevsky or Rimbaud drew
across those links, that to know the crowds and streets and waters that Melville passed through
brings us halfway to knowing him and his art. All we can trace of his world pays, biographically"
(in Hayford files and Leyda Papers, NYU; emphasis added). No materialist would use the word
"milieu" to describe the conditions that any writer encounters, selects, analyzes, and depicts, as if
all elements of the world equally impinge on, and shape, consciousness willy-nilly, as if human
agency and insight were fictions. See Zola essay, excerpted above.

106. See Working Script, 5, 19, folder "Bartleby," Leyda Papers, NYU. After the opera's performance in 1964 (which Leyda, researching German film in East Berlin, did not attend), some
(unspecified) Melville scholars objected to Bartleby's aria (see Walter Aschaffenburg to Leyda,
Nov. 23, 1964). Leyda was apparently pressed by the composer to yield his original vision for the
opera to a more optimistic reading. In one note, Leyda had wanted to end the opera with these
words: "[Bartleby says he will be buried] . . . with kings and counselors who build in the wasteland." On November 22, 1959, the composer wrote to Leyda asking him to rethink the entire concept of the opera; apparently Leyda's concept was too bleak. As Aschaffenburg explained, "The
central theme of B, as I see it is the humanizing of the Lawyer through the vehicle of his encounter
with Bartleby. . . . By the end of the story he has been made aware that he *can* be profoundly affected, shaken, distracted by another human being, a man of such lowly social status that the
Lawyer would hardly have noticed him and for whose welfare he would not have cared less. And
to make the point even more vivid, M has chosen for a vehicle a man in a profession which the
lawyer regards with contempt—a scrivener. To the Lawyer a scrivener is in a way a machine which
does his bidding and of whom he expects only that he do his duty with as little disturbance as possible. M's story then deals with a description of how this change in the Lawyer's character is accomplished, and why." He goes on to say that they have failed to do this: By Act II the lawyer is
already humanized; in other words, Aschaffenburg wants an emphatic conversion narrative. The
"central theme" cannot be the vain hope of social amelioration. But in the draft script, Bartleby's
famous refusal to copy, "I prefer not to," is explained (apparently by Leyda) as, "These are the

words by which Bartleby isolates himself from a world where nobody understands him." The Oberlin press release certainly picked up Leyda's pessimism: "The music . . . explores the dimensions of feeling aroused by man's inability to communicate with his fellows and his resultant loneliness." A journal article or even a dissertation could be devoted to the writing of the opera *Bartleby*, the negotiations between Leyda and Aschaffenburg, and the fashion for modernist despair as a conservative response to the Allied victory and its apparent rehabilitation of the idea of progress.

An undated letter from Leyda (probably 1948) in the Kirstein Papers encloses a plan for the *Bartleby* libretto almost fully developed. Leyda wanted Kirstein to help him find a composer; Aaron Copland had already rejected it, and Leyda did not want Stravinsky. The Kirstein Papers contain correspondence with both Benjamin Britten and E. M. Forster. Leyda had cheered Kirstein on: "I'll bet you'll have a wonderful time both with the BB play and the BB opera." Kirstein's involvement with the Melville Revival deserves more scholarly investigation.

107. See letter James Laughlin of New Directions to Leyda (n.d., but before Apr. 10, 1945; appended); see also letter, Leyda to Powell, July 13, 1949: "You may be relieved to hear that the struggle around the *Log* has been renewed. . . . Harcourt now talks of a luxurious subscription edition, followed by a pared-down trade edition. Does this sound sensible to you?" See also Leyda to Robert Giroux, draft, Leyda Papers, box 24, UCLA, regarding cutting the *Log*: "I have always had faith in the handsome 'gift book' approach that R[eynal] & H[itchcock] started with. And it could still be obligatory and possible buying for every person and library concerned with American literature—aside from the Christmas purchasers."

108. There are numerous letters to dealers and collectors demonstrating Leyda's search for letters and manuscripts, including high-priced items; see, for instance, letter of inquiry to Mary Benjamin, n.d., Leyda Papers, box 7, UCLA. Since Leyda had funded his film *Bronx Morning* through the sale of a folk art item to a Rockefeller, perhaps his entrance into the Melville Revival was partly motivated by the hope that he could fund future artistic endeavors of his own by finding and selling Melville letters and manuscripts, undervalued until the postwar boom.

109. Alfred Kazin, *A Lifetime Burning in Every Moment* (New York: HarperCollins, 1996), 162–63. Kazin was quoting an excerpt from his introduction to the Riverside Press edition of *Moby-Dick*. Compare with the recollection of Lyon Evans; Kazin was Evans's outside reader on the dissertation committee at SUNY-Buffalo (1979–81): "I was literally stunned, when I entered his office . . . to find only one photo on display; the famous 1861 photo of Melville, arms folded-positioned directly above [his] desk on an otherwise bare wall . . . his passion for Melville (which I had not suspected before meeting him) was something to behold" (Ishmail-list, June 7, 1998).

110. This is mentioned by Murray to Leyda, June 15, 1948 (see appendix), and suggested in a letter from the Beverly Hills psychiatrist Robert S. Berns (Nov. 4, 1947) stating that he will support Leyda's claim for continued compensation from the Veterans Administration. See file "Correspondence regarding the Musorgsky Reader," Leyda Papers, box 8, UCLA. The NYU Leyda Papers contain a receipt from Dr. Berns dated January 22, 1947, for $700 that states "Paid in Full." According to his oral history, Leyda had a semi-breakdown after his firing from MoMA in 1940 and a "total" nervous breakdown in a tank after he entered the army. After that he would never drive. See "Reminiscences" 3:110, 111, 164. Was this a real breakdown? Lincoln Kirstein had written to Leyda on August 23, 1943, after the release of *Mission to Moscow* ("the funniest picture I ever saw in my life. I saw it 3 times"): "If you can get out of [the Army] and be legal, do so. This is considered advice. It ain't for the likes of you and me." (This is strange advice, since Kirstein joined the army as a private and wrote poems about his war experiences.) According to his FBI file, Leyda did try to avoid induction, first asking for a change in status because of the movie assignment, then claiming he had to support his wife when the film work was completed.

Leyda's friends were clearly worried about him, and there were attempts to get him transferred to the Signal Corps or to Morale Services. A letter from Howard Koch (screenwriter for *Mission to Moscow*) of January 7, 1944, reassured Leyda that he was not weak but rebelling against the brutalities of war, an "idiotic process." He was really brave in fighting for a world where war won't exist. "Dick" (address "133 W. 12 St., NYC") was alarmed in his January 22, 1943, letter: "The tone of your letters disturbs me something fierce. . . . I will not desert you, nor will your other friends, nor are they . . . *keep a hold on yourself.*" In Chronological Correspondence, 1943 folder, Leyda Papers, NYU. In a letter of February 2, 1944, Harold Leonard of Sweetzer Avenue, Los Angeles, wrote, "Just learned from Sylvia that they are still keeping you in the hospital. Good work. Best place in the world to be so long as you're not by yourself in a private room, and its not costing you money, it can be the easiest way to pass time pleasantly there." On February 20, 1944, Koch told his friend, "We all enjoyed your descriptions of the 'gripings' of an army hospital. I'm glad you've become the father confessor as I think you're admirably equipped—armed as you are with reticence, sense and St. Paul's Epistle." Compare with September 26, 1944, letter from Thomas A. C. Rennie, The Society of the New York Hospital, to Leyda referring him to Dr. Eugene Ziskind, director of a psychiatric clinic in Los Angeles where he can "go for help." On April 25, 1945, Leyda heard from the Veterans Administration, accusing him of fraud in claiming a "vocational handicap" that entitled him to a disability pension. This ruling was protested by Leyda, June 12, 1945; his letter included the information that he had started and stopped school at UCLA.

111. See Forrest G. Robinson, *Love's Story Told: A Life of Henry Murray* (Cambridge, Mass.: Harvard UP, 1992), 320–22, 367, for another account of Leyda's and Murray's conflicted relations, including events treated below.

112. Penciled drafts from Leyda to Murray, on back of Murray's envelope postmarked Mar. 10, 1949, and a library slip, Mar. 14, 1949, Leyda Papers, box 23, UCLA.

113. Paul Jarrico told me he was astonished when his friend Leyda praised the freedom of East Germany, where he had gone after he and Si-Lan fled the Cultural Revolution in China (interview, ca. 1991).

114. In a letter to Henry Allen Moe, secretary of the Guggenheim Foundation, January 27, 1941, Olson reported that he had "resumed the preliminary research for the book and pursued it until a physical breakdown stalled me from May through July [1939]" (Olson Papers). Unless otherwise specified, all other letters quoted in this endnote were written to Leyda and are located in his papers at UCLA. Hayford noted that Leon was "low lately" (Oct. 29, 1949); then, "Leon is fighting to get out of his slump—psychological mostly, but partly due to the corners he has worked himself into in the HM biography. I mean he's up against the poems and needs more information before he can be sure enough to go on" (Nov. 14, 1949). Leon Howard linked the iconoclastic *Log* to the long-suffering Merrell Davis's frightening auto accident: "For the past week or ten days I have been in the midst of Melville, trying to crack a few of the toughest episodic nuts while my mind is free from the disruption of teaching. Your work is going to be monumental and—to a lot of people—devastating. I am delighted to learn that it is going to the publishers so soon. Merrell's long silence was broken yesterday by a post card saying—in explanation—that he had been relieving the pressure of final work on his dissertation by turning over on the highway and totally wrecking his car" (July 23, 1947). Working on the poems, Howard commiserated: "Maybe I am failing mentally. Anyway, like all Melvillians, I am growing intuitive. Jesus . . . I hope you are cured of your jitters" (Jan. 27, 1950). Then: "I still trust that Herman will not remain among my unpublished masterpieces, despite the fact that I got so sick of it while attempting to read it over that I had to stop. . . . I think I am getting old and frail and short of brains" (n.d., but Feb. 21 or 22, 1950). Howard also reported that no one was satisfied with the *Moby-Dick* chapter; and "I have not recovered from the state I was in some months ago when I wrote my 'sad little note'" (n.d.).

William Gilman's complaints seem to reflect the impossible demands of academic life (Nov. 18, 1949), but several remarks—one preceding his reproach that Leyda had published material in *More Books* that he and Davis had "put together" regarding Alexander Bradford (Sept. 13, 1947, appended)—are suggestive: "Until yesterday the dissertation was around my neck." On July 16, 1948, he told Leyda that he was revising his manuscript, and sometimes "I simply can't stand reading it. And trying to gauge the reactions of some other body of readers than those for whom I was aiming at Yale is difficult too." Gilman dismissed the Freudian Arvin: "You undoubtedly know that Newton Arvin is hard at work on his biography of M. He's sent on a few odds and ends that I haven't been able to use . . . all conjectures, in fact, or avenues for further exploration, of which, as we all know there are too many now!" (Aug. 24, 1948).

115. Hayford to Leyda, Aug. 20, 1951, responding to Leyda's letter of July 3, 1951 (signed "Unscrupulous"), leaking the letter "bomb" contained in Eleanor Metcalf's family memoir, an undated letter (ca. 1850) from Sophia Hawthorne to her mother, which no Melvillean had seen; Leyda was reading the manuscript for Harvard University Press (see appendix). In his harshly self-critical letter to Leyda of October 30, 1950, Hayford had already identified himself as an obsessive (Ahab/Bartleby?): "I can't offer any explanation of my long silence except some sort of psychopathic condition which has kept me from writing to anyone at all since last spring. . . . I simply do not know the real reasons, whatever they are. . . . I know I am essentially a very disorderly person. . . . I have a one-track mind and I work at only one thing at a time, and that to the point of blind exhaustion."

116. Howard, *Herman Melville;* William H. Gilman, *Melville's Early Life and "Redburn"* (New York: New York UP, 1951). Walter Kring, co-discoverer of letters disclosing a projected family plan to rescue Melville's wife from crazy Herman, read the *Log* as not disclosing marital unhappiness; see his introduction to *The Endless, Winding Way in Melville: New Charts by Kring and Carey,* ed. Donald Yannella and Hershel Parker (Glassboro, N.J.: The Melville Society, 1981), 4.

117. By Emersonian, I mean radical but antimaterialist. See editorial statement, *American Literature,* Mar. 1929, and my discussion of the *Nation* 1917–19, above.

118. Sealts to author, June 20, 1987. He qualifies this statement with "—at least so some of us thought." Like Thorp, Sealts views Melville as having grown more conservative in his later years, a "democratic aristocrat" as described by J. E. A. Smith. Compare with Olson's assemblage of Melville's images in "The Growth of Herman Melville," 43. Olson associated such formlessness with Melville's (Ahab's) "wandering blood" (38).

119. William Braswell, review of Leyda, *Log,* and Howard, *Herman Melville, American Literature* 24 (1952–53): 245–47.

120. Willard Thorp, review of William H. Gilman, *Melville's Early Life and "Redburn,"* ibid., 391–93.

121. Willard Thorp, review of Geoffrey Stone, *Melville,* ibid. 22 (Nov. 1950): 357.

122. William H. Gilman, review of Lawrance Thompson, *Melville's Quarrel with God,* ibid. 24 (1952–53): 558–61. Harrison Hayford's files contain an important letter (Nov. 12, 1954) from Thompson to Miss Rosenberg, a graduate student of Hayford's. Thompson explained that his book was an attack on Thorp, Vincent, Arvin, Chase, and Murray; they had counterattacked. He now wishes he had read Leo Strauss, *Persecution and the Art of Writing* (1952), which discusses the heretics' expedient of stylistic double-talk to elude captors. He also mentions the fascinating wavering of *Moby-Dick.* Two hundred students turned out at Princeton to hear him defend his views from the criticisms of colleagues.

123. Charles R. Anderson, review of Eleanor Metcalf, *Herman Melville: Cycle and Epicycle, American Literature* 26 (May 1954): 262–64.

124. This sounds like vintage Murray. As her numerous letters in Murray's Melville papers at Harvard show, Eleanor Metcalf was generally restrained and precise, but she was overawed by

Murray's supposed expertise and rarely challenged him. She was so overcome by the "Book" Murray had completed by 1929, then later by Murray's introduction to *Pierre*, that she offered to turn over all her materials to him (in 1949). Murray read a late draft of *Cycles* and commented on it; Metcalf took some suggestions and "compromised" on others (see appendix). Unfortunately, we do not have Murray's side of the correspondence; but there seems to have been no dispute about alcoholism or angry outbursts, since her letters to him do not mention it. See above for the 1920s letters from the Morewoods and Metcalf reporting less serious infractions than the ones quoted by Anderson. Moreover, both "Daniel Orme" and "Billy Budd" suggest that Melville, while no angel and certainly troubled, was more of a victim than a perpetrator.

125. Leyda, *Log* 2:834.

126. Immediately after the assassination of Count Cenci, Beatrice reassures her mother, a collaborator in the deed, who fears discovery; they will tough it out:

BEATRICE.   Mother,
What is done wisely, is done well. Be bold
As thou art just. 'Tis like a truant child
To fear that others know what thou hast done,
Even from thine own strong consciousness, and thus
Write on unsteady eyes and altered cheeks
All thou wouldst hide. Be faithful to thyself,
And fear no other witness but thy fear.
For if, as cannot be, some circumstance
Should rise in accusation, we can blind
Suspicion with such cheap astonishment,
Or overbear it with such guiltless pride,
As murderers cannot feign. The deed is done,
And what may follow now regards not me.
I am as universal as the light;
Free as the earth-surrounding air; as firm
As the world's centre. Consequence to me,
Is as the wind which strikes the solid rock
But shakes it not.   [A cry within and tumult.]
VOICES.   Murder! Murder! Murder! (4.4.34–53)

Beatrice, at one with herself and nature, has stolen the imagery and authority of the Catholic Church: a sensation that immediately elicits the accusation of murder (parricide, not self-defense), exactly Pierre's response after he learns of the insanity and death of his authoritarian mother. See Shelley, *The Cenci* (New York: Phaeton, 1970), 89, 35.

127. The complete libretto is located in the Leyda Papers, NYU, but is undated. It was probably written after completion of *Bartleby*. See Leyda's letter to Walter Aschaffenburg, asking him to be the composer, and the oral history that dates it 1964–65.

9. WHITE ROT IN THE MELVILLE INDUSTRY

1. Murray, draft, chap. 16, "A Little of Much Stabbed At, Not Through, 1849–50," n.d., Murray Papers. The manuscript drafts and notes in Murray's Melville papers are undated unless indicated otherwise.

2. Eleanor Metcalf to Olson, Olson Papers; appended.

3. See, for instance, this entry in Eleanor Melville Metcalf, *Cycle and Epicycle,* 1953: "Melville's strength had been throroughly depleted by the terrific creative strain of writing *Moby Dick.* Yet he must go on writing—where else will bread and butter come from? So *Pierre, or the Ambiguities,* is in process of being infused with driven and flagging energies. Here is a sick man writing of some matters known to be true, some entirely untrue, combined in such a way that the family feared its members and their friends might assume all to be true—that is, factual. Well they knew the description of the soul-searching trials of a young author to be autobiographical. That the young author's story was not autobiographical they also knew: but would others be able to separate fact from invention?" (135). As shown below, Eleanor Metcalf was told of the Isabel letter by Charles Olson; she must be added to those concealing that suggestive document.

4. T. Walter Herbert, Book Review, *Melville Society Extracts* 108 (Mar. 1997): 33–35. Herbert was reviewing Laurie Robertson-Lorant, *Melville,* reporting her judicious positions on the chief gossip items and lauding her treatment of "the whole life, free of the authoritarian defensiveness, obsessive fact-hunting and interminable blandness that so long have marred such work. She treats long-standing shibboleths with eminent good sense, placing Melville's bisexual disposition in the context of the erotic conventions of his time, and brings to bear his experiences of unconventional sexual practice as encountered aboard ship and in Polynesia. The issue of spousal abuse is likewise given even-handed treatment, scrupulously observing the limits placed on conjecture by the surviving documentation, but not shrinking from the more repugnant likelihoods. [She] finds no convincing evidence to support the theory of the illegitimate half-sister, plausibly observing that the two women who approached family after Allan's death might well have been seeking to collect a business debt."

5. Because Allan had died bankrupt, claims were referred to the estate of his late father, Major Thomas Melvill, for whom Shaw was executor. For a full discussion, see Emmers, "Melville's Closet Skeleton."

6. See card in "Morsels" folder, Murray Papers.

7. Hume, *HE* 7:148 (year 1649). The lawful subordination of liberty to order and truth to utility is a constant theme in Hume's history; under such conditions, revolt, though justified, will not lead to civil war when the ruler's behavior is truly outrageous. See also ibid. 6:354 (year 1641) and 8:12–13 (year 1675). Compare with Thomas Paine and other radical liberals for their theory of the social compact.

8. I am not equating Locke's and Freud's maps of the psyche. Locke rejected innate ideas, in effect opting for a history of the imagination, emphasizing experience and environmental conditions in the development of understanding. Freud posited instincts (Eros and Thanatos) and, like Jung, genetically transmitted relics of primitive social organization. Freud's materialism, in its belief in innate aggression, is closer to Hobbes than Locke. However, Freud, like Locke, did believe in the capacity of human reason to penetrate reality and dominate unreason; moreover, he at times demonstrated a similarly sociological imagination, whereas elitist irrationalists distrust the senses and reason entirely, finding social conflicts to originate solely in poor impulse/instinct inhibition, i.e., scapegoating or projection, the habit of the unruly, socially irresponsible, lower orders who illegitimately dominate the modern world.

9. Terence Martin, *Teaching a Novel: Moby-Dick in the Classroom* (New York: College Entrance Examination Board, 1965). Similarly, a Columbia University Teacher's College dissertation of 1983 recommended Cooper's *The Prairie,* Hawthorne's *Scarlet Letter,* and *Moby-Dick* as examples to experimental youth, guiding them away from adolescent folly and toward the higher moderation (abstract appended).

10. Daniel Jonah Goldhagen, *Hitler's Willing Executioners* (New York: Knopf, 1996), 398–99; Primo Levi, *The Periodic Table,* trans. Raymond Rosenthal (New York: Schocken, 1984), 75. Levi

read the Cesare Pavese translation of *Moby-Dick*. I am indebted to Albert Boime for both the Gold-hagen and Levi quotes.

11. Quoted in James Hoopes, *Van Wyck Brooks;* for Brooks's Melville assessments, see pp. 179, 242–43, 291.

12. Melville, *Journal up the Straits, Oct. 11, 1856–May 5, 1857,* ed. and intro. Raymond Weaver (New York: Colophon, 1935), xxii–xxiii, wherein Weaver rejects psychohistory but diagnoses narcissism.

13. In the brief preface to *The Tragedy of Mind,* Sarah Cabot Sedgwick said that she found the manuscript on her husband's desk and completed the editing with the help of Harvard professor Theodore Spencer. Who defined the Isabel problem?

14. Lasswell was the son of a midwestern minister. Entering a project (1928) initiated by others in 1926, Lasswell had played "the primary role" in the shaping of methodology in inter-disciplinary social sciences, against the methods of physical sciences. See Stuart A. Rice, ed., *Methods in Social Science: A Case Book Compiled under the Direction of the Committee on Scientific Method in the Social Sciences of the Social Science Research Council* (Chicago: U of Chicago P, 1931), vii, 732, 734, 737. Lasswell's Appendix B, 740–42, limited scientific studies of social change to the methods of Sumner, Turner, and Spengler.

15. Sidney Hyman, *The Lives of William Benton* (Chicago: U of Chicago P, 1969), 232–33. In his preventive politics, Lasswell was emulating other conservatives, for instance the impor-tant English journalist H. Wickham Steed, editor of the *Times,* and before that head of British war propaganda; see Steed, *Hitler, Whence and Whither?* (London: Nisbet, 1934), 188–89: "German Nazism is the outcome of a morbid national mood, and of propagandistic suggestions working on mass neurasthenia. . . . Great Britain and France have been and are relatively free from this morbid mood, though they are less free from perverse conceptions of democracy, which, by running wild in Italy and Germany, helped to produce a state of mind favourable to the rise of violent totali-tarian dictatorship. We should have a care lest we too, by harbouring perverse and degenerate conceptions of democracy, betray its sound principles and smooth the path of the enslaver."

16. Harold D. Lasswell, *Politics: Who Gets What, When, How* (New York: McGraw-Hill, 1936), 239–42, 236. Commenting on the likely trajectory of romantic fascism, Lasswell warned, "At first private capitalism is preserved; but it seems probable that in the face of the necessity for a united nation, private capitalism will be liquidated in times of military stress. In a military state, the movement for equalization, governmentalization, and monopolization would no doubt proceed."

17. Harold D. Lasswell, *Democracy through Public Opinion* (Menasha, Wisc.: George Banta Book Co. [Chi Omega Research Fund], 1941), 32–34.

18. Talcott Parsons, "Propaganda and Social Control," *Psychiatry* 5 (Nov. 1942): 551–72.

19. Adolf Köberle, the Swabian theology professor quoted in Wolfgang Gerlach, "When the Witnesses Were Silent: The Confessing Church and the Jews," in *The German Public and the Perse-cution of the Jews,* ed. Jorg Wollenberg (Atlantic Highlands, N.J.: Humanities Press, 1996), 161.

20. Richard V. Chase, "New vs. Ordealist," *Kenyon Review* 11 (1949): 12–13, cited again below.

21. See discussion of Madison and the Whigs in Daniel Walker Howe, *Political Culture of the American Whigs* (Chicago: U of Chicago P, 1979), 90–91. As I interpret *The Federalist Papers,* the au-thors (Jay, Hamilton, and Madison) defined their republicanism against all feudal and corporatist entities—the sources of imbecility, war, and anarchy. Liberty was a quality of the rational indi-vidual. Collectivities were fictions necessarily sustained by myth, not political science. Their in-terest groups corresponded to economic interest alone; there was no talk of national identity. The idea of using (irrationalist) propaganda to obtain consensus would or should have been anath-ema. Madison's "Federalist Paper No. 10" does not discuss free speech directly. Addressing men of property alarmed by Shays Rebellion, the Whiskey Rebellion, and demands for several separate

confederacies, the acutely class-conscious essay distinguished the benefits of a balanced republic controlling a large territory as compared with the vulnerabilities of small states and the confiscating propensities of small-scale popular democracies. The more interest groups the better, since no one group, unified by economic interest, could attain a legislative majority to oppress other citizens. Madison's view of human nature does not include moral categories as such: Individuals differ in their capacities to acquire property. Men of property, properly chosen (elected) to represent their constituencies for their inner poise and sense of justice, would be fair to contending parties, abiding by the rule of law—rules that were the same for rich and poor alike. These may be the moderate men interrogated by Melville's dark characters.

22. Erik Homburger Erikson, "Hitler's Imagery and German Youth," *Psychiatry* 5 (Nov. 1942): 475–93. On March 4, 1952, Murray asked for a copy of Erikson's paper "Growth and Crises of the Personality." On November 30, 1952, Murray sent Erikson a copy of his paper on Ahab, *In Nomine Diaboli*. On November 30, 1962, Talcott Parsons invited Erikson to present a study of Max Weber in the style of his Luther psychobiography for the 1964 meeting of the American Sociological Association, noting Weber's "great creative contributions to our culture." See Erikson Papers, bMS Am 2031 (412, 444).

23. The register of the Murray Papers at Harvard states that his analysis of Hitler's psyche was in process beginning in 1938; it is possible that Murray influenced Erikson, not vice versa. See Murray, "Analysis of the personality of Adolph [*sic*] Hitler with predictions of his future behavior and suggestions for dealing with him now and after Germany's surrender," declassified confidential report, FDR Library, Hyde Park, Oct. 1943, 5–7, 31, 46–53, 83, 143, 145, 211, and passim, quoted with permission. Compare with Anton T. Boisen, "The Form and Content of Schizophrenic Thinking," *Psychiatry* 5 (Nov. 1942): 23–33 (the same issue contained the Parsons article on propaganda). Primitives, children, romantic explorers, materialists, individualists, modern artists, and persons undergoing conversion experiences are conflated and diagnosed as anxious, fragmenting (hebephrenic) schizophrenics. Also see Charles Kligerman's diagnosis of Melville's paranoid schizophrenia in "The Psychology of Herman Melville," *Psychoanalytic Review* 40 (Apr. 1953): 125–43.

24. Harold D. Lasswell, *Power and Personality* (New York: Norton, 1948), 222, 211, 186–87.

25. Harold D. Lasswell, *National Security and Individual Freedom* (New York: McGraw-Hill, 1950). Howard B. Myers of CED wrote the brief foreword, explaining that "this report examines the problems that confront us in seeking national security without forfeit of the basic values and principles of American life."

26. Lasswell, Lerner, and de Sola Pool, *The Comparative Study of Symbols*, 24–25. Murray may have gotten the term "apperception" from Goethe's comments on the rigid moralist Dr. Stilling (a.k.a. Jung), an example of a God-intoxicated type, overly impressed by "experience," that Goethe described in his autobiography: "The things sympathetic persons of this kind love most to talk of, are, the so-called awakenings and conversions, to which we will not deny a certain psychological value. They are properly what we call in scientific and poet matters, an '*aperçu*'; the perception of a great maxim, which is always a genius-like operation of the mind; we arrive at it by pure intuition, that is, by reflection, neither by learning or tradition. In the cases before us it is the perception of the moral power, which anchors in faith, and thus feels itself in proud security in the midst of the waves" (*Truth and Poetry* 2:75).

27. See Richard A. Soloway, "Reform or Ruin: English Moral Thought during the First French Republic," *Review of Politics* (Jan. 1963): 110–27.

28. Forrest G. Robinson, *Love's Story Told: A Life of Henry A. Murray* (Cambridge, Mass.: Harvard UP, 1992). According to Robinson, Murray, apparently led by Weaver and Melville's great-nieces, the Morewood sisters, in the mid-1920s, learned that Melville was violent and crazy (133–34); he had also learned from George Eustis Corcoran, June 3, 1926, that a friend who knew

Melville was told by him that *Pierre* was autobiographical; this matter was clinched by Murray's location of the "chair-portrait" of Allan Melvill corresponding to the father's portrait in the novel. It takes Murray an unstated amount of time to figure out the significance of all this, but he "finally revealed what he knew" in his article "Allan Melvill's By-Blow" (in *Melville Society Extracts* 61 [Feb. 1985]: 1–6) (407). Olson is mentioned twice solely as a fan of Murray's published essays. Throughout, Robinson contrasts "mad, moody Melville," a failure, with "Harry": eccentric but not insane, hard drinking but not alcoholic. However, both narcissists were blighted by rejecting, hypochondriacal mothers from whom they could not separate, which accounts for Murray's identification with Melville and Murray's kinky (sadomasochistic/cross-dressing, but not homosexual) sexuality; but whereas Melville (and alcoholic, clinging Christiana) drowned, Murray fulfilled the progressive mission, helping to pluck his followers from the arid wasteland of modernity. Murray's debt to Raymond Weaver (1921) is not acknowledged; instead, Murray's unpublished Melville biography is praised as the greatest ever; Weaver's book is absent from the list of competing psychohistorical interpretations.

29. See above, discussion of Mumford's Melville scholarship.

30. That Murray knew he was making inferences, not relying on either oral or written testimony, may be borne out in a letter written by a Massachusetts television documentarian to Jay Leyda, ca. 1978 (apparently by Ron Nicodemus and/or Bayley Selleck and/or Jean M. Mudge of WGBY-TV, Springfield, Mass.) inviting him to be a consultant. The letter describes the project: a film describing Melville's early years in Pittsfield. Dr. Murray had said it was impossible: "The chances of approximating the factual and/or spiritual turmoil—interpersonal let us say—that marked the first year or so at Arrowhead are very slim indeed, chiefly because the data are *so sparse*. Ninety percent of what was exhibited would have to be invented. The inventor himself would be apt to feel with mystic conviction that his soul had become One with Melville's soul; but at least some of the viewers might be reminded of John Barrymore impersonating Captain Ahab." (This was not given to Leyda as a direct quote from Murray, but it sounds like either a direct quote or a close paraphrase.) In the treatment for the film, Melville is clearly understood as identified with Ahab. See "Correspondence and Film Scripts Mudge & Selleck, Melville Film," Leyda Papers, NYU.

31. Murray asked me, with considerable eagerness, what I thought Melville meant by Billy Budd's last words, "God bless Captain Vere."

32. Charles Olson, Notebook, Winter–Spring 1940; and Olson notes "[Ralph Henry] Gabriel on Am Nat Symbols," Olson Papers.

33. Melville did not, nor am I, specifying any particular economic arrangements. The values come first; the means for institutionalizing those ideals are a separate question.

34. Herman Melville, *White-Jacket* (London: Constable, 1922), 398. Quoted in Murray draft, chap. 16, "A Little of Much Stabbed At, Not Through, 1849–50," Murray Papers.

35. Note that Murray sees Ahab as the writer Pierre here: He sees Ahab's jabs as the spoken memory of abuse (in this case, from the bossy mother) not literal violence; compare with Mumford. Also, Milton is of the devil's party.

36. Murray draft, chap. 16, "A Little of Much Stabbed At," and folder "notes 1849–50" on the radical democratic sentiments of Theo. Parker, W. L. Garrison, Wendell Phillips, Charles Sumner, Robert Rantoul (Murray Papers).

37. Murray, fourteen-page manuscript, "Half-wilful overruling Morbidness." Murray was listing the causes of Melville's moodiness, including the "poisonous pride" of mother, blighted hopes in adolescence, "the wrong wife," and the incestuous passion for Augusta: "His sister was the real object of his love." Earlier in the manuscript he had written, "Chronologically, his emotions, though mature, belonged to the youth of the world; his responses were extreme and

complete; so that when he was overtaken by despondency, his mood was abysmal" (Murray Papers). I agree with Murray's intuition about Augusta, who named his first child.

38. Kenneth M. Stampp, *The Era of Reconstruction 1865–1877* (New York: Knopf, 1965), 139–41. The African Handsome Sailor may also be seen as a reproach to the convictions expressed for instance in the *New York Tribune* (Apr. 7, 1877), "which declared that the Negroes had been given 'ample opportunity to develop their own latent capacities,' and had only succeeded in proving that 'as a race they are idle, ignorant and vicious.'" Quoted in C. Vann Woodward, "The Political Legacy of Reconstruction," in *Reconstruction: An Anthology of Revisionist Writings*, ed. Kenneth M. Stampp and Leon F. Litwack (Baton Rouge: Louisiana State UP, 1969), 530.

39. Schwartz, *From West to East*, 118–22. Besides the dangerous and deadly working conditions (described earlier by Dana and Melville throughout) and the lack of union control over hiring, the union was protesting the practice of boardinghouse keepers who shanghaied not only common sailors but officers. The most notorious "crimp" was John Curtin (whose initials are those of John Claggart). I am not claiming that the Somers mutiny was irrelevant to the tale of Billy Budd; but the condition and militancy of common seamen are central to understanding the response to Melville's writing on their behalf.

40. Louis B. Wright's textbook, *The American Tradition: National Characteristics, Past and Present* (New York: F. S. Crofts, 1941), pushes hard on this point. Wright was a participant in the Rochester conference discussed above.

41. *White-Jacket*, chap. 90. In the catalog of The Direct Book Supply Co. of London, a mail-order lending library, ca. 1950, this book was touted as containing "some of the finest chapters ever written on corporal punishment at sea" for "students of torture and flagellation" seeking "stimulation by punishment." Discovered by a student of Roy Porter and copied to me, 1989.

42. Charles Olson to Henry Murray, Feb. 16, 1952, Olson Papers.

43. Both sides of the Olson-Murray correspondence are located in the Olson Papers. Compare with Clark, *Charles Olson*, 44, who dates Olson's first meeting with Murray at the Metcalf "salon" two years later than the date of this letter.

44. Perhaps Murray was the source for Olson's judgment (*Call Me Ishmael*, 1947) that Christianity was the source of the Melville problem.

45. Note that Olson is concealing the letters from Peter Gansevoort to Thomas Melvill, Jr., first published in Leyda's *Log*, alleging that Allan Melvill was "a Maniac!" during the last stages of his illness. Eleanor Metcalf was angry with Leyda for publishing the letters without comment, as mentioned above.

46. Box "Melville materials, misc. notes 1," folder "Lemuel Shaw papers," Olson Papers. Murray's partly fanciful account of the interactions that produced Olson's footnote is found in a folder pertaining to "The Great Trauma": "Early in 1946, while completing research for *CMI* Charles Olsen [*sic*] gained access to the papers of Lemuel Shaw, then being catalogued by the Massachusetts Historical Society, but not yet open to the public. There, he came upon a letter from TM Jr to Judge Shaw, containing information which suggested that the character of Isabel in *Pierre* may have been inspired [above the line 'engendered'] by an illegitimate daughter of HM's father. Olsen decided to include a footnote reference to his discovery, but 'not to discuss it or weigh it' in relation to the text of *Pierre* because such detailed treatment would be out of place in the work he was pursuing. Instead, he proposed that Murray give the discovery 'its real setting and interpretation' in an introduction to *Pierre* then in composition for the Hendricks House series. As it turned out, Olsen's footnote did not appear. Murray managed only a veiled allusion to the real-life basis for the event that traumatized the hero of M's novel" (Murray Papers; there is a similar version of this draft in folder "Ann Bent Search for A.M.A.," in which Olson "forwarded a copy of the letter to Murray whom he knew was then deep into *Pierre*"). As the Forbes-Olson cor-

respondence and other letters in his papers show, Olson had demanded and received exclusive rights to the Shaw materials.

47. Leyda met Murray in late May 1947 in the Berkshires, or perhaps earlier. See appendix for draft of Leyda's letter to Robinson, 1971. I cannot account for Leyda's blow-up after he read Murray's introduction to *Pierre* (see below), unless Leyda had discussed the Isabel letter with Murray, a matter that never surfaces in his correspondence with Hayford. The Morewood material (owned by three sisters, Agnes, Helen, and Margaret, great-nieces of Melville through his brother Allan) contained psychologically revealing documents: brother Gansevoort's diary and brother Allan's journal, family letters, and letters written by Melville—all reserved for Murray. Leyda was shown most of this material by the Morewood sisters; he then tried to convince Murray (by letter?) to relinquish his monopoly. The prizes included a letter from Maria Gansevoort Melville to Allan rebuking him for standing up to her (tyrannical) brother Peter and a letter from Herman to Allan in blackface minstrel dialect, signing his name "Tawny." Murray was furious with Agnes Morewood for showing Leyda her family's Melville materials, and she apologized abjectly for the betrayal, emphasizing that Leyda had *not* seen the Melville letters and noting that "certainly this Leyda has a way—" that she found hard to resist. Agnes heaped coals on her head after Murray wrote "I trusted you." She replied, "The pain to me is intense and I will never get over it. I only have the man's word to me he will not use any information gained in my house. He asked of Hoadley and of letters of my Grandmothers he already had much. Also I do not like such personal letters printed." See her four agitated letters of 1947: Apr. 27, Apr. 30, May 1, and n.d. 5:45 P.M., in the Murray Papers, Special Correspondence, box 14.

Leyda wrote to Hayford, May 29, 1947: "The Murray meeting came off all right—he's completing (& submitting for publication in the spring) his *first* (of three) volumes (1819 to marriage at present its contents)—& the only things he wants to spring and startle with are in this first vol. So, the 'arrangement' made was that the Log would not precede his vol. I hoard [and J. L. would] have a chance to comb his own collection in September. Now I have to hang on in the East till then, for I don't want to give him any excuse for changing his mind. As his collection contains new stuff in both boyhood and 1850–51, I can't risk it." In his letter of October 17, 1947, Leyda continued, "I didn't say Murray had nothing more to show me. Actually, I saw less than he had promised me under the influence of brandy! He's here in NY now—still finishing the *Pierre* introduction" (Hayford personal files).

48. Folder "Art," Murray Papers.

49. Folder "AMA," box "The Great Trauma," Murray Papers.

50. Weaver, *Mariner and Mystic*, 73, 121, 341.

51. See Carl Jung, "Individual and Mass Psychology," in *Essays on Contemporary Events* (London: Kegan Paul, 1946), xiii–xv, for his view of Hitler as "shadow self" of the uprooted urban mob (excerpt appended). Compare with Henry A. Murray, "Time for a Positive Morality," *Survey Graphic* (Mar. 1947): 195–96, 214–16, hinting that Victorian culture ("scientific criticism") has produced feminized males (i.e., Pierre) unwilling to build "a good world order."

52. Box "Melville materials misc. notes (1)," Olson Papers. Compare with account of Laughlin's project in the Olson-Dahlberg correspondence, *In Love, in Sorrow: The Complete Correspondence of Charles Olson and Edward Dahlberg*, ed. Paul Christensen (New York: Paragon House, 1990), 128–32.

53. I have not found a transcription of the letter in Leyda's copious notes from the Shaw Papers at the Massachusetts Historical Society, nor in any early drafts of the *Log* available to me; samples of his "Specimens" are not complete (see Leyda Papers, box 18, UCLA). See below for implication that he knew he could not publish the Isabel letter or other material: It might have been in the Birss collection, and Birss might not have known Leyda had seen it.

54. This is a revealing slip, since Olson had not mentioned anyone but Murray and himself as charmed. John H. Birss had been compiling a Melville bibliography and a "secret" booklet of letters, according to Leyda (and alluded to by Merrell R. Davis in a letter to Leyda, Nov. 15, 1946, Leyda Papers, UCLA). Birss had seen "Specimens" but had "no enthusiasm" (telegram, Leyda to Olson, Jan. 27, 1946, Olson Papers); this may not be true (see appended letter from Birss to Leyda). As noted above, in 1946 Lincoln Kirstein mentioned materials he had obtained roughly five years before from Birss but could not find. If Birss was withholding primary source documents, then he might be the source for the Isabel letter, coming through Leyda's close friend, who light-heartedly warned (on a small card), "Don't make a move without Lincoln," a message reiterated in his letter of August 25, 1948. I had written to Kirstein, fully disclosing my research and asking for elucidation. He answered on October 24, 1990, "Apart from being senile and losing my memory I really don't care anything about Jay Leyda, or what I can recall of him, or really anything else about Melville. Jay turned on me because I wouldn't do anything about his wife who was an incompetent and very ambitious dancer, for whom I had no use. I'm not very sympathetic to the kind of research you seem to have embroiled yourself in the Melville industry. Jay did a good job on the log, and he should be thanked and left in peace. Let the dead bury the dead." But according to a letter in the Leyda Papers at NYU, Leyda and Kirstein were still on friendly terms in 1971. A letter from the Ballet Society to Si-Lan Chen dated January 22, 1948, rejected her idea for a ballet based on the Turandot legend.

55. Olson Papers.

56. See catalog for memorial retrospective of Leyda's photography by Elena Pinto Simon and David Stirk, "Chronology," in *Jay Leyda: A Life's Work* (New York: Tisch School of the Arts, NYU, 1988), 6.

57. Olson to Allyn Forbes, director of Massachusetts Historical Society, Nov. 12, 1945. From the record of Olson's correspondence with Forbes, only William Charvat is definitely known to have consulted the Shaw Papers between 1934 and the date of Olson's complaint to Forbes. See Charvat's letter to Olson, December 2, 1945, in which Charvat defers to Olson's greater ability to contextualize facts (which are not specified).

Drafts from Olson to Forbes indicate that both Eleanor Metcalf and Murray were informed in 1934 about the Isabel letter, etc.: "This same person [EMM] has known as did the above mentioned biographer [Murray] since 1934. [crossed out:] and have kept them in touch they have, in these intervening years, scrupulously observed my priority." To Charvat, Olson wrote, "If you saw a copy of my letter to Mr. Forbes you will know that I was more disturbed for those two who ten years ago knew of the material and are now both [more] engaged on books on M than I was for myself. I refer to Dr Henry A Murray jr and Mrs E M.M." See box "Melville material misc. 2," folder "Olson-Forbes Dispute," Olson Papers. Harrison Hayford told me in December 1991 that he reviewed the Shaw materials in 1943; however, the alleged Isabel letter was not there. It could have been removed by the curator to protect Olson's interests; but had he seen it, he would not have concluded that it pointed to a real-life half-sister.

58. Olson Papers.

59. Here are a few of the scraps I have found to date in the Murray Papers: Item 1 (folder "AMA"): "early in 1946 . . . [However, faced with a publisher's deadline, Murray postponed ~~thorough scrutiny~~ his intended enterprise leaving the letter to percolate slowly on the backburner along with various other Melville morsels]"; Item 2 (Items 2–8 are in folder "Ann Bent Search for A.M.A."): "Melvillean Charles Olson, the Gloucester poet, was the one, so far as I know, who first gazed with a recognizing eye on the puzzling letter we are presenting here. At the time, 1949, O was searching the LS papers at the MHS, but he was concentrating on his ongoing CMI, in which he had found no place for the letter. Knowing how keen I would be to embrace this critical material, the intelligence of his friendship prompted him to send me an exact copy." Item 3:

Yellow notes: "stalking, digging, surveying, peering through the exhibits—Leaping, stunning disclosure—/ Trauma/ supposition: He has been contributing $ a year to the support of Ann— AM told us he would leave something in the will . . . must be bastard / supporting a bastard." Item 4: "This letter, so far as I know, was first discovered among the Shaw papers at the MHS by Melvillian CO, and copied to oblige me in 1945. The letter reads as follows:" Item 5: Yellow notes: "OLSON. 1st to *recognize significance*—eagle-eye—did not fail to *envisage*/sensational—*one chance in a 1000* one in a million" "Letter—There was no place in the stunning book he was hammering out." Item 6: Three drafts which have no dates for either the discovery or the date of passing it on to Murray. One begins "[CO] once the society's ~~choleric~~ severest critic . . . ." Item 7: "List of some remaining contributions to be posed for MSEx: 1. The Tell-Tale Letter/ A true copy of this letter was given to me by Charles Olson in 1939. A few years later it was rediscovered by Amy Puett Emmers and published rather recently." Item 8: Draft dated 2/6/74, "1. Some 30 years ago I had a copy (sent by Olson, Jan.19, 1947) (found among the Shaw papers at the MHS) written by TM Jr. to Judge LS. Recently, however, a fairly thorough search has revealed neither the original at the Historical Society *nor* my copy of it. But 'to my best recollection' it was a short letter in which T.M. Jr. . . . told LM . . . that he had been visited by Mrs. AMA and Mrs B and was struck by the amazing likeness or resemblance of the latter. . . . 2. In conjunction with other evidence, this letter, if accurately recalled, is a clincher for the thesis that HM's father had a pre-marital amorous affair."

To summarize the various dates of Olson's passing on the letter, Murray has claimed 1939, 1945, 1946, 1947, and 1949; i.e., he concealed his knowledge of the Isabel letter most probably beginning in 1934. But there is more: Item 9: In folder "Morsels," Murray places "Isabel" at top of his list and dates her "1839"; "wild speculation" [HM is voluntarily detained in Boston to see Shaw regarding whereabouts of "illegitimate sister" & wants mother to "meet X"]. Given Murray's strong identification of himself with both Melville and his father, the claims he made to Olson regarding other sexual liaisons in Allan Melvill's biography should be taken with caution.

As of this writing, I have been denied further access to the unpublished Murray biography (or his other papers, with the exception of the correspondence from Eleanor Metcalf, the Morewoods, and Josie Shaw, quoted above); but my brief peeks in 1991 strongly suggested that the biography would suppress the Isabel letter along with Allan Melvill's wild oats. In "Melville Ms. III 6," Murray wrote, "M aimed at aimlessness . . . . [T]he fact that he went that way by choice—following his father who died, he supposed, raving about some girl—was a good sign that he would fail to become an utter wreck" (110). In "Ms. for biography, Chapter 1" there are only vague allusions to the father's premarital escapades.

60. Murray seems to have persisted in his admiration of Allan Melvill, in spite of postwar research disclosing shady business dealings. In an early (prewar) draft of his biography, Murray had disparaged Melville's hypermoralistic "Hebraic ethos": "Did his father's experience teach him nothing? To be sure Allan Melville had not bothered his head about the flagrant discord between the Sermon on the Mount & the practices of merchants; but in his own business dealings, notwithstanding he had been scrupulously honest & the golden rule had been prominently featured. For this reason as much as any he had died a bankrupt" (chap. 16).

61. Later suppressions of the Isabel letter by second-wave scholars are described in my "The 'Melville' Revival, 1919–1953: An Unclosed Case Study in Conservative Enlightenment" (Ph.D. diss., UCLA, 1993). The claim advanced by Hayford and Parker that the women owed Allan Melvill money was considered and rejected by Murray, who noted the secrecy and the lack of bills. See box "The Great Trauma," Murray Papers.

62. These connections are rarely drawn, but they are pervasive in conservative diagnostics of social catastrophes; for instance, see John Allington (a sequestered Divine) in *The Grand Conspiracy of the Members against the Minde, of Jewes against their King* (London, 1653), 33: "An example

strongly convinces me, that even the Law and light of Nature, were it not clouded with carnall and perverse affections, even that glimmering light were enough to teach the minde, that resist we may not against God's ordinance." Or see Axel's remark to Sara in De Lisle's *Axel's Castle:* "The external world! Let us not be gulled by the old slave who sits fettered in broad daylight at our feet and promises the keys of an enchanted palace when his clenched sooty fist hides only a handful of ashes!" Or see this 1937 comment on Krafft-Ebing by Alexander Harwitch in *Aberrations in Sexual Life after the Psychopathio Sexualis . . . A Medico-Legal Study for Doctors and Lawyers* (Springfield, Ill.: Charles Thomas, 1959), 14. "Modern big-city life" and "high civilization" are oversexed: "Episodes displaying moral decline in the lives of nations invariably coincide with periods of decadence, lasciviousness and luxuriousness. The phenomena are only thinkable with an increased demand on the nervous system, which must rise as needs grow higher. As a result of increasing nervous sensitiveness there is an increase in sensuality, and since this leads to excesses among the mass of the people, it undermines the basic props of society, the morality and purity of family life. If excesses, adultery, and luxury undermine this, then collapse, moral and material ruin, are inescapable. Warning examples in this respect are the Roman State, Greece, France and Louis XV and XVI." Or see D. H. Lawrence, *Pornography and Obscenity Handbook for Censors* (Michigan City, Ind.: Fridtjof-Kula Publications, 1958; originally published in *Remember to Remember,* New York: New Directions, 1947), for a diatribe against revolution-inducing masturbation provoked by the wiles of popular culture: For Lawrence, masturbation revived repressed memories (the crab that crawls out from under a rock). Or see Norman Mailer, "Henry Miller: Genius and Lust, Narcissism," *American Review* (Apr. 1976): 1–40, specifically linking Ahab-ish exploration and connection making to (revolting, indispensable) sexual penetration. (This is not the same *American Review* of the mid-1930s, edited by the fascist Seward Collins.)

63. Compare Murray's unbending attack on Melville's "narcism" in his introduction to *Pierre* (1949) with his harsh judgment of unsympathetic readers (i.e., himself) in "Dead to the World: The Passions of Herman Melville" (a speech of 1963). Bartleby's "pathetic state" of "affectlessness" is attributed to "the reception of a host of blockheaded and malicious feedbacks to the publication of his *Pierre.*" In Henry A. Murray, *Endeavors in Psychology: Selections from the Personology of Henry A. Murray,* ed. Edwin S. Shneidman (New York: Harper and Row, 1986), 515.

64. Maurice Bassan, *Hawthorne's Son: The Life and Literary Career of Julian Hawthorne* (Columbus: Ohio State UP, 1970): 191.

65. "Morsels" folder; see also "Miscellaneous" folder in box "The Great Trauma," Murray Papers.

66. These images are from Murray's comparison of Melville with Poe's French detective Dupin ("The Purloined Letter"), in manuscript "Melanophilia," Murray Papers.

67. The frequent resort to corporal punishment (caning) came out in William Gilman's 1951 biography without criticism by the author.

68. Written by staff at the Harvard Psychological Clinic, *Explorations in Personality* (New York: Science Editions, 1938), 226–27. Murray's theory of needs was derived from the social psychology of ultraconservative William McDougall, former chair of the Harvard Department of Psychology. "Infavoidant" referred to the "need" to avoid criticism and humiliation. Murray wrote most of the book, including this passage. The group that formulated the theory of personality included "democrats, fascists, communists, anarchists" (xi).

69. Murray was alluding to *Moby-Dick* (Ishmael's cv): "A whale ship was my Yale College and my Harvard."

70. Compare with Rodney G. Triplet, "Henry A. Murray and the Harvard Psychological Clinic, 1926–1938: A Struggle to Expand the Disciplinary Boundaries of Academic Psychology" (Ph.D. diss., University of New Hampshire, 1983), 205: "Based on his study of [Lawrence] Hen-

derson's *The Order of Nature*, and their collaborative research on the chemical equilibria of the blood, Murray was convinced that the functioning of the human organism was heirarchically [sic] organized to achieve a physical, psychological, and social stability that yet remained flexible enough to allow for growth and adaptation." Harvard liberals considered Henderson a fascist; see the denial by Pareto seminar member Crane Brinton, "Lawrence Joseph Henderson," in *The Saturday Club: A Century Completed 1920–1956*, ed. Edward W. Forbes and John H. Finley, Jr. (Boston: Houghton Mifflin, 1958), 213.

71. Murray to Leyda, May 13, 1977, Leyda Papers, box 4, NYU. The letter reporting the shaving of sailor Herman's beard seems to have been withheld or lost, if it even existed. See Helen Morewood to Jay Leyda, August 12, 1950: "If you want to say, not quoting me the fact that on Melville's return from some years at sea his brother Gansevoort who saw him in N.Y.C. on arrival urged him to shave and change his clothes "before going into his mother's presence"—or before seeing her do so and as soon as possible will copy that letter for you." On November 19, 1950, she wrote again to say that she could not find the letter. Leyda Papers, box 7, UCLA.

72. Jakob M. R. Lenz (1751–1792), a prominent member of the *Sturm und Drang* movement, died insane. Lenz, a playright of interest to Brecht, was later considered a forerunner of naturalism; he was also interested in the effects of electricity as spark to creativity. Compare with Isabel and Frankenstein.

73. Edwin Shneidman told me that Murray circulated this secret: While carving a turkey, Melville would pass the knife under the noses of his sons to terrify them. Compare the story with the slanders directed toward Lord Byron by contemporaries and protested by the nineteenth-century critic George Brandes: "Byron was one of those who permit their imaginative and their reflective powers every possible experiment; he had a strong inclination to brood over, and let his fancy play with, what people in general fear and avoid. The well-known anecdote (which aroused such horror) of his exclaiming, with a knife in his hand: 'I wish I knew what it feels like to have committed a murder,' means this and nothing more. There was the same fascination for him in thinking and working himself into the feeling of guilt which accompanies a criminal attachment as there was in imagining the feelings which accompany a murder. . . . It is not surprising that Byron and Moore should have meditated writing an imaginary biography of Lord Byron in which he was to seduce so many members of the one sex and murder so many of the other, that the scandal-mongers would be outbid and possibly silenced. The project was only relinquished from fear that the public might take the jest as sober, earnest." Georg Brandes, *Naturalism in Nineteenth Century English Literature* (1923; reprint, New York: Russell and Russell, 1957), 306–7.

Speculations about Hitler's possible Jewish blood are found both in the Murray-Allport Harvard worksheet "Hitler, The Man—Notes for a Case History," and in the Murray report to FDR, 1943.

10. AFTER THE REVOLUTION: THE RACIAL DISCOURSE OF ETHNOPLURALISM

1. See two eighteenth-century works, both in Melville's library: Edmund Burke, *A Philosophical Enquiry into the Origin of Our Ideas of the Sublime and the Beautiful*, ed. and intro. Adam Phillips (1757; Oxford: Oxford UP, 1990). In Phillips's opinion, the sublime and the beautiful were not antinomies for Burke: Both were arousing and opposed to indifference and immobility; however, Phillips makes the comparison with rupture and continuity, Thanatos and Eros. Also see Samuel Johnson, *Rasselas* (1759), esp. chap. 17, the remarks on "fancy" (the meteor: transitory, irregular, delusive; i.e., the Melville career as read by conservatives), and chap. 44, "The Dangerous Prevalence of Imagination." Both the pastoral (fantastic delight) and the related visionary utopia

are dangerous and lead to fixed ideas, melancholy, insanity, parricide, and fratricide. *Rasselas* (in subject matter and philosophy likened to Voltaire's *Candide*) was Johnson's most popular work, enjoying 450 editions by 1959. See *Samuel Johnson, LL.D.: An Exhibition of First Editions, Manuscripts, Letters and Portraits to Commemorate the 250th Anniversary of His Birth, and the 200th Anniversary of the Publication of His Rasselas* (New York: Pierpont Morgan Library, 1959). Compare with the attempt by Clark to fasten Paine to this neoclassical literary tradition (*Thomas Paine*, cviii–cxviii).

2. My reference to the mating of unlike things is from Ovid's definition of Chaos that begins *Metamorphoses;* the phrase also appears in Melville's poem "Art." Burke describes the obscurity that results from Milton's description of Satan (and poetry in general) as the consequence of compressing unlike things (a problem not shared by imitative painting), *Philosophical Enquiry*, pt. 2, sect. 4 (cont.):57. "Here is a very noble picture; and in what does this poetical picture consist? in images of a tower, an archangel, the sun rising through the mists, or in an eclipse, the ruin of monarchs, and the revolutions of kingdoms. The mind is hurried out of itself by a croud of great and confused images; which affect because they are crouded and confused. For separate them, and you lose much of the greatness, and join them, and you infallibly lose the clearness."

3. See Piero Camporesi, *The Incorruptible Flesh: Bodily Mutilation and Mortification in Religion and Folklore*, trans. Tania Croft-Murray (Cambridge: Cambridge UP, 1988), chap. 2, "The Impassible Saint."

4. See Denis Diderot, *Memoirs of a Nun*, trans. Frances Birrell (London: Elek Books, 1959).

5. See Heinrich Heine, *Doktor Faust: A Dance Poem*, ed. and trans. Basil Ashmore (London: Peter Nevill, 1952), for the intertwining of the Don Juan/Faust legends and the threat of the autodidact; the conflation of printing with necromancy. Heine wrote in 1851 (the same year *Moby-Dick* was published), "The Church deliberately confused [the historic Faust, a magician, with the inventor of printing] because in its opinion, necromancy has found its most wicked tool in the diffusion of thought by means of printing. To such minds Thought is a terrible menace to that blind credo demanded in the Middle Ages, which requires acceptance of the Church's total authority in matters spiritual and temporal, and keeps the humble charcoal burner [the Carboneri] on his knees. Faust began to *think*. His impious intellect rebelled against the meek acceptance of his forefathers. He was not content to read in dark places and to trifle with simple arts. He longed for scientific knowledge and lusted for worldly power. He demanded to be allowed to think, to act and to enjoy life to its full extent, and so . . . to use the language of the ancients . . . he became an apostate, renounced all hope of heavenly bliss, and turned to Satan and his earthly ways and promises. This single man's revolt was most certainly spread abroad by means of the printer's art, so that his doctrine was very soon assimilated, not merely by a handful of intellectual rebels, but by whole populaces. Small wonder then, that men of God denounced the art of printing as an attribute of Satan" (16–17).

6. See Robert Filmer's classic formulation of stealthily advancing, bloodthirsty, irrational democracies in *Patriarcha*, ed. Peter Laslett (Oxford: Oxford UP, 1949), 89–90.

7. For the invention of "tradition," see Eric J. Hobsbawm, "The Perils of the New Nationalism," *Nation*, Nov. 4, 1991, 537, 555–56.

8. Lewis Mumford, *The Myth of the Machine* (New York: Harcourt Brace Jovanovich, 1967–70), 367–68. At the end of a tirade against modernity, he concluded that junk sculpture may have a prophetic function: "In this light society owes a debt to the anti-art of our period; for it revealed, more than a generation before our scientific instruments of destruction had proliferated and escalated, the irrational promptings and the sterile goals that now characterize Western civilization. If the prophetic nature of this art had been widely understood, it might, taken in sufficiently diluted doses, have served as a timely inoculation to protect us against the disease that is now taking hold of the entire social organism."

9. Willard Thorp, "The Teacher and the New Approaches to American Literature," in *The Teacher and American Literature: Papers Presented at the 1964 Convention of the National Council of Teachers of English*, ed. Lewis Leary (Champaign, Ill.: National Council of Teachers of English, 1965), 3.

10. Matthiessen's contribution to this tradition has been discussed above. See Richard V. Chase, *Herman Melville: A Critical Study* (New York: Macmillan, 1949). Chase's Jungian Melville criticism began with "An Approach to Melville," *Partisan Review* 3 (1947): 285–94; Ahab as False Promethean, correctly diagnosed by D. H. Lawrence, is discussed on pp. 290–91. Not surprisingly, Chase rated Melville "somewhat below Hawthorne and Henry James" (1949, xii).

11. Yvor Winters, *Maule's Curse: Seven Studies in the History of American Obscurantism* (Norfolk, Conn.: New Directions, 1938), 53–89. Winters credits a Stanford student, Achilles Holt, for "details" regarding Melville's symbols, but notes, "I differ radically with Mr. Holt as to his interpretation of the central theme, that is, in regard to the significance of Ahab's character and actions" (53).

12. See also Yvor Winters, "Maule's Curse," *American Review* 9 (Sept. 1937): 339–61. Winters states that Melville was "the greatest of his era and of his nation," unlike his confused contemporaries. The height of clarity is attained in *Moby-Dick* and "Benito Cereno"; *Mardi* and *Pierre*, however, are confused, transmitting the same disastrous intertwining of "New England mysticism" and "Romantic amoralism" characteristic of Emerson and still typically American (359). ("Maule's curse" refers to the germinal event in Hawthorne's *House of the Seven Gables* [1851], written and published while Melville was writing *Moby-Dick*. A humble seventeenth-century "wizard" is destroyed by the determination of the heartless puritan Pyncheon to wrest away his newly cleared land; Maule cursed the progeny, saying they would choke on their own blood.)

13. Newton Arvin, *Herman Melville* (New York: William Sloan, 1950), 174.

14. Richard H. Brodhead, *New Essays on "Moby-Dick"* (Cambridge: Cambridge UP, 1986), 1.

15. Ross J. S. Hoffman, "The Totalitarian Régimes," *American Review* 9 (Sept. 1937): 338, 336–37. There was no explanation for the sudden cessation of *American Review* in 1937. On p. 432, an advertisement appeared alerting readers to the existence of the *American Review* bookshop and lending library at 231 W. 58th Street, NYC; books were also lent by mail.

16. See A. B. R., review of *The Whale, Illustrated London News*, Nov. 1, 1851, quoted above in Hayford and Parker, *Moby-Dick as Doubloon*, 18.

17. Ahab was recognized (but not disapprovingly) as a Jewish communist by actor Roscoe Lee Browne ("what else could he be?") in conversation with me, ca. 1986. (Browne played the role of Babu in the Robert Lowell adaptation of "Benito Cereno.") Ahab was stigmatized by C. L. R. James as a Stalin or Hitler (or Melville) in the first edition of *Mariners, Renegades and Castaways*, in which a Jewish communist named "M" attempts to dupe other detainees on Ellis Island (appended). The UCLA Leyda Papers (box 13) contain Leyda's alteration of the only surviving portrait of Gansevoort, here showing a beaked nose enlarged by Leyda. See page 345 above.

18. Richard V. Chase, "Melville's Confidence Man," *Kenyon Review* 11 (1949): 122–40. Excerpts from Chase's revealing correspondence with prominent New Liberals are appended.

19. During the author's first interview with Edwin Shneidman (1987), he identified Murray as "a left-wing democrat."

20. Melville to Hawthorne, Nov. 17, 1851, *Log*, 434–36.

21. Compare the conclusions in Howard P. Vincent, *The Trying-Out of Moby-Dick* (Boston: Houghton Mifflin, 1949); and Paul C. Metcalf, *Genoa: A Telling of Wonders* (1965; reprint, Albuquerque: U of New Mexico P, 1991). Vincent saw nothing ambiguous about the ending to *Moby-Dick*. As I read it, in Paul Metcalf's "ending" it is not clear that the alienated Michael Mills (Byronically exiled in the attic, a metaphor for his head?) has returned to the family (a

metaphor for a rapprochement with the body?). In correspondence with me, Metcalf has given contradictory accounts: Michael Mills has healed the split in his consciousness; Michael Mills could not have healed because the culture is pathologically divided.

22. See Hawthorne's story "P's Correspondence," in *Mosses from an Old Manse.*

23. Miguel De Cervantes Saavedra, *The First Part of the Life and Achievements of the Renowned Don Quixote De La Mancha,* trans. Peter Motteux (New York: Random House, 1941), 91, 528.

24. Though Andrew Jackson has been cast as a villain in New Left historiography, the constitution of the CPUSA referred to itself as a party in the tradition of "Paine, Jefferson, Jackson and Lincoln."

25. Herman Melville, *Redburn* (NN), chap. 29, 138–40. Weaver's student David Rein (Columbia University, 1933) criticized Melville's weak position on labor, citing *Redburn.* Weaver Papers, Columbia University. Compare with Henry Murray's draft manuscript commenting on the passage I have quoted: "Young, inexperienced and defenseless, M's hero was exposed continuously and at close range to the brutalities of a gross and vulgar lot of men; and these being the chief cause of his misery, the author could not in their case adopt his favorite role and champion the oppressed. These shipmates of his had been more oppressing than oppressed. Indeed it was his intimate first-hand knowledge of foremast hands on merchantmen, whalers and frigates that made it impossible for M to be the romantic utopianist that his nature would otherwise have led him to become. He could not suppose, as idealists are apt to, that the lower classes would make a better job of governing the State than its present leaders. But let the rulers be more humane: this was the sum and substance of his argument. More specifically, he was calling for honesty, unpretentiousness, goodwill, generosity, and sympathy from sea-captains, ship-owners, consuls, commodores, ministers, judges, doctors, kings, and philosophers. As for the common sailors, not much could be expected of them. They would always be kept down by the nature of their work, work that had to be done by someone." Draft, chap. 16, Murray Papers.

26. This passage was marked by Eleanor Metcalf in 13:372 of the Constable edition of Melville's complete works, Berg Collection. Matthiessen would read this as an affirmation of Melville's conservatism; but given the state of politics in post–Civil War America, one can hardly blame him for distancing himself from the stump. Again, the Melville problem is bound to the character of Christianity that Melville held in his heart: radical puritanism or the populist evangelicalism of Father Taylor that pleased Unitarian Boston merchants?

27. The reference to Jackson needs explanation. In my view, Melville was endorsing neither Jackson's militarism nor his extermination of Indians nor his slaveholding, but choosing the conventional symbol of equal opportunity for the common man, also perhaps refuting the Tory youth of *Mardi* mocking the "citizen-kings" who had started the Mexican War and who were likely to repeat the errors of the French Revolution. At this point in the text, he seems to be speaking with the god-centered eloquence of Father Mapple, Ahab, and the paean to republican Chosen People of *White-Jacket.*

28. Melville's lectures of the late 1850s were pieced together from newspaper accounts by Merton M. Sealts, Jr., *Melville as Lecturer* (Cambridge: Harvard UP, 1957). I have used the Sealts version (not identical with NN) because I have commented on his responses to the Tiberius, as seen by Melville.

29. See C. Bradford Welles, "The Hellenistic Orient," in *The Idea of History in the Ancient Near East,* ed. Robert C. Dentan (New Haven: Yale UP, 1953): [Speaking of the historian Hieronymus of Cardia] "Perhaps the quarrelsomeness of the Greeks was deplorable. They were little ready to let go any advantage to another, although this may have been only a consequence and an extension of the qualities which made them unique as a people—their restless and aggressive curiosity, their impatience of authority, and their reluctance to acknowledge a superior" (159).

30. In her marginalia to *Redburn,* Eleanor Metcalf noted Jackson as "forerunner of Claggart?" Ahab was not mentioned in this connection.

31. See Erich Dinkler, "Earliest Christianity," in *The Idea of History in the Ancient Near East,* 187–90.

32. Cowen, "Melville's Marginalia." See Melville's markings in Goethe, *Truth and Poetry,* vol. 2, bk. 16:63–64 (on renunciation) and 66–68. Goethe had been unable to resolve the conflict between Reason and Necessity, so he divided his public and practical side from the privately poetic and natural. There was no reconciliation of the two, no "kindly union" as implied by Carlyle.

33. Pasted to the inside of his laptop writing desk was a slip of paper with a quotation from the politically liberal Schiller: "Keep true to the dreams of thy youth." According to H. Lüdeke, "American Literature in Germany," 170, Schiller was a favorite of American liberals until Goethe was promoted by Carlyle. Revealingly, Goethe does not discuss Schiller in his autobiography; but he has much to say about his friendships with Herder and Lavater.

The Olson Papers contain a long letter from the Swiss scholar Walter M. Weber-Weidig, May 25, 1933, written to Charles R. Anderson but passed on to Olson. Weber-Weidig had heard from Lüdeke that Anderson was working on a Melville biography, and he had numerous questions about influences, including Carlyle's. Weber-Weidig surmised that Melville had read *Sartor Resartus* before writing *Mardi,* prompting the change in style. However, based on Melville's defiance in a letter to Hawthorne (the "No, in thunder" remark), he believed, "Melville detested Carlyle's philosophy, that is why he simply ignores him (like Emerson, Longfellow, etc.). What do you think about this?" Weber-Weidig told Anderson, "You will consider it a matter of national pride and gratefulness towards that fine, deep, almost unknown American writer, to help me making him known more widely in our German language." He did not that think that Hawthorne was as influential as others had claimed. See also Weber-Weidig to Olson, July 1, 1934, expressing the need for studies of "the *material* influences in Melville's works." A letter from K. H. Sundermann to Murray, May 2, 1934, was also forwarded to Olson; Sundermann was clearly hoping to link Melville, "one of the greatest minds of the nineteenth century," to the German romantics.

See also Matthiessen, *American Renaissance,* 119–32, for a discussion of "Ishmael's Loom of Time" that praises (the artist) Ishmael's solution to the problems of freedom and necessity in the image of the woven mat, linking Melville to the seventeenth-century metaphysical poets, Thomas Browne, Coleridge, and others in the antimaterialist right-wing of the romantic movement.

The question of Carlyle's influence on Melville was of the utmost importance to scholars writing in the 1930s, especially since Carlyle's antidemocratic beliefs were well known. See, for instance, H. J. C. Grierson, *Carlyle and Hitler* (1933; reprint, Cambridge: Folcroft Library, 1973), the Adamson Lecture Series at the University of Manchester.

On two things Carlyle seems to me to rest his doctrine of the social need of heroes, the rule of the best: "England will either learn to reverence its heroes and discriminate them from sham-heroes and valets and gas-lighted histrions, and to prize them as God's voices . . . or else England will continue to worship new and ever newer forms of Quackland, and so, with whatever resilience and rebounds, it matters little, go down to the Father of Quacks." The first of these is the natural desire in the heart of the great majority of men to be governed, to be guided, to obey (witness Russia and Italy and Germany today). Nietzsche dwells always on the envy felt by the slave, the weakling, the lower classes, for the great, the strong, the wise; and there is an element of truth in this, had I time to analyse it; but the much more obvious fact is the almost pathetic readiness of the mass of men to accept leadership in things political, intellectual, and spiritual. We in educational circles are always declaring that the end of education is to teach people to think for themselves. But can the majority ever do so? My experience is that eighty percent of a class do not want to think for themselves, or are incapable of doing so. The man who can does so from the beginning. The majority want to be taught what to think, and the practice of Communist Russia and Fascist Italy points to the same conclusion. Men can and must be taught what to think. So the Catholic Church has always taught, and so the Communist and Fascist insist to-day. Freedom of thought and of the Press have had a short and precarious history. Men desire to believe: hero-worship is not only an instinct, it is a need of the human spirit.

The other fact on which Carlyle leans is that, this being the case, and society being a complex organism, the laws of whose being are not open to every man, are only slowly being discovered even by the few; but whose laws, like all the laws of Nature, are relentless and irreversible (make no allowance for ignorance, giving way to repentance); it is folly to suppose that mechanically, through the free play of contending egoisms, or the mechanism of the ballot-box, society can be safely and wisely governed. It can only be done by giving the government to the wise, to those who have what he calls "the seeing eye," which in political as in other practical matters anticipates the findings of science, may guide where, as Pascal taught, science will never be able to lay down fixed principles, because of her abstract character. Life, social and individual, is a conflict in which Justice in the long run will prevail; in the long run, Right and Might will be found to be identical; but this brings us to the difficult question—what did Carlyle mean by the Justice which in the end always prevails, which he had, in the "Everlasting Yea," persuaded himself lies at the heart of the Universe? "Effected it will be," he says, speaking of the just regulation of labour, "unless it were a Demon that made the Universe; which I for my part do at no moment . . . in the least believe"; and again: "All fighting, as we noticed long ago, is the dusty conflict of strengths, each thinking itself the strongest, or, in other words, the justest; —of Mights which do in the long run, and forever will in this just Universe in the long run, mean Rights." (13–15)

. . . He would link the scientific law, or rather fact of cause and effect, with that other conception of Law as imposed by God, so that national prosperity is the reward, national disaster the penalty of disobedience:

> And it shall come to pass, if thou shalt hearken diligently unto the voice of the Lord thy God, to observe to do all his commandments which I command thee this day, that the Lord thy God will set thee on high above all nations of the earth.
> . . . Blessed thou shall be in the city, and blessed shalt thou be in the field. Blessed shall be the fruit of thy body, and fruit of thy ground, and the fruit of thy cattle, the increase of thy kine and the young of thy flock, etc. (15–16)

Grierson refers once to Herman Melville, but not as an epigone of Carlyle: "Dr. Johnson said that he *loved* the University of Salamanca because, when asked by the Pope if it were just to conquer America, that University alone replied, NO. Carlyle would not have agreed, and it is clearly a very difficult question to answer in the abstract whether it had been juster to leave America to contending tribes of Red Indians, or the South Sea Islands to such amiable cannibals as Melville describes in *Omoo*, or to clear them out and to establish such a civilization as that of America to-day with all its complexities of good and evil" (18).

34. Henry A. Murray, *"In Nomine Diaboli," Moby-Dick Centennial Essays*, ed. and intro. Tyrus Hillway and Luther S. Mansfield (Melville Society, 1953), 15. Murray was referring to Hitler and the Nazis as radical inheritors of Byron and Nietzsche.

35. Karl Marx, "The Eighteenth Brumaire of Louis Bonaparte," *The Marx-Engels Reader*, 2d ed., ed. Robert C. Tucker (New York: Norton, 1978), 596, 597–98. The essay was written late 1851–early 1852.

1. The phrase was used by Charles N. Watson, Jr., review of Edward Haviland Miller's psy-chobiography of Melville, *New England Quarterly* 49 (Dec. 1976): 633.

2. Isaiah Berlin aligned Freud with the inheritors of German romanticism in *Vico and Herder* (London: Hogarth Press, 1976), but *Moses and Monotheism* (1939) affirms Freud's ethical universalism: Uplifting of the oppressed is the responsibility of the Chosen People and accounts for their murder by the Nazis.

3. In his response to my dissertation, Harrison Hayford advised that Melville's greatness, not his failure, has been the concern of the Revival. Artists and other nonacademics, however, may have a higher opinion of Melville's achievement than the original revivers or many of their aca-demic followers. At the outset of my research in the mid-1980s, G. Thomas Tanselle (co-editor of the Northwestern-Newberry edition of Melville's complete works and vice president of the Gug-genheim Foundation) cautioned me that Howard Mumford Jones and Harry Hayden Clark, two influential professors of American literature in the 1930s and 1940s, considered Melville to be "over-rated."

4. See Charlotte Weiss Mangold, "Herman Melville in German Criticism from 1900 to 1955" (Ph.D. diss., University of Maryland, 1959). "Benito Cereno" and "Billy Budd" passed through but were restricted to larger, urban libraries, suggesting that there was something dubious about the stance of the author in the minds of the German censors. See also Hershel Parker, *Reading Billy Budd* (Evanston, Ill.: Northwestern UP, 1990), chap. 5, "The Dynamics of the Canonization of *Billy Budd, Foretopman.*" The English critics whom Parker quotes were strongly ideological during the interwar period, ranging from Fabian socialism to Tory, including J. C. Squire, once a Fabian, later a supporter of Italian fascism. There is a letter from Douglas Jerrold to Squire, July 5, 1939, writ-ten on Eyre and Spottiswoode stationery, requesting Squire to front for a pro-Franco group, "Friends of Spain," to build English support for that regime. See Squire Papers.

5. Percy H. Boynton, *A History of American Literature* (Boston: Ginn & Co., 1919), 308, but it was written after the Weaver biography of 1921. Boynton grouped Melville with Stowe in this textbook.

6. Thorp, *Representative Selections,* cxxviii–cxxix; Michael P. Zimmerman, "Herman Melville in the 1920s: A Study in the Origins of the Melville Revival with an Annotated Bibliography" (Ph.D. diss., Columbia University, 1963); Watson G. Branch, ed., *Melville: The Critical Heritage* (London: Routledge and Kegan Paul, 1974), 2; Franklin, *The Victim as Criminal and Artist,* 37; Jeanetta Boswell, *Herman Melville and the Critics: A Checklist of Criticism 1900–1978* (Metuchen, N.J.: Scarecrow Press, 1981), ix. Hershel Parker, Historical Note to *Moby-Dick* (NN), 746–47: Melville's characters are "well-muscled men whose appeal was not diminished by their not always being of the white race and not altogether fluent in the English language." (Parker's biography of Melville elaborates this theme, criticizing the sexualization of the South Sea romancer by hostile religious conservatives in retaliation for his criticisms of missionaries in *Typee* and *Omoo*.) Ibid., 735.

7. See Cain, *The Crisis in Criticism,* 261–62.

8. Paul Lauter, "Melville Climbs the Canon," *American Literature* (Mar. 1994): 20. Though Lauter denies he is conflating Melville and his upper-class champions of the 1920s, he sees Melville as a willfully obscurantist writer, testing the reader's cultural capital. Melvillean profes-sors similarly use Melville as weapons, he argues. Thus Melville is crammed down the throats of defenseless students who really hate this writer, as Lauter's informal polls demonstrate. I am not claiming that the 1920s revivers were left-wing radicals or liberals; for instance, Michael Sadleir's essays and novels entertained apocalyptic fears for civilization after the Bolshevik victory, but also a taste for orphans and low-life, held simultaneously with a hysterical fear of the gutter. Perhaps

as a corrective, in *Excursions in Victorian Bibliography* (London: Chaundy and Cox, 1922) he preferred the tightly crafted "Benito Cereno" to the prolix whale story. Sadleir's ambivalent relations with his father, Michael Ernest Sadleir—a leading Victorian radical, educator, and chief strikebreaker during the Leeds utility strike of 1913—are perhaps central to understanding Sadleir's perfectionist "bibliomania" and his desire to rescue the second-rate, persecuted, and decadent (which he felt he was). See his *Michael Ernest Sadleir, 1861–1943: A Memoir by His Son* (London: Constable, 1949), 257–63, for details of the Leeds strike and its aftermath. In the early 1920s, Constable also published the antisemite Nesta Webster, soon to be a leading British fascist, and today an inspiration to Pat Robertson.

9. For cultural materialists following E. P. Thompson, class is a socially constructed category, as rooted in the moment as its supposedly commensurate siblings, race and gender.

10. Paul Lauter, ed., *Heath Anthology of American Literature* (Lexington, Mass.: D. C. Heath, 1990), xxxiii–xxxv. Lauter suggests that diverse approaches to the writing of introductory material in his anthology empowers students: "These critical differences reflect the very diversity of the literature included here. They may also furnish students with a wider range of models for engaging texts and thus, perhaps, encourage confidence in their own judgments and ways of reading" (xxxviii). Unless students learn to decode the ideology of ethnopluralism, however, I can see no benefit to student self-confidence.

11. William V. Spanos, Jr., *The Errant Art of Moby-Dick: The Canon, the Cold War, and the Struggle for American Studies* (Durham, N.C.: Duke UP, 1995); see also Donald E. Pease, "Melville and Cultural Persuasion," in *Visionary Compacts: American Renaissance Writings in Cultural Context* (Madison: U of Wisconsin P, 1987), 235–75. Hawthorne is the communitarian antidote to Ahab and Ishmael, each of the latter justifying each other's self-interest at the expense of community. Pease's analysis of *Moby-Dick* diverges from the extremist Ahab/moderate Ishmael formulation of postwar Melville studies.

12. See, for instance, Roger Cooter, *The Cultural Meaning of Popular Science: Phrenology and the Organization of Consent in Nineteenth-Century Britain* (Cambridge, England: Cambridge UP, 1984): "Phrenology helped to deflect working people's attention away from material historical forces onto individual pathology. But more than this, by leading them to share the ruling class's image of the nature of cerebral reality, it led them to give tacit consent to the ruling class's right to judge them. Thereby above all did phrenology tighten the corset on working people's ability collectively to determine their own history and reality" (254–55).

13. Kermit Vanderbilt, *American Literature and the Academy: The Roots, Growth and Maturity of a Profession* (Philadelphia: U of Pennsylvania P, 1986), xvi, 14. Van Doren's "model bibliography" of Melville was completed by the end of 1914. A similar line is taken by the multiculturalist Lawrence W. Levine, *The Opening of the American Mind* (Boston: Beacon Press, 1996); however, Levine and the slightly younger 1960s generation are credited with breaking the stranglehold of Anglo-American literature, with only a tiny number of precursors (all followers of German romanticism).

14. Committee on the College Study of American Literature and Culture, *American Literature in the College Curriculum* (Chicago: National Council of Teachers of English, 1948), 20–21.

15. For instance, J. H. Kavanagh, while tracking the popularity of *Moby-Dick*, marked the period 1921–47 as the first phase of the "first Melville revival"; similarly, John Bryant did not correlate the revival with the shifting ideologies of social movements, but used decades to count Melville dissertations, marking the dramatic acceleration during and after the 1960s. See J. H. Kavanagh, "That Hive of Subtlety: 'Benito Cereno' and the Liberal Hero," *Ideology and Classic American Literature*, ed. Sacvan Bercovitch and Myra Jehlen (New York: Cambridge UP, 1986), 378; John Bryant, *Melville Dissertations, 1926–1980* (Westport, Conn.: Greenwood Press, 1983). Even adjusted for rising student enrollments (a roughly 33-percent increase during the 1970s), there is an

acceleration in Melville dissertations during the so-called third wave. Between the wars there were twelve dissertations (1924–39); during the war, eleven (1942–45), postwar, thirteen (1945–50). The figures then take off: 1951–60, 57; 1961–68, 93; 1969–80, 317 (my markings roughly corresponding to ideological shifts and strategies).

16. See Arthur Schlesinger, Jr., to Richard Chase, Jan. 24, 1949, appended. In a letter to me of March 4, 2000, Schlesinger wrote: "I had totally forgotten that Melville wrote about 'that vital centre' in the Epilogue! Maybe it lodged in my unconscious, but I think I had Yeats more in mind ('the centre cannot hold')." Compare with Isaiah Berlin, *Vico and Herder* (London: Hogarth Press, 1976), 196–97, on Herder's concept of the "living centre": "All his talk about the national character, the national genius, the *Volksseele*, the spirit of the people and so forth, comes to this alone. His notion of what it is to belong to a family, to a sect, a place, a period, a style, is the foundation of his populism, and of all the later conscious programmes for self-integration or re-integration among men who feel scattered, exiled, or alienated. The language in which he speaks of his unfortunate fellow countrymen, driven through poverty or the despotic whims of their masters to Russia, or Transylvania, or America to become 'blacks and slaves', is not simply a lament for the material and moral miseries of exile, but is based on the view that to cut men off from the 'living centre'— from the texture to which they naturally belong—or to force them to sit by the rivers of some remote Babylon, and to prostitute their creative faculties for the benefit of strangers, is to degrade, dehumanize, destroy them." Berlin footnoted Herder: "'No Tyrtaeus,' he wrote in 1775, 'will follow our brothers who have been sold to America as soldiers, no Homer will sing of this sad expedition. When religion, people, country, are crushed, when these very notions are grown shadowy, the poet's lyre can yield only muted, strangled sounds'" (quoted from *Die Ursachen des gesunken Geschmacks bei den verschiedenen Völker da er geblühet*).

17. See, for instance, James A. W. Heffernan, ed., *Representing the French Revolution: Literature, Historiography, and Art* (Hanover, N.H.: UP of New England, 1992), ix–x. Heffernan doubts that the Declaration of the Rights of Man and Citizen "potently speaks for the Revolution. During the years of the Revolution itself, its potency seems to have depended on its iconization, on its conversion into an image. For the festival of Châteauvieux in April 1792, a contemporary journalist reported that the Declaration was 'written on two stone tablets as the Decalogue of the Hebrews is represented to us, though it is no match for our declaration.' In a grand procession through Paris from the site of the Bastille to the champs de Mars, we are told, 'four citizens carried this venerable burden on their shoulders.' We may wonder if any of the four grasped the full burden of the iconography they bore, or realized that to associate the Declaration with the ten commandments was plainly to signify the potential for coercion and prohibition that lurked within its ostensibly liberating words. In any case, the ambiguity of this new revolutionary decalogue was exemplified by the centerpiece of the procession. Enthroned in a triumphal chariot was a colossal statue of liberty, mother of the lady who stands in New York Harbor and grandmother of the lady who bravely—though briefly—stood in Beijing's Tiananmen Square in the spring of 1989. But unlike her American and Chinese descendants, this particular statue was seated in a chariot with a prow made of six daggers, and instead of holding up a torch, her hand rested on a bludgeon. The significance of that was certainly not lost on the journalist who reported it. 'We must never forget,' he editorialized, 'that the sceptre of liberty is a bludgeon'. . . ." My book questions all such confident indictments of Hebraic (or maternal) hypocrisy and switching as the source of "red" terror.

18. See William James, "What Pragmatism Means," in *Pragmatism and American Culture*, 17. The essay was written in 1907; volume 13 was part of the series *Problems in American Civilization*, edited by Allan Nevins and organized by the Amherst College history department. Some Marxist-Leninists filter their social analyses through the same German historical lenses as the progressives treated here; there are different Marxisms, reflecting the "traditions" of their locales.

19. This point is clarified by Isaiah Berlin, *Vico and Herder,* in the medieval distinction between *verum* and *factum:* We can comprehend all that is man-made, but God's creation remains mysterious, understood only by himself.

20. Murray, undated draft, chap. 16, "A Little of Much Stabbed At," Murray Papers.

21. See Gunnar Myrdal, *An American Dilemma: The Negro Problem and American Democracy* (New York: Harper & Row, 1944), but especially the extended memoranda written by Ralph J. Bunche for the Carnegie-Myrdal study, deposited at the Schomburg Center, NYPL, and in the Bunche Papers.

22. John Higham, *Strangers in the Land: Patterns of American Nativism, 1860–1925* (New York: Atheneum, 1963). "A whole school of literary traditionalists in the early twenties looked on American literature as a battleground where the old-stock writers were defending the nation's spiritual heritage against onslaught from the spokesmen of alien races. Stuart Pratt Sherman first raised the standard of the nativist critics. Around it rallied Brander Matthews, Gertrude Atherton and John Ferrar, supported by professors of English in many an American college" (276). This pluralist formulation ignores the complex struggle among "old-stock" intellectuals to define the terms of American democracy, a debate expressed in the fight over modernity.

23. See Ceaser, *The Reproduction of America,* 60–61.

24. *Journals* (NN), 97. Was he talking about himself? Melville's Bibles are heavily marked and various passages historicized, with numerous annotations clipped out or erased.

25. Goethe, *Truth and Poetry* 2:64. Although preceding paragraphs were heavily marked by Melville, these despairing proto-existentialist sentences were not.

26. Folder "Moby-Dick," Murray Papers.

27. Ovid, *Metamorphoses,* ed. A. D. Melville (Oxford: Oxford UP, 1978).

28. *John Freeman's Letters,* ed. Gertrude Freeman and Sir John Squire (London: Macmillan, 1936), 46.

29. J. C. Squire, speaking of American poetry to his alma mater, Cambridge University, Oct. 27, 1933.

30. Henry A. Murray and Christiana Morgan, "A Method for Investigating Fantasies: The Thematic Apperception Test," *Archives of Neurology and Psychiatry* 34 (1935): 289–306. In the TAT, the subject is shown a picture, which he then interprets in written form. The progressive Murray, of course, believed he was rescuing the patient from such neuroses as the Icarus complex (social radicalism, itself irrationally motivated).

31. Michael Sadleir, ed., *Studs Lonigan, by James T. Farrell: An Appreciation by Michael Sadleir* (London: Constable, 1936), 4, 5.

32. Carleton Stevens Coons, *The Races of Europe* (New York: Macmillan, 1939), vii–viii, 652. Compare with Lothrop Stoddard, a Harvard Ph.D., urging readers in the early 1920s to halt "the menace of the under-man" and the destruction of the white race by thinking "racially." Stoddard's environmentalism is a "materialism" intended to displace Lockean empiricism. It is of course the same old conservative organicism.

33. J. C. Squire, "Loyalty and Patriotism," undated manuscript, box 5, Squire Papers.

34. Chase Papers.

35. A. Gillies, *Herder* (Oxford: Basil Blackwell, 1945), 83, 135, 136, 134. Gillies's bibliography lists nineteen Herder studies published in Nazi Germany, including a planned new edition in 1939. No comment on the appeal of the antiracist cosmopolitan to Nazis is offered. Though Gillies does not declare it, he promotes the *Kulturnation* as foil to the *Staatsnation,* the humiliating effluent of the French Revolution, "when France was bowing down to the goddess of Reason."

36. Eisenstein Papers, Series B; ellipses in original.

37. Jung, "Individual and Mass Psychology," xiii–xv; originally broadcast on the BBC, Nov. 3, 1946.

38. Olson does not mention his 1942 letter to Leyda, asking him to assist the Office of War Information in compiling a list of foreign-language movie theaters; see Leyda Papers, box 8, UCLA.

39. Murray was worried about "our shocking crime record," "scientific criticism, skepticism" and "cynicism" in the colleges, and the glorification of Huckleberry Finn. Several months later, *Survey Graphic* (Dec. 1947): 701, printed a cartoon depicting another thinker, a tousle-headed adolescent with dark hair and eyeglasses reading Marx and thereby worrying mothers.

40. Would the real Whittaker Chambers have taken Captain Vere's side against Billy Budd? Whittaker Chambers's own account of his character and actions in *Witness* creates yet another context (the Hiss case) for the postwar Melville Revival and its chief actors. Chambers's self-understanding as presented in his book links him to my reading of the Titanic Ahab, of Melville as artist struggling to keep his balance. Chambers located his own character in the tradition of radical puritanism and strict empiricism; he is no monomaniac (530–31).

Adding to the Cold War drama of my study, Henry Murray testified on behalf of Alger Hiss at his second trial for perjury, agreeing with Jungian psychologist Carl Binger in diagnosing Chambers as a "psychopathic personality without symptoms of psychosis or insanity." However, Murray also advised the Hiss lawyers to modify the presentation of Hiss as perfectly virtuous, a "goody-goody." Hiss refused. See Alan Weinstein, *Perjury: The Hiss-Chambers Case* (New York: Knopf, 1978), 492–93n.33, 637. Chambers had his own account of Murray's testimony. (Under interrogation, Chambers had earlier "confessed" that he had never written a book. Note that Murray had not published his Melville biography.) "During the second Hiss trial, one of the defense psychiatrists, Dr. Henry A. Murray, head of Harvard's psychiatry department, was to pick up my literary lapse. He found a dark implication (never, so far as I know, illumined) in the fact that I had never written a book. It is worth pausing a moment over Dr. Murray, because he typifies one important aspect of the Hiss Case. At first Dr. Murray made an impressive witness. Repeatedly, he testified under oath that he had reached his psychiatric conclusions about me wholly and solely from a study of my writings in Time, Life and elsewhere (he had never met me). He named a date when his conclusions had crystallized. In cross-examination Prosecutor Murphy carefully led Dr. Murray to repeat these statements. Then Murphy asked these questions: Was it not true that well before the date on which Dr. Murray said he had made his diagnosis solely on the basis of my writing, he had in person visited a former Time writer to question him about me? Was it not true that he had himself then drawn such a picture of me as a drunken and unstable character that the Time writer had exclaimed: 'But Chambers is not like that at all'? Was it not true that Dr. Murray had then answered angrily, 'Oh, you're just trying to whitewash Chambers'? The distinguished head of Harvard's psychiatry department admitted that it was all true" (524–25). Note: Murray, a Jungian psychoanalyst, was director of the Harvard Clinic; he had no connection with the medical school; also, Weinstein quotes Binger as the source for testimony that the fact Chambers had never written a book was significant. The writer for *Time* was identified as James Agee in Weinstein, *Perjury*, 493–94.

41. Chase to Trilling, Trilling Papers, box 2. Earlier letters from Chase echoed the depression and mental suffering in the 1945 entry above. See letters to Trilling, Aug. 7, 1945 (fearing his "morbid subjectivity"), and Oct. 10, 1946.

42. And yet rigid classifications, e.g., "obdurate Persian dualism" in the tyrant, Freud, were denounced by Murray in 1940 (Shneidman, *Endeavors*, 300–301) and applauded in Mumford in 1948.

43. The Kenyon School of English, June 23–Aug. 6, 1949. Senior Fellows: Matthiessen, John Crowe Ransom, and Lionel Trilling. Fellows: Eric Bentley, Richard Blackmur, Cleanth Brooks, Kenneth Burke, Richard Chase, William Empson, Alfred Kazin, L. C. Knights, Robert Lowell, Philip Rahv, Herbert Read, Philip Blair Rice, Mark Schorer, Allen Tate, Austin B. Warren, Robert Penn Warren, Rene Wellek, Basil Willey, Yvor Winters, and Morton Dauwen Zabel.

44. Chase was revising his Melville manuscript during this period.

45. Compare Elizabeth Melville to Kate Lansing on Herman's fancied rough edges, 1877; also ragged-edged truth in "Billy Budd," both quoted above.

46. In a letter to me of November 8, 1990, Sealts commented, "I realize now that it was written at the end of a college year and at a time when I was tired, discouraged when an expected promotion hadn't come through (it did a year later)."

47. Protested by Leyda, who wanted the publicity department to emphasize "adventure," not "firsts."

48. This is a telling detail, suggesting that Murray told Olson he was responsible for Walter Langer's diagnosis of Hitler as a sexual pervert, demanding that women defecate and urinate on him during sex. See Walter Langer, *The Mind of Adolf Hitler: The Secret Wartime Report* (New York: Basic Books, 1972), 182–84.

49. Draft, Leyda to Murray, n.d. (but 1952), Leyda Papers, box 7, UCLA. Murray would have been angry about the concluding pages of the Howard biography, in which he attacked (but did not name) first-wave scholars who had read Melville as a rebel, not as a post–Civil War convert to skepticism-without-despair—as a democratic pluralist.

50. C. L. R. James, *Mariners, Renegades and Castaways*, 155–59.

51. Murray, review of the Howard and Gilman biographies, *Modern Language Notes* (Jan. 1953): 60–62.

52. Professor Jean Simon of the University of Lille, France, was referring to Chase's review of Melville and his critics in *Profils*.

53. Leyda to Kirstein, Nov. 25, 1953, folder 247, Kirstein Papers.

54. Review by Arthur Loesser, *New York Times*, Mar. 18, 1956, 3, Leyda Papers, NYU.

55. Trilling's letter answered by Chase, Mar. 23, 1957. There was no mention of Ahab versus Starbuck. Chase apologized for discourtesy, but explained, somewhat contradictorily, that he referred to the moralism of Trilling, Blackmur, Leavis, the New Critics, Fiedler, and himself. Trilling, he felt, was more of a centrist than he was. Trilling Papers.

56. A newspaper clipping describes his tragically early death in 1962: "Professor Chase and his family . . . were visiting his parents at Osterville. They went to the pond Sunday, and the professor was taken ill while swimming. He was dead of an apparent heart attack when taken from the water. His body was found in 18 inches of water, only 10 feet from shore, by a nephew, Jonathan Chase, 19, of Cohasset." A letter from Chase's colleague Marjorie Nicolson noted that a close friend also had hypertension and died suddenly, but added, "He [Chase] told me once during the last term that he felt he could not write, that somehow he was drained dry, and I assured him that it was just fatigue, as I knew it was. He had done so much that was important." Chase's letters strongly contradict his public presentation. Harcourt Brace's College Department assured readers, "His control was firm, his candor complete, and his mastery of Melville absolute. The result is that undergraduates have no better place to begin their Melville."

Alfred Kazin told me that New Yorkers assumed Chase's death was a suicide. In response to my question about such rumors, Frances Chase expanded on her husband's medical history in a letter to me, May 5, 1992: "He had poliomyelitis at the age of nine. . . . The viral infection atrophied muscles in the right shoulder and upper arm, and caused a functional heart murmur. High blood pressure was a related on-again, off-again problem. When reserpine . . . was approved by the FDA for lowering blood pressure, it had benefits, but limitations too, for little was known about the side effects. In August 1962 Mr. Chase joined some of the family swimming in a pond at Cape Cod. The Coroner's conclusion was that medication plus shock of the cold water had so reduced blood pressure as to result in a fatal heart attack. As for suicide, I can only hope your commitment to scholarship is such that you won't need to add grist to the rumor mill."

57. *The Unfolding of Moby-Dick: Essays on Evidence by Leon Howard,* ed. James F. Barbour and Thomas Quirk (Glassboro, N.J.: Melville Society, 1987). Kris Lackey has related the following intelligence: "I have a Leon Howard story for you. Long ago I went to a party in Albuquerque, and as so often happened, we graduate students sat on the floor at Leon's feet while he held forth. At one point he said, 'If Melville were to appear in this room tonight, I would fall at his feet and call him Master.' Look at [Melville's Bible] annotations, now, and see if that isn't what Melville had in mind."

58. The report extracted here is taken from the original version of Weiss's shorter article in the *New York Observer;* sent to Joshua Schwartzbach by e-mail, Aug. 20, 1997, and to me by Paul Metcalf, with a note, Sept. 5, 1997, advising "make of it what you will."

Selected Bibliography

ARCHIVAL SOURCES

Berg Collection of American and English Literature. New York Public Library, Astor, Lenox, and Tilden Foundations.

Ralph J. Bunche Papers. Department of Special Collections, Young Research Library, University of California at Los Angeles.

James McKeen Cattell Papers. Rare Book and Manuscript Library, Columbia University.

Richard Volney Chase Papers. Rare Book and Manuscript Library, Columbia University.

Sergei Eisenstein Papers. Museum Archives, The Museum of Modern Art, New York.

Erik Erikson Papers. Houghton Library, Harvard University.

Joseph Freeman Papers. Hoover Institution Archives, Stanford University.

Gansevoort-Lansing Collection. Manuscripts Division, New York Public Library, Astor, Lenox, and Tilden Foundations.

William H. Gilman Papers. Library, University of Rochester.

Lawrence J. Henderson Papers. Harvard University Archives.

Lincoln Kirstein Papers. Dance Division, New York Public Library, Astor, Lenox, and Tilden Foundations.

Jay Leyda Papers. Tamiment Institute Library, New York University.

Jay Leyda Papers. Department of Special Collections, Young Research Library, University of California at Los Angeles.

Frank Otto Matthiessen Papers. Houghton Library, Harvard University.

Carey McWilliams Papers. Department of Special Collections, Young Research Library, University of California at Los Angeles.

Melville Papers. Houghton Library, Harvard University.

Melville's annotated Milton. Rare Books and Special Collections, Princeton University Library.

Perry Miller Papers. Harvard University Archives.

Henry A. Murray Papers. Harvard University Archives.

Charles Olson Papers. Archives and Special Collections, Thomas J. Dodd Research Center, University of Connecticut Libraries.

Parke Benjamin Collection. Rare Book and Manuscript Library, Columbia University.

Franklin Delano Roosevelt Papers. FDR Library, Hyde Park, New York.

Sadomasochism Collection. Department of Special Collections, Young Research Library, University of California at Los Angeles.

William Ellery Sedgwick Papers. Houghton Library, Harvard University.

Edwin S. Shneidman Collection. Department of Special Collections, Young Research Library, University of California at Los Angeles.

J. C. Squire Papers. Department of Special Collections, Young Research Library, University of California at Los Angeles.

James Graham Phelps Stokes Papers. Rare Book and Manuscript Collection, Butler Library, Columbia University.

Lionel Trilling Papers. Rare Book and Manuscript Library, Columbia University.

Mark Van Doren Papers. Rare Book and Manuscript Library, Columbia University.

Raymond Weaver Papers. Rare Book and Manuscript Library, Columbia University.

Raymond Weaver Papers. Department of Special Collections, Young Research Library, University of California at Los Angeles.

PUBLISHED SOURCES

Aaron, Daniel. *Writers on the Left*. New York: Oxford UP, 1977.

Ackerman, Nathan W., and Marie Jahoda. *Anti-Semitism and Emotional Disorder*. New York: Harper, 1950.

Adams, Charles Francis. *Three Episodes of Massachusetts History*. 2 vols. Rev. ed. Boston: Houghton Mifflin, 1903.

Adler, Joyce Sparer. *War in Melville's Imagination*. New York: New York UP, 1981.

Adorno, T. W., Leo Lowenthal, and Paul W. Massing. "Anti-Semitism and Fascist Propaganda." In *Anti-Semitism: A Social Disease*. Ed. Ernst Simmel. New York: International UP, 1946.

Adorno, T. W., et al. *The Authoritarian Personality*. New York: Harper, 1950.

Agulhon, Maurice. *Marianne into Battle: Republican Imagery and Symbolism in France, 1789–1880*. New York: Cambridge UP, 1981.

Alexander, Calvert. *The Catholic Literary Revival*. Milwaukee: Bruce Publishing Co., 1935.

Allport, Gordon W. "Basic Principles in Improving Human Relations." In *Cultural Groups and Human Relations: Twelve Lectures before the Conference on Educational Problems of Special Cultural Groups Held at Teachers College, Columbia University, August 18 to September 7, 1949*. New York: Bureau of Publications, Teachers College, Columbia University, 1951. 8–28.

———. *ABC's of Scapegoating*. 1948. 9th rev. ed. New York: Anti-Defamation League of B'nai Brith, 1983.

Allport, Gordon W., and Henry A. Murray. "Worksheets on Morale: A series of explorations undertaken by a seminar in Psychological Problems in Morale in the Department of Psychology at Harvard University under the direction of Dr. Gordon W. Allport and Dr. H. A. Murray." 1941. Harvard University Archives.

Ament, William S. "Bowdler and the Whale." *American Literature* (March 1932): 39–46.

Anderson, Charles Roberts. "The Romance of Scholarship: Tracking Melville in the South Seas." *Colophon* (Spring 1938): 259–79.

———. *Melville in the South Seas*. 1939. New York: Dover Publications, 1966.

Andress, J. Mace. *Johann Gottfried Herder as an Educator*. New York: G. E. Stechert, 1916.

Appleby, Joyce, Lynn Hunt, and Margaret Jacob. *Telling the Truth in History*. New York: Norton, 1994.

Arvin, Newton. *Hawthorne*. Boston: Little, Brown, 1929.

————. *Herman Melville.* New York: William Sloan, 1950.

Babbitt, Irving. *The New Laokoon: An Essay on the Confusion of the Arts.* Boston: Houghton Mifflin, 1910.

————. *Rousseau and Romanticism.* Boston: Houghton Mifflin, 1919.

Barber, Patricia. "Two New Melville Letters." *American Literature* 49 (1977): 418–21.

Barbour, James F. "Melville Biography." In *A Companion to Melville Studies.* Ed. John Bryant. New York: Greenwood Press, 1986.

Baritz, Loren. *Sources of the American Mind.* New York: John Wiley, 1966.

Bassan, Maurice. *Hawthorne's Son: The Life and Literary Career of Julian Hawthorne.* Columbus: Ohio State UP, 1970.

Bateson, Gregory. "Morale and National Character." In *Civilian Morale: Second Yearbook of the Society for the Psychological Study of Social Issues.* Ed. Goodwin Watson. New York: Houghton Mifflin for Reynal and Hitchcock, 1942. 71–91.

Behrendt, Stephen C. *The Moment of Explosion: Blake and the Illustration of Milton.* Lincoln: U of Nebraska P, 1983.

Belgion, Montgomery. "God Is Mammon." *The Human Parrot and Other Essays.* London: Oxford UP, 1931.

Belloc, Hilaire. *The Great Heresies.* New York: Sheed and Ward, 1938.

Benda, Julien. *The Betrayal of the Intellectuals.* 1928. Boston: Beacon Press, 1955.

Bercaw, Mary K. Introduction to *Melville's Sources.* Evanston: Northwestern UP, 1987.

Bercovitch, Sacvan, and Myra Jehlen, eds. *Ideology and Classic American Literature.* New York: Cambridge UP, 1986.

Berdan, J. M. "American Literature and the High School." *Arena* (April 1903): 337–44.

Berkowitz, Edward, and Kim McQuaid. *Creating the Welfare State: The Political Economy of Twentieth-Century Reform.* New York: Praeger, 1980.

Berlin, Isaiah. *Vico and Herder.* London: Hogarth Press, 1976.

Berthoff, Warner. *The Example of Melville.* Princeton: Princeton UP, 1962.

————, ed. *Great Short Works of Herman Melville.* New York: Harper & Row, 1969.

Bethell, John T. "Harvard and the Arts of War." *Harvard Magazine* (Sept.–Oct. 1995): 32–48.

Bezanson, Walter E. "Herman Melville's *Clarel.*" Ph.D. diss. Yale University, 1943.

————. "Historical and Critical Note." *Clarel.* Evanston and Chicago: Northwestern UP and the Newberry Library, 1991.

Bickman, Martin, ed. *Approaches to Teaching Melville's "Moby-Dick."* New York: MLA, 1985.

Bloom, Harold. *Ahab.* New York: Chelsea House, 1991.

Boer, Charles. *Olson in Connecticut.* Chicago: Swallow Press, 1975.

Boime, Albert. *The Magisterial Gaze: Manifest Destiny in American Landscape Painting ca. 1830–1865.* Washington, D.C.: Smithsonian Institution Press, 1991.

Boisen, Anton T. "The Form and Content of Schizophrenic Thinking." *Psychiatry* 5 (Nov. 1942): 23–33.

Boswell, Jeanetta. *Herman Melville and the Critics: A Checklist of Criticism 1900–1978.* Metuchen, N.J.: Scarecrow Press, 1981.

Bourne, Randolph S. *The History of a Literary Radical and Other Papers.* Ed. and intro. Van Wyck Brooks. New York: B. W. Huebsch, 1920.

Boynton, Percy H. *A History of American Literature.* Boston: Ginn & Co., 1919.

Branch, Watson G., ed. *Melville: The Critical Heritage.* London: Routledge and Kegan Paul, 1974.

Brandes, Georg. *Naturalism in Nineteenth-Century English Literature.* 1923. New York: Russell and Russell, 1957.

————. *Revolution and Reaction in Nineteenth-Century French Literature.* New York: Russell and Russell, 1960.

Brandon, S. G. F. *Jesus and the Zealots: A Study of the Political Factor in Primitive Christianity.* New York: Scribner, 1967.

Braswell, William. *Melville's Religious Thought: An Essay in Interpretation.* Durham, N.C.: Duke UP, 1943.

Brenner, Robert. *Merchants and Revolution.* Princeton: Princeton UP, 1993.

Brinton, Crane. "Lawrence Joseph Henderson." In *The Saturday Club: A Century Completed 1920–1956.* Ed. Edward W. Forbes and John H. Finley, Jr. Boston: Houghton Mifflin, 1958.

Brodhead, Richard H. *New Essays on "Moby-Dick."* Cambridge, Eng.: Cambridge UP, 1986.

———. "Melville, or Aggression." In Bryant and Milder, eds., *Melville's Evermoving Dawn,* 181–91.

Bronner, Stephen Eric. *Socialism Unbound.* New York: Routledge, 1990.

Brooks, Van Wyck. *Letters and Leadership.* New York: B. W. Huebsch, 1918.

———. *An Autobiography.* Foreword John Hall Wheelock. Intro. Malcolm Cowley. New York: E. P. Dutton, 1965.

Brown, Cecil M. "Through a Looking Glass: The White Whale." *Partisan Review* (1969): 453–59.

Bryant, John. *Melville Dissertations, 1926–1980.* Westport, Conn.: Greenwood Press, 1983.

———, ed. *A Companion to Melville Studies.* Westport, Conn.: Greenwood Press, 1986.

Bryant, John, and Robert Milder, eds. *Melville's Evermoving Dawn: Centennial Essays.* Kent, Ohio: Kent State UP, 1997.

Bunche, Ralph J. *A World View of Race.* Washington, D.C.: Associates in Negro Folk Education, 1936.

Burke, Edmund. *A Philosophical Enquiry into the Origin of Our Ideas of the Sublime and the Beautiful.* Ed. and intro. Adam Phillips. 1757. Oxford: Oxford UP, 1990.

Burlingham, Cynthia, and James Cuno. *French Caricature and the French Revolution, 1788–1799.* Los Angeles: Grunwald Center for the Graphic Arts, UCLA, 1988.

Butler, Eliza Marian. *The Fortunes of Faust.* Cambridge, Eng.: Cambridge UP, 1952.

Byron, Lord George Gordon. *Byron.* Ed. Jerome J. McGann. New York: Oxford UP, 1986.

Cain, William E. *The Crisis in Criticism: Theory, Literature, and Reform in English Studies.* Baltimore: Johns Hopkins UP, 1984.

Calverton, V. F. *The Liberation of American Literature.* New York: Scribner, 1932.

Capshew, James H. *Psychologists on the March: Science, Practice, and Professional Identity in America, 1929–1969.* Cambridge, Eng.: Cambridge UP, 1999.

Carlyle, Thomas. *German Romance.* 4 vols. London, 1827.

Cattell, James McKeen. *University Control.* New York: Science Press, 1913.

———. "Academic Slavery." *School and Society,* Oct. 13, 1917, 421–26.

Caute, David. *The Great Fear: The Anti-Communist Purge under Truman and Eisenhower.* New York: Simon and Schuster, 1978.

Ceaser, James W. *The Reproduction of America: The Symbol of America in Modern Thought.* New Haven, Conn.: Yale UP, 1997.

Chambers, Whittaker. *Witness.* New York: Random House, 1952.

Champfleury. "French Images of the Wandering Jew." In *The Wandering Jew: Essays in the Interpretation of a Christian Legend.* Ed. Galit Hasan-Rokem and Alan Dundes. Bloomington: Indiana UP, 1986. 68–75.

Charvat, William. "American Romanticism and the Depression of 1837." *Science & Society* 2 (1937–38): 73.

———. "Melville and the Common Reader." In *The Profession of Authorship in America, 1800–1870.* Ed. Matthew J. Bruccoli. Columbus: Ohio State UP, 1968.

Chase, Richard Volney. "An Approach to Melville." *Partisan Review* 3 (1947): 285–94.

———. "Melville's Confidence Man." *Kenyon Review* 11 (1949): 122–40.

———. "New vs. Ordealist." *Kenyon Review* 11 (1949): 12–13.

————. *Herman Melville: A Critical Study.* New York: Macmillan, 1949.

Christensen, Paul. *Minding the Underworld: Clayton Eshelman and Late Postmodernism.* Santa Rosa: Black Sparrow Press, 1991.

Clark, Harry Hayden, ed. Introduction. *Thomas Paine: Representative Selections.* New York: American Book Co., 1944.

Clark, Tom. *Charles Olson: The Allegory of a Poet's Life.* New York: Norton, 1991.

Clive, John. "Macaulay and the French Revolution." In *The French Revolution and British Culture.* Ed. Ceri Crossley and Ian Small. New York: Oxford UP, 1989.

Cohen, Hennig, and Donald Yannella. *Herman Melville's Malcolm Letter: "Man's Final Lore."* New York: Fordham UP and New York Public Library, 1992.

Cohen, I. B., ed. Introduction. *Puritanism and the Rise of Modern Science: The Merton Thesis.* New Brunswick, N.J.: Rutgers UP, 1990.

Cohn, Norman Rufus Colin. *Warrant for Genocide: The Myth of the Jewish World Conspiracy and the Protocols of the Elders of Zion.* London: Eyre and Spottiswoode, 1967.

Committee on the College Study of American Literature and Culture. *American Literature in the College Curriculum.* Chicago: National Council of Teachers of English, 1948.

Conant, James Bryant. "Education for a Classless Society: The Jeffersonian Tradition." In *Education for Democracy: The Debate over the Report of the President's Commission on Higher Education.* Ed. Gail Kennedy. Boston: D. C. Heath, 1952. 44–52.

Coons, Carleton Stevens. *The Races of Europe.* New York: Macmillan, 1939.

Cooter, Roger. *The Cultural Meaning of Popular Science: Phrenology and the Organization of Consent in Nineteenth-Century Britain.* Cambridge, Eng.: Cambridge UP, 1984.

Coply, Stephen, ed. *Literature and the Social Order in Eighteenth-Century England.* London: Croom Helm, 1984.

Cowen, Wilson Walker. "Melville's Marginalia." 11 vols. Ph.D. diss., Harvard University, 1965.

Crawford, Michael J. "*White-Jacket* and the Navy in Which Melville Served." *Melville Society Extracts* 94 (Sept. 1991): 1–5.

Crossley, Ceri, and Ian Small, eds. *The French Revolution and British Culture.* New York: Oxford UP, 1989.

Crossman, R. H. S. *Plato Today.* London: G. Allen and Unwin, 1937.

Davidson, Donald. "Where Are the Laymen? A Study in Policy-Making." *American Review* 9 (Sept. 1937): 456–81.

Davis, David Brion. *Antebellum American Culture: An Interpretive Anthology.* Lexington, Mass.: D. C. Heath, 1979.

Davis, Merrell R., and William H. Gilman, eds. *Melville's Letters.* New Haven, Conn.: Yale UP, 1962.

Dell, Floyd. *Intellectual Vagabondage.* New York: Doran, 1926.

Demiashkevich, Michael John. *The National Mind: English, French, German.* New York: American Book Co., 1938.

Denny, Margaret, and William H. Gilman, eds. *American Writers and the European Tradition.* 1950. New York: Haskell House, 1968.

Diderot, Denis. *Memoirs of a Nun.* Trans. Frances Birrell. London: Elek Books, 1959.

Dinkler, Erich. "Earliest Christianity." In *The Idea of History in the Ancient Near East.* Ed. Robert C. Dentan. New Haven, Conn.: Yale UP, 1955.

Donald, David Herbert. *Charles Sumner and the Coming of the Civil War.* New York: Knopf, 1960.

Douglas, Ann. *The Feminization of American Culture.* New York: Knopf, 1977.

Douglas, Claire. *Translate This Darkness: The Life of Christiana Morgan.* New York: Simon and Schuster, 1993.

Durham, Philip. "Prelude to the Constable Edition of Melville." *Huntington Library Quarterly* 3 (May 1958): 285–89.

Eisenstein, Sergei. *Beyond the Stars: The Memoirs of Sergei Eisenstein.* Vol. 4. Ed. Richard Taylor, trans. William Powell (London: British Film Institute, 1995).

Eliot, T. S. *After Strange Gods: A Primer of Modern Heresy.* London: Faber and Faber, 1934.

———. "Last Words." *The Criterion* (Jan. 1939): 269–75.

Emmers, Amy Puett. "Melville's Closet Skeleton: A New Letter about the Illegitimacy Incident in *Pierre.*" In *Studies in the American Renaissance 1977.* Ed. Joel Myerson. Boston: Twayne, 1978.

Ergang, Robert Reinhold. *Herder and the Foundations of German Nationalism.* New York: Columbia UP, 1931.

Erikson, Erik Homburger. "Hitler's Imagery and German Youth." *Psychiatry* 5 (Nov. 1942): 475–93.

Evans, Richard I. *Gordon Allport: The Man and His Ideas.* New York: Dutton, 1970.

Fadiman, Clifton. Introduction. *Moby-Dick.* New York: Limited Editions Club, 1943.

Farias, Victor. *Heidegger and Nazism.* Philadelphia: Temple UP, 1989.

Fast, Howard. "American Literature and the Democratic Tradition." *College English* 8 (1947): 279–84.

Feidelson, Charles, Jr., ed. *Moby-Dick.* Indianapolis: Bobbs-Merrill, 1964.

Filler, Louis. *Randolph Bourne.* Washington, D.C.: American Council on Public Affairs, 1943.

Fletcher, John Gould. *The Two Frontiers: A Study in Historical Psychology.* New York: Coward-McCann, 1930.

Foerster, Norman. Introduction. *The Humanities after the War.* Princeton: Princeton UP, 1944.

Foerster, Norman, et al. *Literary Scholarship: Its Aims and Methods.* Chapel Hill: U of North Carolina P, 1941.

Foner, Philip S. *History of the Labor Movement in the United States.* 4 vols. New York: International Publishers, 1947.

Foner, Philip S., and Herbert Shapiro, eds. *Northern Labor and Antislavery: A Documentary History.* Westport, Conn.: Greenwood Press, 1994.

Foster, Charles H. "Something in Emblems: A Reinterpretation of Moby-Dick." *New England Quarterly* (1961): 3–35.

Franklin, H. Bruce. *The Victim as Criminal and Artist: Literature from the Prison.* New York: Oxford UP, 1978.

Fredrickson, George M. *The Inner Civil War: Northern Intellectuals and the Crisis of the Union.* New York: Harper & Row, 1965.

———. *The Black Image in the White Mind: the Debate on Afro-American Character and Destiny, 1817–1914.* New York: Harper & Row, 1971.

Freeman, Ellis. *Conquering the Man in the Street: A Psychological Analysis of Propaganda in War, Fascism, and Politics.* New York: Vanguard Press, 1940.

Freeman, F. Barron. "The Enigma of Melville's 'Daniel Orme.'" *American Literature* 16 (1944): 208–11.

———. *Melville's Billy Budd.* Cambridge, Mass.: Harvard UP, 1948.

Freeman, John. *Herman Melville.* London: Macmillan, 1926.

———. *John Freeman's Letters.* Ed. Gertrude Freeman and Sir John Squire. London: Macmillan, 1936.

Freeman, Joseph. *An American Testament: A Narrative of Rebels and Romantics.* New York: Farrar and Rinehart, 1936.

Freud, Sigmund. *Moses and Monotheism.* New York: Knopf, 1939.

Friedman, John Block. *The Monstrous Races in Medieval Art and Thought.* Cambridge, Mass.: Harvard UP, 1981.

Fuller, E. Torrey. *The Roots of Treason: Ezra Pound and the Secret of Saint Elizabeth's.* New York: McGraw-Hill, 1984.

Gabriel, Ralph Henry. *The Course of American Democratic Thought: An Intellectual History since 1815*. New York: Ronald Press, 1940.

Garner, Stanton. *The Civil War World of Herman Melville*. Lawrence: UP of Kansas, 1993.

Gillies, A. *Herder*. Oxford: Basil Blackwell, 1945.

Gilman, Sander L. *Difference and Pathology: Stereotypes of Sexuality, Race, and Madness*. Ithaca, N.Y.: Cornell UP, 1985.

Gilman, William H. *Melville's Early Life and "Redburn."* New York: New York UP, 1951.

Goethe, Johann Wolfgang von. *The Auto-Biography of Goethe. Truth and Poetry: From My Own Life*. Trans. Rev. A. J. W. Morrison. 2 Vols. London: Henry G. Bohn, 1849.

———. *Faust*. Ed. and trans. Bayard Taylor. 1870. Boston: Houghton Mifflin, 1924.

Golomstock, Igor. *Totalitarian Art in the Soviet Union, the Third Reich, Fascist Italy, and the People's Republic of China*. Trans. Robert Chandler. New York: Icon Editions, 1990.

Gourevitch, Peter Alexis. *Politics in Hard Times: Comparative Responses to International Economic Crises*. Ithaca, N.Y.: Cornell UP, 1986.

Graham, John. "Lavater's Physiognomy in England." *Journal of the History of Ideas* 22 (Oct.–Dec. 1961): 561–72.

Grey, Robin Sandra. "Surmising the Infidel: Interpreting Melville's Annotations on Milton's Poetry." *Milton Quarterly* 26 (Dec. 1992): 103–13.

Grierson, H. J. C. "Lord Byron." *The Nation and Athenaeum*, Apr. 19, 1924, 81–83.

———. *Carlyle and Hitler*. 1933. Cambridge: Folcroft Library, 1973.

Griffiths, Richard. *Fellow Travellers of the Right: British Enthusiasts for Nazi Germany 1933–39*. London: Constable, 1980.

Gross, Paul R., and Norman J. Levitt. *Higher Superstition: The Academic Left and Science*. Baltimore: Johns Hopkins UP, 1994.

Grossinger, Richard, ed. *An Olson-Melville Sourcebook*. Vol. 1. Plainfield, Vt.: North Atlantic Books, 1976.

Gruber, Carol S. *Mars and Minerva: World War I and the Uses of Higher Learning in America*. Baton Rouge: Louisiana State UP, 1975.

Gundolf, Friedrich. "Bismarck's Reflections and Reminiscences as a Literary Monument." *The Criterion* (1939): 179–94.

Hall, H. Lark. *V. L. Parrington: Through the Avenue of Art*. Kent, Ohio: Kent State UP, 1994.

Hall, James B. "*Moby Dick:* Parable of a Dying System." *Western Review* (Spring 1950): 223–26.

Hall, Newton M. "The Study of American Literature in Colleges." *Andover Review* (July–Dec. 1892): 154–62.

Hannay, James. "A Notice of His Life and Times." In *The Poetical Works of Edgar Allan Poe*. London, 1853.

Harris, Abram L. "Sombart and German (National) Socialism." *Journal of Political Economy* 50 (Dec. 1942): 805–35.

Harrison, John R. *The Reactionaries: A Study of the Anti-Democratic Intelligentsia*. New York: Schocken, 1967.

Hart, Henry, ed. *The Writer in a Changing World*. New York: Equinox Press, 1937.

Harvard University. Committee on the Objectives of a General Education in a Free Society. *General Education in a Free Society*. Cambridge, Mass.: Harvard UP, 1945.

Harwitch, Alexander. *Aberrations in Sexual Life after the Psychopathio Sexualis . . . A Medico-Legal Study for Doctors and Lawyers*. Springfield, Ill.: Charles Thomas, 1959.

Haskell, Juliana. *Bayard Taylor's Translation of Goethe's Faust*. New York: Columbia UP, 1908.

Haven, Gilbert, and Thomas Russell. *Father Taylor, the Sailor Preacher*. Boston: H. B. Russell, 1872.

Hawthorne, Julian. *Hawthorne and His Circle*. New York: Harper, 1903.

———. *The Memoirs of Julian Hawthorne.* Ed. Edith Garrigues Hawthorne. New York: Macmillan, 1938.

Hawthorne, Nathaniel. *The Complete Short Stories of Nathaniel Hawthorne.* Garden City, N.J.: Hanover House, 1959.

Hayek, F. A. *Individualism: True and False.* Oxford: Blackwell, 1946.

Hayford, Harrison. "Melville and Hawthorne: A Biographical and Critical Study." Ph.D. diss., Yale University, 1945.

———. *Melville's "Monody" Really for Hawthorne?* Evanston, Ill.: Northwestern UP, 1990.

———. "The Melville Society: A Retrospective." *Melville Society Extracts* 88 (Mar. 1992): 3.

Hayford, Harrison, and Merrell R. Davis. "Herman Melville as Office-Seeker." *Modern Language Quarterly* 10 (June and Sept. 1949): 168–83, 377–88.

Hayford, Harrison, and Hershel Parker, eds. *Moby-Dick as Doubloon: Essays and Extracts (1851–1970).* New York: Norton, 1970.

Hayford, Harrison, and Merton M. Sealts, Jr., eds. *Billy Budd, Sailor (An Inside Narrative): Reading Text and Genetic Text.* Chicago: U of Chicago P, 1962.

Heck, Chester R. "The American Way in Colleges." *Harvard Educational Review* (Mar. 1938): 228–36.

Heffernan, James A. W., ed. *Representing the French Revolution: Literature, Historiography, and Art.* Hanover, N.H.: UP of New England, 1992.

Heffernan, Thomas F. "Melville and Wordsworth." *American Literature* 49 (Nov. 1977): 338–51.

Heimert, Alan. "*Moby-Dick* and American Political Symbolism." *American Quarterly* 15 (1963): 498–534.

Heine, Heinrich. *Doktor Faust: A Dance Poem.* Trans. and ed. Basil Ashmore. London: Peter Nevill, 1952.

Herbert, T. Walter. *"Moby-Dick" and Calvinism: A World Dismantled.* New Brunswick, N.J.: Rutgers UP, 1977.

———. Book Review. *Melville Society Extracts* 108 (Mar. 1997): 33–35.

Herding, Klaus. "Visual Codes in the Graphic Codes of the French Revolution." In Burlingham and Cuno, *French Caricature and the French Revolution.*

Herman, Ellen. *The Romance of American Psychology: Political Culture in the Age of Experts.* Berkeley: U of California P, 1995.

Herzog, Don. *Poisoning the Minds of the Lower Orders.* Princeton: Princeton UP, 1998.

Heyl, Barbara S. "The Harvard 'Pareto' Circle." *Journal of the History of the Behavioral Sciences* 4 (1968): 316–34.

Hicks, Granville. *The Great Tradition.* New York: Macmillan, 1935.

———. "The Literary Opposition to Utilitarianism." *Science & Society* (Summer 1937): 454–72.

Higgins, Brian, and Hershel Parker, eds. *Herman Melville: The Contemporary Reviews.* Cambridge, Eng.: Cambridge UP, 1995.

Higham, John. *Strangers in the Land: Patterns of American Nativism, 1860–1925.* Corrected and new preface. New York: Atheneum, 1963.

Higonnet, Patrice L. R. *Sister Republics: The Origins of French and American Republicanism.* Cambridge, Mass.: Harvard UP, 1988.

Hill, Christopher. *Milton and the English Revolution.* New York: Viking, 1977.

Hobsbawm, Eric J. *Nations and Nationalism since 1780: Programme, Myth, Reality.* Cambridge, Eng.: Cambridge UP, 1990.

———. "The Perils of the New Nationalism." *Nation,* Nov. 4, 1991, 537, 555–56.

Hoffman, Ross J. S. "The Totalitarian Régimes." *American Review* 9 (Sept. 1937): 336–38.

Hofstadter, Richard. *The Age of Reform: From Bryant to F.D.R.* New York: Knopf, 1955.

———. *Anti-Intellectualism in American Life*. New York: Knopf, 1963.

Hogben, Lancelot. "Our Social Heritage." *Science & Society* (Winter 1937): 150–51.

Holliday, Carl. "A Need in the Study of American Literature." *School and Society* 4 (Aug. 5, 1916): 220–22.

Hollinger, David A. *Post-Ethnic America: Beyond Multiculturalism*. New York: Basic Books, 1995.

Hoopes, James. *Van Wyck Brooks: In Search of American Culture*. Amherst: U of Massachusetts P, 1977.

Horsford, Howard C., ed. *Journal of a Visit to Europe and the Levant: 1856–1857*. Princeton: Princeton UP, 1955.

Howard, Leon. *Herman Melville*. Berkeley: U of California P, 1951.

———. Historical Note. *The Writings of Herman Melville*. Vol. 1. Evanston and Chicago: Northwestern University and Newberry Library, 1968.

———. *The Unfolding of Moby-Dick: Essays on Evidence by Leon Howard*. Ed. James Barbour and Thomas Quirk. Glassboro, N.J.: Melville Society, 1987.

Howe, Daniel Walker. *The Political Culture of the American Whigs*. Chicago: U of Chicago P, 1979.

Hughes, H. Stuart. *Consciousness and Society: The Reorientation of European Social Thought 1890–1930*. New York: Random House, 1958.

Hume, David. *The History of England from the Invasion of Julius Caesar to the Revolution of 1688*. 8 vols. London: Dove, 1822.

Huxley, Julian, and A. C. Haddon. *We Europeans*. London: Harper, 1936.

Hyman, Sidney. *The Lives of William Benton*. Chicago: U of Chicago P, 1969.

[William] Jackson Committee Report. "Propaganda and Information Activities in the Free World." *Declassified Documents Catalog: 1988*. Reading, Conn.: Research Associates, ca. 1952. No. 1163.

Jacob, Margaret C. *The Radical Enlightenment: Pantheists, Freemasons, and Republicans*. London: Allen and Unwin, 1981.

Jacoby, Sanford M. *Modern Manors: Welfare Capitalism since the New Deal*. Princeton: Princeton UP, 1997.

James, C. L. R. *Mariners, Renegades and Castaways: The Story of Herman Melville and the World We Live In*. New York: Privately published, 1953.

James, William. "What Pragmatism Means." In *Pragmatism and American Culture*. Ed. Gail Kennedy. Boston: Heath, 1950.

Jameson, Fredric. *Marxism and Form*. Princeton: Princeton UP, 1971.

Jancovich, Mark. *The Cultural Politics of the New Criticism*. New York: Cambridge UP, 1993.

Johnson, Edgar. "Henry Adams, the Last Liberal." *Science & Society* (Spring 1937): 376–77.

Johnson, Samuel. *Rasselas*. London, 1759.

Jones, Howard Mumford. *The Theory of American Literature*. Ithaca, N.Y.: Cornell UP, 1948.

Jung, Carl. "Individual and Mass Psychology." *Essays on Contemporary Events*. London: Kegan Paul, 1946.

Kallen, Horace M. *Culture and Democracy in the United States: Studies in the Group Psychology of the American Peoples*. New York: Boni and Liveright, 1924.

Kaplan, Sidney. "Herman Melville and the American National Sin: The Meaning of 'Benito Cereno.'" *Journal of Negro History* 41 (1956): 311–38, 224–29.

Karanikas, Alexander. *Tillers of a Myth: Southern Agrarians as Social and Literary Critics*. Madison: U of Wisconsin P, 1966.

Karcher, Carolyn L. *Shadow over the Promised Land: Slavery, Race, and Violence in Melville's America*. Baton Rouge: Louisiana State UP, 1980.

———. "Herman Melville 1819–1891." In *The Heath Anthology of American Literature*. Vol. 1. Gen. Ed. Paul Lauter. Lexington, Mass.: Heath, 1990.

Kautsky, Karl. *Social Foundations of Christianity.* Trans. Henry F. Mins. New York: S. A. Russell, 1953.

Kazin, Alfred. *A Lifetime Burning in Every Moment.* New York: HarperCollins, 1996.

Kelley, Wyn. "Melville's Cain." *American Literature* (Mar. 1983): 24–40.

Kenney, Alice P. *The Gansevoorts of Albany: Dutch Patricians in the Upper Hudson Valley.* Syracuse: Syracuse UP, 1969.

[Kingsley, Charles]. *Alton Locke, Tailor and Poet: An Autobiography.* Ed. Elizabeth A. Cripps. Oxford: Oxford UP, 1983.

Klehr, Harvey, John Earl Haynes, and Fridrikh Igorevich Firsov. *The Secret World of American Communism.* New Haven: Yale UP, 1995.

Kligerman, Charles. "The Psychology of Herman Melville." *Psychoanalytic Review* 40 (Apr. 1953): 125–43.

Kring, Walter D. Introduction. *The Endless, Winding Way in Melville: New Charts by Kring and Carey.* Ed. Donald Yannella and Hershel Parker. Glassboro, N.J.: Melville Society, 1981.

Lasswell, Harold D. *Politics: Who Gets What, When, How.* New York: McGraw-Hill, 1936.

———. *Democracy through Public Opinion.* Menasha, Wisc.: George Banta Book Co. (Chi Omega Research Fund), 1941.

———. *Power and Personality.* New York: Norton, 1948.

———. *National Security and Individual Freedom.* New York: McGraw-Hill, 1950.

Lasswell, Harold D., Daniel Lerner, and Ithiel de Sola Pool. *The Comparative Study of Symbols: An Introduction.* Stanford: Hoover Institute, 1952.

Lauter, Paul. "Melville Climbs the Canon." *American Literature* (Mar. 1994): 1–24.

Lavater, J. C. *Physiognomy; or The Corresponding Analogy between the Conformation of the Features, and the Ruling Passions of the Mind.* Trans. Samuel Shaw. London: H. D. Symonds, 1790.

———. *Physiognomical Sketches of Lavater, Engraved from the Original Drawings by John Luffman.* London, 1802.

Lawrence, D. H. *Studies in Classic American Literature.* New York: T. Seltzer, 1923.

———. *Pornography and Obscenity Handbook for Censors.* Michigan City, Ind.: Fridtjof-Kula Publications, 1958.

Lawson, John Howard. *The Hidden Heritage.* New York: Citadel Press, 1950.

Leander, Folke. "The Materialistic and the Humanistic Interpretations of History." *American Review* 9 (Sept. 1937): 380–406.

Lebzelter, Gisela C. *Political Anti-Semitism in England 1918–1939.* London: Macmillan, 1978.

Leisy, Ernest E. "The Significance of Recent Scholarship in American Literature." *College English* (Nov. 1940): 115–24.

Leverenz, David. "Class Conflicts in Teaching *Moby-Dick.*" In Bickman, ed., *Approaches to Teaching Melville's "Moby-Dick."*

———. *Manhood and the American Renaissance.* Ithaca, N.Y.: Cornell UP, 1989.

Levi, Primo. *The Periodic Table.* Trans. Raymond Rosenthal. New York: Schocken, 1984.

Levine, Lawrence W. *The Opening of the American Mind.* Boston: Beacon Press, 1996.

Levinger, Rabbi Lee J. *Anti-Semitism in the United States: Its History and Causes.* New York: Bloch, 1925.

Levitt, Norman J. *Prometheus Bedeviled: Science and the Contradictions of Contemporary Culture.* New Brunswick, N.J.: Rutgers UP, 1999.

Levy, Leonard W. *The Law of the Commonwealth and Chief Justice Shaw.* Cambridge, Mass.: Harvard UP, 1957.

Lewis, David Stephen. *Illusions of Grandeur: Mosley, Fascism and British Society 1931–81.* Manchester: U of Manchester P, 1987.

Lewisohn, Ludwig. "The Weakness of Herman Melville." *This Quarter* 3 (April-June 1931): 610–17.

Leyda, Jay. "The Army of the Potomac Entertains a Poet." *Twice-a-Year* 16 (1948): 259–72.

———, ed. Introduction. *Complete Stories of Herman Melville.* New York: Random House, 1949.

———. *The Melville Log: A Documentary Life of Herman Melville.* New York: Harcourt Brace, 1951.

———, ed. Introduction. *The Portable Melville.* New York: Viking, 1952.

———. "The Reminiscences of Jay Leyda." 2 vols. Columbia University Oral History Collection, 1981.

Litwack, Leon F. *North of Slavery.* Chicago: U of Chicago P, 1961.

Longhurst, Derek. "'Not for all time, but for an Age': An Approach to Shakespeare Studies." In *Re-Reading English.* Ed. Peter Widdowson. London: Methuen, 1982. 150–63.

Lovejoy, Frank O. *The Great Chain of Being: The History of an Idea.* 1936. Cambridge, Mass.: Harvard UP, 1953.

Lowenfish, Lee Elihu. "The American Testament of a Revolutionary." *Columbia University Columns* (Feb. 1978): 3–13.

Lowenthal, Leo. *Literature and the Image of Man.* New Brunswick, N.J.: Transaction, 1986.

Lowman, Moses. *A Dissertation on the Civil Government of the Hebrews. In Which the True Designs and Nature of Their Government are Explained. The Justice, Wisdom and Goodness of the Mosaical Constitutions are vindicated; in particular from some late, unfair and false representations of them in the Moral Philosopher.* London, 1740.

Lüdeke, H. "American Literature in Germany: A Report of Recent Research and Criticism 1931–1933." *American Literature* 6 (1934): 168–75.

Lukács, Georg. *Goethe and His Age.* London: Merlin Press, 1968.

Lynd, Robert S. *Knowledge for What? The Place of Social Science in American Culture.* Princeton: Princeton UP, 1939.

Lynn, Kenneth S. "Lemuel Shaw and Herman Melville." *Constitutional Commentary* 5 (1988): 411–28.

McDougall, William. *Religion and the Sciences of Life, with Other Essays on Allied Topics.* Durham, N.C.: Duke UP, 1934.

McFarland, Gerald W. *Mugwumps, Morals, and Politics, 1884–1920.* Amherst: U of Massachusetts P, 1975.

MacPhee, Lawrence. *Monarch Notes and Study Guide.* New York: Simon and Schuster, 1964.

McPherson, James M. "The Ballot and Land for the Freedmen, 1861–65." In *Reconstruction: An Anthology of Revisionist Writings.* Ed. Kenneth M. Stampp and Leon F. Litwack. Baton Rouge: Louisiana State UP, 1969.

McQuaid, Kim. *Big Business and Presidential Power from FDR to Reagan.* New York: William Morrow, 1982.

Magidoff, Robert. "American Literature in Russia." *Saturday Review of Literature* 2 (Nov. 1946): 271–73.

Mailer, Norman. "Henry Miller: Genius and Lust, Narcissism." *American Review* (Apr. 1976): 1–40.

Malvasi, Mark G. *The Unregenerate South: The Agrarian Thought of John Crowe Ransom, Allen Tate, and Donald Davidson.* Baton Rouge: Louisiana State UP, 1997.

Mangold, Charlotte Weiss. "Herman Melville in German Criticism from 1900 to 1955." Ph.D. diss., University of Maryland, 1959.

Mann, Thomas. Introduction. *The Permanent Goethe.* New York: Dial Press, 1948.

Mansfield, Luther S., and Howard P. Vincent, eds. Introduction and Notes. *Moby-Dick.* By Herman Melville. New York: Hendricks House, 1952.

Markels, Julian. *Melville and the Politics of Identity: From King Lear to Moby-Dick.* Urbana: U of Illinois P, 1993.

Marks, John D. *The Search for the Manchurian Candidate: The CIA and Mind Control.* New York: New York Times Books, 1979.

Martin, Terence. *Teaching a Novel: Moby-Dick in the Classroom.* New York: College Entrance Examination Board, 1965.

Marx, Leo. "The Machine in the Garden." *New England Quarterly* 29 (1956): 27–42.

———. "Double Consciousness and the Cultural Politics of F. O. Matthiessen." *Monthly Review* 34 (1983): 34–56.

Mason, Ronald. *The Spirit above the Dust.* London: John Lehmann, 1951.

Masson, David. *The Three Devils: Luther's, Milton's, and Goethe's.* London: Macmillan, 1874.

Matthews, Brander. "Suggestions for Teachers of American Literature." *Educational Review* (Jan. 1901): 11–16.

Matthiessen, F. O. *American Renaissance: Art and Expression in the Age of Emerson and Whitman.* New York: Oxford UP, 1941.

———. Introduction. *Herman Melville Selected Poems.* New York: Oxford UP, 1944.

———. *From the Heart of Europe.* New York: Oxford UP, 1948.

May, Henry Farnham. *The Divided Heart: Essays on Protestantism and the Enlightenment in America.* New York: Oxford UP, 1991.

Mayer, Arno J. *Wilson vs. Lenin: Political Origins of the New Diplomacy 1917–1918.* Cleveland: Meridian Books, 1964.

Meinecke, Friedrich. *The German Catastrophe.* Trans. Sidney Fay. Boston: Beacon Press, 1950.

Meisel, James H., ed. *Pareto and Mosca.* Englewood Cliffs, N.J.: Prentice-Hall, 1965.

Melville, Herman. *The Works of Herman Melville.* Standard ed. 16 vols. London: Constable, 1922–24.

———. *The Shorter Novels of Herman Melville.* Intro. Raymond Weaver. New York: H. Liveright, 1928.

———. *Journal Up the Straits, Oct. 11, 1856–May 5, 1857.* Ed. and intro. Raymond Weaver. New York: Colophon, 1935.

———. *The Writings.* Ed. Harrison Hayford, Hershel Parker, and G. Thomas Tanselle. Evanston and Chicago: Northwestern University and the Newberry Library, 1968–.

Meredith, George. *The Egoist: A Comedy in Narrative.* London: Kegan Paul, 1879.

Metcalf, Eleanor Melville, ed. *Journal of a Visit to London and the Continent by Herman Melville, 1849–1850.* Cambridge, Mass.: Harvard UP, 1948.

———. *Herman Melville: Cycle and Epicycle.* Cambridge, Mass.: Harvard UP, 1953.

Metcalf, Paul C. *Genoa: A Telling of Wonders.* 1965. Albuquerque: U of New Mexico P, 1991.

———, ed. *Enter Isabel: The Herman Melville Correspondence of Clare Spark and Paul Metcalf.* Ed. and annotated Paul Metcalf. Albuquerque: U of New Mexico P, 1991.

Metzger, Walter P. *Academic Freedom in the Age of the University.* New York: Columbia UP, 1955.

Miller, Donald L. *Lewis Mumford: A Life.* New York: Weidenfeld and Nicolson, 1989.

Miller, Edwin Haviland. *Melville.* New York: Braziller, 1975.

Milton, John. "The Christian Doctrine." In *John Milton: Complete Poems and Major Prose.* Ed. Merritt Y. Hughes. London: Macmillan, 1985.

Mitford, Reverend John. "Life of Milton." *Works.* London, 1851.

Moore, Barrington, Jr. *Political Power and Social Theory: Seven Studies.* New York: Harper Torchbook, 1962.

Morgan, George Allen. *What Nietzsche Means.* Cambridge, Mass.: Harvard UP, 1941.

Morgan, Thomas. *The Moral Philosopher in a Dialogue between Philalethes a Christian Deist, and Theophanes a Christian Jew.* 1659. 2nd ed. London, 1738.

Mosse, George L. *Nazi Culture: Intellectual, Cultural and Social Life in the Third Reich.* New York: Grosset and Dunlap, 1966.

————. *Germans and Jews: The Right, the Left and the Search for a Third Force in Pre-Nazi Germany.* New York: Howard Fertig, 1970.

————. *Toward the Final Solution: A History of European Racism.* New York: Howard Fertig, 1978.

————, ed. *International Facism.* London: Sage, 1979.

————. *Confronting the Nation: Jewish and Western Nationalism.* Waltham: Brandeis UP, 1993.

Mumford, Lewis. *Herman Melville.* New York: Literary Guild, 1929.

————. *The Myth of the Machine.* New York: Harcourt Brace Jovanovich, 1967–70.

————. "Herman Melville." In *Atlantic Brief Lives: A Biographical Companion to the Arts.* Ed. Louis Kronenberger. Boston: Little, Brown, 1971.

————. *My Works and Days: A Personal Chronicle.* New York: Harcourt Brace, 1979.

Murphy, Gardner. "Essentials for a Civilian Morale Program in American Democracy." In *Civilian Morale: Second Yearbook of the Society for the Psychological Study of Social Issues.* New York: Reynal and Hitchcock, 1942.

Murray, Henry A. *Explorations in Personality.* New York: Science Editions, 1938.

————. "What Should Psychologists Do About Psychoanalysis?" *Journal of Abnormal and Social Psychology* 35 (1940): 150–75.

————. "Time for a Positive Morality." *Survey Graphic* (Mar. 1947): 195–96, 214–16.

————. "America's Mission." *Survey Graphic* (Oct. 1948): 411–15.

————. *Assessment of Men: Selection of Personnel for the U.S. Office of Strategic Services.* New York: Rinehart, 1948.

————. Introduction and Notes. *Pierre.* New York: Hendricks House, 1949.

————. "'In Nomine Diaboli.'" In *Moby-Dick Centennial Essays.* Ed. for the Melville Society and intro. Tyrus Hillway and Luther S. Mansfield. Dallas: Southern Methodist UP, 1953.

————. Review of Leon Howard, *Herman Melville* and William H. Gilman, *Melville's Early Life and "Redburn." Modern Language Notes* (Jan. 1953): 60–62.

————. "Bartleby and I." In *Bartleby the Scrivener: A Symposium by Henry A. Murray [and Others].* Ed. Howard P. Vincent. Kent, Ohio: Kent State UP, ca. 1966. 3–24.

————. "Allan Melvill's By-Blow." *Melville Society Extracts* 61 (Feb. 1985): 1–6.

Murray, Henry A., and Christiana Morgan. "A Method for Investigating Fantasies: The Thematic Apperception Test." *Archives of Neurology and Psychiatry* 34 (1935): 289–306.

Myers, Henry Alonzo. *Are Men Equal? An Inquiry into the Meaning of American Democracy.* ca. 1945. Ithaca, N.Y.: Cornell UP, 1955.

New York State Legislature. Joint Committee Investigating Seditious Activities. *Revolutionary radicalism: Its history, purpose and tactics with an exposition and discussion of the steps being taken and required to curb it, being the report of the joint legislative committee investigating seditious activities filed April 24, 1920 in the Senate of the State of New York.* Albany: J. B. Lyon, 1920.

Niebuhr, Reinhold. "The Truth in Myths." In *Evolution and Religion: The Conflict between Science and Theology in Modern America.* Ed. Gail Kennedy. Lexington, Mass.: D. C. Heath, 1957.

Norris, Christopher. *Uncritical Theory: Postmodernism, Intellectuals and the Gulf War.* London: Lawrence and Wishart, 1992.

Nye, Robert C. *The Origins of Crowd Psychology: Gustave Le Bon and Crisis of Mass Democracy in the Third Republic.* London: Sage Publications, 1975.

————. *The Anti-Democratic Sources of Élite Theory: Pareto, Mosca, and Michels.* London: Sage Publications, 1977.

Olson, Charles. "The Growth of Herman Melville, Prose Writer and Poetic Thinker." Master's thesis, Wesleyan University, 1933.

————. "Lear and *Moby-Dick.*" *Twice-a-Year* 1 (1938): 165–89.

————. *Call Me Ishmael.* New York: Reynal and Hitchcock, 1947.

————. *Charles Olson and Ezra Pound: An Encounter at St. Elizabeth's.* Ed. Catherine Seelye. New York: Grossman, 1975.

————. *The Post Office: A Memoir of His Father.* Intro. George F. Butterick. Bolinas, Calif.: Grey Fox Press, 1975.

————. *Charles Olson and Cid Corman: Complete Correspondence 1950–1964.* Ed. George Evans. Orono, Maine: National Poetry Foundation, 1987.

————. *In Love, in Sorrow: The Complete Correspondence of Charles Olson and Edward Dahlberg.* Ed. Paul Christensen. New York: Paragon House, 1990.

Ovid. *Metamorphoses.* Trans. A. D. Melville. Oxford, Eng.: Oxford UP, 1978.

Paltsits, Victor Hugo, ed. *Family Correspondence of Herman Melville 1830–1904 in the Gansevoort-Lansing Collection.* New York: New York Public Library, 1929.

Pareto, Vilfredo. *Sociological Writings.* Selected and intro. S. E. Finer. Trans. Derick Mirfin. London: Pall Mall Press, 1966.

Parker, Bruce R. "Political Thought of the American Renaissance: Melville and Parkman." Ph.D. diss., University of California, Berkeley, 1973.

Parker, Hershel. "Herman Melville and Politics: A Scrutiny of the Political Milieux of Herman Melville's Life and Works." Ph.D. diss., Northwestern University, 1963.

————, ed. *Gansevoort Melville's 1846 London Journal and Letters from England, 1845.* New York: New York Public Library, 1966.

————. *The Recognition of Herman Melville.* Ann Arbor: U of Michigan P, 1967.

————. "Melville and the Berkshires." In *American Literature: The New England Heritage.* Ed. James Nagel and Richard Astro. New York: Garland, 1981.

————. Historical Note. *Moby-Dick.* Evanston and Chicago: Northwestern UP and the Newberry Library, 1988.

————. *Reading Billy Budd.* Evanston, Ill.: Northwestern UP, 1990.

————. *Herman Melville: A Biography, Volume I, 1819–1851.* Baltimore: Johns Hopkins UP, 1996.

Parkes, Henry Bamford. "Poe, Hawthorne, Melville: An Essay in Sociological Criticism." *Partisan Review* 16 (Feb. 1949): 157–66.

Parks, Aileen Wells. "Leviathan: An Essay in Interpretation." *Sewanee Review* 47 (1939): 130–32.

Parsons, Frank. "The Great Coal Strike and Its Lessons." *Arena* (Jan. 1903): 1–7.

Parsons, Talcott. "Propaganda and Social Control." *Psychiatry* 5 (Nov. 1942): 551–72.

Pattee, Fred Lewis. "Herman Melville." *American Mercury,* Jan. 1927, 33–43.

————. *Century Readings in American Literature.* 1919. London, 1932.

Pease, Donald E. "*Moby Dick* and the Cold War." In *The American Renaissance Reconsidered.* Ed. Walter Benn Michaels and Donald E. Pease. Baltimore: Johns Hopkins UP, 1985. 113–55.

————. *Visionary Compacts: American Renaissance Writings in Cultural Context.* Madison: U of Wisconsin P, 1987.

The Pentagon Papers: The Defense Department History of United States Decisionmaking on Vietnam. Ed. Senator Gravel. Boston: Beacon, 1971–72.

Phelps, Leland R. "The Reaction to 'Benito Cereno' and *Billy Budd* in Germany." *Symposium* 13 (1959): 294–99.

Phillips, William, and Philip Rahv. "Some Aspects of Literary Criticism." *Science & Society* 1 (Winter 1937): 212–20.

Picart, Bernard. *The Ceremonies and Religious Customs of the Various Nations of the Known World.* Vol. 5. London, 1736.

Pletcher, David M. *The Diplomacy of Annexation: Texas, Oregon and the Mexican War.* Columbia: U of Missouri P, 1973.

Porter, Roy. "Making Faces: Physiognomy and Fashion in Eighteenth-Century England." *Études Anglaises* (Oct.–Dec. 1985): 385–96.

———. "Seeing the Past." *Past and Present* 118 (Feb. 1988): 186–205.

———. *Enlightenment: Britain and the Creation of the Modern World*. London: Penguin, 2000.

Puett, Amy Elizabeth. "Melville's Wife: A Study of Elizabeth Shaw Melville." Ph.D. diss., Northwestern University, 1970.

Rahv, Philip. "Two Years of Progress—From Waldo Frank to Donald Ogden Stewart." *Partisan Review* 4 (1938): 22–30.

———. "The Cult of Experience." *Partisan Review* (Nov.–Dec.1940): 412–24.

———. "Melville and His Critics." *Partisan Review* 17 (1950): 732–35.

Ransom, John Crowe. "The Aesthetics of Regionalism." *American Review* 2 (1934): 290–310.

Rapaport, Herman. "*Paradise Lost* and the Novel." In *Approaches to Teaching Milton's* Paradise Lost. Ed. Galbraith M. Crump. New York: MLA, 1986.

Rasco, Laven. "The Biographies of Herman Melville." Ph.D. diss., Northwestern University, 1957.

Reichenbach, Hans. *The Rise of Scientific Philosophy*. Berkeley: U of California P, 1951.

Reising, Russell J. *The Unusable Past: Theory and the Study of American Literature*. London: Methuen, 1986.

Renker, Elizabeth. "Melville, Wife-Beating, and the Written Page." *American Literature* (Mar. 1994): 123–50.

Reynolds, Larry J. *European Revolutions and the American Literary Renaissance*. New Haven, Conn.: Yale UP, 1988.

———. "Melville and the New Historicism." *Melville Society Extracts* 95 (Dec. 1993): 17–20.

Rice, Stuart A., ed. *Methods in Social Science: A Case Book Compiled under the Direction of the Committee on Scientific Method in the Social Sciences of the Social Science Research Council*. Chicago: U of Chicago P, 1931.

Riegel, O. W. "The Anatomy of Melville's Fame." *American Literature* 3 (1931): 195–203.

Robertson-Lorant, Laurie. *Melville: A Biography*. New York: Clarkson Potter, 1996.

Robinson, Forrest G. *Love's Story Told: A Life of Henry A. Murray*. Cambridge, Mass.: Harvard UP, 1992.

Rogin, Michael Paul. *Subversive Genealogy: The Politics and Art of Herman Melville*. New York: Knopf, 1983.

Rosenberg, Edgar. *From Shylock to Svengali: Jewish Stereotypes in English Fiction*. Stanford, Calif.: Stanford UP, 1960.

Ross, Steven J. "Struggles for the Screen: Workers, Radicals, and the Political Uses of Silent Film." *American History Review* 96 (Apr. 1991): 333–67.

———. *Working-Class Hollywood: Silent Film and the Shaping of Class in America*. Princeton: Princeton UP, 1998.

Rossiter, Clinton, ed. *The Federalist Papers*. New York: New American Library, 1961.

Rouse, H. Blair. "Democracy, American Literature, and Mr. Fast." *English Journal* 36 (1947): 321–23.

Ruether, Rosemary Radford. *Faith and Fratricide: The Theological Roots of Antisemitism*. New York: Seabury Press, 1974.

Rydell, Robert W. *All the World's a Fair: Visions of Empire at American International Expositions, 1876–1916*. Chicago: U of Chicago P, 1984.

Sadleir, Michael. *Privilege*. New York: G. P. Putnam, 1921.

———. *The Noblest Frailty*. London: Constable, 1925.

———. *Excursions in Victorian Bibliography*. London: Chaundy and Cox, 1922.

———. Introduction. *The Dunciad of Today: A Satire and the Modern Aesop*. By Benjamin Disraeli. London: Ingpen and Grant, 1928.

———. *Studs Lonigan, by James T. Farrell: An Appreciation by Michael Sadleir*. London: Constable, 1936.

———. *Michael Ernest Sadleir, 1861–1943: A Memoir by His Son*. London: Constable, 1949.

———. *The Autobiography of a Bibliomaniac.* Berkeley: University of California Library, 1962.

Schapiro, J. Salwyn. *Condorcet and the Rise of Liberalism.* 1934. New York: Octagon Reprint, 1978.

Schapiro, Meyer. "Looking Forward to Looking Backward." *Partisan Review* (June 1938): 12–24.

Schmidt, Carl Theodore. *The Corporate State in Action: Italy under Fascism.* New York: Oxford UP, 1939.

Schmitt, Carl. "A Note on Europe." *American Review* 9 (1937): 407–10.

Schrecker, Ellen. *No Ivory Tower.* New York: Oxford UP, 1986.

Schultz, Elizabeth A. *Unpainted to the Last: "Moby-Dick" and Twentieth-Century Art.* Lawrence: U of Kansas P, 1995.

Schurz, Carl. *Charles Sumner: An Essay by Carl Schurz.* Ed. Arthur Reed Hogue. Urbana: U of Illinois P, 1951.

Schwartz, Stephen. *Brotherhood of the Sea: A History of the Sailors' Union of the Pacific, 1885–1985.* New Brunswick, N.J.: Transaction, 1986.

———. *From West to East: California and the Making of the American Mind.* New York: Free Press, 1998.

Scudder, H. E. "American Classics in School." *Atlantic Monthly* (July 1887): 85–91.

Sealts, Merton M., Jr. *Early Lives of Melville.* Madison: U of Wisconsin P, 1974.

———. *Melville as Lecturer.* Cambridge, Mass.: Harvard UP, 1957.

———. *Pursuing Melville 1940–1980.* Madison: U of Wisconsin P, 1982.

Sedgwick, William Ellery. *Herman Melville: The Tragedy of Mind.* Cambridge, Mass.: Harvard UP, 1944.

Seton-Watson, Hugh. "The Age of Fascism and Its Legacy." In *International Fascism.* Ed. George L. Mosse. London: Sage, 1979.

Shafer, Robert E. "Teaching Sequences for Hawthorne and Melville." In *The Teacher and American Literature: Papers Presented at the 1964 Convention of the National Council of Teachers of English.* Ed. Lewis Leary. Champaign, Ill.: National Council of Teachers of English, 1965.

Shelley, Percy Bysshe. *The Cenci: A Tragedy in Five Acts.* Intro. Alfred Forman and H. Buxton Forman. Prologue John Todhunter. New York: Phacton Press, 1970.

Shneidman, Edwin S., ed. *Endeavors in Psychology: Selections from the Personology of Henry A. Murray.* New York: Harper & Row, 1981.

Short, R. W. "Melville as Symbolist." In *Interpretations of American Literature.* Ed. Charles Feidelson, Jr,. and Paul Brodtkorb, Jr. New York: Oxford UP, 1959.

Sillen, Samuel. Review of Van Wyck Brooks, *The Flowering of New England. Science & Society* (Winter 1937): 262–65.

Simon, Elena Pinto, and David Stirk. "Chronology." *Jay Leyda: A Life's Work.* New York: New York University Tisch School of the Arts, 1988.

Simon, Jean. *Herman Melville, Marin, Poète, et Métaphysicien.* Paris, 1939.

Slochower, Harry. *Mythopoesis: Mythic Patterns in the Literary Classics.* Detroit: Wayne State UP, 1970.

Sluzki, Carlos E., and Donald C. Ransom, eds. *Double Bind: The Foundation of the Communicational Approach to the Family.* New York: Grune & Stratton, 1976.

Smith, Adam. *The Theory of Moral Sentiments.* London: 1777.

Smith, Bernard, ed. *The Democratic Spirit.* Rev. ed. New York: Knopf, 1945.

Smith, David N. "Authorities, Deities and Commodities." Ph.D. diss., University of Wisconsin, 1988.

Snow, Wilbert. *Codline's Child: The Autobiography of Wilbert Snow.* Middletown, Conn.: Wesleyan UP, 1974.

Sokal, Michael M., ed. *An Education in Psychology: James McKeen Cattell's Journals and Letters from Germany and England, 1880–1888.* Cambridge, Mass.: MIT Press, 1981.

Soloway, Richard A. "Reform or Ruin: English Moral Thought during the First French Republic." *Review of Politics* (Jan. 1963): 110–27.

Spanos, William V., Jr. *The Errant Art of Moby-Dick: The Canon, the Cold War, and the Struggle for American Studies.* Durham, N.C.: Duke UP, 1995.

Spark, Clare L. "The 'Melville' Revival, 1919–1953: An Unclosed Case Study in Conservative Enlightenment." Ph.D. diss., UCLA, 1993.

———. "Klara Hitler's Son: Reading the Langer Report on Hitler's Mind." *Social Thought and Research* 22 (1999): 113–37.

Spiller, Robert E., ed. *The Van Wyck Brooks–Lewis Mumford Letters: The Record of a Literary Friendship, 1921–1963.* New York: Dutton, 1970.

Squire, J. C. *Socialism and Art.* Intro. Walter Crane. London: Twentieth Century Press, 1907.

Stafford, John. *The Literary Criticism of "Young America": A Study in the Relationship of Politics and Literature 1837–1850.* Berkeley: U of California P, 1952.

Stampp, Kenneth M. *The Era of Reconstruction 1865–1877.* New York: Knopf, 1965.

Steed, H. Wickham. *Hitler, Whence and Whither?* London: Nisbet, 1934.

Steel, Ronald. *Walter Lippmann and the American Century.* Boston: Little Brown, 1980.

Stoddard, Lothrop. *The Rising Tide of Color against White World-Supremacy.* New York: Scribner, 1920.

———. *The Revolt against Civilization: The Menace of the Under Man.* New York: Scribner, 1923.

Stokes, Roy. *Michael Sadleir 1888–1957.* Metuchen, N.J.: Scarecrow Press, 1980.

Stone, Geoffrey. "Left Wings over Europe." *American Review* 7 (Oct. 1936): 564–85.

———. "Excelsior." Review of Stephen Spender, *Forward from Liberalism. American Review* 9 (Sept. 1937): 296–305.

———. "The End of Democracy: Ralph Adams Cram's Plea for a New Order." *American Review* 9 (Sept. 1937): 365–79.

———. *Melville.* New York: Sheed and Ward, 1949.

Sudoplatov, Pavel, and Anatoli Sudoplatov, with Jerrold L. and Leona P. Schecter. *Special Tasks.* Boston: Little, Brown, 1994.

Swingewood, Alan. *The Novel and Revolution.* New York: Barnes and Noble Books, 1975.

Thomas, John L. *Alternative America: Henry George, Edward Bellamy, Henry Demarest Lloyd and the Adversary Tradition.* Cambridge, Mass.: Belknap Press, 1983.

Thompson, James Westfall. *A History of Historical Writing.* 2 vols. New York: Macmillan, 1942.

Thompson, Lawrance. *Melville's Quarrel with God.* Princeton: Princeton UP, 1952.

———. Foreword. *Pierre.* By Herman Melville. New York: New American Library, 1964.

Thorp, Willard, ed. *Representative Selections of Herman Melville.* New York: American Book Co., 1938.

———. "The Teacher and the New Approaches to American Literature." In *The Teacher and American Literature: Papers Presented at the 1964 Convention of the National Council of Teachers of English.* Ed. Lewis Leary. Champaign, Ill.: National Council of Teachers of English, 1965.

———. *Literary History of the United States.* Rev. ed. New York: Macmillan, 1974.

Thorpe, James. *Milton Criticism: Selections from Four Centuries.* London: Routledge & Kegan Paul, 1951.

Tillyard, E. M. W. *The Elizabethan World Picture.* New York: Macmillan, 1943.

Todd, Reverend Henry John. *Some Account of the Life and Writings of John Milton.* London, 1809.

Trilling, Diana. "Lionel Trilling: A Jew at Columbia." In *Speaking of Literature and Society.* Ed. Diana Trilling. New York: Harcourt Brace Jovanovich, 1980.

Trilling, Lionel. *The Middle of the Journey.* New York: Viking, 1947.

———. "A Recollection of Raymond Weaver." In *University on the Heights.* Ed. Wesley First. New York: Doubleday, 1958. 5–13.

———. "From the Notebooks of Lionel Trilling." *Partisan Review* 4 (1984): 496–515.

Triplet, Rodney G. "Henry A. Murray and the Harvard Psychological Clinic, 1926–1938: A Struggle to Expand the Disciplinary Boundaries of Academic Psychology." Ph.D. diss., University of New Hampshire, 1983.

Trotter, Wilfred. *Instincts of the Herd in Peace and War.* New York: Macmillan, 1947.

Turner, Frederick Jackson. *The United States 1830–1850.* 1935. New York: Norton, 1965.

Tuveson, Ernest Lee. *Redeemer Nation: The Idea of America's Millennial Role.* Chicago: U of Chicago P, 1968.

Underwood, John C. *Literature and Insurgency: Ten Studies in Racial Evolution.* New York: Mitchell Kennerley, 1914.

Vanderbilt, Kermit. *American Literature and the Academy: The Roots, Growth and Maturity of a Profession.* Philadelphia: University of Pennsylvania Press, 1986.

Van Doren, Carl. Introduction. *White-Jacket.* By Herman Melville. London: Oxford UP, World's Classics, 1929.

Van Doren, Carl, et al., eds. *The Cambridge History of American Literature.* 4 vols. New York: Cambridge UP, 1917.

Vickers, Daniel F. "Maritime Labor in Colonial Massachusetts: A Case Study of the Essex County Cod Fishery and the Whaling Industry of Nantucket, 1630–1775." Ph.D. diss., Princeton University, 1981.

Viereck, Peter. *Metapolitics: The Roots of the Nazi Mind.* New York: Capricorn Books, 1961.

———. "The Philosophical 'New Conservatism.'" In *The Radical Right.* Ed. Daniel Bell. New York: Doubleday, 1964. 185–207.

Vincent, Howard P. *The Trying-Out of Moby-Dick.* Boston: Houghton Mifflin, 1949.

Virgil's Works. Trans. J. W. Mackail. Bk. 2. New York: Modern Library, 1934.

Ware, Caroline F. Introduction. *The Cultural Approach to History.* New York: Columbia UP, 1940.

Warfel, Harry R., Ralph Henry Gabriel, and Stanley T. Williams, eds. *The American Mind: Selections from the Literature of the United States.* New York: American Book Co., 1937.

Watson, E. L. Grant. "Moby Dick." *London Mercury* 3 (1920): 180–86.

———. "Melville's *Pierre.*" *New England Quarterly* 3 (Apr. 1930): 195–234.

Watson, Goodwin. "Five Factors in Morale." *Civilian Morale: Second Yearbook of the Society for the Psychological Study of Social Issues.* New York: Houghton Mifflin for Reynal and Hitchcock, 1942.

Weaks, Mabel. "Long Ago and 'Faraway': Traces of Melville in the Marquesas in the Journal of A. G. Jones, 1854–1855." *Bulletin of the New York Public Library* (July 1948): 362–69.

Weaver, Raymond M. "The Centennial of Herman Melville." *Nation* 109 (Aug. 2, 1919): 145–46.

———. *Herman Melville: Mariner and Mystic.* New York: G. H. Doran, 1921.

———. *Black Valley.* New York: Viking, 1926.

———. Introduction. *The Counterfeiters.* By André Gide. New York: Modern Library, 1931.

Webber, G. C. *The Ideology of the British Right 1918–1939.* London: Croom Helm, 1986.

Weinreich, Max. *Hitler's Professors: The Part of German Scholarship in Germany's Crimes against the Jewish People.* New York: Yiddish Scientific Institute, 1946.

Weinstein, Allen. *Perjury: The Hiss-Chambers Case.* New York: Knopf, 1978.

Weiss, Philip. "Herman-Neutics." *New York Times Magazine,* Dec. 15, 1996, 60–65, 70–72.

Welles, C. Bradford. "The Hellenistic Orient." In *The Idea of History in the Ancient Near East.* Ed. Robert C. Dentan. New Haven, Conn.: Yale UP, 1953.

Wells, Henry W. "Herman Melville's *Clarel.*" *College English* 4 (May 1943): 478–83.

———. *The American Way of Poetry.* New York: Columbia UP, 1943.

———. "An Unobtrusive Democrat: Herman Melville." *South Atlantic Quarterly* (January 1944): 46–51.

White, George Abbott. "Ideology and Literature: American Renaissance and F. O. Matthiessen." In *Literature in Revolution*. Ed. George Abbott White and Charles Newman. New York: Holt, Rinehart, Winston, 1972. 430–500.

Williams, Stanley T. *Studies in Victorian Literature*. New York: Dutton, 1923.

———. "'Follow Your Leader,' Melville's 'Benito Cereno.'" *Virginia Quarterly Review* 23 (1947): 61–76.

Williams, Stanley T., and Nelson Adkins. *Courses of Reading in American Literature with Bibliographies*. New York: Harcourt Brace, 1930.

Winks, Robin W. *Cloak and Gown: Scholars in the Secret War, 1939–1961*. New York: Morrow, 1987.

Winters, Yvor. "Maule's Curse." *American Review* 9 (Sept. 1937): 339–61.

———. *Maule's Curse: Seven Studies in the History of American Obscurantism*. Norfolk, Conn.: New Directions, 1938.

Witcutt, W. P. "The Future of Capitalism: A Note on Werner Sombart." *American Review* 5 (Oct. 1935): 531–35.

Wollstonecraft, Mary. *An Historical and Moral View of the Origin and Progress of the French Revolution and the Effect It Has Produced in Europe*. Vol. 1. London, 1794.

Woodward, C. Vann. "The Political Legacy of Reconstruction." In *Reconstruction: An Anthology of Revisionist Writings*. Ed. Kenneth M. Stampp and Leon F. Litwack. Baton Rouge: Louisiana State UP, 1969.

Wright, Louis B. *The American Tradition: National Characteristics, Past and Present*. New York: F. S. Crofts, 1941.

Wright, Nathalia. "Melville and STW at Yale: Studies under Stanley T. Williams." *Melville Society Extracts* 70 (Sept. 1987): 1–4.

Yerkes, R. M. "Psychology and National Service." *Science*, Aug. 3, 1917, 101–3.

Young, Philip. *The Private Melville*. University Park: Penn State UP, 1991.

Young, Thomas Daniel. *Gentleman in a Dustcoat: A Biography of John Crowe Ransom*. Baton Rouge: Louisiana State UP, 1976.

Zimmerman, Michael P. "Herman Melville in the 1920s: A Study in the Origins of the Melville Revival with an Annotated Bibliography." Ph.D. diss., Columbia University, 1963.

Index

Bateson, Gregory: bipolarity in Western culture, 65–66; double bind in schizophrenia, 65 (*see also* Gorgon). *See also* Morale

Beard, Charles, 47–49

Benito Cereno: in "Benito Cereno," 91, 109, 353

Berthoff, Warner, 110, 133, 596n.55, 600n.84

Bezanson, Walter, 306, 334, 499, 539; life vs. art in *Clarel*, 123, 596n.58, 597n.61, 611n.48, 658n.64; Melville's mental states, 596n.54, 597n.60; Melville's mystery, 85

Billy Budd: in "Billy Budd," 87, 91, 109, 125–27, 178, 399, 411, 598n.73; in Revival, 89, 109–10, 226, 227, 229, 288, 296, 310, 313, 316, 372, 512

Birss, John H., 348, 423, 485–86, 488, 652n.38, 653n.43, 663n.85, 678n.54

Bolshevism, 18, 33, 54–59, 182, 208–9, 253, 316, 340, 433, 434, 572n.41, 578n.60, 607n.28, 617n.6, 687n.8

Bourne, Randolph: as aristocratic radical, 253, 641n.106; as ethnopluralist, 322, 573n.13, 580n.79, 581n.81

Braswell, William, 305, 378, 569n.26, 598n.76, 601n.91, 602n.10, 604n.16, 620n.12

Brodhead, Richard, 182, 197, 438, 616n.34

Brooks, Van Wyck, 249–52, 255, 297, 302, 305, 354–55, 574n.13, 628n.21, 660n.75, 662n.80

Burke, Edmund: aesthetic theory, 432–33, 681n.1, 682n.2; as organic conservative, 12, 35, 45, 85, 132, 310, 398, 436, 599n.82; as proto-progressive, 260, 405, 617n.6

Butler, Nicholas Murray, 46–54

Byron, Lord George Gordon: as Hebraic Ahab/Melville, 7–8, 26, 83, 132, 421, 430, 539, 598n.76, 602n.10; interest in Melville's marginalia to *Poetical Works*, 507, 533; precursor to Melville/Hitler (Murray), 244, 396, 428, 450; as Romantic Wandering Jew/Cain, 28, 117, 180, 182, 197, 390, 681n.73, 683n.21; Titanism transferred to German romantics/Ishmael, 372, 616n.37

Captain Ahab: in *Moby-Dick*, 16–17, 34, 39, 91, 94, 100–101, 108–9, 117, 128, 135–36, 138, 158, 160–61, 171–72, 177, 182–83, 196, 201, 244–45, 262–63, 285–87, 446, 451, 599n.83, 604n.19, 607n.26, 608n.31; in Revival, 7–8, 14, 17–18, 23, 25–27, 32, 34, 44, 52, 55, 59, 66, 74, 84, 137, 150, 180, 186, 197, 201, 207, 209, 221, 227, 237, 253–54, 256–57, 259–63, 268, 270, 285, 287, 291–97, 301, 303–4, 307, 309, 311, 314–15, 318–20, 322–26, 328, 350, 355–56, 369, 371–73, 375,

378, 389–91, 399–400, 405, 413–15, 420, 426–27, 434, 436–37, 446, 461–62, 493–94, 561–62, 569n.25, 570n.32, 582n.82, 589n.19, 592n.32, 600n.88, 602n.9, 604n.18, 605n.20, 606n.23, 607nn.27, 28, 610nn.39, 44, 45–46, 615n.32, 616n.34, 623n.37, 625n.47, 628n.21, 631n.44, 638n.92, 639nn.96, 101, 644n.115, 645n.129, 646nn.130, 1, 5, 675nn.30, 35, 683nn.10–11, 17

Captain Vere: in "Billy Budd," 87, 91, 108–9, 125–28, 234, 399, 407–8; in Revival, 89, 110, 238, 310, 313–14, 316, 323, 355–56, 371, 373, 512, 592n.36, 598n.73, 691n.40

Carlyle, Thomas: affinity to Melville or his narrators, 173, 266, 283, 355, 450, 531, 596n.55, 665n.92, 685n.33; *German Romance*, 180, 190, 447–49, 614n.23; as protofascist, 660n.75, 685n.33; as romantic conservative/anticapitalist, 45, 182, 197, 349, 389, 440

Cattell, James McKeen, 46–54, 575nn.37–38, 576nn.39, 46

Celio: in *Clarel*, 119–20, 124, 419

Cervantes, 442, 443, 444, 452, 497

Charlie Millthorpe: in *Pierre*, 168–69, 171, 440

Chartist agitation: Ahab and Crossthwaite, 192–93; Chartists vs. land reformers, 590n.26, 594n.44; linked to *Moby-Dick*, 182, 191–92

Chase, Richard Volney: anti-Ahab/Amerika Melville criticism/opinions, 7, 26, 400 (letter from Fiedler), 438–40, 447, 515, 516 (letter from Schlesinger Jr.), 524–25, 683n.10; conflicts with Trilling and other critics, 232–33, 502–3, 531, 532–34, 541–42, 548, 551–53, 692n.55; defense of Ezra Pound, 629n.22, 639n.93; distancing from other New Critics (1949), 525–26, 527–29; influence of Taine and Jung, 438; premature death, 553–54, 692n.56; reputation, 238, 305, 325, 513, 533, 538, 541, 545, 553–55 (Trilling eulogy), 670n.122; self-image (as con man, Starbuck, Ishmael, Bartleby), 488–89, 503, 512, 523, 526–27, 529–31, 546–47 (letter from F. W. Dupee), 549 (letter from David Riesman), 691n.41

Christian Socialism, 94, 287, 291, 313, 455–56, 598n.76, 644n.119. *See also Alton Locke, Tailor and Poet*

Civil War and Reconstruction (U.S.), 105, 411; in Melville, 5, 39–40, 106–7, 110, 574n.23; in Revival, 7, 11, 25, 40, 77–78, 86, 215, 267, 301–2, 315–16, 331, 344, 540, 543, 561, 594n.48, 637n.78, 645n.124. *See also* Abolitionism; William Lloyd Garrison; Charles Sumner

Monomania diagnosis: applied to artists, scientists, and technical workers, 61, 62, 96, 187–88, 201, 280, 446, 641n.107, 646n.132; applied to Melville's materialists, 156, 163, 172, 178, 197, 209, 270, 297, 312, 315–16, 355, 407, 413–15, 422, 570n.32, 589n.14, 593n.39, 597n.71; applied to reform movements, 24, 191, 194, 199, 438, 627n.11; pluralism as antidote, 261–68, 560–61

Morale: *Civilian Morale* (1942), 64–67, 583n.88, 584n.90; *Instincts of the Herd in Peace and War*, 250–51; in Melville criticism, 82–86, 261–62, 296–98, 302, 303, 600n.88; OSS personnel assessment screening test, 22, 397–98, 416–20; "Psychological Problems in Morale" (1941), 9–10, 68–72, 319–22, 391–92, 395, 482, 565n.6, 585n.100 (*see also* Gordon Allport; Harold D. Lasswell; Henry A. Murray); radical personality profile, 427; Thematic Apperception Test, 9, 398, 401, 477–78, 584n.93, 628n.20, 690n.30; as threat to corporatist unity/civilian morale, 41–42, 69, 75, 257, 295–303, 321–22, chap. 9; as weapon in science wars/literary theory, 31–32, 145–46, 585n.97, 606n.24, 607n.26, 635nn.60–61, 636n.67, 644n.123, 660n.75 (*see also* Narcissus myth; Charles Olson; Promethean artist)

Morewood, Agnes (great-niece), 217, 219, 220, 472, 525, 543, 553, 557, 622n.28, 677n.47

Morewood, Margaret (great-niece), 218, 219, 300, 472, 473, 531, 622n.29

Mortmain: in *Clarel*, 111, 117–19, 124, 126–27, 315, 597n.64

Multiculturalism, chaps. 1, 2, appendix. *See also* Randolph Bourne; J. G. von Herder; Horace Kallen; Melville Revival, contexts

Mumford, Lewis: communitarian observer of industrial society, 7, 244, 247, 249–53, 354–55, 436, 514–15, 533, 628n.16, 682n.8, 691n.42; Melville criticism, 25, 26, 236, 238, 254–60, 261, 263, 266, 273, 284–85, 289, 305, 307, 309, 315, 320, 323, 324, 356, 365, 367, 368, 400, 421, 447, 484, 501, 540, 549, 627nn.7, 9, 628n.21, 630nn.30, 32, 633n.45, 675n.35

Murphy, Gardner, 65–67

Murray, Henry A.: career as progressive psychologist, 7–10, 66, 391–400, 426–28, 430–31, 503, 513, 514–15, 533, 553, 565nn.5–6, 567n.19, 674nn.22–23, 26, 677n.51, 680nn.68, 70, 690n.40, 691n.42 (*see also* Adolf Hitler; Morale); influence, 295, 595n.51, 596n.56,

623n.33, 676n.44 (*see also* correspondence with Eleanor Melville Metcalf, Charles Olson); interview with author (1987), 220, 399, 400, 427, 428, 561, 617n.3, 625n.58, 675n.31; and Melville's descendants, 211–21, 622nn.27–28, 674n.28, 677n.47 (*see also* Charlotte Hoadley; Eleanor Melville Metcalf; Agnes Morewood; Margaret Morewood; Josephine Shaw); reputation as Melvillean, 288, 387, 498–500, 503–4, 506, 507, 512, 516–17, 518, 543, 544, 555–57, 674n.28, 692n.49 (*see also* correspondence with Jay Leyda, Charles Olson); Edwin Shneidman on Murray (1987), 421–22, 681n.73, 683n.19

—and other Melvilleans, 573n.13, 627n.9; to Jay Leyda, 375, 428, 495–96, 498, 501, 502, 504–5, 509–11, 518–20, 521–23, 531–32, 540–41, 558–59; Leyda to Murray, 376, 520–21, 523–24, 532–33, 556–58 (to Robinson re. Murray, 1971); to Charles Olson, 291, 415–18, 419, 469–70, 481, 487–88, 496, 505–6, 510–11, 513–14, 517–18, 532–33, 540–41, 545–46; Olson to Murray, 416–17, 424–25, 533–34; to Howard P. Vincent, 393, 419, 630n.31; Vincent to Murray, 393, 419; to Weaver, 244, 472

—published Melville criticism: "Bartleby and I," 622n.31; "Dead to the World," 680n.63; *In Nomine Diaboli*, 415, 686n.34; introduction to *Pierre* (1949), 86, 236, 388, 391, 393, 415–22, 599n.79, 630n.31

—unpublished Melville criticism (notes and drafts for psychobiography): antagonism to (puritan) academics, 413, 463; Augusta as Melville's love object, 675n.37; Bulkington as rectified Ahab, 468–69; changing estimation of *Pierre*, 419–20; confusion over narrative voice in *Moby-Dick*, 180; dilution of Melville's class consciousness, 604n.18, 684n.25; disillusion (healthy vs. destructive), 407, 408, 426, 428; exposing Hebraic confidence man/radical democrat (*White-Jacket*), 404–5, 407, 408, 675n.36; hatred of father, 402, 425; Hautia/the unconscious/the People colonizes Melville, 406; Hawthorne as antinomian 599n.78; macabre Melville blighting wife and children (1850s), 401–3, 406, 407; Melville cured by will and insight, 403; Melville as heartless autodidact/Ethan Brand, 407; Melville identified with demonic/macabre characters, 180, 401, 403, 406–7, 413–14, 450, 675n.30 (*see also* Adolf Hitler); Melville as

Organic conservativism, 11–15, 24, 28–29, 35, 79, 635n.66, 636nn.67–68, 644n.116. *See also* Edmund Burke; Thomas Carlyle; Corporatism; J. G. von Herder; J. W. von Goethe; Populist-progressive movement

Osborne, Frances C. (HM's daughter), 213, 220, 620n.16, 622n.32, 662n.82

Ovid (*Metamorphoses*), 101, 288, 433, 466, 470

Paine, Thomas: as radical bourgeois, 11, 141, 178, 349, 373, 389, 404, 428, 601n.91, 603n.14, 608n.31, 645n.126, 653n.40, 672n.7, 684n.24; redefined as New Dealer, 63, 310, 585n.100, 602n.5, 641n.104, 659n.72, 681n.1

Pareto, Vilfredo, 9, 25, 68, 277, 389, 586n.4, 635n.60, 680n.70

Parker, Hershel: comments on Revival, 456, 621n.20, 687nn.4, 6; as Melville biographer and critic, 85, 262, 584n.92, 589n.19, 591n.27, 592n.37, 596n.58, 597n.66, 602n.13, 612n.3, 624nn.41, 43, 642n.109, 654n.44, 665n.92

Parsons, Talcott, 9, 79, 395, 399, 436, 635n.60, 674n.22

Pearson, Norman Holmes, 10, 354, 356, 358, 486, 516, 566n.8, 631n.44, 665n.90

Pelagian heresy, 130–31, 164

Pierre: in *Pierre*, 81–82, 91, 94, 96, 100–102, 108, 120, 128, 133–34, 159–63, 165–69, 171, 176, 192, 196, 242, 446; in Revival, 18, 45, 59, 89, 180, 186, 197, 221, 226–27, 229, 236, 287, 316, 318, 322, 369, 375, 378, 387, 390–91, 420–22, 426–27, 592n.32, 597n.66, 602n.10, 623n.33, 644n.119, 645n.129

Pierrot, 25, 194, 228–34, 303, 328, 344, 377–79, 411–12, 437–38. *See also* Double binds; Middle managers; Raymond M. Weaver

Pip: in *Moby-Dick*, 100, 169–71, 173, 178, 430; in Revival, 430, 610n.45, 642n.109

Pitch: in *Confidence-Man*, 102, 268, 446

Plotinus Plinlimmon: in *Pierre*, 94, 101–2, 114, 170, 437; in Revival, 236, 314–15, 324–25, 631n.44, 639n.101; source, 114, 324, 503–4, 516, 593n.38

Polk, James, 89–91, 150

Popular Front (1935–39), 198, 325, 343–44, 434, 608n.31, 647n.6, 651n.29, 653nn.39–41

Populist-progressive movement, chaps. 1, 2; antifascism in, 61, 67–72, 358, 395–96, 437, 582n.83, 584nn.91, 93; class base, 32–38, 566n.10; disillusion, fear of, 54–56, 395, 405–9, 428, 577n.56, 578n.63; ideology, 11–13, 23,

31–38, 56–61, 566n.12, 571n.34, 573n.8, 578n.61, 579nn.64–70, 580nn.71–74 (*see also* Double bind); pedagogy, 40–44, 63–64, 72, 83–84, 351–52, 407–9, 440, 582n.85, 585n.100, 586n.101, 586n.4, 642n.108, 658n.61. *See also* Modernity; New Deal; Franklin Delano Roosevelt

Positivism, repudiation of: in conservative Enlightenment ideology, 55–56, 62–63, 83–84, 316–18, 349–58, 426–31, 571nn.36–38, 573n.6, 577n.58, 581n.80, 582n.84, 588n.8, 597n.63, 606nn.23–25, 607nn.26–28, 617n.44, 644n.123, 660nn.73, 75–76, 679n.62, 689n.18, 690n.19; the Melville mystery, 82–86, 132–33, 136–38, 151, 425–26, 461–68, 587n.6, 600nn.84, 88, 658n.64. *See also* Monomania diagnosis; Narcissus myth; *Völkisch* ideology

Postmodernism, 10, 13, 145–46, 268, 568n.20, 605n.20, 634n.53

Pound, Ezra, 10, 111, 272, 303, 304, 437 628n.17, 629n.22, 639n.93

Powell, Lawrence Clark, 347, 364, 485, 542, 546, 653n.43, 656n.53, 668n.107

Pragmatism, 8, 25, 58–59, 77, 102, 114, 187, 194, 208, 324, 325, 396, 403, 422, 426, 435, 463–64, 580n.71, 584n.91, 593n.38, 605n.20, 614n.29, 625n.50, 639n.101, 644n.119, 689n.18

Progress: Tory idea of (*see* T. S. Eliot; Excursus; Populist-progressive movement); Whiggish idea of, chap. 1, 54–56, 249, 276, 280, 667n.106

Proletkult, 10, 344

Promethean artist, 7–8, 11, 28, 95–96, 132, 149, 153, 172, 183, 254, 275–76, 283, 285, 288, 294, 314, 319, 374–75, 413, 419, 447, 455, 637n.81

Protestant mission, 13, 21–22, 56, 149–51, 391, 460, 514–15, 605n.20

Psychological Strategy Board, 74–75

Psychological warfare, 8–11, 24, 72, 316–17, 321–23, 388, 585n.100. *See also* Enlightenment, conservative; Jay Leyda; Charles Olson; Morale; Henry A. Murray; Populist-progressive movement; Positivism

Quakers, 15–16, 189, 413, 497, 603n.14, 659n.72

Queequeg: in *Moby-Dick*, 318, 396, 610nn.45, 47, 636n.72

Radical liberals, 11, 141, 267, 373, 464, 638n.86, 672n.8. *See also* Promethean artist

Radical Protestants, 123, 137, 149, 177, 188, 367, 369, 663n.84

Working class: class conflict, 32, 50, 52–58, 266–68, 351; corporatist view of, 4, 10, 12, 15–26, 61–62, 177–80, 195–96, 201, 259, 277–83, 310–11, 325, 406–9, 571n.36, 604n.18, 642n.109, 682n.6 (*see also* Terror-gothic narrative); ethnopluralism as weapon against, 14, 54–72, 110, 432–42, 572n.61; Melville as unorganized worker, 36; Melville's working-class readership, 623n.34; progressive welfare legislation and New Deal concessions, 31–39, 580n.77

—class consciousness in Melville: and abolitionist movement, 40, 103, 590n.26, 594n.44; criticism of abusive authority, 22, 31, 52–53, 75–77, 108–9, 120–22, 133–38, 150–51, 254, 292, 327, 447, 572n.3; images of the People, sailors, and factory workers, 108–9, 121, 122, 135, 178–80, 223, 325, 407–8, 410–11, 443–44, 623n.35, 676n.38; in Revival, 229, 292, 325, 327, 443, 446, 589n.14, 684nn.25, 30 (*see also* Herman Melville, characters; David Rein); perception of structural antagonisms, 149, 254; proletarian Christ, 192, 404–5, 593n.38 (*see also* Herman Melville, writings [marginalia, in Bible])

—labor movement: Depression decade, 266, 351, 658n.60; post–Civil War, 4, 411, 676nn.38–39; pre–Civil War, 21–22; year 1919, 54–58

Zola, Emile, 353–54

Hunting Captain Ahab

was designed by Christine Brooks;

composed by The Bookpage, Inc.

in 10.5/14 Stone Print;

printed on 60# Writers Offset stock;

Smyth sewn and bound over binder's boards,

and wrapped in dust jackets printed in four colors

by Thomson-Shore, Inc. of Dexter, Michigan;

and published by

The Kent State University Press

KENT, OHIO 44242